It's **test-taker friendly** so you can approach the test the way you want.

If you need to **try again...** you can retake the test every **21 days**.

MONTH
21

Skip questions or **change answers!**

Get the **Power of Confidence.** Register at **TakeTheGRE.com**

D0139270

2016 EDITION

Best Grad

SCHOOLS

HOW TO ORDER: Additional copies of U.S.News & World Report's **Best Graduate Schools 2016** guidebook are available for purchase at usnews.com/gradguide or by calling (800) 836-6397.
To order custom reprints, please call (877) 652-5295 or email usnews@wrightsmedia.com.
For permission to republish articles, data or other content from this book, email permissions@usnews.com.

EMORY UNIVERSITY
KENDRICK BRINSON FOR USN&WR

FIND YOUR FUTURE IN GRADUATE SCHOOL

Think Texas — start with seekUT

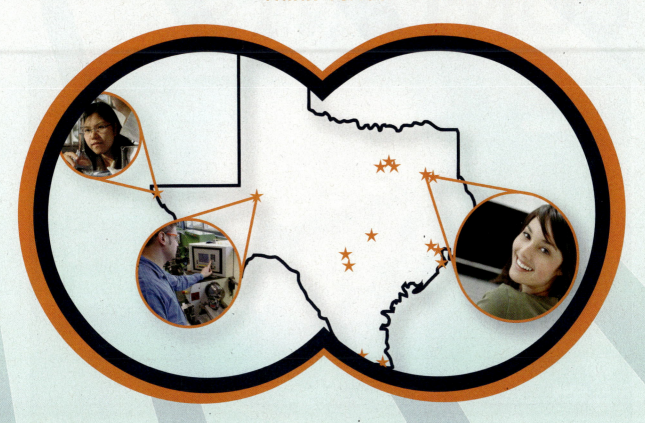

seekUT
FREE Online Resource for College and Career Planning

- Earnings 1, 5, and 10 years after graduation
- Industries that UT graduates are working in
- Occupations by education requirements
- 400 fields of study and descriptions of majors
- Expected job growth by Texas region
- Earnings comparisons across states

UT System
14 Universities. Unlimited Possibilities.

Professional Schools • Dentistry • Law • Medicine • Pharmacy

Graduate Programs • Business • Education • Sciences • Social Sciences • Health • Nursing

REAL GRADUATES
REAL EARNINGS
REALISTIC EXPECTATIONS

utsystem.edu/seekut

THE UNIVERSITY of TEXAS SYSTEM

CONTENTS

20

BRETT ZIEGLER FOR USN&WR

CONTINUED ON PAGE 6

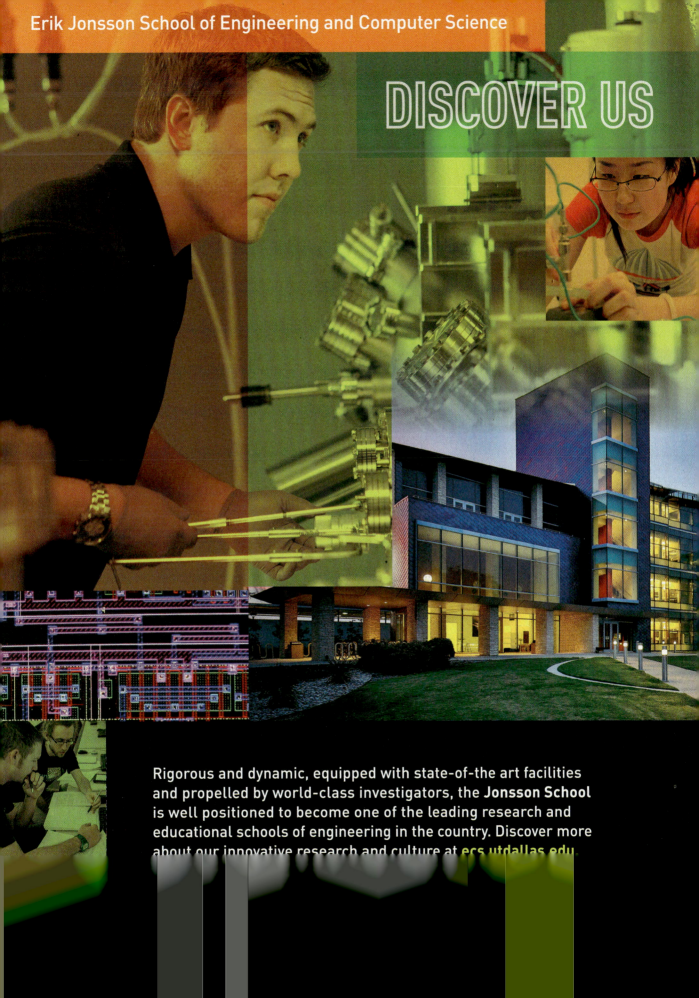

Erik Jonsson School of Engineering and Computer Science

DISCOVER US

Rigorous and dynamic, equipped with state-of-the art facilities and propelled by world-class investigators, the **Jonsson School** is well positioned to become one of the leading research and educational schools of engineering in the country. Discover more about our innovative research and culture at **ecs.utdallas.edu.**

BEST GRAD SCHOOLS
U.S.News & WORLD REPORT
2016

Executive Committee Chairman and Editor-in-Chief
Mortimer B. Zuckerman
Editor and Chief Content Officer Brian Kelly
Executive Editors Margaret Mannix, Tim Smart

BEST GRADUATE SCHOOLS

Managing Editor Anne McGrath
Chief Data Strategist Robert J. Morse
Director of Data Projects Diane Tolis
Senior Data Analyst Samuel Flanigan
Art Director Rebecca Pajak
Director of Photography Avijit Gupta
Photography Editor Brett Ziegler
Designer Michelle Rock
News Editor Elizabeth Whitehead
Contributors Cathie Gandel, Elizabeth Gardner, Christopher J. Gearon,
Katherine Hobson, Beth Howard, Darcy Lewis, Margaret Loftus, Linda Marsa,
Michael Morella, Courtney Rubin, Arlene Weintraub
Research Manager Myke Freeman
Directory Janie S. Price

USNEWS.COM/EDUCATION
Vice President, Education Chris DiCosmo
Managing Editor, Education Anita Narayan
Assistant Education Editor Allison Gualtieri
Reporters/Writers Devon Haynie, Alexandra Pannoni, Kelly Mae Ross
Delece Smith-Barrow, Susannah Snider
Web Producers Briana Boyington, Travis Mitchell
Editorial Project Manager Erica Ryan

ACADEMIC INSIGHTS
General Manager Evan Jones
Account Manager Cale Gosnell
Sales Manager Megan Trudeau
Product Marketing Specialist Taylor Suggs

INFORMATION SERVICES
Vice President, Data and Information Strategy Stephanie Salmon
Data Analysts Eric Brooks, Matthew Mason
Data Collection Joslyn Bloomfield, Geneva Dampare, Alexandra Harris

INFORMATION TECHNOLOGY
Vice President, Information Technology Yingjie Shu
Director of Web Technology Patrick Peak
Director of Engineering Matt Kupferman
Senior Systems Manager Cathy Cacho
Software Team Lead Bethany Morin
Primary Developers José Velazquez, Alex Blum, Jon Lewis, Alan Weinstein
Digital Production Michael A. Brooks, Manager; Michael Fingerhuth

President and Chief Executive Officer William Holiber

ADVERTISING
Publisher and Chief Advertising Officer Kerry Dyer
National Sales Director Ed Hannigan
Director of Strategy and Sales Planning Alexandra Kalaf
Marketing Director Mary Catherine Bain
Health Care Manager Colin Hamilton
Senior Account Executives Steve Hiel, Heather Levine,
Michelle Rosen, Shannon Tkach
Corporate Advocacy Manager Fred Kuhn
Director of Event Sales Peter Bowes
Account Executives Gregg Barton, Christine Savino Fiasconaro,
Laura Gabriel, Taylor Kiefer
Senior Manager, Programmatic and Revenue Platforms Joe Hayden
Senior Manager, Sales Strategy Katie O'Hea
Digital Strategy Manager Rachel Wulfow
Account Managers Katie Harper, Dana Jelen, Ivy Zenati
Sales Planners Rachel Halasz, Liam Kristinnsson, Michael Machado
Sales Strategy Planner Kelly Cohen
Marketing Coordinator Riki Smolen
Executive Assistant to the President Judy David
Executive Assistant to the Publisher Anny Lasso
Sales Administration Coordinator Carmen Caraballo

ADVERTISING OPERATIONS
Director of Advertising Services Phyllis A. Panza
Senior Advertising Operations Manager Cory Nesser
Advertising Operations Coordinator Karolee Jarnecki

Vice President, Manufacturing and Specialty Marketing Mark W. White
Director of Specialty Marketing Abbe Weintraub

Chief Financial Officer Thomas H. Peck
Senior Vice President, Operations Karen S. Chevalier
Senior Vice President, Strategic Development and General Counsel
Peter Dwoskin
Senior Vice President, Human Resources Jeff Zomper
Vice President, Finance Neil Maheshwari

Additional copies of the 2016 edition of U.S.News & World Report's
Best Graduate Schools guidebook are available for purchase at
(800) 836-6397 or online at usnews.com/gradguide. To order custom reprints,
please call (877) 652-5295 or email usnews@wrightsmedia.com.
For all other permissions, email permissions@usnews.com.

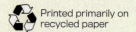 Printed primarily on recycled paper

DAVID BUTOW – REDUX FOR USN&WR

69

CONTINUED ON PAGE 8

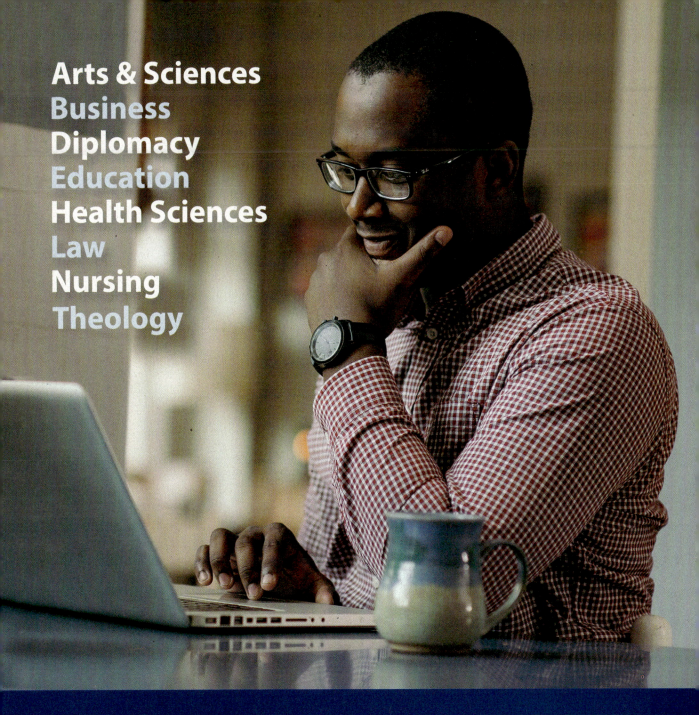

THE RANKINGS

95

Taking THE Tech Track

ACROSS FIELDS, GRAD PROGRAMS ARE ADDING TRAINING IN TECHNOLOGY

By **ARLENE WEINTRAUB**

After Christopher Low graduated from Rensselaer Polytechnic Institute in New York with a bachelor's in industrial engineering in 2012, he spent a year analyzing voter data for a political consulting firm in California. The experience drove home just how central "big data" – and the ability to make sense of it – has become, across a wide range of industries. So when RPI launched a master's of science in business analytics in 2013, he jumped at the chance to join the inaugural class. "Business analytics was a booming field – everyone was talking about it," says Low, 24. After finishing the one-year program last May, he immediately nabbed a job with IBM as a consultant.

RPI is one of dozens of universities answering an insistent call for analytics and other technology experts in all sorts of fields. Some are integrating tech training with the coursework for other advanced degrees, such as MBAs, nursing degrees and J.D.s. Others are rolling out niche degrees in hot specialties such as medical informatics, digital forensics and cybersecurity. Savvy students know that jobs of the future will rely on technology, argues Tim Westerbeck, president of Chicago-based consulting firm Eduvantis. "So higher education institutions are working hard to create these programs."

Indeed, the career opportunities for people with technology creds are expanding rapidly. Big data is becoming so key to strategic decision-making that the consulting group Gartner estimates that 4.4 million jobs in information technology have been created around the world just to support it – and that every one of those jobs has spawned three additional jobs. McKinsey & Co. estimates that by 2018, the U.S. will be short as many as 190,000 people with much-needed deep analytical skills and 1.5 million managers qualified to assess and make decisions based on data. "Tsunamis of data are

being created every day," says Jim Spohrer, director of global university programs for IBM, which works with 1,000 colleges and universities to help shape data science curricula. "Employers want to hire people who can hit the ground running."

And they're willing to compensate them well. Statisticians, for example, were paid an average of $75,560 in 2012, and computer programmers earned $74,280 – both more than double the median for all workers, according to the Bureau of Labor Statistics.

In addition to the new program at RPI, anyone interested in big data as it relates to business can pick from recently launched master's programs at New York University, George Washington University in Washington, D.C., and the University of Southern California, to name a few. These programs are designed to equip students with management, market-

New Cornell Tech master's programs bring computer science and MBA students together.

ing and professional savvy along with expertise in topics like database software and coding, predictive modeling and data analysis. One target audience, says Thomas Begley, dean of the Lally School of Management at RPI, consists of all the college grads in technical fields looking to cultivate the broader array of competencies necessary on the job. Advanced degrees in analytics allow "students with strong quantitative skills to become highly marketable," he says.

Much of the appeal of these degrees to employers is the practical experience graduates gain. Most business analytics degrees build in courses that require students to work in teams to complete real-world projects. In GWU's practicum course, for example, one group of students worked with consulting company Deloitte to analyze data from the U.S. Agency for International Development for insights on how best to promote international trade. Other planned projects range from mining information available on the web to see if it's possible to approximate census stats on more of an ongoing basis to using historical data to predict voting patterns. The first four full-time students to complete GWU's degree graduated in August 2014 and were snapped up by employers such as financial services firm TIAA-CREF and software giant SAS, reports Dustin Pusch, the program's director. Starting salaries ranged from $70,000 to $135,000.

Maybe you'd rather manage technology than work on the

analysis? Several universities now offer "tech MBAs" designed to groom grads for careers as chief information officers or as founders of their own tech startups. Among them: Cornell University in New York and Drexel University in Pennsylvania.

Many of these MBAs operate on traditional two-year schedules, including programs offered by the University of Pittsburgh and the University of Southern California, and cover the full range of business topics beyond technology, from marketing to accounting. Others, like the Johnson Cornell Tech MBA program recently launched in New York City, are intensive one-year experiences. Cornell's program – one of the flagship residents of the NYC tech hub envisioned by

former mayor Michael Bloomberg (story, Page 16) – includes classroom lectures and projects but is largely focused on providing students with work experience. Students spend much of the fall semester working with companies like Google, Qualcomm and MasterCard on technology projects. Then they devise and prototype ideas for tech startups. Drexel's LeBow College of Business, which offers both a master's and an MBA focused on business analytics, requires full-time MBA students to get actual work experience during the summer term. Some students compete for the opportunity to participate in the school's "C-Suite Co-Op," a summer program that puts them in positions in companies such as eBay and software provider SAP, where they work with company leaders on high-level projects.

"Companies can hire a lot of first-rate technologists, or they can go to business schools and hire people who can do a strategic plan and understand customers. What they don't have is people who can cross both disciplines," says Doug Stayman, associate dean of the Johnson Cornell Tech MBA, who believes that the new degree programs serve that need.

For those who want to gain expertise in a fast-growing tech niche, programs are springing up in more narrowly drawn fields from health care informatics to legal protections for digital assets. The University of Maryland University College's mostly online master's of science degree in cyberse-

An MBA? Or an MEM?

To hold their own at a business conference table, fledgling engineers need more than technical skills, says Daniel Moorer, professor of engineering practice at the University of Colorado. In fact, the know-how they need, he says, sounds a lot like an MBA: leadership and management, product development and accounting. At Colorado, though, those skills are also taught in the master's of engineering management program, which is emerging as kind of an MBA-lite for anyone aspiring to a senior role in industries with engineering as their backbone. "An MEM prepares you for technology leadership," says Colin Drummond, a professor at Case Western Reserve in Ohio whose specialty is health care technology and who serves in the organization – ABET – that ac-

credits engineering programs.

How do the degrees differ? The MBA is generally more expensive (a traditional program takes two years, compared to a calendar year for an MEM) and still more recognizable to nonengineers, though that may change. The MBA offers exposure to a more comprehensive menu of business subjects, and greater depth in those. For example, most MBAs require at least two courses in accounting; an MEM might provide just eight weeks' worth. And an MEM will likely skip over such subjects as retail and real estate.

Fifth year. Students typically apply for MBA programs already boasting several years of work experience, whereas an MEM is often referred to as a "fifth year" – a good solution for science majors who re-

alize they don't actually want to be bench scientists.

"Normally, you'd need an MBA to do what I do, but as soon as people hear what my degree is they understand why I chose it," says Timothy Harvey, 29, who earned a degree in cognitive neuroscience at the University of Denver and hopes to run a company some day. He's getting an MEM part-time at the University of Colorado while working as an associate product manager at Terumo BCT, a maker of medical devices. His compensation is in the "upper $70,000s," and benefits include $5,000 per year of tuition reimbursement. "I should graduate with no debt. Whew!" he says.

Harvey's boss, Joy Duemke, notes that Harvey "has to translate customer needs" so products meet them. His degree says he's got both the people skills and technical know-how to do so. –*Courtney Rubin*

Learning the rules on patents in Northwestern's new tech-oriented M.S. in law

curity – six courses plus a "capstone" course in which students apply their newly learned skills to a cybersecurity project in health care, finance or manufacturing, say – currently counts about 1,800 students all over the world. Beyond government agencies concerned about data breaches, says Aric Krause, dean of the graduate school, "the financial and retail industries are moving a mile a minute to try and anticipate and resolve problems."

Employers are on the hunt as well for people equipped to navigate the intersection between law and technology. "There's so much happening, first and foremost in the intellectual property space," says Leslie Oster, clinical associate professor of law at Northwestern University, which launched a Master of Science in Law degree in 2014. "Many companies are reviewing their intellectual property portfolios, exploring the landscape, trying to get a sense of where to innovate and how to value what they currently have. Every major company is beefing up their intellectual property staff."

Northwestern Law's one-year program helps students trained in science and engineering master legal aspects of entrepreneurship and technology, including patenting, regulatory affairs, data privacy and forming a business structure. For example, in a class on patents, students have worked with scientists and engineers at the university to create a patent application for a new invention.

If a full-fledged J.D. is your goal, a dual degree is one way to add tech expertise. Stanford Law School allows students to earn a law degree plus a master's in engineering or computer science and still generally wrap up in three years, for ex-

ample. Or they can opt for a single tech-heavy law program (the Stanford Program in Law, Science & Technology) that offers a large dose of material on big data, intellectual property and contracts.

Students of both programs are offered many opportunities to apply their emerging skills. The law students team up with computer science students, for instance, at CodeX, a center where they work on developing new technology products for the legal industry. Among the projects that have emerged from CodeX is an analytics, search and visualization tool called Ravel that lawyers can use to identify legal cases relevant to their work. In the Juelsgaard Intellectual Property and Innovation Clinic, students help companies to develop intellectual property policies that support innovation. "A team of students operates like a small law firm, representing clients," says Mark Lemley, director of Stanford's Law, Science and Technology program.

Jonathan Mayer, 28, will complete a dual J.D./computer science Ph.D. at Stanford in 2015 and believes the combination of academics and experience – which included helping Mozilla build a new privacy feature into its browser – has opened up opportunities across the technology industry. "There's no doubt the demand is sky-high. I've had a number of unsolicited inquiries about potential jobs," Mayer says.

He isn't alone in believing a technology-tinged advanced degree will convey an advantage. According to Eduvantis, monthly Internet searches around terms like "dual degree" doubled from 2007 to 2014. In the past year, searches for "MBA/computer science" grew by 22 percent, and there was an 86 percent jump in interest in "MBA/engineering." ■

The Next Silicon Valley?

NEW YORK'S TECH HUB IS TAKING SHAPE – AND ENROLLING GRAD STUDENTS

By **KATHERINE HOBSON**

Back in 2010, then-mayor Michael Bloomberg threw down a challenge: New York City would put up $400 million worth of land and infrastructure upgrades to seed a technology hub that would give Silicon Valley a run for its money. Universities would compete for the central role by proposing plans for an applied sciences research facility. The payoff over 30 years, Bloomberg predicted, would be some 400 new companies, billions of dollars in economic activity and nearly 30,000 new jobs.

Today, Bloomberg is back in the business world, running his namesake media company. Meanwhile, Applied Sciences NYC is taking shape

{ **Three programs now have students; ONE is still to open.** }

with not one but four new grad-school options for those interested in applying technological know-how to contemporary problems. All four get a piece of the city's largesse. Three of the programs created by the competition already have students on campus; another could open this year. Here's the lowdown:

1 Cornell Tech, an arm of the Ivy League university and the big official winner, aims to fill "the talent gap of the digital age," says Dean Daniel Huttenlocher. Engineering is integral to almost all aspects of daily life, he says, but the demand for workers with the skills to keep the machinery humming is not being met. The school is temporarily holding classes in Google's downtown Manhattan building and will move to sleek new digs on Roosevelt Island in the East River in 2017. The tech company atmosphere will persist there, with ample studio space to encourage innovation and collaboration and an open floor plan with meeting rooms rather than individual offices for professors.

In the 2014-15 academic year, Cornell Tech has

100 students enrolled in three programs: a one-year master's in computer science and a second in tech-oriented business administration, plus a two-year master's in connective media (focused on the technology behind digital media) through the Jacobs Technion–Cornell Institute, a partnership between Cornell and Israel's Technion-Israel Institute of Technology, which will result in a degree from each university. Future programs include master's degrees for people interested in developing individual technology to drive healthier living (such as mobile devices) and in making buildings and infrastructure more efficient. Cornell Tech expects to have 500 students by 2017.

The computer science and MBA students spend about a third of the curriculum together, in class and working on projects, to ensure that business students hone their tech prowess and the techies learn management and communication skills. In the fall, students collaborate to solve problems at local companies or organizations, and in the spring they work on startup projects.

The entrepreneurial orientation was part of what drew Geoffrey Peterson to the computer science master's. Peterson, 29, graduated from Harvard with a computer science degree but then worked in other fields, most recently in infrastructure policy for the state of Rhode Island. "I was looking for programs that would let me do a career pivot and get back into the tech world," he says. He and several classmates are hoping their startup project, a secure messaging protocol, will lead to jobs – ideally, as their own bosses.

2 New York University's Center for Urban Science and Progress was conceived to address the increasing percentage of the population living in cities and to exploit the massive growth in the ability to collect and analyze data. Created by NYU and a consortium including other academic institutions and companies, CUSP is an effort to use "urban informatics" to improve how cities function, says Constantine Kontokosta, deputy director of academics. Think of city issues like noise, transportation and emergency response, and you'll get a sense of where CUSP is targeting its data analysis power.

There are now 64 students enrolled in a one-year master's and advanced certificate programs in two buildings in downtown Brooklyn. (The

program will move to nearby permanent head-quarters in 2017.) CUSP expects enrollment to hit 500 in about a decade, as more master's students come on board and executive education and Ph.D. programs are added. Master's students work on two-semester deep-dive projects tackling problems faced by a city agency or company – modeling transportation movements and patterns, say, or improving waste management.

The typical student has a quantitative background, but the group represents a wide diversity of academic paths, says JeanCarlo Bonilla, director of enrollment management and student services. The common denominator, he says, is a desire to apply technology to more than making money. "I wanted to use my abilities in a career I thought had more tangible benefits for communities and cities," says Eduardo Franco, 29, a former trader in New York's financial industry with an undergrad degree in industrial engineering from the University of Illinois at Urbana-Champaign.

3 Columbia University's Data Science Institute focuses on six fields: cybersecurity, data science foundations, financial and business analytics, health analytics, new media and smart cities. The availability of data has exploded in these areas in particular, says director Kathleen McKeown, and there's a need for people to smartly analyze it to make predictions. The institute offers a master's in data science as well as a certification for working professionals. The plan

Cornell Tech MBA students gather before class in Google's Manhattan offices.

is to add a data sciences Ph.D. in the fall of 2016 and, by 2017, to be preparing about 75 full-time and 30 part-time students for careers in media, advertising and finance as well as tech.

"This is definitely going to be opening a new door for me," predicts Barbara Welsh, a 31-year-old IT consultant with a math undergrad degree from NYU who was looking to add data analysis to her list of quantitative skills. She is hoping eventually to apply her new knowledge to fields such as energy and health care.

4 Pending curriculum approval by New York state, **Carnegie Mellon's Integrative Media Program** will welcome its first class of about 40 students to Steiner Studios in the Brooklyn Navy Yard this August. The goal is to train students to work in "new creative industries" that bridge technology and the arts, and to include film, social media, games and interactive media. That will happen through four full- and part-time master's programs in emerging media, computational data science, integrated innovation and urban design.

Thanassis Rikakis, CMU's vice provost for design, arts and technology, says creative industries are looking "feverishly" for people who can cross disciplines and tackle challenges like building a brand across media outlets, or designing smart buildings. And artists with the proper technical training can fill those gaps, he says. A theater lighting expert, say, could spend one year working to design a smart home, then develop an app and next turn to a project with Cirque du Soleil. ∎

About the Rankings

OBJECTIVE MEASURES ARE IMPORTANT, AS ARE THE OPINIONS OF PEERS

By **ROBERT J. MORSE** and **SAMUEL FLANIGAN**

Each year, U.S. News ranks professional school programs in business, education, engineering, law and medicine. This year, we also introduce our first annual expanded ranking of master's programs in nursing. The rankings in these six areas are based on two types of data: expert opinions about program excellence and statistical indicators that measure the quality of a school's faculty, research and students. The data come from statistical surveys sent to administrators at nearly 1,900 graduate programs and from reputation surveys sent to more than 13,700 academics and professionals in the disciplines. The surveys were conducted during the fall of 2014 and in early 2015. In each field, we also present rankings of programs in various specialty areas based on reputation data alone.

As you research course offerings and weigh schools' intangible attributes, the information in these pages can help you compare concrete factors such as faculty-student ratio and placement success upon graduation. It's important that you use the rankings to supplement, not substitute for, careful thought and your own research. In each of the six major disciplines, the ranking tables show approximately the top half of the schools that were eligible to be ranked; longer lists and more complete data can be found at usnews.com/grad. Detailed information about the various methodologies can be found there, too, as well as with each ranking in these pages.

Beyond the six disciplines ranked annually, we also periodically rank programs in the sciences, social sciences, humanities, the health arena and many other areas based solely on the ratings of academic experts. This year, new peer assessment surveys were conducted and new rankings are published in five areas in health that were last updated in 2011: health care management, physician assistant, public health, rehabilitation counseling and veterinary medicine. The rankings of programs in the other health fields, as well as those of the Ph.D. programs in the sciences and social sciences and humanities, are based on earlier surveys and are republished.

Full rankings in all categories, plus web-exclusive rankings of schools of public affairs and public policy, fine arts, and library and information studies, are available at our website, usnews.com/grad. (It's a good idea to check back every now and then, as we occasionally add content when we obtain additional data we think useful – whether on job placement, GPA, test scores or other factors – or learn information that changes the data.)

To gather the peer assessment data, we asked deans, program directors and senior faculty to judge the academic quality of programs in their field on a scale of 1 (marginal) to 5 (outstanding). In business, education, engineering, law and medicine, we also surveyed professionals who hire new graduates and have used their three most recent years' responses to calculate the results, up from two previously. Also new this year: The value of jobs held by law graduates that were funded by the law school or the university was discounted, even if the jobs were full-time for at least a year and required bar passage or were roles in which a J.D. degree was an advantage. The value of all other types of school-funded jobs was discounted more than in the past.

Statistical indicators fall into two categories: inputs, or measures of the qualities that students and faculty bring to the educational experience, and outputs, measures of graduates' achievements linked to their degrees. As inputs, for example, we use admission test scores: the LSAT, GMAT, MCAT or GRE. Output measures for the business ranking include starting salaries and grads' ability to find jobs; in law, we look at employment rates at graduation and nine months later, and at state bar exam passage rates.

Our scoring system. To arrive at a school's rank, we examined the data for each indicator. We then standardized the value of each indicator about its mean. The weights applied to each reflect our judgment about the indicators' relative importance, as determined in consultation with experts in each field. Final scores were rescaled so that the highest-scoring school was assigned 100; the other schools' scores were recalculated as a percentage of that top score. The scores were then rounded to the nearest whole number. Schools with a score of 100 did not necessarily top out on every indicator; they accumulated the highest composite score. A school's rank reflects the number of schools that sit above it; if three schools are tied at 1, the next school will be ranked 4, not 2. Tied schools are listed alphabetically. ∎

> Use **the**
> **rankings** to
> **supplement**
> YOUR OWN
> research.

Business

The Wharton School in Philadelphia

THE U.S. NEWS RANKINGS

Inside **3** Top B-Scho

PHOTOGRAPHY BY **BRETT ZIEGLER** FOR USN&WR

ols

Professor Anat Admati's finance class at Stanford

By **MICHAEL MORELLA**

On the surface, the business schools at Stanford, Harvard and the University of Pennsylvania look strikingly similar. Each features state-of-the-art facilities, diverse and high-achieving student populations, vast menus of global excursions and student clubs, and tuition and fees that run more than $61,000 annually. The bread and butter at all three is the two-year, full-time MBA, though a careful look will find some opportunities to specialize, complete joint-degree programs and pursue doctoral and executive business programs. The starting salary for graduates of all three institutions averages more than $142,500, including bonuses. But to hear students tell it, these three elite B-schools are surprisingly different. U.S. News visited each campus to get a sense of what gives each place its distinctive feel.

Stanford, California

Stanford Graduate School of Business

#1 The open-air courtyard at the center of the "GSB" is called Town Square, a fitting nod to what students describe as a close-knit community whose members "are really, really gunning for each other rather than themselves," says second-year MBA student Naomi Bagdonas, 27, who previously worked as a management consultant in San Francisco and a leadership dynamics coach for executives in the U.S. and abroad. Bagdonas recalls the time a year ago when, due to a recruiter's scheduling error, she found out at the last minute that she had an interview for a summer internship early the next morning. She reached out to a classmate who had also applied for the position, and soon was collaborating with several other students preparing to interview.

In part, that openness is a function of the school's size: Each class of MBA candidates numbers only about 400. The more laid-back West Coast ambience plays a role, too; this is a place where students gather weekly in a forum called "Talk" to share stories about their backgrounds and ambitions. Most value the intimate vibe, though the small size can feel a little confining at times, students say.

Located near Palo Alto, the GSB sits on the Stanford campus and features a modern version of Spanish Mission-style architecture. About half of first-year students live in campus housing right next door to

▶ **More on business schools @** usnews.com/bschools

the B-school, and a new residence hall is under construction.

Besides the beauty of its location, a big draw of the Stanford program is that it's so plugged into the Silicon Valley scene. Executives from Adobe, Oracle and Dropbox have taught classes, and many others visit as guest speakers; about a quarter of 2014 grads found jobs in the tech sector. Innovation and entrepreneurial thinking are infused throughout the curriculum, and many students team up with peers from across the university to develop or refine new products and services in the Stanford Venture Studio. But students say it's a misconception that everyone is out to start the next Google. "Being surrounded by a buzz of creativity and the free-flowing discussion of ideas is good for any student," says Whitney Ping, 28, an Olympic table tennis player (the 2004 Games in Athens) who has worked in consulting in Los Angeles and private equity in Boston and finishes up this spring.

A hallmark of Stanford's first-year curriculum is the experiential Leadership Labs course, in which students work in a six-person "squad" to tackle team exercises, group projects and role-playing, taking on the part of executives grappling with staffing

Stanford MBA candidates at work in their "Startup Garage" class

decisions after a merger, for example, or of an entrepreneur pitching to venture capitalists. And many cite "Touchy Feely" (officially Interpersonal Dynamics) as a must-take; the elective focuses on leadership and communication, and students get frequent advice from peers and facilitators. (A common GSB mantra is "Feedback is a gift.")

Part of the first-year curriculum is standardized, but those with backgrounds in finance or economics, say, can take more advanced versions of required courses in these areas. Elective offerings vary with student interests; more than a quarter of those in each recent year have been new, notes acting Dean Madhav Rajan. At least one global study trip is required. Besides the MBA, the GSB offers a one-year master's program for experienced managers. ■

Boston

Harvard Business School

#2 From Day One at Harvard, students step into the shoes of so-called protagonists – business leaders grappling with complex issues such as expanding operations into a new foreign market or addressing social media strategy – and work toward solutions together. During class discussions (participation often counts for half the grade), professors are "more of a facilitator than they are an instructor," says first-year student Ben Zatlin, 27, who worked in engineering and manufacturing roles at Abbott Laboratories before coming to Harvard. This case method of instruction

A taste of the iconic architecture at HBS

has been the cornerstone of the MBA program here for some 90 years, and all told, students work through more than 500 case studies. The highly credentialed faculty includes innovation expert Clayton Christensen and world-renowned strategy pioneer Michael Porter, as well as former executives of companies like General Motors, Amgen and Fidelity.

In 2011, in an effort to inject more experiential learning into what is a standardized first-year program, the school added a yearlong hands-on component, Field Immersion Experiences for Leadership Development, to the curriculum. (While tradition is a vital part of Harvard's DNA, "we can be simultaneously classic and contemporary," says Dean Nitin Nohria.) After some background prep and a course focused on sharpening interpersonal skills, students might spend 10 days in January in India, Brazil or another emerging market developing a car-sharing service for workers, say, or creating a mobile app for a company. Then they work in small teams to develop a microbusiness that their peers

YOU CAN'T CONTROL EVERYTHING

BUT YOU CAN CONTROL YOUR GMAT EXPERIENCE

The GMAT® Exam now has more options to sharpen your prep, preview your scores, and analyze your results to get your best score.

Learn more at **mba.com/controlyourgmat**

Harvard MBA candidate Forrest Funnell studies at the B-school's Baker Library.

Philadelphia
Wharton (University of Pennsylvania)

#3 In 1881, during the second Industrial Revolution, Philadelphia magnate Joseph Wharton founded the nation's first collegiate school of business at the University of Pennsylvania. Today, the Wharton School, based in Huntsman Hall along Penn's tree-lined pedestrian thoroughfare Locust Walk, says it has the world's largest alumni network (more than 93,000 graduates) and boasts the second biggest full-time enrollment (approximately 1,700 MBA students), after Harvard. Unlike Stanford and Harvard, Wharton also enrolls about 2,500 undergraduates.

With more than 5,000 students overall (counting doctoral and executive MBA students), the school can feel like a big place. But "there are a lot of layers to the onion," says second-year student Jake Gorelov, 27, who has worked in consulting in Boston and the Netherlands and media in New York. Cohorts of 70 students take certain core classes – marketing, microeconomics, statistics – together, and

can "invest" in through a simulated stock market.

With more than 1,850 MBA students, Harvard has the highest full-time enrollment of any B-school in the country. To foster community, an entering class is broken into sections of about 90 students who take classes as a group and share in many social activities. More than two-thirds of students live in Harvard-affiliated housing or on the HBS campus in Boston, set on 40 acres just south of the Charles River and about half a mile from the university's Cambridge hub (where they can take classes and pursue joint degrees). That "makes it a lot easier to continue conversations," says second-year student Jennifer Rybak, 27, previously a consultant in New York.

Underground tunnels connect many of the buildings – a real plus in winter – and each of the five coveted residence halls features single rooms, most with private bathrooms, and dry cleaning and laundry facilities. While the close proximity to each other can be an asset, HBS can at times feel "almost like a 24-hour experience," says second-year student Daniel Lennox-Choate, 30, who arrived after serving in the U.S. Army in Iraq and Afghanistan.

It's a competitive culture, students say, but mostly in a good way. "You constantly feel humbled" by

the achievements of classmates, says second-year student Nabil Mohamed, 27, who has an engineering degree and formerly worked at Vodafone in Cairo. But "it lifts you upwards." The school has taken some heat for not being welcoming enough to women, who make up some 41 percent of MBA candidates and 23 percent of the faculty. The administration is intent on adding more female professors and case studies featuring women protagonists. "This is a long march," says Nohria, "and we are committed to that journey." ■

Wharton's off-campus Walnut Street space has plenty of room for study sessions.

Graduate Study at UMass Boston:
Empowered to Change the World

More than 100 innovative doctoral, master's, and graduate certificate programs

World-class faculty and state-of-the-art research facilities

Students from more than 140 countries

Great learning, internship, and career opportunities in our city and across the globe

www.umb.edu/admissions/grad

UMASS BOSTON

WHY I PICKED...

Dartmouth College

Hanover, New Hampshire

E. SELEMON ASFAW, '14
Investment banking associate

▶ Dartmouth's Tuck School of Business has a team orientation. With only 275 classmates, you have to show up and participate and learn how to build relationships with people. I found plenty of opportunities to lead projects without much direction. You get maybe 30 percent of the information you need and then must figure out the rest to execute the project.

Tuck's MBA program prepared me well for my current position at Goldman Sachs, where I find myself in the same kind of team-oriented environment, managing analysts, guiding presentations and interacting with CFOs and VPs at client companies. As was often the case at Tuck, I am responsible for the final deliverable for my team.

cohorts are divided into learning teams of five or six, who work closely on exercises in teamwork and leadership. Each MBA candidate is also linked up with several second-year peers for advice on student life, academics and careers – essentially their "own personal board of directors," says Kembrel Jones, deputy vice dean of student life.

The core requirements offer some flexibility – an operations requirement can be satisfied with a course on innovation or business analytics, say – and students choose their direction from among 18 majors, including health care management and business economics and public policy (or they can design their own). "Our goal is to get all the advantages of the size but enable people to tailor the experience," says finance professor Howard Kaufold, vice dean of the MBA program. While some see the campus culture as quite competitive, most students "champion each other," says former Chicago management consultant Emily Kasavana, 27, class of 2015.

Many Whartonites live in the bustling Center City neighborhood, and the average MBA candidate is involved in nine student-run activities. Students come out in droves for Thursday pub nights and big annual events like the student-choreographed dance per-

formance (no experience required).

Finance figures large in the identity of Wharton, once dubbed "the closest thing that exists to a Wall Street farm team" by The New York Times. (In fact, the original name was the Wharton School of Finance and Economy.) But students are quick to say that times have changed. About 35 percent of 2014 grads went into careers in finance, down from 41 percent in 2012.

Wharton can feel a little insular, but it's "kind of a fluid bubble," notes second-year student Casey Brett, 27, who formerly worked in player development for baseball's Seattle Mariners. Travel options abound, including several-day courses that immerse students in subjects like finance in the Middle East and North Africa and supply chain management in Japan. Last year, Alana Rush, 30, spent a week trekking and camping on an Antarctic island with about 40 peers in one of the popular outdoor expeditions known as Leadership Ventures.

"You're met with challenges you wouldn't normally face," says Rush, who arrived at Wharton after working in education in Boston and as a consultant in Mumbai and Abu Dhabi. "It takes all the things that you learn in a management classroom, and it puts them to use in a very real-world situation." ∎

Learning the art of negotiation in a Wharton B-school class

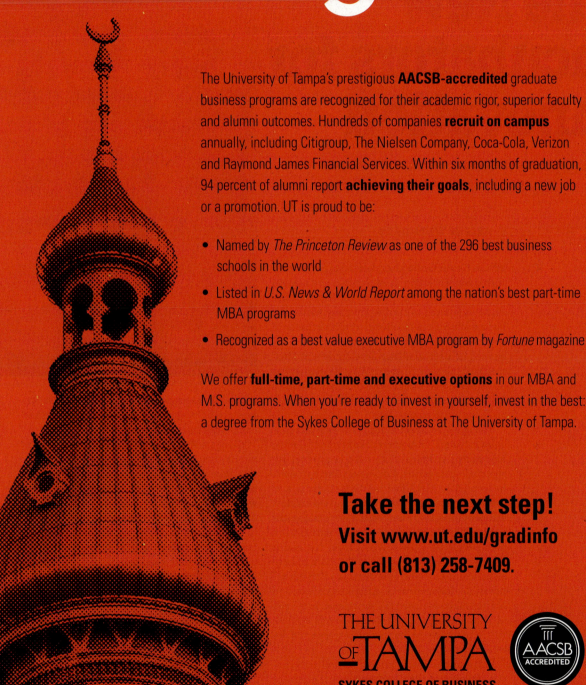

Prestigious

The University of Tampa's prestigious **AACSB-accredited** graduate business programs are recognized for their academic rigor, superior faculty and alumni outcomes. Hundreds of companies **recruit on campus** annually, including Citigroup, The Nielsen Company, Coca-Cola, Verizon and Raymond James Financial Services. Within six months of graduation, 94 percent of alumni report **achieving their goals**, including a new job or a promotion. UT is proud to be:

- Named by *The Princeton Review* as one of the 296 best business schools in the world
- Listed in *U.S. News & World Report* among the nation's best part-time MBA programs
- Recognized as a best value executive MBA program by *Fortune* magazine

We offer **full-time, part-time and executive options** in our MBA and M.S. programs. When you're ready to invest in yourself, invest in the best: a degree from the Sykes College of Business at The University of Tampa.

Take the next step!
Visit www.ut.edu/gradinfo or call (813) 258-7409.

THE UNIVERSITY OF TAMPA

SYKES COLLEGE OF BUSINESS

Offering full-time and part-time options:

MBA | Executive MBA | M.S. in Accounting | M.S. in Finance | M.S. in Marketing | Nonprofit Management Certificate

The New Incubators for Innovation

DO YOU HAVE A GREAT STARTUP IDEA? B-SCHOOLS WANT TO MAKE IT HAPPEN

By **ARLENE WEINTRAUB**

When Kevin Gallagher decided to get an MBA with a concentration in innovation at Carnegie Mellon University in Pittsburgh, it wasn't because he wanted to start a company. Gallagher had a bachelor's in biochemistry with a minor in economics from Boston College and had already worked in medical device development at Massachusetts General Hospital. What he wanted was the expertise he would need to help companies improve their processes and more quickly get new products to the patent stage.

Gallagher, 28, spent much of the two-year program in typical MBA courses like marketing, while also adding technical skills such as product design and engineering. For his capstone project, he teamed up with other master's students, and worked with an international oil and gas services company to develop a new customer-management system. "The program gave me the ability to work with people who are different from me, and it showed me who needs to be in the room to have an educated and informed discussion" about innovation, Gallagher says. After he graduated in May 2014, he parlayed the experience into a job at pharmaceutical giant Bristol-Myers Squibb, where he focuses on improving research and development processes.

Carnegie Mellon is one of several universities stepping up their business-school offerings in innovation. To a large degree, these colleges are responding to demand from students who want to start their own companies: 45 percent of people who graduated from B-school between 2010 and 2013 pursued startups, versus just 7 percent who graduated before 1990, according to the Graduate Management Admission Council.

But as Gallagher's experience shows, inventing new products and services is key to established companies' success as well.

Carnegie Mellon's Integrated Innovation Institute, launched in 2014, brings together faculty from the engineering, design and business schools, and offers the MBA innovation track as well as several master's degrees for students in other fields, like design. Students work in teams to develop new products and services, which so far have included a car that cleans itself with a built-in robot (a project sponsored by Nissan) and a "smart bin" system to automate the distribution of drugs in hospitals. That invention is now being patented by Aesynt, a company focusing on pharmacy automation solutions.

Design a degree. Many of the schools with master's and MBA degrees in innovation permit students to design a program that will most benefit their projected career path. The University of Chicago's Booth School of Business Polsky Center for Entrepreneurship and Innovation, for example, offers courses in a wide range of industries, from real estate to the Internet to global finance. Booth students can also pick from a variety of experiential learning opportunities, such as a new venture lab for those who want to develop

improving the management of electrical grids.

At the University of California–Davis Child Family Institute for Innovation and Entrepreneurship, the curriculum focuses on commercializing advances in science and engineering for social benefit. MBA students follow the whole development process, from evaluating and selecting the most promising product ideas to pitching the winning concept to venture capitalists. More than 500 industry partners include Kraft, Chevron and Pepsi. During the 2013-2014 school year, 14 commercial startups emerged, including one that is developing an irrigation-monitoring device and a biotech company working on fertility treatments.

Added flex. Universities are also increasingly offering their degree programs in more flexible formats. Indiana University's Johnson Center for Entrepreneurship and Innovation offers both full-time on-campus and part-time online MBA programs. And the university recently added an online master's of science program in entrepreneurship and innovation, which allows students to stay in their jobs while gaining graduate-level experience in new venture development. "If you look back to the 1990s, leadership was the big call from companies," says Donald F. Kuratko, chair of entrepreneurship at IU's Kelley School of Business. "Today innovation is the big call."

For students who want to pursue their own ideas, the University of Texas–Dallas has become a startup booster of sorts, matching budding entrepreneurs with any of 90 mentors, some of whom are angel investors. In 2013, the school introduced the Startup Launch Track, in which participating students are given the opportunity to create their businesses while completing their degrees. The program offers office space and seed funding of up to $25,000, no strings attached.

Corey Egan and Swapnil Bora are prime examples of how fruitful these sorts of environments can be. Just four years ago, Egan and Bora came out on top in UT–Dallas' annual Business Idea Competition with their company, ilumi, which makes smart phone-controlled LED light bulbs. In 2014, Egan and Bora appeared on the reality TV program "Shark Tank," catching the attention of co-host and billionaire investor Mark Cuban. He poured $350,000 into ilumi for a 25 percent stake in the company. ∎

their startup ideas and a management lab in new product and strategy development, where students team up with companies and other organizations to complete real-world assignments. One group worked at the university's medical center, where they recommended new processes to reduce emergency room wait times and improve patient discharge.

For Aparna Misra, 26, the two years she spent at Polsky were invaluable for developing her web and mobile app, HighStride, which offers personalized training plans for runners. "I was pretty strong operationally, but I didn't have the selling skills I needed," says Misra, who will graduate from Booth in 2015. So each quarter, she selected at least one class that would give her marketing experience, using her own company as a case study. She reached well over 100,000 downloads in just her first year in the program.

Several schools have designed innovation programs around local industries, including Booth, which in 2010 added the Energy & Cleantech Lab, where students work with energy companies in the Midwest to develop new technologies. The University of California–Berkeley's Cleantech to Market program teams scientists and engineers from the school and the Lawrence Berkeley National Laboratory with business students to commercialize ideas for reducing waste and developing renewable energy sources. The class of 2014 worked on technologies ranging from magnets to make motors more efficient to a mathematical system for

At Carnegie Mellon's innovation institute, students work on ways to improve a delivery service.

THE JOB MARKET | OPERATIONS RESEARCH ANALYST

Using Data to Make the Call

By **CHRISTOPHER J. GEARON**

Electrical engineer Ajay Mehta was working at Union Pacific Railroad in Houston, overseeing two dozen employees charged with testing, installing and maintaining the signal and road-crossing systems, when he decided to get an MBA to broaden his perspective and choices. Armed with a business degree focused on operations research from Boston University School of Management (class of 2012), Mehta today works for Ericsson Consulting in Dallas, helping a range of businesses solve problems and make decisions.

The MBA grounded Mehta in business analytics, which entails mining data and using statistical modeling to inform strategic decisions (story, Page 10). He relies on both to craft the best software and infrastructure solutions for clients to help them increase revenue. While data analytics in the business arena is often associated with tracking customer behavior and improving marketing approaches, "operations is the part of the business where the work actually gets done," Mehta says.

First employed by World War II military planners, operations research has become a key tool in the big data age used by companies and other organizations

Ajay Mehta
Boston University School of
Management, 2012

to better allocate resources, develop production schedules, manage supply chains and set prices. It helps transport companies move freight and manage distribution, allows health care systems to improve the collection and processing of patient lab specimens, and lets supermarkets determine how best to organize products, for example. It used to be that a theme park operator would pair an engineer with a business expert to improve queueing at rides and attractions, notes Robin Keller, a professor of operations and decision technologies at the University of California–Irvine's Paul Merage School of Business. Today, that task is handled by a single person trained in operations research.

The need for such talent has spiked as businesses have felt pressure to more closely scrutinize costs and operations, a legacy of the Great Recession. The Bureau of Labor Statistics projects employment growth of 27 percent for operations research analysts between 2012 and 2022; jobs for logisticians are expected to grow 22 percent – twice the average for all occupations. ∎

... MORE HOT JOBS

Market research analyst

➤ The growing trend of mining the mounds of data on customers to understand their wants and to measure the effectiveness of marketing strategies is increasing demand for these experts. Openings are expected to **grow by nearly one-third** through 2022. While median earnings were **$60,300** in 2012, the top end was much higher. A master's in market research, marketing, statistics or business administration "will give you a leg up," says Roger Moncarz, branch chief in the employment projections program at BLS – potentially to well over **$100,000.**

Health care manager

➤ With health care costs accounting for nearly one-fifth of the U.S. economy, there are plenty of opportunities for people with management skills and an interest in medicine and health. An aging population and emphasis on care coordination and resource management are driving the **23 percent projected growth** in jobs by 2022; the BLS anticipates an added 150,000 openings. Master's degrees in business or public administration are a common credential. The median pay in 2012: **$88,580.** Top earners made over **$150,000.**

Financial analyst

➤ The market for people who guide individual and corporate or mutual-fund investment decisions is projected to **grow 16 percent** by 2022, opening up some 100,000 jobs. Median annual earnings were about **$77,000** in 2012, but salaries can easily hit **$150,000.** A growing range of investment products, the implementation of regulations put in place since the financial meltdown, and the need for in-depth knowledge of other developed and emerging markets are examples of what's driving demand.

Today is the day to stop saying "someday."

———

Every day students are writing their futures at the

University of Nebraska. From an educator named his state's

Teacher of the Year, to the military member earning a degree while

serving his country overseas, to the health care professional combating

global public health issues — no two stories are the same. Our campuses

understand this as we partner with students around the world to turn

someday into today.

———

**Read some of our students' stories and
explore more than 100 programs
at online.nebraska.edu**

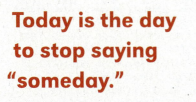

Schools of Business

THE TOP MBA PROGRAMS

Rank School	Overall score	Peer assessment score (5.0=highest)	Recruiter assessment score (5.0=highest)	'14 full-time average undergrad GPA	'14 full-time average GMAT score	'14 full-time acceptance rate	'14 average starting salary and bonus	'14 graduates employed at graduation	'14 Employed 3 months after graduation	'14 out-of-state tuition and fees	'14 total full-time enrollment
1. Stanford University (CA)	100	4.8	4.6	3.74	732	7.1%	$142,834	73.6%	92.1%	$61,875	825
2. Harvard University (MA)	99	4.8	4.6	3.67	726	11.0%	$144,750	76.9%	89.4%	$69,593	1,867
3. University of Pennsylvania (Wharton)	98	4.7	4.5	3.60	728	20.7%	$142,574	84.3%	95.6%	$68,210	1,711
4. University of Chicago (Booth)	97	4.7	4.4	3.60	724	23.5%	$137,615	87.4%	97.2%	$62,561	1,181
5. Massachusetts Institute of Technology (Sloan)	96	4.7	4.5	3.58	713	13.8%	$142,936	79.6%	92.8%	$63,750	812
6. Northwestern University (Kellogg) (IL)	93	4.6	4.4	3.60	713	23.2%	$136,357	80.7%	88.6%	$62,321	1,047
7. University of California–Berkeley (Haas)	91	4.5	4.2	3.62	717	13.2%	$140,935	72.9%	86.7%	$54,066	503
8. Columbia University (NY)	90	4.4	4.2	3.50	716	18.2%	$139,006	75.7%	91.1%	$65,790	1,270
9. Dartmouth College (Tuck) (NH)	89	4.2	4.0	3.54	716	22.1%	$142,489	83.8%	93.8%	$64,680	558
10. University of Virginia (Darden)	87	4.2	4.0	3.50	706	26.0%	$136,474	86.8%	93.4%	$59,268	633
11. New York University (Stern)	86	4.2	4.0	3.52	721	18.1%	$135,933	74.9%	90.4%	$63,168	798
11. University of Michigan–Ann Arbor (Ross)	86	4.4	4.0	3.40	702	N/A	$140,497	81.3%	89.7%	$59,778	886
13. Duke University (Fuqua) (NC)	85	4.3	4.1	3.43	690	25.1%	$137,154	81.8%	89.8%	$60,313	876
13. Yale University (CT)	85	4.1	4.3	3.53	719	23.7%	$126,871	69.4%	88.9%	$60,775	625
15. University of California–Los Angeles (Anderson)	82	4.1	3.8	3.50	715	17.8%	$127,535	69.9%	88.6%	$56,159	708
16. Cornell University (Johnson) (NY)	81	4.2	3.9	3.35	692	30.0%	$132,316	79.6%	89.8%	$60,792	585
17. University of Texas–Austin (McCombs)	80	4.0	4.0	3.40	690	28.5%	$126,160	75.0%	91.3%	$49,532	551
18. U. of North Carolina–Chapel Hill (Kenan-Flagler)	76	3.8	3.6	3.42	697	38.8%	$124,641	75.9%	89.0%	$55,908	562
19. Washington University in St. Louis (Olin)	75	3.7	3.3	3.43	699	26.7%	$111,974	84.5%	96.9%	$52,273	281
20. Carnegie Mellon University (Tepper) (PA)	74	3.9	3.6	3.24	687	31.2%	$131,865	75.5%	88.3%	$59,002	421
21. Emory University (Goizueta) (GA)	73	3.7	3.4	3.30	678	30.7%	$128,347	81.7%	94.8%	$48,634	384
21. Indiana University–Bloomington (Kelley)	73	3.8	3.7	3.34	668	33.1%	$119,581	77.5%	88.1%	$46,560	391
23. University of Washington (Foster)	72	3.5	3.2	3.43	682	22.9%	$125,367	83.1%	95.8%	$44,175	248
24. Georgetown University (McDonough) (DC)	70	3.6	3.5	3.34	691	47.4%	$118,938	70.3%	88.5%	$55,018	528
25. University of Notre Dame (Mendoza) (IN)	69	3.5	3.5	3.38	686	34.8%	$115,694	71.7%	87.7%	$47,450	323
25. University of Southern California (Marshall)	69	3.8	3.3	3.35	684	31.6%	$114,129	64.4%	86.8%	$58,158	431
27. Texas A&M University–College Station (Mays)	68	3.3	3.3	3.47	647	23.6%	$110,219	78.4%	96.1%	$36,376	113

BRETT ZIEGLER FOR USN&WR

Northwestern University, No. 6

▶ More @ usnews.com/grad

THE TOP MBA PROGRAMS continued

Rank	School	Overall score	'14 Peer assessment score (5.0=highest)	'14 Recruiter assessment score (5.0=highest)	'14 full-time average undergrad GPA	'14 full-time average GMAT score	'14 full-time acceptance rate	'14 average starting salary and bonus	'14 graduates employed at graduation	Employed 3 months after graduation	'14 out-of-state tuition and fees	'14 total full-time enrollment
27.	University of Minnesota–Twin Cities (Carlson)	68	3.5	3.3	3.42	683	38.7%	$112,828	72.4%	89.7%	$49,322	220
27.	Vanderbilt University (Owen) (TN)	68	3.5	3.3	3.32	688	41.3%	$113,830	77.1%	90.8%	$48,372	334
30.	Arizona State University (Carey)	67	3.4	3.2	3.46	673	24.5%	$112,884	69.2%	90.4%	$41,736	136
30.	Georgia Institute of Technology (Scheller)	67	3.3	3.3	3.31	676	22.7%	$115,279	78.6%	92.9%	$40,744	127
30.	Ohio State University (Fisher)	67	3.5	3.1	3.48	661	31.2%	$112,883	68.0%	92.8%	$49,099	220
33.	Brigham Young University (Marriott) (UT)	66	3.1	3.3	3.49	667	53.8%	$111,005	80.6%	91.7%	$23,240	301
33.	Rice University (Jones) (TX)	66	3.4	3.0	3.40	676	26.2%	$117,074	74.3%	87.6%	$53,511	214
33.	University of Texas–Dallas	66	2.9	4.2	3.50	673	26.2%	$83,901	75.6%	90.2%	$30,946	128
33.	University of Wisconsin–Madison	66	3.6	3.1	3.35	668	29.0%	$110,411	71.8%	88.2%	$27,815	199
37.	Michigan State University (Broad)	65	3.4	3.1	3.30	666	28.5%	$104,348	76.5%	95.6%	$44,895	150
37.	Pennsylvania State Univ.–University Park (Smeal)	65	3.4	3.3	3.43	649	24.0%	$114,971	75.0%	85.3%	$38,044	157
37.	University of Florida (Hough)	65	3.3	2.8	3.50	687	24.0%	$94,986	79.6%	92.6%	$31,075	117
37.	University of Rochester (Simon) (NY)	65	3.1	3.0	3.55	684	32.1%	$101,961	79.0%	95.0%	$52,696	213
41.	Temple University (Fox) (PA)	62	3.0	3.0	3.61	641	41.5%	$98,380	78.6%	95.2%	$41,862	117
41.	University of Maryland–College Park (Smith)	62	3.4	3.0	3.33	662	28.7%	$102,936	68.5%	88.8%	$49,413	200
43.	Boston University	61	3.1	2.9	3.41	670	30.5%	$108,558	65.3%	89.8%	$46,424	273
43.	University of Iowa (Tippie)	61	3.2	2.8	3.39	669	36.7%	$94,500	72.1%	93.0%	$41,240	118
45.	Boston College (Carroll)	60	3.2	3.1	3.37	664	41.6%	$94,963	67.9%	91.0%	$43,880	193
45.	Wake Forest University (NC)	60	3.2	3.1	3.33	652	39.9%	$94,298	74.1%	92.6%	N/A	95
47.	University of Illinois–Urbana-Champaign	59	3.5	3.1	3.30	659	25.5%	$98,406	58.2%	79.7%	$37,710	169
48.	Rutgers, The State U. of N.J.–Newark & New Brunswick	58	2.9	2.8	3.38	646	41.3%	$105,785	75.8%	93.5%	$47,805	201
48.	Southern Methodist University (Cox) (TX)	58	3.0	3.1	3.22	650	49.0%	$112,071	69.9%	92.5%	$49,370	206
48.	University of California–Davis	58	3.3	2.9	3.27	688	15.3%	$99,952	51.4%	85.7%	$50,663	95
48.	University of Connecticut	58	2.9	2.8	3.49	630	48.3%	$107,852	75.8%	93.9%	$33,326	75
48.	University of Pittsburgh (Katz)	58	3.2	3.1	3.36	620	24.9%	$83,936	73.6%	96.2%	$56,032†	161
53.	Purdue University–West Lafayette (Krannert) (IN)	57	3.4	3.3	3.34	617	28.7%	$108,426	63.8%	75.9%	$43,829	180
53.	University of California–Irvine (Merage)	57	3.3	3.0	3.43	657	22.7%	$88,519	56.2%	82.2%	$47,571	187
53.	University of Georgia (Terry)	57	3.4	3.0	3.32	646	33.7%	$92,432	61.1%	80.6%	$33,054	95
56.	University of Arizona (Eller)	56	3.3	3.1	3.32	646	51.4%	$83,207	62.9%	82.9%	$44,720	81
57.	Northeastern University (MA)	55	2.9	3.1	3.24	655	22.2%	$77,751	70.8%	93.8%	$1,433*	235
58.	Baylor University (Hankamer) (TX)	54	2.9	2.9	3.43	629	37.4%	$74,421	72.2%	94.4%	$38,520	87
58.	George Washington University (DC)	54	3.1	3.1	3.24	648	45.4%	$89,671	56.8%	85.2%	$1,545*	185
58.	University of Alabama (Manderson)	54	2.7	3.2	3.50	659	54.5%	$68,763	63.5%	90.5%	$27,780	164
61.	Tulane University (Freeman) (LA)	53	3.0	2.7	3.38	649	63.5%	$86,925	67.9%	87.5%	$53,405	90
62.	Babson College (Olin) (MA)	52	3.3	3.1	3.13	630	66.8%	$87,057	59.2%	83.4%	$98,144†	378
63.	Case Western Reserve Univ. (Weatherhead) (OH)	51	3.2	2.9	3.32	630	67.9%	$83,465	59.1%	81.8%	$45,140	108
63.	Iowa State University	51	2.7	2.8	3.45	636	52.7%	$61,332	76.2%	95.2%	$23,615	70
63.	Texas Christian University (Neeley)	51	2.7	3.0	3.27	638	48.4%	$90,117	65.8%	92.1%	$46,300	94
63.	University of Arkansas–Fayetteville (Walton)	51	3.1	2.5	3.46	650	60.6%	$66,059	76.0%	84.0%	$40,944	76
63.	University of California–San Diego (Rady)	51	3.0	2.7	3.43	660	41.3%	$75,697	45.9%	86.5%	$54,060	102
63.	University of Oklahoma (Price)	51	2.9	2.9	3.39	628	53.1%	$72,817	70.8%	87.5%	$31,346	76
63.	University of Tennessee–Knoxville	51	3.0	2.9	3.32	605	73.8%	$78,695	73.7%	91.2%	$42,050	145

SPECIALTIES

PROGRAMS RANKED BEST BY BUSINESS SCHOOL DEANS AND MBA PROGRAM DIRECTORS

ACCOUNTING
1. University of Texas–Austin (McCombs)
2. University of Pennsylvania (Wharton)
3. University of Illinois–Urbana-Champaign
4. University of Chicago (Booth)
5. Stanford University (CA)
6. Brigham Young University (Marriott) (UT)
7. University of Michigan–Ann Arbor (Ross)
8. New York University (Stern)
9. University of Southern California (Marshall)
10. Indiana University–Bloomington (Kelley)
10. University of North Carolina–Chapel Hill (Kenan-Flagler)
12. Columbia University (NY)
12. Ohio State University (Fisher)

14. University of Notre Dame (Mendoza) (IN)

ENTREPRENEURSHIP
1. Babson College (Olin) (MA)
2. Stanford University (CA)
3. Massachusetts Institute of Technology (Sloan)
4. Harvard University (MA)
5. University of California–Berkeley (Haas)
6. University of Pennsylvania (Wharton)
7. University of Michigan–Ann Arbor (Ross)
8. University of Texas–Austin (McCombs)
9. Indiana University–Bloomington (Kelley)
10. University of Southern California (Marshall)
11. Northwestern Univ. (Kellogg) (IL)

*Tuition is reported on a per-credit-hour basis. †Total program tuition
Sources: U.S. News and the schools. Assessment data collected by Ipsos Public Affairs.

INSPIRED BY WORLD-RENOWNED RESEARCH.

RECRUITED BY MORE THAN 500 TOP COMPANIES.

ENHANCED BY A LIFELONG PROFESSIONAL COMMUNITY.

Our globally recognized faculty and forward-thinking curriculum provide a phenomenal business education at every level. The sure path for advancing your career starts right here. Now let's begin.

go.wisc.edu/WSB

WISCONSIN SCHOOL OF BUSINESS

UNIVERSITY OF WISCONSIN–MADISON

TOGETHER FORWARD®

SPECIALTIES continued

11. **University of Arizona** (Eller)
13. **Loyola Marymount University** (CA)
13. **Rice University** (Jones) (TX)
13. **University of Virginia** (Darden)

EXECUTIVE MBA
1. **University of Chicago** (Booth)
2. **University of Pennsylvania** (Wharton)
3. **Northwestern Univ.** (Kellogg) (IL)
4. **Duke University** (Fuqua) (NC)
5. **Columbia University** (NY)
6. **University of Michigan–Ann Arbor** (Ross)
7. **New York University** (Stern)
8. **University of California–Los Angeles** (Anderson)
9. **University of California–Berkeley** (Haas)
10. **University of North Carolina– Chapel Hill** (Kenan-Flagler)
11. **University of Virginia** (Darden)
12. **Cornell University** (Johnson) (NY)

FINANCE
1. **University of Pennsylvania** (Wharton)
2. **University of Chicago** (Booth)
3. **New York University** (Stern)
4. **Columbia University** (NY)
5. **Stanford University** (CA)
6. **Massachusetts Institute of Technology** (Sloan)
7. **University of California–Berkeley** (Haas)
8. **University of California–Los Angeles** (Anderson)
9. **Northwestern Univ.** (Kellogg) (IL)
9. **University of Michigan–Ann Arbor** (Ross)

11. **Harvard University** (MA)
12. **University of Rochester** (Simon) (NY)
13. **University of Texas–Austin** (McCombs)
14. **Creighton University** (NE)

INFORMATION SYSTEMS
1. **Massachusetts Institute of Technology** (Sloan)
2. **Carnegie Mellon University** (Tepper) (PA)
3. **University of Arizona** (Eller)
3. **University of Minnesota–Twin Cities** (Carlson)
5. **University of Texas–Austin** (McCombs)
6. **University of Maryland–College Park** (Smith)
7. **New York University** (Stern)
8. **University of Pennsylvania** (Wharton)
9. **Georgia State University** (Robinson)

INTERNATIONAL
1. **University of South Carolina** (Moore)
2. **University of Pennsylvania** (Wharton)
3. **Thunderbird School of Global Management** (AZ)
4. **University of Michigan–Ann Arbor** (Ross)
5. **Columbia University** (NY)
6. **New York University** (Stern)
7. **Harvard University** (MA)
7. **University of California–Berkeley** (Haas)
9. **Stanford University** (CA)

10. **University of Southern California** (Marshall)
11. **Duke University** (Fuqua) (NC)
12. **Georgetown University** (McDonough) (DC)

MANAGEMENT
1. **Harvard University** (MA)
2. **Stanford University** (CA)
3. **University of Michigan–Ann Arbor** (Ross)
4. **University of Pennsylvania** (Wharton)
5. **Northwestern Univ.** (Kellogg) (IL)
6. **Dartmouth College** (Tuck) (NH)
7. **University of Virginia** (Darden)
8. **University of California–Berkeley** (Haas)
9. **Columbia University** (NY)
9. **Duke University** (Fuqua) (NC)
11. **University of Chicago** (Booth)

MARKETING
1. **Northwestern Univ.** (Kellogg) (IL)
2. **University of Pennsylvania** (Wharton)
3. **Stanford University** (CA)
4. **Harvard University** (MA)
5. **Duke University** (Fuqua) (NC)
6. **University of Michigan–Ann Arbor** (Ross)
7. **Columbia University** (NY)
8. **University of Chicago** (Booth)
9. **New York University** (Stern)
10. **University of California–Berkeley** (Haas)
11. **University of Texas–Austin** (McCombs)
12. **University of California–Los Angeles** (Anderson)

NONPROFIT
1. **Yale University** (CT)
2. **Stanford University** (CA)
3. **University of California–Berkeley** (Haas)
4. **Harvard University** (MA)
5. **Northwestern Univ.** (Kellogg) (IL)

PRODUCTION/OPERATIONS
1. **Massachusetts Institute of Technology** (Sloan)
2. **Carnegie Mellon University** (Tepper) (PA)
3. **University of Michigan–Ann Arbor** (Ross)
4. **University of Pennsylvania** (Wharton)
5. **Stanford University** (CA)
6. **Northwestern Univ.** (Kellogg) (IL)
7. **Purdue University–West Lafayette** (Krannert) (IN)
8. **Harvard University** (MA)
9. **Columbia University** (NY)
10. **Ohio State University** (Fisher)

SUPPLY CHAIN/LOGISTICS
1. **Massachusetts Institute of Technology** (Sloan)
2. **Michigan State University** (Broad)
3. **Arizona State University** (Carey)
4. **Ohio State University** (Fisher)
5. **Pennsylvania State University– University Park** (Smeal)
6. **Carnegie Mellon Univ.** (Tepper) (PA)
7. **Stanford University** (CA)
8. **University of Tennessee–Knoxville**
9. **University of Michigan–Ann Arbor** (Ross)
10. **University of Pennsylvania** (Wharton)

METHODOLOGY

The 464 master's programs in business administration accredited by the Association to Advance Collegiate Schools of Business were surveyed; 385 responded, with 126 MBA programs providing the data needed to calculate rankings based on a weighted average of eight indicators:

Quality assessment: Two surveys were conducted in fall 2014. Business school deans and directors of accredited MBA programs were asked to rate the overall academic quality of the MBA programs at each school on a scale from marginal (1) to outstanding (5); 40 percent responded. The average score is weighted by .25

in the ranking model. Corporate recruiters and company contacts who hired MBA grads, whose names were supplied by previously ranked MBA programs, also were asked to rate the programs. The last three years' recruiter responses were averaged and are weighted by .15 in the model.

Placement success (weighted by .35): Based on average starting salary and bonus (40 percent of this measure) and employment rates for full-time 2014 graduates at graduation (20 percent) and three months later (40 percent). Calculations for MBA placement rates exclude those not seeking jobs and those for

whom the school has no information. To be included in the full-time MBA rankings, a program needed 20 or more of its 2014 full-time graduates to be seeking employment. Salary is based on the number of graduates reporting data. Signing bonus is weighted by the proportion of graduates reporting salaries who received a bonus since not everyone with a base salary received a signing bonus.

Student selectivity (.25): The strength of full-time students entering in the fall of 2014 was measured by the average GMAT and GRE scores (65 percent), average undergraduate GPA (30

percent), and the proportion of applicants accepted by the school (5 percent).

Overall rank: Data were standardized about their means, and standardized scores were weighted, totaled and rescaled so that the top school received 100; others received their percentage of the top score.

Specialty rankings: These rankings are based solely on ratings by educators at peer schools. Business school deans and MBA program heads were asked to nominate up to 10 programs for excellence in each specialty. Those receiving the most nominations are listed.

Best Part-Time MBA Programs

Part-time business programs play a vital role for working people who can't go to school full time because of family or financial reasons. The U.S. News part-time MBA ranking is based on five factors: average peer assessment score (50 percent of the overall score); average GMAT score and GRE scores of part-time MBA students entering in the fall of 2014 (15 percent); average undergraduate GPA (5 percent); work experience (15 percent); and the percentage of the fall 2014 MBA enrollment that is part time (15 percent). The average peer assessment score is calculated from a fall 2014 survey that asked business school deans and MBA program directors at each of the nation's 323 part-time MBA programs to rate the other part-time programs on a 5-point scale, from marginal (1) to outstanding (5); 41 percent responded. To be eligible for the part-time ranking, a program needed to be accredited by the Association to Advance Collegiate Schools of Business and have at least 20 students enrolled part time in the fall of 2014; 289 programs met those criteria.

THE TOP PART-TIME PROGRAMS

Rank	School	Overall score	Peer assessment score (5.0=highest)	'14 part-time average GMAT score	'14 part-time acceptance rate	'14 total part-time enrollment
1.	University of California–Berkeley (Haas)	100	4.6	692	43.4%	794
2.	University of Chicago (Booth)	96	4.6	679	N/A	1,378
3.	Northwestern University (Kellogg) (IL)	95	4.6	672	N/A	727
4.	New York University (Stern)	90	4.3	670	60.8%	1,696
5.	University of California–Los Angeles (Anderson)	88	4.2	673	64.1%	920
6.	University of Michigan–Ann Arbor (Ross)	83	4.3	644	N/A	445
7.	Carnegie Mellon University (Tepper) (PA)	79	4.0	654	76.3%	173
7.	University of Texas–Austin (McCombs)	79	4.0	638	77.9%	438
9.	Ohio State University (Fisher)	75	3.8	611	65.2%	318
10.	University of Minnesota–Twin Cities (Carlson)	74	3.7	598	84.7%	1,122
10.	University of Southern California (Marshall)	74	3.9	622	57.8%	620
12.	Indiana University–Bloomington (Kelley)	72	3.9	619	48.1%	304
13.	Georgetown University (McDonough) (DC)	71	3.7	669	57.9%	385
13.	University of Washington (Foster)	71	3.6	632	64.5%	317
15.	Emory University (Goizueta) (GA)	70	3.8	631	75.2%	263
16.	Rice University (Jones) (TX)	69	3.6	627	72.3%	262
16.	University of Massachusetts–Amherst (Isenberg)	69	3.1	563	92.4%	1,185
16.	University of South Carolina (Moore)	69	3.2	617	84.0%	437
16.	Virginia Tech (Pamplin)	69	3.2	610	88.6%	148
20.	Georgia Institute of Technology (Scheller)	68	3.5	623	77.2%	369
20.	Temple University (Fox) (PA)	68	3.1	580	67.2%	510
20.	University of Wisconsin–Madison	68	3.7	606	94.1%	155
20.	Wake Forest University (NC)	68	3.4	583	90.0%	303
24.	University of Iowa (Tippie)	67	3.4	560	87.6%	825
24.	Washington University in St. Louis (Olin)	67	3.8	562	86.7%	362
26.	University of Maryland–College Park (Smith)	66	3.5	590	88.7%	711
27.	Arizona State University (Carey)	65	3.5	576	72.1%	273
27.	University of Florida (Hough)	65	3.4	601	72.4%	377
29.	Case Western Reserve University (Weatherhead) (OH)	64	3.4	588	87.5%	106
29.	University of California–Davis	64	3.3	583	77.5%	438
29.	University of Texas–Dallas	64	3.1	629	66.7%	699
32.	Texas A&M University–College Station (Mays)	63	3.4	607	71.9%	92
33.	Miami University (Farmer) (OH)	62	2.8	556	59.6%	110
33.	University of Arizona (Eller)	62	3.4	524	81.6%	171
35.	Boston University	61	3.3	602	87.9%	678
35.	College of William and Mary (Mason) (VA)	61	3.0	578	92.9%	173
37.	Boston College (Carroll)	60	3.4	586	93.2%	391
37.	Clemson University (SC)	60	2.9	609	87.6%	256
37.	Santa Clara University (Leavey) (CA)	60	3.0	621	71.2%	552
37.	Southern Methodist University (Cox) (TX)	60	3.3	601	66.0%	267
37.	University of California–Irvine (Merage)	60	3.4	567	78.4%	346
37.	University of Georgia (Terry)	60	3.4	530	95.3%	244
37.	Villanova University (PA)	60	2.9	617	74.5%	144
44.	Babson College (Olin) (MA)	59	3.3	580	98.0%	292
44.	Georgia State University (Robinson)	59	3.1	615	50.7%	628
46.	George Washington University (DC)	58	3.2	598	71.1%	336
46.	University of Cincinnati (Lindner)	58	2.8	608	73.3%	145
48.	Colorado State University	57	2.7	562	99.2%	998
48.	Rutgers, The State U. of N.J.–Newark and New Brunswick	57	2.9	589	76.6%	988

▶ More @ usnews.com/grad

Rank School	Overall score	Peer assessment score (5.0=highest)	'14 part-time average GMAT score	'14 part-time acceptance rate	'14 total part-time enrollment
48. University of Delaware (Lerner)	57	2.6	623	88.1%	231
48. University of Houston (Bauer)	57	3.0	595	59.2%	433
52. DePaul University (Kellstadt) (IL)	56	3.0	577	78.0%	887
52. Loyola Marymount University (CA)	56	3.0	569	49.8%	206
52. Loyola University Chicago (Quinlan)	56	2.9	569	47.4%	635
52. Pepperdine University (Graziadio) (CA)	56	3.1	538	87.7%	506
52. University of Colorado–Boulder (Leeds)	56	3.3	590	86.8%	81
52. University of Connecticut	56	3.0	550	76.3%	889
58. CUNY Bernard M. Baruch College (Zicklin)	55	2.9	603	48.5%	810
58. University of California–San Diego (Rady)	55	3.1	573	85.2%	106
58. University of Oklahoma (Price)	55	2.9	601	78.7%	148
61. Purdue University–West Lafayette (Krannert) (IN)	54	3.4	498	79.1%	123
61. Seattle University (Albers)	54	2.8	581	69.2%	585
61. University of Kansas	54	3.1	557	82.1%	168
64. Bentley University (McCallum) (MA)	53	2.8	603	87.4%	248
64. Lehigh University (PA)	53	2.6	615	85.2%	159
64. University of Nebraska–Lincoln	53	3.0	595	72.9%	85
64. University of Pittsburgh (Katz)	53	3.2	554	87.2%	477
64. University of Richmond (Robins) (VA)	53	2.8	591	87.5%	84
69. Florida State University	52	3.0	571	62.0%	54
69. George Mason University (VA)	52	2.8	575	45.6%	251
69. University of Louisville (KY)	52	2.8	573	48.6%	142
69. University of Utah (Eccles)	52	3.0	565	76.5%	338
73. John Carroll University (Boler) (OH)	51	2.5	554	96.5%	117
73. Portland State University (OR)	51	2.5	616	61.0%	47
73. Seton Hall University (Stillman) (NJ)	51	2.6	563	52.3%	372
73. St. Louis University (Cook)	51	3.0	548	90.1%	254

University of Washington offers a full- and a part-time program.

THE TOP PART-TIME PROGRAMS continued

Rank	School	Overall score	Peer assessment score (5.0=highest)	'14 part-time average GMAT score	'14 part-time acceptance rate	'14 total part-time enrollment
73.	University of Alabama–Birmingham	51	2.7	545	86.7%	301
73.	University of Kentucky (Gatton)	51	2.8	648	91.7%	122
73.	University of Rochester (Simon) (NY)	51	3.3	N/A	97.6%	248
73.	University of San Diego	51	2.9	595	75.6%	108
81.	Elon University (Love) (NC)	50	2.5	569	71.2%	121
81.	Gonzaga University (WA)	50	2.8	565	70.7%	168
81.	James Madison University (VA)	50	2.5	548	81.0%	47
81.	University of Portland (Pamplin) (OR)	50	2.6	563	78.3%	65
81.	University of Wisconsin–Milwaukee (Lubar)	50	2.9	550	52.7%	447
86.	Kennesaw State University (Coles) (GA)	49	2.5	567	64.6%	190
86.	Oklahoma State University (Spears)	49	2.7	589	76.9%	124
86.	University of Massachusetts–Lowell	49	2.3	585	86.0%	556
86.	University of North Carolina–Charlotte (Belk)	49	2.6	584	62.5%	301
86.	University of Wisconsin–Eau Claire	49	2.6	536	89.8%	310
91.	Butler University (IN)	48	2.5	579	78.2%	186
91.	Fordham University (NY)	48	2.9	579	85.2%	296
91.	Loyola University Maryland (Sellinger)	48	2.7	549	91.6%	345
91.	University of Colorado–Denver	48	2.8	593	64.9%	549
91.	University of Denver (Daniels)	48	2.8	593	89.7%	138
91.	University of North Carolina–Greensboro (Bryan)	48	2.5	597	81.0%	98
97.	Marquette University (WI)	47	2.9	563	74.3%	263
97.	University of Nebraska–Omaha	47	2.5	581	52.8%	253
99.	American University (Kogod) (DC)	46	2.7	550	89.9%	95
99.	Texas Christian University (Neeley)	46	2.8	546	98.0%	192
99.	University of Missouri–Kansas City (Bloch)	46	2.7	550	55.2%	232
99.	University of New Mexico (Anderson)	46	2.7	605	N/A	200
103.	Creighton University (NE)	45	2.7	530	96.0%	188
103.	North Carolina State University (Jenkins)	45	2.5	565	92.4%	204
103.	University of Nevada–Las Vegas	45	2.4	585	64.6%	160
103.	University of Texas–San Antonio	45	2.6	585	55.6%	164
103.	University of Washington–Bothell	45	2.3	545	64.4%	93
103.	Worcester Polytechnic Institute (MA)	45	2.4	550	66.2%	282
109.	Northeastern University (MA)	44	2.8	567	80.0%	390
109.	San Diego State University	44	2.8	585	51.8%	253
109.	University of Illinois–Chicago (Liautaud)	44	2.8	568	65.6%	175
109.	Xavier University (Williams) (OH)	44	2.6	511	86.2%	493
113.	Claremont Graduate University (Drucker) (CA)	43	3.0	535	100.0%	25
113.	Hofstra University (Zarb) (NY)	43	2.5	559	74.0%	939
113.	Minnesota State University–Mankato	43	2.0	555	73.3%	54
113.	Rutgers, The State University of New Jersey–Camden	43	2.7	500	89.3%	201
113.	St. Joseph's University (Haub) (PA)	43	2.6	537	69.3%	1,211
113.	University of Alabama–Huntsville	43	2.4	549	87.2%	143
113.	University of Michigan–Dearborn	43	2.4	581	70.5%	200
113.	University of St. Thomas (MN)	43	2.6	521	98.0%	708
113.	Virginia Commonwealth University	43	2.5	570	72.3%	180
122.	Grand Valley State University (Seidman) (MI)	42	2.1	573	91.8%	184
122.	Northern Illinois University	42	2.3	500	93.4%	624
122.	Ohio University	42	2.5	N/A	88.4%	101
122.	Old Dominion University (VA)	42	2.4	540	36.5%	172
122.	Queens University of Charlotte (McColl) (NC)	42	2.1	560	82.5%	107
122.	University of Central Florida	42	2.5	N/A	53.9%	252
122.	University of Minnesota–Duluth (Labovitz)	42	2.4	518	71.4%	42
122.	University of Wisconsin–Oshkosh	42	2.1	597	100.0%	391
130.	Boise State University (ID)	41	2.4	583	87.9%	54
130.	California State University–Sacramento	41	2.2	585	55.1%	175
130.	Shippensburg University of Pennsylvania (Grove)	41	1.9	505	88.2%	392
130.	University of Colorado–Colorado Springs	41	2.5	532	61.9%	230
130.	University of Massachusetts–Boston	41	2.6	570	80.8%	188
130.	University of South Florida	41	2.4	553	70.5%	778

Note: The data listed for acceptance rate and enrollment are for informational purposes only and are not used in the computation of the part-time MBA program rankings. N/A=Data were not provided by the school. Sources: U.S. News and the schools. Assessment data collected by Ipsos Public Affairs.

CHAPTER 2

Education

At the University
of Wisconsin–
Madison

THE U.S. NEWS RANKINGS

DARREN HAUCK FOR USNWR

Learning BY Doing

STUDENTS THRIVE ON DISCOVERY, AND FUTURE TEACHERS GET NEEDED PRACTICE

By **CHRISTOPHER J. GEARON**

In Serena Cox's 6th grade science class in Greenville, South Carolina, a visitor can glimpse the future. For a unit on vertebrates, students work busily in teams of three or four, helping the Greenville Zoo bring to life a new exhibit on Earth's varied biomes. Cox, 45, asks each student to select a biome and design signage about animals inhabiting it to be used for the zoo's exhibit. In class, students "meet" zoologists and curators virtually to learn about the animals, conduct their own research and work on assignments. Instruction on vertebrates, which traditionally would take place in a lecture, has been handled instead as homework, taking advantage of PowerPoint, Google Docs and video presentations.

"Flipping the classroom" this way to emphasize group problem-solving gets students more deeply engaged with the material, says Cox, who moves around her room at Dr. Phinnize J. Fisher Middle School observing, redirecting and disci-

plining as needed. "I'm learning more about how to be a teacher-guide," she says, "rather than a teacher-instructor." Cox is earning a certification in science, technology, engineering, arts and math – STEAM – education and project-based learning in a two-year graduate program at Clemson University.

Clemson is one of the forward-looking education schools heeding the call to better arm teachers with the know-how they need to excel in the classroom, particularly in science and math. After years of highly critical report cards on ed schools' performance, citing everything from too little hands-on classroom time to high student dropout rates, the programs training teachers are now being held to higher standards. In November, the administration proposed requiring states to develop rating systems for teacher-prep programs that would rely on graduates' job placement and retention rates as well as the achieve-

ment of the K-12 students graduates teach. That proposal follows closely on the heels of an overhaul of the criteria ed schools must meet to be accredited by the Council for the Accreditation of Educator Preparation. That more rigorous framework, which takes effect in 2016, includes tougher admissions requirements for prospective teachers and much more teaching practice than has been the norm.

The encouraging news is that programs are making great strides, says Melinda George, president of the National Commission on Teaching and America's Future. Still, anybody looking at grad schools today should compare their offerings carefully. It remains "a highly variable landscape," cautions James Cibulka, president of CAEP.

Embracing technology will clearly be one key to emphasizing the in-depth study and analysis – the questioning and discovery – that the Common Core State Standards and Next Generation Science Standards call for. (The goal of the administration's ConnectED effort is to get nearly all schools

wired for next-generation broadband by 2018.) Cox took a digital media and learning course, for example, that taught her to integrate user-friendly tools like the filmmaking program iMovie and PowToon, which allows students to create a digital presentation that uses animation. "With the change in standards and technology access, teachers' roles are changing. The teacher needs to move from being the person who does all of the talking and thinking to putting the students at the center of their learning," says Lisa Dieker, a professor and director of the Ph.D. in Exceptional Education Program at the University of Central Florida.

To that end, a growing number of schools, including UCF, the University of Connecticut and the University of Indianapolis as well as Clemson, have put new emphasis on training would-be teachers to guide students as they learn the material by questioning and experimenting rather than passively absorbing information and turning out projects that simply reflect it. Instead of dressing up for a "frontier feast" at the end of three weeks of lectures and homework assignments

Schools of Education

THE TOP SCHOOLS

Rank School	Overall score	Peer assessment score (5.0=highest)	Administrators/ experts assessment score (5.0=highest)	'14 mean GRE scores (verbal/ quantitative)[1]	'14 doctoral acceptance rate	'14 doctoral students/ faculty[2]	Doctorals granted/ faculty 2013-14	'14 funded research (in millions)	'14 funded research/faculty member (in thousands)	'14 total graduate education enrollment
1. Johns Hopkins University (MD)	100	3.9	4.4	165/164	28.9%	1.1	0.1	$53.6	$825.2	1,869
2. Harvard University (MA)	95	4.2	4.6	164/160	4.7%	4.9	1.0	$34.3	$779.4	876
3. Stanford University (CA)	94	4.6	4.8	163/158	4.6%	3.7	0.7	$27.1	$601.2	379
3. Vanderbilt University (Peabody) (TN)	94	4.4	4.7	163/158	5.7%	2.4	0.7	$41.0	$487.9	934
5. University of Wisconsin–Madison	93	4.3	4.4	155/152	30.7%	4.2	0.7	$66.0	$573.8	1,011
6. University of Washington	89	3.9	4.3	156/150	24.3%	4.8	0.9	$46.8	$883.4	917
7. Northwestern University (IL)	86	3.8	4.1	161/159*	8.1%	2.0	0.2	$23.7	$741.4	294
7. Teachers College, Columbia University (NY)	86	4.2	4.5	159/155	17.8%	4.7	1.3	$50.7	$342.7	4,911
7. University of Pennsylvania	86	3.9	4.2	161/158	5.0%	1.5	0.3	$40.0	$597.8	1,046
10. University of Texas–Austin	84	4.0	4.1	156/152	25.5%	4.4	1.2	$59.8	$559.1	1,124
11. University of Michigan–Ann Arbor	80	4.2	4.4	156/155	11.8%	4.9	0.7	$19.1	$397.9	630
12. University of Oregon	79	3.5	3.8	158/151	10.7%	3.7	0.8	$34.9	$872.0	516
13. Michigan State University	77	4.2	4.3	156/151	36.6%	5.2	0.9	$33.9	$320.0	1,970
13. University of California–Los Angeles	77	4.0	4.3	157/152	27.8%	9.8	1.8	$26.3	$598.6	747
15. Ohio State University	76	3.8	4.1	157/154	44.4%	2.9	0.5	$41.1	$326.4	1,018
15. University of Southern California (Rossier)	76	3.8	4.0	161/157	15.6%	14.0	5.6	$20.8	$1,042.0	1,748
17. Arizona State University	75	3.6	3.8	158/150	31.4%	1.7	0.9	$42.6	$546.7	2,428
17. University of California–Berkeley	75	4.2	4.5	157/152	14.0%	9.2	1.2	$13.8	$474.7	355
17. University of Kansas	75	3.6	4.0	154/152	44.9%	4.7	0.6	$41.6	$539.9	989
20. New York University (Steinhardt)	74	3.7	4.2	160/156	8.6%	3.7	0.8	$30.4	$227.0	3,049
21. University of Minnesota–Twin Cities	72	3.6	4.0	158/153	33.2%	4.7	0.9	$42.6	$340.7	1,749
22. University of Virginia (Curry)	70	3.9	4.2	159/154	15.4%	2.6	0.8	$15.8	$232.8	918
23. Boston College (Lynch)	69	3.7	4.0	160/157	7.1%	2.6	1.0	$15.0	$272.4	689
24. University of Illinois–Urbana-Champaign	67	4.0	4.1	157/154	29.5%	3.6	0.8	$12.4	$153.0	777
25. Indiana University–Bloomington	66	3.8	4.0	154/152	26.4%	3.3	0.7	$23.0	$241.6	934
26. University of Maryland–College Park	65	3.9	4.2	159/156	27.7%	4.2	0.8	$11.4	$126.3	961
27. University of Pittsburgh	64	3.5	3.8	156/153	37.2%	4.1	0.9	$23.8	$448.9	930
27. Virginia Commonwealth University	64	2.9	3.6	157/155	47.6%	1.8	1.3	$28.8	$654.5	898
29. University of Colorado–Boulder	63	3.6	3.7	161/155	16.8%	2.8	0.3	$8.1	$237.3	363
30. University of Florida	62	3.6	3.9	155/152	50.0%	4.1	1.4	$19.8	$324.5	1,106
31. University of California–Irvine	61	3.2	3.7	157/158*	19.0%	3.0	0.3	$8.5	$368.3	238
31. University of Connecticut (Neag)	61	3.6	3.8	160/152	38.7%	1.7	0.6	$14.3	$188.0	671
33. University of Georgia	60	3.8	4.1	153/152	45.4%	3.1	0.6	$16.1	$95.2	1,650
33. University of North Carolina–Chapel Hill	60	3.8	4.3	158/153	49.2%	5.2	0.7	$4.8	$110.5	424
33. Utah State University	60	2.9	3.0	154/153	33.9%	1.1	0.3	$39.7	$289.7	967
36. Pennsylvania State University–University Park	59	3.8	4.1	155/153	39.2%	4.0	0.9	$10.2	$91.1	1,070
37. University of Delaware	57	3.1	3.4	156/158	49.5%	2.6	0.7	$14.7	$407.9	321
38. Purdue University–West Lafayette (IN)	56	3.4	3.8	153/154	42.6%	2.1	0.5	$10.4	$160.4	567
38. University of California–Davis	56	3.4	3.7	157/151	28.8%	4.5	1.2	$6.6	$254.4	446
40. Florida State University	55	3.3	3.7	153/152	43.1%	4.7	0.9	$17.8	$231.0	1,181
40. University of Missouri	55	3.4	3.7	153/149	16.4%	4.1	0.8	$15.0	$162.6	1,507
40. University of Nebraska–Lincoln	55	3.4	3.6	152/152	46.6%	3.2	0.9	$17.6	$202.7	965
43. University of Arizona	54	3.6	3.8	155/153	54.2%	4.0	0.7	$6.7	$113.5	765
43. University of Illinois–Chicago	54	3.4	3.7	153/150	59.4%	4.0	0.6	$11.5	$279.6	726
43. University of Iowa	54	3.4	3.8	154/152	42.4%	5.0	0.6	$11.0	$148.1	720
46. College of William and Mary (VA)	53	3.3	4.1	157/149	54.8%	2.6	0.8	$6.3	$166.0	403
46. George Mason University (VA)	53	3.3	3.6	153/150	42.7%	2.4	0.5	$14.6	$200.5	2,220
46. Lehigh University (PA)	53	2.8	3.5	158/152	22.5%	3.3	0.7	$8.4	$291.2	477
46. Texas A&M University–College Station	53	3.5	3.7	152/151	56.1%	4.0	0.9	$18.2	$176.4	1,432
50. Syracuse University (NY)	52	3.4	3.9	152/148	39.6%	2.6	0.3	$5.9	$104.4	682

▶ More @ usnews.com/grad

Vanderbilt University,
tied at No. 3

Rank	School	Overall score	Peer assessment score (5.0=highest)	Administrators/experts assessment score (5.0=highest)	'14 mean GRE scores (verbal/quantitative)[1]	'14 doctoral acceptance rate	'14 doctoral students/faculty[2]	Doctorals granted/faculty 2013-14	'14 funded research (in millions)	'14 funded research/faculty member (in thousands)	'14 total graduate education enrollment
50.	University of Massachusetts–Amherst	52	3.4	3.8	155/152	47.0%	3.9	0.7	$8.8	$159.9	642
52.	Boston University	51	3.3	4.0	152/146	33.7%	3.1	0.5	$4.0	$119.9	543
52.	George Washington University (DC)	51	3.3	3.7	155/150	48.2%	4.8	1.5	$10.3	$210.7	1,498
52.	North Carolina State University–Raleigh	51	3.1	3.3	156/153	31.9%	3.1	0.8	$12.4	$169.8	1,362
52.	University of Tennessee–Knoxville	51	3.2	3.6	160/155	69.5%	1.7	0.3	$9.5	$89.9	705
56.	Temple University (PA)	50	3.1	3.5	156/151	40.7%	5.1	0.9	$9.7	$224.8	1,109
56.	University at Albany–SUNY	50	3.1	3.5	158/153	35.7%	2.6	0.7	$6.8	$133.5	944
56.	University of Miami (FL)	50	3.2	3.3	154/152	16.1%	3.1	0.5	$5.9	$188.9	322
59.	Fordham University (NY)	49	3.0	3.7	159/151	35.6%	7.2	1.5	$8.1	$253.4	1,082
59.	Loyola Marymount University (CA)	49	2.8	3.6	158/150	31.1%	2.3	0.8	$6.5	$196.6	1,412
59.	Rutgers, The State Univ. of N.J.–New Brunswick	49	3.4	3.6	155/152	41.0%	2.5	0.8	$9.4	$199.3	937
59.	Southern Illinois University–Carbondale	49	2.7	3.1	148/155	30.8%	2.2	0.6	$18.4	$235.7	1,026
59.	University of Kentucky	49	3.2	3.6	152/153	46.0%	3.0	0.4	$11.6	$132.9	726
59.	University of Louisville (KY)	49	3.0	3.7	156/152	31.0%	1.9	0.3	$4.7	$64.1	1,082
59.	University of Utah	49	3.2	3.4	150/151	24.2%	3.0	0.5	$8.4	$167.7	559
59.	Washington University in St. Louis	49	3.2	3.7	N/A/N/A	7.7%	1.1	0.1	$0.0	$0.0	27
67.	University of California–Santa Barbara (Gevirtz)	48	3.1	3.3	157/154	22.0%	5.1	0.8	$3.6	$90.9	327
67.	University of Vermont	48	2.9	3.5	156/149	51.2%	0.7	0.2	$7.2	$181.1	280
69.	Clemson University (Moore) (SC)	47	3.0	3.6	156/151	46.5%	1.3	0.5	$4.7	$71.5	466
69.	University of Oklahoma (Rainbolt)	47	3.0	3.8	153/148	45.7%	2.9	0.7	$5.4	$89.3	790
71.	Georgia State University	46	2.8	3.2	152/147	27.1%	2.4	0.4	$17.2	$159.3	1,592
71.	San Diego State University	46	3.2	3.2	150/144	71.1%	0.9	0.4	$15.6	$208.4	1,178
73.	CUNY–Graduate Center	45	3.0	3.7	155/153	22.2%	12.3	2.2	$1.1	$177.6	74
73.	University of Maine	45	2.7	3.2	154/153	27.3%	1.2	0.4	$5.6	$224.5	378
73.	University of Wisconsin–Milwaukee	45	3.2	3.4	152/148	22.9%	1.5	0.3	$3.2	$47.4	689
76.	Auburn University (AL)	44	3.2	3.8	149/146	38.2%	2.9	0.7	$4.9	$55.2	944
76.	University at Buffalo–SUNY	44	3.0	3.5	153/150	53.1%	4.5	1.2	$4.5	$91.3	1,081
76.	University of California–Riverside	44	3.0	3.5	154/151	46.6%	5.2	0.4	$1.4	$66.5	245
76.	University of Cincinnati	44	3.0	3.3	157/151	26.9%	1.7	0.4	$6.4	$67.2	1,526
76.	University of Hawaii–Manoa	44	2.7	2.8	153/147	50.5%	0.9	0.5	$23.4	$195.3	825
76.	University of Massachusetts–Boston	44	2.9	2.9	156/152	32.7%	1.4	0.4	$5.3	$112.6	985
76.	University of North Carolina–Charlotte	44	3.1	3.5	153/146	54.5%	1.1	0.3	$6.2	$62.1	1,375
83.	Baylor University (TX)	43	2.9	3.5	155/154	45.0%	1.2	0.3	$0.5	$9.9	136
83.	Iowa State University	43	3.1	3.5	154/147	63.2%	1.3	0.5	$3.0	$46.9	524
83.	University of Central Florida	43	3.0	2.9	153/149	53.3%	3.6	1.1	$9.9	$137.1	1,805
83.	University of North Carolina–Greensboro	43	3.1	3.5	156/149	51.0%	3.0	1.0	$4.8	$69.6	957
83.	University of South Florida	43	2.8	3.2	153/150	54.1%	2.9	0.6	$14.8	$136.2	1,372
88.	Boise State University (ID)	42	2.6	2.8	154/149	24.2%	1.1	0.2	$10.1	$154.6	1,292
88.	Brigham Young University–Provo (McKay) (UT)	42	2.8	3.5	156/153	37.1%	1.7	0.2	$1.0	$12.6	328
88.	Kansas State University	42	2.9	3.4	149/149	41.7%	2.1	0.9	$6.1	$141.6	1,004
88.	Louisiana State University–Baton Rouge	42	2.8	3.6	153/145	57.1%	1.8	0.5	$4.3	$72.4	372
88.	University of Alabama	42	3.2	3.7	150/147	56.0%	3.6	0.9	$4.2	$49.3	1,070
88.	University of Arkansas–Fayetteville	42	2.7	3.2	152/149	77.2%	1.9	0.7	$14.0	$170.6	1,123
88.	University of South Carolina	42	3.1	3.6	157/148	57.3%	1.9	0.5	$3.2	$42.2	909
88.	Virginia Tech	42	2.9	3.8	153/149	65.8%	4.6	1.4	$4.4	$91.7	760
96.	Ball State University (IN)	41	2.8	3.5	153/148	17.7%	1.4	0.5	$2.0	$22.7	2,385
96.	University of Colorado–Denver	41	2.9	3.2	N/A/N/A	65.6%	2.3	0.2	$4.6	$136.5	1,381
96.	University of San Diego	41	2.8	3.1	155/151	29.7%	2.0	0.6	$1.5	$55.3	683
99.	Loyola University Chicago	40	3.0	3.3	151/145	29.5%	5.1	0.6	$1.6	$45.8	666
99.	Mississippi State University	40	2.6	3.0	151/151	88.9%	1.3	0.2	$11.1	$125.6	776
99.	Ohio University	40	2.9	3.7	147/144	41.6%	1.8	0.7	$2.6	$48.4	846
99.	Oklahoma State University	40	2.8	3.5	150/145*	29.7%	2.9	0.8	$5.6	$69.3	879
99.	University of California–San Diego	40	3.1	3.1	153/146	51.6%	4.3	1.7	$1.5	$128.5	128
104.	Kent State University (OH)	39	2.8	3.4	152/147	41.5%	3.4	0.4	$4.9	$43.5	1,714
104.	Miami University (OH)	39	3.0	3.6	N/A/N/A	67.7%	0.5	0.1	$1.3	$16.7	686

Rank	School	Overall score	Peer assessment score (5.0=highest)	Administrators/ experts assessment score (5.0=highest)	'14 mean GRE scores (verbal/ quantitative)[1]	'14 doctoral acceptance rate	'14 doctoral students/ faculty[2]	Doctorals granted/ faculty 2013-14	'14 funded research (in millions)	'14 funded research/faculty member (in thousands)	'14 total graduate education enrollment
104.	Towson University (MD)	39	2.4	3.4	153/152	30.1%	0.6	0.1	$3.0	$26.7	1,511
104.	University of Massachusetts–Lowell	39	2.5	3.1	159/151	85.7%	2.4	0.3	$2.9	$222.9	459
104.	University of Mississippi	39	2.7	3.3	149/142	36.9%	1.4	0.4	$7.3	$156.2	596
104.	West Virginia University	39	2.8	3.2	152/148	45.3%	1.8	0.4	$3.5	$53.8	1,073
110.	Illinois State University	38	2.7	3.1	151/148	55.1%	0.9	0.3	$8.6	$86.2	790
110.	Montclair State University (NJ)	38	2.7	2.9	154/147	42.9%	0.6	0.1	$3.8	$33.5	2,037
110.	Old Dominion University (Darden) (VA)	38	2.7	3.1	148/147	48.1%	1.6	0.5	$9.0	$91.8	1,681
110.	University of California–Santa Cruz	38	2.5	2.6	158/152	35.5%	1.9	0.3	$2.9	$194.8	110
110.	University of Houston (TX)	38	2.8	3.2	153/149	38.0%	4.7	0.8	$3.7	$77.0	736
115.	Hofstra University (NY)	37	2.7	3.5	152/149	69.7%	2.6	0.5	$1.6	$35.9	679
115.	Marquette University (WI)	37	2.8	3.2	158/147	75.0%	0.9	0.2	$0.2	$8.3	155
115.	Northern Arizona University	37	2.6	3.2	147/147	59.2%	1.6	0.6	$8.0	$127.4	1,604
115.	Portland State University (OR)	37	2.7	3.2	N/A/N/A	30.8%	1.2	0.6	$4.8	$107.1	1,117
115.	St. John's University (NY)	37	2.6	3.7	151/143	80.0%	2.0	0.9	$4.9	$101.2	1,367
115.	Texas Tech University	37	2.7	3.3	150/146	39.9%	3.6	0.7	$6.8	$92.4	1,089
115.	University of New Hampshire	37	2.8	3.2	N/A/N/A	59.1%	1.2	0.3	N/A	N/A	255
115.	University of New Mexico	37	2.8	3.0	152/146	39.1%	1.6	0.4	$2.9	$29.5	976
115.	University of Northern Iowa	37	2.5	3.3	N/A/N/A	46.2%	0.4	0.1	$1.5	$11.2	619

[1]GRE scores are for doctoral students only, and all those displayed are for exams taken during or after August 2011 using the new 130-170 score scale.
[2]Student/faculty ratio is for all full-time equivalent doctoral students and full-time faculty.
*The school could not break out GRE scores for doctoral students; average scores for all entering students are shown.
N/A=Data were not provided by the school. Sources: U.S. News and the schools. Assessment data collected by Ipsos Public Affairs.

SPECIALTIES

PROGRAMS RANKED BEST BY EDUCATION SCHOOL DEANS

ADMINISTRATION/SUPERVISION
1. Vanderbilt Univ. (Peabody) (TN)
2. University of Wisconsin–Madison
3. University of Texas–Austin
4. Teachers College, Columbia University (NY)
5. Harvard University (MA)
6. Stanford University (CA)
7. Pennsylvania State University–University Park
8. Michigan State University
9. University of Virginia (Curry)
10. University of Washington
11. Ohio State University
12. University of Michigan–Ann Arbor

COUNSELING/PERSONNEL SERVICES
1. University of Maryland–College Park
2. University of North Carolina–Greensboro
3. University of Georgia
4. University of Wisconsin–Madison
5. University of Missouri
6. University of Minnesota–Twin Cities
7. Ohio State University
7. Pennsylvania State University–University Park
9. University of Florida

CURRICULUM/INSTRUCTION
1. University of Wisconsin–Madison
2. Stanford University (CA)
3. Michigan State University
4. Teachers College, Columbia University (NY)
5. University of Michigan–Ann Arbor
6. Vanderbilt Univ. (Peabody) (TN)
7. University of Illinois–Urbana-Champaign
8. Ohio State University
9. University of Georgia

EDUCATION POLICY
1. Stanford University (CA)
2. Vanderbilt Univ. (Peabody) (TN)
3. Harvard University (MA)
4. University of Wisconsin–Madison
5. Teachers College, Columbia University (NY)
6. University of Pennsylvania
7. University of Michigan–Ann Arbor
8. University of California–Berkeley
9. University of California–Los Angeles
10. Pennsylvania State University–University Park

EDUCATIONAL PSYCHOLOGY
1. University of Wisconsin–Madison
2. Stanford University (CA)
3. University of Michigan–Ann Arbor
4. Michigan State University
5. University of Illinois–Urbana-Champaign
5. Vanderbilt Univ. (Peabody) (TN)
7. University of Maryland–College Park
8. University of California–Berkeley
9. University of Minnesota–Twin Cities
10. University of Texas–Austin

ELEMENTARY EDUCATION
1. Michigan State University
2. University of Wisconsin–Madison
3. Teachers College, Columbia University (NY)
4. University of Michigan–Ann Arbor
5. Vanderbilt Univ. (Peabody) (TN)
6. University of Georgia
7. Ohio State University
8. Stanford University (CA)
9. University of Washington

HIGHER EDUCATION ADMINISTRATION
1. University of Michigan–Ann Arbor
2. University of California–Los Angeles

3. University of Southern California (Rossier)
4. Michigan State University
5. University of Pennsylvania
6. University of Georgia
7. Pennsylvania State University–University Park
7. Vanderbilt Univ. (Peabody) (TN)
9. Indiana University–Bloomington
10. University of Maryland–College Park
11. Harvard University (MA)
11. University of Wisconsin–Madison

SECONDARY EDUCATION
1. Michigan State University
2. Stanford University (CA)
3. University of Michigan–Ann Arbor
4. University of Wisconsin–Madison
5. Teachers College, Columbia University (NY)
6. University of Georgia
7. University of Virginia (Curry)
7. University of Washington
7. Vanderbilt Univ. (Peabody) (TN)

SPECIAL EDUCATION
1. Vanderbilt Univ. (Peabody) (TN)
2. University of Kansas
3. University of Oregon
4. University of Texas–Austin
5. University of Florida
6. University of Wisconsin–Madison
7. University of Virginia (Curry)
8. University of Illinois–Urbana-Champaign
9. University of Washington
10. University of Minnesota–Twin Cities

VOCATIONAL/TECHNICAL
1. Pennsylvania State University–University Park
2. Ohio State University
3. University of Georgia

METHODOLOGY

Graduate programs at 357 schools granting education doctoral degrees were surveyed; 253 responded, and 246 provided data needed to calculate rankings based on 10 measures:

Quality assessment: Two surveys were conducted in the fall of 2014. Education school deans and deans of graduate studies were asked to rate program quality from marginal (1) to outstanding (5); 32 percent responded. The resulting score is weighted by .25. Education schools provided names of superintendents, people who hire graduates, and education experts familiar with them, who were also asked to rate programs. The three most recent years' results were averaged and weighted by .15.

Student selectivity (weighted by .18): Combines mean verbal and quantitative GRE scores of doctoral students entering in fall 2014 and the acceptance rate of doctoral applicants for the 2014-2015 academic year (each accounts for one-third of the measure). Where mean GRE scores are not available for doctoral students, mean GRE scores for all entering students may be substituted, if available. Scores for the new and old GRE were converted to a common scale; only new scores are displayed.

Faculty resources (.12): Resources include the 2014 ratio of full-time-equivalent doctoral students to full-time faculty (37.5 percent); average percentage of full-time faculty holding awards or editorships at selected education journals in 2013 and 2014 (20.8 percent); and ratio of doctoral degrees granted to full-time faculty in the 2013-14 school year (41.7 percent).

Research activity (.30): This measure uses average total education school research expenditures (50 percent) and average expenditures per full-time faculty member (50 percent). Expenditures refer to separately funded research, public and private, conducted by the school, averaged over fiscal years 2013 and 2014.

Overall rank: Data were standardized about their means, and standardized scores were weighted, totaled and rescaled so that the top school received 100; other schools received their percentage of the top score.

Specialty rankings: These ratings are based solely on nominations by deans and deans of graduate studies, who were asked to choose up to 10 programs for excellence in each specialty. The top ones are listed.

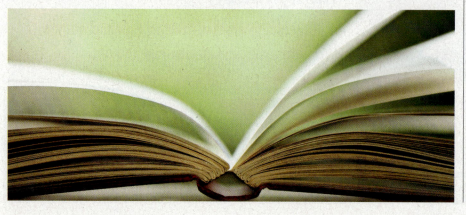

CHAPTER 3

Engineering

In the lab at the
University of Pittsburgh

THE U.S. NEWS RANKINGS

From THE Lab TO THE Market

THE THRILL OF TRANSLATING RESEARCH INTO A PRODUCT

By **CATHIE GANDEL**

A smart phone app that can easily and quickly detect jaundice in newborns. A paste that helps fight periodontal disease. An injection that improves the treatment of glaucoma. A wireless system that helps combat hospital infections. A putty-like substance to repair bone. An inexpensive solar-powered water pump for use in developing countries.

What do all of these innovations have in common? They were developed in the research lab by engineering graduate students, who have delivered or are delivering them to the marketplace.

It was an "awesome experience" to move "from idea to actual product," says Emily Paris, 27, a native of Charlotte, North Carolina, who will receive her master's in civil and environmental engineering from Stanford University in June. Last year, she and her Stanford teammates – a structural engineer, a mechanical engineer and a business school grad student – spent several months in the university's Product Realization Lab using state-of-the-art tools and materials to design prototype after prototype of a solar-powered water pump that could be used to draw water cheaply from below-ground sources in developing countries. Result: a foot-long stainless-steel tube housing a motor that is now helping farmers access water for their crops in Myanmar.

During the winter dry season, the team's on-the-ground partner, Proximity Designs, is overseeing manufacture and distribution of the pump for multiple pilot projects. But "once we are sure we're designing a product that these farmers want and are going to use, we're hoping to form a company, focus on the development of similar products and explore other markets" beginning this summer, says Paris.

The pump is an example of the fruits of "translational re-

▶ More on engineering schools @ usnews.com/engineering

search," or engineering conducted at the lab bench with an eye toward rapidly getting it to customers or, in a medical context, to the bedside. This type of research is gaining ground in engineering schools, reflecting the growing push to tailor graduate study "to be more driven by real-world experience – designing real systems and building things that work," says Christos Cassandras, head of the division of systems engineering at Boston University. "We believe it's crucial to help our students take their research from the classroom to the marketplace," says Gary May, dean of the College of Engineering at the Georgia Institute of Technology. "And our students are demanding this."

Students do indeed welcome the chance to see results. "Why do we do all this research if it's never going any-

ELLEN WEBBER FOR USN&WR

Research that Julia Fleck (right) is working on may improve both traffic flow and cancer care.

where?" wonders Andy Glowacki, 29, who is in the sixth year of his Ph.D. program in chemical and petroleum engineering at the University of Pittsburgh. "Everyone thinks about getting a product to the marketplace."

He himself is hard at work on a substance that would be injected into the pocket between the teeth and gums in people suffering from periodontal disease to help control damaging inflammation. Nicole Ostrowski, a 28-year-old from Warren, Pennsylvania, who got her undergraduate degree in engineering from Pitt and will complete her Ph.D. in bioengineering there this year, has noticed "a sizeable change" in the amount of support students are getting to turn their research into products. Pitt's Innovation Institute, for example, offers a 14-week course called "From Benchtop to Bedside: What Every Scientist Needs to Know" to translate basic research discoveries into drug therapies, medical devices or other clinical uses.

Building in such instruction on the

business and legal processes of bringing an invention to life reflects an understanding that venturing out of the lab takes many engineers "out of their comfort zone," notes Thomas Zurbuchen, associate dean for entrepreneurial programs at the College of Engineering at the University of Michigan. Motivated also by the prospect of research funding for promising technologies and royalties from successful technology transfers, grad schools are adding entrepreneurship and other business classes to the tech curriculum, and lining up collaborating companies or labs inside and outside the university. They're also funding incubators where grad students can develop their ideas and are holding competitions in which they can practice their sales pitch.

At Michigan, for example, the College of Engineering's Center for Entrepreneurship offers classes that range from how to create a prototype to how to obtain a patent. In 2014, the Massachusetts Institute of Technology launched a program called Start6 to teach the nuts and bolts of becoming entrepreneurs. Brown University in Rhode Island features a two-semester course in innovation management and "entrepreneurship engineering." One

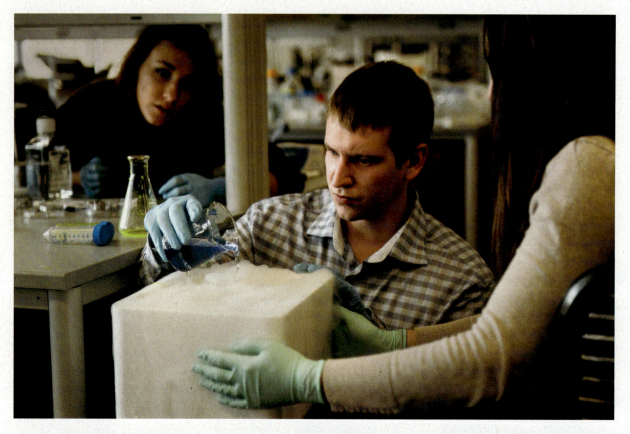

successful startup to come out of it: a company whose app allows patients to connect with their medical providers via text messaging. At New York University, meanwhile, a master's program in biotechnology and entrepreneurship adds electives in finance and project management to the required science.

Teamwork is a big part of the picture, too, both inside and outside the university. Glowacki says he spends "about half his time in other labs," notably at Pitt's Center for Craniofacial Regeneration in the dental school, where he is collaborating with periodontists on his treatment to stop gum disease. He and his dentistry colleagues have successfully performed animal testing, and now Glowacki is starting the process of getting Food and Drug Administration approval to test the substance in people, a necessary step before putting it on the market.

Clinical collaborators have also become an important part of the program at the Georgia Institute of Technology, and Chris Hermann, 30, can attest to their impact. While earning his dual M.D./Ph.D. (in bioengineering) at Emory University and Georgia Tech, Hermann teamed up with a surgeon at Children's Healthcare of Atlanta on a dissertation project to develop a therapy other than surgery to improve the management of babies born with a condition that causes their skull bones to grow too fast. He also happened to mention that he was interested in hand hygiene. An introduction to the head of the hospital's ICU eventually led Hermann to test different wireless technologies to remind medical staff to scrub between patients.

The in-the-trenches feedback he got was invaluable. The original alert was a "beep," but that was no good, staffers said, because the only "beep" they would heed would be one from lifesaving equipment. All other beeps would be ignored. So Hermann substituted a voice that says, "Please foam up." Today Clean Hands Safe Hands is a growing Atlanta-based business, and Hermann is president and CEO while still pursuing his medical degree from Emory. "One of the biggest reasons for our success was that we were

{ Students do indeed welcome the CHANCE to see results. }

able to get out in the real world and work with nurses and physicians," he says.

Sometimes a great engineering idea has multiple applications. Julia Lima Fleck, a 32-year-old from Rio de Janeiro who is in a five-year Ph.D. program in systems engineering at Boston University, started out working with Cassandras and other grad students on a system of "smart" traffic lights, in collaboration with the city of Boston and IBM. Traffic arrival at an intersection is random, the team reasoned; certain events trigger a buildup of cars. The goal is to find a mathematical framework that will switch traffic lights so as to ease congestion and, better yet, to prevent it in the first place.

Then, a seminar in systems biology that

Fleck attended sparked an epiphany. The mathematical model she was developing potentially could apply in treating cancer, also driven by random events. Drugs and medical procedures, like traffic lights, exist to control the disease. Could an engineering framework be applied to help doctors use treatments more effectively? Today, Fleck is collaborating with the Computational Biomedicine group at Boston University School of Medicine to develop software tools to assist oncologists in making decisions. The methodology could potentially be used for other diseases as well, she says.

One good way to get real-world experience as well as feedback on a project's practical applications is to enter a competition, says Cassandras. In 2014, a team from BU won second prize in the annual Smarter Planet Challenge, a national contest sponsored by IBM and the Institute of Electrical and Electronics Engineers for student teams working on solutions to issues such as waste management and greenhouse emissions that plague cities.

Their winning technology: an app that allows cities to detect and classify road bumps and potholes in order to efficiently do repairs. The diverse team involved not only BU systems engineers but also grad students in computer science, environmental science and city planning along with partners such as the city of Boston and a software company. Teams partici-

pating in Columbia University's Engineering Fast Pitch competition have to sell their idea to a panel of judges made up of alumni, venture capitalists and established entrepreneurs in 60 seconds or less. Winning teams split a $5,000 prize pool and get bragging rights. The school offers training in putting together an "elevator pitch" and feedback on a videotaped pitch beforehand.

The support of an incubator can be crucial to helping students navigate the "Valley of Death," the time between doing their research and having a product that will attract investors. Budding entrepreneurs get not only a space to work but also access to experts, mentors and even seed-stage funding. Success stories spawned by Michigan's one-semester TechArb incubator, for instance, include Sidecar, the instant ride-sharing company that recently received a $15 million infusion from investors.

One biotech company getting its start in the University of California–Davis's Engineering Translational Technology Center is developing sensors to be used to monitor patients' vital signs at home. Another is investigating using tobacco plants as "biofactories" of vaccines.

Many students won't see such rapid results, of course, warns Steven Little, chair of the department of chemical and petroleum engineering at Pittsburgh. "My stuff is so preliminary I probably won't see it commercialized," acknowledges Nicole Ostrowski, who is developing a magnesium phosphate-based putty that will facilitate bone regeneration.

Still, she is right where she wants to be – in the middle of the action. "You see the struggles. You see the progress. You see the excitement," she says. Anyone interested in translational research should look for a department and a principal investigator "very supportive of entrepreneurship and commercialization," she recommends.

The need for what Cassandras calls "societal engineers" – the people who can address the multitude of complex challenges looming in health, energy, security and infrastructure – is only going to increase, experts predict. That means expanding opportunity for grad students who want to make the trip from inspiration to concrete change. ∎

Texas A&M
College Station, Texas

CULLY JONES, '12
Environmental Engineer

▶ My master's degree from Dwight Look College of Engineering gave me great preparation for my current job with Chevron, where I focus on regulatory compliance. The school encourages you to take classes with people from other A&M colleges and disciplines, like agriculture and geosciences. You also get to work on projects with cross-functional teams. For example, by helping out with a College of Agriculture rainfall simulation project, I learned to appreciate my teammates' different skill sets and objectives and the need to hear everyone's viewpoint.

A&M also emphasizes technical document writing – a critical skill in a global company spread across many time zones that relies heavily on email communication. Finally, A&M made my education affordable, covering my tuition and fees.

Prepped For 3-D Printing

HOW STUDENTS CAN GET READY FOR THE FUTURE OF MANUFACTURING

By **ELIZABETH GARDNER**

Imagine being able to replace diseased bone with an exact metal copy, but porous so that new tissue can grow inside it. Over time, the metal slowly dissolves, leaving behind healthy bone.

There's no need to imagine it, because such implants are being developed today through "additive manufacturing" techniques such as 3-D printing. "You can get a CT scan of the patient, feed it into the printer, and have the part completely made to fit the patient," says Prashant Kumta, an engineering professor at the University of Pittsburgh.

And the possibilities stretch far beyond medicine to building any custom item, from the parts for cars and planes to clothes to braces for teeth. The consulting firm Wohlers Associates in Fort Collins,

> **New tools and materials demand different SKILLS.**

Colorado, expects worldwide revenues from additive manufacturing techniques to exceed $21 billion by 2020, up from just over $3 billion in 2013. In 2012, the Obama administration provided $50 million to jump-start America Makes, an institute dedicated to growing the nation's competitiveness in additive manufacturing by creating collaborations among businesses, universities, government agencies and nonprofits. The consortium has 100-plus members so far. Little wonder that additive manufacturing is putting a new spin on graduate education in both engineering and industrial design.

Relaxed limits. Historically, the limitations of manufacturing equipment have dictated what parts can be made; 3-D printing can create almost any shape. "What can we design now that all those limitations have been relaxed?" asks Burak Ozdoganlar, director of Carnegie Mellon's Institute for Complex Engineered Systems, one of several academic research centers exploring that question through collaborations of faculty, students and companies. The

combination of new tools and materials demands different engineering and design skills and the ability to collaborate. "You can't deploy this stuff with one specialist," says Chuck Hull, who invented 3-D printing and is now chief technology officer and co-founder of 3D Systems Corp. in Rock Hill, South Carolina, which makes the printers and software as well as prototypes and on-demand parts for customers. "You need teams."

What's the best preparation for someone interested in entering this new field? Hull, who has a bachelor's degree in engineering physics from the University of Colorado, says that if he were starting off today in the field he created, he'd pay a lot more attention to organic chemistry and materials science. "A lot of the technology has to do with how you manipulate materials," he says. Hull also recommends becoming proficient at computer-aided design.

Kumta anticipates that graduate training for additive manufacturing will develop primarily as a subspecialty, and that the educational path will wrap in coursework from materials science, physics, chemistry, biology and bioengineering (depending on the student's specific area of interest), as well as courses from the engineering disciplines. "It's a very interdisciplinary subject," he says, "so creating a specialized department hasn't gathered much steam." Pitt, whose Swanson Center for Product Innovation undertakes projects and research, is incorporating instruction on additive manufacturing into existing core courses and is offering electives focused on specific techniques or materials.

While dedicated programs may be scarce, research opportunities abound. Students who are interested in pursuing graduate level work in the field can check the membership list of America Makes (america-makes.us), which currently boasts about 30 academic institutions, including Carnegie Mellon and the University of Pittsburgh. Others with research centers where students can get experience with additive manufacturing technologies and materials, typically on design and prototyping projects for other researchers, businesses and government agencies, include the Milwaukee School of Engineering and the engineering schools at the University of California–Irvine, the University of Louisville in Kentucky and the University of Texas–El Paso. ■

THE JOB MARKET | PETROLEUM ENGINEER

A Well of Opportunity

By **CATHIE GANDEL**

Kelli Adiaheno always knew she wanted to be an engineer, but an undergrad course in petroleum engineering at the University of Texas–Austin opened the door to her eventual career path. After her sophomore year, she interned at an Oklahoma oil field to see firsthand how oil was extracted from the ground. She liked the interdisciplinary nature of petroleum engineering and the opportunities it opens up. "It involves physics, chemistry, mechanical engineering – you are not pigeonholed," she says. Office and research internships followed and today, after earning a bachelor's, master's and doctorate in petroleum engineering from UT–Austin, Adiaheno, 28, focuses on enhanced oil recovery as a reservoir engineer at Shell International E&P Inc. in Houston. Her role? Using gas-injection technologies that force gasses into a reservoir to push out untapped oil.

Today, the iconic Hollywood image of gushers is obsolete, according to Jon Olson, chair of the Department of Petroleum and Geosystems Engineering at UT–Austin's Cockrell School of Engineering. "All the easy oil has been found." Yet, thanks to new

Kelli Adiaheno
University of Texas–Austin
Cockrell School of Engineering, 2013

engineering approaches, the U.S. has nearly doubled its crude oil production over the past five years. The Bureau of Labor Statistics predicts that jobs in petroleum engineering will grow 26 percent over the decade ending in 2022, though that number might have to be revised if lower oil prices last indefinitely and impact hiring. Still, the industry will always need "people who can create new technology or create new ways to apply existing technology," Olson notes. Besides the type of reservoir engineering that Adiaheno is engaged in, job openings abound in drilling, production, research labs and academia.

Prospective grad students potentially enjoy a big advantage: Because universities receive generous support from the industry and the federal government to encourage engineering breakthroughs and more environmentally friendly extraction techniques, most students can expect to get their studies fully underwritten and even receive a stipend. And median salaries in the field are high: about $130,280. ∎

...MORE HOT JOBS

Biomedical engineer

➤ These engineers are finding futuristic ways to grow new body parts, create targeted drug therapies, and develop individualized drug treatment strategies. This interdisciplinary field combines biological and medical science with mechanical, electronic, chemical and computer engineering. Jobs are concentrated in universities, hospitals, labs, industry and regulatory agencies. The median salary for the profession is roughly **$87,000.** The field is expected to see **10-year growth of 27 percent,** according to the BLS.

Civil engineer

➤ The people focused on infrastructure are in heavy demand. The government expects to see **20 percent more openings by 2022;** median salary now is about **$79,000.** Civil engineers build roads, bridges and railways; are called in after natural disasters; and are tasked to devise disaster prevention strategies such as equipping skyscrapers to withstand earthquakes. Concern about aging infrastructure has led some states to increase gas taxes to help fund transportation projects, and Congress passed legislation authorizing $12.3 billion to modernize dams and levees alone in 2014.

Nuclear engineer

➤ Though the industry was hurt by Japan's 2011 Fukushima Daiichi nuclear power disaster, the BLS predicts **10-year job growth for nuclear engineers of 9 percent** by 2022. Lisa Marshall, director of outreach for the department of nuclear engineering at North Carolina State University, cites a "perfect storm" of variables creating new opportunities. These include increased federal funding for research and development on advanced reactors, security and nuclear waste disposal as well as the growing interest in applying this technology to other sectors, like medicine and agriculture. Median salary in the field was estimated to be **$104,270** in 2012.

Schools of Engineering

THE TOP SCHOOLS

Rank School	Overall score	Peer assessment score (5.0=highest)	Recruiter assessment score (5.0=highest)	'14 average quantitative GRE score[1]	'14 acceptance rate	'14 Ph.D. students/ faculty	'14 faculty membership in National Academy of Engineering	'14 engineering school research expenditures (in millions)	'14 research expenditures per faculty member (in thousands)	Ph.D.s granted 2013-2014	'14 total graduate engineering enrollment
1. Massachusetts Institute of Technology	100	4.9	4.8	166	17.8%	5.5	12.2%	$391.2	$1,026.8	355	3,143
2. Stanford University (CA)	92	4.9	4.6	166	17.1%	7.1	18.3%	$189.4	$823.6	305	3,558
3. University of California–Berkeley	86	4.7	4.5	165	14.4%	5.6	15.1%	$211.1	$851.4	259	1,936
4. Carnegie Mellon University (PA)	79	4.3	4.3	166	26.9%	4.9	11.1%	$207.6	$837.2	226	3,400
5. California Institute of Technology	77	4.6	4.5	166	8.6%	5.5	14.0%	$99.8	$1,121.2	80	537
6. Georgia Institute of Technology	75	4.6	4.3	164	31.1%	4.2	2.6%	$204.1	$401.0	424	6,136
6. Purdue University–West Lafayette (IN)	75	4.2	4.2	164	23.2%	4.9	5.0%	$228.6	$674.4	317	3,409
6. University of Illinois–Urbana-Champaign	75	4.5	4.3	165	25.8%	4.2	3.6%	$229.9	$586.6	304	3,316
6. University of Michigan–Ann Arbor	75	4.4	4.1	165	24.8%	4.3	4.2%	$251.6	$723.0	291	3,212
10. University of Southern California (Viterbi)	71	3.6	3.8	164	23.4%	5.5	10.6%	$187.8	$1,079.3	145	5,142
10. University of Texas–Austin (Cockrell)	71	4.1	4.1	164	16.9%	5.1	8.0%	$187.9	$610.2	271	2,374
12. Texas A&M University–College Station (Look)	70	3.8	3.7	163	24.3%	3.6	2.4%	$293.0	$909.9	241	3,379
13. Cornell University (NY)	69	4.3	4.0	165	27.9%	4.6	11.8%	$141.5	$683.7	139	1,966
14. Columbia University (Fu Foundation) (NY)	67	3.6	3.6	166	22.2%	5.2	13.2%	$149.2	$1,001.5	124	3,038
14. University of California–Los Angeles (Samueli)	67	3.7	3.8	165	28.7%	6.2	19.0%	$101.7	$701.2	177	1,928
14. University of Wisconsin–Madison	67	3.9	3.9	164	11.3%	4.8	3.3%	$204.6	$905.3	154	2,037
17. University of California–San Diego (Jacobs)	66	3.6	3.9	165	21.5%	5.4	11.8%	$151.3	$792.0	142	1,862
18. Princeton University (NJ)	64	4.1	4.1	167	11.2%	4.1	13.4%	$92.8	$713.9	96	583
19. University of Pennsylvania	60	3.6	3.7	166	22.7%	4.1	8.5%	$111.3	$984.6	60	1,596
20. Harvard University (MA)	59	3.6	3.9	166	9.9%	5.1	14.9%	$59.7	$828.9	65	439
21. Northwestern University (McCormick) (IL)	58	3.9	3.9	165	22.9%	4.5	4.3%	$108.4	$576.5	120	1,857
21. Virginia Tech	58	3.8	3.8	163	22.8%	3.3	2.1%	$167.4	$527.9	211	2,045
23. University of California–Santa Barbara	57	3.5	3.6	165	14.4%	3.8	11.8%	$108.4	$827.6	94	690
23. University of Maryland–College Park (Clark)	57	3.6	3.7	163	25.3%	4.0	3.1%	$151.5	$601.0	180	2,217
25. Johns Hopkins University (Whiting) (MD)	56	3.8	4.0	165	24.2%	4.6	1.9%	$105.3	$679.7	94	3,234
25. Pennsylvania State University–University Park	56	3.7	3.8	163	30.0%	3.4	1.6%	$162.7	$460.8	157	1,652
27. University of Washington	55	3.7	3.6	164	19.5%	3.7	4.9%	$133.7	$589.1	134	2,188
28. Duke University (Pratt) (NC)	53	3.6	3.7	164	27.7%	4.1	2.4%	$99.4	$828.5	83	1,041
28. North Carolina State University	53	3.3	3.5	163	17.1%	3.1	4.2%	$165.6	$508.0	182	3,159
28. University of Minnesota–Twin Cities	53	3.6	3.8	165	23.5%	3.8	3.9%	$103.3	$467.6	160	1,867
31. Rice University (Brown) (TX)	51	3.6	3.7	165	20.9%	5.3	7.0%	$53.3	$467.8	85	868
32. Ohio State University	50	3.5	3.5	164	18.3%	3.7	2.3%	$118.8	$484.7	141	1,801
33. University of California–Davis	49	3.4	3.7	162	21.3%	4.2	6.3%	$73.5	$417.8	97	1,159
34. University of Colorado–Boulder	48	3.3	3.4	161	37.8%	4.5	5.1%	$85.4	$550.7	117	1,663
35. Vanderbilt University (TN)	47	3.2	3.5	164	15.6%	4.5	2.2%	$74.4	$835.7	52	492
35. Yale University (CT)	47	3.3	3.7	167	14.0%	3.7	9.3%	$28.4	$556.0	29	211
37. Boston University	46	3.0	3.2	164	24.6%	3.9	6.7%	$98.5	$849.4	78	958
37. University of California–Irvine (Samueli)	46	3.2	3.4	163	20.0%	4.2	3.3%	$82.5	$453.1	122	1,490
39. Rensselaer Polytechnic Institute (NY)	44	3.4	3.7	163	27.1%	3.5	2.0%	$57.7	$372.3	84	733
39. University of Rochester (NY)	44	2.7	3.2	165	35.0%	3.4	4.3%	$87.5	$1,005.9	56	577
39. University of Virginia	44	3.2	3.4	163	18.0%	3.4	3.0%	$67.5	$519.0	96	646
42. Arizona State University (Fulton)	42	3.2	3.3	162	47.5%	3.0	1.9%	$85.2	$387.2	109	3,694
43. Iowa State University	41	3.3	3.3	161	20.9%	2.4	0.8%	$81.8	$354.0	97	1,266
43. Northeastern University (MA)	41	2.9	3.3	161	35.6%	3.8	2.7%	$59.2	$432.4	73	3,182
43. University of Florida	41	3.2	3.3	162	36.6%	3.0	0.4%	$64.3	$247.2	219	2,484
43. University of Pittsburgh (Swanson)	41	3.0	3.1	163	29.5%	3.4	0.7%	$91.0	$654.9	76	1,080
47. Case Western Reserve University (OH)	40	3.2	3.4	164	20.5%	3.1	2.6%	$43.4	$401.6	59	617
47. New York University	40	2.6	3.2	162	37.7%	3.4	10.6%	$20.7	$323.3	43	2,306
49. Brown University (RI)	39	3.2	3.5	164	23.6%	2.7	5.3%	$19.9	$276.1	31	371
49. Lehigh University (Rossin) (PA)	39	3.0	3.4	164	23.4%	5.1	7.1%	$20.9	$191.7	36	802
49. Michigan State University	39	3.1	3.3	162	9.3%	3.1	2.2%	$52.8	$312.2	80	791
49. University of Arizona	39	3.1	3.2	163	42.1%	2.9	5.4%	$59.7	$335.3	83	1,133
49. University of Notre Dame (IN)	39	3.1	3.4	162	22.4%	3.8	2.4%	$45.5	$382.3	71	508
54. University of Delaware	38	2.8	3.2	162	31.9%	4.5	3.9%	$52.5	$391.6	76	873

▶ More @ usnews.com/grad

Photo Credit: Patrick Mansell

GO BEYOND

...the expected and ordinary. Take a long look at what really shapes your graduate school experience—the people, the research, the labs, the partnerships. We are certain you will find what you are looking for at the Penn State College of Engineering.

If you are ready to take that step towards your successful future, the Penn State College of Engineering is ready for you.

www.engr.psu.edu/gobeyond

Degree options in 13 academic areas

New professional 1-year Master's programs

Expansive labs and research facilities

Relaxing and affordable location

PENN STATE
College of Engineering

Rank	School	Overall score	Peer assessment score (5.0=highest)	Recruiter assessment score (5.0=highest)	'14 average quantitative GRE score[1]	'14 acceptance rate	'14 Ph.D. students/ faculty	'14 faculty membership in National Academy of Engineering	'14 engineering school research expenditures (in millions)	'14 research expenditures per faculty member (in thousands)	Ph.D.s granted 2013-2014	'14 total graduate engineering enrollment
54.	Washington University in St. Louis	38	3.2	3.5	165	44.9%	4.1	1.1%	$23.3	$287.5	48	976
56.	Colorado School of Mines	37	3.0	3.5	159	41.3%	2.7	1.6%	$56.6	$320.0	96	1,290
56.	Rutgers, The State Univ. of N.J.–New Brunswick	37	2.9	3.3	163	18.9%	2.1	3.8%	$59.5	$330.5	67	1,229
56.	University of Utah	37	2.8	3.1	162	34.8%	2.6	3.3%	$77.6	$459.1	90	1,209
59.	University at Buffalo–SUNY	36	2.8	3.0	162	24.0%	3.0	1.2%	$59.2	$372.0	84	1,923
59.	University of Massachusetts–Amherst	36	2.8	3.3	162	22.5%	3.3	0.6%	$57.4	$370.4	66	868
61.	Dartmouth College (Thayer) (NH)	35	2.9	3.4	164	21.8%	2.3	2.0%	$18.9	$394.0	21	286
61.	University of Illinois–Chicago	35	2.8	3.3	160	20.5%	4.1	2.1%	$26.8	$285.5	62	1,164
63.	University of Dayton (OH)	34	2.1	2.8	155	35.4%	2.4	N/A	$80.6	$1,491.7	14	845
63.	University of Iowa	34	2.7	3.0	162	22.5%	2.8	1.1%	$51.4	$571.5	40	385
63.	University of Tennessee–Knoxville	34	2.7	3.0	161	31.6%	3.1	2.2%	$58.9	$342.6	101	996
66.	Drexel University (PA)	33	2.9	3.3	160	31.2%	2.8	1.9%	$26.3	$196.5	55	1,257
66.	Stony Brook University–SUNY	33	2.7	3.0	163	31.6%	4.1	2.6%	$29.0	$201.2	71	1,512
68.	Auburn University (Ginn) (AL)	32	2.9	3.0	160	48.0%	2.1	N/A	$60.0	$411.0	63	917
68.	Tufts University (MA)	32	2.8	3.2	162	33.2%	2.7	3.8%	$22.5	$288.6	32	596
68.	University of Connecticut	32	2.7	3.0	162	27.6%	3.4	1.5%	$41.5	$290.3	76	905
71.	Clemson University (SC)	31	2.9	3.1	161	33.7%	2.4	0.5%	$30.8	$146.0	89	1,425
71.	Colorado State University	31	2.7	3.0	160	49.0%	1.0	N/A	$63.3	$614.2	33	758
71.	University of California–Riverside (Bourns)	31	2.2	2.9	161	23.3%	5.2	2.1%	$42.1	$468.1	74	667
74.	Illinois Institute of Technology (Armour)	30	2.6	3.0	161	46.8%	3.1	3.1%	$18.8	$195.6	38	1,704
74.	Syracuse University (NY)	30	2.6	3.1	162	40.3%	3.2	1.5%	$12.0	$168.9	34	1,174
76.	Oregon State University	29	2.6	3.1	160	27.7%	2.5	N/A	$32.1	$214.0	67	1,039
76.	Stevens Institute of Technology (Schaefer) (NJ)	29	2.4	3.1	161	61.4%	2.7	1.3%	$24.2	$326.7	27	1,978
76.	University of Houston (Cullen) (TX)	29	2.4	2.9	161	43.6%	3.5	4.9%	$30.7	$231.1	67	1,437
76.	University of Texas–Dallas (Jonsson)	29	2.3	2.9	160	38.7%	1.8	3.4%	$46.3	$330.6	70	2,550
76.	Washington State University	29	2.7	3.0	161	23.6%	2.7	0.8%	$28.1	$246.3	65	650
81.	Missouri University of Science & Technology	28	2.7	3.2	159	46.4%	2.2	0.6%	$29.3	$177.8	64	1,333
81.	University of Cincinnati	28	2.5	3.0	161	15.4%	3.0	N/A	$23.1	$203.0	71	840
83.	Rochester Institute of Technology (Gleason) (NY)	27	2.8	3.3	158	46.0%	0.7	N/A	$24.7	$206.2	15	1,177
83.	University of North Carolina–Chapel Hill	27	2.7	3.3	158	32.0%	1.9	N/A	$12.1	$376.6	12	112
85.	University of Central Florida	26	2.4	2.7	159	43.0%	4.1	0.8%	$26.8	$207.4	83	1,309
85.	University of New Mexico	26	2.5	2.6	157	57.9%	4.3	1.0%	$29.9	$301.6	61	855
85.	Worcester Polytechnic Institute (MA)	26	2.5	3.3	163	45.9%	1.6	0.9%	$19.7	$167.1	24	1,127
88.	University of California–Santa Cruz (Baskin)	25	2.2	2.7	163	31.5%	3.5	N/A	$31.8	$407.9	29	438
88.	University of Missouri	25	2.5	2.9	161	26.3%	1.4	N/A	$24.7	$223.0	46	634
90.	University of Alabama–Huntsville	24	2.3	2.6	156	70.8%	1.5	N/A	$59.3	$770.7	23	715
90.	University of Kansas	24	2.6	2.9	160	53.0%	1.9	0.9%	$16.8	$158.7	33	680
90.	University of Nebraska–Lincoln	24	2.5	2.8	160	30.3%	2.0	N/A	$31.1	$179.7	46	624
90.	University of Texas–Arlington	24	2.3	2.6	159	55.1%	2.6	N/A	$37.3	$284.8	96	2,646
94.	Kansas State University	23	2.7	2.9	159	38.7%	1.2	N/A	$20.3	$169.2	26	471
94.	Louisiana State University–Baton Rouge	23	2.4	2.7	160	32.5%	2.4	0.8%	$22.5	$187.7	66	659
94.	Mississippi State University (Bagley)	23	2.3	2.7	158	38.4%	1.9	0.9%	$37.1	$325.5	53	588
94.	Texas Tech University (Whitacre)	23	2.3	2.8	160	33.2%	2.3	3.0%	$17.9	$135.7	58	872
94.	University of Kentucky	23	2.4	2.6	160	48.2%	1.8	0.7%	$40.5	$273.9	47	516

SPECIALTIES
PROGRAMS RANKED BEST BY ENGINEERING SCHOOL DEPARTMENT HEADS

Rank	School	Average assessment score (5.0=highest)
AEROSPACE/AERONAUTICAL/ASTRONAUTICAL		
1.	Massachusetts Institute of Technology	4.9
2.	California Institute of Technology	4.7
2.	Stanford University (CA)	4.7
4.	University of Michigan–Ann Arbor	4.6
5.	Georgia Institute of Technology	4.4
6.	Purdue University–West Lafayette (IN)	4.3
7.	University of Illinois–Urbana-Champaign	4.1
8.	Texas A&M University–College Station (Look)	4.0
8.	University of Texas–Austin (Cockrell)	4.0
10.	University of Colorado–Boulder	3.9

Rank	School	Average assessment score (5.0=highest)
BIOLOGICAL/AGRICULTURAL		
1.	Purdue University–West Lafayette (IN)	4.8
2.	Texas A&M University–College Station (Look)	4.5
3.	Iowa State University	4.4
4.	University of Illinois–Urbana-Champaign	4.3
5.	University of Florida	4.1
6.	Cornell University (NY)	4.0
7.	University of California–Davis	3.9
7.	Virginia Tech	3.9
9.	North Carolina State University	3.7
9.	University of Nebraska–Lincoln	3.7

Rank	School	Average assessment score (5.0=highest)
BIOMEDICAL/BIOENGINEERING		
1.	Johns Hopkins University (Whiting) (MD)	4.5
2.	Georgia Institute of Technology	4.4
2.	University of California–San Diego (Jacobs)	4.4
4.	Duke University (Pratt) (NC)	4.3
4.	Massachusetts Institute of Technology	4.3
6.	Stanford University (CA)	4.2
7.	University of California–Berkeley	4.1
7.	University of Pennsylvania	4.1
9.	Boston University	3.9
9.	Rice University (Brown) (TX)	3.9

[1]GRE scores displayed are for master's and Ph.D. students and are only for those GRE exams taken during or after August 2011 using the new 130-170 score scale. N/A=Data were not provided by the school. Sources: U.S. News and the schools. Assessment data collected by Ipsos Public Affairs.

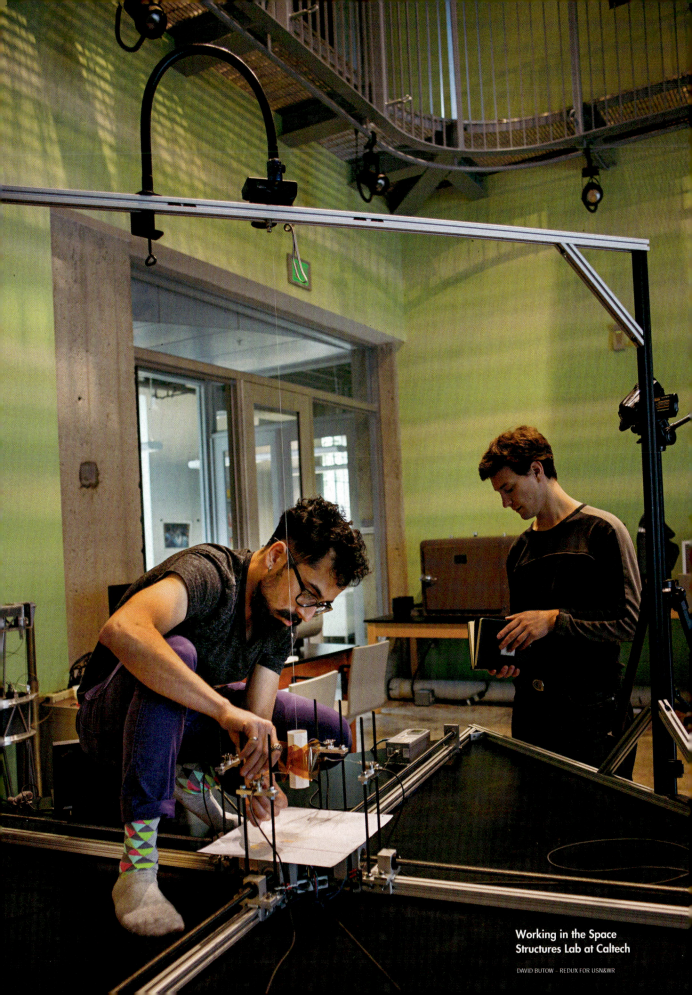

Working in the Space
Structures Lab at Caltech

SPECIALTIES continued

Rank School	Average assessment score (5.0=highest)
9. University of Washington	3.9

CHEMICAL

Rank School	
1. Massachusetts Institute of Technology	4.9
2. University of California–Berkeley	4.7
3. California Institute of Technology	4.6
4. Stanford University (CA)	4.5
5. University of Minnesota–Twin Cities	4.4
6. University of Texas–Austin (Cockrell)	4.3
6. University of Wisconsin–Madison	4.3
8. Princeton University (NJ)	4.2
9. Georgia Institute of Technology	4.1
9. University of California–Santa Barbara	4.1
9. University of Delaware	4.1

CIVIL

Rank School	
1. University of California–Berkeley	4.7
2. University of Illinois–Urbana-Champaign	4.6
3. Stanford University (CA)	4.5
3. University of Texas–Austin (Cockrell)	4.5
5. Georgia Institute of Technology	4.4
6. Purdue University–West Lafayette (IN)	4.2
7. University of Michigan–Ann Arbor	4.1
8. Massachusetts Institute of Technology	4.0
9. Carnegie Mellon University (PA)	3.9
9. Cornell University (NY)	3.9
9. Virginia Tech	3.9

COMPUTER

Rank School	
1. Massachusetts Institute of Technology	5.0
1. Stanford University (CA)	5.0
1. University of California–Berkeley	5.0
4. Carnegie Mellon University (PA)	4.7
5. University of Illinois–Urbana-Champaign	4.6
6. University of Michigan–Ann Arbor	4.4
7. Georgia Institute of Technology	4.3
8. California Institute of Technology	4.2
9. Cornell University (NY)	4.1
9. Princeton University (NJ)	4.1
9. University of Texas–Austin (Cockrell)	4.1

ELECTRICAL/ELECTRONIC/COMMUNICATIONS

Rank School	
1. Massachusetts Institute of Technology	5.0
1. Stanford University (CA)	5.0
3. University of California–Berkeley	4.9
4. University of Illinois–Urbana-Champaign	4.8
5. California Institute of Technology	4.6
6. Georgia Institute of Technology	4.5
7. University of Michigan–Ann Arbor	4.4
8. Carnegie Mellon University (PA)	4.3
8. Princeton University (NJ)	4.3
10. Cornell University (NY)	4.2
10. Purdue University–West Lafayette (IN)	4.2
10. University of Texas–Austin (Cockrell)	4.2

ENVIRONMENTAL/ENVIRONMENTAL HEALTH

Rank School	
1. University of California–Berkeley	4.6
2. Stanford University (CA)	4.5
3. University of Illinois–Urbana-Champaign	4.2
4. Georgia Institute of Technology	4.1
4. University of Michigan–Ann Arbor	4.1
6. University of Texas–Austin (Cockrell)	4.0
7. Carnegie Mellon University (PA)	3.9
8. California Institute of Technology	3.8
8. Johns Hopkins University (Whiting) (MD)	3.8
10. Cornell University (NY)	3.7
10. Massachusetts Institute of Technology	3.7
10. Virginia Tech	3.7

INDUSTRIAL/MANUFACTURING/SYSTEMS

Rank School	
1. Georgia Institute of Technology	4.7
2. University of Michigan–Ann Arbor	4.5
3. University of California–Berkeley	4.4
4. Northwestern University (McCormick) (IL)	4.3
5. Stanford University (CA)	4.2
6. Massachusetts Institute of Technology	4.1
7. Virginia Tech	4.0
8. Cornell University (NY)	3.9
8. Purdue University–West Lafayette (IN)	3.9
10. Pennsylvania State University–University Park	3.8

Rank School	
10. Texas A&M University–College Station (Look)	3.8
10. University of Wisconsin–Madison	3.8

MATERIALS

Rank School	
1. Massachusetts Institute of Technology	4.7
2. University of California–Santa Barbara	4.6
3. Northwestern University (McCormick) (IL)	4.5
4. Stanford University (CA)	4.4
4. University of Illinois–Urbana-Champaign	4.4
6. Georgia Institute of Technology	4.1
6. University of California–Berkeley	4.1
8. California Institute of Technology	3.9
8. Cornell University (NY)	3.9
10. Carnegie Mellon University (PA)	3.8
10. University of Michigan–Ann Arbor	3.8

MECHANICAL

Rank School	
1. Massachusetts Institute of Technology	4.9
2. Stanford University (CA)	4.8
3. California Institute of Technology	4.7
3. University of California–Berkeley	4.7
5. Georgia Institute of Technology	4.6
5. University of Michigan–Ann Arbor	4.6
7. University of Illinois–Urbana-Champaign	4.5
8. Carnegie Mellon University (PA)	4.2
8. Cornell University (NY)	4.2
8. Purdue University–West Lafayette (IN)	4.2

NUCLEAR

Rank School	
1. University of Michigan–Ann Arbor	4.8
2. Massachusetts Institute of Technology	4.7
3. Texas A&M University–College Station (Look)	4.3
3. University of Wisconsin–Madison	4.3
5. Georgia Institute of Technology	3.9
5. Pennsylvania State University–University Park	3.9
5. University of Tennessee–Knoxville	3.9
8. North Carolina State University	3.7
8. University of California–Berkeley	3.7
10. University of Illinois–Urbana-Champaign	3.5

METHODOLOGY

Programs at the 215 engineering schools that grant doctoral degrees were surveyed; 196 responded, and 195 were eligible to be included in the rankings based on a weighted average of 10 indicators described below.

Quality assessment: Two separate surveys were conducted in the fall of 2014. In one, engineering school deans and deans of graduate studies at engineering schools were asked to rate program quality from marginal (1) to outstanding (5); 44 percent responded. The resulting score is weighted by .25 in the overall score. Corporate recruiters and company contacts (names supplied by the engineering schools) who hire engineers with graduate degrees from previously ranked engineering schools were also asked to rate programs. The three most recent years' results were averaged and are weighted by .15.

Student selectivity (weighted by .10): The strength of master's and Ph.D. students entering in fall 2014 was measured by their mean GRE quantitative score (67.5 percent of this measure) and acceptance rate (32.5 percent). Scores for the new and old GRE were converted to a common scale; only new scores are displayed.

Faculty resources (.25): This score is based on the 2014 ratio of full-time doctoral students to full-time faculty (30 percent) and full-time master's students to full-time faculty (15 percent); the proportion of full-time faculty who were members of the National Academy of Engineering in 2014 (30 percent); and the number of engineering doctoral degrees granted in the past school year (25 percent).

Research activity (.25): Based on total externally funded engineering research expenditures (60 percent) and research dollars per full-time tenured and tenure-track engineering faculty member (40 percent). Expenditures refer to separately funded research, public and private, conducted by the school, averaged over fiscal years 2013 and 2014.

Overall rank: Data were standardized about their means, and standardized scores were weighted, totaled and rescaled so the top-scoring school received 100; others received their percentage of the top score.

Specialty rankings: These rankings are based solely on assessments by department heads in each specialty, who rated other schools on a 5-point scale. The top-rated schools in each specialty appear here. Names of department heads surveyed are from the American Society for Engineering Education.

CHAPTER 4

Health &Medicine

UCSF nursing students train at Children's Hospital Oakland.

Medical School GETS A Makeover

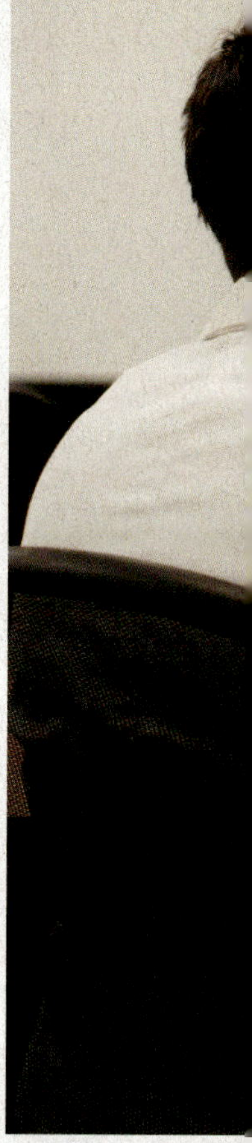

THE DOCTORS OF TOMORROW ARE PREPPING FOR A WHOLE NEW WORLD

By **BETH HOWARD**

When Rolfy Perez Holguin started medical school last fall, he couldn't wait to begin helping people. But he had no idea just how quickly that would happen. Within weeks of tackling his studies at Penn State College of Medicine in Hershey, he was out offering patients guidance and support in a community tuberculosis clinic. "After people are diagnosed with TB, they have to be in isolation for several weeks," says Holguin, 22, who was trained in the new role of "patient navigator" soon after arriving on campus. "But how do they pay the rent if they can't go to work? And what if their kids are infected? You know about challenges patients face, but they don't become real until you actually see them."

Early immersion in the brave new world of patient-centered care, in which doctors consider life circumstances and personal preferences along with symptoms and vital signs, is just one of the trends changing the face of medical education these days. Calls for reform have been issued loud and clear given the monumental shifts taking place in medicine, by groups from the Institute of Medicine to the Carnegie Foundation. And medical schools are responding with innovations at a pace not seen for more than a century, as well as aiming to admit a more diverse set of students armed with people skills along with smarts (box, Page 66).

"The next generation is going to transform the practice of medicine. They need the tools and skills to do it right," says Sherine Gabriel, dean of the Mayo Medical School at the Rochester, Minnesota-based Mayo Clinic. Here are some of the most significant emerging trends:

Face time from the start

Traditionally, the first two years of med school have been spent entirely in the classroom, studying basic medical science. But "people learn much better if they learn a body of knowledge in the context in which it's going to be used," says Bonnie Miller, senior associate dean for health sciences education at Vanderbilt University School of Medicine in Nashville. So first-year Vanderbilt students are "part of the care team," she says, conducting interviews with patients in clinics and helping them understand any new drug prescriptions. Second-year students engage in the transition from hospital to home, helping with discharge arrangements and in some cases following up in house calls.

Also starting in their first year, students at the University of North Texas Health Science Center in Fort Worth are paired with an elderly resident in the area. While visiting the patients in their homes to perform basic medical and nutrition assessments and review medications, students also

▶ **More on medical schools @** usnews.com/medschools

learn to just listen. "Instead of getting a lecture from a geriatrician, they get to hear from seniors themselves what it's like to get old," says Michael Williams, a physician and the school's president. Through such programs, trainees see how putting the focus on the patient prevents costly readmissions and leads to better health outcomes.

Training in multidisciplinary teams

Putting that early training into real-world settings also gives doctors-to-be experience working with other health professionals, a taste of the high-powered team medicine they are expected to practice. "In every other industry – business, aviation, whatever – in order to be more efficient and get good outcomes, you need to take a team approach," says Stephen Klasko, president and CEO of Thomas Jefferson University and Jefferson Health System in Philadelphia. "The only way for that to happen in medicine is to start from the beginning, in school."

Medical students at Jefferson, with students of nursing, pharmacy, physical therapy and other health professions, are assigned to a "health mentor," a patient in the community. The team meets with the person periodically to take histories and create wellness plans. They aren't delivering care per se, but might focus on fixing a safety hazard in a

A team of medical and other students at Thomas Jefferson meets with a patient "health mentor."

mentor's home or check for drug interactions, say, all while beginning to understand what the other experts bring to the table. Claire Sokas, 24, recalls that her team helped their mentor, a woman overwhelmed by a long list of medications and numerous doctors' appointments, figure out how she might cope by, for example, researching mobile apps to keep track of them.

At other schools, groups from different disciplines use training exercises to learn how to interact effectively. At the University of Missouri, medical, nursing, pharmacy and respiratory therapy students take part in a simulation that mimics the chaotic conditions of an emergency room during a flu epidemic. At the University of South Florida, med students gather with peers from the nursing program to simulate such scenarios as treating people injured in a bombing. NYU pairs medical and nursing students to provide care for "virtual" patients with conditions ranging from hip fractures to chronic obstructive pulmonary disease, using electronic health records, or EHRs, and email to communicate.

Developing a sense of social mission

More medical colleges are creating opportunities to help the communities they reside in, particularly underserved popula-

tions. The strategy: to let students see the health consequences of social and economic inequality, an urgent concern among public health experts.

Besides matching students with seniors, UNT dispatches them with doctors and nurses and social workers to disadvantaged neighborhoods in a new mobile pediatric unit to administer screenings and vaccines. "We were able to test her right there on the van," says third-year student Jenifer Gehlsen, 31, recalling a girl with a hearing impairment that had caused her to have difficulty in school; she was immediately referred to a hearing-aid provider. In tiny Eastland, Texas, meanwhile, fourth-year UNT student William Griffin, 28, is completing a rotation in a Rural Osteopathic Medical Education program that has also included stints in several other towns since his first year. "I'm in a unique position to see the whole spectrum of health care," says Griffin, who has helped deliver babies and scrubbed in for surgeries.

At Oakland University William Beaumont School of Medicine in Rochester, Michigan, service-learning opportunities, or experiences that meet community needs and also have an instruc-

New Secrets to Getting In

Near-perfect grades and top MCAT scores once were all the med school gatekeepers cared to see. But seismic shifts in medicine call for a wider set of abilities – such as the people skills needed to navigate in a system where communication is paramount.

That more humanistic focus is reflected in the new MCAT, which adds questions on the social and behavioral sciences and analysis of readings on ethics and philosophy (story, Page 68). And a growing number of schools now base admissions on "holistic review," assessing grades and scores in the context of an applicant's background and experiences and personal qualities. The goal: people who will make compassionate, patient-centered physicians engaged in the community, says Christina Grabowski, assistant dean for admissions and financial services at Oakland University William Beaumont School of Medicine in Michigan.

Interviews, too, are more often being used to size up emotional intelligence. "We might ask something like 'Describe a situation in which you had to disagree with a peer in order to prevent a mistake from being made. What was the outcome?'" says Grabowski. About 30 schools have turned to a tool called the "multiple mini-interview" that rotates candidates through a series of quick interviews, each designed to assess a personal skill or quality, from communication to problem-solving abilities.

More diversity. One aim is to add breadth to the student body. Since

tional purpose, are integrated into the coursework. Students may explore the social problem of food insecurity in one class while learning about its effects on metabolism in another, and then partner with a food bank sending provisions home with schoolkids to put inexpensive nutritious recipes into their backpacks.

Customizable curriculums

No one starts med school with the same knowledge and experience or learns at the same rate, and those variations will only widen as admissions officers look beyond scores and grades. So a growing number of schools are turning to "competency-based" curriculums that allow students to progress not in lock step but after mastering certain skills or reaching defined milestones. These can be specific procedures, such as starting an IV or intubating a patient, or key knowledge, such as the diagnoses to consider for a set of symptoms, says Gabriel.

The idea is to shift from producing doctors who have memorized a lot of information to those who are excellent at what they do and are skilled critical thinkers. At Indiana University School of Medicine, meeting a competency like "professionalism" – which encompasses such concepts as respect for patients, families and other professionals and commitment to serving others – entails, for example, treating donor cadavers

adopting holistic review in 2003, Boston University School of Medicine has seen the proportion of entering students from underrepresented groups grow from 11 to 20 percent, for example. And faculty members have observed that students seem to be more supportive of one another and more engaged in their work. "So far, the classes are just as strong as ever academically," says George Mejicano, senior associate dean for education at Oregon Health & Science University School of Medicine. But "there's greater diversity of thought and experience." –B.H.

with dignity and writing papers on what it means to be a good doctor. Preceptors use checklists of professional behavior to do evaluations.

Students at the Cleveland Clinic Lerner College of Medicine aren't issued grades, but rather assemble an electronic "portfolio" of evidence of progress. This includes feedback from faculty, preceptors and peers, plus self-assessments and essays, grant proposals and other work. "Our goal is to produce doctors who are self-reflective, who are constantly asking 'Could I have done that better? And what am I missing?'" says George Mejicano, Oregon Health & Science University School of Medicine's senior associate dean for education.

A focus on systems of care

The curriculum used to hinge on two things: basic science, or the design and function of the human body, and clinical care, which involves diagnosing and treating bodily ills. Lately schools have focused on a third category of essential intel: system science – how to deliver safe and effective care within a complex system, including everything from reducing errors to understanding costs and how care is financed. "The health care model is completely changing from fee-for-service, based on volume, to pay-for-performance, which is based on value," says Williams. "We haven't been giving students the right skill set to make that adjustment."

To practice being wise stewards of health resources, students on rotations at Mayo use a tool that records the cost of each pill, test and procedure ordered. Later, they reflect back on clinical decisions. "Was that fourth X-ray really needed?" asks Gabriel. "Could the patient have had the same or better outcome with fewer tests and procedures?" Indiana University's new "teaching EHR," a clone of an actual EHR with patient identifiers changed, lets students follow patients from the first to the last day of med school, making treatment decisions and comparing their decisions (and related costs) to the actual ones of physicians in real time.

The medical school of tomorrow clearly is a work in progress. But the revolution is underway – and gaining momentum. ∎

University of Washington
Seattle

LISA MULLEN, '11
Family doctor

▶ UW participates in the WWAMI medical education program that prepares students particularly for rural medical care in communities throughout Washington, Wyoming, Alaska, Montana and Idaho.

I was able to do six-week rotations in four different states and quickly realized how much I loved rural primary care medicine. You get to know patients and their families really well. Specialists aren't always nearby, so you find yourself splinting fractures, delivering babies, doing stress tests and providing end-of-life services. I even took shifts in the local emergency room with my preceptors. The WWAMI program not only provided me with great training for my work in Buffalo, Wyoming, but also took a lot of the stress away by arranging free housing for all my rural rotations.

Get Set For a New MCAT

THE REVISED TEST WILL TARGET PERSONAL QUALITIES AS WELL AS SMARTS

By **DARCY LEWIS**

Being a skilled physician takes more than scientific knowledge, wrote Darrell G. Kirch, president and CEO of the Association of American Medical Colleges, back in 2012 when the association announced plans to launch a revised Medical College Admissions Test in 2015. Also critical in a diverse, patient-centered health care environment, he noted: "good bedside manner, communication skills and an ability to interact with people."

The new test, whose April 2015 launch date affects the class entering in 2016, has been rethought to better identify those qualities. It was developed by a 21-member advisory panel of officials, deans and faculty at academic medical centers, along with other experts, after extensive research, including a survey of more than 2,700 faculty, residents and med students about the competencies students need as soon as they arrive at medical school. The new test will have four sections rather than three, retaining its multiple-choice format, says Karen Mitchell, AAMC's senior director of the admissions testing service, and will better reflect "what people experience in medical school and later as physicians." In a nutshell, MCAT-takers will have to demonstrate knowledge of scientific concepts, scientific reasoning and problem-solving skills, an understanding of research design and execution, and the ability to draw conclusions based on data. They'll get two hours longer to do so, for a total of six and a half hours.

Even as the new test continues to emphasize the natural sciences,

it also includes a section on the behavioral and social sciences for the first time. "We might ask how patients' access to resources affects their well-being," Mitchell says. "That knowledge is extremely relevant to students in a clinical setting." Biochemistry is new to the MCAT, too. "Biochemistry fundamentals are vital to the practice of medicine," says Robert Witzburg, associate dean and director of admissions at Boston University School of Medicine. "Whenever we discuss the management of a diabetic patient, that's biochemistry."

Given the explosive growth of medical knowledge, even the most brilliant physicians can no longer memorize what they need to know to practice. "It's more important to be able to solve problems," Witzburg says. So the new Critical Analysis and Reasoning Skills section has test-takers digest reading passages and answer questions about them, drawing from the humanities and social sciences. No specific subject knowledge is required. "Students who read a newspaper or follow politics and health care reform will learn enough about ethics, philosophy and cultural studies to do well on this section," Witzburg says.

One thing hasn't changed: "Different admissions committees will come to different conclusions about applicants and how much weight to give the MCAT, just as they always have," says Witzburg. "The new test will favor students who are able to draw connections between disciplines and ideas. At BU, we will attach more weight to the new MCAT, because it will be a better, broader test." Aaron Saguil, associate dean for recruitment and admissions at the Uniformed Services University of the Health Sciences medical school in Bethesda, Maryland, predicts that his office will rely more heavily on "other aspects of the applicant's file at least for the first year, and possibly the second as well."

How to prepare for the new MCAT this year? There are few practice materials available from the test-prep industry yet, not to mention a lack of helpful intel from friends who have already taken the exam. The AAMC suggests brushing up on basic probability, confidence intervals, statistical significance levels, graphical presentation of data, hypothesis formulation and testing, independent and dependent variables, and how research is reported. The association offers its own test-prep tools, including some 800 free online tutorials from the nonprofit Khan Academy (khanacademy.org/test-prep/mcat) explaining various concepts, written and narrated by med students. The AAMC also offers sample questions and a sample test; a second will be published in the fall. "It definitely helps to know what the new test looks like," says Saguil. And given the added two hours, he notes, "endurance will be a factor." ∎

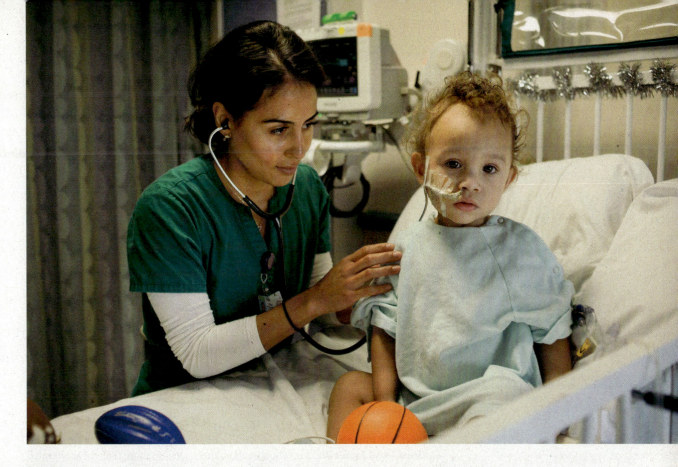

Rx: An Advanced Degree

IT'S A SELLER'S MARKET FOR NURSES WITH A MASTER'S OR DOCTORATE

By **LINDA MARSA**

When Sarah Mobley neared the end of her master's program, she was bombarded with so many calls and emails about potential jobs that she unsubscribed from employment websites. "I got 12 calls in one day alone," says Mobley, who completed a psychiatric nurse practitioner program at the University of Colorado–Denver in December. She ultimately lined up a job at a hospital in Columbus, Ohio, that pays $100,000 a year. "It blows my mind," says Mobley, 27, that she was so marketable.

Mobley's experience is not uncommon these days. The competition for "advanced practice registered nurses," or APRNs (including clinical nurse specialists, certified nurse midwives, nurse practitioners and nurse anesthetists), is growing exponentially. Studies have consistently shown that a more educated work force translates into better care, says Linda Burnes Bolton, vice president for nursing at Cedars-Sinai Medical Center in Los Angeles and vice chair of a 2010 Institute of Medicine study on the future of nursing.

Indeed, people seeking to attain advanced-practice positions soon are apt to be required or strongly encouraged to obtain doctorates. In a decade, newly minted nurse anesthetists will have to

A student in UCSF's accelerated master's nursing program practices at Children's Hospital Oakland.

have a doctorate, and the IOM has called for a doubling of the number of doctorate-level nurses by 2020.

For now, a master's is the main route, though experts expect stiffer credentialing requirements will eventually apply in more areas, as they already do for pharmacists and physical therapists; new entrants to both fields need doctorates. More than 250 schools offer a DNP (doctor of nursing practice) degree, a 2014 RAND Corporation survey showed.

Several factors are fueling the demand, but none more so than the epidemics of diabetes and obesity and the aging of the population. Tending to people with chronic and often multiple conditions, in the home or in outpatient facilities, will account for the lion's share of health care in the 21st century, according to the IOM. "The push now is to get people out of hospitals and bring back house calls, which can be done by nurses," says Vicki Erickson, program director for the master's and DNP programs at Colorado.

Meanwhile, health reform has swept tens of millions of under- and uninsured Americans into a system already strained by a scarcity of family doctors, expected to reach 52,000 vacancies by 2025. Little wonder nurses are increasingly "being given responsibilities that normally flowed to physicians," says Jacqueline Dunbar-Jacob, dean of the school of nursing at the University of Pittsburgh.

Nurses deliver care outside of hospitals that's

WHY I PICKED...

University of Maryland
Baltimore

AYYUB HANIF, '12
Program manager of care coordination

▶ After several years as a transplant nurse, I began my master's in health services leadership and management at UMB's School of Nursing. The program teaches management for the health care setting. This is critical as everything is high stakes in a hospital, from preventing infections to ensuring patients are not served life-threatening foods. We spoke with actual hospital leaders about their management strategies and challenges.

Shortly after completing my master's, I began working in my current position at the University of Maryland Medical Center, focusing on reducing patient readmissions. As someone who hopes to be a hospital executive, I really benefited from the specialized training not generally available in MBA programs.

comparable in quality to a physician's care, according to multiple studies conducted at the University of Pennsylvania and George Washington University, among other research centers, and often at a fraction of the cost. In 2014, British researchers concluded that it's actually safer for healthy women with uncomplicated pregnancies to give birth aided by midwives than by doctors, who are more inclined to use interventions (forceps deliveries or C-sections, say) that cause complications.

Nurse anesthetists – who have been ministering to wounded soldiers since the Civil War – are the sole providers of analgesics in about one-third of all hospitals and close to 100 percent of rural hospitals, assisting in all sorts of surgical and other procedures and providing chronic pain management and emergency care. "If not for them, many of these hospitals in smaller areas couldn't be there," says James Walker, who directs the graduate program for nurse anesthesia at Baylor College of Medicine in Houston. Currently, nurse anesthetists make an average of $150,000 a year.

Nurse practitioners operate in settings from hospitals and HMOs to nursing homes and schools, as well as in private practice. They treat relatively uncomplicated medical problems, provide preventive care and write prescriptions. In 19 states, including Arizona, Colorado and Washington, plus the District of Columbia, nurse practitioners can work without a supervising physician; about a dozen other states, such as Pennsylvania and California, are considering giving them full independence. Clinical nurse specialists work mainly in hospitals, providing specialized care in such areas as geriatrics, cardiac or cancer care. Nurse midwives not only deliver babies but also provide gynecological exams, family planning advice and neonatal care.

Typically, a master's requires 18 to 30 months, while a DNP can take up to three years full-time. Some schools, like the University of Colorado and the University of Pittsburgh, offer Ph.D. programs in nursing, too. The Ph.D., which requires original research and a dissertation, prepares students to become scientists and professors; the DNP, by contrast, emphasizes clinical skills and

involves a so-called practice project but no dissertation.

At Pittsburgh, for instance, DNP students complete about 1,000 hours of mentored clinical practice similar to med school rotations and a capstone project that applies what they've learned. A student might work on upgrading safety in neonatal nursing care, for example, or come up with strategies for helping troubled adolescents in a mental health facility. When choosing a program, experts recommend looking at graduates' pass rates on licensing exams and where they end up. "Placement rates of 94 percent or above are good, and [graduates] should have at least a 90 percent pass rate on exams," suggests Dunbar-Jacob.

A bachelor's in nursing is required to

enter a regular master's program. But there are also more than 60 accelerated programs for people with an undergrad degree in another field who want both a nursing license and an advanced degree. The first year of the University of California–San Francisco's 36-month program for would-be nurse practitioners and clinical nurse specialists, for example, is devoted entirely to nursing courses in preparation for the R.N. boards, taken during the summer. The final two years are dedicated to other courses and clinical preparation. "This is a really intense program, and it's not for everybody," says Kristine Warner, assistant dean and director of the Masters Entry Program in Nursing. "But we have extremely motivated students from all walks of life."

That group includes Steven Foreman, 34, who until recently was a disenchanted chemical engineer working in the oil industry in San Francisco. "I was doing a lot of volunteer work in the gay HIV community and I came in contact with a lot of nurses who had gone through this program, which really turned my head," says Foreman, who gave up his job at a biofuels company and entered what he describes as "R.N. bootcamp" at UCSF last June. "With my experience and technical background, and my desire to give back to my community," he says, the program is "a good fit." His goal: to work as a nurse practitioner. ∎

A Big Piece of Primary Care

By **CHRISTOPHER J. GEARON**

Working as a high school athletic trainer in rural Illinois, Timothy Mangold often teamed up with a local physician assistant specializing in orthopedics. "She was really down to earth, and had a lot of empathy for her patients," Mangold recalls of the experience, which led to his making a late-20s career switch. "It seemed like being a PA would be a great way to help people." Physician assistants examine patients, diagnose injuries and illnesses, and provide treatment under the supervision of a physician or surgeon. Mangold estimates that he can do "80 percent of what a doctor would do."

As a first step, he had to take some undergraduate prerequisites – including organic chemistry and microbiology – that his 2004 bachelor's in athletic training from North Dakota State University did not require. He then entered the University of Iowa's Master of Physician Assistant Studies program (which runs 28 months), often sharing classes with medical students. By his second year, he was seeing patients at the university's hospital and at other facilities in the state. After graduating in 2013, Mangold passed the national certification exam and was hired by the Vinton Family Medical Clinic in Vinton, Iowa, one of Vincent Gay Hospital's outposts.

"I have autonomy, unless I have a question or concern for my supervising physician," says Mangold, 34, who sees about 20 patients daily. He reviews patients'

Timothy Mangold
University of Iowa
Carver College of Medicine, 2013

medical histories, does physical exams, orders and interprets x-rays and other diagnostic tests, treats a whole range of ailments from bronchitis to diabetes, writes prescriptions and removes moles or cysts and performs other office-based procedures.

While one-third of PAs choose a career in primary care, others work in medical specialties, including emergency medicine, orthopedics and psychiatry. Their tasks depend largely on the specialty and what their supervising physician needs them to do. A PA working in surgery, for example, may close incisions and provide care before and after the operation.

As America's population ages, PAs will increasingly be needed to treat the kinds of chronic ailments that come with an older population, like diabetes and heart disease. The Affordable Care Act also has added to the ranks of insured individuals, who now are more able to seek primary care. The Bureau of Labor Statistics projects job growth of 38 percent between 2012 and 2022.

The money is good, too. The median annual wage for PAs was $90,930 in 2012, with the top 10 percent making more than $124,770. ∎

... MORE HOT JOBS

Physical therapist

➤ As the U.S. population expands and baby boomers get creakier, PTs will find plenty of opportunities to help the injured and ill improve their movement and manage their pain. In fact, the government estimates **36 percent growth by 2022** – or nearly 124,000 openings. You'll need a doctor of physical therapy degree, which typically takes three years. The median annual wage for PTs was **$79,860 in 2012**, but leading earners pulled in more than **$112,000**.

Dentist

➤ The demand for dentists is expected to be particularly strong in rural areas in coming years, translating to more than **59,000 positions by 2022**. Dental school requires four years, and specialists like orthodontists and endodontists generally need another two to four years. The hard work pays off, though. The typical general dentist made **$149,310 in 2012** with the top 10 percent boasting **$187,000**.

Optometrist

➤ It's the fading eyesight of America's aging population that is boosting the job market among optometrists, although some specialize in treating infants and children. Optometrists (who must have a doctor of optometry degree) examine, diagnose, treat and manage various eye diseases and injuries. The BLS projects **24 percent growth by 2022**. Median salaries ran about **$97,820 in 2012**, although earnings for some topped **$184,500**.

Best Jobs 2015 Rankings

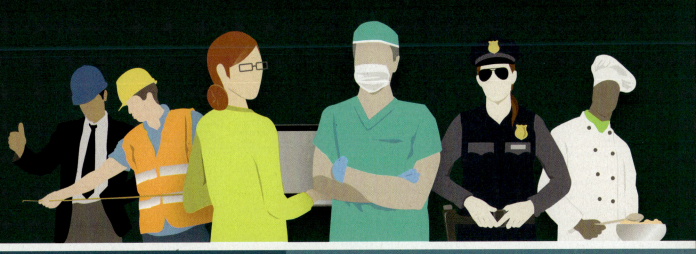

BEST JOBS
U.S.News & WORLD REPORT
RANKINGS

See which jobs are in-demand in the following industries:

- STEM
- Health Care
- Business
- Technology
- Construction
- Social Services
- Creative

Visit **usnews.com/careers**
for rankings and analysis of the greatest occupations of this decade.

Schools of Medicine

THE TOP SCHOOLS - RESEARCH

Rank School	Overall score	Peer assessment score (5.0=highest)	Assessment score, residency directors (5.0=highest)	'14 median undergrad GPA	'14 median MCAT score	'14 acceptance rate	'14 NIH research grants (in millions)	'14 NIH research grants per faculty member (in thousands)	'14 faculty/ student ratio	'14 out-of-state tuition and fees	'14 total medical school enrollment
1. Harvard University (MA)	100	4.8	4.7	3.92	36	3.5%	$1,412.9	$145.5	13.4	$55,785	726
2. Stanford University (CA)	89	4.7	4.6	3.85	37	2.4%	$354.7	$381.8	2.0	$51,356	473
3. Johns Hopkins University (MD)	84	4.8	4.7	3.90	36	5.5%	$528.4	$190.9	6.0	$52,174	461
3. University of California–San Francisco	84	4.7	4.6	3.83	34	3.7%	$549.0	$252.3	3.3	$48,627	664
5. University of Pennsylvania (Perelman)	83	4.5	4.5	3.84	38	4.9%	$550.5	$197.7	4.3	$54,378	655
6. Washington University in St. Louis	78	4.5	4.5	3.87	'38	8.3%	$356.3	$192.5	3.9	$56,212	474
7. Yale University (CT)	77	4.2	4.2	3.83	37	6.5%	$342.9	$242.7	3.4	$54,345	415
8. Columbia University (NY)	76	4.3	4.5	3.82	36	3.9%	$373.2	$198.5	2.9	$59,063	648
8. Duke University (NC)	76	4.5	4.5	3.80	35	3.3%	$324.9	$224.8	3.4	$55,770	430
10. University of Chicago (Pritzker)	74	4.0	4.1	3.87	37	4.0%	$227.4	$255.8	2.5	$52,512	356
10. University of Michigan–Ann Arbor	74	4.3	4.5	3.79	35	6.8%	$350.8	$189.3	2.5	$49,190	727
10. University of Washington	74	4.2	4.3	3.68	31	4.7%	$646.8	$235.3	2.9	$61,356	938
13. University of California–Los Angeles (Geffen)	72	4.0	4.3	3.78	35	3.2%	$416.2	$171.4	3.2	$47,802	749
14. New York University	71	3.6	3.8	3.84	36	6.4%	$340.7	$333.7	1.6	$52,600	650
14. Vanderbilt University (TN)	71	4.1	4.3	3.87	36	3.9%	$337.5	$137.4	5.7	$49,092	429
16. University of Pittsburgh	70	4.0	4.1	3.85	36	6.3%	$369.6	$167.1	3.7	$50,856	601
17. University of California–San Diego	69	4.0	3.9	3.77	34	3.6%	$311.9	$231.4	2.7	$48,329	502
18. Cornell University (Weill) (NY)	68	4.0	4.4	3.82	36	4.1%	$275.8	$117.3	5.8	$53,185	406
19. Northwestern University (Feinberg) (IL)	67	3.8	4.2	3.87	36	6.4%	$283.8	$149.0	2.8	$55,885	687
20. Icahn School of Medicine at Mount Sinai (NY)	65	3.5	3.8	3.78	36	8.5%	$304.8	$206.5	2.7	$50,551	556
21. Baylor College of Medicine (TX)	63	3.5	4.1	3.84	35	4.4%	$260.8	$145.0	2.4	$31,618	738
22. University of North Carolina–Chapel Hill	62	3.9	4.0	3.67	32	4.5%	$297.2	$195.5	1.8	$47,681	827
23. Emory University (GA)	61	3.9	4.1	3.72.	34	5.6%	$237.9	$105.4	4.0	$50,554	560
24. Case Western Reserve University (OH)	60	3.6	3.7	3.74	36	7.9%	$286.2	$113.2	2.9	$57,050	864
25. U. of Texas Southwestern Medical Center	59	4.0	3.9	3.85	34	10.2%	$170.8	$78.2	2.3	$31,693	953
26. University of Virginia	58	3.6	4.0	3.85	35	11.0%	$108.0	$112.0	1.6	$57,044	620
27. Mayo Medical School (MN)	57	3.6	4.0	3.81	33	2.0%	$234.0	$72.6	14.9	$47,470	216
28. University of Wisconsin–Madison	56	3.6	3.8	3.76	32	5.4%	$199.4	$168.4	1.7	$34,841	697
29. University of Iowa (Carver)	55	3.7	3.7	3.76	32	7.6%	$123.9	$127.4	1.6	$51,502	608
30. Boston University	54	3.3	3.5	3.71	34	4.4%	$198.0	$139.7	2.1	$54,678	681
31. Ohio State University	53	3.3	3.6	3.77	34	7.0%	$168.1	$89.3	2.3	$35,947	824
31. Oregon Health and Science University	53	3.5	3.8	3.64	31	4.2%	$231.8	$109.2	4.0	$57,856	526
31. University of Southern California (Keck)	53	3.3	3.7	3.70	35	5.5%	$152.9	$98.9	2.1	$57,091	722
34. University of Rochester (NY)	52	3.5	3.7	3.72	33	5.4%	$141.5	$94.4	3.4	$50,900	435
35. Brown University (Alpert) (RI)	51	3.2	3.7	3.65	33	2.9%	$88.7	$119.5	1.5	$55,421	490
35. University of Colorado	51	3.6	3.6	3.71	33	5.2%	$160.2*	$49.4*	4.8	$62,230	672
37. Dartmouth College (Geisel) (NH)	50	3.3	3.7	3.71	33	5.1%	$83.8	$106.5	2.1	$58,368	368
37. University of Alabama–Birmingham	50	3.6	3.6	3.76	30	8.1%	$156.3	$118.0	1.7	$62,407	781
37. University of Maryland	50	3.2	3.3	3.79	32	6.7%	$151.9*	$121.5*	1.9	$63,466	647
40. University of Cincinnati	49	2.9	3.3	3.74	33	7.9%	$210.9	$123.1	2.6	$50,438	671
40. University of Minnesota	49	3.3	3.6	3.76	31	7.1%	$164.1	$81.3	2.0	$51,607	1,005
40. Yeshiva University (Einstein) (NY)	49	3.2	3.4	3.78	33	4.3%	$160.4	$80.2	2.5	$53,142	793
43. University of California–Davis	48	3.2	3.4	3.62	31	3.9%	$119.4	$162.3	1.7	$52,828	437
43. University of Florida	48	3.1	3.4	3.84	32	5.4%	$115.9	$84.1	2.5	$49,325	543
45. Indiana University–Indianapolis	47	3.4	3.6	3.79	31	10.5%	$101.7*	$50.9*	1.5	$54,158	1,377
45. University of California–Irvine	47	2.9	3.2	3.74	32	4.3%	$103.5	$126.5	1.9	$48,749	420
45. University of Miami (Miller) (FL)	47	3.0	3.4	3.74	33	4.4%	$123.8	$90.5	1.7	$42,610	803
48. University of Utah	46	3.3	3.6	3.72	29	8.6%	$147.5	$94.9	4.2	$65,011	369
49. Georgetown University (DC)	45	3.3	3.6	3.60	31	2.7%	$126.6	$59.2	2.7	$55,136	796

THE TOP SCHOOLS - RESEARCH continued

Rank	School	Overall score	Peer assessment score (5.0=highest)	Assessment score, residency directors (5.0=highest)	'14 median undergrad GPA	'14 median MCAT score	'14 acceptance rate	'14 NIH research grants (in millions)	'14 NIH research grants per faculty member (in thousands)	'14 faculty/ student ratio	'14 out-of-state tuition and fees	'14 total medical school enrollment
49.	Tufts University (MA)	45	3.3	3.5	3.68	32	5.2%	$85.4	$54.5	1.9	$57,920	816
49.	University of Illinois	45	2.9	3.3	3.61	31	12.2%	$139.7	$158.0	0.7	$76,488	1,352
49.	University of Massachusetts–Worcester	45	3.0	3.1	3.70	33	16.5%	$135.2*	$97.2*	2.7	N/A**	508
49.	Wake Forest University (NC)	45	3.0	3.5	3.58	32	2.9%	$102.8	$92.5	2.4	$50,300	469
54.	Medical College of Wisconsin	44	3.0	3.5	3.78	31	6.7%	$87.1	$56.2	1.9	$50,067	817
55.	Temple University (PA)	42	2.6	2.9	3.68	32	4.5%	$89.1	$153.6	0.7	$54,326	879
55.	U. of Texas Health Science Center–San Antonio	42	2.9	3.2	3.77	32	11.4%	$69.4	$64.6	1.3	$33,037	860
57.	Stony Brook University–SUNY	41	2.8	2.9	3.70	32	6.8%	$71.2	$95.7	1.5	$63,180	500
57.	University of Vermont	41	2.8	3.2	3.75	31	4.5%	$63.9	$99.0	1.4	$58,759	465
57.	Univ. of Texas Health Science Center–Houston	41	2.9	3.2	3.79	32	10.4%	$62.0*	$50.8*	1.3	$30,454	960

THE TOP SCHOOLS - PRIMARY CARE

Rank	School	Overall score	Peer assessment score (5.0=highest)	Assessment score, residency directors (5.0=highest)	Selectivity rank	'14 median undergrad GPA	'14 median MCAT score	'14 acceptance rate	% '12-'14 graduates entering primary care	'14 faculty/ student ratio	'14 out-of-state tuition and fees	'14 total medical school enrollment
1.	University of Washington	100	4.0	4.5	65	3.68	31	4.7%	54.3%	2.9	$61,356	938
2.	University of North Carolina–Chapel Hill	98	3.6	4.1	54	3.67	32	4.5%	63.0%	1.8	$47,681	827
3.	University of California–San Francisco	86	3.6	4.5	21	3.83	34	3.7%	42.8%	3.3	$48,627	664
4.	University of Nebraska Medical Center	83	3.1	3.3	54	3.78	31	10.4%	65.0%	1.3	$72,747	515
5.	Oregon Health and Science University	81	3.6	4.1	71	3.64	31	4.2%	46.3%	4.0	$57,856	526
5.	University of Michigan–Ann Arbor	81	3.4	4.2	20	3.79	35	6.8%	43.8%	2.5	$49,190	727
7.	University of California–Los Angeles (Geffen)	80	3.2	4.0	19	3.78	35	3.2%	47.8%	3.2	$47,802	749
8.	University of Colorado	79	3.5	4.0	35	3.71	33	5.2%	44.9%	4.8	$62,230	672
9.	University of Wisconsin–Madison	78	3.5	3.9	38	3.76	32	5.4%	44.9%	1.7	$34,841	697
10.	University of Minnesota	76	3.3	3.8	54	3.76	31	7.1%	48.7%	2.0	$51,607	1,005
11.	Baylor College of Medicine (TX)	75	2.7	4.0	14	3.84	35	4.4%	52.0%	2.4	$31,618	738
12.	Harvard University (MA)	71	2.9	4.1	5	3.92	36	3.5%	41.3%	13.4	$55,785	726
12.	Michigan State U. (Col. of Osteopathic Medicine)	71	2.4	3.1	105	3.56	28	9.3%	79.3%	0.2	$88,784	1,234
12.	University of Massachusetts–Worcester	71	3.0	3.3	45	3.70	33	16.5%	53.1%	2.7	N/A**	508
12.	University of Pennsylvania (Perelman)	71	3.1	4.2	2	3.84	38	4.9%	35.0%	4.3	$54,378	655
16.	University of Iowa (Carver)	70	3.5	4.0	40	3.76	32	7.6%	37.0%	1.6	$51,502	608
17.	University of Alabama–Birmingham	68	3.2	3.8	69	3.76	30	8.1%	44.5%	1.7	$62,407	781
17.	U. of Texas Southwestern Medical Center	68	2.9	3.8	22	3.85	34	10.2%	44.4%	2.3	$31,693	953
19.	University of California–Davis	67	3.2	3.6	73	3.62	31	3.9%	45.4%	1.7	$52,828	437
19.	University of California–San Diego	67	3.0	3.7	23	3.77	34	3.6%	43.0%	2.7	$48,329	502
19.	University of Chicago (Pritzker)	67	2.8	3.8	3	3.87	37	4.0%	41.0%	2.5	$52,512	356
19.	University of Hawaii–Manoa (Burns)	67	3.0	2.9	60	3.71	31	4.6%	55.0%	0.7	$67,912	270
19.	University of Pittsburgh	67	3.1	3.9	10	3.85	36	6.3%	36.0%	3.7	$50,856	601
19.	Washington University in St. Louis	67	3.1	4.0	1	3.87	38	8.3%	32.6%	3.9	$56,212	474
25.	East Carolina University (Brody) (NC)	66	3.0	3.2	95	3.72	28	13.3%	54.6%	1.4	N/A**	313
25.	Stanford University (CA)	66	2.9	4.2	3	3.85	37	2.4%	35.0%	2.0	$51,356	473
25.	University of Kansas Medical Center	66	3.1	3.4	79	3.78	29	8.0%	48.9%	1.1	$58,336	828
25.	Vanderbilt University (TN)	66	3.0	3.9	8	3.87	36	3.9%	36.2%	5.7	$49,092	429
29.	Dartmouth College (Geisel) (NH)	65	3.0	3.6	35	3.71	33	5.1%	43.6%	2.1	$58,368	368
29.	Duke University (NC)	65	3.2	4.1	17	3.80	35	3.3%	32.0%	3.4	$55,770	430
29.	Johns Hopkins University (MD)	65	3.0	4.2	7	3.90	36	5.5%	32.8%	6.0	$52,174	461
29.	Northwestern University (Feinberg) (IL)	65	2.8	3.9	9	3.87	36	6.4%	39.6%	2.8	$55,885	687
29.	University of Vermont	65	3.2	3.5	54	3.75	31	4.5%	43.0%	1.4	$58,759	465
34.	Morehouse School of Medicine (GA)	64	2.8	2.5	114	3.49	26	1.6%	68.0%	0.6	$51,878	398
35.	University of Arkansas for Medical Sciences	63	2.8	3.2	93	3.67	29	8.7%	54.0%	1.9	$50,828	682
35.	University of Missouri	63	3.2	3.4	69	3.76	30	9.1%	43.0%	1.5	$56,872	391
35.	University of New Mexico	63	3.5	3.3	105	3.65	27	10.7%	42.3%	2.1	$49,572	438
35.	University of Rochester (NY)	63	3.2	3.7	33	3.72	33	5.4%	37.0%	3.4	$50,900	435

N/A=Data were not provided by the school. *The medical school's National Institutes of Health grants do not include any grants to affiliated hospitals.
**The school does not accept out-of-state students to its M.D. program. Sources: U.S. News and the schools. Peer assessment data collected by Ipsos Public Affairs.

THE TOP SCHOOLS - PRIMARY CARE continued

Rank	School	Overall score	Peer assessment score (5.0=highest)	Assessment score, residency directors (5.0=highest)	Selectivity rank	'14 median undergrad GPA	'14 median MCAT score	'14 acceptance rate	% '12-'14 graduates entering primary care	'14 faculty/ student ratio	'14 out-of-state tuition and fees	'14 total medical school enrollment
35.	University of Utah	63	3.3	3.8	90	3.72	29	8.6%	37.9%	4.2	$65,011	369
40.	Ohio State University	62	2.8	3.6	25	3.77	34	7.0%	43.3%	2.3	$35,947	824
40.	University of Virginia	62	3.0	3.8	16	3.85	35	11.0%	35.4%	1.6	$57,044	620
42.	Eastern Virginia Medical School	61	2.9	3.0	88	3.55	31	5.1%	52.0%	0.8	$57,802	576
42.	Emory University (GA)	61	2.9	3.8	28	3.72	34	5.6%	38.8%	4.0	$50,554	560
42.	Mayo Medical School (MN)	61	2.8	3.9	27	3.81	33	2.0%	39.0%	14.9	$47,470	216
42.	New York University	61	2.9	3.4	11	3.84	36	6.4%	39.0%	1.6	$52,600	650
42.	University of Arizona	61	2.9	3.3	73	3.70	30	4.2%	48.0%	1.7	$49,437	465
47.	Indiana University–Indianapolis	60	3.3	3.6	49	3.79	31	10.5%	35.0%	1.5	$54,158	1,377
47.	Uniformed Services U. of the Health Sci. (Hebert) (MD)	60	2.7	3.6	76	3.64	31	10.3%	48.0%	5.3	N/A	682
49.	Cornell University (Weill) (NY)	58	2.6	3.7	11	3.82	36	4.1%	39.0%	5.8	$53,185	406
49.	University of Connecticut	58	2.8	3.2	49	3.70	32	8.0%	46.0%	2.8	$65,887	382
49.	Virginia Commonwealth University	58	2.8	3.4	84	3.65	30	4.9%	46.7%	1.8	$47,612	845
52.	Boston University	57	2.8	3.5	29	3.71	34	4.4%	39.9%	2.1	$54,678	681
52.	Columbia University (NY)	57	2.8	3.9	11	3.82	36	3.9%	32.4%	2.9	$59,063	648
52.	Tufts University (MA)	57	2.7	3.5	49	3.68	32	5.2%	44.0%	1.9	$57,920	816
52.	University of Maryland	57	2.9	3.4	37	3.79	32	6.7%	39.3%	1.9	$63,466	647
52.	University of North Texas Health Science Center	57	2.4	2.7	101	3.62	28	15.1%	63.9%	0.5	$34,710	927
57.	Brown University (Alpert) (RI)	56	2.9	3.6	40	3.65	33	2.9%	38.0%	1.5	$55,421	490
57.	Lake Erie College of Osteopathic Medicine (PA)	56	2.3	2.7	113	3.48	27	9.9%	67.9%	0.5	$32,510	2,241
57.	St. Louis University	56	2.7	3.1	25	3.85	33	7.2%	43.8%	0.9	$50,140	730
57.	Yale University (CT)	56	2.7	3.7	6	3.83	37	6.5%	33.8%	3.4	$54,345	415
57.	Yeshiva University (Einstein) (NY)	56	2.6	3.3	29	3.78	33	4.3%	44.0%	2.5	$53,142	793

SPECIALTIES

MEDICAL SCHOOL DEANS AND SENIOR FACULTY SELECT THE BEST PROGRAMS

AIDS
1. University of California–San Francisco
2. Johns Hopkins University (MD)
3. Harvard University (MA)
4. Columbia University (NY)
4. University of Washington
6. University of North Carolina–Chapel Hill
7. University of Pennsylvania (Perelman)
8. University of California–Los Angeles (Geffen)

DRUG/ALCOHOL ABUSE
1. Harvard University (MA)
2. University of California–San Francisco
3. Johns Hopkins University (MD)
3. Yale University (CT)
5. Columbia University (NY)
6. University of Pennsylvania (Perelman)

FAMILY MEDICINE
1. University of Washington

2. University of North Carolina–Chapel Hill
3. Duke University (NC)
4. University of California–San Francisco
5. Oregon Health and Science University
5. University of Wisconsin–Madison
7. University of Colorado
7. University of Michigan–Ann Arbor

GERIATRICS
1. Johns Hopkins University (MD)
2. Icahn School of Medicine at Mount Sinai (NY)
3. University of California–Los Angeles (Geffen)
4. Harvard University (MA)
4. University of Michigan–Ann Arbor
6. Duke University (NC)
6. Yale University (CT)

INTERNAL MEDICINE
1. Johns Hopkins University (MD)

2. Harvard University (MA)
3. University of California–San Francisco
4. Duke University (NC)
5. Washington University in St. Louis
6. University of Pennsylvania (Perelman)
7. University of Michigan–Ann Arbor
8. Columbia University (NY)
8. Stanford University (CA)
8. University of Washington

PEDIATRICS
1. University of Pennsylvania (Perelman)
2. Harvard University (MA)
3. University of Cincinnati
4. Johns Hopkins University (MD)
5. University of Colorado
6. University of California–San Francisco
7. Stanford University (CA)
8. University of Washington
9. Baylor College of Medicine (TX)
9. Washington University in St. Louis

RURAL MEDICINE
1. University of Washington
2. University of North Dakota
3. University of New Mexico
4. University of Minnesota
5. University of North Carolina–Chapel Hill
6. University of South Dakota (Sanford)
6. University of Wisconsin–Madison

WOMEN'S HEALTH
1. Harvard University (MA)
2. University of California–San Francisco
3. Johns Hopkins University (MD)
4. University of Pittsburgh
5. Columbia University (NY)
5. University of Pennsylvania (Perelman)
7. University of Michigan–Ann Arbor
8. Stanford University (CA)
9. Duke University (NC)
9. Northwestern University (Feinberg) (IL)

METHODOLOGY

The 130 medical schools fully accredited in 2014 by the Liaison Committee on Medical Education and the 26 schools of osteopathic medicine fully accredited in 2014 by the American Osteopathic Association were surveyed for the rankings of research medical schools and for top schools in primary care; 118 schools provided the data needed to calculate the two separate rankings. The research model is based on a weighted average of eight indicators, and the primary care model is based on seven indicators. Most indicators are the same for both. The research model factors in NIH research activity; the primary care model uses the proportion of graduates entering primary care specialties.

Quality assessment: Three assessment surveys were conducted in the fall of 2014. In a peer survey, medical and osteopathic school deans, deans of academic affairs, and heads of internal medicine or the directors of admissions were asked to

rate program quality on a scale of marginal (1) to outstanding (5). Respondents were asked to rate research and primary care programs separately. The response rate was 30 percent. Average peer assessment score in the research rankings model is weighted by .20; average score in the primary care model by .25. In two separate surveys, residency program directors were asked to rate programs using the same 5-point scale. One survey dealt with research and was sent to a sample of residency program directors designated by the medical schools as being involved in research. The other survey was sent to residency directors designated by the medical schools as being involved in clinical practice. Residency directors' surveys for the three most recent years were averaged and weighted .20 in the research model and .15 in primary care. Medical schools supplied U.S. News all the names of those residency program directors who were sent either of the residency program director surveys.

Research activity (weighted by .30 in the research model only): Research was measured as the total dollar amount of National Institutes of Health research grants awarded to the medical school and its affiliated hospitals (50 percent of this measure) and the average amount of those grants per full-time medical school science and clinical faculty member (50 percent); for the rankings, both factors were averaged for fiscal years 2013 and 2014. An asterisk indicates schools that reported only NIH research grants going to their medical school in 2014. The NIH figures published are for fiscal year 2014 only.

Primary care rate (.30 in primary care model only): The percentage of medical or osteopathic school graduates entering primary care residencies in the fields of family practice, pediatrics and internal medicine was averaged over the 2012, 2013 and 2014 graduating classes.

Student selectivity (.20 in research model, .15 in primary

care model): Based on three measures describing the class entering in fall 2014: median Medical College Admission Test total score (65 percent of this measure), median undergraduate GPA (30 percent), and the acceptance rate (5 percent).

Faculty resources (.10 in research model, .15 in primary care model): Faculty resources were measured as the ratio of full-time science and clinical faculty to medical or osteopathic students in 2014.

Overall rank: Indicators were standardized about their means, and standardized scores were weighted, totaled and rescaled so that the top school received 100; other schools received their percentage of the top school's score.

Specialty rankings: Based solely on ratings by medical school deans and senior faculty at peer schools, who identified up to 10 schools offering the best programs in each specialty. The top half of programs (by number of nominations) appear.

EXCEED YOUR GOALS.

On the U.S. Army health care team, you can do more than just meet your goals – you can exceed them. By joining the Army team, you can expand your education and explore new areas of your specialty. Army health care professionals are leaders that inspire others to succeed, all while providing outstanding care for Soldiers and their families.

To learn more, call 800-431-6691 or visit healthcare.goarmy.com/at60

U.S. ARMY

Schools of Nursing

THE TOP SCHOOLS - MASTER'S

Rank School	Overall score	Peer assessment score (5.0=highest)	'14 acceptance rate	'14 mean undergrad GPA	'14 student/ faculty ratio	'14 percent of faculty in active nursing practice	'14 master's degrees awarded	'14 NIH and federal research grants (in thousands)	'14 NIH and federal teaching grants (in thousands)	'14 out-of-state tuition and fees	'14 master's program enrollment full-/part-time
1. University of Pennsylvania	100	4.6	55.3%	3.65	7.7	4.9%	249	$8,893.3	$6,572.6	$40,446	203/333
2. Johns Hopkins University (MD)	96	4.5	50.0%	3.55	6.1	50.0%	81	$13,992.9	$2,296.8	$29,970	69/209
2. University of California–San Francisco	96	4.6	31.7%	3.53	10.3	N/A	146	$10,197.7	$5,275.3	$37,037	395/N/A
4. University of Washington	90	4.4	80.9%	N/A	0.6	21.6%	86	$9,532.0	$2,565.3	N/A	13/59
5. University of Pittsburgh	88	4.4	30.0%	3.70	3.5	19.5%	111	$5,245.1	$2,720.3	$43,290	120/69
6. Duke University (NC)	87	4.3	37.8%	3.56	6.5	20.0%	159	$5,282.2	$2,896.0	$1,495*	146/345
6. New York University	87	4.1	67.6%	3.40	8.8	30.8%	186	$6,932.7	$4,182.4	$37,189	34/584
6. University of Maryland–Baltimore	87	4.2	52.7%	3.31	17.3	19.2%	311	$3,011.9	$4,442.9	$1,178*	315/404
6. University of Michigan–Ann Arbor	87	4.3	68.1%	3.56	5.3	17.5%	99	$5,312.8	$2,457.1	$42,182	129/159
10. Emory University (GA)	85	4.2	89.4%	3.46	8.2	16.0%	109	$5,840.8	$1,938.0	$40,934	199/20
11. Columbia University (NY)	84	4.2	81.6%	3.74	23.9	N/A	209	$2,834.6	$1,450.1	$1,366*	209/232
11. Vanderbilt University (TN)	84	4.1	54.5%	3.52	30.0	N/A	407	$5,181.3	$1,069.7	$50,484	441/208
13. University of Alabama–Birmingham	82	4.0	65.7%	3.50	38.2	24.0%	392	$1,129.5	$5,351.1	$476*	616/1,020
13. University of Illinois–Chicago	82	4.2	45.5%	3.40	13.1	N/A	185	$7,824.7	$1,650.6	$35,682	360/280
13. University of Texas–Austin	82	4.0	54.8%	3.46	9.8	95.5%	83	$2,225.2	$1,225.6	$22,655	197/53
16. University of Virginia	81	4.1	55.6%	3.52	6.8	42.3%	94	$1,432.3	$1,784.2	$26,146	123/165
17. Case Western Reserve University (OH)	80	4.2	70.1%	N/A	8.2	16.0%	132	$2,990.6	$1,163.9	$1,818*	165/117
17. U. of North Carolina–Chapel Hill	80	4.2	63.8%	N/A	4.1	13.5%	106	$3,637.3	$1,788.0	$32,822	121/94
19. Indiana Univ.-Purdue Univ.–Indianapolis	79	3.9	61.1%	3.50	3.4	51.2%	120	$3,267.1	$2,152.7	$1,421*	44/287
19. Rush University (IL)	79	4.0	54.4%	3.50	9.5	26.3%	292	$438.2	$3,695.3	$999*	275/118
19. University of California–Los Angeles	79	4.0	45.6%	3.58	12.0	22.2%	153	$6,037.1	$1,461.2	$33,254	325/N/A
22. Ohio State University	78	4.0	58.4%	3.46	10.8	71.9%	129	$1,605.2	$1,154.2	$1,850*	450/150
22. Yale University (CT)	78	4.3	27.9%	3.68	12.7	20.0%	105	$3,230.0	N/A	$38,636	247/18
24. Arizona State University	77	3.8	82.6%	3.57	0.6	72.4%	9	$2,347.7	$1,258.3	$21,030	10/19
25. Rutgers, The State U. of N.J.–Newark/New Brunswick	75	3.4	44.5%	N/A	6.8	60.6%	292	$1,133.1	$39,410.7	$1,081*	61/493
26. University of Utah	72	3.8	100.0%	3.62	1.6	22.9%	30	$2,789.6	$810.5	$33,660	41/11
26. U. of Texas Health Sci. Ctr.–Houston	72	3.8	63.9%	3.53	6.4	36.1%	105	$735.1	$2,771.5	$875*	180/148
28. Medical University of South Carolina	69	3.6	14.4%	3.90	0.4	97.0%	16	$5,337.9	$1,120.2	$32,419	15/9
28. University of Missouri–Kansas City	69	3.4	83.6%	3.66	7.9	22.2%	106	$1,396.2	$6,055.1	$343*	9/186
30. University of Colorado	68	3.8	84.5%	N/A	14.9	4.5%	108	$949.8	$1,625.5	$1,020*	294/103
30. University of Kansas	68	3.7	100.0%	3.05	3.5	54.0%	77	$786.4	$622.5	$14,948	8/149
30. University of Rochester (NY)	68	3.7	70.7%	3.55	3.2	10.5%	58	$2,000.6	$691.9	$23,780	6/166
30. University of San Diego	68	3.6	26.5%	3.45	8.0	50.0%	91	$879.8	$2,302.0	$1,345*	161/44
34. Boston College	67	3.9	58.0%	3.63	6.1	36.7%	105	$51.3	$1,066.4	$25,290	163/64
34. Virginia Commonwealth University	67	3.7	45.6%	3.54	6.2	33.9%	69	$1,600.1	$498.9	$23,262	78/148
36. George Mason University (VA)	66	3.3	43.4%	3.68	8.2	37.5%	56	$2,014.2	$3,192.1	$1,199*	29/109
36. University of Missouri	66	3.8	83.3%	N/A	1.0	4.9%	42	$5,335.7	$150.0	$422*	2/57
38. Penn. State University–University Park	65	3.6	47.7%	3.68	7.5	N/A	36	$1,433.1	$1,069.4	$33,110	66/73
38. University of Arizona	65	3.8	45.0%	N/A	9.3	N/A	83	$1,331.8	$1,849.5	$1,539*	150/247
38. University of South Florida	65	3.5	55.1%	N/A	14.2	34.6%	226	$3,623.8	$565.2	$772*	129/717
41. Uniformed Svces U. of the Hlth. Sci. (MD)	64	3.6	100.0%	3.00	5.3	37.5%	40	$448.7	$117.5	N/A	28/N/A
41. University of Massachusetts–Boston	64	3.6	60.0%	3.80	4.1	23.8%	44	$1,432.0	$548.1	$30,578	42/134
43. University of California–Davis	63	3.5	54.3%	3.29	5.8	N/A	25	$2,928.5	$1,200.7	$37,294	52/N/A
43. University of Connecticut	63	3.7	67.0%	3.40	4.1	26.3%	22	$173.7	$902.7	$34,120	48/92
43. U. of Texas Medical Branch–Galveston	63	3.5	35.5%	N/A	37.6	14.3%	95	$1,568.0	$1,568.0	$639*	144/357
43. Washington State University	63	3.5	58.3%	3.70	0.6	20.0%	82	$1,995.9	$1,388.6	$33,212	6/44
43. Wayne State University (MI)	63	3.5	39.5%	3.71	5.5	N/A	118	$156.9	$3,143.8	$1,698*	59/135
48. Texas Woman's University	62	3.5	59.7%	N/A	6.5	N/A	248	$410.5	$3,030.6	$595*	31/819
48. University of Florida	62	3.7	N/A	N/A	2.3	6.1%	53	$1,259.5	$326.2	$1,253*	27/30

▶ More @ usnews.com/grad

Rank	School	Overall score	Peer assessment score (5.0=highest)	'14 acceptance rate	'14 mean undergrad GPA	'14 student/faculty ratio	'14 percent of faculty in active nursing practice	'14 master's degrees awarded	'14 NIH and federal research grants (in thousands)	'14 NIH and federal teaching grants (in thousands)	'14 out-of-state tuition and fees	'14 master's program enrollment full-/part-time
48.	University of Wisconsin–Milwaukee	62	3.6	70.6%	N/A	3.5	15.4%	55	$734.5	$1,009.4	$24,984	91/N/A
51.	Loyola University Chicago	61	3.5	72.7%	3.61	9.0	N/A	74	$742.7	$1,899.8	$1,020*	134/220
51.	Marquette University (WI)	61	3.5	62.1%	3.37	7.8	26.3%	71	$378.5	$1,165.3	$1,025*	74/223
51.	St. Louis University	61	3.6	75.3%	3.60	10.2	68.0%	85	N/A	$316.2	$1,030*	166/270
54.	Florida International University	60	3.1	37.4%	3.46	36.1	22.2%	164	$3,684.9	$2,188.2	$25,450	308/50
54.	University of Alabama–Huntsville	60	3.3	53.0%	3.49	13.6	77.8%	75	$456.5	$456.5	$1,471*	62/180
54.	University of Cincinnati	60	3.3	45.1%	3.45	37.6	N/A	604	$78.1	$2,083.6	$27,193	229/1,343
54.	University of Massachusetts–Amherst	60	3.5	84.2%	3.50	1.3	40.0%	9	N/A	$965.3	$750*	2/51
58.	George Washington University (DC)	59	3.6	71.7%	3.37	7.0	13.0%	58	N/A	$1,279.1	$920*	37/373
58.	Purdue University–West Lafayette (IN)	59	3.5	100.0%	3.69	2.6	15.0%	15	$158.2	$1,495.4	$28,804	32/6
58.	South Dakota State University	59	3.2	85.2%	3.00	7.0	66.7%	10	$754.0	$744.5	$559*	1/60
61.	CUNY–Hunter College	58	3.4	38.7%	N/A	9.0	50.0%	158	$187.0	$454.0	$18,993	3/530
61.	Michigan State University	58	3.6	38.5%	3.58	4.6	N/A	53	$2,631.3	$78.8	$1,269*	65/110
61.	University of Alabama	58	3.6	55.6%	3.30	3.3	7.7%	39	$192.4	$820.0	$10,226	58/87
61.	University of Miami (FL)	58	3.5	25.0%	3.51	2.5	82.2%	107	$2,001.8	$552.0	$41,782	88/77
61.	Villanova University (PA)	58	3.6	76.9%	3.50	4.8	63.6%	56	N/A	$675.1	$812*	127/94
66.	Texas Christian University	57	3.4	68.0%	3.46	4.7	80.0%	19	N/A	$296.0	$1,340*	46/2
66.	Univ. of South Carolina	57	3.4	86.6%	3.33	4.1	46.7%	63	$1,446.3	$54.0	$1,183*	37/75
68.	California State University–Los Angeles	56	3.3	45.7%	N/A	13.7	30.8%	63	N/A	$9,000.0	$16,830	178/N/A
68.	Pace University (NY)	56	3.4	70.0%	N/A	7.8	35.3%	121	N/A	$467.4	$1,070*	1/396
68.	University of Louisville (KY)	56	3.4	46.6%	3.47	4.0	23.8%	39	$1,205.9	$336.0	$23,764	72/36
68.	University of Vermont	56	3.3	84.6%	3.58	5.6	40.0%	20	$621.1	$343.3	$1,493*	47/27
72.	Baylor University (TX)	55	3.6	N/A	N/A	1.3	66.7%	25	N/A	N/A	$1,437*	5/21
72.	Florida Atlantic University (Lynn)	55	2.9	35.4%	N/A	4.0	39.4%	148	$3,242.8	$2,030.2	$928*	N/A/393
72.	Seton Hall University (NJ)	55	3.3	84.7%	3.30	4.9	20.7%	40	$162.0	$1,700.0	$1,100*	51/134
75.	Duquesne University (PA)	54	3.3	82.0%	3.49	4.6	12.0%	23	$962.0	$384.7	$1,077*	97/55
75.	University of Arkansas	54	3.5	100.0%	N/A	1.3	37.5%	9	N/A	N/A	$388*	3/22
75.	University of Colorado–Colorado Springs	54	3.5	24.1%	N/A	14.8	50.0%	27	N/A	N/A	$20,652	15/133
78.	Thomas Jefferson University (PA)	53	3.3	84.6%	N/A	138.7	N/A	146	N/A	$872.0	$1,054*	N/A/416
78.	University of Missouri–St. Louis	53	3.5	38.3%	N/A	6.3	N/A	79	$112.3	$233.5	$1,024*	N/A/207
78.	University of North Carolina–Greensboro	53	3.3	67.3%	N/A	12.1	10.0%	82	N/A	$1,995.7	$20,612	227/43
78.	University of Southern Indiana	53	3.2	54.8%	N/A	14.5	66.7%	96	N/A	$497.8	$741*	110/321
82.	West Virginia University	52	3.3	76.7%	3.50	4.9	25.9%	38	$137.8	$430.3	$22,212	75/57
83.	East Carolina University (NC)	51	3.1	35.0%	3.35	9.2	39.1%	156	N/A	$1,821.2	$811*	97/347
83.	Pacific Lutheran University (WA)	51	3.4	32.7%	3.53	9.8	33.3%	24	N/A	$318.0	$1,130*	59/N/A
83.	Simmons College (MA)	51	3.2	74.7%	3.13	20.1	100.0%	55	N/A	N/A	$1,246*	94/141
83.	University of Central Florida	51	3.0	46.9%	3.31	3.7	N/A	96	$2,419.7	$700.0	$1,183*	13/171
83.	University of Delaware	51	3.2	79.6%	3.50	2.8	15.8%	46	N/A	$1,131.3	$731*	13/120
83.	University of Hawaii–Manoa	51	3.3	54.5%	N/A	7.7	N/A	58	$803.8	$1,080.4	$1,652*	133/60
83.	University of Scranton (PA)	51	3.1	36.9%	3.52	4.1	90.9%	32	N/A	$395.3	$940*	28/50
90.	The Catholic University of America (DC)	50	3.4	65.0%	3.51	10.4	N/A	15	N/A	$300.0	$40,600	50/69
90.	Drexel University (PA)	50	3.2	49.1%	3.37	56.8	37.5%	222	$249.1	$179.3	$861*	63/1,173
90.	Fairfield University (CT)	50	3.2	62.3%	N/A	1.8	41.2%	39	N/A	$526.0	$850*	1/87
90.	Loyola University New Orleans	50	3.1	75.3%	3.14	28.8	58.3%	185	N/A	$479.5	$818*	316/89
90.	Montana State University	50	3.2	100.0%	3.68	1.0	6.3%	39	$68.3	$845.2	$867*	9/19
90.	Samford University (AL)	50	3.0	68.0%	3.20	16.8	80.0%	107	N/A	$1,090.6	$24,790	250/8
90.	Stony Brook University–SUNY	50	3.0	57.2%	N/A	39.6	100.0%	141	$10.0	$1,533.2	$21,621	38/598
90.	University of Texas–Arlington	50	3.1	60.7%	3.53	48.8	33.3%	227	$258.4	$637.2	$16,100	116/1,409
98.	Georgia Southern University	49	3.1	59.1%	N/A	1.9	38.9%	16	N/A	$2,100.0	$1,155*	35/N/A
98.	University of Indianapolis	49	3.3	54.5%	N/A	4.1	73.9%	57	N/A	N/A	$672*	N/A/280
98.	University of Massachusetts–Dartmouth	49	3.5	100.0%	N/A	1.0	N/A	25	N/A	N/A	$19,980	N/A/30

N/A=Data were not provided by the school. *Tuition is reported on a per-credit-hour basis. Sources: U.S. News and the schools. Peer assessment data collected by Ipsos Public Affairs.

Rank	School	Overall score	Peer assessment score (5.0=highest)	'14 acceptance rate	'14 mean undergrad GPA	'14 student/ faculty ratio	'14 percent of faculty in active nursing practice	'14 master's degrees awarded	'14 NIH and federal research grants (in thousands)	'14 NIH and federal teaching grants (in thousands)	'14 out-of-state tuition and fees	'14 master's program enrollment full-/part-time
98.	Xavier University (OH)	49	3.0	92.5%	3.54	16.2	50.0%	78	N/A	$452.8	$600*	68/185
102.	Clemson University (SC)	48	3.2	85.7%	3.50	4.2	N/A	37	$398.9	$195.3	$20,524	65/17
102.	Creighton University (NE)	48	3.5	50.8%	3.37	2.7	100.0%	37	N/A	$20.5	$780*	62/93
102.	Gonzaga University (WA)	48	3.4	82.2%	3.48	41.2	36.4%	111	N/A	N/A	$900*	391/186
102.	Howard University (DC)	48	2.9	100.0%	3.60	7.9	66.7%	12	N/A	$600.0	$30,323	14/29
102.	University of Maine	48	3.1	100.0%	3.54	2.9	37.5%	8	N/A	$349.8	$1,310*	22/3
102.	University of Southern Mississippi	48	3.0	63.6%	3.27	5.2	42.1%	8	N/A	$1,864.0	$19,190	93/18
102.	University of the Incarnate Word (TX)	48	3.1	87.0%	N/A	0.9	37.5%	8	N/A	$1,294.0	$815*	6/35
109.	Georgia Regents University	47	3.1	45.3%	3.40	20.2	20.0%	144	$262.7	$345.2	$1,181*	292/31
110.	Auburn University (AL)	46	3.2	52.4%	3.18	2.5	40.0%	29	N/A	N/A	$27,366	3/105
110.	MGH Inst. of Health Professions (MA)	46	3.3	50.9%	3.34	N/A	N/A	112	$1,584.4	$309.9	$1,136*	321/21
110.	SUNY Downstate Medical Center	46	3.2	21.1%	N/A	9.4	77.8%	50	N/A	N/A	$20,260	15/209
110.	University of St. Francis (IN)	46	3.0	91.7%	3.60	8.5	100.0%	32	N/A	$350.0	$830*	34/60
110.	Wright State University (OH)	46	3.1	76.8%	3.17	7.8	13.0%	71	$384.0	$384.0	$21,724	143/109
115.	Belmont University (TN)	45	3.0	79.2%	3.67	2.4	77.8%	28	N/A	N/A	N/A	37/20
115.	Brigham Young University (UT)	45	3.3	34.9%	3.86	0.8	55.3%	13	N/A	N/A	$700*	29/N/A
115.	Southeast Missouri State University	45	3.2	38.2%	3.65	1.3	33.3%	16	N/A	$251.0	$482*	12/12
115.	Texas A&M University–Corpus Christi	45	3.0	42.8%	N/A	7.4	14.0%	83	$380.5	$349.9	$734*	N/A/370
115.	University of North Carolina–Charlotte	45	3.3	35.7%	N/A	11.3	7.1%	80	N/A	$300.0	$19,584	133/75
115.	University of St. Francis (IL)	45	3.0	40.1%	3.34	15.6	83.3%	65	N/A	$668.5	N/A	90/293
115.	University of Texas–El Paso	45	2.9	54.5%	N/A	30.8	66.7%	46	N/A	$634.2	$815*	114/212
122.	East Tennessee State University	44	3.0	87.5%	3.51	2.4	100.0%	34	N/A	N/A	$1,258*	45/289
122.	James Madison University (VA)	44	3.1	50.0%	3.46	1.3	29.5%	11	N/A	$350.0	$1,135*	11/45
122.	La Salle University (PA)	44	2.6	65.5%	N/A	6.0	100.0%	72	N/A	$1,571.7	$845*	N/A/344
122.	Northern Arizona University	44	3.0	74.1%	N/A	7.8	50.0%	38	$60.0	$300.0	$1,102*	17/136
122.	Southern Illinois University–Edwardsville	44	3.2	57.4%	3.36	5.8	8.8%	N/A	N/A	$364.8	$7,124	71/181

SPECIALTIES

ADMINISTRATION
1. University of Pennsylvania
2. University of Iowa
2. University of Michigan–Ann Arbor
4. University of Illinois–Chicago
5. Johns Hopkins University (MD)
5. University of Maryland–Baltimore
5. University of Pittsburgh
5. University of North Carolina–Chapel Hill

CLINICAL NURSE LEADER
1. University of Maryland–Baltimore
2. University of Virginia
3. University of Pittsburgh

INFORMATICS
1. University of Maryland–Baltimore
2. University of Minnesota–Twin Cities
3. Columbia University (NY)
3. Duke University (NC)
3. Vanderbilt University (TN)

NURSE ANESTHESIA
1. University of Pittsburgh
2. Rush University (IL)

3. Duke University (NC)
4. Virginia Commonwealth University
5. Uniformed Services University of the Health Sciences (MD)
5. University of Pennsylvania

NURSE MIDWIFERY
1. Frontier Nursing University (KY)
2. University of Pennsylvania
3. Vanderbilt University (TN)
3. Yale University (CT)
5. University of Illinois–Chicago
6. University of California–San Francisco
7. Columbia University (NY)

NURSE PRACTITIONER
ADULT / GERONTOLOGY, ACUTE CARE
1. University of Pennsylvania
2. Duke University (NC)
2. Johns Hopkins University (MD)
4. Rush University (IL)
5. University of Pittsburgh
5. Vanderbilt University (TN)
7. Columbia University (NY)

NURSE PRACTITIONER
ADULT / GERONTOLOGY, PRIMARY CARE
1. University of Pennsylvania
2. New York University
3. University of Michigan–Ann Arbor
4. Columbia University (NY)
4. Rush University (IL)
4. University of Maryland–Baltimore
7. Duke University (NC)
7. Johns Hopkins University (MD)
9. University of California–San Francisco
9. University of Washington

NURSE PRACTITIONER
FAMILY
1. University of Pennsylvania
2. University of California–San Francisco
3. Johns Hopkins University (MD)
3. University of Michigan–Ann Arbor
5. University of Maryland–Baltimore
5. University of Washington
7. Columbia University (NY)
7. Duke University (NC)

7. Vanderbilt University (TN)
10. University of Illinois–Chicago

NURSE PRACTITIONER
PEDIATRIC, PRIMARY CARE
1. University of Pennsylvania
2. Duke University (NC)
3. University of Pittsburgh
3. Yale University (CT)
5. Rush University (IL)
5. University of California–San Francisco
7. Johns Hopkins University (MD)
8. University of Washington

NURSE PRACTITIONER
PSYCHIATRIC / MENTAL HEALTH, ACROSS THE LIFESPAN
1. University of California–San Francisco
1. University of Pennsylvania
3. Rush University (IL)
4. Vanderbilt University (TN)
5. University of Pittsburgh
6. New York University
6. Yale University (CT)

METHODOLOGY

Programs at the 503 nursing schools with master's or doctoral programs accredited by either the Commission on Collegiate Nursing Education or the Accreditation Commission for Education in Nursing were surveyed; 273 responded, and 246 were eligible to be included in the rankings of master's programs based on a weighted average of 13 indicators described below.

Quality assessment:
One survey was conducted in the fall of 2014. Nursing school deans and deans of graduate studies at nursing schools were asked to rate the quality of master's programs from marginal (1) to outstanding (5); 26 percent responded. The resulting score is weighted by .40 in the overall score.

Student selectivity and achievement (weighted by .125): The strength of nursing students entering master's programs in the fall of 2014 was measured by their mean undergraduate grade point average (.05 percent of this measure), and the acceptance rate of master's students in fall 2014 (.025). Achievement was measured by the number of master's degrees awarded for the 2013 graduating class (.05).

Faculty resources (.225): This score is based on the 2014 ratio of full-time master's students to full-time faculty (.05), the proportion of 2014 full-time faculty with doctoral degrees (.05) ; the proportion of full-time faculty with membership in the Institute of Medicine of the National Academies or who are fellows of the National Institutes of Health, fellows of the American Academy of Nursing or fellows of the American Association of Nurse Practitioners in fall 2014 (.025); the proportion of 2014 full-time faculty in active nursing practice (.075); and the number of 2013 master's degrees in nursing awarded per full-time faculty member in the past school year (.025).

Research activity (.25): Based on total National Institutes of Health and other federal research grants to the nursing school (.075); average NIH and other federal research grants per full-time nursing faculty member (.05); total NIH and other federal educational and practical initiative grants to the nursing school (.075); and average NIH and other federal educational and practical initiative grants per full-time nursing faculty member (.05). National Institutes of Health and other federal research grants and educational and practical initiative grants awarded to the nursing school are for fiscal year 2014.

Overall rank: Data were standardized about their means, and standardized scores were weighted, totaled and rescaled so the top-scoring school received 100; others received their percentage of the top score.

Specialty rankings: These rankings are based solely on assessments by nursing school deans and deans of graduate studies who identified up to 10 schools offering the best programs in each specialty area. The top half of ranked programs (based on the number of nominations received) appear.

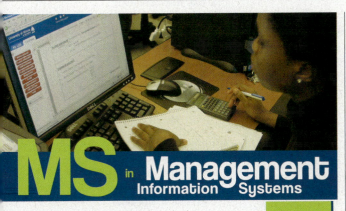

Health Disciplines

SCHOOLS RANKED BEST BY PROGRAM DIRECTORS AND FACULTY

AUDIOLOGY

DOCTORATE Ranked in 2012

Rank	School	Average assessment score (5.0=highest)
1.	Vanderbilt University (TN)	4.5
2.	University of Iowa	4.2
3.	University of North Carolina–Chapel Hill	4.0
3.	University of Texas–Dallas	4.0
3.	University of Washington	4.0
3.	Washington University in St. Louis	4.0
7.	University of Florida	3.9
8.	Northwestern University (IL)	3.7
8.	University of Pittsburgh	3.7
10.	Rush University Medical Center (IL)	3.5
10.	University of Kansas	3.5
12.	Ohio State University	3.4
12.	Purdue Univ.–West Lafayette (IN)	3.4
12.	University of Arizona	3.4
12.	University of Memphis	3.4
12.	University of South Florida	3.4
17.	Arizona State University	3.3
17.	Indiana University–Bloomington	3.3
17.	James Madison University (VA)	3.3
17.	University at Buffalo–SUNY	3.3

CLINICAL PSYCHOLOGY

DOCTORATE Ranked in 2012

Rank	School	Average assessment score (5.0=highest)
1.	University of California–Los Angeles	4.5
2.	University of North Carolina–Chapel Hill	4.4
2.	University of Washington	4.4
2.	University of Wisconsin–Madison	4.4
2.	Yale University (CT)	4.4
6.	Duke University (NC)	4.3
6.	U. of Illinois–Urbana-Champaign	4.3
6.	U. of Kansas (Clin. Child Psych. Prog.)	4.3
6.	University of Minnesota–Twin Cities	4.3
6.	University of Pennsylvania	4.3
11.	Stony Brook University–SUNY	4.2
11.	University of California–Berkeley	4.2
11.	University of Texas–Austin	4.2
14.	Harvard University (MA)	4.1
14.	Northwestern University (IL)	4.1
14.	Vanderbilt University (TN)	4.1
14.	Washington University in St. Louis	4.1
18.	Emory University (GA)	4.0
18.	Indiana University–Bloomington	4.0
18.	Penn. State University–University Park	4.0
18.	University of Colorado–Boulder	4.0

Rank	School	Average assessment score (5.0=highest)
18.	University of Iowa	4.0
18.	University of Pittsburgh	4.0
18.	University of Southern California	4.0
18.	University of Virginia	4.0

HEALTH CARE MANAGEMENT

MASTER'S Ranked in 2015

Rank	School	Average assessment score (5.0=highest)
1.	University of Michigan–Ann Arbor	4.4
2.	University of Alabama–Birmingham	4.3
3.	University of Minnesota–Twin Cities	4.2
3.	Virginia Commonwealth University	4.2
5.	Rush University (IL)	4.0
5.	University of North Carolina–Chapel Hill	4.0
7.	Johns Hopkins University (MD)	3.6
7.	St. Louis University	3.6
7.	U.S. Army-Baylor University (TX)	3.6
10.	Northwestern University (Kellogg) (IL)	3.5
10.	Ohio State University	3.5
10.	Trinity University (TX)	3.5
10.	University of Iowa	3.5
10.	University of Washington	3.5
15.	Cornell University (Sloan) (NY)	3.4
15.	University of California–Los Angeles	3.4
17.	George Washington University (DC)	3.3
18.	Baylor University (TX)	3.2
18.	Boston University	3.2
18.	Medical University of South Carolina	3.2
18.	New York University	3.2
18.	U. of Col.–Denver/Network for Hlthcare Mgmt.	3.2
23.	Columbia University (NY)	3.1
23.	Georgetown University (DC)	3.1
23.	Tulane University (LA)	3.1
23.	University of Colorado–Denver	3.1
23.	University of Southern California	3.1

OCCUPATIONAL THERAPY

MASTER'S/DOCTORATE Ranked in 2012

Rank	School	Average assessment score (5.0=highest)
1.	University of Southern California	4.6
2.	Boston University (Sargent)	4.5

Rank	School	Average assessment score (5.0=highest)
2.	Washington University in St. Louis	4.5
4.	University of Illinois–Chicago	4.3
5.	University of Kansas Medical Center	4.0
6.	Colorado State University	3.9
6.	Thomas Jefferson University (PA)	3.9
6.	Tufts U.-Boston Sch. of Occup. Therapy	3.9
6.	University of Pittsburgh	3.9
10.	New York University	3.8
10.	University of Florida	3.8
10.	University of North Carolina–Chapel Hill	3.8
13.	Columbia University (NY)	3.7
14.	U. of Texas Medical Branch–Galveston	3.6
15.	Creighton University (NE)	3.5
15.	Ohio State University	3.5
15.	Texas Woman's University	3.5
15.	University of Washington	3.5
15.	University of Wisconsin–Madison	3.5
15.	Virginia Commonwealth University	3.5

Note: All schools listed have master's programs; some may not have doctoral programs.

PHARMACY

PHARM.D. Ranked in 2012

Rank	School	Average assessment score (5.0=highest)
1.	University of California–San Francisco	4.6
2.	University of North Carolina–Chapel Hill	4.5
3.	University of Minnesota	4.4
4.	University of Texas–Austin	4.3
5.	University of Kentucky	4.2
5.	University of Wisconsin–Madison	4.2
7.	Ohio State University	4.1
7.	Purdue University (IN)	4.1
7.	University of Michigan–Ann Arbor	4.1
10.	University of Arizona	4.0
10.	University of Southern California	4.0
10.	University of Utah	4.0
10.	University of Washington	4.0
14.	University of Florida	3.9
14.	University of Illinois–Chicago	3.9
14.	University of Pittsburgh	3.9
17.	U. of Tennessee Health Science Center	3.8
17.	University at Buffalo–SUNY	3.8
17.	University of Iowa	3.8
17.	University of Maryland–Baltimore	3.8

▶ More @ usnews.com/grad

PHYSICAL THERAPY

MASTER'S/DOCTORATE Ranked in 2012

Rank	School	Average assessment score (5.0=highest)
1.	University of Southern California	4.3
2.	University of Delaware	4.2
3.	University of Pittsburgh	4.1
3.	Washington University in St. Louis	4.1
5.	University of Iowa	3.9
5.	U.S. Army-Baylor University (TX)	3.9
7.	Emory University (GA)	3.8
7.	MGH Inst. of Health Professions (MA)	3.8
9.	Northwestern University (IL)	3.7
9.	University of Miami (FL)	3.7
9.	University of North Carolina–Chapel Hill	3.7
12.	Marquette University (WI)	3.6
12.	University of Florida	3.6
14.	Arcadia University (PA)	3.5
14.	University of Utah	3.5
16.	Boston University	3.4
16.	Creighton University (NE)	3.4
16.	University of Illinois–Chicago	3.4
19.	Ohio State University	3.3
19.	University of Alabama–Birmingham	3.3
19.	University of Kansas Medical Center	3.3
19.	University of Maryland–Baltimore	3.3
19.	University of Minnesota–Twin Cities	3.3
19.	University of Wisconsin–Madison	3.3
19.	U. of Calif.–San Francisco - S.F. State U.	3.3
19.	Virginia Commonwealth University	3.3

Note: All schools listed have master's programs; some may not have doctoral programs.

PHYSICIAN ASSISTANT

MASTER'S Ranked in 2015

Rank	School	Average assessment score (5.0=highest)
1.	Duke University (NC)	4.4
2.	University of Iowa	4.3
3.	Emory University (GA)	4.1
3.	George Washington University (DC)	4.1
5.	Oregon Health and Sciences University	4.0
5.	Quinnipiac University (CT)	4.0
5.	University of Colorado–Denver	4.0
5.	University of Utah	4.0
9.	University of Nebraska Medical Center	3.9
9.	Wake Forest University (NC)	3.9
11.	Interservice Physician Asst. Prog. (TX)	3.8
11.	University of Washington	3.8
13.	Baylor College of Medicine (TX)	3.7
13.	Drexel University (PA)	3.7
15.	U. of Texas Southwest. Med. Ctr–Dallas	3.6
16.	Rutgers Biomedical and Health Sci. (NJ)	3.5
16.	Shenandoah University (VA)	3.5
16.	Stony Brook University–SUNY	3.5
16.	University of Alabama–Birmingham	3.5
20.	Midwestern University (IL)	3.4

Rank	School	Average assessment score (5.0=highest)
20.	Midwestern University (AZ)	3.4
20.	Northeastern University (MA)	3.4
20.	Rosalind Franklin U. of Med. and Sci. (IL)	3.4
20.	University of Southern California (Keck)	3.4
20.	Yale University (CT)	3.4

PUBLIC HEALTH

MASTER'S/DOCTORATE Ranked in 2015

Rank	School	Average assessment score (5.0=highest)
1.	Johns Hopkins University (MD)	4.8
2.	Harvard University (MA)	4.7
2.	University of North Carolina–Chapel Hill	4.7
4.	University of Michigan–Ann Arbor	4.5
5.	Columbia University (NY)	4.4
6.	University of Washington	4.2
7.	Emory University (GA)	4.1
8.	University of Minnesota–Twin Cities	4.0
9.	University of California–Berkeley	3.9
10.	Boston University	3.6
10.	University of California–Los Angeles	3.6
12.	Tulane University (LA)	3.5
13.	University of Pittsburgh	3.4
14.	George Washington University (DC)	3.2
14.	Yale University (CT)	3.2
16.	University of South Florida	3.1
17.	University of Illinois–Chicago	3.0
17.	University of Iowa	3.0
19.	Ohio State University	2.9
19.	University of Alabama–Birmingham	2.9
21.	U. of Texas–Houston Health Sciences Ctr.	2.8
22.	University of Maryland–College Park	2.7
23.	St. Louis University	2.6
23.	University of South Carolina	2.6

Note: All schools listed have master's programs; some may not have doctoral programs.

REHABILITATION COUNSELING

MASTER'S/DOCTORATE Ranked in 2015

Rank	School	Average assessment score (5.0=highest)
1.	Michigan State University	4.5
1.	University of Wisconsin–Madison	4.5
3.	University of Iowa	4.2
4.	Southern Illinois University–Carbondale	4.0
4.	Virginia Commonwealth University	4.0
6.	George Washington University (DC)	3.8
6.	Penn. State University–University Park	3.8
6.	University of Arizona	3.8
6.	University of Kentucky	3.8
10.	San Diego State University	3.7
10.	University of Wisconsin–Stout	3.7
10.	Utah State University	3.7
13.	Illinois Institute of Technology	3.5
13.	University of Arkansas–Fayetteville	3.5

Rank	School	Average assessment score (5.0=highest)
15.	University of Northern Colorado	3.4
15.	University of North Texas	3.4
15.	University of Texas–Pan American	3.4
18.	East Carolina University (NC)	3.3
18.	Portland State University (OR)	3.3
18.	University of Pittsburgh	3.3
21.	University at Buffalo–SUNY	3.2
21.	University of Memphis	3.2
21.	University of North Carolina–Chapel Hill	3.2

Note: All schools listed have master's programs; some may not have doctoral programs.

SOCIAL WORK

MASTER'S Ranked in 2012

Rank	School	Average assessment score (5.0=highest)
1.	University of Michigan–Ann Arbor	4.4
1.	Washington University in St. Louis	4.4
3.	University of Chicago	4.2
3.	University of Washington	4.2
5.	Columbia University (NY)	4.1
5.	University of North Carolina–Chapel Hill	4.1
7.	University of California–Berkeley	4.0
7.	University of Texas–Austin	4.0
9.	Case Western Reserve University (OH)	3.9
10.	Boston College	3.8
11.	Fordham University (NY)	3.7
11.	University of Pittsburgh	3.7
11.	University of Southern California	3.7
11.	University of Wisconsin–Madison	3.7
11.	Virginia Commonwealth University	3.7
16.	Boston University	3.6
16.	CUNY–Hunter College	3.6
16.	New York University	3.6
16.	Smith College (MA)	3.6
16.	University of California–Los Angeles	3.6
16.	U. of Illinois–Urbana-Champaign	3.6
16.	University of Maryland–Baltimore	3.6
16.	University of Pennsylvania	3.6
24.	University at Albany–SUNY	3.5
24.	University of Illinois–Chicago	3.5

SPEECH–LANGUAGE PATHOLOGY

MASTER'S Ranked in 2012

Rank	School	Average assessment score (5.0=highest)
1.	University of Iowa	4.6
2.	University of Wisconsin–Madison	4.5
3.	University of Washington	4.4
3.	Vanderbilt University (TN)	4.4
5.	Northwestern University (IL)	4.3
5.	Purdue University–West Lafayette (IN)	4.3
5.	University of Arizona	4.3
8.	University of Kansas	4.2
8.	University of Pittsburgh	4.2

SPEECH–LANGUAGE PATHOLOGY Continued

Rank	School	Average assessment score (5.0=highest)
10.	University of Texas–Austin	4.1
11.	Indiana University	4.0
11.	U. of Illinois–Urbana-Champaign	4.0
11.	University of North Carolina–Chapel Hill	4.0
11.	University of Texas–Dallas	4.0
15.	University of Florida	3.9
15.	University of Memphis	3.9
17.	Ohio State University	3.8
17.	University of Maryland–College Park	3.8
17.	University of Minnesota–Twin Cities	3.8
17.	University of Nebraska–Lincoln	3.8
21.	Arizona State University	3.7
21.	Boston University	3.7
21.	Florida State University	3.7
21.	Penn. State University–University Park	3.7

VETERINARY MEDICINE

DOCTOR OF VETERINARY MEDICINE
Ranked in 2015

Rank	School	Average assessment score (5.0=highest)
1.	University of California–Davis	4.5
2.	Cornell University (NY)	4.1
3.	Colorado State University	3.9
3.	North Carolina State University	3.9
5.	Ohio State University	3.7
5.	University of Wisconsin–Madison	3.7
7.	Texas A&M University–College Station	3.6
7.	University of Pennsylvania	3.6
9.	University of Minnesota–Twin Cities	3.4
10.	Tufts University (MA)	3.3
10.	University of Georgia	3.3
12.	Michigan State University	3.2
13.	Iowa State University	3.1

METHODOLOGY

The health rankings are based solely on the results of peer assessment surveys sent to deans, other administrators and/or faculty at accredited degree programs or schools in each discipline. Respondents rated the academic quality of programs on a 5-point scale: outstanding (5 points), strong (4), good (3), adequate (2) or marginal (1). They were instructed to select "don't know" if they did not have enough knowledge to rate a program.

Only fully accredited programs in good standing during the survey period are ranked.

Those with the highest average scores appear.

In the fall of 2011, surveys were conducted for the 2012 rankings of doctor of pharmacy programs accredited by the Accreditation Council for Pharmacy Education (response rate: 39 percent); doctoral programs in clinical psychology accredited by the American Psychological Association (25 percent); graduate programs in occupational therapy accredited by the American Occupational Therapy Association (41 percent); audiology programs and speech-language pathology programs accredited by the American Speech-Language-Hearing Association (55 percent and 31 percent, respectively); physical therapy programs accredited by the Commission on Accreditation in Physical Therapy Education (40 percent); and master of social work programs accredited by the Commission on Accreditation of the Council on Social Work Education (53 percent).

In the fall of 2014, surveys were conducted for 2015 rankings of schools of public health accredited by the Council on Education for Public Health (response rate: 59 percent); health care management programs accredited by the Commission on Accreditation of Healthcare Management Education (57 percent); physician assistant programs accredited by the Accreditation Review Commission on Education for the Physician Assistant (50 percent); rehabilitation counselor education programs accredited by the Commission on Standards and Accreditation: Council on Rehabilitation Education (38 percent); and veterinary schools accredited by the American Veterinary Medical Association (49 percent).

Surveys for both sets of rankings were conducted by research firm Ipsos Public Affairs.

Paging Dr. Ram

We hope you'll answer the page, and join our Rams veterinary family!

The Colorado State DVM Program offers exceptional veterinary teaching, based on world-class research and compassionate clinical care – all in Colorful Colorado. Our veterinary school consistently ranks in the top three in the nation, according to *U.S. News and World Report.*

Colorado State University
COLLEGE OF VETERINARY MEDICINE
AND BIOMEDICAL SCIENCES

www.cvmbs.colostate.edu
dvmadmissions@colostate.edu
970.491.7051

ACADEMIC INSIGHTS
YOUR SCHOOL BY THE NUMBERS

Designed for schools, U.S. News Academic Insights provides instant access to a rich historical archive of undergraduate and graduate school rankings data.

Advanced Visualizations
Take complex data and turn it into six easily understandable and exportable views.

Download Center
Export large data sets from the new Download Center to create custom reports.

Dedicated Account Management
Have access to full analyst support for training, troubleshooting and advanced reporting.

Peer-Group Analysis
Flexibility to create your own peer groups to compare your institution on more than 350 metrics.

Historical Trending
Find out how institutions have performed over time based on more than 350 metrics.

Law

A corporate finance class at Duke Law

THE U.S. NEWS RANKINGS

Want
Law Stude

A DROP IN APPLICATIONS IS SPURRING LAW SCHOOLS TO MAKE CHANGES

By **MARGARET LOFTUS**

After working his way up from teller to branch manager at Wells Fargo, Richard Shreiba, 27, set his sights on becoming an in-house attorney for a bank or financial services firm. Loath to forgo an income for three years, however, he first considered part-time programs. Then he discovered a new J.D. program at Drexel University in Philadelphia that lasts just two calendar years. He'd have to pay the same tuition per credit as a traditional student and take the same number of credits. But saving a year of living expenses clinched the decision, says Shreiba, now a 2L in the inaugural class. "I was more than happy to be the guinea pig," he says.

Accelerated programs are just one of the many innovations that law schools are introducing to woo students into their thinning classes. A radically changed job market since the financial meltdown – in which law firms have retrenched, salaries have fallen, and many new attorneys have struggled to find a job that puts their J.D. to use – has led to a precipitous drop in applications. Enrollment in 2013 was down 24 percent from what it was in 2010, making law school a bit more of a buyer's market (box, Page 92). So even as hiring shows signs of recovery and average starting pay inches up (from the post-crash low of $78,700 for the class of 2011 to about $82,400 for 2013 grads), many schools are dreaming up new ways to make their programs stand out, from condensing coursework and expanding dual and niche degrees to adding more experiential learning.

"You're making a very substantial investment, and a lot of that is made with loans," says Luke Bierman, dean of the Elon University School of Law in North Carolina, which has drastically overhauled its own curriculum. "People are far more sophisticated about return on investment now. They're being much more critical – in a good way. And there are a lot more choices."

As they start their five-week criminal law rotation, 1Ls at Chicago-Kent make a visit to court.

More than a dozen schools now offer some form of compressed program, an innovation pioneered by Northwestern Law in Illinois in 2009. Brooklyn Law School launched a two-year option last summer, for example, in which students start by accumulating six credits over the summer, then take 14 credits in the fall and 15 or 16 each term thereafter, with three-credit intersessions between semesters and an externship during the second summer. At Drexel, two-year students begin with a summer term and then juggle 15 to 17 credits a semester. Other schools offering accelerated programs include Pepperdine University School of Law in California; the University of Dayton School of Law in Ohio; and Gonzaga University School of Law in Washington.

Regardless of how you crunch the credits, the load makes for an intense two years. "It's clearly not for everybody," says Brooklyn Law President and Dean Nick Allard. "It's for highly motivated, highly qualified and mature students." He notes that most of the 30 students in the first class arrived from the work world. It's no coincidence that these programs appeal to a more seasoned student, agrees Drexel Law Dean Roger Dennis, who notes that one aim of starting the program was to appeal to a wider audience. While not required, work experience is strongly preferred for admission to Northwestern's accelerated program. "If you treat it like a full-time job,

ed: nts

Ohio State University
Columbus

LUKE FEDLAM, '13
Sports and entertainment attorney

➤ After representing pro athletes and leading the wealth management division of a sports management boutique, I decided to enroll at OSU Moritz College of Law. A law degree would, I felt, help me protect my clients and their long-term financial security from people who tried to take advantage of them.

OSU allowed me to dive into key subject areas like estate planning and intellectual property, hear prominent attorneys talk about leadership, and build practical skills like reading body language, networking and negotiation in the Program on Law and Leadership. Now, as a sports and entertainment attorney at Kegler Brown Hill + Ritter in Columbus, I can offer my clients the kind of well-rounded support I had hoped to.

momentum in experiential education," says Rodriguez.

Now in its fourth year, Tulane University Law School's January boot camp is an intensive simulation of a lawyer's week, in which students work on cases as if they were on the job. The boot camp joins Tulane's longstanding legal clinics and a semester of training in the nuts and bolts of trial advocacy. Between 80 and 100 lawyers and judges guide the action, which includes tasks like preparing for a deposition and doing all the strategic thinking required when representing clients.

The boot camp offers a real sense of "what you would do in a week's work," says Graham Williams, 24, a 3L who participated in the mock sale of a brewery business from conception to closure, helping to negotiate the buyer's right to terminate long-term employees.

The course has become a showcase for recruiters. Tulane grad Donald Williams, 30, met Lawrance Bohm, the principal of the Bohm Law Group in Sacramento, when Bohm served as an adjunct professor. Williams now works at the firm. Besides providing the job lead, he says the experience – particularly arguing a motion for summary judgment in front of a federal judge and getting feedback – really boosted his confidence.

Other schools have borrowed a page from medicine to incorporate clinical rotations or "residencies." At New York Law School, 3Ls now spend the entire year in three 10-week clinical rotations that have them working with officials at the New York City Law Department and on civil litigation at the Legal Aid Society, for example.

As early as second semester of their first year, students at the Illinois Institute of Technology Chicago-Kent College of Law have the option of doing a clinical rotation with the school's in-house law firm in a handful of different specialties, including criminal defense and family law. "Students can experience different types of law by going on rounds with these clinicians," says the school's dean, Harold Krent. "It gives them an advantage in finding their passion."

In one of the most radical reforms, Elon will introduce a complete overhaul of its curriculum this year. The program

will shift to trimesters so students graduate in two and a half years and can prep for the February bar exam and enter the job market in the spring. The new curriculum is much more intentionally sequenced; shadowing a litigator leads to participation in moot court and then to a residency with a trial and appellate practice firm, for example.

"The real innovation here was to take legal education and make it logically progressive," says Bierman. "We want to make sure students learn each part before they move on."

First-year students will be assigned an

advising team for the duration, including a leadership coach, career development consultant, faculty adviser and a mentor working in their field of interest who will observe them in class and provide feedback on their performance. One-Ls also shadow their mentor for several days. Introductory classes like criminal and property law will be bolstered by labs in which students observe or engage in a simulated plea deal and draft deeds, say.

One full trimester will be spent in a residency, working in a firm, corporate counsel office or judge's chambers, for example. The last trimester will consist of "bridge-to-practice" classes that might simulate a divorce proceeding in which students negotiate, draft motions and argue child custody issues.

While experiential learning is the latest buzzword in legal education, the extent to which students can truly participate in proceedings remains highly regulated by the American Bar Association, which accredits law schools. "You cannot give legal advice to somebody unless you are a licensed attorney," Nebraska's Poser points out. So clinics that serve real clients are typically limited to third-year students certified by their state supreme court to work under the supervision of a lawyer.

The limitations frustrate some educators, who can see the potential for even greater innovation. Rodriguez believes that falling enrollments could jeopardize some law schools, ultimately pressuring the ABA to allow greater freedom of movement. ∎

A Lightened Load

MANY LAW SCHOOLS HELP GRADS IN PUBLIC SERVICE REPAY THEIR LOANS

By **COURTNEY RUBIN**

When Jessica Shulruff applied to law school, she knew she was interested in public-interest law. But she focused on getting into the best law school possible regardless of cost, not thinking about how she would pay back her loans on a public-interest salary.

Shulruff, 32, got lucky. While she was at Duke, the law school beefed up its "loan repayment assistance program," or LRAP, which supports grads going into public service by covering all or part of their loan payments. Participants would now be able to make more than the original ceiling, which was $30,000. At a salary of nearly twice that much as a senior attorney for the nonprofit Americans for Immigrant Justice in Miami, Shulruff today qualifies for her full $485 monthly payment. Without that help, plus a federal program that wipes out outstanding government loans of public servants after 10 years on the job, "it would be a lot harder over time to sustain this kind of career," she says. Currently, Duke grads in the public-interest or nonprofit realm making under $75,000 are eligible, and those earning less than $60,000 can have their payments fully covered.

Roughly half of law schools have LRAPs, and "they should be a significant factor in people choosing where they go to law school," argues Radhika Singh Miller, senior manager of law school engagement and advocacy for Equal Justice Works, a nonprofit in Washington, D.C., that promotes public-interest law. It's worth researching the programs carefully, because they vary greatly, advises Heather Jarvis, an attorney in Wilmington, North Carolina, who is an expert on student indebtedness. Check for time limits on how long after graduation you have to sign up and on how long benefits last, for example. Other questions to research:

● **What jobs are covered?** Most plans are quite specific, requiring law-related work at 501(c)(3) nonprofit organizations or in state or local government. You can't qualify, for example, by teaching in a public school. Many law schools exclude judicial clerkships "because they're prestigious, and people often use them as a launching pad to private employment," Jarvis says.

● **Is there an income cap?** Is income defined as your gross salary only, or as income from all sources – including your spouse? The University of Chicago allows an annual salary of up to $80,000 and disregards a spouse's earnings.

● **Which loans are eligible for benefits?** Private loans in addition to federal ones? Does the program make allowances for undergraduate debt? While not covering undergraduate loans outright, for example, a law school may subtract those payments from your annual income to come up with an award. Duke requires interested grads to have borrowed at least $20,000 for law school and limits its total award to "the total amount borrowed in federal loans for law school enrollment, plus interest that accrues over the period of LRAP eligibility." Month to month, the funds are applied to any federal debt, including undergraduate loans.

● **How is the program funded?** The most reliable funding sources are endowments, not the annual budget.

Rutgers helps 2010 graduate Aarin Michele Williams pay back her loans.

● **How are awards calculated?** Cornell uses a complicated formula that takes into account income, an allowance for the local cost of living, dependents, and an expectation that the grad will kick in a certain amount. Rutgers University School of Law–Newark simply divvies up its available funding among eligible students, averaging roughly 40 percent of their payments over the past several years.

Aarin Michele Williams, 31, a 2010 Rutgers grad and now an assistant deputy public defender in the area, has received about $5,000 per year – a little less than half of what she owes annually – for four years. Rutgers has a five-year cap, so the end is in sight. "I wish it could be more," she says, "but it definitely makes a difference." ■

A Look at 3 Distinct Paths

Prospective attorneys searching for the right fit in a law school might be surprised at the rich variation they find when they delve past a school's rank to the details. Here are three examples of the many ways schools are honing their distinctiveness to offer a special experience along with the legal basics. | *By* **MARGARET LOFTUS**

CORNELL UNIVERSITY The Global Perspective

Interested in practicing in the international arena – or at least gaining a global perspective? Cornell, in Ithaca, New York, has an array of options for students wanting to add international creds to their degree. The joint J.D./ Master of Laws, or LLM degree, in International and Comparative Law is the most rigorous, cramming 20 extra credits into the standard curriculum. An international legal studies specialization, by contrast, requires five extra credits.

Alternately, students may opt for a dual degree adding the law of one of three countries (as long as they are fluent in the language). Those choosing the J.D. Master en Droit, for instance, spend two years at Cornell and two at the Université Paris I Panthéon Sorbonne; there is also a Sorbonne option that can be completed in three years. Students also have dual-degree options in Germany and South Africa. And the simpler semester or summer abroad program, with 28 possible destinations from Cairo to New Delhi, remains the most popular experience by far. Exposure to international law is critical these days even for lawyers who never leave the country, argues Laura Spitz, associate dean for international affairs. "We don't live in a world that's packaged domestically and internationally," she says. "That line is increasingly blurred."

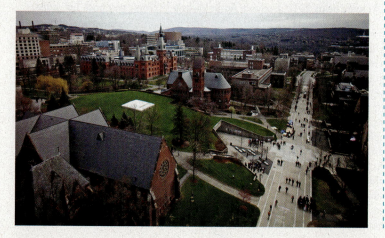

WASHINGTON AND LEE UNIVERSITY
Intensively Experiential

As an extern for a federal judge in Washington, D.C., last fall, Krystal Swendsboe, 27, spent 25 to 30 hours a week in chambers, "far more" than students from other schools, she says. That's because her schedule in the Lexington, Virginia, law school's practice-intensive third year is designed around her real-world workday, shifting the focus from "learning in the classroom to learning in the profession," says Dean Nora Demleitner.

So 3Ls spend most of their year in externships and in clinics built into the curriculum, where work ranges from preparing appeals for coal miners seeking benefits from the federal black lung program to assisting defense counsel in death penalty cases. The pace can be grueling, says Demleitner; faculty tend to treat students like junior partners, calling at all hours if a client is in need.

GONZAGA UNIVERSITY
A Shorter, Skills-Oriented Option

Students in the new accelerated J.D. program at the Spokane, Washington, law school pack 90 credits into two calendar years, the same number required in the school's three-year track. Both reflect a curriculum revamp in 2009 responding to feedback from employers that new hires needed better skills. Along with torts, criminal law and other traditional first-year classes, 1Ls take skills labs in which they draft complaints and contracts, engage in discovery, and conduct client interviews. All students also must take four terms (out of six) of legal research and writing, plus at least 12 credits of experiential learning. Those are earned by doing an externship or by choosing among the eight in-house legal clinics dedicated to such specialties as elder law, Indian law and environmental law.

Jaime Cuevas, 25, says the intensity bonds classmates so they become "war buddies," not competitors. "I was late for class one day," he says, "and I got like five text messages saying, 'Hey, do you want me to take notes for you?'"

Build Your Plan Online

Start Now at USNewsUniversityDirectory.com/Build

Connect
with more than 1,900 top colleges and universities

Target
your search to the schools that best meet your needs

Access
the latest education news from *U.S. News & World Report*

Discover
how to get more financial aid with our free, expert guide

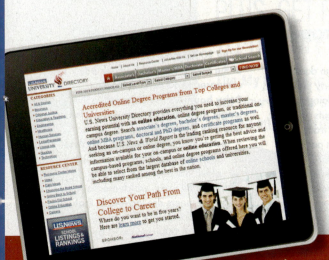

Get Free Assistance
With Your School Search:
855-237-2180

The #1 Authority on the Nation's Best Colleges

THE TOP SCHOOLS continued

Rank School	Overall score	Peer assessment score (5.0=highest)	Assessment score by lawyers/ judges (5.0=highest)	'14 undergrad GPA 25th-75th percentile	'14 LSAT score 25th-75th percentile	'14 acceptance rate	'14 student/ faculty ratio	'13 grads employed at graduation†	Employed 9 months after graduation†	School's bar passage rate in jurisdiction	Jurisdiction's overall bar passage rate
42. University of Utah (Quinney)	55	2.8	3.1	3.36-3.69	158-161	44%	7.7	42.8%	77.9%	90.0%/UT	87%
42. Washington and Lee University (VA)	55	3.1	3.7	3.12-3.55	157-163	43%	8.5	48.3%	63.6%	79.6%/VA	77%
46. Southern Methodist University (Dedman) (TX)	54	2.6	3.2	3.25-3.74	156-163	46%	15.2	55.5%	80.6%	89.6%/TX	85%
47. University of Florida (Levin)	53	3.1	3.4	3.26-3.68	155-161	61%	12.2	37.9%	72.9%	87.2%/FL	78%
47. University of Maryland (Carey)	53	2.9	3.1	3.24-3.68	155-162	47%	10.8	44.7%	67.7%	83.5%/MD	80%
47. Wake Forest University (NC)	53	3.0	3.5	3.37-3.78	157-163	53%	9.7	52.2%	62.3%	75.0%/NC	69%
50. Florida State University	52	2.9	2.9	3.22-3.64	156-161	41%	12.2	32.5%	81.0%	88.4%/FL	78%
50. Tulane University (LA)	52	3.0	3.3	3.18-3.61	157-163	51%	11.2	36.1%	65.2%	66.3%/LA	58%
52. Pepperdine University (CA)	51	2.6	3.3	3.28-3.71	153-162	46%	11.9	36.2%	64.8%	80.9%/CA	65%
52. Temple University (Beasley) (PA)	51	2.6	3.0	3.18-3.66	156-162	42%	9.6	44.1%	70.2%	90.0%/PA	81%
52. University of Richmond (VA)	51	2.5	3.0	3.21-3.62	155-162	34%	9.2	50.7%	71.8%	78.6%/VA	77%
52. University of Tennessee–Knoxville	51	2.6	2.9	3.44-3.85	154-160	40%	9.3	49.1%	76.0%	94.3%/TN	82%
56. Baylor University (TX)	50	2.4	3.3	3.3-3.69	155-162	30%	13.8	35.8%	73.9%	97.0%/TX	85%
56. Georgia State University	50	2.5	2.7	3.12-3.61	155-160	28%	10.4	70.8%	78.5%	94.4%/GA	85%
56. University of Nebraska–Lincoln	50	2.4	3.1	3.41-3.88	152-159	68%	10.5	51.6%	76.6%	86.7%/NE	77%
59. Case Western Reserve University (OH)	49	2.5	3.1	3.24-3.63	157-162	33%	10.6	34.5%	70.7%	87.2%/OH	86%
59. University of California (Hastings)	49	3.1	3.8	3.21-3.62	155-161	49%	14.1	31.4%	47.2%	74.2%/CA	65%
59. University of Houston (TX)	49	2.5	2.7	3.21-3.62	155-161	42%	8.2	51.9%	77.8%	88.2%/TX	85%
59. University of Missouri	49	2.6	3.0	3.08-3.72	154-160	49%	10.4	40.5%	78.6%	93.3%/MO	90%
63. Seton Hall University (NJ)	48	2.3	3.0	3.14-3.71	152-159	50%	10.6	58.3%	77.7%	87.8%/NJ	79%
63. University of Connecticut	48	2.8	2.7	3.15-3.6	155-160	54%	9.6	28.6%	59.9%	84.3%/CT	81%
63. University of Kentucky	48	2.5	3.1	3.22-3.71	152-158	59%	11.1	56.4%	84.2%	90.2%/KY	81%
63. University of Miami (FL)	48	2.7	3.1	3.19-3.63	155-160	51%	12.1	39.3%	70.5%	81.6%/FL	78%
67. University of Denver (Sturm)	47	2.7	3.0	3.1-3.62	153-159	62%	9.5	37.1%	64.8%	85.7%/CO	82%
67. University of Kansas	47	2.6	3.1	3.2-3.69	153-161	57%	10.8	30.1%	76.9%	87.9%/KS	89%
67. University of Nevada–Las Vegas	47	2.3	2.5	3.06-3.62	154-161	35%	10.2	43.9%	71.2%	75.4%/NV	74%
67. University of Oklahoma	47	2.4	3.1	3.24-3.76	155-158	43%	13.9	46.7%	81.0%	88.1%/OK	86%
71. American University (Washington) (DC)	46	2.8	3.2	3.13-3.54	152-158	50%	11.0	50.7%	60.6%	74.6%/NY	76%
71. Pennsylvania State University (Dickinson)	46	2.2	3.1	3.3-3.79	153-160	46%	8.6	29.1%	52.3%	94.3%/PA	81%
71. University of New Mexico	46	2.4	2.7	3.07-3.74	150-157	44%	8.7	57.0%	76.3%	85.4%/NM	91%
71. University of San Diego	46	2.6	2.9	3.23-3.66	155-161	47%	10.8	42.5%	60.1%	75.0%/CA	65%
75. Loyola Marymount University (CA)	45	2.5	3.1	3.21-3.62	156-161	47%	14.8	30.3%	59.1%	84.7%/CA	65%
75. University of Arkansas–Fayetteville	45	2.3	2.9	3.24-3.74	151-157	60%	11.5	40.9%	79.5%	85.7%/AR	76%
75. Yeshiva University (Cardozo) (NY)	45	2.7	2.9	3.25-3.67	155-162	52%	12.9	33.2%	61.6%	84.7%/NY	76%
78. Brooklyn Law School (NY)	44	2.5	2.7	3.05-3.53	153-159	53%	16.0	48.1%	69.0%	92.7%/NY	76%
78. Illinois Institute of Technology (Chicago-Kent)	44	2.5	2.8	3.17-3.62	152-159	62%	10.8	35.8%	67.4%	93.0%/IL	88%
78. Loyola University Chicago	44	2.4	3.1	3.05-3.52	155-159	52%	12.2	38.8%	64.7%	88.3%/IL	88%
78. University of Pittsburgh	44	2.6	3.2	3.09-3.68	152-160	44%	11.9	29.8%	68.2%	80.3%/PA	81%
82. St. John's University (NY)	43	2.2	2.8	3.19-3.64	153-159	46%	13.9	36.6%	67.3%	87.6%/NY	76%
82. University of Cincinnati	43	2.3	2.9	3.22-3.7	151-159	60%	8.4	36.2%	69.1%	89.0%/OH	86%
82. University of Hawaii–Manoa (Richardson)	43	2.4	2.6	3.07-3.6	152-159	38%	7.9	35.8%	71.6%	82.6%/HI	82%
82. University of Oregon	43	2.6	3.2	2.97-3.56	154-159	54%	11.2	27.8%	62.9%	77.6%/OR	80%
82. University of Tulsa (OK)	43	1.9	2.7	3.12-3.73	151-158	33%	9.8	43.8%	78.6%	85.3%/OK	86%
87. Northeastern University (MA)	42	2.3	2.8	3.25-3.68	153-162	38%	12.7	20.2%	55.5%	88.3%/MA	86%
87. Rutgers, The State U. of New Jersey–Newark	42	2.4	2.9	3.05-3.54	153-159	44%	N/A	41.9%	64.8%	70.4%/NJ	79%
87. St. Louis University	42	2.2	3.0	3.19-3.65	151-158	62%	9.2	48.2%	67.4%	91.3%/MO	90%
87. SUNY Buffalo Law School	42	2.2	2.7	3.11-3.66	151-157	56%	10.0	40.3%	71.2%	83.0%/NY	76%
87. Syracuse University (NY)	42	2.2	2.9	3.19-3.55	153-157	56%	10.2	38.7%	66.7%	85.6%/NY	76%
87. University of New Hampshire School of Law	42	1.9	2.6	3.16-3.71	152-158	48%	12.0	49.5%	76.6%	83.7%/NH	76%
87. Villanova University (PA)	42	2.3	3.2	3.33-3.72	152-159	51%	15.4	40.8%	63.3%	86.6%/PA	81%
94. Lewis & Clark College (Northwestern) (OR)	41	2.4	3.0	3-3.58	155-161	67%	10.3	32.0%	66.0%	81.2%/OR	80%
94. Louisiana State Univ.–Baton Rouge (Hebert)	41	2.2	2.8	2.96-3.53	153-158	62%	16.4	45.9%	80.7%	73.4%/LA	58%
94. Michigan State University	41	2.3	2.9	3.25-3.73	150-158	43%	12.7	29.2%	56.8%	81.1%/MI	69%
94. Santa Clara University (CA)	41	2.4	3.1	3.04-3.47	156-160	50%	10.6	25.5%	56.2%	71.9%/CA	65%
94. University of Louisville (Brandeis) (KY)	41	2.1	2.9	3.17-3.62	150-157	70%	12.7	46.9%	80.5%	80.2%/KY	81%

In the reading room
at No. 11 University
of Michigan

Rank School	Overall score	Peer assessment score (5.0=highest)	Assessment score by lawyers/ judges (5.0=highest)	'14 undergrad GPA 25th-75th percentile	'14 LSAT score 25th-75th percentile	'14 acceptance rate	'14 student/ faculty ratio	'13 grads employed at graduation†	Employed 9 months after graduation†	School's bar passage rate in jurisdiction	Jurisdiction's overall bar passage rate
94. University of Mississippi	41	2.2	2.7	3.2-3.66	151-156	44%	10.8	27.9%	72.1%	90.8%/MS	85%
94. University of South Carolina	41	2.3	2.8	2.95-3.54	152-157	57%	13.4	38.7%	75.6%	84.7%/SC	80%
94. West Virginia University	41	2.1	2.7	3.09-3.7	152-156	54%	9.3	33.1%	73.1%	76.9%/WV	76%
102. Florida International University	40	1.7	1.9	3.11-3.76	151-158	27%	10.7	N/A	77.1%	84.8%/FL	78%
102. Indiana University–Indianapolis (McKinney)	40	2.4	3.1	3.02-3.57	148-155	74%	14.5	41.6%	70.8%	81.8%/IN	83%
102. Rutgers, The State U. of New Jersey–Camden	40	2.4	2.9	2.82-3.48	152-158	42%	N/A	52.5%	65.6%	83.8%/NJ	79%
105. Marquette University (WI)	39	2.3	3.0	3.12-3.52	149-155	73%	14.4	38.3%	72.3%	100.0%/WI	88%
105. Stetson University (FL)	39	2.1	2.7	2.97-3.53	152-157	51%	14.3	N/A	70.7%	89.2%/FL	78%
105. Wayne State University (MI)	39	1.9	2.6	2.99-3.52	152-160	49%	9.9	27.6%	62.1%	78.4%/MI	69%
108. The Catholic University of America (DC)	38	2.1	2.9	2.87-3.35	151-157	55%	8.8	46.6%	68.5%	79.2%/MD	80%
108. University of Wyoming	38	2.0	2.7	3.1-3.59	149-155	52%	11.2	52.6%	77.6%	85.0%/WY	84%
110. Gonzaga University (WA)	37	2.0	2.9	3.02-3.55	151-155	67%	14.9	29.2%	72.0%	92.6%/WA	82%
110. Howard University (DC)	37	2.3	2.8	2.95-3.48	148-155	41%	10.3	47.8%	65.9%	67.5%/NY	76%
110. University of Maine	37	2.2	2.8	3.2-3.57	149-157	56%	9.4	41.7%	60.4%	87.5%/ME	81%
113. Creighton University (NE)	36	1.9	2.9	2.91-3.61	148-154	72%	12.5	40.0%	69.6%	73.5%/NE	77%
113. CUNY	36	2.0	2.5	2.97-3.63	151-158	40%	6.6	N/A	55.8%	79.2%/NY	76%
113. Drake University (IA)	36	1.9	2.8	2.97-3.53	148-156	78%	11.0	29.7%	74.6%	94.5%/IA	93%
113. Seattle University	36	2.2	3.0	3.06-3.49	151-157	61%	12.1	N/A	54.7%	82.2%/WA	82%
113. University of Montana	36	1.9	2.4	3.06-3.7	151-158	57%	15.0	45.7%	72.8%	85.9%/MT	89%
118. Duquesne University (PA)	35	1.7	2.7	3.13-3.66	150-155	58%	14.8	33.7%	67.8%	82.2%/PA	81%
118. Mercer University (George) (GA)	35	2.0	2.6	3.05-3.5	147-155	61%	14.5	31.2%	72.0%	86.8%/GA	85%
118. Texas Tech University	35	1.8	2.6	3.17-3.65	151-157	57%	14.7	28.2%	71.0%	86.9%/TX	85%
118. Willamette University (Collins) (OR)	35	2.0	2.8	2.99-3.47	149-155	72%	8.2	25.2%	74.8%	80.6%/OR	80%
122. DePaul University (IL)	34	2.2	2.8	2.98-3.56	148-155	65%	13.1	24.3%	58.5%	87.3%/IL	88%
122. Hofstra University (Deane) (NY)	34	2.1	2.8	3.03-3.55	147-155	61%	14.8	N/A	65.1%	82.6%/NY	76%
122. University of Baltimore	34	2.0	2.6	2.86-3.56	148-154	59%	12.2	47.3%	67.8%	84.9%/MD	80%
122. Vermont Law School	34	2.0	2.7	2.9-3.52	146-156	74%	10.4	29.0%	65.5%	66.7%/NY	76%
122. Washburn University (KS)	34	1.8	2.5	2.96-3.62	148-156	64%	9.6	26.5%	72.8%	86.3%/KS	89%
127. Chapman University (Fowler) (CA)	33	1.8	2.4	3.17-3.56	153-158	52%	9.1	21.5%	45.7%	75.7%/CA	65%
127. Cleveland State Univ. (Cleveland-Marshall)	33	1.7	2.5	2.99-3.54	151-156	55%	10.0	28.3%	67.9%	91.1%/OH	86%
127. Drexel University (Kline) (PA)	33	2.0	2.5	3.05-3.49	151-156	50%	10.5	29.7%	60.1%	80.2%/PA	81%
127. New York Law School	33	1.8	2.6	2.8-3.5	148-154	56%	12.5	31.7%	58.4%	82.4%/NY	76%
127. Quinnipiac University (CT)	33	1.9	2.1	3-3.57	150-155	56%	10.6	23.6%	62.2%	82.2%/CT	81%
127. University of Akron (OH)	33	1.7	2.3	2.93-3.68	147-155	65%	10.7	28.9%	64.5%	83.8%/OH	86%
127. University of Idaho	33	2.0	2.6	2.75-3.52	147-154	61%	11.1	N/A	73.5%	81.1%/ID	83%
127. University of Missouri–Kansas City	33	2.2	2.6	2.96-3.54	150-154	55%	12.8	N/A	60.8%	91.7%/MO	90%
135. Loyola University New Orleans	32	2.1	2.9	2.84-3.47	150-157	58%	10.9	18.0%	58.2%	64.9%/LA	58%
135. University of Arkansas–Little Rock (Bowen)	32	2.1	2.7	3-3.59	146-155	66%	15.2	26.6%	62.9%	69.8%/AR	76%
135. University of St. Thomas (MN)	32	1.8	2.5	3.17-3.61	150-158	73%	13.5	21.5%	62.7%	87.1%/MN	90%
138. Albany Law School (NY)	31	1.7	2.5	2.9-3.51	148-154	61%	14.4	38.3%	68.4%	79.8%/NY	76%
138. Pace University (NY)	31	1.9	2.3	2.9-3.55	148-153	62%	9.8	N/A	52.7%	79.3%/NY	76%
138. University of North Dakota	31	1.9	2.6	2.94-3.61	143-152	54%	13.6	N/A	73.0%	75.9%/ND	80%
138. University of San Francisco	31	2.1	2.9	2.94-3.4	151-156	61%	12.6	25.5%	47.5%	74.1%/CA	65%
142. University of Memphis (Humphreys)	30	1.8	2.2	2.87-3.51	150-157	51%	12.4	23.4%	66.1%	88.0%/TN	82%
142. University of Toledo (OH)	30	1.7	2.3	3.01-3.55	148-154	61%	10.2	22.9%	61.0%	84.6%/OH	86%
142. William Mitchell College of Law (MN)	30	1.8	2.4	2.98-3.59	149-156	72%	20.4	28.3%	71.7%	88.8%/MN	90%
145. Hamline University (MN)	29	1.7	2.4	2.99-3.46	146-155	70%	16.8	23.2%	69.2%	83.7%/MN	90%
145. Ohio Northern University (Pettit)	29	1.5	2.1	2.86-3.58	144-152	49%	11.5	N/A	77.1%	90.3%/OH	86%
145. University of Dayton (OH)	29	1.7	2.5	2.86-3.38	145-151	58%	13.5	N/A	75.3%	78.8%/OH	86%
145. University of South Dakota	29	1.8	2.3	2.71-3.44	144-152	82%	11.6	59.2%	83.1%	97.4%/SD	91%
149. Oklahoma City University	27	1.5	2.3	2.79-3.41	145-151	82%	14.7	N/A	78.2%	82.1%/OK	86%
149. Samford University (Cumberland) (AL)	27	1.7	2.6	2.89-3.52	148-154	76%	16.9	33.8%	65.6%	86.3%/AL	78%
149. Southern Illinois University–Carbondale	27	1.7	2.3	2.71-3.45	144-151	85%	12.1	29.5%	79.1%	88.9%/IL	88%
149. South Texas College of Law	27	1.6	2.1	2.86-3.33	148-153	66%	18.2	N/A	77.3%	88.1%/TX	85%
149. Texas A&M University	27	1.9	2.0	2.93-3.41	152-156	40%	15.3	21.0%	55.1%	86.7%/TX	85%

Other Schools to Consider

The country's other law schools can be considered broadly similar in quality. To be included in the ranking, a law school had to be accredited and fully approved by the American Bar Association, and it had to draw most of its students from the United States.

Remember, as you weigh your options, that you should look not only at a law school's position in the ranking, but also at its many other key characteristics, both tangible and intangible: location, the cost of spending three years there, faculty expertise and the breadth of the course offerings, to name a few – and certainly your prospects of being offered a job upon graduation. More information on all of the law schools is available in the directory at the back of the book, as well as at usnews.com/lawschools.

SECOND TIER (Schools are not ranked, but listed alphabetically.)

School	Peer assessment score (5.0=highest)	Assessment score by lawyers/ judges (5.0=highest)	'14 undergrad GPA 25th-75th percentile	'14 LSAT score 25th-75th percentile	'14 acceptance rate	'14 student/ faculty ratio	'13 grads employed at graduation[1]	Employed 9 months after graduation[1]	School's bar passage rate in jurisdiction	Jurisdiction's overall bar passage rate
Appalachian School of Law[1] (VA)	1.2	1.4	2.57-3.25*	141-148*	67%*	N/A	N/A	55.7%*	59.1%*/VA	77%
Arizona Summit Law School[1]	1.1	1.5	2.56-3.27*	140-149*	69%*	N/A	N/A	56.6%*	70.0%*/AZ	78%
Atlanta's John Marshall Law School[1]	1.3	1.6	2.68-3.21*	146-151*	54%*	N/A	N/A	58.5%*	67.1%*/GA	85%
Ave Maria School of Law (FL)	1.1	1.7	2.66-3.45	139-148	75%	N/A	N/A	48.4%	56.3%/FL	78%
Barry University (FL)	1.2	1.4	2.69-3.3	144-149	62%	N/A	N/A	47.8%*	79.3%/FL	78%
California Western School of Law	1.5	2.2	2.9-3.45	146-153	67%	13.6	N/A	41.6%	70.6%/CA	65%
Campbell University (NC)	1.5	2.1	2.91-3.47	149-156	57%	14.1	20.7%	61.5%	82.4%/NC	69%
Capital University (OH)	1.4	2.1	2.8-3.44	144-152	80%	13.6	N/A	55.1%	86.6%/OH	86%
Charleston School of Law (SC)	1.2	2.0	2.61-3.32	143-151	83%	15.3	N/A	60.4%	75.1%/SC	80%
Charlotte School of Law (NC)	1.2	1.6	2.53-3.18	138-146	75%	19.5	N/A	54.3%	60.6%/NC	69%
Elon University (NC)	1.6	2.4	2.7-3.34	145-151	75%	11.7	23.0%	47.5%	64.5%/NC	69%
Faulkner University[1] (Jones) (AL)	1.3	1.9	2.72-3.34*	142-149*	77%*	N/A	N/A	72.3%*	95.5%*/AL	78%
Florida A&M University[1]	1.3	1.6	2.75-3.3*	144-149*	53%*	N/A	N/A	49.3%*	73.1%*/FL	78%
Florida Coastal School of Law	1.2	1.4	2.63-3.2	140-147	78%	N/A	N/A	37.9%	68.6%/FL	78%
Golden Gate University (CA)	1.6	2.1	2.73-3.24	146-153	65%	12.4	N/A	28.9%	55.7%/CA	65%
Inter-American University[1] (PR)	1.3	1.7	2.98-3.51*	135-141*	52%*	N/A	N/A	30.0%*	N/A	N/A
The John Marshall Law School (IL)	1.7	2.6	2.76-3.34	145-152	73%	16.0	35.0%	64.8%	84.9%/IL	88%
Liberty University (VA)	1.2	1.6	2.74-3.5	148-155	65%	N/A	18.7%	47.3%	66.7%/VA	77%
Mississippi College	1.6	1.9	2.71-3.47	144-153	81%	11.4	26.7%	65.8%	81.5%/MS	85%
New England Law Boston	1.5	2.2	2.85-3.43	146-152	80%	N/A	N/A	55.0%	91.9%/MA	86%
North Carolina Central University	1.4	1.9	2.97-3.5	141-149	54%	13.9	N/A	27.2%	65.6%/NC	69%
Northern Illinois University	1.6	2.2	2.83-3.37	146-153	70%	16.3	N/A	61.5%	87.4%/IL	88%
Northern Kentucky University (Chase)	1.5	2.0	2.87-3.42	146-154	72%	14.5	N/A	61.9%	82.8%/OH	86%
Nova Southeastern University (Broad) (FL)	1.5	1.9	2.84-3.41	146-151	54%	14.8	18.4%	68.8%	81.6%/FL	78%
Pontifical Catholic University of Puerto Rico[1]	1.3	2.2	N/A	131-138*	63%*	N/A	N/A	7.9%*	32.1%*/PR	45%
Regent University (VA)	1.3	1.8	2.96-3.59	148-156	50%	10.9	N/A	64.5%	73.1%/VA	77%
Roger Williams University (RI)	1.6	1.9	2.85-3.41	145-152	72%	13.2	N/A	47.4%	79.1%/MA	86%
Southern University Law Center (LA)	1.4	2.0	2.52-3.2	142-147	65%	15.5	N/A	50.0%	46.6%/LA	58%
Southwestern Law School (CA)	1.9	2.4	2.93-3.43	149-154	61%	14.6	14.0%	52.0%	73.5%/CA	65%
St. Mary's University (TX)	1.6	2.4	2.65-3.32	148-152	70%	14.5	N/A	72.4%	81.5%/TX	85%
St. Thomas University (FL)	1.4	1.7	2.71-3.36	144-151	63%	N/A	N/A	57.4%	71.4%/FL	78%
Suffolk University (MA)	1.8	2.6	2.96-3.43	143-152	89%	17.1	24.0%	50.3%	81.9%/MA	86%
Texas Southern University[1] (Marshall)	1.4	1.8	2.72-3.34*	143-148*	47%*	N/A	N/A	54.7%*	N/A	N/A
Thomas Jefferson School of Law (CA)	1.3	1.8	2.58-3.13	141-149	84%	N/A	18.1%	41.0%	48.9%/CA	65%
Touro College (Fuchsberg) (NY)	1.5	1.7	2.75-3.33	145-149	68%	19.7	N/A	57.4%	66.4%/NY	76%
University of Detroit Mercy	1.4	1.8	2.92-3.35	148-157	54%	12.9	N/A	47.4%	63.0%/MI	69%
University of Puerto Rico[1]	1.5	2.0	3.26-3.81*	142-149*	56%*	N/A	N/A	32.5%*	53.6%*/PR	45%
University of the District of Columbia (Clarke)	1.4	1.6	2.7-3.4	145-153	36%	10.8	N/A	41.3%	54.5%/MD	80%
University of the Pacific (McGeorge) (CA)	1.9	2.6	2.92-3.39	148-155	75%	13.5	21.4%	46.9%	67.5%/CA	65%
Valparaiso University (IN)	1.6	2.6	2.77-3.33	141-149	77%	12.8	N/A	50.6%	76.7%/IN	83%
Western Mich. U. Thomas M. Cooley Law Sch.	1.1	1.7	2.53-3.28	141-149	85%	N/A	N/A	36.3%	58.3%/MI	69%
Western New England University (MA)	1.4	1.7	2.89-3.42	143-149	82%	14.3	N/A	49.6%	68.4%/CT	81%
Western State Col. of Law at Argosy U. (CA)	1.1	1.6	2.86-3.34	146-151	63%	17.1	N/A	43.9%	77.5%/CA	65%
Whittier College (CA)	1.4	2.0	2.62-3.18	143-150	74%	15.2	N/A	30.0%	64.1%/CA	65%
Widener University (DE)	1.7	2.2	2.74-3.34	146-152	63%	10.5	26.8%	60.3%	80.8%/PA	81%

Best Part-Time J.D. Programs

The American Bar Association's latest data reveal that in the fall of 2013, some 18,450 law students, or about 14 percent of the 128,641 total number, were enrolled part time. For many working adults, part-time study is the only way to afford a law degree and still meet other commitments. Fewer than half of the country's law schools offer these programs, which generally require four years to complete. Below, U.S. News presents the top half of accredited law schools offering a part-time pathway. The ranking is based on four factors as described in the methodology below: reputation among deans and faculty at peer schools, LSAT scores and undergraduate GPAs of students entering in the fall of 2014, and the breadth of each school's part-time program.

THE TOP PART-TIME PROGRAMS

Rank School	Overall score	Peer assessment score (5.0=highest)	'14 part-time LSAT score 25th-75th percentile	'14 part-time acceptance rate	'14 part-time enrollment
1. Georgetown University (DC)	100	4.0	160-168	4.9%	247
2. George Washington University (DC)	86	3.3	150-165	29.3%	270
3. Fordham University (NY)	82	3.2	157-163	24.2%	203
4. George Mason University (VA)	71	2.7	158-163	16.4%	150
5. University of Maryland (Carey)	69	2.8	156-162	24.3%	150
6. University of Connecticut	68	2.8	154-160	36.1%	115
7. Southern Methodist University (Dedman) (TX)	65	2.6	153-161	18.6%	228
7. Temple University (Beasley) (PA)	65	2.7	155-161	31.3%	160
9. Lewis & Clark College (Northwestern) (OR)	63	2.4	153-161	49.5%	188
10. University of Denver (Sturm)	62	2.9	151-160	49.6%	138
11. Loyola Marymount University (CA)	60	2.5	154-160	16.9%	194
11. University of Houston (TX)	60	2.6	151-159	21.3%	117
13. University of San Diego	59	2.6	154-162	39.1%	108
14. Georgia State University	57	2.4	153-159	25.9%	46
14. Illinois Institute of Technology (Chicago-Kent)	57	2.6	152-160	42.3%	107
16. American University (Washington) (DC)	55	2.8	152-157	43.6%	249
17. Loyola University Chicago	53	2.5	150-159	37.6%	68
17. Marquette University (WI)	53	2.4	150-161	39.0%	93
19. Brooklyn Law School (NY)	52	2.6	152-159	32.3%	238
19. Rutgers, The State Univ. of New Jersey–Newark	52	2.5	150-157	32.4%	171
21. William Mitchell College of Law (MN)	51	2.1	148-159	34.0%	210
22. University of Nevada–Las Vegas	50	2.3	152-157	29.1%	106
23. Rutgers, The State Univ. of New Jersey–Camden	49	2.4	152-156	22.0%	85
23. Seattle University	49	2.4	150-158	52.4%	163
23. University of Baltimore	49	2.2	149-154	45.0%	297
26. Indiana University–Indianapolis (McKinney)	48	2.4	147-156	73.5%	326
26. Seton Hall University (NJ)	48	2.3	148-156	35.6%	190
26. The Catholic University of America (DC)	48	2.2	150-155	43.8%	164
29. Stetson University (FL)	47	2.1	151-158	33.7%	198
30. University of Hawaii–Manoa (Richardson)	46	2.3	150-159	43.8%	68
31. St. Louis University	45	2.3	150-155	45.1%	72
31. Texas A&M University	45	2.0	151-155	26.9%	244
33. New York Law School	44	2.0	147-152	44.1%	308
34. Southwestern Law School (CA)	43	2.0	148-153	52.3%	361
35. DePaul University (IL)	42	2.3	148-155	47.7%	120
35. Santa Clara University (CA)	42	2.5	155-160	41.2%	165
35. St. John's University (NY)	42	2.1	151-158	28.9%	122
35. University of San Francisco	42	2.1	152-158	45.9%	102
35. University of the Pacific (McGeorge) (CA)	42	2.1	147-154	72.6%	137
35. Wayne State University (MI)	42	2.0	153-161	36.8%	123
41. Hofstra University (Deane) (NY)	41	2.1	144-156	34.6%	24
41. Loyola University New Orleans	41	2.1	150-157	43.5%	99
41. Suffolk University (MA)	41	2.1	143-154	82.9%	461

METHODOLOGY

The ranking of 85 part-time law programs is based on a weighted average of four measures of quality. For a school's program to be eligible for the part-time ranking, it had to have reported at least 20 part-time students enrolled in the fall of 2014 and supplied data on fall 2014 applications and acceptances to its part-time program.

Quality assessment (weighted by .50): In the fall of 2014, deans and three faculty members at each school were asked to rate programs from marginal (1) to outstanding (5); 49 percent responded, and scores for each school were averaged.

Selectivity (weighted by .275): For part-time students entering in 2014, this measure combines median LSAT scores (81.8 percent of this indicator) and undergraduate GPAs (18.2 percent).

Part-time focus (weighted by .225): An index was created from data reported by the schools about their 2014 part-time J.D. programs. Factors used in the creation of this index include the size of part-time first-year sections; the size of part-time first-year small sections; and the number of positions filled by part-time students in seminars, simulation courses, faculty-supervised clinical courses, field placements, law journals, interschool skills competitions and independent study. Schools received credit for reporting data and additional credit for surpassing a threshold value in the various factors used.

Overall rank: Schools' scores on each indicator were standardized, weighted, totaled and rescaled so that the top school received 100, and other schools received a percentage of the top score.

Note: The data listed for acceptance rate and enrollment are for informational purposes only and are not used in the computation of the part-time J.D. program ranking. Only part-time J.D. programs ranked in the top half appear. Sources: U.S. News and the schools. Assessment data collected by Ipsos Public Affairs.

The Rest of the Rankings

The Hearst Memorial Mining Building at UC–Berkeley

THE U.S. NEWS RANKINGS

WHAT CAN
You
BE WITH A
Science
Ph.D.?

THERE'S PLENTY OF OPPORTUNITY OUTSIDE THE IVORY TOWER

- - - - - - - - - - - - - - - - - - -

By **ELIZABETH GARDNER**

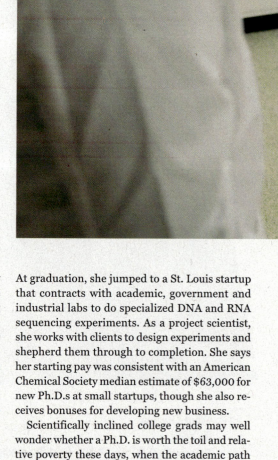

While earning her Ph.D. in chemistry at Washington University in St. Louis, Natalie LaFranzo, 29, spent hours in the lab developing techniques for studying how neurons communicate. Her expenses were fully funded by the university and a grant from the National Institutes of Health. By the time she graduated in 2013, LaFranzo's CV included a respectable list of publications and conference presentations that could well have led to a postdoctoral fellowship and eventually a faculty position.

Except that she didn't want either of those things. "I realized that the academic world wasn't where I was headed," she says; a life of teaching and scrambling for research money just didn't appeal. Instead, she began tailoring her experience for a career in industry, participating in a campus group offering consulting services to biotech startups, adding management skills as a cheerleading coach, and serving on the American Chemical Society's Younger Chemists Committee to strengthen her contacts and get networking experience.

At graduation, she jumped to a St. Louis startup that contracts with academic, government and industrial labs to do specialized DNA and RNA sequencing experiments. As a project scientist, she works with clients to design experiments and shepherd them through to completion. She says her starting pay was consistent with an American Chemical Society median estimate of $63,000 for new Ph.D.s at small startups, though she also receives bonuses for developing new business.

Scientifically inclined college grads may well wonder whether a Ph.D. is worth the toil and relative poverty these days, when the academic path is so narrow and crowded, and unlikely to lead to the tenured professorship traditionally considered the pinnacle of success. (Only 42 percent of people with scientific Ph.D.s today work in academia.) With all sorts of companies clamoring for technical prowess, they can take their quantitative aptitudes directly into the private sector with a master's, or even a bachelor's, and do fine.

But many doctoral students, like LaFranzo, feel

chemistry in 2003 and joined Dow as a researcher.

A key attraction of the business world is the prospect of creating tangible change. "I realized that what motivated me was seeing how my discoveries would relate to helping people now, not years in the future," says Julia Woertink, 34, strategy leader for research and development at Dow, who wrapped up a Ph.D. in chemistry at Stanford University in 2010. Her research there involved the role of copper in biology and the creation of alternative fuels. She has already seen a commercial pay-off for some of her labor at Dow in the form of materials being used in next-generation computer chips.

That Ph.D. gave her a "huge advantage," Woertink says, when it came to demonstrating that she had advanced technical skills along with the ability to think critically and the discipline to carry through a line of inquiry.

In addition to industrial research, opportunities for people with advanced STEM credentials abound in fields like consulting and finance. "One of the nice things about being a mathematician is that so many employers are looking for logical and quantitative skills," says

they get the best of both worlds: They can immerse themselves in the research they're passionate about, usually free of tuition and with a small stipend, and graduate to find companies willing to pay a premium for their advanced research skills, independent thinking and dogged determination.

The most recent stats from the National Science Foundation, which tracks employment in scientific disciplines, show the unemployment rate among Ph.D.s running a third that of the general population (2.1 percent versus 6.3 percent) as of February 2013. Unemployment among Ph.D. mathematicians and statisticians was just 1.2 percent. As for starting salaries, NSF surveys show a median of $98,000 for science and engineering Ph.D.s in private industry, compared with $60,000 in academia. Young math and computer science grads in industry commanded a median of $115,000. Once in the workforce, they can watch their original research turn into products and services rather than journal papers.

"You'll find yourself on the discovery side of new technology," says Andrew Zalusky, a research and development recruiting manager for Dow Chemical Co. in Midland, Michigan. He earned his own doctoral degree in polymer

Dow Chemical strategy leader Julia Woertink talks with associate chemist John Ell.

Ashley Pitlyk, 29, who earned her Ph.D. in math in 2010 from St. Louis University in Missouri, spent one year teaching before deciding to leave academia, and went to work for consulting firm Booz Allen Hamilton in Washington, D.C. "We can go from industry to industry applying them." Some of the firm's engagements require consultants to have Ph.D.s, and even when it's not required, Pitlyk finds that the degree earns her respect from co-workers and clients.

What about physicists, who have perhaps the least obvious nonacademic career path? The data show that more than half of physics Ph.D.s wind up in industry, in fact, while only 1 in 5 stay in education, says Steven Lambert, an industrial physics fellow for the American Physical Society, which tracks the employment status of members. APS research shows that Ph.D. physicists can be found in any number of fields, including manufacturing, engineering, medicine, business and finance, computing and even intellectual property law, where their scientific know-how can help them analyze patents.

Graduate schools are beginning to recognize how widely their students scatter, and are realizing that they need to

Georgia Institute of Technology
Atlanta

MEGAN TONEY, *'14*
Biomechanics associate

► Applied physiology is a smaller program at Georgia Tech, so students have a lot of freedom to explore. The Ph.D. process is project-based. You learn how to define your project, manage your time and prioritize. For example, I studied gait biomechanics to see how the movements of amputees using prosthetics changed in different environments, like walking on ice, compared to nonamputees.

These project-management skills all prepared me well for my current job with Exponent, a technical and engineering company, where I analyze how injuries were caused in car accidents. And because Georgia Tech requires students to regularly make presentations on their work, I am very comfortable explaining complex issues to clients and colleagues – a big part of my job now.

take nonacademic career paths into account when designing their programs. Last year, the Council of Graduate Schools acknowledged that huge numbers of new Ph.D.s take their talents outside academia, and noted somberly: "Our incomplete knowledge of these contributions to U.S. research, scholarship and innovation may prevent us from fully articulating the public and private value of graduate education."

An accompanying survey of students and recent grads showed that more than half thought schools provided inadequate career placement information when they were applying. Ten percent reported receiving no career information at all.

The CGS urges graduate programs to pay attention to what happens to their Ph.D.s, with an eye to improving program design and mentorship for nonacademic careers. Many already are.

Washington University in St. Louis' career center, for example, has earmarked an adviser specifically for students pursuing science Ph.D.s. The University of Wisconsin–Madison recently started a professional development initiative that includes goal-setting, an individualized personal assessment process and career exploration. The University of California–Davis offers grad students workshops and support as they work on core competencies that include public speaking and writing skills and leadership capability – all of those "soft" skills so prized by employers. Other universities that boast similarly muscular professional development programs include Michigan State, Duke, Ohio State, Princeton and the University of California–Santa Cruz.

How do you find a program that will

nurture your aspirations? As with any Ph.D. program, the quality and the value of the experience often rests on finding the right adviser, one who is not biased against a career outside the ivory tower and who preferably collaborates with industrial partners.

"Make sure the professor is doing something that you're interested in and that there's reasonable support for that project, because you can be in trouble if

the money disappears," advises Lambert.

Some universities have forged active industrial partnerships, adding internships or cooperative education experiences and providing access to funding and professional connections. Dow is investing $250 million over 10 years in partnerships with 11 schools, including the California Institute of Technology, the University of California–Santa Barbara, the University of Minnesota, Georgia Institute of Technology and Carnegie Mellon University in Pittsburgh. The funds support new lab space and equipment, graduate student tuition and stipends, and research projects in arenas from electronics to energy storage.

Even if a university doesn't have such formal relationships, individual professors might. Brenda Zhuang, 35, who earned her Ph.D. in manufacturing engineering at Boston University several years ago, recalls benefiting from a consortium of companies organized by a group of BU professors that met every six months to review students' research. "Those poster sessions opened my eyes," she says. "The problems we were solving were actually interesting" to giants like Honeywell as well as small startups. Through those connections, Zhuang found a spot as a software engineer for Mathworks, a scientific computing software company headquartered in Natick, Massachusetts.

Woertink says working in grad school with a variety of partners, both in the U.S. and abroad, has served her well at Dow, where she has to be effective within the global organization as well as with customers. "I would advise anyone interested in an industrial career to get experience with collaboration," she says.

As for scientists who skipped a Ph.D. in favor of a job, they might find they have a chance to go back to school on the company dime, as employers recognize the value of the advanced degree. "They're our biggest feeders into our Ph.D. program," says Karen Panetta, associate dean for graduate education at Tufts University near Boston, of the Lincoln Laboratory at the Massachusetts Institute of Technology, a research and development center. Students have the advantage of being "100 percent funded," she says. "And you have a job when you get out." ∎

The Sciences

PH.D. PROGRAMS RANKED BEST BY DEANS AND DEPARTMENT CHAIRS

BIOLOGICAL SCIENCES Ranked in 2014

Listed schools may have multiple programs.

Rank	School	Average assessment score (5.0=highest)
1.	Harvard University (MA)	4.9
1.	Massachusetts Institute of Technology	4.9
1.	Stanford University (CA)	4.9
4.	University of California–Berkeley	4.8
5.	California Institute of Technology	4.7
5.	Johns Hopkins University (MD)	4.7
7.	University of California–San Francisco	4.6
7.	Yale University (CT)	4.6
9.	Princeton University (NJ)	4.5
9.	Scripps Research Institute (CA)	4.5
11.	Cornell University (NY)	4.4
11.	Duke University (NC)	4.4
11.	Washington University in St. Louis	4.4
14.	Columbia University (NY)	4.3
14.	Rockefeller University (NY)	4.3
14.	University of California–San Diego	4.3
14.	University of Chicago	4.3
18.	University of Wisconsin–Madison	4.2
19.	University of California–Davis	4.1
19.	University of California–Los Angeles	4.1
19.	University of Michigan–Ann Arbor	4.1
19.	University of Pennsylvania	4.1
19.	University of Washington	4.1
19.	U. of Texas Southwest. Med. Ctr.–Dallas	4.1
25.	Baylor College of Medicine (TX)	4.0
26.	Cornell University (Weill) (NY)	3.9
26.	Northwestern University (IL)	3.9
26.	University of North Carolina–Chapel Hill	3.9
26.	Vanderbilt University (TN)	3.9
30.	Emory University (GA)	3.8
30.	University of Colorado–Boulder	3.8
30.	University of Illinois–Urbana-Champaign	3.8
30.	University of Texas–Austin	3.8
34.	Brown University (RI)	3.7
34.	Indiana University–Bloomington	3.7
34.	University of California–Irvine	3.7
34.	University of Minnesota–Twin Cities	3.7
38.	Case Western Reserve University (OH)	3.6
38.	Dartmouth College (NH)	3.6
38.	Mayo Medical School (MN)	3.6
38.	University of Arizona	3.6
42.	Carnegie Mellon University (PA)	3.5
42.	Icahn Sch. of Medicine at Mt. Sinai (NY)	3.5
42.	Ohio State University	3.5
42.	Penn. State University–University Park	3.5
42.	Rice University (TX)	3.5
42.	University of Alabama–Birmingham	3.5
42.	University of Georgia	3.5
42.	University of Pittsburgh	3.5
50.	Michigan State University	3.4
50.	University of California–Santa Barbara	3.4
50.	University of Virginia	3.4
50.	U. of Mass. Medical Center–Worcester	3.4
50.	Yeshiva University (Einstein) (NY)	3.4
55.	Arizona State University	3.3
55.	Brandeis University (MA)	3.3
55.	Georgia Institute of Technology	3.3
55.	Purdue University–West Lafayette (IN)	3.3
55.	Stony Brook University–SUNY	3.3
55.	University of California–Santa Cruz	3.3
55.	University of Florida	3.3
55.	University of Iowa	3.3
55.	University of Maryland–College Park	3.3
55.	University of Massachusetts–Amherst	3.3
55.	University of Oregon	3.3
55.	University of Southern California	3.3
55.	University of Utah	3.3
68.	New York University	3.2
68.	Oregon Health and Science University	3.2
68.	Rutgers, the State U. of N.J.–New Bruns.	3.2
68.	Tufts University (MA)	3.2
68.	University of California–Riverside	3.2
68.	University of Kansas	3.2
68.	University of Rochester (NY)	3.2
75.	Colorado State University	3.1
75.	Iowa State University	3.1
75.	North Carolina State University	3.1
75.	Oregon State University	3.1
75.	Texas A&M University–College Station	3.1
75.	University of Colorado–Denver	3.1
75.	University of Connecticut	3.1
75.	University of Illinois–Chicago	3.1
75.	U. of Texas Health Sci. Ctr.–Houston	3.1

BIOLOGICAL SCIENCES SPECIALTIES

BIOCHEMISTRY/BIOPHYSICS/STRUCTURAL BIOLOGY

1. Harvard University (MA)
1. Stanford University (CA)
3. California Institute of Technology
3. Yale University (CT)

CELL BIOLOGY

1. Yale University (CT)
2. Stanford University (CA)
3. Harvard University (MA)
3. Johns Hopkins University (MD)

ECOLOGY/EVOLUTIONARY BIOLOGY

1. University of California–Berkeley
2. Cornell University (NY)
3. University of California–Davis
4. Stanford University (CA)
4. University of Chicago

GENETICS/GENOMICS/BIOINFORMATICS

1. Harvard University (MA)
1. Stanford University (CA)
3. University of California–Berkeley
3. University of Washington

IMMUNOLOGY/INFECTIOUS DISEASE

1. Johns Hopkins University (MD)
2. University of California–San Francisco
3. Harvard University (MA)

MICROBIOLOGY

1. Harvard University (MA)
2. Stanford University (CA)

MOLECULAR BIOLOGY

1. Harvard University (MA)

1. University of California–Berkeley
3. Johns Hopkins University (MD)
4. Massachusetts Institute of Technology
4. Stanford University (CA)

NEUROSCIENCE/NEUROBIOLOGY

1. Stanford University (CA)
2. University of California–San Diego
3. California Institute of Technology
3. Johns Hopkins University (MD)

CHEMISTRY Ranked in 2014

Rank	School	Average assessment score (5.0=highest)
1.	California Institute of Technology	5.0
1.	Massachusetts Institute of Technology	5.0
1.	University of California–Berkeley	5.0
4.	Harvard University (MA)	4.9
4.	Stanford University (CA)	4.9
6.	University of Illinois–Urbana-Champaign	4.7
7.	Northwestern University (IL)	4.6
7.	Scripps Research Institute (CA)	4.6
9.	University of Wisconsin–Madison	4.5
10.	Columbia University (NY)	4.4
10.	Cornell University (NY)	4.4
12.	University of Chicago	4.3
12.	University of Texas–Austin	4.3
12.	Yale University (CT)	4.3
15.	Princeton University (NJ)	4.2
15.	University of California–Los Angeles	4.2
15.	University of Michigan–Ann Arbor	4.2
15.	University of North Carolina–Chapel Hill	4.2
19.	Texas A&M University–College Station	4.0
19.	University of Pennsylvania	4.0
21.	Penn. State University–University Park	3.9
21.	Purdue University–West Lafayette (IN)	3.9
21.	University of California–San Diego	3.9
24.	Georgia Institute of Technology	3.8
24.	Indiana University–Bloomington	3.8
24.	Johns Hopkins University (MD)	3.8
24.	University of California–Irvine	3.8
24.	University of Colorado–Boulder	3.8
24.	University of Minnesota–Twin Cities	3.8
24.	University of Washington	3.8
31.	Ohio State University	3.7
31.	University of California–San Francisco	3.7
33.	Rice University (TX)	3.6
33.	University of California–Santa Barbara	3.6
35.	Emory University (GA)	3.5
35.	University of California–Davis	3.5
35.	University of Florida	3.5
35.	University of Pittsburgh	3.5
35.	University of Utah	3.5
35.	Washington University in St. Louis	3.5
41.	Duke University (NC)	3.4
41.	University of Arizona	3.4
41.	University of Maryland–College Park	3.4
41.	U. of Texas Southwest. Med. Ct.–Dallas	3.4
45.	Carnegie Mellon University (PA)	3.3
45.	Iowa State University	3.3
45.	Michigan State University	3.3
45.	Vanderbilt University (TN)	3.3
49.	Boston College	3.2
49.	Colorado State University	3.2
49.	Florida State University	3.2
49.	Rockefeller University (NY)	3.2
49.	University of Rochester (NY)	3.2
49.	University of Southern California	3.2
49.	University of Virginia	3.2
56.	North Carolina State University	3.1
56.	Stony Brook University–SUNY	3.1
56.	University of Georgia	3.1
56.	University of Massachusetts–Amherst	3.1
60.	Arizona State University	3.0
60.	Boston University	3.0
60.	Brown University (RI)	3.0
60.	New York University	3.0
60.	Rutgers, the State U. of N.J.–New Bruns.	3.0
60.	University of California–Riverside	3.0
60.	University of Delaware	3.0
60.	University of Iowa	3.0
60.	University of Notre Dame (IN)	3.0
60.	University of Oregon	3.0
60.	Virginia Tech	3.0

CHEMISTRY SPECIALTIES

ANALYTICAL
1. Purdue Univ.–West Lafayette (IN)
2. University of North Carolina–Chapel Hill
3. University of Illinois–Urbana-Champaign
4. University of Texas–Austin
5. Indiana University–Bloomington
6. University of Wisconsin–Madison

BIOCHEMISTRY
1. University of California–Berkeley
2. Scripps Research Institute (CA)
2. University of Wisconsin–Madison
4. Harvard University (MA)
5. University of California–San Francisco
6. Stanford University (CA)
7. Mass. Institute of Technology

INORGANIC
1. Mass. Institute of Technology
2. California Institute of Technology
3. University of California–Berkeley
4. Northwestern University (IL)
5. Texas A&M University–College Station
6. University of Wisconsin–Madison

ORGANIC
1. Harvard University (MA)
2. California Institute of Technology
3. University of California–Berkeley
4. Mass. Institute of Technology
5. Stanford University (CA)
6. Scripps Research Institute (CA)
7. Princeton University (NJ)
8. University of Wisconsin–Madison

PHYSICAL
1. University of California–Berkeley
2. California Institute of Technology
3. Mass. Institute of Technology
4. Stanford University (CA)
5. Northwestern University (IL)
6. University of Chicago

THEORETICAL
1. University of California–Berkeley
2. California Institute of Technology
3. Harvard University (MA)
3. University of Chicago
5. Columbia University (NY)
5. Yale University (CT)
7. Mass. Institute of Technology
7. Stanford University (CA)

COMPUTER SCIENCE Ranked in 2014

Rank	School	Average assessment score (5.0=highest)
1.	Carnegie Mellon University (PA)	5.0
1.	Massachusetts Institute of Technology	5.0
1.	Stanford University (CA)	5.0
1.	University of California–Berkeley	5.0
5.	University of Illinois–Urbana-Champaign	4.6
6.	Cornell University (NY)	4.5
6.	University of Washington	4.5
8.	Princeton University (NJ)	4.4
9.	Georgia Institute of Technology	4.3
9.	University of Texas–Austin	4.3
11.	California Institute of Technology	4.2
11.	University of Wisconsin–Madison	4.2
13.	University of California–Los Angeles	4.1
13.	University of Michigan–Ann Arbor	4.1
15.	Columbia University (NY)	4.0
15.	University of California–San Diego	4.0
15.	University of Maryland–College Park	4.0
18.	Harvard University (MA)	3.9
19.	University of Pennsylvania	3.8
20.	Brown University (RI)	3.7
20.	Purdue University–West Lafayette (IN)	3.7
20.	Rice University (TX)	3.7
20.	University of Southern California	3.7
20.	Yale University (CT)	3.7
25.	Duke University (NC)	3.6
25.	University of Massachusetts–Amherst	3.6
25.	University of North Carolina–Chapel Hill	3.6
28.	Johns Hopkins University (MD)	3.5
29.	New York University	3.4
29.	Penn. State University–University Park	3.4
29.	University of California–Irvine	3.4
29.	University of Minnesota–Twin Cities	3.4
29.	University of Virginia	3.4
34.	Northwestern University (IL)	3.3
34.	Ohio State University	3.3
34.	Rutgers, the State U. of N.J.–New Bruns.	3.3
34.	University of California–Davis	3.3
34.	University of California–Santa Barbara	3.3
34.	University of Chicago	3.3
40.	Dartmouth College (NH)	3.1
40.	Stony Brook University–SUNY	3.1
40.	Texas A&M University–College Station	3.1
40.	University of Arizona	3.1
40.	University of Colorado–Boulder	3.1
40.	University of Utah	3.1
40.	Virginia Tech	3.1
40.	Washington University in St. Louis	3.1
48.	Arizona State University	3.0
48.	Boston University	3.0
48.	North Carolina State University	3.0
48.	University of Florida	3.0

COMPUTER SCIENCE SPECIALTIES

ARTIFICIAL INTELLIGENCE
1. Stanford University (CA)
2. Carnegie Mellon University (PA)
3. Mass. Institute of Technology
4. University of California–Berkeley
5. University of Washington
6. Georgia Institute of Technology
7. University of Illinois–Urbana-Champaign
7. University of Texas–Austin
9. Cornell University (NY)
9. University of California–Los Angeles

PROGRAMMING LANGUAGE
1. Carnegie Mellon University (PA)
2. University of California–Berkeley
3. Stanford University (CA)
4. Mass. Institute of Technology
5. Princeton University (NJ)
6. Cornell University (NY)
7. University of Pennsylvania
8. University of Texas–Austin
9. University of Illinois–Urbana-Champaign
10. University of Wisconsin–Madison

SYSTEMS
1. University of California–Berkeley
2. Mass. Institute of Technology
3. Stanford University (CA)
4. Carnegie Mellon University (PA)
5. University of Washington
6. Georgia Institute of Technology
7. University of Illinois–Urbana-Champaign
8. University of Texas–Austin
8. University of Wisconsin–Madison
10. University of Michigan–Ann Arbor

THEORY
1. University of California–Berkeley
2. Mass. Institute of Technology
3. Stanford University (CA)
4. Princeton University (NJ)
5. Carnegie Mellon University (PA)
6. Cornell University (NY)
7. Harvard University (MA)
8. Georgia Institute of Technology
9. University of Washington

EARTH SCIENCES Ranked in 2014

Rank	School	Average assessment score (5.0=highest)
1.	California Institute of Technology	4.9
2.	Massachusetts Institute of Technology	4.8
3.	Stanford University (CA)	4.6
3.	University of California–Berkeley	4.6
5.	Columbia University (NY)	4.5
6.	Penn. State University–University Park	4.4
7.	University of Arizona	4.3
8.	Harvard University (MA)	4.2
8.	University of Michigan–Ann Arbor	4.2
8.	University of Texas–Austin	4.2
11.	Princeton University (NJ)	4.1
11.	University of Washington	4.1
13.	University of California–Los Angeles	4.0
13.	University of Wisconsin–Madison	4.0
13.	Yale University (CT)	4.0
16.	Brown University (RI)	3.9
16.	Cornell University (NY)	3.9
16.	University of California–San Diego	3.9
16.	University of California–Santa Cruz	3.9
20.	Arizona State University	3.8
20.	University of California–Davis	3.8
20.	University of Chicago	3.8
23.	University of California–Santa Barbara	3.7
23.	University of Colorado–Boulder	3.7
25.	Colorado School of Mines	3.6
25.	Rice University (TX)	3.6
25.	University of Minnesota–Twin Cities	3.6
25.	University of Southern California	3.6
25.	Washington University in St. Louis	3.6
30.	Johns Hopkins University (MD)	3.5
30.	Virginia Tech	3.5
32.	Texas A&M University–College Station	3.4
32.	University of Maryland–College Park	3.4
34.	Northwestern University (IL)	3.3
34.	Ohio State University	3.3
34.	Oregon State University	3.3
34.	Stony Brook University–SUNY	3.3
34.	University of California–Irvine	3.3
34.	University of Hawaii–Manoa	3.3
34.	University of Illinois–Urbana-Champaign	3.3
34.	University of Oregon	3.3

EARTH SCIENCES SPECIALTIES

ENVIRONMENTAL SCIENCES
1. Stanford University (CA)
2. Pennsylvania State University–University Park
3. Columbia University (NY)
3. University of California–Berkeley
5. University of Michigan–Ann Arbor
5. University of Wisconsin–Madison

GEOCHEMISTRY
1. California Institute of Technology
2. Pennsylvania State University–University Park

GEOLOGY
1. Pennsylvania State University–University Park
2. University of Michigan–Ann Arbor
3. Stanford University (CA)
3. University of Arizona
5. California Institute of Technology
5. University of Texas–Austin

GEOPHYSICS AND SEISMOLOGY
1. University of California–Berkeley
2. California Institute of Technology
3. Stanford University (CA)
4. Massachusetts Institute of Technology

PALEONTOLOGY
1. University of Chicago
2. University of California–Berkeley

MATHEMATICS Ranked in 2014

Rank	School	Average assessment score (5.0=highest)
1.	Massachusetts Institute of Technology	5.0
1.	Princeton University (NJ)	5.0
3.	Harvard University (MA)	4.9
3.	University of California–Berkeley	4.9
5.	Stanford University (CA)	4.8
5.	University of Chicago	4.8
7.	California Institute of Technology	4.6
7.	University of California–Los Angeles	4.6
9.	Columbia University (NY)	4.5
9.	New York University	4.5
9.	University of Michigan–Ann Arbor	4.5
9.	Yale University (CT)	4.5
13.	Cornell University (NY)	4.3
14.	Brown University (RI)	4.2
14.	University of Texas–Austin	4.2
14.	University of Wisconsin–Madison	4.2
17.	Duke University (NC)	4.0
17.	Northwestern University (IL)	4.0
17.	University of Illinois–Urbana-Champaign	4.0
17.	University of Maryland–College Park	4.0
17.	University of Minnesota–Twin Cities	4.0
17.	University of Pennsylvania	4.0
23.	Rutgers, the State U. of N.J.–New Bruns.	3.9
23.	University of California–San Diego	3.9
25.	Johns Hopkins University (MD)	3.8
25.	Stony Brook University–SUNY	3.8
25.	University of Washington	3.8
28.	Georgia Institute of Technology	3.7
28.	Ohio State University	3.7
28.	Penn. State University–University Park	3.7
28.	Purdue University–West Lafayette (IN)	3.7
28.	Rice University (TX)	3.7
28.	University of North Carolina–Chapel Hill	3.7
34.	Carnegie Mellon University (PA)	3.6
34.	Indiana University–Bloomington	3.6
34.	University of California–Davis	3.6
34.	University of Illinois–Chicago	3.6
34.	University of Utah	3.6
39.	CUNY Grad School and University Ctr.	3.5
39.	Washington University in St. Louis	3.5
41.	Brandeis University (MA)	3.4
41.	Texas A&M University–College Station	3.4
41.	University of Arizona	3.4
41.	University of California–Irvine	3.4
41.	University of Notre Dame (IN)	3.4
46.	Boston University	3.3
46.	Michigan State University	3.3
46.	University of California–Santa Barbara	3.3
46.	University of Colorado–Boulder	3.3
46.	University of Southern California	3.3
46.	Vanderbilt University (TN)	3.3
52.	Dartmouth College (NH)	3.2
52.	North Carolina State University	3.2
52.	University of Georgia	3.2
52.	University of Virginia	3.2
56.	Rensselaer Polytechnic Institute (NY)	3.1
56.	University of Florida	3.1
56.	University of Iowa	3.1
56.	University of Oregon	3.1

MATHEMATICS SPECIALTIES

ALGEBRA/NUMBER THEORY/ALGEBRAIC GEOMETRY
1. Harvard University (MA)
2. Princeton University (NJ)
3. University of California–Berkeley
4. University of Chicago
5. Mass. Institute of Technology
5. University of California–Los Angeles

ANALYSIS
1. University of California–Los Angeles
2. University of California–Berkeley
3. Princeton University (NJ)
4. University of Chicago
5. Mass. Institute of Technology

6. New York University
6. Stanford University (CA)
8. University of Texas–Austin

APPLIED MATH
1. New York University
2. University of California–Los Angeles
3. California Institute of Technology
4. Mass. Institute of Technology
5. Brown University (RI)
5. University of Minnesota–Twin Cities
7. Princeton University (NJ)

DISCRETE MATHEMATICS AND COMBINATIONS
1. Mass. Institute of Technology

2. Princeton University (NJ)
3. University of California–San Diego
4. Georgia Institute of Technology
5. University of Michigan–Ann Arbor
6. University of California–Berkeley
6. University of California–Los Angeles

GEOMETRY
1. Harvard University (MA)
2. Mass. Institute of Technology
2. Stanford University (CA)
4. Stony Brook University–SUNY
4. University of California–Berkeley
6. Princeton University (NJ)

LOGIC
1. University of California–Berkeley
2. University of California–Los Angeles
3. University of Notre Dame (IN)
4. University of Illinois–Urbana-Champaign
4. University of Wisconsin–Madison

TOPOLOGY
1. University of California–Berkeley
2. Stanford University (CA)
3. Princeton University (NJ)
4. Harvard University (MA)
4. Mass. Institute of Technology
6. University of Chicago

PHYSICS Ranked in 2014

Rank	School	Average assessment score (5.0=highest)
1.	Massachusetts Institute of Technology	5.0
2.	California Institute of Technology	4.9
2.	Harvard University (MA)	4.9
2.	Princeton University (NJ)	4.9
2.	Stanford University (CA)	4.9
2.	University of California–Berkeley	4.9
7.	Cornell University (NY)	4.7
7.	University of Chicago	4.7
9.	University of Illinois–Urbana-Champaign	4.6
10.	University of California–Santa Barbara	4.5
11.	Columbia University (NY)	4.3
11.	University of Michigan–Ann Arbor	4.3
11.	Yale University (CT)	4.3
14.	University of Maryland–College Park	4.2
14.	University of Texas–Austin	4.2
16.	University of California–San Diego	4.1
16.	University of Pennsylvania	4.1
18.	Johns Hopkins University (MD)	4.0
18.	University of California–Los Angeles	4.0
18.	University of Colorado–Boulder	4.0
18.	University of Wisconsin–Madison	4.0
22.	University of Washington	3.9
23.	Ohio State University	3.8
23.	Penn. State University–University Park	3.8
23.	Stony Brook University–SUNY	3.8
26.	Northwestern University (IL)	3.7
26.	Rice University (TX)	3.7
26.	University of Minnesota–Twin Cities	3.7
29.	Brown University (RI)	3.6
29.	Duke University (NC)	3.6
29.	Georgia Institute of Technology	3.6
29.	Michigan State University	3.6
29.	Rutgers, the State U. of N.J.–New Bruns.	3.6
29.	University of California–Davis	3.6
29.	University of California–Irvine	3.6
36.	Carnegie Mellon University (PA)	3.5
36.	New York University	3.5
36.	University of Florida	3.5
39.	Boston University	3.4
39.	Indiana University–Bloomington	3.4
39.	University of Arizona	3.4
39.	University of California–Santa Cruz	3.4
39.	University of North Carolina–Chapel Hill	3.4
44.	Florida State University	3.3
44.	Purdue University–West Lafayette (IN)	3.3
44.	Texas A&M University–College Station	3.3
44.	University of Rochester (NY)	3.3
44.	University of Virginia	3.3
44.	Washington University in St. Louis	3.3
50.	Arizona State University	3.2
50.	Iowa State University	3.2
50.	University of Massachusetts–Amherst	3.2
50.	University of Pittsburgh	3.2

PHYSICS SPECIALTIES

ATOMIC/MOLECULAR/OPTICAL
1. University of Colorado–Boulder
2. Massachusetts Institute of Technology
3. Harvard University (MA)
4. Stanford University (CA)
5. University of California–Berkeley
6. University of Maryland–College Park
6. University of Rochester (NY)
8. California Institute of Technology

CONDENSED MATTER
1. University of Illinois–Urbana-Champaign
2. Stanford University (CA)
3. Massachusetts Institute of Technology
3. University of California–Berkeley
5. University of California–Santa Barbara
6. Cornell University (NY)
7. Harvard University (MA)
8. Princeton University (NJ)
9. California Institute of Technology

COSMOLOGY/RELATIVITY/GRAVITY
1. Princeton University (NJ)
2. California Institute of Technology
3. University of Chicago
4. Harvard University (MA)
5. Stanford University (CA)
5. University of California–Berkeley
7. Massachusetts Institute of Technology
8. University of California–Santa Barbara

ELEMENTARY PARTICLES/FIELDS/STRING THEORY
1. Princeton University (NJ)
2. Harvard University (MA)
3. Stanford University (CA)
4. University of California–Berkeley
5. Massachusetts Institute of Technology
6. California Institute of Technology
7. University of California–Santa Barbara

NUCLEAR
1. Michigan State University
2. University of Washington
3. Massachusetts Institute of Technology
4. Stony Brook University–SUNY
5. Indiana University–Bloomington
6. California Institute of Technology

6. Duke University (NC)
6. University of California–Berkeley
6. Yale University (CT)

PLASMA
1. Princeton University (NJ)
2. University of California–Los Angeles
3. Massachusetts Institute of Technology
3. University of Maryland–College Park
3. University of Texas–Austin
3. University of Wisconsin–Madison

QUANTUM
1. California Institute of Technology
2. Stanford University (CA)
3. Harvard University (MA)
3. Massachusetts Institute of Technology
5. Princeton University (NJ)

STATISTICS Ranked in 2014

Rank	School	Average assessment score (5.0=highest)
1.	Stanford University (CA)	4.9
2.	University of California–Berkeley	4.7
3.	Harvard University (MA)*	4.6
3.	University of Washington*	4.6
5.	Johns Hopkins University (MD)*	4.4
5.	University of Chicago	4.4
7.	Harvard University (MA)	4.3
7.	University of Washington	4.3
9.	Carnegie Mellon University (PA)	4.2
10.	Duke University (NC)	4.1
10.	University of Pennsylvania	4.1
12.	University of Michigan–Ann Arbor*	4.0
12.	University of North Carolina–Chapel Hill*	4.0
12.	University of Wisconsin–Madison	4.0
15.	North Carolina State University	3.9
15.	Texas A&M University–College Station	3.9
15.	University of California–Berkeley*	3.9
15.	University of Michigan–Ann Arbor	3.9
19.	Iowa State University	3.8
20.	Columbia University (NY)	3.7
20.	Pennsylvania State University	3.7
20.	University of Minnesota–Twin Cities	3.7
20.	University of North Carolina–Chapel Hill	3.7
24.	Cornell University (NY)	3.6
24.	Purdue University–West Lafayette (IN)	3.6
24.	University of Minnesota–Twin Cities*	3.6
27.	Ohio State University	3.5
27.	University of California–Davis	3.5
27.	University of Pennsylvania (Perelman)*	3.5

*Denotes a department of biostatistics

METHODOLOGY

Rankings of doctoral programs in the sciences are based on the results of surveys sent to academics in the biological sciences, chemistry, computer science, earth sciences, mathematics, physics and statistics during the fall of 2013. The individuals rated the quality of the program at each institution from marginal (1) to outstanding (5). Individuals who were unfamiliar with a particular school's programs were asked to select "don't know." The schools with the highest average scores were sorted in descending order and appear here. Results from fall 2009 and fall 2013 were averaged to compute the scores; programs had to be rated by at least 10 respondents to be ranked. Surveys were conducted by Ipsos Public Affairs. The universe surveyed in the biological sciences, chemistry, computer science, earth sciences, mathematics and physics consisted of schools that awarded at least five doctoral degrees in 2006 through 2010, according to the National Science Foundation report "Science and Engineering Doctorate Awards." The American Statistical Association provided U.S. News with eligible programs for statistics. In the biological sciences, programs may be offered in a university's medical school or college of arts and sciences. In statistics, programs may be offered through a biostatistics or statistics department. Questionnaires were sent to the department heads and directors of graduate studies at each program in each discipline. Response rates were: for biological sciences, 9 percent; chemistry, 18 percent; computer science, 35 percent; earth sciences, 17 percent; mathematics, 24 percent; physics, 29 percent; and statistics, 39 percent.

Specialty rankings are based solely on nominations by department heads and directors of graduate studies at peer schools. These respondents ranked up to 10 programs in each area. Those with the most votes appear here.

Social Sciences & Humanities

PH.D. PROGRAMS RANKED BEST BY DEPARTMENT CHAIRS AND SENIOR FACULTY

ECONOMICS Ranked in 2013

Rank	School	Average assessment score (5.0=highest)
1.	Harvard University (MA)	5.0
1.	Massachusetts Institute of Technology	5.0
1.	Princeton University (NJ)	5.0
1.	University of Chicago	5.0
5.	Stanford University (CA)	4.9
5.	University of California–Berkeley	4.9
7.	Northwestern University (IL)	4.8
7.	Yale University (CT)	4.8
9.	University of Pennsylvania	4.5
10.	Columbia University (NY)	4.4
11.	New York University	4.3
11.	University of Minnesota–Twin Cities	4.3
13.	University of Michigan–Ann Arbor	4.2
13.	University of Wisconsin–Madison	4.2
15.	California Institute of Technology	4.1
15.	University of California–Los Angeles	4.1
15.	University of California–San Diego	4.1
18.	Cornell University (NY)	3.9

Rank	School	Average assessment score (5.0=highest)
19.	Brown University (RI)	3.8
19.	Carnegie Mellon University (Tepper) (PA)	3.8
19.	Duke University (NC)	3.8
22.	University of Maryland–College Park	3.7
22.	University of Rochester (NY)	3.7
24.	Boston University	3.6
24.	Johns Hopkins University (MD)	3.6
26.	University of Texas–Austin	3.5
27.	Ohio State University	3.4
27.	Penn. State University–University Park	3.4
27.	Washington University in St. Louis	3.4
30.	Michigan State University	3.3
30.	University of Virginia	3.3
32.	Boston College	3.2
32.	University of California–Davis	3.2
32.	University of Illinois–Urbana-Champaign	3.2
32.	University of North Carolina–Chapel Hill	3.2
36.	Arizona State University	3.1

Rank	School	Average assessment score (5.0=highest)
36.	University of Arizona	3.1
36.	University of Pittsburgh	3.1
36.	Vanderbilt University (TN)	3.1
40.	University of Iowa (Tippie)	3.0
40.	University of Washington	3.0
42.	Indiana University–Bloomington	2.9
42.	Purdue–West Lafayette (Krannert) (IN)	2.9
42.	Texas A&M University–College Station	2.9
42.	University of California–Santa Barbara	2.9
46.	Georgetown University (DC)	2.8
46.	University of California–Irvine	2.8
48.	North Carolina State University–Raleigh	2.7
48.	Rice University (TX)	2.7
48.	Rutgers, the State U. of N. J.–New Bruns.	2.7
48.	University of Florida	2.7
48.	University of Southern California	2.7

ECONOMICS SPECIALTIES

DEVELOPMENT ECONOMICS
1. Harvard University (MA)
2. Massachusetts Institute of Tech.
3. Princeton University (NJ)
3. Yale University (CT)
5. University of California–Berkeley

ECONOMETRICS
1. Massachusetts Institute of Tech.
1. Yale University (CT)
3. Princeton University (NJ)
4. University of California–San Diego
5. Harvard University (MA)
6. Northwestern University (IL)
6. University of California–Berkeley

INDUSTRIAL ORGANIZATION
1. Stanford University (CA)
2. Harvard University (MA)
3. Northwestern University (IL)
4. Yale University (CT)
5. University of Chicago
6. Massachusetts Institute of Tech.
6. University of California–Berkeley

INTERNATIONAL ECONOMICS
1. Harvard University (MA)
2. Princeton University (NJ)
3. Columbia University (NY)
4. University of California–Berkeley
5. Massachusetts Institute of Tech.

LABOR ECONOMICS
1. Harvard University (MA)
2. Princeton University (NJ)
3. Massachusetts Institute of Tech.
4. University of California–Berkeley
5. University of Chicago

MACROECONOMICS
1. Harvard University (MA)
2. Massachusetts Institute of Tech.
3. Princeton University (NJ)
4. New York University
5. University of Minnesota–Twin Cities
6. University of Chicago
6. University of Pennsylvania

MICROECONOMICS
1. Stanford University (CA)
2. Massachusetts Institute of Tech.
3. Harvard University (MA)
4. Yale University (CT)
5. Northwestern University (IL)
5. Princeton University (NJ)
7. University of Chicago

PUBLIC FINANCE
1. University of California–Berkeley
2. Harvard University (MA)
2. Massachusetts Institute of Tech.
4. Stanford University (CA)
5. University of Michigan–Ann Arbor

ENGLISH Ranked in 2013

Rank	School	Average assessment score (5.0=highest)
1.	University of California–Berkeley	4.9
2.	Harvard University (MA)	4.8
2.	Stanford University (CA)	4.8
4.	Columbia University (NY)	4.7
4.	Princeton University (NJ)	4.7
4.	University of Pennsylvania	4.7
4.	Yale University (CT)	4.7
8.	Cornell University (NY)	4.6
8.	University of Chicago	4.6
10.	Duke University (NC)	4.4
10.	University of California–Los Angeles	4.4
10.	University of Virginia	4.4

Rank	School	Average assessment score (5.0=highest)
13.	Johns Hopkins University (MD)	4.3
13.	University of Michigan–Ann Arbor	4.3
15.	Brown University (RI)	4.2
15.	University of North Carolina–Chapel Hill	4.2
17.	Rutgers, the State U. of N. J.–New Bruns.	4.1
17.	University of Texas–Austin	4.1
17.	University of Wisconsin–Madison	4.1
20.	New York University	4.0
20.	Northwestern University (IL)	4.0
22.	CUNY Grad School and University Ctr.	3.9
22.	Indiana University–Bloomington	3.9
22.	University of California–Irvine	3.9

Rank	School	Average assessment score (5.0=highest)
22.	University of Illinois–Urbana-Champaign	3.9
26.	Emory University (GA)	3.7
26.	Ohio State University	3.7
26.	Penn. State University–University Park	3.7
26.	University of California–Davis	3.7
26.	University of California–Santa Barbara	3.7
26.	Vanderbilt University (TN)	3.7
32.	University of Iowa	3.6
32.	University of Maryland–College Park	3.6
32.	University of Washington	3.6
32.	Washington University in St. Louis	3.6
36.	Rice University (TX)	3.5

▶ More @ usnews.com/grad

Rank	School	Average assessment score (5.0=highest)
36.	University of Minnesota–Twin Cities	3.5
36.	University of Southern California	3.5
39.	Carnegie Mellon University (PA)	3.4
39.	University of California–San Diego	3.4
39.	University of California–Santa Cruz	3.4

Rank	School	Average assessment score (5.0=highest)
39.	University of Notre Dame (IN)	3.4
39.	University of Pittsburgh	3.4
44.	Boston University	3.3
44.	Brandeis University (MA)	3.3

Rank	School	Average assessment score (5.0=highest)
44.	Claremont Graduate University (CA)	3.3
44.	University at Buffalo–SUNY	3.3
44.	University of California–Riverside	3.3
44.	University of Illinois–Chicago	3.3

ENGLISH SPECIALTIES

AFRICAN-AMERICAN LITERATURE
1. Harvard University (MA)
2. Yale University (CT)
3. Princeton University (NJ)
4. Duke University (NC)
4. University of California–Berkeley
4. Vanderbilt University (TN)

AMERICAN LITERATURE BEFORE 1865
1. University of California–Berkeley
2. Harvard University (MA)
2. University of Pennsylvania
2. Yale University (CT)
5. University of Virginia

AMERICAN LITERATURE AFTER 1865
1. University of California–Berkeley
2. University of Chicago
3. Stanford University (CA)
4. Columbia University (NY)
4. Harvard University (MA)
4. University of Pennsylvania
4. University of Virginia
4. Yale University (CT)

18TH THROUGH 20TH CENTURY BRITISH LITERATURE
1. University of California–Berkeley
2. Harvard University (MA)
2. University of Pennsylvania

2. University of Virginia
5. Stanford University (CA)
6. Columbia University (NY)
6. University of California–Los Angeles
6. Yale University (CT)

GENDER AND LITERATURE
1. University of California–Berkeley
2. Duke University (NC)
3. University of Michigan–Ann Arbor
4. Princeton University (NJ)
4. Stanford University (CA)

LITERARY CRITICISM AND THEORY
1. Duke University (NC)

2. University of California–Berkeley
3. Cornell University (NY)
3. University of California–Irvine
5. Stanford University (CA)
6. Johns Hopkins University (MD)

MEDIEVAL/RENAISSANCE LITERATURE
1. Harvard University (MA)
2. University of California–Berkeley
3. University of Pennsylvania
3. Yale University (CT)
5. Stanford University (CA)
6. University of Notre Dame (IN)

HISTORY Ranked in 2013

Rank	School	Average assessment score (5.0=highest)
1.	Princeton University (NJ)	4.8
1.	University of California–Berkeley	4.8
1.	Yale University (CT)	4.8
4.	Harvard University (MA)	4.7
4.	Stanford University (CA)	4.7
4.	University of Chicago	4.7
7.	Columbia University (NY)	4.6
7.	University of Michigan–Ann Arbor	4.6
9.	University of California–Los Angeles	4.5
9.	University of Pennsylvania	4.5
11.	Cornell University (NY)	4.4
11.	Johns Hopkins University (MD)	4.4

Rank	School	Average assessment score (5.0=highest)
11.	University of North Carolina–Chapel Hill	4.4
14.	Duke University (NC)	4.3
14.	Northwestern University (IL)	4.3
14.	University of Wisconsin–Madison	4.3
17.	University of Texas–Austin	4.2
18.	Brown University (RI)	4.1
18.	New York University	4.1
20.	Rutgers, the State U. of N. J.–New Bruns.	4.0
20.	University of Illinois–Urbana-Champaign	4.0
20.	University of Virginia (Corcoran)	4.0
23.	Indiana University–Bloomington	3.9
24.	Ohio State University	3.8

Rank	School	Average assessment score (5.0=highest)
24.	University of Minnesota–Twin Cities	3.8
24.	Vanderbilt University (TN)	3.8
27.	Emory University (GA)	3.7
27.	Massachusetts Institute of Technology	3.7
27.	University of California–Davis	3.7
30.	CUNY Grad School and University Ctr.	3.6
30.	Georgetown University (DC)	3.6
30.	Rice University (TX)	3.6
30.	University of California–San Diego	3.6
30.	University of Washington	3.6
30.	Washington University in St. Louis	3.6

HISTORY SPECIALTIES

AFRICAN HISTORY
1. University of Wisconsin–Madison
2. University of Michigan–Ann Arbor
3. Michigan State University
4. Northwestern University (IL)
4. University of California–Los Angeles

AFRICAN-AMERICAN HISTORY
1. Yale University (CT)
2. Duke University (NC)
3. University of Michigan–Ann Arbor
4. Harvard University (MA)
5. Columbia University (NY)
6. Princeton University (NJ)
6. Univ. of North Carolina–Chapel Hill

ASIAN HISTORY
1. Harvard University (MA)
1. University of California–Berkeley
3. Yale University (CT)

4. Princeton University (NJ)
4. Stanford University (CA)
4. University of California–Los Angeles

CULTURAL HISTORY
1. University of California–Berkeley
2. University of Michigan–Ann Arbor
3. Yale University (CT)
4. Princeton University (NJ)
5. Columbia University (NY)

EUROPEAN HISTORY
1. University of California–Berkeley
1. Yale University (CT)
3. Harvard University (MA)
3. University of Michigan–Ann Arbor
5. University of Chicago
6. Columbia University (NY)
7. Princeton University (NJ)

LATIN AMERICAN HISTORY
1. University of Texas–Austin
2. Yale University (CT)
3. University of Wisconsin–Madison
4. Duke University (NC)
5. University of California–Los Angeles
6. University of Chicago
6. University of Michigan–Ann Arbor

MODERN U.S. HISTORY
1. Yale University (CT)
2. Harvard University (MA)
2. University of California–Berkeley
4. Columbia University (NY)
4. Princeton University (NJ)
6. University of Michigan–Ann Arbor
6. University of Wisconsin–Madison
8. University of Pennsylvania

U.S. COLONIAL HISTORY
1. Harvard University (MA)
2. University of Pennsylvania
3. Col. of William and Mary (Tyler) (VA)
4. Yale University (CT)
5. University of Virginia (Corcoran)
6. Johns Hopkins University (MD)
7. University of Michigan–Ann Arbor

WOMEN'S HISTORY
1. Rutgers, the State U. of New Jersey–New Brunswick
2. University of Wisconsin–Madison
3. University of Michigan–Ann Arbor
4. University of Pennsylvania
4. Yale University (CT)
6. New York University
7. Univ. of California–Santa Barbara
7. University of Minnesota–Twin Cities

POLITICAL SCIENCE Ranked in 2013

Rank	School	Average assessment score (5.0=highest)
1.	Harvard University (MA)	4.9
2.	Princeton University (NJ)	4.8
2.	Stanford University (CA)	4.8
4.	University of Michigan–Ann Arbor	4.7
4.	Yale University (CT)	4.7
6.	University of California–Berkeley	4.6
7.	Columbia University (NY)	4.4
8.	Massachusetts Institute of Technology	4.3
8.	University of California–San Diego	4.3
10.	Duke University (NC)	4.2
10.	University of California–Los Angeles	4.2
12.	University of Chicago	4.1
13.	University of North Carolina–Chapel Hill	4.0
13.	Washington University in St. Louis	4.0
15.	New York University	3.9
15.	Ohio State University	3.9
15.	University of Rochester (NY)	3.9
15.	University of Wisconsin–Madison	3.9
19.	Cornell University (NY)	3.8
19.	University of Minnesota–Twin Cities	3.8
21.	Northwestern University (IL)	3.6
21.	University of Texas–Austin	3.6
23.	University of California–Davis	3.5
23.	University of Illinois–Urbana-Champaign	3.5
25.	Emory University (GA)	3.4
25.	Indiana University–Bloomington	3.4
25.	Texas A&M University–College Station	3.4
28.	Penn. State University–University Park	3.3
28.	University of Maryland–College Park	3.3
28.	University of Pennsylvania	3.3
28.	University of Washington	3.3
32.	Michigan State University	3.2
32.	Rice University (TX)	3.2
32.	Stony Brook University–SUNY	3.2
32.	University of Iowa	3.2
36.	George Washington University (DC)	3.1
36.	University of Notre Dame (IN)	3.1
36.	University of Virginia	3.1
36.	Vanderbilt University (TN)	3.1
40.	Florida State University	3.0
40.	Georgetown University (DC)	3.0
40.	Johns Hopkins University (MD)	3.0
40.	University of California–Irvine	3.0
40.	University of Pittsburgh	3.0

POLITICAL SCIENCE SPECIALTIES

AMERICAN POLITICS
1. Harvard University (MA)
2. Stanford University (CA)
3. University of Michigan–Ann Arbor
4. Princeton University (NJ)
5. University of California–Berkeley
6. Yale University (CT)
7. Duke University (NC)
8. University of California–Los Angeles
9. Columbia University (NY)

COMPARATIVE POLITICS
1. Harvard University (MA)
2. Stanford University (CA)
3. Princeton University (NJ)
3. University of California–Berkeley
5. Columbia University (NY)
6. Yale University (CT)
7. University of Michigan–Ann Arbor
8. University of California–Los Angeles
9. Duke University (NC)

INTERNATIONAL POLITICS
1. Harvard University (MA)
2. Stanford University (CA)
3. Princeton University (NJ)
4. Columbia University (NY)
5. University of California–San Diego
6. University of Michigan–Ann Arbor
7. New York University
8. Ohio State University
8. Yale University (CT)

POLITICAL METHODOLOGY
1. Harvard University (MA)
2. Stanford University (CA)
3. New York University
3. University of Michigan–Ann Arbor
5. Washington University in St. Louis
6. Princeton University (NJ)
7. University of Rochester (NY)
8. University of California–Berkeley

POLITICAL THEORY
1. Princeton University (NJ)
2. Harvard University (MA)
3. University of Chicago
4. Yale University (CT)
5. Johns Hopkins University (MD)
6. University of California–Berkeley
7. Duke University (NC)
8. Northwestern University (IL)

PSYCHOLOGY Ranked in 2013

Rank	School	Average assessment score (5.0=highest)
1.	Stanford University (CA)	4.8
2.	University of California–Berkeley	4.7
2.	University of California–Los Angeles	4.7
4.	Harvard University (MA)	4.6
4.	University of Michigan–Ann Arbor	4.6
4.	Yale University (CT)	4.6
7.	Princeton University (NJ)	4.5
7.	University of Illinois–Urbana-Champaign	4.5
9.	Massachusetts Institute of Technology	4.4
9.	University of Minnesota–Twin Cities	4.4
9.	University of Wisconsin–Madison	4.4
12.	University of North Carolina–Chapel Hill	4.3
12.	University of Pennsylvania	4.3
14.	Columbia University (NY)	4.2
14.	Cornell University (NY)	4.2
14.	Northwestern University (IL)	4.2
14.	University of California–San Diego	4.2
14.	University of Texas–Austin	4.2
14.	University of Washington	4.2
14.	Washington University in St. Louis	4.2
21.	Carnegie Mellon University (PA)	4.1
21.	Duke University (NC)	4.1
21.	Ohio State University	4.1
21.	University of California–Davis	4.1
21.	University of Chicago	4.1
26.	Brown University (RI)	4.0
26.	Indiana University–Bloomington	4.0
26.	Johns Hopkins University (MD)	4.0
26.	University of Virginia	4.0
30.	New York University	3.9
30.	Penn. State University–University Park	3.9
30.	University of California–Irvine	3.9
30.	University of Colorado–Boulder	3.9
30.	University of Iowa	3.9
30.	University of Oregon	3.9
30.	University of Pittsburgh	3.9
30.	Vanderbilt University (TN)	3.9
38.	Arizona State University	3.8
38.	Emory University (GA)	3.8
40.	University of Arizona	3.7
40.	University of California–Santa Barbara	3.7
40.	University of Florida	3.7
40.	University of Kansas	3.7
40.	University of Maryland–College Park	3.7
40.	University of Southern California	3.7
46.	Boston University	3.6
46.	Dartmouth College (NH)	3.6
46.	Michigan State University	3.6
46.	Purdue University–West Lafayette (IN)	3.6
46.	Stony Brook University–SUNY	3.6
46.	University of Massachusetts–Amherst	3.6
52.	Oregon Health and Science University	3.5
52.	San Diego State - U. of Calif.–San Diego	3.5
52.	Temple University (PA)	3.5
52.	University of Connecticut	3.5
52.	University of Georgia	3.5
52.	University of Miami (FL)	3.5
52.	University of Missouri	3.5
52.	University of Rochester (NY)	3.5
60.	Florida State University	3.4
60.	Rutgers, the State U. of N. J.–New Bruns.	3.4
60.	University of Illinois–Chicago	3.4
63.	Georgia Institute of Technology	3.3
63.	Teachers College, Columbia Univ. (NY)	3.3
63.	University at Buffalo–SUNY	3.3
63.	University of California–Riverside	3.3
67.	Binghamton University–SUNY	3.2
67.	Boston College	3.2
67.	Brandeis University (MA)	3.2
67.	Rice University (TX)	3.2
67.	Rutgers, the State U. of N. J.–Newark	3.2
67.	Texas A&M University–College Station	3.2
67.	Tufts University (MA)	3.2
67.	University of Delaware	3.2
67.	University of Notre Dame (IN)	3.2
67.	University of Utah	3.2
67.	Virginia Tech	3.2

PSYCHOLOGY SPECIALTIES

BEHAVIORAL NEUROSCIENCE
1. University of California–San Diego
2. Massachusetts Institute of Tech.
3. University of Michigan–Ann Arbor
4. Harvard University (MA)
4. University of California–Los Angeles
6. Duke University (NC)
7. Johns Hopkins University (MD)
7. University of California–Berkeley

COGNITIVE PSYCHOLOGY
1. Stanford University (CA)

2. Harvard University (MA)
3. University of California–San Diego
3. Univ. of Illinois–Urbana-Champaign
5. Carnegie Mellon University (PA)
5. University of Michigan–Ann Arbor
5. Yale University (CT)

DEVELOPMENTAL PSYCHOLOGY
1. University of Minnesota–Twin Cities
2. University of Michigan–Ann Arbor
3. Stanford University (CA)
4. Harvard University (MA)

5. Pennsylvania State University–University Park
5. University of California–Berkeley
5. University of California–Los Angeles
5. Univ. of North Carolina–Chapel Hill
5. University of Virginia
5. University of Wisconsin–Madison

INDUSTRIAL AND ORGANIZATIONAL PSYCHOLOGY
1. Michigan State University
1. University of Minnesota–Twin Cities

SOCIAL PSYCHOLOGY
1. Ohio State University
1. University of Michigan–Ann Arbor
3. Harvard University (MA)
3. Princeton University (NJ)
3. Stanford University (CA)
3. University of California–Los Angeles
3. Yale University (CT)

SOCIOLOGY Ranked in 2013

Rank	School	Average assessment score (5.0=highest)
1.	Princeton University (NJ)	4.7
1.	University of California–Berkeley	4.7
1.	University of Wisconsin–Madison	4.7
4.	Stanford University (CA)	4.6
4.	University of Michigan–Ann Arbor	4.6
6.	Harvard University (MA)	4.5
6.	University of Chicago	4.5
6.	University of North Carolina–Chapel Hill	4.5
9.	University of California–Los Angeles	4.4
10.	Northwestern University (IL)	4.3
10.	University of Pennsylvania	4.3
12.	Columbia University (NY)	4.2
12.	Indiana University–Bloomington	4.2
14.	Duke University (NC)	4.1
14.	University of Texas–Austin	4.1
16.	New York University	4.0
17.	Cornell University (NY)	3.9
17.	Ohio State University	3.9
17.	Penn. State University–University Park	3.9
20.	University of Arizona	3.8
20.	University of Minnesota–Twin Cities	3.8
20.	University of Washington	3.8
20.	Yale University (CT)	3.8
24.	University of Maryland–College Park	3.7
25.	Brown University (RI)	3.6
25.	University of California–Irvine	3.6
27.	Johns Hopkins University (MD)	3.5
28.	CUNY Grad School and University Ctr.	3.4
28.	Rutgers, the State U. of N. J.–New Bruns.	3.4
28.	University at Albany–SUNY	3.4
31.	University of California–Davis	3.3
31.	University of California–Santa Barbara	3.3
31.	University of Massachusetts–Amherst	3.3
31.	Vanderbilt University (TN)	3.3
35.	Emory University (GA)	3.2
35.	University of California–San Diego	3.2
35.	University of Iowa	3.2
35.	University of Virginia	3.2
39.	Florida State University	3.1
39.	University of Illinois–Chicago	3.1
39.	University of Southern California	3.1

SOCIOLOGY SPECIALTIES

ECONOMIC SOCIOLOGY
1. Stanford University (CA)
2. Princeton University (NJ)
2. University of California–Berkeley
2. University of Wisconsin–Madison
5. Harvard University (MA)

HISTORICAL SOCIOLOGY
1. Harvard University (MA)
1. University of California–Berkeley

SEX AND GENDER
1. Univ. of California–Santa Barbara
2. University of California–Berkeley
2. University of Wisconsin–Madison
4. Stanford University (CA)

SOCIAL PSYCHOLOGY
1. Stanford University (CA)
2. Indiana University–Bloomington
3. University of Iowa

SOCIAL STRATIFICATION
1. University of Wisconsin–Madison
2. Stanford University (CA)
3. University of California–Los Angeles
3. University of Michigan–Ann Arbor
5. University of California–Berkeley

SOCIOLOGY OF CULTURE
1. Princeton University (NJ)
2. University of California–Berkeley
3. Northwestern University (IL)

SOCIOLOGY OF POPULATION
1. University of Michigan–Ann Arbor
2. University of Wisconsin–Madison
3. Univ. of North Carolina–Chapel Hill
4. University of Pennsylvania
4. University of Texas–Austin
6. Pennsylvania State University–University Park
7. Princeton University (NJ)
7. University of California–Los Angeles

METHODOLOGY

Rankings of doctoral programs in the social sciences and humanities are based solely on the results of peer assessment surveys sent to academics in each discipline. Each school offering a doctoral program was sent two surveys. The questionnaires asked respondents to rate the academic quality of the program at each institution on a 5-point scale: outstanding (5), strong (4), good (3), adequate (2), or marginal (1). Individuals who were unfamiliar with a particular school's programs were asked to select "don't know." Scores for each school were determined by computing a trimmed mean (eliminating the two highest and two lowest responses) of the ratings of all respondents who rated that school for the last two surveys; average scores were then sorted in descending order.

Surveys were conducted in the fall of 2012 by Ipsos Public Affairs. Questionnaires were sent to department heads and directors of graduate studies (or, alternatively, a senior faculty member who teaches graduate students) at schools that had granted a total of five or more doctorates in each discipline during the five-year period from 2005 through 2009, as indicated by the 2010 Survey of Earned Doctorates. The surveys asked about Ph.D. programs in economics (response rate: 25 percent), English (21 percent), history (19 percent), political science (30 percent), psychology (16 percent), and sociology (31 percent). Survey results from fall 2008 and fall 2012 were averaged to compute the scores.

In psychology, a school was listed once on the survey even if it grants a doctoral degree in psychology in multiple departments. Programs in clinical psychology are ranked separately in the health professions section. Specialty rankings are based solely on nominations by department heads and directors of graduate studies at peer schools from the list of schools surveyed. They named up to 10 programs in each area. Those with the most votes appear.

Best Online Programs

For our rankings of online graduate degree programs in business, computer information technology, criminal justice, education, engineering and nursing, U.S. News started by surveying over 900 master's programs at regionally accredited colleges that deliver all required classes predominantly online. Programs were ranked based on their success at promoting student engagement, the training and credentials of their faculty, the selectivity of their admissions processes, the services and technologies available to distance learners, and the opinions of deans and other academics at peer distance-education programs in their disciplines. Although the methodologies used in each discipline rely on varying criteria, individual ranking factors common to all include retention and graduation rates, student indebtedness at graduation, the average undergraduate GPAs of new entrants, proportion of faculty members with terminal degrees, proportion of full-time faculty who are tenured or tenure-track, and whether the program offers support services like career placement assistance and academic advising so they are accessible to students remotely. The top programs in each of the five disciplines are listed below. To find more detail on the methodologies and to see the complete rankings, visit usnews.com/online.

BUSINESS (MBA PROGRAMS)

Rank	School	Overall score	Average peer assessment score (5.0=highest)	'14 total enrollment	'14-'15 total program cost[1]	Entrance test required	'14 average undergrad GPA	'14 acceptance rate	'14 full-time faculty with terminal degree	'14 tenured or tenure-track faculty[2]	'14 retention rate	'14 three-year graduation rate
1.	Indiana University–Bloomington (Kelley)	100	4.1	812	N/A	GMAT or GRE	3.3	76%	100%	74%	97%	72%
1.	Temple University (Fox) (PA)	100	3.2	70	$62,208	GMAT or GRE	3.4	72%	100%	73%	100%	79%
1.	U. of N. Carolina–Chapel Hill (Kenan-Flagler)	100	4.1	640	$96,775	GMAT or GRE	3.3	51%	73%	53%	98%	N/A
4.	Arizona State University (Carey)	96	3.8	415	N/A	GMAT or GRE	3.2	58%	88%	58%	98%	93%
4.	University of Florida (Hough)	96	3.9	372	N/A	GMAT or GRE	3.2	64%	100%	79%	96%	88%
6.	University of Texas–Dallas	90	3.3	318	$37,626	GMAT or GRE	3.5	43%	79%	34%	87%	N/A
7.	Carnegie Mellon University (Tepper) (PA)	85	4.1	29	$116,160	GMAT or GRE	3.3	60%	100%	77%	N/A	N/A
7.	Pennsylvania State University–World Campus	85	3.0	300	$52,608	GMAT or GRE	3.3	81%	100%	92%	96%	92%
9.	North Carolina State University (Jenkins)	83	2.8	111	N/A	GMAT or GRE	3.2	78%	100%	92%	95%	N/A
10.	Auburn University (AL)	82	3.2	159	$28,980	GMAT or GRE	3.2	64%	100%	100%	95%	53%
10.	University of Wisconsin–Eau Claire	82	2.9	261	$20,250	GMAT or GRE	3.2	87%	89%	89%	94%	73%
12.	Arkansas State University–Jonesboro	81	2.2	71	$15,840	GMAT or GRE	3.6	88%	100%	100%	90%	87%
12.	James Madison University (VA)	81	2.9	42	$32,550	GMAT or GRE	3.2	79%	100%	91%	92%	100%
12.	Lehigh University (PA)	81	3.0	215	$37,800	GMAT or GRE	3.3	73%	92%	62%	88%	48%
12.	Univ. of Massachusetts–Amherst (Isenberg)	81	3.3	1,257	$32,175	GMAT or GRE	3.3	90%	92%	62%	96%	53%
16.	Ball State University (Miller) (IN)	80	2.6	256	$13,464	GMAT or GRE	3.4	69%	100%	96%	91%	54%
16.	University of Mississippi	80	3.1	125	N/A	GMAT or GRE	3.3	39%	100%	58%	80%	69%
18.	Georgia Southern University	78	2.7	120	$21,840	GMAT or GRE	3.0	58%	100%	100%	100%	98%
18.	Mississippi State University	78	3.1	295	$11,745	GMAT or GRE	3.2	81%	100%	100%	92%	41%
18.	University of Tennessee–Martin	78	2.4	65	N/A	GMAT	3.1	59%	100%	100%	100%	94%
21.	Thunderbird School of Global Management (AZ)	77	3.2	215	$62,078	GMAT or GRE	3.3	65%	88%	82%	97%	93%
21.	University of Nebraska–Lincoln	77	3.2	192	$25,488	GMAT or GRE	3.3	81%	95%	100%	86%	45%
21.	Washington State University	77	2.9	462	N/A	GMAT	3.5	49%	88%	81%	99%	77%
24.	Pepperdine University (Graziadio) (CA)	76	3.5	106	$83,017	GMAT or GRE	3.1	78%	80%	50%	93%	N/A
25.	Central Michigan University	75	2.6	134	$21,600	GMAT	3.3	41%	88%	82%	91%	44%
25.	Georgia College & State University (Bunting)	75	2.5	53	$21,840	GMAT or GRE	3.2	62%	100%	100%	83%	100%
25.	Rochester Institute of Tech. (Saunders) (NY)	75	3.2	33	N/A	None	2.9	68%	76%	71%	89%	82%
25.	West Virginia University	75	2.8	66	$38,592	GMAT	3.1	65%	96%	91%	96%	93%
29.	Kennesaw State University (Coles) (GA)	74	2.7	134	$21,840	GMAT	3.1	83%	100%	100%	100%	90%
29.	University of Arizona (Eller)	74	3.6	52	$45,000	GMAT	3.3	74%	75%	56%	N/A	N/A
29.	University of Nevada–Reno	74	2.4	31	$24,000	GMAT or GRE	3.1	89%	89%	89%	96%	N/A
32.	University of North Dakota	73	2.8	82	$9,736	GMAT or GRE	3.3	76%	93%	93%	90%	46%
32.	University of South Florida–St. Petersburg	73	2.0	276	$16,617	GMAT or GRE	3.3	51%	100%	73%	90%	77%
32.	West Texas A&M University	73	2.2	300	$13,808	None	3.6	82%	97%	94%	82%	83%
32.	Worcester Polytechnic Institute (MA)	73	2.5	89	$63,600	GMAT or GRE	3.2	54%	82%	82%	95%	N/A
36.	Clarkson University (NY)	72	2.5	38	$58,380	GMAT or GRE	3.2	75%	83%	75%	N/A	92%
36.	George Mason University (VA)	72	3.2	108	N/A	GMAT or GRE	3.2	64%	100%	76%	88%	N/A
36.	Northeastern University (MA)	72	3.2	1,122	$71,650	None	3.2	85%	95%	80%	75%	55%
36.	Southern Illinois University–Carbondale	72	2.9	146	$35,000	GMAT or GRE	3.2	54%	92%	75%	93%	75%
40.	University of Colorado–Colorado Springs	71	2.9	117	$27,576	GMAT or GRE	3.0	84%	100%	94%	70%	50%

N/A=Data were not provided by the school; programs that received insufficient numbers of ratings do not have their peer-assessment scores published.
[1]Tuition is reported for part-time students. [2]Percentage reported of full-time faculty

▶ More @ usnews.com/grad

Rank	School	Overall score	Average peer assessment score (5.0=highest)	'14 total enrollment	'14-'15 total program cost[1]	Entrance test required	'14 average undergrad GPA	'14 acceptance rate	'14 full-time faculty with terminal degree	'14 tenured or tenure-track faculty[2]	'14 retention rate	'14 three-year graduation rate
41.	Hofstra University (Zarb) (NY)	69	2.8	41	N/A	GMAT or GRE	N/A	54%	94%	100%	100%	N/A
41.	Oklahoma State University (Spears)	69	3.1	505	$36,720	GMAT or GRE	N/A	62%	100%	84%	N/A	68%
41.	University of South Dakota	69	2.6	246	$13,695	GMAT	3.3	72%	100%	92%	83%	33%
44.	Cleveland State University (Ahuja) (OH)	68	2.4	42	$37,500	GMAT or GRE	3.3	53%	100%	89%	90%	N/A
44.	George Washington University (DC)	68	3.3	451	$81,113	GMAT or GRE	3.2	70%	100%	82%	84%	66%
44.	University of West Georgia (Richards)	68	2.6	71	N/A	GMAT or GRE	3.1	100%	100%	100%	87%	88%
47.	Columbus State University (Turner) (GA)	67	2.1	31	$21,840	GMAT or GRE	3.0	75%	100%	100%	88%	N/A
47.	Portland State University (OR)	67	2.7	139	$39,600	GMAT or GRE	3.3	78%	75%	0%	95%	89%
47.	Quinnipiac University (CT)	67	2.5	272	$41,170	GMAT or GRE	3.2	86%	93%	93%	83%	46%
47.	University of North Texas	67	2.7	97	$18,012	GMAT	3.4	78%	N/A	N/A	96%	62%
47.	University of Tennessee–Chattanooga	67	2.8	46	$27,348	GMAT or GRE	3.3	45%	100%	100%	N/A	N/A
52.	Baldwin Wallace University (OH)	66	1.8	42	N/A	GMAT	3.2	100%	100%	100%	100%	N/A
52.	Marist College (NY)	66	2.4	244	$22,500	GMAT or GRE	3.2	42%	92%	85%	82%	40%
52.	St. Joseph's University (Haub) (PA)	66	2.4	357	N/A	GMAT or GRE	3.3	74%	88%	85%	80%	70%
55.	Missouri University of Science & Technology	65	2.3	46	N/A	GMAT or GRE	3.4	59%	100%	100%	88%	78%
55.	Wayne State University (MI)	65	2.7	26	N/A	GMAT	3.3	17%	100%	76%	69%	N/A
57.	Colorado State University	63	3.1	1,360	$36,250	GMAT or GRE	3.2	92%	100%	73%	84%	43%
57.	SUNY–Oswego (NY)	63	2.5	94	N/A	GMAT	3.2	97%	89%	100%	N/A	N/A
57.	Syracuse University (Whitman) (NY)	63	3.1	252	N/A	N/A	3.2	90%	86%	68%	93%	39%
57.	University of Louisiana–Monroe	63	2.4	129	$16,842	GMAT or GRE	3.1	100%	78%	78%	61%	35%
57.	University of Michigan–Dearborn	63	2.9	104	N/A	GMAT or GRE	3.4	27%	100%	100%	86%	53%

COMPUTER INFORMATION TECHNOLOGY

Rank	School	Overall score	Average peer assessment score (5.0=highest)	'14 total enrollment	'14-'15 total program cost[1]	Entrance test required	'14 average undergrad GPA	'14 acceptance rate	'14 full-time faculty with terminal degree	'14 tenured or tenure-track faculty[2]	'14 retention rate	'14 three-year graduation rate
1.	University of Southern California	100	4.0	104	$46,062	GRE	3.5	40%	96%	77%	100%	67%
2.	Virginia Tech	88	3.7	413	$27,260	None	3.3	87%	100%	100%	91%	90%
3.	Boston University	79	3.7	816	$32,000	None	3.3	74%	100%	0%	90%	57%
4.	Pennsylvania State University–World Campus	69	3.2	379	N/A	GRE	3.3	80%	70%	37%	86%	62%
5.	Johns Hopkins University (Whiting) (MD)	67	3.4	877	$35,300	None	3.4	93%	N/A	N/A	87%	47%
6.	Auburn University (AL)	61	3.1	28	N/A	GRE	3.5	67%	100%	100%	71%	N/A
7.	North Carolina State University	60	3.6	52	$11,594	GRE	3.6	59%	93%	87%	90%	43%
7.	Sam Houston State University (TX)	60	N/A	48	$8,820	GRE	3.3	82%	100%	100%	78%	N/A
9.	Pace University (NY)	54	2.5	117	N/A	None	3.4	84%	100%	94%	86%	35%
9.	Syracuse University (NY)	54	3.4	77	$48,276	None	3.3	96%	77%	73%	85%	36%
11.	University of Maryland–Baltimore County	52	3.3	177	$27,846	None	N/A	82%	100%	100%	89%	39%
12.	University of North Carolina–Greensboro	51	N/A	73	$14,293	N/A	3.2	86%	100%	100%	N/A	50%
13.	University of Bridgeport (CT)	50	2.8	58	N/A	GRE	3.0	44%	83%	83%	85%	N/A
14.	Mississippi State University (Bagley)	48	2.4	10	$12,920	None	N/A	N/A	100%	98%	100%	N/A
14.	Texas Tech University (Whitacre)	48	3.1	31	$7,888	GRE	3.2	33%	100%	100%	100%	N/A

CRIMINAL JUSTICE

Rank	School	Overall score	Average peer assessment score (5.0=highest)	'14 total enrollment	'14-'15 total program cost[1]	Entrance test required	'14 average undergrad GPA	'14 acceptance rate	'14 full-time faculty with terminal degree	'14 tenured or tenure-track faculty[2]	'14 retention rate	'14 three-year graduation rate
1.	University of California–Irvine	100	N/A	121	N/A	None	3.3	69%	100%	100%	84%	85%
2.	Arizona State University	99	3.5	504	$15,906	None	3.3	87%	58%	50%	88%	62%
2.	Boston University	99	N/A	546	$32,000	None	3.1	77%	100%	0%	88%	70%
2.	Pace University (NY)	99	N/A	20	$31,500	None	3.1	100%	100%	100%	58%	63%
5.	Sam Houston State University (TX)	93	N/A	211	$8,820	None	3.2	78%	100%	100%	85%	55%
6.	Tiffin University (OH)	89	N/A	321	$21,000	None	3.3	80%	67%	0%	79%	68%
7.	Florida State University	81	3.6	92	N/A	GRE	N/A	81%	100%	100%	N/A	N/A
8.	Columbia College (MO)	80	N/A	246	$1,400	None	2.9	94%	100%	100%	74%	35%
9.	University of Colorado–Denver	79	N/A	N/A	$18,324	GRE	N/A	N/A	100%	100%	98%	100%
10.	Indiana University of Pennsylvania	76	N/A	20	$14,337	None	N/A	44%	100%	86%	98%	N/A
11.	Monroe College (NY)	75	N/A	34	$26,748	None	3.2	75%	100%	0%	86%	N/A
11.	Western Kentucky University	75	N/A	20	$19,467	GRE	2.0	N/A	100%	100%	33%	N/A

CRIMINAL JUSTICE continued

Rank	School	Overall score	Average peer assessment score (5.0=highest)	'14 total enrollment	'14-'15 total program cost[1]	Entrance test required	'14 average undergrad GPA	'14 acceptance rate	'14 full-time faculty with terminal degree	'14 tenured or tenure-track faculty[2]	'14 retention rate	'14 three-year graduation rate
13.	College of St. Elizabeth (NJ)	72	N/A	14	N/A	None	N/A	N/A	100%	100%	N/A	N/A
13.	University of Louisville (KY)	72	N/A	44	$24,948	GRE	3.3	93%	100%	57%	N/A	88%
15.	Southeast Missouri State University	69	N/A	24	N/A	None	N/A	N/A	80%	100%	73%	48%
15.	University of Wisconsin–Platteville	69	N/A	166	$18,900	None	N/A	92%	100%	100%	83%	N/A
17.	Bowling Green State University (OH)	67	N/A	13	$14,322	None	N/A	N/A	100%	75%	N/A	93%
18.	Liberty University (VA)	64	N/A	465	$20,340	None	3.2	62%	100%	0%	66%	N/A
19.	Florida International University	63	N/A	248	N/A	GRE	3.4	53%	100%	70%	N/A	N/A
20.	California State University–San Bernardino	62	N/A	N/A	$15,800	None	N/A	N/A	100%	100%	75%	75%
20.	Faulkner University (AL)	62	N/A	51	$14,400	None	3.0	95%	100%	60%	92%	N/A

EDUCATION

Rank	School	Overall score	Average peer assessment score (5.0=highest)	'14 total enrollment	'14-'15 total program cost[1]	Entrance test required	'14 average undergrad GPA	'14 acceptance rate	'14 full-time faculty with terminal degree	'14 tenured or tenure-track faculty[2]	'14 retention rate	'14 three-year graduation rate
1.	University of Houston (TX)	100	3.1	119	N/A	GRE	3.3	75%	100%	68%	94%	100%
2.	Florida State University	94	3.4	162	N/A	GRE	3.4	71%	100%	91%	99%	77%
3.	Northern Illinois University	90	3.3	170	N/A	GRE	3.2	98%	100%	82%	97%	81%
4.	Pennsylvania State University–World Campus	89	3.8	239	$23,520	GRE	3.6	78%	100%	74%	81%	56%
5.	Central Michigan University	88	3.1	496	$16,830	None	3.3	88%	100%	100%	77%	54%
5.	Graceland University (IA)	88	N/A	169	N/A	None	3.4	100%	100%	100%	98%	97%
5.	University of Nebraska–Lincoln	88	3.6	149	$11,700	None	N/A	54%	100%	84%	77%	60%
8.	Auburn University (AL)	87	3.4	149	N/A	GRE	3.2	71%	100%	95%	87%	66%
8.	Ball State University (IN)	87	3.4	2,267	$9,450	None	3.2	74%	95%	72%	87%	75%
8.	George Washington University (DC)	87	3.6	171	N/A	GRE	3.3	69%	100%	33%	82%	79%
11.	Creighton University (NE)	86	3.1	68	$25,488	None	3.7	93%	100%	86%	95%	N/A
11.	Emporia State University (KS)	86	3.0	1,239	$7,272	None	3.4	78%	90%	91%	91%	70%
13.	Michigan State University	84	3.7	873	$22,140	None	3.5	87%	94%	81%	89%	70%
13.	University of Florida	84	3.5	310	N/A	GRE	3.5	69%	100%	37%	95%	N/A
13.	University of Northern Colorado	84	3.3	279	N/A	None	3.6	67%	97%	87%	85%	62%

COURTESY OF ARIZONA STATE UNIVERSITY

Arizona State boasts a few top online programs.

State of Confidence

It's time. All of the reasons you think you can't are reasons you should.
Gain the confidence to do more and be more. Challenge yourself to keep
learning with Colorado's top-ranked MBA program. You're ready.

Colorado State University
COLLEGE OF BUSINESS

EDUCATION continued

Rank	School	Overall score	Average peer assessment score (5.0=highest)	'14 total enrollment	'14-'15 total program cost[1]	Entrance test required	'14 average undergrad GPA	'14 acceptance rate	'14 full-time faculty with terminal degree	'14 tenured or tenure-track faculty[2]	'14 retention rate	'14 three-year graduation rate
13.	University of Scranton (PA)	84	2.6	629	$17,460	None	3.4	98%	100%	100%	87%	54%
13.	Utah State University	84	2.8	87	$14,607	GRE	3.5	100%	73%	55%	85%	N/A
18.	Indiana University–Bloomington	83	3.8	232	N/A	GRE	3.3	89%	100%	100%	77%	65%
18.	University of South Carolina	83	3.1	256	$18,036	GRE	3.3	89%	100%	69%	95%	79%
20.	University of South Florida	81	3.1	N/A	N/A	None	3.4	69%	100%	89%	80%	64%
21.	California State University–Fullerton	80	3.2	220	N/A	None	3.2	79%	100%	95%	N/A	61%
21.	Regent University (VA)	80	2.0	736	$15,525	None	3.1	63%	100%	87%	79%	53%
23.	Arizona State University	79	3.7	1,823	$16,350	None	3.4	93%	92%	58%	91%	71%
23.	New York Institute of Technology	79	N/A	193	N/A	None	3.3	76%	89%	67%	71%	62%
23.	University at Buffalo–SUNY (NY)	79	3.3	81	$16,848	None	3.3	90%	100%	57%	68%	N/A
23.	University of Cincinnati (OH)	79	3.1	751	$19,200	None	3.3	77%	95%	75%	83%	71%
23.	University of Nebraska–Kearney	79	2.8	716	$11,088	None	3.4	90%	100%	84%	95%	57%
28.	Sam Houston State University (TX)	78	2.6	880	N/A	GRE	3.2	90%	100%	100%	66%	56%
28.	University of Georgia	78	3.6	69	$20,196	GRE	3.4	84%	100%	83%	97%	94%
30.	Angelo State University (TX)	77	N/A	448	$2,049	None	3.2	94%	100%	57%	96%	100%
30.	Fort Hays State University (KS)	77	2.8	996	$9,036	None	3.4	97%	92%	83%	95%	22%
30.	University of Alaska–Anchorage	77	N/A	243	$1,209	None	3.4	60%	76%	65%	75%	83%
30.	University of Dayton (OH)	77	2.5	507	$17,550	N/A	3.3	62%	83%	67%	87%	54%
30.	University of Texas–Arlington	77	2.4	1,777	$9,840	GRE	3.0	93%	100%	67%	84%	67%
35.	California University of Pennsylvania	76	N/A	1,247	$15,774	None	N/A	82%	86%	100%	91%	95%
35.	Lamar University (TX)	76	2.5	3,582	N/A	GRE	3.3	91%	94%	72%	82%	73%
35.	North Carolina State University–Raleigh	76	3.2	137	$13,464	GRE	3.4	85%	100%	100%	N/A	N/A
35.	University of Arkansas–Fayetteville	76	3.2	305	$9,312	GRE	N/A	92%	100%	90%	N/A	62%
35.	University of Mississippi	76	3.0	119	$16,200	None	3.3	68%	100%	100%	100%	N/A
35.	University of North Carolina–Wilmington	76	2.8	267	$6,732	GRE	N/A	N/A	100%	95%	N/A	N/A
35.	Western Kentucky University	76	2.8	826	$20,394	GRE	2.7	N/A	94%	97%	81%	56%
42.	Augustana College (SD)	75	2.6	122	$9,900	None	3.5	100%	100%	100%	98%	93%
42.	Brenau University (GA)	75	N/A	66	$10,692	None	3.4	83%	100%	0%	92%	78%
42.	College of St. Scholastica (MN)	75	N/A	58	N/A	None	3.3	84%	83%	83%	83%	70%
42.	Old Dominion University (Darden) (VA)	75	3.2	430	N/A	GRE	N/A	N/A	84%	77%	84%	74%
42.	University of Nevada–Reno	75	3.1	21	$8,448	GRE	3.0	100%	100%	44%	100%	46%
47.	Boise State University (ID)	74	3.3	614	$12,518	None	3.4	85%	100%	86%	90%	51%
47.	Drexel University (PA)	74	2.9	1,114	$37,935	None	3.3	84%	97%	36%	89%	62%
47.	Eastern Kentucky University	74	2.9	323	$14,700	None	3.6	98%	100%	97%	77%	32%
47.	Pittsburg State University (KS)	74	2.7	414	N/A	None	3.5	N/A	54%	100%	86%	65%
47.	St. John's University (NY)	74	3.0	42	N/A	None	3.2	94%	0%	100%	87%	61%
47.	University of Illinois–Urbana-Champaign	74	3.7	285	$13,984	None	3.6	93%	100%	78%	77%	90%
47.	Wright State University (OH)	74	2.5	130	$18,700	GRE	3.4	97%	100%	75%	91%	75%
54.	Concordia University (IL)	73	N/A	1,368	$13,250	None	N/A	N/A	81%	38%	87%	89%
54.	Georgia State University	73	3.2	91	$15,476	GRE	3.3	80%	100%	44%	92%	71%
54.	Purdue University–West Lafayette (IN)	73	3.5	285	N/A	None	3.4	72%	100%	63%	8%	N/A
54.	Regis University (CO)	73	2.6	167	N/A	None	N/A	90%	75%	0%	88%	56%
54.	Rutgers, The State U. of N. J.–New Brunswick	73	3.3	19	N/A	GRE	3.2	72%	100%	100%	100%	40%
54.	Valley City State University (ND)	73	N/A	153	$12,168	None	3.4	91%	100%	100%	75%	57%

ENGINEERING

Rank	School	Overall score	Average peer assessment score (5.0=highest)	'14 total enrollment	'14-'15 total program cost[1]	Entrance test required	'14 average undergrad GPA	'14 acceptance rate	'14 full-time faculty with terminal degree	'14 tenured or tenure-track faculty[2]	'14 retention rate	'14 three-year graduation rate
1.	University of California–Los Angeles (Samueli)	100	3.4	312	$33,000	GRE	3.5	45%	100%	100%	88%	84%
2.	Columbia University (Fu Foundation) (NY)	96	3.8	210	$51,300	GRE	3.6	50%	100%	93%	99%	88%
3.	University of Southern California (Viterbi)	86	4.0	888	$46,062	GRE	3.5	37%	96%	80%	96%	73%
4.	Purdue University–West Lafayette (IN)	80	3.9	731	$34,350	none	3.4	78%	100%	94%	92%	44%
5.	Pennsylvania State University–World Campus	77	3.6	437	N/A	none	3.3	90%	95%	65%	86%	78%
6.	University of Wisconsin–Madison	76	3.9	201	N/A	none	3.3	66%	81%	70%	99%	91%
7.	University of Tennessee–Chattanooga	73	1.9	205	N/A	GRE	3.3	70%	90%	100%	96%	N/A
8.	New York University	68	3.0	138	$44,976	none	3.4	58%	94%	65%	77%	78%

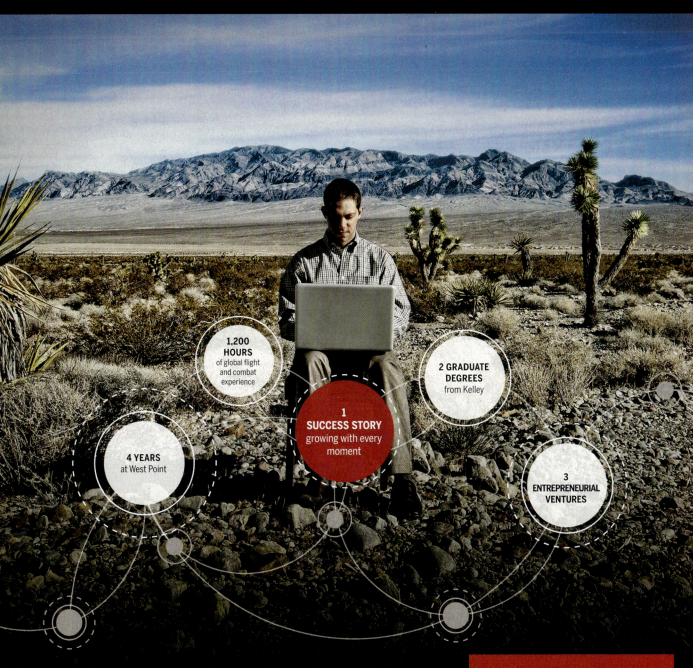

ENGINEERING continued

Rank	School	Overall score	Average peer assessment score (5.0=highest)	'14 total enrollment	'14-'15 total program cost[1]	Entrance test required	'14 average undergrad GPA	'14 acceptance rate	'14 full-time faculty with terminal degree	'14 tenured or tenure-track faculty[2]	'14 retention rate	'14 three-year graduation rate
9.	University of Michigan–Ann Arbor	66	3.9	409	N/A	none	3.4	67%	100%	100%	90%	28%
10.	Cornell University (NY)	64	3.9	88	N/A	GRE	N/A	81%	100%	80%	90%	90%
11.	North Carolina State University	63	3.5	690	$11,594	none	3.5	68%	100%	96%	95%	N/A
12.	Johns Hopkins University (Whiting) (MD)	61	3.3	2,626	$35,300	none	3.4	93%	100%	75%	83%	60%
13.	University of Maryland–College Park (Clark)	60	3.6	329	$30,450	none	3.2	70%	100%	94%	86%	71%
14.	Arizona State University (Fulton)	58	3.2	339	N/A	none	3.3	62%	100%	93%	76%	26%
15.	Virginia Tech	57	3.7	30	N/A	GRE	2.9	46%	100%	100%	100%	N/A
16.	California State University–Fullerton	56	2.6	200	$10,770	none	3.3	74%	100%	100%	91%	76%
17.	Auburn University (AL)	53	3.2	108	N/A	GRE	3.3	57%	100%	100%	91%	17%
17.	University of South Florida	53	2.4	95	N/A	none	3.3	N/A	108%	75%	91%	79%
19.	Ohio State University	52	3.3	28	N/A	none	3.2	93%	100%	71%	95%	N/A
20.	Kansas State University	51	2.6	164	$22,170	none	3.5	0%	100%	96%	89%	69%
20.	Lawrence Technological University (MI)	51	2.3	34	N/A	none	N/A	N/A	100%	100%	61%	52%
20.	Mississippi State University (Bagley)	51	2.7	136	$12,920	none	3.2	88%	100%	98%	98%	16%
20.	Missouri University of Science & Technology	51	2.7	976	N/A	GRE	3.5	91%	97%	33%	84%	71%
20.	Texas Tech University (Whitacre)	51	2.5	120	$7,888	GRE	3.0	47%	100%	100%	82%	56%
20.	University of Colorado–Colorado Springs	51	2.3	62	$20,550	none	3.2	84%	100%	50%	91%	71%

NURSING

Rank	School	Overall score	Average peer assessment score (5.0=highest)	'14 total enrollment	'14-'15 total program cost[1]	Entrance test required	'14 average undergrad GPA	'14 acceptance rate	'14 full-time faculty with terminal degree	'14 tenured or tenure-track faculty[2]	'14 retention rate	'14 three-year graduation rate
1.	Medical University of South Carolina	100	3.6	212	$50,100	None	3.8	31%	90%	100%	98%	83%
2.	St. Xavier University (IL)	99	3.5	263	N/A	None	3.5	87%	75%	100%	98%	91%
3.	Johns Hopkins University (MD)	95	4.2	81	N/A	None	3.4	73%	100%	16%	100%	60%
3.	University of South Carolina	95	3.4	111	N/A	None	3.4	100%	67%	56%	97%	83%
5.	University of Colorado–Denver	94	3.7	155	$17,280	None	3.3	92%	83%	83%	90%	71%
6.	Duke University (NC)	92	4.0	436	N/A	GRE	3.5	50%	98%	49%	98%	84%
6.	Ohio State University	92	3.9	74	$48,490	None	3.5	48%	75%	25%	100%	91%
6.	University of Nevada–Las Vegas	92	3.5	73	$29,706	None	3.6	47%	71%	47%	93%	72%
9.	Duquesne University (PA)	91	3.7	139	N/A	None	3.4	77%	94%	94%	84%	74%
9.	George Washington University (DC)	91	3.6	435	$44,370	None	3.3	67%	91%	77%	92%	69%
9.	Graceland University (MO)	91	3.1	432	$32,665	None	3.7	58%	57%	57%	99%	79%
9.	University of Texas–Tyler	91	3.3	221	$1,850	GRE	3.4	73%	100%	92%	99%	67%
13.	Rush University (IL)	89	4.0	546	N/A	GRE	3.2	82%	79%	53%	93%	79%
13.	Stony Brook University–SUNY (NY)	89	3.3	496	$5,184	None	3.4	59%	86%	19%	95%	70%
15.	Loyola University New Orleans (LA)	88	3.3	1,000	$29,448	None	3.1	95%	100%	71%	84%	66%
15.	University of Massachusetts–Amherst	88	3.5	57	$27,750	None	3.5	86%	100%	70%	86%	73%
15.	University of Texas Medical Branch–Galveston	88	3.5	453	$2,236	None	N/A	30%	55%	22%	97%	79%
18.	East Carolina University (NC)	85	3.4	582	N/A	GRE	3.5	46%	66%	48%	89%	56%
18.	Georgia College & State University	85	3.1	137	$17,486	GRE	3.6	81%	80%	100%	98%	96%
18.	University of Missouri–Kansas City	85	3.5	313	$16,025	None	3.7	69%	72%	11%	95%	71%
21.	Clarion U. of Penn./Edinboro U. of Penn.	84	2.6	72	N/A	None	3.5	79%	100%	100%	86%	81%
21.	Clarkson College (NE)	84	3.1	433	$24,764	None	3.5	57%	80%	0%	90%	53%
21.	University of Pittsburgh (PA)	84	3.7	99	$41,664	GRE	3.7	72%	100%	34%	95%	58%
24.	Ball State University (IN)	83	3.1	476	$13,545	None	3.6	46%	89%	58%	93%	54%
25.	University of Central Florida	82	3.1	135	$13,140	None	3.3	63%	100%	90%	98%	63%
25.	University of Delaware	82	3.2	72	N/A	None	3.0	79%	100%	73%	N/A	85%
25.	University of Kansas	82	3.8	86	$13,373	None	3.4	73%	94%	54%	94%	N/A
28.	Frontier Nursing University (KY)	81	3.5	2,103	$31,720	None	3.5	55%	86%	0%	N/A	73%
28.	Texas A&M University–Corpus Christi	81	3.3	409	$1,363	N/A	3.6	45%	94%	94%	80%	59%
28.	Texas Tech University Health Sciences Center	81	3.7	614	$1,380	None	3.5	58%	83%	39%	N/A	68%
31.	Drexel University (PA)	80	3.5	1,314	$47,355	None	3.3	67%	52%	9%	87%	31%
31.	Georgia Regents University	80	3.0	70	$17,986	GRE	3.2	44%	82%	36%	N/A	100%
31.	Michigan State University	80	3.7	155	$29,070	None	3.7	40%	72%	48%	91%	58%
31.	University of North Carolina–Greensboro	80	3.4	60	N/A	GRE	3.6	N/A	100%	75%	89%	N/A
31.	University of Texas–Arlington	80	3.3	882	$17,800	None	3.5	63%	83%	33%	72%	48%

DIRECTORY OF
GRADUATE
SCHOOLS

Schools are listed alphabetically by state within each discipline; data are accurate as of late February 2015. A key to the terminology used in the directory can be found at the beginning of each area of study.

BUSINESS

The business directory lists all 464 U.S. schools offering master's programs in business accredited by AACSB International–the Association to Advance Collegiate Schools of Business, as of August 2014. Most offer the MBA degree; a few offer the master of business. Three hundred and eighty-five schools responded to the U.S. News survey conducted in the fall of 2014 and early 2015. Schools that did not respond to the survey have abbreviated entries.

KEY TO THE TERMINOLOGY

1. A school whose name is footnoted with the numeral 1 did not return the U.S. News statistical survey; limited data appear in its entry.

N/A. Not available from the school or not applicable.

Email. The address of the admissions office. If instead of an email address a website is given in this field, the website will automatically present an email screen programmed to reach the admissions office.

Application deadline. For fall 2016 enrollment. "Rolling" means there is no application deadline; the school acts on applications as they are received. "Varies" means deadlines vary according to department or whether applicants are U.S. citizens or foreign nationals.

Tuition. For the 2014-15 academic year or for the cost of the total graduate business degree program, if specified. Includes required annual student fees.

Credit hour. The cost per credit hour for the 2014-15 academic year.

Room/board/expenses. For the 2014-15 academic year.

College-funded aid and international student aid. "Yes" means the school provides its own financial aid to students.

Average indebtedness. Computed for 2014 graduates who incurred business school debt.

Enrollment. Full-time and part-time program totals are for fall 2014.

Minorities. For fall 2014, percentage of students who are black or African-American, Asian, American Indian or Alaskan Native, Native Hawaiian or other Pacific Islander, Hispanic/ Latino or two or more races. The minority percentage was reported by each school.

Acceptance rate. Percentage of applicants to the full-time program who were accepted for fall 2014.

Average Graduate Management Admission Test (GMAT) score. Calculated separately for full-time and part-time students who entered in fall 2014.

Average undergraduate grade point average (1.0 to 4.0). For full-time program applicants who entered in fall 2014.

Average age of entrants. Calculated for full-time students who entered in fall 2014.

Average months of work experience. Calculated only for full-time program students who entered in fall 2014. Refers to post-baccalaureate work experience only.

TOEFL requirement. "Yes" means that students from non-English-speaking countries must submit scores for the Test of English as a Foreign Language.

Minimum TOEFL score. The lowest score on the paper TOEFL accepted for admission. (The computer-administered TOEFL is graded on a different scale.)

Most popular departments. Based on highest student demand in the 2014-15 academic year.

Mean starting base salary for 2014 graduates. Calculated only for graduates who were full-time students, had accepted full-time job offers, and reported salary data. Excludes employer-sponsored students, signing bonuses of any kind and other forms of guaranteed compensation, such as stock options.

Employment locations. For the 2014 graduating class. Calculated only for full-time students who had accepted job offers. Abbreviations: **Intl.**, international; **N.E.**, Northeast (Conn., Maine, Mass., N.H., N.J., N.Y., R.I., Vt.); **M.A.**, Middle Atlantic (Del., D.C., Md., Pa., Va., W.Va.); **S.**, South (Ala., Ark., Fla., Ga., Ky., La., Miss., N.C., S.C., Tenn.); **M.W.**, Midwest (Ill., Ind., Iowa, Kan., Mich., Minn., Mo., Neb., N.D., Ohio, S.D., Wis.); **S.W.**, Southwest (Ariz., Colo., N.M., Okla., Texas); **W.**, West (Alaska, Calif., Hawaii, Idaho, Mont., Nev., Ore., Utah, Wash., Wyo.).

ALABAMA

Auburn University (Harbert)
415 W. Magnolia, Suite 503
Auburn, AL 36849-5240
www.business.auburn.edu/mba
Public
Admissions: (334) 844-4060
Email: mbadmis@auburn.edu
Financial aid: (334) 844-4367
Application deadline: 02/01
In-state tuition: total program: $23,291 (full time); part time: N/A
Out-of-state tuition: total program: $49,049 (full time)
Room/board/expenses: $18,964
College-funded aid: Yes
International student aid: Yes
Average student indebtedness at graduation: $34,618
Full-time enrollment: 65
men: 52%; women: 48%;
minorities: 6%; international: 34%
Part-time enrollment: N/A
men: N/A; women: N/A; minorities: N/A; international: N/A
Acceptance rate (full time): 41%
Average GMAT (full time): 616
Average GPA (full time): 3.23
Average age of entrants to full-time program: 26
Average months of prior work experience (full time): 92
TOEFL requirement: Yes
Minimum TOEFL score: 550
Most popular departments: finance, marketing, management information systems, supply chain management, statistics and operations research
Mean starting base salary for 2014 full-time graduates: $56,439
Employment location for 2014 class: Intl. 5%; N.E. 5%; M.A. N/A; S. 82%; M.W. 9%; S.W. N/A; W. N/A

Auburn University-Montgomery
7300 East Drive
Montgomery, AL 36117
www.aum.edu
Public
Admissions: (334) 244-3623
Email: awarren3@aum.edu
Financial aid: (334) 244-3571
Application deadline: rolling
In-state tuition: full time: $348/ credit hour; part time: $348/ credit hour
Out-of-state tuition: full time: $783/ credit hour
Room/board/expenses: N/A
College-funded aid: Yes
International student aid: Yes
Full-time enrollment: 61
men: 51%; women: 49%;
minorities: 56%; international: 46%
Part-time enrollment: 50
men: 52%; women: 48%;
minorities: 34%; international: 8%
Acceptance rate (full time): 88%
Average GMAT (full time): 483
TOEFL requirement: Yes
Minimum TOEFL score: 500

Jacksonville State University[1]
700 Pelham Road N
Jacksonville, AL 36265
www.jsu.edu/ccba/
Public
Admissions: (256) 782-5268
Email: info@jsu.edu
Financial aid: N/A
Tuition: N/A
Room/board/expenses: N/A
Enrollment: N/A

Samford University (Brock)
800 Lakeshore Drive
Birmingham, AL 35229
www.samford.edu/business/
Private
Admissions: (205) 726-2040
Email: gradbusi@samford.edu
Financial aid: (205) 726-2905
Application deadline: 08/01
Tuition: full time: N/A; part time: $744/credit hour
Room/board/expenses: N/A
College-funded aid: Yes
International student aid: No
Full-time enrollment: N/A
men: N/A; women: N/A; minorities: N/A; international: N/A
Part-time enrollment: 77
men: 61%; women: 39%;
minorities: 14%; international: 12%
Average GMAT (part time): 541
TOEFL requirement: Yes
Minimum TOEFL score: N/A

University of Alabama-Birmingham
1720 2nd Avenue South
Birmingham, AL 35294-4460
www.uab.edu/mba
Public
Admissions: (205) 934-8817
Email: cmanning@uab.edu
Financial aid: (205) 934-8223
Application deadline: 07/01
In-state tuition: full time: N/A; part time: $442/credit hour
Out-of-state tuition: full time: N/A
Room/board/expenses: N/A
College-funded aid: Yes
International student aid: No
Full-time enrollment: N/A
men: N/A; women: N/A; minorities: N/A; international: N/A
Part-time enrollment: 301
men: 59%; women: 41%;
minorities: 21%; international: 11%
Average GMAT (part time): 545
TOEFL requirement: Yes
Minimum TOEFL score: N/A
Most popular departments: finance, health care administration, marketing, management information systems

University of Alabama-Huntsville
BAB 202
Huntsville, AL 35899
cba.uah.edu/
Public
Admissions: (256) 824-6681
Email: gradbiz@uah.edu
Financial aid: (256) 824-6241
Application deadline: 07/15

International student aid: Yes
Full-time enrollment: 76
men: 61%; women: 39%;
minorities: 9%; international: 37%
Part-time enrollment: N/A
men: N/A; women: N/A; minorities:
N/A; international: N/A
Acceptance rate (full time): 61%
Average GMAT (full time): 650
Average GPA (full time): 3.46
Average age of entrants to full-time
program: 25
Average months of prior work
experience (full time): 33
TOEFL requirement: Yes
Minimum TOEFL score: 550
Most popular departments:
entrepreneurship, finance,
marketing, non-profit
management, supply chain
management
Mean starting base salary for 2014
full-time graduates: $64,592
Employment location for 2014 class:
Intl. 0%; N.E. 0%; M.A. 5%; S.
86%; M.W. 0%; S.W. 10%; W. 0%

University of Arkansas-Little Rock

2801 S. University Avenue
Little Rock, AR 72204
ualr.edu/cob
Public
Admissions: (501) 569-3356
Email: mbaadvising@ualr.edu
Financial aid: (501) 569-3035
Application deadline: rolling
In-state tuition: full time: $325/
credit hour; part time: $325/
credit hour
Out-of-state tuition: full time: $700/
credit hour
Room/board/expenses: $11,920
College-funded aid: Yes
International student aid: Yes
Average student indebtedness at
graduation: $50,997
Full-time enrollment: 20
men: 55%; women: 45%;
minorities: 20%; international:
15%
Part-time enrollment: 105
men: 59%; women: 41%;
minorities: 19%; international: 5%
Average GMAT (full time): 490
Average GMAT (part time): 510
Average age of entrants to full-time
program: 26
TOEFL requirement: Yes
Minimum TOEFL score: 550

University of Central Arkansas

201 Donaghey
Conway, AR 72035
www.uca.edu/mba
Public
Admissions: (501) 450-5316
Email: mrubach@uca.edu
Financial aid: (501) 450-3140
Application deadline: rolling
In-state tuition: full time: $243/
credit hour; part time: $243/
credit hour
Out-of-state tuition: full time: $486/
credit hour
Room/board/expenses: N/A
College-funded aid: Yes
International student aid: No
Full-time enrollment: 34
men: 59%; women: 41%;
minorities: 12%; international:
29%
Part-time enrollment: 38
men: 68%; women: 32%;
minorities: 11%; international: 8%
Acceptance rate (full time): 79%
Average GMAT (full time): 502
Average GMAT (part time): 548

Average GPA (full time): 3.33
Average age of entrants to full-time
program: 24
TOEFL requirement: Yes
Minimum TOEFL score: 550

CALIFORNIA

California Polytechnic State University-San Luis Obispo (Orfalea)

1 Grand Avenue
San Luis Obispo, CA 93407
www.cob.calpoly.edu/
gradprograms/
Public
Admissions: (805) 756-2311
Email: admissions@calpoly.edu
Financial aid: (805) 756-2927
Application deadline: 04/01
In-state tuition: full time: $23,652;
part time: $18,297
Out-of-state tuition: full time:
$35,556
Room/board/expenses: $15,765
College-funded aid: Yes
International student aid: Yes
Average student indebtedness at
graduation: $19,600
Full-time enrollment: 17
men: 53%; women: 47%;
minorities: N/A; international: 6%
Part-time enrollment: 18
men: 83%; women: 17%;
minorities: N/A; international: N/A
Acceptance rate (full time): 40%
Average GMAT (full time): 610
Average GMAT (part time): 610
Average GPA (full time): 3.47
TOEFL requirement: Yes
Minimum TOEFL score: 550
Most popular departments:
general management, industrial
management, other

California State Polytechnic University-Pomona

3801 W. Temple Avenue
Pomona, CA 91768
www.cpp.edu/~cba
Public
Admissions: (909) 869-3210
Email:
admissions@csupomona.edu
Financial aid: (909) 869-3700
Application deadline: 08/01
In-state tuition: full time: $11,178;
part time: $6,566
Out-of-state tuition: full time:
$17,130
Room/board/expenses: $17,271
College-funded aid: Yes
International student aid: Yes
Full-time enrollment: 39
men: 33%; women: 67%;
minorities: 15%; international:
28%
Part-time enrollment: 37
men: 46%; women: 54%;
minorities: 19%; international: 11%
Average GMAT (part time): 533
TOEFL requirement: Yes
Minimum TOEFL score: 580

California State University-Bakersfield[1]

9001 Stockdale Highway
Bakersfield, CA 93311-1099
www.csub.edu/BPA
Public
Admissions: (661) 664-3036
Email: admissions@csub.edu
Financial aid: N/A
Tuition: N/A

Room/board/expenses: N/A
Enrollment: N/A

California State University-Chico

Tehama Hall 301
Chico, CA 95929-0001
www.csuchico.edu/MBA
Public
Admissions: (530) 898-6880
Email:
graduatestudies@csuchico.edu
Financial aid: (530) 898-6451
Application deadline: 03/01
In-state tuition: total program:
$16,500 (full time); $16,500 (part
time)
Out-of-state tuition: total program:
$27,500 (full time)
Room/board/expenses: $15,000
College-funded aid: Yes
International student aid: Yes
Full-time enrollment: 66
men: 65%; women: 35%;
minorities: N/A; international: N/A
Part-time enrollment: N/A
men: N/A; women: N/A; minorities:
N/A; international: N/A
Acceptance rate (full time): 73%
Average GMAT (full time): 558
Average GPA (full time): 3.16
Average age of entrants to full-time
program: 26
Average months of prior work
experience (full time): 36
TOEFL requirement: Yes
Minimum TOEFL score: 550

California State University-East Bay

25800 Carlos Bee Boulevard
Hayward, CA 94542
www.csueastbay.edu
Public
Admissions: (510) 885-2784
Email:
admissions@csueastbay.edu
Financial aid: (510) 885-2784
Application deadline: 06/30
In-state tuition: full time: $11,886;
part time: $7,026
Out-of-state tuition: full time:
$17,838
Room/board/expenses: $15,000
College-funded aid: Yes
International student aid: No
Average student indebtedness at
graduation: $2,154
Full-time enrollment: N/A
men: N/A; women: N/A; minorities:
N/A; international: N/A
Part-time enrollment: 242
men: 54%; women: 46%;
minorities: 68%; international:
22%
Average GMAT (part time): 540
TOEFL requirement: Yes
Minimum TOEFL score: 550
Most popular departments: finance,
human resources management,
marketing, operations
management, supply chain
management

California State University-Fresno (Craig)[1]

5245 N. Backer Avenue
Fresno, CA 93740-8001
www.craig.csufresno.edu/mba
Public
Admissions: (559) 278-2107
Email: mbainfo@csufresno.edu
Financial aid: N/A
Tuition: N/A
Room/board/expenses: N/A
Enrollment: N/A

California State University-Fullerton (Mihaylo)

PO Box 6848
Fullerton, CA 92834-6848
business.fullerton.edu
Public
Admissions: (657) 278-4035
Email: mba@fullerton.edu
Financial aid: (657) 278-3125
Application deadline: 04/01
In-state tuition: full time: $12,153;
part time: $6,273
Out-of-state tuition: full time:
$18,849
Room/board/expenses: $17,638
College-funded aid: Yes
International student aid: Yes
Full-time enrollment: 23
men: 52%; women: 48%;
minorities: 43%; international:
43%
Part-time enrollment: 292
men: 63%; women: 37%;
minorities: 47%; international:
16%
Acceptance rate (full time): 34%
Average GMAT (full time): 562
Average GMAT (part time): 567
Average GPA (full time): 3.19
Average age of entrants to full-time
program: 23
Average months of prior work
experience (full time): 15
TOEFL requirement: Yes
Minimum TOEFL score: 570
Most popular departments: finance,
general management, marketing,
statistics and operations
research, other

California State University-Long Beach

1250 Bellflower Boulevard
Long Beach, CA 90840-8501
www.csulb.edu/colleges/cba/mba
Public
Admissions: (562) 985-8627
Email: mba@csulb.edu
Financial aid: (562) 985-4141
Application deadline: rolling
In-state tuition: full time: $7,718;
part time: N/A
Out-of-state tuition: full time: N/A
Room/board/expenses: N/A
College-funded aid: Yes
International student aid: Yes
Full-time enrollment: 41
men: 63%; women: 37%;
minorities: 80%; international:
63%
Part-time enrollment: 109
men: 53%; women: 47%;
minorities: 60%; international:
10%
Acceptance rate (full time): 29%
Average GMAT (full time): 563
Average GMAT (part time): 561
Average GPA (full time): 3.31
Average age of entrants to full-time
program: 25
TOEFL requirement: Yes
Minimum TOEFL score: 550

California State University-Los Angeles

5151 State University Drive
Los Angeles, CA 90032-8120
www.calstatela.edu/business/
Public
Admissions: (323) 343-2800
Email: ehsieh@calstatela.edu
Financial aid: (323) 343-6260
Application deadline: rolling
In-state tuition: total program:
$28,000 (full time); part time: N/A

Out-of-state tuition: total program:
$38,000 (full time)
Room/board/expenses: $40,000
College-funded aid: No
International student aid: No
Full-time enrollment: 91
men: 53%; women: 47%;
minorities: 40%; international:
63%
Part-time enrollment: N/A
men: N/A; women: N/A; minorities:
N/A; international: N/A
Acceptance rate (full time): 55%
Average GMAT (full time): 544
Average GPA (full time): 3.12
Average age of entrants to full-time
program: 30
Average months of prior work
experience (full time): 5
TOEFL requirement: Yes
Minimum TOEFL score: 550

California State University-Northridge

18111 Nordhoff Street
Northridge, CA 91330-8380
www.csun.edu/mba/
Public
Admissions: (818) 677-2467
Email: MBA@csun.edu
Financial aid: (818) 677-4085
Application deadline: 05/01
In-state tuition: full time: $12,382;
part time: $8,026
Out-of-state tuition: full time:
$19,078
Room/board/expenses: $17,870
College-funded aid: Yes
International student aid: Yes
Full-time enrollment: N/A
men: N/A; women: N/A; minorities:
N/A; international: N/A
Part-time enrollment: 121
men: 64%; women: 36%;
minorities: 31%; international: 10%
Average GMAT (part time): 561
TOEFL requirement: Yes
Minimum TOEFL score: 550
Most popular departments:
finance, general management,
international business, marketing,
operations management

California State University-Sacramento

6000 J Street
Sacramento, CA 95819-6088
www.csus.edu/cbagrad
Public
Admissions: (916) 278-6772
Email: cbagrad@csus.edu
Financial aid: (916) 278-6554
Application deadline: N/A
In-state tuition: full time: N/A; part
time: $5,082
Out-of-state tuition: full time: N/A
Room/board/expenses: N/A
College-funded aid: No
International student aid: No
Full-time enrollment: N/A
men: N/A; women: N/A; minorities:
N/A; international: N/A
Part-time enrollment: 175
men: 60%; women: 40%;
minorities: 38%; international: 7%
Average GMAT (part time): 585
TOEFL requirement: Yes
Minimum TOEFL score: 550
Most popular departments:
entrepreneurship, finance,
general management, health
care administration, international
business

In-state tuition: full time: $9,180; part time: $665/credit hour
Out-of-state tuition: full time: $20,982
Room/board/expenses: $11,000
College-funded aid: Yes
International student aid: Yes
Average student indebtedness at graduation: $19,482
Full-time enrollment: 47
men: 43%; women: 57%; minorities: 15%; international: 23%
Part-time enrollment: 143
men: 42%; women: 58%; minorities: 17%; international: 2%
Acceptance rate (full time): 89%
Average GMAT (full time): 523
Average GMAT (part time): 549
Average GPA (full time): 3.24
Average age of entrants to full-time program: 28
Average months of prior work experience (full time): 54
TOEFL requirement: Yes
Minimum TOEFL score: 550
Most popular departments: accounting, general management, manufacturing and technology management, supply chain management, technology

University of Alabama (Manderson)

Box 870223
Tuscaloosa, AL 35487
www.manderson.cba.ua.edu
Public
Admissions: (888) 863-2622
Email: mba@cba.ua.edu
Financial aid: (205) 348-6517
Application deadline: 04/15
In-state tuition: full time: $12,656; part time: N/A
Out-of-state tuition: full time: $27,780
Room/board/expenses: N/A
College-funded aid: Yes
International student aid: Yes
Full-time enrollment: 164
men: 67%; women: 33%; minorities: 7%; international: 9%
Part-time enrollment: N/A
men: N/A; women: N/A; minorities: N/A; international: N/A
Acceptance rate (full time): 54%
Average GMAT (full time): 659
Average GPA (full time): 3.50
Average age of entrants to full-time program: 23
Average months of prior work experience (full time): 35
TOEFL requirement: Yes
Minimum TOEFL score: 550
Most popular departments: consulting, finance, management information systems, supply chain management, statistics and operations research
Mean starting base salary for 2014 full-time graduates: $64,893
Employment location for 2014 class: Intl. 0%; N.E. 0%; M.A. 5%; S. 84%; M.W. 5%; S.W. 2%; W. 4%

University of Montevallo

Morgan Hall 201, Station 6540
Montevallo, AL 35115
www.montevallo.edu/grad/
Public
Admissions: (205) 665-6350
Email: graduate@montevallo.edu
Financial aid: (205) 665-6050
Application deadline: 07/15
In-state tuition: full time: $363/credit hour; part time: $363/credit hour

Out-of-state tuition: full time: $747/credit hour
Room/board/expenses: N/A
College-funded aid: Yes
Full-time enrollment: N/A
men: N/A; women: N/A; minorities: N/A; international: N/A
Part-time enrollment: 33
men: 58%; women: 42%; minorities: 24%; international: N/A
TOEFL requirement: Yes
Minimum TOEFL score: 525

University of South Alabama (Mitchell)[1]

307 N. University Boulevard
Mobile, AL 36688
www.southalabama.edu/colleges/mcob/mba/index.html
Public
Admissions: (251) 460-6418
Financial aid: N/A
Tuition: N/A
Room/board/expenses: N/A
Enrollment: N/A

ALASKA

University of Alaska-Anchorage[1]

3211 Providence Drive
Anchorage, AK 99508
www.uaa.alaska.edu/cbpp/
Public
Admissions: (907) 786-1480
Email: admissions@uaa.alaska.edu
Financial aid: N/A
Tuition: N/A
Room/board/expenses: N/A
Enrollment: N/A

University of Alaska-Fairbanks

PO Box 756080
Fairbanks, AK 99775-6080
www.uaf.edu/som/degrees/graduate/mba
Public
Admissions: (800) 478-1823
Email: admissions@uaf.edu
Financial aid: (888) 474-7256
Application deadline: 06/01
In-state tuition: full time: $403/credit hour; part time: $403/credit hour
Out-of-state tuition: full time: $823/credit hour
Room/board/expenses: $12,380
College-funded aid: Yes
International student aid: Yes
Full-time enrollment: 25
men: 68%; women: 32%; minorities: 24%; international: 8%
Part-time enrollment: 39
men: 49%; women: 51%; minorities: 8%; international: 0%
Acceptance rate (full time): 74%
Average GMAT (full time): 493
Average age of entrants to full-time program: 28
TOEFL requirement: Yes
Minimum TOEFL score: 550

ARIZONA

Arizona State University (Carey)

PO Box 874906
Tempe, AZ 85287-4906
wpcarey.asu.edu/mba-programs
Public
Admissions: (480) 965-3332
Email: wpcareymasters@asu.edu
Financial aid: (480) 965-6890

Application deadline: 06/30
In-state tuition: full time: $26,302; part time: $26,552
Out-of-state tuition: full time: $41,736
Room/board/expenses: $18,408
College-funded aid: Yes
International student aid: Yes
Average student indebtedness at graduation: $63,095
Full-time enrollment: 136
men: 71%; women: 29%; minorities: 10%; international: 32%
Part-time enrollment: 273
men: 73%; women: 27%; minorities: 27%; international: 10%
Acceptance rate (full time): 25%
Average GMAT (full time): 673
Average GMAT (part time): 576
Average GPA (full time): 3.46
Average age of entrants to full-time program: 28
Average months of prior work experience (full time): 62
TOEFL requirement: Yes
Minimum TOEFL score: 550
Most popular departments: finance, general management, leadership, marketing, supply chain management
Mean starting base salary for 2014 full-time graduates: $98,093
Employment location for 2014 class: Intl. 2%; N.E. 11%; M.A. 0%; S. 2%; M.W. 4%; S.W. 57%; W. 23%

Northern Arizona University (Franke)

PO Box 15066
Flagstaff, AZ 86011-5066
www.franke.nau.edu/graduateprograms
Public
Admissions: (928) 523-7342
Email: fcb-gradprog@nau.edu
Financial aid: (928) 523-4951
Application deadline: rolling
In-state tuition: total program: $17,475 (full time); part time: N/A
Out-of-state tuition: total program: $28,559 (full time)
Room/board/expenses: N/A
College-funded aid: Yes
International student aid: Yes
Full-time enrollment: 42
men: 62%; women: 38%; minorities: 14%; international: 12%
Part-time enrollment: N/A
men: N/A; women: N/A; minorities: N/A; international: N/A
Acceptance rate (full time): 98%
Average GMAT (full time): 568
Average GPA (full time): 3.34
Average age of entrants to full-time program: 24
Average months of prior work experience (full time): 14
TOEFL requirement: Yes
Minimum TOEFL score: 550

Thunderbird School of Global Management

1 Global Place
Glendale, AZ 85306-6000
www.thunderbird.edu
Private
Admissions: (602) 978-7100
Email: admissions@thunderbird.edu
Financial aid: (602) 978-7130
Application deadline: rolling
Tuition: full time: $1,436/credit hour; part time: N/A
Room/board/expenses: $5,265
College-funded aid: Yes
International student aid: Yes
Average student indebtedness at graduation: $81,367

Full-time enrollment: 283
men: 77%; women: 23%; minorities: 8%; international: 67%
Part-time enrollment: N/A
men: N/A; women: N/A; minorities: N/A; international: N/A
Acceptance rate (full time): 56%
Average GMAT (full time): 605
Average GPA (full time): 3.30
Average age of entrants to full-time program: 28
Average months of prior work experience (full time): 53
TOEFL requirement: Yes
Minimum TOEFL score: 600
Most popular departments: entrepreneurship, finance, general management, international business, marketing
Mean starting base salary for 2014 full-time graduates: $78,123
Employment location for 2014 class: Intl. 27%; N.E. 13%; M.A. 8%; S. 2%; M.W. 15%; S.W. 19%; W. 16%

University of Arizona (Eller)

McClelland Hall, Room 417
Tucson, AZ 85721-0108
ellermba.arizona.edu
Public
Admissions: (520) 621-6227
Email: mba_admissions@eller.arizona.edu
Financial aid: (520) 621-1858
Application deadline: rolling
In-state tuition: full time: $23,238; part time: $22,500
Out-of-state tuition: full time: $40,220
Room/board/expenses: $13,200
College-funded aid: Yes
International student aid: Yes
Average student indebtedness at graduation: $51,918
Full-time enrollment: 81
men: 74%; women: 26%; minorities: 11%; international: 42%
Part-time enrollment: 171
men: 64%; women: 36%; minorities: 23%; international: 1%
Acceptance rate (full time): 51%
Average GMAT (full time): 646
Average GMAT (part time): 524
Average GPA (full time): 3.32
Average age of entrants to full-time program: 27
Average months of prior work experience (full time): 43
TOEFL requirement: Yes
Minimum TOEFL score: 600
Most popular departments: entrepreneurship, finance, health care administration, marketing, management information systems
Mean starting base salary for 2014 full-time graduates: $80,222
Employment location for 2014 class: Intl. 0%; N.E. 10%; M.A. 3%; S. 0%; M.W. 14%; S.W. 55%; W. 17%

ARKANSAS

Arkansas State University-Jonesboro

PO Box 970
State University, AR 72467
www.astate.edu/college/business
Public
Admissions: (870) 972-3029
Email: gradsch@astate.edu
Financial aid: (870) 972-2310
Application deadline: 06/01
In-state tuition: full time: $6,756; part time: $356/credit hour
Out-of-state tuition: full time: $11,712
Room/board/expenses: N/A
College-funded aid: Yes
International student aid: Yes

Average student indebtedness at graduation: $35,000
Full-time enrollment: 129
men: 54%; women: 46%; minorities: 4%; international: 79%
Part-time enrollment: 121
men: 55%; women: 45%; minorities: 18%; international: 18%
Acceptance rate (full time): 87%
Average GMAT (full time): 544
Average GMAT (part time): 522
Average GPA (full time): 3.35
Average age of entrants to full-time program: 29
Average months of prior work experience (full time): 16
TOEFL requirement: Yes
Minimum TOEFL score: 550
Most popular departments: finance, health care administration, international business, management information systems, supply chain management
Mean starting base salary for 2014 full-time graduates: $61,250
Employment location for 2014 class: Intl. 38%; N.E. 6%; M.A. 6%; S. 25%; M.W. 6%; S.W. 16%; W. 3%

Arkansas Tech University[1]

1605 North Coliseum Drive
Russellville, AR 72801
www.atu.edu/business/
Public
Admissions: (479) 968-0398
Email: gradcollege@atu.edu
Financial aid: N/A
Tuition: N/A
Room/board/expenses: N/A
Enrollment: N/A

Henderson State University[1]

1100 Henderson Street, Box 7801
Arkadelphia, AR 71999-0001
www.hsu.edu/Academics/SchoolofBusiness/MBA/index.html
Public
Admissions: N/A
Email: grad@hsu.edu
Financial aid: N/A
Tuition: N/A
Room/board/expenses: N/A
Enrollment: N/A

Southern Arkansas University[1]

100 E. University
Magnolia, AR 71753
web.saumag.edu/graduate/programs/mba/
Public
Admissions: N/A
Financial aid: N/A
Tuition: N/A
Room/board/expenses: N/A
Enrollment: N/A

University of Arkansas-Fayetteville (Walton)

310 Williard J. Walker Hall
Fayetteville, AR 72701
gsb.uark.edu
Public
Admissions: (479) 575-2851
Email: gsb@walton.uark.edu
Financial aid: (479) 575-2711
Application deadline: 04/01
In-state tuition: full time: $17,281; part time: N/A
Out-of-state tuition: full time: $40,883
Room/board/expenses: $19,445
College-funded aid: Yes

Application deadline: 04/15
Tuition: full time: $51,786; part time: $1,644/credit hour
Room/board/expenses: $21,271
College-funded aid: Yes
International student aid: Yes
Full-time enrollment: 431
men: 69%; women: 31%; minorities: 29%; international: 27%
Part-time enrollment: 620
men: 69%; women: 31%; minorities: 51%; international: 3%
Acceptance rate (full time): 32%
Average GMAT (full time): 684
Average GMAT (part time): 622
Average GPA (full time): 3.35
Average age of entrants to full-time program: 28
Average months of prior work experience (full time): 58
TOEFL requirement: Yes
Minimum TOEFL score: 600
Most popular departments: consulting, entrepreneurship, finance, international business, marketing
Mean starting base salary for 2014 full-time graduates: $101,306
Employment location for 2014 class: Intl. 11%; N.E. 6%; M.A. 0%; S. 1%; M.W. 4%; S.W. 2%; W. 77%

University of the Pacific (Eberhardt)

3601 Pacific Avenue
Stockton, CA 95211
www.pacific.edu/mba
Private
Admissions: (209) 946-2629
Email: mba@pacific.edu
Financial aid: (209) 946-2421
Application deadline: 03/01
Tuition: total program: $64,680 (full time); part time: $1,408/credit hour
Room/board/expenses: $24,933
College-funded aid: Yes
International student aid: Yes
Full-time enrollment: 33
men: 45%; women: 55%; minorities: 67%; international: 6%
Part-time enrollment: 5
men: 60%; women: 40%; minorities: 40%; international: 0%
Acceptance rate (full time): 68%
Average GMAT (full time): 648
Average GMAT (part time): 550
Average GPA (full time): 3.45
Average age of entrants to full-time program: 23
Average months of prior work experience (full time): 14
TOEFL requirement: Yes
Minimum TOEFL score: 550
Most popular departments: general management, health care administration
Mean starting base salary for 2014 full-time graduates: $60,400
Employment location for 2014 class: Intl. 33%; N.E. N/A; M.A. N/A; S. N/A; M.W. N/A; S.W. N/A; W. 67%

Woodbury University[1]

7500 N. Glenoaks Boulevard
Burbank, CA 91504
woodbury.edu/
Private
Admissions: (818) 252-5221
Email: business@woodbury.edu
Financial aid: N/A
Tuition: N/A
Room/board/expenses: N/A
Enrollment: N/A

COLORADO

Colorado State University

110 Rockwell Hall West
Fort Collins, CO 80523-1270
www.csumba.com
Public
Admissions: (970) 491-3704
Email: gradadmissions@business.colostate.edu
Financial aid: (970) 491-6321
Application deadline: 07/15
In-state tuition: full time: $673/credit hour; part time: $900/credit hour
Out-of-state tuition: full time: $1,405/credit hour
Room/board/expenses: $13,500
College-funded aid: No
International student aid: No
Average student indebtedness at graduation: $32,812
Full-time enrollment: 95
men: 51%; women: 49%; minorities: 14%; international: 26%
Part-time enrollment: 998
men: 70%; women: 30%; minorities: 24%; international: 1%
Acceptance rate (full time): 77%
Average GMAT (full time): 525
Average GMAT (part time): 562
Average GPA (full time): 3.30
Average age of entrants to full-time program: 26
Average months of prior work experience (full time): 54
TOEFL requirement: Yes
Minimum TOEFL score: 565
Most popular departments: finance, general management, marketing, management information systems, operations management

Colorado State University-Pueblo[1]

2200 Bonforte Boulevard
Pueblo, CO 81001
hsb.colostate-pueblo.edu
Public
Admissions: (719) 549-2461
Email: info@colostate-pueblo.edu
Financial aid: N/A
Tuition: N/A
Room/board/expenses: N/A
Enrollment: N/A

University of Colorado-Boulder (Leeds)

995 Regent Drive 419 UCB
Boulder, CO 80309
leeds.colorado.edu/mba
Public
Admissions: (303) 492-8397
Email: leedsmba@Colorado.edu
Financial aid: (303) 492-8223
Application deadline: 04/15
In-state tuition: full time: $18,610; total program: $49,200 (part time)
Out-of-state tuition: full time: $33,142
Room/board/expenses: $19,286
College-funded aid: Yes
International student aid: Yes
Average student indebtedness at graduation: $51,524
Full-time enrollment: 149
men: 69%; women: 31%; minorities: 9%; international: 17%
Part-time enrollment: 81
men: 59%; women: 41%; minorities: 15%; international: 2%
Acceptance rate (full time): 61%
Average GMAT (full time): 611
Average GMAT (part time): 590

Average GPA (full time): 3.36
Average age of entrants to full-time program: 28
Average months of prior work experience (full time): 57
TOEFL requirement: Yes
Minimum TOEFL score: N/A
Most popular departments: entrepreneurship, finance, marketing, operations management, real estate
Mean starting base salary for 2014 full-time graduates: $72,767
Employment location for 2014 class: Intl. 3%; N.E. 3%; M.A. N/A; S. N/A; M.W. 11%; S.W. 81%; W. 3%

University of Colorado-Colorado Springs

1420 Austin Bluffs Parkway
Colorado Springs, CO 80918
www.uccs.edu/mba
Public
Admissions: (719) 255-3122
Email: mbacred@uccs.edu
Financial aid: (719) 255-3460
Application deadline: 06/15
In-state tuition: full time: $11,558; part time: $4,471
Out-of-state tuition: full time: $20,252
Room/board/expenses: $15,920
College-funded aid: Yes
International student aid: Yes
Full-time enrollment: N/A
men: N/A; women: N/A; minorities: N/A; international: N/A
Part-time enrollment: 230
men: 57%; women: 43%; minorities: 15%; international: 2%
Average GMAT (part time): 532
TOEFL requirement: Yes
Minimum TOEFL score: 550
Most popular departments: accounting, finance, health care administration, marketing, operations management

University of Colorado-Denver

Campus Box 165, PO Box 173364
Denver, CO 80217-3364
www.ucdenver.edu/business/
Public
Admissions: (303) 315-8200
Email: grad.business@ucdenver.edu
Financial aid: (303) 556-2886
Application deadline: rolling
In-state tuition: full time: $7,357; part time: $511/credit hour
Out-of-state tuition: full time: $16,105
Room/board/expenses: $13,059
College-funded aid: Yes
International student aid: Yes
Full-time enrollment: 133
men: 65%; women: 35%; minorities: 17%; international: 5%
Part-time enrollment: 549
men: 61%; women: 39%; minorities: 12%; international: 5%
Acceptance rate (full time): 81%
Average GMAT (full time): 553
Average GMAT (part time): 593
Average age of entrants to full-time program: 35
TOEFL requirement: Yes
Minimum TOEFL score: 560

University of Denver (Daniels)

2101 S. University Boulevard
Denver, CO 80208
www.daniels.du.edu/
Private
Admissions: (303) 871-3416
Email: daniels@du.edu
Financial aid: (303) 871-3416
Application deadline: 05/15
Tuition: full time: $1,142/credit hour; part time: $1,142/credit hour
Room/board/expenses: $16,000
College-funded aid: Yes
International student aid: Yes
Full-time enrollment: 109
men: 57%; women: 43%; minorities: 10%; international: 39%
Part-time enrollment: 138
men: 67%; women: 33%; minorities: 15%; international: 2%
Acceptance rate (full time): 74%
Average GMAT (full time): 581
Average GMAT (part time): 593
Average GPA (full time): 3.29
Average age of entrants to full-time program: 26
Average months of prior work experience (full time): 52
TOEFL requirement: Yes
Minimum TOEFL score: 570
Most popular departments: finance, general management, international business, marketing, other

University of Northern Colorado (Monfort)

800 17th Street
Greeley, CO 80639
mcb.unco.edu/MBA/information.cfm
Public
Admissions: N/A
Financial aid: N/A
Application deadline: N/A
In-state tuition: full time: $11,203; part time: $543/credit hour
Out-of-state tuition: full time: $20,797
Room/board/expenses: N/A
Full-time enrollment: 19
men: 42%; women: 58%; minorities: 21%; international: 5%
Part-time enrollment: 9
men: 89%; women: 11%; minorities: 56%; international: 11%
Minimum TOEFL score: N/A
Most popular departments: accounting, public administration

CONNECTICUT

Central Connecticut State University[1]

1615 Stanley Street
New Britain, CT 06050
www.ccsu.edu/
Public
Admissions: (860) 832-2350
Financial aid: N/A
Tuition: N/A
Room/board/expenses: N/A
Enrollment: N/A

Fairfield University (Dolan)

1073 N. Benson Road
Fairfield, CT 06824
www.fairfield.edu/dsb/graduateprograms/mba/
Private
Admissions: (203) 254-4000
Email: dsbgrad@fairfield.edu
Financial aid: (203) 254-4125

Application deadline: rolling
Tuition: full time: $815/credit hour; part time: $815/credit hour
Room/board/expenses: N/A
College-funded aid: Yes
International student aid: No
Full-time enrollment: 81
men: 57%; women: 43%; minorities: 12%; international: 33%
Part-time enrollment: 51
men: 65%; women: 35%; minorities: 14%; international: 10%
Average GMAT (part time): 528
TOEFL requirement: Yes
Minimum TOEFL score: 550
Most popular departments: accounting, finance, general management, human resources management, marketing

Quinnipiac University

275 Mount Carmel Avenue
Hamden, CT 06518
www.quinnipiac.edu/
Private
Admissions: (800) 462-1944
Email: graduate@quinnipiac.edu
Financial aid: (203) 582-8384
Application deadline: 07/29
Tuition: full time: $920/credit hour; part time: $920/credit hour
Room/board/expenses: $21,242
College-funded aid: Yes
International student aid: Yes
Average student indebtedness at graduation: $37,390
Full-time enrollment: 170
men: 55%; women: 45%; minorities: 17%; international: 6%
Part-time enrollment: 249
men: 55%; women: 45%; minorities: 22%; international: 0%
Acceptance rate (full time): 82%
Average GMAT (full time): 529
Average GMAT (part time): 513
Average GPA (full time): 3.34
Average age of entrants to full-time program: 25
TOEFL requirement: Yes
Minimum TOEFL score: 575
Most popular departments: finance, general management, health care administration, marketing, supply chain management

Sacred Heart University (Welch)

5151 Park Avenue
Fairfield, CT 06825
www.sacredheart.edu/johnfwelchcob.cfm
Private
Admissions: (203) 365-7619
Email: gradstudies@sacredheart.edu
Financial aid: (203) 371-7980
Application deadline: rolling
Tuition: full time: N/A; part time: $825/credit hour
Room/board/expenses: N/A
College-funded aid: Yes
International student aid: Yes
Full-time enrollment: N/A
men: N/A; women: N/A; minorities: N/A; international: N/A
Part-time enrollment: 108
men: 45%; women: 55%; minorities: 26%; international: 4%
Average GMAT (part time): 534
TOEFL requirement: Yes
Minimum TOEFL score: 570
Most popular departments: accounting, finance, general management, human resources management, marketing

University of Connecticut

2100 Hillside Road, Unit 1041
Storrs, CT 06269-1041
www.business.uconn.edu
Public
Admissions: (860) 486-2872
Email: uconnmba@
business.uconn.edu
Financial aid: (860) 486-2819
Application deadline: 04/01
In-state tuition: full time: $13,854;
part time: $750/credit hour
Out-of-state tuition: full time:
$33,326
Room/board/expenses: $25,250
College-funded aid: Yes
International student aid: Yes
**Average student indebtedness at
graduation:** $29,727
Full-time enrollment: 75
men: 69%; women: 31%;
minorities: 13%; international:
55%
Part-time enrollment: 889
men: 72%; women: 28%;
minorities: 17%; international: 1%
Acceptance rate (full time): 48%
Average GMAT (full time): 630
Average GMAT (part time): 550
Average GPA (full time): 3.49
**Average age of entrants to full-time
program:** 27
**Average months of prior work
experience (full time):** 55
TOEFL requirement: Yes
Minimum TOEFL score: 575
Most popular departments: finance,
general management, marketing,
management information
systems, operations management
**Mean starting base salary for 2014
full-time graduates:** $101,562
Employment location for 2014 class:
Intl. N/A; N.E. 87%; M.A. N/A; S.
6%; M.W. N/A; S.W. N/A; W. 6%

University of Hartford (Barney)[1]

200 Bloomfield Avenue
West Hartford, CT 06117
www.hartford.edu/barney
Private
Admissions: N/A
Financial aid: N/A
Tuition: N/A
Room/board/expenses: N/A
Enrollment: N/A

Yale University

165 Whitney Avenue
New Haven, CT 06511-3729
som.yale.edu
Private
Admissions: (203) 432-5635
Email: mba.admissions@yale.edu
Financial aid: (203) 432-5875
Application deadline: N/A
Tuition: full time: $60,775; part
time: N/A
Room/board/expenses: $25,100
College-funded aid: Yes
International student aid: Yes
Full-time enrollment: 625
men: 62%; women: 38%;
minorities: 24%; international:
36%
Part-time enrollment: N/A
men: N/A; women: N/A; minorities:
N/A; international: N/A
Acceptance rate (full time): 24%
Average GMAT (full time): 719
Average GPA (full time): 3.53
**Average age of entrants to full-time
program:** 28
**Average months of prior work
experience (full time):** 62
TOEFL requirement: No
Minimum TOEFL score: N/A

**Mean starting base salary for 2014
full-time graduates:** $109,872
Employment location for 2014 class:
Intl. 9%; N.E. 53%; M.A. 12%; S.
1%; M.W. 4%; S.W. 2%; W. 19%

DELAWARE

Delaware State University

1200 DuPont Highway
Dover, DE 19901
www.desu.edu/business-
administration-mba-program
Public
Admissions: (302) 857-6978
Email: dkim@desu.edu
Financial aid: (302) 857-6250
Application deadline: rolling
In-state tuition: full time: $417/
credit hour; part time: $417/
credit hour
Out-of-state tuition: full time: $920/
credit hour
Room/board/expenses: $18,472
College-funded aid: Yes
International student aid: No
Full-time enrollment: 52
men: 52%; women: 48%;
minorities: 54%; international:
38%
Part-time enrollment: 3
men: 33%; women: 67%;
minorities: 67%; international: 0%
Acceptance rate (full time): 57%
**Average age of entrants to full-time
program:** 32
TOEFL requirement: Yes
Minimum TOEFL score: 550

University of Delaware (Lerner)

103 Alfred Lerner Hall
Newark, DE 19716
www.mba.udel.edu
Public
Admissions: (302) 831-2221
Email: mbaprogram@udel.edu
Financial aid: (302) 831-8761
Application deadline: rolling
In-state tuition: full time: $14,292;
part time: $750/credit hour
Out-of-state tuition: full time:
$24,792
Room/board/expenses: $13,058
College-funded aid: Yes
International student aid: Yes
Full-time enrollment: 117
men: 57%; women: 43%;
minorities: 12%; international:
62%
Part-time enrollment: 231
men: 61%; women: 39%;
minorities: 32%; international: 4%
Acceptance rate (full time): 54%
Average GMAT (full time): 621
Average GMAT (part time): 623
Average GPA (full time): 3.30
**Average age of entrants to full-time
program:** 27
**Average months of prior work
experience (full time):** 42
TOEFL requirement: Yes
Minimum TOEFL score: 600
**Mean starting base salary for 2014
full-time graduates:** $81,125
Employment location for 2014 class:
Intl. N/A; N.E. N/A; M.A. 100%; S.
N/A; M.W. N/A; S.W. N/A; W. N/A

DISTRICT OF COLUMBIA

American University (Kogod)

4400 Massachusetts Avenue NW
Washington, DC 20016
www.kogod.american.edu
Private
Admissions: (202) 885-1913
Email: kogodgrad@american.edu
Financial aid: (202) 885-1907
Application deadline: rolling
Tuition: full time: $1,482/credit
hour; total program: $88,710
(part time)
Room/board/expenses: $20,000
College-funded aid: Yes
International student aid: Yes
Full-time enrollment: 87
men: 54%; women: 46%;
minorities: N/A; international: N/A
Part-time enrollment: 95
men: 45%; women: 55%;
minorities: N/A; international: N/A
Acceptance rate (full time): 70%
Average GMAT (full time): 580
Average GMAT (part time): 550
Average GPA (full time): 3.00
**Average age of entrants to full-time
program:** 27
**Average months of prior work
experience (full time):** 48
TOEFL requirement: Yes
Minimum TOEFL score: N/A
Most popular departments:
consulting, general management
**Mean starting base salary for 2014
full-time graduates:** $74,183
Employment location for 2014 class:
Intl. 0%; N.E. 5%; M.A. 84%; S.
N/A; M.W. 5%; S.W. N/A; W. 5%

Georgetown University (McDonough)

Rafik B. Hariri Building
37th and O Streets NW
Washington, DC 20057
msb.georgetown.edu
Private
Admissions: (202) 687-4200
Email: georgetownmba@
georgetown.edu
Financial aid: (202) 687-4547
Application deadline: N/A
Tuition: full time: $55,018; part
time: $1,618/credit hour
Room/board/expenses: $25,552
College-funded aid: Yes
International student aid: Yes
Full-time enrollment: 528
men: 69%; women: 31%;
minorities: 18%; international:
37%
Part-time enrollment: 385
men: 68%; women: 32%;
minorities: 19%; international: 5%
Acceptance rate (full time): 47%
Average GMAT (full time): 691
Average GMAT (part time): 669
Average GPA (full time): 3.34
**Average age of entrants to full-time
program:** 28
**Average months of prior work
experience (full time):** 57
TOEFL requirement: Yes
Minimum TOEFL score: 600
Most popular departments:
consulting, finance, general
management, international
business, marketing
**Mean starting base salary for 2014
full-time graduates:** $102,096
Employment location for 2014 class:
Intl. 5%; N.E. 32%; M.A. 41%; S.
5%; M.W. 7%; S.W. 5%; W. 4%

George Washington University

2201 G Street NW
Washington, DC 20052
business.gwu.edu/grad/mba/
Private
Admissions: (202) 994-1212
Email: gwmba@gwu.edu
Financial aid: (202) 994-6822
Application deadline: 05/04
Tuition: full time: $1,545/credit
hour; part time: $1,545/credit hour
Room/board/expenses: $23,500
College-funded aid: Yes
International student aid: Yes
**Average student indebtedness at
graduation:** $92,969
Full-time enrollment: 185
men: 59%; women: 41%;
minorities: 15%; international:
46%
Part-time enrollment: 336
men: 55%; women: 45%;
minorities: 32%; international: 6%
Acceptance rate (full time): 45%
Average GMAT (full time): 648
Average GMAT (part time): 598
Average GPA (full time): 3.24
**Average age of entrants to full-time
program:** 30
**Average months of prior work
experience (full time):** 61
TOEFL requirement: Yes
Minimum TOEFL score: 600
Most popular departments:
consulting, international business,
management information
systems, non-profit management,
public policy
**Mean starting base salary for 2014
full-time graduates:** $85,683
Employment location for 2014 class:
Intl. 11%; N.E. 14%; M.A. 55%; S.
2%; M.W. 2%; S.W. 4%; W. 13%

Howard University

2600 Sixth Street NW, Suite 236
Washington, DC 20059
www.bschool.howard.edu
Private
Admissions: (202) 806-1725
Email: MBA_bschool@howard.edu
Financial aid: (202) 806-2820
Application deadline: 04/01
Tuition: full time: $34,399; part
time: $1,840/credit hour
Room/board/expenses: $26,518
College-funded aid: Yes
International student aid: Yes
**Average student indebtedness at
graduation:** $51,924
Full-time enrollment: 57
men: 39%; women: 61%;
minorities: 82%; international:
18%
Part-time enrollment: 26
men: 38%; women: 62%;
minorities: 92%; international: 4%
Acceptance rate (full time): 54%
Average GMAT (full time): 496
Average GPA (full time): 3.35
**Average age of entrants to full-time
program:** 26
**Average months of prior work
experience (full time):** 44
TOEFL requirement: Yes
Minimum TOEFL score: 550
Most popular departments:
finance, general management,
international business, marketing,
supply chain management
**Mean starting base salary for 2014
full-time graduates:** $86,364
Employment location for 2014 class:
Intl. 0%; N.E. 25%; M.A. 46%; S.
0%; M.W. 25%; S.W. 4%; W. 0%

FLORIDA

Barry University

11300 N.E. Second Avenue
Miami Shores, FL 33161-6695
www.barry.edu/mba
Private
Admissions: (305) 899-3146
Email: dfletcher@mail.barry.edu
Financial aid: (305) 899-3673
Application deadline: rolling
Tuition: full time: $990/credit hour;
part time: $990/credit hour
Room/board/expenses: N/A
College-funded aid: Yes
International student aid: Yes
Full-time enrollment: N/A
men: N/A; women: N/A; minorities:
N/A; international: N/A
Part-time enrollment: 82
men: 52%; women: 48%;
minorities: 38%; international:
35%
Average GMAT (part time): 526
TOEFL requirement: Yes
Minimum TOEFL score: 550
Most popular departments:
accounting, finance, general
management, international
business, marketing
**Mean starting base salary for 2014
full-time graduates:** $45,300
Employment location for 2014 class:
Intl. N/A; N.E. N/A; M.A. N/A; S.
100%; M.W. N/A; S.W. N/A; W. N/A

Florida Atlantic University

777 Glades Road
Boca Raton, FL 33431
www.business.fau.edu
Public
Admissions: (561) 297-3624
Email: graduatecollege@fau.edu
Financial aid: (561) 297-3131
Application deadline: rolling
In-state tuition: full time: $304/
credit hour; part time: $304/
credit hour
Out-of-state tuition: full time: $928/
credit hour
Room/board/expenses: $17,044
College-funded aid: Yes
International student aid: Yes
Full-time enrollment: 237
men: 63%; women: 37%;
minorities: 35%; international: 7%
Part-time enrollment: 359
men: 55%; women: 45%;
minorities: 36%; international: 3%
Average GMAT (part time): 535
TOEFL requirement: Yes
Minimum TOEFL score: 600
Most popular departments:
accounting, general management,
health care administration,
international business, tax

Florida Gulf Coast University (Lutgert)

10501 FGCU Boulevard S
Fort Myers, FL 33965-6565
www.fgcu.edu/cob/
Public
Admissions: (239) 590-7988
Email: graduate@fgcu.edu
Financial aid: (239) 590-7920
Application deadline: 06/01
In-state tuition: full time: $8,919;
part time: N/A
Out-of-state tuition: full time:
$30,157
Room/board/expenses: $11,259
College-funded aid: Yes
International student aid: Yes
**Average student indebtedness at
graduation:** $24,381

Full-time enrollment: 29
men: 62%; women: 38%;
minorities: 14%; international: 10%
Part-time enrollment: 97
men: 42%; women: 58%;
minorities: 10%; international: 1%
Average GMAT (full time): 555
Average GMAT (part time): 508
Average GPA (full time): 3.17
Average age of entrants to full-time program: 26
TOEFL requirement: Yes
Minimum TOEFL score: 550
Most popular departments:
accounting, general management

Florida International University
1050 S.W. 112 Avenue, CBC 300
Miami, FL 33199-0001
business.fiu.edu
Public
Admissions: (305) 348-7398
Email: chapman@fiu.edu
Financial aid: (305) 348-7272
Application deadline: 06/03
In-state tuition: total program:
$35,000 (full time); $46,000
(part time)
Out-of-state tuition: total program:
$40,000 (full time)
Room/board/expenses: $18,000
College-funded aid: Yes
International student aid: Yes
Full-time enrollment: 53
men: 62%; women: 38%;
minorities: 45%; international:
43%
Part-time enrollment: 504
men: 41%; women: 59%;
minorities: 82%; international: 4%
Acceptance rate (full time): 34%
Average GMAT (full time): 569
Average GPA (full time): 3.38
Average age of entrants to full-time program: 24
Average months of prior work experience (full time): 35
TOEFL requirement: Yes
Minimum TOEFL score: 550
Most popular departments: finance,
general management, health care
administration, human resources
management, international
business
**Mean starting base salary for 2014
full-time graduates:** $45,000
Employment location for 2014 class:
Intl. 33%; N.E. N/A; M.A. N/A; S.
67%; M.W. N/A; S.W. N/A; W. N/A

Florida Southern College[1]
111 Lake Hollingsworth Drive
Lakeland, FL 33801
www.flsouthern.edu/
Private
Admissions: N/A
Financial aid: N/A
Tuition: N/A
Room/board/expenses: N/A
Enrollment: N/A

Florida State University
Graduate Programs
233 Rovetta Building
Tallahassee, FL 32306-1110
graduatebusiness.fsu.edu
Public
Admissions: (850) 644-1147
Email: graduateprograms@
business.fsu.edu
Financial aid: (850) 644-5716
Application deadline: 06/01
In-state tuition: full time: $480/
credit hour; part time: $480/
credit hour

Out-of-state tuition: full time:
$1,110/credit hour
Room/board/expenses: $52,500
College-funded aid: Yes
International student aid: Yes
Average student indebtedness at graduation: $11,966
Full-time enrollment: 32
men: 69%; women: 31%;
minorities: 19%; international: 0%
Part-time enrollment: 54
men: 70%; women: 30%;
minorities: 13%; international: 0%
Acceptance rate (full time): 56%
Average GMAT (full time): 572
Average GMAT (part time): 571
Average GPA (full time): 3.22
Average age of entrants to full-time program: 23
Average months of prior work experience (full time): 51
TOEFL requirement: Yes
Minimum TOEFL score: 550
Most popular departments:
accounting, finance, general
management, insurance,
marketing
**Mean starting base salary for 2014
full-time graduates:** $57,250
Employment location for 2014 class:
Intl. N/A; N.E. N/A; M.A. N/A; S.
100%; M.W. N/A; S.W. N/A; W. N/A

Jacksonville University
2800 University Blvd N
Jacksonville, FL 32211
www.ju.edu
Private
Admissions: (904) 256-7426
Email: mba@ju.edu
Financial aid: (904) 256-7956
Application deadline: 08/01
Tuition: full time: $695/credit hour;
part time: $695/credit hour
Room/board/expenses: $12,000
College-funded aid: Yes
International student aid: Yes
Average student indebtedness at graduation: $18,092
Full-time enrollment: 45
men: 53%; women: 47%;
minorities: 9%; international: 38%
Part-time enrollment: 156
men: 53%; women: 47%;
minorities: 29%; international: 3%
Acceptance rate (full time): 63%
Average GMAT (full time): 474
Average GMAT (part time): 407
Average GPA (full time): 3.23
Average age of entrants to full-time program: 23
Average months of prior work experience (full time): 64
TOEFL requirement: Yes
Minimum TOEFL score: 540
Most popular departments:
accounting, finance, general
management, leadership
**Mean starting base salary for 2014
full-time graduates:** $43,375
Employment location for 2014 class:
Intl. N/A; N.E. 13%; M.A. N/A; S.
88%; M.W. N/A; S.W. N/A; W. N/A

Rollins College (Crummer)[1]
1000 Holt Avenue
Winter Park, FL 32789-4499
www.rollins.edu/business/
Private
Admissions: N/A
Financial aid: N/A
Tuition: N/A
Room/board/expenses: N/A
Enrollment: N/A

Stetson University
421 N. Woodland Boulevard,
Unit 8398
DeLand, FL 32723
www.stetson.edu/mba
Private
Admissions: (386) 822-7100
Email:
gradadmissions@stetson.edu
Financial aid: (800) 688-7120
Application deadline: rolling
Tuition: full time: $886/credit hour;
part time: $886/credit hour
Room/board/expenses: N/A
College-funded aid: Yes
International student aid: Yes
Average student indebtedness at graduation: $28,865
Full-time enrollment: 102
men: 59%; women: 41%;
minorities: 22%; international: 7%
Part-time enrollment: 42
men: 43%; women: 57%;
minorities: 10%; international: 2%
Acceptance rate (full time): 69%
Average GMAT (full time): 544
Average GPA (full time): 3.38
Average age of entrants to full-time program: 31
TOEFL requirement: Yes
Minimum TOEFL score: 550

University of Central Florida
PO Box 161400
Orlando, FL 32816-1400
www.ucfmba.ucf.edu
Public
Admissions: (407) 823-4723
Email: graduate@mail.ucf.edu
Financial aid: (407) 823-2827
Application deadline: 07/15
In-state tuition: full time: N/A; part
time: $4,435
Out-of-state tuition: full time: N/A
Room/board/expenses: N/A
College-funded aid: Yes
International student aid: Yes
Average student indebtedness at graduation: $21,348
Full-time enrollment: N/A
men: N/A; women: N/A; minorities:
N/A; international: N/A
Part-time enrollment: 252
men: 58%; women: 42%;
minorities: 29%; international: 2%
TOEFL requirement: Yes
Minimum TOEFL score: 575
Most popular departments:
accounting, entrepreneurship,
finance, general management

University of Florida (Hough)
Hough Hall 310
Gainesville, FL 32611-7152
www.floridamba.ufl.edu
Public
Admissions: (352) 392-7992
Email: traditionalmba@
warrington.ufl.edu
Financial aid: (352) 392-1275
Application deadline: 07/01
In-state tuition: full time: $12,682;
part time: $23,096
Out-of-state tuition: full time:
$30,075
Room/board/expenses: $15,610
College-funded aid: Yes
International student aid: Yes
Average student indebtedness at graduation: $34,820
Full-time enrollment: 117
men: 70%; women: 30%;
minorities: 10%; international: 17%
Part-time enrollment: 377
men: 68%; women: 32%;
minorities: 25%; international: 11%

Acceptance rate (full time): 24%
Average GMAT (full time): 687
Average GMAT (part time): 601
Average GPA (full time): 3.50
Average age of entrants to full-time program: 26
Average months of prior work experience (full time): 53
TOEFL requirement: Yes
Minimum TOEFL score: 550
Most popular departments:
consulting, finance, marketing,
real estate, supply chain
management
**Mean starting base salary for 2014
full-time graduates:** $87,445
Employment location for 2014 class:
Intl. 4%; N.E. 6%; M.A. 2%; S.
66%; M.W. 14%; S.W. 8%; W. 0%

University of Miami
PO Box 248027
Coral Gables, FL 33124-6520
www.bus.miami.edu/grad
Private
Admissions: (305) 284-2510
Email: mba@miami.edu
Financial aid: (305) 284-5212
Application deadline: 05/01
Tuition: full time: $1,790/credit
hour; part time: N/A
Room/board/expenses: $20,946
College-funded aid: Yes
International student aid: Yes
Average student indebtedness at graduation: $73,169
Full-time enrollment: 187
men: 67%; women: 33%;
minorities: 38%; international:
24%
Part-time enrollment: N/A
men: N/A; women: N/A; minorities:
N/A; international: N/A
Acceptance rate (full time): 28%
Average GMAT (full time): 621
Average GPA (full time): 3.25
Average age of entrants to full-time program: 26
Average months of prior work experience (full time): 38
TOEFL requirement: Yes
Minimum TOEFL score: 587
Most popular departments:
finance, general management,
marketing, management
information systems, statistics
and operations research
**Mean starting base salary for 2014
full-time graduates:** $71,674
Employment location for 2014 class:
Intl. 0%; N.E. 10%; M.A. 2%; S.
86%; M.W. 0%; S.W. 2%; W. 0%

University of North Florida (Coggin)
1 UNF Drive
Jacksonville, FL 32224-2645
www.unf.edu/coggin
Public
Admissions: (904) 620-1360
Email: i.reigger@unf.edu
Financial aid: (904) 620-5555
Application deadline: 08/01
In-state tuition: full time: $11,841;
part time: $493/credit hour
Out-of-state tuition: full time:
$25,059
Room/board/expenses: $19,989
College-funded aid: Yes
International student aid: Yes
Average student indebtedness at graduation: $28,899
Full-time enrollment: 97
men: 61%; women: 39%;
minorities: 23%; international:
27%
Part-time enrollment: 188
men: 63%; women: 37%;
minorities: 14%; international: 2%

Average GMAT (part time): 588
TOEFL requirement: Yes
Minimum TOEFL score: 550

University of South Florida
4202 Fowler Avenue BSN 3404
Tampa, FL 33620
www.mba.usf.edu
Public
Admissions: (813) 974-3335
Email: bsn-mba@usf.edu
Financial aid: (813) 974-4700
Application deadline: 07/01
In-state tuition: full time: $467/
credit hour; part time: $467/
credit hour
Out-of-state tuition: full time: $913/
credit hour
Room/board/expenses: $17,000
College-funded aid: Yes
International student aid: Yes
Full-time enrollment: 53
men: 57%; women: 43%;
minorities: 13%; international: 6%
Part-time enrollment: 778
men: 63%; women: 37%;
minorities: 19%; international:
43%
Acceptance rate (full time): 84%
Average GMAT (full time): 531
Average GMAT (part time): 553
Average GPA (full time): 3.45
Average age of entrants to full-time program: 23
Average months of prior work experience (full time): 11
TOEFL requirement: Yes
Minimum TOEFL score: 550
Most popular departments:
entrepreneurship, finance,
marketing, management
information systems, other
**Mean starting base salary for 2014
full-time graduates:** $50,742
Employment location for 2014 class:
Intl. N/A; N.E. N/A; M.A. N/A; S.
100%; M.W. N/A; S.W. N/A; W. N/A

University of South Florida-Sarasota-Manatee
8350 N. Tamiami Trail
Sarasota, FL 34243
usfsm.edu/college-of-business
Public
Admissions: N/A
Financial aid: N/A
Application deadline: 07/01
In-state tuition: full time: $380/
credit hour; part time: $380/
credit hour
Out-of-state tuition: full time: $826/
credit hour
Room/board/expenses: $14,500
College-funded aid: Yes
International student aid: Yes
Average student indebtedness at graduation: $43,085
Full-time enrollment: 5
men: 60%; women: 40%;
minorities: 40%; international: 0%
Part-time enrollment: 20
men: 50%; women: 50%;
minorities: 25%; international: 0%
Average GMAT (part time): 535
TOEFL requirement: Yes
Minimum TOEFL score: 550
**Mean starting base salary for 2014
full-time graduates:** $59,166
Employment location for 2014 class:
Intl. N/A; N.E. N/A; M.A. N/A; S.
100%; M.W. N/A; S.W. N/A; W. N/A

University of South Florida-St. Petersburg

140 7th Ave S, BAY III
St. Petersburg, FL 33701
www.usfsp.edu/mba
Public
Admissions: (727) 873-4622
Email: mba@usfsp.edu
Financial aid: (727) 873-4128
Application deadline: 07/01
In-state tuition: full time: $462/credit hour; part time: $462/credit hour
Out-of-state tuition: full time: $907/credit hour
Room/board/expenses: N/A
College-funded aid: Yes
International student aid: Yes
Full-time enrollment: N/A
men: N/A; women: N/A; minorities: N/A; international: N/A
Part-time enrollment: 276
men: 51%; women: 49%;
minorities: 26%; international: 3%
Average GMAT (part time): 547
TOEFL requirement: Yes
Minimum TOEFL score: 550
Most popular departments: accounting, finance, general management, international business, management information systems

University of Tampa (Sykes)

401 W. Kennedy Boulevard
Tampa, FL 33606-1490
grad.ut.edu
Private
Admissions: (813) 257-3642
Email: utgrad@ut.edu
Financial aid: (813) 253-6219
Application deadline: rolling
Tuition: full time: $558/credit hour; part time: $558/credit hour
Room/board/expenses: $19,143
College-funded aid: Yes
International student aid: Yes
Average student indebtedness at graduation: $34,574
Full-time enrollment: 419
men: 56%; women: 44%;
minorities: 11%; international: 50%
Part-time enrollment: 140
men: 59%; women: 41%;
minorities: 17%; international: 1%
Acceptance rate (full time): 27%
Average GMAT (full time): 540
Average GMAT (part time): 560
Average GPA (full time): 3.50
Average age of entrants to full-time program: 26
Average months of prior work experience (full time): 67
TOEFL requirement: Yes
Minimum TOEFL score: 577
Mean starting base salary for 2014 full-time graduates: $54,250
Employment location for 2014 class: Intl. 18%; N.E. 18%; M.A. 10%; S. 44%; M.W. 10%; S.W. 0%; W. 0%

University of West Florida[1]

11000 University Parkway
Pensacola, FL 32514
uwf.edu
Public
Admissions: (850) 474-2230
Email: mba@uwf.edu
Financial aid: N/A
Tuition: N/A
Room/board/expenses: N/A
Enrollment: N/A

GEORGIA

Berry College (Campbell)

PO Box 495024
Mount Berry, GA 30149-5024
www.berry.edu/academics/campbell/
Private
Admissions: (706) 236-2215
Email: admissions@berry.edu
Financial aid: (706) 236-1714
Application deadline: 07/01
Tuition: full time: $550/credit hour; part time: $550/credit hour
Room/board/expenses: N/A
College-funded aid: Yes
International student aid: Yes
Full-time enrollment: 1
men: N/A; women: 100%;
minorities: N/A; international: N/A
Part-time enrollment: 22
men: 32%; women: 68%;
minorities: N/A; international: N/A
Acceptance rate (full time): 33%
Average GMAT (part time): 460
Average GPA (full time): 3.76
Average age of entrants to full-time program: 22
Average months of prior work experience (full time): 12
TOEFL requirement: Yes
Minimum TOEFL score: 550

Clark Atlanta University

223 James P. Brawley Drive SW
Atlanta, GA 30314
www.cau.edu
Private
Admissions: (404) 880-8443
Email: pkamos@cau.edu
Financial aid: (404) 880-6265
Application deadline: rolling
Tuition: full time: $828/credit hour; part time: $828/credit hour
Room/board/expenses: $18,098
College-funded aid: Yes
International student aid: Yes
Full-time enrollment: 69
men: 52%; women: 48%;
minorities: 54%; international: 22%
Part-time enrollment: 9
men: 44%; women: 56%;
minorities: 89%; international: 0%
Acceptance rate (full time): 65%
Average GMAT (full time): 297
Average GMAT (part time): 245
Average GPA (full time): 2.90
Average age of entrants to full-time program: 27
Average months of prior work experience (full time): 18
TOEFL requirement: Yes
Minimum TOEFL score: 500
Mean starting base salary for 2014 full-time graduates: $67,000
Employment location for 2014 class: Intl. N/A; N.E. N/A; M.A. 8%; S. 8%; M.W. 75%; S.W. N/A; W. 8%

Clayton State University[1]

2000 Clayton State Boulevard
Morrow , GA 30260-0285
www.clayton.edu/mba
Public
Admissions: (678) 466-4113
Email: graduate@clayton.edu
Financial aid: N/A
Tuition: N/A
Room/board/expenses: N/A
Enrollment: N/A

Columbus State University (Turner)

4225 University Avenue
Columbus, GA 31907
cobcs.columbusstate.edu
Public
Admissions: (706) 507-8800
Email: lovell_susan@columbusstate.edu
Financial aid: N/A
Application deadline: 06/30
In-state tuition: full time: $245/credit hour; part time: $245/credit hour
Out-of-state tuition: full time: $981/credit hour
Room/board/expenses: N/A
College-funded aid: Yes
International student aid: Yes
Full-time enrollment: 13
men: 69%; women: 31%;
minorities: 15%; international: 15%
Part-time enrollment: 37
men: 43%; women: 57%;
minorities: 26%; international: 3%
Average GMAT (part time): 482
Average GPA (full time): 2.90
TOEFL requirement: Yes
Minimum TOEFL score: 550

Emory University (Goizueta)

1300 Clifton Road NE
Atlanta, GA 30322
www.goizueta.emory.edu
Private
Admissions: (404) 727-6311
Email: mbaadmissions@emory.edu
Financial aid: (404) 727-6039
Application deadline: 03/13
Tuition: full time: $48,634; total program: $73,600 (part time)
Room/board/expenses: $24,416
College-funded aid: Yes
International student aid: Yes
Average student indebtedness at graduation: $72,899
Full-time enrollment: 384
men: 73%; women: 27%;
minorities: 19%; international: 39%
Part-time enrollment: 263
men: 70%; women: 30%;
minorities: 29%; international: 10%
Acceptance rate (full time): 31%
Average GMAT (full time): 678
Average GMAT (part time): 631
Average GPA (full time): 3.30
Average age of entrants to full-time program: 29
Average months of prior work experience (full time): 65
TOEFL requirement: Yes
Minimum TOEFL score: 600
Most popular departments: consulting, finance, general management, marketing, organizational behavior
Mean starting base salary for 2014 full-time graduates: $107,220

Georgia College & State University (Bunting)

Campus Box 019
Milledgeville, GA 31061
mba.gcsu.edu
Public
Admissions: (478) 445-6283
Email: grad-admit@gcsu.edu
Financial aid: (478) 445-5149
Application deadline: 07/01
In-state tuition: full time: $283/credit hour; part time: $283/credit hour

Out-of-state tuition: full time: $1,027/credit hour
Room/board/expenses: $14,520
College-funded aid: Yes
International student aid: Yes
Average student indebtedness at graduation: $13,733
Full-time enrollment: 60
men: 58%; women: 42%;
minorities: 15%; international: 12%
Part-time enrollment: 185
men: 58%; women: 42%;
minorities: 29%; international: 6%
Acceptance rate (full time): 60%
Average GMAT (full time): 530
Average GMAT (part time): 552
Average GPA (full time): 3.38
Average age of entrants to full-time program: 23
TOEFL requirement: Yes
Minimum TOEFL score: 550
Most popular departments: management information systems

Georgia Institute of Technology (Scheller)

800 W. Peachtree Street NW
Atlanta, GA 30332-0520
scheller.gatech.edu
Public
Admissions: (404) 894-8722
Email: mba@scheller.gatech.edu
Financial aid: (404) 894-4160
Application deadline: 05/15
In-state tuition: full time: $29,878; part time: $1,045/credit hour
Out-of-state tuition: full time: $40,744
Room/board/expenses: $15,760
College-funded aid: Yes
International student aid: Yes
Average student indebtedness at graduation: $49,332
Full-time enrollment: 127
men: 28%; women: 72%;
minorities: 13%; international: 28%
Part-time enrollment: 369
men: 25%; women: 75%;
minorities: 28%; international: 7%
Acceptance rate (full time): 23%
Average GMAT (full time): 676
Average GMAT (part time): 623
Average GPA (full time): 3.31
Average age of entrants to full-time program: 29
Average months of prior work experience (full time): 65
TOEFL requirement: Yes
Minimum TOEFL score: 600
Most popular departments: consulting, entrepreneurship, finance, management information systems, supply chain management
Mean starting base salary for 2014 full-time graduates: $105,029
Employment location for 2014 class: Intl. 0%; N.E. 3%; M.A. 2%; S. 73%; M.W. 3%; S.W. 3%; W. 16%

Georgia Regents University[1]

1120 15th Street
Augusta, GA 30912
www.gru.edu/hull/grad/mba.php
Public
Admissions: (706) 737-1418
Email: hull@gru.edu
Financial aid: N/A
Tuition: N/A
Room/board/expenses: N/A
Enrollment: N/A

Georgia Southern University

PO Box 8002
Statesboro, GA 30460-8050
coba.georgiasouthern.edu/mba
Public
Admissions: (912) 478-2357
Email: mba@georgiasouthern.edu
Financial aid: (912) 478-5413
Application deadline: 08/01
In-state tuition: full time: $11,916; part time: $410/credit hour
Out-of-state tuition: full time: $31,804
Room/board/expenses: $16,608
College-funded aid: Yes
International student aid: Yes
Full-time enrollment: N/A
men: N/A; women: N/A; minorities: N/A; international: N/A
Part-time enrollment: 108
men: 48%; women: 52%;
minorities: 33%; international: 6%
Average GMAT (part time): 487
TOEFL requirement: Yes
Minimum TOEFL score: 550

Georgia Southwestern State University[1]

800 Georgia Southwestern State University Drive
Americus, GA 31709
gsw.edu/
Public
Admissions: N/A
Financial aid: N/A
Tuition: N/A
Room/board/expenses: N/A
Enrollment: N/A

Georgia State University (Robinson)

PO Box 3989
Atlanta, GA 30302-3989
robinson.gsu.edu/
Public
Admissions: (404) 413-7167
Email: rcbgradadmissions@gsu.edu
Financial aid: (404) 413-2400
Application deadline: 05/01
In-state tuition: total program: $72,000 (full time); part time: $463/credit hour
Out-of-state tuition: total program: $72,000 (full time)
Room/board/expenses: N/A
College-funded aid: Yes
International student aid: Yes
Full-time enrollment: 35
men: 40%; women: 60%;
minorities: 60%; international: 17%
Part-time enrollment: 628
men: 55%; women: 45%;
minorities: 37%; international: 8%
Acceptance rate (full time): 91%
Average GMAT (part time): 615
Average age of entrants to full-time program: 31
Average months of prior work experience (full time): 68
TOEFL requirement: Yes
Minimum TOEFL score: 610
Most popular departments: finance, general management, health care administration, marketing, organizational behavior

Kennesaw State University (Coles)

MD 3306
Kennesaw, GA 30144-5591
www.kennesaw.edu/graduate/admissions
Public
Admissions: (470) 578-4377

Email: ksugrad@kennesaw.edu
Financial aid: (470) 578-6525
Application deadline: 07/01
In-state tuition: full time: N/A; part time: $329/credit hour
Out-of-state tuition: full time: N/A
Room/board/expenses: N/A
College-funded aid: Yes
International student aid: Yes
Full-time enrollment: 190
men: N/A; women: N/A; minorities: N/A; international: N/A
Part-time enrollment: 190
men: 55%; women: 45%; minorities: 24%; international: 4%
Average GMAT (part time): 567
TOEFL requirement: Yes
Minimum TOEFL score: 550
Most popular departments: economics, finance, general management, marketing, operations management

Mercer University-Atlanta (Stetson)

3001 Mercer University Drive
Atlanta, GA 30341-4155
business.mercer.edu
Private
Admissions: (678) 547-6194
Email: atlbusadm@mercer.edu
Financial aid: (678) 547-6444
Application deadline: rolling
Tuition: full time: $699/credit hour; part time: $699/credit hour
Room/board/expenses: N/A
College-funded aid: No
International student aid: No
Average student indebtedness at graduation: $17,255
Full-time enrollment: 28
men: 57%; women: 43%; minorities: 57%; international: 32%
Part-time enrollment: 324
men: 47%; women: 53%; minorities: 54%; international: 18%
Acceptance rate (full time): 74%
Average GMAT (full time): 499
Average GMAT (part time): 525
Average GPA (full time): 3.19
Average age of entrants to full-time program: 25
Average months of prior work experience (full time): 35
TOEFL requirement: Yes
Minimum TOEFL score: 550
Most popular departments: accounting, economics, finance, health care administration, marketing
Employment location for 2014 class: Intl. N/A; N.E. N/A; M.A. N/A; S. 100%; M.W. N/A; S.W. N/A; W. N/A

Savannah State University

PO Box 20359
Savannah, GA 31404
www.savannahstate.edu/coba/programs-mba.shtml
Public
Admissions: (912) 358-3406
Email: mba@savannahstate.edu
Financial aid: (912) 358-4162
Application deadline: rolling
In-state tuition: full time: N/A; part time: $10,155
Out-of-state tuition: full time: N/A
Room/board/expenses: N/A
College-funded aid: Yes
Full-time enrollment: N/A
men: N/A; women: N/A; minorities: N/A; international: N/A
Part-time enrollment: 40
men: N/A; women: N/A; minorities: N/A; international: N/A

TOEFL requirement: Yes
Minimum TOEFL score: 523

University of Georgia (Terry)

335 Brooks Hall
Athens, GA 30602-6251
mba.terry.uga.edu
Public
Admissions: (706) 542-5671
Email: terrymba@uga.edu
Financial aid: (706) 542-6147
Application deadline: 03/03
In-state tuition: full time: $15,034; total program: $53,400 (part time)
Out-of-state tuition: full time: $33,054
Room/board/expenses: $22,942
College-funded aid: Yes
International student aid: Yes
Average student indebtedness at graduation: $43,043
Full-time enrollment: 95
men: 75%; women: 25%; minorities: 17%; international: 25%
Part-time enrollment: 244
men: 59%; women: 41%; minorities: 33%; international: 5%
Acceptance rate (full time): 34%
Average GMAT (full time): 646
Average GMAT (part time): 530
Average GPA (full time): 3.32
Average age of entrants to full-time program: 28
Average months of prior work experience (full time): 47
TOEFL requirement: Yes
Minimum TOEFL score: N/A
Most popular departments: entrepreneurship, finance, marketing, statistics and operations research, other
Mean starting base salary for 2014 full-time graduates: $84,385
Employment location for 2014 class: Intl. 0%; N.E. 7%; M.A. 3%; S. 72%; M.W. 7%; S.W. 3%; W. 7%

University of North Georgia

82 College Circle
Dahlonega, GA 30597
ung.edu/master-business-administration/
Public
Admissions: (770) 205-5448
Email: mhjordan@northgeorgia.edu
Financial aid: (706) 864-1412
Application deadline: 05/31
In-state tuition: full time: N/A; part time: $509/credit hour
Out-of-state tuition: full time: N/A
Room/board/expenses: N/A
College-funded aid: Yes
International student aid: No
Full-time enrollment: N/A
men: N/A; women: N/A; minorities: N/A; international: N/A
Part-time enrollment: 27
men: 52%; women: 48%; minorities: 19%; international: 0%
Average GMAT (part time): 507
TOEFL requirement: Yes
Minimum TOEFL score: 550

University of West Georgia (Richards)

1601 Maple Street
Carrollton, GA 30118-3000
www.westga.edu/business
Public
Admissions: (678) 839-5355
Email: hudombon@westga.edu
Financial aid: (678) 839-6421

Application deadline: 07/15
In-state tuition: full time: $8,340; part time: $270/credit hour
Out-of-state tuition: full time: $27,122
Room/board/expenses: $11,832
College-funded aid: Yes
International student aid: Yes
Average student indebtedness at graduation: $24,781
Full-time enrollment: 25
men: 28%; women: 72%; minorities: 24%; international: 20%
Part-time enrollment: 112
men: 54%; women: 46%; minorities: 32%; international: 6%
Acceptance rate (full time): 54%
Average GMAT (part time): 416
Average GPA (full time): 3.42
Average age of entrants to full-time program: 28
TOEFL requirement: Yes
Minimum TOEFL score: 550
Most popular departments: accounting, finance, international business

Valdosta State University (Langdale)

1500 N. Patterson Street
Valdosta, GA 31698
www.valdosta.edu/lcoba/grad/
Public
Admissions: (229) 245-3822
Email: mschnake@valdosta.edu
Financial aid: (229) 333-5935
Application deadline: 07/15
In-state tuition: full time: $236/credit hour; part time: $236/credit hour
Out-of-state tuition: full time: $850/credit hour
Room/board/expenses: N/A
College-funded aid: Yes
International student aid: Yes
Full-time enrollment: N/A
men: N/A; women: N/A; minorities: N/A; international: N/A
Part-time enrollment: 38
men: 50%; women: 50%; minorities: 18%; international: 13%
Average GMAT (part time): 473
TOEFL requirement: Yes
Minimum TOEFL score: 523

HAWAII

University of Hawaii-Manoa (Shidler)

2404 Maile Way
Business Administration C-204
Honolulu, HI 96822
www.shidler.hawaii.edu
Public
Admissions: (808) 956-8266
Email: mba@hawaii.edu
Financial aid: (808) 956-7251
Application deadline: rolling
In-state tuition: full time: $20,048; part time: $802/credit hour
Out-of-state tuition: full time: $34,400
Room/board/expenses: $18,000
College-funded aid: Yes
International student aid: Yes
Full-time enrollment: 48
men: 58%; women: 42%; minorities: 71%; international: 23%
Part-time enrollment: 120
men: 54%; women: 46%; minorities: 72%; international: 0%
Acceptance rate (full time): 82%
Average GMAT (full time): 600
Average GMAT (part time): 520
Average GPA (full time): 3.20
Average age of entrants to full-time program: 29
Average months of prior work experience (full time): 63

TOEFL requirement: Yes
Minimum TOEFL score: 600
Most popular departments: accounting, entrepreneurship, finance, international business, marketing

IDAHO

Boise State University

1910 University Drive, MBEB4101
Boise, ID 83725-1600
cobe.boisestate.edu/graduate
Public
Admissions: (208) 426-3116
Email: graduatebusiness@boisestate.edu
Financial aid: (208) 426-1664
Application deadline: rolling
In-state tuition: full time: $7,824; part time: $331/credit hour
Out-of-state tuition: full time: $12,852
Room/board/expenses: $30,876
College-funded aid: Yes
International student aid: Yes
Full-time enrollment: 71
men: 58%; women: 42%; minorities: N/A; international: N/A
Part-time enrollment: 54
men: 65%; women: 35%; minorities: N/A; international: N/A
Acceptance rate (full time): 62%
Average GMAT (full time): 572
Average GMAT (part time): 583
Average GPA (full time): 3.52
Average age of entrants to full-time program: 27
Average months of prior work experience (full time): 23
TOEFL requirement: Yes
Minimum TOEFL score: 587

Idaho State University[1]

921 S. 8th Ave Stop 8020
Pocatello, ID 83209
www.isu.edu/cob/mba.shtml
Public
Admissions: (208) 282-2966
Email: mba@isu.edu
Financial aid: N/A
Tuition: N/A
Room/board/expenses: N/A
Enrollment: N/A

University of Idaho[1]

PO Box 443161
Moscow, ID 83844-3161
www.uidaho.edu
Public
Admissions: (800) 885-4001
Email: graduateadmissions@uidaho.edu
Financial aid: N/A
Tuition: N/A
Room/board/expenses: N/A
Enrollment: N/A

ILLINOIS

Bradley University (Foster)

1501 W. Bradley Avenue
Peoria, IL 61625
www.bradley.edu/mba
Private
Admissions: (309) 677-3714
Email: mba@bradley.edu
Financial aid: (309) 677-3089
Application deadline: rolling
Tuition: full time: N/A; part time: $810/credit hour
Room/board/expenses: N/A
College-funded aid: Yes
International student aid: Yes
Full-time enrollment: N/A
men: N/A; women: N/A; minorities: N/A; international: N/A

Part-time enrollment: 17
men: 76%; women: 24%; minorities: 18%; international: 12%
Average GMAT (part time): 564
TOEFL requirement: Yes
Minimum TOEFL score: 550

DePaul University (Kellstadt)

1 E. Jackson Boulevard
Chicago, IL 60604-2287
www.kellstadt.depaul.edu/
Private
Admissions: (312) 362-8810
Email: kgsb@depaul.edu
Financial aid: (312) 362-8091
Application deadline: 08/01
Tuition: full time: $980/credit hour; part time: $980/credit hour
Room/board/expenses: $15,000
College-funded aid: Yes
International student aid: Yes
Average student indebtedness at graduation: $65,274
Full-time enrollment: 68
men: 59%; women: 41%; minorities: 13%; international: 22%
Part-time enrollment: 887
men: 64%; women: 36%; minorities: 20%; international: 4%
Acceptance rate (full time): 46%
Average GMAT (full time): 622
Average GMAT (part time): 577
Average GPA (full time): 3.19
Average age of entrants to full-time program: 26
Average months of prior work experience (full time): 54
TOEFL requirement: Yes
Minimum TOEFL score: 550
Most popular departments: entrepreneurship, finance, general management, leadership, marketing
Mean starting base salary for 2014 full-time graduates: $65,473
Employment location for 2014 class: Intl. 0%; N.E. 0%; M.A. 0%; S. 0%; M.W. 95%; S.W. 0%; W. 5%

Dominican University (Brennan)[1]

7900 West Division St.
River Forest, IL 60305
business.dom.edu/
Private
Admissions: N/A
Financial aid: N/A
Tuition: N/A
Room/board/expenses: N/A
Enrollment: N/A

Eastern Illinois University (Lumpkin)[1]

600 Lincoln Avenue
Charleston, IL 61920-3099
www.eiu.edu/mba
Public
Admissions: (217) 581-3028
Email: mba@eiu.edu
Financial aid: N/A
Tuition: N/A
Room/board/expenses: N/A
Enrollment: N/A

Illinois Institute of Technology (Stuart)

10 W. 35th St.
Chicago, IL 60616
www.stuart.iit.edu
Private
Admissions: (312) 567-3020
Email: admission@stuart.iit.edu
Financial aid: (312) 567-7219
Application deadline: 04/15

Tuition: full time: $1,675/credit hour; part time: $1,675/credit hour
Room/board/expenses: $18,570
College-funded aid: Yes
International student aid: Yes
Average student indebtedness at graduation: $54,670
Full-time enrollment: 70
men: 53%; women: 47%; minorities: 3%; international: 90%
Part-time enrollment: 24
men: 63%; women: 38%; minorities: 29%; international: 17%
Acceptance rate (full time): 60%
Average GMAT (full time): 540
Average GPA (full time): 3.25
Average age of entrants to full-time program: 25
Average months of prior work experience (full time): 34
TOEFL requirement: Yes
Minimum TOEFL score: 600
Most popular departments: entrepreneurship, finance, marketing, statistics and operations research, technology
Mean starting base salary for 2014 full-time graduates: $36,250
Employment location for 2014 class: Intl. 25%; N.E. N/A; M.A. N/A; S. N/A; M.W. 75%; S.W. N/A; W. N/A

Illinois State University

MBA Program
Campus Box 5570
Normal, IL 61790-5570
www.mba.ilstu.edu/
Public
Admissions: (309) 438-8388
Email: isumba@exchange.cob.ilstu.edu
Financial aid: (309) 438-2231
Application deadline: 07/01
In-state tuition: full time: N/A; part time: N/A
Out-of-state tuition: full time: N/A
Room/board/expenses: N/A
College-funded aid: Yes
International student aid: Yes
Full-time enrollment: 64
men: 63%; women: 38%; minorities: 16%; international: 30%
Part-time enrollment: 78
men: 62%; women: 38%; minorities: 15%; international: 19%
Acceptance rate (full time): 73%
Average GMAT (full time): 529
Average GMAT (part time): 529
Average GPA (full time): 3.46
Average age of entrants to full-time program: 25
Average months of prior work experience (full time): 28
TOEFL requirement: Yes
Minimum TOEFL score: 600
Most popular departments: finance, human resources management, insurance, leadership, marketing

Loyola University Chicago (Quinlan)

820 N. Michigan Avenue
Chicago, IL 60611
www.luc.edu/quinlan/mba/index.shtml
Private
Admissions: (312) 915-8908
Email: quinlangrad@luc.edu
Financial aid: (773) 508-7704
Application deadline: 07/15
Tuition: full time: $1,425/credit hour; part time: $1,425/credit hour
Room/board/expenses: $21,423
College-funded aid: Yes
International student aid: Yes
Full-time enrollment: N/A
men: N/A; women: N/A; minorities: N/A; international: N/A
Part-time enrollment: 635
men: 44%; women: 56%; minorities: 15%; international: 34%
Average GMAT (part time): 569
TOEFL requirement: Yes
Minimum TOEFL score: 577
Most popular departments: accounting, finance, human resources management, marketing, supply chain management

Northern Illinois University

Office of MBA Programs
Barsema Hall 203
De Kalb, IL 60115-2897
www.cob.niu.edu/mbaprograms
Public
Admissions: (866) 648-6221
Email: mba@niu.edu
Financial aid: (815) 753-1395
Application deadline: 07/15
In-state tuition: total program: $43,750 (full time); part time: $670/credit hour
Out-of-state tuition: total program: $59,750 (full time)
Room/board/expenses: $10,000
College-funded aid: Yes
International student aid: Yes
Full-time enrollment: 43
men: 60%; women: 40%; minorities: 7%; international: 47%
Part-time enrollment: 624
men: 69%; women: 31%; minorities: 25%; international: 13%
Acceptance rate (full time): 86%
Average GMAT (full time): 477
Average GMAT (part time): 500
Average GPA (full time): 3.05
Average age of entrants to full-time program: 26
Average months of prior work experience (full time): 72
TOEFL requirement: Yes
Minimum TOEFL score: 550
Most popular departments: finance, international business, leadership, marketing, management information systems

Northwestern University (Kellogg)

2001 Sheridan Road
Evanston, IL 60208-2001
www.kellogg.northwestern.edu
Private
Admissions: (847) 491-3308
Email: mbaadmissions@kellogg.northwestern.edu
Financial aid: (847) 491-3308
Application deadline: 04/01
Tuition: full time: $62,321; part time: $5,969/credit hour
Room/board/expenses: $21,108
College-funded aid: Yes
International student aid: Yes
Full-time enrollment: 1,047
men: 63%; women: 37%; minorities: 20%; international: 40%
Part-time enrollment: 727
men: 70%; women: 30%; minorities: 17%; international: 12%
Acceptance rate (full time): 23%
Average GMAT (full time): 713
Average GMAT (part time): 672
Average GPA (full time): 3.60
Average months of prior work experience (full time): 62
TOEFL requirement: Yes
Minimum TOEFL score: N/A
Most popular departments: entrepreneurship, finance, general management, marketing, organizational behavior
Mean starting base salary for 2014 full-time graduates: $119,202

Southern Illinois University-Carbondale

133 Rehn Hall
Carbondale, IL 62901-4625
mba.business.siu.edu
Public
Admissions: (618) 453-3030
Email: cobgp@business.siu.edu
Financial aid: (618) 453-4334
Application deadline: 06/15
In-state tuition: full time: $453/credit hour; part time: $453/credit hour
Out-of-state tuition: full time: $1,044/credit hour
Room/board/expenses: N/A
College-funded aid: Yes
International student aid: Yes
Full-time enrollment: 74
men: 55%; women: 45%; minorities: 9%; international: 26%
Part-time enrollment: N/A
men: N/A; women: N/A; minorities: N/A; international: N/A
Acceptance rate (full time): 49%
Average GMAT (full time): 564
Average GPA (full time): 3.33
Average age of entrants to full-time program: 25
Average months of prior work experience (full time): 66
TOEFL requirement: Yes
Minimum TOEFL score: 550
Most popular departments: finance, general management, international business, marketing, management information systems

Southern Illinois University-Edwardsville

Box 1051
Edwardsville, IL 62026-1051
www.siue.edu/business
Public
Admissions: (618) 650-3840
Email: mba@siue.edu
Financial aid: (618) 650-3880
Application deadline: rolling
In-state tuition: full time: $279/credit hour; part time: $279/credit hour
Out-of-state tuition: full time: $698/credit hour
Room/board/expenses: $23,500
College-funded aid: Yes
International student aid: Yes
Full-time enrollment: N/A
men: N/A; women: N/A; minorities: N/A; international: N/A
Part-time enrollment: 130
men: 58%; women: 42%; minorities: 15%; international: 4%
Average GMAT (part time): 509
TOEFL requirement: Yes
Minimum TOEFL score: 550

St. Xavier University

3700 West 103rd Street
Chicago, IL 60655
www.sxu.edu/academics/colleges_schools/gsm/
Private
Admissions: (773) 298-3053
Email: graduateadmission@sxu.edu
Financial aid: N/A
Application deadline: N/A
Tuition: full time: $890/credit hour; part time: N/A
Room/board/expenses: N/A
College-funded aid: Yes
International student aid: Yes
Full-time enrollment: 335
men: 53%; women: 47%; minorities: 51%; international: 1%
Part-time enrollment: N/A
men: N/A; women: N/A; minorities: N/A; international: N/A
Acceptance rate (full time): 58%
Average age of entrants to full-time program: 32
Average months of prior work experience (full time): 24
Minimum TOEFL score: N/A
Most popular departments: finance, general management, health care administration, human resources management, marketing

University of Chicago (Booth)

5807 S. Woodlawn Avenue
Chicago, IL 60637
ChicagoBooth.edu
Private
Admissions: (773) 702-7369
Email: admissions@ChicagoBooth.edu
Financial aid: (773) 702-7369
Application deadline: 04/07
Tuition: full time: $62,561; part time: N/A
Room/board/expenses: $25,600
College-funded aid: Yes
International student aid: Yes
Full-time enrollment: 1,181
men: 64%; women: 36%; minorities: 23%; international: 36%
Part-time enrollment: 1,378
men: 76%; women: 24%; minorities: 26%; international: 16%
Acceptance rate (full time): 24%
Average GMAT (full time): 724
Average GMAT (part time): 679
Average GPA (full time): 3.60
Average age of entrants to full-time program: 27
Average months of prior work experience (full time): 55
TOEFL requirement: Yes
Minimum TOEFL score: 600
Most popular departments: economics, entrepreneurship, finance, general management, other
Mean starting base salary for 2014 full-time graduates: $119,104
Employment location for 2014 class: Intl. 13%; N.E. 21%; M.A. 3%; S. 4%; M.W. 35%; S.W. 5%; W. 18%

University of Illinois-Chicago (Liautaud)

601 South Morgan Street
University Hall, 11th Floor
Chicago, IL 60607
www.mba.uic.edu/
Public
Admissions: (312) 996-4573
Email: mba@uic.edu
Financial aid: (312) 996-3126
Application deadline: 06/15
In-state tuition: full time: $23,958; part time: $17,306
Out-of-state tuition: full time: $35,956
Room/board/expenses: $17,545
College-funded aid: Yes
International student aid: Yes
Full-time enrollment: 78
men: 59%; women: 41%; minorities: 23%; international: 22%
Part-time enrollment: 175
men: 65%; women: 35%; minorities: 27%; international: 2%
Acceptance rate (full time): 44%
Average GMAT (full time): 591
Average GMAT (part time): 568
Average GPA (full time): 3.16
Average age of entrants to full-time program: 28
Average months of prior work experience (full time): 46
TOEFL requirement: Yes
Minimum TOEFL score: 550
Mean starting base salary for 2014 full-time graduates: $74,941
Employment location for 2014 class: Intl. 14%; N.E. 5%; M.A. 5%; S. 0%; M.W. 76%; S.W. 0%; W. 0%

University of Illinois-Springfield

1 University Plaza, MS UHB 4000
Springfield , IL 62703
www.uis.edu/admissions
Public
Admissions: (888) 977-4847
Email: admissions@uis.edu
Financial aid: (217) 206-6724
Application deadline: rolling
In-state tuition: full time: $319/credit hour; part time: $319/credit hour
Out-of-state tuition: full time: $665/credit hour
Room/board/expenses: N/A
College-funded aid: Yes
International student aid: Yes
Full-time enrollment: N/A
men: N/A; women: N/A; minorities: N/A; international: N/A
Part-time enrollment: 119
men: 65%; women: 35%; minorities: 13%; international: 13%
Average GMAT (part time): 479
TOEFL requirement: Yes
Minimum TOEFL score: 550

University of Illinois-Urbana-Champaign

515 E. Gregory Drive
3019 BIF, MC 520
Champaign, IL 61820
www.mba.illinois.edu
Public
Admissions: (217) 244-7602
Email: mba@illinois.edu
Financial aid: (217) 333-0100
Application deadline: 05/24
In-state tuition: full time: $26,710; part time: $27,509
Out-of-state tuition: full time: $37,710
Room/board/expenses: $20,992
College-funded aid: Yes
International student aid: Yes
Average student indebtedness at graduation: $62,446
Full-time enrollment: 169
men: 74%; women: 26%; minorities: 23%; international: 42%
Part-time enrollment: N/A
men: N/A; women: N/A; minorities: N/A; international: N/A
Acceptance rate (full time): 25%
Average GMAT (full time): 659
Average GPA (full time): 3.30
Average age of entrants to full-time program: 27
Average months of prior work experience (full time): 50
TOEFL requirement: Yes
Minimum TOEFL score: 550
Most popular departments: consulting, finance, general management, marketing, technology
Mean starting base salary for 2014 full-time graduates: $89,563
Employment location for 2014 class: Intl. 10%; N.E. 10%; M.A. 5%; S. 8%; M.W. 54%; S.W. 3%; W. 11%

More @ www.usnews.com/grad

Western Illinois University

1 University Circle
Macomb, IL 61455
www.wiu.edu/cbt
Public
Admissions: (309) 298-2442
Email: wj-polley@wiu.edu
Financial aid: (309) 298-2446
Application deadline: rolling
In-state tuition: full time: $317/
credit hour; part time: $317/
credit hour
Out-of-state tuition: full time: $635/
credit hour
Room/board/expenses: N/A
College-funded aid: Yes
International student aid: Yes
Full-time enrollment: 38
men: 58%; women: 42%;
minorities: 3%; international: 16%
Part-time enrollment: 30
men: 57%; women: 43%;
minorities: 3%; international: 0%
Acceptance rate (full time): 83%
Average GMAT (full time): 494
Average GMAT (part time): 513
Average GPA (full time): 3.28
Average months of prior work
experience (full time): 73
TOEFL requirement: Yes
Minimum TOEFL score: 550
Most popular departments:
accounting, finance, general
management, international
business, supply chain
management

INDIANA

Ball State University (Miller)

Whitinger Building, 147
Muncie, IN 47306
www.bsu.edu/mba/
Public
Admissions: (765) 285-1931
Email: mba@bsu.edu
Financial aid: (765) 285-5600
Application deadline: 01/07
In-state tuition: total program:
$14,754 (full time); $14,754 (part
time)
Out-of-state tuition: total program:
$34,614 (full time)
Room/board/expenses: $12,340
College-funded aid: Yes
International student aid: Yes
Average student indebtedness at
graduation: $34,096
Full-time enrollment: 44
men: 61%; women: 39%;
minorities: 9%; international: 25%
Part-time enrollment: 15
men: 60%; women: 40%;
minorities: 0%; international: 0%
Acceptance rate (full time): 83%
Average GMAT (full time): 510
Average GMAT (part time): 600
Average GPA (full time): 3.50
Average age of entrants to full-time
program: 24
Average months of prior work
experience (full time): 24
TOEFL requirement: Yes
Minimum TOEFL score: 550
Most popular departments:
entrepreneurship, finance,
general management, health
care administration, operations
management
Mean starting base salary for 2014
full-time graduates: $83,000
Employment location for 2014 class:
Intl. N/A; N.E. N/A; M.A. 11%; S.
N/A; M.W. 89%; S.W. N/A; W. N/A

Butler University

4600 Sunset Avenue
Indianapolis, IN 46208-3485
www.butlermba.com
Private
Admissions: (317) 940-9842
Email: mba@butler.edu
Financial aid: (317) 940-8200
Application deadline: 07/01
Tuition: full time: N/A; part time:
$730/credit hour
Room/board/expenses: N/A
College-funded aid: No
International student aid: No
Full-time enrollment: N/A
men: N/A; women: N/A; minorities:
N/A; international: N/A
Part-time enrollment: 186
men: 71%; women: 29%;
minorities: 4%; international: 3%
Average GMAT (part time): 579
TOEFL requirement: Yes
Minimum TOEFL score: 550
Most popular departments: finance,
international business, leadership,
marketing

Indiana State University

MBA Program
30 N 7th Street
Terre Haute, IN 47809
www.indstate.edu/business/mba/
Public
Admissions: (812) 237-2002
Email: ISU-Gradstudy@
mail.indstate.edu
Financial aid: (812) 237-2215
Application deadline: rolling
In-state tuition: full time: $380/
credit hour; part time: $380/
credit hour
Out-of-state tuition: full time: $747/
credit hour
Room/board/expenses: N/A
College-funded aid: Yes
International student aid: Yes
Full-time enrollment: 59
men: 59%; women: 41%;
minorities: 0%; international: 31%
Part-time enrollment: 38
men: 55%; women: 45%;
minorities: 18%; international: 5%
Acceptance rate (full time): 54%
Average GMAT (full time): 500
Average GPA (full time): 3.00
Average age of entrants to full-time
program: 28
Average months of prior work
experience (full time): 60
TOEFL requirement: Yes
Minimum TOEFL score: 550

Indiana University-Bloomington (Kelley)

1275 E. 10th Street, Suite 2010
Bloomington, IN 47405-1703
kelley.iu.edu/mba
Public
Admissions: (812) 855-8006
Email: iumba@indiana.edu
Financial aid: (812) 855-8006
Application deadline: 04/15
In-state tuition: full time: $27,600;
part time: $728/credit hour
Out-of-state tuition: full time:
$46,560
Room/board/expenses: $18,540
College-funded aid: Yes
International student aid: Yes
Average student indebtedness at
graduation: $63,065
Full-time enrollment: 391
men: 72%; women: 28%;
minorities: 17%; international:
36%

Part-time enrollment: 304
men: 81%; women: 19%;
minorities: 49%; international:
37%
Acceptance rate (full time): 33%
Average GMAT (full time): 668
Average GMAT (part time): 619
Average GPA (full time): 3.34
Average age of entrants to full-time
program: 28
Average months of prior work
experience (full time): 62
TOEFL requirement: Yes
Minimum TOEFL score: 600
Most popular departments:
entrepreneurship, finance,
general management, marketing,
other
Mean starting base salary for 2014
full-time graduates: $103,747
Employment location for 2014 class:
Intl. 0%; N.E. 8%; M.A. 2%; S. 8%;
M.W. 58%; S.W. 11%; W. 13%

Indiana University-Kokomo[1]

2300 S. Washington Street
Kokomo, IN 46904-9003
www.iuk.edu/index.php
Public
Admissions: (765) 455-9275
Financial aid: N/A
Tuition: N/A
Room/board/expenses: N/A
Enrollment: N/A

Indiana University Northwest

3400 Broadway
Gary, IN 46408-1197
www.indiana.edu/~bulletin/iun/
grad/busec.html#pro
Public
Admissions: (219) 980-6635
Email: iunbiz@iun.edu
Financial aid: (219) 980-6778
Application deadline: 08/15
In-state tuition: full time: N/A; part
time: $310/credit hour
Out-of-state tuition: full time: N/A
Room/board/expenses: $0
College-funded aid: Yes
International student aid: No
Full-time enrollment: N/A
men: N/A; women: N/A; minorities:
N/A; international: N/A
Part-time enrollment: 111
men: 56%; women: 44%;
minorities: 44%; international: 0%
Average GMAT (part time): 484
TOEFL requirement: Yes
Minimum TOEFL score: 550

Indiana University-Purdue University-Fort Wayne (Doermer)

2101 E. Coliseum Boulevard
Fort Wayne, IN 46805-1499
www.ipfw.edu/mba
Public
Admissions: (260) 481-6498
Email: mba@ipfw.edu
Financial aid: (260) 481-6820
Application deadline: 06/30
In-state tuition: full time: $621/
credit hour; part time: $327/
credit hour
Out-of-state tuition: full time:
$1,034/credit hour
Room/board/expenses: N/A
College-funded aid: Yes
International student aid: Yes
Full-time enrollment: 26
men: 69%; women: 31%;
minorities: 8%; international: 0%

Part-time enrollment: 14
men: 64%; women: 36%;
minorities: 0%; international: 21%
Acceptance rate (full time): 71%
Average GMAT (part time): 539
Average age of entrants to full-time
program: 33
Average months of prior work
experience (full time): 121
TOEFL requirement: Yes
Minimum TOEFL score: 550

Indiana University-South Bend[1]

1700 Mishawaka Avenue
PO Box 7111
South Bend, IN 46634-7111
www.iusb.edu/buse
Public
Admissions: (574) 520-4497
Email: graduate@iusb.edu
Financial aid: N/A
Tuition: N/A
Room/board/expenses: N/A
Enrollment: N/A

Indiana University-Southeast

4201 Grant Line Road
New Albany, IN 47150
www.ius.edu/graduatebusiness
Public
Admissions: (812) 941-2364
Email: iusmba@ius.edu
Financial aid: (812) 941-2246
Application deadline: 07/20
In-state tuition: full time: N/A; part
time: N/A
Out-of-state tuition: full time: N/A
Room/board/expenses: N/A
College-funded aid: Yes
International student aid: Yes
Full-time enrollment: N/A
men: N/A; women: N/A; minorities:
N/A; international: N/A
Part-time enrollment: 212
men: 58%; women: 42%;
minorities: 13%; international: 1%
Average GMAT (part time): 540
TOEFL requirement: Yes
Minimum TOEFL score: 550

Purdue University-West Lafayette (Krannert)

100 S. Grant Street
Rawls Hall, Room 2020
West Lafayette, IN 47907-2076
www.krannert.purdue.edu/
programs/masters
Public
Admissions: (765) 494-0773
Email:
krannertmasters@purdue.edu
Financial aid: (765) 494-0998
Application deadline: 05/01
In-state tuition: full time: $24,063;
part time: $30,567
Out-of-state tuition: full time:
$43,829
Room/board/expenses: $13,056
College-funded aid: Yes
International student aid: Yes
Average student indebtedness at
graduation: $47,067
Full-time enrollment: 180
men: 76%; women: 24%;
minorities: 19%; international:
49%
Part-time enrollment: 123
men: 81%; women: 19%;
minorities: 20%; international:
10%
Acceptance rate (full time): 29%
Average GMAT (full time): 617
Average GMAT (part time): 498
Average GPA (full time): 3.34

Average age of entrants to full-time
program: 27
Average months of prior work
experience (full time): 48
TOEFL requirement: Yes
Minimum TOEFL score: 600
Most popular departments: finance,
human resources management,
marketing, operations
management, supply chain
management
Mean starting base salary for 2014
full-time graduates: $95,718
Employment location for 2014 class:
Intl. 9%; N.E. 5%; M.A. 6%; S.
14%; M.W. 49%; S.W. 3%; W. 15%

University of Notre Dame (Mendoza)

276 Mendoza College of Business
Notre Dame, IN 46556
mendoza.nd.edu/programs/
mba-programs/two-year-mba/
Private
Admissions: (574) 631-8488
Email: mba.business@nd.edu
Financial aid: (574) 631-6436
Application deadline: rolling
Tuition: full time: $47,450; part
time: N/A
Room/board/expenses: $19,410
College-funded aid: Yes
International student aid: Yes
Average student indebtedness at
graduation: $69,072
Full-time enrollment: 323
men: 73%; women: 27%;
minorities: 13%; international:
25%
Part-time enrollment: N/A
men: N/A; women: N/A; minorities:
N/A; international: N/A
Acceptance rate (full time): 35%
Average GMAT (full time): 686
Average GPA (full time): 3.38
Average age of entrants to full-time
program: 27
Average months of prior work
experience (full time): 59
TOEFL requirement: Yes
Minimum TOEFL score: 600
Most popular departments:
consulting, finance, leadership,
marketing, other
Mean starting base salary for 2014
full-time graduates: $102,404
Employment location for 2014 class:
Intl. 2%; N.E. 17%; M.A. 2%; S. 5%;
M.W. 49%; S.W. 5%; W. 20%

University of Southern Indiana

8600 University Boulevard
Evansville, IN 47712
www.usi.edu/graduatestudies
Public
Admissions: (812) 465-7015
Email: graduate.studeis@usi.edu
Financial aid: (812) 464-1767
Application deadline: rolling
In-state tuition: full time: $325/
credit hour; part time: $325/
credit hour
Out-of-state tuition: full time: $641/
credit hour
Room/board/expenses: $4,514
College-funded aid: Yes
International student aid: Yes
Average student indebtedness at
graduation: $30,564
Full-time enrollment: 22
men: 50%; women: 50%;
minorities: 9%; international: 23%
Part-time enrollment: 92
men: 67%; women: 33%;
minorities: 9%; international: 2%
Acceptance rate (full time): 100%
Average GMAT (full time): 490
Average GMAT (part time): 523

Average GPA (full time): 3.39
Average age of entrants to full-time program: 26
TOEFL requirement: Yes
Minimum TOEFL score: 550

Valparaiso University

Urschel Hall
1909 Chapel Drive
Valparaiso, IN 46383
www.valpo.edu/mba/
Private
Admissions: (219) 465-7952
Email: mba@valpo.edu
Financial aid: (219) 464-5015
Application deadline: 06/24
Tuition: full time: $833/credit hour; part time: $833/credit hour
Room/board/expenses: $16,600
College-funded aid: No
International student aid: No
Average student indebtedness at graduation: $36,516
Full-time enrollment: 11
men: 73%; women: 27%; minorities: 27%; international: 18%
Part-time enrollment: 58
men: 64%; women: 36%; minorities: 10%; international: 2%
Acceptance rate (full time): 74%
Average GMAT (full time): 527
Average GMAT (part time): 507
Average GPA (full time): 3.23
Average age of entrants to full-time program: 25
Average months of prior work experience (full time): 41
TOEFL requirement: Yes
Minimum TOEFL score: 575
Most popular departments: finance, general management, marketing, other
Mean starting base salary for 2014 full-time graduates: $49,667
Employment location for 2014 class: Intl. 0%; N.E. 0%; M.A. 0%; S. 14%; M.W. 86%; S.W. 0%; W. 0%

IOWA

Iowa State University

1360 Gerdin Business Building
Ames, IA 50011-1350
www.business.iastate.edu
Public
Admissions: (515) 294-8118
Email: busgrad@iastate.edu
Financial aid: (515) 294-2223
Application deadline: 07/01
In-state tuition: full time: $10,777; part time: $539/credit hour
Out-of-state tuition: full time: $23,615
Room/board/expenses: N/A
College-funded aid: Yes
International student aid: Yes
Full-time enrollment: 70
men: 69%; women: 31%; minorities: 7%; international: 46%
Part-time enrollment: 63
men: 76%; women: 24%; minorities: 8%; international: 0%
Acceptance rate (full time): 53%
Average GMAT (full time): 636
Average GMAT (part time): 515
Average GPA (full time): 3.45
Average age of entrants to full-time program: 24
TOEFL requirement: Yes
Minimum TOEFL score: 600
Most popular departments: accounting, finance, marketing, supply chain management, technology
Mean starting base salary for 2014 full-time graduates: $59,691
Employment location for 2014 class: Intl. 11%; N.E. 0%; M.A. 0%; S. 5%; M.W. 79%; S.W. 0%; W. 5%

University of Iowa (Tippie)

108 Pappajohn Business Building
Suite W160
Iowa City, IA 52242-1000
tippie.uiowa.edu/mba
Public
Admissions: (319) 335-1039
Email: tippiemba@uiowa.edu
Financial aid: (319) 335-1039
Application deadline: 07/30
In-state tuition: full time: $19,592; part time: $665/credit hour
Out-of-state tuition: full time: $35,950
Room/board/expenses: $17,085
College-funded aid: Yes
International student aid: Yes
Average student indebtedness at graduation: $36,733
Full-time enrollment: 118
men: 74%; women: 26%; minorities: 6%; international: 30%
Part-time enrollment: 825
men: 67%; women: 33%; minorities: 8%; international: 10%
Acceptance rate (full time): 37%
Average GMAT (full time): 669
Average GMAT (part time): 560
Average GPA (full time): 3.39
Average age of entrants to full-time program: 27
Average months of prior work experience (full time): 42
TOEFL requirement: Yes
Minimum TOEFL score: 600
Most popular departments: finance, marketing, operations management, portfolio management, supply chain management
Mean starting base salary for 2014 full-time graduates: $85,586
Employment location for 2014 class: Intl. 5%; N.E. 13%; M.A. 5%; S. 20%; M.W. 43%; S.W. 5%; W. 10%

University of Northern Iowa

Curris Business Building 325
Cedar Falls, IA 50614-0123
www.cba.uni.edu/mba/
Public
Admissions: (319) 273-6243
Email: mba@uni.edu
Financial aid: (319) 273-2700
Application deadline: 05/01
In-state tuition: full time: $10,569; part time: $527/credit hour
Out-of-state tuition: full time: $20,563
Room/board/expenses: $11,650
College-funded aid: Yes
International student aid: No
Full-time enrollment: N/A
men: N/A; women: N/A; minorities: N/A; international: N/A
Part-time enrollment: 61
men: 66%; women: 34%; minorities: 15%; international: 10%
Average GMAT (part time): 568
TOEFL requirement: Yes
Minimum TOEFL score: 550
Most popular departments: accounting, general management

KANSAS

Emporia State University

1 Kellogg Circle
ESU Box 4039
Emporia, KS 66801-5087
emporia.edu/business/programs/mba
Public
Admissions: (800) 950-4723
Email: gradinfo@emporia.edu
Financial aid: (620) 341-5457

Application deadline: rolling
In-state tuition: full time: $227/credit hour; part time: $227/credit hour
Out-of-state tuition: full time: $706/credit hour
Room/board/expenses: N/A
College-funded aid: Yes
International student aid: Yes
Average student indebtedness at graduation: $2,737
Full-time enrollment: 56
men: 48%; women: 52%; minorities: 4%; international: 54%
Part-time enrollment: 80
men: 54%; women: 46%; minorities: 4%; international: 39%
Acceptance rate (full time): 32%
Average GMAT (full time): 514
Average GMAT (part time): 519
Average age of entrants to full-time program: 25
TOEFL requirement: Yes
Minimum TOEFL score: 540
Most popular departments: accounting, general management, other
Employment location for 2014 class: Intl. N/A; N.E. N/A; M.A. N/A; S. N/A; M.W. 100%; S.W. N/A; W. N/A

Kansas State University

112 Calvin Hall
Manhattan, KS 66506-0501
cba.k-state.edu
Public
Admissions: (785) 532-7190
Email: gradbusiness@ksu.edu
Financial aid: (785) 532-6420
Application deadline: 06/01
In-state tuition: full time: $11,600; part time: $368/credit hour
Out-of-state tuition: full time: $22,415
Room/board/expenses: $20,000
College-funded aid: Yes
International student aid: Yes
Full-time enrollment: 45
men: 64%; women: 36%; minorities: 16%; international: 31%
Part-time enrollment: 10
men: N/A; women: 160%; minorities: 50%; international: N/A
Acceptance rate (full time): 75%
Average GMAT (full time): 535
Average GPA (full time): 3.37
Average age of entrants to full-time program: 27
Average months of prior work experience (full time): 63
TOEFL requirement: Yes
Minimum TOEFL score: 550
Most popular departments: finance, marketing, portfolio management, other

Pittsburg State University (Kelce)

1701 S. Broadway
Pittsburg, KS 66762
www.pittstate.edu/kelce/graduate.html
Public
Admissions: (620) 235-4218
Email: grad@pittstate.edu
Financial aid: (620) 235-4240
Application deadline: 07/01
In-state tuition: full time: $8,269; part time: $293/credit hour
Out-of-state tuition: full time: $17,689
Room/board/expenses: $6,734
College-funded aid: Yes
International student aid: Yes
Full-time enrollment: 78
men: 58%; women: 42%; minorities: N/A; international: N/A

Part-time enrollment: 20
men: 50%; women: 50%; minorities: N/A; international: N/A
Acceptance rate (full time): 44%
Average GMAT (full time): 500
Average GMAT (part time): 500
Average age of entrants to full-time program: 26
Average months of prior work experience (full time): 16
TOEFL requirement: Yes
Minimum TOEFL score: 550
Most popular departments: accounting, general management, international business

University of Kansas

1300 Sunnyside Avenue
Lawrence, KS 66045-7585
www.mba.ku.edu
Public
Admissions: (785) 864-7556
Email: bschoolmba@ku.edu
Financial aid: (785) 864-7596
Application deadline: 06/01
In-state tuition: full time: $363/credit hour; part time: $429/credit hour
Out-of-state tuition: full time: $849/credit hour
Room/board/expenses: $14,000
College-funded aid: Yes
International student aid: Yes
Full-time enrollment: 57
men: 72%; women: 28%; minorities: 18%; international: 23%
Part-time enrollment: 168
men: 74%; women: 26%; minorities: 12%; international: 7%
Acceptance rate (full time): 51%
Average GMAT (full time): 594
Average GMAT (part time): 557
Average GPA (full time): 3.32
Average age of entrants to full-time program: 28
Average months of prior work experience (full time): 43
TOEFL requirement: Yes
Minimum TOEFL score: 570
Most popular departments: finance, general management, marketing, supply chain management, other
Mean starting base salary for 2014 full-time graduates: $58,563
Employment location for 2014 class: Intl. 10%; N.E. N/A; M.A. N/A; S. N/A; M.W. 85%; S.W. N/A; W. 5%

Washburn University[1]

1700 S.W. College Avenue
Topeka, KS 66621
www.washburn.edu/business
Public
Admissions: N/A
Financial aid: N/A
Tuition: N/A
Room/board/expenses: N/A
Enrollment: N/A

Wichita State University (Barton)[1]

1845 N. Fairmount, Box 48
Wichita, KS 67260-0048
www.wichita.edu/mba
Public
Admissions: (316) 978-3230
Email: grad.business@wichita.edu
Financial aid: N/A
Tuition: N/A
Room/board/expenses: N/A
Enrollment: N/A

KENTUCKY

Bellarmine University (Rubel)

2001 Newburg Road
Louisville, KY 40205-0671
www.bellarmine.edu/business/
Private
Admissions: N/A
Email: gradadmissions@bellarmine.edu
Financial aid: (502) 452-8124
Application deadline: rolling
Tuition: total program: $33,950 (full time); part time: $730/credit hour
Room/board/expenses: N/A
College-funded aid: Yes
International student aid: Yes
Full-time enrollment: 53
men: 51%; women: 49%; minorities: 19%; international: 2%
Part-time enrollment: 62
men: 47%; women: 53%; minorities: 6%; international: 0%
Average GMAT (full time): 444
Average GMAT (part time): 430
Average GPA (full time): 3.06
Average age of entrants to full-time program: 25
TOEFL requirement: Yes
Minimum TOEFL score: 550

Eastern Kentucky University[1]

521 Lancaster Avenue
Richmond, KY 40475
cbt.eku.edu/
Public
Admissions: (859) 622-1742
Email: graduateschool@eku.edu
Financial aid: N/A
Tuition: N/A
Room/board/expenses: N/A
Enrollment: N/A

Morehead State University[1]

Combs Building 214
Morehead, KY 40351
www.moreheadstate.edu/mba
Public
Admissions: (606) 783-2000
Email: admissions@moreheadstate.edu
Financial aid: N/A
Tuition: N/A
Room/board/expenses: N/A
Enrollment: N/A

Murray State University (Bauernfeind)

109 Business Building
Murray, KY 42071
www.murraystate.edu/business
Public
Admissions: (270) 809-3779
Email: Msu.graduateadmissions@murraystate.edu
Financial aid: (270) 809-2546
Application deadline: rolling
In-state tuition: full time: $425/credit hour; part time: $425/credit hour
Out-of-state tuition: full time: $1,275/credit hour
Room/board/expenses: $15,430
College-funded aid: Yes
International student aid: Yes
Average student indebtedness at graduation: $18,577
Full-time enrollment: 85
men: 59%; women: 41%; minorities: 7%; international: 49%

Part-time enrollment: 150
men: 58%; women: 42%;
minorities: 10%; international: 3%
Acceptance rate (full time): 57%
Average GMAT (full time): 431
Average GMAT (part time): 511
Average age of entrants to full-time program: 26
TOEFL requirement: Yes
Minimum TOEFL score: 527
Most popular departments: accounting, general management

Northern Kentucky University[1]

Suite 401, BEP Center
Highland Heights, KY 41099
cob.nku.edu/
graduatedegrees.html
Public
Admissions: (859) 572-6336
Email: mbusiness@nku.edu
Financial aid: N/A
Tuition: N/A
Room/board/expenses: N/A
Enrollment: N/A

University of Kentucky (Gatton)

145 Gatton College of Business and Economics
Lexington, KY 40506-0034
gatton.uky.edu
Public
Admissions: (859) 257-1306
Email: ukmba@uky.edu
Financial aid: (859) 257-1306
Application deadline: 05/11
In-state tuition: full time: $22,732; part time: $696/credit hour
Out-of-state tuition: full time: $36,110
Room/board/expenses: $13,500
College-funded aid: Yes
International student aid: Yes
Full-time enrollment: 72
men: 68%; women: 32%;
minorities: 1%; international: 13%
Part-time enrollment: 122
men: 63%; women: 37%;
minorities: 7%; international: 2%
Acceptance rate (full time): 83%
Average GMAT (full time): 610
Average GMAT (part time): 648
Average GPA (full time): 3.48
Average age of entrants to full-time program: 24
Average months of prior work experience (full time): 7
TOEFL requirement: Yes
Minimum TOEFL score: 550
Most popular departments: finance, general management, marketing, supply chain management, other
Mean starting base salary for 2014 full-time graduates: $56,980
Employment location for 2014 class: Intl. 0%; N.E. 5%; M.A. 0%; S. 65%; M.W. 27%; S.W. 0%; W. 3%

University of Louisville

Belknap Campus
Louisville, KY 40292
business.louisville.edu/mba
Public
Admissions: (502) 852-7257
Email: mba@louisville.edu
Financial aid: (502) 852-5511
Application deadline: 07/01
In-state tuition: total program: $32,196 (full time); $32,196 (part time)
Out-of-state tuition: total program: $32,196 (full time)
Room/board/expenses: $13,000
College-funded aid: Yes
International student aid: Yes

Average student indebtedness at graduation: $27,507
Full-time enrollment: 47
men: 57%; women: 43%;
minorities: 17%; international: 15%
Part-time enrollment: 142
men: 68%; women: 32%;
minorities: 11%; international: 3%
Acceptance rate (full time): 48%
Average GMAT (full time): 607
Average GMAT (part time): 573
Average GPA (full time): 3.42
Average age of entrants to full-time program: 25
Average months of prior work experience (full time): 17
TOEFL requirement: Yes
Minimum TOEFL score: 550
Most popular departments: consulting, finance, general management, marketing, statistics and operations research
Mean starting base salary for 2014 full-time graduates: $55,720
Employment location for 2014 class: Intl. 3%; N.E. 0%; M.A. 3%; S. 80%; M.W. 14%; S.W. 0%; W. 0%

Western Kentucky University (Ford)

434 A. Grise Hall
Bowling Green, KY 42101-1056
www.wku.edu/mba/
Public
Admissions: (270) 745-2446
Email: mba@wku.edu
Financial aid: (270) 745-2755
Application deadline: rolling
In-state tuition: full time: N/A; part time: N/A
Out-of-state tuition: full time: N/A
Room/board/expenses: N/A
College-funded aid: Yes
International student aid: Yes
Average student indebtedness at graduation: $25,040
Full-time enrollment: 32
men: 41%; women: 59%;
minorities: 3%; international: 41%
Part-time enrollment: 78
men: 58%; women: 42%;
minorities: 14%; international: 14%
Acceptance rate (full time): 46%
Average GMAT (full time): 531
Average GMAT (part time): 509
Average GPA (full time): 3.31
Average age of entrants to full-time program: 26
TOEFL requirement: Yes
Minimum TOEFL score: 550

LOUISIANA

Louisiana State University- Baton Rouge (Ourso)

4000 Business Education Complex
Baton Rouge, LA 70803
mba.lsu.edu
Public
Admissions: (225) 578-8867
Email: busmba@lsu.edu
Financial aid: (225) 578-3103
Application deadline: 05/15
In-state tuition: total program: $31,999 (full time); $52,144 (part time)
Out-of-state tuition: total program: $67,839 (full time)
Room/board/expenses: $20,000
College-funded aid: Yes
International student aid: Yes
Average student indebtedness at graduation: $9,987
Full-time enrollment: 87
men: 47%; women: 53%;
minorities: 9%; international: 20%

Part-time enrollment: 81
men: 70%; women: 30%;
minorities: 19%; international: 0%
Acceptance rate (full time): 43%
Average GMAT (full time): 620
Average GMAT (part time): 506
Average age of entrants to full-time program: 23
Average months of prior work experience (full time): 10
TOEFL requirement: Yes
Minimum TOEFL score: 550
Mean starting base salary for 2014 full-time graduates: $56,656
Employment location for 2014 class: Intl. 2%; N.E. 4%; M.A. N/A; S. 63%; M.W. 2%; S.W. 27%; W. 2%

Louisiana State University-Shreveport

1 University Place
Shreveport, LA 71115
www.lsus.edu/ba/mba
Public
Admissions: (318) 797-5213
Email: bill.bigler@lsus.edu
Financial aid: (318) 797-5363
Application deadline: rolling
In-state tuition: full time: $314/credit hour; part time: $314/credit hour
Out-of-state tuition: full time: $314/credit hour
Room/board/expenses: N/A
College-funded aid: Yes
International student aid: Yes
Full-time enrollment: 113
men: 43%; women: 57%;
minorities: N/A; international: N/A
Part-time enrollment: N/A
men: N/A; women: N/A; minorities: N/A; international: N/A
TOEFL requirement: Yes
Minimum TOEFL score: N/A
Most popular departments: accounting, finance, general management

Louisiana Tech University

PO Box 10318
Ruston, LA 71272
www.latech.edu/graduate_school
Public
Admissions: (318) 257-2924
Email: gschool@latech.edu
Financial aid: (318) 257-2641
Application deadline: 08/01
In-state tuition: full time: $8,025; part time: $6,840
Out-of-state tuition: full time: $16,005
Room/board/expenses: $9,120
College-funded aid: Yes
International student aid: Yes
Full-time enrollment: 71
men: 59%; women: 41%;
minorities: 14%; international: 11%
Part-time enrollment: 27
men: 63%; women: 37%;
minorities: 11%; international: 19%
Acceptance rate (full time): 78%
Average GMAT (full time): 506
Average GMAT (part time): 505
Average GPA (full time): 3.34
TOEFL requirement: Yes
Minimum TOEFL score: 550

Loyola University New Orleans (Butt)

6363 St. Charles Avenue
Campus Box 15
New Orleans, LA 70118
www.business.loyno.edu
Private
Admissions: (504) 864-7953
Email: mba@loyno.edu

Financial aid: (504) 865-3231
Application deadline: 06/30
Tuition: full time: $1,005/credit hour; part time: $1,005/credit hour
Room/board/expenses: N/A
College-funded aid: Yes
International student aid: Yes
Full-time enrollment: 47
men: 57%; women: 43%;
minorities: 15%; international: 13%
Part-time enrollment: 23
men: 48%; women: 52%;
minorities: 30%; international: 0%
Acceptance rate (full time): 97%
Average GMAT (full time): 483
Average GMAT (part time): 494
Average GPA (full time): 3.02
Average age of entrants to full-time program: 28
TOEFL requirement: Yes
Minimum TOEFL score: 580
Most popular departments: entrepreneurship, leadership, marketing, supply chain management, statistics and operations research
Mean starting base salary for 2014 full-time graduates: $52,375

McNeese State University

PO Box 91660
Lake Charles, LA 70609
www.mcneese.edu/colleges/bus
Public
Admissions: (337) 475-5576
Email: mba@mcneese.edu
Financial aid: (337) 475-5065
Application deadline: 12/31
In-state tuition: full time: $6,769; part time: $4,746
Out-of-state tuition: full time: $17,838
Room/board/expenses: $12,688
College-funded aid: Yes
International student aid: No
Full-time enrollment: 51
men: 51%; women: 49%;
minorities: 10%; international: 31%
Part-time enrollment: 1
men: 0%; women: 100%;
minorities: 0%; international: 100%
Acceptance rate (full time): 84%
Average GMAT (full time): 560
Average GPA (full time): 3.36
Average age of entrants to full-time program: 25
TOEFL requirement: Yes
Minimum TOEFL score: 550

Nicholls State University

PO Box 2015
Thibodaux, LA 70310
www.nicholls.edu/business/
Public
Admissions: (985) 448-4507
Email: becky.leblanc-durocher@nicholls.edu
Financial aid: (985) 448-4048
Application deadline: rolling
In-state tuition: full time: $7,547; part time: $4,159
Out-of-state tuition: full time: $17,793
Room/board/expenses: N/A
College-funded aid: Yes
International student aid: Yes
Full-time enrollment: 41
men: 61%; women: 39%;
minorities: N/A; international: N/A
Part-time enrollment: 34
men: 62%; women: 38%;
minorities: N/A; international: N/A
Acceptance rate (full time): 100%
Average GMAT (full time): 508

Average GPA (full time): 3.26
TOEFL requirement: Yes
Minimum TOEFL score: 550

Southeastern Louisiana University

SLU 10735
Hammond, LA 70402
www.selu.edu/acad_research/programs/grad_bus
Public
Admissions: (985) 549-5637
Email: admissions@selu.edu
Financial aid: (985) 549-2244
Application deadline: rolling
In-state tuition: full time: $7,110; part time: $395/credit hour
Out-of-state tuition: full time: $19,674
Room/board/expenses: $11,930
College-funded aid: Yes
International student aid: No
Average student indebtedness at graduation: $25,281
Full-time enrollment: 54
men: 43%; women: 57%;
minorities: 20%; international: 7%
Part-time enrollment: N/A
men: N/A; women: N/A; minorities: N/A; international: N/A
Acceptance rate (full time): 100%
Average GMAT (full time): 505
Average age of entrants to full-time program: 34
TOEFL requirement: Yes
Minimum TOEFL score: 525

Southern University and A&M College[1]

PO Box 9723
Baton Rouge, LA 70813
www.subr.edu/index.cfm/page/121
Public
Admissions: (225) 771-5390
Email: gradschool@subr.edu
Financial aid: N/A
Tuition: N/A
Room/board/expenses: N/A
Enrollment: N/A

Tulane University (Freeman)

7 McAlister Drive
New Orleans, LA 70118-5669
freeman.tulane.edu
Private
Admissions: (504) 865-5410
Email: freeman.admissions@tulane.edu
Financial aid: (504) 865-5410
Application deadline: 05/06
Tuition: full time: $53,405; part time: $1,605/credit hour
Room/board/expenses: $19,140
College-funded aid: Yes
International student aid: Yes
Full-time enrollment: 90
men: 78%; women: 22%;
minorities: 9%; international: 37%
Part-time enrollment: N/A
men: N/A; women: N/A; minorities: N/A; international: N/A
Acceptance rate (full time): 63%
Average GMAT (full time): 649
Average GPA (full time): 3.38
Average age of entrants to full-time program: 28
Average months of prior work experience (full time): 43
TOEFL requirement: Yes
Minimum TOEFL score: 600
Most popular departments: entrepreneurship, finance, general management, international business, other

Mean starting base salary for 2014 full-time graduates: $82,938
Employment location for 2014 class: Intl. 4%; N.E. 4%; M.A. 6%; S. 39%; M.W. 6%; S.W. 37%; W. 4%

University of Louisiana-Lafayette (Moody)
USL Box 44568
Lafayette, LA 70504-4568
gradschool.louisiana.edu/
Public
Admissions: (337) 482-6965
Email: gradschool@louisiana.edu
Financial aid: (337) 482-6506
Application deadline: 06/30
In-state tuition: full time: $6,520; part time: $5,038
Out-of-state tuition: full time: $18,033
Room/board/expenses: $7,000
College-funded aid: Yes
International student aid: Yes
Full-time enrollment: N/A
men: N/A; women: N/A; minorities: N/A; international: N/A
Part-time enrollment: 206
men: 53%; women: 47%; minorities: 15%; international: 8%
Average GMAT (part time): 480
TOEFL requirement: Yes
Minimum TOEFL score: 550

University of Louisiana-Monroe[1]
700 University Avenue
Monroe, LA 71209
www.ulm.edu/cbss/
Public
Admissions: N/A
Financial aid: N/A
Tuition: N/A
Room/board/expenses: N/A
Enrollment: N/A

University of New Orleans
2000 Lakeshore Drive
New Orleans, LA 70148
www.uno.edu/admissions/contact.aspx
Public
Admissions: (504) 280-6595
Email: pec@uno.edu
Financial aid: (504) 280-6603
Application deadline: rolling
In-state tuition: total program: $19,800 (full time); $19,000 (part time)
Out-of-state tuition: total program: $42,000 (full time)
Room/board/expenses: N/A
College-funded aid: Yes
International student aid: Yes
Full-time enrollment: 291
men: N/A; women: N/A; minorities: N/A; international: N/A
Part-time enrollment: N/A
men: N/A; women: N/A; minorities: N/A; international: N/A
Acceptance rate (full time): 78%
Average GMAT (full time): 500
Average GPA (full time): 3.20
TOEFL requirement: Yes
Minimum TOEFL score: 550

MAINE

University of Maine
Donald P. Corbett Business Building
Orono, ME 04469-5723
www.umaine.edu/business/mba
Public
Admissions: (207) 581-1971

Email: mba@maine.edu
Financial aid: (207) 581-1324
Application deadline: rolling
In-state tuition: full time: $8,661; part time: $418/credit hour
Out-of-state tuition: full time: $25,854
Room/board/expenses: $12,520
College-funded aid: Yes
International student aid: Yes
Full-time enrollment: 43
men: N/A; women: N/A; minorities: N/A; international: N/A
Part-time enrollment: N/A
men: N/A; women: N/A; minorities: N/A; international: N/A
Average GMAT (full time): 539
Average GMAT (part time): 539
Average GPA (full time): 3.30
TOEFL requirement: Yes
Minimum TOEFL score: N/A
Most popular departments: accounting, finance, general management, international business, other

University of Southern Maine
PO Box 9300
Portland, ME 04104
www.usm.maine.edu/sb
Public
Admissions: (207) 780-4184
Email: mba@usm.maine.edu
Financial aid: (207) 780-5250
Application deadline: rolling
In-state tuition: full time: N/A; part time: N/A
Out-of-state tuition: full time: N/A
Room/board/expenses: N/A
College-funded aid: Yes
International student aid: Yes
Full-time enrollment: N/A
men: N/A; women: N/A; minorities: N/A; international: N/A
Part-time enrollment: 80
men: 58%; women: 43%; minorities: 3%; international: 1%
Average GMAT (part time): 591
TOEFL requirement: Yes
Minimum TOEFL score: 550

MARYLAND

Frostburg State University
125 Guild Center
101 Braddock Road
Frostburg, MD 21532-2303
www.frostburg.edu/colleges/cob/mba/
Public
Admissions: (301) 687-7053
Email: gradservices@frostburg.edu
Financial aid: (301) 687-4301
Application deadline: rolling
In-state tuition: full time: $357/credit hour; part time: $357/credit hour
Out-of-state tuition: full time: $459/credit hour
Room/board/expenses: N/A
College-funded aid: Yes
International student aid: Yes
Full-time enrollment: 42
men: 71%; women: 29%; minorities: 17%; international: 10%
Part-time enrollment: 235
men: 49%; women: 51%; minorities: 20%; international: 2%
TOEFL requirement: Yes
Minimum TOEFL score: 550

Loyola University Maryland (Sellinger)
4501 N. Charles Street
Baltimore, MD 21210-2699
www.loyola.edu/sellinger/
Private
Admissions: (410) 617-5020
Email: graduate@loyola.edu
Financial aid: (410) 617-2576
Application deadline: 08/15
Tuition: total program: $63,000 (full time); part time: $910/credit hour
Room/board/expenses: N/A
College-funded aid: Yes
International student aid: Yes
Average student indebtedness at graduation: $72,102
Full-time enrollment: 16
men: 81%; women: 19%; minorities: 19%; international: 0%
Part-time enrollment: 345
men: 60%; women: 40%; minorities: 14%; international: 1%
Acceptance rate (full time): 79%
Average GMAT (full time): 546
Average GMAT (part time): 549
Average GPA (full time): 3.20
Average age of entrants to full-time program: 25
Average months of prior work experience (full time): 27
TOEFL requirement: Yes
Minimum TOEFL score: 550
Most popular departments: accounting, finance, general management, international business
Mean starting base salary for 2014 full-time graduates: $64,927
Employment location for 2014 class: Intl. N/A; N.E. 7%; M.A. 93%; S. N/A; M.W. N/A; S.W. N/A; W. N/A

Morgan State University (Graves)[1]
1700 E. Cold Spring Lane
Baltimore, MD 21251
www.morgan.edu/sbm
Public
Admissions: (443) 885-3185
Financial aid: N/A
Tuition: N/A
Room/board/expenses: N/A
Enrollment: N/A

Salisbury University (Perdue)[1]
1101 Camden Avenue
Salisbury, MD 21801-6860
www.salisbury.edu/Schools/perdue/welcome.html
Public
Admissions: (410) 543-6161
Email: admissions@salisbury.edu
Financial aid: N/A
Tuition: N/A
Room/board/expenses: N/A
Enrollment: N/A

University of Baltimore-Towson University
1420 N. Charles Street
Baltimore, MD 21201
mba.ubalt.towson.edu/
Public
Admissions: (410) 837-6565
Email: gradadmissions@ubalt.edu
Financial aid: (410) 837-4763
Application deadline: 08/01
In-state tuition: full time: $705/credit hour; part time: $705/credit hour
Out-of-state tuition: full time: $983/credit hour

Room/board/expenses: N/A
College-funded aid: Yes
International student aid: Yes
Full-time enrollment: N/A
men: N/A; women: N/A; minorities: N/A; international: N/A
Part-time enrollment: 472
men: 52%; women: 48%; minorities: 30%; international: 9%
Average GMAT (part time): 507
TOEFL requirement: Yes
Minimum TOEFL score: 550
Most popular departments: finance, general management, health care administration, leadership, marketing

University of Maryland-College Park (Smith)
2308 Van Munching Hall
College Park, MD 20742
www.rhsmith.umd.edu
Public
Admissions: (301) 405-0202
Email: mba_info@rhsmith.umd.edu
Financial aid: (301) 314-8297
Application deadline: 03/01
In-state tuition: full time: $41,313; part time: $1,465/credit hour
Out-of-state tuition: full time: $49,413
Room/board/expenses: N/A
College-funded aid: Yes
International student aid: Yes
Full-time enrollment: 200
men: 64%; women: 36%; minorities: 22%; international: 36%
Part-time enrollment: 711
men: 66%; women: 34%; minorities: 30%; international: 9%
Acceptance rate (full time): 29%
Average GMAT (full time): 662
Average GMAT (part time): 590
Average GPA (full time): 3.33
Average age of entrants to full-time program: 29
Average months of prior work experience (full time): 68
TOEFL requirement: Yes
Minimum TOEFL score: 600
Most popular departments: consulting, entrepreneurship, finance, general management, marketing
Mean starting base salary for 2014 full-time graduates: $92,781
Employment location for 2014 class: Intl. 3%; N.E. 18%; M.A. 63%; S. N/A; M.W. 10%; S.W. N/A; W. 7%

MASSACHUSETTS

Babson College (Olin)
231 Forest Street
Babson Park, MA 02457-0310
www.babson.edu/graduate
Private
Admissions: (781) 239-4317
Email: mbaadmission@babson.edu
Financial aid: (781) 239-4219
Application deadline: rolling
Tuition: total program: $98,144 (full time); part time: $1,550/credit hour
Room/board/expenses: $50,944
College-funded aid: Yes
International student aid: Yes
Average student indebtedness at graduation: $62,954
Full-time enrollment: 378
men: 67%; women: 33%; minorities: 7%; international: 65%
Part-time enrollment: 292
men: 65%; women: 35%; minorities: 11%; international: 12%
Acceptance rate (full time): 67%

Average GMAT (full time): 630
Average GMAT (part time): 580
Average GPA (full time): 3.13
Average age of entrants to full-time program: 27
Average months of prior work experience (full time): 56
TOEFL requirement: Yes
Minimum TOEFL score: N/A
Most popular departments: entrepreneurship, finance, marketing, other
Mean starting base salary for 2014 full-time graduates: $83,191
Employment location for 2014 class: Intl. 32%; N.E. 56%; M.A. 1%; S. 5%; M.W. 0%; S.W. 2%; W. 5%

Bentley University (McCallum)
175 Forest Street
Waltham, MA 02452-4705
www.bentley.edu/graduate/admission-financial-aid
Private
Admissions: (781) 891-2108
Email: bentleygraduateadmissions@bentley.edu
Financial aid: (781) 891-3441
Application deadline: 03/15
Tuition: full time: $36,487; part time: $1,305/credit hour
Room/board/expenses: $18,810
College-funded aid: Yes
International student aid: Yes
Average student indebtedness at graduation: $40,627
Full-time enrollment: 154
men: 59%; women: 41%; minorities: 11%; international: 59%
Part-time enrollment: 248
men: 60%; women: 40%; minorities: 15%; international: 6%
Acceptance rate (full time): 73%
Average GMAT (full time): 594
Average GMAT (part time): 603
Average GPA (full time): 3.23
Average age of entrants to full-time program: 27
Average months of prior work experience (full time): 70
TOEFL requirement: Yes
Minimum TOEFL score: 600
Most popular departments: accounting, finance, marketing, management information systems, statistics and operations research
Mean starting base salary for 2014 full-time graduates: $76,160
Employment location for 2014 class: Intl. 3%; N.E. 83%; M.A. N/A; S. 5%; M.W. N/A; S.W. 3%; W. 8%

Boston College (Carroll)
140 Commonwealth Avenue
Fulton Hall 320
Chestnut Hill, MA 02467
www.bc.edu/mba
Private
Admissions: (617) 552-3920
Email: bcmba@bc.edu
Financial aid: (800) 294-0294
Application deadline: 04/15
Tuition: full time: $43,880; part time: $1,490/credit hour
Room/board/expenses: $19,560
College-funded aid: Yes
International student aid: Yes
Average student indebtedness at graduation: $64,451
Full-time enrollment: 193
men: 66%; women: 34%; minorities: 11%; international: 30%
Part-time enrollment: 391
men: 64%; women: 36%; minorities: 20%; international: 4%

Acceptance rate (full time): 42%
Average GMAT (full time): 664
Average GMAT (part time): 586
Average GPA (full time): 3.37
Average age of entrants to full-time program: 27
Average months of prior work experience (full time): 45
TOEFL requirement: Yes
Minimum TOEFL score: 600
Most popular departments: accounting, finance, general management, leadership, marketing
Mean starting base salary for 2014 full-time graduates: $94,963
Employment location for 2014 class: Intl. 3%; N.E. 83%; M.A. 0%; S. 4%; M.W. 0%; S.W. 3%; W. 7%

Boston University

595 Commonwealth Avenue
Boston, MA 02215-1704
management.bu.edu
Private
Admissions: (617) 353-2670
Email: mba@bu.edu
Financial aid: (617) 353-2670
Application deadline: N/A
Tuition: full time: $46,424; part time: $1,428/credit hour
Room/board/expenses: $18,254
College-funded aid: Yes
International student aid: Yes
Full-time enrollment: 273
men: 63%; women: 37%;
minorities: 19%; international: 35%
Part-time enrollment: 678
men: 60%; women: 40%;
minorities: 17%; international: 5%
Acceptance rate (full time): 31%
Average GMAT (part time): 602
Average GPA (full time): 3.41
Average age of entrants to full-time program: 28
Average months of prior work experience (full time): 56
TOEFL requirement: Yes
Minimum TOEFL score: 600
Most popular departments: finance, health care administration, marketing, management information systems, non-profit management
Mean starting base salary for 2014 full-time graduates: $99,071
Employment location for 2014 class: Intl. 5%; N.E. 77%; M.A. 3%; S. 0%; M.W. 3%; S.W. 2%; W. 9%

Brandeis University[1]

415 South Street
Waltham, MA 02454-9110
www.brandeis.edu/global
Private
Admissions: (781) 736-4829
Email: admissions@lembergbrandeis.edu
Financial aid: N/A
Tuition: N/A
Room/board/expenses: N/A
Enrollment: N/A

Clark University

950 Main Street
Worcester, MA 01610
www.clarku.edu/gsom
Private
Admissions: (508) 793-7406
Email: gradadmissions@clarku.edu
Financial aid: (508) 793-7373
Application deadline: 06/01
Tuition: full time: $1,325/credit hour; part time: $1,325/credit hour
Room/board/expenses: $13,100
College-funded aid: Yes

International student aid: Yes
Full-time enrollment: 117
men: 56%; women: 44%;
minorities: 9%; international: 44%
Part-time enrollment: 76
men: 63%; women: 37%;
minorities: 9%; international: 3%
Acceptance rate (full time): 30%
Average GMAT (full time): 563
Average GPA (full time): 3.33
Average age of entrants to full-time program: 24
Average months of prior work experience (full time): 36
TOEFL requirement: Yes
Minimum TOEFL score: 577

Harvard University

Dillou House
Boston, MA 02163
www.hbs.edu
Private
Admissions: (617) 495-6128
Email: admissions@hbs.edu
Financial aid: (617) 495-6640
Application deadline: N/A
Tuition: full time: $69,593; part time: N/A
Room/board/expenses: $25,507
College-funded aid: Yes
International student aid: Yes
Average student indebtedness at graduation: $78,991
Full-time enrollment: 1,867
men: 59%; women: 41%;
minorities: 25%; international: 35%
Part-time enrollment: N/A
men: N/A; women: N/A; minorities: N/A; international: N/A
Acceptance rate (full time): 11%
Average GMAT (full time): 726
Average GPA (full time): 3.67
Average age of entrants to full-time program: 27
Average months of prior work experience (full time): 49
TOEFL requirement: Yes
Minimum TOEFL score: N/A
Mean starting base salary for 2014 full-time graduates: $127,236
Employment location for 2014 class: Intl. 16%; N.E. 40%; M.A. 5%; S. 4%; M.W. 8%; S.W. 5%; W. 23%

Massachusetts Institute of Technology (Sloan)

238 Main Street, E48-500
Cambridge, MA 02142
mitsloan.mit.edu/mba
Private
Admissions: (617) 258-5434
Email: mbaadmissions@sloan.mit.edu
Financial aid: (617) 253-4971
Application deadline: N/A
Tuition: full time: $63,750; part time: N/A
Room/board/expenses: $32,264
College-funded aid: Yes
International student aid: Yes
Average student indebtedness at graduation: $106,602
Full-time enrollment: 812
men: 63%; women: 37%;
minorities: 24%; international: 41%
Part-time enrollment: N/A
men: N/A; women: N/A; minorities: N/A; international: N/A
Acceptance rate (full time): 14%
Average GMAT (full time): 713
Average GPA (full time): 3.58
Average age of entrants to full-time program: 28
Average months of prior work experience (full time): 56
TOEFL requirement: No

Minimum TOEFL score: N/A
Most popular departments: entrepreneurship, finance, international business, manufacturing and technology management, operations management
Mean starting base salary for 2014 full-time graduates: $121,277
Employment location for 2014 class: Intl. 14%; N.E. 36%; M.A. 3%; S. 4%; M.W. 6%; S.W. 6%; W. 32%

Northeastern University

360 Huntington Avenue
350 Dodge Hall
Boston, MA 02115
www.mba.northeastern.edu
Private
Admissions: (617) 373-5992
Email: gradbusiness@neu.edu
Financial aid: (617) 373-5899
Application deadline: 04/15
Tuition: full time: $1,433/credit hour; part time: $1,433/credit hour
Room/board/expenses: $25,350
College-funded aid: Yes
International student aid: Yes
Full-time enrollment: 235
men: 63%; women: 37%;
minorities: 13%; international: 28%
Part-time enrollment: 390
men: 61%; women: 39%;
minorities: 21%; international: 2%
Acceptance rate (full time): 22%
Average GMAT (full time): 655
Average GMAT (part time): 567
Average GPA (full time): 3.24
Average age of entrants to full-time program: 26
Average months of prior work experience (full time): 35
TOEFL requirement: Yes
Minimum TOEFL score: 600
Most popular departments: entrepreneurship, finance, international business, marketing, supply chain management
Mean starting base salary for 2014 full-time graduates: $76,038
Employment location for 2014 class: Intl. N/A; N.E. 91%; M.A. 2%; S. 7%; M.W. N/A; S.W. N/A; W. N/A

Simmons College[1]

300 The Fenway
Boston, MA 02115
www.simmons.edu/som
Private
Admissions: N/A
Financial aid: N/A
Tuition: N/A
Room/board/expenses: N/A
Enrollment: N/A

Suffolk University (Sawyer)

8 Ashburton Place
Boston, MA 02108
www.suffolk.edu/business
Private
Admissions: (617) 573-8302
Email: grad.admission@suffolk.edu
Financial aid: (617) 573-8470
Application deadline: rolling
Tuition: full time: $39,288; part time: $1,308/credit hour
Room/board/expenses: $19,880
College-funded aid: Yes
International student aid: Yes
Average student indebtedness at graduation: $66,033
Full-time enrollment: 114
men: 55%; women: 45%;
minorities: 16%; international: 31%

Part-time enrollment: 325
men: 48%; women: 52%;
minorities: 18%; international: 2%
Acceptance rate (full time): 51%
Average GMAT (full time): 488
Average GMAT (part time): 496
Average GPA (full time): 3.22
Average age of entrants to full-time program: 27
Average months of prior work experience (full time): 47
TOEFL requirement: Yes
Minimum TOEFL score: 550
Most popular departments: accounting, finance, marketing, tax
Mean starting base salary for 2014 full-time graduates: $67,800
Employment location for 2014 class: Intl. 16%; N.E. 79%; M.A. 3%; S. N/A; M.W. N/A; S.W. N/A; W. 3%

University of Massachusetts-Amherst (Isenberg)

121 Presidents Drive
Amherst, MA 01003
www.isenberg.umass.edu/mba
Public
Admissions: (413) 545-5608
Email: mba@isenberg.umass.edu
Financial aid: (413) 577-0555
Application deadline: 12/01
In-state tuition: full time: $2,640; part time: $825/credit hour
Out-of-state tuition: full time: $9,937
Room/board/expenses: $27,625
College-funded aid: Yes
International student aid: Yes
Average student indebtedness at graduation: $28,240
Full-time enrollment: 45
men: 64%; women: 36%;
minorities: 13%; international: 33%
Part-time enrollment: 1,185
men: 73%; women: 27%;
minorities: 19%; international: 6%
Acceptance rate (full time): 25%
Average GMAT (full time): 648
Average GMAT (part time): 563
Average GPA (full time): 3.40
Average age of entrants to full-time program: 28
Average months of prior work experience (full time): 51
TOEFL requirement: Yes
Minimum TOEFL score: 600
Most popular departments: entrepreneurship, finance, health care administration, marketing, sports business
Mean starting base salary for 2014 full-time graduates: $81,583
Employment location for 2014 class: Intl. 0%; N.E. 58%; M.A. 17%; S. 0%; M.W. 17%; S.W. 0%; W. 8%

University of Massachusetts-Boston

100 Morrissey Boulevard
Boston, MA 02125-3393
www.umb.edu/cmgrad
Public
Admissions: (617) 287-7720
Email: gradcm@umb.edu
Financial aid: (617) 287-6300
Application deadline: 06/01
In-state tuition: full time: $625/credit hour; part time: $625/credit hour
Out-of-state tuition: full time: $1,212/credit hour
Room/board/expenses: $14,989
College-funded aid: Yes
International student aid: Yes

Full-time enrollment: 238
men: 53%; women: 47%;
minorities: 16%; international: 58%
Part-time enrollment: 188
men: 64%; women: 36%;
minorities: 17%; international: 0%
Acceptance rate (full time): 74%
Average GMAT (full time): 587
Average GMAT (part time): 570
Average GPA (full time): 3.30
Average age of entrants to full-time program: 26
Average months of prior work experience (full time): 39
TOEFL requirement: Yes
Minimum TOEFL score: 600
Most popular departments: finance, health care administration, international business, leadership, marketing
Mean starting base salary for 2014 full-time graduates: $61,173
Employment location for 2014 class: Intl. 13%; N.E. 57%; M.A. 4%; S. 9%; M.W. 9%; S.W. 0%; W. 9%

University of Massachusetts-Dartmouth

285 Old Westport Road
North Dartmouth, MA 02747-2300
www.umassd.edu/charlton/
Public
Admissions: (508) 999-8604
Email: graduate@umassd.edu
Financial aid: (508) 999-8643
Application deadline: 07/01
In-state tuition: full time: $13,952; part time: $86/credit hour
Out-of-state tuition: full time: $19,980
Room/board/expenses: $14,286
College-funded aid: Yes
International student aid: Yes
Full-time enrollment: 147
men: 53%; women: 47%;
minorities: 2%; international: 86%
Part-time enrollment: 154
men: 49%; women: 51%;
minorities: 12%; international: 23%
Acceptance rate (full time): 80%
Average GMAT (full time): 481
Average GMAT (part time): 512
Average GPA (full time): 3.27
Average age of entrants to full-time program: 28
TOEFL requirement: Yes
Minimum TOEFL score: 500
Most popular departments: accounting, finance, general management, marketing, supply chain management

University of Massachusetts-Lowell

1 University Avenue
Lowell, MA 01854
www.uml.edu/grad
Public
Admissions: (978) 934-2381
Email: graduate_school@uml.edu
Financial aid: (978) 934-4220
Application deadline: rolling
In-state tuition: full time: $1,637; part time: $91/credit hour
Out-of-state tuition: full time: $6,425
Room/board/expenses: $18,200
College-funded aid: Yes
International student aid: Yes
Full-time enrollment: 104
men: 66%; women: 34%;
minorities: 10%; international: 65%
Part-time enrollment: 556
men: 68%; women: 32%;
minorities: 22%; international: 3%

Acceptance rate (full time): 86%
Average GMAT (full time): 530
Average GMAT (part time): 585
Average GPA (full time): 3.37
Average age of entrants to full-time program: 25
Average months of prior work experience (full time): 44
TOEFL requirement: Yes
Minimum TOEFL score: 600
Most popular departments: accounting, entrepreneurship, finance, general management, management information systems

Western New England University

1215 Wilbraham Road
Springfield, MA 01119-2684
www1.wne.edu/business/
Private
Admissions: (800) 325-1122
Email: study@wne.edu
Financial aid: (413) 796-2080
Application deadline: rolling
Tuition: full time: N/A; part time: $771/credit hour
Room/board/expenses: N/A
College-funded aid: No
International student aid: No
Full-time enrollment: N/A
men: N/A; women: N/A; minorities: N/A; international: N/A
Part-time enrollment: 176
men: 48%; women: 52%;
minorities: 8%; international: 3%
Average GMAT (part time): 505
TOEFL requirement: Yes
Minimum TOEFL score: 550
Most popular departments: accounting, general management, leadership

Worcester Polytechnic Institute

100 Institute Road
Worcester, MA 01609
business.wpi.edu
Private
Admissions: (508) 831-4665
Email: business@wpi.edu
Financial aid: (508) 831-5469
Application deadline: 07/01
Tuition: full time: $1,325/credit hour; part time: $1,325/credit hour
Room/board/expenses: $14,000
College-funded aid: Yes
International student aid: Yes
Full-time enrollment: 123
men: 37%; women: 63%;
minorities: 2%; international: 87%
Part-time enrollment: 282
men: 69%; women: 31%;
minorities: 10%; international: 15%
Acceptance rate (full time): 39%
Average GMAT (full time): 628
Average GMAT (part time): 550
Average GPA (full time): 3.50
Average age of entrants to full-time program: 24
Average months of prior work experience (full time): 23
TOEFL requirement: Yes
Minimum TOEFL score: 563
Most popular departments: entrepreneurship, marketing, management information systems, operations management, technology

MICHIGAN

Central Michigan University[1]

252 ABSC - Grawn Hall
Mount Pleasant, MI 48859
www.cmich.edu/colleges/cba/Pages/default.aspx
Public
Admissions: (989) 774-4723
Email: grad@cmich.edu
Financial aid: N/A
Tuition: N/A
Room/board/expenses: N/A
Enrollment: N/A

Eastern Michigan University

404 Gary M. Owen Building
Ypsilanti, MI 48197
www.cob.emich.edu
Public
Admissions: (734) 487-4444
Email: cob.graduate@emich.edu
Financial aid: (734) 487-0455
Application deadline: 05/15
In-state tuition: full time: $649/credit hour; part time: $649/credit hour
Out-of-state tuition: full time: $1,116/credit hour
Room/board/expenses: $9,000
College-funded aid: Yes
International student aid: Yes
Full-time enrollment: N/A
men: N/A; women: N/A; minorities: N/A; international: N/A
Part-time enrollment: 191
men: 59%; women: 41%;
minorities: 36%; international: 12%
Average GMAT (part time): 500
TOEFL requirement: Yes
Minimum TOEFL score: 550
Most popular departments: accounting, entrepreneurship, general management, human resources management, supply chain management

Grand Valley State University (Seidman)

50 Front Ave. SW
Grand Rapids, MI 49504-6424
www.gvsu.edu
Public
Admissions: (616) 331-7400
Email: go2gvmba@gvsu.edu
Financial aid: (616) 331-3234
Application deadline: 08/01
In-state tuition: total program: $36,927 (full time); part time: $589/credit hour
Out-of-state tuition: total program: $44,907 (full time)
Room/board/expenses: $12,600
College-funded aid: Yes
International student aid: Yes
Average student indebtedness at graduation: $45,457
Full-time enrollment: 13
men: 62%; women: 38%;
minorities: 0%; international: 15%
Part-time enrollment: 184
men: 26%; women: 74%;
minorities: 5%; international: 4%
Acceptance rate (full time): 100%
Average GMAT (full time): 571
Average GMAT (part time): 573
Average GPA (full time): 3.50
Average age of entrants to full-time program: 24
Average months of prior work experience (full time): 24
TOEFL requirement: Yes
Minimum TOEFL score: 550

Most popular departments: finance, general management, manufacturing and technology management
Mean starting base salary for 2014 full-time graduates: $56,166
Employment location for 2014 class: Intl. N/A; N.E. N/A; M.A. N/A; S. 7%; M.W. 93%; S.W. N/A; W. N/A

Michigan State University (Broad)

Eppley Center
645 N. Shaw Lane, Rm 211
East Lansing, MI 48824-1121
www.mba.msu.edu
Public
Admissions: (517) 355-7604
Email: mba@msu.edu
Financial aid: (517) 355-7604
Application deadline: N/A
In-state tuition: full time: $28,313; part time: N/A
Out-of-state tuition: full time: $44,895
Room/board/expenses: $20,030
College-funded aid: Yes
International student aid: Yes
Average student indebtedness at graduation: $56,504
Full-time enrollment: 150
men: 73%; women: 27%;
minorities: 12%; international: 39%
Part-time enrollment: N/A
men: N/A; women: N/A; minorities: N/A; international: N/A
Acceptance rate (full time): 29%
Average GMAT (full time): 666
Average GPA (full time): 3.30
Average age of entrants to full-time program: 28
Average months of prior work experience (full time): 50
TOEFL requirement: Yes
Minimum TOEFL score: 600
Most popular departments: finance, general management, human resources management, marketing, supply chain management
Mean starting base salary for 2014 full-time graduates: $91,647
Employment location for 2014 class: Intl. 2%; N.E. 6%; M.A. 2%; S. 9%; M.W. 55%; S.W. 8%; W. 18%

Michigan Technological University

1400 Townsend Drive
Houghton, MI 49931-1295
www.mba.mtu.edu
Public
Admissions: (906) 487-3055
Email: mba@mtu.edu
Financial aid: (906) 487-3055
Application deadline: 07/01
In-state tuition: full time: $821/credit hour; part time: $821/credit hour
Out-of-state tuition: full time: $821/credit hour
Room/board/expenses: $13,347
College-funded aid: Yes
International student aid: Yes
Full-time enrollment: 24
men: 63%; women: 38%;
minorities: 4%; international: 25%
Part-time enrollment: N/A
men: N/A; women: N/A; minorities: N/A; international: N/A
Acceptance rate (full time): 32%
Average GMAT (full time): 568
Average GPA (full time): 3.30
Average age of entrants to full-time program: 31
Average months of prior work experience (full time): 142

TOEFL requirement: Yes
Minimum TOEFL score: 590
Most popular departments: entrepreneurship, manufacturing and technology management, technology

Northern Michigan University

1401 Presque Isle Avenue
Marquette, MI 49855
www.nmu.edu/graduatestudies
Public
Admissions: (906) 227-2300
Email: gradapp@nmu.edu
Financial aid: (906) 227-2327
Application deadline: 07/01
In-state tuition: full time: $623/credit hour; part time: $623/credit hour
Out-of-state tuition: full time: $623/credit hour
Room/board/expenses: $8,954
College-funded aid: Yes
International student aid: Yes
Average student indebtedness at graduation: $21,125
Full-time enrollment: 23
men: 43%; women: 57%;
minorities: 9%; international: 9%
Part-time enrollment: 2
men: 0%; women: 100%;
minorities: 0%; international: 0%
Acceptance rate (full time): 93%
Average GMAT (full time): 504
Average GPA (full time): 3.37
Average age of entrants to full-time program: 26
Average months of prior work experience (full time): 61
TOEFL requirement: Yes
Minimum TOEFL score: 550
Most popular departments: general management
Mean starting base salary for 2014 full-time graduates: $44,875
Employment location for 2014 class: Intl. 0%; N.E. 0%; M.A. 0%; S. 13%; M.W. 75%; S.W. 13%; W. 0%

Oakland University

238 Elliott Hall
Rochester, MI 48309-4493
www.oakland.edu/business/grad
Public
Admissions: (248) 370-3287
Email: gbp@lists.oakland.edu
Financial aid: (248) 370-2550
Application deadline: 07/15
In-state tuition: full time: $637/credit hour; part time: $637/credit hour
Out-of-state tuition: full time: $1,027/credit hour
Room/board/expenses: $12,200
College-funded aid: Yes
International student aid: Yes
Full-time enrollment: N/A
men: N/A; women: N/A; minorities: N/A; international: N/A
Part-time enrollment: 313
men: 68%; women: 32%;
minorities: 15%; international: 9%
Average GMAT (part time): 482
TOEFL requirement: Yes
Minimum TOEFL score: 550

Saginaw Valley State University

7400 Bay Road
University Center, MI 48710
www.svsu.edu/cbm/
Public
Admissions: (989) 964-4064
Email: cbmdean@svsu.edu
Financial aid: (989) 964-4103
Application deadline: rolling

In-state tuition: full time: $498/credit hour; part time: $498/credit hour
Out-of-state tuition: full time: $949/credit hour
Room/board/expenses: $13,117
College-funded aid: Yes
International student aid: Yes
Full-time enrollment: N/A
men: N/A; women: N/A; minorities: N/A; international: N/A
Part-time enrollment: 103
men: 65%; women: 35%;
minorities: 9%; international: 42%
TOEFL requirement: Yes
Minimum TOEFL score: 550

University of Detroit Mercy

4001 W. McNichols Road
Detroit, MI 48221-3038
business.udmercy.edu
Private
Admissions: (800) 635-5020
Email: admissions@udmercy.edu
Financial aid: N/A
Application deadline: 08/01
Tuition: full time: $1,439/credit hour; part time: $1,439/credit hour
Room/board/expenses: N/A
College-funded aid: Yes
International student aid: Yes
Average student indebtedness at graduation: $59,600
Full-time enrollment: 43
men: 58%; women: 42%;
minorities: 23%; international: 23%
Part-time enrollment: 81
men: 43%; women: 57%;
minorities: 28%; international: 2%
Acceptance rate (full time): 84%
Average GMAT (full time): 540
Average GPA (full time): 3.30
Average age of entrants to full-time program: 29
TOEFL requirement: No
Minimum TOEFL score: N/A
Most popular departments: accounting, general management, health care administration, leadership, organizational behavior

University of Michigan-Ann Arbor (Ross)

701 Tappan Street
Ann Arbor, MI 48109-1234
michiganross.umich.edu/
Public
Admissions: (734) 763-5796
Email: rossmba@umich.edu
Financial aid: (734) 764-5796
Application deadline: 03/23
In-state tuition: full time: $54,778; part time: $1,796/credit hour
Out-of-state tuition: full time: $59,778
Room/board/expenses: $19,556
College-funded aid: Yes
International student aid: Yes
Average student indebtedness at graduation: $101,107
Full-time enrollment: 886
men: 68%; women: 32%;
minorities: 24%; international: 31%
Part-time enrollment: 445
men: 80%; women: 20%;
minorities: 12%; international: 18%
Average GMAT (full time): 702
Average GMAT (part time): 644
Average GPA (full time): 3.40
Average age of entrants to full-time program: 27
Average months of prior work experience (full time): 64
TOEFL requirement: Yes

Minimum TOEFL score: N/A
Most popular departments: consulting, entrepreneurship, finance, marketing, operations management
Mean starting base salary for 2014 full-time graduates: $115,309
Employment location for 2014 class: Intl. 7%; N.E. 21%; M.A. 3%; S. 4%; M.W. 36%; S.W. 7%; W. 22%

University of Michigan-Dearborn
19000 Hubbard Drive
Dearborn, MI 48126-2638
umdearborn.edu/cob
Public
Admissions: (313) 593-5460
Email: umd-gradbusiness@umich.edu
Financial aid: (313) 593-5300
Application deadline: 08/01
In-state tuition: full time: N/A; part time: $613/credit hour
Out-of-state tuition: full time: N/A
Room/board/expenses: N/A
College-funded aid: Yes
International student aid: Yes
Full-time enrollment: N/A
men: N/A; women: N/A; minorities: N/A; international: N/A
Part-time enrollment: 200
men: 65%; women: 36%; minorities: 16%; international: 4%
Average GMAT (part time): 581
TOEFL requirement: Yes
Minimum TOEFL score: 560
Most popular departments: finance, general management, international business, marketing, management information systems

University of Michigan-Flint
303 E. Kearsley Street
Flint, MI 48502-1950
mba.umflint.edu
Public
Admissions: (810) 762-3171
Email: graduate@umflint.edu.
Financial aid: (810) 762-3444
Application deadline: 08/01
In-state tuition: full time: $11,601; part time: $621/credit hour
Out-of-state tuition: full time: $14,296
Room/board/expenses: $10,866
College-funded aid: Yes
International student aid: No
Full-time enrollment: N/A
men: N/A; women: N/A; minorities: N/A; international: N/A
Part-time enrollment: 169
men: 61%; women: 39%; minorities: 20%; international: 13%
Average GMAT (part time): 519
TOEFL requirement: Yes
Minimum TOEFL score: 560
Most popular departments: accounting, finance, health care administration, international business, marketing

Wayne State University
5201 Cass Avenue
Prentis Building
Detroit, MI 48202
www.business.wayne.edu
Public
Admissions: (313) 577-4511
Email: gradbusiness@wayne.edu
Financial aid: (313) 577-2100
Application deadline: 06/01
In-state tuition: full time: $664/credit hour; part time: $664/credit hour

Out-of-state tuition: full time: $1,329/credit hour
Room/board/expenses: $16,431
College-funded aid: Yes
International student aid: Yes
Full-time enrollment: N/A
men: N/A; women: N/A; minorities: N/A; international: N/A
Part-time enrollment: 490
men: 61%; women: 39%; minorities: 27%; international: 6%
Average GMAT (part time): 471
TOEFL requirement: Yes
Minimum TOEFL score: 550
Most popular departments: finance, general management, marketing, management information systems, supply chain management

Western Michigan University (Haworth)
1903 W. Michigan Avenue
Kalamazoo, MI 49008-5480
www.wmich.edu/mba
Public
Admissions: (269) 387-5133
Email: mba-advising@wmich.edu
Financial aid: (269) 387-6000
Application deadline: rolling
In-state tuition: full time: N/A; part time: $514/credit hour
Out-of-state tuition: full time: N/A
Room/board/expenses: N/A
College-funded aid: Yes
International student aid: No
Full-time enrollment: N/A
men: N/A; women: N/A; minorities: N/A; international: N/A
Part-time enrollment: 381
men: 67%; women: 33%; minorities: 10%; international: 13%
Average GMAT (part time): 533
TOEFL requirement: Yes
Minimum TOEFL score: 550
Most popular departments: finance, general management, health care administration, marketing, management information systems

MINNESOTA

Minnesota State University-Mankato
120 Morris Hall
Mankato, MN 56001
grad.mnsu.edu
Public
Admissions: (507) 389-2321
Financial aid: (507) 389-1419
Application deadline: 06/01
In-state tuition: full time: N/A; part time: $566/credit hour
Out-of-state tuition: full time: N/A
Room/board/expenses: N/A
College-funded aid: Yes
International student aid: No
Full-time enrollment: N/A
men: N/A; women: N/A; minorities: N/A; international: N/A
Part-time enrollment: 54
men: 74%; women: 26%; minorities: 6%; international: 13%
Average GMAT (part time): 555
TOEFL requirement: Yes
Minimum TOEFL score: 500

Minnesota State University-Moorhead[1]
1104 7th Ave South
Moorhead, MN 56563
www.mnstate.edu/
Public
Admissions: (218) 477-2134
Email: graduate@mnstate.edu
Financial aid: N/A
Tuition: N/A
Room/board/expenses: N/A
Enrollment: N/A

St. Cloud State University (Herberger)[1]
720 Fourth Avenue S
St. Cloud, MN 56301-4498
www.stcloudstate.edu/mba
Public
Admissions: (320) 308-3212
Email: mba@stcloudstate.edu
Financial aid: N/A
Tuition: N/A
Room/board/expenses: N/A
Enrollment: N/A

University of Minnesota-Duluth (Labovitz)
1318 Kirby Drive
Duluth, MN 55812-2496
https://lsbe.d.umn.edu/mba/mba.php
Public
Admissions: (218) 726-8839
Email: grad@d.umn.edu
Financial aid: (218) 726-8000
Application deadline: rolling
In-state tuition: full time: N/A; part time: $1,189/credit hour
Out-of-state tuition: full time: N/A
Room/board/expenses: N/A
College-funded aid: Yes
International student aid: No
Full-time enrollment: N/A
men: N/A; women: N/A; minorities: N/A; international: N/A
Part-time enrollment: 42
men: 52%; women: 48%; minorities: 14%; international: 0%
Average GMAT (part time): 518
TOEFL requirement: Yes
Minimum TOEFL score: 550

University of Minnesota-Twin Cities (Carlson)
321 19th Avenue S, Office 4-300
Minneapolis, MN 55455
www.carlsonschool.umn.edu/mba
Public
Admissions: (612) 625-5555
Email: mba@umn.edu
Financial aid: (612) 624-1111
Application deadline: 04/01
In-state tuition: full time: $39,582; part time: $1,270/credit hour
Out-of-state tuition: full time: $49,322
Room/board/expenses: $17,000
College-funded aid: Yes
International student aid: Yes
Average student indebtedness at graduation: $62,769
Full-time enrollment: 220
men: 72%; women: 28%; minorities: 13%; international: 25%
Part-time enrollment: 1,122
men: 68%; women: 32%; minorities: 9%; international: 5%
Acceptance rate (full time): 39%
Average GMAT (full time): 683
Average GMAT (part time): 598
Average GPA (full time): 3.42
Average age of entrants to full-time program: 28
Average months of prior work experience (full time): 57
TOEFL requirement: Yes
Minimum TOEFL score: 580
Most popular departments: finance, general management, health care administration, marketing, supply chain management
Mean starting base salary for 2014 full-time graduates: $99,955

Employment location for 2014 class: Intl. 4%; N.E. 3%; M.A. 0%; S. 4%; M.W. 72%; S.W. 13%; W. 4%

University of St. Thomas
1000 LaSalle Avenue SCH200
Minneapolis, MN 55403
www.stthomas.edu/business
Private
Admissions: (651) 962-8800
Email: ustmba@stthomas.edu
Financial aid: (651) 962-6550
Application deadline: 06/15
Tuition: full time: $32,400; part time: $1,005/credit hour
Room/board/expenses: $16,328
College-funded aid: Yes
International student aid: Yes
Average student indebtedness at graduation: $45,952
Full-time enrollment: 93
men: 59%; women: 41%; minorities: 28%; international: 16%
Part-time enrollment: 708
men: 59%; women: 41%; minorities: 17%; international: 2%
Acceptance rate (full time): 77%
Average GMAT (full time): 557
Average GMAT (part time): 521
Average GPA (full time): 3.30
Average age of entrants to full-time program: 28
Average months of prior work experience (full time): 55
TOEFL requirement: Yes
Minimum TOEFL score: 550
Most popular departments: accounting, entrepreneurship, finance, general management, marketing
Mean starting base salary for 2014 full-time graduates: $74,370
Employment location for 2014 class: Intl. N/A; N.E. N/A; M.A. N/A; S. N/A; M.W. 88%; S.W. 8%; W. 4%

MISSISSIPPI

Jackson State University (Moore)[1]
1400 J.R. Lynch Street
Jackson, MS 39217
www.jsums.edu/business
Public
Admissions: N/A
Financial aid: N/A
Tuition: N/A
Room/board/expenses: N/A
Enrollment: N/A

Millsaps College (Else)[1]
1701 N. State Street
Jackson, MS 39210
millsaps.edu/esom
Private
Admissions: N/A
Financial aid: N/A
Tuition: N/A
Room/board/expenses: N/A
Enrollment: N/A

Mississippi State University
PO Box 5288
Mississippi State, MS 39762
www.business.msstate.edu/gsb
Public
Admissions: (662) 325-1891
Email: gsb@cobilan.msstate.edu
Financial aid: (662) 325-2450
Application deadline: 03/01
In-state tuition: total program: $9,030 (full time); part time: $371/credit hour

Out-of-state tuition: total program: $22,614 (full time)
Room/board/expenses: $9,220
College-funded aid: Yes
International student aid: Yes
Average student indebtedness at graduation: $24,453
Full-time enrollment: 36
men: 58%; women: 42%; minorities: 14%; international: 11%
Part-time enrollment: N/A
men: N/A; women: N/A; minorities: N/A; international: N/A
Acceptance rate (full time): 55%
Average GMAT (full time): 566
Average GPA (full time): 3.61
Average age of entrants to full-time program: 24
TOEFL requirement: Yes
Minimum TOEFL score: 575
Mean starting base salary for 2014 full-time graduates: $43,347
Employment location for 2014 class: Intl. N/A; N.E. N/A; M.A. 90%; S. N/A; M.W. N/A; S.W. 5%; W. 5%

University of Mississippi
253 Holman Hall
University, MS 38677
www.olemissbusiness.com/mba
Public
Admissions: (662) 915-5483
Email: ajones@bus.olemiss.edu
Financial aid: (800) 891-4596
Application deadline: 01/07
In-state tuition: total program: $15,970 (full time); part time: $529/credit hour
Out-of-state tuition: total program: $39,055 (full time)
Room/board/expenses: $19,098
College-funded aid: Yes
International student aid: Yes
Average student indebtedness at graduation: $21,081
Full-time enrollment: 75
men: 71%; women: 29%; minorities: 11%; international: 1%
Part-time enrollment: N/A
men: N/A; women: N/A; minorities: N/A; international: N/A
Acceptance rate (full time): 42%
Average GMAT (full time): 521
Average GPA (full time): 3.29
Average age of entrants to full-time program: 24
TOEFL requirement: Yes
Minimum TOEFL score: 600
Employment location for 2014 class: Intl. N/A; N.E. N/A; M.A. N/A; S. 100%; M.W. N/A; S.W. N/A; W. N/A

University of Southern Mississippi
118 College Drive, #5096
Hattiesburg, MS 39406-5096
www.usm.edu/business
Public
Admissions: (601) 266-5137
Email: gc-business@usm.edu
Financial aid: (601) 266-4774
Application deadline: 04/01
In-state tuition: full time: $388/credit hour; part time: $388/credit hour
Out-of-state tuition: full time: $865/credit hour
Room/board/expenses: N/A
College-funded aid: Yes
International student aid: Yes
Full-time enrollment: 22
men: 50%; women: 50%; minorities: 14%; international: 18%
Part-time enrollment: 46
men: 67%; women: 33%; minorities: 4%; international: 4%
Acceptance rate (full time): 78%

Average GMAT (full time): 486
Average GMAT (part time): 488
Average GPA (full time): 3.41
Average age of entrants to full-time program: 26
Average months of prior work experience (full time): 63
TOEFL requirement: Yes
Minimum TOEFL score: 550

MISSOURI

Drury University

900 North Benton Avenue
Springfield, MO 65802
www.drury.edu/mba/
Private
Admissions: (417) 873-6948
Email: grad@drury.edu
Financial aid: (417) 873-7312
Application deadline: N/A
Tuition: full time: N/A; part time: N/A
Room/board/expenses: N/A
College-funded aid: Yes
International student aid: Yes
Full-time enrollment: 56
men: 52%; women: 48%; minorities: N/A; international: 14%
Part-time enrollment: N/A
men: N/A; women: N/A; minorities: N/A; international: N/A
Acceptance rate (full time): 44%
Average GMAT (full time): 540
Average GPA (full time): 3.60
Average age of entrants to full-time program: 27
Average months of prior work experience (full time): 36
TOEFL requirement: Yes
Minimum TOEFL score: 550

Missouri State University

901 S. National Avenue
Glass Hall 400
Springfield, MO 65897
www.mba.missouristate.edu
Public
Admissions: (417) 836-5331
Email: graduatecollege@missouristate.edu
Financial aid: (417) 836-5262
Application deadline: rolling
In-state tuition: full time: $282/credit hour; part time: $282/credit hour
Out-of-state tuition: full time: $533/credit hour
Room/board/expenses: $7,678
College-funded aid: Yes
International student aid: Yes
Full-time enrollment: 359
men: 53%; women: 47%; minorities: 23%; international: 31%
Part-time enrollment: N/A
men: N/A; women: N/A; minorities: N/A; international: N/A
Acceptance rate (full time): 75%
Average GMAT (full time): 504
Average GPA (full time): 3.28
Average age of entrants to full-time program: 30
TOEFL requirement: Yes
Minimum TOEFL score: 550
Most popular departments: finance, general management, leadership, marketing, management information systems

Missouri University of Science & Technology

1870 Miner Circle
Rolla, MO
bit.mst.edu/
Public
Admissions: (573) 341-4165

Email: admissions@mst.edu
Financial aid: N/A
Application deadline: 07/01
In-state tuition: full time: $376/credit hour; part time: $376/credit hour
Out-of-state tuition: full time: $1,013/credit hour
Room/board/expenses: $11,802
College-funded aid: Yes
International student aid: Yes
Average student indebtedness at graduation: $10,143
Full-time enrollment: 66
men: 68%; women: 32%; minorities: 5%; international: 89%
Part-time enrollment: 41
men: 68%; women: 32%; minorities: 12%; international: 39%
Average GMAT (full time): 550
Average GPA (full time): 3.54
Average age of entrants to full-time program: 24
TOEFL requirement: Yes
Minimum TOEFL score: 570
Most popular departments: general management, leadership, management information systems, statistics and operations research, technology

Rockhurst University (Helzberg)

1100 Rockhurst Road
Kansas City, MO 64110
www.rockhurst.edu/hsom/
Private
Admissions: (816) 501-4632
Email: mba@rockhurst.edu
Financial aid: N/A
Application deadline: rolling
Tuition: full time: N/A; part time: $625/credit hour
Room/board/expenses: N/A
College-funded aid: Yes
International student aid: Yes
Full-time enrollment: N/A
men: N/A; women: N/A; minorities: N/A; international: N/A
Part-time enrollment: 303
men: 64%; women: 36%; minorities: 16%; international: 2%
Average GMAT (part time): 521
TOEFL requirement: Yes
Minimum TOEFL score: 550
Most popular departments: accounting, general management, health care administration, international business, statistics and operations research

Southeast Missouri State University (Harrison)

1 University Plaza, MS 5890
Cape Girardeau, MO 63701
www.semo.edu/mba
Public
Admissions: (573) 651-2590
Email: mba@semo.edu
Financial aid: (573) 651-2039
Application deadline: rolling
In-state tuition: full time: $258/credit hour; part time: $258/credit hour
Out-of-state tuition: full time: $482/credit hour
Room/board/expenses: $11,335
College-funded aid: Yes
International student aid: Yes
Full-time enrollment: 63
men: 59%; women: 41%; minorities: 2%; international: 68%
Part-time enrollment: 118
men: 58%; women: 42%; minorities: 6%; international: 12%
Acceptance rate (full time): 49%
Average GMAT (full time): 486

Average GMAT (part time): 473
Average GPA (full time): 3.37
Average age of entrants to full-time program: 26
TOEFL requirement: Yes
Minimum TOEFL score: 550
Most popular departments: accounting, finance, general management, international business, other

St. Louis University (Cook)

3674 Lindell Boulevard
St. Louis, MO 63108
www.business.slu.edu
Private
Admissions: (314) 977-2125
Email: gradbiz@slu.edu
Financial aid: (314) 977-2350
Application deadline: 08/01
Tuition: full time: $54,801; part time: $975/credit hour
Room/board/expenses: $18,158
College-funded aid: Yes
International student aid: Yes
Average student indebtedness at graduation: $50,980
Full-time enrollment: 35
men: 57%; women: 43%; minorities: 6%; international: 31%
Part-time enrollment: 254
men: 61%; women: 39%; minorities: 15%; international: 6%
Acceptance rate (full time): 65%
Average GMAT (full time): 563
Average GMAT (part time): 548
Average GPA (full time): 3.30
Average age of entrants to full-time program: 27
Average months of prior work experience (full time): 39
TOEFL requirement: Yes
Minimum TOEFL score: 570
Most popular departments: finance, general management, international business, marketing, supply chain management
Mean starting base salary for 2014 full-time graduates: $65,563
Employment location for 2014 class: Intl. N/A; N.E. 6%; M.A. N/A; S. N/A; M.W. 94%; S.W. N/A; W. N/A

Truman State University

100 E. Normal
Kirksville, MO 63501
gradstudies.truman.edu
Public
Admissions: (660) 785-4109
Email: gradinfo@truman.edu
Financial aid: (660) 785-4130
Application deadline: rolling
In-state tuition: full time: N/A; part time: N/A
Out-of-state tuition: full time: N/A
Room/board/expenses: N/A
College-funded aid: Yes
International student aid: Yes
Full-time enrollment: 33
men: 36%; women: 64%; minorities: 0%; international: 15%
Part-time enrollment: N/A
men: N/A; women: N/A; minorities: N/A; international: N/A
Acceptance rate (full time): 85%
Average GMAT (full time): 573
Average GPA (full time): 3.47
Average age of entrants to full-time program: 22
TOEFL requirement: Yes
Minimum TOEFL score: 550
Mean starting base salary for 2014 full-time graduates: $51,000

University of Central Missouri (Harmon)

Ward Edwards 1600
Warrensburg, MO 64093
www.ucmo.edu/mba
Public
Admissions: (660) 543-8617
Email: mba@ucmo.edu
Financial aid: (800) 729-2678
Application deadline: rolling
In-state tuition: full time: $276/credit hour; part time: N/A
Out-of-state tuition: full time: $553/credit hour
Room/board/expenses: N/A
College-funded aid: Yes
International student aid: Yes
Full-time enrollment: 110
men: N/A; women: N/A; minorities: N/A; international: N/A
Part-time enrollment: N/A
men: N/A; women: N/A; minorities: N/A; international: N/A
TOEFL requirement: Yes
Minimum TOEFL score: 550

University of Missouri-Kansas City (Bloch)

5100 Rockhill Road
Kansas City, MO 64110
www.bloch.umkc.edu/graduate-program/mba
Public
Admissions: (816) 235-5254
Email: bloch@umkc.edu
Financial aid: (816) 235-1154
Application deadline: rolling
In-state tuition: full time: $343/credit hour; part time: $343/credit hour
Out-of-state tuition: full time: $884/credit hour
Room/board/expenses: $18,888
College-funded aid: Yes
International student aid: Yes
Full-time enrollment: N/A
men: N/A; women: N/A; minorities: N/A; international: N/A
Part-time enrollment: 232
men: 64%; women: 36%; minorities: 12%; international: 9%
Average GMAT (part time): 550
TOEFL requirement: Yes
Minimum TOEFL score: 600
Most popular departments: entrepreneurship, finance, general management, leadership, marketing

University of Missouri-St. Louis[1]

1 University Boulevard
St. Louis, MO 63121
mba.umsl.edu
Public
Admissions: N/A
Financial aid: N/A
Tuition: N/A
Room/board/expenses: N/A
Enrollment: N/A

University of Missouri (Trulaske)

213 Cornell Hall
Columbia, MO 65211
mba.missouri.edu
Public
Admissions: (573) 882-2750
Email: mba@missouri.edu
Financial aid: (573) 882-2750
Application deadline: 07/31
In-state tuition: total program: $26,950 (full time); part time: $347/credit hour

Out-of-state tuition: total program: $59,030 (full time)
Room/board/expenses: $19,556
College-funded aid: Yes
International student aid: Yes
Average student indebtedness at graduation: $21,383
Full-time enrollment: 158
men: 72%; women: 28%; minorities: 4%; international: 28%
Part-time enrollment: N/A
men: N/A; women: N/A; minorities: N/A; international: N/A
Acceptance rate (full time): 43%
Average GMAT (full time): 647
Average GPA (full time): 3.48
Average age of entrants to full-time program: 25
Average months of prior work experience (full time): 27
TOEFL requirement: Yes
Minimum TOEFL score: 550
Most popular departments: entrepreneurship, finance, general management, marketing, other
Mean starting base salary for 2014 full-time graduates: $57,219
Employment location for 2014 class: Intl. 0%; N.E. 2%; M.A. 4%; S. 10%; M.W. 65%; S.W. 10%; W. 8%

Washington University in St. Louis (Olin)

1 Brookings Drive
Campus Box 1133
St. Louis, MO 63130-4899
www.olin.wustl.edu/academicprograms/MBA/Pages/default.aspx
Private
Admissions: (314) 935-7301
Email: mba@wustl.edu
Financial aid: (314) 935-7301
Application deadline: 04/01
Tuition: full time: $52,273; part time: $1,500/credit hour
Room/board/expenses: $24,568
College-funded aid: Yes
International student aid: Yes
Average student indebtedness at graduation: $64,524
Full-time enrollment: 281
men: 73%; women: 27%; minorities: 18%; international: 38%
Part-time enrollment: 362
men: 72%; women: 28%; minorities: 25%; international: 6%
Acceptance rate (full time): 27%
Average GMAT (full time): 699
Average GMAT (part time): 562
Average GPA (full time): 3.43
Average age of entrants to full-time program: 27
Average months of prior work experience (full time): 48
TOEFL requirement: Yes
Minimum TOEFL score: N/A
Most popular departments: consulting, entrepreneurship, finance, marketing, supply chain management
Mean starting base salary for 2014 full-time graduates: $98,297
Employment location for 2014 class: Intl. 3%; N.E. 7%; M.A. 3%; S. 6%; M.W. 56%; S.W. 15%; W. 9%

MONTANA

University of Montana[1]

32 Campus Drive
Missoula, MT 59812-6808
www.business.umt.edu/
Public
Admissions: N/A
Email: mba@business.umt.edu
Financial aid: N/A
Tuition: N/A

Room/board/expenses: N/A
Enrollment: N/A

NEBRASKA

Creighton University
2500 California Plaza
Omaha, NE 68178-0130
business.creighton.edu
Private
Admissions: (402) 280-2841
Email:
busgradadmit@creighton.edu
Financial aid: (402) 280-2731
Application deadline: rolling
Tuition: full time: N/A; part time:
$780/credit hour
Room/board/expenses: N/A
College-funded aid: Yes
International student aid: Yes
Full-time enrollment: N/A
men: N/A; women: N/A; minorities:
N/A; international: N/A
Part-time enrollment: 188
men: 69%; women: 31%;
minorities: 11%; international: 6%
Average GMAT (part time): 530
TOEFL requirement: Yes
Minimum TOEFL score: 550
Most popular departments:
accounting, finance, leadership,
management information
systems, portfolio management

University of Nebraska-Kearney[1]
905 West 25th Street
Kearney, NE 68849
www.unk.edu
Public
Admissions: (800) 717-7881
Email: gradstudies@unk.edu
Financial aid: N/A
Tuition: N/A
Room/board/expenses: N/A
Enrollment: N/A

University of Nebraska-Lincoln
P.O. Box 880405
Lincoln, NE 68588-0405
www.mba.unl.edu
Public
Admissions: (402) 472-2338
Email: cbagrad@unl.edu
Financial aid: (402) 472-2030
Application deadline: 07/01
In-state tuition: full time: N/A; part
time: $353/credit hour
Out-of-state tuition: full time: N/A
Room/board/expenses: N/A
College-funded aid: Yes
International student aid: Yes
Full-time enrollment: N/A
men: N/A; women: N/A; minorities:
N/A; international: N/A
Part-time enrollment: 85
men: 68%; women: 32%;
minorities: 5%; international: 34%
Average GMAT (part time): 595
TOEFL requirement: Yes
Minimum TOEFL score: 550
Most popular departments: finance,
international business, marketing,
supply chain management,
statistics and operations
research

University of Nebraska-Omaha
6708 Pine St
Omaha, NE 68182-0048
mba.unomaha.edu
Public
Admissions: (402) 554-2303
Email: mba@unomaha.edu
Financial aid: (402) 554-2327

Application deadline: 07/01
In-state tuition: full time: N/A; part
time: $278/credit hour
Out-of-state tuition: full time: N/A
Room/board/expenses: N/A
College-funded aid: Yes
International student aid: Yes
Full-time enrollment: N/A
men: N/A; women: N/A; minorities:
N/A; international: N/A
Part-time enrollment: 253
men: 66%; women: 34%;
minorities: 11%; international: 7%
Average GMAT (part time): 581
TOEFL requirement: Yes
Minimum TOEFL score: 550
Most popular departments: finance,
health care administration,
human resources management,
international business, other

NEVADA

University of Nevada-Las Vegas
4505 Maryland Parkway
PO Box 456031
Las Vegas, NV 89154-6031
business.unlv.edu
Public
Admissions: (702) 895-3655
Email: lbsmba@unlv.edu
Financial aid: (702) 895-3682
Application deadline: 06/01
In-state tuition: full time: $364/
credit hour; part time: $364/
credit hour
Out-of-state tuition: full time:
$22,646
Room/board/expenses: N/A
College-funded aid: Yes
International student aid: Yes
Full-time enrollment: N/A
men: N/A; women: N/A; minorities:
N/A; international: N/A
Part-time enrollment: 160
men: 64%; women: 36%;
minorities: 29%; international: 11%
Average GMAT (part time): 585
TOEFL requirement: Yes
Minimum TOEFL score: 550
Most popular departments:
accounting, entrepreneurship,
finance, hotel administration,
management information systems

University of Nevada-Reno
1664 N. Virginia Street
Reno, NV 89557
www.coba.unr.edu
Public
Admissions: (775) 784-4912
Email: vkrentz@unr.edu
Financial aid: (775) 784-4666
Application deadline: 03/15
In-state tuition: full time: N/A; part
time: $365/credit hour
Out-of-state tuition: full time: N/A
Room/board/expenses: N/A
College-funded aid: Yes
International student aid: Yes
Full-time enrollment: N/A
men: N/A; women: N/A; minorities:
N/A; international: N/A
Part-time enrollment: 218
men: 63%; women: 37%;
minorities: 9%; international: 3%
Average GMAT (part time): 528
TOEFL requirement: Yes
Minimum TOEFL score: 550
Most popular departments:
accounting, entrepreneurship,
finance, general management,
marketing

NEW HAMPSHIRE

Dartmouth College (Tuck)
100 Tuck Hall
Hanover, NH 03755-9000
www.tuck.dartmouth.edu
Private
Admissions: (603) 646-3162
Email: tuck.admissions@
dartmouth.edu
Financial aid: (603) 646-0640
Application deadline: 04/03
Tuition: full time: $64,680; part
time: N/A
Room/board/expenses: $29,925
College-funded aid: Yes
International student aid: Yes
Full-time enrollment: 558
men: 68%; women: 32%;
minorities: 15%; international:
33%
Part-time enrollment: N/A
men: N/A; women: N/A; minorities:
N/A; international: N/A
Acceptance rate (full time): 22%
Average GMAT (full time): 716
Average GPA (full time): 3.54
Average age of entrants to full-time
program: 28
TOEFL requirement: Yes
Minimum TOEFL score: N/A
Mean starting base salary for 2014
full-time graduates: $117,860
Employment location for 2014 class:
Intl. 14%; N.E. 45%; M.A. 5%; S.
4%; M.W. 8%; S.W. 3%; W. 20%

University of New Hampshire (Paul)
10 Garrison Avenue
Durham, NH 03824
www.mba.unh.edu
Public
Admissions: (603) 862-1367
Email: info.mba@unh.edu
Financial aid: (603) 862-3600
Application deadline: rolling
In-state tuition: total program:
$29,214 (full time); part time:
$880/credit hour
Out-of-state tuition: total program:
$42,214 (full time)
Room/board/expenses: $12,385
College-funded aid: Yes
International student aid: Yes
Full-time enrollment: 22
men: 50%; women: 50%;
minorities: 0%; international: 18%
Part-time enrollment: 37
men: 68%; women: 32%;
minorities: 19%; international: 0%
Acceptance rate (full time): 81%
Average GMAT (full time): 543
Average GMAT (part time): 573
Average GPA (full time): 3.29
Average age of entrants to full-time
program: 25
TOEFL requirement: Yes
Minimum TOEFL score: 550

NEW JERSEY

Fairleigh Dickinson University (Silberman)[1]
1000 River Road
Teaneck, NJ 07666
www.fduinfo.com/depts/
sctab.php
Private
Admissions: (201) 692-2554
Email: grad@fdu.edu
Financial aid: N/A
Tuition: N/A
Room/board/expenses: N/A
Enrollment: N/A

Monmouth University
400 Cedar Avenue
West Long Branch, NJ 07764
www.monmouth.edu
Private
Admissions: (732) 571-3452
Email: gradadm@monmouth.edu
Financial aid: (732) 571-3463
Application deadline: 07/15
Tuition: full time: $1,004/credit
hour; part time: $1,004/credit
hour
Room/board/expenses: $17,897
College-funded aid: Yes
International student aid: Yes
Average student indebtedness at
graduation: $17,387
Full-time enrollment: 13
men: 62%; women: 38%;
minorities: 0%; international: 0%
Part-time enrollment: 171
men: 61%; women: 39%;
minorities: 16%; international: 5%
Acceptance rate (full time): 100%
Average GMAT (full time): 605
Average GMAT (part time): 482
Average GPA (full time): 3.42
Average age of entrants to full-time
program: 23
Average months of prior work
experience (full time): 78
TOEFL requirement: Yes
Minimum TOEFL score: 550

Montclair State University
Partridge Hall
1 Normal Avenue
Montclair, NJ 07043
www.montclair.edu/mba
Public
Admissions: (973) 655-5147
Email: graduate.school@
montclair.edu
Financial aid: (973) 655-4461
Application deadline: rolling
In-state tuition: full time: $671/
credit hour; part time: $671/
credit hour
Out-of-state tuition: full time: $671/
credit hour
Room/board/expenses: $19,711
College-funded aid: Yes
International student aid: Yes
Average student indebtedness at
graduation: $34,879
Full-time enrollment: N/A
men: N/A; women: N/A; minorities:
N/A; international: N/A
Part-time enrollment: 333
men: 55%; women: 45%;
minorities: 41%; international: 10%
TOEFL requirement: Yes
Minimum TOEFL score: 380

New Jersey Institute of Technology
University Heights
Newark, NJ 07102
management.njit.edu/
Public
Admissions: (973) 596-3300
Email: admissions@njit.edu
Financial aid: (973) 596-3479
Application deadline: rolling
In-state tuition: full time: $18,066;
part time: $982/credit hour
Out-of-state tuition: full time:
$26,458
Room/board/expenses: $16,780
College-funded aid: Yes
International student aid: Yes
Average student indebtedness at
graduation: $32,606
Full-time enrollment: 115
men: 63%; women: 37%;
minorities: 20%; international:
68%

Part-time enrollment: 146
men: 71%; women: 29%;
minorities: 54%; international: 5%
Acceptance rate (full time): 68%
Average GMAT (full time): 560
Average GMAT (part time): 510
Average age of entrants to full-time
program: 24
TOEFL requirement: Yes
Minimum TOEFL score: 550
Mean starting base salary for 2014
full-time graduates: $67,692
Employment location for 2014 class:
Intl. N/A; N.E. 97%; M.A. N/A; S.
N/A; M.W. N/A; S.W. N/A; W. 3%

Rider University
2083 Lawrenceville Road
Lawrenceville, NJ 08648-3099
www.rider.edu/mba
Private
Admissions: (609) 896-5036
Email: gradadm@rider.edu
Financial aid: (609) 896-5360
Application deadline: 08/01
Tuition: full time: N/A; part time:
N/A
Room/board/expenses: N/A
College-funded aid: Yes
International student aid: Yes
Full-time enrollment: N/A
men: N/A; women: N/A; minorities:
N/A; international: N/A
Part-time enrollment: 161
men: 52%; women: 48%;
minorities: 15%; international: 18%
Average GMAT (part time): 502
TOEFL requirement: Yes
Minimum TOEFL score: 550

Rowan University (Rohrer)
201 Mullica Hill Road
Glassboro, NJ 08028
www.rowancge.com
Public
Admissions: (856) 256-5435
Email:
cgceadmissions@rowan.edu
Financial aid: (856) 256-5186
Application deadline:
In-state tuition: full time: $700/
credit hour; part time: $700/
credit hour
Out-of-state tuition: full time: $700/
credit hour
Room/board/expenses: $16,412
College-funded aid: Yes
International student aid: No
Average student indebtedness at
graduation: $7,755
Full-time enrollment: 22
men: 59%; women: 41%;
minorities: 32%; international:
14%
Part-time enrollment: 84
men: 62%; women: 38%;
minorities: 12%; international: 1%
Average GMAT (part time): 509
TOEFL requirement: Yes
Minimum TOEFL score: 550

Rutgers, The State University of New Jersey-Camden
227 Penn Street
Camden, NJ 08102
business.camden.rutgers.edu
Public
Admissions: (856) 225-6104
Email:
camden@camuga.rutgers.edu
Financial aid: (856) 225-6039
Application deadline: rolling
In-state tuition: full time: $918/
credit hour; part time: $918/
credit hour

Out-of-state tuition: full time: $1,541/credit hour
Room/board/expenses: N/A
College-funded aid: Yes
International student aid: Yes
Full-time enrollment: N/A
men: N/A; women: N/A; minorities: N/A; international: N/A
Part-time enrollment: 201
men: 64%; women: 36%;
minorities: 34%; international: 6%
Average GMAT (part time): 500
TOEFL requirement: Yes
Minimum TOEFL score: 550

Rutgers, The State University of New Jersey-Newark and New Brunswick
1 Washington Park
Newark, NJ 07102-3122
www.business.rutgers.edu
Public
Admissions: (973) 353-1234
Email: admit@business.rutgers.edu
Financial aid: (973) 353-5151
Application deadline: 05/01
In-state tuition: full time: $29,958; part time: $1,034/credit hour
Out-of-state tuition: full time: $47,805
Room/board/expenses: $29,500
College-funded aid: Yes
International student aid: No
Average student indebtedness at graduation: $42,500
Full-time enrollment: 201
men: 60%; women: 40%;
minorities: 35%; international: 26%
Part-time enrollment: 988
men: 63%; women: 37%;
minorities: 45%; international: 2%
Acceptance rate (full time): 41%
Average GMAT (full time): 646
Average GMAT (part time): 589
Average GPA (full time): 3.38
Average age of entrants to full-time program: 28
Average months of prior work experience (full time): 55
TOEFL requirement: Yes
Minimum TOEFL score: 600
Most popular departments: entrepreneurship, finance, marketing, supply chain management, other
Mean starting base salary for 2014 full-time graduates: $94,887
Employment location for 2014 class: Intl. 2%; N.E. 71%; M.A. 5%; S. 0%; M.W. 2%; S.W. 11%; W. 9%

Seton Hall University (Stillman)
400 S. Orange Avenue
South Orange, NJ 07079
www.shu.edu/academics/business/
Private
Admissions: (973) 761-9262
Email: mba@shu.edu
Financial aid: (973) 761-9350
Application deadline: 05/31
Tuition: full time: N/A; part time: $1,184/credit hour
Room/board/expenses: $17,600
College-funded aid: Yes
International student aid: Yes
Full-time enrollment: N/A
men: N/A; women: N/A; minorities: N/A; international: N/A
Part-time enrollment: 372
men: 62%; women: 38%;
minorities: 4%; international: 26%
Average GMAT (part time): 563
TOEFL requirement: Yes
Minimum TOEFL score: 607

William Paterson University (Cotsakos)
1600 Valley Road
Wayne, NJ 07474
www.wpunj.edu/cob/
Public
Admissions: (973) 720-2237
Email: graduate@wpunj.edu
Financial aid: (973) 720-2928
Application deadline: rolling
In-state tuition: full time: $523/credit hour; part time: $523/credit hour
Out-of-state tuition: full time: $890/credit hour
Room/board/expenses: $14,770
College-funded aid: Yes
International student aid: Yes
Average student indebtedness at graduation: $22,250
Full-time enrollment: 41
men: 49%; women: 51%;
minorities: 17%; international: 24%
Part-time enrollment: 85
men: 53%; women: 47%;
minorities: 32%; international: 1%
Average GMAT (part time): 450
TOEFL requirement: Yes
Minimum TOEFL score: 550

NEW MEXICO

New Mexico State University
P.O. Box 30001, MSC 3GSP
Las Cruces, NM 88003
business.nmsu.edu/mba
Public
Admissions: (505) 646-8003
Email: mba@nmsu.edu
Financial aid: (505) 646-4105
Application deadline: 07/15
In-state tuition: full time: $4,822; part time: $221/credit hour
Out-of-state tuition: full time: $14,691
Room/board/expenses: $13,068
College-funded aid: Yes
International student aid: Yes
Full-time enrollment: N/A
men: N/A; women: N/A; minorities: N/A; international: N/A
Part-time enrollment: 134
men: 53%; women: 47%;
minorities: 41%; international: 13%
Average GMAT (part time): 490
TOEFL requirement: Yes
Minimum TOEFL score: 550

University of New Mexico (Anderson)
MSC05 3090
1 University of New Mexico
Albuquerque, NM 87131-0001
www.mgt.unm.edu
Public
Admissions: (505) 277-3290
Email: andersonadvising@unm.edu
Financial aid: (505) 277-8900
Application deadline: 04/01
In-state tuition: full time: $431/credit hour; part time: $431/credit hour
Out-of-state tuition: full time: $1,023/credit hour
Room/board/expenses: N/A
College-funded aid: Yes
International student aid: Yes
Full-time enrollment: 184
men: 57%; women: 43%;
minorities: 44%; international: 14%

Part-time enrollment: 200
men: 52%; women: 48%;
minorities: 55%; international: 2%
Average GMAT (full time): 534
Average GMAT (part time): 605
Average GPA (full time): 3.53
Average age of entrants to full-time program: 26
TOEFL requirement: Yes
Minimum TOEFL score: 550
Most popular departments: accounting, finance, marketing, management information systems, operations management
Mean starting base salary for 2014 full-time graduates: $43,517
Employment location for 2014 class: Intl. 0%; N.E. 0%; M.A. 3%; S. 6%; M.W. 0%; S.W. 89%; W. 3%

NEW YORK

Adelphi University
1 South Avenue
Garden City, NY 11530
www.adelphi.edu
Private
Admissions: (516) 877-3050
Email: admissions@adelphi.edu
Financial aid: (516) 877-3080
Application deadline: rolling
Tuition: full time: N/A; part time: N/A
Room/board/expenses: N/A
College-funded aid: Yes
International student aid: Yes
Full-time enrollment: N/A
men: N/A; women: N/A; minorities: N/A; international: N/A
Part-time enrollment: 363
men: 49%; women: 51%;
minorities: 24%; international: 39%
Average GMAT (part time): 501
TOEFL requirement: Yes
Minimum TOEFL score: 550

Alfred University
Saxon Drive
Alfred, NY 14802
business.alfred.edu/mba
Private
Admissions: (800) 541-9229
Email: gradinquiry@alfred.edu
Financial aid: (607) 871-2159
Application deadline: 08/01
Tuition: full time: $38,970; part time: $810/credit hour
Room/board/expenses: $13,090
College-funded aid: Yes
International student aid: Yes
Full-time enrollment: 17
men: 47%; women: 53%;
minorities: 29%; international: 12%
Part-time enrollment: 17
men: 71%; women: 29%;
minorities: 6%; international: N/A
Acceptance rate (full time): 100%
Average GMAT (full time): 320
Average GPA (full time): 3.22
Average age of entrants to full-time program: 24
TOEFL requirement: Yes
Minimum TOEFL score: 590
Employment location for 2014 class: Intl. N/A; N.E. 100%; M.A. N/A; S. N/A; M.W. N/A; S.W. N/A; W. N/A

Binghamton University-SUNY
PO Box 6000
Binghamton, NY 13902-6000
www2.binghamton.edu/som/
Public
Admissions: (607) 777-2317
Email: somadvis@binghamton.edu
Financial aid: (607) 777-2470
Application deadline: 03/01

In-state tuition: full time: $15,224; part time: $551/credit hour
Out-of-state tuition: full time: $24,174
Room/board/expenses: $15,000
College-funded aid: Yes
International student aid: Yes
Average student indebtedness at graduation: $26,947
Full-time enrollment: 81
men: 67%; women: 33%;
minorities: 4%; international: 49%
Part-time enrollment: 5
men: 60%; women: 40%;
minorities: 20%; international: 0%
Acceptance rate (full time): 60%
Average GMAT (full time): 606
Average GPA (full time): 3.37
Average age of entrants to full-time program: 23
Average months of prior work experience (full time): 42
TOEFL requirement: Yes
Minimum TOEFL score: 590
Most popular departments: marketing, management information systems
Mean starting base salary for 2014 full-time graduates: $68,000
Employment location for 2014 class: Intl. 0%; N.E. 100%; M.A. 0%; S. 0%; M.W. 0%; S.W. 0%; W. 0%

Canisius College (Wehle)
2001 Main Street
Buffalo, NY 14208
www.canisius.edu/business/graduate_programs.asp
Public
Admissions: (800) 950-2505
Email: gradbus@canisius.edu
Financial aid: (716) 888-2300
Application deadline: rolling
In-state tuition: total program: $37,950 (full time); part time: $765/credit hour
Out-of-state tuition: total program: $37,950 (full time)
Room/board/expenses: $15,016
College-funded aid: Yes
International student aid: Yes
Full-time enrollment: 20
men: 55%; women: 45%;
minorities: 25%; international: 5%
Part-time enrollment: 233
men: 59%; women: 41%;
minorities: 10%; international: 4%
Acceptance rate (full time): 60%
Average GMAT (full time): 444
Average GMAT (part time): 485
Average GPA (full time): 3.70
Average age of entrants to full-time program: 24
TOEFL requirement: Yes
Minimum TOEFL score: 550
Most popular departments: marketing
Mean starting base salary for 2014 full-time graduates: $51,150
Employment location for 2014 class: Intl. N/A; N.E. 100%; M.A. N/A; S. N/A; M.W. N/A; S.W. N/A; W. N/A

Clarkson University
Snell Hall 322E, Box 5770
Potsdam, NY 13699-5770
www.clarkson.edu/business/graduate
Private
Admissions: (315) 268-6613
Email: busgrad@clarkson.edu
Financial aid: (315) 268-7699
Application deadline: rolling
Tuition: full time: $53,410; part time: $1,390/credit hour
Room/board/expenses: $18,295
College-funded aid: Yes
International student aid: Yes

Average student indebtedness at graduation: $42,273
Full-time enrollment: 64
men: 58%; women: 42%;
minorities: 8%; international: 42%
Part-time enrollment: N/A
men: N/A; women: N/A; minorities: N/A; international: N/A
Acceptance rate (full time): 64%
Average GMAT (full time): 548
Average GPA (full time): 3.29
Average age of entrants to full-time program: 25
Average months of prior work experience (full time): 28
TOEFL requirement: Yes
Minimum TOEFL score: 550
Most popular departments: accounting, entrepreneurship, general management, supply chain management, other
Mean starting base salary for 2014 full-time graduates: $58,164
Employment location for 2014 class: Intl. 6%; N.E. 65%; M.A. 6%; S. 0%; M.W. 12%; S.W. 6%; W. 6%

College at Brockport-SUNY[1]
119 Hartwell Hall
Brockport, NY 14420
www.brockport.edu/business
Public
Admissions: N/A
Financial aid: N/A
Tuition: N/A
Room/board/expenses: N/A
Enrollment: N/A

Columbia University
3022 Broadway
216 Uris Hall
New York, NY 10027
www.gsb.columbia.edu
Private
Admissions: (212) 854-1961
Email: apply@gsb.columbia.edu
Financial aid: (212) 854-4057
Application deadline: 04/13
Tuition: full time: $65,790; part time: N/A
Room/board/expenses: $26,397
College-funded aid: Yes
International student aid: Yes
Full-time enrollment: 1,270
men: 63%; women: 37%;
minorities: 23%; international: 33%
Part-time enrollment: N/A
men: N/A; women: N/A; minorities: N/A; international: N/A
Acceptance rate (full time): 18%
Average GMAT (full time): 716
Average GPA (full time): 3.50
Average age of entrants to full-time program: 28
Average months of prior work experience (full time): 60
TOEFL requirement: Yes
Minimum TOEFL score: N/A
Most popular departments: entrepreneurship, finance, general management, leadership, marketing
Mean starting base salary for 2014 full-time graduates: $118,719

Cornell University (Johnson)
Sage Hall, Cornell University
Ithaca, NY 14853-6201
www.johnson.cornell.edu
Private
Admissions: (607) 255-0600
Email: mba@cornell.edu
Financial aid: (607) 255-6116
Application deadline: 03/11

Tuition: full time: $60,792; part time: N/A
Room/board/expenses: $21,700
College-funded aid: Yes
International student aid: Yes
Average student indebtedness at graduation: $106,200
Full-time enrollment: 585
men: 70%; women: 30%; minorities: 30%; international: 28%
Part-time enrollment: N/A
men: N/A; women: N/A; minorities: N/A; international: N/A
Acceptance rate (full time): 30%
Average GMAT (full time): 692
Average GPA (full time): 3.35
Average age of entrants to full-time program: 28
Average months of prior work experience (full time): 58
TOEFL requirement: Yes
Minimum TOEFL score: 600
Most popular departments: consulting, finance, leadership, marketing, technology
Mean starting base salary for 2014 full-time graduates: $110,872
Employment location for 2014 class: Intl. 6%; N.E. 54%; M.A. 6%; S. 5%; M.W. 5%; S.W. 7%; W. 18%

CUNY Bernard M. Baruch College (Zicklin)
1 Bernard Baruch Way
New York, NY 10010
zicklin.baruch.cuny.edu
Public
Admissions: (646) 312-1300
Email: zicklingradadmissions@baruch.cuny.edu
Financial aid: (646) 312-1370
Application deadline: rolling
In-state tuition: full time: $14,190; part time: $635/credit hour
Out-of-state tuition: full time: $29,100
Room/board/expenses: N/A
College-funded aid: Yes
International student aid: Yes
Full-time enrollment: 115
men: 69%; women: 31%; minorities: 17%; international: 35%
Part-time enrollment: 810
men: 61%; women: 39%; minorities: 34%; international: 1%
Acceptance rate (full time): 34%
Average GMAT (full time): 630
Average GMAT (part time): 603
Average GPA (full time): 3.24
Average age of entrants to full-time program: 28
Average months of prior work experience (full time): 56
TOEFL requirement: Yes
Minimum TOEFL score: N/A
Most popular departments: accounting, finance, general management, marketing, management information systems
Mean starting base salary for 2014 full-time graduates: $77,000
Employment location for 2014 class: Intl. 3%; N.E. 76%; M.A. 6%; S. 3%; M.W. 3%; S.W. 3%; W. 6%

Fordham University
113 W. 60th Street, Room 624
New York, NY 10023
www.bnet.fordham.edu
Private
Admissions: (212) 636-6200
Email: admissionsgb@fordham.edu
Financial aid: (212) 636-6700
Application deadline: 06/01

Tuition: full time: $1,306/credit hour; part time: $1,306/credit hour
Room/board/expenses: $28,835
College-funded aid: Yes
International student aid: Yes
Average student indebtedness at graduation: $66,664
Full-time enrollment: 328
men: 54%; women: 46%; minorities: 18%; international: 32%
Part-time enrollment: 296
men: 65%; women: 35%; minorities: 20%; international: 7%
Acceptance rate (full time): 51%
Average GMAT (full time): 613
Average GMAT (part time): 579
Average GPA (full time): 3.20
Average age of entrants to full-time program: 28
Average months of prior work experience (full time): 56
TOEFL requirement: Yes
Minimum TOEFL score: N/A
Most popular departments: accounting, finance, general management, marketing, management information systems
Mean starting base salary for 2014 full-time graduates: $70,000
Employment location for 2014 class: Intl. 2%; N.E. 91%; M.A. 4%; S. N/A; M.W. N/A; S.W. N/A; W. 4%

Hofstra University (Zarb)
300 Weller Hall
Hempstead, NY 11549
www.hofstra.edu/graduate
Private
Admissions: (800) 463-7872
Email: gradstudent@hofstra.edu
Financial aid: (516) 463-4335
Application deadline: rolling
Tuition: full time: $1,170/credit hour; part time: $1,170/credit hour
Room/board/expenses: $21,740
College-funded aid: Yes
International student aid: Yes
Full-time enrollment: 80
men: 65%; women: 35%; minorities: 11%; international: 66%
Part-time enrollment: 939
men: 51%; women: 49%; minorities: 11%; international: 61%
Acceptance rate (full time): 43%
Average GMAT (full time): 598
Average GMAT (part time): 559
Average GPA (full time): 3.07
Average age of entrants to full-time program: 24
Average months of prior work experience (full time): 25
TOEFL requirement: Yes
Minimum TOEFL score: 550
Most popular departments: accounting, finance, general management, health care administration, marketing
Mean starting base salary for 2014 full-time graduates: $56,669
Employment location for 2014 class: Intl. 5%; N.E. 89%; M.A. 0%; S. 0%; M.W. 0%; S.W. 0%; W. 5%

Iona College (Hagan)
715 North Avenue
New Rochelle, NY 10801
www.iona.edu/hagan
Private
Admissions: (914) 633-2288
Email: FBoughner@iona.edu
Financial aid: (914) 633-2497
Application deadline: rolling
Tuition: full time: N/A; part time: $985/credit hour
Room/board/expenses: N/A
College-funded aid: Yes
International student aid: Yes

Full-time enrollment: N/A
men: N/A; women: N/A; minorities: N/A; international: N/A
Part-time enrollment: 324
men: 53%; women: 47%; minorities: 19%; international: 8%
Average GMAT (part time): 372
TOEFL requirement: Yes
Minimum TOEFL score: 580
Most popular departments: accounting, finance, general management, marketing, management information systems

Ithaca College
953 Danby Road
Ithaca, NY 14850-7000
www.ithaca.edu/gps
Private
Admissions: (607) 274-3527
Email: gps@ithaca.edu
Financial aid: (607) 274-3131
Application deadline: 05/15
Tuition: full time: $877/credit hour; part time: $877/credit hour
Room/board/expenses: N/A
College-funded aid: Yes
International student aid: Yes
Full-time enrollment: 23
men: 78%; women: 22%; minorities: 13%; international: 13%
Part-time enrollment: 4
men: 25%; women: 75%; minorities: 0%; international: 0%
Acceptance rate (full time): 78%
Average GPA (full time): 3.61
Average age of entrants to full-time program: 24
TOEFL requirement: Yes
Minimum TOEFL score: 550

Le Moyne College
1419 Salt Springs Road
Syracuse, NY 13214-1301
www.lemoyne.edu/mba
Private
Admissions: (315) 445-5444
Email: business@lemoyne.edu
Financial aid: (315) 445-4400
Application deadline: 07/01
Tuition: full time: $755/credit hour; part time: $755/credit hour
Room/board/expenses: N/A
College-funded aid: Yes
International student aid: Yes
Average student indebtedness at graduation: $16,583
Full-time enrollment: 25
men: 68%; women: 32%; minorities: 16%; international: 0%
Part-time enrollment: 89
men: 53%; women: 47%; minorities: 3%; international: 2%
Acceptance rate (full time): 100%
Average GMAT (part time): 479
Average GPA (full time): 3.00
Average age of entrants to full-time program: 23
TOEFL requirement: Yes
Minimum TOEFL score: 550

LIU Post
720 Northern Boulevard
Brookville, NY 11548-1300
www.liu.edu/postmba
Private
Admissions: (516) 299-2900
Email: enroll@cwpost.liu.edu
Financial aid: (516) 299-2338
Application deadline: rolling
Tuition: full time: $1,132/credit hour; part time: $1,132/credit hour
Room/board/expenses: $18,564
College-funded aid: Yes
International student aid: Yes
Full-time enrollment: 88
men: 59%; women: 41%; minorities: 40%; international: 75%

Part-time enrollment: 58
men: 76%; women: 24%; minorities: 17%; international: 0%
Acceptance rate (full time): 99%
Average GMAT (full time): 460
Average GMAT (part time): 460
Average GPA (full time): 3.24
Average age of entrants to full-time program: 24
Average months of prior work experience (full time): 41
TOEFL requirement: Yes
Minimum TOEFL score: 563

Marist College
127 Dyson Center
Poughkeepsie, NY 12601
www.marist.edu/mba
Private
Admissions: (845) 575-3800
Email: graduate@marist.edu
Financial aid: (845) 575-3230
Application deadline: rolling
Tuition: full time: N/A; part time: $750/credit hour
Room/board/expenses: N/A
College-funded aid: Yes
International student aid: No
Full-time enrollment: N/A
men: N/A; women: N/A; minorities: N/A; international: N/A
Part-time enrollment: 189
men: 56%; women: 44%; minorities: 19%; international: 0%
Average GMAT (part time): 520
TOEFL requirement: Yes
Minimum TOEFL score: 550
Most popular departments: finance, general management, health care administration, international business, leadership

New York University (Stern)
44 W. Fourth Street
New York, NY 10012-1126
www.stern.nyu.edu
Private
Admissions: (212) 998-0600
Email: sternmba@stern.nyu.edu
Financial aid: (212) 998-0790
Application deadline: 03/15
Tuition: full time: $63,168; part time: $1,930/credit hour
Room/board/expenses: $37,310
College-funded aid: Yes
International student aid: Yes
Average student indebtedness at graduation: $116,533
Full-time enrollment: 798
men: 62%; women: 38%; minorities: 26%; international: 26%
Part-time enrollment: 1,696
men: 67%; women: 33%; minorities: 27%; international: 12%
Acceptance rate (full time): 18%
Average GMAT (full time): 721
Average GMAT (part time): 670
Average GPA (full time): 3.52
Average age of entrants to full-time program: 28
Average months of prior work experience (full time): 52
TOEFL requirement: Yes
Minimum TOEFL score: N/A
Most popular departments: economics, entrepreneurship, finance, general management, marketing
Mean starting base salary for 2014 full-time graduates: $112,096
Employment location for 2014 class: Intl. 12%; N.E. 70%; M.A. 3%; S. 1%; M.W. 4%; S.W. 1%; W. 9%

Niagara University
PO Box 1909
Niagara University, NY 14109
mba.niagara.edu
Private
Admissions: (716) 286-8051
Email: mbadirector@niagara.edu
Financial aid: (716) 286-8686
Application deadline: rolling
Tuition: full time: $835/credit hour; part time: $835/credit hour
Room/board/expenses: $13,816
College-funded aid: Yes
International student aid: Yes
Full-time enrollment: 137
men: 59%; women: 41%; minorities: 9%; international: 29%
Part-time enrollment: 60
men: 53%; women: 47%; minorities: 12%; international: 13%
Average age of entrants to full-time program: 26
TOEFL requirement: Yes
Minimum TOEFL score: 550
Most popular departments: accounting, finance, general management, marketing, operations management

Pace University (Lubin)
1 Pace Plaza
New York, NY 10038
www.pace.edu/lubin/
Private
Admissions: (212) 346-1531
Email: gradnyc@pace.edu
Financial aid: (914) 773-3751
Application deadline: 08/01
Tuition: full time: $1,120/credit hour; part time: $1,120/credit hour
Room/board/expenses: $20,064
College-funded aid: Yes
International student aid: Yes
Average student indebtedness at graduation: $38,011
Full-time enrollment: 281
men: 51%; women: 49%; minorities: 22%; international: 46%
Part-time enrollment: 186
men: 52%; women: 48%; minorities: 31%; international: 15%
Acceptance rate (full time): 61%
Average GMAT (full time): 550
Average GMAT (part time): 544
Average GPA (full time): 3.37
Average age of entrants to full-time program: 24
TOEFL requirement: Yes
Minimum TOEFL score: 600
Most popular departments: accounting, finance, human resources management, marketing, tax
Mean starting base salary for 2014 full-time graduates: $57,000
Employment location for 2014 class: Intl. N/A; N.E. 100%; M.A. N/A; S. N/A; M.W. N/A; S.W. N/A; W. N/A

Rensselaer Polytechnic Institute (Lally)
110 Eighth Street
Pittsburgh Building 5202
Troy, NY 12180-3590
lallyschool.rpi.edu
Private
Admissions: (518) 276-6565
Email: lallymba@rpi.edu
Financial aid: (518) 276-6565
Application deadline: 04/15
Tuition: full time: $48,915; part time: N/A
Room/board/expenses: $17,265
College-funded aid: Yes
International student aid: Yes

Full-time enrollment: 24
men: 63%; women: 38%;
minorities: 8%; international: 54%
Part-time enrollment: 55
men: 75%; women: 25%;
minorities: N/A; international: N/A
Acceptance rate (full time): 54%
Average GMAT (full time): 625
Average GPA (full time): 3.27
Average age of entrants to full-time
program: 25
Average months of prior work
experience (full time): 17
TOEFL requirement: Yes
Minimum TOEFL score: 577
Most popular departments:
entrepreneurship, finance,
marketing, supply chain
management, technology
Mean starting base salary for 2014
full-time graduates: $64,300
Employment location for 2014 class:
Intl. 24%; N.E. 59%; M.A. 6%; S.
6%; M.W. N/A; S.W. N/A; W. 6%

Rochester Institute of Technology (Saunders)

105 Lomb Memorial Drive
Rochester, NY 14623-5608
saunders.rit.edu
Private
Admissions: (585) 475-7284
Email: gradinfo@rit.edu
Financial aid: (585) 475-2186
Application deadline: rolling
Tuition: full time: $38,948; part
time: $1,612/credit hour
Room/board/expenses: $13,593
College-funded aid: Yes
International student aid: Yes
Full-time enrollment: 133
men: 56%; women: 44%;
minorities: 9%; international: 52%
Part-time enrollment: 80
men: 60%; women: 40%;
minorities: 4%; international: 29%
Acceptance rate (full time): 49%
Average GMAT (full time): 532
Average GMAT (part time): 543
Average GPA (full time): 3.31
Average age of entrants to full-time
program: 26
Average months of prior work
experience (full time): 30
TOEFL requirement: Yes
Minimum TOEFL score: 580
Most popular departments:
accounting, entrepreneurship,
finance, leadership, marketing
Mean starting base salary for 2014
full-time graduates: $48,932
Employment location for 2014 class:
Intl. 4%; N.E. 77%; M.A. 9%; S. 1%;
M.W. 1%; S.W. 3%; W. 4%

Siena College[1]

515 Loudon Road
Loudonville, NY 12211-1462
https://www.siena.edu/
Private
Admissions: N/A
Financial aid: N/A
Tuition: N/A
Room/board/expenses: N/A
Enrollment: N/A

St. Bonaventure University

3261 West State Road
St. Bonaventure, NY 14778
www.sbu.edu/admission-aid/
graduate-admissions
Private
Admissions: (716) 375-2021
Email: gradsch@sbu.edu
Financial aid: (716) 375-2528
Application deadline: rolling

Tuition: full time: $711/credit hour;
part time: $711/credit hour
Room/board/expenses: $13,486
College-funded aid: Yes
International student aid: Yes
Average student indebtedness at
graduation: $23,570
Full-time enrollment: 46
men: 59%; women: 41%;
minorities: 13%; international: 9%
Part-time enrollment: 36
men: 44%; women: 56%;
minorities: 0%; international: 0%
Average GMAT (full time): 506
Average GMAT (part time): 465
Average GPA (full time): 3.39
Average age of entrants to full-time
program: 24
TOEFL requirement: Yes
Minimum TOEFL score: 550

St. John Fisher College

3690 East Avenue
Rochester, NY 14618
www.sjfc.edu/academics/
business/about/index.dot
Private
Admissions: (585) 385-8161
Email: grad@sjfc.edu
Financial aid: (585) 385-8042
Application deadline: rolling
Tuition: full time: $950/credit hour;
part time: $950/credit hour
Room/board/expenses: N/A
College-funded aid: Yes
International student aid: Yes
Full-time enrollment: 64
men: 61%; women: 39%;
minorities: 6%; international: 2%
Part-time enrollment: 74
men: 49%; women: 51%;
minorities: 12%; international: 0%
Acceptance rate (full time): 79%
Average GMAT (full time): 467
Average GMAT (part time): 483
Average GPA (full time): 3.42
Average age of entrants to full-time
program: 23
Average months of prior work
experience (full time): 48
TOEFL requirement: Yes
Minimum TOEFL score: 575

St. John's University (Tobin)

8000 Utopia Parkway
Queens, NY 11439
www.stjohns.edu/tobin
Private
Admissions: (718) 990-1345
Email: tobingradnyc@stjohns.edu
Financial aid: (718) 990-2000
Application deadline: 05/01
Tuition: full time: $1,155/credit
hour; part time: $1,155/credit hour
Room/board/expenses: $22,610
College-funded aid: Yes
International student aid: Yes
Average student indebtedness at
graduation: $28,789
Full-time enrollment: 400
men: 46%; women: 55%;
minorities: 19%; international:
58%
Part-time enrollment: 218
men: 55%; women: 45%;
minorities: 36%; international:
17%
Acceptance rate (full time): 74%
Average GMAT (full time): 546
Average GMAT (part time): 561
Average GPA (full time): 3.29
Average age of entrants to full-time
program: 24
Average months of prior work
experience (full time): 14
TOEFL requirement: Yes
Minimum TOEFL score: 600

Most popular departments:
accounting, finance, general
management, international
business, marketing
Employment location for 2014 class:
Intl. 6%; N.E. 89%; M.A. 1%; S.
2%; M.W. 1%; S.W. 1%; W. 1%

SUNY-Geneseo[1]

1 College Circle
Geneseo, NY 14454
www.geneseo.edu/business
Public
Admissions: N/A
Financial aid: N/A
Tuition: N/A
Room/board/expenses: N/A
Enrollment: N/A

SUNY-New Paltz

1 Hawk Drive
New Paltz, NY
www.newpaltz.edu/graduate
Public
Admissions: (845) 257-3947
Email: gradschool@newpaltz.edu
Financial aid: N/A
Application deadline: rolling
In-state tuition: full time: $14,455;
part time: $551/credit hour
Out-of-state tuition: full time:
$23,405
Room/board/expenses: N/A
College-funded aid: Yes
International student aid: No
Full-time enrollment: 44
men: 52%; women: 48%;
minorities: 9%; international: 30%
Part-time enrollment: 31
men: 45%; women: 55%;
minorities: 29%; international:
19%
Acceptance rate (full time): 92%
Average GMAT (full time): 469
Average GPA (full time): 3.38
Average age of entrants to full-time
program: 25
TOEFL requirement: Yes
Minimum TOEFL score: 550

SUNY-Oswego

138 Rich Hall
Oswego, NY 13126
www.oswego.edu/academics/
colleges_and_departments/
business/index.html
Public
Admissions: (315) 312-3152
Email: gradoff@oswego.edu
Financial aid: (315) 312-2248
Application deadline: rolling
In-state tuition: full time: $13,220;
part time: $551/credit hour
Out-of-state tuition: full time:
$22,170
Room/board/expenses: $16,093
College-funded aid: Yes
International student aid: Yes
Average student indebtedness at
graduation: $13,890
Full-time enrollment: 84
men: 55%; women: 45%;
minorities: 12%; international: 7%
Part-time enrollment: 125
men: 69%; women: 31%;
minorities: 9%; international: 1%
Acceptance rate (full time): 84%
Average GMAT (full time): 536
Average GMAT (part time): 510
Average GPA (full time): 3.60
Average age of entrants to full-time
program: 25
TOEFL requirement: Yes
Minimum TOEFL score: 560
Most popular departments:
accounting, general management,
health care administration,
marketing, tax

SUNY Polytechnic Institute

100 Seymour Road
Utica, NY 13502
www.sunyit.edu/programs/
graduate/mbatm
Public
Admissions: (315) 792-7347
Email: gradcenter@sunyit.edu
Financial aid: (315) 792-7210
Application deadline: N/A
In-state tuition: full time: $14,490;
part time: $551/credit hour
Out-of-state tuition: full time:
$23,440
Room/board/expenses: $15,975
College-funded aid: Yes
International student aid: Yes
Full-time enrollment: 28
men: 50%; women: 50%;
minorities: 36%; international: 4%
Part-time enrollment: 88
men: 69%; women: 31%;
minorities: 11%; international: 0%
Acceptance rate (full time): 33%
Average GMAT (full time): 530
Average GMAT (part time): 507
Average GPA (full time): 3.49
Average age of entrants to full-time
program: 31
TOEFL requirement: Yes
Minimum TOEFL score: 550
Most popular departments:
accounting, finance, human
resources management,
marketing, other

Syracuse University (Whitman)

721 University Avenue, Suite 315
Syracuse, NY 13244-2450
whitman.syr.edu/mba/fulltime
Private
Admissions: (315) 443-9214
Email: busgrad@syr.edu
Financial aid: (315) 443-3727
Application deadline: 04/19
Tuition: full time: $41,404; part
time: $1,341/credit hour
Room/board/expenses: $19,456
College-funded aid: Yes
International student aid: Yes
Average student indebtedness at
graduation: $49,252
Full-time enrollment: 73
men: 66%; women: 34%;
minorities: 11%; international: 70%
Part-time enrollment: N/A
men: N/A; women: N/A; minorities:
N/A; international: N/A
Acceptance rate (full time): 53%
Average GMAT (full time): 639
Average GPA (full time): 3.33
Average age of entrants to full-time
program: 25
Average months of prior work
experience (full time): 31
TOEFL requirement: Yes
Minimum TOEFL score: 600
Most popular departments:
entrepreneurship, finance,
general management, marketing,
supply chain management
Mean starting base salary for 2014
full-time graduates: $66,648
Employment location for 2014 class:
Intl. 5%; N.E. 85%; M.A. 5%; S.
N/A; M.W. N/A; S.W. 5%; W. N/A

Union Graduate College[1]

80 Nott Terrace
Schenectady, NY 12308-3107
www.uniongraduatecollege.edu/
management
Private
Admissions: (518) 631-9831
Financial aid: N/A
Tuition: N/A

Room/board/expenses: N/A
Enrollment: N/A

University at Albany-SUNY

1400 Washington Avenue
Albany, NY 12222
www.albany.edu/business
Public
Admissions: (518) 442-4961
Email: busweb@uamail.albany.edu
Financial aid: (518) 442-5757
Application deadline: 03/01
In-state tuition: full time: $8,160;
part time: $551/credit hour
Out-of-state tuition: full time:
$12,635
Room/board/expenses: N/A
College-funded aid: Yes
International student aid: No
Full-time enrollment: 77
men: 53%; women: 47%;
minorities: 5%; international: 22%
Part-time enrollment: 210
men: 61%; women: 39%;
minorities: N/A; international: 1%
Acceptance rate (full time): 39%
Average GMAT (full time): 565
Average GMAT (part time): 556
Average GPA (full time): 3.44
Average months of prior work
experience (full time): 36
TOEFL requirement: Yes
Minimum TOEFL score: 600
Most popular departments:
human resources management,
management information systems

University at Buffalo-SUNY

203 Alfiero Center
Buffalo, NY 14260-4010
www.mgt.buffalo.edu
Public
Admissions: (716) 645-3204
Email: som-apps@buffalo.edu
Financial aid: (716) 645-2450
Application deadline: 05/01
In-state tuition: full time: $16,804;
part time: $725/credit hour
Out-of-state tuition: full time:
$25,754
Room/board/expenses: $19,000
College-funded aid: Yes
International student aid: Yes
Full-time enrollment: 206
men: 64%; women: 36%;
minorities: 18%; international:
33%
Part-time enrollment: 185
men: 68%; women: 32%;
minorities: 9%; international: 4%
Acceptance rate (full time): 48%
Average GMAT (full time): 614
Average GMAT (part time): 549
Average GPA (full time): 3.38
Average age of entrants to full-time
program: 25
Average months of prior work
experience (full time): 25
TOEFL requirement: Yes
Minimum TOEFL score: 570
Most popular departments:
consulting, finance, health care
administration, marketing,
management information systems
Mean starting base salary for 2014
full-time graduates: $63,044
Employment location for 2014 class:
Intl. 2%; N.E. 70%; M.A. 11%; S.
2%; M.W. 2%; S.W. 9%; W. 5%

University of Rochester (Simon)

Schlegel Hall
Rochester, NY 14627
www.simon.rochester.edu
Private
Admissions: (585) 275-3533
Email: admissions@
simon.rochester.edu
Financial aid: (585) 275-3533
Application deadline: 05/15
Tuition: full time: $52,696; part
time: $1,694/credit hour
Room/board/expenses: $17,715
College-funded aid: Yes
International student aid: Yes
**Average student indebtedness at
graduation:** $45,144
Full-time enrollment: 213
men: 70%; women: 30%;
minorities: 21%; international: 51%
Part-time enrollment: 248
men: 71%; women: 29%;
minorities: 10%; international: 7%
Acceptance rate (full time): 32%
Average GMAT (full time): 684
Average GPA (full time): 3.55
**Average age of entrants to full-time
program:** 27
**Average months of prior work
experience (full time):** 56
TOEFL requirement: Yes
Minimum TOEFL score: N/A
Most popular departments:
accounting, consulting,
finance, marketing, operations
management
**Mean starting base salary for 2014
full-time graduates:** $91,543
Employment location for 2014 class:
Intl. 7%; N.E. 50%; M.A. 4%; S.
8%; M.W. 13%; S.W. 9%; W. 10%

Yeshiva University (Syms)

500 West 185th Street
New York, NY 10033
www.yu.edu/syms/
Private
Admissions: N/A
Financial aid: N/A
Application deadline: N/A
Tuition: full time: $1,060/credit
hour; part time: $1,060/credit
hour
Room/board/expenses: N/A
Full-time enrollment: 24
men: 67%; women: 33%;
minorities: N/A; international: 8%
Part-time enrollment: 4
men: 50%; women: 50%;
minorities: N/A; international: 75%
Minimum TOEFL score: N/A

NORTH CAROLINA

Appalachian State University (Walker)

Box 32037
Boone, NC 28608-2037
www.business.appstate.edu/
grad/mba.asp
Public
Admissions: (828) 262-2130
Email: mba@appstate.edu
Financial aid: (828) 262-2190
Application deadline: 07/01
In-state tuition: full time: N/A; part
time: N/A
Out-of-state tuition: full time: N/A
Room/board/expenses: N/A
College-funded aid: Yes
International student aid: Yes
Full-time enrollment: 86
men: N/A; women: N/A; minorities:
N/A; international: N/A
Part-time enrollment: 7
men: N/A; women: N/A;
minorities: N/A; international: N/A

TOEFL requirement: Yes
Minimum TOEFL score: 550

Duke University (Fuqua)

100 Fuqua Drive, Box 90120
Durham, NC 27708-0120
www.fuqua.duke.edu
Private
Admissions: (919) 660-7705
Email: admissions-info@
fuqua.duke.edu
Financial aid: (919) 660-7687
Application deadline: 03/19
Tuition: full time: $60,313; part
time: N/A
Room/board/expenses: $20,772
College-funded aid: Yes
International student aid: Yes
**Average student indebtedness at
graduation:** $115,201
Full-time enrollment: 876
men: 67%; women: 33%;
minorities: 19%; international:
39%
Part-time enrollment: N/A
men: N/A; women: N/A; minorities:
N/A; international: N/A
Acceptance rate (full time): 25%
Average GMAT (full time): 690
Average GPA (full time): 3.43
**Average age of entrants to full-time
program:** 29
**Average months of prior work
experience (full time):** 66
TOEFL requirement: Yes
Minimum TOEFL score: N/A
Most popular departments:
consulting, finance, health care
administration, marketing,
statistics and operations
research
**Mean starting base salary for 2014
full-time graduates:** $114,109
Employment location for 2014 class:
Intl. 14%; N.E. 24%; M.A. 8%; S.
16%; M.W. 15%; S.W. 7%; W. 16%

East Carolina University

3203 Bate Building
Greenville, NC 27858-4353
www.business.ecu.edu/grad/
Public
Admissions: (252) 328-6970
Email: gradbus@ecu.edu
Financial aid: (252) 328-6610
Application deadline: 06/01
In-state tuition: full time: $301/
credit hour; part time: $332/
credit hour
Out-of-state tuition: full time: $814/
credit hour
Room/board/expenses: N/A
College-funded aid: Yes
International student aid: Yes
**Average student indebtedness at
graduation:** $37,899
Full-time enrollment: 172
men: 52%; women: 48%;
minorities: 34%; international: 8%
Part-time enrollment: 513
men: 60%; women: 40%;
minorities: 23%; international: 2%
Acceptance rate (full time): 85%
Average GMAT (full time): 513
Average GMAT (part time): 528
Average GPA (full time): 3.21
**Average age of entrants to full-time
program:** 26
TOEFL requirement: Yes
Minimum TOEFL score: 550
Most popular departments: finance,
health care administration, hotel
administration, management
information systems, supply chain
management

Elon University (Love)

100 Campus Drive
Elon, NC 27244-2010
elon.edu/mba
Private
Admissions: (336) 278-7600
Email: gradadm@elon.edu
Financial aid: (336) 278-7600
Application deadline: rolling
Tuition: full time: N/A; part time:
$827/credit hour
Room/board/expenses: N/A
College-funded aid: No
International student aid: No
Full-time enrollment: N/A
men: N/A; women: N/A; minorities:
N/A; international: N/A
Part-time enrollment: 121
men: 62%; women: 38%;
minorities: 23%; international: 7%
Average GMAT (part time): 569
TOEFL requirement: Yes
Minimum TOEFL score: 550
Most popular departments:
entrepreneurship, general
management, human resources
management, leadership,
marketing

Fayetteville State University

1200 Murchison Road
Newbold Station
Fayetteville, NC 28301-1033
mba.uncfsu.edu/
Public
Admissions: (910) 672-1197
Email: mbaprogram@uncfsu.edu
Financial aid: (910) 672-1325
Application deadline: rolling
In-state tuition: full time: $3,190;
part time: $199/credit hour
Out-of-state tuition: full time:
$14,039
Room/board/expenses: N/A
College-funded aid: Yes
International student aid: No
Full-time enrollment: N/A
men: N/A; women: N/A; minorities:
N/A; international: N/A
Part-time enrollment: 107
men: 50%; women: 50%;
minorities: 50%; international: N/A
Average GMAT (part time): 498
TOEFL requirement: Yes
Minimum TOEFL score: 550
Most popular departments:
entrepreneurship, finance,
general management, health
care administration, operations
management

Meredith College

3800 Hillsborough St.
Raleigh, NC 27607
www.meredith.edu/mba
Private
Admissions: (919) 760-8212
Email: mba@meredith.edu
Financial aid: (919) 760-8565
Application deadline: rolling
Tuition: full time: N/A; part time:
$11,730
Room/board/expenses: N/A
College-funded aid: Yes
International student aid: Yes
**Average student indebtedness at
graduation:** $0
Full-time enrollment: N/A
men: N/A; women: N/A; minorities:
N/A; international: N/A
Part-time enrollment: 68
men: 16%; women: 84%;
minorities: 28%; international: 6%
TOEFL requirement: Yes
Minimum TOEFL score: 550

North Carolina A&T State University

1601 E. Market Street
Greensboro, NC 27411
www.ncat.edu/academics/
schools-colleges1/grad/index.html
Admissions: (336) 334-7920
Email: jjtaylor@ncat.edu
Financial aid: (336) 334-7973
Application deadline: 06/01
In-state tuition: full time: $6,718;
part time: $272/credit hour
Out-of-state tuition: full time:
$19,122
Room/board/expenses: $10,500
College-funded aid: Yes
International student aid: Yes
**Average student indebtedness at
graduation:** $40,000
Full-time enrollment: 24
men: 42%; women: 58%;
minorities: 0%; international: 17%
Part-time enrollment: 13
men: 46%; women: 54%;
minorities: 92%; international: 0%
Acceptance rate (full time): 6%
Average GMAT (full time): 503
Average GPA (full time): 3.42
**Average age of entrants to full-time
program:** 27
**Average months of prior work
experience (full time):** 11
TOEFL requirement: Yes
Minimum TOEFL score: 550
**Mean starting base salary for 2014
full-time graduates:** $40,000
Employment location for 2014 class:
Intl. 0%; N.E. 0%; M.A. 0%; S.
100%; M.W. 0%; S.W. 0%; W. 0%

North Carolina Central University[1]

1801 Fayetteville Street
Durham, NC 27707
www.nccu.edu/academics/
business/index.cfm
Public
Admissions: (919) 530-6405
Email: mba@nccu.edu
Financial aid: N/A
Tuition: N/A
Room/board/expenses: N/A
Enrollment: N/A

North Carolina State University (Jenkins)

2130 Nelson Hall
Campus Box 8114
Raleigh, NC 27695-8114
www.mba.ncsu.edu
Public
Admissions: (919) 515-5584
Email: mba@ncsu.edu
Financial aid: (919) 515-2866
Application deadline: 03/02
In-state tuition: total program:
$42,534 (full time); part time:
$932/credit hour
Out-of-state tuition: total program:
$70,878 (full time)
Room/board/expenses: $18,683
College-funded aid: Yes
International student aid: Yes
**Average student indebtedness at
graduation:** $36,946
Full-time enrollment: 86
men: 60%; women: 40%;
minorities: 38%; international:
29%
Part-time enrollment: 204
men: 64%; women: 36%;
minorities: 35%; international: 8%
Acceptance rate (full time): 45%
Average GMAT (full time): 639
Average GMAT (part time): 565
Average GPA (full time): 3.26

**Average age of entrants to full-time
program:** 27
**Average months of prior work
experience (full time):** 63
TOEFL requirement: Yes
Minimum TOEFL score: N/A
Most popular departments:
entrepreneurship, marketing,
supply chain management, other
**Mean starting base salary for 2014
full-time graduates:** $78,204
Employment location for 2014 class:
Intl. N/A; N.E. 4%; M.A. N/A; S.
86%; M.W. 4%; S.W. 4%; W. 4%

Queens University of Charlotte (McColl)

1900 Selwyn Avenue
Charlotte, NC 28274
mccoll.queens.edu/
Private
Admissions: (704) 337-2224
Email: MBA@Queens.edu
Financial aid: (704) 337-2225
Application deadline: rolling
Tuition: full time: N/A; part time:
$1,060/credit hour
Room/board/expenses: N/A
College-funded aid: Yes
International student aid: Yes
Full-time enrollment: N/A
men: N/A; women: N/A; minorities:
N/A; international: N/A
Part-time enrollment: 107
men: 53%; women: 47%;
minorities: 17%; international: 17%
Average GMAT (part time): 560
TOEFL requirement: Yes
Minimum TOEFL score: 550

University of North Carolina–Chapel Hill (Kenan-Flagler)

CB 3490, McColl Building
Chapel Hill, NC 27599-3490
www.kenan-flagler.unc.edu
Public
Admissions: (919) 962-3236
Email: mba_info@unc.edu
Financial aid: (919) 962-9096
Application deadline: 03/13
In-state tuition: full time: $37,453;
part time: N/A
Out-of-state tuition: full time:
$55,908
Room/board/expenses: $24,682
College-funded aid: Yes
International student aid: Yes
**Average student indebtedness at
graduation:** $87,533
Full-time enrollment: 562
men: 73%; women: 27%;
minorities: 18%; international: 31%
Part-time enrollment: N/A
men: N/A; women: N/A; minorities:
N/A; international: N/A
Acceptance rate (full time): 39%
Average GMAT (full time): 697
Average GPA (full time): 3.42
**Average age of entrants to full-time
program:** 28
**Average months of prior work
experience (full time):** 59
TOEFL requirement: Yes
Minimum TOEFL score: N/A
Most popular departments:
consulting, finance, general
management, marketing, real
estate
**Mean starting base salary for 2014
full-time graduates:** $104,286
Employment location for 2014 class:
Intl. 7%; N.E. 14%; M.A. 9%; S.
37%; M.W. 6%; S.W. 9%; W. 16%

University of North Carolina-Charlotte (Belk)

9201 University City Boulevard
Charlotte, NC 28223
www.mba.uncc.edu
Public
Admissions: (704) 687-7566
Email: mba@uncc.edu
Financial aid: (704) 687-2461
Application deadline: rolling
In-state tuition: full time: $12,263; part time: $8,740
Out-of-state tuition: full time: $24,550
Room/board/expenses: N/A
College-funded aid: Yes
International student aid: Yes
Full-time enrollment: N/A
men: N/A; women: N/A; minorities: N/A; international: N/A
Part-time enrollment: 301
men: 64%; women: 36%; minorities: 20%; international: 15%
Average GMAT (part time): 584
TOEFL requirement: Yes
Minimum TOEFL score: 557
Most popular departments: finance, general management, marketing, real estate, other

University of North Carolina-Greensboro (Bryan)

PO Box 26170
Greensboro, NC 27402-6170
mba.uncg.edu
Public
Admissions: (336) 334-5390
Email: mba@uncg.edu
Financial aid: (336) 334-5702
Application deadline: 07/01
In-state tuition: full time: $9,441; part time: $780/credit hour
Out-of-state tuition: full time: $22,890
Room/board/expenses: $11,524
College-funded aid: Yes
International student aid: Yes
Full-time enrollment: 44
men: 34%; women: 66%; minorities: 23%; international: 32%
Part-time enrollment: 98
men: 69%; women: 31%; minorities: 9%; international: 1%
Acceptance rate (full time): 74%
Average GMAT (full time): 597
Average GMAT (part time): 597
Average GPA (full time): 3.55
Average age of entrants to full-time program: 23
Average months of prior work experience (full time): 6
TOEFL requirement: Yes
Minimum TOEFL score: 550
Most popular departments: accounting, finance, marketing, management information systems, supply chain management
Mean starting base salary for 2014 full-time graduates: $54,000
Employment location for 2014 class: Intl. 12%; N.E. 6%; M.A. N/A; S. 71%; M.W. N/A; S.W. 6%; W. 6%

University of North Carolina-Pembroke

PO Box 1510, One University Drive
Pembroke, NC 28372
www.uncp.edu/grad
Public
Admissions: (910) 521-6271
Email: grad@uncp.edu

Financial aid: (910) 521-6255
Application deadline: 12/31
In-state tuition: full time: N/A; part time: N/A
Out-of-state tuition: full time: N/A
Room/board/expenses: N/A
College-funded aid: Yes
Average student indebtedness at graduation: $0
Full-time enrollment: 24
men: 25%; women: 75%; minorities: 29%; international: 8%
Part-time enrollment: 17
men: 47%; women: 53%; minorities: 29%; international: 0%
Acceptance rate (full time): 93%
Average GMAT (full time): 580
Average GPA (full time): 3.54
Average age of entrants to full-time program: 29
TOEFL requirement: Yes
Minimum TOEFL score: 550

University of North Carolina-Wilmington (Cameron)

601 S. College Road
Wilmington, NC 28403-5680
www.csb.uncw.edu/gradprograms
Public
Admissions: (910) 962-3903
Email: barnhillk@uncw.edu
Financial aid: (910) 962-3177
Application deadline: 06/01
In-state tuition: total program: $18,125 (full time); $8,466 (part time)
Out-of-state tuition: total program: $18,125 (full time)
Room/board/expenses: N/A
College-funded aid: Yes
International student aid: Yes
Average student indebtedness at graduation: $27,934
Full-time enrollment: 28
men: 46%; women: 54%; minorities: 11%; international: 36%
Part-time enrollment: 34
men: 74%; women: 26%; minorities: 6%; international: 0%
Acceptance rate (full time): 87%
Average GMAT (full time): 531
Average GMAT (part time): 507
Average GPA (full time): 3.40
Average age of entrants to full-time program: 23
Average months of prior work experience (full time): 32
TOEFL requirement: Yes
Minimum TOEFL score: 550
Most popular departments: consulting, finance, general management, marketing, supply chain management

Wake Forest University

PO Box 7659
Winston-Salem, NC 27109-7659
www.business.wfu.edu
Private
Admissions: (336) 758-5422
Email: busadmissions@wfu.edu
Financial aid: (336) 758-4424
Application deadline: rolling
Tuition: full time: N/A; part time: $36,561
Room/board/expenses: N/A
College-funded aid: Yes
International student aid: Yes
Full-time enrollment: 95
men: 74%; women: 26%; minorities: 19%; international: 21%
Part-time enrollment: 303
men: 70%; women: 30%; minorities: 22%; international: 2%
Acceptance rate (full time): 40%
Average GMAT (full time): 652

Average GMAT (part time): 583
Average GPA (full time): 3.33
Average age of entrants to full-time program: 28
Average months of prior work experience (full time): 51
TOEFL requirement: Yes
Minimum TOEFL score: 600
Most popular departments: finance, general management, marketing, operations management, statistics and operations research
Mean starting base salary for 2014 full-time graduates: $84,911
Employment location for 2014 class: Intl. 0%; N.E. 12%; M.A. 2%; S. 58%; M.W. 4%; S.W. 12%; W. 12%

Western Carolina University

Forsyth Building
Cullowhee, NC 28723
grad.wcu.edu
Public
Admissions: (828) 227-3174
Email: gradsch@email.wcu.edu
Financial aid: (828) 227-7290
Application deadline: 04/01
In-state tuition: full time: $9,238; part time: $7,990
Out-of-state tuition: full time: $20,545
Room/board/expenses: N/A
College-funded aid: Yes
International student aid: No
Full-time enrollment: 50
men: 44%; women: 56%; minorities: 22%; international: 2%
Part-time enrollment: 181
men: 62%; women: 38%; minorities: 23%; international: 2%
Average GMAT (full time): 483
Average GMAT (part time): 467
Average GPA (full time): 3.33
Average age of entrants to full-time program: 27
TOEFL requirement: Yes
Minimum TOEFL score: 550

Winston-Salem State University[1]

RJR Center Suite 109
Winston-Salem, NC 27110
www.wssu.edu/
Public
Admissions: (336) 750-3045
Email: graduate@wssu.edu
Financial aid: N/A
Tuition: N/A
Room/board/expenses: N/A
Enrollment: N/A

NORTH DAKOTA

North Dakota State University[1]

NDSU Department 2400
PO Box 6050
Fargo, ND 58108-6050
www.ndsu.edu/
Public
Admissions: N/A
Financial aid: N/A
Tuition: N/A
Room/board/expenses: N/A
Enrollment: N/A

University of North Dakota[1]

293 Centennial Drive, Stop 8098
Grand Forks, ND 58202-8098
business.und.edu/
Public
Admissions: N/A
Financial aid: N/A

Tuition: N/A
Room/board/expenses: N/A
Enrollment: N/A

OHIO

Bowling Green State University

371 Business Administration Building
Bowling Green, OH 43403-0001
www.bgsumba.com
Public
Admissions: (800) 247-8622
Email: mba@bgsu.edu
Financial aid: (419) 372-2651
Application deadline: 02/10
In-state tuition: total program: $17,997 (full time); $17,997 (part time)
Out-of-state tuition: total program: $28,959 (full time)
Room/board/expenses: N/A
College-funded aid: Yes
International student aid: Yes
Full-time enrollment: 35
men: 66%; women: 34%; minorities: 9%; international: 37%
Part-time enrollment: 77
men: 74%; women: 26%; minorities: 13%; international: 0%
Acceptance rate (full time): 45%
Average GMAT (full time): 526
Average GMAT (part time): 536
Average GPA (full time): 3.28
Average age of entrants to full-time program: 25
Average months of prior work experience (full time): 18
TOEFL requirement: Yes
Minimum TOEFL score: 550
Most popular departments: accounting, finance, supply chain management

Case Western Reserve University (Weatherhead)

Peter B. Lewis Building
10900 Euclid Avenue
Cleveland, OH 44106-7235
www.weatherhead.case.edu
Private
Admissions: (216) 368-6702
Email: wsomadmissions@case.edu
Financial aid: (216) 368-5033
Application deadline: 06/01
Tuition: full time: $45,140; part time: $1,870/credit hour
Room/board/expenses: $14,800
College-funded aid: Yes
International student aid: Yes
Average student indebtedness at graduation: $65,952
Full-time enrollment: 108
men: 64%; women: 36%; minorities: 12%; international: 47%
Part-time enrollment: 106
men: 62%; women: 38%; minorities: 13%; international: 8%
Acceptance rate (full time): 68%
Average GMAT (full time): 630
Average GMAT (part time): 588
Average GPA (full time): 3.32
Average age of entrants to full-time program: 28
Average months of prior work experience (full time): 65
TOEFL requirement: Yes
Minimum TOEFL score: 600
Mean starting base salary for 2014 full-time graduates: $79,027
Employment location for 2014 class: Intl. 0%; N.E. 12%; M.A. 9%; S. 3%; M.W. 74%; S.W. 0%; W. 3%

Cleveland State University (Ahuja)

1860 E. 18th Street, BU420
Cleveland, OH 44115
www.csuohio.edu/business/
Public
Admissions: (216) 687-5599
Email: cbacsu@csuohio.edu
Financial aid: (216) 687-3764
Application deadline: 08/15
In-state tuition: full time: $569/credit hour; part time: $569/credit hour
Out-of-state tuition: full time: $1,074/credit hour
Room/board/expenses: $15,818
College-funded aid: Yes
International student aid: Yes
Average student indebtedness at graduation: $36,766
Full-time enrollment: 206
men: 55%; women: 45%; minorities: 24%; international: 29%
Part-time enrollment: 392
men: 57%; women: 43%; minorities: 19%; international: 7%
Acceptance rate (full time): 80%
Average GMAT (full time): 480
Average GMAT (part time): 480
Average GPA (full time): 3.20
Average age of entrants to full-time program: 28
Average months of prior work experience (full time): 37
TOEFL requirement: Yes
Minimum TOEFL score: 550
Most popular departments: accounting, finance, health care administration, marketing, supply chain management
Employment location for 2014 class: Intl. 4%; N.E. N/A; M.A. N/A; S. N/A; M.W. 96%; S.W. N/A; W. N/A

John Carroll University (Boler)

1 John Carroll Boulevard
University Heights, OH 44118
www.jcu.edu/mba
Private
Admissions: (216) 397-1970
Email: gradbusiness@jcu.edu
Financial aid: (216) 397-4248
Application deadline: 07/15
Tuition: full time: N/A; part time: $855/credit hour
Room/board/expenses: N/A
College-funded aid: Yes
International student aid: Yes
Full-time enrollment: N/A
men: N/A; women: N/A; minorities: N/A; international: N/A
Part-time enrollment: 117
men: 55%; women: 45%; minorities: 11%; international: 7%
Average GMAT (part time): 554
TOEFL requirement: Yes
Minimum TOEFL score: 550
Most popular departments: accounting, finance, human resources management, international business, marketing

Kent State University

PO Box 5190
Kent, OH 44242-0001
www.kent.edu/business/grad
Public
Admissions: (330) 672-2282
Email: gradbus@kent.edu
Financial aid: (330) 672-2972
Application deadline: 04/01
In-state tuition: full time: $11,852; part time: $485/credit hour
Out-of-state tuition: full time: $19,368
Room/board/expenses: $11,000
College-funded aid: Yes

International student aid: Yes
Full-time enrollment: 58
men: 57%; women: 43%;
minorities: 5%; international: 41%
Part-time enrollment: 77
men: 56%; women: 44%;
minorities: 6%; international: 0%
Acceptance rate (full time): 70%
Average GMAT (full time): 556
Average GMAT (part time): 560
Average GPA (full time): 3.29
Average age of entrants to full-time
program: 25
Average months of prior work
experience (full time): 19
TOEFL requirement: Yes
Minimum TOEFL score: 550
Most popular departments:
accounting, finance, human
resources management,
international business, marketing
Mean starting base salary for 2014
full-time graduates: $43,333
Employment location for 2014 class:
Intl. N/A; N.E. N/A; M.A. N/A; S.
N/A; M.W. 100%; S.W. N/A; W. N/A

Miami University (Farmer)

800 E. High Street
Oxford, OH 45056
mba.muohio.edu
Public
Admissions: (513) 895-8876
Email: miamimba@muohio.edu
Financial aid: (513) 529-8710
Application deadline: rolling
In-state tuition: full time: N/A; total
program: $29,700 (part time)
Out-of-state tuition: full time: N/A
Room/board/expenses: N/A
College-funded aid: No
International student aid: No
Full-time enrollment: N/A
men: N/A; women: N/A; minorities:
N/A; international: N/A
Part-time enrollment: 110
men: 69%; women: 31%;
minorities: 14%; international: 1%
Average GMAT (part time): 556
TOEFL requirement: Yes
Minimum TOEFL score: 550
Most popular departments: finance,
general management, marketing

Ohio State University (Fisher)

100 Gerlach Hall
2108 Neil Avenue
Columbus, OH 43210-1144
fisher.osu.edu/master
Public
Admissions: (614) 292-8511
Email: mba@fisher.osu.edu
Financial aid: (614) 292-8511
Application deadline: 04/15
In-state tuition: full time: $30,555;
part time: $1,514/credit hour
Out-of-state tuition: full time:
$49,099
Room/board/expenses: $17,296
College-funded aid: Yes
International student aid: Yes
Full-time enrollment: 220
men: 68%; women: 32%;
minorities: 11%; international: 33%
Part-time enrollment: 318
men: 70%; women: 30%;
minorities: 14%; international: 11%
Acceptance rate (full time): 31%
Average GMAT (full time): 661
Average GMAT (part time): 611
Average GPA (full time): 3.48
Average age of entrants to full-time
program: 28
Average months of prior work
experience (full time): 60
TOEFL requirement: Yes
Minimum TOEFL score: 600

Most popular departments:
consulting, finance, marketing,
operations management, supply
chain management
Mean starting base salary for 2014
full-time graduates: $100,307
Employment location for 2014 class:
Intl. 3%; N.E. 7%; M.A. 1%; S. 3%;
M.W. 73%; S.W. 1%; W. 11%

Ohio University

514 Copeland Hall
Athens, OH 45701
www.cob.ohiou.edu
Public
Admissions: (740) 593-2053
Email: rossj@ohio.edu
Financial aid: (740) 593-4141
Application deadline: 01/01
In-state tuition: total program:
$20,910 (full time) $39,743 (part
time)
Out-of-state tuition: total program:
$32,898 (full time)
Room/board/expenses: N/A
College-funded aid: Yes
International student aid: Yes
Full-time enrollment: 9
men: 67%; women: 33%;
minorities: 0%; international: 11%
Part-time enrollment: 101
men: 71%; women: 29%;
minorities: 11%; international: 0%
Acceptance rate (full time): 61%
Average GMAT (full time): 526
Average GPA (full time): 3.48
Average age of entrants to full-time
program: 23
Average months of prior work
experience (full time): 24
TOEFL requirement: Yes
Minimum TOEFL score: 600

University of Akron

CBA 412
Akron, OH 44325-4805
mba.uakron.edu
Public
Admissions: (330) 972-7043
Email: gradcba@uakron.edu
Financial aid: (330) 972-7032
Application deadline: 07/15
In-state tuition: full time: N/A; part
time: $461/credit hour
Out-of-state tuition: full time: N/A
Room/board/expenses: N/A
College-funded aid: Yes
International student aid: Yes
Full-time enrollment: N/A
men: N/A; women: N/A; minorities:
N/A; international: N/A
Part-time enrollment: 289
men: 58%; women: 42%;
minorities: 8%; international: 20%
Average GMAT (part time): 549
TOEFL requirement: Yes
Minimum TOEFL score: 550
Most popular departments: finance,
general management, health care
administration, marketing, supply
chain management

University of Cincinnati (Lindner)

606 Lindner Hall
Cincinnati, OH 45221-0020
business.uc.edu/graduate/
mba.html
Public
Admissions: (513) 556-7024
Email: graduate@uc.edu
Financial aid: (513) 556-6982
Application deadline: rolling
In-state tuition: total program:
$31,437 (full time); part time:
$890/credit hour
Out-of-state tuition: total program:
$38,694 (full time)

Room/board/expenses: $25,000
College-funded aid: Yes
International student aid: Yes
Average student indebtedness at
graduation: $26,961
Full-time enrollment: 100
men: 54%; women: 46%;
minorities: 14%; international:
32%
Part-time enrollment: 145
men: 63%; women: 37%;
minorities: 12%; international: 2%
Acceptance rate (full time): 70%
Average GMAT (full time): 622
Average GMAT (part time): 608
Average GPA (full time): 3.50
Average age of entrants to full-time
program: 24
Average months of prior work
experience (full time): 42
TOEFL requirement: Yes
Minimum TOEFL score: 600
Most popular departments: finance,
international business, marketing,
operations management,
statistics and operations
research
Mean starting base salary for 2014
full-time graduates: $58,428
Employment location for 2014 class:
Intl. 6%; N.E. 4%; M.A. 1%; S. 7%;
M.W. 78%; S.W. 0%; W. 3%

University of Dayton

300 College Park Avenue
Dayton, OH 45469-2234
business.udayton.edu/mba
Private
Admissions: (937) 229-3733
Email: mba@udayton.edu
Financial aid: (937) 229-4311
Application deadline: rolling
Tuition: full time: $923/credit hour;
part time: $923/credit hour
Room/board/expenses: N/A
College-funded aid: Yes
International student aid: Yes
Full-time enrollment: 109
men: 57%; women: 43%;
minorities: 8%; international: 41%
Part-time enrollment: 71
men: 62%; women: 38%;
minorities: 8%; international: 10%
Acceptance rate (full time): 25%
Average GMAT (full time): 540
Average GMAT (part time): 540
Average GPA (full time): 3.30
Average age of entrants to full-time
program: 25
TOEFL requirement: Yes
Minimum TOEFL score: 550

University of Toledo

Stranahan Hall North, Room 3130
Toledo, OH 43606-3390
utoledo.edu/business/
gradprograms/
Public
Admissions: (419) 530-2087
Email: COBladvising@utoledo.edu
Financial aid: (419) 530-5800
Application deadline: rolling
In-state tuition: full time: $543/
credit hour; part time: $543/
credit hour
Out-of-state tuition: full time: $970/
credit hour
Room/board/expenses: $10,275
College-funded aid: Yes
International student aid: Yes
Full-time enrollment: N/A
men: N/A; women: N/A; minorities:
N/A; international: N/A
Part-time enrollment: 408
men: 55%; women: 45%;
minorities: 6%; international: 48%
Average GMAT (part time): 428
Average GPA (full time): 3.34
TOEFL requirement: Yes
Minimum TOEFL score: 550

Mean starting base salary for 2014
full-time graduates: $52,547
Employment location for 2014 class:
Intl. 4%; N.E. 2%; M.A. 0%; S. 6%;
M.W. 84%; S.W. 2%; W. 2%

Wright State University (Soin)[1]

3640 Colonel Glenn Highway
Dayton, OH 45435-0001
www.wright.edu/business
Public
Admissions: (937) 775-2437
Email: mba@wright.edu
Financial aid: N/A
Tuition: N/A
Room/board/expenses: N/A
Enrollment: N/A

Xavier University (Williams)

1002 Francis Xavier Way
Cincinnati, OH 45207-1221
www.xavier.edu/MBA
Private
Admissions: (513) 745-3525
Email: xumba@xu.edu
Financial aid: (513) 745-3142
Application deadline: 08/01
Tuition: full time: $780/credit hour;
part time: $780/credit hour
Room/board/expenses: $3,200
College-funded aid: Yes
International student aid: Yes
Average student indebtedness at
graduation: $28,646
Full-time enrollment: N/A
men: N/A; women: N/A; minorities:
N/A; international: N/A
Part-time enrollment: 493
men: 69%; women: 31%;
minorities: 16%; international: 4%
Average GMAT (part time): 511
TOEFL requirement: Yes
Minimum TOEFL score: 550

Youngstown State University (Williamson)[1]

1 University Plaza
Youngstown, OH 44555
web.ysu.edu/mba
Public
Admissions: N/A
Email: graduateschool@ysu.edu
Financial aid: N/A
Tuition: N/A
Room/board/expenses: N/A
Enrollment: N/A

OKLAHOMA

Oklahoma City University

2501 N Blackwelder
Oklahoma City, OK 73106
www.okcu.edu/mba/
Private
Admissions: N/A
Financial aid: N/A
Application deadline: rolling
Tuition: full time: N/A; part time:
N/A
Room/board/expenses: N/A
Full-time enrollment: 171
men: N/A; women: N/A; minorities:
N/A; international: N/A
Part-time enrollment: 232
men: N/A; women: N/A; minorities:
N/A; international: N/A
Minimum TOEFL score: N/A

Oklahoma State University (Spears)

102 Gundersen
Stillwater, OK 74078-4022
spears.okstate.edu/
Public
Admissions: (405) 744-2951
Email:
spearsmasters@okstate.edu
Financial aid: (405) 744-6604
Application deadline: 04/15
In-state tuition: full time: $187/
credit hour; part time: $187/
credit hour
Out-of-state tuition: full time: $765/
credit hour
Room/board/expenses: $9,350
College-funded aid: Yes
International student aid: No
Full-time enrollment: 63
men: 67%; women: 33%;
minorities: 13%; international:
30%
Part-time enrollment: 124
men: 65%; women: 35%;
minorities: 15%; international: 2%
Acceptance rate (full time): 94%
Average GMAT (full time): 511
Average GMAT (part time): 589
Average GPA (full time): 3.25
Average age of entrants to full-time
program: 25
Average months of prior work
experience (full time): 59
TOEFL requirement: Yes
Minimum TOEFL score: 575
Mean starting base salary for 2014
full-time graduates: $65,929
Employment location for 2014 class:
Intl. 20%; N.E. 0%; M.A. 0%; S.
0%; M.W. 80%; S.W. 80%; W. 0%

Southeastern Oklahoma State University

1405 N. Fourth Avenue, PMB 4205
Durant, OK 74701-0609
www.se.edu/bus/
Public
Admissions: N/A
Email: kluke@se.edu
Financial aid: (580) 745-2186
Application deadline: rolling
In-state tuition: full time: $212/
credit hour; part time: $212/
credit hour
Out-of-state tuition: full time: $532/
credit hour
Room/board/expenses: $500
College-funded aid: Yes
International student aid: Yes
Full-time enrollment: 21
men: 29%; women: 71%;
minorities: 57%; international: 0%
Part-time enrollment: 35
men: 63%; women: 37%;
minorities: 66%; international: 3%
Acceptance rate (full time): 100%
Average age of entrants to full-time
program: 32
TOEFL requirement: Yes
Minimum TOEFL score: 550

University of Oklahoma (Price)

Price Hall
1003 Asp Avenue, Suite 1040
Norman, OK 73019-4302
ou.edu/mba
Public
Admissions: (405) 325-5623
Email: rebecca_watts@ou.edu
Financial aid: (405) 325-4521
Application deadline: 05/15
In-state tuition: full time: $183/
credit hour; part time: $183/
credit hour

Out-of-state tuition: full time: $707/credit hour
Room/board/expenses: $14,000
College-funded aid: Yes
International student aid: Yes
Full-time enrollment: 76
men: 67%; women: 33%; minorities: 13%; international: 17%
Part-time enrollment: 148
men: 78%; women: 22%; minorities: 6%; international: 1%
Acceptance rate (full time): 53%
Average GMAT (full time): 628
Average GMAT (part time): 601
Average GPA (full time): 3.39
Average age of entrants to full-time program: 26
Average months of prior work experience (full time): 34
TOEFL requirement: Yes
Minimum TOEFL score: 600
Most popular departments: entrepreneurship, finance, management information systems, other
Mean starting base salary for 2014 full-time graduates: $69,300
Employment location for 2014 class: Intl. 2%; N.E. 0%; M.A. 2%; S. 5%; M.W. 5%; S.W. 83%; W. 2%

University of Tulsa (Collins)

800 S. Tucker Drive
Tulsa, OK 74104-9700
business.utulsa.edu/academics/graduate-business
Private
Admissions: (918) 631-2242
Email: graduate-business@utulsa.edu
Financial aid: (918) 631-2526
Application deadline: 07/01
Tuition: full time: $1,120/credit hour; part time: $1,120/credit hour
Room/board/expenses: $15,138
College-funded aid: Yes
International student aid: Yes
Average student indebtedness at graduation: $10,522
Full-time enrollment: 42
men: 45%; women: 55%; minorities: 12%; international: 26%
Part-time enrollment: 34
men: 35%; women: 65%; minorities: 21%; international: 6%
Acceptance rate (full time): 58%
Average GMAT (full time): 566
Average GMAT (part time): 568
Average GPA (full time): 3.71
Average age of entrants to full-time program: 26
Average months of prior work experience (full time): 25
TOEFL requirement: Yes
Minimum TOEFL score: 575
Mean starting base salary for 2014 full-time graduates: $61,055
Employment location for 2014 class: Intl. 0%; N.E. 6%; M.A. 0%; S. 6%; M.W. 11%; S.W. 78%; W. 0%

OREGON

Oregon State University

Bexell Hall 200
Corvallis, OR 97331
business.oregonstate.edu/mba/
Public
Admissions: (541) 737-5510
Email: osumba@bus.oregonstate.edu
Financial aid: (541) 737-2241
Application deadline: rolling
In-state tuition: total program: $18,960 (full time); part time: $761/credit hour

Out-of-state tuition: total program: $31,050 (full time)
Room/board/expenses: $15,237
College-funded aid: Yes
International student aid: Yes
Average student indebtedness at graduation: $32,719
Full-time enrollment: 177
men: 53%; women: 47%; minorities: 5%; international: 60%
Part-time enrollment: 12
men: 58%; women: 42%; minorities: 8%; international: 8%
Acceptance rate (full time): 65%
Average GMAT (full time): 576
Average GPA (full time): 3.22
Average age of entrants to full-time program: 27
Average months of prior work experience (full time): 33
TOEFL requirement: Yes
Minimum TOEFL score: 575
Most popular departments: accounting, finance, leadership, management information systems, supply chain management

Portland State University

PO Box 751
Portland, OR 97207-0751
www.pdx.edu/sba/master-of-business-administration
Public
Admissions: (503) 725-3714
Email: gradinfo@sba.pdx.edu
Financial aid: (503) 725-5442
Application deadline: 05/01
In-state tuition: full time: $580/credit hour; part time: $580/credit hour
Out-of-state tuition: full time: $699/credit hour
Room/board/expenses: $20,000
College-funded aid: Yes
International student aid: Yes
Full-time enrollment: 30
men: 63%; women: 37%; minorities: 13%; international: 30%
Part-time enrollment: 47
men: 55%; women: 45%; minorities: 23%; international: 6%
Acceptance rate (full time): 46%
Average GMAT (full time): 630
Average GMAT (part time): 616
Average GPA (full time): 3.31
Average age of entrants to full-time program: 29
Average months of prior work experience (full time): 69
TOEFL requirement: Yes
Minimum TOEFL score: 550
Mean starting base salary for 2014 full-time graduates: $61,333
Employment location for 2014 class: Intl. N/A; N.E. N/A; M.A. N/A; S. N/A; M.W. N/A; S.W. N/A; W. 100%

University of Oregon (Lundquist)

1208 University of Oregon
Eugene, OR 97403-1208
business.uoregon.edu/mba
Public
Admissions: (541) 346-3306
Email: mbainfo@uoregon.edu
Financial aid: (541) 346-3221
Application deadline: 03/15
In-state tuition: full time: $26,958; part time: N/A
Out-of-state tuition: full time: $36,642
Room/board/expenses: $14,322
College-funded aid: Yes
International student aid: Yes
Average student indebtedness at graduation: $38,237

Full-time enrollment: 74
men: 70%; women: 30%; minorities: 16%; international: 19%
Part-time enrollment: N/A
men: N/A; women: N/A; minorities: N/A; international: N/A
Acceptance rate (full time): 63%
Average GMAT (full time): 628
Average GPA (full time): 3.36
Average age of entrants to full-time program: 28
Average months of prior work experience (full time): 60
TOEFL requirement: Yes
Minimum TOEFL score: 600
Most popular departments: entrepreneurship, finance, marketing, sports business, other
Mean starting base salary for 2014 full-time graduates: $71,831
Employment location for 2014 class: Intl. N/A; N.E. 8%; M.A. N/A; S. N/A; M.W. 4%; S.W. N/A; W. 88%

University of Portland (Pamplin)

5000 N. Willamette Boulevard
Portland, OR 97203-5798
business.up.edu
Private
Admissions: (503) 943-7225
Email: mba-up@up.edu
Financial aid: (503) 943-7311
Application deadline: 07/15
Tuition: full time: $1,120/credit hour; part time: $1,120/credit hour
Room/board/expenses: $10,000
College-funded aid: Yes
International student aid: Yes
Average student indebtedness at graduation: $47,749
Full-time enrollment: 49
men: 63%; women: 37%; minorities: 29%; international: 37%
Part-time enrollment: 65
men: 65%; women: 35%; minorities: 17%; international: 3%
Acceptance rate (full time): 75%
Average GMAT (full time): 530
Average GMAT (part time): 563
Average GPA (full time): 3.25
Average age of entrants to full-time program: 29
Average months of prior work experience (full time): 72
TOEFL requirement: Yes
Minimum TOEFL score: 570
Most popular departments: entrepreneurship, finance, marketing, operations management, other

Willamette University (Atkinson)

900 State Street
Salem, OR 97301-3922
www.willamette.edu/mba
Private
Admissions: (503) 370-6167
Email: mba-admission@willamette.edu
Financial aid: (503) 370-6273
Application deadline: 05/01
Tuition: full time: $36,320; total program: $66,000 (part time)
Room/board/expenses: $13,000
College-funded aid: Yes
International student aid: Yes
Average student indebtedness at graduation: $60,626
Full-time enrollment: 192
men: 57%; women: 43%; minorities: 13%; international: 43%
Part-time enrollment: 90
men: 59%; women: 41%; minorities: 20%; international: 0%
Acceptance rate (full time): 73%

Average GMAT (full time): 587
Average GMAT (part time): 514
Average GPA (full time): 3.23
Average age of entrants to full-time program: 25
Average months of prior work experience (full time): 22
TOEFL requirement: Yes
Minimum TOEFL score: 570
Most popular departments: accounting, entrepreneurship, finance, marketing, statistics and operations research
Mean starting base salary for 2014 full-time graduates: $51,466
Employment location for 2014 class: Intl. 17%; N.E. 6%; M.A. 0%; S. 0%; M.W. 2%; S.W. 6%; W. 69%

PENNSYLVANIA

Bloomsburg University of Pennsylvania

Sutliff Hall, Room 212
400 Second Street
Bloomsburg, PA 17815-1301
www.bloomu.edu/gradschool/mba
Public
Admissions: (570) 389-4394
Financial aid: (570) 389-4297
Application deadline: rolling
In-state tuition: full time: N/A; part time: $454/credit hour
Out-of-state tuition: full time: N/A
Room/board/expenses: N/A
College-funded aid: Yes
International student aid: Yes
Full-time enrollment: N/A
men: N/A; women: N/A; minorities: N/A; international: N/A
Part-time enrollment: 33
men: 67%; women: 33%; minorities: 6%; international: 21%
Average GMAT (part time): 500
TOEFL requirement: Yes
Minimum TOEFL score: 550

Carnegie Mellon University (Tepper)

5000 Forbes Avenue
Pittsburgh, PA 15213
www.tepper.cmu.edu
Private
Admissions: (412) 268-2272
Email: mba-admissions@andrew.cmu.edu
Financial aid: (412) 268-7581
Application deadline: 03/15
Tuition: full time: $58,300; part time: $1,815/credit hour
Room/board/expenses: $21,002
College-funded aid: Yes
International student aid: Yes
Average student indebtedness at graduation: $86,443
Full-time enrollment: 421
men: 75%; women: 25%; minorities: 28%; international: 33%
Part-time enrollment: 173
men: 86%; women: 14%; minorities: 11%; international: 12%
Acceptance rate (full time): 31%
Average GMAT (full time): 687
Average GMAT (part time): 654
Average GPA (full time): 3.24
Average age of entrants to full-time program: 28
Average months of prior work experience (full time): 59
TOEFL requirement: Yes
Minimum TOEFL score: 600
Most popular departments: entrepreneurship, finance, marketing, operations management, statistics and operations research
Mean starting base salary for 2014 full-time graduates: $109,982

Employment location for 2014 class: Intl. 6%; N.E. 27%; M.A. 18%; S. 2%; M.W. 12%; S.W. 6%; W. 29%

Clarion University of Pennsylvania

840 Wood Street
Clarion, PA 16214
www.clarion.edu/admissions/graduate
Public
Admissions: (814) 393-2337
Email: gradstudies@clarion.edu
Financial aid: (800) 672-7171
Application deadline: 07/15
In-state tuition: full time: $454/credit hour; part time: $454/credit hour
Out-of-state tuition: full time: $681/credit hour
Room/board/expenses: N/A
College-funded aid: Yes
International student aid: Yes
Average student indebtedness at graduation: $26,315
Full-time enrollment: 19
men: 47%; women: 53%; minorities: 0%; international: 0%
Part-time enrollment: 83
men: 46%; women: 54%; minorities: 10%; international: 0%
Acceptance rate (full time): 100%
Average GMAT (full time): 460
Average GMAT (part time): 530
Average GPA (full time): 3.50
Average age of entrants to full-time program: 25
Average months of prior work experience (full time): 3
TOEFL requirement: Yes
Minimum TOEFL score: 550
Most popular departments: accounting, economics, general management, marketing

Drexel University (LeBow)

3141 Chestnut Street
Philadelphia, PA 19104
www.lebow.drexel.edu/
Private
Admissions: (215) 895-6804
Email: mba@drexel.edu
Financial aid: N/A
Application deadline: 09/16
Tuition: total program: $64,000 (full time); part time: $1,106/credit hour
Room/board/expenses: N/A
College-funded aid: Yes
International student aid: Yes
Full-time enrollment: 65
men: 57%; women: 43%; minorities: 12%; international: 43%
Part-time enrollment: 339
men: 61%; women: 39%; minorities: 29%; international: 9%
Acceptance rate (full time): 48%
Average GMAT (full time): 581
Average GMAT (part time): 523
Average GPA (full time): 3.20
Average age of entrants to full-time program: 29
Average months of prior work experience (full time): 63
TOEFL requirement: Yes
Minimum TOEFL score: 600
Most popular departments: entrepreneurship, finance, health care administration, marketing, other
Mean starting base salary for 2014 full-time graduates: $72,881
Employment location for 2014 class: Intl. 11%; N.E. 7%; M.A. 67%; S. 4%; M.W. 7%; S.W. N/A; W. 4%

Duquesne University (Donahue)

704 Rockwell Hall
Pittsburgh, PA 15282
www.duq.edu/business/grad
Private
Admissions: (412) 396-6276
Email: grad-bus@duq.edu
Financial aid: (412) 396-6607
Application deadline: 07/01
Tuition: total program: $51,039 (full time); part time: $1,049/credit hour
Room/board/expenses: $13,634
College-funded aid: Yes
International student aid: Yes
Average student indebtedness at graduation: $43,768
Full-time enrollment: 32
men: 34%; women: 66%; minorities: 9%; international: 19%
Part-time enrollment: 231
men: 60%; women: 40%; minorities: 5%; international: 15%
Acceptance rate (full time): 84%
Average GMAT (full time): 550
Average GMAT (part time): 521
Average GPA (full time): 3.31
Average age of entrants to full-time program: 25
Average months of prior work experience (full time): 37
TOEFL requirement: Yes
Minimum TOEFL score: 577
Most popular departments: accounting, finance, marketing, management information systems, supply chain management

Indiana University of Pennsylvania (Eberly)

664 Pratt Drive, Room 402
Indiana, PA 15705
www.iup.edu/business
Public
Admissions: (724) 357-2522
Email: iup-mba@iup.edu
Financial aid: (724) 357-2218
Application deadline: rolling
In-state tuition: full time: $11,143; part time: $478/credit hour
Out-of-state tuition: full time: $15,444
Room/board/expenses: $14,296
College-funded aid: Yes
International student aid: Yes
Full-time enrollment: 106
men: 71%; women: 29%; minorities: 3%; international: 84%
Part-time enrollment: 52
men: 63%; women: 37%; minorities: 0%; international: 88%
Acceptance rate (full time): 32%
Average GMAT (full time): 480
Average GMAT (part time): 505
Average age of entrants to full-time program: 25
TOEFL requirement: Yes
Minimum TOEFL score: 540

King's College (McGowan)[1]

133 N. River Street
Wilkes-Barre, PA 18711
www.kings.edu/academics/colleges_and_programs/business
Private
Admissions: (570) 208-5991
Email: gradprograms@kings.edu
Financial aid: N/A
Tuition: N/A
Room/board/expenses: N/A
Enrollment: N/A

La Salle University

1900 W. Olney Avenue
Philadelphia, PA 19141
www.lasalle.edu/mba
Private
Admissions: (215) 951-1057
Email: mba@lasalle.edu
Financial aid: (215) 951-1070
Application deadline: rolling
Tuition: full time: $22,170; part time: $910/credit hour
Room/board/expenses: N/A
College-funded aid: Yes
International student aid: Yes
Average student indebtedness at graduation: $25,875
Full-time enrollment: 72
men: 50%; women: 50%; minorities: 21%; international: 28%
Part-time enrollment: 394
men: 52%; women: 48%; minorities: 18%; international: 2%
Acceptance rate (full time): 78%
Average GMAT (full time): 465
Average GMAT (part time): 448
Average GPA (full time): 3.32
Average age of entrants to full-time program: 27
TOEFL requirement: Yes
Minimum TOEFL score: 573

Lehigh University

621 Taylor Street
Bethlehem, PA 18015
www.lehigh.edu/mba
Private
Admissions: (610) 758-5280
Email: mba.admissions@lehigh.edu
Financial aid: (610) 758-4450
Application deadline: 07/15
Tuition: full time: $1,050/credit hour; part time: $1,050/credit hour
Room/board/expenses: $17,000
College-funded aid: Yes
International student aid: Yes
Average student indebtedness at graduation: $25,207
Full-time enrollment: 25
men: 52%; women: 48%; minorities: 8%; international: 48%
Part-time enrollment: 159
men: 71%; women: 29%; minorities: 16%; international: 4%
Acceptance rate (full time): 44%
Average GMAT (full time): 611
Average GMAT (part time): 615
Average GPA (full time): 3.36
Average age of entrants to full-time program: 29
Average months of prior work experience (full time): 44
TOEFL requirement: Yes
Minimum TOEFL score: 600
Most popular departments: entrepreneurship, finance, marketing, supply chain management, other
Employment location for 2014 class: Intl. 25%; N.E. 50%; M.A. 25%; S. N/A; M.W. N/A; S.W. N/A; W. N/A

Pennsylvania State University-Erie, The Behrend College (Black)

5101 Jordan Road
Erie, PA 16563
www.pennstatebehrend.psu.edu
Public
Admissions: (814) 898-7255
Email: behrend.admissions@psu.edu
Financial aid: (814) 898-6162
Application deadline: 06/15

In-state tuition: full time: N/A; part time: $811/credit hour
Out-of-state tuition: full time: N/A
Room/board/expenses: $21,600
College-funded aid: Yes
International student aid: Yes
Average student indebtedness at graduation: $36,551
Full-time enrollment: N/A
men: N/A; women: N/A; minorities: N/A; international: N/A
Part-time enrollment: 127
men: 68%; women: 32%; minorities: 6%; international: 2%
Average GMAT (part time): 520
TOEFL requirement: Yes
Minimum TOEFL score: 550
Mean starting base salary for 2014 full-time graduates: $45,000
Employment location for 2014 class: Intl. N/A; N.E. N/A; M.A. N/A; S. N/A; M.W. 100%; S.W. N/A; W. N/A

Pennsylvania State University-Great Valley[1]

30 E. Swedesford Road
Malvern, PA 19355
www.sgps.psu.edu
Public
Admissions: (610) 648-3242
Email: gvadmiss@psu.edu
Financial aid: N/A
Tuition: N/A
Room/board/expenses: N/A
Enrollment: N/A

Pennsylvania State University-Harrisburg

777 W. Harrisburg Pike
Middletown, PA 17057-4898
harrisburg.psu.edu/business-adminstration
Public
Admissions: (717) 948-6250
Email: mbahbg@psu.edu
Financial aid: (717) 948-6307
Application deadline: rolling
In-state tuition: full time: N/A; part time: $792/credit hour
Out-of-state tuition: full time: N/A
Room/board/expenses: N/A
College-funded aid: Yes
International student aid: Yes
Full-time enrollment: N/A
men: N/A; women: N/A; minorities: N/A; international: N/A
Part-time enrollment: 124
men: 65%; women: 35%; minorities: 14%; international: 5%
Average GMAT (part time): 551
TOEFL requirement: Yes
Minimum TOEFL score: 550
Most popular departments: accounting, finance, general management, management information systems, supply chain management

Pennsylvania State University-University Park (Smeal)

220 Business Building
University Park, PA 16802-3000
www.smeal.psu.edu/mba
Public
Admissions: (814) 863-0474
Email: smealmba@psu.edu
Financial aid: (814) 865-6301
Application deadline: 04/01
In-state tuition: full time: $24,162; part time: N/A
Out-of-state tuition: full time: $38,044
Room/board/expenses: $19,900
College-funded aid: Yes

International student aid: Yes
Average student indebtedness at graduation: $38,137
Full-time enrollment: 157
men: 71%; women: 29%; minorities: 17%; international: 37%
Part-time enrollment: N/A
men: N/A; women: N/A; minorities: N/A; international: N/A
Acceptance rate (full time): 24%
Average GMAT (full time): 649
Average GPA (full time): 3.43
Average age of entrants to full-time program: 26
Average months of prior work experience (full time): 48
TOEFL requirement: Yes
Minimum TOEFL score: 600
Most popular departments: entrepreneurship, finance, leadership, marketing, supply chain management
Mean starting base salary for 2014 full-time graduates: $101,044
Employment location for 2014 class: Intl. 2%; N.E. 25%; M.A. 27%; S. 9%; M.W. 9%; S.W. 7%; W. 21%

Robert Morris University

6001 University Boulevard
Moon Township, PA 15108-1189
mba.rmu.edu/
Private
Admissions: (800) 762-0097
Email: enrollmentoffice@rmu.edu
Financial aid: (412) 397-6250
Application deadline: 05/01
Tuition: full time: N/A; part time: $850/credit hour
Room/board/expenses: N/A
College-funded aid: Yes
International student aid: Yes
Full-time enrollment: N/A
men: N/A; women: N/A; minorities: N/A; international: N/A
Part-time enrollment: 225
men: 60%; women: 40%; minorities: 5%; international: 2%
TOEFL requirement: Yes
Minimum TOEFL score: 550
Most popular departments: general management, human resources management

Shippensburg University of Pennsylvania (Grove)

1871 Old Main Drive
Shippensburg, PA 17257
www.ship.edu/mba
Public
Admissions: (717) 477-1231
Email: admiss@ship.edu
Financial aid: (717) 477-1131
Application deadline: rolling
In-state tuition: full time: $454/credit hour; part time: $454/credit hour
Out-of-state tuition: full time: $681/credit hour
Room/board/expenses: $6,747
College-funded aid: Yes
International student aid: Yes
Full-time enrollment: 35
men: 74%; women: 26%; minorities: 6%; international: 57%
Part-time enrollment: 392
men: 60%; women: 40%; minorities: 10%; international: 1%
Acceptance rate (full time): 84%
Average GMAT (full time): 500
Average GMAT (part time): 505
Average GPA (full time): 2.85
Average age of entrants to full-time program: 27
Average months of prior work experience (full time): 20
TOEFL requirement: Yes

Minimum TOEFL score: 500
Most popular departments: general management, management information systems, supply chain management

St. Joseph's University (Haub)

5600 City Avenue
Philadelphia, PA 19131
www.sju.edu/haubmba
Private
Admissions: (610) 660-1690
Email: sjumba@sju.edu
Financial aid: (610) 660-2000
Application deadline: 07/15
Tuition: full time: $946/credit hour; part time: $946/credit hour
Room/board/expenses: N/A
College-funded aid: Yes
International student aid: Yes
Full-time enrollment: N/A
men: N/A; women: N/A; minorities: N/A; international: N/A
Part-time enrollment: 1,211
men: 56%; women: 44%; minorities: 16%; international: 25%
Average GMAT (part time): 537
TOEFL requirement: Yes
Minimum TOEFL score: 550
Most popular departments: finance, general management, human resources management, marketing, management information systems

Temple University (Fox)

Alter Hall
1801 Liacouras Walk, Suite A701
Philadelphia, PA 19122-6083
sbm.temple.edu/
Public
Admissions: (215) 204-7678
Email: foxinfo@temple.edu
Financial aid: (215) 204-7678
Application deadline: 12/10
In-state tuition: full time: $30,144; part time: $1,077/credit hour
Out-of-state tuition: full time: $41,862
Room/board/expenses: $18,148
College-funded aid: Yes
International student aid: Yes
Average student indebtedness at graduation: $49,855
Full-time enrollment: 117
men: 56%; women: 44%; minorities: N/A; international: 27%
Part-time enrollment: 510
men: 62%; women: 38%; minorities: N/A; international: 15%
Acceptance rate (full time): 41%
Average GMAT (full time): 641
Average GMAT (part time): 580
Average GPA (full time): 3.61
Average age of entrants to full-time program: 27
Average months of prior work experience (full time): 52
TOEFL requirement: Yes
Minimum TOEFL score: 600
Most popular departments: finance, general management, health care administration, marketing, management information systems
Mean starting base salary for 2014 full-time graduates: $89,361
Employment location for 2014 class: Intl. 8%; N.E. 15%; M.A. 70%; S. N/A; M.W. N/A; S.W. N/A; W. 8%

University of Pennsylvania (Wharton)

420 Jon M. Huntsman Hall
3730 Walnut Street
Philadelphia, PA 19104
www.wharton.edu
Private
Admissions: (215) 898-6183
Email: mbaadmiss@
wharton.upenn.edu
Financial aid: (215) 898-8728
Application deadline: 03/26
Tuition: full time: $68,210; part
time: N/A
Room/board/expenses: $29,332
College-funded aid: Yes
International student aid: Yes
Full-time enrollment: 1,711
men: 59%; women: 41%;
minorities: N/A; international: 33%
Part-time enrollment: N/A
men: N/A; women: N/A; minorities:
N/A; international: N/A
Acceptance rate (full time): 21%
Average GMAT (full time): 728
Average GPA (full time): 3.60
Average age of entrants to full-time
program: 28
Average months of prior work
experience (full time): 60
TOEFL requirement: Yes
Minimum TOEFL score: N/A
Most popular departments:
entrepreneurship, finance,
general management, health care
administration, other
Mean starting base salary for 2014
full-time graduates: $123,431
Employment location for 2014 class:
Intl. 20%; N.E. 34%; M.A. 9%; S.
4%; M.W. 5%; S.W. 4%; W. 23%

University of Pittsburgh (Katz)

372 Mervis Hall
Pittsburgh, PA 15260
www.business.pitt.edu/katz
Public
Admissions: (412) 648-1700
Email: mba@katz.pitt.edu
Financial aid: (412) 648-1700
Application deadline: 04/01
In-state tuition: total program:
$48,964 (full time); part time:
$1,189/credit hour
Out-of-state tuition: total program:
$63,632 (full time)
Room/board/expenses: $35,476
College-funded aid: Yes
International student aid: Yes
Full-time enrollment: 161
men: 70%; women: 30%;
minorities: 19%; international:
33%
Part-time enrollment: 477
men: 66%; women: 34%;
minorities: 15%; international: 3%
Acceptance rate (full time): 25%
Average GMAT (full time): 620
Average GMAT (part time): 554
Average GPA (full time): 3.36
Average age of entrants to full-time
program: 27
Average months of prior work
experience (full time): 44
TOEFL requirement: Yes
Minimum TOEFL score: N/A
Most popular departments:
finance, marketing, management
information systems, operations
management, supply chain
management
Mean starting base salary for 2014
full-time graduates: $80,096
Employment location for 2014 class:
Intl. 0%; N.E. 6%; M.A. 42%; S.
6%; M.W. 26%; S.W. 2%; W. 18%

University of Scranton

800 Linden Street
Scranton, PA 18510-4632
www.scranton.edu
Private
Admissions: (570) 941-7540
Email: robackj2@scranton.edu
Financial aid: (570) 941-7700
Application deadline: rolling
Tuition: full time: $940/credit hour;
part time: $940/credit hour
Room/board/expenses: N/A
College-funded aid: Yes
International student aid: Yes
Full-time enrollment: N/A
men: N/A; women: N/A; minorities:
N/A; international: N/A
Part-time enrollment: 130
men: 72%; women: 28%;
minorities: 3%; international: 45%
Average GMAT (part time): 532
TOEFL requirement: Yes
Minimum TOEFL score: 500
Most popular departments:
accounting, finance, general
management, marketing,
management information systems

Villanova University

Bartley Hall
800 Lancaster Avenue
Villanova, PA 19085
mba.villanova.edu
Private
Admissions: (610) 519-4336
Email: meredith.lockyer@
villanova.edu
Financial aid: (610) 519-4010
Application deadline: N/A
Tuition: full time: N/A; part time:
$1,035/credit hour
Room/board/expenses: N/A
College-funded aid: Yes
International student aid: Yes
Full-time enrollment: N/A
men: N/A; women: N/A; minorities:
N/A; international: N/A
Part-time enrollment: 144
men: 65%; women: 35%;
minorities: 16%; international: 2%
Average GMAT (part time): 617
TOEFL requirement: Yes
Minimum TOEFL score: 550
Most popular departments:
finance, general management,
international business, marketing,
real estate

West Chester University of Pennsylvania

1160 McDermott Drive
West Chester, PA 19383
www.wcmba.org/
Public
Admissions: (610) 436-2943
Email: gradstudy@wcupa.edu
Financial aid: (610) 436-2627
Application deadline: rolling
In-state tuition: full time: N/A; part
time: $454/credit hour
Out-of-state tuition: full time: N/A
Room/board/expenses: N/A
College-funded aid: Yes
International student aid: Yes
Full-time enrollment: 9
men: 44%; women: 56%;
minorities: 0%; international: 33%
Part-time enrollment: 109
men: 74%; women: 26%;
minorities: 16%; international: 1%
Acceptance rate (full time): 100%
Average GMAT (part time): 557
Average age of entrants to full-time
program: 27
TOEFL requirement: Yes
Minimum TOEFL score: 550

Widener University

1 University Place
Chester, PA 19013
www.widener.edu/sba
Private
Admissions: (610) 499-4305
Email:
sbagradv@mail.widener.edu
Financial aid: (610) 499-4174
Application deadline: rolling
Tuition: full time: $950/credit hour;
part time: $950/credit hour
Room/board/expenses: N/A
College-funded aid: Yes
International student aid: Yes
Full-time enrollment: 34
men: 47%; women: 53%;
minorities: 12%; international:
35%
Part-time enrollment: 48
men: 54%; women: 46%;
minorities: 8%; international: 2%
Acceptance rate (full time): 57%
Average age of entrants to full-time
program: 23
TOEFL requirement: Yes
Minimum TOEFL score: 587

RHODE ISLAND

Bryant University

1150 Douglas Pike
Smithfield, RI 02917
www.bryant.edu/
Private
Admissions: (401) 232-6230
Email: gradprog@bryant.edu
Financial aid: (401) 232-6020
Application deadline: 04/15
Tuition: full time: $1,118/credit
hour; part time: $1,118/credit hour
Room/board/expenses: $31,824
College-funded aid: Yes
International student aid: Yes
Average student indebtedness at
graduation: $43,465
Full-time enrollment: 21
men: 71%; women: 29%;
minorities: 14%; international: 19%
Part-time enrollment: 38
men: 66%; women: 34%;
minorities: 5%; international: 0%
Acceptance rate (full time): 57%
Average GMAT (full time): 470
Average GMAT (part time): 507
Average GPA (full time): 3.31
Average age of entrants to full-time
program: 25
TOEFL requirement: Yes
Minimum TOEFL score: 580
Most popular departments:
finance, general management,
international business, supply
chain management, other

Providence College

One Cunningham Square
Providence, RI 02918
providence.edu/mba
Private
Admissions: (401) 865-2294
Email: mba@providence.edu
Financial aid: (401) 865-2286
Application deadline: 06/01
Tuition: full time: $10,800; part
time: $7,200
Room/board/expenses: $11,600
College-funded aid: Yes
International student aid: No
Average student indebtedness at
graduation: $23,342
Full-time enrollment: N/A
men: N/A; women: N/A; minorities:
N/A; international: N/A
Part-time enrollment: 142
men: 68%; women: 32%;
minorities: 7%; international: 5%
Average GMAT (part time): 529
TOEFL requirement: Yes
Minimum TOEFL score: N/A

University of Rhode Island

7 Lippitt Road
Kingston, RI 02881
web.uri.edu/business/
Public
Admissions: (401) 874-2842
Email: gradadm@etal.uri.edu
Financial aid: N/A
Application deadline: 06/30
In-state tuition: total program:
$15,378 (full time); part time: $641/
credit hour
Out-of-state tuition: total program:
$31,472 (full time)
Room/board/expenses: N/A
College-funded aid: No
International student aid: No
Full-time enrollment: 21
men: N/A; women: N/A; minorities:
N/A; international: N/A
Part-time enrollment: 206
men: N/A; women: N/A; minorities:
N/A; international: N/A
Acceptance rate (full time): 74%
Average age of entrants to full-time
program: 24
TOEFL requirement: Yes
Minimum TOEFL score: 575
Most popular departments: finance,
general management, marketing,
supply chain management

SOUTH CAROLINA

The Citadel

171 Moultrie Street
Charleston, SC 29409
www.citadel.edu/csba/
Public
Admissions: (843) 953-5089
Email: cgc@citadel.edu
Financial aid: (843) 953-5187
Application deadline: rolling
In-state tuition: full time: $538/
credit hour; part time: $538/
credit hour
Out-of-state tuition: full time: $896/
credit hour
Room/board/expenses: $17,388
College-funded aid: Yes
International student aid: Yes
Average student indebtedness at
graduation: $24,770
Full-time enrollment: 23
men: 83%; women: 17%;
minorities: 13%; international: 4%
Part-time enrollment: 182
men: 59%; women: 41%;
minorities: 11%; international: 1%
Acceptance rate (full time): 100%
Average GMAT (full time): 448
Average GMAT (part time): 428
Average GPA (full time): 3.34
Average age of entrants to full-time
program: 29
Average months of prior work
experience (full time): 176
TOEFL requirement: Yes
Minimum TOEFL score: 550

Clemson University

55 East Camperdown Way
Greenville, SC 29601
www.clemson.edu/cbbs/
departments/mba
Public
Admissions: (864) 656-8173
Email: mba@clemson.edu
Financial aid: (864) 656-2280
Application deadline: 07/01
In-state tuition: full time: $10,296;
part time: $638/credit hour
Out-of-state tuition: full time:
$20,524
Room/board/expenses: $13,450
College-funded aid: Yes
International student aid: Yes
Full-time enrollment: 115
men: 71%; women: 29%;
minorities: 11%; international: 29%
Part-time enrollment: 256
men: 67%; women: 33%;
minorities: 14%; international: 2%
Acceptance rate (full time): 66%
Average GMAT (full time): 587
Average GMAT (part time): 609
Average GPA (full time): 3.27
Average age of entrants to full-time
program: 28
Average months of prior work
experience (full time): 57
TOEFL requirement: Yes
Minimum TOEFL score: 580
Most popular departments:
entrepreneurship, general
management
Mean starting base salary for 2014
full-time graduates: $53,500
Employment location for 2014 class:
Intl. 0%; N.E. 6%; M.A. 13%; S.
81%; M.W. 0%; S.W. 0%; W. 0%

Coastal Carolina University

PO Box 261954
Conway, SC 29528-6054
www.coastal.edu/admissions
Public
Admissions: (843) 349-2026
Email: admissions@coastal.edu
Financial aid: (843) 349-2313
Application deadline: 06/15
In-state tuition: full time: $15,955;
part time: $521/credit hour
Out-of-state tuition: full time:
$28,675
Room/board/expenses: $4,932
College-funded aid: Yes
International student aid: Yes
Average student indebtedness at
graduation: $27,499
Full-time enrollment: 61
men: 69%; women: 31%;
minorities: 34%; international:
15%
Part-time enrollment: 41
men: 34%; women: 66%;
minorities: 7%; international: 12%
Acceptance rate (full time): 82%
Average GMAT (full time): 495
Average GPA (full time): 3.38
Average age of entrants to full-time
program: 24
TOEFL requirement: Yes
Minimum TOEFL score: 575
Employment location for 2014 class:
Intl. N/A; N.E. 9%; M.A. 24%; S.
50%; M.W. 7%; S.W. 7%; W. 4%

College of Charleston

Randolph Hall 310
Charleston, SC 29424
sb.cofc.edu/
Public
Admissions: (843) 953-5614
Email: gradsch@cofc.edu
Financial aid: (843) 953-5540
Application deadline: 05/01
In-state tuition: full time: $25,000;
part time: N/A
Out-of-state tuition: full time:
$25,000
Room/board/expenses: N/A
College-funded aid: Yes
International student aid: Yes
Average student indebtedness at
graduation: $14,200
Full-time enrollment: 36
men: 33%; women: 67%;
minorities: 3%; international: 11%
Part-time enrollment: N/A
men: N/A; women: N/A; minorities:
N/A; international: N/A
Acceptance rate (full time): 58%

Average GMAT (full time): 591
Average GPA (full time): 3.40
Average age of entrants to full-time program: 26
Average months of prior work experience (full time): 38
TOEFL requirement: Yes
Minimum TOEFL score: N/A
Most popular departments: finance, general management, hotel administration, marketing, other
Mean starting base salary for 2014 full-time graduates: $62,000
Employment location for 2014 class: Intl. 11%; N.E. 11%; M.A. 11%; S. 63%; M.W. 5%; S.W. N/A; W. N/A

Francis Marion University[1]
Box 100547
Florence, SC 29501
www.fmarion.edu/academics/mba
Public
Admissions: (843) 661-1281
Email: graduate@fmarion.edu
Financial aid: N/A
Tuition: N/A
Room/board/expenses: N/A
Enrollment: N/A

South Carolina State University
300 College Street NE
Orangeburg, SC 29117
www.scsu.edu/schoolofgraduatestudies
Public
Admissions: (803) 536-7133
Email: graduateschool@scsu.edu
Financial aid: (803) 536-7067
Application deadline: rolling
In-state tuition: full time: $11,403; part time: $560/credit hour
Out-of-state tuition: full time: $21,171
Room/board/expenses: N/A
College-funded aid: Yes
International student aid: Yes
Full-time enrollment: 16
men: 56%; women: 44%; minorities: 100%; international: 0%
Part-time enrollment: 4
men: 100%; women: 0%; minorities: 100%; international: 0%
Acceptance rate (full time): 100%
Average age of entrants to full-time program: 25
TOEFL requirement: Yes
Minimum TOEFL score: 550

University of South Carolina (Moore)
1014 Greene Street
Columbia, SC 29208
moore.sc.edu/
Public
Admissions: (803) 777-4346
Email: gradinfo@moore.sc.edu
Financial aid: (803) 777-8134
Application deadline: rolling
In-state tuition: total program: $44,422 (full time); part time: $634/credit hour
Out-of-state tuition: total program: $72,860 (full time)
Room/board/expenses: $7,345
College-funded aid: Yes
International student aid: Yes
Average student indebtedness at graduation: $47,484
Full-time enrollment: 83
men: 76%; women: 24%; minorities: 22%; international: 17%

Part-time enrollment: 437
men: 75%; women: 25%; minorities: 20%; international: 2%
Acceptance rate (full time): 62%
Average GMAT (full time): 666
Average GMAT (part time): 617
Average GPA (full time): 3.28
Average age of entrants to full-time program: 29
Average months of prior work experience (full time): 60
TOEFL requirement: Yes
Minimum TOEFL score: 600
Mean starting base salary for 2014 full-time graduates: $85,732
Employment location for 2014 class: Intl. 7%; N.E. 9%; M.A. 7%; S. 51%; M.W. 7%; S.W. 13%; W. 7%

Winthrop University[1]
Thurmond Building
Rock Hill, SC 29733
www.winthrop.edu/cba
Public
Admissions: (803) 323-2204
Email: gradschool@winthrop.edu
Financial aid: N/A
Tuition: N/A
Room/board/expenses: N/A
Enrollment: N/A

SOUTH DAKOTA

Black Hills State University[1]
1200 University Street
Spearfish, SD 57799
www.bhsu.edu/
Public
Admissions: (800) 255-2478
Email: BHSUGraduateStudies@bhsu.edu
Financial aid: N/A
Tuition: N/A
Room/board/expenses: N/A
Enrollment: N/A

University of South Dakota
414 E. Clark Street
Vermillion, SD 57069
www.usd.edu/mba
Public
Admissions: (605) 677-5232
Email: mba@usd.edu
Financial aid: (605) 677-5446
Application deadline: 06/01
In-state tuition: full time: $210/credit hour; part time: $414/credit hour
Out-of-state tuition: full time: $445/credit hour
Room/board/expenses: N/A
College-funded aid: Yes
International student aid: Yes
Full-time enrollment: 27
men: 59%; women: 41%; minorities: 0%; international: 15%
Part-time enrollment: 228
men: 67%; women: 33%; minorities: 5%; international: 7%
Acceptance rate (full time): 89%
Average GMAT (full time): 539
Average GMAT (part time): 545
Average GPA (full time): 3.46
Average age of entrants to full-time program: 27
Average months of prior work experience (full time): 55
TOEFL requirement: Yes
Minimum TOEFL score: 550
Most popular departments: general management, health care administration, other
Mean starting base salary for 2014 full-time graduates: $46,193

Employment location for 2014 class: Intl. N/A; N.E. N/A; M.A. N/A; S. N/A; M.W. 100%; S.W. N/A; W. N/A

TENNESSEE

Belmont University (Massey)
1900 Belmont Boulevard
Nashville, TN 37212
www.belmont.edu/business/masseyschool
Private
Admissions: (615) 460-6480
Email: masseyadmissions@belmont.edu
Financial aid: (615) 460-6403
Application deadline: 07/01
Tuition: total program: $50,150 (full time) / $50,150 (part time)
Room/board/expenses: N/A
College-funded aid: Yes
International student aid: Yes
Full-time enrollment: 24
men: 42%; women: 58%; minorities: 8%; international: 8%
Part-time enrollment: 112
men: 59%; women: 41%; minorities: 15%; international: 4%
Acceptance rate (full time): 100%
Average GMAT (full time): 526
Average GMAT (part time): 526
Average GPA (full time): 3.40
Average age of entrants to full-time program: 23
TOEFL requirement: Yes
Minimum TOEFL score: 550
Most popular departments: finance, general management, health care administration, marketing, other
Mean starting base salary for 2014 full-time graduates: $47,363
Employment location for 2014 class: Intl. N/A; N.E. N/A; M.A. N/A; S. 92%; M.W. N/A; S.W. 8%; W. N/A

East Tennessee State University[1]
PO Box 70699
Johnson City, TN 37614
www.etsu.edu/cbat
Public
Admissions: (423) 439-5314
Email: business@etsu.edu
Financial aid: N/A
Tuition: N/A
Room/board/expenses: N/A
Enrollment: N/A

Middle Tennessee State University[1]
PO Box 290
Murfreesboro, TN 37132
www.mtsu.edu
Public
Admissions: (615) 898-2840
Email: graduate@mtsu.edu
Financial aid: N/A
Tuition: N/A
Room/board/expenses: N/A
Enrollment: N/A

Tennessee State University[1]
330 N. 10th Avenue
Nashville, TN 37203
www.tnstate.edu/business
Public
Admissions: (615) 963-5145
Email: cobinfo@tnstate.edu
Financial aid: N/A
Tuition: N/A
Room/board/expenses: N/A
Enrollment: N/A

Tennessee Technological University
Box 5023
Cookeville, TN 38505
www.tntech.edu/mba
Public
Admissions: (931) 372-3600
Email: mbastudies@tntech.edu
Financial aid: (931) 372-3073
Application deadline: 07/01
In-state tuition: full time: $492/credit hour; part time: $492/credit hour
Out-of-state tuition: full time: $1,179/credit hour
Room/board/expenses: N/A
College-funded aid: Yes
International student aid: Yes
Average student indebtedness at graduation: $11,103
Full-time enrollment: 57
men: 49%; women: 51%; minorities: 5%; international: 18%
Part-time enrollment: 107
men: 64%; women: 36%; minorities: 4%; international: 3%
Acceptance rate (full time): 72%
Average GMAT (full time): 533
Average GMAT (part time): 531
Average GPA (full time): 3.33
Average age of entrants to full-time program: 30
TOEFL requirement: Yes
Minimum TOEFL score: 550
Most popular departments: accounting, finance, general management, human resources management, management information systems

Union University[1]
1050 Union University Drive
Jackson, TN 38305
www.uu.edu/
Private
Admissions: N/A
Financial aid: N/A
Tuition: N/A
Room/board/expenses: N/A
Enrollment: N/A

University of Memphis (Fogelman)
3675 Central Avenue
Memphis, TN 38152
fcbe.memphis.edu/
Public
Admissions: (901) 678-3721
Email: krishnan@memphis.edu
Financial aid: (901) 678-4825
Application deadline: rolling
In-state tuition: full time: $461/credit hour; part time: $461/credit hour
Out-of-state tuition: full time: $949/credit hour
Room/board/expenses: N/A
College-funded aid: Yes
International student aid: Yes
Average student indebtedness at graduation: $33,248
Full-time enrollment: 52
men: 44%; women: 56%; minorities: 38%; international: 42%
Part-time enrollment: 117
men: 62%; women: 38%; minorities: 34%; international: 4%
Acceptance rate (full time): 58%
Average GMAT (full time): 598
Average GMAT (part time): 592
Average GPA (full time): 3.32
TOEFL requirement: Yes
Minimum TOEFL score: 550
Most popular departments: accounting, finance, international business, marketing, management information systems

University of Tennessee-Chattanooga
615 McCallie Avenue
Chattanooga, TN 37403
www.utc.edu/Academic/Business/
Public
Admissions: (423) 425-4210
Email: Michael-Owens@utc.edu
Financial aid: (423) 425-4677
Application deadline: 07/01
In-state tuition: full time: N/A; part time: $428/credit hour
Out-of-state tuition: full time: N/A
Room/board/expenses: N/A
College-funded aid: Yes
International student aid: No
Full-time enrollment: N/A
men: N/A; women: N/A; minorities: N/A; international: N/A
Part-time enrollment: 246
men: 64%; women: 36%; minorities: 8%; international: 1%
Average GMAT (part time): 492
TOEFL requirement: Yes
Minimum TOEFL score: 550
Most popular departments: accounting, finance, general management, human resources management, marketing

University of Tennessee-Knoxville
504 Haslam Business Building
Knoxville, TN 37996-0552
mba.utk.edu
Public
Admissions: (865) 974-5033
Email: mba@utk.edu
Financial aid: (865) 974-3131
Application deadline: 02/01
In-state tuition: full time: $22,602; part time: N/A
Out-of-state tuition: full time: $41,050
Room/board/expenses: $16,000
College-funded aid: Yes
International student aid: Yes
Average student indebtedness at graduation: $39,500
Full-time enrollment: 145
men: 79%; women: 21%; minorities: 8%; international: 14%
Part-time enrollment: N/A
men: N/A; women: N/A; minorities: N/A; international: N/A
Acceptance rate (full time): 74%
Average GMAT (full time): 605
Average GPA (full time): 3.32
Average age of entrants to full-time program: 27
Average months of prior work experience (full time): 40
TOEFL requirement: Yes
Minimum TOEFL score: 600
Mean starting base salary for 2014 full-time graduates: $76,351
Employment location for 2014 class: Intl. 0%; N.E. 8%; M.A. 0%; S. 58%; M.W. 13%; S.W. 13%; W. 8%

University of Tennessee-Martin
103 Business Administration Building
Martin, TN 38238
www.utm.edu/departments/cbga/mba
Public
Admissions: (731) 881-7012
Email: jcunningham@utm.edu
Financial aid: (731) 881-7040
Application deadline: rolling
In-state tuition: full time: $518/credit hour; part time: $518/credit hour

Out-of-state tuition: full time:
$1,293/credit hour
Room/board/expenses: N/A
College-funded aid: Yes
International student aid: Yes
Full-time enrollment: 5
men: 80%; women: 20%;
minorities: 40%; international:
40%
Part-time enrollment: 12
men: 58%; women: 42%;
minorities: 33%; international: 8%
Acceptance rate (full time): 58%
Average GMAT (full time): 420
Average GMAT (part time): 545
Average GPA (full time): 3.35
Average age of entrants to full-time
program: 23
Average months of prior work
experience (full time): 3
TOEFL requirement: Yes
Minimum TOEFL score: 525

Vanderbilt University (Owen)
401 21st Avenue S
Nashville, TN 37203
www.owen.vanderbilt.edu
Private
Admissions: (615) 322-6469
Email: mba@owen.vanderbilt.edu
Financial aid: (615) 322-3591
Application deadline: 05/05
Tuition: full time: $48,372; part
time: N/A
Room/board/expenses: $24,806
College-funded aid: Yes
International student aid: Yes
Average student indebtedness at
graduation: $82,998
Full-time enrollment: 334
men: 51%; women: 49%;
minorities: 12%; international: 18%
Part-time enrollment: N/A
men: N/A; women: N/A; minorities:
N/A; international: N/A
Acceptance rate (full time): 41%
Average GMAT (full time): 688
Average GPA (full time): 3.32
Average age of entrants to full-time
program: 28
Average months of prior work
experience (full time): 62
TOEFL requirement: Yes
Minimum TOEFL score: N/A
Most popular departments:
consulting, finance, health care
administration, marketing,
organizational behavior
Mean starting base salary for 2014
full-time graduates: $100,513
Employment location for 2014 class:
Intl. 4%; N.E. 12%; M.A. 4%; S.
44%; M.W. 7%; S.W. 14%; W. 14%

TEXAS

Abilene Christian University[1]
ACU Box 29300
Abilene, TX 79699-9300
www.acu.edu/academics/coba/
index.html
Private
Admissions: (800) 460-6228
Email: info@admissions.acu.edu
Financial aid: N/A
Tuition: N/A
Room/board/expenses: N/A
Enrollment: N/A

Baylor University (Hankamer)
1 Bear Place, #98013
Waco, TX 76798-8013
www.baylor.edu/mba
Private
Admissions: (254) 710-3718

Email: mba_info@baylor.edu
Financial aid: (254) 710-2611
Application deadline: 06/15
Tuition: full time: $38,520; part
time: N/A
Room/board/expenses: $19,504
College-funded aid: Yes
International student aid: Yes
Average student indebtedness at
graduation: $21,480
Full-time enrollment: 87
men: 68%; women: 32%;
minorities: 18%; international: 14%
Part-time enrollment: N/A
men: N/A; women: N/A; minorities:
N/A; international: N/A
Acceptance rate (full time): 37%
Average GMAT (full time): 629
Average GPA (full time): 3.43
Average age of entrants to full-time
program: 25
Average months of prior work
experience (full time): 23
TOEFL requirement: Yes
Minimum TOEFL score: 600
Most popular departments:
entrepreneurship, finance,
general management, health care
administration, management
information systems
Mean starting base salary for 2014
full-time graduates: $71,840
Employment location for 2014 class:
Intl. 0%; N.E. 3%; M.A. 0%; S. 3%;
M.W. 6%; S.W. 85%; W. 3%

Lamar University
4400 Martin Luther King Parkway
Beaumont, TX 77710
mba.lamar.edu
Public
Admissions: (409) 880-8888
Email: gradmissions@lamar.edu
Financial aid: (409) 880-8450
Application deadline: 07/01
In-state tuition: full time: $12,950;
part time: $10,088
Out-of-state tuition: full time:
$22,724
Room/board/expenses: N/A
College-funded aid: Yes
International student aid: Yes
Full-time enrollment: 123
men: 58%; women: 42%;
minorities: N/A; international: 36%
Part-time enrollment: N/A
men: N/A; women: N/A; minorities:
N/A; international: N/A
Acceptance rate (full time): 82%
Average GMAT (full time): 469
Average GPA (full time): 3.18
Average age of entrants to full-time
program: 27
TOEFL requirement: Yes
Minimum TOEFL score: 550
Mean starting base salary for 2014
full-time graduates: $62,000

Midwestern State University[1]
3410 Taft Boulevard
Wichita Falls, TX 76308
www.mwsu.edu
Public
Admissions: N/A
Financial aid: N/A
Tuition: N/A
Room/board/expenses: N/A
Enrollment: N/A

Prairie View A&M University
PO Box 519; MS 2300
Prairie View, TX 77446
pvamu.edu/business
Public
Admissions: (936) 261-9215
Email: mba@pvamu.edu

Financial aid: N/A
Application deadline: rolling
In-state tuition: full time: $249/
credit hour; part time: $249/
credit hour
Out-of-state tuition: full time: $609/
credit hour
Room/board/expenses: $1,448
College-funded aid: Yes
International student aid: Yes
Full-time enrollment: 54
men: 37%; women: 63%;
minorities: 70%; international:
20%
Part-time enrollment: 165
men: 44%; women: 56%;
minorities: 95%; international: 1%
Acceptance rate (full time): 76%
Average GPA (full time): 2.92
Average age of entrants to full-time
program: 28
TOEFL requirement: Yes
Minimum TOEFL score: 500

Rice University (Jones)
PO Box 2932
Houston, TX 77252-2932
business.rice.edu
Private
Admissions: (713) 348-4918
Email: ricemba@rice.edu
Financial aid: (713) 348-4958
Application deadline: 04/04
Tuition: full time: $53,511; total
program: $95,500 (part time)
Room/board/expenses: $29,500
College-funded aid: Yes
International student aid: Yes
Average student indebtedness at
graduation: $69,884
Full-time enrollment: 214
men: 65%; women: 35%;
minorities: 24%; international:
32%
Part-time enrollment: 262
men: 79%; women: 21%;
minorities: 27%; international:
10%
Acceptance rate (full time): 26%
Average GMAT (full time): 676
Average GMAT (part time): 627
Average GPA (full time): 3.40
Average age of entrants to full-time
program: 28
Average months of prior work
experience (full time): 60
TOEFL requirement: Yes
Minimum TOEFL score: 600
Most popular departments:
accounting, entrepreneurship,
finance, health care
administration, other
Mean starting base salary for 2014
full-time graduates: $102,740
Employment location for 2014 class:
Intl. 1%; N.E. 1%; M.A. 2%; S. 0%;
M.W. 0%; S.W. 91%; W. 4%

Sam Houston State University
PO Box 2056
Huntsville, TX 77341
coba.shsu.edu/
Public
Admissions: (936) 294-1246
Email: busgrad@shsu.edu
Financial aid: (936) 294-1724
Application deadline: 08/01
In-state tuition: full time: $254/
credit hour; part time: $254/
credit hour
Out-of-state tuition: full time: $616/
credit hour
Room/board/expenses: N/A
College-funded aid: Yes
International student aid: Yes
Full-time enrollment: 82
men: 57%; women: 43%;
minorities: 27%; international:
10%

Part-time enrollment: 232
men: 58%; women: 42%;
minorities: 31%; international: 1%
Acceptance rate (full time): 78%
Average GMAT (full time): 520
Average GPA (full time): 3.39
Average age of entrants to full-time
program: 27
TOEFL requirement: Yes
Minimum TOEFL score: 550
Most popular departments:
economics, finance, general
management

Southern Methodist University (Cox)
PO Box 750333
Dallas, TX 75275-0333
www.coxmba.com
Private
Admissions: (214) 768-1214
Email: mbainfo@cox.smu.edu
Financial aid: (214) 768-2371
Application deadline: 05/05
Tuition: full time: $49,370; part
time: $46,066
Room/board/expenses: $17,220
College-funded aid: Yes
International student aid: Yes
Full-time enrollment: 206
men: 69%; women: 31%;
minorities: 14%; international: 27%
Part-time enrollment: 267
men: 71%; women: 29%;
minorities: 23%; international: 7%
Acceptance rate (full time): 49%
Average GMAT (full time): 650
Average GMAT (part time): 601
Average GPA (full time): 3.22
Average age of entrants to full-time
program: 27
Average months of prior work
experience (full time): 50
TOEFL requirement: Yes
Minimum TOEFL score: 600
Most popular departments:
consulting, entrepreneurship,
finance, marketing, real estate
Mean starting base salary for 2014
full-time graduates: $97,804
Employment location for 2014 class:
Intl. 1%; N.E. 9%; M.A. 1%; S. 0%;
M.W. 4%; S.W. 74%; W. 9%

Stephen F. Austin State University[1]
PO Box 13004, SFA Station
Nacogdoches, TX 75962-3004
www.sfasu.edu/cob/
Public
Admissions: (936) 468-2807
Email: gschool@titan.sfasu.edu
Financial aid: N/A
Tuition: N/A
Room/board/expenses: N/A
Enrollment: N/A

St. Mary's University (Greehey)
1 Camino Santa Maria
San Antonio, TX 78228-8607
www.stmarytx.edu/mba
Private
Admissions: (210) 436-3708
Email: ebroughton@stmarytx.edu
Financial aid: (210) 436-3141
Application deadline: 08/01
Tuition: full time: $800/credit hour;
part time: $800/credit hour
Room/board/expenses: $17,030
College-funded aid: Yes
International student aid: Yes
Full-time enrollment: 33
men: 70%; women: 30%;
minorities: 39%; international:
24%
Part-time enrollment: 28
men: 61%; women: 39%;
minorities: 39%; international: 7%

Acceptance rate (full time): 57%
Average GMAT (full time): 543
Average GMAT (part time): 534
Average GPA (full time): 3.16
Average age of entrants to full-time
program: 28
TOEFL requirement: Yes
Minimum TOEFL score: 570
Most popular departments:
accounting, general management,
other

Texas A&M International University
5201 University Boulevard
Western Hemispheric Trade
Center, Suite 203
Laredo, TX 78041-1900
www.tamiu.edu
Public
Admissions: (956) 326-2200
Email: adms@tamiu.edu
Financial aid: (956) 326-2225
Application deadline: 04/30
In-state tuition: full time: $77/credit
hour; part time: $77/credit hour
Out-of-state tuition: full time: $439/
credit hour
Room/board/expenses: $7,865
College-funded aid: Yes
International student aid: Yes
Average student indebtedness at
graduation: $21,062
Full-time enrollment: 95
men: 53%; women: 47%;
minorities: 47%; international: 51%
Part-time enrollment: 151
men: 58%; women: 42%;
minorities: 72%; international:
28%
Acceptance rate (full time): 99%
Average GMAT (full time): 473
Average GPA (full time): 2.98
Average age of entrants to full-time
program: 24
Average months of prior work
experience (full time): 32
TOEFL requirement: Yes
Minimum TOEFL score: 550
Most popular departments:
accounting, finance, general
management, international
business, management
information systems

Texas A&M University- College Station (Mays)
4117 TAMU, 390 Wehner Building
College Station, TX 77843-4117
ftmba.tamu.edu
Public
Admissions: (979) 845-4714
Email: ftmba@tamu.edu
Financial aid: (979) 845-3236
Application deadline: 04/15
In-state tuition: full time: $23,986;
total program: $79,500 (part time)
Out-of-state tuition: full time:
$36,376
Room/board/expenses: $14,963
College-funded aid: Yes
International student aid: Yes
Average student indebtedness at
graduation: $37,859
Full-time enrollment: 113
men: 75%; women: 25%;
minorities: 18%; international:
26%
Part-time enrollment: 92
men: 78%; women: 22%;
minorities: 30%; international: 5%
Acceptance rate (full time): 24%
Average GMAT (full time): 647
Average GMAT (part time): 607
Average GPA (full time): 3.47

Average age of entrants to full-time program: 29
Average months of prior work experience (full time): 67
TOEFL requirement: Yes
Minimum TOEFL score: 600
Most popular departments: accounting, finance, human resources management, marketing, management information systems
Mean starting base salary for 2014 full-time graduates: $98,313
Employment location for 2014 class: Intl. 0%; N.E. 0%; M.A. 0%; S. 10%; M.W. 4%; S.W. 76%; W. 10%

Texas A&M University-Commerce[1]

PO Box 3011
Commerce, TX 75429-3011
www.tamuc.edu
Public
Admissions: N/A
Financial aid: N/A
Tuition: N/A
Room/board/expenses: N/A
Enrollment: N/A

Texas A&M University-Corpus Christi

6300 Ocean Drive
Corpus Christi, TX 78412-5807
www.cob.tamucc.edu/prstudents/graduate.html
Public
Admissions: (361) 825-2177
Email: maria.martinez@tamucc.edu
Financial aid: (361) 825-2338
Application deadline: 07/15
In-state tuition: full time: $208/credit hour; part time: $213/credit hour
Out-of-state tuition: full time: $570/credit hour
Room/board/expenses: N/A
College-funded aid: Yes
International student aid: Yes
Full-time enrollment: N/A
men: N/A; women: N/A; minorities: N/A; international: N/A
Part-time enrollment: 382
men: N/A; women: N/A; minorities: N/A; international: N/A
TOEFL requirement: Yes
Minimum TOEFL score: 550
Most popular departments: finance, health care administration, international business

Texas Christian University (Neeley)

PO Box 298540
Fort Worth, TX 76129
www.mba.tcu.edu
Private
Admissions: (817) 257-7531
Email: mbainfo@tcu.edu
Financial aid: (817) 257-7531
Application deadline: 11/01
Tuition: full time: $46,300; part time: $30,220
Room/board/expenses: $13,000
College-funded aid: Yes
International student aid: Yes
Average student indebtedness at graduation: $42,798
Full-time enrollment: 94
men: 78%; women: 22%; minorities: 7%; international: 27%
Part-time enrollment: 192
men: 71%; women: 29%; minorities: 16%; international: 2%
Acceptance rate (full time): 48%
Average GMAT (full time): 638

Average GMAT (part time): 546
Average GPA (full time): 3.27
Average age of entrants to full-time program: 28
Average months of prior work experience (full time): 49
TOEFL requirement: Yes
Minimum TOEFL score: 600
Most popular departments: finance, marketing, portfolio management, supply chain management, other
Mean starting base salary for 2014 full-time graduates: $85,367
Employment location for 2014 class: Intl. 9%; N.E. 0%; M.A. 0%; S. 3%; M.W. 6%; S.W. 80%; W. 3%

Texas Southern University (Jones)

3100 Cleburne Avenue
Houston, TX 77004
www.tsu.edu/academics/colleges_schools/Jesse_H_Jones_School_of_Business/
Public
Admissions: (713) 313-7590
Email: haidern@tsu.edu
Financial aid: (713) 313-7480
Application deadline: rolling
In-state tuition: full time: N/A; part time: N/A
Out-of-state tuition: full time: N/A
Room/board/expenses: N/A
College-funded aid: Yes
International student aid: Yes
Full-time enrollment: 204
men: 49%; women: 51%; minorities: 87%; international: 10%
Part-time enrollment: N/A
men: N/A; women: N/A; minorities: N/A; international: N/A
Acceptance rate (full time): 52%
Average GMAT (full time): 329
Average GPA (full time): 3.09
Average age of entrants to full-time program: 29
Average months of prior work experience (full time): 18
TOEFL requirement: Yes
Minimum TOEFL score: 550
Most popular departments: accounting, finance, general management, health care administration, management information systems

Texas State University (McCoy)

601 University Drive
San Marcos, TX 78666-4616
www.txstate.edu
Public
Admissions: (512) 245-3591
Email: gradcollege@txstate.edu
Financial aid: (512) 245-2315
Application deadline: 06/01
In-state tuition: full time: N/A; total program: $16,976 (part time)
Out-of-state tuition: full time: N/A
Room/board/expenses: N/A
College-funded aid: Yes
International student aid: Yes
Full-time enrollment: N/A
men: N/A; women: N/A; minorities: N/A; international: N/A
Part-time enrollment: 303
men: 58%; women: 42%; minorities: 31%; international: 7%
Average GMAT (part time): 530
TOEFL requirement: Yes
Minimum TOEFL score: 550
Most popular departments: general management, health care administration, human resources management, international business, manufacturing and technology management

Texas Tech University (Rawls)

PO Box 42101
Lubbock, TX 79409-2101
www.depts.ttu.edu/rawlsbusiness/graduate/mba/index.php
Public
Admissions: (806) 742-3184
Email: rawlsgrad@ttu.edu
Financial aid: (806) 742-0454
Application deadline: rolling
In-state tuition: full time: $263/credit hour; part time: $263/credit hour
Out-of-state tuition: full time: $625/credit hour
Room/board/expenses: $15,225
College-funded aid: Yes
International student aid: Yes
Average student indebtedness at graduation: $17,575
Full-time enrollment: 214
men: 69%; women: 31%; minorities: 39%; international: 8%
Part-time enrollment: 8
men: 88%; women: 13%; minorities: 50%; international: 0%
Acceptance rate (full time): 63%
Average GMAT (full time): 559
Average GPA (full time): 3.39
Average age of entrants to full-time program: 25
TOEFL requirement: Yes
Minimum TOEFL score: 550
Most popular departments: general management, health care administration, other
Mean starting base salary for 2014 full-time graduates: $57,107
Employment location for 2014 class: Intl. 8%; N.E. N/A; M.A. N/A; S. 4%; M.W. N/A; S.W. 85%; W. 4%

Texas Wesleyan University[1]

1201 Wesleyan Street
Fort Worth, TX 76105
https://txwes.edu/
Private
Admissions: (817) 531-4930
Email: graduate@txwes.edu
Financial aid: N/A
Tuition: N/A
Room/board/expenses: N/A
Enrollment: N/A

University of Dallas

1845 East Northgate Drive
Irving, TX 75062
www.udallas.edu/cob/
Private
Admissions: N/A
Email: admiss@udallas.edu
Financial aid: N/A
Application deadline: rolling
Tuition: full time: $1,225/credit hour; part time: $1,225/credit hour
Room/board/expenses: $21,640
College-funded aid: Yes
International student aid: Yes
Average student indebtedness at graduation: $49,601
Full-time enrollment: N/A
men: N/A; women: N/A; minorities: N/A; international: N/A
Part-time enrollment: 900
men: 63%; women: 37%; minorities: 42%; international: 27%
Average GMAT (part time): 463
TOEFL requirement: Yes
Minimum TOEFL score: N/A
Most popular departments: accounting, finance, management information systems, technology

University of Houston (Bauer)

334 Melcher Hall, Suite 330
Houston, TX 77204-6021
www.bauer.uh.edu/graduate
Public
Admissions: (713) 743-4638
Email: houstonmba@uh.edu
Financial aid: (713) 743-2062
Application deadline: 06/01
In-state tuition: full time: $23,094; part time: $14,238
Out-of-state tuition: full time: $36,954
Room/board/expenses: $17,500
College-funded aid: Yes
International student aid: Yes
Full-time enrollment: 97
men: 62%; women: 38%; minorities: 21%; international: 36%
Part-time enrollment: 433
men: 72%; women: 28%; minorities: 33%; international: 20%
Acceptance rate (full time): 41%
Average GMAT (full time): 601
Average GMAT (part time): 595
Average GPA (full time): 3.35
Average age of entrants to full-time program: 28
Average months of prior work experience (full time): 50
TOEFL requirement: Yes
Minimum TOEFL score: 603
Mean starting base salary for 2014 full-time graduates: $65,559
Employment location for 2014 class: Intl. 0%; N.E. 0%; M.A. 0%; S. 3%; M.W. 0%; S.W. 97%; W. 0%

University of Houston-Clear Lake

2700 Bay Area Boulevard, Box 71
Houston, TX 77058
www.uhcl.edu/admissions
Public
Admissions: (281) 283-2500
Email: admissions@uhcl.edu
Financial aid: (281) 283-2480
Application deadline: 08/01
In-state tuition: full time: N/A; part time: $392/credit hour
Out-of-state tuition: full time: N/A
Room/board/expenses: N/A
College-funded aid: Yes
International student aid: Yes
Full-time enrollment: N/A
men: N/A; women: N/A; minorities: N/A; international: N/A
Part-time enrollment: 272
men: 57%; women: 43%; minorities: 35%; international: 18%
Average GMAT (part time): 494
TOEFL requirement: Yes
Minimum TOEFL score: 550
Most popular departments: finance, human resources management, international business, leadership, management information systems

University of Houston-Downtown

One Main St.
Houston, TX 77002
uhd.edu/admissions/graduate.htm
Public
Admissions: (713) 221-8093
Email: gradadmissions@uhd.edu
Financial aid: (713) 221-8041
Application deadline: 07/15
In-state tuition: full time: N/A; part time: $408/credit hour
Out-of-state tuition: full time: N/A
Room/board/expenses: $16,505
College-funded aid: Yes
International student aid: Yes

Full-time enrollment: N/A
men: N/A; women: N/A; minorities: N/A; international: N/A
Part-time enrollment: 314
men: 45%; women: 55%; minorities: 79%; international: 4%
Average GMAT (part time): 402
TOEFL requirement: Yes
Minimum TOEFL score: 550
Most popular departments: finance, general management, human resources management, leadership, supply chain management

University of Houston-Victoria

University West Room 214
3007 N. Ben Wilson
Victoria, TX 77901
www.uhv.edu/bus/default.asp
Public
Admissions: (361) 570-4110
Email: admissions@uhv.edu
Financial aid: (361) 570-4131
Application deadline: rolling
In-state tuition: full time: $286/credit hour; part time: $286/credit hour
Out-of-state tuition: full time: $648/credit hour
Room/board/expenses: $8,000
College-funded aid: Yes
International student aid: No
Average student indebtedness at graduation: $30,727
Full-time enrollment: 180
men: 46%; women: 54%; minorities: 68%; international: 20%
Part-time enrollment: 549
men: 54%; women: 46%; minorities: 66%; international: 10%
Acceptance rate (full time): 79%
Average GMAT (full time): 392
Average GMAT (part time): 459
Average GPA (full time): 2.89
Average age of entrants to full-time program: 30
TOEFL requirement: Yes
Minimum TOEFL score: 550
Most popular departments: accounting, finance, general management, international business, marketing

University of North Texas

1155 Union Circle #311160
Denton, TX 76203-5017
www.cob.unt.edu
Public
Admissions: (940) 369-8977
Email: mbacob@unt.edu
Financial aid: (940) 565-2302
Application deadline: 07/15
In-state tuition: full time: $303/credit hour; part time: $303/credit hour
Out-of-state tuition: full time: $665/credit hour
Room/board/expenses: $11,892
College-funded aid: Yes
International student aid: Yes
Average student indebtedness at graduation: $31,752
Full-time enrollment: 261
men: 56%; women: 44%; minorities: 38%; international: 6%
Part-time enrollment: 312
men: 62%; women: 38%; minorities: 16%; international: 2%
Acceptance rate (full time): 66%
Average GMAT (full time): 532
Average GMAT (part time): 520
Average GPA (full time): 3.28
Average age of entrants to full-time program: 26

Average months of prior work experience (full time): 70
TOEFL requirement: Yes
Minimum TOEFL score: 550
Most popular departments: accounting, finance, general management, marketing, tax

University of St. Thomas-Houston

3800 Montrose Blvd.
Houston, TX 77006
www.stthom.edu/bschool
Private
Admissions: (713) 525-2100
Email: cameron@stthom.edu
Financial aid: (713) 525-2170
Application deadline: 07/15
Tuition: full time: N/A; part time: N/A
Room/board/expenses: N/A
College-funded aid: Yes
International student aid: Yes
Full-time enrollment: 267
men: 48%; women: 52%;
minorities: 39%; international: 34%
Part-time enrollment: N/A
men: N/A; women: N/A; minorities: N/A; international: N/A
Acceptance rate (full time): 88%
Average GMAT (full time): 433
Average GPA (full time): 3.25
Average age of entrants to full-time program: 31
TOEFL requirement: Yes
Minimum TOEFL score: 550
Most popular departments: finance, general management, international business, marketing, management information systems

University of Texas-Arlington

UTA Box 19377
Arlington, TX 76019-0376
wweb.uta.edu/business/gradbiz
Public
Admissions: (817) 272-3004
Financial aid: (817) 272-3561
Application deadline: 06/01
In-state tuition: full time: $8,918; part time: $6,112
Out-of-state tuition: full time: $16,168
Room/board/expenses: $14,374
College-funded aid: Yes
International student aid: Yes
Average student indebtedness at graduation: $39,928
Full-time enrollment: 663
men: 50%; women: 50%;
minorities: 38%; international: 27%
Part-time enrollment: N/A
men: N/A; women: N/A; minorities: N/A; international: N/A
Acceptance rate (full time): 71%
Average GMAT (full time): 505
Average GPA (full time): 3.23
Average age of entrants to full-time program: 28
TOEFL requirement: Yes
Minimum TOEFL score: 550
Most popular departments: accounting, finance, general management, marketing, other

University of Texas-Austin (McCombs)

MBA Program
2110 Speedway, Stop B6004
Austin, TX 78712-1750
www.mccombs.utexas.edu/mba/full-time
Public
Admissions: (512) 471-7698
Email: Texas MBA@mccombs.utexas.edu
Financial aid: (512) 471-7698
Application deadline: 03/22
In-state tuition: total program: $65,716 (full time); $99,700 (part time)
Out-of-state tuition: total program: $96,046 (full time)
Room/board/expenses: $19,394
College-funded aid: Yes
International student aid: Yes
Average student indebtedness at graduation: $69,409
Full-time enrollment: 551
men: 71%; women: 29%;
minorities: 21%; international: 22%
Part-time enrollment: 438
men: 76%; women: 24%;
minorities: 30%; international: 11%
Acceptance rate (full time): 29%
Average GMAT (full time): 690
Average GMAT (part time): 638
Average GPA (full time): 3.40
Average age of entrants to full-time program: 28
Average months of prior work experience (full time): 63
TOEFL requirement: Yes
Minimum TOEFL score: 620
Most popular departments: consulting, entrepreneurship, finance, marketing, management information systems
Mean starting base salary for 2014 full-time graduates: $107,272
Employment location for 2014 class: Intl. 2%; N.E. 5%; M.A. 3%; S. 4%; M.W. 5%; S.W. 63%; W. 16%

University of Texas-Brownsville[1]

80 Fort Brown
Brownsville, TX 78520
www.utb.edu/
Public
Admissions: (956) 882-6552
Email: graduate.school@utb.edu
Financial aid: N/A
Tuition: N/A
Room/board/expenses: N/A
Enrollment: N/A

University of Texas-Dallas

800 W. Campbell Road
Richardson, TX 75080-3021
jindal.utdallas.edu/academic-programs/mba-programs/
Public
Admissions: (972) 883-6191
Email: mba@utdallas.edu
Financial aid: (972) 883-2941
Application deadline: 07/01
In-state tuition: full time: $15,242; part time: $12,714
Out-of-state tuition: full time: $30,866
Room/board/expenses: $15,000
College-funded aid: Yes
International student aid: Yes
Full-time enrollment: 128
men: 69%; women: 31%;
minorities: 16%; international: 41%
Part-time enrollment: 699
men: 60%; women: 40%;
minorities: 31%; international: 31%
Acceptance rate (full time): 26%
Average GMAT (full time): 673
Average GMAT (part time): 629
Average GPA (full time): 3.50
Average age of entrants to full-time program: 28
Average months of prior work experience (full time): 61
TOEFL requirement: Yes
Minimum TOEFL score: 550

Most popular departments: finance, marketing, management information systems, operations management, supply chain management
Mean starting base salary for 2014 full-time graduates: $80,081
Employment location for 2014 class: Intl. 0%; N.E. 10%; M.A. 0%; S. 6%; M.W. 3%; S.W. 74%; W. 6%

University of Texas-El Paso

500 W. University Avenue
El Paso, TX 79968
mba.utep.edu
Public
Admissions: (915) 747-7726
Email: mba@utep.edu
Financial aid: (915) 747-5204
Application deadline: 07/15
In-state tuition: full time: $248/credit hour; part time: N/A
Out-of-state tuition: full time: $599/credit hour
Room/board/expenses: N/A
College-funded aid: Yes
International student aid: Yes
Average student indebtedness at graduation: $31,737
Full-time enrollment: 151
men: 53%; women: 47%;
minorities: 65%; international: 18%
Part-time enrollment: 1
men: 100%; women: N/A;
minorities: 100%; international: N/A
Acceptance rate (full time): 71%
Average GMAT (full time): 478
Average GPA (full time): 3.31
Average age of entrants to full-time program: 30
Average months of prior work experience (full time): 100
TOEFL requirement: Yes
Minimum TOEFL score: 600
Most popular departments: accounting, finance, general management, human resources management, international business
Mean starting base salary for 2014 full-time graduates: $65,364
Employment location for 2014 class: Intl. N/A; N.E. 9%; M.A. 9%; S. 9%; M.W. N/A; S.W. 64%; W. 9%

University of Texas of the Permian Basin[1]

4901 E. University
Odessa, TX 79762
www.utpb.edu/
Public
Admissions: N/A
Financial aid: N/A
Tuition: N/A
Room/board/expenses: N/A
Enrollment: N/A

University of Texas-Pan American

1201 W. University Drive
Edinburg, TX 78539
portal.utpa.edu/utpa_main/daa_home/coba_new_home/coba_degrees/coba_graduate/coba_mba
Public
Admissions: (956) 381-3313
Email: mbaprog@utpa.edu
Financial aid: (956) 381-5372
Application deadline: rolling
In-state tuition: full time: $552/credit hour; part time: $568/credit hour
Out-of-state tuition: full time: $1,293/credit hour

Room/board/expenses: N/A
College-funded aid: Yes
International student aid: Yes
Full-time enrollment: 138
men: 63%; women: 37%;
minorities: 79%; international: 21%
Part-time enrollment: 148
men: 61%; women: 39%;
minorities: 95%; international: 5%
Acceptance rate (full time): 88%
TOEFL requirement: Yes
Minimum TOEFL score: 500
Most popular departments: accounting, finance, general management, health care administration, human resources management

University of Texas-San Antonio

1 UTSA Circle
San Antonio, TX 78249
www.graduateschool.utsa.edu
Public
Admissions: (210) 458-4331
Email: graduateadmissions@utsa.edu
Financial aid: (210) 458-8000
Application deadline: 07/01
In-state tuition: full time: $310/credit hour; part time: $310/credit hour
Out-of-state tuition: full time: $1,051/credit hour
Room/board/expenses: N/A
College-funded aid: Yes
International student aid: Yes
Full-time enrollment: 65
men: 75%; women: 25%;
minorities: 31%; international: 12%
Part-time enrollment: 164
men: 71%; women: 29%;
minorities: 31%; international: 2%
Acceptance rate (full time): 38%
Average GMAT (full time): 581
Average GMAT (part time): 585
Average GPA (full time): 3.24
Average age of entrants to full-time program: 28
Average months of prior work experience (full time): 35
TOEFL requirement: Yes
Minimum TOEFL score: 550
Most popular departments: finance, general management, health care administration, statistics and operations research, other
Mean starting base salary for 2014 full-time graduates: $54,126
Employment location for 2014 class: Intl. 11%; N.E. N/A; M.A. N/A; S. N/A; M.W. N/A; S.W. 89%; W. N/A

University of Texas-Tyler[1]

3900 University Boulevard
Tyler, TX 75799
www.uttyler.edu/cbt/
Public
Admissions: (903) 566-7360
Email: cbtinfo@uttyler.edu
Financial aid: N/A
Tuition: N/A
Room/board/expenses: N/A
Enrollment: N/A

West Texas A&M University

WTAMU Box 60768
Canyon, TX 79016
www.wtamu.edu/academics/online-mba.aspx
Public
Admissions: (806) 651-2501
Email: lmills@wtamu.edu
Financial aid: (806) 651-2055
Application deadline: rolling

In-state tuition: total program: $15,500 (full time); $17,000 (part time)
Out-of-state tuition: total program: $17,500 (full time)
Room/board/expenses: $15,000
College-funded aid: Yes
International student aid: Yes
Average student indebtedness at graduation: $18,000
Full-time enrollment: 114
men: 44%; women: 56%;
minorities: 32%; international: 26%
Part-time enrollment: 186
men: 54%; women: 46%;
minorities: 30%; international: 1%
Acceptance rate (full time): 67%
Average GMAT (full time): 550
Average GMAT (part time): 520
Average GPA (full time): 3.65
Average age of entrants to full-time program: 25
Average months of prior work experience (full time): 16
TOEFL requirement: Yes
Minimum TOEFL score: 525
Most popular departments: finance, health care administration, marketing, management information systems, organizational behavior
Mean starting base salary for 2014 full-time graduates: $62,000
Employment location for 2014 class: Intl. 7%; N.E. N/A; M.A. N/A; S. N/A; M.W. 14%; S.W. 71%; W. 7%

UTAH

Brigham Young University (Marriott)

W-437 TNRB
Provo, UT 84602
mba.byu.edu
Private
Admissions: (801) 422-3500
Email: mba@byu.edu
Financial aid: (801) 422-5195
Application deadline: 05/01
Tuition: full time: $11,620; part time: N/A
Room/board/expenses: $20,400
College-funded aid: Yes
International student aid: Yes
Average student indebtedness at graduation: $28,386
Full-time enrollment: 301
men: 80%; women: 20%;
minorities: 9%; international: 17%
Part-time enrollment: N/A
men: N/A; women: N/A; minorities: N/A; international: N/A
Acceptance rate (full time): 54%
Average GMAT (full time): 667
Average GPA (full time): 3.49
Average age of entrants to full-time program: 29
Average months of prior work experience (full time): 52
TOEFL requirement: Yes
Minimum TOEFL score: 590
Most popular departments: entrepreneurship, finance, human resources management, marketing, supply chain management
Mean starting base salary for 2014 full-time graduates: $96,673
Employment location for 2014 class: Intl. 2%; N.E. 7%; M.A. 2%; S. 8%; M.W. 21%; S.W. 19%; W. 42%

Southern Utah University

351 W. University Boulevard
Cedar City, UT 84720
www.suu.edu/business
Public
Admissions: (435) 586-5462
Financial aid: (435) 586-7735

Application deadline: 03/01
In-state tuition: total program:
$12,846 (full time); part time:
$382/credit hour
Out-of-state tuition: total program:
$35,394 (full time)
Room/board/expenses: $9,900
College-funded aid: Yes
International student aid: No
Average student indebtedness at
graduation: $26,350
Full-time enrollment: 36
men: 67%; women: 33%;
minorities: 14%; international: 8%
Part-time enrollment: 22
men: 73%; women: 27%;
minorities: 5%; international: 0%
Acceptance rate (full time): 95%
Average GMAT (full time): 536
Average GMAT (part time): 554
Average GPA (full time): 3.53
Average age of entrants to full-time
program: 28
TOEFL requirement: Yes
Minimum TOEFL score: 525
Most popular departments:
accounting, general management
Employment location for 2014 class:
Intl. 0%; N.E. 0%; M.A. 3%; S. 0%;
M.W. 3%; S.W. 0%; W. 94%

University of Utah (Eccles)

1655 E. Campus Center Drive
Room 1113
Salt Lake City, UT 84112-9301
www.business.utah.edu
Public
Admissions: (801) 581-7785
Email: mastersinfo@
business.utah.edu
Financial aid: (801) 581-7785
Application deadline: 03/01
In-state tuition: total program:
$50,717 (full time) / $56,050 (part
time)
Out-of-state tuition: total program:
$92,850 (full time)
Room/board/expenses: $24,096
College-funded aid: Yes
International student aid: Yes
Average student indebtedness at
graduation: $53,434
Full-time enrollment: 117
men: 79%; women: 21%;
minorities: 9%; international: 5%
Part-time enrollment: 338
men: 79%; women: 21%;
minorities: 6%; international: 1%
Acceptance rate (full time): 55%
Average GMAT (full time): 596
Average GMAT (part time): 565
Average GPA (full time): 3.44
Average age of entrants to full-time
program: 27
Average months of prior work
experience (full time): 33
TOEFL requirement: Yes
Minimum TOEFL score: 600
Most popular departments:
entrepreneurship, general
management, health care
administration, management
information systems, operations
management
Mean starting base salary for 2014
full-time graduates: $77,900
Employment location for 2014 class:
Intl. 2%; N.E. 0%; M.A. 0%; S. 4%;
M.W. 4%; S.W. 9%; W. 80%

Utah State University (Huntsman)[1]

3500 Old Main Hill
Logan, UT 84322-3500
www.huntsman.usu.edu/mba/
Public
Admissions: (435) 797-3624
Email: HuntsmanMBA@usu.edu

Financial aid: N/A
Tuition: N/A
Room/board/expenses: N/A
Enrollment: N/A

Utah Valley University[1]

800 W. University Parkway
Orem, UT 84058
www.uvu.edu/woodbury
Public
Admissions: (801) 863-8367
Financial aid: N/A
Tuition: N/A
Room/board/expenses: N/A
Enrollment: N/A

Weber State University (Goddard)

2750 N. University Park
Boulevard, MC102
Layton, UT 84041-9099
weber.edu/mba
Public
Admissions: (801) 395-3528
Email: mba@weber.edu
Financial aid: (801) 626-7569
Application deadline: 05/08
In-state tuition: full time: N/A; part
time: $637/credit hour
Out-of-state tuition: full time: N/A
Room/board/expenses: N/A
College-funded aid: Yes
International student aid: Yes
Full-time enrollment: N/A
men: N/A; women: N/A; minorities:
N/A; international: N/A
Part-time enrollment: 177
men: 80%; women: 20%;
minorities: N/A; international: 6%
Average GMAT (part time): 562
TOEFL requirement: Yes
Minimum TOEFL score: 550
Most popular departments: health
care administration, management
information systems, other

VERMONT

University of Vermont

55 Colchester Avenue
Burlington, VT 05405
www.uvm.edu/business
Public
Admissions: (802) 656-0794
Email: mba@uvm.edu
Financial aid: N/A
Application deadline: 02/16
In-state tuition: total program:
$28,750 (full time); part time: N/A
Out-of-state tuition: total program:
$66,618 (full time)
Room/board/expenses: $10,000
College-funded aid: Yes
International student aid: Yes
Full-time enrollment: 20
men: 45%; women: 55%;
minorities: 5%; international: 10%
Part-time enrollment: N/A
men: N/A; women: N/A; minorities:
N/A; international: N/A
Acceptance rate (full time): 84%
Average GMAT (full time): 558
Average GPA (full time): 3.50
Average age of entrants to full-time
program: 31
Average months of prior work
experience (full time): 96
TOEFL requirement: Yes
Minimum TOEFL score: 577
Most popular departments:
entrepreneurship, other

VIRGINIA

College of William and Mary (Mason)

PO Box 8795
Williamsburg, VA 23187-8795
mason.wm.edu
Public
Admissions: (757) 221-2900
Email: admissions@
mason.wm.edu
Financial aid: (757) 221-2944
Application deadline: 07/15
In-state tuition: full time: $31,058;
part time: $750/credit hour
Out-of-state tuition: full time:
$41,514
Room/board/expenses: $17,130
College-funded aid: Yes
International student aid: Yes
Average student indebtedness at
graduation: $65,438
Full-time enrollment: 189
men: 70%; women: 30%;
minorities: 24%; international:
42%
Part-time enrollment: 173
men: 64%; women: 36%;
minorities: 25%; international: 3%
Acceptance rate (full time): 58%
Average GMAT (full time): 611
Average GMAT (part time): 578
Average GPA (full time): 3.30
Average age of entrants to full-time
program: 28
Average months of prior work
experience (full time): 57
TOEFL requirement: Yes
Minimum TOEFL score: 600
Most popular departments:
entrepreneurship, finance,
general management, marketing,
supply chain management
Mean starting base salary for 2014
full-time graduates: $76,520
Employment location for 2014 class:
Intl. 34%; N.E. 15%; M.A. 32%; S.
4%; M.W. 3%; S.W. 4%; W. 7%

George Mason University

4400 University Drive
Fairfax, VA 22030
business.gmu.edu
Public
Admissions: (703) 993-2136
Email: mba@gmu.edu
Financial aid: (703) 993-2353
Application deadline: rolling
In-state tuition: full time: $896/
credit hour; part time: $869/
credit hour
Out-of-state tuition: full time:
$1,604/credit hour
Room/board/expenses: N/A
College-funded aid: Yes
International student aid: Yes
Average student indebtedness at
graduation: $46,369
Full-time enrollment: N/A
men: N/A; women: N/A; minorities:
N/A; international: N/A
Part-time enrollment: 251
men: 58%; women: 42%;
minorities: 24%; international: 3%
Average GMAT (part time): 575
TOEFL requirement: Yes
Minimum TOEFL score: 570
Most popular departments:
accounting, entrepreneurship,
finance, general management,
leadership

James Madison University

Showker Hall
Harrisonburg, VA 22807
www.jmu.edu/cob/mba
Public
Admissions: (540) 568-3236
Email: busingme@jmu.edu
Financial aid: (540) 568-3139
Application deadline: 06/01
In-state tuition: full time: N/A; part
time: $415/credit hour
Out-of-state tuition: full time: N/A
Room/board/expenses: N/A
College-funded aid: Yes
International student aid: Yes
Full-time enrollment: N/A
men: N/A; women: N/A; minorities:
N/A; international: N/A
Part-time enrollment: 47
men: 64%; women: 36%;
minorities: 11%; international: 6%
Average GMAT (part time): 548
TOEFL requirement: Yes
Minimum TOEFL score: 570
Most popular departments:
leadership, technology

Longwood University[1]

201 High Street
Farmville, VA 23909
www.longwood.edu/business/
Public
Admissions: (877) 267-7883
Email: graduate@longwood.edu
Financial aid: N/A
Tuition: N/A
Room/board/expenses: N/A
Enrollment: N/A

Old Dominion University

1026 Constant Hall
Norfolk, VA 23529
odu.edu/mba
Public
Admissions: (757) 683-3585
Email: mbainfo@odu.edu
Financial aid: (757) 683-3683
Application deadline: 06/01
In-state tuition: full time: $437/
credit hour; part time: $437/
credit hour
Out-of-state tuition: full time:
$1,089/credit hour
Room/board/expenses: $17,500
College-funded aid: Yes
International student aid: Yes
Full-time enrollment: N/A
men: N/A; women: N/A; minorities:
N/A; international: N/A
Part-time enrollment: 172
men: 52%; women: 48%;
minorities: 20%; international: 8%
Average GMAT (part time): 540
TOEFL requirement: Yes
Minimum TOEFL score: 550
Most popular departments:
accounting, general management,
health care administration, public
administration, other

Radford University

PO Box 6956
Radford, VA 24142
www.radford.edu
Public
Admissions: (540) 831-6296
Email: gradcoll@radford.edu
Financial aid: (540) 831-5408
Application deadline: 06/01
In-state tuition: full time: $299/
credit hour; part time: $299/
credit hour
Out-of-state tuition: full time: $683/
credit hour

Room/board/expenses: $19,814
College-funded aid: Yes
International student aid: Yes
Full-time enrollment: 27
men: 67%; women: 33%;
minorities: 19%; international:
33%
Part-time enrollment: 23
men: 57%; women: 43%;
minorities: 4%; international: 4%
Average GMAT (full time): 491
Average GMAT (part time): 410
Average GPA (full time): 3.35
Average age of entrants to full-time
program: 26
Average months of prior work
experience (full time): 24
TOEFL requirement: Yes
Minimum TOEFL score: 550
Employment location for 2014 class:
Intl. N/A; N.E. N/A; M.A. 100%; S.
N/A; M.W. N/A; S.W. N/A; W. N/A

Shenandoah University (Byrd)

Halpin Harrison, Room 103
Winchester, VA 22601
www.su.edu/
Private
Admissions: (540) 665-4581
Email: admit@su.edu
Financial aid: (540) 665-4621
Application deadline: 05/01
Tuition: full time: $15,254; part
time: $813/credit hour
Room/board/expenses: $14,228
College-funded aid: Yes
International student aid: Yes
Average student indebtedness at
graduation: $104,800
Full-time enrollment: 53
men: 49%; women: 51%;
minorities: 47%; international: 21%
Part-time enrollment: 40
men: 48%; women: 53%;
minorities: 10%; international: 10%
Acceptance rate (full time): 43%
Average GPA (full time): 2.32
Average age of entrants to full-time
program: 26
TOEFL requirement: Yes
Minimum TOEFL score: 550

University of Richmond (Robins)

1 Gateway Road
Richmond, VA 23173
robins.richmond.edu/mba/
Private
Admissions: (804) 289-8553
Email: mba@richmond.edu
Financial aid: (804) 289-8438
Application deadline: rolling
Tuition: full time: N/A; part time:
$1,350/credit hour
Room/board/expenses: N/A
College-funded aid: Yes
International student aid: Yes
Full-time enrollment: N/A
men: N/A; women: N/A; minorities:
N/A; international: N/A
Part-time enrollment: 84
men: 62%; women: 38%;
minorities: 14%; international: 2%
Average GMAT (part time): 591
TOEFL requirement: Yes
Minimum TOEFL score: 600

University of Virginia (Darden)

PO Box 6550
Charlottesville, VA 22906-6550
www.darden.virginia.edu
Public
Admissions: (434) 924-7281
Email: darden@virginia.edu
Financial aid: (434) 924-7739
Application deadline: N/A

In-state tuition: full time: $56,950; part time: N/A
Out-of-state tuition: full time: $59,268
Room/board/expenses: $25,215
College-funded aid: Yes
International student aid: Yes
Average student indebtedness at graduation: $102,122
Full-time enrollment: 633
men: 69%; women: 31%; minorities: 16%; international: 29%
Part-time enrollment: N/A
men: N/A; women: N/A; minorities: N/A; international: N/A
Acceptance rate (full time): 26%
Average GMAT (full time): 706
Average GPA (full time): 3.50
Average age of entrants to full-time program: 27
Average months of prior work experience (full time): 58
TOEFL requirement: No
Minimum TOEFL score: N/A
Most popular departments: consulting, entrepreneurship, finance, general management, marketing
Mean starting base salary for 2014 full-time graduates: $112,257
Employment location for 2014 class: Intl. 8%; N.E. 25%; M.A. 20%; S. 13%; M.W. 10%; S.W. 9%; W. 14%

Virginia Commonwealth University

301 W. Main Street
Richmond, VA 23284-4000
www.business.vcu.edu/graduate
Public
Admissions: (804) 828-4622
Email: gsib@vcu.edu
Financial aid: (804) 828-6669
Application deadline: 07/01
In-state tuition: full time: $13,172; part time: $570/credit hour
Out-of-state tuition: full time: $24,005
Room/board/expenses: $19,200
College-funded aid: Yes
International student aid: Yes
Full-time enrollment: N/A
men: N/A; women: N/A; minorities: N/A; international: N/A
Part-time enrollment: 180
men: 69%; women: 31%; minorities: 16%; international: 11%
Average GMAT (part time): 570
TOEFL requirement: Yes
Minimum TOEFL score: 600
Most popular departments: entrepreneurship, finance, general management, international business, management information systems

Virginia Tech (Pamplin)

1044 Pamplin Hall (0209)
Blacksburg, VA 24061
www.mba.vt.edu
Public
Admissions: (703) 538-8410
Email: mba@vt.edu
Financial aid: (540) 231-5179
Application deadline: 08/01
In-state tuition: full time: N/A; part time: $717/credit hour
Out-of-state tuition: full time: N/A
Room/board/expenses: N/A
College-funded aid: Yes
International student aid: Yes
Full-time enrollment: N/A
men: N/A; women: N/A; minorities: N/A; international: N/A

Part-time enrollment: 148
men: 63%; women: 37%; minorities: 27%; international: 3%
Average GMAT (part time): 610
TOEFL requirement: Yes
Minimum TOEFL score: 550
Most popular departments: finance, general management, international business, leadership, technology

WASHINGTON

Eastern Washington University[1]

668 N. Riverpoint Boulevard
Suite A
Spokane, WA 99202-1677
www.ewu.edu/mba
Public
Admissions: (509) 828-1248
Email: mbaprogram@ewu.edu
Financial aid: N/A
Tuition: N/A
Room/board/expenses: N/A
Enrollment: N/A

Gonzaga University

502 E. Boone Avenue
Spokane, WA 99258-0009
www.gonzaga.edu/mba
Private
Admissions: (509) 313-4622
Email: chatman@gonzaga.edu
Financial aid: (509) 313-6581
Application deadline: rolling
Tuition: full time: $900/credit hour; part time: $900/credit hour
Room/board/expenses: $14,850
College-funded aid: Yes
International student aid: Yes
Average student indebtedness at graduation: $32,000
Full-time enrollment: N/A
men: N/A; women: N/A; minorities: N/A; international: N/A
Part-time enrollment: 168
men: 60%; women: 40%; minorities: 14%; international: 11%
Average GMAT (part time): 565
TOEFL requirement: Yes
Minimum TOEFL score: 570

Pacific Lutheran University

Morken Center for Learning and Technology, Room 176
Tacoma, WA 98447
www.plu.edu/mba/home.php
Private
Admissions: (253) 535-7330
Email: plumba@plu.edu
Financial aid: (253) 535-7134
Application deadline: rolling
Tuition: full time: N/A; total program: $52,200 (part time)
Room/board/expenses: $5,489
College-funded aid: Yes
International student aid: Yes
Full-time enrollment: N/A
men: N/A; women: N/A; minorities: N/A; international: N/A
Part-time enrollment: 43
men: 63%; women: 37%; minorities: 19%; international: 12%
Average GMAT (part time): 444
TOEFL requirement: Yes
Minimum TOEFL score: 570
Most popular departments: entrepreneurship, general management, health care administration, technology

Seattle Pacific University

3307 Third Avenue W, Suite 201
Seattle, WA 98119-1950
www.spu.edu/sbe
Private
Admissions: (206) 281-2753
Email: drj@spu.edu
Financial aid: (206) 281-2469
Application deadline: 02/01
Tuition: full time: N/A; part time: $792/credit hour
Room/board/expenses: N/A
College-funded aid: No
International student aid: No
Full-time enrollment: N/A
men: N/A; women: N/A; minorities: N/A; international: N/A
Part-time enrollment: 72
men: 57%; women: 43%; minorities: 29%; international: 14%
Average GMAT (part time): 438
TOEFL requirement: Yes
Minimum TOEFL score: 565

Seattle University (Albers)

901 12th Avenue
PO Box 222000
Seattle, WA 98122-1090
www.seattleu.edu/albers/gradoverview/
Private
Admissions: (206) 296-5708
Email: millardj@seattleu.edu
Financial aid: (206) 220-8020
Application deadline: 08/20
Tuition: full time: N/A; part time: $800/credit hour
Room/board/expenses: N/A
College-funded aid: Yes
International student aid: Yes
Full-time enrollment: N/A
men: N/A; women: N/A; minorities: N/A; international: N/A
Part-time enrollment: 585
men: 53%; women: 47%; minorities: 24%; international: 22%
Average GMAT (part time): 581
TOEFL requirement: Yes
Minimum TOEFL score: 580
Most popular departments: accounting, entrepreneurship, finance, marketing, management information systems

University of Washington–Bothell

18115 Campus Way NW
Box 358533
Bothell, WA 98011
www.uwb.edu/mba/mbaadmissions
Public
Admissions: (425) 352-5394
Email: vtolbert@uwb.edu
Financial aid: N/A
Application deadline: 05/01
In-state tuition: full time: N/A; part time: $23,202
Out-of-state tuition: full time: N/A
Room/board/expenses: N/A
College-funded aid: Yes
Full-time enrollment: N/A
men: N/A; women: N/A; minorities: N/A; international: N/A
Part-time enrollment: 93
men: 61%; women: 39%; minorities: 39%; international: 8%
Average GMAT (part time): 545
TOEFL requirement: Yes
Minimum TOEFL score: 580
Most popular departments: consulting, entrepreneurship, leadership, technology

University of Washington (Foster)

PO Box 353200
Seattle, WA 98195-3200
foster.washington.edu/mba
Public
Admissions: (206) 543-4661
Email: mba@uw.edu
Financial aid: (206) 543-4661
Application deadline: 03/15
In-state tuition: full time: $30,339; part time: $23,169
Out-of-state tuition: full time: $44,175
Room/board/expenses: $23,590
College-funded aid: Yes
International student aid: Yes
Average student indebtedness at graduation: $29,720
Full-time enrollment: 248
men: 67%; women: 33%; minorities: 15%; international: 35%
Part-time enrollment: 317
men: 71%; women: 29%; minorities: 35%; international: 6%
Acceptance rate (full time): 23%
Average GMAT (full time): 682
Average GMAT (part time): 632
Average GPA (full time): 3.43
Average age of entrants to full-time program: 30
Average months of prior work experience (full time): 76
TOEFL requirement: Yes
Minimum TOEFL score: 600
Most popular departments: entrepreneurship, finance, international business, marketing, supply chain management
Mean starting base salary for 2014 full-time graduates: $105,680
Employment location for 2014 class: Intl. N/A; N.E. N/A; M.A. N/A; S. N/A; M.W. 2%; S.W. 2%; W. 96%

University of Washington–Tacoma

1900 Commerce Street
Box 358420
Tacoma, WA 98402
www.tacoma.uw.edu/milgard-school-business/master-business
Public
Admissions: (253) 692-5630
Email: uwtmba@uw.edu
Financial aid: (253) 692-4374
Application deadline: 06/01
In-state tuition: full time: N/A; part time: $27,632
Out-of-state tuition: full time: N/A
Room/board/expenses: N/A
College-funded aid: Yes
International student aid: Yes
Full-time enrollment: N/A
men: N/A; women: N/A; minorities: N/A; international: N/A
Part-time enrollment: 56
men: 70%; women: 30%; minorities: 21%; international: 0%
Average GMAT (part time): 501
TOEFL requirement: Yes
Minimum TOEFL score: 580

Washington State University

PO Box 644744
Pullman, WA 99164-4744
www.business.wsu.edu/graduate
Public
Admissions: (509) 335-7617
Email: mba@wsu.edu
Financial aid: (509) 335-9711
Application deadline: 01/10
In-state tuition: total program: $21,000 (full time); part time: $890/credit hour
Out-of-state tuition: total program: $40,000 (full time)

Room/board/expenses: $14,518
College-funded aid: Yes
International student aid: Yes
Average student indebtedness at graduation: $45,476
Full-time enrollment: 25
men: 56%; women: 44%; minorities: 24%; international: 20%
Part-time enrollment: 441
men: 68%; women: 32%; minorities: 23%; international: 4%
Acceptance rate (full time): 35%
Average GMAT (full time): 538
Average GMAT (part time): 583
Average GPA (full time): 3.44
Average age of entrants to full-time program: 24
Average months of prior work experience (full time): 46
TOEFL requirement: Yes
Minimum TOEFL score: 580

Western Washington University[1]

516 High Street, MS 9072
Bellingham, WA 98225-9072
www.cbe.wwu.edu/mba/
Public
Admissions: (360) 650-3898
Email: mba@wwu.edu
Financial aid: N/A
Tuition: N/A
Room/board/expenses: N/A
Enrollment: N/A

WEST VIRGINIA

Marshall University (Lewis)

1 John Marshall Drive
Huntington, WV 25755-2020
www.marshall.edu/lcob/
Public
Admissions: (800) 642-9842
Email: johnson73@marshall.edu
Financial aid: (800) 438-5390
Application deadline: rolling
In-state tuition: full time: $8,246; part time: $409/credit hour
Out-of-state tuition: full time: $18,290
Room/board/expenses: N/A
College-funded aid: Yes
International student aid: Yes
Full-time enrollment: 137
men: 65%; women: 35%; minorities: 11%; international: 36%
Part-time enrollment: 34
men: 62%; women: 38%; minorities: 3%; international: 3%
Acceptance rate (full time): 88%
Average GPA (full time): 3.30
Average age of entrants to full-time program: 25
TOEFL requirement: Yes
Minimum TOEFL score: 550

West Virginia University

PO Box 6027
Morgantown, WV 26506
www.be.wvu.edu
Public
Admissions: (304) 293-7937
Email: mba@wvu.edu
Financial aid: (304) 293-5242
Application deadline: 03/01
In-state tuition: total program: $24,876 (full time); part time: N/A
Out-of-state tuition: total program: $58,500 (full time)
Room/board/expenses: $14,712
College-funded aid: Yes
International student aid: Yes

Full-time enrollment: 41
men: 68%; women: 32%;
minorities: 20%; international:
41%
Part-time enrollment: N/A
men: N/A; women: N/A; minorities:
N/A; international: N/A
Acceptance rate (full time): 49%
Average GMAT (full time): 617
Average GPA (full time): 3.37
Average age of entrants to full-time
program: 24
Average months of prior work
experience (full time): 15
TOEFL requirement: Yes
Minimum TOEFL score: 580
Most popular departments:
accounting, finance, general
management, human resources
management
Mean starting base salary for 2014
full-time graduates: $45,000
Employment location for 2014 class:
Intl. N/A; N.E. 10%; M.A. 75%; S.
5%; M.W. N/A; S.W. 5%; W. 5%

WISCONSIN

Marquette University
PO Box 1881
Milwaukee, WI 53201-1881
www.marquette.edu/gsm
Private
Admissions: (414) 288-7145
Email: mba@Marquette.edu
Financial aid: (414) 288-7137
Application deadline: rolling
Tuition: full time: $1,025/credit
hour; part time: $1,025/credit hour
Room/board/expenses: $16,306
College-funded aid: Yes
International student aid: Yes
Full-time enrollment: 180
men: 37%; women: 63%;
minorities: 6%; international: 46%
Part-time enrollment: 263
men: 70%; women: 30%;
minorities: 7%; international: 2%
Acceptance rate (full time): 55%
Average GMAT (full time): 630
Average GMAT (part time): 563
Average age of entrants to full-time
program: 23
TOEFL requirement: Yes
Minimum TOEFL score: 550
Most popular departments:
accounting, economics, finance,
human resources management,
international business

University of
Wisconsin-Eau Claire
Schneider Hall 215
Eau Claire, WI 54702-4004
www.uwec.edu/COB/graduate/
index.htm
Public
Admissions: (715) 836-5415
Email: uwecmba@uwec.edu
Financial aid: (715) 836-3373
Application deadline: rolling

In-state tuition: full time: $521/
credit hour; part time: $521/
credit hour
Out-of-state tuition: full time:
$1,030/credit hour
Room/board/expenses: $9,374
College-funded aid: Yes
International student aid: Yes
Full-time enrollment: 9
men: 56%; women: 44%;
minorities: 0%; international: 11%
Part-time enrollment: 310
men: 55%; women: 45%;
minorities: 6%; international: 2%
Acceptance rate (full time): 81%
Average GMAT (part time): 536
Average age of entrants to full-time
program: 28
TOEFL requirement: Yes
Minimum TOEFL score: 550
Most popular departments:
accounting, general management,
health care administration,
marketing, management
information systems

University of
Wisconsin-La Crosse
1725 State Street
La Crosse, WI 54601
www.uwlax.edu
Public
Admissions: (608) 785-8939
Email: admissions@uwlax.edu
Financial aid: (608) 785-8604
Application deadline: rolling
In-state tuition: total program:
$12,000 (full time); part time:
$506/credit hour
Out-of-state tuition: total program:
$24,220 (full time)
Room/board/expenses: N/A
College-funded aid: Yes
International student aid: Yes
Full-time enrollment: 43
men: 79%; women: 21%;
minorities: N/A; international: 35%
Part-time enrollment: N/A
men: N/A; women: N/A; minorities:
N/A; international: N/A
Average months of prior work
experience (full time): 46
TOEFL requirement: Yes
Minimum TOEFL score: 550
Most popular departments: finance,
general management, health care
administration, marketing

University of
Wisconsin-Madison
2450 Grainger Hall
975 University Avenue
Madison, WI 53706-1323
www.bus.wisc.edu/mba
Public
Admissions: (608) 262-4000
Email: mba@bus.wisc.edu
Financial aid: (608) 262-4000
Application deadline: rolling
In-state tuition: full time: $14,320;
part time: $17,835

Out-of-state tuition: full time:
$27,815
Room/board/expenses: $16,895
College-funded aid: Yes
International student aid: Yes
Full-time enrollment: 199
men: 64%; women: 36%;
minorities: 15%; international:
20%
Part-time enrollment: 155
men: 66%; women: 34%;
minorities: 10%; international: 7%
Acceptance rate (full time): 29%
Average GMAT (full time): 668
Average GMAT (part time): 606
Average age of entrants to full-time
program: 29
Average months of prior work
experience (full time): 62
TOEFL requirement: Yes
Minimum TOEFL score: N/A

University of
Wisconsin-
Milwaukee (Lubar)
PO Box 742
Milwaukee, WI 53201-9863
lubar.uwm.edu/programs
Public
Admissions: (414) 229-5403
Email: mba-ms@uwm.edu
Financial aid: (414) 229-4541
Application deadline: 08/01
In-state tuition: full time: $16,304;
part time: $13,226
Out-of-state tuition: full time:
$31,974
Room/board/expenses: $13,500
College-funded aid: Yes
International student aid: Yes
Full-time enrollment: 18
men: 44%; women: 56%;
minorities: 22%; international: 0%
Part-time enrollment: 447
men: 62%; women: 38%;
minorities: 11%; international: 17%
Acceptance rate (full time): 96%
Average GMAT (part time): 550
Average GPA (full time): 3.33
Average age of entrants to full-time
program: 25
Average months of prior work
experience (full time): 36
TOEFL requirement: Yes
Minimum TOEFL score: 550
Mean starting base salary for 2014
full-time graduates: $40,642

University of
Wisconsin-Oshkosh
800 Algoma Boulevard
Oshkosh, WI 54901
www.uwosh.edu/coba/
Public
Admissions: (800) 633-1430
Email: mba@uwosh.edu
Financial aid: (920) 424-3377
Application deadline: rolling
In-state tuition: full time: N/A; total
program: $24,500 (part time)
Out-of-state tuition: full time: N/A

Room/board/expenses: N/A
College-funded aid: Yes
International student aid: Yes
Full-time enrollment: 10
men: 80%; women: 20%;
minorities: 20%; international:
50%
Part-time enrollment: 391
men: 56%; women: 44%;
minorities: 5%; international: 1%
Acceptance rate (full time): 100%
Average GMAT (full time): 620
Average GMAT (part time): 597
Average GPA (full time): 3.47
Average age of entrants to full-time
program: 25
Average months of prior work
experience (full time): 48
TOEFL requirement: Yes
Minimum TOEFL score: 550
Most popular departments: finance,
health care administration,
international business,
management information
systems, other

University of
Wisconsin-Parkside
PO Box 2000
Kenosha, WI 53141-2000
www.uwp.edu/departments/
business
Public
Admissions: (262) 595-2280
Email: mba@uwp.edu
Financial aid: (262) 595-2574
Application deadline: rolling
In-state tuition: full time: $482/
credit hour; part time: $482/
credit hour
Out-of-state tuition: full time: $989/
credit hour
Room/board/expenses: $9,000
College-funded aid: Yes
International student aid: Yes
Full-time enrollment: 13
men: 46%; women: 54%;
minorities: 8%; international: 54%
Part-time enrollment: 77
men: 62%; women: 38%;
minorities: 16%; international: 12%
Acceptance rate (full time): 77%
Average GMAT (full time): 421
Average GMAT (part time): 455
Average GPA (full time): 3.41
Average age of entrants to full-time
program: 30
Average months of prior work
experience (full time): 48
TOEFL requirement: Yes
Minimum TOEFL score: 550

University of
Wisconsin-River Falls
410 S. Third Street
River Falls, WI 54022-5001
www.uwrf.edu/mba
Public
Admissions: (715) 425-3335
Email: mbacbe@uwrf.edu
Financial aid: (715) 425-4111
Application deadline: rolling

In-state tuition: full time: $692/
credit hour; part time: $692/
credit hour
Out-of-state tuition: full time: $692/
credit hour
Room/board/expenses: N/A
College-funded aid: Yes
International student aid: Yes
Full-time enrollment: 17
men: 71%; women: 29%;
minorities: 0%; international: 24%
Part-time enrollment: 65
men: 48%; women: 52%;
minorities: 8%; international: 2%
Acceptance rate (full time): 100%
Average GMAT (full time): 461
Average GMAT (part time): 441
Average GPA (full time): 3.15
Average age of entrants to full-time
program: 28
Average months of prior work
experience (full time): 9
TOEFL requirement: Yes
Minimum TOEFL score: 550

University of
Wisconsin-
Whitewater
800 W. Main Street
Whitewater, WI 53190
www.uww.edu/
Public
Admissions: (262) 472-1945
Email: smithL@uww.edu
Financial aid: (262) 472-1130
Application deadline: 07/15
In-state tuition: full time: $9,118;
part time: $507/credit hour
Out-of-state tuition: full time:
$18,274
Room/board/expenses: $6,400
College-funded aid: Yes
International student aid: Yes
Full-time enrollment: 227
men: 56%; women: 44%;
minorities: N/A; international: N/A
Part-time enrollment: 341
men: 37%; women: 63%;
minorities: N/A; international: N/A
Average GPA (full time): 3.23
TOEFL requirement: Yes
Minimum TOEFL score: 550
Most popular departments: finance,
general management, marketing,
technology, other

WYOMING

University of
Wyoming[1]
PO Box 3275
Laramie, WY 82071-3275
www.uwyo.edu/business/
Public
Admissions: N/A
Financial aid: N/A
Tuition: N/A
Room/board/expenses: N/A
Enrollment: N/A

EDUCATION

Here you'll find information on 357 schools nationwide that offer doctoral programs in education. Two hundred fifty-three responded to the U.S. News survey, which was conducted in the fall of 2014 and early 2015. They provided information on matters of interest to applicants such as entrance requirements, enrollment, costs, location and specialties. Schools that did not respond to the survey have abbreviated entries.

KEY TO THE TERMINOLOGY

1. A school whose name has been footnoted with the numeral 1 did not return the U.S. News statistical survey; limited data appear in its entry.
N/A. Not available from the school or not applicable.
Admissions. The admissions office phone number.
Email. The address of the admissions office. If instead of an email address a website is listed, the website will automatically present an email screen programmed to reach the admissions office.
Financial aid. The financial aid office phone number.
Application deadline. For fall 2016 enrollment. "Rolling" means there is no deadline; the school acts on applications as they are received. "Varies" means deadlines vary according to department or whether applicants are U.S. citizens or foreign nationals.
Tuition. For the 2014-15 academic year. Includes fees.
Credit hour. The cost per credit hour for the 2014-15 academic year.
Room/board/expenses. For the 2014-15 academic year.
Enrollment. Full-time and part-time graduate-level enrollment at the education school for fall 2014.
Minorities. Full-time and part-time graduate-level minority enrollment percentage for fall 2014. It is the share of students who are black or African-American, Asian, American Indian or Alaskan Native, Native Hawaiian or other Pacific Islander, Hispanic/ Latino or two or more races. The minority percentage was reported by each school.
Acceptance rate. Percentage of applicants who were accepted among those who applied for fall 2014 for both master's and doctoral programs.

Entrance test required. GRE means that scores on the Graduate Record Examination are required by some or all departments. GRE scores displayed are for both the master's and Ph.D. students and are only for those GRE exams taken by the fall 2014 entering students during or after August 2011 using the new GRE 130-170 score scale. MAT means that the Miller Analogies Test is required by some or all departments. GRE or MAT means that some or all departments require either the GRE or MAT.
Average GRE scores. Average verbal and quantitative scores for students who entered in fall 2014. Averages are based on the number of students who provided the school with scores. That number may be less than the total number of students who entered in fall 2014. (The GRE scores published in the ranking table refer to the scores of a school's entering doctoral students and may not be the same as the average GRE scores for the overall entering class printed in the directory.)
Total research assistantships. For the 2014-15 academic year.
Students reporting specialty. The percentage of graduate students, both full and part time, reporting a program specialization in fall 2014. If a school's figure is less than 50 percent, then its directory entry does not include this information or an enumeration of student specialties.
Student specialties. Proportion of students in the specialty-reporting population (not necessarily the entire student body) who are enrolled in a particular specialty. Numbers may not add up to 100 percent because of rounding or students enrolled in multiple specialties. The largest specialty areas in graduate education are listed.

ALABAMA

Alabama State University
915 S. Jackson Street
Montgomery, AL 36101
www.alasu.edu/Education/
Public
Admissions: (334) 229-4275
Financial aid: (334) 229-4324
Application deadline: rolling
In-state tuition: full time: $343/ credit hour; part time: $343/ credit hour
Out-of-state tuition: full time: $686/ credit hour
Room/board/expenses: $7,802
Full-time enrollment: 84
doctoral students: 27%; master's students: 69%; education specialists: 4%; men: 26%; women: 74%; minorities: 96%; international: N/A
Part-time enrollment: 309
doctoral students: 11%; master's students: 76%; education specialists: 13%; men: 29%; women: 71%; minorities: 95%; international: N/A
Acceptance rate (master's): 56%
Acceptance rate (doctoral): 38%
Entrance test required: GRE
Avg. GRE (of all entering students with scores): quantitative: 141; verbal: 142
Students reporting specialty: 48%
Students specializing in: N/A

Auburn University
3084 Haley Center
Auburn, AL 36849-5218
www.auburn.edu/
Public
Admissions: (334) 844-4700
Email: gradadm@auburn.edu
Financial aid: (334) 844-4634
Application deadline: rolling
In-state tuition: full time: $10,194; part time: $477/credit hour
Out-of-state tuition: full time: $27,366
Room/board/expenses: $18,964
Full-time enrollment: 427
doctoral students: 41%; master's students: 58%; education specialists: 2%; men: 33%; women: 67%; minorities: 26%; international: 4%
Part-time enrollment: 515
doctoral students: 46%; master's students: 43%; education specialists: 12%; men: 34%; women: 66%; minorities: 23%; international: 1%
Acceptance rate (master's): 69%
Acceptance rate (doctoral): 38%
Entrance test required: GRE
Avg. GRE (of all entering students with scores): quantitative: 146; verbal: 149
Research assistantships: 30
Students reporting specialty: 100%
Students specializing in: admin.: 11%; instructional media design: 1%; educational psych: 7%; elementary: 5%; higher education admin.: 12%; secondary: 8%; special: 9%; counseling: 10%; technical (vocational): 6%; other: 31%

Samford University (Beeson)
800 Lakeshore Drive
Birmingham, AL 35229
education.samford.edu
Private
Admissions: (205) 726-2451
Email: lsennis@samford.edu
Financial aid: (205) 726-2905
Application deadline: 07/31
Tuition: full time: $744/credit hour; part time: $744/credit hour
Room/board/expenses: $1,100
Full-time enrollment: 201
doctoral students: 25%; master's students: 64%; education specialists: 10%; men: 26%; women: 74%; minorities: 22%; international: 0%
Part-time enrollment: 89
doctoral students: 67%; master's students: 31%; education specialists: 1%; men: 29%; women: 71%; minorities: 20%; international: N/A
Acceptance rate (master's): 64%
Acceptance rate (doctoral): 52%
Entrance test required: GRE
Avg. GRE (of all entering students with scores): quantitative: 145; verbal: 145
Research assistantships: 0
Students reporting specialty: 100%
Students specializing in: admin.: 65%; elementary: 2%; secondary: 19%; special: 10%; other: 4%

University of Alabama
Box 870231
Tuscaloosa, AL 35487-0231
graduate.ua.edu
Public
Admissions: (205) 348-5921
Email: gradschool@ua.edu
Financial aid: (205) 348-7949
Application deadline: rolling
In-state tuition: full time: $9,826; part time: N/A
Out-of-state tuition: full time: $24,950
Room/board/expenses: $12,457
Full-time enrollment: 367
doctoral students: 49%; master's students: 48%; education specialists: 4%; men: 30%; women: 70%; minorities: 22%; international: 8%
Part-time enrollment: 660
doctoral students: 54%; master's students: 33%; education specialists: 12%; men: 29%; women: 71%; minorities: 21%; international: 3%
Acceptance rate (master's): 53%
Acceptance rate (doctoral): 56%
Entrance test required: GRE
Avg. GRE (of all entering students with scores): quantitative: 147; verbal: 149
Research assistantships: 51
Students reporting specialty: 100%
Students specializing in: admin.: 33%; evaluation/research/ statistics: 2%; educational psych: 9%; elementary: 5%; higher education admin.: 14%; secondary: 13%; special: 6%; counseling: 3%; other: 18%

University of Alabama-Birmingham

1530 Third Avenue S, EB 217
Birmingham, AL 35294-1250
www.uab.edu/graduate
Public
Admissions: (205) 934-8227
Email: gradschool@uab.edu
Financial aid: (205) 934-8223
Application deadline: rolling
In-state tuition: full time: $7,090;
part time: $370/credit hour
Out-of-state tuition: full time:
$16,072
Room/board/expenses: $14,409
Full-time enrollment: 188
doctoral students: 5%; master's
students: 94%; education
specialists: 1%; men: 23%;
women: 77%; minorities: 23%;
international: 3%
Part-time enrollment: 584
doctoral students: 11%; master's
students: 75%; education
specialists: 14%; men: 23%;
women: 77%; minorities: 26%;
international: 1%
Acceptance rate (master's): 96%
Acceptance rate (doctoral): 82%
Entrance test required: GRE
**Avg. GRE (of all entering students
with scores):** quantitative: 148;
verbal: 149
Research assistantships: 7
Students reporting specialty: 100%
Students specializing in:
curriculum/instr.: 9%; admin.:
19%; evaluation/research/
statistics: 3%; elementary: 6%;
secondary: 14%; special: 8%;
counseling: 12%; other: 29%

University of South Alabama[1]

UCOM 3600
Mobile, AL 36688
www.southalabama.edu/
Public
Admissions: N/A
Financial aid: N/A
Tuition: N/A
Room/board/expenses: N/A
Enrollment: N/A

ARIZONA

Arizona State University

PO Box 37100
MC 1252
Phoenix, AZ 85069-7100
www.asu.edu/graduate
Public
Admissions: (480) 965-6113
Email: grad-ges@asu.edu
Financial aid: (480) 965-3355
Application deadline: rolling
In-state tuition: full time: $11,303;
part time: $758/credit hour
Out-of-state tuition: full time:
$26,737
Room/board/expenses: $18,408
Full-time enrollment: 752
doctoral students: 14%; master's
students: 86%; education
specialists: N/A; men: 29%;
women: 71%; minorities: 29%;
international: 6%
Part-time enrollment: 1,579
doctoral students: 10%; master's
students: 90%; education
specialists: N/A; men: 19%;
women: 81%; minorities: 29%;
international: 5%
Acceptance rate (master's): 87%
Acceptance rate (doctoral): 31%
Entrance test required: GRE

**Avg. GRE (of all entering students
with scores):** quantitative: 149;
verbal: 154
Research assistantships: 81
Students reporting specialty: 100%
Students specializing in:
curriculum/instr.: 50%; admin.:
13%; policy: 2%; instructional
media design: 3%; educational
psych: 1%; elementary: 6%;
higher education admin.: 5%;
secondary: 8%; special: 4%;
other: 8%

Grand Canyon University[1]

3300 W. Camelback Road
Phoenix, AZ 85017
www.gcu.edu
Private
Admissions: N/A
Financial aid: N/A
Tuition: N/A
Room/board/expenses: N/A
Enrollment: N/A

Northern Arizona University

PO Box 5774
Flagstaff, AZ 86011-5774
nau.edu/GradCol/Welcome/
Public
Admissions: (928) 523-4348
Email: Graduate@nau.edu
Financial aid: (928) 523-4951
Application deadline: rolling
In-state tuition: full time: $8,838;
part time: $410/credit hour
Out-of-state tuition: full time:
$20,102
Room/board/expenses: $15,058
Full-time enrollment: 567
doctoral students: 10%; master's
students: 85%; education
specialists: 5%; men: 32%;
women: 68%; minorities: 31%;
international: 2%
Part-time enrollment: 990
doctoral students: 13%; master's
students: 87%; education
specialists: 1%; men: 29%;
women: 71%; minorities: 36%;
international: 0%
Acceptance rate (master's): 75%
Acceptance rate (doctoral): 59%
Entrance test required: GRE
**Avg. GRE (of all entering students
with scores):** quantitative: 146;
verbal: 150
Research assistantships: 2
Students reporting specialty: 100%
Students specializing in:
curriculum/instr.: 3%; admin.:
46%; educational psych:
2%; educational tech.: 4%;
elementary: 9%; secondary: 1%;
special: 3%; counseling: 20%;
technical (vocational): 0%; other:
12%

Prescott College[1]

220 Grove Ave.
Prescott, AZ 86301
www.prescott.edu/learn/
index.html
Private
Admissions: N/A
Financial aid: N/A
Tuition: N/A
Room/board/expenses: N/A
Enrollment: N/A

University of Arizona

Box 210069
1430 E. Second Street
Tucson, AZ 85721-0069
grad.arizona.edu/admissions
Public
Admissions: (520) 626-8851
Email: gradadmissions@
grad.arizona.edu
Financial aid: (520) 621-5200
Application deadline: rolling
In-state tuition: full time: $12,758;
part time: $766/credit hour
Out-of-state tuition: full time:
$29,740
Room/board/expenses: $17,000
Full-time enrollment: 461
doctoral students: 44%; master's
students: 52%; education
specialists: 3%; men: 30%;
women: 70%; minorities: 41%;
international: 9%
Part-time enrollment: 301
doctoral students: 36%; master's
students: 56%; education
specialists: 8%; men: 24%;
women: 76%; minorities: 35%;
international: 2%
Acceptance rate (master's): 61%
Acceptance rate (doctoral): 54%
Entrance test required: GRE
**Avg. GRE (of all entering students
with scores):** quantitative: 150;
verbal: 153
Research assistantships: 27
Students reporting specialty: 88%
Students specializing in:
curriculum/instr.: 20%; admin.:
9%; policy: 6%; evaluation/
research/statistics: 0%;
educational psych: 6%;
elementary: 2%; higher
education admin.: 14%; junior
high: 2%; secondary: 7%; social/
philosophical foundations: 7%;
special: 16%; counseling: 7%;
other: 10%

ARKANSAS

Arkansas State University-Jonesboro[1]

PO Box 10
State University, AR 72467
www.astate.edu/college/
graduate-school/
Public
Admissions: N/A
Financial aid: N/A
Tuition: N/A
Room/board/expenses: N/A
Enrollment: N/A

Harding University

Box 12234
Searcy, AR 72149
www.harding.edu/education/
grad.html
Private
Admissions: (501) 279-4315
Email:
gradstudiesedu@harding.edu
Financial aid: (501) 279-4081
Application deadline: N/A
Tuition: full time: N/A; part time:
N/A
Room/board/expenses: N/A
Full-time enrollment: 118
doctoral students: 0%; master's
students: 93%; education
specialists: 7%; men: 25%;
women: 75%; minorities: 13%;
international: 9%
Part-time enrollment: 337
doctoral students: 11%; master's
students: 81%; education
specialists: 8%; men: 30%;
women: 70%; minorities: 18%;
international: 1%
Acceptance rate (master's): 100%

Acceptance rate (doctoral): 100%
Entrance test required: GRE
**Avg. GRE (of all entering students
with scores):** quantitative: N/A;
verbal: N/A
Research assistantships: 0
Students reporting specialty: 0%
Students specializing in: N/A

University of Arkansas-Fayetteville

324 Graduate Education Building
Fayetteville, AR 72701
coehp.uark.edu
Public
Admissions: (479) 575-6247
Email: gradinfo@uark.edu
Financial aid: (479) 575-3276
Application deadline: 08/01
In-state tuition: full time: $388/
credit hour; part time: $388/
credit hour
Out-of-state tuition: full time: $919/
credit hour
Room/board/expenses: $14,856
Full-time enrollment: 522
doctoral students: 20%; master's
students: 79%; education
specialists: 0%; men: 28%;
women: 72%; minorities: 13%;
international: 8%
Part-time enrollment: 480
doctoral students: 33%; master's
students: 62%; education
specialists: 5%; men: 32%;
women: 68%; minorities: 19%;
international: 0%
Acceptance rate (master's): 79%
Acceptance rate (doctoral): 77%
Entrance test required: GRE
**Avg. GRE (of all entering students
with scores):** quantitative: 149;
verbal: 151
Research assistantships: 53
Students reporting specialty: 100%
Students specializing in:
curriculum/instr.: 6%; admin.:
10%; evaluation/research/
statistics: 1%; instructional
media design: 4%; elementary:
7%; higher education admin.:
8%; secondary: 4%; social/
philosophical foundations: 2%;
special: 3%; counseling: 9%;
other: 47%

University of Arkansas-Little Rock[1]

2801 S. University Avenue
Little Rock, AR 72204
ualr.edu/www/
Public
Admissions: N/A
Financial aid: N/A
Tuition: N/A
Room/board/expenses: N/A
Enrollment: N/A

CALIFORNIA

Alliant International University

1 Beach Street
San Francisco, CA 94133-1221
www.alliant.edu/
Private
Admissions: (866) 825-5426
Email: admissions@alliant.edu
Financial aid: (858) 635-4559
Application deadline: rolling
Tuition: full time: $615/credit hour;
part time: $615/credit hour
Room/board/expenses: $23,100
Full-time enrollment: 125
doctoral students: 22%; master's
students: 78%; education
specialists: N/A; men: 32%;
women: 68%; minorities: 54%;
international: 13%

Part-time enrollment: 160
doctoral students: 51%; master's
students: 49%; education
specialists: N/A; men: 33%;
women: 67%; minorities: 50%;
international: 9%
Acceptance rate (master's): N/A
Acceptance rate (doctoral): N/A
Entrance test required: N/A
**Avg. GRE (of all entering students
with scores):** quantitative: N/A;
verbal: N/A
Students reporting specialty: 100%
Students specializing in:
curriculum/instr.: 13%; admin.:
12%; educational psych: 31%;
elementary: 1%; higher education
admin.: 1%; secondary: 4%;
special: 3%; counseling: 4%;
other: 31%

Azusa Pacific University

PO Box 7000
Azusa, CA 91702
www.apu.edu
Private
Admissions: N/A
Financial aid: N/A
Application deadline: 08/01
Tuition: full time: $622/credit hour;
part time: $622/credit hour
Room/board/expenses: N/A
Full-time enrollment: 574
doctoral students: 11%; master's
students: 89%; education
specialists: N/A; men: 26%;
women: 74%; minorities: 42%;
international: 1%
Part-time enrollment: 544
doctoral students: 13%; master's
students: 87%; education
specialists: N/A; men: 30%;
women: 70%; minorities: 44%;
international: N/A
Acceptance rate (master's): 94%
Acceptance rate (doctoral): N/A
Entrance test required: GRE
**Avg. GRE (of all entering students
with scores):** quantitative: N/A;
verbal: N/A
Students reporting specialty: 100%
Students specializing in: admin.:
13%; educational psych:
5%; educational tech.: 1%;
elementary: 13%; secondary:
18%; special: 28%; counseling:
11%; other: 9%

California Lutheran University[1]

60 West Olsen Road
Thousand Oaks, CA 91360
www.callutheran.edu/
Private
Admissions: N/A
Financial aid: N/A
Tuition: N/A
Room/board/expenses: N/A
Enrollment: N/A

California State University-East Bay[1]

25800 Carlos Bee Boulevard
Hayward, CA 94542
www.csueastbay.edu
Public
Admissions: N/A
Financial aid: N/A
Tuition: N/A
Room/board/expenses: N/A
Enrollment: N/A

California State University-Fresno[1]
5150 N. Maple
Fresno, CA 93740
www.fresnostate.edu
Public
Admissions: N/A
Financial aid: N/A
Tuition: N/A
Room/board/expenses: N/A
Enrollment: N/A

California State University-Fullerton[1]
800 N. State College Boulevard
Fullerton, CA 92831-3599
ed.fullerton.edu/
Public
Admissions: N/A
Financial aid: N/A
Tuition: N/A
Room/board/expenses: N/A
Enrollment: N/A

California State University-Long Beach
1250 Bellflower Boulevard
Long Beach, CA 90840
www.ced.csulb.edu
Public
Admissions: (562) 985-4547
Email: nmcgloth@csulb.edu
Financial aid: (562) 985-8403
Application deadline: rolling
In-state tuition: full time: $7,718;
part time: N/A
Out-of-state tuition: full time: N/A
Room/board/expenses: N/A
Full-time enrollment: 249
doctoral students: 1%; master's
students: 97%; education
specialists: 2%; men: 20%;
women: 80%; minorities: 68%;
international: 7%
Part-time enrollment: 348
doctoral students: 22%; master's
students: 73%; education
specialists: 5%; men: 27%;
women: 73%; minorities: 70%;
international: 3%
Acceptance rate (master's): 37%
Acceptance rate (doctoral): 45%
Entrance test required: GRE
**Avg. GRE (of all entering students
with scores):** quantitative: N/A;
verbal: N/A
Students reporting specialty: 100%
Students specializing in:
curriculum/instr.: 2%; admin.:
17%; instructional media design:
2%; educational psych: 0%;
elementary: 12%; secondary:
39%; social/philosophical
foundations: 3%; special: 1%;
counseling: 8%; other: 15%

California State University-Los Angeles[1]
5151 State University Drive
Los Angeles, CA 90032
www.calstatela.edu/academic/ccoe/
Public/
Admissions: N/A
Financial aid: N/A
Tuition: N/A
Room/board/expenses: N/A
Enrollment: N/A

CaliforniaState University-Northridge[1]
18111 Nordhoff Street
Northridge, CA 91330-8265
www.csun.edu/
Public
Admissions: N/A
Financial aid: N/A
Tuition: N/A
Room/board/expenses: N/A
Enrollment: N/A

California State University-Sacramento[1]
6000 J Street
Sacramento, CA 95819-2694
www.csus.edu/
Public
Admissions: N/A
Financial aid: N/A
Tuition: N/A
Room/board/expenses: N/A
Enrollment: N/A

California State University-San Bernardino[1]
5500 University Parkway
San Bernardino, CA 92407
www.csusb.edu/
Public
Admissions: N/A
Financial aid: N/A
Tuition: N/A
Room/board/expenses: N/A
Enrollment: N/A

California State University-Stanislaus[1]
801 W. Monte Vista Avenue
Turlock, CA 95382
www.csustan.edu/
Public
Admissions: N/A
Financial aid: N/A
Tuition: N/A
Room/board/expenses: N/A
Enrollment: N/A

Chapman University
1 University Drive
Orange, CA 92866
www.chapman.edu/ces
Private
Admissions: (888) 282-7759
Email: admit@chapman.edu
Financial aid: (714) 997-6741
Application deadline: N/A
Tuition: full time: $824/credit hour;
part time: $824/credit hour
Room/board/expenses: $1,450
Full-time enrollment: 244
doctoral students: 5%; master's
students: 77%; education
specialists: 17%; men: 19%;
women: 81%; minorities: 41%;
international: 3%
Part-time enrollment: 173
doctoral students: 35%; master's
students: 55%; education
specialists: 9%; men: 24%;
women: 76%; minorities: 44%;
international: 2%
Acceptance rate (master's): 29%
Acceptance rate (doctoral): 69%
Entrance test required: GRE
**Avg. GRE (of all entering students
with scores):** quantitative: N/A;
verbal: N/A
Research assistantships: 31
Students reporting specialty: 100%
Students specializing in:
curriculum/instr.: 6%; educational
psych: 15%; elementary: 13%;

higher education admin.: 4%;
secondary: 15%; special: 18%;
counseling: 7%; other: 23%

Claremont Graduate University
150 E. 10th Street
Claremont, CA 91711
www.cgu.edu/pages/267.asp
Private
Admissions: (909) 621-8263
Email: admiss@cgu.edu
Financial aid: (909) 621-8337
Application deadline: rolling
Tuition: full time: $42,384; part
time: $1,741/credit hour
Room/board/expenses: $26,000
Full-time enrollment: 77
doctoral students: 82%; master's
students: 18%; education
specialists: N/A; men: 23%;
women: 77%; minorities: 55%;
international: 6%
Part-time enrollment: 310
doctoral students: 84%; master's
students: 16%; education
specialists: N/A; men: 30%;
women: 70%; minorities: 49%;
international: 2%
Acceptance rate (master's): 97%
Acceptance rate (doctoral): 81%
Entrance test required: GRE
**Avg. GRE (of all entering students
with scores):** quantitative: 146;
verbal: 151
Research assistantships: 13
Students reporting specialty: 100%
Students specializing in:
curriculum/instr.: 21%; admin.:
16%; policy: 4%; evaluation/
research/statistics: 2%;
elementary: 7%; higher education
admin.: 17%; secondary: 9%;
special: 8%; other: 15%

Fielding Graduate University
2020 De La Vina Street
Santa Barbara, CA 93105
www.fielding.edu/programs/
education/default.aspx
Private
Admissions: (800) 340-1099
Email: admission@fielding.edu
Financial aid: (805) 898-4009
Application deadline: N/A
Tuition: full time: $46,590; part
time: $46,590
Room/board/expenses: $24,000
Full-time enrollment: 146
doctoral students: 89%; master's
students: 11%; education
specialists: N/A; men: 29%;
women: 71%; minorities: 30%;
international: 1%
Part-time enrollment: 7
doctoral students: 71%; master's
students: 29%; education
specialists: N/A; men: 57%;
women: 43%; minorities: 100%;
international: N/A
Acceptance rate (master's): 94%
Acceptance rate (doctoral): 98%
Entrance test required: N/A
**Avg. GRE (of all entering students
with scores):** quantitative: N/A;
verbal: N/A
Research assistantships: 0
Students reporting specialty: 100%
Students specializing in: admin.:
100%

La Sierra University[1]
4700 Pierce Street
Riverside, CA 92515
lasierra.edu
Private
Admissions: N/A
Financial aid: N/A

Tuition: N/A
Room/board/expenses: N/A
Enrollment: N/A

Loyola Marymount University
1 LMU Drive
Los Angeles, CA 90045
soe.lmu.edu
Private
Admissions: (310) 338-7845
Email: soeinfo@lmu.edu
Financial aid: (310) 338-2753
Application deadline: 06/15
Tuition: full time: $1,074/credit
hour; part time: $1,074/credit hour
Room/board/expenses: $21,012
Full-time enrollment: 967
doctoral students: 7%; master's
students: 88%; education
specialists: 5%; men: 26%;
women: 74%; minorities: 60%;
international: 4%
Part-time enrollment: 135
doctoral students: 0%; master's
students: 100%; education
specialists: 0%; men: 25%;
women: 75%; minorities: 58%;
international: 5%
Acceptance rate (master's): 32%
Acceptance rate (doctoral): 31%
Entrance test required: GRE
**Avg. GRE (of all entering students
with scores):** quantitative: 149;
verbal: 153
Research assistantships: 19
Students reporting specialty: 100%
Students specializing in: admin.:
12%; educational psych: 3%;
elementary: 23%; secondary:
26%; special: 14%; counseling:
13%; other: 13%

Mills College
5000 MacArthur Boulevard
Oakland, CA 94613
www.mills.edu/
Private
Admissions: (510) 430-3309
Email: grad-studies@mills.edu
Financial aid: (510) 430-2000
Application deadline: 12/15
Tuition: full time: $32,056; part
time: $7,726/credit hour
Room/board/expenses: $16,496
Full-time enrollment: 152
doctoral students: 16%; master's
students: 84%; education
specialists: N/A; men: 13%;
women: 88%; minorities: 43%;
international: 1%
Part-time enrollment: 68
doctoral students: 46%; master's
students: 54%; education
specialists: N/A; men: 18%;
women: 82%; minorities: 43%;
international: N/A
Acceptance rate (master's): 91%
Acceptance rate (doctoral): 70%
Entrance test required: N/A
**Avg. GRE (of all entering students
with scores):** quantitative: N/A;
verbal: N/A
Research assistantships: 1
Students reporting specialty: 84%
Students specializing in: admin.:
45%; elementary: 12%;
secondary: 15%; special: 9%;
other: 28%

Pepperdine University
6100 Center Drive, Fifth Floor
Los Angeles, CA 90045-4301
gsep.pepperdine.edu/
Private
Admissions: (310) 568-5744
Email: barbara.moore@
pepperdine.edu
Financial aid: (310) 568-5735

Application deadline: rolling
Tuition: full time: $1,110/credit
hour; part time: $1,110/credit hour
Room/board/expenses: $10,200
Full-time enrollment: 696
doctoral students: 68%; master's
students: 32%; education
specialists: N/A; men: 32%;
women: 68%; minorities: 36%;
international: 8%
Part-time enrollment: N/A
doctoral students: N/A; master's
students: N/A; education
specialists: N/A; men: N/A;
women: N/A; minorities: N/A;
international: N/A
Acceptance rate (master's): 68%
Acceptance rate (doctoral): 63%
Entrance test required: GRE
**Avg. GRE (of all entering students
with scores):** quantitative: 148;
verbal: 150
Research assistantships: 26
Students reporting specialty: 99%
Students specializing in:
curriculum/instr.: 23%; policy:
11%; evaluation/research/
statistics: 5%; educational
psych: 20%; educational tech.:
13%; elementary: 14%; higher
education admin.: 10%; junior
high: 23%; secondary: 9%; social/
philosophical foundations: 5%;
special: 23%; other: 43%

San Diego State University
5500 Campanile Drive
San Diego, CA 92182
edweb.sdsu.edu/
Public
Admissions: (619) 594-6336
Email: barata@mail.sdsu.edu
Financial aid: (619) 594-6323
Application deadline: N/A
In-state tuition: full time: $8,132;
part time: $5,300
Out-of-state tuition: full time: $372/
credit hour
Room/board/expenses: $15,535
Full-time enrollment: 381
doctoral students: 9%; master's
students: 78%; education
specialists: 13%; men: 27%;
women: 73%; minorities: 58%;
international: 6%
Part-time enrollment: 270
doctoral students: 29%; master's
students: 71%; education
specialists: 0%; men: 26%;
women: 74%; minorities: 49%;
international: 6%
Acceptance rate (master's): 62%
Acceptance rate (doctoral): 71%
Entrance test required: GRE
**Avg. GRE (of all entering students
with scores):** quantitative: 145;
verbal: 149
Research assistantships: 26
Students reporting specialty: 93%
Students specializing in:
curriculum/instr.: 4%; admin.:
7%; policy: 0%; elementary:
17%; higher education admin.:
9%; secondary: 14%; social/
philosophical foundations: 3%;
special: 13%; counseling: 10%;
other: 23%

San Francisco State University[1]
1600 Holloway Avenue
San Francisco, CA 94132
www.sfsu.edu/
Public
Admissions: N/A
Financial aid: N/A
Tuition: N/A
Room/board/expenses: N/A
Enrollment: N/A

Stanford University

485 Lasuen Mall
Stanford, CA 94305-3096
ed.stanford.edu
Private
Admissions: (650) 723-4794
Email: info@gse.stanford.edu
Financial aid: (650) 723-4794
Application deadline: N/A
Tuition: full time: $44,757; part time: N/A
Room/board/expenses: $22,905
Full-time enrollment: 379
doctoral students: 47%; master's students: 53%; education specialists: N/A; men: 33%; women: 67%; minorities: 36%; international: 14%
Part-time enrollment: N/A
doctoral students: N/A; master's students: N/A; education specialists: N/A; men: N/A; women: N/A; minorities: N/A; international: N/A
Acceptance rate (master's): 22%
Acceptance rate (doctoral): 5%
Entrance test required: GRE
Avg. GRE (of all entering students with scores): quantitative: 158; verbal: 162
Research assistantships: 560
Students reporting specialty: 100%
Students specializing in: curriculum/instr.: 11%; admin.: 3%; policy: 17%; evaluation/research/ statistics: 9%; instructional media design: 8%; educational psych.: 8%; educational tech.: 6%; elementary: 6%; higher education admin.: 0%; secondary: 17%; social/philosophical foundations: 6%; other: 8%

St. Mary's College of California[1]

1928 St. Mary's Road
Moraga, CA 94556
www.stmarys-ca.edu
Private
Admissions: N/A
Financial aid: N/A
Tuition: N/A
Room/board/expenses: N/A
Enrollment: N/A

University of California-Berkeley

1600 Tolman Hall, MC #1670
Berkeley, CA 94720-1670
gse.berkeley.edu
Public
Admissions: (510) 642-0841
Email: gse_info@berkeley.edu
Financial aid: (510) 643-1720
Application deadline: 12/01
In-state tuition: full time: $15,321; part time: N/A
Out-of-state tuition: full time: $30,423
Room/board/expenses: $23,814
Full-time enrollment: 355
doctoral students: 70%; master's students: 30%; education specialists: N/A; men: 29%; women: 71%; minorities: 46%; international: 11%
Part-time enrollment: N/A
doctoral students: N/A; master's students: N/A; education specialists: N/A; men: N/A; women: N/A; minorities: N/A; international: N/A
Acceptance rate (master's): 33%
Acceptance rate (doctoral): 14%
Entrance test required: GRE
Avg. GRE (of all entering students with scores): quantitative: 152; verbal: 157
Research assistantships: 75

Students reporting specialty: 100%
Students specializing in: admin.: 17%; policy: 9%; evaluation/ research/statistics: 6%; educational psych: 15%; elementary: 5%; secondary: 12%; social/philosophical foundations: 9%; special: 5%; other: 20%

University of California-Davis

School of Education
1 Shields Avenue
Davis, CA 95616
education.ucdavis.edu
Public
Admissions: (530) 752-5887
Email: eduadvising@ucdavis.edu
Financial aid: (530) 752-2396
Application deadline: N/A
In-state tuition: full time: $26,218; part time: $20,608
Out-of-state tuition: full time: $41,320
Room/board/expenses: $21,206
Full-time enrollment: 127
doctoral students: 94%; master's students: 6%; education specialists: N/A; men: 34%; women: 66%; minorities: 45%; international: 2%
Part-time enrollment: 156
doctoral students: 15%; master's students: 85%; education specialists: N/A; men: 20%; women: 80%; minorities: 44%; international: N/A
Acceptance rate (master's): 54%
Acceptance rate (doctoral): 29%
Entrance test required: GRE
Avg. GRE (of all entering students with scores): quantitative: 150; verbal: 157
Research assistantships: 108
Students reporting specialty: 0%
Students specializing in: N/A

University of California-Irvine

3200 Education
Irvine, CA 92697-5500
education.uci.edu
Public
Admissions: (949) 824-7465
Email: judi.conroy@uci.edu
Financial aid: (949) 824-5337
Application deadline: rolling
In-state tuition: full time: $16,035; part time: $10,425
Out-of-state tuition: full time: $31,137
Room/board/expenses: $18,405
Full-time enrollment: 170
doctoral students: 40%; master's students: 60%; education specialists: N/A; men: 24%; women: 76%; minorities: 56%; international: 6%
Part-time enrollment: 1
doctoral students: N/A; master's students: 100%; education specialists: N/A; men: 100%; women: N/A; minorities: 100%; international: N/A
Acceptance rate (master's): 87%
Acceptance rate (doctoral): 19%
Entrance test required: GRE
Avg. GRE (of all entering students with scores): quantitative: 152; verbal: 154
Research assistantships: 29
Students reporting specialty: 100%
Students specializing in: other: 100%

University of California-Los Angeles

1009 Moore Hall
MB 951521
Los Angeles, CA 90095-1521
www.gseis.ucla.edu
Public
Admissions: (310) 825-8326
Email: info@gseis.ucla.edu
Financial aid: (310) 206-0400
Application deadline: 12/01
In-state tuition: full time: $15,582; part time: N/A
Out-of-state tuition: full time: $30,684
Room/board/expenses: $20,334
Full-time enrollment: 747
doctoral students: 55%; master's students: 45%; education specialists: N/A; men: 30%; women: 70%; minorities: 59%; international: 6%
Part-time enrollment: N/A
doctoral students: N/A; master's students: N/A; education specialists: N/A; men: N/A; women: N/A; minorities: N/A; international: N/A
Acceptance rate (master's): 65%
Acceptance rate (doctoral): 28%
Entrance test required: GRE
Avg. GRE (of all entering students with scores): quantitative: 151; verbal: 155
Research assistantships: 129
Students reporting specialty: 99%
Students specializing in: curriculum/instr.: 3%; admin.: 16%; policy: 17%; evaluation/ research/statistics: 6%; instructional media design: 2%; educational psych: 6%; elementary: 12%; higher education admin.: 15%; secondary: 21%; social/philosophical foundations: 12%; special: 3%; counseling: 2%

University of California-Riverside

1207 Sproul Hall
Riverside, CA 92521
www.education.ucr.edu
Public
Admissions: (951) 827-6362
Email: edgrad@ucr.edu
Financial aid: (951) 827-3878
Application deadline: N/A
In-state tuition: full time: $16,197; part time: N/A
Out-of-state tuition: full time: $31,299
Room/board/expenses: $16,400
Full-time enrollment: 213
doctoral students: 46%; master's students: 54%; education specialists: N/A; men: 25%; women: 75%; minorities: 56%; international: 9%
Part-time enrollment: N/A
doctoral students: N/A; master's students: N/A; education specialists: N/A; men: N/A; women: N/A; minorities: N/A; international: N/A
Acceptance rate (master's): 67%
Acceptance rate (doctoral): 47%
Entrance test required: GRE
Avg. GRE (of all entering students with scores): quantitative: 152; verbal: 153
Research assistantships: 20
Students reporting specialty: 100%
Students specializing in: admin.: 1%; educational psych: 11%; elementary: 16%; higher education admin.: 12%; secondary: 22%; special: 16%; counseling: 11%; other: 13%

University of California-San Diego

9500 Gilman Drive
La Jolla, CA 92093
eds.ucsd.edu
Public
Admissions: (858) 534-2958
Email: gvanluit@ucsd.edu
Financial aid: (858) 534-3898
Application deadline: rolling
In-state tuition: full time: $16,129; part time: $10,519
Out-of-state tuition: full time: $31,231
Room/board/expenses: $18,121
Full-time enrollment: 128
doctoral students: 44%; master's students: 48%; education specialists: 9%; men: 28%; women: 72%; minorities: 49%; international: 1%
Part-time enrollment: N/A
doctoral students: N/A; master's students: N/A; education specialists: N/A; men: N/A; women: N/A; minorities: N/A; international: N/A
Acceptance rate (master's): 80%
Acceptance rate (doctoral): 52%
Entrance test required: GRE
Avg. GRE (of all entering students with scores): quantitative: 151; verbal: 153
Research assistantships: 2
Students reporting specialty: 100%
Students specializing in: curriculum/instr.: 48%; admin.: 30%; elementary: 28%; higher education admin.: 10%; junior high: 28%; secondary: 28%; special: 9%

University of California-Santa Barbara (Gevirtz)

Education Building
Santa Barbara, CA 93106-9490
www.education.ucsb.edu
Public
Admissions: (805) 893-2137
Email: sao@education.ucsb.edu
Financial aid: (805) 893-2432
Application deadline: N/A
In-state tuition: full time: $15,754; part time: N/A
Out-of-state tuition: full time: $30,856
Room/board/expenses: $20,021
Full-time enrollment: 327
doctoral students: 69%; master's students: 28%; education specialists: 3%; men: 23%; women: 77%; minorities: 45%; international: 9%
Part-time enrollment: N/A
doctoral students: N/A; master's students: N/A; education specialists: N/A; men: N/A; women: N/A; minorities: N/A; international: N/A
Acceptance rate (master's): 59%
Acceptance rate (doctoral): 22%
Entrance test required: GRE
Avg. GRE (of all entering students with scores): quantitative: 152; verbal: 155
Research assistantships: 32
Students reporting specialty: 100%
Students specializing in: curriculum/instr.: 11%; admin.: 1%; policy: 5%; evaluation/research/ statistics: 2%; elementary: 11%; secondary: 11%; social/ philosophical foundations: 9%; special: 7%; counseling: 25%; other: 18%

University of California-Santa Cruz

1156 High Street
Santa Cruz, CA 95064
www.graddiv.ucsc.edu/
Public
Admissions: (831) 459-5905
Email: gradadm@ucsc.edu
Financial aid: (831) 459-2963
Application deadline: N/A
In-state tuition: full time: $16,959; part time: $11,349
Out-of-state tuition: full time: $32,061
Room/board/expenses: $22,545
Full-time enrollment: 107
doctoral students: 26%; master's students: 74%; education specialists: N/A; men: 28%; women: 72%; minorities: 45%; international: 1%
Part-time enrollment: 3
doctoral students: 67%; master's students: 33%; education specialists: N/A; men: N/A; women: 100%; minorities: 33%; international: N/A
Acceptance rate (master's): 81%
Acceptance rate (doctoral): 35%
Entrance test required: GRE
Avg. GRE (of all entering students with scores): quantitative: 151; verbal: 158
Research assistantships: 7
Students reporting specialty: 99%
Students specializing in: elementary: 38%; secondary: 36%; other: 27%

University of La Verne

1950 Third Street
La Verne, CA 91750
www.laverne.edu/academics/education/
Private
Admissions: (877) 468-6858
Email: gradadmt@ulv.edu
Financial aid: (800) 649-0160
Application deadline: rolling
Tuition: full time: $660/credit hour; part time: $660/credit hour
Room/board/expenses: N/A
Full-time enrollment: 407
doctoral students: 34%; master's students: 65%; education specialists: 1%; men: 22%; women: 78%; minorities: 44%; international: 1%
Part-time enrollment: 439
doctoral students: 13%; master's students: 78%; education specialists: 9%; men: 21%; women: 79%; minorities: 53%; international: 0%
Acceptance rate (master's): 52%
Acceptance rate (doctoral): 74%
Entrance test required: N/A
Avg. GRE (of all entering students with scores): quantitative: N/A; verbal: N/A
Research assistantships: 0
Students reporting specialty: 100%
Students specializing in: admin.: 22%; elementary: 13%; secondary: 9%; special: 8%; counseling: 18%; other: 29%

University of Redlands

PO Box 3080
Redlands, CA 92373
www.redlands.edu
Private
Admissions: (909) 748-8064
Email: education@redlands.edu
Financial aid: (909) 748-8047
Application deadline: rolling
Tuition: full time: $685/credit hour; part time: $685/credit hour
Room/board/expenses: N/A

Full-time enrollment: 293
doctoral students: 9%; master's
students: 84%; education
specialists: 7%; men: 25%;
women: 75%; minorities: 55%;
international: N/A
Part-time enrollment: 40
doctoral students: 33%; master's
students: 40%; education
specialists: 28%; men: 28%;
women: 73%; minorities: 70%;
international: N/A
Acceptance rate (master's): N/A
Acceptance rate (doctoral): N/A
Entrance test required: N/A
Avg. GRE (of all entering students
with scores): quantitative: N/A;
verbal: N/A
Students reporting specialty: 0%
Students specializing in: N/A

University of
San Diego
5998 Alcala Park
San Diego, CA 92110-2492
www.sandiego.edu/soles/
Private
Admissions: (619) 260-4524
Email: grads@sandiego.edu
Financial aid: (619) 260-2700
Application deadline: 07/01
Tuition: full time: $1,325/credit
hour; part time: $1,325/credit hour
Room/board/expenses: $16,821
Full-time enrollment: 335
doctoral students: 16%; master's
students: 84%; education
specialists: N/A; men: 24%;
women: 76%; minorities: 43%;
international: 9%
Part-time enrollment: 312
doctoral students: 11%; master's
students: 89%; education
specialists: N/A; men: 23%;
women: 77%; minorities: 40%;
international: 2%
Acceptance rate (master's): 59%
Acceptance rate (doctoral): 30%
Entrance test required: GRE
Avg. GRE (of all entering students
with scores): quantitative: 149;
verbal: 153
Research assistantships: 21
Students reporting specialty: 100%
Students specializing in:
curriculum/instr.: 23%; admin.:
20%; instructional media
design: 2%; elementary: 6%;
higher education admin.: 18%;
secondary: 14%; special: 5%;
counseling: 7%; other: 23%

University of
San Francisco
2130 Fulton Street
San Francisco, CA 94117-1080
www.usfca.edu
Private
Admissions: (415) 422-6563
Email: graduate@usfca.edu
Financial aid: (415) 422-6303
Application deadline:
Tuition: full time: $1,080/credit
hour; part time: $1,080/credit
hour
Room/board/expenses: $20,510
Full-time enrollment: 858
doctoral students: 13%; master's
students: 87%; education
specialists: N/A; men: 25%;
women: 75%; minorities: 45%;
international: 6%
Part-time enrollment: 211
doctoral students: 43%; master's
students: 57%; education
specialists: N/A; men: 25%;
women: 75%; minorities: 33%;
international: 4%
Acceptance rate (master's): 73%
Acceptance rate (doctoral): 77%

Entrance test required: GRE
Avg. GRE (of all entering students
with scores): quantitative: N/A;
verbal: N/A
Research assistantships: 30
Students reporting specialty: 100%
Students specializing in:
curriculum/instr.: 4%; admin.: 3%;
evaluation/research/statistics:
5%; instructional media design:
2%; educational tech.: 3%;
elementary: 5%; higher education
admin.: 4%; secondary: 5%;
special: 3%; counseling: 1%;
other: 64%

University of
Southern California
(Rossier)
3470 Trousdale Parkway
Waite Phillips Hall
Los Angeles, CA 90089-0031
rossier.usc.edu
Private
Admissions: (213) 740-0224
Email: soeinfo@usc.edu
Financial aid: (213) 740-1111
Application deadline: rolling
Tuition: full time: $1,602/credit
hour; part time: $1,602/credit hour
Room/board/expenses: $18,936
Full-time enrollment: 644
doctoral students: 9%; master's
students: 91%; education
specialists: N/A; men: 27%;
women: 73%; minorities: 49%;
international: 9%
Part-time enrollment: 1,095
doctoral students: 60%; master's
students: 40%; education
specialists: N/A; men: 32%;
women: 68%; minorities: 56%;
international: 6%
Acceptance rate (master's): 81%
Acceptance rate (doctoral): 16%
Entrance test required: GRE
Avg. GRE (of all entering students
with scores): quantitative: 151;
verbal: 152
Research assistantships: 48
Students reporting specialty: 100%
Students specializing in: admin.:
42%; policy: 3%; instructional
media design: 1%; elementary:
9%; higher education admin.: 5%;
secondary: 17%; special: 0%;
counseling: 3%; other: 19%

University of
the Pacific[1]
3601 Pacific Avenue
Stockton, CA 95211
www.pacific.edu
Private
Admissions: N/A
Financial aid: N/A
Tuition: N/A
Room/board/expenses: N/A
Enrollment: N/A

COLORADO

Colorado State
University
1588 Campus Delivery
Fort Collins, CO 80523-1588
www.colostate.edu/
Public
Admissions: (970) 491-6909
Email:
gschool@grad.colostate.edu
Financial aid: (970) 491-6321
Application deadline: rolling
In-state tuition: full time: $6,355;
part time: $504/credit hour
Out-of-state tuition: full time:
$12,942

Room/board/expenses: $14,502
Full-time enrollment: 145
doctoral students: 6%; master's
students: 94%; education
specialists: N/A; men: 32%;
women: 68%; minorities: 26%;
international: 5%
Part-time enrollment: 532
doctoral students: 42%; master's
students: 58%; education
specialists: N/A; men: 36%;
women: 64%; minorities: 20%;
international: 1%
Acceptance rate (master's): 48%
Acceptance rate (doctoral): 51%
Entrance test required: GRE
Avg. GRE (of all entering students
with scores): quantitative: 147;
verbal: 153
Research assistantships: 2
Students reporting specialty: 100%
Students specializing in: admin.:
8%; elementary: 1%; higher
education admin.: 32%; junior
high: 4%; secondary: 4%;
counseling: 7%; technical
(vocational): 0%; other: 48%

Jones International
University[1]
9697 East Mineral Avenue
Centennial, CO 80112
www.jiu.edu/academics/
education
Private
Admissions: N/A
Financial aid: N/A
Tuition: N/A
Room/board/expenses: N/A
Enrollment: N/A

University of
Colorado-Boulder
Campus Box 249
Boulder, CO 80309-0249
www.colorado.edu/education
Public
Admissions: (303) 492-6555
Email: edadvise@colorado.edu
Financial aid: (303) 492-5091
Application deadline: 12/15
In-state tuition: full time: $11,974;
part time: $568/credit hour
Out-of-state tuition: full time:
$29,272
Room/board/expenses: $19,236
Full-time enrollment: 203
doctoral students: 42%; master's
students: 58%; education
specialists: N/A; men: 31%;
women: 69%; minorities: 30%;
international: 2%
Part-time enrollment: 160
doctoral students: 4%; master's
students: 96%; education
specialists: N/A; men: 18%;
women: 83%; minorities: 26%;
international: 1%
Acceptance rate (master's): 77%
Acceptance rate (doctoral): 17%
Entrance test required: GRE
Avg. GRE (of all entering students
with scores): quantitative: 155;
verbal: 161
Research assistantships: 120
Students reporting specialty: 100%
Students specializing in:
curriculum/instr.: 27%;
evaluation/research/statistics:
2%; educational psych:
6%; secondary: 7%; social/
philosophical foundations: 65%;
special: 19%; other: 52%

University of
Colorado-
Colorado Springs
PO Box 7150
Colorado Springs, CO 80933
www.uccs.edu/~coe/
Public
Admissions: (719) 255-4996
Email: education@uccs.edu
Financial aid: (719) 255-3460
Application deadline: rolling
In-state tuition: full time: $10,928;
part time: $4,261
Out-of-state tuition: full time:
$18,992
Room/board/expenses: $15,920
Full-time enrollment: 211
doctoral students: 24%; master's
students: 76%; education
specialists: N/A; men: 33%;
women: 67%; minorities: 17%;
international: 5%
Part-time enrollment: 217
doctoral students: 0%; master's
students: 100%; education
specialists: N/A; men: 30%;
women: 70%; minorities: 23%;
international: 5%
Acceptance rate (master's): 82%
Acceptance rate (doctoral): 74%
Entrance test required: GRE
Avg. GRE (of all entering students
with scores): quantitative: 145;
verbal: 151
Students reporting specialty: 95%
Students specializing in:
curriculum/instr.: 23%; higher
education admin.: 36%; special:
12%; counseling: 29%

University of
Colorado-Denver
PO Box 173364
Campus Box 106
Denver, CO 80217-3364
www.ucdenver.edu/education
Public
Admissions: (303) 315-6300
Email: education@ucdenver.edu
Financial aid: (303) 556-2886
Application deadline: rolling
In-state tuition: full time: $360/
credit hour; part time: $360/
credit hour
Out-of-state tuition: full time:
$1,219/credit hour
Room/board/expenses: $20,652
Full-time enrollment: 1,007
doctoral students: 9%; master's
students: 81%; education
specialists: 10%; men: 20%;
women: 80%; minorities: 17%;
international: 2%
Part-time enrollment: 362
doctoral students: 4%; master's
students: 92%; education
specialists: 4%; men: 20%;
women: 80%; minorities: 14%;
international: 1%
Acceptance rate (master's): 66%
Acceptance rate (doctoral): 66%
Entrance test required: GRE
Avg. GRE (of all entering students
with scores): quantitative: N/A;
verbal: N/A
Research assistantships: 35
Students reporting specialty: 100%
Students specializing in:
curriculum/instr.: 9%; admin.:
15%; policy: 0%; evaluation/
research/statistics: 2%;
instructional media design:
1%; educational psych:
14%; educational tech.: 8%;
elementary: 19%; secondary:
12%; special: 11%; counseling: 7%;
other: 26%

University of
Denver (Morgridge)
Ruffatto Hall
1999 East Evans Avenue
Denver, CO 80208
www.du.edu/education/
Private
Admissions: (303) 871-2509
Email: edinfo@du.edu
Financial aid: (303) 871-2509
Application deadline: rolling
Tuition: full time: $1,142/credit
hour; part time: $1,142/credit hour
Room/board/expenses: N/A
Full-time enrollment: 572
doctoral students: 22%; master's
students: 68%; education
specialists: 10%; men: 26%;
women: 74%; minorities: 22%;
international: 4%
Part-time enrollment: 193
doctoral students: 70%; master's
students: 30%; education
specialists: 0%; men: 27%;
women: 73%; minorities: 26%;
international: 1%
Acceptance rate (master's): 79%
Acceptance rate (doctoral): 49%
Entrance test required: GRE
Avg. GRE (of all entering students
with scores): quantitative: 152;
verbal: 153
Research assistantships: 23
Students reporting specialty: 100%
Students specializing in:
curriculum/instr.: 26%; admin.:
19%; evaluation/research/
statistics: 5%; higher education
admin.: 12%; special: 3%; other:
37%

University of
Northern Colorado
McKee 125
Greeley, CO 80639
www.unco.edu/grad/index.html
Public
Admissions: (970) 351-2831
Email: gradsch@unco.edu
Financial aid: (970) 351-2502
Application deadline: rolling
In-state tuition: full time: $9,637;
part time: $456/credit hour
Out-of-state tuition: full time:
$19,573
Room/board/expenses: $14,194
Full-time enrollment: 543
doctoral students: 24%; master's
students: 70%; education
specialists: 6%; men: 23%;
women: 77%; minorities: 12%;
international: 11%
Part-time enrollment: 793
doctoral students: 26%; master's
students: 65%; education
specialists: 9%; men: 23%;
women: 77%; minorities: 14%;
international: 6%
Acceptance rate (master's): 87%
Acceptance rate (doctoral): 43%
Entrance test required: GRE
Avg. GRE (of all entering students
with scores): quantitative: 148;
verbal: 153
Students reporting specialty: 100%
Students specializing in: admin.:
12%; evaluation/research/
statistics: 3%; educational psych:
6%; educational tech.: 4%;
elementary: 2%; higher education
admin.: 7%; special: 23%;
counseling: 6%; other: 37%

CONNECTICUT

Central Connecticut State University
1615 Stanley Street
New Britain, CT 06050
web.ccsu.edu/gradstudies/
default.asp
Public
Admissions: (860) 832-2350
Email: graduateadmissions@
mail.ccsu.edu
Financial aid: (860) 832-2200
Application deadline: 06/01
In-state tuition: full time: $9,941;
part time: $534/credit hour
Out-of-state tuition: full time:
$20,175
Room/board/expenses: $14,072
Full-time enrollment: 200
doctoral students: 1%; master's
students: 100%; education
specialists: N/A; men: 15%;
women: 85%; minorities: 29%;
international: 3%
Part-time enrollment: 585
doctoral students: 7%; master's
students: 93%; education
specialists: N/A; men: 26%;
women: 74%; minorities: 14%;
international: 1%
Acceptance rate (master's): 64%
Acceptance rate (doctoral): N/A
Entrance test required: GRE
**Avg. GRE (of all entering students
with scores):** quantitative: N/A;
verbal: N/A
Students reporting specialty: 100%
Students specializing in: admin.:
8%; instructional media design:
4%; elementary: 2%; secondary:
6%; social/philosophical
foundations: 2%; special: 18%;
counseling: 22%; other: 38%

Southern Connecticut State University[1]
501 Crescent Street
New Haven, CT 06515
www.southernct.edu/
Public
Admissions: (203) 392-5240
Email: GradInfo@southernCT.edu
Financial aid: (203) 392-5222
Tuition: N/A
Room/board/expenses: N/A
Enrollment: N/A

University of Bridgeport
126 Park Avenue
Bridgeport, CT 06604
www.bridgeport.edu/
Private
Admissions: (203) 576-4552
Email: admit@bridgeport.edu
Financial aid: (203) 576-4568
Application deadline: rolling
Tuition: full time: $670/credit hour;
part time: $670/credit hour
Room/board/expenses: $15,810
Full-time enrollment: 205
doctoral students: 8%; master's
students: 84%; education
specialists: 8%; men: 30%;
women: 70%; minorities: 26%;
international: 3%
Part-time enrollment: 293
doctoral students: 6%; master's
students: 57%; education
specialists: 37%; men: 25%;
women: 75%; minorities: 23%;
international: 2%
Acceptance rate (master's): 45%
Acceptance rate (doctoral): 43%
Entrance test required: N/A
**Avg. GRE (of all entering students
with scores):** quantitative: N/A;
verbal: N/A

Students reporting specialty: 100%
Students specializing in:
curriculum/instr.: 4%; admin.:
25%; elementary: 39%; junior
high: 2%; secondary: 14%;
counseling: 17%

University of Connecticut (Neag)
249 Glenbrook Road
Storrs, CT 06269-2064
www.grad.uconn.edu
Public
Admissions: (860) 486-3617
Email: gradschool@uconn.edu
Financial aid: (860) 486-2819
Application deadline: rolling
In-state tuition: full time: $14,472;
part time: $678/credit hour
Out-of-state tuition: full time:
$33,944
Room/board/expenses: $18,728
Full-time enrollment: 399
doctoral students: 22%; master's
students: 78%; education
specialists: N/A; men: 31%;
women: 69%; minorities: 16%;
international: 6%
Part-time enrollment: 149
doctoral students: 54%; master's
students: 46%; education
specialists: N/A; men: 28%;
women: 72%; minorities: 22%;
international: 3%
Acceptance rate (master's): 43%
Acceptance rate (doctoral): 39%
Entrance test required: GRE
**Avg. GRE (of all entering students
with scores):** quantitative: 152;
verbal: 157
Research assistantships: 80
Students reporting specialty: 98%
Students specializing in:
curriculum/instr.: 6%; admin.:
15%; policy: 0%; evaluation/
research/statistics: 4%;
instructional media design:
1%; educational psych.: 15%;
elementary: 6%; higher education
admin.: 6%; secondary: 18%;
special: 13%; counseling: 8%;
other: 8%

University of Hartford
200 Bloomfield Avenue
West Hartford, CT 06117
www.hartford.edu/enhp
Private
Admissions: (860) 768-4371
Email: gradstudy@hartford.edu
Financial aid: (860) 768-4296
Application deadline: rolling
Tuition: full time: $11,754; part
time: $532/credit hour
Room/board/expenses: N/A
Full-time enrollment: 95
doctoral students: 55%; master's
students: 45%; education
specialists: N/A; men: 27%;
women: 73%; minorities: 17%;
international: 5%
Part-time enrollment: 104
doctoral students: 29%; master's
students: 71%; education
specialists: N/A; men: 26%;
women: 74%; minorities: 14%;
international: 1%
Acceptance rate (master's): 55%
Acceptance rate (doctoral): 62%
Entrance test required: GRE
**Avg. GRE (of all entering students
with scores):** quantitative: 145;
verbal: 152
Research assistantships: 13
Students reporting specialty: 97%
Students specializing in: admin.:
18%; elementary: 14%; higher
education admin.: 39%; other:
28%

Western Connecticut State University[1]
181 White Street
Danbury, CT 06810
www.wcsu.edu
Public
Admissions: N/A
Financial aid: N/A
Tuition: N/A
Room/board/expenses: N/A
Enrollment: N/A

DELAWARE

Delaware State University[1]
1200 N. DuPont Highway
Dover, DE 19901
www.desu.edu
Public
Admissions: N/A
Financial aid: N/A
Tuition: N/A
Room/board/expenses: N/A
Enrollment: N/A

University of Delaware
113 Willard Hall Education Building
Newark, DE 19716
www.education.udel.edu
Public
Admissions: (302) 831-2129
Email: marym@udel.edu
Financial aid: (302) 831-2129
Application deadline: N/A
In-state tuition: full time: $1,625/
credit hour; part time: $1,625/
credit hour
Out-of-state tuition: full time:
$1,625/credit hour
Room/board/expenses: $14,194
Full-time enrollment: 114
doctoral students: 43%; master's
students: 48%; education
specialists: 9%; men: 19%;
women: 82%; minorities: 14%;
international: 30%
Part-time enrollment: 207
doctoral students: 63%; master's
students: 32%; education
specialists: 5%; men: 35%;
women: 65%; minorities: 16%;
international: 1%
Acceptance rate (master's): 67%
Acceptance rate (doctoral): 50%
Entrance test required: GRE
**Avg. GRE (of all entering students
with scores):** quantitative: 154;
verbal: 156
Research assistantships: 12
Students reporting specialty: 0%
Students specializing in: N/A

Wilmington University[1]
320 DuPont Highway
Wilmington, DE 19720
www.wilmu.edu
Private
Admissions: N/A
Financial aid: N/A
Tuition: N/A
Room/board/expenses: N/A
Enrollment: N/A

DISTRICT OF COLUMBIA

American University[1]
4400 Massachusetts Avenue NW
Washington, DC 20016-8030
www.american.edu/cas/seth/
Private
Admissions: N/A
Financial aid: N/A
Tuition: N/A
Room/board/expenses: N/A
Enrollment: N/A

The Catholic University of America
Cardinal Station
Washington, DC 20064
admissions.cua.edu/graduate/
Private
Admissions: (800) 673-2772
Email: cua-admissions@cua.edu
Financial aid: (202) 319-5307
Application deadline: rolling
Tuition: full time: $40,600; part
time: $1,600/credit hour
Room/board/expenses: $20,454
Full-time enrollment: 5
doctoral students: N/A; master's
students: 100%; education
specialists: N/A; men: 40%;
women: 60%; minorities: N/A;
international: N/A
Part-time enrollment: 39
doctoral students: 46%; master's
students: 44%; education
specialists: 10%; men: 28%;
women: 72%; minorities: 13%;
international: 3%
Acceptance rate (master's): 71%
Acceptance rate (doctoral): 55%
Entrance test required: GRE
**Avg. GRE (of all entering students
with scores):** quantitative: N/A;
verbal: N/A
Research assistantships: 12
Students reporting specialty: 100%
Students specializing in:
secondary: 13%; special: 15%;
other: 72%

Gallaudet University
800 Florida Avenue NE
Washington, DC 20002-3695
gradschool.gallaudet.edu
Private
Admissions: (202) 651-5717
Email:
graduate.school@gallaudet.edu
Financial aid: (202) 651-5290
Application deadline: rolling
Tuition: full time: $16,482; part
time: $886/credit hour
Room/board/expenses: $19,564
Full-time enrollment: 68
doctoral students: 9%; master's
students: 71%; education
specialists: 21%; men: 18%;
women: 82%; minorities: 28%;
international: 10%
Part-time enrollment: 29
doctoral students: 31%; master's
students: 52%; education
specialists: 17%; men: 24%;
women: 76%; minorities: 14%;
international: 3%
Acceptance rate (master's): 37%
Acceptance rate (doctoral): 0%
Entrance test required: GRE
**Avg. GRE (of all entering students
with scores):** quantitative: N/A;
verbal: N/A
Research assistantships: 0
Students reporting specialty: 87%
Students specializing in: special:
71%; counseling: 15%; other: 44%

George Washington University
2134 G Street NW
Washington, DC 20052
gsehd.gwu.edu
Private
Admissions: (202) 994-9283
Email: gsehdadm@gwu.edu
Financial aid: (202) 994-6822
Application deadline: rolling
Tuition: full time: $1,475/credit
hour; part time: $1,475/credit hour
Room/board/expenses: $23,500
Full-time enrollment: 407
doctoral students: 26%; master's
students: 70%; education

specialists: 4%; men: 24%;
women: 76%; minorities: 27%;
international: 14%
Part-time enrollment: 878
doctoral students: 50%; master's
students: 45%; education
specialists: 6%; men: 28%;
women: 72%; minorities: 33%;
international: 3%
Acceptance rate (master's): 71%
Acceptance rate (doctoral): 48%
Entrance test required: GRE
**Avg. GRE (of all entering students
with scores):** quantitative: 151;
verbal: 155
Research assistantships: 27
Students reporting specialty: 99%
Students specializing in:
curriculum/instr.: 4%; admin.:
20%; instructional media design:
3%; educational tech.: 3%;
elementary: 1%; higher education
admin.: 8%; secondary: 3%;
special: 16%; counseling: 32%;
other: 10%

Howard University
2441 Fourth Street NW
Washington, DC 20059
www.howard.edu/
schooleducation
Private
Admissions: (202) 806-7523
Email:
hugsadmission@howard.edu
Financial aid: (202) 806-2820
Application deadline: rolling
Tuition: full time: $33,211; part
time: $1,700/credit hour
Room/board/expenses: $25,587
Full-time enrollment: 140
doctoral students: 68%; master's
students: 32%; education
specialists: N/A; men: 23%;
women: 77%; minorities: 74%;
international: 18%
Part-time enrollment: 115
doctoral students: 68%; master's
students: 32%; education
specialists: N/A; men: 30%;
women: 70%; minorities: 73%;
international: 16%
Acceptance rate (master's): 61%
Acceptance rate (doctoral): 51%
Entrance test required: GRE
**Avg. GRE (of all entering students
with scores):** quantitative: 142;
verbal: 145
Research assistantships: 22
Students reporting specialty: 100%
Students specializing in:
curriculum/instr.: 11%; admin.:
32%; policy: 32%; educational
psych.: 7%; elementary: 8%;
secondary: 2%; special: 2%;
counseling: 50%

FLORIDA

Barry University (Dominican)[1]
11300 N.E. Second Avenue
Miami Shores, FL 33161-6695
www.barry.edu/
Private
Admissions: N/A
Financial aid: N/A
Tuition: N/A
Room/board/expenses: N/A
Enrollment: N/A

Florida A&M University
Gore Education Center
Tallahassee, FL 32307
www.famu.edu/education/
Public
Admissions: (850) 599-3315
Email: adm@famu.edu

Financial aid: (850) 599-3730
Application deadline: 05/01
In-state tuition: full time: $406/credit hour; part time: $406/credit hour
Out-of-state tuition: full time: $1,022/credit hour
Room/board/expenses: $15,138
Full-time enrollment: 49
doctoral students: 61%; master's students: 39%; education specialists: N/A; men: 22%; women: 78%; minorities: 98%; international: N/A
Part-time enrollment: 49
doctoral students: 55%; master's students: 45%; education specialists: N/A; men: 24%; women: 76%; minorities: 98%; international: N/A
Acceptance rate (master's): 59%
Acceptance rate (doctoral): 69%
Entrance test required: GRE
Avg. GRE (of all entering students with scores): quantitative: 141; verbal: 144
Research assistantships: 0
Students reporting specialty: 100%
Students specializing in: curriculum/instr.: 7%; admin.: 73%; counseling: 19%

Florida Atlantic University

777 Glades Road
PO Box 3091
Boca Raton, FL 33431-0991
www.coe.fau.edu/menu.htm
Public
Admissions: (561) 297-3624
Email: gradadm@fau.edu
Financial aid: (561) 297-3131
Application deadline: rolling
In-state tuition: full time: $369/credit hour; part time: $369/credit hour
Out-of-state tuition: full time: $1,024/credit hour
Room/board/expenses: $17,040
Full-time enrollment: 348
doctoral students: 17%; master's students: 81%; education specialists: 2%; men: 26%; women: 74%; minorities: 34%; international: 5%
Part-time enrollment: 473
doctoral students: 41%; master's students: 53%; education specialists: 6%; men: 25%; women: 75%; minorities: 37%; international: 1%
Acceptance rate (master's): 37%
Acceptance rate (doctoral): 35%
Entrance test required: GRE
Avg. GRE (of all entering students with scores): quantitative: 146; verbal: 150
Research assistantships: 46
Students reporting specialty: 99%
Students specializing in: curriculum/instr.: 18%; admin.: 38%; elementary: 4%; social/philosophical foundations: 1%; special: 5%; counseling: 15%; other: 19%

Florida Gulf Coast University

10501 FGCU Boulevard, S
Fort Myers, FL 33965
coe.fgcu.edu/
Public
Admissions: N/A
Email: graduate@fgcu.edu
Financial aid: N/A
Application deadline: 05/01
In-state tuition: full time: $8,919; part time: N/A
Out-of-state tuition: full time: $30,157

Room/board/expenses: $11,259
Full-time enrollment: 28
doctoral students: 14%; master's students: 86%; education specialists: N/A; men: 18%; women: 82%; minorities: 21%; international: 4%
Part-time enrollment: 267
doctoral students: 22%; master's students: 78%; education specialists: N/A; men: 20%; women: 80%; minorities: 24%; international: 0%
Acceptance rate (master's): 73%
Acceptance rate (doctoral): 69%
Entrance test required: GRE
Avg. GRE (of all entering students with scores): quantitative: 145; verbal: 149
Research assistantships: 15
Students reporting specialty: 92%
Students specializing in: curriculum/instr.: 16%; admin.: 20%; instructional media design: 5%; special: 4%; counseling: 32%; other: 22%

Florida Institute of Technology

150 W. University Boulevard
Melbourne, FL 32901
www.fit.edu
Private
Admissions: (800) 944-4348
Email: grad-admissions@fit.edu
Financial aid: (321) 674-8070
Application deadline: rolling
Tuition: full time: $1,179/credit hour; part time: $1,179/credit hour
Room/board/expenses: $17,310
Full-time enrollment: 35
doctoral students: 54%; master's students: 46%; education specialists: N/A; men: 46%; women: 54%; minorities: 14%; international: 51%
Part-time enrollment: 34
doctoral students: 35%; master's students: 65%; education specialists: N/A; men: 35%; women: 65%; minorities: 12%; international: 47%
Acceptance rate (master's): 48%
Acceptance rate (doctoral): 56%
Entrance test required: N/A
Avg. GRE (of all entering students with scores): quantitative: N/A; verbal: N/A
Research assistantships: 0
Students reporting specialty: 100%
Students specializing in: secondary: 1%; other: 99%

Florida International University

11200 S.W. Eighth Street
Miami, FL 33199
education.fiu.edu
Public
Admissions: (305) 348-7442
Email: gradadm@fiu.edu
Financial aid: (305) 348-7272
Application deadline: rolling
In-state tuition: full time: $11,277; part time: $454/credit hour
Out-of-state tuition: full time: $24,382
Room/board/expenses: $25,528
Full-time enrollment: 401
doctoral students: 12%; master's students: 83%; education specialists: 5%; men: 25%; women: 75%; minorities: 67%; international: 13%
Part-time enrollment: 590
doctoral students: 20%; master's students: 75%; education specialists: 6%; men: 22%; women: 78%; minorities: 80%; international: 1%

Acceptance rate (master's): 67%
Acceptance rate (doctoral): 49%
Entrance test required: GRE
Avg. GRE (of all entering students with scores): quantitative: 146; verbal: 149
Research assistantships: 8
Students reporting specialty: 98%
Students specializing in: curriculum/instr.: 20%; admin.: 8%; higher education admin.: 13%; special: 7%; counseling: 13%; other: 38%

Florida State University

Suite 1100 Stone Building
1114 W. Call Street
Tallahassee, FL 32306-4450
www.coe.fsu.edu
Public
Admissions: (850) 644-6200
Email: admissions@admin.fsu.edu
Financial aid: (850) 644-0539
Application deadline: rolling
In-state tuition: full time: $404/credit hour; part time: $404/credit hour
Out-of-state tuition: full time: $1,035/credit hour
Room/board/expenses: $15,922
Full-time enrollment: 733
doctoral students: 41%; master's students: 50%; education specialists: 9%; men: 35%; women: 65%; minorities: 20%; international: 26%
Part-time enrollment: 442
doctoral students: 37%; master's students: 57%; education specialists: 6%; men: 30%; women: 70%; minorities: 27%; international: 8%
Acceptance rate (master's): 60%
Acceptance rate (doctoral): 43%
Entrance test required: GRE
Avg. GRE (of all entering students with scores): quantitative: 149; verbal: 151
Research assistantships: 128
Students reporting specialty: 99%
Students specializing in: curriculum/instr.: 12%; admin.: 7%; policy: 3%; evaluation/research/statistics: 3%; instructional media design: 11%; educational psych: 7%; elementary: 3%; higher education admin.: 9%; secondary: 5%; social/philosophical foundations: 3%; special: 4%; counseling: 10%; other: 22%

Lynn University

3601 North Military Trail
Boca Raton, FL 33431
www.lynn.edu
Private
Admissions: (561) 237-7834
Email: admission@lynn.edu
Financial aid: (561) 237-7816
Application deadline: rolling
Tuition: full time: $675/credit hour; part time: $675/credit hour
Room/board/expenses: N/A
Full-time enrollment: 44
doctoral students: 23%; master's students: 77%; education specialists: N/A; men: 32%; women: 68%; minorities: 18%; international: 14%
Part-time enrollment: 40
doctoral students: 68%; master's students: 33%; education specialists: N/A; men: 48%; women: 53%; minorities: 33%; international: 3%
Acceptance rate (master's): 90%
Acceptance rate (doctoral): 83%
Entrance test required: N/A

Avg. GRE (of all entering students with scores): quantitative: N/A; verbal: N/A
Research assistantships: 0
Students reporting specialty: 100%
Students specializing in: admin.: 79%; special: 21%

Nova Southeastern University (Fischler)

3301 College Avenue
Fort Lauderdale, FL 33314
www.schoolofed.nova.edu
Private
Admissions: (954) 262-8500
Financial aid: (954) 262-3380
Application deadline: rolling
Tuition: full time: N/A; part time: N/A
Room/board/expenses: N/A
Full-time enrollment: N/A
doctoral students: N/A; master's students: N/A; education specialists: N/A; men: N/A; women: N/A; minorities: N/A; international: N/A
Part-time enrollment: N/A
doctoral students: N/A; master's students: N/A; education specialists: N/A; men: N/A; women: N/A; minorities: N/A; international: N/A
Acceptance rate (master's): N/A
Acceptance rate (doctoral): N/A
Entrance test required: GRE
Avg. GRE (of all entering students with scores): quantitative: N/A; verbal: N/A
Students reporting specialty: 0%
Students specializing in: N/A

University of Central Florida

4000 Central Florida Boulevard
Orlando, FL 32816-1250
www.graduate.ucf.edu
Public
Admissions: (407) 823-0549
Email: graduate@mail.ucf.edu
Financial aid: (407) 823-2827
Application deadline: N/A
In-state tuition: full time: $359/credit hour; part time: $359/credit hour
Out-of-state tuition: full time: $1,183/credit hour
Room/board/expenses: $15,532
Full-time enrollment: 756
doctoral students: 28%; master's students: 66%; education specialists: 7%; men: 24%; women: 76%; minorities: 31%; international: 4%
Part-time enrollment: 846
doctoral students: 15%; master's students: 83%; education specialists: 1%; men: 24%; women: 76%; minorities: 28%; international: N/A
Acceptance rate (master's): 65%
Acceptance rate (doctoral): 53%
Entrance test required: GRE
Avg. GRE (of all entering students with scores): quantitative: 149; verbal: 152
Research assistantships: 10
Students reporting specialty: 100%
Students specializing in: curriculum/instr.: 5%; admin.: 20%; instructional media design: 5%; educational psych: 2%; educational tech.: 1%; elementary: 4%; higher education admin.: 6%; junior high: 1%; secondary: 4%; special: 9%; counseling: 3%; technical (vocational): 2%; other: 36%

University of Florida

140 Norman Hall
PO Box 117040
Gainesville, FL 32611-7040
education.ufl.edu/
Public
Admissions: (352) 273-4116
Email: tla@coe.ufl.edu
Financial aid: (352) 392-1275
Application deadline: rolling
In-state tuition: full time: $449/credit hour; part time: $449/credit hour
Out-of-state tuition: full time: $1,253/credit hour
Room/board/expenses: $15,610
Full-time enrollment: 538
doctoral students: 30%; master's students: 49%; education specialists: 21%; men: 17%; women: 83%; minorities: 22%; international: 17%
Part-time enrollment: 509
doctoral students: 55%; master's students: 36%; education specialists: 9%; men: 25%; women: 75%; minorities: 27%; international: 4%
Acceptance rate (master's): 61%
Acceptance rate (doctoral): 50%
Entrance test required: GRE
Avg. GRE (of all entering students with scores): quantitative: 152; verbal: 153
Research assistantships: 75
Students reporting specialty: 100%
Students specializing in: curriculum/instr.: 32%; admin.: 11%; evaluation/research/statistics: 2%; elementary: 8%; higher education admin.: 6%; special: 8%; counseling: 10%; other: 23%

University of Miami

PO Box 248212
Coral Gables, FL 33124
www.education.miami.edu
Private
Admissions: (305) 284-2167
Email: soegradadmissions@miami.edu
Financial aid: (305) 284-5212
Application deadline: rolling
Tuition: full time: $1,790/credit hour; part time: $1,790/credit hour
Room/board/expenses: $18,640
Full-time enrollment: 222
doctoral students: 45%; master's students: 55%; education specialists: 0%; men: 34%; women: 66%; minorities: 42%; international: 14%
Part-time enrollment: 97
doctoral students: 1%; master's students: 99%; education specialists: 0%; men: 19%; women: 81%; minorities: 60%; international: 1%
Acceptance rate (master's): 68%
Acceptance rate (doctoral): 16%
Entrance test required: GRE
Avg. GRE (of all entering students with scores): quantitative: 151; verbal: 153
Research assistantships: 26
Students reporting specialty: 100%
Students specializing in: admin.: 5%; evaluation/research/statistics: 3%; higher education admin.: 18%; special: 7%; other: 68%

University of North Florida

1 UNF Drive
Jacksonville, FL 32224-2676
www.unf.edu/graduatestudies
Public
Admissions: (904) 620-1360
Email: graduatestudies@unf.edu
Financial aid: (904) 620-5555
Application deadline: rolling
In-state tuition: full time: $493/
credit hour; part time: $493/
credit hour
Out-of-state tuition: full time:
$1,043/credit hour
Room/board/expenses: $14,632
Full-time enrollment: 145
doctoral students: 6%; master's
students: 94%; education
specialists: N/A; men: 14%;
women: 86%; minorities: 37%;
international: 8%
Part-time enrollment: 353
doctoral students: 27%; master's
students: 73%; education
specialists: N/A; men: 25%;
women: 75%; minorities: 25%;
international: N/A
Acceptance rate (master's): 64%
Acceptance rate (doctoral): 62%
Entrance test required: GRE
**Avg. GRE (of all entering students
with scores):** quantitative: 145;
verbal: 148
Research assistantships: 6
Students reporting specialty: 83%
Students specializing in: admin.:
59%; elementary: 8%; secondary:
4%; special: 14%; counseling:
10%; other: 6%

University of South Florida

4202 E. Fowler Avenue
EDU 105
Tampa, FL 33620
www.grad.usf.edu
Public
Admissions: (813) 974-8800
Email: admissions@grad.usf.edu
Financial aid: (813) 974-4700
Application deadline: rolling
In-state tuition: full time: $431/
credit hour; part time: $431/
credit hour
Out-of-state tuition: full time: $877/
credit hour
Room/board/expenses: $15,500
Full-time enrollment: 541
doctoral students: 35%; master's
students: 64%; education
specialists: 1%; men: 29%;
women: 71%; minorities: 25%;
international: 15%
Part-time enrollment: 831
doctoral students: 41%; master's
students: 58%; education
specialists: 2%; men: 25%;
women: 75%; minorities: 28%;
international: 2%
Acceptance rate (master's): 55%
Acceptance rate (doctoral): 54%
Entrance test required: GRE
**Avg. GRE (of all entering students
with scores):** quantitative: 148;
verbal: 151
Research assistantships: 12
Students reporting specialty: 100%
Students specializing in: admin.:
8%; evaluation/research/
statistics: 3%; educational
psych.: 4%; educational tech.:
6%; elementary: 6%; higher
education admin.: 6%; junior high:
1%; secondary: 12%; special:
6%; counseling: 9%; technical
(vocational): other: 36%

University of West Florida[1]

11000 University Parkway
Pensacola, FL 32514-5750
uwf.edu
Public
Admissions: N/A
Financial aid: N/A
Tuition: N/A
Room/board/expenses: N/A
Enrollment: N/A

GEORGIA

Clark Atlanta University

223 James P. Brawley Drive SW
Atlanta, GA 30314
www.cau.edu/
Private
Admissions: (404) 880-6605
Email: cauadmissions@cau.edu
Financial aid: (404) 880-8992
Application deadline: rolling
Tuition: full time: $828/credit hour;
part time: $828/credit hour
Room/board/expenses: $17,241
Full-time enrollment: 88
doctoral students: 34%; master's
students: 65%; education
specialists: 1%; men: 25%;
women: 75%; minorities: 85%;
international: 2%
Part-time enrollment: 58
doctoral students: 52%; master's
students: 45%; education
specialists: 3%; men: 36%;
women: 64%; minorities: 86%;
international: 7%
Acceptance rate (master's): 81%
Acceptance rate (doctoral): 85%
Entrance test required: GRE
**Avg. GRE (of all entering students
with scores):** quantitative: N/A;
verbal: N/A
Students reporting specialty: 100%
Students specializing in: admin.:
60%; secondary: 1%; special: 5%;
counseling: 17%; other: 16%

Columbus State University

4225 University Ave.
Columbus, GA 31907
www.columbusstate.edu
Public
Admissions: (706) 507-8800
Financial aid: (706) 507-8800
Application deadline: rolling
In-state tuition: full time: $196/
credit hour; part time: $196/
credit hour
Out-of-state tuition: full time: $782/
credit hour
Room/board/expenses: N/A
Full-time enrollment: 207
doctoral students: 2%; master's
students: 65%; education
specialists: 33%; men: 28%;
women: 72%; minorities: 40%;
international: 1%
Part-time enrollment: 431
doctoral students: 17%; master's
students: 51%; education
specialists: 32%; men: 28%;
women: 72%; minorities: 51%;
international: 1%
Acceptance rate (master's): 60%
Acceptance rate (doctoral): 61%
Entrance test required: GRE
**Avg. GRE (of all entering students
with scores):** quantitative: 144;
verbal: 146
Research assistantships: 2
Students reporting specialty: 97%
Students specializing in:
curriculum/instr.: 6%; admin.:
39%; instructional media design:
1%; elementary: 8%; higher

Georgia Southern University

U.S. Highway 301, S
P.O. Box 8033
Statesboro, GA 30460
coe.georgiasouthern.edu/ger/
Public
Admissions: (912) 478-5648
Email: GradAdmissions@
georgiasouthern.edu
Financial aid: (912) 478-5413
Application deadline: rolling
In-state tuition: full time: $302/
credit hour; part time: $302/
credit hour
Out-of-state tuition: full time:
$1,130/credit hour
Room/board/expenses: $16,608
Full-time enrollment: 348
doctoral students: 11%; master's
students: 78%; education
specialists: 11%; men: 20%;
women: 80%; minorities: 45%;
international: 1%
Part-time enrollment: 860
doctoral students: 30%; master's
students: 54%; education
specialists: 16%; men: 22%;
women: 78%; minorities: 41%;
international: 0%
Acceptance rate (master's): 82%
Acceptance rate (doctoral): 62%
Entrance test required: GRE
**Avg. GRE (of all entering students
with scores):** quantitative: 151;
verbal: 154
Research assistantships: 1
Students reporting specialty: 100%
Students specializing in:
curriculum/instr.: 13%; admin.:
16%; instructional media design:
13%; higher education admin.:
11%; junior high: 2%; secondary:
5%; counseling: 7%; other: 32%

Georgia State University

PO Box 3980
Atlanta, GA 30302-3980
education.gsu.edu/coe/
Public
Admissions: (404) 413-8000
Email: educadmissions@gsu.edu
Financial aid: (404) 413-2400
Application deadline: rolling
In-state tuition: full time: $8,644;
part time: $362/credit hour
Out-of-state tuition: full time:
$24,142
Room/board/expenses: $14,967
Full-time enrollment: 929
doctoral students: 20%; master's
students: 73%; education
specialists: 7%; men: 25%;
women: 75%; minorities: 47%;
international: 5%
Part-time enrollment: 502
doctoral students: 45%; master's
students: 51%; education
specialists: 4%; men: 30%;
women: 70%; minorities: 48%;
international: 6%
Acceptance rate (master's): 42%
Acceptance rate (doctoral): 27%
Entrance test required: GRE
**Avg. GRE (of all entering students
with scores):** quantitative: 148;
verbal: 152
Research assistantships: 427
Students reporting specialty: 67%
Students specializing in:
curriculum/instr.: 2%; admin.:
7%; evaluation/research/
statistics: 1%; educational psych:
5%; educational tech.: 4%;
elementary: 20%; junior high:

education admin.: 3%; junior high:
4%; secondary: 6%; special: 11%;
counseling: 4%; other: 19%

3%; secondary: 24%; social/
philosophical foundations: 1%;
special: 17%; counseling: 16%

Kennesaw State University[1]

1000 Chastain Road
Campus Box 0123
Kennesaw, GA 30144
www.kennesaw.edu
Public
Admissions: N/A
Financial aid: N/A
Tuition: N/A
Room/board/expenses: N/A
Enrollment: N/A

Mercer University[1]

1400 Coleman Avenue
Macon, GA 31207
www.mercer.edu/
Private
Admissions: N/A
Financial aid: N/A
Tuition: N/A
Room/board/expenses: N/A
Enrollment: N/A

Piedmont College[1]

165 Central Avenue
PO Box 10
Demorest, GA 30535
www.piedmont.edu
Private
Admissions: N/A
Financial aid: N/A
Tuition: N/A
Room/board/expenses: N/A
Enrollment: N/A

University of Georgia

G-3 Aderhold Hall
Athens, GA 30602-7101
www.coe.uga.edu/
Public
Admissions: (706) 542-1739
Email: gradadm@uga.edu
Financial aid: (706) 542-6147
Application deadline: 07/01
In-state tuition: full time: $10,334;
part time: $337/credit hour
Out-of-state tuition: full time:
$25,634
Room/board/expenses: $12,208
Full-time enrollment: 930
doctoral students: 45%; master's
students: 54%; education
specialists: 2%; men: 32%;
women: 68%; minorities: 20%;
international: 20%
Part-time enrollment: 655
doctoral students: 40%; master's
students: 47%; education
specialists: 13%; men: 28%;
women: 72%; minorities: 29%;
international: 3%
Acceptance rate (master's): 49%
Acceptance rate (doctoral): 45%
Entrance test required: GRE
**Avg. GRE (of all entering students
with scores):** quantitative: 151;
verbal: 152
Research assistantships: 199
Students reporting specialty: 96%
Students specializing in: admin.:
2%; policy: 2%; evaluation/
research/statistics: 1%;
instructional media design:
2%; educational psych:
7%; educational tech.: 5%;
elementary: 8%; higher
education admin.: 3%; junior
high: 1%; secondary: 23%; social/
philosophical foundations: 1%;
special: 4%; counseling: 19%;
technical (vocational): 2%; other:
21%

University of West Georgia

1601 Maple Street
Carrollton, GA 30118
www.westga.edu/coegrad/
Public
Admissions: (678) 839-5430
Email: coegrads@westga.edu
Financial aid: (678) 839-6421
Application deadline: rolling
In-state tuition: full time: $6,734;
part time: $204/credit hour
Out-of-state tuition: full time:
$20,810
Room/board/expenses: $10,032
Full-time enrollment: 338
doctoral students: 2%; master's
students: 89%; education
specialists: 9%; men: 20%;
women: 80%; minorities: 36%;
international: 1%
Part-time enrollment: 789
doctoral students: 12%; master's
students: 56%; education
specialists: 32%; men: 20%;
women: 80%; minorities: 43%;
international: 1%
Acceptance rate (master's): 62%
Acceptance rate (doctoral): 56%
Entrance test required: GRE
**Avg. GRE (of all entering students
with scores):** quantitative: 145;
verbal: 149
Students reporting specialty: 100%
Students specializing in: admin.:
2%; instructional media design:
24%; elementary: 8%; secondary:
1%; special: 9%; counseling: 18%;
other: 38%

Valdosta State University

1500 N. Patterson Street
Valdosta, GA 31698
www.valdosta.edu/
Public
Admissions: (229) 333-5694
Email: rlwaters@valdosta.edu
Financial aid: (229) 333-5935
Application deadline: rolling
In-state tuition: full time: $236/
credit hour; part time: $236/
credit hour
Out-of-state tuition: full time: $850/
credit hour
Room/board/expenses: $10,724
Full-time enrollment: 348
doctoral students: 3%; master's
students: 75%; education
specialists: 21%; men: 21%;
women: 79%; minorities: 31%;
international: 1%
Part-time enrollment: 927
doctoral students: 38%; master's
students: 35%; education
specialists: 28%; men: 28%;
women: 72%; minorities: 29%;
international: 1%
Acceptance rate (master's): 40%
Acceptance rate (doctoral): 58%
Entrance test required: GRE
**Avg. GRE (of all entering students
with scores):** quantitative: 146;
verbal: 150
Students reporting specialty: 100%
Students specializing in:
curriculum/instr.: 7%; admin.:
32%; instructional media design:
9%; junior high: 4%; secondary:
2%; special: 6%; counseling: 2%;
other: 38%

DIRECTORY

HAWAII

University of Hawaii-Manoa
1776 University Avenue
Everly Hall 128
Honolulu, HI 96822
manoa.hawaii.edu/graduate/
Public
Admissions: (808) 956-8544
Email: graduate.education@
hawaii.edu
Financial aid: (808) 956-7251
Application deadline: 03/01
In-state tuition: full time: $552/
credit hour; part time: $522/
credit hour
Out-of-state tuition: full time:
$1,334/credit hour
Room/board/expenses: $16,212
Full-time enrollment: 197
doctoral students: 18%; master's
students: 82%; education
specialists: N/A; men: 27%;
women: 73%; minorities: 60%;
international: 12%
Part-time enrollment: 528
doctoral students: 40%; master's
students: 60%; education
specialists: N/A; men: 28%;
women: 72%; minorities: 71%;
international: 2%
Acceptance rate (master's): 70%
Acceptance rate (doctoral): 50%
Entrance test required: GRE
**Avg. GRE (of all entering students
with scores):** quantitative: 147;
verbal: 150
Research assistantships: 25
Students reporting specialty: 100%
Students specializing in:
curriculum/instr.: 17%; admin.:
5%; policy: 1%; educational
psych: 8%; educational tech.:
13%; elementary: 4%; higher
education admin.: 5%; secondary:
9%; social/philosophical
foundations: 8%; special: 11%;
other: 18%

IDAHO

Boise State University
1910 University Drive
Boise, ID 83725-1700
www.boisestate.edu/
Public
Admissions: (208) 426-3903
Email: gradcoll@boisestate.edu
Financial aid: (800) 824-7017
Application deadline: 03/01
In-state tuition: full time: $7,825;
part time: $331/credit hour
Out-of-state tuition: full time:
$20,677
Room/board/expenses: $11,978
Full-time enrollment: 105
doctoral students: 25%; master's
students: 75%; education
specialists: 0%; men: 22%;
women: 78%; minorities: 12%;
international: 7%
Part-time enrollment: 686
doctoral students: 11%; master's
students: 88%; education
specialists: 1%; men: 40%;
women: 60%; minorities: 10%;
international: 3%
Acceptance rate (master's): 92%
Acceptance rate (doctoral): 24%
Entrance test required: GRE
**Avg. GRE (of all entering students
with scores):** quantitative: 149;
verbal: 154
Research assistantships: 28
Students reporting specialty: 7%
Students specializing in: N/A

Idaho State University[1]
921 S. Eighth Avenue
Pocatello, ID 83209-8059
ed.isu.edu/
Public
Admissions: N/A
Financial aid: N/A
Tuition: N/A
Room/board/expenses: N/A
Enrollment: N/A

University of Idaho
PO Box 443080
Moscow, ID 83844-3080
www.uidaho.edu/ed
Public
Admissions: (208) 885-4001
Email: graduateadmissions@
uidaho.edu
Financial aid: N/A
Application deadline: N/A
In-state tuition: full time: $7,882;
part time: $7,008
Out-of-state tuition: full time:
$21,412
Room/board/expenses: N/A
Full-time enrollment: 108
doctoral students: 26%; master's
students: 73%; education
specialists: 1%; men: 35%;
women: 65%; minorities: 2%;
international: 1%
Part-time enrollment: 280
doctoral students: 23%; master's
students: 59%; education
specialists: 18%; men: 40%;
women: 60%; minorities: 3%;
international: 1%
Acceptance rate (master's): N/A
Acceptance rate (doctoral): N/A
Entrance test required: GRE
**Avg. GRE (of all entering students
with scores):** quantitative: N/A;
verbal: N/A
Students reporting specialty: 48%
Students specializing in: N/A

ILLINOIS

Argosy University[1]
225 N. Michigan Avenue
Chicago, IL 60601
www.argosy.edu/colleges/
education/default.aspx
Private
Admissions: N/A
Financial aid: N/A
Tuition: N/A
Room/board/expenses: N/A
Enrollment: N/A

Aurora University[1]
347 S. Gladstone Avenue
Aurora, IL 60506-4892
www.aurora.edu
Private
Admissions: N/A
Financial aid: N/A
Tuition: N/A
Room/board/expenses: N/A
Enrollment: N/A

Benedictine University[1]
5700 College Road
Lisle, IL 60532
www.ben.edu
Private
Admissions: N/A
Financial aid: N/A
Tuition: N/A
Room/board/expenses: N/A
Enrollment: N/A

Chicago State University
9501 S. King Drive
ED 320
Chicago, IL 60628
www.csu.edu/
Public
Admissions: N/A
Financial aid: N/A
Application deadline: 12/31
In-state tuition: full time: $8,020;
part time: $5,070
Out-of-state tuition: full time:
$12,880
Room/board/expenses: $14,170
Full-time enrollment: 68
doctoral students: 0%; master's
students: 100%; education
specialists: 0%; men: 31%;
women: 69%; minorities: 81%;
international: 1%
Part-time enrollment: 244
doctoral students: 23%; master's
students: 77%; education
specialists: 0%; men: 32%;
women: 68%; minorities: 86%;
international: N/A
Acceptance rate (master's): N/A
Acceptance rate (doctoral): N/A
Entrance test required: N/A
**Avg. GRE (of all entering students
with scores):** quantitative: N/A;
verbal: N/A
Students reporting specialty: 0%
Students specializing in: N/A

Concordia University[1]
7400 Augusta Street
River Forest, IL 60305-1499
www.cuchicago.edu
Private
Admissions: N/A
Financial aid: N/A
Tuition: N/A
Room/board/expenses: N/A
Enrollment: N/A

DePaul University
1 E. Jackson Boulevard
Chicago, IL 60604-2287
education.depaul.edu
Private
Admissions: (773) 325-4405
Email:
edgradadmissions@depaul.edu
Financial aid: (312) 362-8610
Application deadline: rolling
Tuition: full time: $600/credit hour;
part time: $600/credit hour
Room/board/expenses: $13,526
Full-time enrollment: 584
doctoral students: 8%; master's
students: 92%; education
specialists: N/A; men: 22%;
women: 78%; minorities: 30%;
international: 3%
Part-time enrollment: 355
doctoral students: 21%; master's
students: 79%; education
specialists: N/A; men: 21%;
women: 79%; minorities: 34%;
international: 2%
Acceptance rate (master's): 79%
Acceptance rate (doctoral): 66%
Entrance test required: GRE
**Avg. GRE (of all entering students
with scores):** quantitative: N/A;
verbal: N/A
Research assistantships: 10
Students reporting specialty: 97%
Students specializing in:
curriculum/instr.: 8%; admin.:
14%; elementary: 13%; secondary:
14%; social/philosophical
foundations: 3%; special: 9%;
counseling: 26%; other: 13%

Illinois State University
Campus Box 5300
Normal, IL 61790-5300
www.illinoisstate.edu
Public
Admissions: (309) 438-2181
Email:
admissions@illinoisstate.edu
Financial aid: (309) 438-2231
Application deadline: rolling
In-state tuition: full time: $360/
credit hour; part time: $360/
credit hour
Out-of-state tuition: full time: $747/
credit hour
Room/board/expenses: $14,752
Full-time enrollment: 208
doctoral students: 22%; master's
students: 72%; education
specialists: 6%; men: 17%;
women: 83%; minorities: 22%;
international: 4%
Part-time enrollment: 562
doctoral students: 37%; master's
students: 58%; education
specialists: 5%; men: 26%;
women: 74%; minorities: 13%;
international: 1%
Acceptance rate (master's): 33%
Acceptance rate (doctoral): 55%
Entrance test required: GRE
**Avg. GRE (of all entering students
with scores):** quantitative: 149;
verbal: 152
Research assistantships: 102
Students reporting specialty: 100%
Students specializing in:
curriculum/instr.: 16%; admin.:
19%; educational psych: 6%;
educational tech.: 3%; special:
11%; counseling: 7%; other: 39%

Lewis University[1]
One University Parkway
Romeoville, IL 60446
www.lewisu.edu/
Private
Admissions: N/A
Financial aid: N/A
Tuition: N/A
Room/board/expenses: N/A
Enrollment: N/A

Loyola University Chicago
820 N. Michigan Avenue
Chicago, IL 60611
www.luc.edu/education/
Private
Admissions: (312) 915-6722
Email: schleduc@luc.edu
Financial aid: (773) 508-7704
Application deadline: N/A
Tuition: full time: $930/credit hour;
part time: $930/credit hour
Room/board/expenses: $24,698
Full-time enrollment: 404
doctoral students: 40%; master's
students: 48%; education
specialists: 12%; men: 23%;
women: 77%; minorities: 33%;
international: 3%
Part-time enrollment: 230
doctoral students: 43%; master's
students: 57%; education
specialists: 0%; men: 27%;
women: 73%; minorities: 34%;
international: 1%
Acceptance rate (master's): 66%
Acceptance rate (doctoral): 29%
Entrance test required: GRE
**Avg. GRE (of all entering students
with scores):** quantitative: 148;
verbal: 152
Research assistantships: 74
Students reporting specialty: 100%

National-Louis University
122 S. Michigan Avenue
Chicago, IL 60603
www.nl.edu
Private
Admissions: N/A
Financial aid: N/A
Application deadline: N/A
Tuition: full time: $9,753; part time:
$521/credit hour
Room/board/expenses: N/A
Full-time enrollment: 753
doctoral students: 1%; master's
students: 93%; education
specialists: 6%; men: 27%;
women: 73%; minorities: 36%;
international: 1%
Part-time enrollment: 1,300
doctoral students: 12%; master's
students: 79%; education
specialists: 8%; men: 18%;
women: 82%; minorities: 36%;
international: 0%
Acceptance rate (master's): N/A
Acceptance rate (doctoral): N/A
Entrance test required: N/A
**Avg. GRE (of all entering students
with scores):** quantitative: N/A;
verbal: N/A
Students reporting specialty: 71%
Students specializing in:
curriculum/instr.: 26%; admin.:
25%; educational psych: 3%;
elementary: 17%; secondary: 14%;
special: 14%

Northern Illinois University[1]
321 Graham Hall
DeKalb, IL 60115
www.niu.edu
Public
Admissions: N/A
Financial aid: N/A
Tuition: N/A
Room/board/expenses: N/A
Enrollment: N/A

Northwestern University
2120 Campus Drive
Evanston, IL 60208
www.sesp.northwestern.edu
Private
Admissions: (847) 467-2789
Email: sesp@northwestern.edu
Financial aid: (847) 467-2789
Application deadline: rolling
Tuition: full time: $47,236; part
time: $5,555/credit hour
Room/board/expenses: N/A
Full-time enrollment: 170
doctoral students: 37%; master's
students: 63%; education
specialists: N/A; men: 28%;
women: 72%; minorities: 26%;
international: 12%
Part-time enrollment: 102
doctoral students: 0%; master's
students: 100%; education
specialists: N/A; men: 23%;
women: 77%; minorities: 13%;
international: 2%
Acceptance rate (master's): 66%
Acceptance rate (doctoral): 8%
Entrance test required: GRE

Students specializing in:
curriculum/instr.: 8%; admin.:
16%; policy: 3%; evaluation/
research/statistics: 3%;
educational psych: 4%;
elementary: 4%; higher education
admin.: 21%; secondary: 2%;
social/philosophical foundations:
6%; special: 2%; counseling: 16%;
other: 17%

Avg. GRE (of all entering students with scores): quantitative: 157; verbal: 161
Research assistantships: 29
Students reporting specialty: 73%
Students specializing in: elementary: 8%; higher education admin.: 29%; secondary: 21%; other: 41%

Roosevelt University[1]
430 S. Michigan Avenue
Chicago, IL 60605
www.roosevelt.edu
Private
Admissions: N/A
Financial aid: N/A
Tuition: N/A
Room/board/expenses: N/A
Enrollment: N/A

Southern Illinois University-Carbondale
Wham Building 115
Carbondale, IL 62901-4624
web.coehs.siu.edu/Public/
Public
Admissions: (618) 536-7791
Email: gradschl@siu.edu
Financial aid: (618) 453-4334
Application deadline: rolling
In-state tuition: full time: $1,154/credit hour; part time: $1,154/credit hour
Out-of-state tuition: full time: $1,745/credit hour
Room/board/expenses: $17,105
Full-time enrollment: 553
doctoral students: 18%; master's students: 82%; education specialists: N/A; men: 33%; women: 67%; minorities: 21%; international: 15%
Part-time enrollment: 473
doctoral students: 37%; master's students: 63%; education specialists: N/A; men: 34%; women: 66%; minorities: 20%; international: 7%
Acceptance rate (master's): 43%
Acceptance rate (doctoral): 31%
Entrance test required: GRE
Avg. GRE (of all entering students with scores): quantitative: 150; verbal: 147
Research assistantships: 133
Students reporting specialty: 100%
Students specializing in: curriculum/instr.: 15%; admin.: 6%; educational psych: 5%; higher education admin.: 4%; special: 1%; other: 70%

Southern Illinois University-Edwardsville
Campus Box 1049
Edwardsville, IL 62026
www.siue.edu/education/
Public
Admissions: N/A
Financial aid: N/A
Application deadline: rolling
In-state tuition: full time: $6,710; part time: $5,034
Out-of-state tuition: full time: $14,250
Room/board/expenses: $12,396
Full-time enrollment: 28
doctoral students: 7%; master's students: 93%; education specialists: 0%; men: 11%; women: 89%; minorities: 29%; international: 11%
Part-time enrollment: 292
doctoral students: 5%; master's students: 77%; education specialists: 17%; men: 33%; women: 67%; minorities: 21%; international: 0%

Acceptance rate (master's): 55%
Acceptance rate (doctoral): 93%
Entrance test required: GRE
Avg. GRE (of all entering students with scores): quantitative: 147; verbal: 151
Research assistantships: 12
Students reporting specialty: 93%
Students specializing in: curriculum/instr.: 11%; admin.: 28%; educational psych: 3%; educational tech.: 19%; higher education admin.: 7%; special: 13%; other: 19%

University of Illinois-Chicago
1040 W. Harrison Street
Chicago, IL 60607-7133
www.education.uic.edu
Public
Admissions: (312) 996-4532
Email: jeisen@uic.edu
Financial aid: (312) 996-3126
Application deadline: rolling
In-state tuition: full time: $14,304; part time: $10,552
Out-of-state tuition: full time: $26,302
Room/board/expenses: $17,958
Full-time enrollment: 149
doctoral students: 51%; master's students: 49%; education specialists: N/A; men: 21%; women: 79%; minorities: 42%; international: 11%
Part-time enrollment: 545
doctoral students: 46%; master's students: 54%; education specialists: N/A; men: 26%; women: 74%; minorities: 38%; international: 3%
Acceptance rate (master's): 89%
Acceptance rate (doctoral): 59%
Entrance test required: GRE
Avg. GRE (of all entering students with scores): quantitative: 151; verbal: 154
Research assistantships: 63
Students reporting specialty: 100%
Students specializing in: curriculum/instr.: 10%; admin.: 14%; policy: 3%; evaluation/research/statistics: 12%; educational psych: 12%; elementary: 5%; secondary: 4%; social/philosophical foundations: 3%; special: 15%; other: 23%

University of Illinois-Urbana-Champaign
1310 S. Sixth Street
Champaign, IL 61820
education.illinois.edu
Public
Admissions: (217) 333-2800
Email: saao@education.illinois.edu
Financial aid: (217) 333-2800
Application deadline: N/A
In-state tuition: full time: $15,560; part time: $11,620
Out-of-state tuition: full time: $29,282
Room/board/expenses: $17,701
Full-time enrollment: 317
doctoral students: 71%; master's students: 29%; education specialists: N/A; men: 30%; women: 70%; minorities: 42%; international: 22%
Part-time enrollment: 457
doctoral students: 41%; master's students: 59%; education specialists: N/A; men: 30%; women: 70%; minorities: 28%; international: 7%
Acceptance rate (master's): 66%
Acceptance rate (doctoral): 29%
Entrance test required: GRE

Avg. GRE (of all entering students with scores): quantitative: N/A; verbal: N/A
Research assistantships: 140
Students reporting specialty: 100%
Students specializing in: curriculum/instr.: 17%; admin.: 12%; policy: 20%; evaluation/research/statistics: 2%; educational psych.: 11%; educational tech.: 2%; elementary: 1%; higher education admin.: 9%; junior high: 6%; secondary: 2%; social/philosophical foundations: 30%; special: 9%; counseling: 2%; other: 14%

Western Illinois University[1]
1 University Circle
Macomb, IL 61455
www.wiu.edu
Public
Admissions: N/A
Financial aid: N/A
Tuition: N/A
Room/board/expenses: N/A
Enrollment: N/A

INDIANA

Ball State University
2000 W. University Avenue
Muncie, IN 47306
www.bsu.edu/gradschool/
Public
Admissions: (765) 285-1297
Email: gradschool@bsu.edu
Financial aid: (765) 285-5600
Application deadline: 08/08
In-state tuition: full time: $378/credit hour; part time: $378/credit hour
Out-of-state tuition: full time: $1,040/credit hour
Room/board/expenses: $13,304
Full-time enrollment: 597
doctoral students: 12%; master's students: 86%; education specialists: 2%; men: 22%; women: 78%; minorities: 9%; international: 6%
Part-time enrollment: 1,557
doctoral students: 10%; master's students: 90%; education specialists: 1%; men: 21%; women: 79%; minorities: 9%; international: 2%
Acceptance rate (master's): 78%
Acceptance rate (doctoral): 18%
Entrance test required: GRE
Avg. GRE (of all entering students with scores): quantitative: 148; verbal: 153
Research assistantships: 61
Students reporting specialty: 100%
Students specializing in: curriculum/instr.: 0%; admin.: 24%; instructional media design: 0%; educational psych: 2%; educational tech.: 2%; elementary: 4%; junior high: 0%; secondary: 1%; special: 85%; counseling: 2%; technical (vocational): 1%; other: 27%

Indiana State University
401 N. Seventh Street
Terre Haute, IN 47809
www.coe.indstate.edu/
Public
Admissions: (800) 444-4723
Email: grdstudy@indstate.edu
Financial aid: (800) 841-4744
Application deadline: rolling

In-state tuition: full time: $380/credit hour; part time: $380/credit hour
Out-of-state tuition: full time: $747/credit hour
Room/board/expenses: $12,649
Full-time enrollment: 267
doctoral students: 54%; master's students: 44%; education specialists: 2%; men: 32%; women: 68%; minorities: 15%; international: 26%
Part-time enrollment: 313
doctoral students: 68%; master's students: 24%; education specialists: 8%; men: 42%; women: 58%; minorities: 16%; international: 11%
Acceptance rate (master's): 23%
Acceptance rate (doctoral): 41%
Entrance test required: GRE
Avg. GRE (of all entering students with scores): quantitative: N/A; verbal: N/A
Research assistantships: 2
Students reporting specialty: 100%
Students specializing in: curriculum/instr.: 20%; admin.: 35%; instructional media design: 2%; educational psych: 2%; elementary: 1%; higher education admin.: 12%; special: 9%; counseling: 18%

Indiana University-Bloomington
201 N. Rose Avenue
Bloomington, IN 47405-1006
education.indiana.edu/
Public
Admissions: (812) 856-8504
Email: educate@indiana.edu
Financial aid: (812) 855-3278
Application deadline: rolling
In-state tuition: full time: $413/credit hour; part time: $413/credit hour
Out-of-state tuition: full time: $1,202/credit hour
Room/board/expenses: $22,142
Full-time enrollment: 420
doctoral students: 52%; master's students: 44%; education specialists: 4%; men: 30%; women: 70%; minorities: 19%; international: 31%
Part-time enrollment: 481
doctoral students: 54%; master's students: 44%; education specialists: 2%; men: 33%; women: 67%; minorities: 14%; international: 24%
Acceptance rate (master's): 35%
Acceptance rate (doctoral): 26%
Entrance test required: GRE
Avg. GRE (of all entering students with scores): quantitative: 152; verbal: 153
Research assistantships: 94
Students reporting specialty: 100%
Students specializing in: curriculum/instr.: 30%; admin.: 8%; policy: 5%; evaluation/research/statistics: 2%; instructional media design: 11%; educational psych: 9%; elementary: 4%; higher education admin.: 10%; secondary: 2%; social/philosophical foundations: 0%; special: 3%; counseling: 17%; other: 1%

Oakland City University[1]
143 N. Lucretia Street
Oakland City, IN 47660
www.oak.edu
Private
Admissions: N/A
Financial aid: N/A

Tuition: N/A
Room/board/expenses: N/A
Enrollment: N/A

Purdue University-West Lafayette
100 N. University Street
West Lafayette, IN 47907-2098
www.education.purdue.edu/
Public
Admissions: (765) 494-2345
Email: education-gradoffice@purdue.edu
Financial aid: (765) 494-5050
Application deadline: rolling
In-state tuition: full time: $10,002; part time: $348/credit hour
Out-of-state tuition: full time: $28,804
Room/board/expenses: $13,060
Full-time enrollment: 185
doctoral students: 68%; master's students: 31%; education specialists: 1%; men: 33%; women: 67%; minorities: 15%; international: 34%
Part-time enrollment: 337
doctoral students: 23%; master's students: 77%; education specialists: 0%; men: 29%; women: 71%; minorities: 18%; international: 5%
Acceptance rate (master's): 79%
Acceptance rate (doctoral): 43%
Entrance test required: GRE
Avg. GRE (of all entering students with scores): quantitative: 152; verbal: 153
Research assistantships: 47
Students reporting specialty: 100%
Students specializing in: curriculum/instr.: 22%; admin.: 9%; educational psych: 9%; educational tech.: 39%; higher education admin.: 1%; social/philosophical foundations: 1%; special: 8%; counseling: 8%; technical (vocational): 2%

IOWA

Drake University
3206 University Avenue
Des Moines, IA 50311-4505
www.drake.edu/soe/
Private
Admissions: (515) 271-2552
Email: soegradadmission@drake.edu
Financial aid: (515) 271-2905
Application deadline: rolling
Tuition: full time: $450/credit hour; part time: $450/credit hour
Room/board/expenses: $10,146
Full-time enrollment: 86
doctoral students: 1%; master's students: 97%; education specialists: 2%; men: 23%; women: 77%; minorities: 6%; international: 2%
Part-time enrollment: 406
doctoral students: 13%; master's students: 80%; education specialists: 7%; men: 27%; women: 73%; minorities: 6%; international: 1%
Acceptance rate (master's): 76%
Acceptance rate (doctoral): 96%
Entrance test required: GRE
Avg. GRE (of all entering students with scores): quantitative: 152; verbal: 155
Research assistantships: 2
Students reporting specialty: 99%
Students specializing in: curriculum/instr.: 14%; admin.: 16%; elementary: 7%; secondary: 10%; special: 1%; counseling: 19%; other: 34%

Iowa State University

E262 Lagomarcino Hall
Ames, IA 50011
www.grad-college.iastate.edu/
Public
Admissions: (515) 294-5836
Email: admissions@iastate.edu
Financial aid: (515) 294-2223
Application deadline: rolling
In-state tuition: full time: $8,818;
part time: $444/credit hour
Out-of-state tuition: full time:
$21,632
Room/board/expenses: $12,303
Full-time enrollment: 226
doctoral students: 21%; master's
students: 79%; education
specialists: N/A; men: 38%;
women: 62%; minorities: 17%;
international: 12%
Part-time enrollment: 231
doctoral students: 38%; master's
students: 62%; education
specialists: N/A; men: 32%;
women: 68%; minorities: 11%;
international: 2%
Acceptance rate (master's): 64%
Acceptance rate (doctoral): 63%
Entrance test required: GRE
Avg. GRE (of all entering students
with scores): quantitative: 150;
verbal: 154
Research assistantships: 17
Students reporting specialty: 87%
Students specializing in:
curriculum/instr.: 7%; admin.: 8%;
evaluation/research/statistics:
1%; educational tech.: 14%; higher
education admin.: 48%; junior
high: 4%; secondary: 4%; social/
philosophical foundations: 3%;
special: 2%; other: 14%

University of Iowa

Lindquist Center
Iowa City, IA 52242
www.education.uiowa.edu
Public
Admissions: (319) 335-5359
Email: edu-educationservices@
uiowa.edu
Financial aid: (319) 335-1450
Application deadline: rolling
In-state tuition: full time: $11,043;
part time: $544/credit hour
Out-of-state tuition: full time:
$27,953
Room/board/expenses: $18,195
Full-time enrollment: 449
doctoral students: 62%; master's
students: 37%; education
specialists: 0%; men: 32%;
women: 68%; minorities: 14%;
international: 20%
Part-time enrollment: 210
doctoral students: 58%; master's
students: 38%; education
specialists: 4%; men: 43%;
women: 57%; minorities: 12%;
international: 10%
Acceptance rate (master's): 53%
Acceptance rate (doctoral): 42%
Entrance test required: GRE
Avg. GRE (of all entering students
with scores): quantitative: 150;
verbal: 152
Research assistantships: 209
Students reporting specialty: 100%
Students specializing in: admin.:
10%; evaluation/research/
statistics: 10%; educational
psych: 5%; higher education
admin.: 11%; secondary: 18%;
social/philosophical foundations:
5%; special: 14%; counseling: 7%;
other: 24%

University of Northern Iowa

205 Schindler Center
Cedar Falls, IA 50614-0610
www.uni.edu/coe
Public
Admissions: (319) 273-2623
Email: registrar@uni.edu
Financial aid: (800) 772-2736
Application deadline: rolling
In-state tuition: full time: $9,013;
part time: $440/credit hour
Out-of-state tuition: full time:
$19,007
Room/board/expenses: $11,150
Full-time enrollment: 149
doctoral students: 13%; master's
students: 78%; education
specialists: 9%; men: 36%;
women: 64%; minorities: 8%;
international: 13%
Part-time enrollment: 407
doctoral students: 20%; master's
students: 80%; education
specialists: 0%; men: 33%;
women: 67%; minorities: 6%;
international: 6%
Acceptance rate (master's): 57%
Acceptance rate (doctoral): 46%
Entrance test required: GRE
Avg. GRE (of all entering students
with scores): quantitative: N/A;
verbal: N/A
Research assistantships: 13
Students reporting specialty: 89%
Students specializing in:
curriculum/instr.: 12%; admin.:
26%; instructional media
design: 6%; educational psych:
4%; elementary: 4%; social/
philosophical foundations: 3%;
special: 7%; counseling: 7%;
other: 32%

KANSAS

Baker University

PO Box 65
Baldwin City, KS 66006
www.bakeru.edu/soe-
prospective-students2
Private
Admissions: (913) 491-4432
Email: education@bakeru.edu
Financial aid: N/A
Application deadline: rolling
Tuition: full time: N/A; part time:
N/A
Room/board/expenses: N/A
Full-time enrollment: 561
doctoral students: 40%; master's
students: 60%; education
specialists: N/A; men: 28%;
women: 72%; minorities: 13%;
international: N/A
Part-time enrollment: N/A
doctoral students: N/A; master's
students: N/A; education
specialists: N/A; men: N/A;
women: N/A; minorities: N/A;
international: N/A
Acceptance rate (master's): N/A
Acceptance rate (doctoral): 88%
Entrance test required: N/A
Avg. GRE (of all entering students
with scores): quantitative: N/A;
verbal: N/A
Students reporting specialty: 14%
Students specializing in: N/A

Kansas State University

18 Bluemont Hall
Manhattan, KS 66506
www.ksu.edu/
Public
Admissions: (785) 532-5595
Email: coegrads@ksu.edu
Financial aid: (785) 532-6420
Application deadline: rolling
In-state tuition: full time: $463/
credit hour; part time: $463/
credit hour
Out-of-state tuition: full time: $925/
credit hour
Room/board/expenses: $14,826
Full-time enrollment: 224
doctoral students: 18%; master's
students: 82%; education
specialists: N/A; men: 38%;
women: 63%; minorities: 20%;
international: 24%
Part-time enrollment: 602
doctoral students: 26%; master's
students: 74%; education
specialists: N/A; men: 32%;
women: 68%; minorities: 18%;
international: 1%
Acceptance rate (master's): 76%
Acceptance rate (doctoral): 42%
Entrance test required: GRE
Avg. GRE (of all entering students
with scores): quantitative: 149;
verbal: 149
Research assistantships: 10
Students reporting specialty: 98%
Students specializing in:
curriculum/instr.: 24%; admin.:
9%; special: 4%; counseling: 45%;
other: 18%

University of Kansas

217 Joseph R. Pearson Hall
Lawrence, KS 66045
www.soe.ku.edu
Public
Admissions: (785) 864-4510
Email: khuggett@ku.edu
Financial aid: (785) 864-4700
Application deadline: N/A
In-state tuition: full time: $363/
credit hour; part time: $363/
credit hour
Out-of-state tuition: full time: $849/
credit hour
Room/board/expenses: N/A
Full-time enrollment: 547
doctoral students: 62%; master's
students: 34%; education
specialists: 3%; men: 36%;
women: 64%; minorities: 15%;
international: 22%
Part-time enrollment: 391
doctoral students: 20%; master's
students: 80%; education
specialists: 0%; men: 21%;
women: 79%; minorities: 13%;
international: 2%
Acceptance rate (master's): 73%
Acceptance rate (doctoral): 45%
Entrance test required: GRE
Avg. GRE (of all entering students
with scores): quantitative: 151;
verbal: 154
Research assistantships: 74
Students reporting specialty: 100%
Students specializing in:
curriculum/instr.: 20%; admin.:
9%; policy: 1%; evaluation/
research/statistics: 5%;
educational psych: 4%;
educational tech.: 5%;
higher education admin.:
12%; secondary: 1%; social/
philosophical foundations: 2%;
special: 24%; counseling: 7%;
other: 10%

Wichita State University[1]

1845 N. Fairmount
Wichita, KS 67260-0131
www.wichita.edu
Public
Admissions: N/A
Financial aid: N/A
Tuition: N/A
Room/board/expenses: N/A
Enrollment: N/A

KENTUCKY

Eastern Kentucky University

521 Lancaster Avenue
Richmond, KY 40475
www.eku.edu
Public
Admissions: N/A
Financial aid: N/A
Application deadline: 10/01
In-state tuition: full time: $8,550;
part time: $475/credit hour
Out-of-state tuition: full time:
$14,490
Room/board/expenses: $11,828
Full-time enrollment: 207
doctoral students: 5%; master's
students: 89%; education
specialists: 5%; men: 17%;
women: 83%; minorities: 10%;
international: 1%
Part-time enrollment: 562
doctoral students: 17%; master's
students: 74%; education
specialists: 10%; men: 21%;
women: 79%; minorities: 9%;
international: 0%
Acceptance rate (master's): 79%
Acceptance rate (doctoral): 96%
Entrance test required: GRE
Avg. GRE (of all entering students
with scores): quantitative: 146;
verbal: 149
Research assistantships: 22
Students reporting specialty: 100%
Students specializing in:
curriculum/instr.: 2%; admin.:
31%; elementary: 5%; higher
education admin.: 4%; junior high:
5%; secondary: 6%; special: 15%;
counseling: 19%; other: 18%

Morehead State University[1]

Ginger Hall 100
Morehead, KY 40351
www.moreheadstate.edu/
education/
Public
Admissions: N/A
Financial aid: N/A
Tuition: N/A
Room/board/expenses: N/A
Enrollment: N/A

Northern Kentucky University[1]

Nunn Drive
Highland Heights, KY 41099
www.nku.edu
Public
Admissions: N/A
Financial aid: N/A
Tuition: N/A
Room/board/expenses: N/A
Enrollment: N/A

Spalding University[1]

851 S. Fourth Street
Louisville, KY 40203
spalding.edu/
Private
Admissions: N/A
Financial aid: N/A
Tuition: N/A
Room/board/expenses: N/A
Enrollment: N/A

University of Kentucky

103 Dickey Hall
Lexington, KY 40506-0033
www.gradschool.uky.edu/
Public
Admissions: (859) 257-4905
Email: Brian.Jackson@uky.edu
Financial aid: (859) 257-3172
Application deadline: rolling
In-state tuition: full time: $12,525;
part time: $596/credit hour
Out-of-state tuition: full time:
$25,857
Room/board/expenses: $14,888
Full-time enrollment: 497
doctoral students: 47%; master's
students: 48%; education
specialists: 5%; men: 34%;
women: 66%; minorities: 21%;
international: 5%
Part-time enrollment: 207
doctoral students: 43%; master's
students: 51%; education
specialists: 6%; men: 33%;
women: 67%; minorities: 13%;
international: N/A
Acceptance rate (master's): 71%
Acceptance rate (doctoral): 46%
Entrance test required: GRE
Avg. GRE (of all entering students
with scores): quantitative: 149;
verbal: 150
Research assistantships: 56
Students reporting specialty: 97%
Students specializing in:
curriculum/instr.: 3%; admin.:
9%; policy: 3%; instructional
media design: 1%; educational
psych: 8%; educational tech.: 0%;
higher education admin.: 13%;
junior high: 0%; secondary: 8%;
social/philosophical foundations:
11%; special: 17%; counseling:
8%; technical (vocational): 0%;
other: 19%

University of Louisville

Cardinal Boulevard and
First Street
Louisville, KY 40292
www.louisville.edu/education
Public
Admissions: (502) 852-3101
Email: gradadm@louisville.edu
Financial aid: (502) 852-5511
Application deadline: rolling
In-state tuition: full time: $11,522;
part time: $630/credit hour
Out-of-state tuition: full time:
$23,764
Room/board/expenses: $15,326
Full-time enrollment: 380
doctoral students: 23%; master's
students: 76%; education
specialists: 1%; men: 34%;
women: 66%; minorities: 20%;
international: 4%
Part-time enrollment: 614
doctoral students: 19%; master's
students: 74%; education
specialists: 7%; men: 31%;
women: 69%; minorities: 22%;
international: 0%
Acceptance rate (master's): 64%
Acceptance rate (doctoral): 31%
Entrance test required: GRE
Avg. GRE (of all entering students
with scores): quantitative: 148;
verbal: 151
Research assistantships: 33
Students reporting specialty: 100%
Students specializing in:
curriculum/instr.: 4%; admin.:
13%; elementary: 3%; higher
education admin.: 6%; special:
5%; counseling: 21%; other: 48%

Western Kentucky University

1906 College Heights Boulevard
Bowling Green, KY 42101
www.wku.edu/cebs
Public
Admissions: (270) 745-2446
Email: graduate.studies@wku.edu
Financial aid: (270) 745-2755
Application deadline: rolling

In-state tuition: full time: $515/credit hour; part time: $515/credit hour
Out-of-state tuition: full time: $691/credit hour
Room/board/expenses: $10,907
Full-time enrollment: 160
doctoral students: 1%; master's students: 89%; education specialists: 10%; men: 10%; women: 90%; minorities: 6%; international: 4%
Part-time enrollment: 492
doctoral students: 7%; master's students: 91%; education specialists: 2%; men: 16%; women: 84%; minorities: 13%; international: N/A
Acceptance rate (master's): 45%
Acceptance rate (doctoral): 100%
Entrance test required: GRE
Avg. GRE (of all entering students with scores): quantitative: 146; verbal: 152
Research assistantships: 40
Students reporting specialty: 100%
Students specializing in: admin.: 8%; elementary: 11%; junior high: 3%; secondary: 8%; special: 10%; other: 60%

LOUISIANA

Grambling State University[1]
GSU Box 4305
Grambling, LA 71245
www.gram.edu/
Public
Admissions: N/A
Financial aid: N/A
Tuition: N/A
Room/board/expenses: N/A
Enrollment: N/A

Louisiana State University-Baton Rouge
223 Peabody Hall
Baton Rouge, LA 70803
www.lsu.edu/coe
Public
Admissions: (225) 578-1641
Email: graddeanoffice@lsu.edu
Financial aid: (225) 578-3103
Application deadline: rolling
In-state tuition: full time: $9,441; part time: $5,390
Out-of-state tuition: full time: $27,272
Room/board/expenses: $14,380
Full-time enrollment: 237
doctoral students: 27%; master's students: 73%; education specialists: 0%; men: 20%; women: 80%; minorities: 29%; international: 2%
Part-time enrollment: 135
doctoral students: 66%; master's students: 27%; education specialists: 7%; men: 19%; women: 81%; minorities: 35%; international: 1%
Acceptance rate (master's): 69%
Acceptance rate (doctoral): 57%
Entrance test required: GRE
Avg. GRE (of all entering students with scores): quantitative: 147; verbal: 152
Research assistantships: 25
Students reporting specialty: 100%
Students specializing in: curriculum/instr.: 16%; admin.: 7%; evaluation/research/statistics: 3%; educational psych: 6%; educational tech.: 1%; elementary: 9%; higher education admin.: 24%; secondary: 6%; special: 3%; counseling: 8%; other: 17%

Louisiana Tech University
PO Box 3163
Ruston, LA 71272-0001
www.latech.edu/education/
Public
Admissions: (318) 257-2924
Email: gschool@latech.edu
Financial aid: (318) 257-2641
Application deadline: rolling
In-state tuition: full time: $8,025; part time: $6,840
Out-of-state tuition: full time: $16,005
Room/board/expenses: $12,720
Full-time enrollment: 236
doctoral students: 30%; master's students: 70%; education specialists: N/A; men: 30%; women: 70%; minorities: 12%; international: 3%
Part-time enrollment: 199
doctoral students: 27%; master's students: 73%; education specialists: N/A; men: 28%; women: 72%; minorities: 20%; international: 1%
Acceptance rate (master's): 66%
Acceptance rate (doctoral): 28%
Entrance test required: GRE
Avg. GRE (of all entering students with scores): quantitative: 151; verbal: 154
Research assistantships: 20
Students reporting specialty: 30%
Students specializing in: N/A

Southeastern Louisiana University
SLU 10671
Hammond, LA 70402
www.southeastern.edu/
Public
Admissions: N/A
Email: admissions@selu.edu
Financial aid: (985) 549-2244
Application deadline: rolling
In-state tuition: full time: $7,110; part time: $395/credit hour
Out-of-state tuition: full time: $19,674
Room/board/expenses: $11,930
Full-time enrollment: 68
doctoral students: 1%; master's students: 99%; education specialists: N/A; men: 9%; women: 91%; minorities: 26%; international: N/A
Part-time enrollment: 321
doctoral students: 20%; master's students: 80%; education specialists: N/A; men: 17%; women: 83%; minorities: 31%; international: 0%
Acceptance rate (master's): N/A
Acceptance rate (doctoral): N/A
Entrance test required: GRE
Avg. GRE (of all entering students with scores): quantitative: N/A; verbal: N/A
Students reporting specialty: 83%
Students specializing in: curriculum/instr.: 5%; admin.: 44%; special: 12%; other: 39%

Southern University and A&M College[1]
JC Clark Administration Building
4th Floor
Baton Rouge, LA 70813
www.subr.edu/
Public
Admissions: N/A
Financial aid: N/A
Tuition: N/A
Room/board/expenses: N/A
Enrollment: N/A

University of Louisiana-Lafayette
PO Drawer 44872
Lafayette, LA 70504-4872
www.louisiana.edu
Public
Admissions: N/A
Financial aid: N/A
Application deadline: rolling
In-state tuition: full time: $7,346; part time: $408/credit hour
Out-of-state tuition: full time: $19,746
Room/board/expenses: $15,910
Full-time enrollment: 101
doctoral students: 9%; master's students: 91%; education specialists: N/A; men: 22%; women: 78%; minorities: 31%; international: 1%
Part-time enrollment: 181
doctoral students: 55%; master's students: 45%; education specialists: N/A; men: 23%; women: 77%; minorities: 29%; international: 1%
Acceptance rate (master's): 40%
Acceptance rate (doctoral): 57%
Entrance test required: GRE
Avg. GRE (of all entering students with scores): quantitative: N/A; verbal: N/A
Students reporting specialty: 100%
Students specializing in: curriculum/instr.: 6%; admin.: 36%; elementary: 4%; higher education admin.: 5%; secondary: 3%; special: 4%; counseling: 28%; other: 14%

University of Louisiana-Monroe
Strauss Hall
Monroe, LA 71209-0001
www.ulm.edu
Public
Admissions: (318) 342-5252
Email: admissions@ulm.edu
Financial aid: (318) 342-5320
Application deadline: rolling
In-state tuition: full time: $9,264; part time: $7,320
Out-of-state tuition: full time: $18,862
Room/board/expenses: $9,824
Full-time enrollment: 172
doctoral students: 24%; master's students: 76%; education specialists: N/A; men: 23%; women: 77%; minorities: 31%; international: 8%
Part-time enrollment: 51
doctoral students: 43%; master's students: 57%; education specialists: N/A; men: 25%; women: 75%; minorities: 18%; international: N/A
Acceptance rate (master's): N/A
Acceptance rate (doctoral): N/A
Entrance test required: GRE
Avg. GRE (of all entering students with scores): quantitative: N/A; verbal: N/A
Research assistantships: 2
Students reporting specialty: 92%
Students specializing in: curriculum/instr.: 35%; admin.: 17%; instructional media design: 6%; educational tech.: 5%; elementary: 19%; secondary: 12%; special: 15%

University of New Orleans[1]
2000 Lakeshore Drive
New Orleans, LA 70148
coehd.uno.edu/
Public
Admissions: N/A

Financial aid: N/A
Tuition: N/A
Room/board/expenses: N/A
Enrollment: N/A

MAINE

University of Maine
Shibles Hall
Orono, ME 04469-5766
www.umaine.edu/edhd/
Public
Admissions: (207) 581-3219
Email: graduate@maine.edu
Financial aid: (207) 581-1324
Application deadline: rolling
In-state tuition: full time: $418/credit hour; part time: $418/credit hour
Out-of-state tuition: full time: $1,310/credit hour
Room/board/expenses: $15,760
Full-time enrollment: 140
doctoral students: 15%; master's students: 78%; education specialists: 7%; men: 27%; women: 73%; minorities: 11%; international: 4%
Part-time enrollment: 215
doctoral students: 11%; master's students: 63%; education specialists: 26%; men: 25%; women: 75%; minorities: 3%; international: 1%
Acceptance rate (master's): 63%
Acceptance rate (doctoral): 27%
Entrance test required: GRE
Avg. GRE (of all entering students with scores): quantitative: 148; verbal: 152
Research assistantships: 0
Students reporting specialty: 100%
Students specializing in: curriculum/instr.: 9%; admin.: 18%; educational tech.: 6%; higher education admin.: 7%; secondary: 1%; special: 13%; counseling: 15%; other: 32%

MARYLAND

Bowie State University
14000 Jericho Park Road
Bowie, MD 20715-9465
www.bowiestate.edu/academics-research/the-graduate-school/
Public
Admissions: (301) 860-3415
Email: gradadmissions@bowiestate.edu
Financial aid: (301) 860-3540
Application deadline: N/A
In-state tuition: full time: $372/credit hour; part time: $372/credit hour
Out-of-state tuition: full time: $674/credit hour
Room/board/expenses: $12,392
Full-time enrollment: 106
doctoral students: 1%; master's students: 99%; education specialists: N/A; men: 20%; women: 80%; minorities: 22%; international: 3%
Part-time enrollment: 265
doctoral students: 14%; master's students: 86%; education specialists: N/A; men: 23%; women: 77%; minorities: 93%; international: 2%
Acceptance rate (master's): 52%
Acceptance rate (doctoral): 83%
Entrance test required: GRE
Avg. GRE (of all entering students with scores): quantitative: N/A; verbal: N/A
Students reporting specialty: 43%
Students specializing in: N/A

Johns Hopkins University
2800 N. Charles Street
Baltimore, MD 21218
education.jhu.edu/admission/
Private
Admissions: (877) 548-7631
Email: soe.admissions@jhu.edu
Financial aid: (410) 516-9808
Application deadline: 04/01
Tuition: full time: $1,000/credit hour; part time: $720/credit hour
Room/board/expenses: N/A
Full-time enrollment: 224
doctoral students: 8%; master's students: 92%; education specialists: N/A; men: 29%; women: 71%; minorities: 37%; international: 6%
Part-time enrollment: 1,407
doctoral students: 11%; master's students: 89%; education specialists: N/A; men: 25%; women: 75%; minorities: 38%; international: 2%
Acceptance rate (master's): 76%
Acceptance rate (doctoral): 29%
Entrance test required: GRE
Avg. GRE (of all entering students with scores): quantitative: 154; verbal: 158
Research assistantships: 1
Students reporting specialty: 100%
Students specializing in: curriculum/instr.: 1%; admin.: 9%; evaluation/research/statistics: 1%; educational tech.: 4%; elementary: 16%; secondary: 26%; special: 9%; counseling: 15%; other: 27%

Morgan State University[1]
1700 E. Cold Spring Lane
Baltimore, MD 21251
www.morgan.edu/
Public
Admissions: N/A
Financial aid: N/A
Tuition: N/A
Room/board/expenses: N/A
Enrollment: N/A

Towson University
8000 York Road
Towson, MD 21252
www.grad.towson.edu
Public
Admissions: (410) 704-2501
Email: grads@towson.edu
Financial aid: (410) 704-4236
Application deadline: rolling
In-state tuition: full time: $365/credit hour; part time: $365/credit hour
Out-of-state tuition: full time: $755/credit hour
Room/board/expenses: $15,436
Full-time enrollment: 286
doctoral students: 22%; master's students: 78%; education specialists: N/A; men: 18%; women: 82%; minorities: 15%; international: 2%
Part-time enrollment: 1,057
doctoral students: 2%; master's students: 98%; education specialists: N/A; men: 16%; women: 84%; minorities: 13%; international: 1%
Acceptance rate (master's): 47%
Acceptance rate (doctoral): 30%
Entrance test required: GRE
Avg. GRE (of all entering students with scores): quantitative: 150; verbal: 153
Research assistantships: 1
Students reporting specialty: 100%

Students specializing in: admin.: 16%; instructional media design: 7%; educational psych: 3%; educational tech.: 6%; elementary: 2%; junior high: 0%; secondary: 5%; special: 14%; other: 47%

University of Maryland-College Park

3119 Benjamin Building
College Park, MD 20742-1121
www.education.umd.edu/GraduatePrograms
Public
Admissions: (301) 405-5609
Email: pdowdell@umd.edu
Financial aid: (301) 314-9000
Application deadline: rolling
In-state tuition: full time: $602/credit hour; part time: $602/credit hour
Out-of-state tuition: full time: $1,298/credit hour
Room/board/expenses: $14,925
Full-time enrollment: 630
doctoral students: 58%; master's students: 42%; education specialists: 0%; men: 24%; women: 76%; minorities: 32%; international: 13%
Part-time enrollment: 315
doctoral students: 16%; master's students: 84%; education specialists: 0%; men: 19%; women: 81%; minorities: 36%; international: 4%
Acceptance rate (master's): 58%
Acceptance rate (doctoral): 28%
Entrance test required: GRE
Avg. GRE (of all entering students with scores): quantitative: 155; verbal: 158
Research assistantships: 51
Students reporting specialty: 100%
Students specializing in: admin.: 9%; policy: 7%; evaluation/research/statistics: 6%; educational psych: 7%; elementary: 5%; higher education admin.: 4%; junior high: 4%; secondary: 35%; social/philosophical foundations: 1%; special: 11%; counseling: 10%

University of Maryland-Eastern Shore[1]

1 Backbone Road
Princess Anne, MD 21853
www.umes.edu
Public
Admissions: N/A
Financial aid: N/A
Tuition: N/A
Room/board/expenses: N/A
Enrollment: N/A

MASSACHUSETTS

American International College

1000 State Street
Springfield, MA 01109
www.aic.edu
Private
Admissions: (413) 205-3275
Email: janelle.holmboe@aic.edu
Financial aid: (413) 205-3280
Application deadline: rolling
Tuition: full time: $419/credit hour; part time: $419/credit hour
Room/board/expenses: $13,645
Full-time enrollment: 1,224
doctoral students: 6%; master's students: 94%; education specialists: N/A; men: 20%;

women: 80%; minorities: 14%; international: N/A
Part-time enrollment: 210
doctoral students: 0%; master's students: 100%; education specialists: N/A; men: 24%; women: 76%; minorities: 16%; international: N/A
Acceptance rate (master's): 74%
Acceptance rate (doctoral): 79%
Entrance test required: N/A
Avg. GRE (of all entering students with scores): quantitative: N/A; verbal: N/A
Research assistantships: 0
Students reporting specialty: 73%
Students specializing in: curriculum/instr.: 2%; admin.: 17%; educational psych: 0%; elementary: 16%; junior high: 11%; secondary: 14%; special: 37%; counseling: 4%

Boston College (Lynch)

Campion Hall
Chestnut Hill, MA 02467-3813
www.bc.edu/schools/lsoe/gradadmission
Private
Admissions: (617) 552-4214
Email: gsoe@bc.edu
Financial aid: (617) 552-3300
Application deadline: 12/01
Tuition: full time: $1,260/credit hour; part time: $1,260/credit hour
Room/board/expenses: $22,193
Full-time enrollment: 432
doctoral students: 26%; master's students: 74%; education specialists: N/A; men: 25%; women: 75%; minorities: 23%; international: 12%
Part-time enrollment: 257
doctoral students: 40%; master's students: 60%; education specialists: N/A; men: 26%; women: 74%; minorities: 18%; international: 8%
Acceptance rate (master's): 70%
Acceptance rate (doctoral): 7%
Entrance test required: GRE
Avg. GRE (of all entering students with scores): quantitative: 151; verbal: 154
Research assistantships: 374
Students reporting specialty: 99%
Students specializing in: curriculum/instr.: 21%; admin.: 7%; evaluation/research/statistics: 7%; educational psych: 5%; elementary: 3%; higher education admin.: 17%; secondary: 8%; special: 6%; counseling: 25%; other: 1%

Boston University

2 Silber Way
Boston, MA 02215
www.bu.edu/sed
Private
Admissions: (617) 353-4237
Email: sedgrad@bu.edu
Financial aid: (617) 353-4238
Application deadline: rolling
Tuition: full time: $46,342; part time: $714/credit hour
Room/board/expenses: $19,917
Full-time enrollment: 237
doctoral students: 29%; master's students: 71%; education specialists: 0%; men: 32%; women: 68%; minorities: 19%; international: 19%
Part-time enrollment: 306
doctoral students: 22%; master's students: 75%; education specialists: 4%; men: 26%; women: 74%; minorities: 20%; international: 3%

Acceptance rate (master's): 59%
Acceptance rate (doctoral): 34%
Entrance test required: GRE
Avg. GRE (of all entering students with scores): quantitative: 151; verbal: 154
Research assistantships: 8
Students reporting specialty: 99%
Students specializing in: curriculum/instr.: 27%; admin.: 2%; policy: 7%; elementary: 4%; higher education admin.: 10%; junior high: 22%; secondary: 22%; social/philosophical foundations: 5%; special: 6%; counseling: 13%; other: 6%

Cambridge College[1]

1000 Massachusetts Avenue
Cambridge, MA 02138
www.cambridgecollege.edu/
Private
Admissions: N/A
Financial aid: N/A
Tuition: N/A
Room/board/expenses: N/A
Enrollment: N/A

Harvard University

Appian Way
Cambridge, MA 02138
www.gse.harvard.edu
Private
Admissions: (617) 495-3414
Email: gseadmissions@harvard.edu
Financial aid: (617) 495-3416
Application deadline: 12/14
Tuition: full time: $44,974; part time: $24,166
Room/board/expenses: $22,870
Full-time enrollment: 801
doctoral students: 26%; master's students: 74%; education specialists: N/A; men: 28%; women: 72%; minorities: 27%; international: 18%
Part-time enrollment: 75
doctoral students: 5%; master's students: 95%; education specialists: N/A; men: 32%; women: 68%; minorities: 28%; international: 3%
Acceptance rate (master's): 51%
Acceptance rate (doctoral): 5%
Entrance test required: GRE
Avg. GRE (of all entering students with scores): quantitative: 156; verbal: 160
Research assistantships: 105
Students reporting specialty: 100%
Students specializing in: curriculum/instr.: 5%; admin.: 20%; policy: 23%; evaluation/research/statistics: 3%; educational tech.: 6%; higher education admin.: 8%; secondary: 3%; counseling: 5%; other: 40%

Lesley University[1]

29 Everett Street
Cambridge, MA 02138-2790
www.lesley.edu/soe.html
Private
Admissions: N/A
Financial aid: N/A
Tuition: N/A
Room/board/expenses: N/A
Enrollment: N/A

Northeastern University[1]

360 Huntington Avenue
50 Nightingale Hall
Boston, MA 02115
www.northeastern.edu/
Private
Admissions: N/A

Financial aid: N/A
Tuition: N/A
Room/board/expenses: N/A
Enrollment: N/A

Tufts University[1]

Paige Hall
12 Upper Campus Road
Medford, MA 02155
www.tufts.edu/
Private
Admissions: N/A
Financial aid: N/A
Tuition: N/A
Room/board/expenses: N/A
Enrollment: N/A

University of Massachusetts-Amherst

Furcolo Hall
813 N. Pleasant Street
Amherst, MA 01003-9308
www.umass.edu/education
Public
Admissions: (413) 545-0722
Email: gradadm@grad.umass.edu
Financial aid: (413) 545-0801
Application deadline: 01/01
In-state tuition: full time: $110/credit hour; part time: $110/credit hour
Out-of-state tuition: full time: $414/credit hour
Room/board/expenses: $13,700
Full-time enrollment: 382
doctoral students: 46%; master's students: 53%; education specialists: 1%; men: 27%; women: 73%; minorities: 16%; international: 23%
Part-time enrollment: 259
doctoral students: 60%; master's students: 35%; education specialists: 5%; men: 29%; women: 71%; minorities: 21%; international: 7%
Acceptance rate (master's): 52%
Acceptance rate (doctoral): 47%
Entrance test required: GRE
Avg. GRE (of all entering students with scores): quantitative: 152; verbal: 154
Research assistantships: 162
Students reporting specialty: 94%
Students specializing in: curriculum/instr.: 28%; admin.: 6%; policy: 8%; evaluation/research/statistics: 4%; educational psych: 7%; educational tech.: 3%; elementary: 4%; higher education admin.: 15%; junior high: 3%; secondary: 9%; social/philosophical foundations: 6%; special: 6%; counseling: 12%; other: 4%

University of Massachusetts-Boston

100 Morrissey Blvd
Boston, MA 02125-3393
www.umb.edu/academics/graduate?nossi
Public
Admissions: (617) 287-6400
Email: bos.gadm@umb.edu
Financial aid: (617) 287-6300
Application deadline: N/A
In-state tuition: full time: $15,013; part time: $12,531
Out-of-state tuition: full time: $22,181
Room/board/expenses: $14,240
Full-time enrollment: 408
doctoral students: 9%; master's students: 90%; education

specialists: 1%; men: 24%; women: 76%; minorities: 26%; international: 7%
Part-time enrollment: 485
doctoral students: 20%; master's students: 69%; education specialists: 12%; men: 27%; women: 73%; minorities: 25%; international: 1%
Acceptance rate (master's): 74%
Acceptance rate (doctoral): 33%
Entrance test required: GRE
Avg. GRE (of all entering students with scores): quantitative: 148; verbal: 153
Research assistantships: 76
Students reporting specialty: 100%
Students specializing in: admin.: 3%; educational psych: 4%; elementary: 10%; higher education admin.: 19%; special: 7%; counseling: 7%; other: 49%

University of Massachusetts-Lowell

510 O'Leary Library
61 Wilder Street
Lowell, MA 01854
www.uml.edu
Public
Admissions: (978) 934-2373
Email: Graduate_Admissions@uml.edu
Financial aid: (978) 934-2000
Application deadline: 08/01
In-state tuition: full time: $711/credit hour; part time: $711/credit hour
Out-of-state tuition: full time: $1,277/credit hour
Room/board/expenses: $1,150
Full-time enrollment: 55
doctoral students: 0%; master's students: 80%; education specialists: 20%; men: 20%; women: 80%; minorities: 5%; international: 2%
Part-time enrollment: 332
doctoral students: 29%; master's students: 60%; education specialists: 11%; men: 28%; women: 72%; minorities: 8%; international: 1%
Acceptance rate (master's): 88%
Acceptance rate (doctoral): 86%
Entrance test required: GRE
Avg. GRE (of all entering students with scores): quantitative: 148; verbal: 153
Research assistantships: 0
Students reporting specialty: 66%
Students specializing in: curriculum/instr.: 34%; admin.: 16%; elementary: 5%; higher education admin.: 7%; secondary: 18%; other: 20%

MICHIGAN

Andrews University

Berrien Springs, MI 49104-0103
www.andrews.edu/
Private
Admissions: (800) 253-2874
Email: enroll@andrews.edu
Financial aid: (269) 471-3334
Application deadline: 07/15
Tuition: full time: $1,156/credit hour; part time: $1,156/credit hour
Room/board/expenses: $15,756
Full-time enrollment: 183
doctoral students: 58%; master's students: 35%; education specialists: 7%; men: 37%; women: 63%; minorities: 44%; international: 29%
Part-time enrollment: 114
doctoral students: 51%; master's students: 45%; education specialists: 4%; men: 39%;

women: 61%; minorities: 44%;
international: 25%
Acceptance rate (master's): 89%
Acceptance rate (doctoral): 90%
Entrance test required: GRE
**Avg. GRE (of all entering students
with scores):** quantitative: 138;
verbal: 144
Research assistantships: 5
Students reporting specialty: 100%
Students specializing in:
curriculum/instr.: 13%; admin.:
7%; evaluation/research:
statistics: 5%; educational psych:
12%; elementary: 1%; higher
education admin.: 4%; secondary:
2%; special: 3%; counseling: 24%;
other: 29%

Central Michigan University[1]
105 Warriner
Mount Pleasant, MI 48859
www.cmich.edu/
Public
Admissions: N/A
Financial aid: N/A
Tuition: N/A
Room/board/expenses: N/A
Enrollment: N/A

Eastern Michigan University
310 Porter Building
Ypsilanti, MI 48197
www.emich.edu/coe/
Public
Admissions: (734) 487-3400
Email: graduate.admissions@
emich.edu
Financial aid: (734) 487-0455
Application deadline: rolling
In-state tuition: full time: $481/
credit hour; part time: $481/
credit hour
Out-of-state tuition: full time: $948/
credit hour
Room/board/expenses: $13,144
Full-time enrollment: 204
doctoral students: 6%; master's
students: 93%; education
specialists: 1%; men: 20%;
women: 80%; minorities: 16%;
international: 9%
Part-time enrollment: 871
doctoral students: 17%; master's
students: 79%; education
specialists: 5%; men: 24%;
women: 76%; minorities: 19%;
international: 1%
Acceptance rate (master's): 52%
Acceptance rate (doctoral): 40%
Entrance test required: GRE
**Avg. GRE (of all entering students
with scores):** quantitative: 147;
verbal: 151
Research assistantships: 3
Students reporting specialty: 100%
Students specializing in: admin.:
27%; instructional media
design: 3%; educational psych:
4%; elementary: 2%; higher
education admin.: 11%; junior
high: 0%; secondary: 4%; social/
philosophical foundations: 1%;
special: 23%; counseling: 5%;
other: 19%

Ferris State University[1]
1349 Cramer Circle
Bishop 421
Big Rapids, MI 49307
www.ferris.edu/education/
education/
Public
Admissions: N/A
Financial aid: N/A
Tuition: N/A

Room/board/expenses: N/A
Enrollment: N/A

Michigan State University
620 Farm Lane, Room 501
East Lansing, MI 48824-1034
www.educ.msu.edu
Public
Admissions: (517) 355-8332
Email: admis@msu.edu
Financial aid: (517) 353-5940
Application deadline: 12/01
In-state tuition: full time: $679/
credit hour; part time: $679/
credit hour
Out-of-state tuition: full time:
$1,302/credit hour
Room/board/expenses: $13,418
Full-time enrollment: 1,046
doctoral students: 54%; master's
students: 44%; education
specialists: 2%; men: 33%;
women: 67%; minorities: 20%;
international: 15%
Part-time enrollment: 397
doctoral students: 16%; master's
students: 83%; education
specialists: 1%; men: 22%;
women: 78%; minorities: 11%;
international: 4%
Acceptance rate (master's): 36%
Acceptance rate (doctoral): 37%
Entrance test required: GRE
**Avg. GRE (of all entering students
with scores):** quantitative: 152;
verbal: 156
Research assistantships: 285
Students reporting specialty: 74%
Students specializing in:
curriculum/instr.: 28%; admin.:
8%; policy: 4%; evaluation/
research/statistics: 2%;
educational psych: 3%;
educational tech.: 10%;
elementary: 3%; higher education
admin.: 16%; secondary: 2%;
social/philosophical foundations:
1%; special: 8%; counseling: 7%;
other: 8%

Oakland University
415 Pawley Hall
Rochester, MI 48309-4494
www.oakland.edu/grad
Public
Admissions: (248) 370-3167
Email: gradmail@oakland.edu
Financial aid: (248) 370-2550
Application deadline: rolling
In-state tuition: full time: $15,294;
part time: $637/credit hour
Out-of-state tuition: full time:
$24,648
Room/board/expenses: $11,673
Full-time enrollment: 320
doctoral students: 10%; master's
students: 90%; education
specialists: 0%; men: 15%;
women: 85%; minorities: 16%;
international: 7%
Part-time enrollment: 738
doctoral students: 16%; master's
students: 70%; education
specialists: 14%; men: 21%;
women: 79%; minorities: 13%;
international: 1%
Acceptance rate (master's): 56%
Acceptance rate (doctoral): 28%
Entrance test required: N/A
**Avg. GRE (of all entering students
with scores):** quantitative: N/A;
verbal: N/A
Students reporting specialty: 100%
Students specializing in:
curriculum/instr.: 1%; admin.:
16%; elementary: 6%; higher
education admin.: 1%; secondary:
7%; special: 14%; counseling:
24%; other: 31%

University of Michigan-Ann Arbor
610 E. University Street
Ann Arbor, MI 48109-1259
www.soe.umich.edu/
Public
Admissions: (734) 615-1528
Email: ed.grad.admit@umich.edu
Financial aid: (734) 615-1528
Application deadline: N/A
In-state tuition: full time: $20,798;
part time: $1,459/credit hour
Out-of-state tuition: full time:
$41,712
Room/board/expenses: $19,032
Full-time enrollment: 408
doctoral students: 59%; master's
students: 41%; education
specialists: N/A; men: 32%;
women: 68%; minorities: 28%;
international: 16%
Part-time enrollment: 47
doctoral students: 6%; master's
students: 94%; education
specialists: N/A; men: 21%;
women: 79%; minorities: 23%;
international: N/A
Acceptance rate (master's): 70%
Acceptance rate (doctoral): 12%
Entrance test required: GRE
**Avg. GRE (of all entering students
with scores):** quantitative: 153;
verbal: 157
Research assistantships: 155
Students reporting specialty: 72%
Students specializing in:
curriculum/instr.: 22%;
admin.: 4%; policy: 10%;
evaluation/research/statistics:
1%; educational psych:
8%; educational tech.: 3%;
elementary: 6%; higher education
admin.: 26%; secondary: 10%;
social/philosophical foundations:
6%; other: 5%

Wayne State University
5425 Gullen Mall
Detroit, MI 48202-3489
www.coe.wayne.edu/
Public
Admissions: (313) 577-1605
Email:
gradadmissions@wayne.edu
Financial aid: (313) 577-2100
Application deadline: rolling
In-state tuition: full time: $572/
credit hour; part time: $572/
credit hour
Out-of-state tuition: full time:
$1,239/credit hour
Room/board/expenses: $16,431
Full-time enrollment: 593
doctoral students: 24%; master's
students: 72%; education
specialists: 4%; men: 24%;
women: 76%; minorities: 32%;
international: 8%
Part-time enrollment: 909
doctoral students: 12%; master's
students: 75%; education
specialists: 12%; men: 24%;
women: 76%; minorities: 45%;
international: 1%
Acceptance rate (master's): 48%
Acceptance rate (doctoral): 14%
Entrance test required: GRE
**Avg. GRE (of all entering students
with scores):** quantitative: 148;
verbal: 149
Research assistantships: 12
Students reporting specialty: 100%
Students specializing in:
curriculum/instr.: 5%; admin.:
12%; policy: 1%; evaluation/
research/statistics: 3%;
instructional media design:
9%; educational psych: 6%;
elementary: 5%; secondary: 8%;

special: 9%; counseling: 16%;
technical (vocational): 1%; other:
29%

Western Michigan University
1903 W. Michigan Avenue
Kalamazoo, MI 49008-5229
www.wmich.edu/education/
Public
Admissions: (269) 387-2000
Email: ask-wmu@wmich.edu
Financial aid: (269) 387-6000
Application deadline: rolling
In-state tuition: full time: $514/
credit hour; part time: $514/
credit hour
Out-of-state tuition: full time:
$1,089/credit hour
Room/board/expenses: $13,413
Full-time enrollment: 695
doctoral students: 15%; master's
students: 85%; education
specialists: 0%; men: 32%;
women: 68%; minorities: 20%;
international: 13%
Part-time enrollment: 750
doctoral students: 22%; master's
students: 78%; education
specialists: 1%; men: 31%;
women: 69%; minorities: 22%;
international: 2%
Acceptance rate (master's): 63%
Acceptance rate (doctoral): 37%
Entrance test required: GRE
**Avg. GRE (of all entering students
with scores):** quantitative: 147;
verbal: 147
Research assistantships: 64
Students reporting specialty: 100%
Students specializing in: admin.:
18%; evaluation/research/
statistics: 4%; instructional media
design: 4%; higher education
admin.: 4%; secondary: 1%;
social/philosophical foundations:
1%; special: 5%; counseling:
14%; technical (vocational): 2%;
other: 50%

MINNESOTA

Bethel University[1]
3900 Bethel Drive
St. Paul, MN 55112-6999
gs.bethel.edu
Private
Admissions: N/A
Financial aid: N/A
Tuition: N/A
Room/board/expenses: N/A
Enrollment: N/A

Capella University[1]
225 South 6th Street
Minneapolis, MN 55402
www.capella.edu
Private
Admissions: N/A
Financial aid: N/A
Tuition: N/A
Room/board/expenses: N/A
Enrollment: N/A

Hamline University
1536 Hewitt Avenue
St. Paul, MN 55104-1284
www.hamline.edu
Private
Admissions: (651) 523-2900
Email: gradprog@hamline.edu
Financial aid: N/A
Application deadline: rolling
Tuition: full time: $405/credit hour;
part time: $405/credit hour
Room/board/expenses: $11,178

Full-time enrollment: 307
doctoral students: 3%; master's
students: 97%; education
specialists: N/A; men: 28%;
women: 72%; minorities: 7%;
international: 2%
Part-time enrollment: 525
doctoral students: 6%; master's
students: 94%; education
specialists: N/A; men: 25%;
women: 75%; minorities: 6%;
international: 0%
Acceptance rate (master's): 87%
Acceptance rate (doctoral): 100%
Entrance test required: N/A
**Avg. GRE (of all entering students
with scores):** quantitative: N/A;
verbal: N/A
Research assistantships: 0
Students reporting specialty: 90%
Students specializing in: admin.:
17%; elementary: 35%; higher
education admin.: 4%; junior high:
32%; secondary: 36%; special:
1%; other: 11%

Minnesota State University-Mankato[1]
118 Armstrong Hall
Mankato, MN 56001
www.mnsu.edu
Public
Admissions: N/A
Financial aid: N/A
Tuition: N/A
Room/board/expenses: N/A
Enrollment: N/A

St. Cloud State University[1]
720 S. Fourth Avenue
St. Cloud, MN 56301
www.stclousdstate.edu
Public
Admissions: N/A
Financial aid: N/A
Tuition: N/A
Room/board/expenses: N/A
Enrollment: N/A

St. Mary's University of Minnesota[1]
700 Terrace Heights
Winona, MN 55987-1700
www.smumn.edu
Private
Admissions: N/A
Financial aid: N/A
Tuition: N/A
Room/board/expenses: N/A
Enrollment: N/A

University of Minnesota-Duluth
1207 Ordean Court
Duluth, MN 55812
www.d.umn.edu/grad/
graduate-programs.php
Public
Admissions: (218) 726-7523
Email: grad@d.umn.edu
Financial aid: N/A
Application deadline: N/A
In-state tuition: full time: $628/
credit hour; part time: $628/
credit hour
Out-of-state tuition: full time: $986/
credit hour
Room/board/expenses: $10,204
Full-time enrollment: 80
doctoral students: 21%; master's
students: 79%; education
specialists: N/A; men: 35%;
women: 65%; minorities: 21%;
international: 5%

Part-time enrollment: 49
doctoral students: 24%; master's
students: 76%; education
specialists: N/A; men: 35%;
women: 65%; minorities: 18%;
international: 2%
Acceptance rate (master's): 90%
Acceptance rate (doctoral): 100%
Entrance test required: GRE
Avg. GRE (of all entering students
with scores): quantitative: N/A;
verbal: N/A
Research assistantships: 4
Students reporting specialty: 100%
Students specializing in: special:
1%; other: 99%

University of Minnesota-Twin Cities
104 Burton Hall
178 Pillsbury Drive SE
Minneapolis, MN 55455
www.cehd.umn.edu
Public
Admissions: (612) 625-3339
Email: cehdinfo@umn.edu
Financial aid: (612) 624-1111
Application deadline: rolling
In-state tuition: full time: $16,522;
part time: $1,288/credit hour
Out-of-state tuition: full time:
$24,744
Room/board/expenses: $13,926
Full-time enrollment: 882
doctoral students: 53%; master's
students: 46%; education
specialists: 1%; men: 32%;
women: 68%; minorities: 16%;
international: 15%
Part-time enrollment: 484
doctoral students: 61%; master's
students: 38%; education
specialists: 1%; men: 33%;
women: 67%; minorities: 17%;
international: 8%
Acceptance rate (master's): 57%
Acceptance rate (doctoral): 33%
Entrance test required: GRE
Avg. GRE (of all entering students
with scores): quantitative: 155;
verbal: 157
Research assistantships: 231
Students reporting specialty: 100%
Students specializing in:
curriculum/instr.: 11%; admin.:
5%; evaluation/research/
statistics: 2%; educational psych:
6%; educational tech.: 3%;
elementary: 7%; higher education
admin.: 7%; secondary: 13%;
social/philosophical foundations:
5%; special: 7%; counseling: 6%;
other: 27%

University of St. Thomas
1000 LaSalle Avenue
Minneapolis, MN 55403
www.stthomas.edu/education
Private
Admissions: (651) 962-4550
Email: education@stthomas.edu
Financial aid: (651) 962-6550
Application deadline: rolling
Tuition: full time: $794/credit hour;
part time: $794/credit hour
Room/board/expenses: $1,200
Full-time enrollment: 472
doctoral students: 6%; master's
students: 78%; education
specialists: 17%; men: 35%;
women: 65%; minorities: 14%;
international: 10%
Part-time enrollment: 453
doctoral students: 28%; master's
students: 63%; education
specialists: 9%; men: 32%;
women: 68%; minorities: 15%;
international: 3%
Acceptance rate (master's): 99%

Acceptance rate (doctoral): 100%
Entrance test required: N/A
Avg. GRE (of all entering students
with scores): quantitative: N/A;
verbal: N/A
Research assistantships: 3
Students reporting specialty: 83%
Students specializing in:
curriculum/instr.: 5%; admin.:
38%; elementary: 4%; higher
education admin.: 6%; junior high:
0%; secondary: 7%; special: 40%

MISSISSIPPI

Delta State University
1003 W. Sunflower Road
Cleveland, MS 38733
www.deltastate.edu/pages/
251.asp
Public
Admissions: (662) 846-4875
Email: grad-info@deltastate.edu
Financial aid: (662) 846-4670
Application deadline: rolling
In-state tuition: full time: $6,562;
part time: $334/credit hour
Out-of-state tuition: full time:
$6,562
Room/board/expenses: $12,025
Full-time enrollment: 110
doctoral students: 1%; master's
students: 87%; education
specialists: 12%; men: 35%;
women: 65%; minorities: 54%;
international: 1%
Part-time enrollment: 364
doctoral students: 27%; master's
students: 44%; education
specialists: 29%; men: 21%;
women: 79%; minorities: 57%;
international: N/A
Acceptance rate (master's): 90%
Acceptance rate (doctoral): 100%
Entrance test required: GRE
Avg. GRE (of all entering students
with scores): quantitative: N/A;
verbal: N/A
Students reporting specialty: 100%
Students specializing in: admin.:
20%; elementary: 19%;
secondary: 3%; special: 6%;
counseling: 19%; other: 32%

Jackson State University[1]
1400 John R. Lynch Street
Administration Tower
Jackson, MS 39217
www.jsums.edu/
Public
Admissions: N/A
Financial aid: N/A
Tuition: N/A
Room/board/expenses: N/A
Enrollment: N/A

Mississippi College[1]
P.O. Box 4026
Clinton, MS 39058
www.mc.edu/
Private
Admissions: N/A
Financial aid: N/A
Tuition: N/A
Room/board/expenses: N/A
Enrollment: N/A

Mississippi State University
PO Box 9710
Mississippi State, MS 39762
www.educ.msstate.edu/
Public
Admissions: (662) 325-2224
Email: grad@grad.msstate.edu
Financial aid: (662) 325-2450
Application deadline: rolling

In-state tuition: full time: $7,040;
part time: $392/credit hour
Out-of-state tuition: full time:
$18,378
Room/board/expenses: $18,010
Full-time enrollment: 291
doctoral students: 16%; master's
students: 78%; education
specialists: 5%; men: 40%;
women: 60%; minorities: 27%;
international: 2%
Part-time enrollment: 485
doctoral students: 45%; master's
students: 48%; education
specialists: 7%; men: 25%;
women: 75%; minorities: 41%;
international: N/A
Acceptance rate (master's): 94%
Acceptance rate (doctoral): 89%
Entrance test required: GRE
Avg. GRE (of all entering students
with scores): quantitative: 146;
verbal: 148
Research assistantships: 18
Students reporting specialty: 100%
Students specializing in:
curriculum/instr.: 5%; admin.:
23%; educational psych: 5%;
elementary: 2%; junior high:
7%; secondary: 14%; special:
2%; counseling: 18%; technical
(vocational): 1%; other: 23%

University of Mississippi
222 Guyton Hall
University, MS 38677
education.olemiss.edu
Public
Admissions: (662) 915-7226
Email: admissions@olemiss.edu
Financial aid: (662) 915-5788
Application deadline: 03/01
In-state tuition: full time: $389/
credit hour; part time: $389/
credit hour
Out-of-state tuition: full time:
$1,058/credit hour
Room/board/expenses: $19,598
Full-time enrollment: 279
doctoral students: 15%; master's
students: 82%; education
specialists: 3%; men: 17%;
women: 83%; minorities: 24%;
international: N/A
Part-time enrollment: 317
doctoral students: 25%; master's
students: 53%; education
specialists: 22%; men: 24%;
women: 76%; minorities: 42%;
international: N/A
Acceptance rate (master's): 35%
Acceptance rate (doctoral): 37%
Entrance test required: GRE
Avg. GRE (of all entering students
with scores): quantitative: 143;
verbal: 148
Research assistantships: 13
Students reporting specialty: 97%
Students specializing in:
curriculum/instr.: 40%; admin.:
18%; higher education admin.:
23%; counseling: 19%

University of Southern Mississippi[1]
118 College Drive, Box 5023
Hattiesburg, MS 39406
www.usm.edu
Public
Admissions: N/A
Financial aid: N/A
Tuition: N/A
Room/board/expenses: N/A
Enrollment: N/A

MISSOURI

Lindenwood University
209 S. Kings Highway
St. Charles, MO 63301
www.lindenwood.edu
Private
Admissions: (636) 949-4933
Email: eveningadmissions@
lindenwood.edu
Financial aid: (636) 949-4923
Application deadline: rolling
Tuition: full time: $15,580; part
time: $440/credit hour
Room/board/expenses: $12,560
Full-time enrollment: 294
doctoral students: 4%; master's
students: 91%; education
specialists: 5%; men: 25%;
women: 75%; minorities: 20%;
international: 2%
Part-time enrollment: 1,305
doctoral students: 25%; master's
students: 64%; education
specialists: 11%; men: 26%;
women: 74%; minorities: 26%;
international: 1%
Acceptance rate (master's): 79%
Acceptance rate (doctoral): 90%
Entrance test required: GRE
Avg. GRE (of all entering students
with scores): quantitative: N/A;
verbal: N/A
Research assistantships: 0
Students reporting specialty: 100%
Students specializing in: admin.:
41%; educational tech.: 2%;
elementary: 11%; junior high: 1%;
secondary: 2%; special: 4%;
counseling: 13%; other: 26%

Maryville University of St. Louis
650 Maryville University Drive
St. Louis, MO 63141
maryville.edu
Private
Admissions: (314) 529-9350
Email: admissions@maryville.edu
Financial aid: (314) 529-9361
Application deadline: rolling
Tuition: full time: $25,884; part
time: $740/credit hour
Room/board/expenses: $9,711
Full-time enrollment: 21
doctoral students: 5%; master's
students: 95%; education
specialists: N/A; men: 19%;
women: 81%; minorities: 19%;
international: 10%
Part-time enrollment: 228
doctoral students: 72%; master's
students: 28%; education
specialists: N/A; men: 26%;
women: 74%; minorities: 24%;
international: 1%
Acceptance rate (master's): N/A
Acceptance rate (doctoral): N/A
Entrance test required: N/A
Avg. GRE (of all entering students
with scores): quantitative: N/A;
verbal: N/A
Students reporting specialty: 100%
Students specializing in:
curriculum/instr.: 9%; admin.:
53%; elementary: 2%; higher
education admin.: 15%; junior
high: 0%; other: 20%

Missouri Baptist University[1]
1 College Park Drive
St. Louis, MO 63141
www.mobap.edu/academics/
graduate-education-division/
Private
Admissions: N/A
Financial aid: N/A

Tuition: N/A
Room/board/expenses: N/A
Enrollment: N/A

St. Louis University
3500 Lindell Boulevard
St. Louis, MO 63103-3412
www.slu.edu/x7039.xml
Private
Admissions: (314) 977-3939
Email: achamb10@slu.edu
Financial aid: (314) 977-2350
Application deadline: rolling
Tuition: full time: $1,030/credit
hour; part time: $1,030/credit
hour
Room/board/expenses: $18,158
Full-time enrollment: 60
doctoral students: 88%; master's
students: 12%; education
specialists: 0%; men: 43%;
women: 57%; minorities: 12%;
international: 23%
Part-time enrollment: 188
doctoral students: 89%; master's
students: 9%; education
specialists: 2%; men: 37%;
women: 63%; minorities: 18%;
international: 7%
Acceptance rate (master's): 73%
Acceptance rate (doctoral): 69%
Entrance test required: GRE
Avg. GRE (of all entering students
with scores): quantitative: N/A;
verbal: N/A
Research assistantships: 18
Students reporting specialty: 39%
Students specializing in: N/A

University of Central Missouri[1]
Lovinger 2190
Warrensburg, MO 64093
www.ucmo.edu/graduate
Public
Admissions: N/A
Financial aid: N/A
Tuition: N/A
Room/board/expenses: N/A
Enrollment: N/A

University of Missouri
118 Hill Hall
Columbia, MO 65211
education.missouri.edu/
Public
Admissions: (573) 882-7832
Email: chvalkb@missouri.edu
Financial aid: (573) 882-7506
Application deadline: rolling
In-state tuition: full time: $347/
credit hour; part time: $347/
credit hour
Out-of-state tuition: full time: $910/
credit hour
Room/board/expenses: $16,862
Full-time enrollment: 680
doctoral students: 46%; master's
students: 51%; education
specialists: 4%; men: 33%;
women: 67%; minorities: 14%;
international: 9%
Part-time enrollment: 827
doctoral students: 20%; master's
students: 68%; education
specialists: 12%; men: 35%;
women: 65%; minorities: 9%;
international: 3%
Acceptance rate (master's): 53%
Acceptance rate (doctoral): 16%
Entrance test required: GRE
Avg. GRE (of all entering students
with scores): quantitative: 149;
verbal: 155
Research assistantships: 135
Students reporting specialty: 100%

Students specializing in: curriculum/instr.: 26%; admin.: 24%; evaluation/research/statistics: 2%; educational tech.: 7%; special: 3%; counseling: 25%; technical (vocational): 1%; other: 14%

University of Missouri-Kansas City

5100 Rockhill Road
Kansas City, MO 64110-2499
www.umkc.edu/
Public
Admissions: (816) 235-1111
Email: admit@umkc.edu
Financial aid: (816) 235-1154
Application deadline: rolling
In-state tuition: full time: $334/credit hour; part time: $334/credit hour
Out-of-state tuition: full time: $884/credit hour
Room/board/expenses: $18,888
Full-time enrollment: 203
doctoral students: 16%; master's students: 81%; education specialists: 2%; men: 27%; women: 73%; minorities: 21%; international: 9%
Part-time enrollment: 369
doctoral students: 23%; master's students: 64%; education specialists: 13%; men: 27%; women: 73%; minorities: 24%; international: 2%
Acceptance rate (master's): 71%
Acceptance rate (doctoral): 18%
Entrance test required: GRE
Avg. GRE (of all entering students with scores): quantitative: 148; verbal: 152
Research assistantships: 14
Students reporting specialty: 0%
Students specializing in: N/A

University of Missouri-St. Louis

1 University Boulevard
St. Louis, MO 63121
coe.umsl.edu
Public
Admissions: (314) 516-5458
Email: gradadm@umsl.edu
Financial aid: (314) 516-5508
Application deadline: rolling
In-state tuition: full time: $415/credit hour; part time: $415/credit hour
Out-of-state tuition: full time: $1,024/credit hour
Room/board/expenses: $12,018
Full-time enrollment: 173
doctoral students: 14%; master's students: 73%; education specialists: 13%; men: 21%; women: 79%; minorities: 20%; international: 12%
Part-time enrollment: 1,091
doctoral students: 24%; master's students: 73%; education specialists: 3%; men: 25%; women: 75%; minorities: 29%; international: 1%
Acceptance rate (master's): 86%
Acceptance rate (doctoral): 68%
Entrance test required: GRE
Avg. GRE (of all entering students with scores): quantitative: 150; verbal: 153
Research assistantships: 24
Students reporting specialty: 100%
Students specializing in: admin.: 13%; evaluation/research/statistics: 0%; elementary: 14%; secondary: 20%; special: 7%; counseling: 16%; other: 31%

Washington University in St. Louis

1 Brookings Drive, Box 1183
St. Louis, MO 63130-4899
education.wustl.edu
Private
Admissions: (314) 935-6791
Email: nkolk@artsci.wustl.edu
Financial aid: (314) 935-6880
Application deadline: N/A
Tuition: full time: $47,352; part time: $1,904/credit hour
Room/board/expenses: N/A
Full-time enrollment: 21
doctoral students: 48%; master's students: 52%; education specialists: N/A; men: 24%; women: 76%; minorities: 29%; international: 10%
Part-time enrollment: 1
doctoral students: 0%; master's students: 100%; education specialists: N/A; men: N/A; women: 100%; minorities: N/A; international: N/A
Acceptance rate (master's): 52%
Acceptance rate (doctoral): 8%
Entrance test required: GRE
Avg. GRE (of all entering students with scores): quantitative: 152; verbal: 156
Research assistantships: 1
Students reporting specialty: 100%
Students specializing in: policy: 37%; elementary: 22%; secondary: 41%

William Woods University

One University Ave
Fulton, MO 65251
https://www.williamwoods.edu/academics/graduate/education_graduate/index.html
Private
Admissions: N/A
Financial aid: N/A
Application deadline: rolling
Tuition: full time: $300/credit hour; part time: $300/credit hour
Room/board/expenses: N/A
Full-time enrollment: 33
doctoral students: 9%; master's students: 67%; education specialists: 24%; men: 33%; women: 67%; minorities: 9%; international: N/A
Part-time enrollment: 776
doctoral students: 14%; master's students: 65%; education specialists: 22%; men: 35%; women: 65%; minorities: 3%; international: 1%
Acceptance rate (master's): 57%
Acceptance rate (doctoral): 17%
Entrance test required: N/A
Avg. GRE (of all entering students with scores): quantitative: N/A; verbal: N/A
Research assistantships: 15
Students reporting specialty: 97%
Students specializing in: curriculum/instr.: 13%; admin.: 77%; instructional media design: 10%

MONTANA

Montana State University

215 Reid Hall
Bozeman, MT 59717
www.montana.edu/wwweduc/
Public
Admissions: (406) 994-4145
Email: gradstudy@montana.edu
Financial aid: (406) 994-2845
Application deadline: 04/01

In-state tuition: full time: $5,200; part time: $267/credit hour
Out-of-state tuition: full time: $15,100
Room/board/expenses: $9,330
Full-time enrollment: 13
doctoral students: 46%; master's students: 46%; education specialists: 8%; men: 54%; women: 46%; minorities: 154%; international: 23%
Part-time enrollment: 306
doctoral students: 26%; master's students: 74%; education specialists: 0%; men: 33%; women: 67%; minorities: 10%; international: N/A
Acceptance rate (master's): 89%
Acceptance rate (doctoral): 100%
Entrance test required: GRE
Avg. GRE (of all entering students with scores): quantitative: 150; verbal: 149
Research assistantships: 2
Students reporting specialty: 61%
Students specializing in: curriculum/instr.: 31%; admin.: 50%; instructional media design: 11%; higher education admin.: 19%

University of Montana

PJWEC Room 321
Missoula, MT 59812
www.coehs.umt.edu
Public
Admissions: (406) 243-2572
Email: grad.school@umontana.edu
Financial aid: (406) 243-5373
Application deadline: rolling
In-state tuition: full time: $6,902; part time: N/A
Out-of-state tuition: full time: $19,646
Room/board/expenses: $14,433
Full-time enrollment: 171
doctoral students: 11%; master's students: 89%; education specialists: 0%; men: 23%; women: 77%; minorities: 12%; international: 4%
Part-time enrollment: 143
doctoral students: 45%; master's students: 53%; education specialists: 1%; men: 31%; women: 69%; minorities: 7%; international: 3%
Acceptance rate (master's): 26%
Acceptance rate (doctoral): 95%
Entrance test required: GRE
Avg. GRE (of all entering students with scores): quantitative: 149; verbal: 153
Research assistantships: 5
Students reporting specialty: 93%
Students specializing in: curriculum/instr.: 34%; admin.: 27%; counseling: 22%; other: 17%

NEBRASKA

College of St. Mary

7000 Mercy Road
Omaha, NE 68106
www.csm.edu
Private
Admissions: (800) 926-5534
Financial aid: N/A
Application deadline: rolling
Tuition: full time: $590/credit hour; part time: $590/credit hour
Room/board/expenses: $12,832
Full-time enrollment: 83
doctoral students: 0%; master's students: 100%; education specialists: N/A; men: 11%; women: 89%; minorities: 16%; international: N/A
Part-time enrollment: 67
doctoral students: 75%; master's students: 25%; education

specialists: N/A; men: 7%; women: 93%; minorities: 10%; international: N/A
Acceptance rate (master's): 72%
Acceptance rate (doctoral): 82%
Entrance test required: N/A
Avg. GRE (of all entering students with scores): quantitative: N/A; verbal: N/A
Research assistantships: 0
Students reporting specialty: 100%
Students specializing in: curriculum/instr.: 3%; admin.: 11%; elementary: 19%; secondary: 30%; special: 15%; other: 22%

University of Nebraska-Lincoln

233 Mabel Lee Hall
Lincoln, NE 68588-0234
cehs.unl.edu
Public
Admissions: (402) 472-2878
Email: graduate@unl.edu
Financial aid: (402) 472-2030
Application deadline: rolling
In-state tuition: full time: $285/credit hour; part time: $285/credit hour
Out-of-state tuition: full time: $816/credit hour
Room/board/expenses: $12,059
Full-time enrollment: 380
doctoral students: 43%; master's students: 56%; education specialists: 1%; men: 22%; women: 78%; minorities: 13%; international: 15%
Part-time enrollment: 500
doctoral students: 58%; master's students: 40%; education specialists: 2%; men: 36%; women: 64%; minorities: 9%; international: 3%
Acceptance rate (master's): 56%
Acceptance rate (doctoral): 47%
Entrance test required: GRE
Avg. GRE (of all entering students with scores): quantitative: 152; verbal: 153
Research assistantships: 116
Students reporting specialty: 91%
Students specializing in: curriculum/instr.: 23%; admin.: 23%; evaluation/research/statistics: 5%; instructional media design: 2%; educational psych: 7%; educational tech.: 1%; elementary: 2%; higher education admin.: 22%; secondary: 1%; special: 7%; counseling: 3%; other: 11%

University of Nebraska-Omaha

6001 Dodge Street
Omaha, NE 68182
www.unomaha.edu
Public
Admissions: (402) 554-2936
Email: graduate@unomaha.edu
Financial aid: (402) 554-3408
Application deadline: rolling
In-state tuition: full time: $245/credit hour; part time: $245/credit hour
Out-of-state tuition: full time: $685/credit hour
Room/board/expenses: $13,154
Full-time enrollment: 77
doctoral students: 12%; master's students: 71%; education specialists: 17%; men: 13%; women: 87%; minorities: 12%; international: 5%
Part-time enrollment: 571
doctoral students: 13%; master's students: 85%; education specialists: 2%; men: 18%;

women: 82%; minorities: 12%; international: 0%
Acceptance rate (master's): 33%
Acceptance rate (doctoral): 64%
Entrance test required: GRE
Avg. GRE (of all entering students with scores): quantitative: 148; verbal: 151
Research assistantships: 14
Students reporting specialty: 100%
Students specializing in: admin.: 19%; elementary: 20%; secondary: 14%; special: 17%; counseling: 7%; other: 23%

NEVADA

University of Nevada-Las Vegas

4505 Maryland Parkway
Box 453001
Las Vegas, NV 89154-3001
graduatecollege.unlv.edu/admissions/
Public
Admissions: (702) 895-3320
Email: GradAdmissions@unlv.edu
Financial aid: (702) 895-3424
Application deadline: rolling
In-state tuition: full time: $8,524; part time: $264/credit hour
Out-of-state tuition: full time: $22,434
Room/board/expenses: $20,850
Full-time enrollment: 451
doctoral students: 10%; master's students: 87%; education specialists: 2%; men: 27%; women: 73%; minorities: 40%; international: 2%
Part-time enrollment: 543
doctoral students: 24%; master's students: 75%; education specialists: 1%; men: 27%; women: 73%; minorities: 34%; international: 3%
Acceptance rate (master's): 87%
Acceptance rate (doctoral): 72%
Entrance test required: GRE
Avg. GRE (of all entering students with scores): quantitative: 142; verbal: 146
Research assistantships: 40
Students reporting specialty: 95%
Students specializing in: curriculum/instr.: 51%; educational psych: 6%; special: 24%; counseling: 11%; other: 9%

University of Nevada-Reno

MS278
Reno, NV 89557-0278
www.unr.edu/grad
Public
Admissions: (775) 784-6869
Email: gradadmissions@unr.edu
Financial aid: (775) 784-4666
Application deadline: rolling
In-state tuition: full time: $264/credit hour; part time: $264/credit hour
Out-of-state tuition: full time: $14,288
Room/board/expenses: $19,700
Full-time enrollment: 229
doctoral students: 19%; master's students: 81%; education specialists: N/A; men: 27%; women: 73%; minorities: 1%; international: 2%
Part-time enrollment: 308
doctoral students: 27%; master's students: 73%; education specialists: N/A; men: 35%; women: 65%; minorities: 20%; international: 2%
Acceptance rate (master's): 82%
Acceptance rate (doctoral): 83%
Entrance test required: GRE

Avg. GRE (of all entering students with scores): quantitative: 146; verbal: 150
Research assistantships: 16
Students reporting specialty: 50%
Students specializing in: admin.: 19%; elementary: 12%; higher education admin.: 8%; secondary: 17%; special: 17%; counseling: 14%; other: 12%

NEW HAMPSHIRE

Plymouth State University[1]
17 High Street MSC 11
Plymouth, NH 03264
www.plymouth.edu/
Public
Admissions: N/A
Financial aid: N/A
Tuition: N/A
Room/board/expenses: N/A
Enrollment: N/A

Rivier University[1]
420 Main Street
Nashua, NH 03060
www.rivier.edu/
Private
Admissions: N/A
Financial aid: N/A
Tuition: N/A
Room/board/expenses: N/A
Enrollment: N/A

University of New Hampshire
Morrill Hall
Durham, NH 03824-3595
www.unh.edu/education/
Public
Admissions: (603) 862-2381
Financial aid: (603) 862-3600
Application deadline: rolling
In-state tuition: full time: $15,288; part time: $750/credit hour
Out-of-state tuition: full time: $28,248
Room/board/expenses: $21,950
Full-time enrollment: 104
doctoral students: 25%; master's students: 75%; education specialists: 0%; men: 22%; women: 78%; minorities: 7%; international: 5%
Part-time enrollment: 148
doctoral students: 11%; master's students: 80%; education specialists: 9%; men: 28%; women: 72%; minorities: 4%; international: 1%
Acceptance rate (master's): 83%
Acceptance rate (doctoral): 59%
Entrance test required: GRE
Avg. GRE (of all entering students with scores): quantitative: 150; verbal: 160
Research assistantships: 1
Students reporting specialty: 100%
Students specializing in: admin.: 8%; policy: 2%; elementary: 19%; higher education admin.: 17%; secondary: 33%; special: 9%; counseling: 11%; other: 1%

NEW JERSEY

College of St. Elizabeth
2 Convent Road
Morristown, NJ 07960-6989
www.cse.edu
Private
Admissions: (800) 210-7900
Email: apply@cse.edu
Financial aid: (973) 290-4432
Application deadline: rolling

Tuition: full time: $19,152; part time: $1,064/credit hour
Room/board/expenses: N/A
Full-time enrollment: 95
doctoral students: 18%; master's students: 82%; education specialists: N/A; men: 72%; women: 28%; minorities: 23%; international: N/A
Part-time enrollment: 35
doctoral students: 66%; master's students: 34%; education specialists: N/A; men: 51%; women: 49%; minorities: 83%; international: N/A
Acceptance rate (master's): 91%
Acceptance rate (doctoral): 70%
Entrance test required: N/A
Avg. GRE (of all entering students with scores): quantitative: N/A; verbal: N/A
Students reporting specialty: 100%
Students specializing in: admin.: 48%; elementary: 52%

Kean University[1]
1000 Morris Avenue
Union, NJ 07083
www.kean.edu/
Public
Admissions: N/A
Financial aid: N/A
Tuition: N/A
Room/board/expenses: N/A
Enrollment: N/A

Montclair State University
1 Normal Avenue
Upper Montclair, NJ 07043
cehs.montclair.edu/
Public
Admissions: (973) 655-5147
Email: Graduate.School@montclair.edu
Financial aid: (973) 655-4461
Application deadline: rolling
In-state tuition: full time: $553/credit hour; part time: $553/credit hour
Out-of-state tuition: full time: $837/credit hour
Room/board/expenses: N/A
Full-time enrollment: 605
doctoral students: 6%; master's students: 94%; education specialists: N/A; men: 26%; women: 74%; minorities: 31%; international: 3%
Part-time enrollment: 1,098
doctoral students: 8%; master's students: 92%; education specialists: N/A; men: 23%; women: 77%; minorities: 28%; international: 0%
Acceptance rate (master's): 72%
Acceptance rate (doctoral): 43%
Entrance test required: GRE
Avg. GRE (of all entering students with scores): quantitative: 146; verbal: 149
Research assistantships: 82
Students reporting specialty: 100%
Students specializing in: admin.: 16%; evaluation/research/statistics: 0%; special: 8%; counseling: 20%; other: 55%

Rowan University
201 Mullica Hill Road
Glassboro, NJ 08028
www.rowan.edu/
Public
Admissions: (856) 256-4050
Email: gradoffice@rowan.edu
Financial aid: (856) 256-4250
Application deadline: rolling
In-state tuition: full time: $648/credit hour; part time: $648/credit hour

Out-of-state tuition: full time: $648/credit hour
Room/board/expenses: N/A
Full-time enrollment: 162
doctoral students: 0%; master's students: 86%; education specialists: 14%; men: 24%; women: 76%; minorities: 13%; international: 2%
Part-time enrollment: 548
doctoral students: 41%; master's students: 56%; education specialists: 3%; men: 27%; women: 73%; minorities: 21%; international: N/A
Acceptance rate (master's): 46%
Acceptance rate (doctoral): 84%
Entrance test required: GRE
Avg. GRE (of all entering students with scores): quantitative: 145; verbal: 147
Research assistantships: 3
Students reporting specialty: 100%
Students specializing in: admin.: 46%; special: 9%; counseling: 11%; other: 34%

Rutgers, The State University of New Jersey-New Brunswick
10 Seminary Place
New Brunswick, NJ 08901-1183
www.gse.rutgers.edu
Public
Admissions: (732) 932-7711
Email: gradadm@rci.rutgers.edu
Financial aid: (848) 932-2622
Application deadline: 02/01
In-state tuition: full time: $17,610; part time: $662/credit hour
Out-of-state tuition: full time: $28,458
Room/board/expenses: $17,666
Full-time enrollment: 354
doctoral students: 13%; master's students: 87%; education specialists: N/A; men: 24%; women: 76%; minorities: 30%; international: 7%
Part-time enrollment: 380
doctoral students: 56%; master's students: 44%; education specialists: N/A; men: 27%; women: 73%; minorities: 24%; international: 2%
Acceptance rate (master's): 58%
Acceptance rate (doctoral): 41%
Entrance test required: GRE
Avg. GRE (of all entering students with scores): quantitative: 149; verbal: 152
Research assistantships: 0
Students reporting specialty: 100%
Students specializing in: admin.: 12%; policy: 1%; evaluation/research/statistics: 2%; instructional media design: 2%; educational psych: 5%; educational tech.: 1%; elementary: 10%; higher education admin.: 6%; junior high: 3%; secondary: 26%; social/philosophical foundations: 5%; special: 25%; counseling: 3%; other: 11%

Seton Hall University[1]
400 S. Orange Avenue
South Orange, NJ 07079
www.shu.edu/academics/education/
Private
Admissions: N/A
Financial aid: N/A
Tuition: N/A
Room/board/expenses: N/A
Enrollment: N/A

NEW MEXICO

New Mexico State University
PO Box 30001, MSC 3AC
Las Cruces, NM 88003-8001
education.nmsu.edu
Public
Admissions: (575) 646-3121
Email: admissions@nmsu.edu
Financial aid: (505) 646-4105
Application deadline: rolling
In-state tuition: full time: $4,822; part time: $221/credit hour
Out-of-state tuition: full time: $14,691
Room/board/expenses: $13,068
Full-time enrollment: 305
doctoral students: 25%; master's students: 69%; education specialists: 7%; men: 24%; women: 76%; minorities: 52%; international: 10%
Part-time enrollment: 474
doctoral students: 31%; master's students: 67%; education specialists: 2%; men: 22%; women: 78%; minorities: 58%; international: 3%
Acceptance rate (master's): 52%
Acceptance rate (doctoral): 28%
Entrance test required: GRE
Avg. GRE (of all entering students with scores): quantitative: 143; verbal: 147
Research assistantships: 35
Students reporting specialty: 97%
Students specializing in: curriculum/instr.: 43%; admin.: 17%; educational psych: 3%; elementary: 1%; secondary: 1%; special: 18%; counseling: 8%; other: 10%

University of New Mexico
MSC05 3040
Albuquerque, NM 87131-0001
www.unm.edu
Public
Admissions: (505) 277-2447
Financial aid: (505) 277-8900
Application deadline: rolling
In-state tuition: full time: $5,488; part time: $302/credit hour
Out-of-state tuition: full time: $16,047
Room/board/expenses: $15,285
Full-time enrollment: 385
doctoral students: 27%; master's students: 70%; education specialists: 3%; men: 32%; women: 68%; minorities: 44%; international: 11%
Part-time enrollment: 591
doctoral students: 29%; master's students: 68%; education specialists: 2%; men: 23%; women: 77%; minorities: 45%; international: 5%
Acceptance rate (master's): 51%
Acceptance rate (doctoral): 39%
Entrance test required: GRE
Avg. GRE (of all entering students with scores): quantitative: 148; verbal: 151
Research assistantships: 40
Students reporting specialty: 100%
Students specializing in: curriculum/instr.: 1%; admin.: 11%; educational psych: 3%; elementary: 11%; secondary: 8%; social/philosophical foundations: 16%; special: 14%; counseling: 9%; other: 27%

NEW YORK

Binghamton University-SUNY[1]
PO Box 6000
Binghamton, NY 13902-6000
gse.binghamton.edu
Public
Admissions: N/A
Financial aid: N/A
Tuition: N/A
Room/board/expenses: N/A
Enrollment: N/A

Cornell University[1]
Kennedy Hall
Ithaca, NY 14853
www.cornell.edu
Private
Admissions: N/A
Financial aid: N/A
Tuition: N/A
Room/board/expenses: N/A
Enrollment: N/A

CUNY-Graduate Center
365 Fifth Avenue
New York, NY 10016
www.gc.cuny.edu
Public
Admissions: (212) 817-7470
Email: admissions@gc.cuny.edu
Financial aid: (212) 817-7460
Application deadline: N/A
In-state tuition: full time: $8,995; part time: $490/credit hour
Out-of-state tuition: full time: $835/credit hour
Room/board/expenses: $25,046
Full-time enrollment: 74
doctoral students: 100%; master's students: N/A; education specialists: N/A; men: 22%; women: 78%; minorities: 23%; international: N/A
Part-time enrollment: N/A
doctoral students: N/A; master's students: N/A; education specialists: N/A; men: N/A; women: N/A; minorities: N/A; international: N/A
Acceptance rate (master's): N/A
Acceptance rate (doctoral): 22%
Entrance test required: GRE
Avg. GRE (of all entering students with scores): quantitative: 153; verbal: 155
Research assistantships: 11
Students reporting specialty: 100%
Students specializing in: policy: 7%; educational psych: 100%

Dowling College
Idle Hour Boulevard
Oakdale Long Island, NY 11769
www.dowling.edu/school-education/index.shtm
Private
Admissions: (631) 244-3303
Financial aid: (631) 244-3220
Application deadline: rolling
Tuition: full time: $1,220/credit hour; part time: $1,220/credit hour
Room/board/expenses: $15,572
Full-time enrollment: 159
doctoral students: 55%; master's students: 45%; education specialists: N/A; men: 33%; women: 67%; minorities: 8%; international: 9%
Part-time enrollment: 202
doctoral students: N/A; master's students: 100%; education specialists: N/A; men: 31%; women: 69%; minorities: 5%; international: 0%
Acceptance rate (master's): 71%
Acceptance rate (doctoral): N/A

Entrance test required: GRE
Avg. GRE (of all entering students with scores): quantitative: N/A; verbal: N/A
Research assistantships: 0
Students reporting specialty: 2%
Students specializing in: N/A

D'Youville College

1 D'Youville Square
320 Porter Avenue
Buffalo, NY 14201-1084
www.dyc.edu/academics/
education/index.asp
Private
Admissions: (716) 829-7676
Email: graduateadmissions@
dyc.edu
Financial aid: (716) 829-7500
Application deadline: rolling
Tuition: full time: $852/credit hour;
part time: N/A
Room/board/expenses: $10,832
Full-time enrollment: 60
doctoral students: 10%; master's
students: 90%; education
specialists: N/A; men: 23%;
women: 77%; minorities: 20%;
international: 63%
Part-time enrollment: 63
doctoral students: 27%; master's
students: 73%; education
specialists: N/A; men: 43%;
women: 57%; minorities: 14%;
international: 56%
Acceptance rate (master's): N/A
Acceptance rate (doctoral): N/A
Entrance test required: N/A
Avg. GRE (of all entering students with scores): quantitative: N/A; verbal: N/A
Students reporting specialty: 0%
Students specializing in: N/A

Fordham University

113 W. 60th Street
New York, NY 10023
www.fordham.edu/gse
Private
Admissions: (212) 636-6400
Email: gse_admiss@fordham.edu
Financial aid: (212) 636-6400
Application deadline: rolling
Tuition: full time: $1,240/credit
hour; part time: $1,240/credit hour
Room/board/expenses: $23,500
Full-time enrollment: 703
doctoral students: 23%; master's
students: 69%; education
specialists: 7%; men: 21%;
women: 79%; minorities: 28%;
international: 6%
Part-time enrollment: 379
doctoral students: 46%; master's
students: 49%; education
specialists: 5%; men: 25%;
women: 75%; minorities: 26%;
international: N/A
Acceptance rate (master's): 80%
Acceptance rate (doctoral): 36%
Entrance test required: GRE
Avg. GRE (of all entering students with scores): quantitative: N/A;
verbal: N/A
Research assistantships: 97
Students reporting specialty: 100%
Students specializing in:
curriculum/instr.: 1%; admin.:
24%; educational psych: 1%;
elementary: 10%; secondary:
18%; special: 9%; counseling:
28%; other: 9%

Hofstra University

Hagedorn Hall
Hempstead, NY 11549
www.hofstra.edu/graduate
Private
Admissions: (800) 463-7872
Email: gradstudent@hofstra.edu

Financial aid: (516) 463-6680
Application deadline: rolling
Tuition: full time: $1,145/credit
hour; part time: $1,145/credit hour
Room/board/expenses: $21,740
Full-time enrollment: 288
doctoral students: 19%; master's
students: 81%; education
specialists: N/A; men: 18%;
women: 82%; minorities: 21%;
international: 7%
Part-time enrollment: 329
doctoral students: 39%; master's
students: 61%; education
specialists: N/A; men: 32%;
women: 68%; minorities: 26%;
international: 0%
Acceptance rate (master's): 90%
Acceptance rate (doctoral): 70%
Entrance test required: GRE
Avg. GRE (of all entering students with scores): quantitative: N/A;
verbal: N/A
Research assistantships: 17
Students reporting specialty: 100%
Students specializing in: admin.:
10%; instructional media design:
1%; elementary: 4%; higher
education admin.: 6%; junior
high: 0%; secondary: 1%; social/
philosophical foundations: 0%;
special: 18%; other: 57%

LIU Post[1]

720 Northern Boulevard
Brookville, NY 11548
www.liu.edu/post/Academics/
schools/CEIS
Private
Admissions: N/A
Financial aid: N/A
Tuition: N/A
Room/board/expenses: N/A
Enrollment: N/A

New York University (Steinhardt)

82 Washington Square E
Fourth Floor
New York, NY 10003
www.steinhardt.nyu.edu/
Private
Admissions: (212) 998-5030
Email: steinhardt.gradadmission@
nyu.edu
Financial aid: (212) 998-4444
Application deadline: rolling
Tuition: full time: $37,848; part
time: $1,479/credit hour
Room/board/expenses: $33,208
Full-time enrollment: 2,017
doctoral students: 17%; master's
students: 83%; education
specialists: N/A; men: 25%;
women: 75%; minorities: 24%;
international: 29%
Part-time enrollment: 1,032
doctoral students: 15%; master's
students: 85%; education
specialists: N/A; men: 23%;
women: 77%; minorities: 27%;
international: 13%
Acceptance rate (master's): 49%
Acceptance rate (doctoral): 9%
Entrance test required: GRE
Avg. GRE (of all entering students with scores): quantitative: 156;
verbal: 155
Research assistantships: 30
Students reporting specialty: 100%
Students specializing in:
curriculum/instr.: 6%; admin.: 3%;
policy: 5%; evaluation/research/
statistics: 0%; instructional media
design: 3%; educational tech.: 1%;
elementary: 1%; higher education
admin.: 4%; secondary: 6%;
social/philosophical foundations:
1%; special: 2%; counseling: 6%;
other: 63%

The Sage Colleges[1]

65 1st Street
Troy, NY 12180
www.sage.edu/academics/
education/
Private
Admissions: N/A
Financial aid: N/A
Tuition: N/A
Room/board/expenses: N/A
Enrollment: N/A

St. John's University

8000 Utopia Parkway
Queens, NY 11439
www.stjohns.edu/academics/
graduate/education
Private
Admissions: (718) 990-2304
Email: graded@stjohns.edu
Financial aid: (718) 990-2000
Application deadline: 08/17
Tuition: full time: $1,145/credit
hour; part time: $1,145/credit hour
Room/board/expenses: $1,700
Full-time enrollment: 281
doctoral students: 6%; master's
students: 92%; education
specialists: 2%; men: 16%;
women: 84%; minorities: 37%;
international: 13%
Part-time enrollment: 1,084
doctoral students: 22%; master's
students: 63%; education
specialists: 15%; men: 27%;
women: 73%; minorities: 37%;
international: 2%
Acceptance rate (master's): 91%
Acceptance rate (doctoral): 80%
Entrance test required: GRE
Avg. GRE (of all entering students with scores): quantitative: N/A;
verbal: N/A
Research assistantships: 0
Students reporting specialty: 100%
Students specializing in:
curriculum/instr.: 8%; admin.:
23%; elementary: 3%; secondary:
5%; special: 18%; counseling: 3%;
other: 40%

Syracuse University

230 Huntington Hall
Syracuse, NY 13244-2340
soe.syr.edu
Private
Admissions: (315) 443-2505
Email: gradrcrt@gwmail.syr.edu
Financial aid: (315) 443-1513
Application deadline: rolling
Tuition: full time: $1,341/credit
hour; part time: $1,341/credit hour
Room/board/expenses: $17,328
Full-time enrollment: 376
doctoral students: 31%; master's
students: 69%; education
specialists: N/A; men: 28%;
women: 72%; minorities: 24%;
international: 16%
Part-time enrollment: 214
doctoral students: 44%; master's
students: 56%; education
specialists: N/A; men: 35%;
women: 65%; minorities: 15%;
international: 6%
Acceptance rate (master's): 70%
Acceptance rate (doctoral): 40%
Entrance test required: GRE
Avg. GRE (of all entering students with scores): quantitative: 148;
verbal: 152
Research assistantships: 10
Students reporting specialty: 100%
Students specializing in:
curriculum/instr.: 8%; admin.:
13%; instructional media design:
9%; educational tech.: 1%;
elementary: 2%; higher education
admin.: 15%; secondary: 9%;

social/philosophical foundations:
13%; special: 11%; counseling:
15%; other: 5%

Teachers College, Columbia University

525 W. 120th Street
New York, NY 10027
www.tc.columbia.edu/
Private
Admissions: (212) 678-3710
Email: tcinfo@tc.columbia.edu
Financial aid: (212) 678-3714
Application deadline: rolling
Tuition: full time: $1,398/credit
hour; part time: $1,398/credit hour
Room/board/expenses: $26,800
Full-time enrollment: 1,750
doctoral students: 20%; master's
students: 80%; education
specialists: N/A; men: 23%;
women: 77%; minorities: 30%;
international: 26%
Part-time enrollment: 3,161
doctoral students: 31%; master's
students: 69%; education
specialists: N/A; men: 24%;
women: 76%; minorities: 35%;
international: 15%
Acceptance rate (master's): 55%
Acceptance rate (doctoral): 18%
Entrance test required: GRE
Avg. GRE (of all entering students with scores): quantitative: 155;
verbal: 156
Research assistantships: 110
Students reporting specialty: 96%
Students specializing in:
curriculum/instr.: 11%; admin.: 6%;
policy: 2%; evaluation/research/
statistics: 1%; instructional media
design: 2%; educational psych:
6%; educational tech.: 2%;
elementary: 9%; higher education
admin.: 5%; secondary: 13%;
social/philosophical foundations:
12%; special: 3%; counseling:
20%; other: 10%

University at Albany-SUNY

1400 Washington Avenue
ED 212
Albany, NY 12222
www.albany.edu/education
Public
Admissions: (518) 442-3980
Email:
graduate@uamail.albany.edu
Financial aid: (518) 442-5757
Application deadline: N/A
In-state tuition: full time: $11,880;
part time: $432/credit hour
Out-of-state tuition: full time:
$21,700
Room/board/expenses: $13,100
Full-time enrollment: 405
doctoral students: 22%; master's
students: 72%; education
specialists: 6%; men: 21%;
women: 79%; minorities: 15%;
international: 11%
Part-time enrollment: 539
doctoral students: 37%; master's
students: 57%; education
specialists: 6%; men: 23%;
women: 77%; minorities: 10%;
international: 5%
Acceptance rate (master's): 73%
Acceptance rate (doctoral): 36%
Entrance test required: GRE
Avg. GRE (of all entering students with scores): quantitative: N/A;
verbal: N/A
Research assistantships: 79
Students reporting specialty: 100%
Students specializing in:
curriculum/instr.: 11%; admin.: 6%;
policy: 3%; evaluation/research/
statistics: 2%; instructional

media design: 3%; educational
psych: 6%; educational tech.: 6%;
elementary: 7%; higher education
admin.: 6%; secondary: 6%;
special: 10%; counseling: 5%;
other: 29%

University at Buffalo-SUNY

367 Baldy Hall
Buffalo, NY 14260-1000
www.gse.buffalo.edu
Public
Admissions: (716) 645-2110
Email: gseinfo@buffalo.edu
Financial aid: (716) 645-8232
Application deadline: rolling
In-state tuition: full time: $12,490;
part time: $432/credit hour
Out-of-state tuition: full time:
$22,310
Room/board/expenses: $17,504
Full-time enrollment: 488
doctoral students: 31%; master's
students: 69%; education
specialists: N/A; men: 25%;
women: 75%; minorities: 27%;
international: 20%
Part-time enrollment: 476
doctoral students: 41%; master's
students: 59%; education
specialists: N/A; men: 28%;
women: 72%; minorities: 10%;
international: 5%
Acceptance rate (master's): 76%
Acceptance rate (doctoral): 53%
Entrance test required: GRE
Avg. GRE (of all entering students with scores): quantitative: 149;
verbal: 152
Research assistantships: 89
Students reporting specialty: 99%
Students specializing in:
curriculum/instr.: 13%; admin.:
8%; educational psych: 2%;
educational tech.: 1%; elementary:
8%; higher education admin.:
9%; secondary: 8%; social/
philosophical foundations: 3%;
special: 1%; counseling: 9%;
other: 39%

University of Rochester (Warner)[1]

2-147 Dewey Hall
Rochester, NY 14627
www.rochester.edu/warner/
Private
Admissions: N/A
Financial aid: N/A
Tuition: N/A
Room/board/expenses: N/A
Enrollment: N/A

Yeshiva University (Azrieli)[1]

245 Lexington Avenue
New York, NY 10016
www.yu.edu/azrieli/
Private
Admissions: N/A
Financial aid: N/A
Tuition: N/A
Room/board/expenses: N/A
Enrollment: N/A

NORTH CAROLINA

Appalachian State University

College of Education Building
Boone, NC 28608-2068
www.graduate.appstate.edu
Public
Admissions: (828) 262-2130
Email: KrauseSL@appstate.edu
Financial aid: (828) 262-2190

Application deadline: rolling
In-state tuition: full time: $7,084; part time: $235/credit hour
Out-of-state tuition: full time: $19,029
Room/board/expenses: N/A
Full-time enrollment: 303
doctoral students: 4%; master's students: 96%; education specialists: 0%; men: 16%; women: 84%; minorities: 7%; international: 1%
Part-time enrollment: 591
doctoral students: 13%; master's students: 77%; education specialists: 10%; men: 21%; women: 79%; minorities: 7%; international: 0%
Acceptance rate (master's): 48%
Acceptance rate (doctoral): 60%
Entrance test required: GRE
Avg. GRE (of all entering students with scores): quantitative: 147; verbal: 152
Students reporting specialty: 100%
Students specializing in: curriculum/instr.: 3%; admin.: 26%; instructional media design: 12%; educational psych: 2%; elementary: 0%; higher education admin.: 12%; special: 1%; counseling: 13%; other: 30%

East Carolina University

E. Fifth Street
Greenville, NC 27858
www.ecu.edu/gradschool/
Public
Admissions: (252) 328-6012
Email: gradschool@ecu.edu
Financial aid: (252) 737-6610
Application deadline: N/A
In-state tuition: full time: $6,342; part time: $4,230
Out-of-state tuition: full time: $18,659
Room/board/expenses: $13,022
Full-time enrollment: 203
doctoral students: 28%; master's students: 72%; education specialists: N/A; men: 29%; women: 71%; minorities: 25%; international: 0%
Part-time enrollment: 725
doctoral students: 10%; master's students: 87%; education specialists: 3%; men: 20%; women: 80%; minorities: 21%; international: 0%
Acceptance rate (master's): 78%
Acceptance rate (doctoral): 89%
Entrance test required: GRE
Avg. GRE (of all entering students with scores): quantitative: 149; verbal: 150
Research assistantships: 40
Students reporting specialty: 62%
Students specializing in: admin.: 49%; instructional media design: 18%; elementary: 4%; junior high: 2%; special: 4%; technical (vocational): 1%; other: 21%

Fayetteville State University[1]

1200 Murchison Road
Fayetteville, NC 28301
www.uncfsu.edu/
Public
Admissions: N/A
Financial aid: N/A
Tuition: N/A
Room/board/expenses: N/A
Enrollment: N/A

Gardner-Webb University

110 S. Main Street
Boiling Springs, NC 28017
www.gardner-webb.edu
Private
Admissions: (800) 492-4723
Email: gradschool@gardner-webb.edu
Financial aid: (704) 406-3271
Application deadline: rolling
Tuition: full time: $391/credit hour; part time: $391/credit hour
Room/board/expenses: $11,793
Full-time enrollment: N/A
doctoral students: N/A; master's students: N/A; education specialists: N/A; men: N/A; women: N/A; minorities: N/A; international: N/A
Part-time enrollment: 845
doctoral students: 37%; master's students: 58%; education specialists: 4%; men: 26%; women: 74%; minorities: 33%; international: 0%
Acceptance rate (master's): 61%
Acceptance rate (doctoral): 40%
Entrance test required: GRE
Avg. GRE (of all entering students with scores): quantitative: N/A; verbal: N/A
Students reporting specialty: 100%
Students specializing in: curriculum/instr.: 27%; admin.: 65%; elementary: 2%; junior high: 2%; counseling: 3%; other: 2%

North Carolina State University-Raleigh

Campus Box 7801
Raleigh, NC 27695-7801
ced.ncsu.edu/
Public
Admissions: (919) 515-2872
Email: graduate_admissions@ncsu.edu
Financial aid: (919) 515-3325
Application deadline: rolling
In-state tuition: full time: $11,039; part time: $6,363
Out-of-state tuition: full time: $25,238
Room/board/expenses: $17,664
Full-time enrollment: 362
doctoral students: 31%; master's students: 69%; education specialists: N/A; men: 23%; women: 77%; minorities: 27%; international: 7%
Part-time enrollment: 648
doctoral students: 52%; master's students: 48%; education specialists: N/A; men: 28%; women: 72%; minorities: 25%; international: 1%
Acceptance rate (master's): 44%
Acceptance rate (doctoral): 32%
Entrance test required: GRE
Avg. GRE (of all entering students with scores): quantitative: 151; verbal: 154
Research assistantships: 36
Students reporting specialty: 70%
Students specializing in: curriculum/instr.: 13%; admin.: 28%; policy: 10%; evaluation/research/statistics: 11%; instructional media design: 5%; educational psych: 3%; elementary: 2%; higher education admin.: 6%; junior high: 1%; secondary: 7%; special: 1%; counseling: 11%; technical (vocational): 2%

University of North Carolina-Chapel Hill

CB#3500
101 Peabody Hall
Chapel Hill, NC 27599-3500
soe.unc.edu
Public
Admissions: (919) 966-1346
Email: ed@unc.edu
Financial aid: (919) 966-1346
Application deadline: rolling
In-state tuition: full time: $10,594; part time: $8,421
Out-of-state tuition: full time: $27,805
Room/board/expenses: $24,920
Full-time enrollment: 311
doctoral students: 62%; master's students: 38%; education specialists: N/A; men: 29%; women: 71%; minorities: 33%; international: 10%
Part-time enrollment: 106
doctoral students: 40%; master's students: 60%; education specialists: N/A; men: 20%; women: 80%; minorities: 31%; international: 5%
Acceptance rate (master's): 73%
Acceptance rate (doctoral): 49%
Entrance test required: GRE
Avg. GRE (of all entering students with scores): quantitative: N/A; verbal: N/A
Students reporting specialty: 100%
Students specializing in: curriculum/instr.: 27%; admin.: 65%; elementary: 2%; junior high: 2%; secondary: 4%; social/philosophical foundations: 11%; special: 3%; counseling: 6%; other: 19%

University of North Carolina-Charlotte

9201 University City Boulevard
Charlotte, NC 28223
education.uncc.edu/
Public
Admissions: (704) 687-3366
Email: gradadm@uncc.edu
Financial aid: (704) 687-5547
Application deadline: 05/15
In-state tuition: full time: $6,763; part time: $5,761
Out-of-state tuition: full time: $19,050
Room/board/expenses: $14,033
Full-time enrollment: 185
doctoral students: 37%; master's students: 63%; education specialists: N/A; men: 18%; women: 82%; minorities: 31%; international: 3%
Part-time enrollment: 527
doctoral students: 24%; master's students: 76%; education specialists: N/A; men: 22%; women: 78%; minorities: 27%; international: 1%
Acceptance rate (master's): 76%
Acceptance rate (doctoral): 54%
Entrance test required: GRE
Avg. GRE (of all entering students with scores): quantitative: 145; verbal: 149
Research assistantships: 30
Students reporting specialty: 100%
Students specializing in: curriculum/instr.: 4%; admin.: 11%; instructional media design: 2%; elementary: 1%; special: 8%; counseling: 15%; other: 61%

University of North Carolina-Greensboro

School of Education Building
P.O. Box 26170
Greensboro, NC 27402-6170
www.uncg.edu/grs
Public
Admissions: (336) 334-5596
Email: inquiries@uncg.edu
Financial aid: (336) 334-5702
Application deadline: rolling
In-state tuition: full time: $7,151; part time: $4,831
Out-of-state tuition: full time: $20,600
Room/board/expenses: $10,576
Full-time enrollment: 636
doctoral students: 27%; master's students: 64%; education specialists: 9%; men: 23%; women: 77%; minorities: 27%; international: 4%
Part-time enrollment: 190
doctoral students: 47%; master's students: 51%; education specialists: 2%; men: 25%; women: 75%; minorities: 26%; international: 2%
Acceptance rate (master's): 59%
Acceptance rate (doctoral): 51%
Entrance test required: GRE
Avg. GRE (of all entering students with scores): quantitative: 148; verbal: 153
Research assistantships: 12
Students reporting specialty: 94%
Students specializing in: curriculum/instr.: 20%; admin.: 15%; evaluation/research/statistics: 6%; educational tech.: 0%; elementary: 4%; higher education admin.: 6%; junior high: 2%; secondary: 2%; special: 8%; counseling: 12%; other: 33%

University of North Carolina-Wilmington[1]

601 S. College Road
Wilmington, NC 28403
uncw.edu/
Public
Admissions: N/A
Financial aid: N/A
Tuition: N/A
Room/board/expenses: N/A
Enrollment: N/A

Western Carolina University

Killian Building, Room 204
Cullowhee, NC 28723
www.wcu.edu/
Public
Admissions: (828) 227-7398
Email: grad@wcu.edu
Financial aid: (828) 227-7290
Application deadline: rolling
In-state tuition: full time: $12,578; part time: $719/credit hour
Out-of-state tuition: full time: $22,985
Room/board/expenses: $14,066
Full-time enrollment: 250
doctoral students: 2%; master's students: 92%; education specialists: 6%; men: 23%; women: 77%; minorities: 12%; international: N/A
Part-time enrollment: 78
doctoral students: 40%; master's students: 56%; education specialists: 4%; men: 27%; women: 73%; minorities: 8%; international: N/A
Acceptance rate (master's): 63%
Acceptance rate (doctoral): 50%

Entrance test required: GRE
Avg. GRE (of all entering students with scores): quantitative: 145; verbal: 149
Research assistantships: 17
Students reporting specialty: 100%
Students specializing in: admin.: 29%; educational psych: 4%; junior high: 1%; special: 15%; counseling: 6%; other: 44%

Wingate University[1]

220 North Camden Road
Wingate, NC 28174
www.wingate.edu/matthews/grad-ed
Private
Admissions: N/A
Financial aid: N/A
Tuition: N/A
Room/board/expenses: N/A
Enrollment: N/A

NORTH DAKOTA

North Dakota State University

Box 6050
Department 2600
Fargo, ND 58108-6050
www.ndsu.edu/gradschool/
Public
Admissions: (702) 231-7033
Email: ndsu.grad.school@ndsu.edu
Financial aid: (701) 231-6200
Application deadline: rolling
In-state tuition: full time: $345/credit hour; part time: $345/credit hour
Out-of-state tuition: full time: $345/credit hour
Room/board/expenses: N/A
Full-time enrollment: 44
doctoral students: 30%; master's students: 70%; education specialists: N/A; men: 23%; women: 77%; minorities: 18%; international: 7%
Part-time enrollment: 207
doctoral students: 42%; master's students: 56%; education specialists: 2%; men: 27%; women: 73%; minorities: 7%; international: 3%
Acceptance rate (master's): 72%
Acceptance rate (doctoral): 59%
Entrance test required: GRE
Avg. GRE (of all entering students with scores): quantitative: N/A; verbal: N/A
Research assistantships: 5
Students reporting specialty: 100%
Students specializing in: curriculum/instr.: 24%; admin.: 11%; evaluation/research/statistics: 15%; higher education admin.: 16%; secondary: 8%; counseling: 8%; other: 18%

University of North Dakota[1]

Box 7189
Grand Forks, ND 58202-7189
und.edu/
Public
Admissions: N/A
Financial aid: N/A
Tuition: N/A
Room/board/expenses: N/A
Enrollment: N/A

OHIO

Ashland University (Schar)[1]
401 College Avenue
Ashland, OH 44805
www.ashland.edu
Private
Admissions: N/A
Financial aid: N/A
Tuition: N/A
Room/board/expenses: N/A
Enrollment: N/A

Bowling Green State University
444 Education Building
Bowling Green, OH 43403
www.bgsu.edu/colleges/edhd/
Public
Admissions: (419) 372-BGSU
Email: prospct@bgsu.edu
Financial aid: (419) 372-2651
Application deadline: rolling
In-state tuition: full time: $12,016; part time: $424/credit hour
Out-of-state tuition: full time: $19,318
Room/board/expenses: $14,711
Full-time enrollment: 338
doctoral students: 12%; master's students: 88%; education specialists: 0%; men: 30%; women: 70%; minorities: 13%; international: 12%
Part-time enrollment: 373
doctoral students: 16%; master's students: 78%; education specialists: 6%; men: 24%; women: 76%; minorities: 9%; international: 2%
Acceptance rate (master's): 45%
Acceptance rate (doctoral): 46%
Entrance test required: GRE
Avg. GRE (of all entering students with scores): quantitative: N/A; verbal: N/A
Research assistantships: 52
Students reporting specialty: 100%
Students specializing in: curriculum/instr.: 9%; admin.: 14%; educational tech.: 8%; higher education admin.: 6%; special: 13%; counseling: 20%; other: 33%

Cleveland State University
2121 Euclid Avenue
JH 210
Cleveland, OH 44115
www.csuohio.edu/cehs/
Public
Admissions: (216) 687-5599
Email: graduate.admissions@csuohio.edu
Financial aid: (216) 687-5411
Application deadline: 05/15
In-state tuition: full time: $13,866; part time: $531/credit hour
Out-of-state tuition: full time: $26,021
Room/board/expenses: $14,358
Full-time enrollment: 1,124
doctoral students: 10%; master's students: 89%; education specialists: 1%; men: 23%; women: 77%; minorities: 28%; international: 8%
Part-time enrollment: N/A
doctoral students: N/A; master's students: N/A; education specialists: N/A; men: N/A; women: N/A; minorities: N/A; international: N/A
Acceptance rate (master's): 82%
Acceptance rate (doctoral): 41%
Entrance test required: GRE

Avg. GRE (of all entering students with scores): quantitative: 146; verbal: 152
Research assistantships: 40
Students reporting specialty: 100%
Students specializing in: N/A

Kent State University
PO Box 5190
Kent, OH 44242-0001
www.ehhs.kent.edu
Public
Admissions: (330) 672-2576
Email: ogs@kent.edu
Financial aid: (330) 672-2972
Application deadline: rolling
In-state tuition: full time: $8,730; part time: $485/credit hour
Out-of-state tuition: full time: $14,886
Room/board/expenses: $17,116
Full-time enrollment: 887
doctoral students: 38%; master's students: 59%; education specialists: 3%; men: 27%; women: 73%; minorities: 13%; international: 9%
Part-time enrollment: 522
doctoral students: 23%; master's students: 75%; education specialists: 2%; men: 23%; women: 77%; minorities: 11%; international: 5%
Acceptance rate (master's): 47%
Acceptance rate (doctoral): 42%
Entrance test required: GRE
Avg. GRE (of all entering students with scores): quantitative: 147; verbal: 151
Research assistantships: 99
Students reporting specialty: 100%
Students specializing in: curriculum/instr.: 7%; admin.: 2%; evaluation/research/statistics: 2%; instructional media design: 4%; educational psych: 3%; higher education admin.: 9%; junior high: 1%; secondary: 1%; social/philosophical foundations: 3%; special: 8%; counseling: 15%; technical (vocational): 2%; other: 42%

Miami University
207 McGuffey Hall
Oxford, OH 45056
www.miami.muohio.edu/graduate-studies/index.html
Public
Admissions: (513) 529-3734
Email: gradschool@muohio.edu
Financial aid: (513) 529-8734
Application deadline: rolling
In-state tuition: full time: $13,533; part time: $537/credit hour
Out-of-state tuition: full time: $29,640
Room/board/expenses: $16,366
Full-time enrollment: 211
doctoral students: 14%; master's students: 83%; education specialists: 3%; men: 21%; women: 79%; minorities: 22%; international: 8%
Part-time enrollment: 434
doctoral students: 10%; master's students: 89%; education specialists: 1%; men: 23%; women: 77%; minorities: 13%; international: 1%
Acceptance rate (master's): 97%
Acceptance rate (doctoral): 68%
Entrance test required: GRE
Avg. GRE (of all entering students with scores): quantitative: N/A; verbal: N/A
Research assistantships: 19
Students reporting specialty: 37%
Students specializing in: N/A

Ohio State University
1945 N. High Street
Columbus, OH 43210-1172
ehe.osu.edu/
Public
Admissions: (614) 292-9444
Email: domestic.grad@osu.edu
Financial aid: (614) 292-0300
Application deadline: rolling
In-state tuition: full time: $12,803; part time: $723/credit hour
Out-of-state tuition: full time: $31,347
Room/board/expenses: $18,618
Full-time enrollment: 690
doctoral students: 51%; master's students: 47%; education specialists: 2%; men: 26%; women: 74%; minorities: 18%; international: 23%
Part-time enrollment: 218
doctoral students: 28%; master's students: 68%; education specialists: 4%; men: 29%; women: 71%; minorities: 14%; international: 2%
Acceptance rate (master's): 49%
Acceptance rate (doctoral): 44%
Entrance test required: GRE
Avg. GRE (of all entering students with scores): quantitative: 152; verbal: 155
Research assistantships: 65
Students reporting specialty: 100%
Students specializing in: curriculum/instr.: 12%; admin.: 12%; policy: 1%; evaluation/research/statistics: 1%; educational psych: 2%; educational tech.: 3%; elementary: 11%; higher education admin.: 9%; junior high: 3%; secondary: 12%; social/philosophical foundations: 5%; special: 8%; counseling: 13%; technical (vocational): 8%; other: 14%

Ohio University
133 McCracken Hall
Athens, OH 45701-2979
www.ohio.edu/education/
Public
Admissions: (740) 593-2800
Email: graduate@ohio.edu
Financial aid: (740) 593-4141
Application deadline: rolling
In-state tuition: full time: $10,536; part time: $583/credit hour
Out-of-state tuition: full time: $19,500
Room/board/expenses: $15,310
Full-time enrollment: 349
doctoral students: 20%; master's students: 80%; education specialists: N/A; men: 35%; women: 65%; minorities: 10%; international: 19%
Part-time enrollment: 497
doctoral students: 25%; master's students: 75%; education specialists: N/A; men: 58%; women: 42%; minorities: 21%; international: 5%
Acceptance rate (master's): 64%
Acceptance rate (doctoral): 42%
Entrance test required: GRE
Avg. GRE (of all entering students with scores): quantitative: 144; verbal: 147
Research assistantships: 27
Students reporting specialty: 100%
Students specializing in: curriculum/instr.: 17%; admin.: 12%; evaluation/research/statistics: 3%; educational tech.: 8%; higher education admin.: 13%; secondary: 2%; counseling: 11%; other: 34%

University of Akron
302 Buchtel Common
Akron, OH 44325-4201
www.uakron.edu/admissions/graduate
Public
Admissions: (330) 972-7663
Email: gradschool@uakron.edu
Financial aid: (330) 972-5858
Application deadline: rolling
In-state tuition: full time: $414/credit hour; part time: $413/credit hour
Out-of-state tuition: full time: $707/credit hour
Room/board/expenses: $14,068
Full-time enrollment: 166
doctoral students: 7%; master's students: 93%; education specialists: N/A; men: 39%; women: 61%; minorities: 11%; international: 19%
Part-time enrollment: 326
doctoral students: 15%; master's students: 85%; education specialists: N/A; men: 26%; women: 74%; minorities: 16%; international: 3%
Acceptance rate (master's): 87%
Acceptance rate (doctoral): 27%
Entrance test required: GRE
Avg. GRE (of all entering students with scores): quantitative: N/A; verbal: N/A
Research assistantships: 12
Students reporting specialty: 100%
Students specializing in: admin.: 9%; evaluation/research/statistics: 4%; instructional media design: 12%; elementary: 4%; higher education admin.: 10%; junior high: 1%; secondary: 13%; social/philosophical foundations: 1%; special: 15%; technical (vocational): 4%; other: 27%

University of Cincinnati
PO Box 210002
Cincinnati, OH 45221-0002
www.cech.uc.edu
Public
Admissions: (513) 556-1427
Email: kendalce@ucmail.uc.edu
Financial aid: (513) 556-4170
Application deadline: rolling
In-state tuition: full time: $14,468; part time: $724/credit hour
Out-of-state tuition: full time: $26,210
Room/board/expenses: $16,238
Full-time enrollment: 294
doctoral students: 35%; master's students: 59%; education specialists: 5%; men: 24%; women: 76%; minorities: 8%; international: 15%
Part-time enrollment: 822
doctoral students: 11%; master's students: 88%; education specialists: 1%; men: 18%; women: 82%; minorities: 3%; international: 19%
Acceptance rate (master's): 56%
Acceptance rate (doctoral): 27%
Entrance test required: GRE
Avg. GRE (of all entering students with scores): quantitative: 150; verbal: 156
Research assistantships: 47
Students reporting specialty: 96%
Students specializing in: curriculum/instr.: 19%; admin.: 5%; evaluation/research/statistics: 0%; junior high: 0%; secondary: 0%; social/philosophical foundations: 6%; special: 6%; counseling: 1%; other: 71%

University of Dayton
300 College Park
Fitz Hall
Dayton, OH 45469-2969
www.udayton.edu/education/
Private
Admissions: (937) 229-4411
Email: gradadmission@udayton.edu
Financial aid: (937) 229-2751
Application deadline: rolling
Tuition: full time: $585/credit hour; part time: $585/credit hour
Room/board/expenses: N/A
Full-time enrollment: 594
doctoral students: 28%; master's students: 70%; education specialists: 2%; men: 28%; women: 72%; minorities: 12%; international: 12%
Part-time enrollment: 320
doctoral students: 0%; master's students: 95%; education specialists: 5%; men: 26%; women: 74%; minorities: 11%; international: 6%
Acceptance rate (master's): 75%
Acceptance rate (doctoral): 46%
Entrance test required: GRE
Avg. GRE (of all entering students with scores): quantitative: 148; verbal: 151
Research assistantships: 21
Students reporting specialty: 100%
Students specializing in: admin.: 37%; instructional media design: 1%; higher education admin.: 2%; junior high: 1%; secondary: 3%; special: 5%; counseling: 10%; other: 43%

University of Toledo[1]
2801 W. Bancroft Street
Toledo, OH 43606
www.utoledo.edu/education/index.html
Public
Admissions: N/A
Financial aid: N/A
Tuition: N/A
Room/board/expenses: N/A
Enrollment: N/A

Youngstown State University[1]
1 University Plaza
Youngstown, OH 44555
bcoe.ysu.edu/bcoe
Public
Admissions: N/A
Financial aid: N/A
Tuition: N/A
Room/board/expenses: N/A
Enrollment: N/A

OKLAHOMA

Oklahoma State University
325 Willard Hall
Stillwater, OK 74078-4033
www.okstate.edu/education/
Public
Admissions: (405) 744-6368
Email: grad-i@okstate.edu
Financial aid: (405) 744-6604
Application deadline: rolling
In-state tuition: full time: $187/credit hour; part time: $187/credit hour
Out-of-state tuition: full time: $795/credit hour
Room/board/expenses: $7,150
Full-time enrollment: 375
doctoral students: 41%; master's students: 56%; education specialists: 3%; men: 35%; women: 65%; minorities: 23%; international: 9%

Part-time enrollment: 504
doctoral students: 53%; master's students: 47%; education specialists: 0%; men: 33%; women: 67%; minorities: 18%; international: 2%
Acceptance rate (master's): 55%
Acceptance rate (doctoral): 30%
Entrance test required: GRE
Avg. GRE (of all entering students with scores): quantitative: 145; verbal: 150
Research assistantships: 15
Students reporting specialty: 100%
Students specializing in: curriculum/instr.: 6%; admin.: 9%; policy: 5%; evaluation/research/statistics: 1%; instructional media design: 1%; educational psych: 8%; educational tech.: 2%; elementary: 1%; higher education admin.: 8%; junior high: 1%; secondary: 2%; social/philosophical foundations: 2%; special: 4%; counseling: 11%; technical (vocational): 7%; other: 31%

Oral Roberts University
7777 S. Lewis Avenue
Tulsa, OK 74171
www.oru.edu/
Private
Admissions: (918) 495-6553
Email: gradedu@oru.edu
Financial aid: (918) 495-6602
Application deadline: rolling
Tuition: full time: N/A; part time: N/A
Room/board/expenses: N/A
Full-time enrollment: N/A
doctoral students: N/A; master's students: N/A; education specialists: N/A; men: N/A; women: N/A; minorities: N/A; international: N/A
Part-time enrollment: N/A
doctoral students: N/A; master's students: N/A; education specialists: N/A; men: N/A; women: N/A; minorities: N/A; international: N/A
Acceptance rate (master's): 100%
Acceptance rate (doctoral): 89%
Entrance test required: GRE
Avg. GRE (of all entering students with scores): quantitative: N/A; verbal: N/A
Students reporting specialty: 0%
Students specializing in: N/A

University of Oklahoma (Rainbolt)
820 Van Vleet Oval, No. 100
Norman, OK 73019-2041
www.ou.edu/education
Public
Admissions: (405) 325-2252
Email: admrec@ou.edu
Financial aid: (405) 325-4521
Application deadline: rolling
In-state tuition: full time: $8,183; part time: $183/credit hour
Out-of-state tuition: full time: $20,759
Room/board/expenses: $17,220
Full-time enrollment: 536
doctoral students: 27%; master's students: 73%; education specialists: N/A; men: 33%; women: 67%; minorities: 28%; international: 5%
Part-time enrollment: 234
doctoral students: 59%; master's students: 41%; education specialists: N/A; men: 25%; women: 75%; minorities: 21%; international: 3%
Acceptance rate (master's): 84%
Acceptance rate (doctoral): 46%
Entrance test required: GRE
Avg. GRE (of all entering students with scores): quantitative: 148; verbal: 153
Research assistantships: 194
Students reporting specialty: 100%
Students specializing in: curriculum/instr.: 23%; admin.: 24%; evaluation/research/statistics: 6%; higher education admin.: 27%; social/philosophical foundations: 4%; special: 7%; counseling: 8%; other: 3%

OREGON

George Fox University[1]
414 N. Meridian Street
Newberg, OR 97132
www.georgefox.edu
Private
Admissions: N/A
Financial aid: N/A
Tuition: N/A
Room/board/expenses: N/A
Enrollment: N/A

Lewis & Clark College
0615 S.W. Palatine Hill Road
Portland, OR 97219-7899
graduate.lclark.edu
Private
Admissions: (503) 768-6200
Email: gseadmit@lclark.edu
Financial aid: (503) 768-7090
Application deadline: rolling
Tuition: full time: N/A; part time: N/A
Room/board/expenses: $7,275
Full-time enrollment: 161
doctoral students: 1%; master's students: 80%; education specialists: 20%; men: 34%; women: 66%; minorities: 14%; international: 1%
Part-time enrollment: 98
doctoral students: 35%; master's students: 41%; education specialists: 24%; men: 24%; women: 76%; minorities: 16%; international: N/A
Acceptance rate (master's): 88%
Acceptance rate (doctoral): 92%
Entrance test required: GRE
Avg. GRE (of all entering students with scores): quantitative: N/A; verbal: N/A
Research assistantships: 0
Students reporting specialty: 100%
Students specializing in: curriculum/instr.: 5%; admin.: 40%; educational psych: 12%; elementary: 6%; higher education admin.: 3%; secondary: 13%; special: 3%; counseling: 14%; other: 4%

Oregon State University
104 Furman Hall
Corvallis, OR 97331-3502
oregonstate.edu/education/
Public
Admissions: (541) 737-4411
Email: osuadmit@oregonstate.edu
Financial aid: (541) 737-2241
Application deadline: 06/01
In-state tuition: full time: $13,379; part time: $441/credit hour
Out-of-state tuition: full time: $21,425
Room/board/expenses: $15,693
Full-time enrollment: 179
doctoral students: 16%; master's students: 84%; education specialists: N/A; men: 29%; women: 71%; minorities: 16%; international: 1%
Part-time enrollment: 265
doctoral students: 49%; master's students: 51%; education specialists: N/A; men: 28%; women: 72%; minorities: 22%; international: N/A
Acceptance rate (master's): 48%
Acceptance rate (doctoral): 38%
Entrance test required: N/A
Avg. GRE (of all entering students with scores): quantitative: N/A; verbal: N/A
Research assistantships: 10
Students reporting specialty: 100%
Students specializing in: elementary: 6%; higher education admin.: 8%; secondary: 28%; counseling: 32%; other: 25%

Portland State University
PO Box 751
Portland, OR 97207-0751
www.ed.pdx.edu/admissions.shtml
Public
Admissions: (503) 725-3511
Email: adm@pdx.edu
Financial aid: (503) 725-3461
Application deadline: rolling
In-state tuition: full time: $10,594; part time: $345/credit hour
Out-of-state tuition: full time: $15,832
Room/board/expenses: $15,507
Full-time enrollment: 475
doctoral students: 7%; master's students: 93%; education specialists: N/A; men: 28%; women: 72%; minorities: 23%; international: 3%
Part-time enrollment: 511
doctoral students: 12%; master's students: 88%; education specialists: N/A; men: 25%; women: 75%; minorities: 22%; international: 3%
Acceptance rate (master's): 63%
Acceptance rate (doctoral): 31%
Entrance test required: N/A
Avg. GRE (of all entering students with scores): quantitative: N/A; verbal: N/A
Research assistantships: 4
Students reporting specialty: 100%
Students specializing in: curriculum/instr.: 21%; admin.: 23%; instructional media design: 1%; elementary: 10%; higher education admin.: 2%; junior high: 11%; secondary: 0%; social/philosophical foundations: 5%; special: 14%; counseling: 14%; other: 1%

University of Oregon
1215 University of Oregon
Eugene, OR 97403-1215
education.uoregon.edu/
Public
Admissions: (541) 346-3201
Email: uoadmit@uoregon.edu
Financial aid: (541) 346-3221
Application deadline: rolling
In-state tuition: full time: $17,760; part time: $539/credit hour
Out-of-state tuition: full time: $24,480
Room/board/expenses: $14,322
Full-time enrollment: 383
doctoral students: 34%; master's students: 66%; education specialists: N/A; men: 22%; women: 78%; minorities: 21%; international: 4%
Part-time enrollment: 133
doctoral students: 34%; master's students: 66%; education specialists: N/A; men: 33%; women: 67%; minorities: 17%; international: 21%
Acceptance rate (master's): 50%
Acceptance rate (doctoral): 11%
Entrance test required: GRE
Avg. GRE (of all entering students with scores): quantitative: 149; verbal: 156
Students reporting specialty: 100%
Students specializing in: admin.: 17%; policy: 7%; evaluation/research/statistics: 5%; elementary: 12%; secondary: 9%; social/philosophical foundations: 5%; special: 18%; other: 27%

PENNSYLVANIA

Arcadia University
450 S. Easton Road
Glenside, PA 19038-3295
www.arcadia.edu/
Private
Admissions: (877) 272-2342
Email: admiss@arcadia.edu
Financial aid: (215) 572-2980
Application deadline: rolling
Tuition: full time: $720/credit hour; part time: $720/credit hour
Room/board/expenses: N/A
Full-time enrollment: 31
doctoral students: 3%; master's students: 87%; education specialists: 10%; men: 26%; women: 74%; minorities: 23%; international: 6%
Part-time enrollment: 382
doctoral students: 13%; master's students: 76%; education specialists: 11%; men: 19%; women: 81%; minorities: 19%; international: 1%
Acceptance rate (master's): 60%
Acceptance rate (doctoral): 76%
Entrance test required: N/A
Avg. GRE (of all entering students with scores): quantitative: N/A; verbal: N/A
Students reporting specialty: 78%
Students specializing in: instructional media design: 4%; educational psych: 18%; elementary: 3%; junior high: 4%; secondary: 24%; special: 33%; other: 79%

Drexel University
3141 Chestnut Street
Philadelphia, PA 19104
goodwin.drexel.edu/soe
Private
Admissions: (215) 895-2400
Email: admissions@drexel.edu
Financial aid: (215) 895-1627
Application deadline: rolling
Tuition: full time: $1,123/credit hour; part time: $1,123/credit hour
Room/board/expenses: N/A
Full-time enrollment: 42
doctoral students: 12%; master's students: 64%; education specialists: 24%; men: 21%; women: 79%; minorities: 21%; international: 2%
Part-time enrollment: 849
doctoral students: 31%; master's students: 64%; education specialists: 5%; men: 26%; women: 74%; minorities: 27%; international: 2%
Acceptance rate (master's): 86%
Acceptance rate (doctoral): 57%
Entrance test required: GRE
Avg. GRE (of all entering students with scores): quantitative: N/A; verbal: N/A
Research assistantships: 6
Students reporting specialty: 97%
Students specializing in: curriculum/instr.: 11%; admin.: 12%; policy: 4%; evaluation/research/statistics: 27%; instructional media design: 5%; educational tech.: 5%; elementary: 15%; higher education admin.: 22%; secondary: 14%; social/philosophical foundations: 2%; special: 9%; counseling: 9%; other: 2%

Duquesne University
600 Forbes Avenue
Pittsburgh, PA 15282
www.duq.edu/education/
Private
Admissions: (412) 396-6091
Email: black@duq.edu
Financial aid: (412) 396-6607
Application deadline: rolling
Tuition: full time: $1,049/credit hour; part time: $1,049/credit hour
Room/board/expenses: $13,634
Full-time enrollment: 513
doctoral students: 44%; master's students: 56%; education specialists: N/A; men: 25%; women: 75%; minorities: 17%; international: 7%
Part-time enrollment: 76
doctoral students: 5%; master's students: 95%; education specialists: N/A; men: 18%; women: 82%; minorities: 14%; international: 1%
Acceptance rate (master's): 51%
Acceptance rate (doctoral): 42%
Entrance test required: GRE
Avg. GRE (of all entering students with scores): quantitative: 147; verbal: 150
Students reporting specialty: 100%
Students specializing in: admin.: 8%; evaluation/research/statistics: 2%; educational psych: 16%; educational tech.: 10%; elementary: 7%; junior high: 1%; secondary: 6%; special: 2%; counseling: 32%; other: 17%

East Stroudsburg University of Pennsylvania
200 Prospect Street
East Stroudsburg, PA 18301-2999
www.esu.edu
Public
Admissions: (570) 422-3536
Email: grad@po-box.esu.edu
Financial aid: N/A
Application deadline: 08/19
In-state tuition: full time: $454/credit hour; part time: $454/credit hour
Out-of-state tuition: full time: $681/credit hour
Room/board/expenses: N/A
Full-time enrollment: 28
doctoral students: N/A; master's students: 100%; education specialists: 0%; men: 39%; women: 61%; minorities: 18%; international: 14%
Part-time enrollment: 129
doctoral students: N/A; master's students: 95%; education specialists: 5%; men: 24%; women: 76%; minorities: 9%; international: 1%
Acceptance rate (master's): 75%
Acceptance rate (doctoral): N/A
Entrance test required: GRE
Avg. GRE (of all entering students with scores): quantitative: N/A; verbal: N/A
Students reporting specialty: 79%
Students specializing in: admin.: 4%; educational tech.: 22%; elementary: 5%; secondary: 37%; special: 32%

More @ www.usnews.com/grad

Immaculata University[1]

1145 King Road
Immaculata, PA 19345
www.immaculata.edu
Private
Admissions: N/A
Financial aid: N/A
Tuition: N/A
Room/board/expenses: N/A
Enrollment: N/A

Indiana University of Pennsylvania

104 Stouffer Hall
Indiana, PA 15705-1083
www.iup.edu/graduate
Public
Admissions: (724) 357-4511
Email: graduate-admissions@
iup.edu
Financial aid: (724) 357-2218
Application deadline: rolling
In-state tuition: full time: $10,648;
part time: $454/credit hour
Out-of-state tuition: full time:
$14,734
Room/board/expenses: $14,152
Full-time enrollment: 292
doctoral students: 7%; master's
students: 93%; education
specialists: 0%; men: 27%;
women: 73%; minorities: 10%;
international: 4%
Part-time enrollment: 414
doctoral students: 54%; master's
students: 44%; education
specialists: 2%; men: 29%;
women: 71%; minorities: 11%;
international: 3%
Acceptance rate (master's): 42%
Acceptance rate (doctoral): 66%
Entrance test required: GRE
**Avg. GRE (of all entering students
with scores):** quantitative: 147;
verbal: 149
Students reporting specialty: 100%
Students specializing in: admin.:
15%; educational psych: 3%;
elementary: 14%; special: 4%;
counseling: 16%; other: 48%

Lehigh University

111 Research Drive
Bethlehem, PA 18015
coe.lehigh.edu/
Private
Admissions: (610) 758-3231
Email: ineduc@lehigh.edu
Financial aid: (610) 758-3181
Application deadline: rolling
Tuition: full time: $565/credit hour;
part time: $565/credit hour
Room/board/expenses: $19,820
Full-time enrollment: 170
doctoral students: 39%; master's
students: 54%; education
specialists: 7%; men: 18%;
women: 82%; minorities: 15%;
international: 16%
Part-time enrollment: 271
doctoral students: 29%; master's
students: 70%; education
specialists: 0%; men: 38%;
women: 62%; minorities: 10%;
international: 6%
Acceptance rate (master's): 68%
Acceptance rate (doctoral): 23%
Entrance test required: GRE
**Avg. GRE (of all entering students
with scores):** quantitative: 151;
verbal: 155
Research assistantships: 30
Students reporting specialty: 100%
Students specializing in: admin.:
25%; instructional media design:
8%; educational psych: 15%;
elementary: 3%; secondary: 5%;
special: 10%; counseling: 14%;
other: 19%

Neumann University[1]

1 Neumann Drive
Aston, PA 19014
www.neumann.edu
Private
Admissions: N/A
Financial aid: N/A
Tuition: N/A
Room/board/expenses: N/A
Enrollment: N/A

Pennsylvania State University-Harrisburg

777 W. Harrisburg Pike
Middletown, PA 17057
hbg.psu.edu/admissions/
index.php
Public
Admissions: (717) 948-6250
Email: hbgadmit@psu.edu
Financial aid: (717) 948-6307
Application deadline: rolling
In-state tuition: full time: $19,746;
part time: $784/credit hour
Out-of-state tuition: full time:
$25,862
Room/board/expenses: $18,662
Full-time enrollment: 13
doctoral students: 23%; master's
students: 77%; education
specialists: 0%; men: 15%;
women: 85%; minorities: 38%;
international: 8%
Part-time enrollment: 235
doctoral students: 12%; master's
students: 66%; education
specialists: 23%; men: 15%;
women: 85%; minorities: 9%;
international: N/A
Acceptance rate (master's): 97%
Acceptance rate (doctoral): 100%
Entrance test required: GRE
**Avg. GRE (of all entering students
with scores):** quantitative: N/A;
verbal: N/A
Research assistantships: 2
Students reporting specialty: 78%
Students specializing in:
curriculum/instr.: 44%;
secondary: 4%; other: 52%

Pennsylvania State University-University Park

274 Chambers Building
University Park, PA 16802-3206
www.ed.psu.edu
Public
Admissions: (814) 865-1795
Email: gadm@psu.edu
Financial aid: (814) 863-1489
Application deadline: rolling
In-state tuition: full time: $19,746;
part time: $784/credit hour
Out-of-state tuition: full time:
$33,110
Room/board/expenses: $17,952
Full-time enrollment: 540
doctoral students: 71%; master's
students: 29%; education
specialists: N/A; men: 29%;
women: 71%; minorities: 17%;
international: 29%
Part-time enrollment: 460
doctoral students: 38%; master's
students: 62%; education
specialists: N/A; men: 31%;
women: 69%; minorities: 14%;
international: 5%
Acceptance rate (master's): 51%
Acceptance rate (doctoral): 39%
Entrance test required: GRE
**Avg. GRE (of all entering students
with scores):** quantitative: 151;
verbal: 153
Research assistantships: 85
Students reporting specialty: 100%

Students specializing in:
curriculum/instr.: 18%; admin.:
24%; policy: 5%; evaluation/
research/statistics: 1%;
instructional media design:
6%; educational psych:
3%; educational tech.: 9%;
elementary: 2%; higher education
admin.: 11%; secondary: 0%;
social/philosophical foundations:
4%; special: 7%; counseling:
14%; technical (vocational): 3%;
other: 24%

Robert Morris University

6001 University Boulevard
Moon Township, PA 15108-1189
www.rmu.edu
Private
Admissions: (412) 397-5200
Email: admissions@rmu.edu
Financial aid: (412) 262-8212
Application deadline: 05/01
Tuition: full time: N/A; part time:
$790/credit hour
Room/board/expenses: N/A
Full-time enrollment: N/A
doctoral students: N/A; master's
students: N/A; education
specialists: N/A; men: N/A;
women: N/A; minorities: N/A;
international: N/A
Part-time enrollment: 171
doctoral students: 47%; master's
students: 53%; education
specialists: N/A; men: 41%;
women: 59%; minorities: 14%;
international: 1%
Acceptance rate (master's): 34%
Acceptance rate (doctoral): 70%
Entrance test required: N/A
**Avg. GRE (of all entering students
with scores):** quantitative: N/A;
verbal: N/A
Students reporting specialty: 100%
Students specializing in:
curriculum/instr.: 73%; admin.:
2%; higher education admin.:
6%; secondary: 7%; special:
4%; technical (vocational): 3%;
other: 6%

St. Joseph's University[1]

5600 City Avenue
Philadelphia, PA 19131
www.sju.edu
Private
Admissions: N/A
Financial aid: N/A
Tuition: N/A
Room/board/expenses: N/A
Enrollment: N/A

Temple University

OSS RA238
Philadelphia, PA 19122
www.temple.edu/
Public
Admissions: (215) 204-8011
Email: educate@temple.edu
Financial aid: (215) 204-1492
Application deadline: rolling
In-state tuition: full time: $805/
credit hour; part time: $805/
credit hour
Out-of-state tuition: full time:
$1,103/credit hour
Room/board/expenses: $18,200
Full-time enrollment: 324
doctoral students: 54%; master's
students: 40%; education
specialists: 6%; men: 30%;
women: 70%; minorities: 22%;
international: 9%
Part-time enrollment: 480
doctoral students: 39%; master's
students: 61%; education

specialists: 0%; men: 40%;
women: 60%; minorities: 17%;
international: 18%
Acceptance rate (master's): 61%
Acceptance rate (doctoral): 41%
Entrance test required: GRE
**Avg. GRE (of all entering students
with scores):** quantitative: 150;
verbal: 155
Research assistantships: 23
Students reporting specialty: 99%
Students specializing in:
curriculum/instr.: 22%; admin.:
8%; instructional media design:
1%; educational psych: 5%;
higher education admin.: 8%;
junior high: 1%; secondary: 5%;
social/philosophical foundations:
5%; special: 6%; counseling:
9%; technical (vocational): 9%;
other: 21%

University of Pennsylvania

3700 Walnut Street
Philadelphia, PA 19104-6216
www.gse.upenn.edu
Private
Admissions: (215) 898-6455
Email: admissions@gse.upenn.edu
Financial aid: (215) 898-6455
Application deadline: 12/15
Tuition: full time: $48,154; part
time: $5,696/credit hour
Room/board/expenses: $26,426
Full-time enrollment: 827
doctoral students: 12%; master's
students: 88%; education
specialists: N/A; men: 24%;
women: 76%; minorities: 32%;
international: 32%
Part-time enrollment: 175
doctoral students: 5%; master's
students: 95%; education
specialists: N/A; men: 33%;
women: 67%; minorities: 26%;
international: 11%
Acceptance rate (master's): 66%
Acceptance rate (doctoral): 5%
Entrance test required: GRE
**Avg. GRE (of all entering students
with scores):** quantitative: 155;
verbal: 155
Research assistantships: 98
Students reporting specialty: 100%
Students specializing in:
curriculum/instr.: 35%; admin.:
4%; policy: 7%; evaluation/
research/statistics: 3%;
educational psych: 4%;
elementary: 4%; higher
education admin.: 9%; junior
high: 3%; secondary: 9%; social/
philosophical foundations: 4%;
special: 4%; counseling: 14%

University of Pittsburgh

5601 Wesley W. Posvar Hall
Pittsburgh, PA 15260
www.education.pitt.edu
Public
Admissions: (412) 648-2230
Email: soeinfo@pitt.edu
Financial aid: (412) 648-2230
Application deadline: rolling
In-state tuition: full time: $21,542;
part time: $838/credit hour
Out-of-state tuition: full time:
$34,760
Room/board/expenses: $17,362
Full-time enrollment: 466
doctoral students: 35%; master's
students: 65%; education
specialists: N/A; men: 26%;
women: 74%; minorities: 15%;
international: 20%
Part-time enrollment: 363
doctoral students: 43%; master's
students: 57%; education

specialists: N/A; men: 23%;
women: 77%; minorities: 14%;
international: 2%
Acceptance rate (master's): 80%
Acceptance rate (doctoral): 37%
Entrance test required: GRE
**Avg. GRE (of all entering students
with scores):** quantitative: 153;
verbal: 152
Research assistantships: 31
Students reporting specialty: 100%
Students specializing in:
curriculum/instr.: 1%; admin.: 11%;
policy: 1%; evaluation/research/
statistics: 3%; educational
psych: 8%; elementary: 7%;
higher education admin.:
12%; secondary: 18%; social/
philosophical foundations: 10%;
special: 18%; other: 16%

Widener University[1]

1 University Place
Chester, PA 19013-5792
www.widener.edu
Private
Admissions: N/A
Financial aid: N/A
Tuition: N/A
Room/board/expenses: N/A
Enrollment: N/A

Wilkes University[1]

84 W. South Street
Wilkes-Barre, PA 18766
www.wilkes.edu
Private
Admissions: N/A
Financial aid: N/A
Tuition: N/A
Room/board/expenses: N/A
Enrollment: N/A

RHODE ISLAND

Johnson & Wales University[1]

8 Abbott Park Place
Providence, RI 02903-3703
www.jwu.edu
Private
Admissions: N/A
Financial aid: N/A
Tuition: N/A
Room/board/expenses: N/A
Enrollment: N/A

University of Rhode Island-Rhode Island College (Feinstein)[1]

600 Mount Pleasant Avenue
Providence, RI 02908
www.uri.edu/prov
Public
Admissions: N/A
Financial aid: N/A
Tuition: N/A
Room/board/expenses: N/A
Enrollment: N/A

SOUTH CAROLINA

Clemson University (Moore)

102 Tillman Hall
Clemson, SC 29634-0702
www.grad.clemson.edu
Public
Admissions: (864) 656-3195
Email: grdapp@clemson.edu
Financial aid: (864) 656-2280
Application deadline: rolling
In-state tuition: full time: $3,566;
part time: $384/credit hour

Out-of-state tuition: full time: $7,093
Room/board/expenses: $0
Full-time enrollment: 249 doctoral students: 22%; master's students: 76%; education specialists: 2%; men: 26%; women: 74%; minorities: 24%; international: 4%
Part-time enrollment: 217 doctoral students: 35%; master's students: 50%; education specialists: 15%; men: 24%; women: 76%; minorities: 17%; international: 1%
Acceptance rate (master's): 65%
Acceptance rate (doctoral): 47%
Entrance test required: GRE
Avg. GRE (of all entering students with scores): quantitative: 149; verbal: 153
Research assistantships: 4
Students reporting specialty: 100%
Students specializing in: curriculum/instr.: 9%; admin.: 24%; junior high: 9%; secondary: 3%; special: 1%; counseling: 32%; other: 23%

Columbia International University[1]

7435 Monticello Road
Columbia, SC 29203
www.ciu.edu/
Private
Admissions: N/A
Financial aid: N/A
Tuition: N/A
Room/board/expenses: N/A
Enrollment: N/A

South Carolina State University

PO Box 7298
300 College Street NE
Orangeburg, SC 29117
www.scsu.edu/
schoolofgraduatestudies.aspx
Public
Admissions: (803) 536-7133
Email: graduateschool@scsu.edu
Financial aid: (803) 536-7067
Application deadline: rolling
In-state tuition: full time: $10,088; part time: $560/credit hour
Out-of-state tuition: full time: $19,856
Room/board/expenses: N/A
Full-time enrollment: 95 doctoral students: 2%; master's students: 95%; education specialists: 3%; men: 35%; women: 65%; minorities: 99%; international: 2%
Part-time enrollment: 178 doctoral students: 46%; master's students: 38%; education specialists: 16%; men: 21%; women: 79%; minorities: 96%; international: 1%
Acceptance rate (master's): 96%
Acceptance rate (doctoral): 82%
Entrance test required: GRE
Avg. GRE (of all entering students with scores): quantitative: N/A; verbal: N/A
Students reporting specialty: 100%
Students specializing in: admin.: 42%; elementary: 8%; secondary: 8%; special: 0%; counseling: 33%; other: 9%

University of South Carolina

Wardlaw Building
Columbia, SC 29208
www.ed.sc.edu
Public
Admissions: (803) 777-4243
Email: gradapp@mailbox.sc.edu
Financial aid: (803) 777-8134
Application deadline: rolling
In-state tuition: full time: $12,424; part time: $501/credit hour
Out-of-state tuition: full time: $26,170
Room/board/expenses: $17,000
Full-time enrollment: 406 doctoral students: 18%; master's students: 73%; education specialists: 9%; men: 26%; women: 74%; minorities: 21%; international: 4%
Part-time enrollment: 486 doctoral students: 48%; master's students: 45%; education specialists: 7%; men: 26%; women: 74%; minorities: 26%; international: 2%
Acceptance rate (master's): 78%
Acceptance rate (doctoral): 57%
Entrance test required: GRE
Avg. GRE (of all entering students with scores): quantitative: 147; verbal: 152
Research assistantships: 33
Students reporting specialty: 100%
Students specializing in: curriculum/instr.: 4%; admin.: 24%; evaluation/research/statistics: 3%; instructional media design: 1%; elementary: 2%; higher education admin.: 3%; secondary: 5%; social/philosophical foundations: 1%; special: 7%; counseling: 19%; other: 30%

SOUTH DAKOTA

University of South Dakota

414 E. Clark Street
Vermillion, SD 57069
www.usd.edu/grad
Public
Admissions: (605) 677-6240
Email: grad@usd.edu
Financial aid: (605) 677-5446
Application deadline: rolling
In-state tuition: full time: $210/credit hour; part time: $210/credit hour
Out-of-state tuition: full time: $445/credit hour
Room/board/expenses: $11,295
Full-time enrollment: 185 doctoral students: 18%; master's students: 69%; education specialists: 13%; men: 32%; women: 68%; minorities: 11%; international: 3%
Part-time enrollment: 364 doctoral students: 44%; master's students: 39%; education specialists: 18%; men: 39%; women: 61%; minorities: 9%; international: 1%
Acceptance rate (master's): 80%
Acceptance rate (doctoral): 82%
Entrance test required: GRE
Avg. GRE (of all entering students with scores): quantitative: 148; verbal: 151
Research assistantships: 17
Students reporting specialty: 100%
Students specializing in: curriculum/instr.: 7%; admin.: 34%; instructional media design: 1%; educational psych: 11%; elementary: 2%; higher education

admin.: 19%; secondary: 2%; special: 5%; counseling: 13%; other: 7%

TENNESSEE

East Tennessee State University (Clemmer)

PO Box 70720
Johnson City, TN 37614-0720
www.etsu.edu/coe/
Public
Admissions: (423) 439-4221
Email: gradsch@etsu.edu
Financial aid: (423) 439-4300
Application deadline: rolling
In-state tuition: full time: $8,951; part time: $422/credit hour
Out-of-state tuition: full time: $22,469
Room/board/expenses: $15,482
Full-time enrollment: 285 doctoral students: 14%; master's students: 86%; education specialists: 0%; men: 39%; women: 61%; minorities: 8%; international: 5%
Part-time enrollment: 346 doctoral students: 60%; master's students: 38%; education specialists: 2%; men: 29%; women: 71%; minorities: 11%; international: 1%
Acceptance rate (master's): 50%
Acceptance rate (doctoral): 54%
Entrance test required: GRE
Avg. GRE (of all entering students with scores): quantitative: N/A; verbal: N/A
Research assistantships: 28
Students reporting specialty: 100%
Students specializing in: admin.: 39%; instructional media design: 7%; elementary: 2%; secondary: 2%; special: 2%; counseling: 11%; other: 37%

Lincoln Memorial University[1]

6965 Cumberland Gap Parkway
Harrogateq, TN 37752
www.lmunet.edu/
Private
Admissions: N/A
Financial aid: N/A
Tuition: N/A
Room/board/expenses: N/A
Enrollment: N/A

Middle Tennessee State University

1301 E. Main Street
CAB Room 205
Murfreesboro, TN 37132
www.mtsu.edu/education/index.php
Public
Admissions: N/A
Financial aid: N/A
Application deadline: rolling
In-state tuition: full time: $420/credit hour; part time: $420/credit hour
Out-of-state tuition: full time: $1,163/credit hour
Room/board/expenses: $13,580
Full-time enrollment: 168 doctoral students: 8%; master's students: 91%; education specialists: 1%; men: 30%; women: 70%; minorities: 21%; international: 20%
Part-time enrollment: 330 doctoral students: 14%; master's students: 70%; education specialists: 16%; men: 17%; women: 83%; minorities: 15%; international: 3%

Acceptance rate (master's): 55%
Acceptance rate (doctoral): 80%
Entrance test required: N/A
Avg. GRE (of all entering students with scores): quantitative: N/A; verbal: N/A
Students reporting specialty: 100%
Students specializing in: curriculum/instr.: 42%; admin.: 26%; evaluation/research/statistics: 6%; special: 3%; counseling: 15%; other: 9%

Tennessee State University[1]

3500 John A. Merritt Boulevard
Nashville, TN 37209-1561
www.tnstate.edu
Public
Admissions: N/A
Financial aid: N/A
Tuition: N/A
Room/board/expenses: N/A
Enrollment: N/A

Tennessee Technological University

Box 5012
Cookeville, TN 38505-0001
www.tntech.edu/
Public
Admissions: (931) 372-3233
Email: gradstudies@tntech.edu
Financial aid: (931) 372-3073
Application deadline: 07/01
In-state tuition: full time: $13,725; part time: $492/credit hour
Out-of-state tuition: full time: $36,107
Room/board/expenses: $16,300
Full-time enrollment: 148 doctoral students: 7%; master's students: 88%; education specialists: 5%; men: 33%; women: 67%; minorities: 14%; international: 3%
Part-time enrollment: 242 doctoral students: 10%; master's students: 67%; education specialists: 22%; men: 27%; women: 73%; minorities: 8%; international: 3%
Acceptance rate (master's): 77%
Acceptance rate (doctoral): 64%
Entrance test required: GRE
Avg. GRE (of all entering students with scores): quantitative: N/A; verbal: N/A
Research assistantships: 2
Students reporting specialty: 98%
Students specializing in: curriculum/instr.: 24%; admin.: 7%; evaluation/research/statistics: 9%; educational psych: 3%; educational tech.: 4%; elementary: 6%; secondary: 11%; special: 7%; counseling: 17%; other: 13%

Trevecca Nazarene University[1]

333 Murfreesboro Road
Nashville, TN 37210
www.trevecca.edu/academics/schools-colleges/education/
Private
Admissions: N/A
Financial aid: N/A
Tuition: N/A
Room/board/expenses: N/A
Enrollment: N/A

Union University

1050 Union University Drive
Jackson, TN 38305
www.uu.edu/
Private
Admissions: (731) 661-5928
Email: crbrown@uu.edu
Financial aid: (731) 661-5015
Application deadline: rolling
Tuition: full time: $470/credit hour; part time: $470/credit hour
Room/board/expenses: N/A
Full-time enrollment: N/A doctoral students: N/A; master's students: N/A; education specialists: N/A; men: N/A; women: N/A; minorities: N/A; international: N/A
Part-time enrollment: N/A doctoral students: N/A; master's students: N/A; education specialists: N/A; men: N/A; women: N/A; minorities: N/A; international: N/A
Acceptance rate (master's): N/A
Acceptance rate (doctoral): N/A
Entrance test required: GRE
Avg. GRE (of all entering students with scores): quantitative: N/A; verbal: N/A
Research assistantships: 1
Students reporting specialty: 93%
Students specializing in: admin.: 26%; higher education admin.: 8%; other: 65%

University of Memphis

215 Ball Hall
Memphis, TN 38152-6015
www.memphis.edu/admissions.htm
Public
Admissions: (901) 678-2911
Email: admissions@memphis.edu
Financial aid: (901) 678-4825
Application deadline: rolling
In-state tuition: full time: $452/credit hour; part time: $566/credit hour
Out-of-state tuition: full time: $990/credit hour
Room/board/expenses: $10,910
Full-time enrollment: 297 doctoral students: 26%; master's students: 72%; education specialists: 2%; men: 26%; women: 74%; minorities: 36%; international: 5%
Part-time enrollment: 517 doctoral students: 43%; master's students: 53%; education specialists: 4%; men: 30%; women: 70%; minorities: 42%; international: 2%
Acceptance rate (master's): 69%
Acceptance rate (doctoral): 54%
Entrance test required: GRE
Avg. GRE (of all entering students with scores): quantitative: N/A; verbal: N/A
Students reporting specialty: 36%
Students specializing in: N/A

University of Tennessee-Chattanooga

615 McCallie Avenue
Chattanooga, TN 37403
www.utc.edu/graduate-school
Public
Admissions: (423) 425-4666
Financial aid: (423) 425-4677
Application deadline: rolling
In-state tuition: full time: $9,416; part time: $680/credit hour
Out-of-state tuition: full time: $25,526
Room/board/expenses: $10,854

Full-time enrollment: 103
doctoral students: 1%; master's students: 74%; education specialists: 25%; men: 13%; women: 87%; minorities: 20%; international: 2%
Part-time enrollment: 211
doctoral students: 43%; master's students: 50%; education specialists: 7%; men: 31%; women: 69%; minorities: 18%; international: N/A
Acceptance rate (master's): 42%
Acceptance rate (doctoral): 44%
Entrance test required: GRE
Avg. GRE (of all entering students with scores): quantitative: N/A; verbal: N/A
Research assistantships: 10
Students reporting specialty: 100%
Students specializing in: admin.: 36%; elementary: 8%; secondary: 21%; special: 6%; counseling: 17%; other: 13%

University of Tennessee–Knoxville

335 Claxton Complex
Knoxville, TN 37996-3400
cehhs.utk.edu
Public
Admissions: (865) 974-3251
Email: nfox@utk.edu
Financial aid: (865) 974-3131
Application deadline: rolling
In-state tuition: full time: $11,601; part time: $563/credit hour
Out-of-state tuition: full time: $29,790
Room/board/expenses: $19,080
Full-time enrollment: 364
doctoral students: 35%; master's students: 62%; education specialists: 4%; men: 20%; women: 80%; minorities: 16%; international: 5%
Part-time enrollment: 264
doctoral students: 55%; master's students: 37%; education specialists: 8%; men: 26%; women: 74%; minorities: 16%; international: 2%
Acceptance rate (master's): 65%
Acceptance rate (doctoral): 70%
Entrance test required: GRE
Avg. GRE (of all entering students with scores): quantitative: 152; verbal: 157
Research assistantships: 81
Students reporting specialty: 89%
Students specializing in: admin.: 5%; policy: 7%; evaluation/research/statistics: 1%; educational psych: 9%; educational tech.: 5%; elementary: 12%; higher education admin.: 6%; junior high: 1%; secondary: 13%; social/philosophical foundations: 1%; special: 6%; counseling: 10%; other: 26%

Vanderbilt University (Peabody)

PO Box 227
Nashville, TN 37203-9418
peabody.vanderbilt.edu
Private
Admissions: (615) 322-8410
Email: peabody.admissions@vanderbilt.edu
Financial aid: (615) 322-8400
Application deadline: rolling
Tuition: full time: $1,782/credit hour; part time: $1,782/credit hour
Room/board/expenses: $20,717
Full-time enrollment: 700
doctoral students: 25%; master's students: 75%; education specialists: N/A; men: 21%;

women: 79%; minorities: 17%; international: 8%
Part-time enrollment: 210
doctoral students: 30%; master's students: 70%; education specialists: N/A; men: 34%; women: 66%; minorities: 20%; international: 9%
Acceptance rate (master's): 60%
Acceptance rate (doctoral): 6%
Entrance test required: GRE
Avg. GRE (of all entering students with scores): quantitative: 158; verbal: 161
Research assistantships: 207
Students reporting specialty: 100%
Students specializing in: curriculum/instr.: 13%; admin.: 5%; policy: 12%; evaluation/research/statistics: 13%; elementary: 3%; higher education admin.: 10%; secondary: 5%; special: 14%; counseling: 10%; other: 15%

TEXAS

Baylor University

1 Bear Place #97304
Waco, TX 76798-7304
www.baylor.edu/SOE/
Private
Admissions: (254) 710-3584
Email: graduate_school@baylor.edu
Financial aid: (254) 710-2611
Application deadline: rolling
Tuition: full time: $1,437/credit hour; part time: $1,437/credit hour
Room/board/expenses: $11,058
Full-time enrollment: 98
doctoral students: 30%; master's students: 49%; education specialists: 21%; men: 16%; women: 84%; minorities: 22%; international: 7%
Part-time enrollment: 38
doctoral students: 34%; master's students: 66%; education specialists: 0%; men: 24%; women: 76%; minorities: 26%; international: 3%
Acceptance rate (master's): 63%
Acceptance rate (doctoral): 45%
Entrance test required: GRE
Avg. GRE (of all entering students with scores): quantitative: 152; verbal: 155
Research assistantships: 29
Students reporting specialty: 100%
Students specializing in: curriculum/instr.: 32%; admin.: 28%; educational psych: 40%

Dallas Baptist University (Bush)[1]

3000 Mountain Creek Parkway
Dallas, TX 75211-9299
www.dbu.edu/
Private
Admissions: N/A
Financial aid: N/A
Tuition: N/A
Room/board/expenses: N/A
Enrollment: N/A

Lamar University

PO Box 10034
Lamar University Station
Beaumont, TX 77710
dept.lamar.edu/education/
Public
Admissions: (409) 880-8356
Email: gradmissions@hal.lamar.edu
Financial aid: (409) 880-8450
Application deadline: 07/01
In-state tuition: full time: $7,664; part time: $308/credit hour

Out-of-state tuition: full time: $14,180
Room/board/expenses: $13,410
Full-time enrollment: 114
doctoral students: 45%; master's students: 55%; education specialists: N/A; men: 24%; women: 76%; minorities: 36%; international: 15%
Part-time enrollment: 3,141
doctoral students: 7%; master's students: 93%; education specialists: N/A; men: 23%; women: 77%; minorities: 40%; international: 0%
Acceptance rate (master's): 91%
Acceptance rate (doctoral): 100%
Entrance test required: GRE
Avg. GRE (of all entering students with scores): quantitative: N/A; verbal: N/A
Students reporting specialty: 100%
Students specializing in: curriculum/instr.: 6%; admin.: 37%; educational tech.: 5%; special: 2%; counseling: 32%; other: 18%

Prairie View A&M University[1]

PO Box 3089
Office of Admissions and Records
Prarie View, TX 77446-0188
www.pvamu.edu/
Public
Admissions: N/A
Financial aid: N/A
Tuition: N/A
Room/board/expenses: N/A
Enrollment: N/A

Sam Houston State University

PO Box 2119
Huntsville, TX 77341
www.shsu.edu/~grs_www
Public
Admissions: (936) 294-1971
Email: graduate@shsu.edu
Financial aid: (936) 294-1724
Application deadline: 08/01
In-state tuition: full time: $254/credit hour; part time: $254/credit hour
Out-of-state tuition: full time: $616/credit hour
Room/board/expenses: $11,238
Full-time enrollment: 143
doctoral students: 7%; master's students: 78%; education specialists: 15%; men: 19%; women: 81%; minorities: 31%; international: 5%
Part-time enrollment: 1,082
doctoral students: 19%; master's students: 81%; education specialists: 0%; men: 17%; women: 83%; minorities: 33%; international: 2%
Acceptance rate (master's): 91%
Acceptance rate (doctoral): 58%
Entrance test required: GRE
Avg. GRE (of all entering students with scores): quantitative: 151; verbal: 152
Research assistantships: 15
Students reporting specialty: 100%
Students specializing in: curriculum/instr.: 16%; admin.: 23%; educational psych: 2%; educational tech.: 3%; higher education admin.: 5%; special: 9%; counseling: 19%; other: 24%

Southern Methodist University[1]

PO Box 750181
Dallas, TX 75275-0181
www.smu.edu/
Private
Admissions: N/A
Financial aid: N/A
Tuition: N/A
Room/board/expenses: N/A
Enrollment: N/A

Stephen F. Austin State University

PO Box 13024
SFA Station
Nacogdoches, TX 75962
www.sfasu.edu/graduate
Public
Admissions: (936) 468-2807
Email: gschool@sfasu.edu
Financial aid: (936) 468-2403
Application deadline: rolling
In-state tuition: full time: $251/credit hour; part time: $251/credit hour
Out-of-state tuition: full time: $613/credit hour
Room/board/expenses: $11,614
Full-time enrollment: 268
doctoral students: 15%; master's students: 85%; education specialists: N/A; men: 28%; women: 72%; minorities: 33%; international: 3%
Part-time enrollment: 767
doctoral students: 6%; master's students: 94%; education specialists: N/A; men: 21%; women: 79%; minorities: 29%; international: 1%
Acceptance rate (master's): N/A
Acceptance rate (doctoral): N/A
Entrance test required: GRE
Avg. GRE (of all entering students with scores): quantitative: N/A; verbal: N/A
Research assistantships: 26
Students reporting specialty: 100%
Students specializing in: admin.: 29%; elementary: 11%; secondary: 5%; special: 17%; counseling: 1%; other: 38%

Tarleton State University

Box T-0350
Stephenville, TX 76402
www.tarleton.edu
Public
Admissions: N/A
Financial aid: N/A
Application deadline: 08/23
In-state tuition: full time: $204/credit hour; part time: $204/credit hour
Out-of-state tuition: full time: $566/credit hour
Room/board/expenses: N/A
Full-time enrollment: 160
doctoral students: 38%; master's students: 63%; education specialists: N/A; men: 28%; women: 73%; minorities: 26%; international: 1%
Part-time enrollment: 427
doctoral students: 8%; master's students: 92%; education specialists: N/A; men: 25%; women: 75%; minorities: 30%; international: 0%
Acceptance rate (master's): N/A
Acceptance rate (doctoral): N/A
Entrance test required: GRE
Avg. GRE (of all entering students with scores): quantitative: N/A; verbal: N/A
Students reporting specialty: 100%

Students specializing in: curriculum/instr.: 20%; admin.: 30%; educational psych: 28%; special: 2%; counseling: 10%; other: 11%

Texas A&M University–College Station

4222 TAMUS
College Station, TX 77843-4222
www.cehd.tamu.edu/
Public
Admissions: (979) 845-1071
Email: admissions@tamu.edu
Financial aid: (979) 845-3236
Application deadline: rolling
In-state tuition: full time: $308/credit hour; part time: $308/credit hour
Out-of-state tuition: full time: $670/credit hour
Room/board/expenses: $14,526
Full-time enrollment: 628
doctoral students: 51%; master's students: 49%; education specialists: N/A; men: 31%; women: 69%; minorities: 26%; international: 28%
Part-time enrollment: 796
doctoral students: 38%; master's students: 62%; education specialists: N/A; men: 27%; women: 73%; minorities: 37%; international: 2%
Acceptance rate (master's): 71%
Acceptance rate (doctoral): 56%
Entrance test required: GRE
Avg. GRE (of all entering students with scores): quantitative: 151; verbal: 151
Research assistantships: 90
Students reporting specialty: 99%
Students specializing in: curriculum/instr.: 28%; admin.: 16%; educational psych: 12%; educational tech.: 2%; special: 4%; counseling: 3%; other: 35%

Texas A&M University-Commerce[1]

PO Box 3011
Commerce, TX 75429-3011
www.tamuc.edu/
Public
Admissions: N/A
Financial aid: N/A
Tuition: N/A
Room/board/expenses: N/A
Enrollment: N/A

Texas A&M University–Corpus Christi

6300 Ocean Drive
Corpus Christi, TX 78412
gradschool.tamucc.edu
Public
Admissions: (361) 825-2177
Email: gradweb@tamucc.edu
Financial aid: (361) 825-2332
Application deadline: rolling
In-state tuition: full time: N/A; part time: N/A
Out-of-state tuition: full time: N/A
Room/board/expenses: N/A
Full-time enrollment: 159
doctoral students: 21%; master's students: 79%; education specialists: N/A; men: 27%; women: 73%; minorities: 39%; international: 11%
Part-time enrollment: 354
doctoral students: 32%; master's students: 68%; education specialists: N/A; men: 18%; women: 82%; minorities: 56%; international: 2%

Acceptance rate (master's): 82%
Acceptance rate (doctoral): 68%
Entrance test required: GRE
Avg. GRE (of all entering students with scores): quantitative: N/A; verbal: N/A
Students reporting specialty: 100%
Students specializing in: curriculum/instr.: 14%; admin.: 20%; educational tech.: 3%; elementary: 5%; secondary: 4%; special: 5%; counseling: 34%; other: 15%

Texas A&M University-Kingsville

700 University Boulevard
Kingsville, TX 78363
www.tamuk.edu
Public
Admissions: (361) 593-2811
Email: admissions@tamuk.edu
Financial aid: (361) 593-3911
Application deadline: rolling
In-state tuition: full time: $7,554; part time: $694/credit hour
Out-of-state tuition: full time: $15,226
Room/board/expenses: $14,206
Full-time enrollment: 133
doctoral students: 29%; master's students: 71%; education specialists: N/A; men: 31%; women: 69%; minorities: 71%; international: 12%
Part-time enrollment: 285
doctoral students: 27%; master's students: 73%; education specialists: N/A; men: 25%; women: 75%; minorities: 78%; international: 5%
Acceptance rate (master's): 92%
Acceptance rate (doctoral): 73%
Entrance test required: GRE
Avg. GRE (of all entering students with scores): quantitative: 144; verbal: 146
Students reporting specialty: 36%
Students specializing in: N/A

Texas Christian University

3000 Bellaire Drive N
Fort Worth, TX 76129
www.coe.tcu.edu
Private
Admissions: (817) 257-7661
Financial aid: (817) 257-7872
Application deadline: 03/01
Tuition: full time: $1,340/credit hour; part time: $1,340/credit hour
Room/board/expenses: $15,900
Full-time enrollment: 156
doctoral students: 36%; master's students: 64%; education specialists: N/A; men: 20%; women: 80%; minorities: 32%; international: 4%
Part-time enrollment: 33
doctoral students: 55%; master's students: 45%; education specialists: N/A; men: 30%; women: 70%; minorities: 24%; international: 3%
Acceptance rate (master's): 79%
Acceptance rate (doctoral): 91%
Entrance test required: GRE
Avg. GRE (of all entering students with scores): quantitative: N/A; verbal: N/A
Students reporting specialty: 100%
Students specializing in: curriculum/instr.: 5%; admin.: 43%; elementary: 5%; higher education admin.: 12%; secondary: 3%; social/philosophical foundations: 1%; special: 7%; counseling: 23%; other: 14%

Texas Southern University

3100 Cleburne Street
Houston, TX 77004
www.tsu.edu/academics/colleges_schools/The_Graduate_School/admissions.php
Public
Admissions: (713) 313-7435
Email: graduateadmissions@tsu.edu
Financial aid: (713) 313-7071
Application deadline: 07/15
In-state tuition: full time: $6,106; part time: $100/credit hour
Out-of-state tuition: full time: $11,722
Room/board/expenses: $16,659
Full-time enrollment: 149
doctoral students: 28%; master's students: 72%; education specialists: N/A; men: 37%; women: 63%; minorities: 97%; international: 2%
Part-time enrollment: 193
doctoral students: 49%; master's students: 51%; education specialists: N/A; men: 25%; women: 75%; minorities: 96%; international: 1%
Acceptance rate (master's): 52%
Acceptance rate (doctoral): 50%
Entrance test required: GRE
Avg. GRE (of all entering students with scores): quantitative: N/A; verbal: N/A
Students reporting specialty: 100%
Students specializing in: curriculum/instr.: 15%; admin.: 32%; counseling: 34%; other: 19%

Texas State University

601 University Drive
San Marcos, TX 78666
www.txstate.edu
Public
Admissions: (512) 245-2581
Email: gradcollege@txstate.edu
Financial aid: (512) 245-2315
Application deadline: rolling
In-state tuition: full time: $6,814; part time: $289/credit hour
Out-of-state tuition: full time: $13,330
Room/board/expenses: $11,760
Full-time enrollment: 533
doctoral students: 10%; master's students: 82%; education specialists: 8%; men: 24%; women: 76%; minorities: 36%; international: 4%
Part-time enrollment: 619
doctoral students: 17%; master's students: 80%; education specialists: 2%; men: 24%; women: 76%; minorities: 40%; international: 1%
Acceptance rate (master's): 61%
Acceptance rate (doctoral): 58%
Entrance test required: GRE
Avg. GRE (of all entering students with scores): quantitative: 147; verbal: 151
Research assistantships: 62
Students reporting specialty: 100%
Students specializing in: admin.: 22%; instructional media design: 3%; educational psych: 22%; elementary: 15%; higher education admin.: 3%; secondary: 7%; special: 5%; counseling: 0%; other: 23%

Texas Tech University

Box 41071
Lubbock, TX 79409-1071
www.educ.ttu.edu/
Public
Admissions: (806) 742-2787
Email: gradschool@ttu.edu
Financial aid: (806) 742-3681
Application deadline: rolling
In-state tuition: full time: $263/credit hour; part time: $263/credit hour
Out-of-state tuition: full time: $625/credit hour
Room/board/expenses: $14,705
Full-time enrollment: 276
doctoral students: 43%; master's students: 57%; education specialists: N/A; men: 26%; women: 74%; minorities: 28%; international: 21%
Part-time enrollment: 705
doctoral students: 53%; master's students: 47%; education specialists: N/A; men: 26%; women: 74%; minorities: 31%; international: 3%
Acceptance rate (master's): 61%
Acceptance rate (doctoral): 40%
Entrance test required: GRE
Avg. GRE (of all entering students with scores): quantitative: 145; verbal: 149
Research assistantships: 72
Students reporting specialty: 100%
Students specializing in: curriculum/instr.: 18%; admin.: 8%; evaluation/research/statistics: 15%; instructional media design: 7%; educational psych: 5%; elementary: 0%; secondary: 0%; special: 24%; counseling: 12%; other: 12%

Texas Woman's University[1]

PO Box 425769
Denton, TX 76204-5769
www.twu.edu/
Public
Admissions: N/A
Financial aid: N/A
Tuition: N/A
Room/board/expenses: N/A
Enrollment: N/A

University of Houston

4800 Calhoun Road
Farish Hall
Houston, TX 77204-5023
www.coe.uh.edu/
Public
Admissions: (713) 743-4997
Email: coegrad@uh.edu
Financial aid: (713) 743-1010
Application deadline: rolling
In-state tuition: full time: $8,757; part time: $405/credit hour
Out-of-state tuition: full time: $16,560
Room/board/expenses: $15,600
Full-time enrollment: 352
doctoral students: 52%; master's students: 48%; education specialists: N/A; men: 19%; women: 81%; minorities: 41%; international: 18%
Part-time enrollment: 321
doctoral students: 54%; master's students: 46%; education specialists: N/A; men: 26%; women: 74%; minorities: 54%; international: 2%
Acceptance rate (master's): 65%
Acceptance rate (doctoral): 38%
Entrance test required: GRE
Avg. GRE (of all entering students with scores): quantitative: 149; verbal: 152

Research assistantships: 40
Students reporting specialty: 91%
Students specializing in: curriculum/instr.: 40%; admin.: 23%; educational psych: 11%; higher education admin.: 5%; special: 2%; counseling: 12%; other: 7%

University of Houston-Clear Lake[1]

2700 Bay Area Boulevard
Houston, TX 77058
www.uhcl.edu
Public
Admissions: N/A
Financial aid: N/A
Tuition: N/A
Room/board/expenses: N/A
Enrollment: N/A

University of Mary Hardin-Baylor[1]

UMHB Box 8017
900 College Street
Belton, TX 76513
www.umhb.edu/
Private
Admissions: N/A
Financial aid: N/A
Tuition: N/A
Room/board/expenses: N/A
Enrollment: N/A

University of North Texas

1155 Union Circle, #311337
Denton, TX 76203-1337
tsgs.unt.edu/overview
Public
Admissions: (940) 565-2383
Email: gradsch@unt.edu
Financial aid: (940) 565-2302
Application deadline: rolling
In-state tuition: full time: $303/credit hour; part time: $303/credit hour
Out-of-state tuition: full time: $664/credit hour
Room/board/expenses: $11,766
Full-time enrollment: 346
doctoral students: 30%; master's students: 70%; education specialists: N/A; men: 27%; women: 73%; minorities: 28%; international: 13%
Part-time enrollment: 755
doctoral students: 38%; master's students: 62%; education specialists: N/A; men: 28%; women: 72%; minorities: 33%; international: 2%
Acceptance rate (master's): 34%
Acceptance rate (doctoral): 39%
Entrance test required: GRE
Avg. GRE (of all entering students with scores): quantitative: 147; verbal: 151
Research assistantships: 15
Students reporting specialty: 65%
Students specializing in: curriculum/instr.: 13%; admin.: 4%; evaluation/research/statistics: 8%; educational psych: 3%; higher education admin.: 18%; secondary: 1%; special: 14%; counseling: 8%

University of Texas-Arlington

701 S. Nedderman Drive
Arlington, TX 76019
www.uta.edu
Public
Admissions: N/A
Financial aid: N/A
Application deadline: 01/06

In-state tuition: full time: $8,198; part time: $4,170
Out-of-state tuition: full time: $15,448
Room/board/expenses: $14,374
Full-time enrollment: 53
doctoral students: 17%; master's students: 83%; education specialists: N/A; men: 23%; women: 77%; minorities: 42%; international: 9%
Part-time enrollment: 1,553
doctoral students: 5%; master's students: 95%; education specialists: N/A; men: 20%; women: 80%; minorities: 43%; international: 1%
Acceptance rate (master's): 64%
Acceptance rate (doctoral): 38%
Entrance test required: GRE
Avg. GRE (of all entering students with scores): quantitative: 148; verbal: 152
Research assistantships: 6
Students reporting specialty: 98%
Students specializing in: curriculum/instr.: 56%; admin.: 39%; educational psych: 2%; educational tech.: 3%

University of Texas-Austin

1 University Station, D5000
Sanchez Building, Room 210
Austin, TX 78712
www.edb.utexas.edu/education/
Public
Admissions: (512) 475-7398
Email: adgrd@utxdp.dp.utexas.edu
Financial aid: (512) 475-6282
Application deadline: rolling
In-state tuition: full time: $8,402; part time: $8,066
Out-of-state tuition: full time: $16,338
Room/board/expenses: $18,810
Full-time enrollment: 791
doctoral students: 53%; master's students: 47%; education specialists: N/A; men: 29%; women: 71%; minorities: 28%; international: 16%
Part-time enrollment: 328
doctoral students: 52%; master's students: 48%; education specialists: N/A; men: 32%; women: 68%; minorities: 37%; international: 7%
Acceptance rate (master's): 53%
Acceptance rate (doctoral): 25%
Entrance test required: GRE
Avg. GRE (of all entering students with scores): quantitative: 151; verbal: 154
Research assistantships: 311
Students reporting specialty: 100%
Students specializing in: curriculum/instr.: 26%; admin.: 7%; policy: 5%; evaluation/research/statistics: 3%; educational psych: 13%; educational tech.: 4%; higher education admin.: 10%; special: 12%; counseling: 4%; other: 16%

University of Texas-Brownsville[1]

80 Fort Brown
Brownsville, TX 78520
www.utb.edu/
Public
Admissions: N/A
Financial aid: N/A
Tuition: N/A
Room/board/expenses: N/A
Enrollment: N/A

University of Texas-El Paso[1]

500 W. University Avenue
El Paso, TX 79968
www.utep.edu/
Public
Admissions: N/A
Financial aid: N/A
Tuition: N/A
Room/board/expenses: N/A
Enrollment: N/A

University of Texas-Pan American

1201 W. University Drive
Edinburg, TX 78541-2999
www.utpa.edu/colleges/coe/
Public
Admissions: (956) 665-3661
Email: admissions@utpa.edu
Financial aid: (956) 665-2501
Application deadline: 08/01
In-state tuition: full time: $5,488;
part time: $233/credit hour
Out-of-state tuition: full time:
$12,568
Room/board/expenses: $11,170
Full-time enrollment: 98
doctoral students: 14%; master's
students: 86%; education
specialists: N/A; men: 24%;
women: 76%; minorities: 96%;
international: 3%
Part-time enrollment: 650
doctoral students: 6%; master's
students: 94%; education
specialists: N/A; men: 26%;
women: 74%; minorities: 95%;
international: 1%
Acceptance rate (master's): N/A
Acceptance rate (doctoral): N/A
Entrance test required: GRE
**Avg. GRE (of all entering students
with scores):** quantitative: N/A;
verbal: N/A
Students reporting specialty: 0%
Students specializing in: N/A

University of Texas-San Antonio

1 UTSA Circle
San Antonio, TX 78249-0617
www.graduateschool.utsa.edu
Public
Admissions: (210) 458-4331
Email: graduatestudies@usta.edu
Financial aid: (210) 458-8000
Application deadline: N/A
In-state tuition: full time: $260/
credit hour; part time: $260/
credit hour
Out-of-state tuition: full time:
$1,001/credit hour
Room/board/expenses: $14,919
Full-time enrollment: 419
doctoral students: 12%; master's
students: 88%; education
specialists: N/A; men: 22%;
women: 78%; minorities: 55%;
international: 5%
Part-time enrollment: 922
doctoral students: 17%; master's
students: 83%; education
specialists: N/A; men: 24%;
women: 76%; minorities: 65%;
international: 2%
Acceptance rate (master's): 91%
Acceptance rate (doctoral): 62%
Entrance test required: GRE
**Avg. GRE (of all entering students
with scores):** quantitative: 145;
verbal: 150
Research assistantships: 29
Students reporting specialty: 74%
Students specializing in: admin.:
21%; policy: 26%; educational
psych: 7%; educational tech.: 4%;
elementary: 4%; higher education
admin.: 7%; special: 6%;
counseling: 10%; other: 47%

University of the Incarnate Word

4301 Broadway
San Antonio, TX 78209
www.uiw.edu
Private
Admissions: (210) 829-6005
Email: admis@uiwtx.edu
Financial aid: (210) 829-6008
Application deadline: rolling
Tuition: full time: $815/credit hour;
part time: $815/credit hour
Room/board/expenses: $12,262
Full-time enrollment: 38
doctoral students: 29%; master's
students: 71%; education
specialists: N/A; men: 24%;
women: 76%; minorities: 32%;
international: 66%
Part-time enrollment: 205
doctoral students: 69%; master's
students: 31%; education
specialists: N/A; men: 33%;
women: 67%; minorities: 60%;
international: 7%
Acceptance rate (master's): 64%
Acceptance rate (doctoral): 86%
Entrance test required: GRE
**Avg. GRE (of all entering students
with scores):** quantitative: 144;
verbal: 143
Research assistantships: 20
Students reporting specialty: 100%
Students specializing in:
elementary: 7%; secondary: 3%;
other: 91%

UTAH

Brigham Young University-Provo (McKay)

301 MCKB
Provo, UT 84602
www.byu.edu/gradstudies
Private
Admissions: (801) 422-4091
Email: admissions@byu.edu
Financial aid: (801) 422-4104
Application deadline: N/A
Tuition: full time: $6,757; part
time: $1,147
Room/board/expenses: $15,712
Full-time enrollment: 248
doctoral students: 56%; master's
students: 33%; education
specialists: 11%; men: 48%;
women: 52%; minorities: 13%;
international: 3%
Part-time enrollment: 78
doctoral students: 8%; master's
students: 83%; education
specialists: 9%; men: 27%;
women: 73%; minorities: 9%;
international: 4%
Acceptance rate (master's): 48%
Acceptance rate (doctoral): 37%
Entrance test required: GRE
**Avg. GRE (of all entering students
with scores):** quantitative: 151;
verbal: 154
Research assistantships: 99
Students reporting specialty: 78%
Students specializing in: admin.:
14%; evaluation/research/
statistics: 4%; instructional media
design: 15%; educational psych:
27%; higher education admin.:
19%; special: 5%; counseling:
15%; other: 2%

University of Utah

1721 E. Campus Center Drive
Salt Lake City, UT 84112-9251
admissions.utah.edu
Public
Admissions: (801) 581-7281
Email: admissions@utah.edu
Financial aid: (801) 581-6211

Application deadline: 04/01
In-state tuition: full time: $8,271;
part time: $242/credit hour
Out-of-state tuition: full time:
$22,353
Room/board/expenses: $16,022
Full-time enrollment: 373
doctoral students: 37%; master's
students: 63%; education
specialists: N/A; men: 28%;
women: 72%; minorities: 20%;
international: 3%
Part-time enrollment: 165
doctoral students: 52%; master's
students: 48%; education
specialists: N/A; men: 30%;
women: 70%; minorities: 28%;
international: 1%
Acceptance rate (master's): 57%
Acceptance rate (doctoral): 24%
Entrance test required: GRE
**Avg. GRE (of all entering students
with scores):** quantitative: 150;
verbal: 152
Research assistantships: 12
Students reporting specialty: 72%
Students specializing in: admin.:
14%; policy: 7%; educational
psych: 11%; educational
tech.: 10%; elementary: 1%;
higher education admin.:
20%; secondary: 6%; social/
philosophical foundations: 16%;
special: 10%; counseling: 7%

Utah State University

2800 Old Main Hill
Logan, UT 84322-2800
www.rgs.usu.edu/graduateschool
Public
Admissions: (435) 797-1189
Email: graduateschool@usu.edu
Financial aid: (435) 797-0173
Application deadline: rolling
In-state tuition: full time: $5,837;
part time: $5,356
Out-of-state tuition: full time:
$18,321
Room/board/expenses: $11,690
Full-time enrollment: 296
doctoral students: 30%; master's
students: 65%; education
specialists: 5%; men: 31%;
women: 69%; minorities: 7%;
international: 7%
Part-time enrollment: 576
doctoral students: 29%; master's
students: 70%; education
specialists: 1%; men: 38%;
women: 62%; minorities: 7%;
international: 2%
Acceptance rate (master's): 46%
Acceptance rate (doctoral): 34%
Entrance test required: GRE
**Avg. GRE (of all entering students
with scores):** quantitative: 150;
verbal: 155
Research assistantships: 91
Students reporting specialty: 61%
Students specializing in:
curriculum/instr.: 16%; admin.:
12%; instructional media design:
27%; elementary: 6%; junior high:
0%; secondary: 7%; special: 11%;
counseling: 21%

VERMONT

University of Vermont

309 Waterman Building
Burlington, VT 05405-0160
www.uvm.edu/~gradcoll
Public
Admissions: (802) 656-2699
Email: graduate.admissions@
uvm.edu
Financial aid: (802) 656-3156
Application deadline: 02/15
In-state tuition: full time: $15,988;
part time: $591/credit hour

Out-of-state tuition: full time:
$37,636
Room/board/expenses: $15,594
Full-time enrollment: 98
doctoral students: 16%; master's
students: 38%; education
specialists: 46%; men: 35%;
women: 65%; minorities: 22%;
international: 4%
Part-time enrollment: 177
doctoral students: 25%; master's
students: 23%; education
specialists: 53%; men: 29%;
women: 71%; minorities: 8%;
international: 2%
Acceptance rate (master's): 36%
Acceptance rate (doctoral): 51%
Entrance test required: GRE
**Avg. GRE (of all entering students
with scores):** quantitative: 149;
verbal: 155
Research assistantships: 5
Students reporting specialty: 100%
Students specializing in:
curriculum/instr.: 11%; admin.:
9%; policy: 21%; higher education
admin.: 11%; junior high: 3%;
secondary: 5%; special: 16%;
counseling: 14%; other: 11%

VIRGINIA

College of William and Mary

PO Box 8795
Williamsburg, VA 23187-8795
education.wm.edu/
Public
Admissions: (757) 221-2317
Email: GradEd@wm.edu
Financial aid: (757) 221-2317
Application deadline: 01/15
In-state tuition: full time: $12,778;
part time: $430/credit hour
Out-of-state tuition: full time:
$27,721
Room/board/expenses: $19,300
Full-time enrollment: 216
doctoral students: 21%; master's
students: 75%; education
specialists: 4%; men: 18%;
women: 82%; minorities: 13%;
international: 5%
Part-time enrollment: 187
doctoral students: 72%; master's
students: 23%; education
specialists: 5%; men: 25%;
women: 75%; minorities: 24%;
international: 1%
Acceptance rate (master's): 58%
Acceptance rate (doctoral): 55%
Entrance test required: GRE
**Avg. GRE (of all entering students
with scores):** quantitative: 152;
verbal: 157
Students reporting specialty: 100%
Students specializing in:
curriculum/instr.: 22%; admin.:
52%; counseling: 19%; other: 7%

George Mason University

4400 University Drive
MSN 2F1
Fairfax, VA 22030-4444
cehd.gmu.edu
Public
Admissions: (703) 993-2892
Email: cehdgrad@gmu.edu
Financial aid: (703) 993-2349
Application deadline: rolling
In-state tuition: full time: $322/
credit hour; part time: $322/
credit hour
Out-of-state tuition: full time: $558/
credit hour
Room/board/expenses: $23,344
Full-time enrollment: 397
doctoral students: 20%; master's
students: 80%; education

specialists: N/A; men: 18%;
women: 82%; minorities: 25%;
international: 5%
Part-time enrollment: 1,823
doctoral students: 15%; master's
students: 85%; education
specialists: N/A; men: 20%;
women: 80%; minorities: 22%;
international: 1%
Acceptance rate (master's): 80%
Acceptance rate (doctoral): 43%
Entrance test required: GRE
**Avg. GRE (of all entering students
with scores):** quantitative: 150;
verbal: 153
Research assistantships: 55
Students reporting specialty: 84%
Students specializing in:
curriculum/instr.: 52%; admin.:
14%; educational psych: 2%;
special: 28%; counseling: 4%

Liberty University

1971 University Boulevard
Lynchburg, VA 24502
www.liberty.edu/academics/
graduate
Private
Admissions: (800) 424-9596
Email:
gradadmissions@liberty.edu
Financial aid: (434) 582-2270
Application deadline: rolling
Tuition: full time: $520/credit hour;
part time: $565/credit hour
Room/board/expenses: N/A
Full-time enrollment: 2,037
doctoral students: 19%; master's
students: 54%; education
specialists: 31%; men: 26%;
women: 74%; minorities: 25%;
international: 0%
Part-time enrollment: 4,324
doctoral students: 19%; master's
students: 71%; education
specialists: 10%; men: 24%;
women: 76%; minorities: 26%;
international: 0%
Acceptance rate (master's): 50%
Acceptance rate (doctoral): 14%
Entrance test required: GRE
**Avg. GRE (of all entering students
with scores):** quantitative: N/A;
verbal: N/A
Students reporting specialty: 100%
Students specializing in:
curriculum/instr.: 10%; admin.:
41%; instructional media design:
6%; elementary: 12%; junior high:
1%; secondary: 6%; special: 8%;
counseling: 15%; other: 2%

Old Dominion University (Darden)

Education Building, Room 218
Norfolk, VA 23529
education.odu.edu
Public
Admissions: (757) 683-3685
Email: admit@odu.edu
Financial aid: (757) 683-3683
Application deadline: rolling
In-state tuition: full time: $437/
credit hour; part time: $437/
credit hour
Out-of-state tuition: full time:
$1,089/credit hour
Room/board/expenses: $13,271
Full-time enrollment: 604
doctoral students: 13%; master's
students: 87%; education
specialists: 2%; men: 19%;
women: 81%; minorities: 18%;
international: 3%
Part-time enrollment: 783
doctoral students: 29%; master's
students: 60%; education
specialists: 11%; men: 28%;
women: 72%; minorities: 21%;
international: 2%

Acceptance rate (master's): 61%
Acceptance rate (doctoral): 48%
Entrance test required: GRE
Avg. GRE (of all entering students with scores): quantitative: 146; verbal: 149
Research assistantships: 24
Students reporting specialty: 85%
Students specializing in: admin.: 25%; elementary: 18%; secondary: 8%; special: 7%; counseling: 13%; other: 29%

Regent University

1000 Regent University Drive
Virginia Beach, VA 23464
www.regent.edu/acad/schedu
Private
Admissions: (888) 713-1595
Email: education@regent.edu
Financial aid: (757) 352-4125
Application deadline: N/A
Tuition: full time: $575/credit hour; part time: $575/credit hour
Room/board/expenses: $20,060
Full-time enrollment: 92
doctoral students: 0%; master's students: 100%; education specialists: 0%; men: 20%; women: 80%; minorities: 34%; international: N/A
Part-time enrollment: 707
doctoral students: 25%; master's students: 69%; education specialists: 6%; men: 21%; women: 79%; minorities: 34%; international: 1%
Acceptance rate (master's): 58%
Acceptance rate (doctoral): 43%
Entrance test required: GRE
Avg. GRE (of all entering students with scores): quantitative: 142; verbal: 143
Research assistantships: 0
Students reporting specialty: 0%
Students specializing in: N/A

Shenandoah University

1460 University Drive
Winchester, VA 22601
www.su.edu
Private
Admissions: (540) 665-4581
Email: admit@su.edu
Financial aid: (540) 665-4621
Application deadline: rolling
Tuition: full time: $9,404; part time: $488/credit hour
Room/board/expenses: $14,228
Full-time enrollment: 19
doctoral students: 5%; master's students: 95%; education specialists: N/A; men: 32%; women: 68%; minorities: 21%; international: 37%
Part-time enrollment: 321
doctoral students: 31%; master's students: 69%; education specialists: N/A; men: 28%; women: 72%; minorities: 14%; international: 2%
Acceptance rate (master's): 92%
Acceptance rate (doctoral): 95%
Entrance test required: N/A
Avg. GRE (of all entering students with scores): quantitative: N/A; verbal: N/A
Research assistantships: 0
Students reporting specialty: 100%
Students specializing in: admin.: 31%; elementary: 6%; junior high: 1%; secondary: 3%; special: 3%; other: 68%

University of Virginia (Curry)

405 Emmet Street S
Charlottesville, VA 22903-2495
curry.virginia.edu
Public
Admissions: (434) 924-0742
Email: curry-admissions@virginia.edu
Financial aid: (434) 982-6000
Application deadline: N/A
In-state tuition: full time $16,778; part time: $769/credit hour
Out-of-state tuition: full time: $26,102
Room/board/expenses: $20,635
Full-time enrollment: 559
doctoral students: 30%; master's students: 70%; education specialists: 0%; men: 22%; women: 78%; minorities: 18%; international: 5%
Part-time enrollment: 294
doctoral students: 27%; master's students: 60%; education specialists: 13%; men: 24%; women: 76%; minorities: 8%; international: 0%
Acceptance rate (master's): 48%
Acceptance rate (doctoral): 15%
Entrance test required: GRE
Avg. GRE (of all entering students with scores): quantitative: 152; verbal: 156
Research assistantships: 41
Students reporting specialty: 100%
Students specializing in: curriculum/instr.: 16%; admin.: 10%; policy: 1%; evaluation/research/statistics: 1%; educational psych: 3%; educational tech.: 2%; elementary: 8%; higher education admin.: 8%; secondary: 13%; social/philosophical foundations: 8%; special: 8%; counseling: 4%; other: 18%

Virginia Commonwealth University

1015 W. Main Street
PO Box 842020
Richmond, VA 23284-2020
www.soe.vcu.edu
Public
Admissions: (804) 828-3382
Email: htclark@vcu.edu
Financial aid: (804) 828-6181
Application deadline: 02/01
In-state tuition: full time: $12,399; part time: $567/credit hour
Out-of-state tuition: full time: $23,232
Room/board/expenses: $15,108
Full-time enrollment: 354
doctoral students: 10%; master's students: 90%; education specialists: 0%; men: 23%; women: 77%; minorities: 23%; international: 1%
Part-time enrollment: 317
doctoral students: 41%; master's students: 51%; education specialists: 8%; men: 23%; women: 77%; minorities: 21%; international: 1%
Acceptance rate (master's): 61%
Acceptance rate (doctoral): 48%
Entrance test required: GRE
Avg. GRE (of all entering students with scores): quantitative: 149; verbal: 152
Research assistantships: 10
Students reporting specialty: 100%
Students specializing in: curriculum/instr.: 3%; admin.: 4%; policy: 3%; evaluation/research/statistics: 1%; educational psych: 2%; educational tech.: 3%;

elementary: 15%; secondary: 6%; special: 8%; counseling: 12%; other: 42%

Virginia State University

1 Hayden Street
Petersburg, VA 23806
www.vsu.edu/
Public
Admissions: (804) 524-5985
Email: gradadmiss@vsu.edu
Financial aid: N/A
Application deadline: N/A
In-state tuition: full time $10,282; part time: $494/credit hour
Out-of-state tuition: full time: $19,038
Room/board/expenses: $12,803
Full-time enrollment: 88
doctoral students: 31%; master's students: 69%; education specialists: N/A; men: 45%; women: 55%; minorities: 90%; international: 3%
Part-time enrollment: 144
doctoral students: 21%; master's students: 79%; education specialists: N/A; men: 33%; women: 67%; minorities: 87%; international: N/A
Acceptance rate (master's): N/A
Acceptance rate (doctoral): 80%
Entrance test required: GRE
Avg. GRE (of all entering students with scores): quantitative: N/A; verbal: N/A
Research assistantships: 6
Students reporting specialty: 100%
Students specializing in: curriculum/instr.: 24%; admin.: 35%; special: 0%; counseling: 41%

Virginia Tech

226 War Memorial Hall (0313)
Blacksburg, VA 24061
www.graduateschool.vt.edu/
Public
Admissions: (540) 231-8636
Email: gradappl@vt.edu
Financial aid: (540) 231-4558
Application deadline: rolling
In-state tuition: full time: $13,585; part time: $648/credit hour
Out-of-state tuition: full time: $25,280
Room/board/expenses: $13,722
Full-time enrollment: 356
doctoral students: 42%; master's students: 56%; education specialists: 2%; men: 30%; women: 70%; minorities: 17%; international: 10%
Part-time enrollment: 404
doctoral students: 49%; master's students: 45%; education specialists: 6%; men: 34%; women: 66%; minorities: 21%; international: 2%
Acceptance rate (master's): 72%
Acceptance rate (doctoral): 66%
Entrance test required: GRE
Avg. GRE (of all entering students with scores): quantitative: 149; verbal: 153
Research assistantships: 8
Students reporting specialty: 100%
Students specializing in: curriculum/instr.: 48%; admin.: 37%; evaluation/research/statistics: 3%; counseling: 9%; other: 4%

Seattle Pacific University[1]

3307 Third Avenue W
Seattle, WA 98119-1997
www.spu.edu
Private
Admissions: N/A
Financial aid: N/A
Tuition: N/A
Room/board/expenses: N/A
Enrollment: N/A

Seattle University

901 12th Avenue
Seattle, WA 98122
www.seattleu.edu/education
Private
Admissions: (206) 296-2000
Email: grad-admissions@seattleu.edu
Financial aid: (206) 296-2000
Application deadline: rolling
Tuition: full time: $610/credit hour; part time: $610/credit hour
Room/board/expenses: N/A
Full-time enrollment: 386
doctoral students: 10%; master's students: 77%; education specialists: 13%; men: 24%; women: 76%; minorities: 33%; international: 3%
Part-time enrollment: 121
doctoral students: 27%; master's students: 51%; education specialists: 21%; men: 27%; women: 73%; minorities: 31%; international: 1%
Acceptance rate (master's): 73%
Acceptance rate (doctoral): 89%
Entrance test required: GRE
Avg. GRE (of all entering students with scores): quantitative: N/A; verbal: N/A
Students reporting specialty: 99%
Students specializing in: admin.: 8%; evaluation/research/statistics: 14%; educational psych: 13%; elementary: 8%; higher education admin.: 11%; secondary: 8%; special: 3%; counseling: 23%; other: 12%

University of Washington

PO Box 353600
206 Miller
Seattle, WA 98195-3600
education.uw.edu/home
Public
Admissions: (206) 543-7834
Email: edinfo@u.washington.edu
Financial aid: (206) 543-7834
Application deadline: N/A
In-state tuition: full time: $16,104; part time: $694/credit hour
Out-of-state tuition: full time: $28,929
Room/board/expenses: $18,843
Full-time enrollment: 661
doctoral students: 35%; master's students: 59%; education specialists: 6%; men: 26%; women: 74%; minorities: 29%; international: 8%
Part-time enrollment: 157
doctoral students: 42%; master's students: 58%; education specialists: 0%; men: 18%; women: 82%; minorities: 32%; international: 3%
Acceptance rate (master's): 65%
Acceptance rate (doctoral): 24%
Entrance test required: GRE
Avg. GRE (of all entering students with scores): quantitative: 150; verbal: 154
Research assistantships: 82
Students reporting specialty: 92%

Students specializing in: curriculum/instr.: 22%; admin.: 26%; policy: 25%; evaluation/research/statistics: 2%; educational psych: 17%; elementary: 10%; higher education admin.: 5%; secondary: 5%; social/philosophical foundations: 8%; special: 19%; counseling: 7%

Washington State University[1]

PO Box 642114
Pullman, WA 99164-2114
www.wsu.edu/
Public
Admissions: N/A
Financial aid: N/A
Tuition: N/A
Room/board/expenses: N/A
Enrollment: N/A

Marshall University[1]

100 Angus E. Peyton Drive
South Charleston, WV 25303
www.marshall.edu/gsepd/
Public
Admissions: N/A
Financial aid: N/A
Tuition: N/A
Room/board/expenses: N/A
Enrollment: N/A

West Virginia University

802 Allen Hall
PO Box 6122
Morgantown, WV 26506-6122
www.wvu.edu
Public
Admissions: (304) 293-2124
Email: graded@mail.wvu.edu
Financial aid: (304) 293-5242
Application deadline: rolling
In-state tuition: full time: $8,352; part time: $464/credit hour
Out-of-state tuition: full time: $21,906
Room/board/expenses: $12,491
Full-time enrollment: 495
doctoral students: 15%; master's students: 85%; education specialists: N/A; men: 18%; women: 82%; minorities: 7%; international: 4%
Part-time enrollment: 475
doctoral students: 22%; master's students: 78%; education specialists: N/A; men: 19%; women: 81%; minorities: 7%; international: 0%
Acceptance rate (master's): 56%
Acceptance rate (doctoral): 45%
Entrance test required: GRE
Avg. GRE (of all entering students with scores): quantitative: 148; verbal: 151
Research assistantships: 32
Students reporting specialty: 60%
Students specializing in: admin.: 1%; instructional media design: 3%; educational psych: 4%; elementary: 20%; higher education admin.: 4%; secondary: 19%; special: 42%; counseling: 8%

Cardinal Stritch University

6801 N. Yates Road
Milwaukee, WI 53217
www.stritch.edu/
Private
Admissions: N/A

Financial aid: N/A
Application deadline: rolling
Tuition: full time: $11,684; part time: $725/credit hour
Room/board/expenses: N/A
Full-time enrollment: 454
doctoral students: 29%; master's students: 71%; education specialists: N/A; men: 34%; women: 66%; minorities: 26%; international: 1%
Part-time enrollment: 132
doctoral students: 24%; master's students: 76%; education specialists: N/A; men: 31%; women: 69%; minorities: 16%; international: 1%
Acceptance rate (master's): 99%
Acceptance rate (doctoral): 100%
Entrance test required: GRE
Avg. GRE (of all entering students with scores): quantitative: N/A; verbal: N/A
Research assistantships: 0
Students reporting specialty: 100%
Students specializing in: admin.: 47%; instructional media design: 2%; elementary: 14%; secondary: 6%; special: 13%; other: 18%

Edgewood College

1000 Edgewood College Drive
Madison, WI 53711
www.edgewood.edu
Private
Admissions: (608) 663-3297
Email: gps@edgewood.edu
Financial aid: (608) 663-4300
Application deadline: rolling
Tuition: full time: $836/credit hour; part time: $836/credit hour
Room/board/expenses: N/A
Full-time enrollment: 165
doctoral students: 68%; master's students: 32%; education specialists: N/A; men: 38%; women: 62%; minorities: 19%; international: 10%

Part-time enrollment: 187
doctoral students: 20%; master's students: 80%; education specialists: N/A; men: 21%; women: 79%; minorities: 17%; international: 6%
Acceptance rate (master's): N/A
Acceptance rate (doctoral): N/A
Entrance test required: N/A
Avg. GRE (of all entering students with scores): quantitative: N/A; verbal: N/A
Students reporting specialty: 0%
Students specializing in: N/A

Marquette University

Schroeder Complex, Box 1881
Milwaukee, WI 53201
www.grad.marquette.edu
Private
Admissions: (414) 288-7137
Email: mugs@marquette.edu
Financial aid: (414) 288-5325
Application deadline: rolling
Tuition: full time: $765/credit hour; part time: $765/credit hour
Room/board/expenses: $16,306
Full-time enrollment: 50
doctoral students: 6%; master's students: 94%; education specialists: N/A; men: 14%; women: 86%; minorities: 12%; international: 2%
Part-time enrollment: 86
doctoral students: 24%; master's students: 76%; education specialists: N/A; men: 33%; women: 67%; minorities: 10%; international: 1%
Acceptance rate (master's): 79%
Acceptance rate (doctoral): 75%
Entrance test required: GRE
Avg. GRE (of all entering students with scores): quantitative: 150; verbal: 155
Research assistantships: 5
Students reporting specialty: 100%

Students specializing in: curriculum/instr.: 1%; admin.: 14%; policy: 15%; elementary: 3%; higher education admin.: 23%; junior high: 31%; secondary: 28%; social/philosophical foundations: 25%; counseling: 8%

University of Wisconsin-Madison

1000 Bascom Mall, Suite 377
Madison, WI 53706-1326
www.education.wisc.edu
Public
Admissions: (608) 262-2433
Email: gradamiss@grad.wisc.edu
Financial aid: (608) 262-2087
Application deadline: rolling
In-state tuition: full time: $11,864; part time: $786/credit hour
Out-of-state tuition: full time: $25,191
Room/board/expenses: $13,014
Full-time enrollment: 714
doctoral students: 64%; master's students: 36%; education specialists: N/A; men: 30%; women: 70%; minorities: 25%; international: 18%
Part-time enrollment: 297
doctoral students: 42%; master's students: 58%; education specialists: N/A; men: 32%; women: 68%; minorities: 21%; international: 8%
Acceptance rate (master's): 28%
Acceptance rate (doctoral): 31%
Entrance test required: GRE
Avg. GRE (of all entering students with scores): quantitative: 153; verbal: 156
Research assistantships: 10
Students reporting specialty: 100%
Students specializing in: curriculum/instr.: 28%; admin.: 25%; policy: 7%; educational psych: 12%; special: 3%; counseling: 7%; other: 18%

University of Wisconsin-Milwaukee

PO Box 413
Milwaukee, WI 53201
www.graduateschool.uwm.edu
Public
Admissions: (414) 229-4495
Email: gradschool@uwm.edu
Financial aid: (414) 229-4541
Application deadline: rolling
In-state tuition: full time: $12,986; part time: $1,065/credit hour
Out-of-state tuition: full time: $25,452
Room/board/expenses: $11,836
Full-time enrollment: 272
doctoral students: 35%; master's students: 61%; education specialists: 4%; men: 26%; women: 74%; minorities: 28%; international: 5%
Part-time enrollment: 373
doctoral students: 13%; master's students: 83%; education specialists: 3%; men: 24%; women: 76%; minorities: 27%; international: 1%
Acceptance rate (master's): 51%
Acceptance rate (doctoral): 23%
Entrance test required: GRE
Avg. GRE (of all entering students with scores): quantitative: 148; verbal: 153
Research assistantships: 27
Students reporting specialty: 100%
Students specializing in: curriculum/instr.: 13%; admin.: 44%; policy: 0%; educational psych: 29%; social/philosophical foundations: 7%; special: 5%; other: 2%

University of Wyoming

Department 3374
1000 E. University Avenue
Laramie, WY 82071
www.uwyo.edu/education/
Public
Admissions: (307) 766-5160
Email: admissions@uwyo.edu
Financial aid: N/A
Application deadline: N/A
In-state tuition: full time: $221/credit hour; part time: $221/credit hour
Out-of-state tuition: full time: $660/credit hour
Room/board/expenses: $16,599
Full-time enrollment: 149
doctoral students: 37%; master's students: 63%; education specialists: N/A; men: 28%; women: 72%; minorities: 9%; international: 8%
Part-time enrollment: 396
doctoral students: 40%; master's students: 60%; education specialists: N/A; men: 39%; women: 61%; minorities: 10%; international: 2%
Acceptance rate (master's): 83%
Acceptance rate (doctoral): 71%
Entrance test required: GRE
Avg. GRE (of all entering students with scores): quantitative: 152; verbal: 154
Research assistantships: 18
Students reporting specialty: 100%
Students specializing in: curriculum/instr.: 2%; admin.: 4%; special: 1%; counseling: 11%; other: 82%

ENGINEERING

The engineering directory lists the country's 215 schools offering doctoral programs. One hundred ninety-six schools responded to the U.S. News survey conducted in the fall of 2014 and early 2015. Information about entrance requirements, enrollment and costs is reported. Institutions that did not respond to the survey have abbreviated entries.

KEY TO THE TERMINOLOGY

1. A school footnoted with the numeral 1 did not return the U.S. News statistical survey; limited data appear in its entry.

N/A. Not available from the school or not applicable.

Admissions. The admissions office phone number.

Email. The address of the admissions office. If instead of an email address a website is listed, the website will automatically present an email screen programmed to reach the admissions office.

Financial aid. The financial aid office phone number.

Application deadline. For fall 2016 enrollment. "Rolling" means there is no deadline; the school acts on applications as they are received. "Varies" means deadlines vary according to department or whether applicants are U.S. citizens or foreign nationals.

Tuition. For the 2014-15 academic year. Includes fees.

Credit hour. The cost per credit hour for the 2014-15 academic year.

Room/board/expenses. For the 2014-15 academic year.

Enrollment. Full and part time for fall 2014. The total is the combination of master's and doctoral students if the school offers both degrees. Where available, the breakdown for men, women, minorities and international students is provided. Percentages for men and women may not add up to 100 because of rounding.

Minorities. For fall 2014, the percentage of students who are black or African-American, Asian, American Indian or Alaskan Native, Native Hawaiian or other Pacific Islander, Hispanic/Latino or two or more races. The minority percentage was reported by each school.

Acceptance rate. Percentage of applicants who were accepted for fall 2014, including both master's and doctoral degree programs.

GRE requirement. "Yes" means Graduate Record Examination scores are required by some or all departments.

Average GRE scores. Combined for both master's and doctoral degree students who entered in fall 2014. GRE scores displayed are for fall 2014 entering master's and Ph.D. students and are only for those GRE exams taken during or after August 2011 using the new 130-170 score scale.

TOEFL requirement. "Yes" means that students from non-English-speaking countries must submit scores for the Test of English as a Foreign Language.

Minimum TOEFL score. The score listed is the minimum acceptable score for the paper TOEFL. (The computer-administered TOEFL is graded on a different scale.)

Total fellowships, teaching assistantships and research assistantships. The number of student appointments for the 2014-15 academic year. Students may hold multiple appointments and would therefore be counted more than once.

Student specialties. Proportion of master's and doctoral students, both full and part time, in the specialty-reporting population (not necessarily the entire student body) who were enrolled in a particular specialty in fall 2014. Specialty fields listed are aerospace/aeronautical/astronautical; biological/agricultural; architectural engineering; bioengineering/biomedical; chemical; civil; computer engineering; computer science; electrical/electronic/communications; engineering management; engineering science and physics; environmental/environmental health; industrial/manufacturing/systems; materials; mechanical; mining; nuclear; petroleum; and other. Numbers may not add up to 100 percent from rounding or because students are enrolled in multiple specialties.

ALABAMA

Auburn University (Ginn)
1301 Shelby Center
Auburn University, AL 36849
www.grad.auburn.edu
Public
Admissions: (334) 844-4700
Email: gradadm@auburn.edu
Financial aid: (334) 844-4367
Application deadline: rolling
In-state tuition: full time: $10,194; part time: $477/credit hour
Out-of-state tuition: full time: $27,366
Room/board/expenses: $18,964
Full-time enrollment: 619
men: 78%; women: 22%; minorities: 4%; international: 77%
Part-time enrollment: 298
men: 79%; women: 21%; minorities: 12%; international: 21%
Acceptance rate: 48%
GRE requirement: Yes
Avg. GRE: quantitative: 160
TOEFL requirement: Yes
Minimum TOEFL score: 550
Fellowships: 91
Teaching assistantships: 234
Research assistantships: 326
Students specializing in:
aerospace: 5%; agriculture: 3%; chemical: 9%; civil: 12%; computer science: 12%; electrical: 21%; industrial: 17%; materials: 3%; mechanical: 15%; other: 1%

Tuskegee University[1]
202 Engineering Building
Tuskegee, AL 36088-1920
www.tuskegee.edu
Private
Admissions: (334) 727-8500
Email: adm@tuskegee.edu
Financial aid: N/A
Tuition: N/A
Room/board/expenses: N/A
Enrollment: N/A

University of Alabama
Box 870200
Tuscaloosa, AL 35487-0200
www.coeweb.eng.ua.edu/
Public
Admissions: (205) 348-5921
Email: gradschool@ua.edu
Financial aid: (205) 348-2976
Application deadline: rolling
In-state tuition: full time: $9,826; part time: N/A
Out-of-state tuition: full time: $24,950
Room/board/expenses: $12,457
Full-time enrollment: 279
men: 81%; women: 19%; minorities: 8%; international: 51%
Part-time enrollment: 69
men: 94%; women: 6%; minorities: 10%; international: 28%
Acceptance rate: 35%
GRE requirement: Yes
Avg. GRE: quantitative: 160
TOEFL requirement: Yes
Minimum TOEFL score: 550
Fellowships: 0
Teaching assistantships: 98
Research assistantships: 29
Students specializing in:
aerospace: 15%; chemical: 7%; civil: 18%; computer science: 15%; electrical: 16%; materials: 10%; mechanical: 20%; other: 3%

University of Alabama–Birmingham
1720 2nd Avenue S
HOEN 100
Birmingham, AL 35294-4440
www.uab.edu/engineering
Public
Admissions: (205) 934-8232
Email: gradschool@uab.edu
Financial aid: (205) 934-8132
Application deadline: 07/01
In-state tuition: full time: $7,090; part time: $370/credit hour
Out-of-state tuition: full time: $16,072
Room/board/expenses: $10,840
Full-time enrollment: 131
men: 19%; women: 81%; minorities: 18%; international: 54%
Part-time enrollment: 341
men: 18%; women: 82%; minorities: 32%; international: 6%
Acceptance rate: 83%
GRE requirement: Yes
Avg. GRE: quantitative: 158
TOEFL requirement: Yes
Minimum TOEFL score: 550
Fellowships: 19
Teaching assistantships: 7
Research assistantships: 56
Students specializing in:
biomedical: 10%; civil: 10%; computer: 3%; electrical: 5%; management: 53%; environmental: 0%; materials: 7%; mechanical: 5%; other: 8%

University of Alabama–Huntsville
301 Sparkman Drive
EB 102
Huntsville, AL 35899
www.uah.edu
Public
Admissions: (256) 824-6198
Email: berkowd@uah.edu
Financial aid: (256) 824-6241
Application deadline: rolling
In-state tuition: full time: $9,180; part time: $6,676
Out-of-state tuition: full time: $21,232
Room/board/expenses: $11,324
Full-time enrollment: 268
men: 72%; women: 28%; minorities: 7%; international: 60%
Part-time enrollment: 447
men: 81%; women: 19%; minorities: 12%; international: 5%
Acceptance rate: 71%
GRE requirement: Yes
Avg. GRE: quantitative: 156
TOEFL requirement: Yes
Minimum TOEFL score: N/A
Teaching assistantships: 91
Research assistantships: 75
Students specializing in:
aerospace: 10%; biomedical: 4%; chemical: 1%; civil: 3%; computer: 6%; computer science: 16%; electrical: 19%; management: 4%; industrial: 13%; materials: 1%; mechanical: 15%; other: 7%

ALASKA

University of Alaska–Fairbanks
PO Box 755960
Fairbanks, AK 99775-5960
www.uaf.edu/cem
Public
Admissions: (800) 478-1823
Email: admissions@uaf.edu
Financial aid: (888) 474-7256

Application deadline: 06/01
In-state tuition: full time: $403/credit hour; part time: $403/credit hour
Out-of-state tuition: full time: $823/credit hour
Room/board/expenses: $12,380
Full-time enrollment: 85
men: 74%; women: 26%; minorities: 9%; international: 54%
Part-time enrollment: 42
men: 81%; women: 19%; minorities: 12%; international: 12%
Acceptance rate: 27%
GRE requirement: Yes
Avg. GRE: quantitative: N/A
TOEFL requirement: Yes
Minimum TOEFL score: 550
Teaching assistantships: 37
Research assistantships: 33
Students specializing in: civil: 9%; computer: 1%; computer science: 4%; electrical: 12%; management: 4%; mechanical: 6%; mining: 5%; petroleum: 27%; other: 29%

ARIZONA

Arizona State University (Fulton)

Box 879309
Tempe, AZ 85287-9309
engineering.asu.edu
Public
Admissions: (480) 965-6113
Email: grad-ges@asu.edu
Financial aid: (480) 965-3355
Application deadline: rolling
In-state tuition: full time: $12,103; part time: $1,022/credit hour
Out-of-state tuition: full time: $27,537
Room/board/expenses: $11,872
Full-time enrollment: 2,863
men: 77%; women: 23%; minorities: 6%; international: 82%
Part-time enrollment: 831
men: 80%; women: 20%; minorities: 21%; international: 38%
Acceptance rate: 47%
GRE requirement: Yes
Avg. GRE: quantitative: 162
TOEFL requirement: Yes
Minimum TOEFL score: 550
Fellowships: 298
Teaching assistantships: 292
Research assistantships: 604
Students specializing in: aerospace: 2%; biomedical: 5%; chemical: 2%; civil: 5%; computer: 5%; computer science: 22%; electrical: 28%; environmental: 2%; industrial: 7%; materials: 4%; mechanical: 11%; other: 7%

University of Arizona

Civil Engineering Building
Room 100
Tucson, AZ 85721-0072
grad.arizona.edu
Public
Admissions: (520) 621-3471
Email: gradadmission@grad.arizona.edu
Financial aid: (520) 621-1858
Application deadline: rolling
In-state tuition: full time: $11,738; part time: $766/credit hour
Out-of-state tuition: full time: $28,720
Room/board/expenses: $17,000
Full-time enrollment: 843
men: 76%; women: 24%; minorities: 13%; international: 56%
Part-time enrollment: 290
men: 79%; women: 21%; minorities: 25%; international: 22%
Acceptance rate: 42%
GRE requirement: Yes
Avg. GRE: quantitative: 163
TOEFL requirement: Yes
Minimum TOEFL score: 550

Fellowships: 47
Teaching assistantships: 87
Research assistantships: 324
Students specializing in: aerospace: 3%; agriculture: 2%; biomedical: 3%; chemical: 4%; civil: 4%; computer science: 6%; electrical: 24%; management: 3%; environmental: 4%; industrial: 6%; materials: 4%; mechanical: 5%; mining: 2%; other: 30%

ARKANSAS

University of Arkansas-Fayetteville

Bell Engineering Center
Room 4183
Fayetteville, AR 72701
www.engr.uark.edu
Public
Admissions: (479) 575-4401
Email: gradinfo@uark.edu
Financial aid: (479) 575-3806
Application deadline: 08/01
In-state tuition: full time: $388/credit hour; part time: $388/credit hour
Out-of-state tuition: full time: $919/credit hour
Room/board/expenses: $12,464
Full-time enrollment: 320
men: 78%; women: 22%; minorities: 8%; international: 60%
Part-time enrollment: 143
men: 83%; women: 17%; minorities: 23%; international: 20%
Acceptance rate: 34%
GRE requirement: Yes
Avg. GRE: quantitative: 159
TOEFL requirement: Yes
Minimum TOEFL score: 550
Fellowships: 49
Teaching assistantships: 83
Research assistantships: 151
Students specializing in: agriculture: 5%; biomedical: 4%; chemical: 6%; civil: 10%; computer: 7%; computer science: 7%; electrical: 26%; industrial: 13%; mechanical: 9%; other: 13%

University of Arkansas-Little Rock[1]

2801 S University Avenue
Little Rock, AR 72204
ualr.edu/eit/
Public
Admissions: (501) 569-3127
Email: admissions@ualr.edu
Financial aid: N/A
Tuition: N/A
Room/board/expenses: N/A
Enrollment: N/A

CALIFORNIA

California Institute of Technology

1200 E. California Boulevard
Pasadena, CA 91125-4400
www.gradoffice.caltech.edu
Private
Admissions: (626) 395-6346
Email: gradofc@its.caltech.edu
Financial aid: (626) 395-6346
Application deadline: 12/15
Tuition: full time: $43,230; part time: N/A
Room/board/expenses: $29,391
Full-time enrollment: 537
men: 80%; women: 20%; minorities: 6%; international: 51%
Part-time enrollment: N/A
men: N/A; women: N/A; minorities: N/A; international: N/A
Acceptance rate: 9%
GRE requirement: Yes
Avg. GRE: quantitative: 166
TOEFL requirement: Yes
Minimum TOEFL score: N/A
Fellowships: 202
Teaching assistantships: 94

Research assistantships: 353
Students specializing in: aerospace: 13%; biomedical: 1%; chemical: 11%; civil: 3%; computer science: 8%; electrical: 24%; science and physics: 11%; environmental: 5%; materials: 13%; mechanical: 11%

California State University-Long Beach

1250 Bellflower Boulevard
Long Beach, CA 90840-8306
www.csulb.edu/colleges/coe/
Public
Admissions: (562) 985-5121
Email: coe-gr@csulb.edu
Financial aid: N/A
Application deadline: 04/15
In-state tuition: full time: $7,718; part time: $4,886
Out-of-state tuition: full time: $14,414
Room/board/expenses: $16,000
Full-time enrollment: 383
men: 83%; women: 17%; minorities: 8%; international: 86%
Part-time enrollment: 368
men: 80%; women: 20%; minorities: 15%; international: 43%
Acceptance rate: 31%
GRE requirement: Yes
Avg. GRE: quantitative: 157
TOEFL requirement: Yes
Minimum TOEFL score: 550
Fellowships: 12
Teaching assistantships: 6
Research assistantships: 14
Students specializing in: aerospace: 4%; civil: 8%; computer: 5%; computer science: 27%; electrical: 41%; industrial: 2%; mechanical: 9%; other: 5%

Naval Postgraduate School[1]

1 University Circle
Monterey, CA 93943-5001
www.nps.edu/Academics/Schools/GSEAS/
Public
Admissions: (831) 656-3093
Email: grad-ed@nps.edu
Financial aid: N/A
Tuition: N/A
Room/board/expenses: N/A
Enrollment: N/A

Northwestern Polytechnic University[1]

47671 Westinghouse Drive
Fremont, CA 94539
www.npu.edu
Private
Admissions: (510) 592-9688
Email: admission@npu.edu
Financial aid: N/A
Tuition: N/A
Room/board/expenses: N/A
Enrollment: N/A

San Diego State University

5500 Campanile Drive
San Diego, CA 92182
engineering.sdsu.edu
Public
Admissions: (619) 594-6061
Email: admissions@sdsu.edu
Financial aid: (619) 594-6323
Application deadline: N/A
In-state tuition: full time: $8,132; part time: $5,300
Out-of-state tuition: full time: $372/credit hour
Room/board/expenses: $17,568

Full-time enrollment: 249
men: 65%; women: 35%; minorities: 14%; international: 61%
Part-time enrollment: 187
men: 77%; women: 23%; minorities: 55%; international: 28%
Acceptance rate: 49%
GRE requirement: Yes
Avg. GRE: quantitative: 157
TOEFL requirement: Yes
Minimum TOEFL score: 550
Teaching assistantships: 25
Students specializing in: aerospace: 10%; biomedical: 8%; civil: 17%; electrical: 52%; science and physics: 5%; environmental: 5%; mechanical: 3%; other: 1%

Santa Clara University

500 El Camino Real
Santa Clara, CA 95053-0583
www.scu.edu/engineering/graduate
Private
Admissions: (408) 554-4313
Email: gradengineer@scu.edu
Financial aid: (408) 554-4505
Application deadline: rolling
Tuition: full time: $862/credit hour; part time: $862/credit hour
Room/board/expenses: N/A
Full-time enrollment: 579
men: 59%; women: 41%; minorities: 87%; international: 79%
Part-time enrollment: 321
men: 72%; women: 28%; minorities: 65%; international: 25%
Acceptance rate: 50%
GRE requirement: Yes
Avg. GRE: quantitative: 159
TOEFL requirement: Yes
Minimum TOEFL score: N/A
Teaching assistantships: 32
Research assistantships: 17
Students specializing in: biomedical: 3%; civil: 3%; computer: 54%; electrical: 14%; management: 12%; environmental: 2%; mechanical: 11%; other: 1%

Stanford University

Huang Engineering Center
Suite 226
Stanford, CA 94305-4121
engineering.stanford.edu
Private
Admissions: (650) 723-4291
Email: gradadmissions@stanford.edu
Financial aid: (650) 723-3058
Application deadline: N/A
Tuition: full time: $47,745; part time: N/A
Room/board/expenses: $27,156
Full-time enrollment: 3,266
men: 72%; women: 28%; minorities: 24%; international: 45%
Part-time enrollment: 292
men: 77%; women: 23%; minorities: 35%; international: 25%
Acceptance rate: 17%
GRE requirement: Yes
Avg. GRE: quantitative: 166
TOEFL requirement: Yes
Minimum TOEFL score: 575
Fellowships: 1,179
Teaching assistantships: 548
Research assistantships: 1,069
Students specializing in: aerospace: 6%; biomedical: 4%; chemical: 4%; civil: 12%; computer science: 15%; electrical: 23%; management: 9%; materials: 5%; mechanical: 15%; petroleum: 1%; other: 5%

University of California-Berkeley

320 McLaughlin Hall, # 1700
Berkeley, CA 94720-1700
www.grad.berkeley.edu/
Public
Admissions: (510) 642-7405
Email: gradadm@berkeley.edu
Financial aid: (510) 642-6442
Application deadline: 02/10
In-state tuition: full time: $16,210; part time: N/A
Out-of-state tuition: full time: $31,312
Room/board/expenses: $20,812
Full-time enrollment: 1,850
men: 73%; women: 27%; minorities: 22%; international: 41%
Part-time enrollment: 86
men: 64%; women: 36%; minorities: 34%; international: 17%
Acceptance rate: 14%
GRE requirement: Yes
Avg. GRE: quantitative: 165
TOEFL requirement: Yes
Minimum TOEFL score: 570
Fellowships: 834
Teaching assistantships: 378
Research assistantships: 677
Students specializing in: biomedical: 11%; chemical: 7%; civil: 17%; computer: 11%; electrical: 18%; industrial: 4%; materials: 5%; mechanical: 19%; nuclear: 4%; other: 2%

University of California-Davis

1050 Kemper Hall
1 Shields Avenue
Davis, CA 95616-5294
engineering.ucdavis.edu
Public
Admissions: (530) 752-1473
Email: gradadmit@ucdavis.edu
Financial aid: (530) 752-8864
Application deadline: N/A
In-state tuition: full time: $13,109; part time: $7,499
Out-of-state tuition: full time: $28,211
Room/board/expenses: $21,206
Full-time enrollment: 1,114
men: 73%; women: 27%; minorities: 21%; international: 41%
Part-time enrollment: 45
men: 76%; women: 24%; minorities: 31%; international: 7%
Acceptance rate: 21%
GRE requirement: Yes
Avg. GRE: quantitative: 162
TOEFL requirement: Yes
Minimum TOEFL score: 550
Fellowships: 240
Teaching assistantships: 252
Research assistantships: 472
Students specializing in: aerospace: 15%; agriculture: 4%; biomedical: 10%; chemical: 5%; civil: 19%; computer: 18%; computer science: 18%; electrical: 18%; science and physics: 1%; environmental: 19%; materials: 6%; mechanical: 15%; other: 4%

University of California-Irvine (Samueli)

305 EH 5200
Irvine, CA 92697-2700
www.eng.uci.edu
Public
Admissions: (949) 824-4334
Email: gradengr@uci.edu
Financial aid: (949) 824-4889
Application deadline: 01/15
In-state tuition: full time: $16,035; part time: $10,425
Out-of-state tuition: full time: $31,137
Room/board/expenses: $18,405

Full-time enrollment: 1,386
men: 72%; women: 28%;
minorities: 17%; international: 62%
Part-time enrollment: 104
men: 76%; women: 24%;
minorities: 36%; international:
38%
Acceptance rate: 20%
GRE requirement: Yes
Avg. GRE: quantitative: 163
TOEFL requirement: Yes
Minimum TOEFL score: 550
Fellowships: 746
Teaching assistantships: 375
Research assistantships: 672
Students specializing in:
aerospace: 4%; biomedical:
9%; chemical: 5%; civil: 10%;
computer: 10%; computer
science: 23%; electrical: 16%;
management: 1%; environmental:
5%; industrial: 2%; materials: 4%;
mechanical: 8%; other: 2%

University of California-Los Angeles (Samueli)

6426 Boelter Hall
Box 951601
Los Angeles, CA 90095-1601
www.engineer.ucla.edu
Public
Admissions: (310) 825-2514
Email: gradadm@seas.ucla.edu
Financial aid: (310) 206-0400
Application deadline: 12/01
In-state tuition: full time: $12,571;
part time: N/A
Out-of-state tuition: full time:
$27,673
Room/board/expenses: $19,788
Full-time enrollment: 1,928
men: 78%; women: 22%;
minorities: 25%; international:
54%
Part-time enrollment: N/A
men: N/A; women: N/A; minorities:
N/A; international: N/A
Acceptance rate: 29%
GRE requirement: Yes
Avg. GRE: quantitative: 165
TOEFL requirement: Yes
Minimum TOEFL score: 560
Fellowships: 680
Teaching assistantships: 609
Research assistantships: 1,400
Students specializing in:
aerospace: 3%; biomedical: 9%;
chemical: 5%; civil: 7%; computer
science: 19%; electrical: 25%;
materials: 8%; mechanical: 13%;
other: 10%

University of California-Merced

5200 North Lake Road
Merced, CA 95343
engineering.ucmerced.edu/
Public
Admissions: (202) 228-4400
Email: engineering@ucmerced.edu
Financial aid: N/A
Application deadline: N/A
In-state tuition: full time: $12,829;
part time: $7,219
Out-of-state tuition: full time:
$27,931
Room/board/expenses: N/A
Full-time enrollment: 128
men: 72%; women: 28%;
minorities: 9%; international: 56%
Part-time enrollment: 2
men: 100%; women: 0%;
minorities: 50%; international: 0%
Acceptance rate: 39%
GRE requirement: Yes
Avg. GRE: quantitative: 159
TOEFL requirement: Yes
Minimum TOEFL score: 550
Fellowships: 1
Teaching assistantships: 58
Research assistantships: 26

Students specializing in:
biomedical: 18%; computer
science: 28%; environmental:
33%; mechanical: 21%

University of California-Riverside (Bourns)

University Office Building
Riverside, CA 92521-0208
www.graddiv.ucr.edu
Public
Admissions: (951) 827-3313
Email: grdadmis@ucr.edu
Financial aid: (951) 827-3387
Application deadline: 01/05
In-state tuition: full time: $16,198;
part time: $10,588
Out-of-state tuition: full time:
$31,300
Room/board/expenses: $20,900
Full-time enrollment: 667
men: 76%; women: 24%;
minorities: 24%; international:
50%
Part-time enrollment: N/A
men: N/A; women: N/A; minorities:
N/A; international: N/A
Acceptance rate: 23%
GRE requirement: Yes
Avg. GRE: quantitative: 161
TOEFL requirement: Yes
Minimum TOEFL score: 550
Fellowships: 133
Teaching assistantships: 245
Research assistantships: 483
Students specializing in:
biomedical: 14%; chemical: 15%;
computer: 4%; computer science:
25%; electrical: 21%; materials:
11%; mechanical: 10%; other: 0%

University of California-San Diego (Jacobs)

9500 Gilman Drive
La Jolla, CA 92093-0403
www.jacobsschool.ucsd.edu
Public
Admissions: (858) 534-3555
Email: gradadmissions@ucsd.edu
Financial aid: (858) 534-4480
Application deadline: N/A
In-state tuition: full time: $12,928;
part time: $7,318
Out-of-state tuition: full time:
$28,030
Room/board/expenses: $21,322
Full-time enrollment: 1,762
men: 78%; women: 22%;
minorities: 22%; international:
54%
Part-time enrollment: 100
men: 80%; women: 20%;
minorities: 42%; international: 17%
Acceptance rate: 22%
GRE requirement: Yes
Avg. GRE: quantitative: 165
TOEFL requirement: Yes
Minimum TOEFL score: 550
Fellowships: 430
Teaching assistantships: 550
Research assistantships: 1,020
Students specializing in:
aerospace: 1%; biomedical:
14%; chemical: 2%; civil: 9%;
computer: 5%; computer science:
20%; electrical: 24%; science
and physics: 2%; materials: 8%;
mechanical: 10%; other: 5%

University of California-Santa Barbara

Harold Frank Hall, #1038
Santa Barbara, CA 93106-5130
www.engineering.ucsb.edu
Public
Admissions: (805) 893-2277
Email: gradadmissions@
graddiv.ucsb.edu
Financial aid: (805) 893-2277
Application deadline: N/A

In-state tuition: full time: $13,114;
part time: N/A
Out-of-state tuition: full time:
$29,138
Room/board/expenses: $16,541
Full-time enrollment: 690
men: 79%; women: 21%;
minorities: 10%; international:
47%
Part-time enrollment: N/A
men: N/A; women: N/A; minorities:
N/A; international: N/A
Acceptance rate: 14%
GRE requirement: Yes
Avg. GRE: quantitative: 165
TOEFL requirement: Yes
Minimum TOEFL score: 600
Fellowships: 154
Teaching assistantships: 117
Research assistantships: 392
Students specializing in: chemical:
12%; computer science: 20%;
electrical: 39%; materials: 20%;
mechanical: 10%

University of California-Santa Cruz (Baskin)

1156 High Street
Santa Cruz, CA 95064
ga.soe.ucsc.edu/
Public
Admissions: (831) 459-5905
Email: soegradadm@soe.ucsc.edu
Financial aid: (831) 459-2963
Application deadline: N/A
In-state tuition: full time: $16,959;
part time: $11,349
Out-of-state tuition: full time:
$32,061
Room/board/expenses: $22,545
Full-time enrollment: 400
men: 73%; women: 28%;
minorities: 18%; international:
26%
Part-time enrollment: 38
men: 84%; women: 16%;
minorities: 34%; international: 11%
Acceptance rate: 32%
GRE requirement: Yes
Avg. GRE: quantitative: 163
TOEFL requirement: Yes
Minimum TOEFL score: 570
Fellowships: 103
Teaching assistantships: 288
Research assistantships: 365
Students specializing in:
biomedical: 11%; computer: 19%;
computer science: 31%; electrical:
21%; other: 18%

University of Southern California (Viterbi)

University Park
Olin Hall 200
Los Angeles, CA 90089-1450
viterbi.usc.edu
Private
Admissions: (213) 740-4530
Email: viterbi.gradadmission@
usc.edu
Financial aid: (213) 740-0119
Application deadline: 01/15
Tuition: full time: $32,747; part
time: $1,706/credit hour
Room/board/expenses: $21,792
Full-time enrollment: 3,330
men: 72%; women: 28%;
minorities: 8%; international: 83%
Part-time enrollment: 1,812
men: 73%; women: 27%;
minorities: 18%; international:
60%
Acceptance rate: 23%
GRE requirement: Yes
Avg. GRE: quantitative: 164
TOEFL requirement: Yes
Minimum TOEFL score: N/A
Fellowships: 288
Teaching assistantships: 638
Research assistantships: 1,128

Students specializing in:
aerospace: 5%; biomedical: 5%;
chemical: 3%; civil: 5%; computer:
2%; computer science: 30%;
electrical: 25%; management: 2%;
environmental: 1%; industrial: 5%;
materials: 3%; mechanical: 6%;
petroleum: 4%; other: 4%

COLORADO

Colorado School of Mines

1500 Illinois Street
Golden, CO 80401-1887
gradschool.mines.edu
Public
Admissions: (303) 384-2221
Email: grad-school@mines.edu
Financial aid: (303) 273-3207
Application deadline: 07/01
In-state tuition: full time: $16,918;
part time: $822/credit hour
Out-of-state tuition: full time:
$33,598
Room/board/expenses: $19,800
Full-time enrollment: 1,128
men: 72%; women: 28%;
minorities: 8%; international: 36%
Part-time enrollment: 162
men: 79%; women: 21%;
minorities: 18%; international: 7%
Acceptance rate: 41%
GRE requirement: Yes
Avg. GRE: quantitative: 159
TOEFL requirement: Yes
Minimum TOEFL score: 550
Fellowships: 65
Teaching assistantships: 164
Research assistantships: 509
Students specializing in: chemical:
11%; civil: 11%; electrical: 8%;
science and physics: 6%;
materials: 10%; mechanical:
10%; mining: 4%; petroleum: 7%;
other: 32%

Colorado State University

Campus Delivery 1301
Fort Collins, CO 80523-1301
www.engr.colostate.edu
Public
Admissions: (970) 491-6817
Email:
gschool@grad.colostate.edu
Financial aid: (970) 491-6321
Application deadline: 02/01
In-state tuition: full time: $11,104;
part time: $674/credit hour
Out-of-state tuition: full time:
$24,276
Room/board/expenses: $14,502
Full-time enrollment: 372
men: 73%; women: 27%;
minorities: 5%; international: 51%
Part-time enrollment: 386
men: 73%; women: 27%;
minorities: 7%; international: 42%
Acceptance rate: 49%
GRE requirement: Yes
Avg. GRE: quantitative: 160
TOEFL requirement: Yes
Minimum TOEFL score: 550
Fellowships: 37
Teaching assistantships: 46
Research assistantships: 212
Students specializing in:
biomedical: 6%; chemical: 3%;
civil: 32%; electrical: 32%;
industrial: 2%; mechanical: 13%;
other: 12%

University of Colorado-Boulder

422 UCB
Boulder, CO 80309-0422
www.colorado.edu/engineering
Public
Admissions: (303) 492-5071
Financial aid: (303) 492-5091
Application deadline: 01/15
In-state tuition: full time: $14,955;
part time: $10,457

Out-of-state tuition: full time:
$31,302
Room/board/expenses: $25,712
Full-time enrollment: 1,431
men: 75%; women: 25%;
minorities: 12%; international: 37%
Part-time enrollment: 232
men: 79%; women: 21%;
minorities: 13%; international: 12%
Acceptance rate: 38%
GRE requirement: Yes
Avg. GRE: quantitative: 161
TOEFL requirement: Yes
Minimum TOEFL score: 600
Fellowships: 108
Teaching assistantships: 109
Research assistantships: 487
Students specializing in:
aerospace: 15%; architectural:
2%; chemical: 6%; civil: 14%;
computer science: 13%; electrical:
16%; management: 11%; materials:
1%; mechanical: 11%; other: 11%

University of Colorado-Colorado Springs

1420 Austin Bluffs Parkway
Colorado Springs, CO 80918
www.uccs.edu
Public
Admissions: (719) 255-3383
Email: admrec@uccs.edu
Financial aid: (719) 255-3460
Application deadline: rolling
In-state tuition: full time: $11,358;
part time: $4,271
Out-of-state tuition: full time:
$20,052
Room/board/expenses: $15,920
Full-time enrollment: 130
men: 83%; women: 17%;
minorities: 10%; international:
49%
Part-time enrollment: 192
men: 81%; women: 19%;
minorities: 17%; international: 29%
Acceptance rate: 65%
GRE requirement: Yes
Avg. GRE: quantitative: 155
TOEFL requirement: Yes
Minimum TOEFL score: 550
Students specializing in: computer
science: 22%; electrical: 15%;
management: 54%; mechanical:
9%

University of Colorado-Denver

PO Box 173364
Campus Box 104
Denver, CO 80217-3364
www.ucdenver.edu/
Public
Admissions: (303) 556-2704
Email: admissions@ucdenver.edu
Financial aid: (303) 556-2886
Application deadline: rolling
In-state tuition: full time: $5,687;
part time: $446/credit hour
Out-of-state tuition: full time:
$13,415
Room/board/expenses: $16,504
Full-time enrollment: 397
men: 71%; women: 29%;
minorities: 10%; international:
63%
Part-time enrollment: 151
men: 82%; women: 18%;
minorities: 10%; international:
20%
Acceptance rate: 53%
GRE requirement: No
Avg. GRE: quantitative: N/A
TOEFL requirement: Yes
Minimum TOEFL score: 500
Students specializing in:
biomedical: 11%; civil: 26%;
computer science: 26%;
electrical: 20%; science and
physics: 7%; mechanical: 10%

University of Denver

2135 E. Wesley Avenue
Denver, CO 80208
www.du.edu/secs/
Private
Admissions: (303) 871-2831
Email: grad-info@du.edu
Financial aid: (303) 871-4020
Application deadline: 02/01
Tuition: full time $41,889; part time: $1,142/credit hour
Room/board/expenses: $14,778
Full-time enrollment: 158
men: 79%; women: 21%; minorities: 4%; international: 68%
Part-time enrollment: 71
men: 85%; women: 15%; minorities: 23%; international: 1%
Acceptance rate: 78%
GRE requirement: Yes
Avg. GRE: quantitative: 159
TOEFL requirement: Yes
Minimum TOEFL score: 550
Fellowships: 0
Teaching assistantships: 31
Research assistantships: 28
Students specializing in:
biomedical: 4%; computer: 3%; computer science: 23%; electrical: 22%; materials: 4%; mechanical: 13%; other: 30%

CONNECTICUT

University of Bridgeport

221 University Avenue
Bridgeport, CT 06604
www.bridgeport.edu/sed
Private
Admissions: (203) 576-4552
Email: admit@bridgeport.edu
Financial aid: (203) 576-4568
Application deadline: rolling
Tuition: full time: $775/credit hour; part time: $775/credit hour
Room/board/expenses: $15,810
Full-time enrollment: 433
men: 78%; women: 22%; minorities: 21%; international: 97%
Part-time enrollment: 215
men: 81%; women: 19%; minorities: 12%; international: 76%
Acceptance rate: 52%
GRE requirement: No
Avg. GRE: quantitative: N/A
TOEFL requirement: Yes
Minimum TOEFL score: 550
Teaching assistantships: 22
Research assistantships: 34
Students specializing in:
biomedical: 11%; computer: 4%; computer science: 38%; electrical: 24%; management: 11%; mechanical: 13%

University of Connecticut

261 Glenbrook Road, Unit 3237
Storrs, CT 06269-3237
www.uconn.edu
Public
Admissions: (860) 486-0974
Email: gradadmissions@uconn.edu
Financial aid: (860) 486-2819
Application deadline: rolling
In-state tuition: full time: $14,472; part time: $678/credit hour
Out-of-state tuition: full time: $33,944
Room/board/expenses: $20,428
Full-time enrollment: 641
men: 72%; women: 28%; minorities: 10%; international: 65%
Part-time enrollment: 264
men: 83%; women: 17%; minorities: 17%; international: 11%
Acceptance rate: 28%
GRE requirement: Yes
Avg. GRE: quantitative: 162
TOEFL requirement: Yes
Minimum TOEFL score: 550
Fellowships: 174

Teaching assistantships: 45
Research assistantships: 351
Students specializing in:
biomedical: 13%; chemical: 7%; civil: 10%; computer: 14%; computer science: 14%; electrical: 18%; environmental: 4%; materials: 8%; mechanical: 23%; other: 3%

Yale University

226 Dunham Lab
10 Hillhouse Avenue
New Haven, CT 06520
www.seas.yale.edu
Private
Admissions: (203) 432-2771
Email: graduate.admissions@yale.edu
Financial aid: (203) 432-2739
Application deadline: 01/02
Tuition: full time: $37,600; part time: $4,700/credit hour
Room/board/expenses: $27,393
Full-time enrollment: 208
men: 70%; women: 30%; minorities: 14%; international: 52%
Part-time enrollment: 3
men: 100%; women: 0%; minorities: 0%; international: 33%
Acceptance rate: 14%
GRE requirement: Yes
Avg. GRE: quantitative: 167
TOEFL requirement: Yes
Minimum TOEFL score: 590
Fellowships: 75
Teaching assistantships: 140
Research assistantships: 112
Students specializing in:
biomedical: 31%; chemical: 29%; electrical: 21%; mechanical: 17%; other: 1%

DELAWARE

University of Delaware

102 DuPont Hall
Newark, DE 19716-3101
www.engr.udel.edu
Public
Admissions: (302) 831-2129
Email: gradadmissions@udel.edu
Financial aid: (302) 831-8189
Application deadline: rolling
In-state tuition: full time: $1,625/credit hour; part time: $1,625/credit hour
Out-of-state tuition: full time: $1,625/credit hour
Room/board/expenses: $15,100
Full-time enrollment: 756
men: 73%; women: 27%; minorities: 10%; international: 59%
Part-time enrollment: 117
men: 85%; women: 15%; minorities: 16%; international: 9%
Acceptance rate: 32%
GRE requirement: Yes
Avg. GRE: quantitative: 162
TOEFL requirement: Yes
Minimum TOEFL score: 570
Fellowships: 30
Teaching assistantships: 51
Research assistantships: 418
Students specializing in:
biomedical: 5%; chemical: 17%; civil: 12%; computer: 20%; computer science: 15%; electrical: 20%; environmental: 18%; materials: 9%; mechanical: 10%; other: 6%

DISTRICT OF COLUMBIA

The Catholic University of America

620 Michigan Avenue NE
Washington, DC 20064
admissions.cua.edu/graduate/
Private
Admissions: (800) 673-2772
Email: cua-admissions@cua.edu
Financial aid: (202) 319-5307

Application deadline: 07/15
Tuition: full time: $41,100; part time: $1,600/credit hour
Room/board/expenses: $20,454
Full-time enrollment: 83
men: 66%; women: 34%; minorities: 14%; international: 77%
Part-time enrollment: 103
men: 71%; women: 29%; minorities: 24%; international: 35%
Acceptance rate: 70%
GRE requirement: No
Avg. GRE: quantitative: N/A
TOEFL requirement: Yes
Minimum TOEFL score: 580
Students specializing in:
biomedical: 14%; civil: 15%; electrical: 31%; management: 19%; materials: 5%; mechanical: 16%

George Washington University

725 23rd Street NW
Tompkins Hall
Washington, DC 20052
www.seas.gwu.edu/
Private
Admissions: (202) 994-8675
Email: engineering@gwu.edu
Financial aid: (202) 994-6822
Application deadline: 01/15
Tuition: full time: $1,490/credit hour; part time: $1,490/credit hour
Room/board/expenses: $23,500
Full-time enrollment: 575
men: 72%; women: 28%; minorities: 8%; international: 79%
Part-time enrollment: 1,039
men: 74%; women: 26%; minorities: 30%; international: 15%
Acceptance rate: 38%
GRE requirement: Yes
Avg. GRE: quantitative: 161
TOEFL requirement: Yes
Minimum TOEFL score: 550
Fellowships: 150
Teaching assistantships: 88
Research assistantships: 66
Students specializing in:
biomedical: 1%; civil: 3%; computer: 1%; computer science: 26%; electrical: 11%; management: 51%; mechanical: 8%

Howard University

2366 Sixth Street NW, Suite 100
Washington, DC 20059
www.gs.howard.edu
Private
Email: hugsadmissions@howard.edu
Financial aid: (202) 806-2820
Application deadline: N/A
Tuition: full time: $33,211; part time: $1,700/credit hour
Room/board/expenses: $25,587
Full-time enrollment: 48
men: 73%; women: 27%; minorities: 85%; international: 25%
Part-time enrollment: 19
men: 63%; women: 37%; minorities: 79%; international: 16%
Acceptance rate: 63%
GRE requirement: Yes
Avg. GRE: quantitative: N/A
TOEFL requirement: Yes
Minimum TOEFL score: 550
Fellowships: 10
Teaching assistantships: 4
Research assistantships: 12
Students specializing in: chemical: 7%; civil: 10%; computer science: 27%; electrical: 40%; mechanical: 15%

FLORIDA

Embry-Riddle Aeronautical University

600 S. Clyde Morris Boulevard
Daytona Beach, FL 32114
daytonabeach.erau.edu/admissions/index.html
Private
Admissions: (800) 388-3728
Email: graduate.admissions@erau.edu
Financial aid: (855) 661-7968
Application deadline: 07/01
Tuition: full time: $1,280/credit hour; part time: $1,280/credit hour
Room/board/expenses: $15,634
Full-time enrollment: 292
men: 81%; women: 19%; minorities: 10%; international: 64%
Part-time enrollment: 60
men: 87%; women: 13%; minorities: 7%; international: 42%
Acceptance rate: 51%
GRE requirement: Yes
Avg. GRE: quantitative: 156
TOEFL requirement: Yes
Minimum TOEFL score: 550
Fellowships: 10
Teaching assistantships: 38
Research assistantships: 3
Students specializing in:
aerospace: 43%; computer science: 0%; electrical: 10%; science and physics: 10%; mechanical: 21%; other: 16%

Florida A&M University-Florida State University

2525 Pottsdamer Street
Tallahassee, FL 32310
www.eng.fsu.edu
Public
Admissions: (850) 410-6423
Email: perry@eng.fsu.edu
Financial aid: (850) 410-6423
Application deadline: 04/01
In-state tuition: full time: $404/credit hour; part time: $404/credit hour
Out-of-state tuition: full time: $1,005/credit hour
Room/board/expenses: $15,092
Full-time enrollment: 324
men: 80%; women: 20%; minorities: 66%; international: 50%
Part-time enrollment: N/A
men: N/A; women: N/A; minorities: N/A; international: N/A
Acceptance rate: 39%
GRE requirement: Yes
Avg. GRE: quantitative: 157
TOEFL requirement: Yes
Minimum TOEFL score: 550
Fellowships: 30
Teaching assistantships: 77
Research assistantships: 171
Students specializing in:
biomedical: 4%; chemical: 8%; civil: 16%; electrical: 26%; industrial: 23%; mechanical: 23%

Florida Atlantic University

777 Glades Road
Boca Raton, FL 33431-0991
www.eng.fau.edu
Public
Admissions: (561) 297-3642
Email: graduatecollege@fau.edu
Financial aid: (561) 297-3530
Application deadline: 07/01
In-state tuition: full time: $370/credit hour; part time: $370/credit hour
Out-of-state tuition: full time: $1,025/credit hour
Room/board/expenses: $15,294

Full-time enrollment: 126
men: 75%; women: 25%; minorities: 27%; international: 37%
Part-time enrollment: 173
men: 79%; women: 21%; minorities: 41%; international: 17%
Acceptance rate: 32%
GRE requirement: Yes
Avg. GRE: quantitative: 155
TOEFL requirement: Yes
Minimum TOEFL score: 550
Fellowships: 4
Teaching assistantships: 40
Research assistantships: 43
Students specializing in:
biomedical: 7%; civil: 11%; computer: 13%; computer science: 28%; electrical: 19%; mechanical: 9%; other: 14%

Florida Institute of Technology

150 W. University Boulevard
Melbourne, FL 32901-6975
www.fit.edu
Private
Admissions: (800) 944-4348
Email: grad-admissions@fit.edu
Financial aid: (321) 674-8070
Application deadline: rolling
Tuition: full time: $1,179/credit hour; part time: $1,179/credit hour
Room/board/expenses: $17,310
Full-time enrollment: 663
men: 77%; women: 23%; minorities: 4%; international: 82%
Part-time enrollment: 305
men: 77%; women: 23%; minorities: 16%; international: 41%
Acceptance rate: 51%
GRE requirement: Yes
Avg. GRE: quantitative: 154
TOEFL requirement: Yes
Minimum TOEFL score: 550
Fellowships: 0
Teaching assistantships: 71
Research assistantships: 40
Students specializing in:
aerospace: 7%; biomedical: 5%; chemical: 2%; civil: 6%; computer: 11%; computer science: 46%; electrical: 26%; management: 5%; environmental: 3%; mechanical: 12%

Florida International University

10555 W. Flagler Street
Miami, FL 33174
www.eng.fiu.edu/
Public
Admissions: (305) 348-7442
Email: gradadm@fiu.edu
Financial aid: (305) 348-7272
Application deadline: 02/15
In-state tuition: full time: $11,277; part time: $454/credit hour
Out-of-state tuition: full time: $24,382
Room/board/expenses: $25,528
Full-time enrollment: 607
men: 74%; women: 26%; minorities: 22%; international: 72%
Part-time enrollment: 296
men: 78%; women: 22%; minorities: 61%; international: 23%
Acceptance rate: 55%
GRE requirement: Yes
Avg. GRE: quantitative: 156
TOEFL requirement: Yes
Minimum TOEFL score: 550
Fellowships: 15
Teaching assistantships: 144
Research assistantships: 119
Students specializing in:
biomedical: 5%; civil: 13%; computer: 4%; computer science: 21%; electrical: 17%; management: 15%; environmental: 1%; materials: 4%; mechanical: 5%; other: 16%

University of Central Florida

4000 Central Florida Boulevard
Orlando, FL 32816-2993
www.cecs.ucf.edu/graduate.php
Public
Admissions: (407) 823-2455
Email: gradengr@ucf.edu
Financial aid: (407) 823-2827
Application deadline: 07/15
In-state tuition: full time: $359/
credit hour; part time: $359/
credit hour
Out-of-state tuition: full time:
$1,183/credit hour
Room/board/expenses: $15,532
Full-time enrollment: 828
men: 78%; women: 22%;
minorities: 12%; international:
64%
Part-time enrollment: 481
men: 79%; women: 21%;
minorities: 33%; international: 0%
Acceptance rate: 43%
GRE requirement: Yes
Avg. GRE: quantitative: 159
TOEFL requirement: Yes
Minimum TOEFL score: 560
Fellowships: 50
Teaching assistantships: 156
Research assistantships: 250
Students specializing in:
aerospace: 2%; civil: 12%;
computer: 6%; computer
science: 24%; electrical: 16%;
management: 6%; environmental:
3%; industrial: 16%; materials:
4%; mechanical: 12%

University of Florida

300 Weil Hall
Gainesville, FL 32611-6550
www.eng.ufl.edu
Public
Admissions: (352) 392-0943
Email: admissions@eng.ufl.edu
Financial aid: (352) 392-0943
Application deadline: 06/01
In-state tuition: full time: $12,682;
part time: $528/credit hour
Out-of-state tuition: full time:
$30,075
Room/board/expenses: $15,610
Full-time enrollment: 1,915
men: 76%; women: 24%;
minorities: 11%; international: 69%
Part-time enrollment: 569
men: 79%; women: 21%;
minorities: 21%; international:
25%
Acceptance rate: 37%
GRE requirement: Yes
Avg. GRE: quantitative: 162
TOEFL requirement: Yes
Minimum TOEFL score: 550
Fellowships: 168
Teaching assistantships: 132
Research assistantships: 642
Students specializing in:
aerospace: 4%; agriculture:
2%; biomedical: 5%; chemical:
8%; civil: 9%; computer:
9%; computer science: 9%;
electrical: 18%; management: 3%;
environmental: 6%; industrial: 3%;
materials: 9%; mechanical: 14%;
nuclear: 1%

University of Miami

1251 Memorial Drive
Coral Gables, FL 33146
www.miami.edu/engineering
Private
Admissions: (305) 284-2942
Email: gradadm.eng@miami.edu
Financial aid: (305) 284-5212
Application deadline: 12/01
Tuition: full time: $1,790/credit
hour; part time: $1,790/credit hour
Room/board/expenses: $18,640
Full-time enrollment: 253
men: 76%; women: 24%;
minorities: 21%; international:
56%

Part-time enrollment: 18
men: 67%; women: 33%;
minorities: 61%; international: 17%
Acceptance rate: 45%
GRE requirement: Yes
Avg. GRE: quantitative: 158
TOEFL requirement: Yes
Minimum TOEFL score: 550
Fellowships: 11
Teaching assistantships: 33
Research assistantships: 65
Students specializing in:
biomedical: 25%; civil: 11%;
computer science: 7%; electrical:
19%; industrial: 25%; mechanical:
13%

University of South Florida

4202 E. Fowler Avenue
ENB118
Tampa, FL 33620
admissions.grad.usf.edu/
Public
Admissions: (813) 974-8800
Email: admissions@grad.usf.edu
Financial aid: (813) 974-4700
Application deadline: 02/15
In-state tuition: full time: $10,502;
part time: $431/credit hour
Out-of-state tuition: full time:
$21,200
Room/board/expenses: $15,650
Full-time enrollment: 816
men: 72%; women: 28%;
minorities: 13%; international:
63%
Part-time enrollment: 161
men: 83%; women: 17%;
minorities: 37%; international: 0%
Acceptance rate: 46%
GRE requirement: Yes
Avg. GRE: quantitative: 157
TOEFL requirement: Yes
Minimum TOEFL score: 550
Fellowships: 64
Teaching assistantships: 204
Research assistantships: 197
Students specializing in:
biomedical: 5%; chemical:
4%; civil: 13%; computer: 9%;
computer science: 13%; electrical:
31%; management: 11%; science
and physics: 1%; environmental:
4%; industrial: 4%; materials: 1%;
mechanical: 10%

GEORGIA

Georgia Institute of Technology

225 North Avenue
Atlanta, GA 30332-0360
www.gradadmiss.gatech.edu/
Public
Admissions: (404) 894-1610
Email: gradstudies@gatech.edu
Financial aid: (404) 894-4160
Application deadline: rolling
In-state tuition: full time: $14,736;
part time: $515/credit hour
Out-of-state tuition: full time:
$29,992
Room/board/expenses: $15,760
Full-time enrollment: 3,953
men: 78%; women: 22%;
minorities: 14%; international:
58%
Part-time enrollment: 2,183
men: 87%; women: 13%;
minorities: 25%; international:
19%
Acceptance rate: 31%
GRE requirement: Yes
Avg. GRE: quantitative: 164
TOEFL requirement: Yes
Minimum TOEFL score: 550
Fellowships: 830
Teaching assistantships: 452
Research assistantships: 1,944
Students specializing in:
aerospace: 9%; biomedical: 3%;
chemical: 3%; civil: 4%; computer
science: 34%; electrical: 22%;
science and physics: 0%;
environmental: 2%; industrial: 6%;

materials: 3%; mechanical: 13%;
nuclear: 1%; other: 1%

University of Georgia

Paul D. Coverdell Center
Athens, GA 30602
grad.uga.edu
Public
Admissions: (706) 542-1739
Email: gradadm@uga.edu
Financial aid: (706) 542-6147
Application deadline: 12/31
In-state tuition: full time: $337/
credit hour; part time: $337/
credit hour
Out-of-state tuition: full time: $975/
credit hour
Room/board/expenses: $12,150
Full-time enrollment: 72
men: 78%; women: 22%;
minorities: 56%; international:
56%
Part-time enrollment: 5
men: 60%; women: 40%;
minorities: 40%; international:
40%
Acceptance rate: 43%
GRE requirement: Yes
Avg. GRE: quantitative: 161
TOEFL requirement: Yes
Minimum TOEFL score: N/A
Fellowships: 0
Teaching assistantships: 13
Research assistantships: 53
Students specializing in:
agriculture: 42%; biomedical:
10%; science and physics: 44%;
environmental: 4%

HAWAII

University of Hawaii-Manoa

2540 Dole Street
Holmes Hall 240
Honolulu, HI 96822
www.eng.hawaii.edu/
current-students/
graduate-students
Public
Admissions: (808) 956-8544
Email: gradadm@hawaii.edu
Financial aid: (808) 956-7251
Application deadline: 03/01
In-state tuition: full time: $9,632;
part time: $552/credit hour
Out-of-state tuition: full time:
$22,144
Room/board/expenses: $16,212
Full-time enrollment: 176
men: 74%; women: 26%;
minorities: 21%; international:
39%
Part-time enrollment: 15
men: 87%; women: 13%;
minorities: 80%; international: 0%
Acceptance rate: 63%
GRE requirement: Yes
Avg. GRE: quantitative: 162
TOEFL requirement: Yes
Minimum TOEFL score: 500
Fellowships: 4
Teaching assistantships: 22
Research assistantships: 85
Students specializing in: civil: 31%;
electrical: 35%; mechanical: 24%;
other: 11%

IDAHO

Boise State University

1910 University Drive
Boise, ID 83725
graduatecollege.boisestate.edu
Public
Admissions: (208) 426-3903
Email:
gradcollege@boisestate.edu
Financial aid: (208) 426-1664
Application deadline: 05/15
In-state tuition: full time: $7,825;
part time: $331/credit hour
Out-of-state tuition: full time:
$20,677
Room/board/expenses: $11,978

Full-time enrollment: 90
men: 76%; women: 24%;
minorities: 6%; international: 31%
Part-time enrollment: 44
men: 89%; women: 11%;
minorities: 5%; international: 7%
Acceptance rate: 37%
GRE requirement: Yes
Avg. GRE: quantitative: 158
TOEFL requirement: Yes
Minimum TOEFL score: 587
Fellowships: 12
Teaching assistantships: 4
Research assistantships: 39
Students specializing in: civil: 7%;
computer: 4%; electrical: 37%;
materials: 43%; mechanical: 10%

Idaho State University[1]

921 S. Eighth Street
MS 8060
Pocatello, ID 83209-8060
www.isu.edu/cse
Public
Admissions: (208) 282-2150
Email: graddean@isu.edu
Financial aid: N/A
Tuition: N/A
Room/board/expenses: N/A
Enrollment: N/A

University of Idaho[1]

PO Box 441011
Moscow, ID 83844-1011
www.engr.uidaho.edu/
Public
Admissions: (208) 885-4001
Email: gadms@uidaho.edu
Financial aid: N/A
Tuition: N/A
Room/board/expenses: N/A
Enrollment: N/A

ILLINOIS

Illinois Institute of Technology (Armour)

10 West 33rd Street
Perlstein Hall, Suite 224
Chicago, IL 60616
www.iit.edu/engineering
Private
Admissions: (312) 567-3020
Email: gradstu@iit.edu
Financial aid: (312) 567-7219
Application deadline: 08/01
Tuition: full time: $1,250/credit
hour; part time: $1,250/credit hour
Room/board/expenses: $16,800
Full-time enrollment: 1,396
men: 76%; women: 24%;
minorities: 2%; international: 92%
Part-time enrollment: 308
men: 81%; women: 19%;
minorities: 10%; international:
55%
Acceptance rate: 47%
GRE requirement: Yes
Avg. GRE: quantitative: 161
TOEFL requirement: Yes
Minimum TOEFL score: 550
Fellowships: 25
Teaching assistantships: 92
Research assistantships: 251
Students specializing in:
aerospace: 10%; agriculture: 1%;
architectural: 1%; biomedical: 3%;
chemical: 8%; civil: 9%; computer:
7%; computer science: 33%;
electrical: 26%; environmental:
3%; industrial: 0%; materials: 2%;
mechanical: 10%

Northwestern University (McCormick)

2145 Sheridan Road
Evanston, IL 60208
www.tgs.northwestern.edu/
Private
Admissions: (847) 491-5279
Email:
gradapp@northwestern.edu

Financial aid: (847) 491-8495
Application deadline: 12/31
Tuition: full time: $47,166; part
time: $5,555/credit hour
Room/board/expenses: $22,590
Full-time enrollment: 1,560
men: 69%; women: 31%;
minorities: 16%; international:
52%
Part-time enrollment: 297
men: 73%; women: 27%;
minorities: 23%; international:
41%
Acceptance rate: 23%
GRE requirement: Yes
Avg. GRE: quantitative: 165
TOEFL requirement: Yes
Minimum TOEFL score: 577
Fellowships: 195
Teaching assistantships: 85
Research assistantships: 517
Students specializing in:
biomedical: 8%; chemical:
7%; civil: 5%; computer:
2%; computer science: 10%;
electrical: 9%; management: 7%;
environmental: 2%; industrial: 3%;
materials: 12%; mechanical: 8%;
other: 26%

Southern Illinois University-Carbondale

900 S. Normal Avenue
Mailcode 4716
Carbondale, IL 62901-6603
gradschool.siuc.edu/
Public
Admissions: (618) 536-7791
Email: gradschl@siu.edu
Financial aid: (618) 453-4334
Application deadline: rolling
In-state tuition: full time: $394/
credit hour; part time: $394/
credit hour
Out-of-state tuition: full time: $985/
credit hour
Room/board/expenses: $17,105
Full-time enrollment: 334
men: 80%; women: 20%;
minorities: 4%; international: 87%
Part-time enrollment: 78
men: 79%; women: 21%;
minorities: 10%; international:
62%
Acceptance rate: 47%
GRE requirement: Yes
Avg. GRE: quantitative: 156
TOEFL requirement: Yes
Minimum TOEFL score: 550
Fellowships: 10
Teaching assistantships: 168
Research assistantships: 116
Students specializing in:
biomedical: 4%; civil: 10%;
computer: 69%; electrical: 69%;
environmental: 10%; mechanical:
13%; mining: 4%

University of Illinois-Chicago

851 S. Morgan Street
Chicago, IL 60607-7043
www.uic.edu/
Public
Admissions: (312) 996-5133
Email: uicgrad@uic.edu
Financial aid: (312) 996-3126
Application deadline: 05/15
In-state tuition: full time: $17,590;
part time: $12,742
Out-of-state tuition: full time:
$29,588
Room/board/expenses: $17,958
Full-time enrollment: 943
men: 73%; women: 27%;
minorities: 9%; international: 79%
Part-time enrollment: 221
men: 77%; women: 23%;
minorities: 27%; international:
25%
Acceptance rate: 21%
GRE requirement: Yes
Avg. GRE: quantitative: 160
TOEFL requirement: Yes
Minimum TOEFL score: 550
Fellowships: 18

Teaching assistantships: 210
Research assistantships: 207
Students specializing in:
biomedical: 12%; chemical: 5%;
civil: 9%; computer science: 20%;
electrical: 24%; mechanical: 26%;
other: 5%

University of Illinois-Urbana-Champaign

1308 W. Green
Urbana, IL 61801
engineering.illinois.edu
Public
Admissions: (217) 333-0035
Email: engineering@illinois.edu
Financial aid: (217) 333-0100
Application deadline: rolling
In-state tuition: full time: $20,862;
part time: $15,154
Out-of-state tuition: full time:
$34,584
Room/board/expenses: $17,701
Full-time enrollment: 3,135
men: 77%; women: 23%;
minorities: 12%; international:
63%
Part-time enrollment: 181
men: 84%; women: 16%;
minorities: 16%; international:
34%
Acceptance rate: 26%
GRE requirement: Yes
Avg. GRE: quantitative: 165
TOEFL requirement: Yes
Minimum TOEFL score: 550
Fellowships: 338
Teaching assistantships: 801
Research assistantships: 1,752
Students specializing in:
aerospace: 4%; agriculture:
2%; biomedical: 2%; chemical:
3%; civil: 18%; computer: 16%;
computer science: 16%; electrical:
16%; science and physics: 8%;
environmental: 4%; industrial: 5%;
materials: 6%; mechanical: 13%;
nuclear: 2%

INDIANA

Indiana University-Purdue University-Indianapolis

799 W. Michigan Street, ET 219
Indianapolis, IN 46202-5160
engr.iupui.edu
Public
Admissions: (317) 278-4960
Email: gradengr@iupui.edu
Financial aid: N/A
Application deadline: 06/01
In-state tuition: full time: $366/
credit hour; part time: $366/
credit hour
Out-of-state tuition: full time:
$1,048/credit hour
Room/board/expenses: $2,481
Full-time enrollment: 225
men: 78%; women: 22%;
minorities: 8%; international: 77%
Part-time enrollment: 59
men: 90%; women: 10%;
minorities: 10%; international: 15%
Acceptance rate: 58%
GRE requirement: Yes
Avg. GRE: quantitative: 158
TOEFL requirement: Yes
Minimum TOEFL score: 550
Fellowships: 5
Teaching assistantships: 14
Research assistantships: 57
Students specializing in:
biomedical: 10%; computer: 19%;
electrical: 29%; mechanical: 42%

Purdue University-West Lafayette

701 W. Stadium Avenue
Suite 3000 ARMS
West Lafayette, IN 47907-2045
engineering.purdue.edu
Public
Admissions: (765) 494-2598

Email: gradinfo@purdue.edu
Financial aid: (765) 494-2598
Application deadline: rolling
In-state tuition: full time: $11,076;
part time: $329/credit hour
Out-of-state tuition: full time:
$29,888
Room/board/expenses: $13,420
Full-time enrollment: 2,716
men: 78%; women: 22%;
minorities: 8%; international: 68%
Part-time enrollment: 693
men: 79%; women: 21%;
minorities: 16%; international: 19%
Acceptance rate: 23%
GRE requirement: Yes
Avg. GRE: quantitative: 164
TOEFL requirement: Yes
Minimum TOEFL score: 550
Fellowships: 314
Teaching assistantships: 529
Research assistantships: 1,285
Students specializing in:
aerospace: 12%; agriculture:
3%; biomedical: 2%; chemical:
4%; civil: 12%; computer:
5%; computer science: 8%;
electrical: 18%; environmental:
1%; industrial: 5%; materials: 3%;
mechanical: 16%; nuclear: 2%;
other: 12%

University of Notre Dame

257 Fitzpatrick Hall of Engineering
Notre Dame, IN 46556
www.nd.edu
Private
Admissions: (574) 631-7706
Email: gradad@nd.edu
Financial aid: (574) 631-7706
Application deadline: rolling
Tuition: full time: $46,075; part
time: $2,534/credit hour
Room/board/expenses: $19,410
Full-time enrollment: 506
men: 76%; women: 24%;
minorities: 9%; international: 52%
Part-time enrollment: 2
men: 100%; women: 0%;
minorities: 50%; international: 0%
Acceptance rate: 22%
GRE requirement: Yes
Avg. GRE: quantitative: 162
TOEFL requirement: Yes
Minimum TOEFL score: 0
Fellowships: 45
Teaching assistantships: 46
Research assistantships: 375
Students specializing in:
biomedical: 4%; chemical: 17%;
civil: 17%; computer science:
22%; electrical: 22%; mechanical:
19%; other: 0%

IOWA

Iowa State University

4565 Memorial Union
Ames, IA 50011-1130
www.engineering.iastate.edu/
Public
Admissions: (800) 262-3810
Email:
grad_admissions@iastate.edu
Financial aid: (515) 294-2223
Application deadline: rolling
In-state tuition: full time: $10,509;
part time: $512/credit hour
Out-of-state tuition: full time:
$23,285
Room/board/expenses: $11,747
Full-time enrollment: 1,266
men: 77%; women: 23%;
minorities: 8%; international: 55%
Part-time enrollment: N/A
men: N/A; women: N/A; minorities:
N/A; international: N/A
Acceptance rate: 21%
GRE requirement: Yes
Avg. GRE: quantitative: 161
TOEFL requirement: Yes
Minimum TOEFL score: 550
Fellowships: 45
Teaching assistantships: 210
Research assistantships: 602

Students specializing in:
aerospace: 7%; agriculture:
4%; chemical: 5%; civil: 15%;
computer: 9%; electrical: 21%;
industrial: 15%; materials: 5%;
mechanical: 17%; other: 2%

University of Iowa

3100 Seamans Center
Iowa City, IA 52242-1527
www.uiowa.edu/admissions/
graduate/index.html
Public
Admissions: (319) 335-1525
Email: admissions@uiowa.edu
Financial aid: (319) 335-1450
Application deadline: rolling
In-state tuition: full time: $9,901;
part time: N/A
Out-of-state tuition: full time:
$26,783
Room/board/expenses: $16,125
Full-time enrollment: 385
men: 75%; women: 25%;
minorities: 9%; international: 51%
Part-time enrollment: N/A
men: N/A; women: N/A; minorities:
N/A; international: N/A
Acceptance rate: 22%
GRE requirement: Yes
Avg. GRE: quantitative: 162
TOEFL requirement: Yes
Minimum TOEFL score: 550
Fellowships: 28
Teaching assistantships: 82
Research assistantships: 221
Students specializing in:
biomedical: 19%; chemical: 9%;
civil: 19%; computer science:
18%; electrical: 17%; industrial:
5%; mechanical: 13%

KANSAS

Kansas State University

1046 Rathbone Hall
Manhattan, KS 66506-5201
www.engg.ksu.edu/
Public
Admissions: (785) 532-6191
Email: grad@ksu.edu
Financial aid: (785) 532-6420
Application deadline: rolling
In-state tuition: full time: $368/
credit hour; part time: $368/
credit hour
Out-of-state tuition: full time: $830/
credit hour
Room/board/expenses: $11,010
Full-time enrollment: 265
men: 71%; women: 29%;
minorities: 5%; international: 59%
Part-time enrollment: 206
men: 83%; women: 17%;
minorities: 20%; international:
12%
Acceptance rate: 39%
GRE requirement: Yes
Avg. GRE: quantitative: 159
TOEFL requirement: Yes
Minimum TOEFL score: 550
Fellowships: 13
Teaching assistantships: 81
Research assistantships: 119
Students specializing in:
agriculture: 7%; architectural:
2%; chemical: 7%; civil: 16%;
computer science: 18%; electrical:
17%; industrial: 19%; mechanical:
10%; nuclear: 4%

University of Kansas

1 Eaton Hall
1520 W. 15th Street
Lawrence, KS 66045-7621
www.engr.ku.edu
Public
Admissions: (785) 864-3881
Email: kuengr@ku.edu
Financial aid: (785) 864-5491
Application deadline: rolling
In-state tuition: full time: $363/
credit hour; part time: $363/
credit hour

Out-of-state tuition: full time: $849/
credit hour
Room/board/expenses: $16,394
Full-time enrollment: 436
men: 71%; women: 29%;
minorities: 5%; international: 63%
Part-time enrollment: 244
men: 80%; women: 20%;
minorities: 14%; international: 14%
Acceptance rate: 53%
GRE requirement: Yes
Avg. GRE: quantitative: 160
TOEFL requirement: Yes
Minimum TOEFL score: 530
Fellowships: 117
Teaching assistantships: 106
Research assistantships: 147
Students specializing in:
aerospace: 7%; architectural:
1%; biomedical: 8%; chemical:
5%; civil: 15%; computer: 2%;
computer science: 15%; electrical:
13%; management: 16%;
environmental: 3%; mechanical:
9%; petroleum: 1%; other: 4%

Wichita State University

1845 N. Fairmount
Wichita, KS 67260-0044
www.wichita.edu/engineering
Public
Admissions: (316) 978-3095
Email: jordan.oleson@wichita.edu
Financial aid: (316) 978-3430
Application deadline: 07/15
In-state tuition: full time: $264/
credit hour; part time: $264/
credit hour
Out-of-state tuition: full time: $649/
credit hour
Room/board/expenses: $12,675
Full-time enrollment: 576
men: 77%; women: 23%;
minorities: 4%; international: 91%
Part-time enrollment: 315
men: 84%; women: 16%;
minorities: 18%; international:
50%
Acceptance rate: 58%
GRE requirement: Yes
Avg. GRE: quantitative: 152
TOEFL requirement: Yes
Minimum TOEFL score: 550
Fellowships: 0
Teaching assistantships: 83
Research assistantships: 166
Students specializing in:
aerospace: 16%; computer
science: 12%; electrical: 21%;
management: 4%; industrial: 15%;
mechanical: 12%; other: 20%

KENTUCKY

University of Kentucky

351 Ralph G. Anderson Building
Lexington, KY 40506-0503
www.engr.uky.edu
Public
Admissions: (859) 257-4905
Email: grad.admit@uky.edu
Financial aid: (859) 257-3172
Application deadline: 07/15
In-state tuition: full time: $11,312;
part time: $596/credit hour
Out-of-state tuition: full time:
$24,664
Room/board/expenses: $10,889
Full-time enrollment: 447
men: 79%; women: 21%;
minorities: 7%; international: 58%
Part-time enrollment: 69
men: 88%; women: 12%;
minorities: 14%; international:
29%
Acceptance rate: 48%
GRE requirement: Yes
Avg. GRE: quantitative: 160
TOEFL requirement: Yes
Minimum TOEFL score: 550
Fellowships: 36
Teaching assistantships: 88
Research assistantships: 164

Students specializing in:
agriculture: 6%; biomedical:
9%; chemical: 8%; civil: 12%;
computer science: 19%; electrical:
17%; industrial: 1%; materials: 5%;
mechanical: 18%; mining: 5%

University of Louisville (Speed)

2301 S. Third Street
Louisville, KY 40292
louisville.edu/speed/
Public
Admissions: (502) 852-3101
Email: gradadm@louisville.edu
Financial aid: (502) 852-5511
Application deadline: rolling
In-state tuition: full time: $11,522;
part time: $630/credit hour
Out-of-state tuition: full time:
$23,764
Room/board/expenses: $13,912
Full-time enrollment: 409
men: 78%; women: 22%;
minorities: 8%; international: 43%
Part-time enrollment: 258
men: 81%; women: 19%;
minorities: 18%; international: 17%
Acceptance rate: 61%
GRE requirement: Yes
Avg. GRE: quantitative: 159
TOEFL requirement: Yes
Minimum TOEFL score: 550
Fellowships: 20
Teaching assistantships: 46
Research assistantships: 53
Students specializing in:
biomedical: 3%; chemical:
6%; civil: 7%; computer: 11%;
computer science: 9%; electrical:
14%; management: 18%;
industrial: 14%; mechanical: 17%

LOUISIANA

Louisiana State University-Baton Rouge

3304 Patrick F. Taylor Building
Baton Rouge, LA 70803
www.eng.lsu.edu
Public
Admissions: (225) 578-1641
Email: graddeanoffice@lsu.edu
Financial aid: (225) 578-3103
Application deadline: rolling
In-state tuition: full time: $9,441;
part time: $5,390
Out-of-state tuition: full time:
$27,272
Room/board/expenses: $14,380
Full-time enrollment: 535
men: 79%; women: 21%;
minorities: 7%; international: 73%
Part-time enrollment: 124
men: 84%; women: 16%;
minorities: 17%; international: 23%
Acceptance rate: 32%
GRE requirement: Yes
Avg. GRE: quantitative: 160
TOEFL requirement: Yes
Minimum TOEFL score: 550
Fellowships: 21
Teaching assistantships: 110
Research assistantships: 229
Students specializing in:
agriculture: 2%; chemical: 8%;
civil: 17%; computer science:
13%; electrical: 17%; science
and physics: 10%; industrial: 7%;
mechanical: 12%; petroleum: 10%;
other: 10%

Louisiana Tech University

PO Box 10348
Ruston, LA 71272
www.latech.edu/tech/engr
Public
Admissions: (318) 257-2924
Email: gschool@latech.edu
Financial aid: (318) 257-2641
Application deadline: 08/01

In-state tuition: full time: $8,025;
part time: $6,840
Out-of-state tuition: full time:
$16,005
Room/board/expenses: $12,720
Full-time enrollment: 294
men: 76%; women: 24%;
minorities: 7%; international: 68%
Part-time enrollment: 87
men: 83%; women: 17%;
minorities: 14%; international:
28%
Acceptance rate: 71%
GRE requirement: Yes
Avg. GRE: quantitative: 157
TOEFL requirement: Yes
Minimum TOEFL score: 550
Fellowships: 16
Teaching assistantships: 73
Research assistantships: 69
Students specializing in:
biomedical: 15%; chemical: 9%;
civil: 6%; computer science: 12%;
electrical: 13%; management:
27%; science and physics: 6%;
industrial: 3%; mechanical: 10%

Tulane University

201 Lindy Boggs Building
New Orleans, LA 70118
tulane.edu/sse/academics/
graduate/index.cfm
Private
Admissions: (504) 865-5764
Email: segrad@tulane.edu
Financial aid: (504) 865-5764
Application deadline: rolling
Tuition: full time: $48,305; part
time: $2,618/credit hour
Room/board/expenses: $18,300
Full-time enrollment: 86
men: 60%; women: 40%;
minorities: 9%; international: 49%
Part-time enrollment: N/A
men: N/A; women: N/A; minorities:
N/A; international: N/A
Acceptance rate: 27%
GRE requirement: Yes
Avg. GRE: quantitative: 161
TOEFL requirement: Yes
Minimum TOEFL score: 600
Fellowships: 8
Teaching assistantships: 17
Research assistantships: 35
Students specializing in:
biomedical: 52%; chemical: 48%

University of
Louisiana-Lafayette

PO Box 42251
Lafayette, LA 70504
engineering.louisiana.edu/
Public
Admissions: (337) 482-6467
Email: gradschool@louisiana.edu
Financial aid: (337) 482-6506
Application deadline: rolling
In-state tuition: full time: $7,346;
part time: $408/credit hour
Out-of-state tuition: full time:
$19,746
Room/board/expenses: $15,910
Full-time enrollment: 288
men: 79%; women: 21%;
minorities: 7%; international: 79%
Part-time enrollment: 57
men: 79%; women: 21%;
minorities: 16%; international:
46%
Acceptance rate: 32%
GRE requirement: Yes
Avg. GRE: quantitative: 157
TOEFL requirement: Yes
Minimum TOEFL score: 550
Fellowships: 3
Teaching assistantships: 17
Research assistantships: 44
Students specializing in: chemical:
2%; civil: 5%; computer: 16%;
computer science: 43%;
management: 9%; industrial: 2%;
mechanical: 4%; petroleum: 17%

University of
New Orleans

2000 Lakeshore Drive
New Orleans, LA 70148
www.uno.edu
Public
Admissions: (504) 280-6595
Email: pec@uno.edu
Financial aid: (504) 280-6603
Application deadline: 07/01
In-state tuition: full time: $7,734;
part time: $4,700
Out-of-state tuition: full time:
$21,344
Room/board/expenses: $13,621
Full-time enrollment: 116
men: 84%; women: 16%;
minorities: 4%; international: 57%
Part-time enrollment: 68
men: 81%; women: 19%;
minorities: 9%; international: 25%
Acceptance rate: 43%
GRE requirement: Yes
Avg. GRE: quantitative: 157
TOEFL requirement: Yes
Minimum TOEFL score: 550
Students specializing in: N/A

MAINE

University of Maine

Advanced Manufacturing Center
Orono, ME 04469
www.engineering.umaine.edu/
Public
Admissions: (207) 581-3291
Email: graduate@maine.edu
Financial aid: (207) 581-1324
Application deadline: rolling
In-state tuition: full time: $418/
credit hour; part time: $418/
credit hour
Out-of-state tuition: full time:
$1,310/credit hour
Room/board/expenses: $15,760
Full-time enrollment: 137
men: 78%; women: 22%;
minorities: 7%; international: 34%
Part-time enrollment: 23
men: 83%; women: 17%;
minorities: 4%; international: 4%
Acceptance rate: 59%
GRE requirement: Yes
Avg. GRE: quantitative: 157
TOEFL requirement: Yes
Minimum TOEFL score: 550
Fellowships: 6
Teaching assistantships: 22
Research assistantships: 44
Students specializing in:
biomedical: 3%; chemical:
11%; civil: 24%; computer: 4%;
computer science: 11%; electrical:
11%; science and physics: 1%;
mechanical: 15%; other: 22%

MARYLAND

Johns Hopkins
University (Whiting)

3400 N. Charles Street
Baltimore, MD 21218
engineering.jhu.edu
Private
Admissions: (410) 516-8174
Email: graduateadmissions@
jhu.edu
Financial aid: (410) 516-8028
Application deadline: N/A
Tuition: full time: $47,560; part
time: $1,570/credit hour
Room/board/expenses: $17,300
Full-time enrollment: 1,155
men: 71%; women: 29%;
minorities: 14%; international:
55%
Part-time enrollment: 2,079
men: 77%; women: 23%;
minorities: 28%; international: 2%
Acceptance rate: 24%
GRE requirement: Yes
Avg. GRE: quantitative: 165
TOEFL requirement: Yes
Minimum TOEFL score: 600
Fellowships: 154

Teaching assistantships: 101
Research assistantships: 553
Students specializing in:
aerospace: 0%; biomedical: 6%;
chemical: 3%; civil: 2%; computer
science: 19%; electrical: 13%;
management: 1%; environmental:
3%; materials: 3%; mechanical:
6%; other: 43%

Morgan State
University (Mitchell)

1700 E. Coldspring Lane
Baltimore, MD 21251
www.morgan.edu/
Prospective_Grad_Students.html
Public
Admissions: (443) 885-3185
Email: mark.garrison@morgan.edu
Financial aid: (443) 885-3170
Application deadline: 07/10
In-state tuition: full time: $371/
credit hour; part time: $371/
credit hour
Out-of-state tuition: full time: $726/
credit hour
Room/board/expenses: $14,892
Full-time enrollment: 67
men: 75%; women: 25%;
minorities: 48%; international:
48%
Part-time enrollment: 72
men: 76%; women: 24%;
minorities: 82%; international: 11%
Acceptance rate: 90%
GRE requirement: Yes
Avg. GRE: quantitative: N/A
TOEFL requirement: Yes
Minimum TOEFL score: 550
Fellowships: 7
Teaching assistantships: 5
Research assistantships: 8
Students specializing in: N/A

University of
Maryland-
Baltimore County

1000 Hilltop Circle
Baltimore, MD 21250
www.umbc.edu/gradschool/
Public
Admissions: (410) 455-2537
Email: umbcgrad@umbc.edu
Financial aid: (410) 455-2387
Application deadline: 06/01
In-state tuition: full time: $557/
credit hour; part time: $557/
credit hour
Out-of-state tuition: full time: $922/
credit hour
Room/board/expenses: $15,465
Full-time enrollment: 301
men: 73%; women: 27%;
minorities: 15%; international:
57%
Part-time enrollment: 332
men: 78%; women: 22%;
minorities: 33%; international: 7%
Acceptance rate: 42%
GRE requirement: Yes
Avg. GRE: quantitative: 159
TOEFL requirement: Yes
Minimum TOEFL score: 550
Fellowships: 2
Teaching assistantships: 63
Research assistantships: 91
Students specializing in: chemical:
3%; computer: 5%; computer
science: 26%; electrical: 8%;
management: 13%; environmental:
3%; mechanical: 11%; other: 30%

University of
Maryland-
College Park (Clark)

3110 Jeong H. Kim Engineering
Building
College Park, MD 20742-2831
www.eng.umd.edu
Public
Admissions: (301) 405-0376
Email: gradschool@umd.edu
Financial aid: (301) 314-9000

Application deadline: N/A
In-state tuition: full time: $13,530;
part time: $602/credit hour
Out-of-state tuition: full time:
$27,450
Room/board/expenses: $17,250
Full-time enrollment: 1,641
men: 77%; women: 23%;
minorities: 12%; international:
64%
Part-time enrollment: 576
men: 84%; women: 16%;
minorities: 32%; international: 9%
Acceptance rate: 25%
GRE requirement: Yes
Avg. GRE: quantitative: 163
TOEFL requirement: Yes
Minimum TOEFL score: 574
Fellowships: 123
Teaching assistantships: 128
Research assistantships: 653
Students specializing in:
aerospace: 8%; biomedical:
4%; chemical: 3%; civil: 16%;
computer science: 11%; electrical:
18%; materials: 4%; mechanical:
14%; other: 22%

MASSACHUSETTS

Boston University

44 Cummington Street
Boston, MA 02215
www.bu.edu/eng
Private
Admissions: (617) 353-9760
Email: enggrad@bu.edu
Financial aid: (617) 353-9760
Application deadline: 12/15
Tuition: full time: $46,362; part
time: $1,428/credit hour
Room/board/expenses: $18,040
Full-time enrollment: 825
men: 71%; women: 29%;
minorities: 14%; international:
54%
Part-time enrollment: 133
men: 72%; women: 28%;
minorities: 24%; international:
32%
Acceptance rate: 25%
GRE requirement: Yes
Avg. GRE: quantitative: 164
TOEFL requirement: Yes
Minimum TOEFL score: 550
Fellowships: 97
Teaching assistantships: 84
Research assistantships: 414
Students specializing in:
biomedical: 23%; computer: 11%;
computer science: 9%; electrical:
22%; industrial: 0%; materials:
6%; mechanical: 15%; other: 12%

Harvard University

29 Oxford Street, Room 217A,
Pierce Hall
Cambridge, MA 02138
www.gsas.harvard.edu
Private
Admissions: (617) 495-5315
Email: admiss@fas.harvard.edu
Financial aid: (617) 495-5396
Application deadline: 12/15
Tuition: full time: $43,774; part
time: N/A
Room/board/expenses: $26,500
Full-time enrollment: 434
men: 75%; women: 25%;
minorities: 16%; international:
45%
Part-time enrollment: 5
men: 100%; women: 0%;
minorities: 40%; international:
20%
Acceptance rate: 10%
GRE requirement: Yes
Avg. GRE: quantitative: 166
TOEFL requirement: Yes
Minimum TOEFL score: N/A
Fellowships: 172
Teaching assistantships: 67
Research assistantships: 265

Students specializing in:
biomedical: 10%; computer
science: 26%; electrical: 8%;
environmental: 7%; materials: 4%;
mechanical: 7%; other: 38%

Massachusetts
Institute of Technology

77 Massachusetts Avenue
Room 1-206
Cambridge, MA 02139-4307
web.mit.edu/admissions/
graduate/
Private
Admissions: (617) 253-3400
Email: mitgrad@mit.edu
Financial aid: (617) 253-4971
Application deadline: N/A
Tuition: full time: $45,016; part
time: N/A
Room/board/expenses: $30,980
Full-time enrollment: 3,088
men: 72%; women: 28%;
minorities: 21%; international:
43%
Part-time enrollment: 55
men: 71%; women: 29%;
minorities: 27%; international: 13%
Acceptance rate: 18%
GRE requirement: Yes
Avg. GRE: quantitative: 166
Minimum TOEFL score: N/A
Fellowships: 607
Teaching assistantships: 284
Research assistantships: 1,667
Students specializing in:
aerospace: 7%; biomedical: 8%;
chemical: 8%; civil: 4%; computer
science: 14%; electrical: 12%;
management: 10%; environmental:
2%; materials: 6%; mechanical:
17%; nuclear: 4%; petroleum: 0%;
other: 6%

Northeastern
University

130 Snell Engineering Center
Boston, MA 02115-5000
www.coe.neu.edu/gse
Private
Admissions: (617) 373-2711
Email: grad-eng@coe.neu.edu
Financial aid: (617) 373-3190
Application deadline: 08/01
Tuition: full time: $1,354/credit
hour; part time: $1,354/credit hour
Room/board/expenses: $18,900
Full-time enrollment: 2,970
men: 71%; women: 29%;
minorities: 4%; international: 87%
Part-time enrollment: 212
men: 78%; women: 22%;
minorities: 20%; international: 7%
Acceptance rate: 36%
GRE requirement: Yes
Avg. GRE: quantitative: 161
TOEFL requirement: Yes
Minimum TOEFL score: 550
Fellowships: 88
Teaching assistantships: 120
Research assistantships: 321
Students specializing in:
biomedical: 1%; chemical:
2%; civil: 6%; computer: 2%;
computer science: 23%;
electrical: 15%; management: 8%;
industrial: 11%; mechanical: 8%;
other: 24%

Tufts University

Anderson Hall
Medford, MA 02155
engineering.tufts.edu
Private
Admissions: (617) 627-3395
Email: gradschool@ase.tufts.edu
Financial aid: (617) 627-2000
Application deadline: 01/15
Tuition: full time: $29,422; part
time: $4,644/credit hour
Room/board/expenses: $22,956
Full-time enrollment: 518
men: 66%; women: 34%;
minorities: 15%; international:
33%

Part-time enrollment: 78
men: 78%; women: 22%;
minorities: 18%; international: 6%
Acceptance rate: 33%
GRE requirement: Yes
Avg. GRE: quantitative: 162
TOEFL requirement: Yes
Minimum TOEFL score: 550
Fellowships: 21
Teaching assistantships: 68
Research assistantships: 149
Students specializing in:
biomedical: 15%; chemical: 8%;
civil: 4%; computer science: 11%;
electrical: 13%; management:
28%; environmental: 10%;
mechanical: 8%; other: 3%

University of Massachusetts-Amherst

Room 125, Marston Hall
Amherst, MA 01003
www.umass.edu/gradschool
Public
Admissions: (413) 545-0722
Email: gradadm@grad.umass.edu
Financial aid: (413) 577-0555
Application deadline: 01/15
In-state tuition: full time: $14,504;
part time: $110/credit hour
Out-of-state tuition: full time:
$21,801
Room/board/expenses: $13,957
Full-time enrollment: 868
men: 69%; women: 31%;
minorities: 8%; international: 61%
Part-time enrollment: N/A
men: N/A; women: N/A; minorities:
N/A; international: N/A
Acceptance rate: 22%
GRE requirement: Yes
Avg. GRE: quantitative: 162
TOEFL requirement: Yes
Minimum TOEFL score: 550
Fellowships: 42
Teaching assistantships: 69
Research assistantships: 491
Students specializing in: chemical:
7%; civil: 14%; computer
science: 26%; electrical: 27%;
management: 1%; industrial: 2%;
materials: 12%; mechanical: 10%

University of Massachusetts-Dartmouth

285 Old Westport Road
North Dartmouth, MA 02747-2300
www.umassd.edu/graduate
Public
Admissions: (508) 999-8604
Email: graduate@umassd.edu
Financial aid: (508) 999-8632
Application deadline: 02/15
In-state tuition: full time: $13,952;
part time: $86/credit hour
Out-of-state tuition: full time:
$19,980
Room/board/expenses: $14,286
Full-time enrollment: 150
men: 71%; women: 29%;
minorities: 4%; international: 77%
Part-time enrollment: 85
men: 84%; women: 16%;
minorities: 11%; international: 36%
Acceptance rate: 61%
GRE requirement: Yes
Avg. GRE: quantitative: 154
TOEFL requirement: Yes
Minimum TOEFL score: 550
Fellowships: 0
Teaching assistantships: 27
Research assistantships: 27
Students specializing in:
biomedical: 9%; civil: 4%;
computer: 1%; computer
science: 34%; electrical: 21%;
science and physics: 9%;
mechanical: 8%

University of Massachusetts-Lowell (Francis)

1 University Avenue
Lowell, MA 01854
www.uml.edu/grad
Public
Admissions: (978) 934-2390
Email: graduate_school@uml.edu
Financial aid: (978) 934-4226
Application deadline: rolling
In-state tuition: full time: $12,799;
part time: $711/credit hour
Out-of-state tuition: full time:
$22,978
Room/board/expenses: $12,578
Full-time enrollment: 539
men: 77%; women: 23%;
minorities: 8%; international: 66%
Part-time enrollment: 401
men: 82%; women: 18%;
minorities: 23%; international:
15%
Acceptance rate: 65%
GRE requirement: Yes
Avg. GRE: quantitative: 157
TOEFL requirement: Yes
Minimum TOEFL score: 550
Fellowships: 4
Teaching assistantships: 90
Research assistantships: 199
Students specializing in:
biomedical: 13%; chemical:
4%; civil: 9%; computer: 8%;
computer science: 19%; electrical:
17%; environmental: 2%;
materials: 13%; mechanical: 13%;
nuclear: 0%; other: 4%

Worcester Polytechnic Institute

100 Institute Road
Worcester, MA 01609-2280
grad.wpi.edu/
Private
Admissions: (508) 831-5301
Email: grad@wpi.edu
Financial aid: (508) 831-5469
Application deadline: rolling
Tuition: full time: $23,910; part
time: $1,325/credit hour
Room/board/expenses: $22,941
Full-time enrollment: 445
men: 78%; women: 22%;
minorities: 6%; international: 65%
Part-time enrollment: 682
men: 79%; women: 21%;
minorities: 14%; international:
23%
Acceptance rate: 46%
GRE requirement: Yes
Avg. GRE: quantitative: 163
TOEFL requirement: Yes
Minimum TOEFL score: 563
Fellowships: 20
Teaching assistantships: 97
Research assistantships: 137
Students specializing in:
biomedical: 4%; chemical: 3%;
civil: 4%; computer science: 12%;
electrical: 25%; environmental:
2%; industrial: 2%; materials: 8%;
mechanical: 12%; other: 27%

MICHIGAN

Lawrence Technological University

21000 W. Ten Mile Road
Southfield, MI 48075
www.ltu.edu
Private
Admissions: (248) 204-3160
Email: admissions@ltu.edu
Financial aid: (248) 204-2126
Application deadline: rolling
Tuition: full time: $14,850; part
time: $8,550
Room/board/expenses: $14,499
Full-time enrollment: 16
men: 63%; women: 38%;
minorities: 50%; international:
19%

Part-time enrollment: 475
men: 85%; women: 15%;
minorities: 60%; international: 7%
Acceptance rate: 60%
GRE requirement: No
Avg. GRE: quantitative: N/A
TOEFL requirement: Yes
Minimum TOEFL score: 550
Fellowships: 0
Teaching assistantships: 0
Research assistantships: 3
Students specializing in:
architectural: 2%; civil: 10%;
electrical: 19%; management: 8%;
industrial: 10%; mechanical: 29%;
other: 25%

Michigan State University

428 S.Shaw Lane
3410 Engineering Building
East Lansing, MI 48824
www.egr.msu.edu
Public
Admissions: (517) 355-8332
Email: egrgrad@egr.msu.edu
Financial aid: (517) 353-5940
Application deadline: 12/01
In-state tuition: full time: $646/
credit hour; part time: $646/
credit hour
Out-of-state tuition: full time:
$1,269/credit hour
Room/board/expenses: $14,196
Full-time enrollment: 791
men: 77%; women: 23%;
minorities: 7%; international: 63%
Part-time enrollment: N/A
men: N/A; women: N/A; minorities:
N/A; international: N/A
Acceptance rate: 9%
GRE requirement: Yes
Avg. GRE: quantitative: 162
TOEFL requirement: Yes
Minimum TOEFL score: 550
Fellowships: 185
Teaching assistantships: 131
Research assistantships: 326
Students specializing in:
agriculture: 6%; chemical: 8%;
civil: 9%; computer science: 17%;
electrical: 29%; environmental:
5%; materials: 7%; mechanical:
19%

Michigan Technological University

1400 Townsend Drive
Houghton, MI 49931-1295
www.mtu.edu/gradschool/
Public
Admissions: (906) 487-2327
Email: gradadms@mtu.edu
Financial aid: (906) 487-2622
Application deadline: rolling
In-state tuition: full time: $16,817;
part time: $821/credit hour
Out-of-state tuition: full time:
$16,817
Room/board/expenses: $13,347
Full-time enrollment: 770
men: 76%; women: 24%;
minorities: 3%; international: 74%
Part-time enrollment: 204
men: 81%; women: 19%;
minorities: 11%; international: 44%
Acceptance rate: 30%
GRE requirement: Yes
Avg. GRE: quantitative: N/A
TOEFL requirement: Yes
Minimum TOEFL score: 550
Fellowships: 36
Teaching assistantships: 100
Research assistantships: 153
Students specializing in:
biomedical: 3%; chemical: 5%;
civil: 8%; computer: 1%; computer
science: 4%; electrical: 26%;
environmental: 11%; materials:
3%; mechanical: 33%; mining: 0%;
other: 6%

Oakland University

2200 Squirrel Road
Rochester, MI 48309
oakland.edu/secs/
Public
Admissions: (248) 370-2700
Email: gradinfo@oakland.edu
Financial aid: (248) 370-2550
Application deadline: 07/15
In-state tuition: full time: $637/
credit hour; part time: $637/
credit hour
Out-of-state tuition: full time:
$1,027/credit hour
Room/board/expenses: $11,410
Full-time enrollment: 228
men: 73%; women: 27%;
minorities: 9%; international: 52%
Part-time enrollment: 346
men: 84%; women: 16%;
minorities: 14%; international: 17%
Acceptance rate: 25%
GRE requirement: Yes
Avg. GRE: quantitative: N/A
TOEFL requirement: Yes
Minimum TOEFL score: 550
Teaching assistantships: 40
Research assistantships: 41
Students specializing in: computer:
5%; computer science: 16%;
electrical: 25%; management:
12%; industrial: 3%; mechanical:
30%; other: 8%

University of Detroit Mercy

4001 W. McNichols
Detroit, MI 48221-3038
www.udmercy.edu
Private
Admissions: (313) 993-1592
Email: admissions@udmercy.edu
Financial aid: N/A
Application deadline: 08/01
Tuition: full time: $1,465/credit
hour; part time: $1,465/credit hour
Room/board/expenses: N/A
Full-time enrollment: 94
men: 87%; women: 13%;
minorities: 2%; international: 87%
Part-time enrollment: 60
men: 80%; women: 20%;
minorities: 17%; international: 25%
Acceptance rate: 42%
GRE requirement: No
Avg. GRE: quantitative: N/A
TOEFL requirement: No
Minimum TOEFL score: N/A
Students specializing in: civil: 18%;
computer: 19%; electrical: 4%;
management: 5%; environmental:
19%; mechanical: 14%; other: 22%

University of Michigan-Ann Arbor

Robert H. Lurie Engineering
Center
Ann Arbor, MI 48109-2102
www.engin.umich.edu/
academics/gradprograms
Public
Admissions: (734) 647-7090
Email: grad-ed@engin.umich.edu
Financial aid: (734) 647-7090
Application deadline: rolling
In-state tuition: full time: $23,057;
part time: $1,231/credit hour
Out-of-state tuition: full time:
$43,213
Room/board/expenses: $19,248
Full-time enrollment: 2,895
men: 78%; women: 22%;
minorities: 14%; international:
55%
Part-time enrollment: 317
men: 83%; women: 17%;
minorities: 10%; international:
38%
Acceptance rate: 25%
GRE requirement: Yes
Avg. GRE: quantitative: 165
TOEFL requirement: Yes
Minimum TOEFL score: 560

Students specializing in:
aerospace: 6%; biomedical: 7%;
chemical: 5%; civil: 4%; computer:
4%; computer science: 5%;
electrical: 19%; environmental:
2%; industrial: 5%; materials: 4%;
mechanical: 14%; nuclear: 4%;
other: 23%

University of Michigan-Dearborn

4901 Evergreen Road
Dearborn, MI 48128
www.engin.umd.umich.edu/
Public
Admissions: (313) 593-1494
Email: umdgrad@umd.umich.edu
Financial aid: (517) 353-5940
Application deadline: 08/01
In-state tuition: full time: $707/
credit hour; part time: $707/
credit hour
Out-of-state tuition: full time:
$1,209/credit hour
Room/board/expenses: $10,520
Full-time enrollment: 273
men: 75%; women: 25%;
minorities: 3%; international: 92%
Part-time enrollment: 631
men: 78%; women: 22%;
minorities: 19%; international:
29%
Acceptance rate: 55%
GRE requirement: Yes
Avg. GRE: quantitative: 159
TOEFL requirement: Yes
Minimum TOEFL score: 560
Teaching assistantships: 9
Research assistantships: 32
Students specializing in: computer:
3%; computer science: 6%;
electrical: 18%; management:
8%; science and physics: 21%;
industrial: 7%; mechanical: 26%;
other: 12%

Wayne State University

5050 Anthony Wayne Drive
Detroit, MI 48202
engineering.wanye.edu
Public
Admissions: (313) 577-2170
Email:
gradadmissions@wayne.edu
Financial aid: (313) 577-2100
Application deadline: 06/01
In-state tuition: full time: $664/
credit hour; part time: $664/
credit hour
Out-of-state tuition: full time:
$1,329/credit hour
Room/board/expenses: $16,431
Full-time enrollment: 841
men: 79%; women: 21%;
minorities: 7%; international: 78%
Part-time enrollment: 362
men: 77%; women: 23%;
minorities: 25%; international:
29%
Acceptance rate: 45%
GRE requirement: Yes
Avg. GRE: quantitative: 156
TOEFL requirement: Yes
Minimum TOEFL score: 550
Fellowships: 22
Teaching assistantships: 84
Research assistantships: 86
Students specializing in:
biomedical: 9%; chemical:
3%; civil: 8%; computer: 3%;
computer science: 17%; electrical:
11%; management: 5%; industrial:
17%; materials: 2%; mechanical:
20%; other: 4%

Western Michigan University

1903 W. Michigan Avenue
Kalamazoo, MI 49008-5314
www.wmich.edu/engineer/
Public
Admissions: (269) 387-2000
Email: ask-wmu@wmich.edu

Financial aid: (269) 387-6000
Application deadline: rolling
In-state tuition: full time: $514/credit hour; part time: $514/credit hour
Out-of-state tuition: full time: $1,089/credit hour
Room/board/expenses: $13,413
Full-time enrollment: 475
men: 83%; women: 17%; minorities: 4%; international: 85%
Part-time enrollment: 121
men: 88%; women: 12%; minorities: 10%; international: 36%
Acceptance rate: 61%
GRE requirement: Yes
Avg. GRE: quantitative: 152
TOEFL requirement: Yes
Minimum TOEFL score: 550
Fellowships: 0
Teaching assistantships: 48
Research assistantships: 36
Students specializing in: chemical: 2%; civil: 13%; computer: 3%; computer science: 19%; electrical: 27%; management: 7%; industrial: 11%; mechanical: 15%; other: 5%

MINNESOTA

Mayo Graduate School

200 First Street SW
Rochester, MN 55905
www.mayo.edu/mgs/
Private
Admissions: N/A
Financial aid: N/A
Application deadline: 12/01
Tuition: full time: N/A; part time: N/A
Room/board/expenses: N/A
Full-time enrollment: 27
men: 52%; women: 48%; minorities: 0%; international: 33%
Part-time enrollment: N/A
men: N/A; women: N/A; minorities: N/A; international: N/A
Avg. GRE: quantitative: N/A
TOEFL requirement: Yes
Minimum TOEFL score: N/A
Students specializing in: N/A

University of Minnesota-Twin Cities

117 Pleasant Street SE
Minneapolis, MN 55455
www.cse.umn.edu
Public
Admissions: (612) 625-3014
Email: gsquest@umn.edu
Financial aid: (612) 624-1111
Application deadline: 12/01
In-state tuition: full time: $17,030; part time: $1,288/credit hour
Out-of-state tuition: full time: $25,252
Room/board/expenses: $14,800
Full-time enrollment: 1,495
men: 76%; women: 24%; minorities: 8%; international: 57%
Part-time enrollment: 372
men: 80%; women: 20%; minorities: 11%; international: 34%
Acceptance rate: 24%
GRE requirement: Yes
Avg. GRE: quantitative: 165
TOEFL requirement: Yes
Minimum TOEFL score: 550
Fellowships: 208
Teaching assistantships: 334
Research assistantships: 628
Students specializing in: aerospace: 5%; biomedical: 8%; chemical: 7%; civil: 7%; computer science: 20%; electrical: 24%; management: 2%; industrial: 3%; materials: 4%; mechanical: 14%; other: 5%

MISSISSIPPI

Jackson State University

1400 John R. Lynch Street
Jackson, MS 39217
www.jsums.edu/
Public
Admissions: N/A
Email: graduate@jsums.edu
Financial aid: N/A
Application deadline: rolling
In-state tuition: full time: $6,602; part time: $367/credit hour
Out-of-state tuition: full time: $16,174
Room/board/expenses: $9,087
Full-time enrollment: 18
men: 78%; women: 22%; minorities: 89%; international: 83%
Part-time enrollment: 61
men: 74%; women: 26%; minorities: 72%; international: 25%
Acceptance rate: 30%
GRE requirement: Yes
Avg. GRE: quantitative: N/A
Minimum TOEFL score: 525
Fellowships: 1
Teaching assistantships: 4
Research assistantships: 4
Students specializing in: N/A

Mississippi State University (Bagley)

PO Box 9544
Mississippi State, MS 39762
www.bagley.msstate.edu/
Public
Admissions: (662) 325-7400
Email: gradapps@grad.msstate.edu
Financial aid: (662) 325-2450
Application deadline: 07/01
In-state tuition: full time: $7,140; part time: $392/credit hour
Out-of-state tuition: full time: $18,478
Room/board/expenses: $18,010
Full-time enrollment: 337
men: 79%; women: 21%; minorities: 10%; international: 52%
Part-time enrollment: 251
men: 78%; women: 22%; minorities: 26%; international: 8%
Acceptance rate: 38%
GRE requirement: Yes
Avg. GRE: quantitative: 158
TOEFL requirement: Yes
Minimum TOEFL score: 550
Fellowships: 30
Teaching assistantships: 66
Research assistantships: 208
Students specializing in: aerospace: 6%; agriculture: 2%; biomedical: 3%; chemical: 4%; civil: 17%; computer science: 11%; electrical: 17%; science and physics: 7%; industrial: 13%; mechanical: 14%; other: 5%

University of Mississippi

Brevard Hall, Room 227
University, MS 38677-1848
www.engineering.olemiss.edu/
Public
Admissions: (662) 915-7474
Email: gschool@olemiss.edu
Financial aid: (800) 891-4596
Application deadline: rolling
In-state tuition: full time: $7,002; part time: $389/credit hour
Out-of-state tuition: full time: $19,044
Room/board/expenses: $19,098
Full-time enrollment: 137
men: 77%; women: 23%; minorities: 9%; international: 59%
Part-time enrollment: 24
men: 83%; women: 17%; minorities: 21%; international: 8%
Acceptance rate: 26%

GRE requirement: Yes
Avg. GRE: quantitative: 155
TOEFL requirement: Yes
Minimum TOEFL score: 550
Fellowships: 1
Teaching assistantships: 68
Research assistantships: 18
Students specializing in: N/A

University of Southern Mississippi[1]

118 College Drive, #5050
Hattiesburg, MS 39406
www.usm.edu/graduate-school
Public
Admissions: (601) 266-4369
Financial aid: N/A
Tuition: N/A
Room/board/expenses: N/A
Enrollment: N/A

MISSOURI

Missouri University of Science & Technology

500 W. 16th Street
110 ERL
Rolla, MO 65409-0840
www.mst.edu
Public
Admissions: (800) 522-0938
Email: admissions@mst.edu
Financial aid: (800) 522-0938
Application deadline: 07/15
In-state tuition: full time: $7,849; part time: $376/credit hour
Out-of-state tuition: full time: $19,316
Room/board/expenses: $11,802
Full-time enrollment: 943
men: 81%; women: 19%; minorities: 3%; international: 69%
Part-time enrollment: 390
men: 84%; women: 16%; minorities: 13%; international: 25%
Acceptance rate: 46%
GRE requirement: Yes
Avg. GRE: quantitative: 159
TOEFL requirement: Yes
Minimum TOEFL score: 550
Fellowships: 21
Teaching assistantships: 159
Research assistantships: 351
Students specializing in: N/A

St. Louis University (Parks)

3450 Lindell Boulevard
St. Louis, MO 63103
parks.slu.edu
Private
Admissions: (314) 977-8547
Email: parksgraduateprograms@slu.edu
Financial aid: (314) 977-2350
Application deadline: 06/30
Tuition: full time: $1,030/credit hour; part time: $1,030/credit hour
Room/board/expenses: $18,158
Full-time enrollment: 54
men: 74%; women: 26%; minorities: 19%; international: 39%
Part-time enrollment: 34
men: 68%; women: 32%; minorities: 18%; international: 18%
Acceptance rate: 65%
GRE requirement: Yes
Avg. GRE: quantitative: N/A
TOEFL requirement: Yes
Minimum TOEFL score: 550
Fellowships: 3
Teaching assistantships: 0
Research assistantships: 20
Students specializing in: aerospace: 20%; biomedical: 20%; civil: 23%; computer: 4%; electrical: 4%; mechanical: 25%; other: 3%

University of Missouri

W1025 Thomas and Nell Lafferre Hall
Columbia, MO 65211
www.missouri.edu/
Public
Admissions: (573) 882-7786
Email: gradadmin@missouri.edu
Financial aid: (573) 882-2751
Application deadline: rolling
In-state tuition: full time: $6,548; part time: $347/credit hour
Out-of-state tuition: full time: $9,006
Room/board/expenses: $16,862
Full-time enrollment: 355
men: 75%; women: 25%; minorities: 4%; international: 71%
Part-time enrollment: 279
men: 78%; women: 22%; minorities: 3%; international: 76%
Acceptance rate: 26%
GRE requirement: Yes
Avg. GRE: quantitative: 161
TOEFL requirement: Yes
Minimum TOEFL score: 500
Fellowships: 38
Teaching assistantships: 105
Research assistantships: 194
Students specializing in: biomedical: 9%; chemical: 5%; civil: 11%; computer: 3%; computer science: 20%; electrical: 21%; industrial: 6%; mechanical: 16%; nuclear: 7%; other: 3%

University of Missouri–Kansas City

534 R. H. Flarsheim Hall
5100 Rockhill Road
Kansas City, MO 64110-2499
www.umkc.edu/sce
Public
Admissions: (816) 235-1111
Email: graduate@umkc.edu
Financial aid: (816) 235-1154
Application deadline: rolling
In-state tuition: full time: $343/credit hour; part time: $343/credit hour
Out-of-state tuition: full time: $884/credit hour
Room/board/expenses: $18,888
Full-time enrollment: 505
men: 71%; women: 29%; minorities: 1%; international: 96%
Part-time enrollment: 178
men: 79%; women: 21%; minorities: 8%; international: 58%
Acceptance rate: 46%
GRE requirement: Yes
Avg. GRE: quantitative: N/A
TOEFL requirement: Yes
Minimum TOEFL score: 550
Teaching assistantships: 20
Research assistantships: 28
Students specializing in: N/A

Washington University in St. Louis

1 Brookings Drive
Campus Box 1100
St. Louis, MO 63130
www.engineering.wustl.edu/
Private
Admissions: (314) 935-7974
Email: gradengineering@seas.wustl.edu
Financial aid: (314) 935-5900
Application deadline: 01/15
Tuition: full time: $46,030; part time: $1,904/credit hour
Room/board/expenses: $25,604
Full-time enrollment: 638
men: 73%; women: 27%; minorities: 8%; international: 64%
Part-time enrollment: 338
men: 77%; women: 23%; minorities: 25%; international: 4%
Acceptance rate: 45%
GRE requirement: Yes
Avg. GRE: quantitative: 165
TOEFL requirement: Yes

Minimum TOEFL score: 550
Fellowships: 50
Teaching assistantships: 3
Research assistantships: 304
Students specializing in: aerospace: 4%; biomedical: 14%; computer: 3%; computer science: 12%; electrical: 17%; management: 12%; industrial: 1%; materials: 1%; mechanical: 12%; other: 23%

MONTANA

Montana State University[1]

212 Roberts Hall
PO Box 173820
Bozeman, MT 59717-3820
www.montana.edu/wwwdg
Public
Admissions: (406) 994-4145
Email: gradstudy@montana.edu
Financial aid: (406) 994-2845
Tuition: N/A
Room/board/expenses: N/A
Enrollment: N/A

NEBRASKA

University of Nebraska-Lincoln

114 Othmer Hall
Lincoln, NE 68588-0642
www.engineering.unl.edu/graduate-programs
Public
Admissions: (402) 472-2875
Email: graduate@unl.edu
Financial aid: (402) 472-2030
Application deadline: rolling
In-state tuition: full time: $394/credit hour; part time: $394/credit hour
Out-of-state tuition: full time: $1,052/credit hour
Room/board/expenses: $12,839
Full-time enrollment: 519
men: 78%; women: 22%; minorities: 4%; international: 65%
Part-time enrollment: 105
men: 85%; women: 15%; minorities: 11%; international: 18%
Acceptance rate: 30%
GRE requirement: Yes
Avg. GRE: quantitative: 160
TOEFL requirement: Yes
Minimum TOEFL score: 550
Fellowships: 2
Teaching assistantships: 125
Research assistantships: 270
Students specializing in: agriculture: 6%; architectural: 9%; biomedical: 2%; chemical: 3%; civil: 17%; computer: 5%; computer science: 18%; electrical: 14%; science and physics: 5%; environmental: 2%; materials: 4%; mechanical: 10%; other: 4%

NEVADA

University of Nevada-Las Vegas (Hughes)

4505 Maryland Parkway
Box 544005
Las Vegas, NV 89154-4005
go.unlv.edu/
Public
Admissions: (702) 895-3320
Email: gradcollege@unlv.edu
Financial aid: (702) 895-3697
Application deadline: 06/01
In-state tuition: full time: $9,148; part time: $264/credit hour
Out-of-state tuition: full time: $23,276
Room/board/expenses: $17,400
Full-time enrollment: 175
men: 72%; women: 28%; minorities: 21%; international: 56%

Part-time enrollment: 51
men: 71%; women: 29%;
minorities: 31%; international: 6%
Acceptance rate: 62%
GRE requirement: Yes
Avg. GRE: quantitative: 154
TOEFL requirement: Yes
Minimum TOEFL score: 550
Fellowships: 1
Teaching assistantships: 71
Research assistantships: 51
Students specializing in:
biomedical: 2%; civil: 35%;
computer science: 22%;
electrical: 21%; mechanical: 17%;
nuclear: 2%; other: 1%

University of Nevada-Reno

Mail Stop 0256
Reno, NV 89557-0256
www.unr.edu/grad/admissions
Public
Admissions: (775) 784-6869
Email: gradadmissions@unr.edu
Financial aid: (775) 784-4666
Application deadline: rolling
In-state tuition: full time: $371/
credit hour; part time: $371/
credit hour
Out-of-state tuition: full time:
$1,289/credit hour
Room/board/expenses: $20,100
Full-time enrollment: 191
men: 76%; women: 24%;
minorities: 16%; international:
62%
Part-time enrollment: 62
men: 79%; women: 21%;
minorities: 16%; international: 27%
Acceptance rate: 58%
GRE requirement: Yes
Avg. GRE: quantitative: 158
TOEFL requirement: Yes
Minimum TOEFL score: 500
Fellowships: 10
Teaching assistantships: 63
Research assistantships: 95
Students specializing in:
biomedical: 4%; chemical:
4%; civil: 34%; computer:
29%; computer science: 29%;
electrical: 8%; environmental:
32%; materials: 7%; mechanical:
14%

NEW HAMPSHIRE

Dartmouth College (Thayer)

14 Engineering Drive
Hanover, NH 03755
engineering.dartmouth.edu
Private
Admissions: (603) 646-2606
Email: engineering.admissions@
dartmouth.edu
Financial aid: (603) 646-3844
Application deadline: 01/01
Tuition: full time: $47,143; part
time: N/A
Room/board/expenses: $24,963
Full-time enrollment: 285
men: 73%; women: 27%;
minorities: 13%; international:
60%
Part-time enrollment: 1
men: 100%; women: 0%;
minorities: 0%; international: 0%
Acceptance rate: 22%
GRE requirement: Yes
Avg. GRE: quantitative: 164
TOEFL requirement: Yes
Minimum TOEFL score: 600
Fellowships: 47
Teaching assistantships: 29
Research assistantships: 94
Students specializing in: computer
science: 34%; science and
physics: 66%

University of New Hampshire

Kingsbury Hall
33 College Road
Durham, NH 03824
www.gradschool.unh.edu/
Public
Admissions: (603) 862-3000
Email: grad.school@unh.edu
Financial aid: (603) 862-3600
Application deadline: 02/15
In-state tuition: full time: $15,288;
part time: $750/credit hour
Out-of-state tuition: full time:
$28,248
Room/board/expenses: $16,200
Full-time enrollment: 135
men: 76%; women: 24%;
minorities: 4%; international: 45%
Part-time enrollment: 140
men: 78%; women: 22%;
minorities: 9%; international: 24%
Acceptance rate: 62%
GRE requirement: Yes
Avg. GRE: quantitative: 160
TOEFL requirement: Yes
Minimum TOEFL score: 550
Fellowships: 6
Teaching assistantships: 69
Research assistantships: 47
Students specializing in: chemical:
7%; civil: 26%; computer science:
25%; electrical: 13%; materials:
2%; mechanical: 22%; other: 5%

NEW JERSEY

New Jersey Institute of Technology

University Heights
Newark, NJ 07102-1982
www.njit.edu/
Public
Admissions: (973) 596-3300
Email: admissions@njit.edu
Financial aid: (973) 596-3479
Application deadline: rolling
In-state tuition: full time: $20,572;
part time: $982/credit hour
Out-of-state tuition: full time:
$28,964
Room/board/expenses: $16,780
Full-time enrollment: 1,439
men: 72%; women: 28%;
minorities: 13%; international:
80%
Part-time enrollment: 814
men: 76%; women: 24%;
minorities: 48%; international: 7%
Acceptance rate: 59%
GRE requirement: Yes
Avg. GRE: quantitative: N/A
TOEFL requirement: Yes
Minimum TOEFL score: 550
Fellowships: 16
Teaching assistantships: 63
Research assistantships: 53
Students specializing in:
biomedical: 6%; chemical:
4%; civil: 9%; computer: 2%;
computer science: 34%;
electrical: 15%; management:
8%; science and physics: 0%;
environmental: 2%; industrial: 2%;
materials: 2%; mechanical: 5%;
other: 9%

Princeton University

C230 Engineering Quadrangle
Princeton, NJ 08544-5263
engineering.princeton.edu
Private
Admissions: (609) 258-3034
Email: gsadmit@princeton.edu
Financial aid: (609) 258-3037
Application deadline: N/A
Tuition: full time: $43,720; part
time: N/A
Room/board/expenses: $27,450
Full-time enrollment: 583
men: 75%; women: 25%;
minorities: 12%; international:
56%

Part-time enrollment: N/A
men: N/A; women: N/A; minorities:
N/A; international: N/A
Acceptance rate: 11%
GRE requirement: Yes
Avg. GRE: quantitative: 167
TOEFL requirement: Yes
Minimum TOEFL score: N/A
Fellowships: 169
Teaching assistantships: 108
Research assistantships: 302
Students specializing in: chemical:
14%; civil: 10%; computer science:
21%; electrical: 31%; mechanical:
17%; other: 7%

Rutgers Biomedical and Health Sciences[1]

185 South Orange Avenue
Newark, NJ 07103
gsbs.rutgers.edu/
Public
Admissions: (973) 972-4511
Email:
gsbsnadm@gsbs.rutgers.edu
Financial aid: N/A
Tuition: N/A
Room/board/expenses: N/A
Enrollment: N/A

Rutgers, The State University of New Jersey-New Brunswick

98 Brett Road
Piscataway, NJ 08854-8058
gradstudy.rutgers.edu
Public
Admissions: (732) 932-7711
Email: gradadm@rci.rutgers.edu
Financial aid: (732) 932-7057
Application deadline: rolling
In-state tuition: full time: $17,922;
part time: $662/credit hour
Out-of-state tuition: full time:
$28,770
Room/board/expenses: $17,584
Full-time enrollment: 828
men: 77%; women: 23%;
minorities: 9%; international: 75%
Part-time enrollment: 401
men: 76%; women: 24%;
minorities: 17%; international:
53%
Acceptance rate: 19%
GRE requirement: Yes
Avg. GRE: quantitative: 163
TOEFL requirement: Yes
Minimum TOEFL score: 550
Fellowships: 100
Teaching assistantships: 156
Research assistantships: 174
Students specializing in:
biomedical: 8%; chemical: 15%;
civil: 8%; computer science: 16%;
electrical: 28%; industrial: 6%;
materials: 5%; mechanical: 14%

Stevens Institute of Technology (Schaefer)

Castle Point on Hudson
Hoboken, NJ 07030
www.stevens.edu/ses/index.php
Private
Admissions: (201) 216-5197
Email:
gradadmissions@stevens.edu
Financial aid: (201) 216-8143
Application deadline: rolling
Tuition: full time: $32,020; part
time: $1,400/credit hour
Room/board/expenses: $14,000
Full-time enrollment: 1,464
men: 74%; women: 26%;
minorities: 2%; international: 88%
Part-time enrollment: 514
men: 75%; women: 25%;
minorities: 18%; international: 0%
Acceptance rate: 61%
GRE requirement: Yes
Avg. GRE: quantitative: 161
TOEFL requirement: Yes
Minimum TOEFL score: 537

Fellowships: 40
Teaching assistantships: 120
Research assistantships: 130
Students specializing in:
biomedical: 2%; chemical:
2%; civil: 3%; computer: 4%;
computer science: 18%; electrical:
17%; management: 4%; science
and physics: 0%; environmental:
2%; materials: 2%; mechanical:
10%; other: 36%

NEW MEXICO

New Mexico Institute of Mining and Technology

801 Leroy Place
Socorro, NM 87801
www.nmt.edu
Public
Admissions: (505) 835-5513
Email: graduate@nmt.edu
Financial aid: (505) 835-5333
Application deadline: 02/15
In-state tuition: full time: $6,472;
part time: $307/credit hour
Out-of-state tuition: full time:
$19,243
Room/board/expenses: $13,238
Full-time enrollment: 119
men: 78%; women: 22%;
minorities: 17%; international: 45%
Part-time enrollment: 71
men: 87%; women: 13%;
minorities: 30%; international: 11%
Acceptance rate: 45%
GRE requirement: Yes
Avg. GRE: quantitative: 157
TOEFL requirement: Yes
Minimum TOEFL score: 540
Fellowships: 5
Teaching assistantships: 39
Research assistantships: 42
Students specializing in: computer
science: 11%; electrical: 5%;
management: 8%; environmental:
3%; materials: 14%; mechanical:
27%; mining: 11%; petroleum: 21%

New Mexico State University

PO Box 30001
Department 3449
Las Cruces, NM 88003
www.nmsu.edu
Public
Admissions: (575) 646-3121
Email: admissions@nmsu.edu
Financial aid: (505) 646-4105
Application deadline: rolling
In-state tuition: full time: $4,822;
part time: $221/credit hour
Out-of-state tuition: full time:
$14,691
Room/board/expenses: $13,068
Full-time enrollment: 357
men: 75%; women: 25%;
minorities: 16%; international:
69%
Part-time enrollment: 188
men: 84%; women: 16%;
minorities: 38%; international:
18%
Acceptance rate: 51%
GRE requirement: Yes
Avg. GRE: quantitative: 156
TOEFL requirement: Yes
Minimum TOEFL score: 550
Fellowships: 19
Teaching assistantships: 72
Research assistantships: 116
Students specializing in:
aerospace: 2%; chemical: 10%;
civil: 11%; computer science: 18%;
electrical: 26%; environmental:
3%; industrial: 23%; mechanical:
7%

University of New Mexico

MSC 01 1140
1 University of New Mexico
Albuquerque, NM 87131
admissions.unm.edu/graduate
Public
Admissions: (505) 277-8900
Email: chat@studentinfo.unm.edu
Financial aid: (505) 277-8900
Application deadline: 07/15
In-state tuition: full time: $6,753;
part time: $247/credit hour
Out-of-state tuition: full time:
$21,322
Room/board/expenses: $15,285
Full-time enrollment: 855
men: 79%; women: 21%;
minorities: 20%; international:
38%
Part-time enrollment: N/A
men: N/A; women: N/A; minorities:
N/A; international: N/A
Acceptance rate: 58%
GRE requirement: Yes
Avg. GRE: quantitative: 157
TOEFL requirement: Yes
Minimum TOEFL score: 550
Fellowships: 10
Teaching assistantships: 50
Research assistantships: 344
Students specializing in:
biomedical: 3%; chemical:
2%; civil: 11%; computer:
8%; computer science: 24%;
electrical: 21%; industrial: 1%;
mechanical: 14%; nuclear: 6%;
other: 10%

NEW YORK

Alfred University-New York State College of Ceramics (Inamori)

2 Pine Street
Alfred, NY 14802-1296
nyscc.alfred.edu
Public
Admissions: (800) 541-9229
Email: admwww@alfred.edu
Financial aid: (607) 871-2159
Application deadline: rolling
In-state tuition: full time: $23,470;
part time: $810/credit hour
Out-of-state tuition: full time:
$23,470
Room/board/expenses: $14,980
Full-time enrollment: 37
men: 73%; women: 27%;
minorities: 0%; international: 41%
Part-time enrollment: 25
men: 64%; women: 36%;
minorities: 0%; international: 20%
Acceptance rate: 66%
GRE requirement: No
Avg. GRE: quantitative: N/A
TOEFL requirement: Yes
Minimum TOEFL score: 590
Fellowships: 1
Teaching assistantships: 8
Research assistantships: 19
Students specializing in: N/A

Binghamton University-SUNY (Watson)

PO Box 6000
Binghamton, NY 13902-6000
watson.binghamton.edu
Public
Admissions: (607) 777-2151
Email: gradsch@binghamton.edu
Financial aid: (607) 777-2428
Application deadline: rolling
In-state tuition: full time: $14,266;
part time: $432/credit hour
Out-of-state tuition: full time:
$24,086
Room/board/expenses: $17,478
Full-time enrollment: 673
men: 77%; women: 23%;
minorities: 9%; international: 77%

Part-time enrollment: 317
men: 83%; women: 17%;
minorities: 8%; international: 59%
Acceptance rate: 49%
GRE requirement: Yes
Avg. GRE: quantitative: 159
TOEFL requirement: Yes
Minimum TOEFL score: 550
Fellowships: 5
Teaching assistantships: 85
Research assistantships: 132
Students specializing in:
biomedical: 5%; computer:
0%; computer science: 36%;
electrical: 22%; industrial: 22%;
materials: 2%; mechanical: 10%;
other: 4%

Clarkson University

8 Clarkson Avenue
Box 5700
Potsdam, NY 13699
www.clarkson.edu/engineering/
graduate/index.html
Private
Admissions: (315) 268-7929
Email: enggrad@clarkson.edu
Financial aid: (315) 268-7929
Application deadline: rolling
Tuition: full time: $1,390/credit
hour; part time: $1,390/credit
hour
Room/board/expenses: $13,724
Full-time enrollment: 184
men: 78%; women: 22%;
minorities: 5%; international: 59%
Part-time enrollment: 9
men: 78%; women: 22%;
minorities: 0%; international: 0%
Acceptance rate: 66%
GRE requirement: Yes
Avg. GRE: quantitative: 160
TOEFL requirement: Yes
Minimum TOEFL score: 550
Fellowships: 10
Teaching assistantships: 48
Research assistantships: 67
Students specializing in: chemical:
12%; civil: 16%; electrical:
22%; science and physics: 4%;
environmental: 14%; materials:
5%; mechanical: 26%

Columbia University (Fu Foundation)

500 W. 120th Street
Room 510 Mudd
New York, NY 10027
www.engineering.columbia.edu
Private
Admissions: (212) 854-6438
Email: seasgradmit@columbia.edu
Financial aid: (212) 854-6438
Application deadline: 12/15
Tuition: full time: $45,845; part
time: $1,710/credit hour
Room/board/expenses: $25,900
Full-time enrollment: 1,948
men: 70%; women: 30%;
minorities: 13%; international:
73%
Part-time enrollment: 1,090
men: 70%; women: 30%;
minorities: 11%; international: 70%
Acceptance rate: 22%
GRE requirement: Yes
Avg. GRE: quantitative: 166
TOEFL requirement: Yes
Minimum TOEFL score: 590
Fellowships: 109
Teaching assistantships: 183
Research assistantships: 466
Students specializing in:
biomedical: 5%; chemical:
6%; civil: 9%; computer: 2%;
computer science: 20%;
electrical: 17%; management:
5%; science and physics: 2%;
environmental: 3%; industrial:
19%; materials: 3%; mechanical:
8%; other: 2%

Cornell University

242 Carpenter Hall
Ithaca, NY 14853
www.engineering.cornell.edu
Private
Admissions: (607) 255-5820
Email: engr_grad@cornell.edu
Financial aid: (607) 255-5820
Application deadline: N/A
Tuition: full time: $29,581; part
time: $1,960/credit hour
Room/board/expenses: $23,470
Full-time enrollment: 1,864
men: 68%; women: 32%;
minorities: 16%; international:
54%
Part-time enrollment: 102
men: 84%; women: 16%;
minorities: 31%; international: 2%
Acceptance rate: 28%
GRE requirement: Yes
Avg. GRE: quantitative: 165
TOEFL requirement: Yes
Minimum TOEFL score: N/A
Fellowships: 354
Teaching assistantships: 209
Research assistantships: 456
Students specializing in:
aerospace: 2%; agriculture:
3%; biomedical: 9%; chemical:
10%; civil: 7%; computer:
16%; computer science: 16%;
management: 2%; science and
physics: 4%; industrial: 8%;
materials: 5%; mechanical: 8%;
other: 10%

CUNY-City College (Grove)

Convent Avenue at 138th Street
New York, NY 10031
www.ccny.cuny.edu/Admissions/
index.cfm
Public
Admissions: (212) 650-6853
Email: graduateadmissions@
ccny.cuny.edu
Financial aid: (212) 650-6656
Application deadline: 12/31
In-state tuition: full time: $11,581;
part time: $480/credit hour
Out-of-state tuition: full time: $830/
credit hour
Room/board/expenses: $25,400
Full-time enrollment: 345
men: 68%; women: 32%;
minorities: 24%; international:
50%
Part-time enrollment: 240
men: 78%; women: 23%;
minorities: 52%; international:
16%
Acceptance rate: 55%
GRE requirement: Yes
Avg. GRE: quantitative: 159
TOEFL requirement: Yes
Minimum TOEFL score: 550
Fellowships: 118
Teaching assistantships: 33
Research assistantships: 144
Students specializing in:
biomedical: 11%; chemical:
11%; civil: 20%; computer
science: 23%; electrical: 21%;
environmental: 2%; mechanical:
13%

New York University

6 MetroTech Center
Brooklyn, NY 11201
engineering.nyu.edu/
Private
Admissions: (718) 260-3200
Email: gradinfo@poly.edu
Financial aid: (718) 260-3182
Application deadline: N/A
Tuition: full time: $1,452/credit
hour; part time: $1,452/credit hour
Room/board/expenses: $29,890
Full-time enrollment: 1,789
men: 74%; women: 26%;
minorities: 5%; international: 88%
Part-time enrollment: 517
men: 74%; women: 26%;
minorities: 31%; international:
32%

Acceptance rate: 38%
GRE requirement: Yes
Avg. GRE: quantitative: 162
TOEFL requirement: Yes
Minimum TOEFL score: 550
Fellowships: 25
Teaching assistantships: 46
Research assistantships: 144
Students specializing in:
biomedical: 5%; chemical:
2%; civil: 9%; computer: 5%;
computer science: 34%;
electrical: 23%; management:
13%; environmental: 1%;
industrial: 4%; mechanical: 4%

Rensselaer Polytechnic Institute

Jonsson Engineering Center 3004
Troy, NY 12180-3590
www.rpi.edu
Private
Admissions: (518) 276-6216
Email: admissions@rpi.edu
Financial aid: (518) 276-6813
Application deadline: 01/01
Tuition: full time: $48,915; part
time: $1,945/credit hour
Room/board/expenses: $15,765
Full-time enrollment: 573
men: 78%; women: 22%;
minorities: 11%; international: 54%
Part-time enrollment: 160
men: 85%; women: 15%;
minorities: 9%; international: 14%
Acceptance rate: 27%
GRE requirement: Yes
Avg. GRE: quantitative: 163
TOEFL requirement: Yes
Minimum TOEFL score: 570
Fellowships: 38
Teaching assistantships: 203
Research assistantships: 315
Students specializing in:
aerospace: 5%; biomedical:
8%; chemical: 10%; civil: 4%;
computer: 2%; computer
science: 15%; electrical: 15%;
management: 2%; science and
physics: 2%; environmental: 1%;
materials: 8%; mechanical: 25%;
nuclear: 4%

Rochester Institute of Technology (Gleason)

77 Lomb Memorial Drive
Rochester, NY 14623
www.rit.edu
Private
Admissions: (585) 475-2229
Email: gradinfo@rit.edu
Financial aid: (585) 475-5520
Application deadline: rolling
Tuition: full time: $38,948; part
time: $1,612/credit hour
Room/board/expenses: $13,593
Full-time enrollment: 908
men: 77%; women: 23%;
minorities: 3%; international: 79%
Part-time enrollment: 269
men: 81%; women: 19%;
minorities: 9%; international: 36%
Acceptance rate: 46%
GRE requirement: No
Avg. GRE: quantitative: 158
TOEFL requirement: Yes
Minimum TOEFL score: 550
Fellowships: 5
Teaching assistantships: 43
Research assistantships: 114
Students specializing in: computer:
5%; computer science: 40%;
electrical: 22%; management:
2%; science and physics: 0%;
industrial: 5%; mechanical: 11%;
other: 22%

Stony Brook University-SUNY

Engineering Room 100
Stony Brook, NY 11794-2200
www.grad.stonybrook.edu
Public
Admissions: (631) 632-7035

Email: gradadmissions@
stonybrook.edu
Financial aid: (631) 632-6840
Application deadline: 01/15
In-state tuition: full time: $11,801;
part time: $432/credit hour
Out-of-state tuition: full time:
$21,621
Room/board/expenses: $18,432
Full-time enrollment: 1,285
men: 74%; women: 26%;
minorities: 9%; international: 80%
Part-time enrollment: 227
men: 73%; women: 27%;
minorities: 8%; international: 52%
Acceptance rate: 32%
GRE requirement: Yes
Avg. GRE: quantitative: 163
TOEFL requirement: Yes
Minimum TOEFL score: N/A
Fellowships: 32
Teaching assistantships: 177
Research assistantships: 262
Students specializing in:
biomedical: 6%; computer:
2%; computer science: 33%;
electrical: 11%; materials: 10%;
mechanical: 14%; other: 28%

SUNY College of Environmental Science and Forestry[1]

227 Bray Hall
Syracuse, NY 13210
www.esf.edu/
Public
Admissions: N/A
Email: esfgrad@esf.edu
Financial aid: N/A
Tuition: N/A
Room/board/expenses: N/A
Enrollment: N/A

Syracuse University

223 Link Hall
Syracuse, NY 13244-1240
www.lcs.syr.edu/
Private
Admissions: (315) 443-4492
Financial aid: (315) 443-1513
Application deadline: rolling
Tuition: full time: $41,886; part
time: $1,757/credit hour
Room/board/expenses: $20,318
Full-time enrollment: 1,053,
men: 74%; women: 26%;
minorities: 3%; international: 90%
Part-time enrollment: 121
men: 80%; women: 20%;
minorities: 18%; international:
30%
Acceptance rate: 40%
GRE requirement: Yes
Avg. GRE: quantitative: 162
TOEFL requirement: Yes
Minimum TOEFL score: 550
Fellowships: 29
Teaching assistantships: 89
Research assistantships: 78
Students specializing in:
aerospace: 6%; biomedical: 7%;
chemical: 4%; civil: 9%; computer:
18%; computer science: 15%;
electrical: 13%; management: 5%;
environmental: 2%; mechanical:
11%; other: 11%

University at Buffalo-SUNY

208 Davis Hall
Buffalo, NY 14260-1900
www.eng.buffalo.edu
Public
Admissions: (716) 645-2771
Email: seasgrad@buffalo.edu
Financial aid: (716) 645-2450
Application deadline: rolling
In-state tuition: full time: $12,485;
part time: $583/credit hour
Out-of-state tuition: full time:
$22,305
Room/board/expenses: $17,504

Full-time enrollment: 1,835
men: 79%; women: 21%;
minorities: 3%; international: 88%
Part-time enrollment: 88
men: 88%; women: 13%;
minorities: 19%; international: 0%
Acceptance rate: 24%
GRE requirement: Yes
Avg. GRE: quantitative: 162
TOEFL requirement: Yes
Minimum TOEFL score: 550
Fellowships: 38
Teaching assistantships: 185
Research assistantships: 215
Students specializing in:
aerospace: 2%; biomedical: 3%;
chemical: 6%; civil: 9%; computer
science: 37%; electrical: 21%;
science and physics: 0%;
industrial: 12%; mechanical: 10%

University of Rochester

Lattimore Hall
Box 270076
Rochester, NY 14627-0076
www.Hajim.rochester.edu
Private
Admissions: (585) 275-2059
Email: graduate.admissions@
rochester.edu
Financial aid: (585) 275-3226
Application deadline: N/A
Tuition: full time: $1,442/credit
hour; part time: $1,442/credit hour
Room/board/expenses: $17,010
Full-time enrollment: 550
men: 73%; women: 27%;
minorities: 4%; international: 62%
Part-time enrollment: 27
men: 81%; women: 19%;
minorities: 4%; international: 19%
Acceptance rate: 35%
GRE requirement: Yes
Avg. GRE: quantitative: 165
TOEFL requirement: Yes
Minimum TOEFL score: 600
Fellowships: 100
Teaching assistantships: 60
Research assistantships: 177
Students specializing in:
biomedical: 14%; chemical: 10%;
computer science: 12%; electrical:
25%; materials: 7%; mechanical:
7%; other: 26%

NORTH CAROLINA

Duke University (Pratt)

305 Teer Building
Durham, NC 27708-0271
www.pratt.duke.edu
Private
Admissions: (919) 684-3913
Email: grad-admissions@duke.edu
Financial aid: (919) 681-1552
Application deadline: 12/08
Tuition: full time: $50,142; part
time: $2,765/credit hour
Room/board/expenses: $24,412
Full-time enrollment: 980
men: 67%; women: 33%;
minorities: 12%; international:
60%
Part-time enrollment: 61
men: 77%; women: 23%;
minorities: 16%; international: 8%
Acceptance rate: 28%
GRE requirement: Yes
Avg. GRE: quantitative: 164
TOEFL requirement: Yes
Minimum TOEFL score: 577
Fellowships: 218
Teaching assistantships: 14
Research assistantships: 294
Students specializing in:
biomedical: 21%; civil: 5%;
computer science: 8%; electrical:
22%; management: 29%;
mechanical: 8%; other: 8%

North Carolina A&T State University

1601 E. Market Street
651 McNair Hall
Greensboro, NC 27411
www.ncat.edu/academics/
schools-colleges1/grad/
admissions/index.html
Public
Admissions: (336) 285-2366
Email: grad@ncat.edu
Financial aid: (336) 334-7973
Application deadline: rolling
In-state tuition: full time: $5,535;
part time: $136/credit hour
Out-of-state tuition: full time:
$18,295
Room/board/expenses: $10,755
Full-time enrollment: 223
men: 69%; women: 31%;
minorities: 49%; international:
39%
Part-time enrollment: 104
men: 82%; women: 18%;
minorities: 47%; international:
44%
Acceptance rate: 84%
GRE requirement: Yes
Avg. GRE: quantitative: 153
TOEFL requirement: Yes
Minimum TOEFL score: 550
Fellowships: 17
Teaching assistantships: 71
Research assistantships: 105
Students specializing in:
biomedical: 4%; chemical:
5%; civil: 9%; computer: 11%;
computer science: 19%; electrical:
20%; industrial: 17%; mechanical:
14%

North Carolina State University

PO Box 7901
Raleigh, NC 27695
www.engr.ncsu.edu/
Public
Admissions: (919) 515-2872
Email: graduate_application@
ncsu.edu
Financial aid: (919) 515-2421
Application deadline: 06/25
In-state tuition: full time: $10,006;
part time: $8,100
Out-of-state tuition: full time:
$23,694
Room/board/expenses: $18,605
Full-time enrollment: 2,303
men: 75%; women: 25%;
minorities: 5%; international: 70%
Part-time enrollment: 856
men: 81%; women: 19%;
minorities: 17%; international: 22%
Acceptance rate: 17%
GRE requirement: Yes
Avg. GRE: quantitative: 163
TOEFL requirement: Yes
Minimum TOEFL score: 550
Fellowships: 198
Teaching assistantships: 279
Research assistantships: 849
Students specializing in:
aerospace: 3%; agriculture:
2%; biomedical: 3%; chemical:
5%; civil: 10%; computer:
4%; computer science: 22%;
electrical: 19%; environmental:
1%; industrial: 6%; materials: 4%;
mechanical: 10%; nuclear: 3%;
other: 8%

University of North Carolina-Chapel Hill

CB #7431
166 Rosenau Hall
Chapel Hill, NC 27599-7431
www.sph.unc.edu/envr
Public
Admissions: (919) 966-3844
Email: jack_whaley@unc.edu
Financial aid: (919) 966-3844
Application deadline: 04/14
In-state tuition: full time: $11,855;
part time: $797/credit hour
Out-of-state tuition: full time:
$27,909
Room/board/expenses: $24,920
Full-time enrollment: 112
men: 41%; women: 59%;
minorities: 10%; international:
27%
Part-time enrollment: N/A
men: N/A; women: N/A; minorities:
N/A; international: N/A
Acceptance rate: 32%
GRE requirement: Yes
Avg. GRE: quantitative: 158
TOEFL requirement: Yes
Minimum TOEFL score: 550
Fellowships: 18
Teaching assistantships: 15
Research assistantships: 33
Students specializing in:
environmental: 100%

University of North Carolina-Charlotte (Lee)

Duke Centennial Hall
9201 University City Boulevard
Charlotte, NC 28223-0001
graduateschool.uncc.edu
Public
Admissions: (704) 687-5503
Email: gradadm@uncc.edu
Financial aid: (704) 687-5504
Application deadline: 03/01
In-state tuition: full time: $8,663;
part time: $5,759
Out-of-state tuition: full time:
$20,950
Room/board/expenses: $14,346
Full-time enrollment: 421
men: 80%; women: 20%;
minorities: 5%; international: 75%
Part-time enrollment: 189
men: 76%; women: 24%;
minorities: 20%; international:
33%
Acceptance rate: 45%
GRE requirement: Yes
Avg. GRE: quantitative: 159
TOEFL requirement: Yes
Minimum TOEFL score: 557
Fellowships: 7
Teaching assistantships: 84
Research assistantships: 135
Students specializing in: civil: 9%;
electrical: 45%; management:
13%; environmental: 8%;
mechanical: 19%; other: 9%

NORTH DAKOTA

North Dakota State University

NDSU Department 2450
PO Box 6050
Fargo, ND 58108-6050
www.ndsu.nodak.edu/ndsu/cea/
Public
Admissions: (701) 231-7033
Email:
ndsu.grad.school@ndsu.edu
Financial aid: (701) 231-7533
Application deadline: rolling
In-state tuition: full time: $374/
credit hour; part time: $374/
credit hour
Out-of-state tuition: full time: $913/
credit hour
Room/board/expenses: $10,002
Full-time enrollment: 73
men: 86%; women: 14%;
minorities: 77%; international:
79%
Part-time enrollment: 124
men: 81%; women: 19%;
minorities: 56%; international:
47%
Acceptance rate: 31%
GRE requirement: Yes
Avg. GRE: quantitative: 158
TOEFL requirement: Yes
Minimum TOEFL score: 525
Fellowships: 8
Teaching assistantships: 65

Research assistantships: 79
Students specializing in:
agriculture: 7%; civil: 19%;
electrical: 29%; environmental:
3%; industrial: 9%; mechanical:
13%; other: 20%

University of North Dakota[1]

243 Centennial Drive
Stop 8155
Grand Forks, ND 58202-8155
und.edu/
Public
Admissions: (701) 777-2945
Email: questions@
gradschool.und.edu
Financial aid: N/A
Tuition: N/A
Room/board/expenses: N/A
Enrollment: N/A

OHIO

Air Force Institute of Technology[1]

AFIT/RRA, 2950 P Street
Wright Patterson AFB, OH 45433
www.afit.edu
Public
Admissions: (800) 211-5097
Email: counselors@afit.edu
Financial aid: N/A
Tuition: N/A
Room/board/expenses: N/A
Enrollment: N/A

Case Western Reserve University

500 Nord Hall
10900 Euclid Avenue
Cleveland, OH 44106-7220
gradstudies.case.edu
Private
Admissions: (216) 368-4390
Email: gradstudies@case.edu
Financial aid: (216) 368-4530
Application deadline: rolling
Tuition: full time: $39,874; part
time: $1,660/credit hour
Room/board/expenses: $16,420
Full-time enrollment: 544
men: 71%; women: 29%;
minorities: 11%; international: 61%
Part-time enrollment: 73
men: 71%; women: 29%;
minorities: 16%; international: 16%
Acceptance rate: 21%
GRE requirement: Yes
Avg. GRE: quantitative: 164
TOEFL requirement: Yes
Minimum TOEFL score: 577
Fellowships: 50
Teaching assistantships: 24
Research assistantships: 235
Students specializing in:
aerospace: 1%; biomedical:
20%; chemical: 19%; civil: 3%;
computer: 3%; computer science:
8%; electrical: 18%; management:
6%; materials: 6%; mechanical:
14%; other: 1%

Cleveland State University

2121 Euclid Avenue, FH 104
Cleveland, OH 44115-2425
www.csuohio.edu/engineering/
Public
Admissions: (216) 687-5599
Email: graduate.admissions@
csuohio.edu
Financial aid: (216) 687-3764
Application deadline: 07/01
In-state tuition: full time: $531/
credit hour; part time: $531/
credit hour
Out-of-state tuition: full time: $999/
credit hour
Room/board/expenses: $16,326

Full-time enrollment: 131
men: 85%; women: 15%;
minorities: 1%; international: 77%
Part-time enrollment: 428
men: 79%; women: 21%;
minorities: 9%; international: 57%
Acceptance rate: 39%
GRE requirement: Yes
Avg. GRE: quantitative: 142
TOEFL requirement: Yes
Minimum TOEFL score: 525
Fellowships: 0
Teaching assistantships: 58
Research assistantships: 51
Students specializing in:
biomedical: 11%; chemical:
6%; civil: 11%; electrical: 46%;
environmental: 1%; industrial: 2%;
mechanical: 17%; other: 6%

Ohio State University

2070 Neil Avenue
Columbus, OH 43210-1278
engineering.osu.edu/
Public
Admissions: (614) 292-9444
Email: gradadmissions@osu.edu
Financial aid: (614) 292-0300
Application deadline: rolling
In-state tuition: full time: $12,935;
part time: $746/credit hour
Out-of-state tuition: full time:
$31,479
Room/board/expenses: $15,174
Full-time enrollment: 1,673
men: 77%; women: 23%;
minorities: 6%; international: 64%
Part-time enrollment: 128
men: 79%; women: 21%;
minorities: 16%; international:
24%
Acceptance rate: 18%
GRE requirement: Yes
Avg. GRE: quantitative: 164
TOEFL requirement: Yes
Minimum TOEFL score: 550
Fellowships: 124
Teaching assistantships: 192
Research assistantships: 684
Students specializing in:
aerospace: 3%; agriculture:
3%; biomedical: 4%; chemical:
5%; civil: 6%; computer: 19%;
electrical: 26%; management: 0%;
environmental: 1%; industrial: 9%;
materials: 9%; mechanical: 12%;
nuclear: 2%

Ohio University (Russ)

150 Stocker Center
Athens, OH 45701
www.ohio.edu/engineering
Public
Admissions: (740) 593-2800
Email: graduate@ohio.edu
Financial aid: (740) 593-4141
Application deadline: rolling
In-state tuition: full time: $9,810;
part time: $505/credit hour
Out-of-state tuition: full time:
$17,802
Room/board/expenses: $11,500
Full-time enrollment: 223
men: 75%; women: 25%;
minorities: 3%; international: 60%
Part-time enrollment: 284
men: 82%; women: 18%;
minorities: 19%; international: 18%
Acceptance rate: 36%
GRE requirement: Yes
Avg. GRE: quantitative: 159
TOEFL requirement: Yes
Minimum TOEFL score: 550
Fellowships: 20
Teaching assistantships: 94
Research assistantships: 205
Students specializing in:
biomedical: 2%; chemical: 10%;
civil: 18%; computer science: 7%;
electrical: 17%; management:
29%; industrial: 8%; mechanical:
9%

University of Akron

201 ASEC
Akron, OH 44325-3901
www.uakron.edu/gradsch/
Public
Admissions: (330) 972-7663
Email: gradschool@uakron.edu
Financial aid: (330) 972-7663
Application deadline: rolling
In-state tuition: full time: $9,435;
part time: $421/credit hour
Out-of-state tuition: full time:
$14,833
Room/board/expenses: $14,958
Full-time enrollment: 291
men: 80%; women: 20%;
minorities: 3%; international: 75%
Part-time enrollment: 97
men: 78%; women: 22%;
minorities: 6%; international: 28%
Acceptance rate: 49%
GRE requirement: Yes
Avg. GRE: quantitative: 160
TOEFL requirement: Yes
Minimum TOEFL score: 550
Fellowships: 1
Teaching assistantships: 132
Research assistantships: 160
Students specializing in:
biomedical: 8%; chemical:
21%; civil: 25%; computer: 1%;
electrical: 19%; management: 3%;
mechanical: 24%; other: 1%

University of Cincinnati

PO Box 210077
Cincinnati, OH 45221-0077
www.eng.uc.edu
Public
Admissions: (513) 556-6347
Email: engrgrad@uc.edu
Financial aid: (513) 556-3647
Application deadline: 01/31
In-state tuition: full time: $17,604;
part time: $640/credit hour
Out-of-state tuition: full time:
$29,346
Room/board/expenses: $12,819
Full-time enrollment: 808
men: 76%; women: 24%;
minorities: 3%; international: 67%
Part-time enrollment: 32
men: 91%; women: 9%; minorities:
19%; international: 0%
Acceptance rate: 15%
GRE requirement: Yes
Avg. GRE: quantitative: 161
TOEFL requirement: Yes
Minimum TOEFL score: 550
Fellowships: 30
Teaching assistantships: 164
Research assistantships: 378
Students specializing in:
aerospace: 16%; biomedical: 3%;
chemical: 5%; civil: 7%; computer:
10%; computer science: 12%;
electrical: 12%; environmental:
1%; materials: 9%; mechanical:
25%

University of Dayton

300 College Park
Dayton, OH 45469-0254
www.udayton.edu/apply
Private
Admissions: (937) 229-4411
Email:
gradadmission@udayton.edu
Financial aid: (937) 229-4311
Application deadline: rolling
Tuition: full time: $923/credit hour;
part time: $923/credit hour
Room/board/expenses: $15,033
Full-time enrollment: 673
men: 78%; women: 22%;
minorities: 5%; international: 71%
Part-time enrollment: 172
men: 81%; women: 19%;
minorities: 9%; international: 31%
Acceptance rate: 35%
GRE requirement: Yes
Avg. GRE: quantitative: 155
TOEFL requirement: Yes
Minimum TOEFL score: 550

Fellowships: 1
Teaching assistantships: 28
Research assistantships: 65
Students specializing in:
aerospace: 5%; biomedical: 1%;
chemical: 5%; civil: 3%; electrical:
30%; management: 14%;
materials: 9%; mechanical: 16%;
other: 17%

University of Toledo

2801 W. Bancroft
Toledo, OH 43606
www.eng.utoledo.edu/coe/
grad_studies/
Public
Admissions: (419) 530-4723
Email: gradoff@eng.utoledo.edu
Financial aid: (419) 530-8700
Application deadline: rolling
In-state tuition: full time: $13,166;
part time: $549/credit hour
Out-of-state tuition: full time:
$23,502
Room/board/expenses: $14,960
Full-time enrollment: 81
men: 79%; women: 21%;
minorities: 5%; international: 68%
Part-time enrollment: 308
men: 80%; women: 20%;
minorities: 2%; international: 75%
Acceptance rate: 76%
GRE requirement: Yes
Avg. GRE: quantitative: 158
TOEFL requirement: Yes
Minimum TOEFL score: 550
Fellowships: 3
Teaching assistantships: 104
Research assistantships: 85
Students specializing in:
biomedical: 9%; chemical: 11%;
civil: 10%; computer science: 12%;
electrical: 26%; industrial: 7%;
mechanical: 22%; other: 7%

Wright State University

3640 Colonel Glenn Highway
Dayton, OH 45435
www.wright.edu/sogs/
Public
Admissions: (937) 775-2976
Email: wsugrad@wright.edu
Financial aid: (937) 775-5721
Application deadline: rolling
In-state tuition: full time: $12,788;
part time: $590/credit hour
Out-of-state tuition: full time:
$21,724
Room/board/expenses: $14,000
Full-time enrollment: 854
men: 72%; women: 28%;
minorities: 6%; international: 76%
Part-time enrollment: 195
men: 76%; women: 24%;
minorities: 13%; international:
46%
Acceptance rate: 44%
GRE requirement: Yes
Avg. GRE: quantitative: 156
TOEFL requirement: Yes
Minimum TOEFL score: 550
Fellowships: 0
Teaching assistantships: 64
Research assistantships: 136
Students specializing in:
biomedical: 5%; computer:
6%; computer science: 27%;
electrical: 35%; management:
2%; industrial: 6%; materials: 2%;
mechanical: 9%; other: 9%

OKLAHOMA

Oklahoma State University

201 ATRC
Stillwater, OK 74078-0535
gradcollege.okstate.edu
Public
Admissions: (405) 744-6368
Email: grad-i@okstate.edu
Financial aid: (405) 744-6604
Application deadline: rolling

In-state tuition: full time: $187/
credit hour; part time: $187/
credit hour
Out-of-state tuition: full time: $765/
credit hour
Room/board/expenses: $14,300
Full-time enrollment: 401
men: N/A; women: N/A; minorities:
5%; international: 82%
Part-time enrollment: 477
men: N/A; women: N/A; minorities:
13%; international: 43%
Acceptance rate: 22%
GRE requirement: Yes
Avg. GRE: quantitative: N/A
TOEFL requirement: Yes
Minimum TOEFL score: 550
Fellowships: 39
Teaching assistantships: 152
Research assistantships: 186
Students specializing in: N/A

University of Oklahoma

202 W. Boyd, CEC 107
Norman, OK 73019
www.ou.edu/coe
Public
Admissions: (405) 325-2252
Email: admrec@ou.edu
Financial aid: (405) 325-4521
Application deadline: rolling
In-state tuition: full time: $183/
credit hour; part time: $183/
credit hour
Out-of-state tuition: full time: $707/
credit hour
Room/board/expenses: $15,687
Full-time enrollment: 414
men: 78%; women: 22%;
minorities: 7%; international: 69%
Part-time enrollment: 216
men: 75%; women: 25%;
minorities: 12%; international:
54%
Acceptance rate: 34%
GRE requirement: Yes
Avg. GRE: quantitative: 160
TOEFL requirement: Yes
Minimum TOEFL score: 550
Fellowships: 27
Teaching assistantships: 108
Research assistantships: 166
Students specializing in:
aerospace: 2%; biomedical: 3%;
chemical: 9%; civil: 7%; computer
science: 16%; electrical: 24%;
science and physics: 1%;
environmental: 3%; industrial:
11%; mechanical: 7%; petroleum:
17%; other: 6%

University of Tulsa

800 S. Tucker Drive
Tulsa, OK 74104-3189
www.utulsa.edu
Private
Admissions: (918) 631-2336
Email: grad@utulsa.edu
Financial aid: (918) 631-2526
Application deadline: rolling
Tuition: full time: $1,120/credit
hour; part time: $1,120/credit hour
Room/board/expenses: $14,938
Full-time enrollment: 227
men: 79%; women: 21%;
minorities: 3%; international: 73%
Part-time enrollment: 14
men: 79%; women: 21%;
minorities: 14%; international: 0%
Acceptance rate: 24%
GRE requirement: Yes
Avg. GRE: quantitative: 164
TOEFL requirement: Yes
Minimum TOEFL score: 550
Fellowships: 13
Teaching assistantships: 42
Research assistantships: 91
Students specializing in: chemical:
8%; computer: 1%; computer
science: 22%; electrical: 5%;
mechanical: 20%; petroleum: 45%

OREGON

Oregon Health and Science University[1]

3181 SW Sam Jackson Park Road
MC: L102GS
Portland, OR 97239
www.ohsu.edu/som/graduate
Public
Admissions: (503) 494-6222
Email: somgrad@ohsu.edu
Financial aid: N/A
Tuition: N/A
Room/board/expenses: N/A
Enrollment: N/A

Oregon State University

101 Covell Hall
Corvallis, OR 97331-2409
engr.oregonstate.edu/
Public
Admissions: (541) 737-4411
Email: osuadmit@orst.edu
Financial aid: (541) 737-2241
Application deadline: 01/15
In-state tuition: full time: $15,359;
part time: $496/credit hour
Out-of-state tuition: full time:
$23,405
Room/board/expenses: $15,693
Full-time enrollment: 880
men: 80%; women: 20%;
minorities: 7%; international: 56%
Part-time enrollment: 159
men: 78%; women: 22%;
minorities: 10%; international: 31%
Acceptance rate: 28%
GRE requirement: Yes
Avg. GRE: quantitative: 160
TOEFL requirement: Yes
Minimum TOEFL score: 550
Fellowships: 35
Teaching assistantships: 210
Research assistantships: 291
Students specializing in:
agriculture: 1%; chemical: 7%;
civil: 16%; computer science: 16%;
electrical: 18%; environmental:
4%; industrial: 6%; materials: 4%;
mechanical: 15%; nuclear: 4%;
other: 9%

Portland State University (Maseeh)

PO Box 751
Portland, OR 97207
www.pdx.edu/cecs
Public
Admissions: (503) 725-5525
Email: askadm@pdx.edu
Financial aid: (503) 725-3461
Application deadline: rolling
In-state tuition: full time: $11,934;
part time: $289/credit hour
Out-of-state tuition: full time:
$17,172
Room/board/expenses: $15,507
Full-time enrollment: 474
men: 72%; women: 28%;
minorities: 5%; international: 72%
Part-time enrollment: 301
men: 78%; women: 22%;
minorities: 21%; international:
25%
Acceptance rate: 42%
GRE requirement: Yes
Avg. GRE: quantitative: N/A
TOEFL requirement: Yes
Minimum TOEFL score: 550
Fellowships: 0
Teaching assistantships: 71
Research assistantships: 65
Students specializing in: civil: 14%;
computer science: 17%; electrical:
42%; management: 16%;
mechanical: 10%; other: 0%

PENNSYLVANIA

Carnegie Mellon University

5000 Forbes Avenue
Pittsburgh, PA 15213
www.cit.cmu.edu/
Private
Admissions: (412) 268-2478
Financial aid: (412) 268-2482
Application deadline: rolling
Tuition: full time: $41,746; part
time: $1,708/credit hour
Room/board/expenses: $27,150
Full-time enrollment: 3,122
men: 73%; women: 27%;
minorities: 8%; international: 71%
Part-time enrollment: 278
men: 71%; women: 29%;
minorities: 13%; international:
67%
Acceptance rate: 27%
GRE requirement: Yes
Avg. GRE: quantitative: 166
TOEFL requirement: Yes
Minimum TOEFL score: N/A
Fellowships: 432
Teaching assistantships: 78
Research assistantships: 957
Students specializing in:
biomedical: 3%; chemical: 6%;
civil: 9%; computer science: 37%;
electrical: 23%; materials: 4%;
mechanical: 9%; other: 11%

Drexel University

3141 Chestnut Street
Philadelphia, PA 19104
www.drexel.edu/engineering
Private
Admissions: (215) 895-6700
Email: enroll@drexel.edu
Financial aid: (215) 895-1600
Application deadline: rolling
Tuition: full time: $31,161; part
time: $1,123/credit hour
Room/board/expenses: $21,839
Full-time enrollment: 769
men: 71%; women: 29%;
minorities: 55%; international:
49%
Part-time enrollment: 488
men: 76%; women: 24%;
minorities: 25%; international: 3%
Acceptance rate: 31%
GRE requirement: Yes
Avg. GRE: quantitative: 160
TOEFL requirement: Yes
Minimum TOEFL score: 600
Fellowships: 264
Teaching assistantships: 167
Research assistantships: 48
Students specializing in:
architectural: 1%; biomedical:
18%; chemical: 4%; civil: 5%;
computer: 2%; computer science:
7%; electrical: 21%; management:
6%; environmental: 3%; materials:
7%; mechanical: 13%; other: 14%

Lehigh University (Rossin)

19 Memorial Drive W
Bethlehem, PA 18015
www.lehigh.edu/engineering
Private
Admissions: (610) 758-6310
Email: ineas@lehigh.edu
Financial aid: (610) 758-3181
Application deadline: 01/15
Tuition: full time: $1,340/credit
hour; part time: $1,340/credit hour
Room/board/expenses: $12,800
Full-time enrollment: 730
men: 75%; women: 25%;
minorities: 7%; international: 64%
Part-time enrollment: 72
men: 69%; women: 31%;
minorities: 19%; international: 3%
Acceptance rate: 23%
GRE requirement: Yes
Avg. GRE: quantitative: 164
TOEFL requirement: Yes
Minimum TOEFL score: 550
Fellowships: 32

Teaching assistantships: 82
Research assistantships: 203
Students specializing in:
biomedical: 1%; chemical:
9%; civil: 9%; computer:
2%; computer science: 5%;
electrical: 7%; management: 2%;
environmental: 1%; industrial:
29%; materials: 6%; mechanical:
21%; other: 5%

Pennsylvania State University- University Park

101 Hammond Building
University Park, PA 16802
www.gradsch.psu.edu
Public
Admissions: (814) 865-1795
Email: gswww@psu.edu
Financial aid: (814) 865-6301
Application deadline: rolling
In-state tuition: full time: $20,812;
part time: $828/credit hour
Out-of-state tuition: full time:
$34,316
Room/board/expenses: $14,274
Full-time enrollment: 1,453
men: 77%; women: 23%;
minorities: 6%; international: 65%
Part-time enrollment: 199
men: 79%; women: 21%;
minorities: 7%; international: 25%
Acceptance rate: 30%
GRE requirement: Yes
Avg. GRE: quantitative: 163
TOEFL requirement: Yes
Minimum TOEFL score: 550
Fellowships: 43
Teaching assistantships: 297
Research assistantships: 765
Students specializing in:
aerospace: 6%; agriculture: 2%;
architectural: 3%; biomedical: 3%;
chemical: 7%; civil: 6%; computer:
10%; electrical: 14%; science and
physics: 5%; environmental: 2%;
industrial: 12%; materials: 9%;
mechanical: 12%; nuclear: 5%;
other: 4%

Philadelphia University[1]

4201 Henry Avenue
Philadelphia, PA 19144
www.philau.edu
Private
Admissions: (215) 951-2943
Email: gradadm@philau.edu
Financial aid: N/A
Tuition: N/A
Room/board/expenses: N/A
Enrollment: N/A

Temple University

1947 N. 12th Street
Philadelphia, PA 19122
www.temple.edu/engineering/
academic-programs/
graduate-programs/
Public
Admissions: (215) 204-7800
Email: gradengr@temple.edu
Financial aid: (215) 204-2244
Application deadline: 03/01
In-state tuition: full time: $913/
credit hour; part time: $913/
credit hour
Out-of-state tuition: full time:
$1,210/credit hour
Room/board/expenses: $19,250
Full-time enrollment: 217
men: 69%; women: 31%;
minorities: 8%; international: 70%
Part-time enrollment: 62
men: 68%; women: 32%;
minorities: 6%; international: 27%
Acceptance rate: 61%
GRE requirement: Yes
Avg. GRE: quantitative: 158
TOEFL requirement: Yes
Minimum TOEFL score: 550
Fellowships: 4
Teaching assistantships: 58

Research assistantships: 60
Students specializing in:
biomedical: 7%; civil: 4%;
computer science: 41%;
electrical: 11%; management: 2%;
environmental: 5%; mechanical:
4%; other: 26%

University of Pennsylvania

107 Towne Building
Philadelphia, PA 19104
www.seas.upenn.edu/grad
Private
Admissions: (215) 898-4542
Email:
gradstudies@seas.upenn.edu
Financial aid: (215) 898-1988
Application deadline: 11/15
Tuition: full time: $29,890; part
time: $5,598/credit hour
Room/board/expenses: $21,710
Full-time enrollment: 1,354
men: 68%; women: 32%;
minorities: 15%; international:
59%
Part-time enrollment: 242
men: 64%; women: 36%;
minorities: 21%; international:
42%
Acceptance rate: 23%
GRE requirement: Yes
Avg. GRE: quantitative: 166
TOEFL requirement: Yes
Minimum TOEFL score: 600
Fellowships: 134
Teaching assistantships: 0
Research assistantships: 340
Students specializing in:
biomedical: 18%; chemical:
7%; computer science: 26%;
electrical: 12%; industrial: 2%;
materials: 9%; mechanical: 11%;
other: 16%

University of Pittsburgh (Swanson)

109 Benedum Hall
Pittsburgh, PA 15261
www.engineering.pitt.edu
Public
Admissions: (412) 624-9800
Email: ssoeadm@pitt.edu
Financial aid: (412) 624-7488
Application deadline: 03/01
In-state tuition: full time: $24,608;
part time: $1,130/credit hour
Out-of-state tuition: full time:
$39,790
Room/board/expenses: $20,425
Full-time enrollment: 796
men: 74%; women: 26%;
minorities: 9%; international: 66%
Part-time enrollment: 284
men: 84%; women: 16%;
minorities: 8%; international: 12%
Acceptance rate: 30%
GRE requirement: Yes
Avg. GRE: quantitative: 163
TOEFL requirement: Yes
Minimum TOEFL score: 550
Fellowships: 66
Teaching assistantships: 159
Research assistantships: 241
Students specializing in:
biomedical: 16%; chemical:
6%; civil: 14%; computer: 0%;
computer science: 9%; electrical:
15%; industrial: 10%; materials:
6%; mechanical: 19%; nuclear:
1%; petroleum: 3%; other: 1%

Villanova University[1]

800 E. Lancaster Avenue
Villanova, PA 19085
www.villanova.edu
Private
Admissions: N/A
Email: engineering.grad@
villanova.edu
Financial aid: N/A
Tuition: N/A
Room/board/expenses: N/A
Enrollment: N/A

Brown University

Box D
Providence, RI 02912
www.brown.edu/academics/
gradschool
Private
Admissions: (401) 863-2600
Email: Admission_Graduate@
brown.edu
Financial aid: (401) 863-2721
Application deadline: rolling
Tuition: full time: $47,434; part
time: $12,628
Room/board/expenses: $16,190
Full-time enrollment: 355
men: 74%; women: 26%;
minorities: 9%; international: 59%
Part-time enrollment: 16
men: 75%; women: 25%;
minorities: 6%; international: 19%
Acceptance rate: 24%
GRE requirement: Yes
Avg. GRE: quantitative: 164
TOEFL requirement: Yes
Minimum TOEFL score: 577
Fellowships: 67
Teaching assistantships: 40
Research assistantships: 168
Students specializing in: computer
science: 36%; other: 64%

University of Rhode Island

102 Bliss Hall
Kingston, RI 02881
www.uri.edu/gsadmis/
Public
Admissions: (401) 874-2872
Email: gradadm@etal.uri.edu
Financial aid: (401) 874-2314
Application deadline: rolling
In-state tuition: full time: $12,974;
part time: $641/credit hour
Out-of-state tuition: full time:
$25,057
Room/board/expenses: $22,650
Full-time enrollment: 138
men: 77%; women: 23%;
minorities: 4%; international: 18%
Part-time enrollment: 120
men: 83%; women: 17%;
minorities: 13%; international: 17%
Acceptance rate: 55%
GRE requirement: Yes
Avg. GRE: quantitative: N/A
TOEFL requirement: Yes
Minimum TOEFL score: 550
Fellowships: 0
Teaching assistantships: 28
Research assistantships: 36
Students specializing in: chemical:
10%; civil: 12%; computer science:
16%; electrical: 21%; industrial:
9%; mechanical: 20%; other: 13%

Clemson University

Room 109, Riggs Hall
Clemson, SC 29634-0901
www.grad.clemson.edu/
Public
Admissions: (864) 656-4172
Email: grdapp@clemson.edu
Financial aid: (864) 656-2280
Application deadline: rolling
In-state tuition: full time: $10,548;
part time: $638/credit hour
Out-of-state tuition: full time:
$20,776
Room/board/expenses: $15,500
Full-time enrollment: 1,178
men: 77%; women: 23%;
minorities: 4%; international: 69%
Part-time enrollment: 247
men: 79%; women: 21%;
minorities: 11%; international: 26%
Acceptance rate: 34%
GRE requirement: Yes
Avg. GRE: quantitative: 161
TOEFL requirement: Yes
Minimum TOEFL score: N/A
Fellowships: 61
Teaching assistantships: 286

Research assistantships: 421
Students specializing in:
biomedical: 9%; chemical:
2%; civil: 10%; computer: 4%;
computer science: 12%; electrical:
10%; environmental: 5%;
industrial: 16%; materials: 4%;
mechanical: 13%; other: 15%

University of South Carolina

Swearingen Engineering Center
Columbia, SC 29208
www.cec.sc.edu
Public
Admissions: (803) 777-4243
Email: gradapp@mailbox.sc.edu
Financial aid: (803) 777-8134
Application deadline: N/A
In-state tuition: full time: $12,400;
part time: $501/credit hour
Out-of-state tuition: full time:
$26,200
Room/board/expenses: $10,418
Full-time enrollment: 331
men: 77%; women: 23%;
minorities: 49%; international:
59%
Part-time enrollment: 162
men: 83%; women: 17%;
minorities: 36%; international:
46%
Acceptance rate: 40%
GRE requirement: Yes
Avg. GRE: quantitative: 161
TOEFL requirement: Yes
Minimum TOEFL score: 570
Fellowships: 15
Teaching assistantships: 92
Research assistantships: 231
Students specializing in:
aerospace: 3%; biomedical:
4%; chemical: 14%; civil: 15%;
computer: 20%; electrical: 19%;
management: 2%; mechanical:
16%; nuclear: 6%; other: 1%

South Dakota School of Mines and Technology

501 E. St. Joseph Street
Rapid City, SD 57701-3995
www.sdsmt.edu/
Public
Admissions: (605) 394-2341
Email: graduate.admissions@
sdsmt.edu
Financial aid: (605) 394-2400
Application deadline: rolling
In-state tuition: full time: $210/
credit hour; part time: $210/
credit hour
Out-of-state tuition: full time: $470/
credit hour
Room/board/expenses: $11,370
Full-time enrollment: 147
men: 73%; women: 27%;
minorities: 51%; international:
44%
Part-time enrollment: 88
men: 78%; women: 22%;
minorities: 23%; international:
13%
Acceptance rate: 45%
GRE requirement: Yes
Avg. GRE: quantitative: 158
TOEFL requirement: Yes
Minimum TOEFL score: 520
Fellowships: 30
Teaching assistantships: 65
Research assistantships: 129
Students specializing in:
biomedical: 5%; chemical: 9%;
civil: 8%; computer science: 4%;
electrical: 8%; management: 18%;
materials: 12%; mechanical: 11%;
mining: 7%; other: 20%

South Dakota State University

CEH 201, Box 2219
Brookings, SD 57007-0096
www3.sdstate.edu/
Public
Admissions: (605) 688-4181
Email: gradschl@adm.sdstate.edu
Financial aid: (605) 688-4695
Application deadline: 04/15
In-state tuition: full time: $210/
credit hour; part time: $210/
credit hour
Out-of-state tuition: full time: $445/
credit hour
Room/board/expenses: $8,038
Full-time enrollment: 307
men: 77%; women: 23%;
minorities: 4%; international: 64%
Part-time enrollment: N/A
men: N/A; women: N/A; minorities:
N/A; international: N/A
Acceptance rate: 53%
GRE requirement: No
Avg. GRE: quantitative: N/A
TOEFL requirement: Yes
Minimum TOEFL score: 550
Fellowships: 7
Teaching assistantships: 65
Research assistantships: 83
Students specializing in:
agriculture: 7%; civil: 16%;
computer science: 17%;
electrical: 17%; management: 8%;
mechanical: 13%; other: 24%

University of South Dakota

414 E Clark Street
Vermillion, SD 57069
www.usd.edu/
Public
Admissions: N/A
Email: grad@usd.edu
Financial aid: N/A
Application deadline: 08/08
In-state tuition: full time: $210/
credit hour; part time: $210/
credit hour
Out-of-state tuition: full time: $445/
credit hour
Room/board/expenses: $9,000
Full-time enrollment: 835
men: 39%; women: 61%;
minorities: N/A; international: 11%
Part-time enrollment: 1,256
men: 43%; women: 57%;
minorities: N/A; international: 2%
Acceptance rate: 16%
Avg. GRE: quantitative: N/A
TOEFL requirement: Yes
Minimum TOEFL score: 550
Students specializing in: N/A

Tennessee State University[1]

3500 John Merritt Boulevard
Nashville, TN 37209-1651
www.tnstate.edu/
Public
Admissions: (615) 963-5107
Email: gradschool@tnstate.edu
Financial aid: N/A
Tuition: N/A
Room/board/expenses: N/A
Enrollment: N/A

Tennessee Technological University[1]

N. Dixie Avenue
Cookeville, TN 38505
www.tntech.edu/engineering
Public
Admissions: (931) 372-3233
Email: g_admissions@tntech.edu
Financial aid: (931) 372-3073
Application deadline: 07/01
In-state tuition: full time: $10,145;
part time: $492/credit hour

Out-of-state tuition: full time:
$22,945
Room/board/expenses: $15,950
Full-time enrollment: 112
men: 82%; women: 18%;
minorities: 2%; international: 63%
Part-time enrollment: 63
men: 76%; women: 24%;
minorities: 8%; international: 51%
Acceptance rate: 40%
GRE requirement: No
Avg. GRE: quantitative: 155
TOEFL requirement: Yes
Minimum TOEFL score: 550
Fellowships: 3
Teaching assistantships: 44
Research assistantships: 68
Students specializing in: chemical:
19%; civil: 16%; computer
science: 13%; electrical: 23%;
mechanical: 29%

University of Memphis (Herff)

201 Engineering Administration
Building
Memphis, TN 38152
www.memphis.edu/herff/
index.php
Public
Admissions: (901) 678-2111
Email: recruitment@memphis.edu
Financial aid: (901) 678-4825
Application deadline: rolling
In-state tuition: full time: $9,867;
part time: $461/credit hour
Out-of-state tuition: full time:
$18,651/credit hour
Room/board/expenses: $15,571
Full-time enrollment: 107
men: 73%; women: 27%;
minorities: 16%; international:
57%
Part-time enrollment: 52
men: 75%; women: 25%;
minorities: 17%; international: 31%
Acceptance rate: 57%
GRE requirement: Yes
Avg. GRE: quantitative: 157
TOEFL requirement: Yes
Minimum TOEFL score: 550
Fellowships: 31
Teaching assistantships: 2
Research assistantships: 77
Students specializing in:
biomedical: 22%; civil: 13%;
computer: 20%; electrical: 20%;
science and physics: 37%;
mechanical: 8%

University of Tennessee-Chattanooga

615 McCallie Avenue
Chattanooga, TN 37403
www.utc.edu/college-
engineering-computer-science/
Public
Admissions: N/A
Financial aid: N/A
Application deadline: rolling
In-state tuition: full time: $9,416;
part time: $428/credit hour
Out-of-state tuition: full time:
$25,534
Room/board/expenses: $16,680
Full-time enrollment: 97
men: 75%; women: 25%;
minorities: 68%; international:
71%
Part-time enrollment: 111
men: 80%; women: 20%;
minorities: 30%; international:
14%
Acceptance rate: 29%
GRE requirement: Yes
Avg. GRE: quantitative: N/A
TOEFL requirement: Yes
Minimum TOEFL score: 550
Research assistantships: 70
Students specializing in: chemical:
4%; civil: 3%; computer
science: 20%; electrical: 12%;
management: 37%; industrial: 1%;
mechanical: 6%; other: 17%

University of Tennessee-Knoxville

124 Perkins Hall
Knoxville, TN 37996-2000
graduateadmissions.utk.edu/
Public
Admissions: (865) 974-3251
Email: graduateadmissions@utk.edu
Financial aid: (865) 974-3131
Application deadline: 02/01
In-state tuition: full time: $11,602; part time: $563/credit hour
Out-of-state tuition: full time: $30,050
Room/board/expenses: $20,744
Full-time enrollment: 748
men: 78%; women: 22%; minorities: 5%; international: 45%
Part-time enrollment: 248
men: 88%; women: 13%; minorities: 7%; international: 10%
Acceptance rate: 32%
GRE requirement: Yes
Avg. GRE: quantitative: 161
TOEFL requirement: Yes
Minimum TOEFL score: 550
Fellowships: 72
Teaching assistantships: 221
Research assistantships: 522
Students specializing in: aerospace: 3%; agriculture: 2%; biomedical: 3%; chemical: 6%; civil: 13%; computer: 4%; computer science: 6%; electrical: 13%; management: 0%; science and physics: 1%; environmental: 1%; industrial: 13%; materials: 9%; mechanical: 10%; nuclear: 13%; other: 5%

Vanderbilt University

VU Station B 351826
2301 Vanderbilt Place
Nashville, TN 37235
engineering.vanderbilt.edu
Private
Admissions: (615) 322-0236
Email: apply@vanderbilt.edu
Financial aid: (615) 322-3591
Application deadline: 01/15
Tuition: full time: $1,782/credit hour; part time: $1,782/credit hour
Room/board/expenses: $23,678
Full-time enrollment: 469
men: 70%; women: 30%; minorities: 9%; international: 41%
Part-time enrollment: 23
men: 70%; women: 30%; minorities: 13%; international: 9%
Acceptance rate: 16%
GRE requirement: Yes
Avg. GRE: quantitative: 164
TOEFL requirement: Yes
Minimum TOEFL score: N/A
Fellowships: 35
Teaching assistantships: 113
Research assistantships: 220
Students specializing in: biomedical: 15%; chemical: 11%; civil: 10%; computer science: 17%; electrical: 19%; environmental: 8%; materials: 7%; mechanical: 12%

TEXAS

Baylor University

One Bear Place, #97356
Waco, TX 76798
www.ecs.baylor.edu/
Private
Admissions: (254) 710-4060
Email: Graduate_Admissions@baylor.edu
Financial aid: N/A
Application deadline: 12/31
Tuition: full time: $28,702; part time: $1,437/credit hour
Room/board/expenses: $9,337
Full-time enrollment: 68
men: 82%; women: 18%; minorities: 13%; international: 40%
Part-time enrollment: N/A
men: N/A; women: N/A; minorities: N/A; international: N/A
Acceptance rate: 29%
GRE requirement: Yes
Avg. GRE: quantitative: 162
TOEFL requirement: Yes
Minimum TOEFL score: 540
Teaching assistantships: 21
Research assistantships: 30
Students specializing in: biomedical: 4%; computer science: 26%; electrical: 41%; mechanical: 26%; other: 1%

Lamar University

4400 Martin Luther King Boulevard
Beaumont, TX 77710
dept.lamar.edu/engineering/coe/
Public
Admissions: (409) 880-8888
Email: admissions@hal.lamar.edu
Financial aid: (409) 880-8450
Application deadline: 04/15
In-state tuition: full time: $7,664; part time: $308/credit hour
Out-of-state tuition: full time: $14,180
Room/board/expenses: $13,410
Full-time enrollment: 622
men: 83%; women: 17%; minorities: 3%; international: 95%
Part-time enrollment: 121
men: 81%; women: 19%; minorities: 7%; international: 86%
Acceptance rate: 92%
GRE requirement: Yes
Avg. GRE: quantitative: 155
TOEFL requirement: Yes
Minimum TOEFL score: 550
Fellowships: 42
Teaching assistantships: 9
Research assistantships: 12
Students specializing in: chemical: 17%; civil: 12%; computer science: 13%; electrical: 26%; industrial: 14%; mechanical: 18%

Prairie View A&M University

PO Box 519
MS 2500
Prairie View, TX 77446
www.pvamu.edu
Public
Admissions: (936) 261-2131
Email: graduateadmissions@pvamu.edu
Financial aid: (936) 261-1000
Application deadline: 07/01
In-state tuition: full time: $249/credit hour; part time: $249/credit hour
Out-of-state tuition: full time: $609/credit hour
Room/board/expenses: $13,035
Full-time enrollment: 113
men: 59%; women: 41%; minorities: 39%; international: 46%
Part-time enrollment: 55
men: 58%; women: 42%; minorities: 51%; international: 38%
Acceptance rate: 80%
GRE requirement: Yes
Avg. GRE: quantitative: 151
TOEFL requirement: Yes
Minimum TOEFL score: 500
Students specializing in: computer science: 38%; electrical: 24%; mechanical: 38%

Rice University (Brown)

PO Box 1892, MS 364
Houston, TX 77251-1892
engr.rice.edu
Private
Admissions: (713) 348-4002
Email: graduate@rice.edu
Financial aid: (713) 348-4958
Application deadline: N/A
Tuition: full time: $40,414; part time: $2,216/credit hour
Room/board/expenses: $16,000
Full-time enrollment: 818
men: 71%; women: 29%; minorities: 15%; international: 60%
Part-time enrollment: 50
men: 70%; women: 30%; minorities: 14%; international: 76%
Acceptance rate: 21%
GRE requirement: Yes
Avg. GRE: quantitative: 165
TOEFL requirement: Yes
Minimum TOEFL score: 600
Fellowships: 295
Teaching assistantships: 38
Research assistantships: 305
Students specializing in: biomedical: 18%; chemical: 12%; civil: 3%; computer science: 15%; electrical: 23%; environmental: 4%; materials: 6%; mechanical: 7%; other: 13%

Southern Methodist University (Lyle)

3145 Dyer Street
Dallas, TX 75275-0335
www.engr.smu.edu
Private
Admissions: (214) 768-3484
Email: valerin@engr.smu.edu
Financial aid: (214) 768-3484
Application deadline: 07/01
Tuition: full time: $1,165/credit hour; part time: $1,165/credit hour
Room/board/expenses: $25,890
Full-time enrollment: 455
men: 74%; women: 26%; minorities: 7%; international: 79%
Part-time enrollment: 608
men: 76%; women: 24%; minorities: 31%; international: 17%
Acceptance rate: 70%
GRE requirement: Yes
Avg. GRE: quantitative: 160
TOEFL requirement: Yes
Minimum TOEFL score: 550
Fellowships: 0
Teaching assistantships: 63
Research assistantships: 68
Students specializing in: civil: 3%; computer: 2%; computer science: 16%; electrical: 29%; management: 18%; environmental: 4%; industrial: 5%; mechanical: 5%; other: 19%

Texas A&M University-College Station (Look)

Jack K. Williams Administration Building, Suite 312
College Station, TX 77843-3126
engineering.tamu.edu/graduate
Public
Admissions: (979) 845-7200
Email: gradengineer@tamu.edu
Financial aid: (979) 845-3236
Application deadline: rolling
In-state tuition: full time: $227/credit hour; part time: $227/credit hour
Out-of-state tuition: full time: $581/credit hour
Room/board/expenses: $14,664
Full-time enrollment: 2,768
men: 78%; women: 22%; minorities: 9%; international: 72%
Part-time enrollment: 611
men: 79%; women: 21%; minorities: 21%; international: 38%
Acceptance rate: 24%
GRE requirement: Yes
Avg. GRE: quantitative: 163
TOEFL requirement: Yes
Minimum TOEFL score: 550
Fellowships: 444
Teaching assistantships: 384
Research assistantships: 1,185
Students specializing in: aerospace: 3%; agriculture: 2%; biomedical: 3%; chemical: 5%; civil: 14%; computer science: 9%; electrical: 21%; industrial: 8%; materials: 3%; mechanical: 13%; nuclear: 4%; petroleum: 13%; other: 0%

Texas A&M University-Kingsville (Dotterweich)

MSC 188
Kingsville, TX 78363
www.engineer.tamuk.edu
Public
Admissions: (361) 593-2315
Financial aid: (361) 593-3911
Application deadline: 08/11
In-state tuition: full time: $7,554; part time: $694/credit hour
Out-of-state tuition: full time: $15,226
Room/board/expenses: $14,206
Full-time enrollment: 1,253
men: 81%; women: 19%; minorities: 3%; international: 96%
Part-time enrollment: 285
men: 76%; women: 24%; minorities: 12%; international: 83%
Acceptance rate: 78%
GRE requirement: Yes
Avg. GRE: quantitative: 152
TOEFL requirement: Yes
Minimum TOEFL score: 550
Fellowships: 1
Teaching assistantships: 8
Research assistantships: 39
Students specializing in: chemical: 3%; civil: 5%; computer science: 38%; electrical: 28%; environmental: 4%; industrial: 6%; mechanical: 11%; petroleum: 3%; other: 2%

Texas Tech University (Whitacre)

Box 43103
Lubbock, TX 79409-3103
www.depts.ttu.edu/coe/
Public
Admissions: (806) 742-2787
Email: gradschool@ttu.edu
Financial aid: (806) 742-3681
Application deadline: rolling
In-state tuition: full time: $263/credit hour; part time: $263/credit hour
Out-of-state tuition: full time: $625/credit hour
Room/board/expenses: $14,705
Full-time enrollment: 697
men: 76%; women: 24%; minorities: 8%; international: 75%
Part-time enrollment: 175
men: 84%; women: 16%; minorities: 18%; international: 29%
Acceptance rate: 33%
GRE requirement: Yes
Avg. GRE: quantitative: 160
TOEFL requirement: Yes
Minimum TOEFL score: 550
Fellowships: 0
Teaching assistantships: 100
Research assistantships: 158
Students specializing in: biomedical: 1%; chemical: 9%; civil: 8%; computer science: 13%; electrical: 26%; environmental: 2%; industrial: 8%; mechanical: 15%; petroleum: 7%; other: 11%

University of Houston (Cullen)

E421 Engineering Building 2
Houston, TX 77204-4007
www.egr.uh.edu
Public
Admissions: (713) 743-4200
Email: grad-admit@egr.uh.edu
Financial aid: (713) 743-9090
Application deadline: 02/01
In-state tuition: full time: $459/credit hour; part time: $459/credit hour
Out-of-state tuition: full time: $921/credit hour
Room/board/expenses: $15,288
Full-time enrollment: 1,158
men: 73%; women: 27%; minorities: 6%; international: 87%
Part-time enrollment: 279
men: 77%; women: 23%; minorities: 34%; international: 35%
Acceptance rate: 44%
GRE requirement: Yes
Avg. GRE: quantitative: 161
TOEFL requirement: Yes
Minimum TOEFL score: 550
Fellowships: 558
Teaching assistantships: 74
Research assistantships: 362
Students specializing in: aerospace: 0%; biomedical: 4%; chemical: 10%; civil: 10%; computer: 3%; computer science: 16%; electrical: 17%; environmental: 2%; industrial: 11%; materials: 3%; mechanical: 11%; petroleum: 8%; other: 5%

University of North Texas

1155 Union Circle, #310440
Denton, TX 76203-5017
tsgs.unt.edu/overview
Public
Admissions: (940) 565-2383
Email: gradsch@unt.edu
Financial aid: (940) 565-2302
Application deadline: 07/15
In-state tuition: full time: $228/credit hour; part time: $228/credit hour
Out-of-state tuition: full time: $590/credit hour
Room/board/expenses: $13,160
Full-time enrollment: 380
men: 74%; women: 26%; minorities: 8%; international: 83%
Part-time enrollment: 152
men: 80%; women: 20%; minorities: 24%; international: 49%
Acceptance rate: 42%
GRE requirement: Yes
Avg. GRE: quantitative: 158
TOEFL requirement: Yes
Minimum TOEFL score: 550
Fellowships: 9
Teaching assistantships: 45
Research assistantships: 82
Students specializing in: computer: 24%; computer science: 40%; electrical: 14%; materials: 17%; mechanical: 6%; other: 15%

University of Texas-Arlington

UTA Box 19019
Arlington, TX 76019
www.uta.edu/engineering/
Public
Admissions: (817) 272-2380
Email: graduate.school@uta.edu
Financial aid: (817) 272-3561
Application deadline: 06/01
In-state tuition: full time: $8,558; part time: $5,810
Out-of-state tuition: full time: $15,808
Room/board/expenses: $14,374
Full-time enrollment: 2,022
men: 76%; women: 24%; minorities: 4%; international: 92%
Part-time enrollment: 624
men: 78%; women: 22%; minorities: 18%; international: 55%
Acceptance rate: 55%
GRE requirement: Yes
Avg. GRE: quantitative: 159
TOEFL requirement: Yes
Minimum TOEFL score: 550
Fellowships: 327
Teaching assistantships: 332
Research assistantships: 125

More @ www.usnews.com/grad

Students specializing in: aerospace: 5%; biomedical: 6%; civil: 12%; computer: 1%; computer science: 24%; electrical: 20%; management: 3%; industrial: 11%; materials: 2%; mechanical: 15%

University of Texas-Austin (Cockrell)

301 E. Dean Keeton Street
Stop C2100
Austin, TX 78712-2100
www.engr.utexas.edu/
Public
Admissions: (512) 475-7391
Email: adgrd@utxdp.its.utexas.edu
Financial aid: (512) 475-6282
Application deadline: rolling
In-state tuition: full time: $9,564; part time: N/A
Out-of-state tuition: full time: $17,506
Room/board/expenses: $18,810
Full-time enrollment: 2,010
men: 80%; women: 20%; minorities: 12%; international: 58%
Part-time enrollment: 364
men: 83%; women: 17%; minorities: 29%; international: 26%
Acceptance rate: 17%
GRE requirement: Yes
Avg. GRE: quantitative: 164
TOEFL requirement: Yes
Minimum TOEFL score: 550
Fellowships: 714
Teaching assistantships: 481
Research assistantships: 974
Students specializing in: aerospace: 6%; architectural: 1%; biomedical: 3%; chemical: 8%; civil: 13%; computer: 15%; computer science: 11%; electrical: 14%; management: 3%; environmental: 2%; industrial: 3%; materials: 3%; mechanical: 11%; petroleum: 9%

University of Texas-Dallas (Jonsson)

800 W. Campbell Road
Mail Station EC32
Richardson, TX 75080-3021
www.utdallas.edu
Public
Admissions: (972) 883-2270
Email: interest@utdallas.edu
Financial aid: (972) 883-2941
Application deadline: 07/01
In-state tuition: full time: $11,940; part time: N/A
Out-of-state tuition: full time: $22,282
Room/board/expenses: $14,464
Full-time enrollment: 1,997
men: 74%; women: 26%; minorities: 4%; international: 90%
Part-time enrollment: 553
men: 71%; women: 29%; minorities: 14%; international: 69%
Acceptance rate: 39%
GRE requirement: Yes
Avg. GRE: quantitative: 160
TOEFL requirement: Yes
Minimum TOEFL score: 550
Fellowships: 46
Teaching assistantships: 189
Research assistantships: 275
Students specializing in: biomedical: 3%; computer: 5%; computer science: 45%; electrical: 33%; management: 2%; materials: 2%; mechanical: 6%; other: 5%

University of Texas-El Paso[1]

500 W. University Avenue
El Paso, TX 79968
www.utep.edu/graduate
Public
Admissions: (915) 747-5491
Email: gradschool@utep.edu
Financial aid: (915) 747-5204
Tuition: N/A
Room/board/expenses: N/A
Enrollment: N/A

University of Texas Health Science Center-San Antonio[1]

7703 Floyd Curl Drive
San Antonio, TX 78229
gsbs.uthscsa.edu/
Public
Admissions: N/A
Email: gsbsinquiry@uthscsa.edu
Financial aid: N/A
Tuition: N/A
Room/board/expenses: N/A
Enrollment: N/A

University of Texas-San Antonio

1 UTSA Circle
San Antonio, TX 78249-0665
www.graduateschool.utsa.edu
Public
Admissions: (210) 458-4330
Email: gradstudies@utsa.edu
Financial aid: (210) 458-8000
Application deadline: N/A
In-state tuition: full time: $260/credit hour; part time: $260/credit hour
Out-of-state tuition: full time: $1,001/credit hour
Room/board/expenses: $14,919
Full-time enrollment: 478
men: 72%; women: 28%; minorities: 15%; international: 72%
Part-time enrollment: 229
men: 79%; women: 21%; minorities: 35%; international: 27%
Acceptance rate: 72%
GRE requirement: Yes
Avg. GRE: quantitative: 157
TOEFL requirement: Yes
Minimum TOEFL score: 550
Fellowships: 72
Teaching assistantships: 94
Research assistantships: 123
Students specializing in: biomedical: 11%; civil: 5%; computer: 6%; computer science: 20%; electrical: 37%; environmental: 3%; industrial: 4%; materials: 2%; mechanical: 12%

University of Texas Southwestern Medical Center-Dallas[1]

5323 Harry Hines Boulevard
Dallas, TX 75390
www.utsouthwestern.edu/education/index.html
Public
Admissions: (214) 648-5617
Email: admissions@utsouthwestern.edu
Financial aid: N/A
Tuition: N/A
Room/board/expenses: N/A
Enrollment: N/A

UTAH

Brigham Young University (Fulton)

270 CB
Provo, UT 84602
www.byu.edu/gradstudies
Private
Admissions: (801) 422-4091
Email: gradstudies@byu.edu
Financial aid: (801) 422-4104
Application deadline: 01/15
Tuition: full time: $6,310; part time: $350/credit hour
Room/board/expenses: $19,616
Full-time enrollment: 371
men: 89%; women: 11%; minorities: 6%; international: 18%
Part-time enrollment: N/A
men: N/A; women: N/A; minorities: N/A; international: N/A
Acceptance rate: 68%
GRE requirement: Yes
Avg. GRE: quantitative: 161
TOEFL requirement: Yes
Minimum TOEFL score: 580
Fellowships: 31
Teaching assistantships: 197
Research assistantships: 591
Students specializing in: chemical: 13%; civil: 20%; computer science: 19%; electrical: 19%; mechanical: 30%

University of Utah

72 S. Central Campus Drive
1650 WEB
Salt Lake City, UT 84112-9200
www.utah.edu
Public
Admissions: (801) 581-7281
Email: admissions@sa.utah.edu
Financial aid: (801) 581-6211
Application deadline: 04/01
In-state tuition: full time: $7,070; part time: $5,250
Out-of-state tuition: full time: $19,269
Room/board/expenses: $17,066
Full-time enrollment: 918
men: 81%; women: 19%; minorities: 6%; international: 52%
Part-time enrollment: 291
men: 86%; women: 14%; minorities: 9%; international: 26%
Acceptance rate: 35%
GRE requirement: Yes
Avg. GRE: quantitative: 162
TOEFL requirement: Yes
Minimum TOEFL score: 550
Fellowships: 63
Teaching assistantships: 152
Research assistantships: 454
Students specializing in: biomedical: 13%; chemical: 10%; civil: 11%; computer science: 35%; electrical: 21%; materials: 4%; mechanical: 18%; mining: 2%; nuclear: 2%; other: 6%

Utah State University

4100 Old Main Hill
Logan, UT 84322-4100
www.engineering.usu.edu/
Public
Admissions: (435) 797-1189
Email: grad.admissions@aggiemail.usu.edu
Financial aid: (435) 797-0173
Application deadline: rolling
In-state tuition: full time: $6,380; part time: $5,568
Out-of-state tuition: full time: $18,488
Room/board/expenses: $11,490
Full-time enrollment: 300
men: 84%; women: 16%; minorities: 9%; international: 48%
Part-time enrollment: 95
men: 81%; women: 19%; minorities: 11%; international: 36%
GRE requirement: Yes
Avg. GRE: quantitative: 162
TOEFL requirement: Yes
Minimum TOEFL score: 550
Fellowships: 19

Teaching assistantships: 43
Research assistantships: 188
Students specializing in: aerospace: 4%; agriculture: 10%; civil: 25%; computer: 3%; computer science: 19%; electrical: 21%; mechanical: 16%; other: 3%

VERMONT

University of Vermont[1]

109 Votey Hall
Burlington, VT 05405
www.cems.uvm.edu
Public
Admissions: (802) 656-2699
Email: graduate.admissions@uvm.edu
Financial aid: N/A
Tuition: N/A
Room/board/expenses: N/A
Enrollment: N/A

VIRGINIA

George Mason University (Volgenau)

4400 University Drive, MS4A3
Fairfax, VA 22030-4444
volgenau.gmu.edu/
Public
Admissions: (703) 993-1512
Email: vsegadm@gmu.edu
Financial aid: (703) 993-2353
Application deadline: 01/15
In-state tuition: full time: $15,014; part time: $617/credit hour
Out-of-state tuition: full time: $29,798
Room/board/expenses: $23,344
Full-time enrollment: 684
men: 71%; women: 29%; minorities: 12%; international: 70%
Part-time enrollment: 843
men: 79%; women: 21%; minorities: 31%; international: 10%
Acceptance rate: 54%
GRE requirement: Yes
Avg. GRE: quantitative: 158
TOEFL requirement: Yes
Minimum TOEFL score: 570
Fellowships: 0
Teaching assistantships: 150
Research assistantships: 87
Students specializing in: civil: 5%; computer: 5%; computer science: 31%; electrical: 29%; industrial: 9%; other: 20%

Old Dominion University[1]

102 Kaufman Hall
Norfolk, VA 23529
www.admissions.odu.edu
Public
Admissions: (757) 683-3685
Email: gradadmit@odu.edu
Financial aid: N/A
Tuition: N/A
Room/board/expenses: N/A
Enrollment: N/A

University of Virginia

Thornton Hall
Charlottesville, VA 22904-4246
www.seas.virginia.edu/
Public
Admissions: (434) 924-3897
Email: seas-grad-admission@virginia.edu
Financial aid: (434) 924-3897
Application deadline: 01/15
In-state tuition: full time: $18,000; part time: $769/credit hour
Out-of-state tuition: full time: $27,324
Room/board/expenses: $20,635
Full-time enrollment: 586
men: 74%; women: 26%; minorities: 13%; international: 45%

Part-time enrollment: 60
men: 77%; women: 23%; minorities: 23%; international: 2%
Acceptance rate: 18%
GRE requirement: Yes
Avg. GRE: quantitative: 163
TOEFL requirement: Yes
Minimum TOEFL score: 600
Fellowships: 350
Teaching assistantships: 106
Research assistantships: 440
Students specializing in: biomedical: 10%; chemical: 7%; civil: 8%; computer: 5%; computer science: 9%; electrical: 15%; science and physics: 2%; materials: 11%; mechanical: 15%; other: 17%

Virginia Commonwealth University

PO Box 843068
Richmond, VA 23284-3068
www.egr.vcu.edu/
Public
Admissions: (804) 828-1087
Email: josephl@vcu.edu
Financial aid: (804) 828-3925
Application deadline: 06/01
In-state tuition: full time: $12,956; part time: $470/credit hour
Out-of-state tuition: full time: $24,129
Room/board/expenses: $23,316
Full-time enrollment: 197
men: 76%; women: 24%; minorities: 13%; international: 61%
Part-time enrollment: 68
men: 75%; women: 25%; minorities: 22%; international: 22%
Acceptance rate: 52%
GRE requirement: Yes
Avg. GRE: quantitative: 157
TOEFL requirement: Yes
Minimum TOEFL score: 550
Fellowships: 6
Teaching assistantships: 59
Research assistantships: 66
Students specializing in: biomedical: 22%; chemical: 11%; computer: 20%; computer science: 20%; electrical: 20%; mechanical: 28%; nuclear: 28%

Virginia Tech

3046 Torgersen Hall
Blacksburg, VA 24061-0217
www.grads.vt.edu
Public
Admissions: (540) 231-8636
Email: gradappl@vt.edu
Financial aid: (540) 231-5179
Application deadline: 01/01
In-state tuition: full time: $16,915; part time: $647/credit hour
Out-of-state tuition: full time: $29,124
Room/board/expenses: $15,500
Full-time enrollment: 1,697
men: 77%; women: 23%; minorities: 9%; international: 59%
Part-time enrollment: 348
men: 84%; women: 16%; minorities: 18%; international: 24%
Acceptance rate: 23%
GRE requirement: Yes
Avg. GRE: quantitative: 163
TOEFL requirement: Yes
Minimum TOEFL score: 565
Fellowships: 118
Teaching assistantships: 373
Research assistantships: 922
Students specializing in: aerospace: 7%; agriculture: 2%; biomedical: 7%; chemical: 2%; civil: 16%; computer science: 12%; electrical: 26%; industrial: 7%; materials: 3%; mechanical: 15%; mining: 2%; other: 2%

WASHINGTON

University of Washington

371 Loew Hall
Box 352180
Seattle, WA 98195-2180
www.engr.washington.edu
Public
Admissions: (206) 685-2630
Email: uwgrad@uw.edu
Financial aid: (206) 543-6101
Application deadline: N/A
In-state tuition: full time: $17,040;
part time: $760/credit hour
Out-of-state tuition: full time:
$29,514
Room/board/expenses: $18,843
Full-time enrollment: 1,441
men: 70%; women: 30%;
minorities: 14%; international:
43%
Part-time enrollment: 747
men: 74%; women: 26%;
minorities: 30%; international:
13%
Acceptance rate: 20%
GRE requirement: Yes
Avg. GRE: quantitative: 164
TOEFL requirement: Yes
Minimum TOEFL score: 580
Fellowships: 200
Teaching assistantships: 245
Research assistantships: 649
Students specializing in:
aerospace: 10%; biomedical:
7%; chemical: 4%; civil: 17%;
computer: 17%; electrical: 16%;
industrial: 4%; materials: 4%;
mechanical: 11%; other: 8%

Washington State University

PO Box 642714
Pullman, WA 99164-2714
www.vcea.wsu.edu
Public
Admissions: (509) 335-1446
Email: gradsch@wsu.edu
Financial aid: (509) 335-9711
Application deadline: 01/10
In-state tuition: full time: $12,728;
part time: $587/credit hour
Out-of-state tuition: full time:
$26,160
Room/board/expenses: $15,952

Full-time enrollment: 460
men: 71%; women: 29%;
minorities: 8%; international: 68%
Part-time enrollment: 190
men: 78%; women: 22%;
minorities: 17%; international: 19%
Acceptance rate: 24%
GRE requirement: Yes
Avg. GRE: quantitative: 161
TOEFL requirement: Yes
Minimum TOEFL score: 550
Fellowships: 33
Teaching assistantships: 113
Research assistantships: 176
Students specializing in:
agriculture: 11%; chemical:
12%; civil: 10%; computer: 1%;
computer science: 9%; electrical:
16%; management: 12%; science
and physics: 0%; environmental:
3%; materials: 10%; mechanical:
15%

WEST VIRGINIA

West Virginia University

PO Box 6070
Morgantown, WV 26506-6070
www.statler.wvu.edu
Public
Admissions: (304) 293-2121
Email: graduateadmissions@
mail.wvu.edu
Financial aid: (304) 293-5242
Application deadline: 08/01
In-state tuition: full time: $8,112;
part time: $338/credit hour
Out-of-state tuition: full time:
$22,128
Room/board/expenses: $12,194
Full-time enrollment: 520
men: 77%; women: 23%;
minorities: 5%; international: 59%
Part-time enrollment: 169
men: 79%; women: 21%;
minorities: 14%; international: 31%
Acceptance rate: 38%
GRE requirement: Yes
Avg. GRE: quantitative: 160
TOEFL requirement: Yes
Minimum TOEFL score: 550
Fellowships: 9
Teaching assistantships: 92
Research assistantships: 253

Students specializing in:
aerospace: 4%; chemical:
6%; civil: 8%; computer: 2%;
computer science: 11%; electrical:
17%; industrial: 6%; mechanical:
18%; mining: 4%; petroleum: 7%;
other: 18%

WISCONSIN

Marquette University

PO Box 1881
Milwaukee, WI 53201-1881
www.grad.marquette.edu
Private
Admissions: (414) 288-7137
Email: mugs@mu.edu
Financial aid: (414) 288-5325
Application deadline: rolling
Tuition: full time: $1,025/credit
hour; part time: $1,025/credit hour
Room/board/expenses: $16,306
Full-time enrollment: 118
men: 75%; women: 25%;
minorities: 9%; international: 38%
Part-time enrollment: 77
men: 74%; women: 26%;
minorities: 17%; international: 16%
Acceptance rate: 54%
GRE requirement: Yes
Avg. GRE: quantitative: 160
TOEFL requirement: Yes
Minimum TOEFL score: 590
Fellowships: 12
Teaching assistantships: 34
Research assistantships: 54
Students specializing in:
biomedical: 22%; civil: 17%;
electrical: 30%; mechanical: 25%;
other: 6%

University of Wisconsin-Madison

2610 Engineering Hall
Madison, WI 53706
www.engr.wisc.edu/
Public
Admissions: (608) 262-2433
Email: gradadmiss@
bascom.wisc.edu
Financial aid: (608) 262-3060
Application deadline: N/A
In-state tuition: full time: $13,001;
part time: $786/credit hour
Out-of-state tuition: full time:
$26,327

Room/board/expenses: $17,426
Full-time enrollment: 1,586
men: 81%; women: 19%;
minorities: 5%; international: 56%
Part-time enrollment: 451
men: 85%; women: 15%;
minorities: 6%; international: 29%
Acceptance rate: 11%
GRE requirement: Yes
Avg. GRE: quantitative: 164
TOEFL requirement: Yes
Minimum TOEFL score: 580
Fellowships: 61
Teaching assistantships: 251
Research assistantships: 899
Students specializing in:
agriculture: 2%; biomedical: 5%;
chemical: 5%; civil: 6%; computer
science: 15%; electrical: 22%;
environmental: 1%; industrial: 9%;
materials: 6%; mechanical: 19%;
nuclear: 8%; other: 1%

University of Wisconsin-Milwaukee

PO Box 784
Milwaukee, WI 53201-0784
www.uwm.edu/CEAS
Public
Admissions: (414) 229-6169
Email: bwarras@uwm.edu
Financial aid: (414) 229-4541
Application deadline: 04/01
In-state tuition: full time: $11,596;
part time: $1,023/credit hour
Out-of-state tuition: full time:
$24,061
Room/board/expenses: $10,136
Full-time enrollment: 341
men: 75%; women: 25%;
minorities: 7%; international: 71%
Part-time enrollment: 70
men: 84%; women: 16%;
minorities: 20%; international: 0%
Acceptance rate: 57%
GRE requirement: Yes
Avg. GRE: quantitative: 157
TOEFL requirement: Yes
Minimum TOEFL score: 550
Fellowships: 42
Teaching assistantships: 128
Research assistantships: 58
Students specializing in:
biomedical: 8%; civil: 14%;
computer science: 20%;
electrical: 21%; industrial: 11%;
materials: 8%; mechanical: 18%

WYOMING

University of Wyoming

Department 3295
1000 E. University Avenue
Laramie, WY 82071
www.uwyo.edu/ceas/
Public
Admissions: (307) 766-5160
Email: why-wyo@uwyo.edu
Financial aid: (307) 766-2116
Application deadline: rolling
In-state tuition: full time: $221/
credit hour; part time: $221/
credit hour
Out-of-state tuition: full time: $660/
credit hour
Room/board/expenses: $16,599
Full-time enrollment: 150
men: 76%; women: 24%;
minorities: 4%; international: 57%
Part-time enrollment: 77
men: 73%; women: 27%;
minorities: 1%; international: 58%
Acceptance rate: 31%
GRE requirement: Yes
Avg. GRE: quantitative: 160
TOEFL requirement: Yes
Minimum TOEFL score: 550
Fellowships: 6
Teaching assistantships: 57
Research assistantships: 200
Students specializing in: chemical:
12%; civil: 15%; computer
science: 13%; electrical: 11%;
environmental: 4%; mechanical:
19%; petroleum: 19%; other: 9%

LAW

The law directory lists the 201 schools in the country offering the J.D. degree that were fully or provisionally accredited by the American Bar Association in August 2014. One hundred ninety schools responded to the U.S. News survey conducted in the fall of 2014 and early 2015, and their data are reported here. Nonresponders have abbreviated entries.

KEY TO THE TERMINOLOGY

1. A school whose name is footnoted with the numeral 1 did not return the U.S. News statistical survey; limited data appear in its entry.

N/A. Not available from the school or not applicable.

Admissions. The admissions office phone number.

Email. The address of the admissions office. If instead of an email address a website is listed, the website will automatically present an email screen programmed to reach the admissions office.

Financial aid. The financial aid office phone number.

Application deadline. For fall 2016 enrollment. "Rolling" means there is no deadline; the school acts on applications as they are received. "Varies" means deadlines vary according to department or whether applicants are U.S. citizens or foreign nationals.

Tuition. For the 2014-15 academic year. Includes fees.

Credit hour. The cost per credit hour for the 2014-15 academic year.

Room/board/expenses. For the 2014-15 academic year.

Median grant. The median value of grants to full-time students enrolled in 2014-15. This is calculated for all full-time students (not just those in the first year) who received grants and scholarships from internal sources.

Average law school indebtedness. For 2014 graduates, the average law school debt for those taking out at least one educational loan while in school.

Enrollment. Full and part time, fall 2014. Gender figure is for full and part time.

Minorities. For fall 2014, the percentage of full-time and part-time U.S. students who are black or African-American, Asian, American Indian or Alaskan Native, Native Hawaiian or other Pacific Islander, Hispanic/Latino or two or more races.

Acceptance rate. Percentage of applicants who were accepted for the fall 2014 full-time J.D. program.

Midrange Law School Admission Test (LSAT) score. For full-time students who entered in fall 2014. The first number is the 25th percentile test score for the class; the second, the 75th percentile.

Midrange undergraduate grade point average. For full-time students who entered in fall 2014. The first number is the 25th percentile GPA for the class; the second is the 75th percentile.

Midrange of full-time private sector starting salaries. For the 2013 graduating class, the starting salary is for those employed full time in the private sector in law firms, business, industry or other jobs. The first number is the starting salary at the 25th percentile of the graduating class; the second number is the starting salary at the 75th percentile. When a school has the same salary at the 25th and 75th percentiles, it means that the starting salaries for private sector jobs were the same for a large proportion of the class.

Job classifications. For 2013 graduates, this represents the breakdown for the following types of employment: in law firms, business and industry (legal and nonlegal), government, public interest, judicial clerkship, academia and unknown. Numbers may not add up to 100 percent because of rounding.

Employment locations. For the 2013 graduating class. Abbreviations: **Intl.,** international; **N.E.,** New England (Conn., Maine, Mass., N.H., R.I., Vt.); **M.A.,** Middle Atlantic (N.J., N.Y., Pa.); **S.A.,** South Atlantic (Del., D.C., Fla., Ga., Md., N.C., S.C., Va., W.Va.); **E.N.C.,** East North Central (Ill., Ind., Mich., Ohio, Wis.); **W.N.C.,** West North Central (Iowa, Kan., Minn., Mo., Neb., N.D., S.D.); **E.S.C.,** East South Central (Ala., Ky., Miss., Tenn.); **W.S.C.,** West South Central (Ark., La., Okla., Texas); **Mt.,** Mountain (Ariz., Colo., Idaho, Mont., Nev., N.M., Utah, Wyo.); **Pac.,** Pacific (Alaska, Calif., Hawaii, Ore., Wash.).

ALABAMA

Faulkner University (Jones)[1]
5345 Atlanta Highway
Montgomery, AL 36109
www.faulkner.edu/law
Private
Admissions: (334) 386-7210
Email: law@faulkner.edu
Financial aid: N/A
Tuition: N/A
Room/board/expenses: N/A
Enrollment: N/A

Samford University (Cumberland)
800 Lakeshore Drive
Birmingham, AL 35229
www.samford.edu/cumberlandlaw/
Private
Admissions: (205) 726-2702
Email: law.admissions@samford.edu
Financial aid: (205) 726-2905
Application deadline: 04/01
Tuition: full time: $36,734; part time: $21,673
Room/board/expenses: $16,274
Median grant: $15,000
Average student indebtedness at graduation: $124,106
Enrollment: full time: 401; part time: 25
men: 54%; women: 46%; minorities: 11%
Acceptance rate (full time): 76%
Midrange LSAT (full time): 148-154
Midrange undergraduate GPA (full time): 2.89-3.52
Midrange of full-time private-sector salaries of 2013 grads: $46,500-$70,000
2013 grads employed in: law firms: 64%; business and industry: 12%; government: 16%; public interest: 3%; judicial clerk: 3%; academia: 2%; unknown: 0%
Employment location for 2013 class: Intl. N/A; N.E. %; M.A. 0%; E.N.C. 0%; W.N.C. 0%; S.A. 26%; E.S.C. 71%; W.S.C. 1%; Mt. 1%; Pac. 1%; unknown 0%

University of Alabama
Box 870382
Tuscaloosa, AL 35487
www.law.ua.edu
Public
Admissions: (205) 348-5440
Email: admissions@law.ua.edu
Financial aid: (205) 348-6756
Application deadline: rolling
In-state tuition: full time: $21,624; part time: N/A
Out-of-state tuition: full time: $36,304
Room/board/expenses: $18,235
Median grant: $15,000
Average student indebtedness at graduation: $69,440
Enrollment: full time: 420; part time: N/A
men: 57%; women: 43%; minorities: 15%
Acceptance rate (full time): 27%
Midrange LSAT (full time): 157-165
Midrange undergraduate GPA (full time): 3.37-3.94

Midrange of full-time private-sector salaries of 2013 grads: $95,000-$110,000
2013 grads employed in: law firms: 48%; business and industry: 17%; government: 11%; public interest: 4%; judicial clerk: 17%; academia: 3%; unknown: 0%
Employment location for 2013 class: Intl. N/A; N.E. %; M.A. 3%; E.N.C. 1%; W.N.C. 1%; S.A. 18%; E.S.C. 66%; W.S.C. 9%; Mt. 1%; Pac. 1%; unknown 0%

ARIZONA

Arizona State University (O'Connor)
1100 S. McAllister Avenue
Tempe, AZ 85287-7906
www.law.asu.edu
Public
Admissions: (480) 965-1474
Email: law.admissions@asu.edu
Financial aid: (480) 965-1474
Application deadline: 02/01
In-state tuition: full time: $26,753; part time: N/A
Out-of-state tuition: full time: $41,751
Room/board/expenses: $21,388
Median grant: $15,000
Average student indebtedness at graduation: $97,431
Enrollment: full time: 576; part time: N/A
men: 60%; women: 40%; minorities: 26%
Acceptance rate (full time): 44%
Midrange LSAT (full time): 157-163
Midrange undergraduate GPA (full time): 3.37-3.78
Midrange of full-time private-sector salaries of 2013 grads: $65,000-$112,500
2013 grads employed in: law firms: 56%; business and industry: 13%; government: 19%; public interest: 2%; judicial clerk: 5%; academia: 6%; unknown: 1%
Employment location for 2013 class: Intl. N/A; N.E. %; M.A. 1%; E.N.C. 1%; W.N.C. 1%; S.A. 3%; E.S.C. 0%; W.S.C. 2%; Mt. 90%; Pac. 4%; unknown 0%

Arizona Summit Law School[1]
One North Central Avenue
Phoenix, AZ 85004
www.azsummitlaw.edu/
Private
Admissions: (602) 682-6800
Email: admissions@AZSummitLaw.edu
Financial aid: N/A
Tuition: N/A
Room/board/expenses: N/A
Enrollment: N/A

University of Arizona (Rogers)
PO Box 210176
Tucson, AZ 85721-0176
www.law.arizona.edu
Public
Admissions: (520) 621-7666
Email: admissions@law.arizona.edu

Financial aid: (520) 626-1832
Application deadline: 02/15
In-state tuition: full time: $24,607;
part time: N/A
Out-of-state tuition: full time:
$29,000
Room/board/expenses: $20,900
Median grant: $12,850
**Average student indebtedness at
graduation:** $95,533
Enrollment: full time: 379; part
time: N/A
men: 60%; women: 40%;
minorities: 22%
Acceptance rate (full time): 39%
Midrange LSAT (full time): 156-163
**Midrange undergraduate GPA (full
time):** 3.25-3.72
**Midrange of full-time private-sector
salaries of 2013 grads:** $72,000-
$120,000
2013 grads employed in: law firms:
38%; business and industry: 16%;
government: 15%; public interest:
6%; judicial clerk: 25%; academia:
0%; unknown: 0%
Employment location for 2013 class:
Intl. N/A; N.E. %; M.A. 1%; E.N.C.
0%; W.N.C. 2%; S.A. 7%; E.S.C.
1%; W.S.C. 1%; Mt. 82%; Pac. 5%;
unknown 0%

ARKANSAS

University of
Arkansas-Fayetteville

Robert A. Leflar Law Center
Fayetteville, AR 72701
law.uark.edu/
Public
Admissions: (479) 575-3102
Email: jkmiller@uark.edu
Financial aid: (479) 575-3806
Application deadline: 04/15
In-state tuition: full time: $14,508;
part time: N/A
Out-of-state tuition: full time:
$30,028
Room/board/expenses: $18,528
Median grant: $5,000
**Average student indebtedness at
graduation:** $63,541
Enrollment: full time: 361; part
time: N/A
men: 61%; women: 39%;
minorities: 19%
Acceptance rate (full time): 60%
Midrange LSAT (full time): 151-157
**Midrange undergraduate GPA (full
time):** 3.24-3.74
**Midrange of full-time private-sector
salaries of 2013 grads:** $55,000-
$80,000
2013 grads employed in: law firms:
50%; business and industry: 25%;
government: 10%; public interest:
5%; judicial clerk: 7%; academia:
3%; unknown: 0%
Employment location for 2013 class:
Intl. N/A; N.E. %; M.A. 1%; E.N.C.
2%; W.N.C. 3%; S.A. 4%; E.S.C.
1%; W.S.C. 77%; Mt. 4%; Pac. 1%;
unknown 5%

University of
Arkansas-Little Rock
(Bowen)

1201 McMath Avenue
Little Rock, AR 72202-5142
www.law.ualr.edu/
Public
Admissions: (501) 324-9439
Email: lawadm@ualr.edu
Financial aid: (501) 569-3035
Application deadline: 03/15
In-state tuition: full time: $13,996;
part time: $9,374

Out-of-state tuition: full time:
$28,342
Room/board/expenses: $15,138
Median grant: $7,000
**Average student indebtedness at
graduation:** $69,532
Enrollment: full time: 306; part
time: 118
men: 58%; women: 42%;
minorities: 16%
Acceptance rate (full time): 61%
Midrange LSAT (full time): 146-155
**Midrange undergraduate GPA (full
time):** 3.02-3.69
**Midrange of full-time private-sector
salaries of 2013 grads:** $45,000-
$65,000
2013 grads employed in: law firms:
50%; business and industry: 27%;
government: 10%; public interest:
5%; judicial clerk: 3%; academia:
3%; unknown: 1%
Employment location for 2013 class:
Intl. N/A; N.E. %; M.A. 0%; E.N.C.
0%; W.N.C. 1%; S.A. 7%; E.S.C.
3%; W.S.C. 88%; Mt. 1%; Pac. 1%;
unknown 0%

CALIFORNIA

California Western
School of Law

225 Cedar Street
San Diego, CA 92101-3090
www.cwsl.edu
Private
Admissions: (619) 525-1401
Email: admissions@cwsl.edu
Financial aid: (619) 525-7060
Application deadline: 04/01
Tuition: full time: $45,900; part
time: $32,100
Room/board/expenses: $24,028
Median grant: $18,054
**Average student indebtedness at
graduation:** $151,197
Enrollment: full time: 525; part
time: 142
men: 41%; women: 59%;
minorities: 37%
Acceptance rate (full time): 69%
Midrange LSAT (full time): 146-153
**Midrange undergraduate GPA (full
time):** 2.90-3.46
**Midrange of full-time private-sector
salaries of 2013 grads:** $45,000-
$65,000
2013 grads employed in: law firms:
56%; business and industry: 26%;
government: 7%; public interest:
9%; judicial clerk: 2%; academia:
1%; unknown: 0%
Employment location for 2013 class:
Intl. N/A; N.E. %; M.A. 1%; E.N.C.
0%; W.N.C. 0%; S.A. 5%; E.S.C.
0%; W.S.C. 0%; Mt. 6%; Pac.
79%; unknown 8%

Chapman
University (Fowler)

1 University Drive
Orange, CA 92866
www.chapman.edu/law
Private
Admissions: (714) 628-2500
Email: lawadm@chapman.edu
Financial aid: (714) 628-2510
Application deadline: 04/15
Tuition: full time: $46,766; part
time: $37,131
Room/board/expenses: $26,800
Median grant: $26,707
**Average student indebtedness at
graduation:** $148,429
Enrollment: full time: 444; part
time: 29
men: 50%; women: 50%;
minorities: 33%

Acceptance rate (full time): 54%
Midrange LSAT (full time): 153-158
**Midrange undergraduate GPA (full
time):** 3.18-3.57
**Midrange of full-time private-sector
salaries of 2013 grads:** $60,000-
$79,500
2013 grads employed in: law firms:
59%; business and industry: 31%;
government: 6%; public interest:
1%; judicial clerk: 2%; academia:
1%; unknown: 0%
Employment location for 2013 class:
Intl. N/A; N.E. %; M.A. 2%; E.N.C.
0%; W.N.C. 0%; S.A. 2%; E.S.C.
0%; W.S.C. 0%; Mt. 2%; Pac.
94%; unknown 0%

Golden Gate University

536 Mission Street
San Francisco, CA 94105
www.law.ggu.edu
Private
Admissions: (415) 442-6630
Email: lawadmit@ggu.edu
Financial aid: (415) 442-6635
Application deadline: 04/05
Tuition: full time: $45,350; part
time: $34,850
Room/board/expenses: $25,364
Median grant: $15,000
**Average student indebtedness at
graduation:** $146,288
Enrollment: full time: 301; part
time: 148
men: 45%; women: 55%;
minorities: 44%
Acceptance rate (full time): 66%
Midrange LSAT (full time): 146-153
**Midrange undergraduate GPA (full
time):** 2.75-3.23
**Midrange of full-time private-sector
salaries of 2013 grads:** $50,000-
$80,000
2013 grads employed in: law firms:
44%; business and industry: 29%;
government: 14%; public interest:
11%; judicial clerk: 1%; academia:
2%; unknown: 1%
Employment location for 2013 class:
Intl. N/A; N.E. %; M.A. 2%; E.N.C.
2%; W.N.C. 0%; S.A. 4%; E.S.C.
0%; W.S.C. 1%; Mt. 2%; Pac. 89%;
unknown 2%

Loyola Marymount
University

919 Albany Street
Los Angeles, CA 90015-1211
www.lls.edu
Private
Admissions: (213) 736-1074
Email: Admissions@lls.edu
Financial aid: (213) 736-1140
Application deadline: 02/02
Tuition: full time: $47,750; part
time: $31,975
Room/board/expenses: $29,350
Median grant: $23,000
**Average student indebtedness at
graduation:** $147,701
Enrollment: full time: 900; part
time: 194
men: 46%; women: 54%;
minorities: 40%
Acceptance rate (full time): 47%
Midrange LSAT (full time): 156-161
**Midrange undergraduate GPA (full
time):** 3.21-3.62
**Midrange of full-time private-sector
salaries of 2013 grads:** $60,000-
$114,400
2013 grads employed in: law firms:
60%; business and industry: 17%;
government: 8%; public interest:
9%; judicial clerk: 3%; academia:
3%; unknown: 0%

Employment location for 2013 class:
Intl. N/A; N.E. %; M.A. 0%; E.N.C.
0%; W.N.C. 1%; S.A. 0%; E.S.C.
0%; W.S.C. 1%; Mt. 1%; Pac. 97%;
unknown 0%

Pepperdine University

24255 Pacific Coast Highway
Malibu, CA 90263
law.pepperdine.edu
Private
Admissions: (310) 506-4631
Email: soladmis@pepperdine.edu
Financial aid: (310) 506-4633
Application deadline: 02/01
Tuition: full time: $49,030; part
time: N/A
Room/board/expenses: $27,970
Median grant: $22,000
**Average student indebtedness at
graduation:** $145,525
Enrollment: full time: 605; part
time: N/A
men: 50%; women: 50%;
minorities: 28%
Acceptance rate (full time): 46%
Midrange LSAT (full time): 153-162
**Midrange undergraduate GPA (full
time):** 3.28-3.71
**Midrange of full-time private-sector
salaries of 2013 grads:** $64,480-
$100,000
2013 grads employed in: law firms:
59%; business and industry: 18%;
government: 6%; public interest:
3%; judicial clerk: 7%; academia:
8%; unknown: 0%
Employment location for 2013 class:
Intl. N/A; N.E. %; M.A. 2%; E.N.C.
3%; W.N.C. 0%; S.A. 4%; E.S.C.
2%; W.S.C. 7%; Mt. 5%; Pac. 76%;
unknown 0%

Santa Clara University

500 El Camino Real
Santa Clara, CA 95053-0421
www.scu.edu/law
Private
Admissions: (408) 554-4800
Email: lawadmissions@scu.edu
Financial aid: (408) 554-4447
Application deadline: 02/02
Tuition: full time: $1,568/credit
hour; part time: $1,568/credit hour
Room/board/expenses: $23,280
Median grant: $13,000
**Average student indebtedness at
graduation:** $136,990
Enrollment: full time: 478; part
time: 165
men: 52%; women: 48%;
minorities: 42%
Acceptance rate (full time): 50%
Midrange LSAT (full time): 156-160
**Midrange undergraduate GPA (full
time):** 3.06-3.47
**Midrange of full-time private-sector
salaries of 2013 grads:** $70,000-
$160,000
2013 grads employed in: law firms:
55%; business and industry: 28%;
government: 8%; public interest:
4%; judicial clerk: 0%; academia:
6%; unknown: 0%
Employment location for 2013 class:
Intl. N/A; N.E. %; M.A. 1%; E.N.C.
0%; W.N.C. 0%; S.A. 2%; E.S.C.
0%; W.S.C. 0%; Mt. 2%; Pac.
90%; unknown 0%

Southwestern
Law School

3050 Wilshire Boulevard
Los Angeles, CA 90010-1106
www.swlaw.edu
Private
Admissions: (213) 738-6717
Email: admissions@swlaw.edu
Financial aid: (213) 738-6719
Application deadline: 04/01
Tuition: full time: $47,100; part
time: $31,470
Room/board/expenses: $30,290
Median grant: $20,000
Enrollment: full time: 687; part
time: 361
men: 42%; women: 58%;
minorities: 44%
Acceptance rate (full time): 62%
Midrange LSAT (full time): 150-155
**Midrange undergraduate GPA (full
time):** 2.99-3.45
**Midrange of full-time private-sector
salaries of 2013 grads:** $50,000-
$86,250
2013 grads employed in: law firms:
61%; business and industry: 27%;
government: 4%; public interest:
3%; judicial clerk: 3%; academia:
2%; unknown: 0%
Employment location for 2013 class:
Intl. N/A; N.E. %; M.A. 3%; E.N.C.
0%; W.N.C. 0%; S.A. 2%; E.S.C.
0%; W.S.C. 0%; Mt. 3%; Pac.
90%; unknown 2%

Stanford University

Crown Quadrangle
559 Nathan Abbott Way
Stanford, CA 94305-8610
www.law.stanford.edu/
Private
Admissions: (650) 723-4985
Email:
admissions@law.stanford.edu
Financial aid: (650) 723-9247
Application deadline: 02/01
Tuition: full time: $54,366; part
time: N/A
Room/board/expenses: $28,395
Median grant: $23,060
**Average student indebtedness at
graduation:** $128,137
Enrollment: full time: 577; part
time: N/A
men: 55%; women: 45%;
minorities: 35%
Acceptance rate (full time): 9%
Midrange LSAT (full time): 169-174
**Midrange undergraduate GPA (full
time):** 3.80-3.97
**Midrange of full-time private-sector
salaries of 2013 grads:** $160,000-
$160,000
2013 grads employed in: law firms:
52%; business and industry: 7%;
government: 2%; public interest:
5%; judicial clerk: 32%; academia:
2%; unknown: 0%
Employment location for 2013 class:
Intl. N/A; N.E. %; M.A. 18%; E.N.C.
4%; W.N.C. 2%; S.A. 11%; E.S.C.
1%; W.S.C. 8%; Mt. 5%; Pac. 49%;
unknown 0%

Thomas Jefferson
School of Law

1155 Island Avenue
San Diego, CA 92101
www.tjsl.edu
Private
Admissions: (619) 297-9700
Email: info@tjsl.edu
Financial aid: (619) 297-9700
Application deadline: 08/01
Tuition: full time: $44,900; part
time: $33,000

Room/board/expenses: $23,070
Median grant: $18,000
Average student indebtedness at graduation: $172,445
Enrollment: full time: 518; part time: 247
men: 47%; women: 53%; minorities: 47%
Acceptance rate (full time): 85%
Midrange LSAT (full time): 142-149
Midrange undergraduate GPA (full time): 2.57-3.07
Midrange of full-time private-sector salaries of 2013 grads: $39,200-$65,500
2013 grads employed in: law firms: 59%; business and industry: 27%; government: 7%; public interest: 2%; judicial clerk: 4%; academia: 2%; unknown: 0%
Employment location for 2013 class: Intl. N/A; N.E. %; M.A. 3%; E.N.C. 5%; W.N.C. 1%; S.A. 1%; E.S.C. 0%; W.S.C. 2%; Mt. 13%; Pac. 72%; unknown 0%

University of California-Berkeley
Boalt Hall
Berkeley, CA 94720-7200
www.law.berkeley.edu
Public
Admissions: (510) 642-2274
Email: admissions@law.berkeley.edu
Financial aid: (510) 642-1563
Application deadline: 02/01
In-state tuition: full time: $48,166; part time: N/A
Out-of-state tuition: full time: $52,117
Room/board/expenses: $27,692
Median grant: $19,906
Average student indebtedness at graduation: $143,546
Enrollment: full time: 890; part time: 4
men: 46%; women: 54%; minorities: 39%
Acceptance rate (full time): 20%
Midrange LSAT (full time): 164-169
Midrange undergraduate GPA (full time): 3.67-3.88
Midrange of full-time private-sector salaries of 2013 grads: $160,000-$160,000
2013 grads employed in: law firms: 60%; business and industry: 3%; government: 8%; public interest: 17%; judicial clerk: 11%; academia: 2%; unknown: 0%
Employment location for 2013 class: Intl. N/A; N.E. %; M.A. 13%; E.N.C. 2%; W.N.C. 0%; S.A. 10%; E.S.C. 0%; W.S.C. 5%; Mt. 1%; Pac. 68%; unknown 0%

University of California-Davis
400 Mrak Hall Drive
Davis, CA 95616-5201
www.law.ucdavis.edu/jd
Public
Admissions: (530) 752-6477
Email: admissions@law.ucdavis.edu
Financial aid: (530) 752-6573
Application deadline: 03/15
In-state tuition: full time: $47,286; part time: N/A
Out-of-state tuition: full time: $56,537
Room/board/expenses: $17,634
Median grant: $25,000
Average student indebtedness at graduation: $93,498

Enrollment: full time: 513; part time: N/A
men: 47%; women: 53%; minorities: 37%
Acceptance rate (full time): 35%
Midrange LSAT (full time): 160-164
Midrange undergraduate GPA (full time): 3.33-3.75
Midrange of full-time private-sector salaries of 2013 grads: $72,000-$145,000
2013 grads employed in: law firms: 52%; business and industry: 8%; government: 15%; public interest: 5%; judicial clerk: 6%; academia: 13%; unknown: 1%
Employment location for 2013 class: Intl. N/A; N.E. %; M.A. 2%; E.N.C. 1%; W.N.C. 0%; S.A. 2%; E.S.C. 0%; W.S.C. 2%; Mt. 2%; Pac. 89%; unknown 0%

University of California (Hastings)
200 McAllister Street
San Francisco, CA 94102
www.uchastings.edu
Public
Admissions: (415) 565-4623
Email: admiss@uchastings.edu
Financial aid: (415) 565-4624
Application deadline: 03/01
In-state tuition: full time: $48,335; part time: N/A
Out-of-state tuition: full time: $54,335
Room/board/expenses: $23,613
Median grant: $15,800
Average student indebtedness at graduation: $129,178
Enrollment: full time: 930; part time: 3
men: 48%; women: 52%; minorities: 47%
Acceptance rate (full time): 49%
Midrange LSAT (full time): 155-161
Midrange undergraduate GPA (full time): 3.21-3.62
Midrange of full-time private-sector salaries of 2013 grads: $72,500-$160,000
2013 grads employed in: law firms: 47%; business and industry: 14%; government: 22%; public interest: 11%; judicial clerk: 4%; academia: 2%; unknown: 0%
Employment location for 2013 class: Intl. N/A; N.E. %; M.A. 0%; E.N.C. 0%; W.N.C. 0%; S.A. 4%; E.S.C. 0%; W.S.C. 1%; Mt. 3%; Pac. 89%; unknown 0%

University of California-Irvine
401 East Peltason Drive
Suite 1000
Irvine, CA 92697-8000
www.law.uci.edu/
Public
Admissions: (949) 824-4545
Email: lawadmit@law.uci.edu
Financial aid: (949) 824-8080
Application deadline: 03/31
In-state tuition: full time: $44,717; part time: N/A
Out-of-state tuition: full time: $51,211
Room/board/expenses: $25,386
Median grant: $23,654
Average student indebtedness at graduation: $102,891
Enrollment: full time: 326; part time: N/A
men: 52%; women: 48%; minorities: 43%
Acceptance rate (full time): 22%
Midrange LSAT (full time): 162-166

Midrange undergraduate GPA (full time): 3.27-3.70
Midrange of full-time private-sector salaries of 2013 grads: $73,500-$160,000
2013 grads employed in: law firms: 42%; business and industry: 6%; government: 16%; public interest: 5%; judicial clerk: 27%; academia: 3%; unknown: 0%
Employment location for 2013 class: Intl. N/A; N.E. %; M.A. 2%; E.N.C. 3%; W.N.C. 2%; S.A. 2%; E.S.C. 2%; W.S.C. 2%; Mt. 3%; Pac. 82%; unknown 0%

University of California-Los Angeles
71 Dodd Hall
PO Box 951445
Los Angeles, CA 90095-1445
www.law.ucla.edu
Public
Admissions: (310) 825-2260
Email: admissions@law.ucla.edu
Financial aid: (310) 825-2459
Application deadline: 02/01
In-state tuition: full time: $45,226; part time: N/A
Out-of-state tuition: full time: $51,720
Room/board/expenses: $26,136
Median grant: $20,000
Average student indebtedness at graduation: $121,066
Enrollment: full time: 992; part time: N/A
men: 52%; women: 48%; minorities: 32%
Acceptance rate (full time): 28%
Midrange LSAT (full time): 163-169
Midrange undergraduate GPA (full time): 3.56-3.90
Midrange of full-time private-sector salaries of 2013 grads: $99,000-$160,000
2013 grads employed in: law firms: 56%; business and industry: 10%; government: 9%; public interest: 14%; judicial clerk: 10%; academia: 2%; unknown: 0%
Employment location for 2013 class: Intl. N/A; N.E. %; M.A. 5%; E.N.C. 1%; W.N.C. 0%; S.A. 4%; E.S.C. 0%; W.S.C. 2%; Mt. 2%; Pac. 85%; unknown 0%

University of La Verne[1]
320 E. D Street
Ontario, CA 91764
law.laverne.edu
Private
Admissions: (909) 460-2006
Email: lawadm@laverne.edu
Financial aid: N/A
Tuition: N/A
Room/board/expenses: N/A
Enrollment: N/A

University of San Diego
5998 Alcala Park
San Diego, CA 92110-2492
www.law.sandiego.edu
Private
Admissions: (619) 260-4528
Email: jdinfo@SanDiego.edu
Financial aid: (619) 260-4570
Application deadline: rolling
Tuition: full time: $47,490; part time: $35,190
Room/board/expenses: $21,999
Median grant: $21,000
Average student indebtedness at graduation: $128,477

Enrollment: full time: 632; part time: 108
men: 50%; women: 50%; minorities: 30%
Acceptance rate (full time): 47%
Midrange LSAT (full time): 155-161
Midrange undergraduate GPA (full time): 3.30-3.68
Midrange of full-time private-sector salaries of 2013 grads: $65,000-$130,000
2013 grads employed in: law firms: 58%; business and industry: 20%; government: 13%; public interest: 4%; judicial clerk: 1%; academia: 5%; unknown: 0%
Employment location for 2013 class: Intl. N/A; N.E. %; M.A. 1%; E.N.C. 0%; W.N.C. 1%; S.A. 1%; E.S.C. 0%; W.S.C. 2%; Mt. 5%; Pac. 86%; unknown 1%

University of San Francisco
2130 Fulton Street
San Francisco, CA 94117-1080
www.usfca.edu/law
Private
Admissions: (415) 422-6586
Email: lawadmissions@usfca.edu
Financial aid: (415) 422-6210
Application deadline: 02/01
Tuition: full time: $45,542; part time: $32,465
Room/board/expenses: $27,800
Median grant: $20,000
Average student indebtedness at graduation: $154,321
Enrollment: full time: 424; part time: 102
men: 45%; women: 55%; minorities: 47%
Acceptance rate (full time): 62%
Midrange LSAT (full time): 150-156
Midrange undergraduate GPA (full time): 3.00-3.40
Midrange of full-time private-sector salaries of 2013 grads: $65,000-$110,000
2013 grads employed in: law firms: 54%; business and industry: 18%; government: 13%; public interest: 12%; judicial clerk: 0%; academia: 1%; unknown: 2%
Employment location for 2013 class: Intl. N/A; N.E. %; M.A. 3%; E.N.C. 1%; W.N.C. 0%; S.A. 2%; E.S.C. 1%; W.S.C. 4%; Mt. 1%; Pac. 82%; unknown 4%

University of Southern California (Gould)
699 Exposition Boulevard
Los Angeles, CA 90089-0071
lawweb.usc.edu
Private
Admissions: (213) 740-2523
Email: admissions@law.usc.edu
Financial aid: (213) 740-6314
Application deadline: 02/01
Tuition: full time: $57,507; part time: N/A
Room/board/expenses: $24,092
Median grant: $20,000
Average student indebtedness at graduation: $137,163
Enrollment: full time: 604; part time: 2
men: 53%; women: 47%; minorities: 38%
Acceptance rate (full time): 28%
Midrange LSAT (full time): 163-167
Midrange undergraduate GPA (full time): 3.55-3.86

Midrange of full-time private-sector salaries of 2013 grads: $85,625-$160,000
2013 grads employed in: law firms: 62%; business and industry: 16%; government: 6%; public interest: 8%; judicial clerk: 6%; academia: 3%; unknown: 0%
Employment location for 2013 class: Intl. N/A; N.E. %; M.A. 2%; E.N.C. 1%; W.N.C. 0%; S.A. 4%; E.S.C. 0%; W.S.C. 1%; Mt. 2%; Pac. 86%; unknown 0%

University of the Pacific (McGeorge)
3200 Fifth Avenue
Sacramento, CA 95817
www.mcgeorge.edu
Private
Admissions: (916) 739-7105
Email: admissionsmcgeorge@pacific.edu
Financial aid: (916) 739-7158
Application deadline: 04/01
Tuition: full time: $46,462; part time: $30,858
Room/board/expenses: $22,578
Median grant: $13,096
Average student indebtedness at graduation: $140,517
Enrollment: full time: 416; part time: 137
men: 48%; women: 52%; minorities: 35%
Acceptance rate (full time): 75%
Midrange LSAT (full time): 148-155
Midrange undergraduate GPA (full time): 2.96-3.39
Midrange of full-time private-sector salaries of 2013 grads: $50,000-$77,500
2013 grads employed in: law firms: 53%; business and industry: 18%; government: 17%; public interest: 5%; judicial clerk: 3%; academia: 4%; unknown: 1%
Employment location for 2013 class: Intl. N/A; N.E. %; M.A. 1%; E.N.C. 1%; W.N.C. 0%; S.A. 2%; E.S.C. 0%; W.S.C. 1%; Mt. 7%; Pac. 88%; unknown 1%

Western State College of Law at Argosy University
1111 N. State College Boulevard
Fullerton, CA 92831
www.wsulaw.edu
Private
Admissions: (714) 459-1101
Email: adm@wsulaw.edu
Financial aid: (714) 459-1120
Application deadline: 06/01
Tuition: full time: $42,102; part time: $28,310
Room/board/expenses: $23,467
Median grant: $15,846
Average student indebtedness at graduation: $120,350
Enrollment: full time: 220; part time: 133
men: 47%; women: 53%; minorities: 48%
Acceptance rate (full time): 65%
Midrange LSAT (full time): 146-151
Midrange undergraduate GPA (full time): 2.91-3.38
Midrange of full-time private-sector salaries of 2013 grads: $48,000-$80,000
2013 grads employed in: law firms: 61%; business and industry: 26%; government: 5%; public interest: 2%; judicial clerk: 1%; academia: 5%; unknown: 0%

Employment location for 2013 class: Intl. N/A; N.E. %; M.A. 0%; E.N.C. 1%; W.N.C. 0%; S.A. 1%; E.S.C. 0%; W.S.C. 1%; Mt. 1%; Pac. 94%; unknown 0%

Whittier College

3333 Harbor Boulevard
Costa Mesa, CA 92626-1501
www.law.whittier.edu
Private
Admissions: (800) 808-8188
Email: info@law.whittier.edu
Financial aid: (714) 444-4141
Application deadline: 07/31
Tuition: full time: $42,400; part time: $28,300
Room/board/expenses: $30,380
Median grant: $20,780
Average student indebtedness at graduation: $151,602
Enrollment: full time: 409; part time: 127
men: 44%; women: 56%; minorities: 48%
Acceptance rate (full time): 75%
Midrange LSAT (full time): 143-150
Midrange undergraduate GPA (full time): 2.62-3.19
Midrange of full-time private-sector salaries of 2013 grads: $42,000-$75,000
2013 grads employed in: law firms: 56%; business and industry: 32%; government: 7%; public interest: 3%; judicial clerk: 1%; academia: 0%; unknown: 1%
Employment location for 2013 class: Intl. N/A; N.E. %; M.A. 3%; E.N.C. 1%; W.N.C. 0%; S.A. 6%; E.S.C. 0%; W.S.C. 1%; Mt. 3%; Pac. 81%; unknown 5%

COLORADO

University of Colorado-Boulder

Box 401
Boulder, CO 80309-0401
www.colorado.edu/law/
Public
Admissions: (303) 492-7203
Email: lawadmin@colorado.edu
Financial aid: (303) 492-0647
Application deadline: 03/15
In-state tuition: full time: $31,886; part time: N/A
Out-of-state tuition: full time: $38,672
Room/board/expenses: $19,286
Median grant: $10,000
Average student indebtedness at graduation: $116,280
Enrollment: full time: 509; part time: N/A
men: 54%; women: 46%; minorities: 18%
Acceptance rate (full time): 47%
Midrange LSAT (full time): 156-163
Midrange undergraduate GPA (full time): 3.34-3.76
Midrange of full-time private-sector salaries of 2013 grads: $60,000-$95,000
2013 grads employed in: law firms: 32%; business and industry: 13%; government: 18%; public interest: 14%; judicial clerk: 19%; academia: 4%; unknown: 0%
Employment location for 2013 class: Intl. N/A; N.E. %; M.A. 1%; E.N.C. 1%; W.N.C. 0%; S.A. 2%; E.S.C. 1%; W.S.C. 3%; Mt. 84%; Pac. 8%; unknown 2%

University of Denver (Sturm)

2255 E. Evans Avenue
Denver, CO 80208
www.law.du.edu
Private
Admissions: (303) 871-6135
Email: admissions@law.du.edu
Financial aid: (303) 871-6362
Application deadline: rolling
Tuition: full time: $42,370; part time: $31,106
Room/board/expenses: $18,581
Median grant: $21,000
Average student indebtedness at graduation: $132,083
Enrollment: full time: 725; part time: 138
men: 48%; women: 52%; minorities: 17%
Acceptance rate (full time): 63%
Midrange LSAT (full time): 153-159
Midrange undergraduate GPA (full time): 3.14-3.62
Midrange of full-time private-sector salaries of 2013 grads: $50,250-$98,750
2013 grads employed in: law firms: 36%; business and industry: 21%; government: 19%; public interest: 3%; judicial clerk: 16%; academia: 6%; unknown: 0%
Employment location for 2013 class: Intl. N/A; N.E. %; M.A. 2%; E.N.C. 3%; W.N.C. 2%; S.A. 2%; E.S.C. 0%; W.S.C. 3%; Mt. 86%; Pac. 1%; unknown 0%

CONNECTICUT

Quinnipiac University

275 Mount Carmel Avenue
Hamden, CT 06518
law.quinnipiac.edu
Private
Admissions: (203) 582-3400
Email: ladm@quinnipiac.edu
Financial aid: (203) 582-3405
Application deadline: rolling
Tuition: full time: $47,101; part time: $33,241
Room/board/expenses: $19,410
Median grant: $25,000
Average student indebtedness at graduation: $119,956
Enrollment: full time: 229; part time: 59
men: 44%; women: 56%; minorities: 16%
Acceptance rate (full time): 58%
Midrange LSAT (full time): 151-155
Midrange undergraduate GPA (full time): 3.03-3.68
Midrange of full-time private-sector salaries of 2013 grads: $45,000-$80,000
2013 grads employed in: law firms: 47%; business and industry: 27%; government: 16%; public interest: 2%; judicial clerk: 5%; academia: 3%; unknown: 0%
Employment location for 2013 class: Intl. N/A; N.E. %; M.A. 9%; E.N.C. 0%; W.N.C. 0%; S.A. 2%; E.S.C. 1%; W.S.C. 2%; Mt. 0%; Pac. 2%; unknown 2%

University of Connecticut

55 Elizabeth Street
Hartford, CT 06105-2296
www.law.uconn.edu
Public
Admissions: (860) 570-5100
Email: law.admissions@uconn.edu
Financial aid: (860) 570-5147
Application deadline: 07/15

In-state tuition: full time: $26,224; part time: $18,296
Out-of-state tuition: full time: $54,248
Room/board/expenses: $17,510
Median grant: $11,300
Average student indebtedness at graduation: $70,139
Enrollment: full time: 385; part time: 115
men: 52%; women: 48%; minorities: 25%
Acceptance rate (full time): 57%
Midrange LSAT (full time): 155-160
Midrange undergraduate GPA (full time): 3.18-3.62
Midrange of full-time private-sector salaries of 2013 grads: $60,000-$120,000
2013 grads employed in: law firms: 39%; business and industry: 32%; government: 10%; public interest: 5%; judicial clerk: 10%; academia: 4%; unknown: 0%
Employment location for 2013 class: Intl. N/A; N.E. %; M.A. 10%; E.N.C. 1%; W.N.C. 0%; S.A. 3%; E.S.C. 0%; W.S.C. 1%; Mt. 0%; Pac. 2%; unknown 0%

Yale University

PO Box 208215
New Haven, CT 06520-8215
www.law.yale.edu
Private
Admissions: (203) 432-4995
Email: admissions.law@yale.edu
Financial aid: (203) 432-1688
Application deadline: 02/29
Tuition: full time: $56,200; part time: N/A
Room/board/expenses: $20,202
Median grant: $22,090
Average student indebtedness at graduation: $117,093
Enrollment: full time: 607; part time: 1
men: 52%; women: 48%; minorities: 30%
Acceptance rate (full time): 9%
Midrange LSAT (full time): 170-176
Midrange undergraduate GPA (full time): 3.82-3.97
Midrange of full-time private-sector salaries of 2013 grads: $160,000-$160,000
2013 grads employed in: law firms: 34%; business and industry: 3%; government: 5%; public interest: 13%; judicial clerk: 41%; academia: 3%; unknown: 0%
Employment location for 2013 class: Intl. N/A; N.E. %; M.A. 32%; E.N.C. 5%; W.N.C. 1%; S.A. 26%; E.S.C. 2%; W.S.C. 4%; Mt. 3%; Pac. 15%; unknown 0%

DELAWARE

Widener University

PO Box 7474
Wilmington, DE 19803-0474
law.widener.edu
Private
Admissions: (302) 477-2162
Email: law.admissions@law.widener.edu
Financial aid: (302) 477-2272
Application deadline: 05/15
Tuition: full time: $1,354/credit hour; part time: $1,354/credit hour
Room/board/expenses: $20,539
Median grant: $10,000
Average student indebtedness at graduation: $139,229

Enrollment: full time: 503; part time: 255
men: 52%; women: 48%; minorities: 22%
Acceptance rate (full time): 67%
Midrange LSAT (full time): 147-152
Midrange undergraduate GPA (full time): 2.78-3.35
Midrange of full-time private-sector salaries of 2013 grads: $50,000-$87,500
2013 grads employed in: law firms: 42%; business and industry: 21%; government: 17%; public interest: 1%; judicial clerk: 19%; academia: 1%; unknown: 0%
Employment location for 2013 class: Intl. N/A; N.E. %; M.A. 74%; E.N.C. 1%; W.N.C. 0%; S.A. 24%; E.S.C. 0%; W.S.C. 0%; Mt. 1%; Pac. 0%; unknown 0%

DISTRICT OF COLUMBIA

American University (Washington)

4801 Massachusetts Avenue NW
Washington, DC 20016-8192
www.wcl.american.edu
Private
Admissions: (202) 274-4101
Email: wcladmit@wcl.american.edu
Financial aid: (202) 274-4040
Application deadline: 03/01
Tuition: full time: $49,542; part time: $34,750
Room/board/expenses: $23,460
Median grant: $10,000
Average student indebtedness at graduation: $159,316
Enrollment: full time: 1,117; part time: 249
men: 42%; women: 58%; minorities: 36%
Acceptance rate (full time): 50%
Midrange LSAT (full time): 152-159
Midrange undergraduate GPA (full time): 3.15-3.54
Midrange of full-time private-sector salaries of 2013 grads: $60,000-$150,000
2013 grads employed in: law firms: 35%; business and industry: 17%; government: 16%; public interest: 17%; judicial clerk: 12%; academia: 3%; unknown: 0%
Employment location for 2013 class: Intl. N/A; N.E. %; M.A. 8%; E.N.C. 2%; W.N.C. 1%; S.A. 75%; E.S.C. 0%; W.S.C. 3%; Mt. 2%; Pac. 3%; unknown 0%

The Catholic University of America

3600 John McCormack Road NE
Washington, DC 20064
www.law.edu
Private
Admissions: (202) 319-5151
Email: admissions@law.edu
Financial aid: (202) 319-5143
Application deadline: 06/30
Tuition: full time: $45,375; part time: $1,625/credit hour
Room/board/expenses: $25,735
Median grant: $12,500
Average student indebtedness at graduation: $144,737
Enrollment: full time: 291; part time: 164
men: 51%; women: 49%; minorities: 20%
Acceptance rate (full time): 58%
Midrange LSAT (full time): 152-157
Midrange undergraduate GPA (full time): 2.99-3.35

Midrange of full-time private-sector salaries of 2013 grads: $60,000-$147,500
2013 grads employed in: law firms: 30%; business and industry: 26%; government: 27%; public interest: 5%; judicial clerk: 12%; academia: 0%; unknown: 0%
Employment location for 2013 class: Intl. N/A; N.E. %; M.A. 9%; E.N.C. 2%; W.N.C. 1%; S.A. 80%; E.S.C. 1%; W.S.C. 2%; Mt. 2%; Pac. 1%; unknown 0%

Georgetown University

600 New Jersey Avenue NW
Washington, DC 20001-2075
www.law.georgetown.edu
Private
Admissions: (202) 662-9015
Email: admis@law.georgetown.edu
Financial aid: (202) 662-9210
Application deadline: 03/01
Tuition: full time: $53,130; part time: $37,500
Room/board/expenses: $26,670
Median grant: $20,000
Average student indebtedness at graduation: $150,529
Enrollment: full time: 1,719; part time: 247
men: 53%; women: 47%; minorities: 16%
Acceptance rate (full time): 29%
Midrange LSAT (full time): 163-168
Midrange undergraduate GPA (full time): 3.52-3.85
Midrange of full-time private-sector salaries of 2013 grads: $71,250-$160,000
2013 grads employed in: law firms: 55%; business and industry: 6%; government: 12%; public interest: 16%; judicial clerk: 10%; academia: 2%; unknown: 0%
Employment location for 2013 class: Intl. N/A; N.E. %; M.A. 28%; E.N.C. 3%; W.N.C. 1%; S.A. 49%; E.S.C. 0%; W.S.C. 2%; Mt. 2%; Pac. 9%; unknown 1%

George Washington University

2000 H Street NW
Washington, DC 20052
www.law.gwu.edu
Private
Admissions: (202) 994-7230
Email: jdadmit@law.gwu.edu
Financial aid: (202) 994-6592
Application deadline: 03/01
Tuition: full time: $52,033; part time: $38,430
Room/board/expenses: $26,007
Median grant: $16,000
Average student indebtedness at graduation: $141,346
Enrollment: full time: 1,376; part time: 270
men: 50%; women: 50%; minorities: 25%
Acceptance rate (full time): 46%
Midrange LSAT (full time): 160-166
Midrange undergraduate GPA (full time): 3.43-3.81
Midrange of full-time private-sector salaries of 2013 grads: $145,000-$160,000
2013 grads employed in: law firms: 49%; business and industry: 12%; government: 22%; public interest: 8%; judicial clerk: 9%; academia: 1%; unknown: 0%

Employment location for 2013 class: Intl. N/A; N.E. %; M.A. 15%; E.N.C. 3%; W.N.C. 1%; S.A. 64%; E.S.C. 1%; W.S.C. 2%; Mt. 2%; Pac. 7%; unknown 0%

Howard University
2900 Van Ness Street NW
Washington, DC 20008
www.law.howard.edu
Private
Admissions: (202) 806-8009
Email: admissions@law.howard.edu
Financial aid: (202) 806-8005
Application deadline: 03/15
Tuition: full time: $33,732; part time: N/A
Room/board/expenses: $24,508
Median grant: $12,000
Average student indebtedness at graduation: $24,021
Enrollment: full time: 412; part time: N/A
men: 36%; women: 64%; minorities: 94%
Acceptance rate (full time): 41%
Midrange LSAT (full time): 148-155
Midrange undergraduate GPA (full time): 2.95-3.48
Midrange of full-time private-sector salaries of 2013 grads: $60,000-$160,000
2013 grads employed in: law firms: 23%; business and industry: 27%; government: 26%; public interest: 6%; judicial clerk: 14%; academia: 4%; unknown: 0%
Employment location for 2013 class: Intl. N/A; N.E. %; M.A. 23%; E.N.C. 4%; W.N.C. 3%; S.A. 62%; E.S.C. 0%; W.S.C. 2%; Mt. 0%; Pac. 3%; unknown 0%

University of the District of Columbia (Clarke)
4200 Connecticut Avenue NW
Building 38 & 52
Washington, DC 20008
www.law.udc.edu
Public
Admissions: (202) 274-7341
Email: vcanty@udc.edu
Financial aid: (202) 274-7337
Application deadline: 03/15
In-state tuition: full time: $11,383; part time: $369/credit hour
Out-of-state tuition: full time: $22,136.
Room/board/expenses: $26,200
Median grant: $5,000
Average student indebtedness at graduation: $73,175
Enrollment: full time: 162; part time: 144
men: 41%; women: 59%; minorities: 59%
Acceptance rate (full time): 30%
Midrange LSAT (full time): 145-155
Midrange undergraduate GPA (full time): 2.65-3.32
Midrange of full-time private-sector salaries of 2013 grads: $25,000-$60,000
2013 grads employed in: law firms: 34%; business and industry: 26%; government: 14%; public interest: 16%; judicial clerk: 7%; academia: 3%; unknown: 0%
Employment location for 2013 class: Intl. N/A; N.E. %; M.A. 2%; E.N.C. 0%; W.N.C. 0%; S.A. 86%; E.S.C. 2%; W.S.C. 0%; Mt. 3%; Pac. 5%; unknown 0%

FLORIDA

Ave Maria School of Law
1025 Commons Circle
Naples, FL 34119
www.avemarialaw.edu
Private
Admissions: (239) 687-5420
Email: info@avemarialaw.edu
Financial aid: (239) 687-5335
Application deadline: 07/01
Tuition: full time: $40,136; part time: N/A
Room/board/expenses: $21,799
Median grant: $15,000
Average student indebtedness at graduation: $132,236
Enrollment: full time: 267; part time: 2
men: 48%; women: 52%; minorities: 36%
Acceptance rate (full time): 75%
Midrange LSAT (full time): 139-148
Midrange undergraduate GPA (full time): 2.66-3.45
Midrange of full-time private-sector salaries of 2013 grads: $35,000-$58,000
2013 grads employed in: law firms: 43%; business and industry: 25%; government: 17%; public interest: 4%; judicial clerk: 6%; academia: 4%; unknown: 1%
Employment location for 2013 class: Intl. N/A; N.E. %; M.A. 14%; E.N.C. 13%; W.N.C. 1%; S.A. 64%; E.S.C. 2%; W.S.C. 1%; Mt. 3%; Pac. 2%; unknown N/A

Barry University
6441 E. Colonial Drive
Orlando, FL 32807
www.barry.edu/law/
Private
Admissions: (866) 532-2779
Email: lawadmissions@barry.edu
Financial aid: (321) 206-5621
Application deadline: 05/01
Tuition: full time: $35,844; part time: $27,070
Room/board/expenses: $26,050
Median grant: $8,000
Average student indebtedness at graduation: $149,175
Enrollment: full time: 517; part time: 265
men: 42%; women: 58%; minorities: 47%
Acceptance rate (full time): 63%
Midrange LSAT (full time): 144-150
Midrange undergraduate GPA (full time): 2.69-3.33
Midrange of full-time private-sector salaries of 2013 grads: N/A-N/A
2013 grads employed in: law firms: 56%; business and industry: 13%; government: 18%; public interest: 4%; judicial clerk: 1%; academia: 5%; unknown: 3%
Employment location for 2013 class: Intl. N/A; N.E. %; M.A. 4%; E.N.C. 1%; W.N.C. 2%; S.A. 90%; E.S.C. 1%; W.S.C. 1%; Mt. 0%; Pac. 1%; unknown 0%

Florida A&M University[1]
201 Beggs Avenue
Orlando, FL 32801
law.famu.edu/
Public
Admissions: (407) 254-3263
Email: famulaw.admissions@famu.edu
Financial aid: N/A
Tuition: N/A

Room/board/expenses: N/A
Enrollment: N/A

Florida Coastal School of Law
8787 Baypine Road
Jacksonville, FL 32256
www.fcsl.edu
Private
Admissions: (904) 680-7710
Email: admissions@fcsl.edu
Financial aid: (904) 680-7717
Application deadline: rolling
Tuition: full time: $42,906; part time: $34,778
Room/board/expenses: $18,396
Median grant: $12,500
Average student indebtedness at graduation: $162,785
Enrollment: full time: 924; part time: 191
men: 44%; women: 56%; minorities: 44%
Acceptance rate (full time): 79%
Midrange LSAT (full time): 140-147
Midrange undergraduate GPA (full time): 2.64-3.20
Midrange of full-time private-sector salaries of 2013 grads: $36,000-$54,000
2013 grads employed in: law firms: 50%; business and industry: 18%; government: 12%; public interest: 13%; judicial clerk: 3%; academia: 4%; unknown: 0%
Employment location for 2013 class: Intl. N/A; N.E. %; M.A. 5%; E.N.C. 3%; W.N.C. 2%; S.A. 80%; E.S.C. 1%; W.S.C. 3%; Mt. 3%; Pac. 2%; unknown 0%

Florida International University
Modesto A. Maidique Campus
RDB 2015
Miami, FL 33199
law.fiu.edu
Public
Admissions: (305) 348-8006
Email: lawadmit@fiu.edu
Financial aid: (305) 348-8006
Application deadline: 05/31
In-state tuition: full time: $21,345; part time: 14,460
Out-of-state tuition: full time: $35,590
Room/board/expenses: $27,588
Median grant: $5,000
Average student indebtedness at graduation: $89,815
Enrollment: full time: 356; part time: 131
men: 47%; women: 53%; minorities: 63%
Acceptance rate (full time): 29%
Midrange LSAT (full time): 151-158
Midrange undergraduate GPA (full time): 3.17-3.79
Midrange of full-time private-sector salaries of 2013 grads: N/A-N/A
2013 grads employed in: law firms: 59%; business and industry: 18%; government: 14%; public interest: 5%; judicial clerk: 1%; academia: 3%; unknown: 0%
Employment location for 2013 class: Intl. N/A; N.E. %; M.A. 1%; E.N.C. 1%; W.N.C. N/A; S.A. 96%; E.S.C. 0%; W.S.C. 0%; Mt. 1%; Pac. 1%; unknown 0%

Florida State University
425 W. Jefferson Street
Tallahassee, FL 32306-1601
www.law.fsu.edu
Public
Admissions: (850) 644-3787
Email: admissions@law.fsu.edu
Financial aid: (850) 644-5716
Application deadline: 05/01
In-state tuition: full time: $20,683; part time: N/A
Out-of-state tuition: full time: $40,695
Room/board/expenses: $17,700
Median grant: $5,000
Average student indebtedness at graduation: $80,375
Enrollment: full time: 614; part time: 30
men: 57%; women: 43%; minorities: 24%
Acceptance rate (full time): 41%
Midrange LSAT (full time): 156-161
Midrange undergraduate GPA (full time): 3.22-3.64
Midrange of full-time private-sector salaries of 2013 grads: $50,000-$80,000
2013 grads employed in: law firms: 44%; business and industry: 15%; government: 29%; public interest: 3%; judicial clerk: 6%; academia: 2%; unknown: 0%
Employment location for 2013 class: Intl. N/A; N.E. %; M.A. 2%; E.N.C. 1%; W.N.C. 2%; S.A. 90%; E.S.C. 1%; W.S.C. 1%; Mt. 1%; Pac. 0%; unknown 0%

Nova Southeastern University (Broad)
3305 College Avenue
Fort Lauderdale, FL 33314-7721
www.nsulaw.nova.edu/
Private
Admissions: (954) 262-6117
Email: admission@nsu.law.nova.edu
Financial aid: (954) 262-7412
Application deadline: 05/01
Tuition: full time: $36,906; part time: $27,912
Room/board/expenses: $26,017
Median grant: $10,000
Average student indebtedness at graduation: $136,450
Enrollment: full time: 618; part time: 191
men: 45%; women: 55%; minorities: 48%
Acceptance rate (full time): 56%
Midrange LSAT (full time): 147-151
Midrange undergraduate GPA (full time): 2.84-3.40
Midrange of full-time private-sector salaries of 2013 grads: $50,000-$65,000
2013 grads employed in: law firms: 64%; business and industry: 17%; government: 9%; public interest: 7%; judicial clerk: 2%; academia: 2%; unknown: 0%
Employment location for 2013 class: Intl. N/A; N.E. %; M.A. 3%; E.N.C. 0%; W.N.C. 1%; S.A. 92%; E.S.C. 0%; W.S.C. 1%; Mt. 0%; Pac. 0%; unknown 0%

Stetson University
1401 61st Street S
Gulfport, FL 33707
www.law.stetson.edu
Private
Admissions: (727) 562-7802
Email: lawadmit@law.stetson.edu
Financial aid: (727) 562-7813

Application deadline: 05/15
Tuition: full time: $38,904; part time: $26,960
Room/board/expenses: $15,588
Median grant: $10,000
Average student indebtedness at graduation: $148,394
Enrollment: full time: 667; part time: 198
men: 50%; women: 50%; minorities: 23%
Acceptance rate (full time): 52%
Midrange LSAT (full time): 152-157
Midrange undergraduate GPA (full time): 2.98-3.52
Midrange of full-time private-sector salaries of 2013 grads: $45,000-$75,000
2013 grads employed in: law firms: 53%; business and industry: 15%; government: 25%; public interest: 5%; judicial clerk: 1%; academia: 1%; unknown: 0%
Employment location for 2013 class: Intl. N/A; N.E. %; M.A. 2%; E.N.C. 1%; W.N.C. 1%; S.A. 92%; E.S.C. 1%; W.S.C. 1%; Mt. 0%; Pac. 2%; unknown 0%

St. Thomas University
16401 N.W. 37th Avenue
Miami Gardens, FL 33054
www.stu.edu
Private
Admissions: (305) 623-2310
Email: admitme@stu.edu
Financial aid: (305) 474-2409
Application deadline: 05/01
Tuition: full time: $38,458; part time: N/A
Room/board/expenses: $26,624
Median grant: $10,000
Average student indebtedness at graduation: $140,808
Enrollment: full time: 643; part time: N/A
men: 45%; women: 55%; minorities: 77%
Acceptance rate (full time): 63%
Midrange LSAT (full time): 144-151
Midrange undergraduate GPA (full time): 2.71-3.36
Midrange of full-time private-sector salaries of 2013 grads: $40,000-$60,000
2013 grads employed in: law firms: 60%; business and industry: 18%; government: 19%; public interest: 1%; judicial clerk: 1%; academia: 2%; unknown: 0%
Employment location for 2013 class: Intl. N/A; N.E. %; M.A. 6%; E.N.C. 1%; W.N.C. 0%; S.A. 88%; E.S.C. 1%; W.S.C. 1%; Mt. 1%; Pac. 1%; unknown 0%

University of Florida (Levin)
PO Box 117620
Gainesville, FL 32611-7620
www.law.ufl.edu
Public
Admissions: (352) 273-0890
Email: admissions@law.ufl.edu
Financial aid: (352) 273-0628
Application deadline: 03/15
In-state tuition: full time: $22,230; part time: N/A
Out-of-state tuition: full time: $38,830
Room/board/expenses: $16,170
Median grant: $7,500
Average student indebtedness at graduation: $82,410
Enrollment: full time: 944; part time: N/A
men: 58%; women: 42%; minorities: 30%

Acceptance rate (full time): 61%
Midrange LSAT (full time): 155-161
Midrange undergraduate GPA (full time): 3.26-3.68
Midrange of full-time private-sector salaries of 2013 grads: $52,500-$95,000
2013 grads employed in: law firms: 58%; business and industry: 10%; government: 18%; public interest: 4%; judicial clerk: 6%; academia: 4%; unknown: 0%
Employment location for 2013 class: Intl. N/A; N.E. %; M.A. 2%; E.N.C. 0%; W.N.C. 1%; S.A. 92%; E.S.C. 1%; W.S.C. 1%; Mt. 0%; Pac. 2%; unknown 0%

University of Miami
PO Box 248087
Coral Gables, FL 33124-8087
www.law.miami.edu
Private
Admissions: (305) 284-2795
Email: admissions@law.miami.edu
Financial aid: (305) 284-3115
Application deadline: 07/31
Tuition: full time: $46,166; part time: $1,615/credit hour
Room/board/expenses: $26,350
Median grant: $22,333
Average student indebtedness at graduation: $143,845
Enrollment: full time: 972; part time: 39
men: 53%; women: 47%; minorities: 38%
Acceptance rate (full time): 51%
Midrange LSAT (full time): 155-160
Midrange undergraduate GPA (full time): 3.19-3.63
Midrange of full-time private-sector salaries of 2013 grads: $51,929-$89,368
2013 grads employed in: law firms: 58%; business and industry: 24%; government: 11%; public interest: 4%; judicial clerk: 2%; academia: 1%; unknown: 0%
Employment location for 2013 class: Intl. N/A; N.E. %; M.A. 5%; E.N.C. 4%; W.N.C. 0%; S.A. 83%; E.S.C. 2%; W.S.C. 1%; Mt. 1%; Pac. 1%; unknown 0%

GEORGIA

Atlanta's John Marshall Law School[1]
1422 W. Peachtree Street, NW
Atlanta, GA 30309
www.johnmarshall.edu
Private
Admissions: (404) 872-3593
Email: admissions@johnmarshall.edu
Financial aid: N/A
Tuition: N/A
Room/board/expenses: N/A
Enrollment: N/A

Emory University
1301 Clifton Road
Atlanta, GA 30322-2770
www.law.emory.edu
Private
Admissions: (404) 727-6802
Email: lawinfo@law.emory.edu
Financial aid: (404) 727-6039
Application deadline: 03/01
Tuition: full time: $49,734; part time: N/A
Room/board/expenses: $25,982
Median grant: $20,000
Average student indebtedness at graduation: $108,690

Enrollment: full time: 819; part time: N/A
men: 50%; women: 50%; minorities: 30%
Acceptance rate (full time): 37%
Midrange LSAT (full time): 158-166
Midrange undergraduate GPA (full time): 3.30-3.85
Midrange of full-time private-sector salaries of 2013 grads: $88,125-$157,500
2013 grads employed in: law firms: 48%; business and industry: 15%; government: 15%; public interest: 5%; judicial clerk: 8%; academia: 8%; unknown: 0%
Employment location for 2013 class: Intl. N/A; N.E. %; M.A. 15%; E.N.C. 4%; W.N.C. 0%; S.A. 66%; E.S.C. 3%; W.S.C. 2%; Mt. 0%; Pac. 6%; unknown 0%

Georgia State University
PO Box 4049
Atlanta, GA 30302-4049
law.gsu.edu
Public
Admissions: (404) 651-2048
Email: admissions@gsulaw.gsu.edu
Financial aid: (404) 651-2227
Application deadline: 03/15
In-state tuition: full time: $16,378; part time: $12,844
Out-of-state tuition: full time: $35,986
Room/board/expenses: $15,438
Median grant: $7,500
Average student indebtedness at graduation: $69,822
Enrollment: full time: 140; part time: 46
men: 53%; women: 47%; minorities: 24%
Acceptance rate (full time): 29%
Midrange LSAT (full time): 156-161
Midrange undergraduate GPA (full time): 3.12-3.60
Midrange of full-time private-sector salaries of 2013 grads: $55,000-$90,000
2013 grads employed in: law firms: 51%; business and industry: 19%; government: 15%; public interest: 4%; judicial clerk: 7%; academia: 4%; unknown: 0%
Employment location for 2013 class: Intl. N/A; N.E. %; M.A. 2%; E.N.C. 1%; W.N.C. 0%; S.A. 92%; E.S.C. 2%; W.S.C. 1%; Mt. 1%; Pac. 1%; unknown 0%

Mercer University (George)
1021 Georgia Avenue
Macon, GA 31207-0001
www.law.mercer.edu
Private
Admissions: (478) 301-2605
Email: admissions@law.mercer.edu
Financial aid: (478) 301-5902
Application deadline: 03/15
Tuition: full time: $37,260; part time: N/A
Room/board/expenses: $20,540
Median grant: $12,000
Average student indebtedness at graduation: $125,301
Enrollment: full time: 427; part time: 1
men: 49%; women: 51%; minorities: 25%
Acceptance rate (full time): 61%
Midrange LSAT (full time): 147-155
Midrange undergraduate GPA (full time): 3.05-3.50

Midrange of full-time private-sector salaries of 2013 grads: $50,000-$70,000
2013 grads employed in: law firms: 59%; business and industry: 12%; government: 13%; public interest: 3%; judicial clerk: 10%; academia: 2%; unknown: 0%
Employment location for 2013 class: Intl. N/A; N.E. %; M.A. 0%; E.N.C. 1%; W.N.C. 0%; S.A. 91%; E.S.C. 5%; W.S.C. 2%; Mt. 1%; Pac. 1%; unknown 0%

University of Georgia
Herty Drive
Athens, GA 30602
www.law.uga.edu
Public
Admissions: (706) 542-7060
Email: ugajd@uga.edu
Financial aid: (706) 542-6147
Application deadline: 06/01
In-state tuition: full time: $19,140; part time: N/A
Out-of-state tuition: full time: $36,810
Room/board/expenses: $16,000
Median grant: $5,000
Average student indebtedness at graduation: $88,825
Enrollment: full time: 583; part time: N/A
men: 55%; women: 45%; minorities: 19%
Acceptance rate (full time): 31%
Midrange LSAT (full time): 158-164
Midrange undergraduate GPA (full time): 3.42-3.80
Midrange of full-time private-sector salaries of 2013 grads: $60,000-$130,000
2013 grads employed in: law firms: 49%; business and industry: 17%; government: 9%; public interest: 7%; judicial clerk: 17%; academia: 3%; unknown: 0%
Employment location for 2013 class: Intl. N/A; N.E. %; M.A. 2%; E.N.C. 1%; W.N.C. 1%; S.A. 92%; E.S.C. 2%; W.S.C. 1%; Mt. 1%; Pac. 1%; unknown 0%

HAWAII

University of Hawaii-Manoa (Richardson)
2515 Dole Street
Honolulu, HI 96822-2328
www.law.hawaii.edu/
Public
Admissions: (808) 956-5557
Email: lawadm@hawaii.edu
Financial aid: (808) 956-7966
Application deadline: 02/02
In-state tuition: full time: $19,464; part time: $811/credit hour
Out-of-state tuition: full time: $39,192
Room/board/expenses: $16,212
Median grant: $4,000
Average student indebtedness at graduation: $56,266
Enrollment: full time: 257; part time: 68
men: 46%; women: 54%; minorities: 65%
Acceptance rate (full time): 37%
Midrange LSAT (full time): 153-159
Midrange undergraduate GPA (full time): 3.11-3.62
Midrange of full-time private-sector salaries of 2013 grads: $41,616-$74,750

2013 grads employed in: law firms: 30%; business and industry: 9%; government: 23%; public interest: 8%; judicial clerk: 29%; academia: 2%; unknown: 0%
Employment location for 2013 class: Intl. N/A; N.E. N/A; M.A. N/A; E.N.C. N/A; W.N.C. N/A; S.A. N/A; E.S.C. N/A; W.S.C. N/A; Mt. N/A; Pac. N/A; unknown N/A

IDAHO

University of Idaho
875 Perimeter Drive MS2321
Moscow, ID 83844-2321
www.uidaho.edu/law/admissions
Public
Admissions: (208) 885-2300
Email: lawadmit@uidaho.edu
Financial aid: (208) 885-6312
Application deadline: 03/15
In-state tuition: full time: $16,480; part time: N/A
Out-of-state tuition: full time: $30,010
Room/board/expenses: $15,816
Median grant: $7,000
Average student indebtedness at graduation: $92,732
Enrollment: full time: 351; part time: 2
men: 60%; women: 40%; minorities: 18%
Acceptance rate (full time): 61%
Midrange LSAT (full time): 158-164
Midrange undergraduate GPA (full time): 3.42-3.80
Midrange of full-time private-sector salaries of 2013 grads: $40,000-$62,000
2013 grads employed in: law firms: 45%; business and industry: 19%; government: 16%; public interest: 2%; judicial clerk: 16%; academia: 1%; unknown: 2%
Employment location for 2013 class: Intl. N/A; N.E. %; M.A. 0%; E.N.C. 1%; W.N.C. 2%; S.A. 5%; E.S.C. 1%; W.S.C. 1%; Mt. 69%; Pac. 20%; unknown 0%

ILLINOIS

DePaul University
25 E. Jackson Boulevard
Chicago, IL 60604
www.law.depaul.edu
Private
Admissions: (312) 362-6831
Email: lawinfo@depaul.edu
Financial aid: (312) 362-8091
Application deadline: 03/01
Tuition: full time: $44,999; part time: $29,414
Room/board/expenses: $20,932
Median grant: $15,000
Average student indebtedness at graduation: $125,895
Enrollment: full time: 642; part time: 120
men: 43%; women: 57%; minorities: 24%
Acceptance rate (full time): 67%
Midrange LSAT (full time): 149-155
Midrange undergraduate GPA (full time): 2.98-3.57
Midrange of full-time private-sector salaries of 2013 grads: $50,000-$80,000
2013 grads employed in: law firms: 50%; business and industry: 27%; government: 10%; public interest: 7%; judicial clerk: 3%; academia: 3%; unknown: 0%
Employment location for 2013 class: Intl. N/A; N.E. %; M.A. 2%; E.N.C. 88%; W.N.C. 1%; S.A. 3%; E.S.C. 2%; W.S.C. 1%; Mt. 1%; Pac. 1%; unknown 0%

Illinois Institute of Technology (Chicago-Kent)
565 W. Adams Street
Chicago, IL 60661-3691
www.kentlaw.iit.edu/
Private
Admissions: (312) 906-5020
Email: admissions@kentlaw.iit.edu
Financial aid: (312) 906-5180
Application deadline: 03/15
Tuition: full time: $45,472; part time: $33,220
Room/board/expenses: $19,454
Median grant: $20,000
Average student indebtedness at graduation: $119,884
Enrollment: full time: 692; part time: 107
men: 53%; women: 47%; minorities: 28%
Acceptance rate (full time): 64%
Midrange LSAT (full time): 152-159
Midrange undergraduate GPA (full time): 3.20-3.62
Midrange of full-time private-sector salaries of 2013 grads: $55,000-$107,000
2013 grads employed in: law firms: 62%; business and industry: 24%; government: 8%; public interest: 3%; judicial clerk: 3%; academia: 0%; unknown: 0%
Employment location for 2013 class: Intl. N/A; N.E. %; M.A. 2%; E.N.C. 89%; W.N.C. 3%; S.A. 2%; E.S.C. 0%; W.S.C. 1%; Mt. 1%; Pac. 1%; unknown 0%

The John Marshall Law School
315 S. Plymouth Court
Chicago, IL 60604
www.jmls.edu
Private
Admissions: (800) 537-4280
Email: admission@jmls.edu
Financial aid: (800) 537-4280
Application deadline: 04/01
Tuition: full time: $45,074; part time: $31,619
Room/board/expenses: $26,814
Median grant: $10,000
Average student indebtedness at graduation: $143,518
Enrollment: full time: 835; part time: 303
men: 50%; women: 50%; minorities: 30%
Acceptance rate (full time): 75%
Midrange LSAT (full time): 146-151
Midrange undergraduate GPA (full time): 2.80-3.35
Midrange of full-time private-sector salaries of 2013 grads: $45,000-$70,000
2013 grads employed in: law firms: 63%; business and industry: 17%; government: 14%; public interest: 2%; judicial clerk: 2%; academia: 2%; unknown: %
Employment location for 2013 class: Intl. N/A; N.E. %; M.A. 1%; E.N.C. 90%; W.N.C. 2%; S.A. 3%; E.S.C. 1%; W.S.C. 1%; Mt. 1%; Pac. 1%; unknown 0%

Loyola University Chicago
25 E. Pearson Street
Chicago, IL 60611
www.luc.edu/law/
Private
Admissions: (312) 915-7170
Email: law-admissions@luc.edu
Financial aid: (312) 915-7170
Application deadline: 03/01

Tuition: full time: $44,180; part time: $33,360
Room/board/expenses: $23,386
Median grant: $12,000
Average student indebtedness at graduation: $134,968
Enrollment: full time: 656; part time: 68
men: 47%; women: 53%; minorities: 27%
Acceptance rate (full time): 53%
Midrange LSAT (full time): 155-159
Midrange undergraduate GPA (full time): 3.06-3.52
Midrange of full-time private-sector salaries of 2013 grads: $50,000-$120,000
2013 grads employed in: law firms: 53%; business and industry: 25%; government: 9%; public interest: 7%; judicial clerk: 4%; academia: 1%; unknown: 0%
Employment location for 2013 class: Intl. N/A; N.E. %; M.A. 2%; E.N.C. 86%; W.N.C. 1%; S.A. 5%; E.S.C. 1%; W.S.C. 0%; Mt. 1%; Pac. 3%; unknown 0%

Northern Illinois University
Swen Parson Hall, Room 276
De Kalb, IL 60115
niu.edu/law
Public
Admissions: (815) 753-8595
Email: lawadm@niu.edu
Financial aid: (815) 753-8595
Application deadline: 04/01
In-state tuition: full time: $21,764; part time: $1,005/credit hour
Out-of-state tuition: full time: $37,700
Room/board/expenses: $18,800
Median grant: $7,812
Average student indebtedness at graduation: $77,182
Enrollment: full time: 265; part time: 12
men: 53%; women: 47%; minorities: 26%
Acceptance rate (full time): 72%
Midrange LSAT (full time): 146-153
Midrange undergraduate GPA (full time): 2.83-3.37
Midrange of full-time private-sector salaries of 2013 grads: $42,000-$55,000
2013 grads employed in: law firms: 62%; business and industry: 16%; government: 18%; public interest: 1%; judicial clerk: 0%; academia: 2%; unknown 0%
Employment location for 2013 class: Intl. N/A; N.E. %; M.A. N/A; E.N.C. 84%; W.N.C. 1%; S.A. 1%; E.S.C. N/A; W.S.C. N/A; Mt. 2%; Pac. 1%; unknown 10%

Northwestern University
375 E. Chicago Avenue
Chicago, IL 60611
www.law.northwestern.edu
Private
Admissions: (312) 503-8465
Email: admissions@law.northwestern.edu
Financial aid: (312) 503-8465
Application deadline: 02/15
Tuition: full time: $56,434; part time: N/A
Room/board/expenses: $21,680
Median grant: $20,000
Average student indebtedness at graduation: $163,065

Enrollment: full time: 737; part time: N/A
men: 53%; women: 47%; minorities: 33%
Acceptance rate (full time): 25%
Midrange LSAT (full time): 162-170
Midrange undergraduate GPA (full time): 3.53-3.83
Midrange of full-time private-sector salaries of 2013 grads: $145,000-$160,000
2013 grads employed in: law firms: 65%; business and industry: 15%; government: 4%; public interest: 5%; judicial clerk: 10%; academia: 0%; unknown: 0%
Employment location for 2013 class: Intl. N/A; N.E. %; M.A. 24%; E.N.C. 41%; W.N.C. 2%; S.A. 8%; E.S.C. 1%; W.S.C. 4%; Mt. 2%; Pac. 16%; unknown 0%

Southern Illinois University-Carbondale
Lesar Law Building
Carbondale, IL 62901
www.law.siu.edu
Public
Admissions: (800) 739-9187
Email: lawadmit@siu.edu
Financial aid: (618) 453-4334
Application deadline: rolling
In-state tuition: full time: $18,153; part time: N/A
Out-of-state tuition: full time: $40,803
Room/board/expenses: $17,155
Median grant: $5,500
Enrollment: full time: 348; part time: 1
men: 60%; women: 40%; minorities: 20%
Acceptance rate (full time): 85%
Midrange LSAT (full time): 144-151
Midrange undergraduate GPA (full time): 2.71-3.45
Midrange of full-time private-sector salaries of 2013 grads: $45,000-$60,000
2013 grads employed in: law firms: 60%; business and industry: 11%; government: 18%; public interest: 3%; judicial clerk: 3%; academia: 0%; unknown: 4%
Employment location for 2013 class: Intl. N/A; N.E. %; M.A. 1%; E.N.C. 64%; W.N.C. 15%; S.A. 4%; E.S.C. 6%; W.S.C. 0%; Mt. 6%; Pac. 3%; unknown 0%

University of Chicago
1111 E. 60th Street
Chicago, IL 60637
www.law.uchicago.edu
Private
Admissions: (773) 702-9484
Email: admissions@law.uchicago.edu
Financial aid: (773) 702-9484
Application deadline: 02/01
Tuition: full time: $55,503; part time: N/A
Room/board/expenses: $23,634
Median grant: $15,000
Average student indebtedness at graduation: $144,695
Enrollment: full time: 604; part time: N/A
men: 57%; women: 43%; minorities: 28%
Acceptance rate (full time): 18%
Midrange LSAT (full time): 166-172
Midrange undergraduate GPA (full time): 3.79-3.96
Midrange of full-time private-sector salaries of 2013 grads: $160,000-$160,000

2013 grads employed in: law firms: 69%; business and industry: 4%; government: 6%; public interest: 6%; judicial clerk: 13%; academia: 2%; unknown: 0%
Employment location for 2013 class: Intl. N/A; N.E. %; M.A. 17%; E.N.C. 35%; W.N.C. 3%; S.A. 13%; E.S.C. 2%; W.S.C. 6%; Mt. 1%; Pac. 20%; unknown 0%

University of Illinois-Urbana-Champaign
504 E. Pennsylvania Avenue
Champaign, IL 61820
www.law.illinois.edu
Public
Admissions: (217) 244-6415
Email: law-admissions@illinois.edu
Financial aid: (217) 244-6415
Application deadline: 03/15
In-state tuition: full time: $41,294; part time: N/A
Out-of-state tuition: full time: $49,044
Room/board/expenses: $17,701
Median grant: $18,550
Average student indebtedness at graduation: $89,852
Enrollment: full time: 510; part time: N/A
men: 58%; women: 42%; minorities: 31%
Acceptance rate (full time): 42%
Midrange LSAT (full time): 158-163
Midrange undergraduate GPA (full time): 3.15-3.63
Midrange of full-time private-sector salaries of 2013 grads: $60,000-$160,000
2013 grads employed in: law firms: 60%; business and industry: 9%; government: 15%; public interest: 6%; judicial clerk: 6%; academia: 5%; unknown: 0%
Employment location for 2013 class: Intl. N/A; N.E. %; M.A. 8%; E.N.C. 74%; W.N.C. 3%; S.A. 5%; E.S.C. 1%; W.S.C. 2%; Mt. 3%; Pac. 4%; unknown 0%

INDIANA

Indiana University-Bloomington (Maurer)
211 S. Indiana Avenue
Bloomington, IN 47405-1001
www.law.indiana.edu
Public
Admissions: (812) 855-4765
Email: lawadmis@indiana.edu
Financial aid: (812) 855-7746
Application deadline: rolling
In-state tuition: full time: $31,121; part time: N/A
Out-of-state tuition: full time: $49,927
Room/board/expenses: $19,784
Median grant: $24,936
Average student indebtedness at graduation: $89,785
Enrollment: full time: 586; part time: N/A
men: 55%; women: 45%; minorities: 22%
Acceptance rate (full time): 62%
Midrange LSAT (full time): 154-163
Midrange undergraduate GPA (full time): 3.30-3.88
Midrange of full-time private-sector salaries of 2013 grads: $70,000-$120,000
2013 grads employed in: law firms: 44%; business and industry: 20%; government: 16%; public interest: 5%; judicial clerk: 11%; academia: 3%; unknown: 0%

Employment location for 2013 class: Intl. N/A; N.E. %; M.A. 5%; E.N.C. 59%; W.N.C. 5%; S.A. 11%; E.S.C. 3%; W.S.C. 6%; Mt. 1%; Pac. 6%; unknown 0%

Indiana University-Indianapolis (McKinney)
530 W. New York Street
Indianapolis, IN 46202-3225
mckinneylaw.iu.edu
Public
Admissions: (317) 274-2459
Email: pkkinney@iupui.edu
Financial aid: (317) 278-2880
Application deadline: 07/31
In-state tuition: full time: $24,892; part time: $18,927
Out-of-state tuition: full time: $45,193
Room/board/expenses: $16,076
Median grant: $13,000
Average student indebtedness at graduation: $96,651
Enrollment: full time: 531; part time: 326
men: 54%; women: 46%; minorities: 16%
Acceptance rate (full time): 75%
Midrange LSAT (full time): 148-155
Midrange undergraduate GPA (full time): 3.09-3.61
Midrange of full-time private-sector salaries of 2013 grads: $60,750-$103,750
2013 grads employed in: law firms: 45%; business and industry: 23%; government: 20%; public interest: 2%; judicial clerk: 4%; academia: 5%; unknown: 0%
Employment location for 2013 class: Intl. N/A; N.E. %; M.A. 1%; E.N.C. 91%; W.N.C. 0%; S.A. 1%; E.S.C. 2%; W.S.C. 0%; Mt. 1%; Pac. 1%; unknown 1%

University of Notre Dame
PO Box 780
Notre Dame, IN 46556-0780
law.nd.edu
Private
Admissions: (574) 631-6626
Email: lawadmit@nd.edu
Financial aid: (574) 631-6626
Application deadline: 03/15
Tuition: full time: $50,520; part time: N/A
Room/board/expenses: $19,410
Median grant: $18,000
Average student indebtedness at graduation: $111,310
Enrollment: full time: 549; part time: N/A
men: 58%; women: 42%; minorities: 23%
Acceptance rate (full time): 37%
Midrange LSAT (full time): 160-165
Midrange undergraduate GPA (full time): 3.44-3.78
Midrange of full-time private-sector salaries of 2013 grads: $75,000-$160,000
2013 grads employed in: law firms: 58%; business and industry: 11%; government: 16%; public interest: 3%; judicial clerk: 11%; academia: 1%; unknown: 0%
Employment location for 2013 class: Intl. N/A; N.E. %; M.A. 10%; E.N.C. 35%; W.N.C. 3%; S.A. 19%; E.S.C. 2%; W.S.C. 8%; Mt. 8%; Pac. 9%; unknown 0%

Valparaiso University
656 S. Greenwich Street
Wesemann Hall
Valparaiso, IN 46383
www.valpo.edu/law
Private
Admissions: (219) 465-7821
Email: law.admissions@valpo.edu
Financial aid: (219) 465-7818
Application deadline: 07/15
Tuition: full time: $39,612; part time: $1,520/credit hour
Room/board/expenses: $12,350
Median grant: $19,370
Average student indebtedness at graduation: $132,010
Enrollment: full time: 448; part time: 24
men: 50%; women: 50%; minorities: 38%
Acceptance rate (full time): 77%
Midrange LSAT (full time): 142-150
Midrange undergraduate GPA (full time): 2.80-3.37
Midrange of full-time private-sector salaries of 2013 grads: $40,000-$55,000
2013 grads employed in: law firms: 50%; business and industry: 19%; government: 19%; public interest: 1%; judicial clerk: 5%; academia: 7%; unknown: 0%
Employment location for 2013 class: Intl. N/A; N.E. %; M.A. 0%; E.N.C. 84%; W.N.C. 1%; S.A. 9%; E.S.C. 1%; W.S.C. 0%; Mt. 2%; Pac. 2%; unknown 0%

IOWA

Drake University
2507 University Avenue
Des Moines, IA 50311
www.law.drake.edu/
Private
Admissions: (515) 271-2782
Email: lawadmit@drake.edu
Financial aid: (515) 271-2782
Application deadline: 04/01
Tuition: full time: $38,106; part time: $1,310/credit hour
Room/board/expenses: $20,040
Median grant: $18,275
Average student indebtedness at graduation: $108,857
Enrollment: full time: 325; part time: 8
men: 54%; women: 46%; minorities: 8%
Acceptance rate (full time): 78%
Midrange LSAT (full time): 148-156
Midrange undergraduate GPA (full time): 2.97-3.53
Midrange of full-time private-sector salaries of 2013 grads: $50,000-$84,500
2013 grads employed in: law firms: 52%; business and industry: 29%; government: 7%; public interest: 3%; judicial clerk: 6%; academia: 4%; unknown: 0%
Employment location for 2013 class: Intl. N/A; N.E. %; M.A. 1%; E.N.C. 2%; W.N.C. 84%; S.A. 2%; E.S.C. 1%; W.S.C. 2%; Mt. 5%; Pac. 1%; unknown 0%

University of Iowa
320 Melrose Avenue
Iowa City, IA 52242
www.law.uiowa.edu
Public
Admissions: (319) 335-9095
Email: law-admissions@uiowa.edu
Financial aid: (319) 335-9142
Application deadline: 04/01

In-state tuition: full time: $23,760; part time: N/A
Out-of-state tuition: full time: $41,296
Room/board/expenses: $16,892
Median grant: $23,453
Average student indebtedness at graduation: $92,373
Enrollment: full time: 388; part time: 2
men: 56%; women: 44%; minorities: 17%
Acceptance rate (full time): 41%
Midrange LSAT (full time): 157-162
Midrange undergraduate GPA (full time): 3.51-3.77
Midrange of full-time private-sector salaries of 2013 grads: $55,000-$117,500
2013 grads employed in: law firms: 49%; business and industry: 18%; government: 8%; public interest: 5%; judicial clerk: 19%; academia: 1%; unknown: 0%
Employment location for 2013 class: Intl. N/A; N.E. %; M.A. 1%; E.N.C. 17%; W.N.C. 58%; S.A. 6%; E.S.C. 1%; W.S.C. 4%; Mt. 5%; Pac. 3%; unknown 0%

KANSAS

University of Kansas
Green Hall
1535 W. 15th Street
Lawrence, KS 66045-7608
www.law.ku.edu
Public
Admissions: (866) 220-3654
Email: admitlaw@ku.edu
Financial aid: (785) 864-4700
Application deadline: 04/01
In-state tuition: full time: $19,985; part time: N/A
Out-of-state tuition: full time: $34,089
Room/board/expenses: $16,994
Median grant: $5,600
Average student indebtedness at graduation: $74,890
Enrollment: full time: 376; part time: N/A
men: 58%; women: 42%; minorities: 14%
Acceptance rate (full time): 57%
Midrange LSAT (full time): 153-161
Midrange undergraduate GPA (full time): 3.20-3.69
Midrange of full-time private-sector salaries of 2013 grads: $52,250-$105,000
2013 grads employed in: law firms: 57%; business and industry: 19%; government: 11%; public interest: 4%; judicial clerk: 4%; academia: 3%; unknown: 0%
Employment location for 2013 class: Intl. N/A; N.E. %; M.A. 3%; E.N.C. 1%; W.N.C. 76%; S.A. 3%; E.S.C. 1%; W.S.C. 3%; Mt. 6%; Pac. 4%; unknown 0%

Washburn University
1700 S.W. College Avenue
Topeka, KS 66621
washburnlaw.edu
Public
Admissions: (785) 670-1185
Email: admissions@washburnlaw.edu
Financial aid: (785) 670-1151
Application deadline: 04/01
In-state tuition: full time: $19,094; part time: N/A
Out-of-state tuition: full time: $29,766
Room/board/expenses: $15,299
Median grant: $14,392

Average student indebtedness at graduation: $83,396
Enrollment: full time: 323; part time: N/A
men: 64%; women: 36%; minorities: 14%
Acceptance rate (full time): 64%
Midrange LSAT (full time): 148-156
Midrange undergraduate GPA (full time): 2.96-3.62
Midrange of full-time private-sector salaries of 2013 grads: $44,500-$69,250
2013 grads employed in: law firms: 48%; business and industry: 11%; government: 18%; public interest: 2%; judicial clerk: 4%; academia: 1%; unknown: 0%
Employment location for 2013 class: Intl. N/A; N.E. %; M.A. 2%; E.N.C. 5%; W.N.C. 0%; S.A. 10%; E.S.C. 76%; W.S.C. 1%; Mt. 2%; Pac. 2%; unknown 0%

KENTUCKY

Northern Kentucky University (Chase)
Nunn Hall
Highland Heights, KY 41099-6031
chaselaw.nku.edu
Public
Admissions: (859) 572-5841
Email: chaseadmissions@nku.edu
Financial aid: (859) 572-6437
Application deadline: 06/01
In-state tuition: full time: $17,414; part time: $12,094
Out-of-state tuition: full time: $27,944
Room/board/expenses: $13,934
Median grant: $12,000
Average student indebtedness at graduation: $82,989
Enrollment: full time: 287; part time: 136
men: 59%; women: 41%; minorities: 11%
Acceptance rate (full time): 73%
Midrange LSAT (full time): 147-155
Midrange undergraduate GPA (full time): 2.93-3.43
Midrange of full-time private-sector salaries of 2013 grads: $40,000-$62,000
2013 grads employed in: law firms: 46%; business and industry: 30%; government: 12%; public interest: 5%; judicial clerk: 5%; academia: 2%; unknown: 0%
Employment location for 2013 class: Intl. N/A; N.E. %; M.A. 1%; E.N.C. 54%; W.N.C. 0%; S.A. 3%; E.S.C. 40%; W.S.C. 0%; Mt. 1%; Pac. 0%; unknown 1%

University of Kentucky
209 Law Building
Lexington, KY 40506-0048
www.law.uky.edu
Public
Admissions: (859) 218-1699
Email: uklawadmissions@uky.edu
Financial aid: (859) 257-3172
Application deadline: 03/15
In-state tuition: full time: $20,988; part time: N/A
Out-of-state tuition: full time: $38,508
Room/board/expenses: $14,912
Median grant: $6,000
Average student indebtedness at graduation: $76,746
Enrollment: full time: 388; part time: N/A
men: 57%; women: 43%; minorities: 9%

Acceptance rate (full time): 59%
Midrange LSAT (full time): 152-158
Midrange undergraduate GPA (full time): 3.22-3.71
Midrange of full-time private-sector salaries of 2013 grads: $47,500-$86,500
2013 grads employed in: law firms: 49%; business and industry: 11%; government: 13%; public interest: 4%; judicial clerk: 20%; academia: 2%; unknown: 0%
Employment location for 2013 class: Intl. N/A; N.E. %; M.A. 2%; E.N.C. 5%; W.N.C. 0%; S.A. 10%; E.S.C. 76%; W.S.C. 1%; Mt. 2%; Pac. 2%; unknown 0%

University of Louisville (Brandeis)
2301 S. Third Street
Louisville, KY 40292
www.law.louisville.edu
Public
Admissions: (502) 852-6365
Email: lawadmissions@louisville.edu
Financial aid: (502) 852-6391
Application deadline: 04/15
In-state tuition: full time: $19,702; part time: $15,049
Out-of-state tuition: full time: $36,538
Room/board/expenses: $18,464
Median grant: $10,000
Average student indebtedness at graduation: $90,195
Enrollment: full time: 336; part time: 15
men: 53%; women: 47%; minorities: 11%
Acceptance rate (full time): 72%
Midrange LSAT (full time): 150-157
Midrange undergraduate GPA (full time): 3.16-3.61
Midrange of full-time private-sector salaries of 2013 grads: $45,000-$70,000
2013 grads employed in: law firms: 54%; business and industry: 19%; government: 12%; public interest: 7%; judicial clerk: 7%; academia: 1%; unknown: 0%
Employment location for 2013 class: Intl. N/A; N.E. %; M.A. 1%; E.N.C. 8%; W.N.C. 1%; S.A. 7%; E.S.C. 81%; W.S.C. 1%; Mt. 0%; Pac. 1%; unknown 0%

LOUISIANA

Louisiana State University-Baton Rouge (Hebert)
400 Paul M. Hebert Law Center
Baton Rouge, LA 70803
www.law.lsu.edu
Public
Admissions: (225) 578-8646
Email: admissions@law.lsu.edu
Financial aid: (225) 578-3103
Application deadline: 03/01
In-state tuition: full time: $20,998; part time: N/A
Out-of-state tuition: full time: $40,348/credit hour
Room/board/expenses: $20,042
Median grant: $8,952
Average student indebtedness at graduation: $89,471
Enrollment: full time: 551; part time: 29
men: 58%; women: 42%; minorities: 22%
Acceptance rate (full time): 62%
Midrange LSAT (full time): 153-158
Midrange undergraduate GPA (full time): 2.96-3.53

Midrange of full-time private-sector salaries of 2013 grads: $57,250-$75,000
2013 grads employed in: law firms: 51%; business and industry: 18%; government: 11%; public interest: 2%; judicial clerk: 14%; academia: 4%; unknown: 0%
Employment location for 2013 class: Intl. N/A; N.E. %; M.A. 1%; E.N.C. 1%; W.N.C. 1%; S.A. 5%; E.S.C. 3%; W.S.C. 85%; Mt. 1%; Pac. 3%; unknown 0%

Loyola University New Orleans
7214 St. Charles Avenue
PO Box 901
New Orleans, LA 70118
law.loyno.edu/
Private
Admissions: (504) 861-5575
Email: ladmit@loyno.edu
Financial aid: (504) 865-3231
Application deadline: rolling
Tuition: full time: $43,150; part time: $32,650
Room/board/expenses: $21,644
Median grant: $20,000
Average student indebtedness at graduation: $117,892
Enrollment: full time: 503; part time: 99
men: 50%; women: 50%; minorities: 23%
Acceptance rate (full time): 60%
Midrange LSAT (full time): 150-157
Midrange undergraduate GPA (full time): 2.84-3.43
Midrange of full-time private-sector salaries of 2013 grads: $80,000-$107,500
2013 grads employed in: law firms: 57%; business and industry: 15%; government: 9%; public interest: 4%; judicial clerk: 12%; academia: 1%; unknown: 2%
Employment location for 2013 class: Intl. N/A; N.E. %; M.A. 2%; E.N.C. 1%; W.N.C. 0%; S.A. 7%; E.S.C. 4%; W.S.C. 79%; Mt. 2%; Pac. 4%; unknown 1%

Southern University Law Center
PO Box 9294
Baton Rouge, LA 70813
www.sulc.edu/index_v3.htm
Public
Admissions: (225) 771-5340
Email: Admission@sulc.edu
Financial aid: (225) 771-2141
Application deadline: 02/28
In-state tuition: full time: $12,014; part time: $10,478
Out-of-state tuition: full time: $20,078
Room/board/expenses: $20,020
Median grant: $3,750
Average student indebtedness at graduation: $77,067
Enrollment: full time: 509; part time: 134
men: 48%; women: 52%; minorities: 59%
Acceptance rate (full time): 68%
Midrange LSAT (full time): 143-147
Midrange undergraduate GPA (full time): 2.57-3.21
Midrange of full-time private-sector salaries of 2013 grads: $40,000-$66,000
2013 grads employed in: law firms: 44%; business and industry: 21%; government: 16%; public interest: 3%; judicial clerk: 7%; academia: 5%; unknown: 4%

Employment location for 2013 class: Intl. N/A; N.E. N/A; M.A. N/A; E.N.C. N/A; W.N.C. N/A; S.A. N/A; E.S.C. N/A; W.S.C. N/A; Mt. N/A; Pac. N/A; unknown 0%

Tulane University
6329 Freret Street
John Giffen Weinmann Hall
New Orleans, LA 70118-6231
www.law.tulane.edu
Private
Admissions: (504) 865-5930
Email: admissions@law.tulane.edu
Financial aid: (504) 865-5931
Application deadline: rolling
Tuition: full time: $48,576; part time: N/A
Room/board/expenses: $22,140
Median grant: $20,000
Average student indebtedness at graduation: $140,965
Enrollment: full time: 622; part time: 2
men: 52%; women: 48%; minorities: 20%
Acceptance rate (full time): 51%
Midrange LSAT (full time): 157-163
Midrange undergraduate GPA (full time): 3.18-3.61
Midrange of full-time private-sector salaries of 2013 grads: $60,000-$147,500
2013 grads employed in: law firms: 50%; business and industry: 27%; government: 8%; public interest: 4%; judicial clerk: 8%; academia: 3%; unknown: 0%
Employment location for 2013 class: Intl. N/A; N.E. %; M.A. 13%; E.N.C. 2%; W.N.C. 1%; S.A. 16%; E.S.C. 4%; W.S.C. 50%; Mt. 2%; Pac. 5%; unknown 3%

MAINE

University of Maine
246 Deering Avenue
Portland, ME 04102
mainelaw.maine.edu
Public
Admissions: (207) 780-4341
Email: lawadmissions@maine.edu
Financial aid: (207) 780-5250
Application deadline: 04/15
In-state tuition: full time: $23,666; part time: N/A
Out-of-state tuition: full time: $34,736
Room/board/expenses: $15,796
Median grant: $6,000
Average student indebtedness at graduation: $101,749
Enrollment: full time: 252; part time: N/A
men: 51%; women: 49%; minorities: 10%
Acceptance rate (full time): 56%
Midrange LSAT (full time): 149-157
Midrange undergraduate GPA (full time): 3.20-3.57
Midrange of full-time private-sector salaries of 2013 grads: $31,200-$60,000
2013 grads employed in: law firms: 49%; business and industry: 21%; government: 15%; public interest: 5%; judicial clerk: 10%; academia: 0%; unknown: 0%
Employment location for 2013 class: Intl. N/A; N.E. %; M.A. 1%; E.N.C. 0%; W.N.C. 0%; S.A. 6%; E.S.C. 0%; W.S.C. 1%; Mt. 1%; Pac. 4%; unknown 0%

MARYLAND

University of Baltimore
1420 N. Charles Street
Baltimore, MD 21201-5779
law.ubalt.edu
Public
Admissions: (410) 837-4459
Email: lawadmissions@ubalt.edu
Financial aid: (410) 837-4763
Application deadline: 07/15
In-state tuition: full time: $27,884; part time: $20,810
Out-of-state tuition: full time: $41,044
Room/board/expenses: $19,950
Median grant: $10,000
Average student indebtedness at graduation: $114,725
Enrollment: full time: 567; part time: 297
men: 51%; women: 49%; minorities: 27%
Acceptance rate (full time): 63%
Midrange LSAT (full time): 148-155
Midrange undergraduate GPA (full time): 2.93-3.60
Midrange of full-time private-sector salaries of 2013 grads: $50,000-$80,750
2013 grads employed in: law firms: 40%; business and industry: 14%; government: 17%; public interest: 5%; judicial clerk: 18%; academia: 5%; unknown: 0%
Employment location for 2013 class: Intl. N/A; N.E. %; M.A. 3%; E.N.C. 0%; W.N.C. 0%; S.A. 93%; E.S.C. 1%; W.S.C. 0%; Mt. 1%; Pac. 0%; unknown 0%

University of Maryland (Carey)
500 W. Baltimore Street
Baltimore, MD 21201-1786
www.law.umaryland.edu
Public
Admissions: (410) 706-3492
Email: admissions@law.umaryland.edu
Financial aid: (410) 706-0873
Application deadline: 04/01
In-state tuition: full time: $28,657; part time: $22,000
Out-of-state tuition: full time: $41,464
Room/board/expenses: $23,075
Median grant: $7,000
Average student indebtedness at graduation: $102,183
Enrollment: full time: 560; part time: 150
men: 49%; women: 51%; minorities: 45%
Acceptance rate (full time): 49%
Midrange LSAT (full time): 154-162
Midrange undergraduate GPA (full time): 3.26-3.68
Midrange of full-time private-sector salaries of 2013 grads: $60,000-$110,000
2013 grads employed in: law firms: 33%; business and industry: 21%; government: 12%; public interest: 6%; judicial clerk: 21%; academia: 5%; unknown: 1%
Employment location for 2013 class: Intl. N/A; N.E. %; M.A. 4%; E.N.C. 1%; W.N.C. 0%; S.A. 88%; E.S.C. 0%; W.S.C. 2%; Mt. 0%; Pac. 2%; unknown 0%

MASSACHUSETTS

Boston College
885 Centre Street
Newton, MA 02459-1154
www.bc.edu/lawschool
Private
Admissions: (617) 552-4351
Email: bclawadm@bc.edu
Financial aid: (617) 552-4243
Application deadline: 03/31
Tuition: full time: $46,790; part time: N/A
Room/board/expenses: $19,360
Median grant: $20,000
Average student indebtedness at graduation: $97,006
Enrollment: full time: 698; part time: N/A
men: 54%; women: 46%; minorities: 25%
Acceptance rate (full time): 44%
Midrange LSAT (full time): 159-164
Midrange undergraduate GPA (full time): 3.32-3.64
Midrange of full-time private-sector salaries of 2013 grads: $80,000-$160,000
2013 grads employed in: law firms: 59%; business and industry: 12%; government: 14%; public interest: 5%; judicial clerk: 7%; academia: 4%; unknown: 0%
Employment location for 2013 class: Intl. N/A; N.E. %; M.A. 17%; E.N.C. 2%; W.N.C. 1%; S.A. 7%; E.S.C. 0%; W.S.C. 3%; Mt. 2%; Pac. 4%; unknown 0%

Boston University
765 Commonwealth Avenue
Boston, MA 02215
www.bu.edu/law/
Private
Admissions: (617) 353-3100
Email: bulawadm@bu.edu
Financial aid: (617) 353-3160
Application deadline: 04/01
Tuition: full time: $47,188; part time: N/A
Room/board/expenses: $18,142
Median grant: $20,000
Average student indebtedness at graduation: $107,850
Enrollment: full time: 645; part time: 1
men: 45%; women: 55%; minorities: 27%
Acceptance rate (full time): 39%
Midrange LSAT (full time): 160-165
Midrange undergraduate GPA (full time): 3.42-3.74
Midrange of full-time private-sector salaries of 2013 grads: $90,000-$160,000
2013 grads employed in: law firms: 47%; business and industry: 14%; government: 16%; public interest: 17%; judicial clerk: 6%; academia: 0%; unknown: 0%
Employment location for 2013 class: Intl. N/A; N.E. %; M.A. 21%; E.N.C. 3%; W.N.C. 1%; S.A. 9%; E.S.C. 0%; W.S.C. 2%; Mt. 2%; Pac. 6%; unknown 0%

Harvard University
1563 Massachusetts Avenue
Cambridge, MA 02138
www.law.harvard.edu
Private
Admissions: (617) 495-3109
Email: jdadmiss@law.harvard.edu
Financial aid: (617) 495-4606
Application deadline: 02/01
Tuition: full time: $55,842; part time: N/A
Room/board/expenses: $26,058
Median grant: $18,760
Average student indebtedness at graduation: $137,599
Enrollment: full time: 1,752; part time: N/A
men: 50%; women: 50%; minorities: 32%
Acceptance rate (full time): 15%
Midrange LSAT (full time): 170-175
Midrange undergraduate GPA (full time): 3.75-3.95
Midrange of full-time private-sector salaries of 2013 grads: $160,000-$160,000
2013 grads employed in: law firms: 59%; business and industry: 5%; government: 5%; public interest: 8%; judicial clerk: 22%; academia: 1%; unknown: 0%
Employment location for 2013 class: Intl. N/A; N.E. %; M.A. 38%; E.N.C. 7%; W.N.C. 1%; S.A. 16%; E.S.C. 1%; W.S.C. 3%; Mt. 2%; Pac. 15%; unknown 0%

New England Law Boston[1]
154 Stuart Street
Boston, MA 02116
www.nesl.edu
Private
Admissions: (617) 422-7210
Email: admit@nesl.edu
Financial aid: (617) 422-7298
Tuition: N/A
Room/board/expenses: N/A
Enrollment: N/A

Northeastern University
416 Huntington Avenue
Boston, MA 02115
northeastern.edu/law
Private
Admissions: (617) 373-2395
Email: lawadmissions@neu.edu
Financial aid: (617) 373-4620
Application deadline: 03/01
Tuition: full time: $45,000; part time: N/A
Room/board/expenses: $19,599
Median grant: $10,000
Average student indebtedness at graduation: $134,918
Enrollment: full time: 473; part time: N/A
men: 39%; women: 61%; minorities: 31%
Acceptance rate (full time): 38%
Midrange LSAT (full time): 153-162
Midrange undergraduate GPA (full time): 3.25-3.68
Midrange of full-time private-sector salaries of 2013 grads: $54,000-$110,000
2013 grads employed in: law firms: 34%; business and industry: 16%; government: 12%; public interest: 17%; judicial clerk: 6%; academia: 15%; unknown: 1%
Employment location for 2013 class: Intl. N/A; N.E. %; M.A. 7%; E.N.C. 3%; W.N.C. 1%; S.A. 7%; E.S.C. 0%; W.S.C. 0%; Mt. 2%; Pac. 4%; unknown 0%

Suffolk University
120 Tremont Street
Boston, MA 02108
www.law.suffolk.edu/
Private
Admissions: (617) 573-8144
Email: lawadm@suffolk.edu
Financial aid: (617) 573-8147
Application deadline: 04/01
Tuition: full time: $46,042; part time: $34,530
Room/board/expenses: $16,433
Median grant: $20,000
Average student indebtedness at graduation: $120,993
Enrollment: full time: 953; part time: 461
men: 44%; women: 56%; minorities: 22%
Acceptance rate (full time): 88%
Midrange LSAT (full time): 142-151
Midrange undergraduate GPA (full time): 2.94-3.40
Midrange of full-time private-sector salaries of 2013 grads: $46,800-$98,000
2013 grads employed in: law firms: 51%; business and industry: 27%; government: 11%; public interest: 2%; judicial clerk: 7%; academia: 2%; unknown: 0%
Employment location for 2013 class: Intl. N/A; N.E. %; M.A. 7%; E.N.C. 1%; W.N.C. 0%; S.A. 3%; E.S.C. 0%; W.S.C. 1%; Mt. 1%; Pac. 1%; unknown 1%

University of Massachusetts-Dartmouth
333 Faunce Corner Road
North Dartmouth, MA 02747
www.umassd.edu/law/admissions
Public
Admissions: (508) 985-1110
Email: lawadmissions@umassd.edu
Financial aid: (508) 985-1187
Application deadline: 06/30
In-state tuition: full time: $24,178; part time: $18,252
Out-of-state tuition: full time: $31,870
Room/board/expenses: $17,886
Median grant: $11,649
Average student indebtedness at graduation: $105,415
Enrollment: full time: 126; part time: 88
men: 49%; women: 51%; minorities: 25%
Acceptance rate (full time): 68%
Midrange LSAT (full time): 145-151
Midrange undergraduate GPA (full time): 2.76-3.22
Midrange of full-time private-sector salaries of 2013 grads: $33,975-$51,500
2013 grads employed in: law firms: 31%; business and industry: 31%; government: 22%; public interest: 5%; judicial clerk: 8%; academia: 3%; unknown: 0%
Employment location for 2013 class: Intl. N/A; N.E. %; M.A. 4%; E.N.C. 0%; W.N.C. 1%; S.A. 1%; E.S.C. 0%; W.S.C. 1%; Mt. 0%; Pac. 1%; unknown 0%

Western New England University
1215 Wilbraham Road
Springfield, MA 01119-2684
www.law.wne.edu
Private
Admissions: (413) 782-1406
Email: admissions@law.wne.edu
Financial aid: (413) 796-2080
Application deadline: rolling
Tuition: full time: $40,954; part time: $30,298
Room/board/expenses: $23,695
Median grant: $14,000
Average student indebtedness at graduation: $130,124

MICHIGAN

Michigan State University
648 N. Shaw Lane, Room 368
East Lansing, MI 48824-1300
www.law.msu.edu
Private
Admissions: (517) 432-0222
Email: law@law.msu.edu
Financial aid: (517) 432-6810
Application deadline: 04/30
Tuition: full time: $37,294; part time: $28,292
Room/board/expenses: $14,220
Median grant: $27,033
Average student indebtedness at graduation: $95,494
Enrollment: full time: 699; part time: 127
men: 55%; women: 45%; minorities: 23%
Acceptance rate (full time): 43%
Midrange LSAT (full time): 152-158
Midrange undergraduate GPA (full time): 3.30-3.75
Midrange of full-time private-sector salaries of 2013 grads: $50,000-$86,000
2013 grads employed in: law firms: 41%; business and industry: 23%; government: 12%; public interest: 15%; judicial clerk: 2%; academia: 5%; unknown: 1%
Employment location for 2013 class: Intl. N/A; N.E. %; M.A. 9%; E.N.C. 62%; W.N.C. 2%; S.A. 9%; E.S.C. 1%; W.S.C. 4%; Mt. 4%; Pac. 6%; unknown 0%

University of Detroit Mercy
651 E. Jefferson Avenue
Detroit, MI 48226
www.law.udmercy.edu
Private
Admissions: (313) 596-0264
Email: udmlawao@udmercy.edu
Financial aid: (313) 596-0214
Application deadline: 04/01
Tuition: full time: $40,502; part time: $32,408
Room/board/expenses: $23,117
Median grant: $10,000
Average student indebtedness at graduation: $132,245
Enrollment: full time: 431; part time: 92
men: 46%; women: 54%; minorities: 15%
Acceptance rate (full time): 54%
Midrange LSAT (full time): 148-157
Midrange undergraduate GPA (full time): 2.93-3.35

Enrollment: full time: 239; part time: 101
men: 45%; women: 55%; minorities: 25%
Acceptance rate (full time): 84%
Midrange LSAT (full time): 143-148
Midrange undergraduate GPA (full time): 2.92-3.53
Midrange of full-time private-sector salaries of 2013 grads: $39,000-$65,000
2013 grads employed in: law firms: 38%; business and industry: 23%; government: 16%; public interest: 5%; judicial clerk: 13%; academia: 5%; unknown: 0%
Employment location for 2013 class: Intl. N/A; N.E. %; M.A. 20%; E.N.C. 0%; W.N.C. 0%; S.A. 2%; E.S.C. 0%; W.S.C. 1%; Mt. 0%; Pac. 1%; unknown 0%

Midrange of full-time private-sector salaries of 2013 grads: $38,500-$100,000

2013 grads employed in: law firms: 61%; business and industry: 18%; government: 10%; public interest: 6%; judicial clerk: 2%; academia: 3%; unknown: 0%

Employment location for 2013 class: Intl. N/A; N.E. %; M.A. 2%; E.N.C. 62%; W.N.C. 0%; S.A. 3%; E.S.C. 1%; W.S.C. 1%; Mt. 1%; Pac. 1%; unknown 0%

University of Michigan-Ann Arbor

625 S. State Street
Ann Arbor, MI 48109-1215
www.law.umich.edu/
Public
Admissions: (734) 764-0537
Email: law.jd.admissions@umich.edu
Financial aid: (734) 764-5289
Application deadline: 02/15
In-state tuition: full time: $51,398; part time: N/A
Out-of-state tuition: full time: $54,398
Room/board/expenses: $18,030
Median grant: $15,000
Average student indebtedness at graduation: $132,473
Enrollment: full time: 1,000; part time: 1
men: 55%; women: 45%; minorities: 23%
Acceptance rate (full time): 27%
Midrange LSAT (full time): 165-169
Midrange undergraduate GPA (full time): 3.57-3.83
Midrange of full-time private-sector salaries of 2013 grads: $130,000-$160,000
2013 grads employed in: law firms: 65%; business and industry: 4%; government: 9%; public interest: 8%; judicial clerk: 13%; academia: 2%; unknown: 0%
Employment location for 2013 class: Intl. N/A; N.E. %; M.A. 22%; E.N.C. 33%; W.N.C. 3%; S.A. 13%; E.S.C. 1%; W.S.C. 3%; Mt. 3%; Pac. 16%; unknown 1%

Wayne State University

471 W. Palmer Street
Detroit, MI 48202
www.law.wayne.edu
Public
Admissions: (313) 577-3937
Email: lawinquire@wayne.edu
Financial aid: (313) 577-7731
Application deadline: 06/30
In-state tuition: full time: $30,025; part time: $16,825
Out-of-state tuition: full time: $32,808
Room/board/expenses: $21,990
Median grant: $23,785
Average student indebtedness at graduation: $79,881
Enrollment: full time: 296; part time: 123
men: 58%; women: 42%; minorities: 14%
Acceptance rate (full time): 51%
Midrange LSAT (full time): 152-160
Midrange undergraduate GPA (full time): 3.03-3.55
Midrange of full-time private-sector salaries of 2013 grads: $50,000-$100,000
2013 grads employed in: law firms: 61%; business and industry: 17%;

government: 7%; public interest: 7%; judicial clerk: 4%; academia: 4%; unknown: 0%
Employment location for 2013 class: Intl. N/A; N.E. %; M.A. 2%; E.N.C. 91%; W.N.C. 1%; S.A. 4%; E.S.C. 0%; W.S.C. 0%; Mt. 0%; Pac. 0%; unknown 0%

Western Michigan University Thomas M. Cooley Law School

300 S. Capitol Avenue
Lansing, MI 48933
www.cooley.edu
Private
Admissions: (517) 371-5140
Email: admissions@cooley.edu
Financial aid: (517) 371-5140
Application deadline: 09/01
Tuition: full time: $44,990; part time: $27,940
Room/board/expenses: $17,584
Median grant: $15,469
Enrollment: full time: 303; part time: 1,439
men: 46%; women: 54%; minorities: 34%
Midrange LSAT (full time): 146-154
Midrange undergraduate GPA (full time): 2.66-3.41
Midrange of full-time private-sector salaries of 2013 grads: $38,000-$60,000
2013 grads employed in: law firms: 49%; business and industry: 30%; government: 10%; public interest: 4%; judicial clerk: 5%; academia: 2%; unknown: 0%
Employment location for 2013 class: Intl. N/A; N.E. %; M.A. 11%; E.N.C. 59%; W.N.C. 3%; S.A. 10%; E.S.C. 2%; W.S.C. 3%; Mt. 4%; Pac. 4%; unknown 0%

MINNESOTA

Hamline University

1536 Hewitt Avenue
St. Paul, MN 55104-1284
www.hamline.edu/law
Private
Admissions: (651) 523-2461
Email: lawadm@hamline.edu
Financial aid: (651) 523-3000
Application deadline: 08/01
Tuition: full time: $39,536; part time: $28,768
Room/board/expenses: $19,972
Median grant: $18,484
Average student indebtedness at graduation: $113,173
Enrollment: full time: 219; part time: 102
men: 48%; women: 52%; minorities: 19%
Acceptance rate (full time): 71%
Midrange LSAT (full time): 146-154
Midrange undergraduate GPA (full time): 2.99-3.47
Midrange of full-time private-sector salaries of 2013 grads: $47,000-$70,000
2013 grads employed in: law firms: 33%; business and industry: 35%; government: 14%; public interest: 4%; judicial clerk: 13%; academia: 1%; unknown: 1%
Employment location for 2013 class: Intl. N/A; N.E. %; M.A. 1%; E.N.C. 4%; W.N.C. 83%; S.A. 2%; E.S.C. 1%; W.S.C. 1%; Mt. 4%; Pac. 2%; unknown 1%

University of Minnesota-Twin Cities

229 19th Avenue S
Minneapolis, MN 55455
www.law.umn.edu
Public
Admissions: (612) 625-3487
Email: umnlsadm@umn.edu
Financial aid: (612) 625-3487
Application deadline: rolling
In-state tuition: full time: $41,222; part time: N/A
Out-of-state tuition: full time: $48,710
Room/board/expenses: $15,626
Median grant: $20,000
Average student indebtedness at graduation: $104,733
Enrollment: full time: 681; part time: 17
men: 57%; women: 43%; minorities: 19%
Acceptance rate (full time): 41%
Midrange LSAT (full time): 157-166
Midrange undergraduate GPA (full time): 3.42-3.85
Midrange of full-time private-sector salaries of 2013 grads: $54,850-$110,000
2013 grads employed in: law firms: 44%; business and industry: 15%; government: 8%; public interest: 13%; judicial clerk: 20%; academia: 0%; unknown: 0%
Employment location for 2013 class: Intl. N/A; N.E. %; M.A. 7%; E.N.C. 7%; W.N.C. 71%; S.A. 5%; E.S.C. 0%; W.S.C. 1%; Mt. 3%; Pac. 5%; unknown 0%

University of St. Thomas

MSL 411
1000 LaSalle Avenue
Minneapolis, MN 55403-2015
www.stthomas.edu/law
Private
Admissions: (651) 962-4895
Email: lawschool@stthomas.edu
Financial aid: (651) 962-4895
Application deadline: 07/01
Tuition: full time: $37,185; part time: N/A
Room/board/expenses: $19,963
Median grant: $20,000
Average student indebtedness at graduation: $100,401
Enrollment: full time: 368; part time: 8
men: 52%; women: 48%; minorities: 13%
Acceptance rate (full time): 73%
Midrange LSAT (full time): 150-158
Midrange undergraduate GPA (full time): 3.17-3.61
Midrange of full-time private-sector salaries of 2013 grads: $50,000-$76,000
2013 grads employed in: law firms: 34%; business and industry: 30%; government: 11%; public interest: 6%; judicial clerk: 16%; academia: 2%; unknown: 2%
Employment location for 2013 class: Intl. N/A; N.E. %; M.A. 1%; E.N.C. 5%; W.N.C. 81%; S.A. 2%; E.S.C. 2%; W.S.C. 2%; Mt. 1%; Pac. 3%; unknown 0%

William Mitchell College of Law

875 Summit Avenue
St. Paul, MN 55105-3076
www.wmitchell.edu
Private
Admissions: (651) 290-6476
Email: admissions@wmitchell.edu

Financial aid: (651) 290-6403
Application deadline: 08/01
Tuition: full time: $38,660; part time: $28,030
Room/board/expenses: $19,450
Median grant: $20,585
Average student indebtedness at graduation: $110,738
Enrollment: full time: 455; part time: 210
men: 46%; women: 54%; minorities: 14%
Acceptance rate (full time): 72%
Midrange LSAT (full time): 149-156
Midrange undergraduate GPA (full time): 3.01-3.60
Midrange of full-time private-sector salaries of 2013 grads: $45,000-$72,500
2013 grads employed in: law firms: 44%; business and industry: 25%; government: 13%; public interest: 2%; judicial clerk: 15%; academia: 0%; unknown: 0%
Employment location for 2013 class: Intl. N/A; N.E. %; M.A. 1%; E.N.C. 5%; W.N.C. 86%; S.A. 3%; E.S.C. 1%; W.S.C. 0%; Mt. 1%; Pac. 1%; unknown 2%

MISSISSIPPI

Mississippi College

151 E. Griffith Street
Jackson, MS 39201
www.law.mc.edu
Private
Admissions: (601) 925-7153
Email: kflowers@mc.edu
Financial aid: (601) 925-7110
Application deadline: 07/01
Tuition: full time: $32,680; part time: $1,037/credit hour
Room/board/expenses: $21,225
Median grant: $20,000
Average student indebtedness at graduation: $130,700
Enrollment: full time: 409; part time: 23
men: 55%; women: 45%; minorities: 22%
Acceptance rate (full time): 82%
Midrange LSAT (full time): 144-153
Midrange undergraduate GPA (full time): 2.71-3.47
Midrange of full-time private-sector salaries of 2013 grads: $47,500-$87,500
2013 grads employed in: law firms: 52%; business and industry: 15%; government: 21%; public interest: 2%; judicial clerk: 9%; academia: 0%; unknown: 0%
Employment location for 2013 class: Intl. N/A; N.E. %; M.A. 2%; E.N.C. 2%; W.N.C. 2%; S.A. 11%; E.S.C. 63%; W.S.C. 16%; Mt. 2%; Pac. 1%; unknown 1%

University of Mississippi

PO Box 1848
University, MS 38677
law.olemiss.edu
Public
Admissions: (662) 915-6910
Email: lawmiss@olemiss.edu
Financial aid: (800) 891-4569
Application deadline: 04/14
In-state tuition: full time: $14,688; part time: N/A
Out-of-state tuition: full time: $31,688
Room/board/expenses: $19,198
Median grant: $9,846
Average student indebtedness at graduation: $73,003

Enrollment: full time: 386; part time: N/A
men: 60%; women: 40%; minorities: 21%
Acceptance rate (full time): 44%
Midrange LSAT (full time): 151-156
Midrange undergraduate GPA (full time): 3.20-3.66
Midrange of full-time private-sector salaries of 2013 grads: $52,000-$100,000
2013 grads employed in: law firms: 57%; business and industry: 16%; government: 13%; public interest: 2%; judicial clerk: 10%; academia: 2%; unknown: 0%
Employment location for 2013 class: Intl. N/A; N.E. %; M.A. 1%; E.N.C. 2%; W.N.C. 2%; S.A. 16%; E.S.C. 68%; W.S.C. 7%; Mt. 2%; Pac. 1%; unknown 0%

MISSOURI

St. Louis University

100 N. Tucker
St. Louis, MO 63101
law.slu.edu
Private
Admissions: (314) 977-2800
Email: admissions@law.slu.edu
Financial aid: (314) 977-3369
Application deadline: rolling
Tuition: full time: $38,435; part time: $27,975
Room/board/expenses: $18,158
Median grant: $17,000
Average student indebtedness at graduation: $128,764
Enrollment: full time: 461; part time: 72
men: 50%; women: 50%; minorities: 16%
Acceptance rate (full time): 63%
Midrange LSAT (full time): 151-159
Midrange undergraduate GPA (full time): 3.23-3.67
Midrange of full-time private-sector salaries of 2013 grads: $55,000-$95,000
2013 grads employed in: law firms: 54%; business and industry: 26%; government: 14%; public interest: 3%; judicial clerk: 3%; academia: 0%; unknown: 0%
Employment location for 2013 class: Intl. N/A; N.E. %; M.A. 1%; E.N.C. 15%; W.N.C. 72%; S.A. 6%; E.S.C. 1%; W.S.C. 2%; Mt. 2%; Pac. 1%; unknown 0%

University of Missouri

203 Hulston Hall
Columbia, MO 65211-4300
www.law.missouri.edu
Public
Admissions: (573) 882-6042
Email: mulawadmissions@missouri.edu
Financial aid: (573) 882-1383
Application deadline: 03/15
In-state tuition: full time: $19,832; part time: N/A
Out-of-state tuition: full time: $37,462
Room/board/expenses: $12,368
Median grant: $9,000
Average student indebtedness at graduation: $67,289
Enrollment: full time: 351; part time: 17
men: 61%; women: 39%; minorities: 16%
Acceptance rate (full time): 49%
Midrange LSAT (full time): 154-160
Midrange undergraduate GPA (full time): 3.08-3.72

Midrange of full-time private-sector salaries of 2013 grads: $52,000-$100,000

2013 grads employed in: law firms: 39%; business and industry: 20%; government: 21%; public interest: 7%; judicial clerk: 7%; academia: 6%; unknown: 0%

Employment location for 2013 class: Intl. N/A; N.E. %; M.A. 2%; E.N.C. 5%; W.N.C. 80%; S.A. 5%; E.S.C. 0%; W.S.C. 1%; Mt. 1%; Pac. 5%; unknown 1%

University of Missouri-Kansas City

500 East 52nd Street
Kansas City, MO 64110
www.law.umkc.edu
Public
Admissions: (816) 235-1644
Email: law@umkc.edu
Financial aid: (816) 235-1154
Application deadline: 03/01
In-state tuition: full time: $18,320; part time: $11,162
Out-of-state tuition: full time: $34,832
Room/board/expenses: $15,911
Median grant: $8,942
Enrollment: full time: 399; part time: 69
men: 59%; women: 41%; minorities: 15%
Acceptance rate (full time): 56%
Midrange of full-time private-sector salaries of 2013 grads: $42,000-$60,000
2013 grads employed in: law firms: 46%; business and industry: 31%; government: 11%; public interest: 3%; judicial clerk: 8%; academia: 2%; unknown: 0%
Employment location for 2013 class: Intl. N/A; N.E. %; M.A. 1%; E.N.C. 0%; W.N.C. 94%; S.A. 2%; E.S.C. 1%; W.S.C. 0%; Mt. 2%; Pac. 0%; unknown 0%

Washington University in St. Louis

1 Brookings Drive, Box 1120
St. Louis, MO 63130
www.law.wustl.edu
Private
Admissions: (314) 935-4525
Email: admiss@wulaw.wustl.edu
Financial aid: (314) 935-4605
Application deadline: 08/01
Tuition: full time: $50,152; part time: N/A
Room/board/expenses: $22,700
Median grant: $26,000
Average student indebtedness at graduation: $111,345
Enrollment: full time: 749; part time: 4
men: 56%; women: 44%; minorities: 22%
Acceptance rate (full time): 30%
Midrange LSAT (full time): 162-167
Midrange undergraduate GPA (full time): 3.20-3.76
Midrange of full-time private-sector salaries of 2013 grads: $95,000-$160,000
2013 grads employed in: law firms: 55%; business and industry: 16%; government: 14%; public interest: 5%; judicial clerk: 7%; academia: 3%; unknown: 0%
Employment location for 2013 class: Intl. N/A; N.E. %; M.A. 15%; E.N.C. 19%; W.N.C. 29%; S.A. 14%; E.S.C. 1%; W.S.C. 6%; Mt. 0%; Pac. 9%; unknown 0%

MONTANA

University of Montana

32 Campus Drive
Missoula, MT 59812
www.umt.edu/law
Public
Admissions: (406) 243-2698
Email: lori.freeman@umontana.edu
Financial aid: (406) 243-5524
Application deadline: 03/15
In-state tuition: full time: $11,335; part time: N/A
Out-of-state tuition: full time: $29,328
Room/board/expenses: $14,683
Median grant: $3,500
Average student indebtedness at graduation: $71,216
Enrollment: full time: 247; part time: N/A
men: 57%; women: 43%; minorities: 11%
Acceptance rate (full time): 57%
Midrange LSAT (full time): 151-158
Midrange undergraduate GPA (full time): 3.06-3.70
Midrange of full-time private-sector salaries of 2013 grads: $45,000-$60,000
2013 grads employed in: law firms: 43%; business and industry: 6%; government: 7%; public interest: 12%; judicial clerk: 30%; academia: 1%; unknown: 0%
Employment location for 2013 class: Intl. N/A; N.E. %; M.A. 0%; E.N.C. 0%; W.N.C. 0%; S.A. 1%; E.S.C. 0%; W.S.C. 1%; Mt. 91%; Pac. 4%; unknown 0%

NEBRASKA

Creighton University

2500 California Plaza
Omaha, NE 68178
www.creighton.edu/law
Private
Admissions: (800) 282-5835
Email: lawadmit@creighton.edu
Financial aid: (402) 280-2352
Application deadline: 08/01
Tuition: full time: $35,530; part time: $1,130/credit hour
Room/board/expenses: $16,900
Median grant: $16,500
Average student indebtedness at graduation: $126,586
Enrollment: full time: 354; part time: 7
men: 62%; women: 38%; minorities: 18%
Acceptance rate (full time): 73%
Midrange LSAT (full time): 148-154
Midrange undergraduate GPA (full time): 2.91-3.61
Midrange of full-time private-sector salaries of 2013 grads: $49,500-$75,000
2013 grads employed in: law firms: 46%; business and industry: 34%; government: 9%; public interest: 5%; judicial clerk: 5%; academia: 0%; unknown: 0%
Employment location for 2013 class: Intl. N/A; N.E. %; M.A. 2%; E.N.C. 2%; W.N.C. 79%; S.A. 3%; E.S.C. 0%; W.S.C. 1%; Mt. 8%; Pac. 4%; unknown 0%

University of Nebraska-Lincoln

PO Box 830902
Lincoln, NE 68583-0902
law.unl.edu
Public
Admissions: (402) 472-8333
Email: lawadm@unl.edu
Financial aid: (402) 472-8333
Application deadline: 03/01
In-state tuition: full time: $14,479; part time: N/A
Out-of-state tuition: full time: $32,852
Room/board/expenses: $15,400
Median grant: $14,000
Average student indebtedness at graduation: $62,985
Enrollment: full time: 359; part time: 1
men: 55%; women: 45%; minorities: 8%
Acceptance rate (full time): 68%
Midrange LSAT (full time): 152-159
Midrange undergraduate GPA (full time): 3.41-3.88
Midrange of full-time private-sector salaries of 2013 grads: $45,000-$70,000
2013 grads employed in: law firms: 51%; business and industry: 20%; government: 14%; public interest: 9%; judicial clerk: 4%; academia: 3%; unknown: 0%
Employment location for 2013 class: Intl. N/A; N.E. %; M.A. 1%; E.N.C. 2%; W.N.C. 84%; S.A. 1%; E.S.C. 0%; W.S.C. 2%; Mt. 8%; Pac. 1%; unknown 0%

NEVADA

University of Nevada-Las Vegas

4505 S. Maryland Parkway
Box 451003
Las Vegas, NV 89154-1003
www.law.unlv.edu/
Public
Admissions: (702) 895-2440
Email: elizabeth.jost@unlv.edu
Financial aid: (702) 895-4107
Application deadline: 03/15
In-state tuition: full time: $24,749; part time: $18,713
Out-of-state tuition: full time: $35,749
Room/board/expenses: $22,796
Median grant: $15,950
Average student indebtedness at graduation: $99,678
Enrollment: full time: 288; part time: 106
men: 55%; women: 45%; minorities: 33%
Acceptance rate (full time): 36%
Midrange LSAT (full time): 156-161
Midrange undergraduate GPA (full time): 3.06-3.65
Midrange of full-time private-sector salaries of 2013 grads: $56,000-$80,000
2013 grads employed in: law firms: 49%; business and industry: 14%; government: 9%; public interest: 4%; judicial clerk: 23%; academia: 2%; unknown: 0%
Employment location for 2013 class: Intl. N/A; N.E. %; M.A. 0%; E.N.C. 0%; W.N.C. 0%; S.A. 1%; E.S.C. 0%; W.S.C. 0%; Mt. 93%; Pac. 5%; unknown 0%

NEW HAMPSHIRE

University of New Hampshire School of Law

2 White Street
Concord, NH 03301
www.law.unh.edu
Public
Admissions: (603) 513-5300
Email: admissions@law.unh.edu
Financial aid: (603) 228-1541
Application deadline: 04/01
In-state tuition: full time: $37,378; part time: N/A
Out-of-state tuition: full time: $41,378
Room/board/expenses: $21,872
Median grant: $15,000
Average student indebtedness at graduation: $121,469
Enrollment: full time: 217; part time: 2
men: 60%; women: 40%; minorities: 11%
Acceptance rate (full time): 48%
Midrange LSAT (full time): 152-158
Midrange undergraduate GPA (full time): 3.16-3.71
Midrange of full-time private-sector salaries of 2013 grads: $70,000-$140,000
2013 grads employed in: law firms: 55%; business and industry: 24%; government: 13%; public interest: 3%; judicial clerk: 2%; academia: 2%; unknown: 0%
Employment location for 2013 class: Intl. N/A; N.E. %; M.A. 10%; E.N.C. 9%; W.N.C. 1%; S.A. 14%; E.S.C. 0%; W.S.C. 3%; Mt. 2%; Pac. 5%; unknown 0%

NEW JERSEY

Rutgers, The State University of New Jersey-Camden

217 N. Fifth Street
Camden, NJ 08102-1203
camlaw.rutgers.edu
Public
Admissions: (800) 466-7561
Email: admissions@camlaw.rutgers.edu
Financial aid: (856) 225-6039
Application deadline: 03/15
In-state tuition: full time: $26,101; part time: $21,904
Out-of-state tuition: full time: $38,068
Room/board/expenses: $13,661
Median grant: $10,000
Enrollment: full time: 415; part time: 85
men: 62%; women: 38%; minorities: 22%
Acceptance rate (full time): 44%
Midrange LSAT (full time): 153-158
Midrange undergraduate GPA (full time): 2.83-3.41
Midrange of full-time private-sector salaries of 2013 grads: $60,000-$120,000
2013 grads employed in: law firms: 29%; business and industry: 16%; government: 6%; public interest: 0%; judicial clerk: 47%; academia: 1%; unknown: 0%
Employment location for 2013 class: Intl. N/A; N.E. %; M.A. 92%; E.N.C. 1%; W.N.C. 0%; S.A. 4%; E.S.C. 1%; W.S.C. 1%; Mt. 0%; Pac. 0%; unknown 0%

Rutgers, The State University of New Jersey-Newark

123 Washington Street
Newark, NJ 07102
law.newark.rutgers.edu
Public
Admissions: (973) 353-5554
Email: lawinfo@andromeda.rutgers.edu
Financial aid: (973) 353-1702
Application deadline: 03/15
In-state tuition: full time: $26,062; part time: $18,943
Out-of-state tuition: full time: $38,029
Room/board/expenses: $18,023
Median grant: $10,000
Average student indebtedness at graduation: $89,507
Enrollment: full time: 501; part time: 171
men: 59%; women: 41%; minorities: 37%
Acceptance rate (full time): 46%
Midrange LSAT (full time): 153-159
Midrange undergraduate GPA (full time): 3.07-3.54
Midrange of full-time private-sector salaries of 2013 grads: $60,000-$160,000
2013 grads employed in: law firms: 35%; business and industry: 22%; government: 9%; public interest: 2%; judicial clerk: 29%; academia: 4%; unknown: 0%
Employment location for 2013 class: Intl. N/A; N.E. %; M.A. 94%; E.N.C. 0%; W.N.C. 0%; S.A. 5%; E.S.C. 0%; W.S.C. 0%; Mt. 0%; Pac. 0%; unknown 0%

Seton Hall University

1 Newark Center
Newark, NJ 07102-5210
law.shu.edu
Private
Admissions: (888) 415-7271
Email: admitme@shu.edu
Financial aid: (973) 642-8850
Application deadline: 04/01
Tuition: full time: $50,034; part time: $37,736
Room/board/expenses: $22,146
Median grant: $25,000
Average student indebtedness at graduation: $128,100
Enrollment: full time: 381; part time: 190
men: 47%; women: 53%; minorities: 25%
Acceptance rate (full time): 54%
Midrange LSAT (full time): 156-161
Midrange undergraduate GPA (full time): 3.29-3.72
Midrange of full-time private-sector salaries of 2013 grads: $65,000-$145,000
2013 grads employed in: law firms: 32%; business and industry: 15%; government: 8%; public interest: 1%; judicial clerk: 43%; academia: 2%; unknown: 0%
Employment location for 2013 class: Intl. N/A; N.E. %; M.A. 89%; E.N.C. 1%; W.N.C. 0%; S.A. 4%; E.S.C. 0%; W.S.C. 1%; Mt. 0%; Pac. 1%; unknown 1%

NEW MEXICO

University of New Mexico

1117 Stanford Drive NE
MSC11 6070
Albuquerque, NM 87131-0001
lawschool.unm.edu
Public
Admissions: (505) 277-0958
Email: admissions@law.unm.edu
Financial aid: (505) 277-9035
Application deadline: 02/15
In-state tuition: full time: $16,251; part time: N/A
Out-of-state tuition: full time: $34,521
Room/board/expenses: $15,333
Median grant: $5,675
Average student indebtedness at graduation: $71,029
Enrollment: full time: 344; part time: 3
men: 51%; women: 49%; minorities: 49%
Acceptance rate (full time): 44%
Midrange LSAT (full time): 150-157
Midrange undergraduate GPA (full time): 3.07-3.74
Midrange of full-time private-sector salaries of 2013 grads: $46,000-$70,000
2013 grads employed in: law firms: 49%; business and industry: 10%; government: 22%; public interest: 4%; judicial clerk: 14%; academia: 1%; unknown: 1%
Employment location for 2013 class: Intl. N/A; N.E. %; M.A. 1%; E.N.C. 0%; W.N.C. 0%; S.A. 0%; E.S.C. 1%; W.S.C. 4%; Mt. 89%; Pac. 4%; unknown 0%

NEW YORK

Albany Law School

80 New Scotland Avenue
Albany, NY 12208-3494
www.albanylaw.edu
Private
Admissions: (518) 445-2326
Email: admissions@albanylaw.edu
Financial aid: (518) 445-2357
Application deadline: 06/01
Tuition: full time: $43,398; part time: $32,586
Room/board/expenses: $16,330
Median grant: $20,000
Average student indebtedness at graduation: $130,184
Enrollment: full time: 420; part time: 46
men: 51%; women: 49%; minorities: 15%
Acceptance rate (full time): 61%
Midrange LSAT (full time): 148-154
Midrange undergraduate GPA (full time): 2.90-3.51
Midrange of full-time private-sector salaries of 2013 grads: $46,750-$77,500
2013 grads employed in: law firms: 48%; business and industry: 19%; government: 22%; public interest: 4%; judicial clerk: 4%; academia: 2%; unknown: 0%
Employment location for 2013 class: Intl. N/A; N.E. %; M.A. 91%; E.N.C. 2%; W.N.C. 0%; S.A. 2%; E.S.C. 0%; W.S.C. 0%; Mt. 1%; Pac. 2%; unknown 0%

Brooklyn Law School

250 Joralemon Street
Brooklyn, NY 11201
www.brooklaw.edu
Private
Admissions: (718) 780-7906
Email: admitq@brooklaw.edu
Financial aid: (718) 780-7915
Application deadline: rolling
Tuition: full time: $1,795/credit hour; part time: $1,795/credit hour
Room/board/expenses: $24,458
Median grant: $30,600
Average student indebtedness at graduation: $114,953
Enrollment: full time: 881; part time: 238
men: 54%; women: 46%; minorities: 27%
Acceptance rate (full time): 56%
Midrange LSAT (full time): 153-159
Midrange undergraduate GPA (full time): 3.05-3.53
Midrange of full-time private-sector salaries of 2013 grads: $54,800-$105,000
2013 grads employed in: law firms: 42%; business and industry: 24%; government: 15%; public interest: 10%; judicial clerk: 7%; academia: 1%; unknown: 1%
Employment location for 2013 class: Intl. N/A; N.E. %; M.A. 91%; E.N.C. 0%; W.N.C. 0%; S.A. 2%; E.S.C. 0%; W.S.C. 0%; Mt. 0%; Pac. 2%; unknown 1%

Columbia University

435 W. 116th Street
New York, NY 10027
www.law.columbia.edu
Private
Admissions: (212) 854-2670
Email: admissions@law.columbia.edu
Financial aid: (212) 854-7730
Application deadline: rolling
Tuition: full time: $60,274; part time: N/A
Room/board/expenses: $22,868
Median grant: $15,000
Average student indebtedness at graduation: $154,076
Enrollment: full time: 1,170; part time: N/A
men: 54%; women: 46%; minorities: 34%
Acceptance rate (full time): 19%
Midrange LSAT (full time): 170-174
Midrange undergraduate GPA (full time): 3.58-3.81
Midrange of full-time private-sector salaries of 2013 grads: $160,000-$160,000
2013 grads employed in: law firms: 78%; business and industry: 2%; government: 5%; public interest: 8%; judicial clerk: 6%; academia: 0%; unknown: 0%
Employment location for 2013 class: Intl. N/A; N.E. %; M.A. 69%; E.N.C. 2%; W.N.C. 0%; S.A. 8%; E.S.C. 1%; W.S.C. 2%; Mt. 1%; Pac. 11%; unknown 0%

Cornell University

Myron Taylor Hall
Ithaca, NY 14853-4901
www.lawschool.cornell.edu
Private
Admissions: (607) 255-5141
Email: jdadmissions@cornell.edu
Financial aid: (607) 255-5141
Application deadline: 02/01
Tuition: full time: $59,360; part time: N/A
Room/board/expenses: $20,069
Median grant: $15,000

Average student indebtedness at graduation: $135,000

Enrollment: full time: 595; part time: N/A
men: 54%; women: 46%; minorities: 35%
Acceptance rate (full time): 30%
Midrange LSAT (full time): 166-169
Midrange undergraduate GPA (full time): 3.55-3.76
Midrange of full-time private-sector salaries of 2013 grads: $160,000-$160,000
2013 grads employed in: law firms: 69%; business and industry: 3%; government: 5%; public interest: 7%; judicial clerk: 15%; academia: 0%; unknown: 1%
Employment location for 2013 class: Intl. N/A; N.E. %; M.A. 68%; E.N.C. 3%; W.N.C. 1%; S.A. 10%; E.S.C. 1%; W.S.C. 3%; Mt. 1%; Pac. 8%; unknown 0%

CUNY

2 Court Square
Long Island City, NY 11101-4356
www.law.cuny.edu/
Public
Admissions: (718) 340-4210
Email: admissions@law.cuny.edu
Financial aid: (718) 340-4284
Application deadline: 06/15
In-state tuition: full time: $15,193; part time: N/A
Out-of-state tuition: full time: $24,073
Room/board/expenses: $19,984
Median grant: $4,000
Average student indebtedness at graduation: $82,415
Enrollment: full time: 322; part time: 5
men: 35%; women: 65%; minorities: 43%
Acceptance rate (full time): 40%
Midrange LSAT (full time): 151-158
Midrange undergraduate GPA (full time): 2.97-3.63
Midrange of full-time private-sector salaries of 2013 grads: $36,400-$60,000
2013 grads employed in: law firms: 17%; business and industry: 10%; government: 16%; public interest: 42%; judicial clerk: 12%; academia: 1%; unknown: 2%
Employment location for 2013 class: Intl. N/A; N.E. %; M.A. 84%; E.N.C. 0%; W.N.C. 0%; S.A. 6%; E.S.C. 0%; W.S.C. 0%; Mt. 5%; Pac. 4%; unknown 1%

Fordham University

150 W. 62nd Street
New York, NY 10023-7485
law.fordham.edu
Private
Admissions: (212) 636-6810
Email: lawadmissions@law.fordham.edu
Financial aid: (212) 636-6815
Application deadline: 03/15
Tuition: full time: $52,532; part time: $39,472
Room/board/expenses: $25,408
Median grant: $12,500
Average student indebtedness at graduation: $140,577
Enrollment: full time: 1,005; part time: 203
men: 52%; women: 48%; minorities: 25%
Acceptance rate (full time): 37%
Midrange LSAT (full time): 161-165
Midrange undergraduate GPA (full time): 3.35-3.67

Midrange of full-time private-sector salaries of 2013 grads: $80,000-$160,000

2013 grads employed in: law firms: 56%; business and industry: 15%; government: 8%; public interest: 8%; judicial clerk: 8%; academia: 4%; unknown: 0%
Employment location for 2013 class: Intl. N/A; N.E. %; M.A. 91%; E.N.C. 0%; W.N.C. 0%; S.A. 3%; E.S.C. 0%; W.S.C. 1%; Mt. 0%; Pac. 1%; unknown 0%

Hofstra University (Deane)

121 Hofstra University
Hempstead, NY 11549
law.hofstra.edu
Private
Admissions: (516) 463-5916
Email: lawadmissions@hofstra.edu
Financial aid: (516) 463-5929
Application deadline: 04/15
Tuition: full time: $52,190; part time: $39,070
Room/board/expenses: $24,079
Median grant: $25,000
Average student indebtedness at graduation: $143,646
Enrollment: full time: 769; part time: 24
men: 49%; women: 51%; minorities: 28%
Acceptance rate (full time): 64%
Midrange LSAT (full time): 147-155
Midrange undergraduate GPA (full time): 3.02-3.55
Midrange of full-time private-sector salaries of 2013 grads: $50,000-$77,500
2013 grads employed in: law firms: 58%; business and industry: 19%; government: 12%; public interest: 5%; judicial clerk: 1%; academia: 2%; unknown: 2%
Employment location for 2013 class: Intl. N/A; N.E. %; M.A. 84%; E.N.C. 0%; W.N.C. 0%; S.A. 7%; E.S.C. 0%; W.S.C. 1%; Mt. 1%; Pac. 0%; unknown 4%

New York Law School

185 W. Broadway
New York, NY 10013-2960
www.nyls.edu
Private
Admissions: (212) 431-2888
Email: admissions@nyls.edu
Financial aid: (212) 431-2828
Application deadline: 07/01
Tuition: full time: $49,240; part time: $37,880
Room/board/expenses: $23,663
Median grant: $14,672
Average student indebtedness at graduation: $166,622
Enrollment: full time: 660; part time: 308
men: 47%; women: 53%; minorities: 33%
Acceptance rate (full time): 58%
Midrange LSAT (full time): 148-154
Midrange undergraduate GPA (full time): 2.90-3.53
Midrange of full-time private-sector salaries of 2013 grads: $50,000-$90,000
2013 grads employed in: law firms: 45%; business and industry: 34%; government: 10%; public interest: 3%; judicial clerk: 4%; academia: 3%; unknown: 0%

New York University

40 Washington Square S
New York, NY 10012
www.law.nyu.edu
Private
Admissions: (212) 998-6060
Email: law.moreinfo@nyu.edu
Financial aid: (212) 998-6050
Application deadline: 02/15
Tuition: full time: $56,838; part time: N/A
Room/board/expenses: $26,884
Median grant: $20,000
Average student indebtedness at graduation: $147,744
Enrollment: full time: 1,423; part time: 2
men: 54%; women: 46%; minorities: 29%
Acceptance rate (full time): 30%
Midrange LSAT (full time): 167-172
Midrange undergraduate GPA (full time): 3.56-3.87
Midrange of full-time private-sector salaries of 2013 grads: $160,000-$160,000
2013 grads employed in: law firms: 66%; business and industry: 2%; government: 8%; public interest: 12%; judicial clerk: 12%; academia: 0%; unknown: 0%
Employment location for 2013 class: Intl. N/A; N.E. %; M.A. 70%; E.N.C. 2%; W.N.C. 0%; S.A. 9%; E.S.C. 1%; W.S.C. 3%; Mt. 2%; Pac. 9%; unknown 0%

Pace University

78 N. Broadway
White Plains, NY 10603
www.law.pace.edu
Private
Admissions: (914) 422-4210
Email: admissions@law.pace.edu
Financial aid: (914) 422-4050
Application deadline: 06/01
Tuition: full time: $45,376; part time: $34,034
Room/board/expenses: $18,580
Median grant: $16,000
Average student indebtedness at graduation: $122,180
Enrollment: full time: 443; part time: 64
men: 42%; women: 58%; minorities: 28%
Acceptance rate (full time): 65%
Midrange LSAT (full time): 148-153
Midrange undergraduate GPA (full time): 2.91-3.55
Midrange of full-time private-sector salaries of 2013 grads: $48,000-$90,000
2013 grads employed in: law firms: 45%; business and industry: 27%; government: 11%; public interest: 6%; judicial clerk: 3%; academia: 6%; unknown: 1%
Employment location for 2013 class: Intl. N/A; N.E. %; M.A. 85%; E.N.C. 0%; W.N.C. 0%; S.A. 4%; E.S.C. 0%; W.S.C. 1%; Mt. 1%; Pac. 2%; unknown 1%

St. John's University

8000 Utopia Parkway
Jamaica, NY 11439
www.law.stjohns.edu/
Private
Admissions: (718) 990-6474
Email: lawinfo@stjohns.edu
Financial aid: (718) 990-1485

Application deadline: 04/01
Tuition: full time: $51,490; part time: $38,630
Room/board/expenses: $25,124
Median grant: $30,000
Average student indebtedness at graduation: $111,959
Enrollment: full time: 620; part time: 122
men: 54%; women: 46%; minorities: 29%
Acceptance rate (full time): 49%
Midrange LSAT (full time): 154-160
Midrange undergraduate GPA (full time): 3.22-3.65
Midrange of full-time private-sector salaries of 2013 grads: $52,000-$90,000
2013 grads employed in: law firms: 53%; business and industry: 21%; government: 16%; public interest: 5%; judicial clerk: 2%; academia: 3%; unknown: 0%
Employment location for 2013 class: Intl. N/A; N.E. %; M.A. 93%; E.N.C. 0%; W.N.C. 0%; S.A. 4%; E.S.C. 0%; W.S.C. 0%; Mt. 1%; Pac. 0%; unknown 0%

SUNY Buffalo Law School
John Lord O'Brian Hall
Buffalo, NY 14260
www.law.buffalo.edu
Public
Admissions: (716) 645-2907
Email: law-admissions@buffalo.edu
Financial aid: (716) 645-7324
Application deadline: rolling
In-state tuition: full time: $26,097; part time: N/A
Out-of-state tuition: full time: $43,987
Room/board/expenses: $20,920
Median grant: $5,000
Average student indebtedness at graduation: $76,010
Enrollment: full time: 552; part time: 5
men: 50%; women: 50%; minorities: 16%
Acceptance rate (full time): 56%
Midrange LSAT (full time): 151-157
Midrange undergraduate GPA (full time): 3.11-3.66
Midrange of full-time private-sector salaries of 2013 grads: $50,000-$85,000
2013 grads employed in: law firms: 55%; business and industry: 22%; government: 14%; public interest: 4%; judicial clerk: 3%; academia: 2%; unknown: 0%
Employment location for 2013 class: Intl. N/A; N.E. %; M.A. 89%; E.N.C. 1%; W.N.C. 0%; S.A. 4%; E.S.C. 0%; W.S.C. 2%; Mt. 1%; Pac. 0%; unknown 2%

Syracuse University
Suite 440
Syracuse, NY 13244-1030
www.law.syr.edu
Private
Admissions: (315) 443-1962
Email: admissions@law.syr.edu
Financial aid: (315) 443-1963
Application deadline: 04/01
Tuition: full time: $46,064; part time: N/A
Room/board/expenses: $18,636
Median grant: $13,500
Average student indebtedness at graduation: $129,249

Enrollment: full time: 539; part time: 1
men: 59%; women: 41%; minorities: 17%
Acceptance rate (full time): 56%
Midrange LSAT (full time): 153-157
Midrange undergraduate GPA (full time): 3.19-3.55
Midrange of full-time private-sector salaries of 2013 grads: $50,000-$90,000
2013 grads employed in: law firms: 42%; business and industry: 27%; government: 19%; public interest: 5%; judicial clerk: 4%; academia: 2%; unknown: 1%
Employment location for 2013 class: Intl. N/A; N.E. %; M.A. 60%; E.N.C. 4%; W.N.C. 1%; S.A. 15%; E.S.C. 4%; W.S.C. 3%; Mt. 1%; Pac. 5%; unknown 0%

Touro College (Fuchsberg)
225 Eastview Drive
Central Islip, NY 11722
www.tourolaw.edu
Private
Admissions: (631) 761-7010
Email: admissions@tourolaw.edu
Financial aid: (631) 761-7020
Application deadline: 08/01
Tuition: full time: $44,520; part time: $33,220
Room/board/expenses: $28,258
Median grant: $9,000
Average student indebtedness at graduation: $154,855
Enrollment: full time: 383; part time: 204
men: 45%; women: 55%; minorities: 36%
Acceptance rate (full time): 71%
Midrange LSAT (full time): 145-149
Midrange undergraduate GPA (full time): 2.80-3.33
Midrange of full-time private-sector salaries of 2013 grads: $45,000-$65,000
2013 grads employed in: law firms: 57%; business and industry: 27%; government: 10%; public interest: 3%; judicial clerk: 1%; academia: 2%; unknown: 0%
Employment location for 2013 class: Intl. N/A; N.E. %; M.A. 98%; E.N.C. 0%; W.N.C. 0%; S.A. 2%; E.S.C. 0%; W.S.C. 0%; Mt. 0%; Pac. 0%; unknown 0%

Yeshiva University (Cardozo)
55 Fifth Avenue, 10th Floor
New York, NY 10003
www.cardozo.yu.edu
Private
Admissions: (212) 790-0274
Email: lawinfo@yu.edu
Financial aid: (212) 790-0392
Application deadline: 04/01
Tuition: full time: $53,570; part time: $53,570
Room/board/expenses: $26,401
Median grant: $30,000
Average student indebtedness at graduation: $121,644
Enrollment: full time: 947; part time: 75
men: 49%; women: 51%; minorities: 26%
Acceptance rate (full time): 49%
Midrange LSAT (full time): 157-163
Midrange undergraduate GPA (full time): 3.27-3.67
Midrange of full-time private-sector salaries of 2013 grads: $50,000-$133,000

2013 grads employed in: law firms: 49%; business and industry: 25%; government: 10%; public interest: 11%; judicial clerk: 5%; academia: 0%; unknown: 0%
Employment location for 2013 class: Intl. N/A; N.E. %; M.A. 88%; E.N.C. 2%; W.N.C. 1%; S.A. 2%; E.S.C. 0%; W.S.C. 0%; Mt. 0%; Pac. 3%; unknown 0%

NORTH CAROLINA

Campbell University
225 Hillsborough Street, Suite 401
Raleigh, NC 27603
www.law.campbell.edu
Private
Admissions: (919) 865-5989
Email: admissions@law.campbell.edu
Financial aid: (919) 865-5990
Application deadline: 05/01
Tuition: full time: $38,645; part time: $19,745
Room/board/expenses: $26,665
Median grant: $12,500
Average student indebtedness at graduation: $90,065
Enrollment: full time: 421; part time: 21
men: 51%; women: 49%; minorities: 14%
Acceptance rate (full time): 58%
Midrange LSAT (full time): 150-156
Midrange undergraduate GPA (full time): 2.93-3.47
Midrange of full-time private-sector salaries of 2013 grads: $45,000-$80,000
2013 grads employed in: law firms: 43%; business and industry: 34%; government: 12%; public interest: 4%; judicial clerk: 7%; academia: 1%; unknown: 0%
Employment location for 2013 class: Intl. N/A; N.E. %; M.A. 0%; E.N.C. 0%; W.N.C. 1%; S.A. 98%; E.S.C. 0%; W.S.C. 1%; Mt. 0%; Pac. 0%; unknown 0%

Charlotte School of Law
201 South College Street
Suite 400
Charlotte, NC 28244
www.charlottelaw.edu/
Private
Admissions: (704) 971-8500
Email: admissions@charlottelaw.edu
Financial aid: (704) 971-8386
Application deadline: rolling
Tuition: full time: $41,348; part time: $33,448
Room/board/expenses: $22,620
Median grant: $15,000
Average student indebtedness at graduation: $140,528
Enrollment: full time: 957; part time: 310
men: 40%; women: 60%; minorities: 48%
Acceptance rate (full time): 75%
Midrange LSAT (full time): 140-147
Midrange undergraduate GPA (full time): 2.59-3.21
Midrange of full-time private-sector salaries of 2013 grads: $45,000-$65,500
2013 grads employed in: law firms: 39%; business and industry: 33%; government: 7%; public interest: 10%; judicial clerk: 2%; academia: 8%; unknown: 0%

Employment location for 2013 class: Intl. N/A; N.E. %; M.A. 3%; E.N.C. 3%; W.N.C. 2%; S.A. 85%; E.S.C. 1%; W.S.C. 1%; Mt. 3%; Pac. 1%; unknown 0%

Duke University
210 Science Drive
Box 90362
Durham, NC 27708-0362
www.law.duke.edu
Private
Admissions: (919) 613-7020
Email: admissions@law.duke.edu
Financial aid: (919) 613-7026
Application deadline: 02/15
Tuition: full time: $55,588; part time: N/A
Room/board/expenses: $18,705
Median grant: $18,000
Average student indebtedness at graduation: $125,406
Enrollment: full time: 643; part time: 20
men: 57%; women: 43%; minorities: 26%
Acceptance rate (full time): 21%
Midrange LSAT (full time): 166-170
Midrange undergraduate GPA (full time): 3.66-3.85
Midrange of full-time private-sector salaries of 2013 grads: $145,000-$160,000
2013 grads employed in: law firms: 66%; business and industry: 6%; government: 7%; public interest: 4%; judicial clerk: 17%; academia: 1%; unknown: 0%
Employment location for 2013 class: Intl. N/A; N.E. %; M.A. 28%; E.N.C. 7%; W.N.C. 1%; S.A. 37%; E.S.C. 0%; W.S.C. 10%; Mt. 3%; Pac. 8%; unknown 0%

Elon University
201 N. Greene Street
Greensboro, NC 27401
law.elon.edu
Private
Admissions: (336) 279-9200
Email: law@elon.edu
Financial aid: (336) 278-2000
Application deadline: rolling
Tuition: full time: $37,924; part time: N/A
Room/board/expenses: $25,718
Median grant: $12,500
Average student indebtedness at graduation: $132,444
Enrollment: full time: 281; part time: N/A
men: 47%; women: 53%; minorities: 21%
Acceptance rate (full time): 75%
Midrange LSAT (full time): 145-151
Midrange undergraduate GPA (full time): 2.70-3.34
Midrange of full-time private-sector salaries of 2013 grads: $43,700-$55,000
2013 grads employed in: law firms: 43%; business and industry: 30%; government: 7%; public interest: 9%; judicial clerk: 3%; academia: 7%; unknown: 0%
Employment location for 2013 class: Intl. N/A; N.E. %; M.A. 0%; E.N.C. 2%; W.N.C. 0%; S.A. 94%; E.S.C. 2%; W.S.C. 1%; Mt. 0%; Pac. 0%; unknown 0%

North Carolina Central University
640 Nelson Street
Durham, NC 27707
law.nccu.edu
Public
Admissions: (919) 530-5243
Email: recruiter@nccu.edu
Financial aid: (919) 530-6365
Application deadline: 03/31
In-state tuition: full time: $12,655; part time: $12,655
Out-of-state tuition: full time: $27,696
Room/board/expenses: $22,908
Median grant: $6,294
Average student indebtedness at graduation: $58,061
Enrollment: full time: 495; part time: 100
men: 40%; women: 60%; minorities: 63%
Acceptance rate (full time): 55%
Midrange LSAT (full time): 141-148
Midrange undergraduate GPA (full time): 2.97-3.45
Midrange of full-time private-sector salaries of 2013 grads: N/A-N/A
2013 grads employed in: law firms: 37%; business and industry: 29%; government: 6%; public interest: 8%; judicial clerk: 5%; academia: 14%; unknown: 1%
Employment location for 2013 class: Intl. N/A; N.E. %; M.A. 3%; E.N.C. 1%; W.N.C. 3%; S.A. 89%; E.S.C. 3%; W.S.C. 0%; Mt. 1%; Pac. 0%; unknown 1%

University of North Carolina–Chapel Hill
Van Hecke-Wettach Hall
CB No. 3380
Chapel Hill, NC 27599-3380
www.law.unc.edu
Public
Admissions: (919) 962-5109
Email: law_admission@unc.edu
Financial aid: (919) 962-8396
Application deadline: 08/01
In-state tuition: full time: $22,560; part time: N/A
Out-of-state tuition: full time: $39,191
Room/board/expenses: $24,910
Median grant: $2,628
Average student indebtedness at graduation: $92,475
Enrollment: full time: 667; part time: N/A
men: 50%; women: 50%; minorities: 24%
Acceptance rate (full time): 40%
Midrange LSAT (full time): 157-163
Midrange undergraduate GPA (full time): 3.33-3.66
Midrange of full-time private-sector salaries of 2013 grads: $70,000-$145,000
2013 grads employed in: law firms: 52%; business and industry: 18%; government: 10%; public interest: 6%; judicial clerk: 10%; academia: 4%; unknown: 0%
Employment location for 2013 class: Intl. N/A; N.E. %; M.A. 10%; E.N.C. 2%; W.N.C. 0%; S.A. 81%; E.S.C. 0%; W.S.C. 1%; Mt. 1%; Pac. 2%; unknown 0%

Wake Forest University

Reynolda Station
PO Box 7206
Winston-Salem, NC 27109
www.law.wfu.edu
Private
Admissions: (336) 758-5437
Email: lawadmissions@wfu.edu
Financial aid: (336) 758-5437
Application deadline: 03/15
Tuition: full time: $42,276; part time: N/A
Room/board/expenses: $21,129
Median grant: $20,000
Average student indebtedness at graduation: $107,532
Enrollment: full time: 486; part time: 15
men: 53%; women: 47%; minorities: 21%
Acceptance rate (full time): 53%
Midrange LSAT (full time): 157-163
Midrange undergraduate GPA (full time): 3.37-3.78
Midrange of full-time private-sector salaries of 2013 grads: $65,000-$130,000
2013 grads employed in: law firms: 58%; business and industry: 10%; government: 18%; public interest: 4%; judicial clerk: 8%; academia: 2%; unknown: 1%
Employment location for 2013 class: Intl. N/A; N.E. %; M.A. 5%; E.N.C. 2%; W.N.C. 1%; S.A. 78%; E.S.C. 4%; W.S.C. 7%; Mt. 1%; Pac. 2%; unknown 0%

NORTH DAKOTA

University of North Dakota

215 Centennial Drive
Stop 9003
Grand Forks, ND 58202
www.law.und.edu
Public
Admissions: (701) 777-2260
Email: benjamin.hoffman@law.und.edu
Financial aid; (701) 777-3121
Application deadline: 07/15
In-state tuition: full time: $10,925; part time: N/A
Out-of-state tuition: full time: $24,249
Room/board/expenses: $19,019
Median grant: $2,418
Average student indebtedness at graduation: $64,818
Enrollment: full time: 229; part time: N/A
men: 54%; women: 46%; minorities: 11%
Acceptance rate (full time): 54%
Midrange LSAT (full time): 143-152
Midrange undergraduate GPA (full time): 2.94-3.61
Midrange of full-time private-sector salaries of 2013 grads: $45,000-$58,250
2013 grads employed in: law firms: 41%; business and industry: 16%; government: 10%; public interest: 5%; judicial clerk: 23%; academia: 5%; unknown: 0%
Employment location for 2013 class: Intl. N/A; N.E. %; M.A. 0%; E.N.C. 3%; W.N.C. 84%; S.A. 5%; E.S.C. 2%; W.S.C. 0%; Mt. 2%; Pac. 0%; unknown 0%

OHIO

Capital University

303 E. Broad Street
Columbus, OH 43215-3200
www.law.capital.edu
Private
Admissions: (614) 236-6310
Email: admissions@law.capital.edu
Financial aid: (614) 236-6350
Application deadline: rolling
Tuition: full time: $1,185/credit hour; part time: $1,185/credit hour
Room/board/expenses: $18,070
Median grant: $10,000
Average student indebtedness at graduation: $113,434
Enrollment: full time: 291; part time: 184
men: 54%; women: 46%; minorities: 21%
Acceptance rate (full time): 82%
Midrange LSAT (full time): 145-152
Midrange undergraduate GPA (full time): 2.80-3.49
Midrange of full-time private-sector salaries of 2013 grads: $40,000-$78,000
2013 grads employed in: law firms: 51%; business and industry: 25%; government: 21%; public interest: 1%; judicial clerk: 1%; academia: 0%; unknown: 0%
Employment location for 2013 class: Intl. N/A; N.E. %; M.A. 0%; E.N.C. 91%; W.N.C. 1%; S.A. 4%; E.S.C. 1%; W.S.C. 1%; Mt. 2%; Pac. 0%; unknown 0%

Case Western Reserve University

11075 E. Boulevard
Cleveland, OH 44106-7148
www.law.case.edu
Private
Admissions: (800) 756-0036
Email: lawadmissions@case.edu
Financial aid: (877) 889-4279
Application deadline: 04/01
Tuition: full time: $47,728; part time: N/A
Room/board/expenses: $22,644
Median grant: $27,000
Average student indebtedness at graduation: $131,724
Enrollment: full time: 397; part time: 1
men: 52%; women: 48%; minorities: 18%
Acceptance rate (full time): 33%
Midrange LSAT (full time): 157-162
Midrange undergraduate GPA (full time): 3.24-3.63
Midrange of full-time private-sector salaries of 2013 grads: $58,139-$110,000
2013 grads employed in: law firms: 46%; business and industry: 20%; government: 16%; public interest: 11%; judicial clerk: 5%; academia: 2%; unknown: 0%
Employment location for 2013 class: Intl. N/A; N.E. %; M.A. 10%; E.N.C. 64%; W.N.C. 1%; S.A. 11%; E.S.C. 1%; W.S.C. 3%; Mt. 3%; Pac. 3%; unknown 0%

Cleveland State University (Cleveland-Marshall)

2121 Euclid Avenue, LB 138
Cleveland, OH 44115-2214
www.law.csuohio.edu
Public
Admissions: (216) 687-2304
Email: law.admissions@csuohio.edu
Financial aid: (216) 687-2304
Application deadline: 05/01
In-state tuition: full time: $24,887; part time: $20,101
Out-of-state tuition: full time: $34,174
Room/board/expenses: $18,344
Median grant: $5,954
Average student indebtedness at graduation: $89,879
Enrollment: full time: 314; part time: 91
men: 58%; women: 42%; minorities: 16%
Acceptance rate (full time): 56%
Midrange LSAT (full time): 151-156
Midrange undergraduate GPA (full time): 3.02-3.56
Midrange of full-time private-sector salaries of 2013 grads: $50,000-$80,000
2013 grads employed in: law firms: 53%; business and industry: 27%; government: 16%; public interest: 4%; judicial clerk: 1%; academia: 0%; unknown: 0%
Employment location for 2013 class: Intl. N/A; N.E. %; M.A. 4%; E.N.C. 90%; W.N.C. 0%; S.A. 3%; E.S.C. 0%; W.S.C. 0%; Mt. 0%; Pac. 2%; unknown 0%

Ohio Northern University (Pettit)

525 S. Main Street
Ada, OH 45810-1599
www.law.onu.edu
Private
Admissions: (877) 452-9668
Email: lawadmissions@onu.edu
Financial aid: (419) 772-2272
Application deadline: 08/15
Tuition: full time: $24,800; part time: N/A
Room/board/expenses: $19,543
Median grant: $22,000
Average student indebtedness at graduation: $107,764
Enrollment: full time: 206; part time: N/A
men: 52%; women: 48%; minorities: 15%
Acceptance rate (full time): 49%
Midrange LSAT (full time): 144-152
Midrange undergraduate GPA (full time): 2.86-3.58
Midrange of full-time private-sector salaries of 2013 grads: $38,000-$120,000
2013 grads employed in: law firms: 62%; business and industry: 17%; government: 13%; public interest: 4%; judicial clerk: 4%; academia: 0%; unknown: 1%
Employment location for 2013 class: Intl. N/A; N.E. %; M.A. 18%; E.N.C. 51%; W.N.C. 0%; S.A. 12%; E.S.C. 3%; W.S.C. 5%; Mt. 10%; Pac. 1%; unknown 0%

Ohio State University (Moritz)

55 W. 12th Avenue
Columbus, OH 43210
www.moritzlaw.osu.edu
Public
Admissions: (614) 292-8810
Email: lawadmit@osu.edu
Financial aid: (614) 292-8807
Application deadline: 03/31
In-state tuition: full time: $28,577; part time: N/A
Out-of-state tuition: full time: $43,508
Room/board/expenses: $19,287
Median grant: $11,000
Average student indebtedness at graduation: $97,021
Enrollment: full time: 532; part time: N/A
men: 54%; women: 46%; minorities: 19%
Acceptance rate (full time): 50%
Midrange LSAT (full time): 156-162
Midrange undergraduate GPA (full time): 3.44-3.79
Midrange of full-time private-sector salaries of 2013 grads: $52,000-$110,000
2013 grads employed in: law firms: 40%; business and industry: 27%; government: 17%; public interest: 7%; judicial clerk: 5%; academia: 4%; unknown: 0%
Employment location for 2013 class: Intl. N/A; N.E. %; M.A. 5%; E.N.C. 80%; W.N.C. 0%; S.A. 6%; E.S.C. 0%; W.S.C. 2%; Mt. 2%; Pac. 4%; unknown 0%

University of Akron

C. Blake McDowell Law Center
Akron, OH 44325-2901
www.uakron.edu/law
Public
Admissions: (800) 425-7668
Email: lawadmissions@uakron.edu
Financial aid: (800) 621-3847
Application deadline: 03/31
In-state tuition: full time: $24,340; part time: $14,947
Out-of-state tuition: full time: $24,440
Room/board/expenses: $16,524
Median grant: $12,000
Average student indebtedness at graduation: $82,322
Enrollment: full time: 274; part time: 170
men: 57%; women: 43%; minorities: 13%
Acceptance rate (full time): 63%
Midrange LSAT (full time): 146-155
Midrange undergraduate GPA (full time): 3.14-3.77
Midrange of full-time private-sector salaries of 2013 grads: $45,000-$75,000
2013 grads employed in: law firms: 52%; business and industry: 26%; government: 16%; public interest: 2%; judicial clerk: 0%; academia: 2%; unknown: 1%
Employment location for 2013 class: Intl. N/A; N.E. %; M.A. 4%; E.N.C. 84%; W.N.C. 0%; S.A. 5%; E.S.C. 0%; W.S.C. 1%; Mt. 2%; Pac. 2%; unknown 1%

University of Cincinnati

PO Box 210040
Cincinnati, OH 45221-0040
www.law.uc.edu
Public
Admissions: (513) 556-6805
Email: admissions@law.uc.edu
Financial aid: (513) 556-0078
Application deadline: 03/15
In-state tuition: full time: $24,010; part time: N/A
Out-of-state tuition: full time: $29,010
Room/board/expenses: $18,336
Median grant: $6,500
Average student indebtedness at graduation: $76,663
Enrollment: full time: 293; part time: N/A
men: 60%; women: 40%; minorities: 13%
Acceptance rate (full time): 60%
Midrange LSAT (full time): 151-159
Midrange undergraduate GPA (full time): 3.22-3.70
Midrange of full-time private-sector salaries of 2013 grads: $55,000-$105,000
2013 grads employed in: law firms: 44%; business and industry: 20%; government: 21%; public interest: 5%; judicial clerk: 5%; academia: 5%; unknown: 2%
Employment location for 2013 class: Intl. N/A; N.E. %; M.A. 2%; E.N.C. 73%; W.N.C. 1%; S.A. 9%; E.S.C. 7%; W.S.C. 3%; Mt. 2%; Pac. 3%; unknown 0%

University of Dayton

300 College Park
Dayton, OH 45469-2772
www.udayton.edu/law
Private
Admissions: (937) 229-3555
Email: lawinfo@udayton.edu
Financial aid: (937) 229-3555
Application deadline: 05/01
Tuition: full time: $35,273; part time: N/A
Room/board/expenses: $17,500
Median grant: $10,000
Average student indebtedness at graduation: $113,486
Enrollment: full time: 276; part time: N/A
men: 52%; women: 48%; minorities: 19%
Acceptance rate (full time): 58%
Midrange LSAT (full time): 145-151
Midrange undergraduate GPA (full time): 2.86-3.38
Midrange of full-time private-sector salaries of 2013 grads: $50,000-$70,000
2013 grads employed in: law firms: 67%; business and industry: 9%; government: 15%; public interest: 5%; judicial clerk: 0%; academia: 4%; unknown: 0%
Employment location for 2013 class: Intl. N/A; N.E. %; M.A. 2%; E.N.C. 75%; W.N.C. 1%; S.A. 11%; E.S.C. 6%; W.S.C. 1%; Mt. 2%; Pac. 2%; unknown 0%

University of Toledo

2801 W. Bancroft
Toledo, OH 43606
utoledo.edu/law/admissions
Public
Admissions: (419) 530-4131
Email: utoledo.edu/law
Financial aid: (419) 530-7929
Application deadline: 08/03
In-state tuition: full time: $22,203;
part time: $925/credit hour
Out-of-state tuition: full time:
$33,752
Room/board/expenses: $19,468
Median grant: $12,510
**Average student indebtedness at
graduation:** $96,924
Enrollment: full time: 233; part
time: 66
men: 56%; women: 44%;
minorities: 16%
Acceptance rate (full time): 62%
Midrange LSAT (full time): 148-154
**Midrange undergraduate GPA (full
time):** 3.02-3.55
**Midrange of full-time private-sector
salaries of 2013 grads:** $45,000-
$72,500
2013 grads employed in: law firms:
47%; business and industry: 25%;
government: 10%; public interest:
8%; judicial clerk: 7%; academia:
2%; unknown: 0%
Employment location for 2013 class:
Intl: N/A; N.E. %; M.A. 4%; E.N.C.
78%; W.N.C. 0%; S.A. 5%; E.S.C.
1%; W.S.C. 0%; Mt. 0%; Pac. 9%;
unknown 0%

OKLAHOMA

Oklahoma City University

2501 N. Blackwelder Avenue
Oklahoma City, OK 73106-1493
www.law.okcu.edu
Private
Admissions: (866) 529-6281
Email: lawquestions@okcu.edu
Financial aid: (800) 633-7242
Application deadline: 08/01
Tuition: full time: $1,065/credit
hour; part time: $1,065/credit
hour
Room/board/expenses: $20,738
Median grant: $16,000
**Average student indebtedness at
graduation:** $121,476
Enrollment: full time: 399; part
time: 54
men: 53%; women: 47%;
minorities: 32%
Acceptance rate (full time): 83%
Midrange LSAT (full time): 145-152
**Midrange undergraduate GPA (full
time):** 2.81-3.39
**Midrange of full-time private-sector
salaries of 2013 grads:** $45,000-
$65,000
2013 grads employed in: law firms:
55%; business and industry: 24%;
government: 16%; public interest:
2%; judicial clerk: 1%; academia:
3%; unknown: 0%
Employment location for 2013 class:
Intl: N/A; N.E. %; M.A. 1%; E.N.C.
1%; W.N.C. 5%; S.A. 2%; E.S.C.
1%; W.S.C. 83%; Mt. 6%; Pac. 1%;
unknown 0%

University of Oklahoma

Andrew M. Coats Hall
300 Timberdell Road
Norman, OK 73019-5081
www.law.ou.edu
Public
Admissions: (405) 325-4728
Email: admissions@law.ou.edu
Financial aid: (405) 325-4521
Application deadline: 03/15
In-state tuition: full time: $19,973;
part time: N/A
Out-of-state tuition: full time:
$30,398
Room/board/expenses: $17,860
Median grant: $5,560
**Average student indebtedness at
graduation:** $81,789
Enrollment: full time: 475; part
time: N/A
men: 56%; women: 44%;
minorities: 24%
Acceptance rate (full time): 43%
Midrange LSAT (full time): 155-158
**Midrange undergraduate GPA (full
time):** 3.24-3.76
**Midrange of full-time private-sector
salaries of 2013 grads:** $47,000-
$79,000
2013 grads employed in: law firms:
56%; business and industry: 23%;
government: 16%; public interest:
3%; judicial clerk: 1%; academia:
1%; unknown: 0%
Employment location for 2013 class:
Intl: N/A; N.E. %; M.A. 1%; E.N.C.
1%; W.N.C. 1%; S.A. 2%; E.S.C.
0%; W.S.C. 90%; Mt. 4%; Pac.
2%; unknown 0%

University of Tulsa

3120 E. Fourth Place
Tulsa, OK 74104
www.utulsa.edu/law
Private
Admissions: (918) 631-2709
Email: lawadmissions@utulsa.edu
Financial aid: (918) 631-2526
Application deadline: 07/31
Tuition: full time: $34,490; part
time: N/A
Room/board/expenses: $19,560
Median grant: $18,000
**Average student indebtedness at
graduation:** $99,305
Enrollment: full time: 244; part
time: 22
men: 52%; women: 48%;
minorities: 21%
Acceptance rate (full time): 32%
Midrange LSAT (full time): 151-158
**Midrange undergraduate GPA (full
time):** 3.12-3.73
**Midrange of full-time private-sector
salaries of 2013 grads:** $53,000-
$75,000
2013 grads employed in: law firms:
48%; business and industry: 29%;
government: 9%; public interest:
8%; judicial clerk: 2%; academia:
4%; unknown: 0%
Employment location for 2013 class:
Intl: N/A; N.E. %; M.A. 0%; E.N.C.
2%; W.N.C. 3%; S.A. 4%; E.S.C.
0%; W.S.C. 82%; Mt. 6%; Pac.
3%; unknown 0%

OREGON

Lewis & Clark College (Northwestern)

10015 S.W. Terwilliger Boulevard
Portland, OR 97219
law.lclark.edu
Private
Admissions: (503) 768-6613
Email: lawadmss@lclark.edu
Financial aid: (503) 768-7090
Application deadline: 03/15
Tuition: full time: $40,114; part
time: $30,084
Room/board/expenses: $22,600
Median grant: $16,000
**Average student indebtedness at
graduation:** $127,064
Enrollment: full time: 437; part
time: 188
men: 54%; women: 46%;
minorities: 22%
Acceptance rate (full time): 68%
Midrange LSAT (full time): 155-161
**Midrange undergraduate GPA (full
time):** 3.00-3.59
**Midrange of full-time private-sector
salaries of 2013 grads:** $48,000-
$75,000
2013 grads employed in: law firms:
38%; business and industry:
16%; government: 15%; public
interest: 15%; judicial clerk: 13%;
academia: 2%; unknown: 0%
Employment location for 2013 class:
Intl: N/A; N.E. %; M.A. 1%; E.N.C.
1%; W.N.C. 0%; S.A. 2%; E.S.C.
1%; W.S.C. 1%; Mt. 4%; Pac. 85%;
unknown 0%

University of Oregon

1221 University of Oregon
Eugene, OR 97403-1221
www.law.uoregon.edu
Public
Admissions: (541) 346-3846
Email:
admissions@law.uoregon.edu
Financial aid: (800) 760-6953
Application deadline: 03/01
In-state tuition: full time: $30,586;
part time: N/A
Out-of-state tuition: full time:
$38,056
Room/board/expenses: $14,322
Median grant: $10,000
**Average student indebtedness at
graduation:** $105,900
Enrollment: full time: 372; part
time: N/A
men: 59%; women: 41%;
minorities: 20%
Acceptance rate (full time): 54%
Midrange LSAT (full time): 154-159
**Midrange undergraduate GPA (full
time):** 2.97-3.56
**Midrange of full-time private-sector
salaries of 2013 grads:** $53,750-
$102,500
2013 grads employed in: law firms:
40%; business and industry:
11%; government: 11%; public
interest: 12%; judicial clerk: 21%;
academia: 5%; unknown: 0%
Employment location for 2013 class:
Intl: N/A; N.E. %; M.A. 0%; E.N.C.
2%; W.N.C. 0%; S.A. 2%; E.S.C.
0%; W.S.C. 2%; Mt. 12%; Pac.
81%; unknown 0%

Willamette University (Collins)

245 Winter Street SE
Salem, OR 97301
www.willamette.edu/wucl
Private
Admissions: (503) 370-6282
Email:
law-admission@willamette.edu
Financial aid: (503) 370-6273
Application deadline: 03/01
Tuition: full time: $37,625; part
time: $26,064
Room/board/expenses: $17,210
Median grant: $10,500
**Average student indebtedness at
graduation:** $136,099
Enrollment: full time: 312; part
time: 6
men: 55%; women: 45%;
minorities: 17%
Acceptance rate (full time): 74%
Midrange LSAT (full time): 149-155
**Midrange undergraduate GPA (full
time):** 2.96-3.49
**Midrange of full-time private-sector
salaries of 2013 grads:** $45,000-
$71,000
2013 grads employed in: law firms:
50%; business and industry: 22%;
government: 14%; public interest:
5%; judicial clerk: 4%; academia:
2%; unknown: 3%
Employment location for 2013 class:
Intl: N/A; N.E. %; M.A. 0%; E.N.C.
0%; W.N.C. 1%; S.A. 1%; E.S.C.
0%; W.S.C. 1%; Mt. 4%; Pac. 93%;
unknown 0%

PENNSYLVANIA

Drexel University (Kline)

3320 Market Street, Suite 400
Philadelphia, PA 19104
www.drexel.edu/law/admissions/
overview/
Private
Admissions: (215) 895-1529
Email: lawadmissions@drexel.edu
Financial aid: (215) 895-1044
Application deadline: rolling
Tuition: full time: $1,354/credit
hour; part time: N/A
Room/board/expenses: $21,382
Median grant: $20,000
**Average student indebtedness at
graduation:** $91,915
Enrollment: full time: 394; part
time: 10
men: 54%; women: 46%;
minorities: 14%
Acceptance rate (full time): 50%
Midrange LSAT (full time): 151-156
**Midrange undergraduate GPA (full
time):** 3.05-3.49
**Midrange of full-time private-sector
salaries of 2013 grads:** $40,000-
$115,000
2013 grads employed in: law firms:
43%; business and industry: 24%;
government: 10%; public interest:
7%; judicial clerk: 13%; academia:
3%; unknown: 0%
Employment location for 2013 class:
Intl: N/A; N.E. %; M.A. 78%; E.N.C.
2%; W.N.C. 0%; S.A. 15%; E.S.C.
0%; W.S.C. 1%; Mt. 0%; Pac. 2%;
unknown 1%

Duquesne University

600 Forbes Avenue
Pittsburgh, PA 15282
www.duq.edu/law
Private
Admissions: (412) 396-6296
Email: lawadmissions@duq.edu
Financial aid: (412) 396-6607
Application deadline: 03/01
Tuition: full time: $38,420; part
time: $29,706
Room/board/expenses: $14,928
Median grant: $8,000
**Average student indebtedness at
graduation:** $107,496
Enrollment: full time: 310; part
time: 114
men: 52%; women: 48%;
minorities: 8%
Acceptance rate (full time): 58%
Midrange LSAT (full time): 151-155
**Midrange undergraduate GPA (full
time):** 3.18-3.71
**Midrange of full-time private-sector
salaries of 2013 grads:** $50,000-
$90,000
2013 grads employed in: law firms:
50%; business and industry: 29%;
government: 9%; public interest:
1%; judicial clerk: 9%; academia:
1%; unknown: 1%
Employment location for 2013 class:
Intl: N/A; N.E. %; M.A. 95%; E.N.C.
0%; W.N.C. 1%; S.A. 4%; E.S.C.
0%; W.S.C. 1%; Mt. 0%; Pac. 0%;
unknown 0%

Pennsylvania State University (Dickinson)

Lewis Katz Building
University Park, PA 16802
Public
Admissions: N/A
Financial aid: N/A
Application deadline: rolling
In-state tuition: full time: $43,700;
part time: N/A
Out-of-state tuition: full time:
$43,700
Room/board/expenses: $22,236
Median grant: $14,700
**Average student indebtedness at
graduation:** $123,842
Enrollment: full time: 479; part
time: N/A
men: 55%; women: 45%;
minorities: 17%
Acceptance rate (full time): 46%
Midrange LSAT (full time): 153-160
**Midrange undergraduate GPA (full
time):** 3.30-3.79
**Midrange of full-time private-sector
salaries of 2013 grads:** $53,500-
$92,800
2013 grads employed in: law firms:
34%; business and industry: 22%;
government: 14%; public interest:
3%; judicial clerk: 19%; academia:
5%; unknown: 2%
Employment location for 2013 class:
Intl: N/A; N.E. %; M.A. 52%; E.N.C.
6%; W.N.C. 1%; S.A. 17%; E.S.C.
0%; W.S.C. 2%; Mt. 3%; Pac. 6%;
unknown 9%

Temple University (Beasley)

1719 N. Broad Street
Philadelphia, PA 19122
www.law.temple.edu
Public
Admissions: (800) 560-1428
Email: lawadmis@temple.edu
Financial aid: (800) 560-1428
Application deadline: 03/01
In-state tuition: full time: $21,646; part time: $17,466
Out-of-state tuition: full time: $34,772
Room/board/expenses: $22,464
Median grant: $10,000
Average student indebtedness at graduation: $97,323
Enrollment: full time: 563; part time: 160
men: 55%; women: 45%; minorities: 25%
Acceptance rate (full time): 44%
Midrange LSAT (full time): 157-162
Midrange undergraduate GPA (full time): 3.25-3.67
Midrange of full-time private-sector salaries of 2013 grads: $55,000-$115,000
2013 grads employed in: law firms: 43%; business and industry: 21%; government: 11%; public interest: 10%; judicial clerk: 14%; academia: 2%; unknown: 0%
Employment location for 2013 class: Intl. N/A; N.E. %; M.A. 84%; E.N.C. 1%; W.N.C. 0%; S.A. 8%; E.S.C. 0%; W.S.C. 0%; Mt. 2%; Pac. 3%; unknown 0%

University of Pennsylvania

3501 Sansom Street
Philadelphia, PA 19104-6204
www.law.upenn.edu
Private
Admissions: (215) 898-7400
Email: contactadmissions@law.upenn.edu
Financial aid: (215) 898-7400
Application deadline: 03/01
Tuition: full time: $56,916; part time: N/A
Room/board/expenses: $22,444
Median grant: $18,000
Average student indebtedness at graduation: $130,002
Enrollment: full time: 756; part time: N/A
men: 55%; women: 45%; minorities: 28%
Acceptance rate (full time): 16%
Midrange LSAT (full time): 164-170
Midrange undergraduate GPA (full time): 3.52-3.95
Midrange of full-time private-sector salaries of 2013 grads: $160,000-$160,000
2013 grads employed in: law firms: 66%; business and industry: 8%; government: 4%; public interest: 6%; judicial clerk: 16%; academia: 1%; unknown: 0%
Employment location for 2013 class: Intl. N/A; N.E. %; M.A. 58%; E.N.C. 2%; W.N.C. 0%; S.A. 23%; E.S.C. 0%; W.S.C. 3%; Mt. 2%; Pac. 7%; unknown 0%

University of Pittsburgh

3900 Forbes Avenue
Pittsburgh, PA 15260
www.law.pitt.edu
Public
Admissions: (412) 648-1415

Email: admissions@law.pitt.edu
Financial aid: (412) 648-1415
Application deadline: 04/01
In-state tuition: full time: $31,616; part time: N/A
Out-of-state tuition: full time: $39,100
Room/board/expenses: $18,392
Median grant: $14,000
Average student indebtedness at graduation: $103,461
Enrollment: full time: 526; part time: 3
men: 56%; women: 44%; minorities: 18%
Acceptance rate (full time): 44%
Midrange LSAT (full time): 152-160
Midrange undergraduate GPA (full time): 3.09-3.68
Midrange of full-time private-sector salaries of 2013 grads: $56,250-$105,000
2013 grads employed in: law firms: 42%; business and industry: 27%; government: 9%; public interest: 7%; judicial clerk: 13%; academia: 3%; unknown: 0%
Employment location for 2013 class: Intl. N/A; N.E. %; M.A. 79%; E.N.C. 2%; W.N.C. 0%; S.A. 10%; E.S.C. 0%; W.S.C. 2%; Mt. 2%; Pac. 4%; unknown 0%

Villanova University

299 N. Spring Mill Road
Villanova, PA 19085
www.law.villanova.edu/
Private
Admissions: (610) 519-7010
Email: admissions@law.villanova.edu
Financial aid: (610) 519-7015
Application deadline: 04/01
Tuition: full time: $41,250; part time: N/A
Room/board/expenses: $22,732
Median grant: $25,000
Average student indebtedness at graduation: $95,297
Enrollment: full time: 536; part time: N/A
men: 51%; women: 49%; minorities: 17%
Acceptance rate (full time): 51%
Midrange LSAT (full time): 152-159
Midrange undergraduate GPA (full time): 3.33-3.72
Midrange of full-time private-sector salaries of 2013 grads: $55,000-$125,000
2013 grads employed in: law firms: 50%; business and industry: 19%; government: 8%; public interest: 4%; judicial clerk: 16%; academia: 2%; unknown: 1%
Employment location for 2013 class: Intl. N/A; N.E. %; M.A. 71%; E.N.C. 2%; W.N.C. 2%; S.A. 15%; E.S.C. 1%; W.S.C. 1%; Mt. 2%; Pac. 2%; unknown 0%

PUERTO RICO

Inter-American University[1]

PO Box 70351
San Juan, PR 00936-8351
www.metro.inter.edu
Private
Admissions: (787) 765-1270
Financial aid: N/A
Tuition: N/A
Room/board/expenses: N/A
Enrollment: N/A

Pontifical Catholic University of Puerto Rico[1]

2250 Avenida Las Americas
Suite 584
Ponce, PR 00717-0777
www.pucpr.edu
Private
Admissions: (787) 841-2000
Email: admisiones@pucpr.edu
Financial aid: N/A
Tuition: N/A
Room/board/expenses: N/A
Enrollment: N/A

University of Puerto Rico[1]

PO Box 23303
Estacion Universidad
Rio Piedras, PR 00931-3302
www.upr.edu
Public
Admissions: (787) 764-0000
Email: admisiones@upr.edu
Financial aid: N/A
Tuition: N/A
Room/board/expenses: N/A
Enrollment: N/A

RHODE ISLAND

Roger Williams University

10 Metacom Avenue
Bristol, RI 02809-5171
law.rwu.edu
Private
Admissions: (401) 254-4555
Email: Admissions@rwu.edu
Financial aid: (401) 254-4510
Application deadline: 04/01
Tuition: full time: $33,792; part time: N/A
Room/board/expenses: $17,386
Median grant: $20,000
Average student indebtedness at graduation: $128,543
Enrollment: full time: 370; part time: N/A
men: 51%; women: 49%; minorities: 18%
Acceptance rate (full time): 72%
Midrange LSAT (full time): 145-152
Midrange undergraduate GPA (full time): 2.85-3.41
Midrange of full-time private-sector salaries of 2013 grads: $39,000-$60,000
2013 grads employed in: law firms: 50%; business and industry: 23%; government: 8%; public interest: 5%; judicial clerk: 13%; academia: 2%; unknown: 0%
Employment location for 2013 class: Intl. N/A; N.E. %; M.A. 13%; E.N.C. 2%; W.N.C. 1%; S.A. 9%; E.S.C. 0%; W.S.C. 1%; Mt. 1%; Pac. 2%; unknown 0%

SOUTH CAROLINA

Charleston School of Law

PO Box 535
Charleston, SC 29402
www.charlestonlaw.edu
Private
Admissions: (843) 377-2143
Email: info@charlestonlaw.edu
Financial aid: (843) 377-1102
Application deadline: 03/01
Tuition: full time: $39,216; part time: $31,532
Room/board/expenses: $22,388
Median grant: $8,500

Average student indebtedness at graduation: $147,031
Enrollment: full time: 362; part time: 92
men: 55%; women: 45%; minorities: 17%
Acceptance rate (full time): 83%
Midrange LSAT (full time): 144-152
Midrange undergraduate GPA (full time): 2.63-3.31
Midrange of full-time private-sector salaries of 2013 grads: $35,000-$67,000
2013 grads employed in: law firms: 55%; business and industry: 18%; government: 10%; public interest: 4%; judicial clerk: 10%; academia: 2%; unknown: 2%
Employment location for 2013 class: Intl. N/A; N.E. %; M.A. 2%; E.N.C. 1%; W.N.C. 0%; S.A. 90%; E.S.C. 3%; W.S.C. 1%; Mt. 2%; Pac. 1%; unknown 0%

University of South Carolina

701 S. Main Street
Columbia, SC 29208
www.law.sc.edu/admissions
Public
Admissions: (803) 777-6605
Email: usclaw@law.sc.edu
Financial aid: (803) 777-6605
Application deadline: 03/01
In-state tuition: full time: $23,074; part time: N/A
Out-of-state tuition: full time: $46,180
Room/board/expenses: $17,947
Median grant: $20,564
Average student indebtedness at graduation: $84,590
Enrollment: full time: 619; part time: 2
men: 56%; women: 44%; minorities: 18%
Acceptance rate (full time): 57%
Midrange LSAT (full time): 152-157
Midrange undergraduate GPA (full time): 2.85-3.54
Midrange of full-time private-sector salaries of 2013 grads: $54,750-$92,500
2013 grads employed in: law firms: 47%; business and industry: 15%; government: 11%; public interest: 6%; judicial clerk: 21%; academia: 1%; unknown: 0%
Employment location for 2013 class: Intl. N/A; N.E. %; M.A. 1%; E.N.C. 2%; W.N.C. 0%; S.A. 95%; E.S.C. 1%; W.S.C. 0%; Mt. 1%; Pac. 0%; unknown 0%

SOUTH DAKOTA

University of South Dakota

414 E. Clark Street
Vermillion, SD 57069-2390
www.usd.edu/law/
Public
Admissions: (605) 677-6358
Email: law@usd.edu
Financial aid: (605) 677-5446
Application deadline: 07/15
In-state tuition: full time: $13,904; part time: $464/credit hour
Out-of-state tuition: full time: $29,518
Room/board/expenses: $14,364
Median grant: $1,930
Average student indebtedness at graduation: $78,963
Enrollment: full time: 198; part time: 4
men: 60%; women: 40%; minorities: 12%

Acceptance rate (full time): 83%
Midrange LSAT (full time): 144-152
Midrange undergraduate GPA (full time): 2.71-3.44
Midrange of full-time private-sector salaries of 2013 grads: $0-$0
2013 grads employed in: law firms: 42%; business and industry: 19%; government: 10%; public interest: 2%; judicial clerk: 23%; academia: 5%; unknown: 0%
Employment location for 2013 class: Intl. N/A; N.E. %; M.A. 0%; E.N.C. 3%; W.N.C. 81%; S.A. 2%; E.S.C. 2%; W.S.C. 0%; Mt. 13%; Pac. 0%; unknown 0%

TENNESSEE

Belmont University[1]

1900 Belmont Blvd.
Nashville, TN 37212
www.belmont.edu/law/
Private
Admissions: (615) 460-8400
Email: law@belmont.edu
Financial aid: N/A
Tuition: N/A
Room/board/expenses: N/A
Enrollment: N/A

University of Memphis (Humphreys)

1 North Front Street
Memphis, TN 38103-2189
www.memphis.edu/law
Public
Admissions: (901) 678-5403
Email: lawadmissions@memphis.edu
Financial aid: (901) 678-2743
Application deadline: 03/15
In-state tuition: full time: $17,927; part time: $850/credit hour
Out-of-state tuition: full time: $25,632
Room/board/expenses: $16,641
Median grant: $8,250
Average student indebtedness at graduation: $78,030
Enrollment: full time: 312; part time: 22
men: 60%; women: 40%; minorities: 25%
Acceptance rate (full time): 49%
Midrange LSAT (full time): 150-157
Midrange undergraduate GPA (full time): 2.93-3.50
Midrange of full-time private-sector salaries of 2013 grads: $40,000-$70,000
2013 grads employed in: law firms: 55%; business and industry: 16%; government: 12%; public interest: 6%; judicial clerk: 10%; academia: 2%; unknown: 0%
Employment location for 2013 class: Intl. N/A; N.E. %; M.A. 0%; E.N.C. 1%; W.N.C. 1%; S.A. 7%; E.S.C. 86%; W.S.C. 4%; Mt. 0%; Pac. 0%; unknown 0%

University of Tennessee-Knoxville

1505 W. Cumberland Avenue
Knoxville, TN 37996-1810
www.law.utk.edu
Public
Admissions: (865) 974-4131
Email: lawadmit@utk.edu
Financial aid: (865) 974-4131
Application deadline: 03/01
In-state tuition: full time: $19,048; part time: N/A
Out-of-state tuition: full time: $37,752

Room/board/expenses: $20,900
Median grant: $5,000
Average student indebtedness at graduation: $66,201
Enrollment: full time: 390; part time: N/A
men: 59%; women: 41%; minorities: 19%
Acceptance rate (full time): 40%
Midrange LSAT (full time): 154-160
Midrange undergraduate GPA (full time): 3.44-3.85
Midrange of full-time private-sector salaries of 2013 grads: $52,500-$92,500
2013 grads employed in: law firms: 59%; business and industry: 16%; government: 13%; public interest: 3%; judicial clerk: 7%; academia: 1%; unknown: 0%
Employment location for 2013 class: Intl. N/A; N.E. %; M.A. 1%; E.N.C. 3%; W.N.C. 1%; S.A. 17%; E.S.C. 73%; W.S.C. 2%; Mt. 4%; Pac. 0%; unknown 0%

Vanderbilt University
131 21st Avenue S
Nashville, TN 37203-1181
www.vanderbilt.edu/law/
Private
Admissions: (615) 322-6452
Email: admissions@law.vanderbilt.edu
Financial aid: (615) 322-6452
Application deadline: 04/01
Tuition: full time: $49,722; part time: N/A
Room/board/expenses: $24,382
Median grant: $20,000
Average student indebtedness at graduation: $122,327
Enrollment: full time: 525; part time: N/A
men: 54%; women: 46%; minorities: 21%
Acceptance rate (full time): 35%
Midrange LSAT (full time): 162-168
Midrange undergraduate GPA (full time): 3.45-3.84
Midrange of full-time private-sector salaries of 2013 grads: $60,000-$146,250
2013 grads employed in: law firms: 58%; business and industry: 10%; government: 10%; public interest: 7%; judicial clerk: 13%; academia: 2%; unknown: 0%
Employment location for 2013 class: Intl. N/A; N.E. %; M.A. 16%; E.N.C. 7%; W.N.C. 3%; S.A. 24%; E.S.C. 27%; W.S.C. 7%; Mt. 4%; Pac. 8%; unknown 2%

TEXAS

Baylor University
1114 S. University Parks Drive
1 Bear Place, # 97288
Waco, TX 76798-7288
www.baylor.edu/law/
Private
Admissions: (254) 710-3239
Email: nicole_neeley@baylor.edu
Financial aid: (254) 710-2611
Application deadline: 03/01
Tuition: full time: $52,400; part time: $1,268/credit hour
Room/board/expenses: $20,820
Median grant: $20,000
Average student indebtedness at graduation: $116,666
Enrollment: full time: 376; part time: 6
men: 58%; women: 42%; minorities: 23%
Acceptance rate (full time): 30%
Midrange LSAT (full time): 155-162

Midrange undergraduate GPA (full time): 3.30-3.69
Midrange of full-time private-sector salaries of 2013 grads: $60,000-$100,000
2013 grads employed in: law firms: 70%; business and industry: 11%; government: 12%; public interest: 1%; judicial clerk: 3%; academia: 3%; unknown: 0%
Employment location for 2013 class: Intl. N/A; N.E. %; M.A. 1%; E.N.C. 1%; W.N.C. 1%; S.A. 1%; E.S.C. 1%; W.S.C. 90%; Mt. 2%; Pac. 1%; unknown 1%

Southern Methodist University (Dedman)
PO Box 750116
Dallas, TX 75275-0116
www.law.smu.edu
Private
Admissions: (214) 768-2540
Email: lawadmit@mail.smu.edu
Financial aid: (214) 768-4119
Application deadline: 02/15
Tuition: full time: $48,796; part time: $36,597
Room/board/expenses: $20,238
Median grant: $23,000
Average student indebtedness at graduation: $124,617
Enrollment: full time: 537; part time: 228
men: 55%; women: 45%; minorities: 20%
Acceptance rate (full time): 44%
Midrange LSAT (full time): 157-164
Midrange undergraduate GPA (full time): 3.30-3.76
Midrange of full-time private-sector salaries of 2013 grads: $65,000-$160,000
2013 grads employed in: law firms: 65%; business and industry: 26%; government: 5%; public interest: 1%; judicial clerk: 3%; academia: 0%; unknown: 0%
Employment location for 2013 class: Intl. N/A; N.E. %; M.A. 1%; E.N.C. 1%; W.N.C. 0%; S.A. 2%; E.S.C. 0%; W.S.C. 92%; Mt. 0%; Pac. 1%; unknown 0%

South Texas College of Law
1303 San Jacinto Street
Houston, TX 77002-7006
www.stcl.edu
Private
Admissions: (713) 646-1810
Email: admissions@stcl.edu
Financial aid: (713) 646-1820
Application deadline: 03/15
Tuition: full time: $28,680; part time: $19,320
Room/board/expenses: $21,900
Median grant: $4,600
Average student indebtedness at graduation: $113,748
Enrollment: full time: 850; part time: 266
men: 54%; women: 46%; minorities: 38%
Acceptance rate (full time): 68%
Midrange LSAT (full time): 148-154
Midrange undergraduate GPA (full time): 2.90-3.32
Midrange of full-time private-sector salaries of 2013 grads: $51,250-$109,000
2013 grads employed in: law firms: 66%; business and industry: 23%; government: 8%; public interest: 1%; judicial clerk: 1%; academia: 2%; unknown: 0%

Employment location for 2013 class: Intl. N/A; N.E. %; M.A. 0%; E.N.C. 1%; W.N.C. 0%; S.A. 1%; E.S.C. 0%; W.S.C. 95%; Mt. 0%; Pac. 1%; unknown 2%

St. Mary's University
1 Camino Santa Maria
San Antonio, TX 78228-8602
www.stmarytx.edu/law
Private
Email: lawadmissions@stmarytx.edu
Financial aid: (210) 431-6743
Application deadline: 03/01
Tuition: full time: $33,100; part time: $17,248
Room/board/expenses: $19,688
Median grant: $3,491
Average student indebtedness at graduation: $116,782
Enrollment: full time: 592; part time: 172
men: 57%; women: 43%; minorities: 51%
Acceptance rate (full time): 74%
Midrange LSAT (full time): 148-152
Midrange undergraduate GPA (full time): 2.70-3.32
Midrange of full-time private-sector salaries of 2013 grads: $49,500-$75,000
2013 grads employed in: law firms: 64%; business and industry: 17%; government: 12%; public interest: 4%; judicial clerk: 2%; academia: 0%; unknown: 0%
Employment location for 2013 class: Intl. N/A; N.E. %; M.A. 0%; E.N.C. 0%; W.N.C. 0%; S.A. 1%; E.S.C. 0%; W.S.C. 96%; Mt. 1%; Pac. 0%; unknown 0%

Texas A&M University
1515 Commerce Street
Fort Worth, TX 76102
law.tamu.edu/
Public
Admissions: (817) 212-4040
Email: law-admissions@law.tamu.edu
Financial aid: (817) 212-4090
Application deadline: rolling
In-state tuition: full time: $33,092; part time: $24,069
Out-of-state tuition: full time: $33,092
Room/board/expenses: $21,828
Median grant: $1,288
Average student indebtedness at graduation: $103,500
Enrollment: full time: 458; part time: 244
men: 52%; women: 48%; minorities: 28%
Acceptance rate (full time): 42%
Midrange LSAT (full time): 152-156
Midrange undergraduate GPA (full time): 2.92-3.41
Midrange of full-time private-sector salaries of 2013 grads: $50,000-$72,000
2013 grads employed in: law firms: 52%; business and industry: 35%; government: 8%; public interest: 1%; judicial clerk: 1%; academia: 2%; unknown: 2%
Employment location for 2013 class: Intl. N/A; N.E. %; M.A. 0%; E.N.C. 0%; W.N.C. 2%; S.A. 2%; E.S.C. 0%; W.S.C. 92%; Mt. 1%; Pac. 1%; unknown 2%

Texas Southern University (Marshall)[1]
3100 Cleburne Street
Houston, TX 77004
www.tsulaw.edu
Public
Admissions: (713) 313-7114
Email: lawadmit@tsulaw.edu
Financial aid: N/A
Tuition: N/A
Room/board/expenses: N/A
Enrollment: N/A

Texas Tech University
1802 Hartford Avenue
Lubbock, TX 79409-0004
www.law.ttu.edu
Public
Admissions: (806) 834-5024
Email: admissions.law@ttu.edu
Financial aid: (806) 834-3875
Application deadline: 03/01
In-state tuition: full time: $22,733; part time: N/A
Out-of-state tuition: full time: $32,693
Room/board/expenses: $16,060
Median grant: $10,000
Average student indebtedness at graduation: $84,272
Enrollment: full time: 629; part time: N/A
men: 52%; women: 48%; minorities: 28%
Acceptance rate (full time): 57%
Midrange LSAT (full time): 151-157
Midrange undergraduate GPA (full time): 3.17-3.65
Midrange of full-time private-sector salaries of 2013 grads: $53,051-$84,576
2013 grads employed in: law firms: 55%; business and industry: 21%; government: 14%; public interest: 2%; judicial clerk: 6%; academia: 2%; unknown: 0%
Employment location for 2013 class: Intl. N/A; N.E. %; M.A. 0%; E.N.C. 1%; W.N.C. 1%; S.A. 2%; E.S.C. 0%; W.S.C. 90%; Mt. 5%; Pac. 2%; unknown 0%

University of Houston
100 Law Center
Houston, TX 77204-6060
www.law.uh.edu
Public
Admissions: (713) 743-2280
Email: lawadmissions@uh.edu
Financial aid: (713) 743-2269
Application deadline: 02/15
In-state tuition: full time: $29,748; part time: $20,448
Out-of-state tuition: full time: $43,176
Room/board/expenses: $19,200
Median grant: $5,000
Average student indebtedness at graduation: $88,664
Enrollment: full time: 615; part time: 117
men: 53%; women: 47%; minorities: 34%
Acceptance rate (full time): 46%
Midrange LSAT (full time): 156-161
Midrange undergraduate GPA (full time): 3.28-3.62
Midrange of full-time private-sector salaries of 2013 grads: $80,000-$160,000
2013 grads employed in: law firms: 62%; business and industry: 23%; government: 8%; public interest: 3%; judicial clerk: 2%; academia: 2%; unknown: 0%
Employment location for 2013 class: Intl. N/A; N.E. %; M.A. 1%; E.N.C. 1%; W.N.C. 1%; S.A. 9%; E.S.C. 0%; W.S.C. 9%; Mt. 65%; Pac. 12%; unknown 0%

Employment location for 2013 class: Intl. N/A; N.E. %; M.A. 1%; E.N.C. 0%; W.N.C. 0%; S.A. 1%; E.S.C. 0%; W.S.C. 93%; Mt. 0%; Pac. 3%; unknown 0%

University of Texas-Austin
727 E. Dean Keeton Street
Austin, TX 78705-3299
www.utexas.edu/law
Public
Admissions: (512) 232-1200
Email: admissions@law.utexas.edu
Financial aid: (512) 232-1130
Application deadline: 03/01
In-state tuition: full time: $33,162; part time: N/A
Out-of-state tuition: full time: $49,244
Room/board/expenses: $19,370
Median grant: $9,700
Average student indebtedness at graduation: $100,868
Enrollment: full time: 1,025; part time: 6
men: 56%; women: 44%; minorities: 32%
Acceptance rate (full time): 24%
Midrange LSAT (full time): 163-168
Midrange undergraduate GPA (full time): 3.43-3.82
Midrange of full-time private-sector salaries of 2013 grads: $100,000-$160,000
2013 grads employed in: law firms: 60%; business and industry: 9%; government: 11%; public interest: 5%; judicial clerk: 14%; academia: 0%; unknown: 0%
Employment location for 2013 class: Intl. N/A; N.E. %; M.A. 7%; E.N.C. 2%; W.N.C. 1%; S.A. 6%; E.S.C. 2%; W.S.C. 73%; Mt. 2%; Pac. 5%; unknown 0%

UTAH

Brigham Young University (Clark)
243 JRCB
Provo, UT 84602-8000
www.law.byu.edu
Private
Admissions: (801) 422-4277
Email: kulbethm@law.byu.edu
Financial aid: (801) 422-6386
Application deadline: rolling
Tuition: full time: $11,620; part time: N/A
Room/board/expenses: $20,400
Median grant: $5,000
Average student indebtedness at graduation: $54,203
Enrollment: full time: 394; part time: 12
men: 60%; women: 40%; minorities: 18%
Acceptance rate (full time): 36%
Midrange LSAT (full time): 156-164
Midrange undergraduate GPA (full time): 3.52-3.85
Midrange of full-time private-sector salaries of 2013 grads: $60,000-$120,000
2013 grads employed in: law firms: 48%; business and industry: 19%; government: 15%; public interest: 2%; judicial clerk: 13%; academia: 2%; unknown: 0%
Employment location for 2013 class: Intl. N/A; N.E. %; M.A. 1%; E.N.C. 1%; W.N.C. 1%; S.A. 9%; E.S.C. 0%; W.S.C. 9%; Mt. 65%; Pac. 12%; unknown 0%

University of Utah (Quinney)

332 S. 1400 E, Room 101
Salt Lake City, UT 84112
www.law.utah.edu
Public
Admissions: (801) 581-7479
Email: admissions@law.utah.edu
Financial aid: (801) 581-6211
Application deadline: 02/15
In-state tuition: full time: $24,797; part time: N/A
Out-of-state tuition: full time: $47,170
Room/board/expenses: $20,664
Median grant: $7,034
Average student indebtedness at graduation: $78,725
Enrollment: full time: 332; part time: N/A
men: 63%; women: 37%; minorities: 11%
Acceptance rate (full time): 44%
Midrange LSAT (full time): 158-161
Midrange undergraduate GPA (full time): 3.36-3.69
Midrange of full-time private-sector salaries of 2013 grads: $52,000-$99,000
2013 grads employed in: law firms: 42%; business and industry: 24%; government: 18%; public interest: 2%; judicial clerk: 12%; academia: 2%; unknown: 0%
Employment location for 2013 class: Intl. N/A; N.E. %; M.A. 0%; E.N.C. 0%; W.N.C. 1%; S.A. 2%; E.S.C. 0%; W.S.C. 1%; Mt. 90%; Pac. 6%; unknown 0%

VERMONT

Vermont Law School

Chelsea Street
South Royalton, VT 05068-0096
www.vermontlaw.edu
Private
Admissions: (888) 277-5985
Email: admiss@vermontlaw.edu
Financial aid: (888) 277-5985
Application deadline: 04/15
Tuition: full time: $47,135; part time: N/A
Room/board/expenses: $24,934
Median grant: $15,000
Average student indebtedness at graduation: $156,713
Enrollment: full time: 424; part time: N/A
men: 44%; women: 56%; minorities: 20%
Acceptance rate (full time): 74%
Midrange LSAT (full time): 146-156
Midrange undergraduate GPA (full time): 2.90-3.52
Midrange of full-time private-sector salaries of 2013 grads: $48,000-$65,000
2013 grads employed in: law firms: 24%; business and industry: 20%; government: 15%; public interest: 24%; judicial clerk: 15%; academia: 1%; unknown: 0%
Employment location for 2013 class: Intl. N/A; N.E. %; M.A. 11%; E.N.C. 8%; W.N.C. 3%; S.A. 20%; E.S.C. 3%; W.S.C. 1%; Mt. 9%; Pac. 10%; unknown 0%

VIRGINIA

Appalachian School of Law[1]

1169 Edgewater Drive
Grundy, VA 24614-2825
www.asl.edu
Private
Admissions: (800) 895-7411
Email: aslinfo@asl.edu
Financial aid: N/A
Tuition: N/A
Room/board/expenses: N/A
Enrollment: N/A

College of William and Mary (Marshall-Wythe)

PO Box 8795
Williamsburg, VA 23187-8795
law.wm.edu/
Public
Admissions: (757) 221-3785
Email: lawadm@wm.edu
Financial aid: (757) 221-2420
Application deadline: 03/01
In-state tuition: full time: $29,800; part time: N/A
Out-of-state tuition: full time: $38,800
Room/board/expenses: $17,150
Median grant: $10,000
Average student indebtedness at graduation: $98,487
Enrollment: full time: 631; part time: N/A
men: 48%; women: 52%; minorities: 13%
Acceptance rate (full time): 32%
Midrange LSAT (full time): 157-165
Midrange undergraduate GPA (full time): 3.53-3.89
Midrange of full-time private-sector salaries of 2013 grads: $80,000-$150,000
2013 grads employed in: law firms: 42%; business and industry: 8%; government: 29%; public interest: 9%; judicial clerk: 9%; academia: 2%; unknown: 0%
Employment location for 2013 class: Intl. N/A; N.E. %; M.A. 16%; E.N.C. 4%; W.N.C. 1%; S.A. 64%; E.S.C. 2%; W.S.C. 4%; Mt. 1%; Pac. 4%; unknown 0%

George Mason University

3301 Fairfax Drive
Arlington, VA 22201-4426
www.law.gmu.edu
Public
Admissions: (703) 993-8010
Email: lawadmit@gmu.edu
Financial aid: (703) 993-2353
Application deadline: 04/01
In-state tuition: full time: $25,351; part time: $905/credit hour
Out-of-state tuition: full time: $40,737
Room/board/expenses: $23,549
Median grant: $10,000
Average student indebtedness at graduation: $126,723
Enrollment: full time: 340; part time: 150
men: 57%; women: 43%; minorities: 19%
Acceptance rate (full time): 38%
Midrange LSAT (full time): 155-162
Midrange undergraduate GPA (full time): 3.27-3.71
Midrange of full-time private-sector salaries of 2013 grads: $62,500-$140,000

2013 grads employed in: law firms: 36%; business and industry: 17%; government: 22%; public interest: 9%; judicial clerk: 8%; academia: 9%; unknown: 0%
Employment location for 2013 class: Intl. N/A; N.E. %; M.A. 5%; E.N.C. 4%; W.N.C. 0%; S.A. 80%; E.S.C. 1%; W.S.C. 2%; Mt. 3%; Pac. 2%; unknown 0%

Liberty University

1971 University Boulevard
Lynchburg, VA 24515
law.liberty.edu
Private
Admissions: (434) 592-5300
Email: lawadmissions@liberty.edu
Financial aid: (434) 592-5300
Application deadline: 06/01
Tuition: full time: $31,562; part time: N/A
Room/board/expenses: $16,800
Median grant: $18,238
Average student indebtedness at graduation: $69,475
Enrollment: full time: 205; part time: N/A
men: 62%; women: 38%; minorities: 20%
Acceptance rate (full time): 65%
Midrange LSAT (full time): 148-155
Midrange undergraduate GPA (full time): 2.74-3.50
Midrange of full-time private-sector salaries of 2013 grads: N/A-N/A
2013 grads employed in: law firms: 42%; business and industry: 18%; government: 21%; public interest: 6%; judicial clerk: 6%; academia: 6%; unknown: 0%
Employment location for 2013 class: Intl. N/A; N.E. %; M.A. 5%; E.N.C. 5%; W.N.C. 5%; S.A. 74%; E.S.C. 3%; W.S.C. 2%; Mt. 2%; Pac. 5%; unknown 0%

Regent University

1000 Regent University Drive
Virginia Beach, VA 23464-9880
www.regent.edu/law/admissions
Private
Admissions: (757) 226-4584
Email: lawschool@regent.edu
Financial aid: (757) 352-4559
Application deadline: rolling
Tuition: full time: $1,125/credit hour; part time: $1,125/credit hour
Room/board/expenses: $20,760
Median grant: $9,500
Average student indebtedness at graduation: $125,158
Enrollment: full time: 287; part time: 25
men: 47%; women: 53%; minorities: 18%
Acceptance rate (full time): 52%
Midrange LSAT (full time): 148-156
Midrange undergraduate GPA (full time): 2.96-3.59
Midrange of full-time private-sector salaries of 2013 grads: $45,750-$72,500
2013 grads employed in: law firms: 42%; business and industry: 15%; government: 23%; public interest: 9%; judicial clerk: 7%; academia: 2%; unknown: 1%
Employment location for 2013 class: Intl. N/A; N.E. %; M.A. 4%; E.N.C. 3%; W.N.C. 4%; S.A. 67%; E.S.C. 5%; W.S.C. 6%; Mt. 5%; Pac. 6%; unknown 1%

University of Richmond

28 Westhampton Way
Richmond, VA 23173
law.richmond.edu
Private
Admissions: (804) 289-8189
Email: mrahman@richmond.edu
Financial aid: (804) 289-8438
Application deadline: 03/31
Tuition: full time: $39,200; part time: $2,180/credit hour
Room/board/expenses: $16,040
Median grant: $20,000
Average student indebtedness at graduation: $110,380
Enrollment: full time: 455; part time: 3
men: 53%; women: 47%; minorities: 12%
Acceptance rate (full time): 34%
Midrange LSAT (full time): 155-162
Midrange undergraduate GPA (full time): 3.21-3.62
Midrange of full-time private-sector salaries of 2013 grads: $50,000-$90,000
2013 grads employed in: law firms: 42%; business and industry: 25%; government: 8%; public interest: 8%; judicial clerk: 18%; academia: 0%; unknown: 0%
Employment location for 2013 class: Intl. N/A; N.E. %; M.A. 4%; E.N.C. 1%; W.N.C. 0%; S.A. 92%; E.S.C. 1%; W.S.C. 0%; Mt. 1%; Pac. 1%; unknown 0%

University of Virginia

580 Massie Road
Charlottesville, VA 22903-1738
www.law.virginia.edu
Public
Admissions: (434) 924-7354
Email: lawadmit@virginia.edu
Financial aid: (434) 924-7805
Application deadline: 03/01
In-state tuition: full time: $51,800; part time: N/A
Out-of-state tuition: full time: $54,800
Room/board/expenses: $21,023
Median grant: $25,000
Average student indebtedness at graduation: $132,182
Enrollment: full time: 1,005; part time: N/A
men: 59%; women: 41%; minorities: 20%
Acceptance rate (full time): 18%
Midrange LSAT (full time): 166-170
Midrange undergraduate GPA (full time): 3.57-3.93
Midrange of full-time private-sector salaries of 2013 grads: $145,000-$160,000
2013 grads employed in: law firms: 56%; business and industry: 2%; government: 15%; public interest: 6%; judicial clerk: 20%; academia: 1%; unknown: 0%
Employment location for 2013 class: Intl. N/A; N.E. %; M.A. 21%; E.N.C. 4%; W.N.C. 1%; S.A. 49%; E.S.C. 2%; W.S.C. 6%; Mt. 3%; Pac. 8%; unknown 0%

Washington and Lee University

Sydney Lewis Hall
Lexington, VA 24450-0303
law.wlu.edu
Private
Admissions: (540) 458-8504
Email: lawadm@wlu.edu
Financial aid: (540) 458-8729
Application deadline: 03/01

Tuition: full time: $45,597; part time: N/A
Room/board/expenses: $19,143
Median grant: $20,000
Average student indebtedness at graduation: $109,422
Enrollment: full time: 370; part time: N/A
men: 55%; women: 45%; minorities: 21%
Acceptance rate (full time): 43%
Midrange LSAT (full time): 157-163
Midrange undergraduate GPA (full time): 3.12-3.55
Midrange of full-time private-sector salaries of 2013 grads: $62,500-$140,000
2013 grads employed in: law firms: 51%; business and industry: 14%; government: 11%; public interest: 10%; judicial clerk: 12%; academia: 2%; unknown: 0%
Employment location for 2013 class: Intl. N/A; N.E. %; M.A. 15%; E.N.C. 2%; W.N.C. 0%; S.A. 62%; E.S.C. 3%; W.S.C. 8%; Mt. 0%; Pac. 6%; unknown 0%

WASHINGTON

Gonzaga University

PO Box 3528
Spokane, WA 99220-3528
www.law.gonzaga.edu
Private
Admissions: (800) 793-1710
Email: admissions@ lawschool.gonzaga.edu
Financial aid: (800) 448-2138
Application deadline: 04/15
Tuition: full time: $36,510; part time: N/A
Room/board/expenses: $16,689
Median grant: $13,500
Average student indebtedness at graduation: $121,281
Enrollment: full time: 339; part time: N/A
men: 58%; women: 42%; minorities: 17%
Acceptance rate (full time): 67%
Midrange LSAT (full time): 151-155
Midrange undergraduate GPA (full time): 3.02-3.55
Midrange of full-time private-sector salaries of 2013 grads: $47,800-$60,000
2013 grads employed in: law firms: 58%; business and industry: 17%; government: 13%; public interest: 4%; judicial clerk: 6%; academia: 1%; unknown: 0%
Employment location for 2013 class: Intl. N/A; N.E. %; M.A. 1%; E.N.C. 1%; W.N.C. 0%; S.A. 1%; E.S.C. 0%; W.S.C. 1%; Mt. 25%; Pac. 70%; unknown 0%

Seattle University

901 12th Avenue
Seattle, WA 98122-1090
www.law.seattleu.edu
Private
Admissions: (206) 398-4200
Email: lawadmis@seattleu.edu
Financial aid: (206) 398-4250
Application deadline: rolling
Tuition: full time: $41,088; part time: $35,598
Room/board/expenses: $23,545
Median grant: $11,500
Average student indebtedness at graduation: $131,414
Enrollment: full time: 630; part time: 163
men: 49%; women: 51%; minorities: 33%

Acceptance rate (full time): 62%
Midrange LSAT (full time): 152–157
Midrange undergraduate GPA (full time): 3.09–3.47
Midrange of full-time private-sector salaries of 2013 grads: $50,000–$82,000
2013 grads employed in: law firms: 51%; business and industry: 24%; government: 11%; public interest: 4%; judicial clerk: 6%; academia: 2%; unknown: 0%
Employment location for 2013 class: Intl. N/A; N.E. %; M.A. 1%; E.N.C. 0%; W.N.C. 0%; S.A. 2%; E.S.C. 1%; W.S.C. 2%; Mt. 1%; Pac. 90%; unknown 0%

University of Washington

Campus Box 353020
Seattle, WA 98195-3020
www.law.washington.edu
Public
Admissions: (206) 543-4078
Email: lawadm@u.washington.edu
Financial aid: (206) 543-4078
Application deadline: 03/15
In-state tuition: full time: $31,980; part time: N/A
Out-of-state tuition: full time: $45,021
Room/board/expenses: $18,843
Median grant: $8,000
Average student indebtedness at graduation: $105,990
Enrollment: full time: 516; part time: N/A
men: 52%; women: 48%; minorities: 27%
Acceptance rate (full time): 26%
Midrange LSAT (full time): 160–166
Midrange undergraduate GPA (full time): 3.51–3.84
Midrange of full-time private-sector salaries of 2013 grads: $72,750–$120,000

2013 grads employed in: law firms: 45%; business and industry: 8%; government: 17%; public interest: 9%; judicial clerk: 15%; academia: 6%; unknown: 1%
Employment location for 2013 class: Intl. N/A; N.E. %; M.A. 4%; E.N.C. 0%; W.N.C. 0%; S.A. 5%; E.S.C. 1%; W.S.C. 0%; Mt. 1%; Pac. 85%; unknown 0%

WEST VIRGINIA

West Virginia University

PO Box 6130
Morgantown, WV 26506-6130
law.wvu.edu/
Public
Admissions: (304) 293-5304
Email: wvulaw.admissions@mail.wvu.edu
Financial aid: (304) 293-5302
Application deadline: 03/01
In-state tuition: full time: $18,234; part time: $1,013/credit hour
Out-of-state tuition: full time: $34,524
Room/board/expenses: $15,881
Median grant: $17,250
Average student indebtedness at graduation: $84,727
Enrollment: full time: 344; part time: 3
men: 60%; women: 40%; minorities: 9%
Acceptance rate (full time): 54%
Midrange LSAT (full time): 152–156
Midrange undergraduate GPA (full time): 3.09–3.70
Midrange of full-time private-sector salaries of 2013 grads: $50,000–$73,000
2013 grads employed in: law firms: 52%; business and industry: 21%; government: 10%; public interest: 8%; judicial clerk: 6%; academia: 3%; unknown: 0%

Employment location for 2013 class: Intl. N/A; N.E. %; M.A. 10%; E.N.C. 1%; W.N.C. 0%; S.A. 81%; E.S.C. 1%; W.S.C. 3%; Mt. 1%; Pac. 2%; unknown 1%

WISCONSIN

Marquette University

Eckstein Hall
PO Box 1881
Milwaukee, WI 53201-1881
law.marquette.edu
Private
Admissions: (414) 288-6767
Email: law.admission@marquette.edu
Financial aid: (414) 288-7390
Application deadline: 04/01
Tuition: full time: $41,040; part time: $24,450
Room/board/expenses: $20,358
Median grant: $8,000
Average student indebtedness at graduation: $134,533
Enrollment: full time: 572; part time: 93
men: 58%; women: 42%; minorities: 17%
Acceptance rate (full time): 76%
Midrange LSAT (full time): 149–155
Midrange undergraduate GPA (full time): 3.12–3.52
Midrange of full-time private-sector salaries of 2013 grads: $50,000–$95,000
2013 grads employed in: law firms: 56%; business and industry: 25%; government: 7%; public interest: 5%; judicial clerk: 2%; academia: 4%; unknown: 0%
Employment location for 2013 class: Intl. N/A; N.E. %; M.A. 1%; E.N.C. 85%; W.N.C. 3%; S.A. 2%; E.S.C. 1%; W.S.C. 2%; Mt. 3%; Pac. 1%; unknown 0%

University of Wisconsin-Madison

975 Bascom Mall
Madison, WI 53706-1399
www.law.wisc.edu
Public
Admissions: (608) 262-5914
Email: admissions@law.wisc.edu
Financial aid: (608) 262-5914
Application deadline: 04/01
In-state tuition: full time: $21,372; part time: $1,875/credit hour
Out-of-state tuition: full time: $40,068
Room/board/expenses: $19,676
Median grant: $10,000
Average student indebtedness at graduation: $79,373
Enrollment: full time: 525; part time: 48
men: 57%; women: 43%; minorities: 19%
Acceptance rate (full time): 50%
Midrange LSAT (full time): 157–163
Midrange undergraduate GPA (full time): 3.30–3.76
Midrange of full-time private-sector salaries of 2013 grads: $62,000–$135,000
2013 grads employed in: law firms: 49%; business and industry: 17%; government: 14%; public interest: 9%; judicial clerk: 6%; academia: 3%; unknown: 1%
Employment location for 2013 class: Intl. N/A; N.E. %; M.A. 5%; E.N.C. 72%; W.N.C. 5%; S.A. 4%; E.S.C. 0%; W.S.C. 1%; Mt. 4%; Pac. 6%; unknown 0%

WYOMING

University of Wyoming

Department 3035
1000 E. University Avenue
Laramie, WY 82071
www.uwyo.edu/law
Public
Admissions: (307) 766-6416
Email: lawadmis@uwyo.edu
Financial aid: (307) 766-2116
Application deadline: 03/01
In-state tuition: full time: $14,455; part time: N/A
Out-of-state tuition: full time: $29,245
Room/board/expenses: $16,599
Median grant: $5,600
Average student indebtedness at graduation: $67,087
Enrollment: full time: 226; part time: N/A
men: 56%; women: 44%; minorities: 12%
Acceptance rate (full time): 52%
Midrange LSAT (full time): 149–155
Midrange undergraduate GPA (full time): 3.10–3.59
Midrange of full-time private-sector salaries of 2013 grads: $51,000–$62,500
2013 grads employed in: law firms: 53%; business and industry: 9%; government: 27%; public interest: 0%; judicial clerk: 11%; academia: 0%; unknown: 0%
Employment location for 2013 class: Intl. N/A; N.E. %; M.A. 0%; E.N.C. 0%; W.N.C. 5%; S.A. 2%; E.S.C. 2%; W.S.C. 0%; Mt. 78%; Pac. 5%; unknown 8%

MEDICINE

This directory lists the 130 schools offering M.D. degrees that were accredited by the Liaison Committee on Medical Education in 2014, plus the 26 schools that offer D.O. degrees and were accredited by the American Osteopathic Association in 2014. Of those, 102 M.D.-granting schools and 16 D.O.-granting schools responded to the U.S. News survey, conducted in the fall of 2014 and early 2015. Their data are reported below. Schools that did not respond have abbreviated entries.

KEY TO THE TERMINOLOGY

1. A school whose name is footnoted with the numeral 1 did not return the U.S. News statistical survey; limited data appear in its entry.
N/A. Not available from the school or not applicable.
Admissions. The admissions office phone number.
Email. The address of the admissions office. If instead of an email address a website is listed, the website will automatically present an email screen programmed to reach the admissions office.
Financial aid. The financial aid office phone number.
Application deadline. For fall 2016 enrollment.
Tuition. For the 2014-15 academic year. Includes fees.
Room/board/expenses. For the 2014-15 academic year.
Students receiving grants. The percentage of the entire student body during the 2013-14 academic year that received grants or scholarships.
Average indebtedness. For 2013 graduates who incurred medical school-related debt.
Enrollment. Total doctor of medicine (M.D.) or doctor of osteopathy (D.O.) degree program enrollment for fall 2014.
Minorities. For fall 2014, percentage of U.S. students who fall in one of these groups: black or African-American, Asian, American Indian or Alaskan Native, Native Hawaiian or other Pacific Islander, Hispanic/Latino or two or more races. The minority percentage was reported by the school.
Underrepresented minorities. For fall 2014, percentage of U.S. students who are black or African-American, American Indian or Alaskan Native, Native Hawaiian or other Pacific Islander, Hispanic/Latino or two or more races. (This category is used only for medical schools. The underrepresented minority percentage was reported by the school.)
Acceptance rate. Percentage of applicants who were accepted for fall 2014 to an M.D. or D.O. degree program.
Median Medical College Admission Test (MCAT) total score. For M.D. or D.O. students who entered the medical or osteopathic program in the fall of 2014. The median total score of verbal reasoning and physical sciences and biological sciences MCAT scores. (These three separate MCAT scores are reported to test-takers on a scale of 1 to 15.)
Median undergraduate grade point average (GPA). For M.D. or D.O. students who entered in the fall of 2014.
Most popular undergraduate majors. For students who entered in the fall of 2014. The main areas are biological sciences, including microbiology; physical sciences, including chemistry; nonsciences, including the humanities; and other, including double majors, mixed disciplines and other health professions like nursing and pharmacy.
Graduates entering primary care specialties. This is the three-year average percentage of all medical or osteopathic school graduates entering primary care residencies in the fields of family practice, general pediatrics or general internal medicine during 2012, 2013 and 2014.

ALABAMA

University of Alabama-Birmingham
Medical Student Services
VH Suite 100
Birmingham, AL 35294-0019
www.uab.edu/medicine/
admissions
Public
Admissions: (205) 934-2433
Email: medschool@uab.edu
Financial aid: (205) 934-8223
Application deadline: 11/01
In-state tuition: $29,307
Out-of-state tuition: $62,407
Room/board/expenses: $21,502
Percent receiving grants: 39%
Average student indebtedness at graduation: $138,727
Enrollment: 781
men: 58%; women: 42%; minorities: 23%; underrepresented minorities: 11%; in state: 92%
Acceptance rate: 8%
Median MCAT total score: 30
Median GPA: 3.76
Most popular undergraduate majors: biological sciences: 34%; physical sciences: 19%; nonsciences: 8%; other: 39%
Percent of graduates entering primary-care specialties: 44.5%

University of South Alabama[1]
307 University Boulevard
170 CSAB
Mobile, AL 36688
www.usahealthsystem.com/com
Public
Admissions: (251) 460-7176
Financial aid: N/A
Tuition: N/A
Room/board/expenses: N/A
Enrollment: N/A

ARIZONA

University of Arizona
1501 N. Campbell Avenue
Tucson, AZ 85724
www.medicine.arizona.edu/
Public
Admissions: (520) 626-6214
Email: admissions@
medicine.arizona.edu
Financial aid: (520) 626-7145
Application deadline: 11/01
In-state tuition: $30,279
Out-of-state tuition: $49,437
Room/board/expenses: $13,000
Percent receiving grants: 85%
Average student indebtedness at graduation: $149,357
Enrollment: 465
men: 47%; women: 53%; minorities: 36%; underrepresented minorities: 14%; in state: 93%
Acceptance rate: 4%
Median MCAT total score: 30
Median GPA: 3.70
Most popular undergraduate majors: biological sciences: 56%; physical sciences: 17%; nonsciences: 10%; other: 17%
Percent of graduates entering primary-care specialties: 48.0%

ARKANSAS

University of Arkansas for Medical Sciences
4301 W. Markham Street, Slot 551
Little Rock, AR 72205
www.uams.edu
Public
Admissions: (501) 686-5354
Email: southtomg@uams.edu
Financial aid: (501) 686-5451
Application deadline: 11/02
In-state tuition: $26,694
Out-of-state tuition: $50,828
Room/board/expenses: $0
Average student indebtedness at graduation: $145,888
Enrollment: 682
men: 65%; women: 35%; minorities: 20%; underrepresented minorities: 12%; in state: 92%
Acceptance rate: 9%
Median MCAT total score: 29
Median GPA: 3.67
Most popular undergraduate majors: biological sciences: 43%; physical sciences: 34%; nonsciences: 15%; other: 8%
Percent of graduates entering primary-care specialties: 54.0%

CALIFORNIA

Loma Linda University[1]
Loma Linda, CA 92350
www.llu.edu/medicine/index.page
Private
Admissions: (909) 558-4467
Email: admissions.sm@llu.edu
Financial aid: N/A
Tuition: N/A
Room/board/expenses: N/A
Enrollment: N/A

Stanford University
300 Pasteur Drive, Suite M121
Stanford, CA 94305
med.stanford.edu
Private
Admissions: (650) 723-6861
Email: mdadmissions@stanford.edu
Financial aid: (650) 723-6958
Application deadline: 10/15
Tuition: $51,356
Room/board/expenses: $27,231
Percent receiving grants: 71%
Average student indebtedness at graduation: $96,385
Enrollment: 473
men: 52%; women: 48%; minorities: 58%; underrepresented minorities: 16%; in state: 41%
Acceptance rate: 2%
Median MCAT total score: 37
Median GPA: 3.85
Most popular undergraduate majors: biological sciences: 44%; physical sciences: 41%; nonsciences: 7%; other: 8%
Percent of graduates entering primary-care specialties: 35.0%

University of California-Davis

4610 X Street
Sacramento, CA 95817
www.ucdmc.ucdavis.edu/
medschool/
Public
Admissions: (916) 734-4800
Email: medadmsinfo@ucdavis.edu
Financial aid: (916) 734-4120
Application deadline: 10/01
In-state tuition: $40,583
Out-of-state tuition: $52,828
Room/board/expenses: $15,574
Percent receiving grants: 94%
Average student indebtedness at graduation: $146,756
Enrollment: 437
men: 45%; women:
55%; minorities: 61%;
underrepresented minorities:
26%; in state: 100%
Acceptance rate: 4%
Median MCAT total score: 31
Median GPA: 3.62
Most popular undergraduate majors: biological sciences:
53%; physical sciences: 9%;
nonsciences: 18%; other: 20%
Percent of graduates entering primary-care specialties: 45.4%

University of California-Irvine

252 Irvine Hall
Irvine, CA 92697-3950
www.som.uci.edu
Public
Admissions: (949) 824-5388
Email: medadmit@uci.edu
Financial aid: (949) 824-6476
Application deadline: 11/01
In-state tuition: $36,704
Out-of-state tuition: $48,749
Room/board/expenses: $13,310
Percent receiving grants: 51%
Average student indebtedness at graduation: $139,899
Enrollment: 420
men: 50%; women:
50%; minorities: 48%;
underrepresented minorities:
17%; in state: 94%
Acceptance rate: 4%
Median MCAT total score: 32
Median GPA: 3.74
Most popular undergraduate majors: biological sciences:
66%; physical sciences: 14%;
nonsciences: 12%; other: 8%
Percent of graduates entering primary-care specialties: 42.0%

University of California-Los Angeles (Geffen)

12-138 CHS
10833 Le Conte Avenue
Los Angeles, CA 90095-1720
www.medsch.ucla.edu
Public
Admissions: (310) 825-6081
Email: somadmiss@
mednet.ucla.edu
Financial aid: (310) 825-4181
Application deadline: 11/01
In-state tuition: $35,557
Out-of-state tuition: $47,802
Room/board/expenses: $17,250
Percent receiving grants: 93%
Average student indebtedness at graduation: $107,549
Enrollment: 749
men: 51%; women:
49%; minorities: 62%;
underrepresented minorities:
29%; in state: 93%
Acceptance rate: 3%
Median MCAT total score: 35
Median GPA: 3.78

Most popular undergraduate majors: biological sciences:
40%; physical sciences: 17%;
nonsciences: 15%; other: 28%
Percent of graduates entering primary-care specialties: 47.8%

University of California-San Diego

9500 Gilman Drive
La Jolla, CA 92093-0602
meded.ucsd.edu/
Public
Admissions: (858) 534-3880
Email: somadmissions@ucsd.edu
Financial aid: (858) 534-4664
Application deadline: 11/01
In-state tuition: $36,084
Out-of-state tuition: $48,329
Room/board/expenses: $11,727
Percent receiving grants: 64%
Average student indebtedness at graduation: $104,100
Enrollment: 502
men: 51%; women:
49%; minorities: 52%;
underrepresented minorities:
18%; in state: 90%
Acceptance rate: 4%
Median MCAT total score: 34
Median GPA: 3.77
Most popular undergraduate majors: biological sciences:
66%; physical sciences: 20%;
nonsciences: 10%; other: 4%
Percent of graduates entering primary-care specialties: 43.0%

University of California-San Francisco

513 Parnassus Avenue
Room S224
San Francisco, CA 94143-0410
medschool.ucsf.edu/
Public
Admissions: (415) 476-4044
Email: admissions@
medsch.ucsf.edu
Financial aid: (415) 476-4181
Application deadline: 10/13
In-state tuition: $36,382
Out-of-state tuition: $48,627
Room/board/expenses: $22,407
Percent receiving grants: 81%
Average student indebtedness at graduation: $118,216
Enrollment: 664
men: 48%; women:
52%; minorities: 54%;
underrepresented minorities:
26%; in state: 93%
Acceptance rate: 4%
Median MCAT total score: 34
Median GPA: 3.83
Most popular undergraduate majors: biological sciences:
54%; physical sciences: 13%;
nonsciences: 17%; other: 16%
Percent of graduates entering primary-care specialties: 42.8%

University of Southern California (Keck)

1975 Zonal Avenue, KAM 500
Los Angeles, CA 90033
www.usc.edu/keck
Private
Admissions: (323) 442-2552
Email: medadmit@usc.edu
Financial aid: (213) 740-5462
Application deadline: 11/02
Tuition: $57,091
Room/board/expenses: $18,783
Percent receiving grants: 27%
Average student indebtedness at graduation: $219,473

Enrollment: 722
men: 52%; women:
48%; minorities: 50%;
underrepresented minorities:
14%; in state: 77%
Acceptance rate: 6%
Median MCAT total score: 35
Median GPA: 3.70
Most popular undergraduate majors: biological sciences:
52%; physical sciences: 10%;
nonsciences: 16%; other: 22%
Percent of graduates entering primary-care specialties: 32.6%

COLORADO

University of Colorado

13001 E. 17th Place, MS C290
Aurora, CO 80045
medschool.ucdenver.edu/
admissions
Public
Admissions: (303) 724-8025
Email: somadmin@ucdenver.edu
Financial aid: (303) 724-8039
Application deadline: 11/02
In-state tuition: $36,275
Out-of-state tuition: $62,230
Room/board/expenses: $18,240
Percent receiving grants: 35%
Average student indebtedness at graduation: $157,868
Enrollment: 672
men: 52%; women:
48%; minorities: 47%;
underrepresented minorities:
32%; in state: 81%
Acceptance rate: 5%
Median MCAT total score: 33
Median GPA: 3.71
Most popular undergraduate majors: biological sciences:
42%; physical sciences: 25%;
nonsciences: 15%; other: 18%
Percent of graduates entering primary-care specialties: 44.9%

CONNECTICUT

University of Connecticut

263 Farmington Avenue
Farmington, CT 06030-1905
medicine.uchc.edu
Public
Admissions: (860) 679-4713
Email: admissions@uchc.edu
Financial aid: (860) 679-1364
Application deadline: 11/15
In-state tuition: $37,033
Out-of-state tuition: $65,887
Room/board/expenses: $20,625
Percent receiving grants: 49%
Average student indebtedness at graduation: $115,994
Enrollment: 382
men: 48%; women:
52%; minorities: 35%;
underrepresented minorities:
16%; in state: 93%
Acceptance rate: 8%
Median MCAT total score: 32
Median GPA: 3.70
Most popular undergraduate majors: biological sciences:
36%; physical sciences: 18%;
nonsciences: 16%; other: 30%
Percent of graduates entering primary-care specialties: 46.0%

Yale University

333 Cedar Street
PO Box 208055
New Haven, CT 06520-8055
medicine.yale.edu
Private
Admissions: (203) 785-2643
Email: medical.admissions@
yale.edu

Financial aid: (203) 785-2645
Application deadline: 10/15
Tuition: $54,345
Room/board/expenses: $12,920
Percent receiving grants: 59%
Average student indebtedness at graduation: $123,910
Enrollment: 415
men: 52%; women:
48%; minorities: 64%;
underrepresented minorities:
18%; in state: 7%
Acceptance rate: 6%
Median MCAT total score: 37
Median GPA: 3.83
Most popular undergraduate majors: biological sciences:
40%; physical sciences: 35%;
nonsciences: 16%; other: 9%
Percent of graduates entering primary-care specialties: 33.8%

DISTRICT OF COLUMBIA

Georgetown University

3900 Reservoir Road NW
Med-Dent Building
Washington, DC 20007
som.georgetown.edu/
Private
Admissions: (202) 687-1154
Email: medicaladmissions@
georgetown.edu
Financial aid: (202) 687-1693
Application deadline: 11/02
Tuition: $55,136
Room/board/expenses: $19,250
Percent receiving grants: 48%
Average student indebtedness at graduation: $224,000
Enrollment: 796
men: 49%; women:
51%; minorities: 30%;
underrepresented minorities:
12%; in state: 3%
Acceptance rate: 3%
Median MCAT total score: 31
Median GPA: 3.60
Most popular undergraduate majors: biological sciences:
27%; physical sciences: 12%;
nonsciences: 18%; other: 43%
Percent of graduates entering primary-care specialties: 39.0%

George Washington University

2300 Eye Street NW, Room 708W
Washington, DC 20037
smhs.gwu.edu
Private
Admissions: (202) 994-3506
Email: medadmit@gwu.edu
Financial aid: (202) 994-2960
Application deadline: 12/01
Tuition: N/A
Room/board/expenses: N/A
Average student indebtedness at graduation: $218,356
Enrollment: 707
men: 45%; women:
55%; minorities: 42%;
underrepresented minorities:
16%; in state: 0%
Acceptance rate: 3%
Median MCAT total score: 30
Median GPA: 3.68
Most popular undergraduate majors: biological sciences:
39%; physical sciences: 10%;
nonsciences: 29%; other: 22%
Percent of graduates entering primary-care specialties: 37.6%

Howard University

520 W. Street NW
Washington, DC 20059
healthsciences.howard.edu/
education/schools-and-
academics/medicine
Private
Admissions: (202) 806-6279
Email:
sharmon.jones@howard.edu
Financial aid: N/A
Application deadline: 12/15
Tuition: $46,838
Room/board/expenses: N/A
Percent receiving grants: 57%
Average student indebtedness at graduation: $169,030
Enrollment: 456
men: 52%; women:
48%; minorities: 73%;
underrepresented minorities:
62%; in state: 40%
Acceptance rate: 3%
Median MCAT total score: 37
Median GPA: 3.47
Most popular undergraduate majors: biological sciences:
50%; physical sciences: 17%;
nonsciences: 12%; other: 21%
Percent of graduates entering primary-care specialties: 38.0%

FLORIDA

Florida International University (Wertheim)[1]

11200 SW 8th Street
Miami, FL 33199
medicine.fiu.edu/
Public
Admissions: (305) 348-0644
Email: med.admissions@fiu.edu
Financial aid: N/A
Tuition: N/A
Room/board/expenses: N/A
Enrollment: N/A

Florida State University

1115 W. Call Street
Tallahassee, FL 32306-4300
www.med.fsu.edu/
Public
Admissions: (850) 644-7904
Email: medadmissions@
med.fsu.edu
Financial aid: (850) 645-7270
Application deadline: 12/01
In-state tuition: $24,779
Out-of-state tuition: $59,330
Room/board/expenses: $15,104
Percent receiving grants: 72%
Average student indebtedness at graduation: $146,720
Enrollment: 485
men: 51%; women:
49%; minorities: 44%;
underrepresented minorities:
36%; in state: 100%
Acceptance rate: 4%
Median MCAT total score: 27
Median GPA: 3.67
Most popular undergraduate majors: biological sciences:
63%; physical sciences: 15%;
nonsciences: 7%; other: 15%
Percent of graduates entering primary-care specialties: 47.4%

University of Central Florida

6850 Lake Nona Boulevard
Orlando, FL 32827
med.ucf.edu/
Public
Admissions: (407) 266-1350
Email: mdadmissions@ucf.edu
Financial aid: (407) 266-1000
Application deadline: 11/16
In-state tuition: $29,680

DIRECTORY

Out-of-state tuition: $31,063
Room/board/expenses: $13,850
Percent receiving grants: 100%
Average student indebtedness at graduation: $13,902
Enrollment: 420
men: 52%; women: 48%; minorities: 49%; underrepresented minorities: 20%; in state: 75%
Median MCAT total score: 32
Median GPA: 3.76
Most popular undergraduate majors: biological sciences: 50%; physical sciences: 29%; nonsciences: 9%; other: 12%
Percent of graduates entering primary-care specialties: N/A

University of Florida

Box 100216 UFHSC
Gainesville, FL 32610-0216
www.med.ufl.edu
Public
Admissions: (352) 273-7990
Email: med-admissions@ufl.edu
Financial aid: (352) 273-7939
Application deadline: 12/16
In-state tuition: $37,069
Out-of-state tuition: $49,325
Room/board/expenses: $12,645
Percent receiving grants: 73%
Average student indebtedness at graduation: $139,600
Enrollment: 543
men: 54%; women: 46%; minorities: 44%; underrepresented minorities: 29%; in state: 97%
Acceptance rate: 5%
Median MCAT total score: 32
Median GPA: 3.84
Most popular undergraduate majors: biological sciences: 55%; physical sciences: 16%; nonsciences: 10%; other: 20%
Percent of graduates entering primary-care specialties: 35.8%

University of Miami (Miller)

1120 N.W. 14 Street
Miami, FL 33136
www.med.miami.edu
Private
Admissions: (305) 243-3234
Email: med.admissions@miami.edu
Financial aid: (305) 243-6211
Application deadline: 12/01
Tuition: $35,892
Room/board/expenses: $27,314
Percent receiving grants: 32%
Average student indebtedness at graduation: $165,689
Enrollment: 803
men: 51%; women: 49%; minorities: 38%; underrepresented minorities: 17%; in state: 55%
Acceptance rate: 4%
Median MCAT total score: 33
Median GPA: 3.74
Most popular undergraduate majors: biological sciences: 78%; physical sciences: 12%; nonsciences: 2%; other: 8%
Percent of graduates entering primary-care specialties: 32.5%

University of South Florida

12901 Bruce B. Downs Boulevard
MDC 2
Tampa, FL 33612
www.health.usf.edu/medicine/home.html
Public
Admissions: (813) 974-2229
Email: md-admissions@health.usf.edu

Financial aid: (813) 974-2068
Application deadline: 11/16
In-state tuition: $33,726
Out-of-state tuition: $54,915
Room/board/expenses: $12,250
Percent receiving grants: 52%
Average student indebtedness at graduation: $148,291
Enrollment: 657
men: 57%; women: 43%; minorities: 41%; underrepresented minorities: 17%; in state: 84%
Acceptance rate: 8%
Median MCAT total score: 31
Median GPA: 3.69
Most popular undergraduate majors: biological sciences: 45%; physical sciences: 15%; nonsciences: 10%; other: 30%
Percent of graduates entering primary-care specialties: 44.0%

GEORGIA

Emory University

100 Woodruff Circle NE
Atlanta, GA 30322
www.med.emory.edu
Private
Admissions: (404) 727-5660
Email: medadmiss@emory.edu
Financial aid: (404) 727-6039
Application deadline: 10/15
Tuition: $50,554
Room/board/expenses: $23,704
Percent receiving grants: 49%
Average student indebtedness at graduation: $148,941
Enrollment: 560
men: 48%; women: 52%; minorities: 33%; underrepresented minorities: 13%; in state: 31%
Acceptance rate: 6%
Median MCAT total score: 34
Median GPA: 3.72
Most popular undergraduate majors: biological sciences: 31%; physical sciences: 26%; nonsciences: 19%; other: 24%
Percent of graduates entering primary-care specialties: 38.8%

Georgia Regents University

1120 15th Street
Augusta, GA 30912-4750
www.gru.edu/medicine/admit/
Public
Admissions: (706) 721-3186
Email: stdadmin@gru.edu
Financial aid: (706) 721-4901
Application deadline: 11/01
In-state tuition: $30,224
Out-of-state tuition: $58,028
Room/board/expenses: $22,566
Percent receiving grants: 20%
Average student indebtedness at graduation: $108,214
Enrollment: 921
men: 59%; women: 41%; minorities: 36%; underrepresented minorities: 15%; in state: 97%
Acceptance rate: 13%
Median MCAT total score: 31
Median GPA: 3.73
Most popular undergraduate majors: biological sciences: 46%; physical sciences: 28%; nonsciences: 13%; other: 13%
Percent of graduates entering primary-care specialties: 31.0%

Mercer University[1]

1550 College Street
Macon, GA 31207
medicine.mercer.edu
Private
Admissions: (478) 301-2542
Email: admissions@med.mercer.edu
Financial aid: N/A
Tuition: N/A
Room/board/expenses: N/A
Enrollment: N/A

Morehouse School of Medicine

720 Westview Drive SW
Atlanta, GA 30310
www.msm.edu
Private
Admissions: (404) 752-1650
Email: mdadmissions@msm.edu
Financial aid: (404) 752-1655
Application deadline: 12/01
Tuition: $51,878
Room/board/expenses: N/A
Percent receiving grants: 42%
Average student indebtedness at graduation: $203,007
Enrollment: 398
men: 37%; women: 63%; minorities: 95%; underrepresented minorities: 85%; in state: N/A
Acceptance rate: 2%
Median MCAT total score: 26
Median GPA: 3.49
Most popular undergraduate majors: biological sciences: 40%; physical sciences: 38%; nonsciences: 12%; other: 10%
Percent of graduates entering primary-care specialties: 68.0%

HAWAII

University of Hawaii-Manoa (Burns)

651 Ilalo Street
Honolulu, HI 96813
jabsom.hawaii.edu
Public
Admissions: (808) 692-1000
Email: medadmin@hawaii.edu
Financial aid: (808) 956-7251
Application deadline: 11/01
In-state tuition: $33,928
Out-of-state tuition: $67,912
Room/board/expenses: $16,236
Average student indebtedness at graduation: $130,749
Enrollment: 270
men: 47%; women: 53%; minorities: 84%; underrepresented minorities: 12%; in state: 85%
Acceptance rate: 5%
Median MCAT total score: 31
Median GPA: 3.71
Most popular undergraduate majors: biological sciences: 49%; physical sciences: 26%; nonsciences: 20%; other: 5%
Percent of graduates entering primary-care specialties: 55.0%

ILLINOIS

Loyola University Chicago (Stritch)[1]

2160 S. First Avenue, Building 120
Maywood, IL 60153
www.meddean.luc.edu/
Private
Admissions: (708) 216-3229
Email: ssom-admissions@lumc.edu
Financial aid: N/A
Tuition: N/A
Room/board/expenses: N/A
Enrollment: N/A

Northwestern University (Feinberg)

420 E. Superior Street
Rubloff Building, 12th Floor
Chicago, IL 60611
www.feinberg.northwestern.edu
Private
Admissions: (312) 503-8206
Email: med-admissions@northwestern.edu
Financial aid: (312) 503-8722
Application deadline: 11/01
Tuition: $55,885
Room/board/expenses: $18,282
Percent receiving grants: 44%
Average student indebtedness at graduation: $146,490
Enrollment: 687
men: 55%; women: 45%; minorities: 47%; underrepresented minorities: 18%; in state: 20%
Acceptance rate: 6%
Median MCAT total score: 36
Median GPA: 3.87
Most popular undergraduate majors: biological sciences: 40%; physical sciences: 18%; nonsciences: 23%; other: 19%
Percent of graduates entering primary-care specialties: 39.6%

Rosalind Franklin University of Medicine and Science[1]

3333 Green Bay Road
North Chicago, IL 60064
www.rosalindfranklin.edu/cms/
Private
Admissions: (847) 578-3204
Email: cms.admissions@rosalindfranklin.edu
Financial aid: N/A
Tuition: N/A
Room/board/expenses: N/A
Enrollment: N/A

Rush University

600 S. Paulina Street
Chicago, IL 60612
www.rushu.rush.edu/medcol/
Private
Admissions: N/A
Email: RMC_Admissions@rush.edu
Financial aid: (312) 942-6256
Application deadline: 11/02
Tuition: $49,997
Room/board/expenses: $8,676
Percent receiving grants: 54%
Average student indebtedness at graduation: $201,359
Enrollment: 510
men: 50%; women: 50%; minorities: 36%; underrepresented minorities: 16%; in state: 53%
Acceptance rate: 4%
Median MCAT total score: 31
Median GPA: 3.62
Most popular undergraduate majors: biological sciences: 42%; physical sciences: 17%; nonsciences: 21%; other: 20%
Percent of graduates entering primary-care specialties: 40.3%

Southern Illinois University-Springfield[1]

801 N. Rutledge
PO Box 19620
Springfield, IL 62794-9620
www.siumed.edu/
Public
Admissions: (217) 545-6013
Email: admissions@siumed.edu
Financial aid: N/A
Tuition: N/A
Room/board/expenses: N/A
Enrollment: N/A

University of Chicago (Pritzker)

5841 S. Maryland Avenue
MC 1000
Chicago, IL 60637-5416
pritzker.bsd.uchicago.edu
Private
Admissions: (773) 702-1937
Email: pritzkeradmissions@bsd.uchicago.edu
Financial aid: (773) 702-1938
Application deadline: 10/15
Tuition: $52,512
Room/board/expenses: $16,800
Percent receiving grants: 89%
Average student indebtedness at graduation: $117,790
Enrollment: 356
men: 52%; women: 48%; minorities: 37%; underrepresented minorities: 17%; in state: 25%
Acceptance rate: 4%
Median MCAT total score: 37
Median GPA: 3.87
Most popular undergraduate majors: biological sciences: 28%; physical sciences: 23%; nonsciences: 17%; other: 32%
Percent of graduates entering primary-care specialties: 41.0%

University of Illinois

1853 W. Polk Street, M/C 784
Chicago, IL 60612
www.medicine.uic.edu
Public
Admissions: (312) 996-5635
Email: medadmit@uic.edu
Financial aid: (312) 413-0127
Application deadline: 11/01
In-state tuition: $39,488
Out-of-state tuition: $76,488
Room/board/expenses: $14,464
Percent receiving grants: 48%
Average student indebtedness at graduation: $203,709
Enrollment: 1,352
men: 53%; women: 47%; minorities: 51%; underrepresented minorities: 33%; in state: 76%
Acceptance rate: 12%
Median MCAT total score: 31
Median GPA: 3.61
Most popular undergraduate majors: biological sciences: 34%; physical sciences: 15%; nonsciences: 25%; other: 26%
Percent of graduates entering primary-care specialties: 37.2%

INDIANA

Indiana University-Indianapolis

340 W. 10th Street, Suite 6200
Indianapolis, IN 46202
www.medicine.iu.edu
Public
Admissions: (317) 274-3772
Email: inmedadm@iupui.edu
Financial aid: (317) 274-1967
Application deadline: 11/15
In-state tuition: $33,804
Out-of-state tuition: $54,158
Room/board/expenses: $11,646
Percent receiving grants: 32%
Average student indebtedness at graduation: $171,212
Enrollment: 1,377
men: 55%; women: 45%; minorities: 26%; underrepresented minorities: 15%; in state: 82%
Acceptance rate: 11%
Median MCAT total score: 31
Median GPA: 3.79

Most popular undergraduate majors: biological sciences: 42%; physical sciences: 23%; nonsciences: 7%; other: 28%
Percent of graduates entering primary-care specialties: 35.0%

IOWA

University of Iowa (Carver)

200 CMAB
Iowa City, IA 52242-1101
www.medicine.uiowa.edu
Public
Admissions: (319) 335-8052
Email: medical-admissions@uiowa.edu
Financial aid: (319) 335-8059
Application deadline: 10/15
In-state tuition: $34,724
Out-of-state tuition: $51,502
Room/board/expenses: $10,260
Percent receiving grants: 60%
Average student indebtedness at graduation: $156,012
Enrollment: 608
men: 57%; women: 43%; minorities: 25%; underrepresented minorities: 11%; in state: 68%
Acceptance rate: 8%
Median MCAT total score: 32
Median GPA: 3.76
Most popular undergraduate majors: biological sciences: 66%; physical sciences: 9%; nonsciences: 9%; other: 16%
Percent of graduates entering primary-care specialties: 37.0%

KANSAS

University of Kansas Medical Center

3901 Rainbow Boulevard
Kansas City, KS 66160
medicine.kumc.edu
Public
Admissions: (913) 588-5245
Email: premedinfo@kumc.edu
Financial aid: (913) 588-5170
Application deadline: 10/15
In-state tuition: $33,276
Out-of-state tuition: $58,336
Room/board/expenses: $15,500
Percent receiving grants: 88%
Average student indebtedness at graduation: $150,649
Enrollment: 828
men: 56%; women: 44%; minorities: 23%; underrepresented minorities: 13%; in state: 89%
Acceptance rate: 8%
Median MCAT total score: 29
Median GPA: 3.78
Most popular undergraduate majors: biological sciences: 61%; physical sciences: 15%; nonsciences: 8%; other: 16%
Percent of graduates entering primary-care specialties: 48.9%

KENTUCKY

University of Kentucky

138 Leader Avenue
Lexington, KY 40506-9983
www.med.uky.edu
Public
Admissions: (859) 323-6161
Email: kymedap@uky.edu
Financial aid: (859) 257-1652
Application deadline: 11/01
In-state tuition: $34,983
Out-of-state tuition: $64,043
Room/board/expenses: $13,500
Percent receiving grants: 47%

Average student indebtedness at graduation: $185,483
Enrollment: 509
men: 60%; women: 40%; minorities: 21%; underrepresented minorities: 7%; in state: 74%
Acceptance rate: 9%
Median MCAT total score: 32
Median GPA: 3.69
Most popular undergraduate majors: biological sciences: 52%; physical sciences: 21%; nonsciences: 11%; other: 16%
Percent of graduates entering primary-care specialties: 38.3%

University of Louisville

Abell Administration Center
H.S.C.
Louisville, KY 40202
www.louisville.edu
Public
Admissions: (502) 852-5193
Email: medadm@louisville.edu
Financial aid: (502) 852-5187
Application deadline: 10/15
In-state tuition: $36,363
Out-of-state tuition: $54,763
Room/board/expenses: $10,550
Percent receiving grants: 29%
Average student indebtedness at graduation: $156,177
Enrollment: 635
men: 57%; women: 43%; minorities: 18%; underrepresented minorities: 7%; in state: 76%
Acceptance rate: 9%
Median MCAT total score: 29
Median GPA: 3.60
Most popular undergraduate majors: biological sciences: 50%; physical sciences: 20%; nonsciences: 15%; other: 15%
Percent of graduates entering primary-care specialties: 39.7%

LOUISIANA

Louisiana State University Health Sciences Center-New Orleans[1]

Admissions Office
1901 Perdido Street
New Orleans, LA 70112-1393
www.medschool.lsuhsc.edu/
Public
Admissions: (504) 568-6262
Email: ms-admissions@lsuhsc.edu
Financial aid: N/A
Tuition: N/A
Room/board/expenses: N/A
Enrollment: N/A

Louisiana State University Health Sciences Center-Shreveport[1]

PO Box 33932
1501 Kings Highway
Shreveport, LA 71130-3932
www.lsuhscshreveport.edu/
Education/SchoolofMedicine.aspx
Public
Admissions: (318) 675-5190
Email: shvadm@lsuhsc.edu
Financial aid: N/A
Tuition: N/A
Room/board/expenses: N/A
Enrollment: N/A

Tulane University[1]

1430 Tulane Avenue, SL67
New Orleans, LA 70112-2699
tulane.edu/som/
Private
Admissions: (504) 988-5187
Email: medsch@tulane.edu
Financial aid: N/A
Tuition: N/A
Room/board/expenses: N/A
Enrollment: N/A

MARYLAND

Johns Hopkins University

733 N. Broadway
Baltimore, MD 21205
www.hopkinsmedicine.org
Private
Admissions: (410) 955-3182
Email: somadmiss@jhmi.edu
Financial aid: (410) 955-1324
Application deadline: 10/15
Tuition: $52,174
Room/board/expenses: $22,270
Percent receiving grants: 61%
Average student indebtedness at graduation: $113,144
Enrollment: 461
men: 49%; women: 51%; minorities: 52%; underrepresented minorities: 19%; in state: 17%
Acceptance rate: 6%
Median MCAT total score: 36
Median GPA: 3.90
Most popular undergraduate majors: biological sciences: 49%; physical sciences: 25%; nonsciences: 21%; other: 5%
Percent of graduates entering primary-care specialties: 32.8%

Uniformed Services University of the Health Sciences (Hebert)

4301 Jones Bridge Road
Bethesda, MD 20814
www.usuhs.edu
Public
Admissions: (800) 772-1743
Email: admissions@usuhs.edu
Financial aid: N/A
Application deadline: 11/15
In-state tuition: $0
Out-of-state tuition: $0
Room/board/expenses: $0
Percent receiving grants: 0%
Average student indebtedness at graduation: $0
Enrollment: 682
men: 68%; women: 32%; minorities: 28%; underrepresented minorities: 9%; in state: 11%
Acceptance rate: 10%
Median MCAT total score: 31
Median GPA: 3.64
Most popular undergraduate majors: biological sciences: 41%; physical sciences: 31%; nonsciences: 13%; other: 15%
Percent of graduates entering primary-care specialties: 48.0%

University of Maryland

655 W. Baltimore Street
Room 14-029
Baltimore, MD 21201-1559
medschool.umaryland.edu
Public
Admissions: (410) 706-7478
Email: admissions@som.umaryland.edu
Financial aid: (410) 706-7347
Application deadline: 11/01
In-state tuition: $36,873

Out-of-state tuition: $63,466
Room/board/expenses: $21,500
Percent receiving grants: 67%
Average student indebtedness at graduation: $152,626
Enrollment: 647
men: 43%; women: 57%; minorities: 35%; underrepresented minorities: 9%; in state: 85%
Acceptance rate: 7%
Median MCAT total score: 32
Median GPA: 3.79
Most popular undergraduate majors: biological sciences: 53%; physical sciences: 17%; nonsciences: 20%; other: 10%
Percent of graduates entering primary-care specialties: 39.3%

MASSACHUSETTS

Boston University

72 E. Concord Street, L-103
Boston, MA 02118
www.bumc.bu.edu
Private
Admissions: (617) 638-4630
Email: medadms@bu.edu
Financial aid: (617) 638-5130
Application deadline: 11/01
Tuition: $54,678
Room/board/expenses: $10,500
Percent receiving grants: 62%
Average student indebtedness at graduation: $188,193
Enrollment: 681
men: 50%; women: 50%; minorities: 47%; underrepresented minorities: 20%; in state: 19%
Acceptance rate: 4%
Median MCAT total score: 34
Median GPA: 3.71
Most popular undergraduate majors: biological sciences: 39%; physical sciences: 27%; nonsciences: 12%; other: 24%
Percent of graduates entering primary-care specialties: 39.9%

Harvard University

25 Shattuck Street
Boston, MA 02115-6092
hms.harvard.edu
Private
Admissions: (617) 432-1550
Email: admissions_office@hms.harvard.edu
Financial aid: (617) 432-0449
Application deadline: 10/22
Tuition: $55,785
Room/board/expenses: $14,280
Percent receiving grants: 73%
Average student indebtedness at graduation: $97,290
Enrollment: 726
men: 50%; women: 50%; minorities: 52%; underrepresented minorities: 21%; in state: N/A
Acceptance rate: 3%
Median MCAT total score: 36
Median GPA: 3.92
Most popular undergraduate majors: biological sciences: 57%; physical sciences: 16%; nonsciences: 6%; other: 21%
Percent of graduates entering primary-care specialties: 41.3%

Tufts University

136 Harrison Avenue
Boston, MA 02111
md.tufts.edu/med
Private
Admissions: (617) 636-6571
Email: med-admissions@tufts.edu
Financial aid: (617) 636-6574
Application deadline: 08/15
Tuition: $57,920

Room/board/expenses: $14,620
Percent receiving grants: 39%
Average student indebtedness at graduation: $191,207
Enrollment: 816
men: 49%; women: 51%; minorities: 32%; underrepresented minorities: 13%; in state: 30%
Acceptance rate: 5%
Median MCAT total score: 32
Median GPA: 3.68
Most popular undergraduate majors: biological sciences: 50%; physical sciences: 15%; nonsciences: 21%; other: 14%
Percent of graduates entering primary-care specialties: 44.0%

University of Massachusetts-Worcester

55 Lake Avenue N
Worcester, MA 01655
www.umassmed.edu
Public
Admissions: (508) 856-2323
Email: admissions@umassmed.edu
Financial aid: (508) 856-2265
Application deadline: 11/01
In-state tuition: $23,350
Out-of-state tuition: N/A
Room/board/expenses: $13,792
Percent receiving grants: 42%
Average student indebtedness at graduation: $117,733
Enrollment: 508
men: 46%; women: 54%; minorities: 28%; underrepresented minorities: 8%; in state: 98%
Acceptance rate: 16%
Median MCAT total score: 33
Median GPA: 3.70
Most popular undergraduate majors: biological sciences: 38%; physical sciences: 16%; nonsciences: 13%; other: 33%
Percent of graduates entering primary-care specialties: 53.1%

MICHIGAN

Michigan State University (College of Human Medicine)

15 Michigan St. NE
Grand Rapids, MI 49503
humanmedicine.msu.edu
Public
Admissions: (517) 353-9620
Email: MDadmissions@msu.edu
Financial aid: (517) 353-5940
Application deadline: 11/02
In-state tuition: $31,349
Out-of-state tuition: $62,845
Room/board/expenses: $14,616
Percent receiving grants: 32%
Average student indebtedness at graduation: $214,952
Enrollment: 853
men: 47%; women: 53%; minorities: 33%; underrepresented minorities: 16%; in state: 82%
Acceptance rate: 4%
Median MCAT total score: 28
Median GPA: 3.56
Most popular undergraduate majors: biological sciences: 65%; physical sciences: 7%; nonsciences: 14%; other: 14%
Percent of graduates entering primary-care specialties: 45.1%

University of Michigan-Ann Arbor

1301 Catherine Road
Ann Arbor, MI 48109-0624
www.med.umich.edu/medschool/
Public
Admissions: (734) 764-6317
Email:
umichmedadmiss@umich.edu
Financial aid: (734) 763-4147
Application deadline: 09/30
In-state tuition: $31,482
Out-of-state tuition: $49,190
Room/board/expenses: $22,525
Percent receiving grants: 55%
Average student indebtedness at
graduation: $119,177
Enrollment: 727
men: 49%; women:
51%; minorities: 36%;
underrepresented minorities:
13%; in state: 51%
Acceptance rate: 7%
Median MCAT total score: 35
Median GPA: 3.79
Most popular undergraduate
majors: biological sciences:
36%; physical sciences: 37%;
nonsciences: 6%; other: 21%
Percent of graduates entering
primary-care specialties: 43.8%

Wayne State University

540 E. Canfield
Detroit, MI 48201
admissions.med.wayne.edu/
Public
Admissions: (313) 577-1466
Email:
admissions@med.wayne.edu
Financial aid: (313) 577-7731
Application deadline: 12/15
In-state tuition: $32,426
Out-of-state tuition: $65,346
Room/board/expenses: $13,000
Percent receiving grants: 57%
Average student indebtedness at
graduation: $162,258
Enrollment: 1,220
men: 55%; women:
45%; minorities: 27%;
underrepresented minorities: 7%;
in state: 81%
Acceptance rate: 11%
Median MCAT total score: 32
Median GPA: 3.74
Most popular undergraduate
majors: biological sciences:
50%; physical sciences: 20%;
nonsciences: 10%; other: 20%
Percent of graduates entering
primary-care specialties: 33.6%

MINNESOTA

Mayo Medical School

200 First Street SW
Rochester, MN 55905
www.mayo.edu/mms/
Private
Admissions: (507) 284-3671
Email: medschooladmissions@
mayo.edu
Financial aid: (507) 284-4839
Application deadline: 12/31
Tuition: $47,470
Room/board/expenses: $18,048
Percent receiving grants: 96%
Average student indebtedness at
graduation: $65,339
Enrollment: 216
men: 51%; women:
49%; minorities: 34%;
underrepresented minorities:
13%; in state: 12%
Acceptance rate: 2%
Median MCAT total score: 33
Median GPA: 3.81

Most popular undergraduate
majors: biological sciences:
37%; physical sciences: 25%;
nonsciences: 14%; other: 24%
Percent of graduates entering
primary-care specialties: 39.0%

University of Minnesota

420 Delaware Street SE
MMC 293
Minneapolis, MN 55455
www.med.umn.edu
Public
Admissions: (612) 625-7977
Email: meded@umn.edu
Financial aid: (612) 625-4998
Application deadline: 11/15
In-state tuition: $39,712
Out-of-state tuition: $51,607
Room/board/expenses: $13,658
Percent receiving grants: 63%
Average student indebtedness at
graduation: $185,818
Enrollment: 1,005
men: 51%; women:
49%; minorities: 20%;
underrepresented minorities: 11%;
in state: 90%
Acceptance rate: 7%
Median MCAT total score: 31
Median GPA: 3.76
Most popular undergraduate
majors: biological sciences:
47%; physical sciences: 17%;
nonsciences: 9%; other: 27%
Percent of graduates entering
primary-care specialties: 48.7%

MISSISSIPPI

University of Mississippi[1]

2500 N. State Street
Jackson, MS 39216-4505
www.umc.edu/som/
Public
Admissions: (601) 984-5010
Email: AdmitMD@umc.edu
Financial aid: N/A
Tuition: N/A
Room/board/expenses: N/A
Enrollment: N/A

MISSOURI

St. Louis University

1402 S. Grand Boulevard
St. Louis, MO 63104
medschool.slu.edu
Private
Admissions: (314) 977-9870
Email: slumd@slu.edu
Financial aid: (314) 977-9840
Application deadline: 12/15
Tuition: $50,140
Room/board/expenses: $11,530
Percent receiving grants: 56%
Average student indebtedness at
graduation: $187,266
Enrollment: 730
men: 52%; women:
48%; minorities: 40%;
underrepresented minorities:
10%; in state: 40%
Acceptance rate: 7%
Median MCAT total score: 33
Median GPA: 3.85
Most popular undergraduate
majors: biological sciences:
51%; physical sciences: 18%;
nonsciences: 6%; other: 25%
Percent of graduates entering
primary-care specialties: 43.8%

University of Missouri

One Hospital Drive
Columbia, MO 65212
medicine.missouri.edu
Public
Admissions: (573) 882-9219
Email: MizzouMed@missouri.edu
Financial aid: (573) 882-2923
Application deadline: 10/15
In-state tuition: $29,778
Out-of-state tuition: $56,872
Room/board/expenses: $10,920
Percent receiving grants: 62%
Average student indebtedness at
graduation: $137,113
Enrollment: 391
men: 55%; women: 45%;
minorities: 17%; underrepresented
minorities: 6%; in state: 83%
Acceptance rate: 9%
Median MCAT total score: 30
Median GPA: 3.76
Most popular undergraduate
majors: biological sciences:
48%; physical sciences: 17%;
nonsciences: 15%; other: 20%
Percent of graduates entering
primary-care specialties: 43.0%

University of Missouri-Kansas City[1]

2411 Holmes
Kansas City, MO 64108
www.med.umkc.edu
Public
Admissions: (816) 235-1870
Email: medicine@umkc.edu
Financial aid: N/A
Tuition: N/A
Room/board/expenses: N/A
Enrollment: N/A

Washington University in St. Louis

660 S. Euclid Avenue
St. Louis, MO 63110
medadmissions.wustl.edu
Private
Admissions: (314) 362-6858
Email: wumscoa@wustl.edu
Financial aid: (314) 362-6671
Application deadline: 12/01
Tuition: $56,212
Room/board/expenses: $12,306
Percent receiving grants: 75%
Average student indebtedness at
graduation: $100,308
Enrollment: 474
men: 49%; women:
51%; minorities: 47%;
underrepresented minorities:
12%; in state: 10%
Acceptance rate: 8%
Median MCAT total score: 38
Median GPA: 3.87
Most popular undergraduate
majors: biological sciences:
34%; physical sciences: 29%;
nonsciences: 7%; other: 29%
Percent of graduates entering
primary-care specialties: 32.6%

NEBRASKA

Creighton University

2500 California Plaza
Omaha, NE 68178
medicine.creighton.edu
Private
Admissions: (402) 280-2799
Email:
medadmissions@creighton.edu
Financial aid: (402) 280-2731
Application deadline: 11/01
Tuition: $53,352
Room/board/expenses: $14,400
Percent receiving grants: 53%
Average student indebtedness at
graduation: $211,699

Enrollment: 620
men: 48%; women:
52%; minorities: 13%;
underrepresented minorities: 7%;
in state: 10%
Acceptance rate: 6%
Median MCAT total score: 30
Median GPA: 3.77
Most popular undergraduate
majors: biological sciences:
50%; physical sciences: 18%;
nonsciences: 14%; other: 18%
Percent of graduates entering
primary-care specialties: 39.3%

University of Nebraska Medical Center

985527 Nebraska Medical Center
Omaha, NE 68198-5527
www.unmc.edu/com/
admissions.htm
Public
Admissions: (402) 559-2259
Email: grrogers@unmc.edu
Financial aid: (402) 559-4199
Application deadline: 11/01
In-state tuition: $31,107
Out-of-state tuition: $72,747
Room/board/expenses: $15,300
Percent receiving grants: 44%
Average student indebtedness at
graduation: $155,262
Enrollment: 515
men: 60%; women:
40%; minorities: 13%;
underrepresented minorities: 3%;
in state: 83%
Acceptance rate: 10%
Median MCAT total score: 31
Median GPA: 3.78
Most popular undergraduate
majors: biological sciences:
38%; physical sciences: 18%;
nonsciences: 7%; other: 37%
Percent of graduates entering
primary-care specialties: 65.0%

NEVADA

University of Nevada

Pennington Building, Mailstop 357
Reno, NV 89557-0357
www.medicine.nevada.edu
Public
Admissions: (775) 784-6063
Email: asa@medicine.nevada.edu
Financial aid: (775) 682-8358
Application deadline: N/A
In-state tuition: $27,794
Out-of-state tuition: $59,078
Room/board/expenses: $15,340
Percent receiving grants: 82%
Average student indebtedness at
graduation: $141,639
Enrollment: 265
men: 57%; women:
43%; minorities: 42%;
underrepresented minorities:
17%; in state: 93%
Acceptance rate: 8%
Median MCAT total score: 31
Median GPA: 3.73
Most popular undergraduate
majors: biological sciences:
N/A; physical sciences: N/A;
nonsciences: N/A; other: N/A
Percent of graduates entering
primary-care specialties: 48.0%

NEW HAMPSHIRE

Dartmouth College (Geisel)

1 Rope Ferry Road
Hanover, NH 03755-1404
geiselmed.dartmouth.edu
Private
Admissions: (603) 650-1505
Email: geisel.admissions@
dartmouth.edu

Financial aid: (603) 650-1919
Application deadline: 11/01
Tuition: $58,368
Room/board/expenses: $10,750
Percent receiving grants: 59%
Average student indebtedness at
graduation: $142,047
Enrollment: 368
men: 45%; women:
55%; minorities: 43%;
underrepresented minorities:
24%; in state: 5%
Acceptance rate: 5%
Median MCAT total score: 33
Median GPA: 3.71
Most popular undergraduate
majors: biological sciences:
32%; physical sciences: 26%;
nonsciences: 8%; other: 34%
Percent of graduates entering
primary-care specialties: 43.6%

NEW JERSEY

Rutgers Biomedical and Health Sciences

185 S. Orange Avenue
Newark, NJ 07101-1709
www.njms.rutgers.edu
Public
Admissions: (973) 972-4631
Email:
njmsadmiss@njms.rutgers.edu
Financial aid: (973) 972-4376
Application deadline: 12/01
In-state tuition: $39,160
Out-of-state tuition: $59,024
Room/board/expenses: $17,870
Percent receiving grants: 39%
Average student indebtedness at
graduation: $151,924
Enrollment: 743
men: 62%; women:
38%; minorities: 62%;
underrepresented minorities:
19%; in state: 100%
Acceptance rate: 10%
Median MCAT total score: 32
Median GPA: 3.63
Most popular undergraduate
majors: biological sciences:
45%; physical sciences: 19%;
nonsciences: 20%; other: 16%
Percent of graduates entering
primary-care specialties: 34.9%

Rutgers Robert Wood Johnson Medical School

125 Paterson Street
New Brunswick, NJ 08903-0019
rwjms.umdnj.edu
Public
Admissions: (732) 235-4576
Email: rwjapadm@umdnj.edu
Financial aid: (732) 235-4689
Application deadline: 12/01
In-state tuition: $41,681
Out-of-state tuition: $61,545
Room/board/expenses: $14,160
Percent receiving grants: 26%
Average student indebtedness at
graduation: $141,667
Enrollment: 586
men: 43%; women:
57%; minorities: 44%;
underrepresented minorities:
13%; in state: 97%
Acceptance rate: 7%
Median MCAT total score: 31
Median GPA: 3.68
Most popular undergraduate
majors: biological sciences:
53%; physical sciences: 12%;
nonsciences: 16%; other: 19%
Percent of graduates entering
primary-care specialties: 44.9%

NEW MEXICO

University of New Mexico

Reginald Heber Fitz Hall
Room 107
Albuquerque, NM 87131
som.unm.edu
Public
Admissions: (505) 272-4766
Email: somadmissions@
salud.unm.edu
Financial aid: (505) 272-8008
Application deadline: 11/01
In-state tuition: $19,395
Out-of-state tuition: $49,572
Room/board/expenses: $15,722
Percent receiving grants: 67%
Average student indebtedness at graduation: $127,491
Enrollment: 438
men: 47%; women:
53%; minorities: 56%;
underrepresented minorities:
49%; in state: 84%
Acceptance rate: 11%
Median MCAT total score: 27
Median GPA: 3.65
Most popular undergraduate majors: biological sciences:
40%; physical sciences: 26%;
nonsciences: 8%; other: 26%
Percent of graduates entering primary-care specialties: 42.3%

NEW YORK

Albany Medical College[1]

47 New Scotland Avenue
Albany, NY 12208
www.amc.edu/Academic/
Private
Admissions: (518) 262-5521
Email: admissions@mail.amc.edu
Financial aid: N/A
Tuition: N/A
Room/board/expenses: N/A
Enrollment: N/A

Columbia University

630 W. 168th Street
New York, NY 10032
ps.columbia.edu
Private
Admissions: (212) 305-3595
Email:
psadmissions@columbia.edu
Financial aid: (212) 305-4100
Application deadline: 10/15
Tuition: $59,063
Room/board/expenses: $16,718
Percent receiving grants: 62%
Average student indebtedness at graduation: $132,220
Enrollment: 648
men: 49%; women:
51%; minorities: 38%;
underrepresented minorities:
22%; in state: 33%
Acceptance rate: 4%
Median MCAT total score: 36
Median GPA: 3.82
Most popular undergraduate majors: biological sciences:
37%; physical sciences: 16%;
nonsciences: 26%; other: 21%
Percent of graduates entering primary-care specialties: 32.4%

Cornell University (Weill)

1300 York Avenue
New York, NY 10065
www.weill.cornell.edu
Private
Admissions: (212) 746-1067
Email: wcmc-admissions@
med.cornell.edu
Financial aid: (212) 746-1066
Application deadline: 10/15
Tuition: $53,185
Room/board/expenses: $12,580
Percent receiving grants: 61%
Average student indebtedness at graduation: $142,938
Enrollment: 406
men: 53%; women:
47%; minorities: 42%;
underrepresented minorities:
19%; in state: 31%
Acceptance rate: 4%
Median MCAT total score: 36
Median GPA: 3.82
Most popular undergraduate majors: biological sciences:
26%; physical sciences: 16%;
nonsciences: 10%; other: 49%
Percent of graduates entering primary-care specialties: 39.0%

Icahn School of Medicine at Mount Sinai

1 Gustave L. Levy Place
PO Box 1217
New York, NY 10029
www.icahn.mssm.edu
Private
Admissions: (212) 241-6696
Email: admissions@mssm.edu
Financial aid: (212) 241-5245
Application deadline: 10/15
Tuition: $50,551
Room/board/expenses: $12,687
Percent receiving grants: 37%
Average student indebtedness at graduation: $129,453
Enrollment: 556
men: 52%; women:
48%; minorities: 42%;
underrepresented minorities:
17%; in state: 32%
Acceptance rate: 8%
Median MCAT total score: 36
Median GPA: 3.78
Most popular undergraduate majors: biological sciences:
40%; physical sciences: 19%;
nonsciences: 26%; other: 15%
Percent of graduates entering primary-care specialties: 37.3%

New York Medical College

40 Sunshine Cottage Road
Valhalla, NY 10595
www.nymc.edu
Private
Admissions: (914) 594-4507
Email: mdadmit@nymc.edu
Financial aid: (914) 594-4491
Application deadline: 12/15
Tuition: $54,246
Room/board/expenses: $18,920
Percent receiving grants: 52%
Average student indebtedness at graduation: $216,631
Enrollment: 818
men: 52%; women:
48%; minorities: 43%;
underrepresented minorities:
20%; in state: 31%
Acceptance rate: 6%
Median MCAT total score: 31
Median GPA: 3.58
Most popular undergraduate majors: biological sciences:
53%; physical sciences: 15%;
nonsciences: 10%; other: 22%
Percent of graduates entering primary-care specialties: 40.0%

SUNY Downstate Medical Center[1]

450 Clarkson Avenue, Box 60
Brooklyn, NY 11203
www.downstate.edu/
college_of_medicine/
Public
Admissions: (718) 270-2446
Email: medadmissions@
downstate.edu
Financial aid: N/A
Tuition: N/A
Room/board/expenses: N/A
Enrollment: N/A

SUNY-Syracuse[1]

766 Irving Avenue
Syracuse, NY 13210
www.upstate.edu/com/
Public
Admissions: (315) 464-4570
Email: admiss@upstate.edu
Financial aid: N/A
Tuition: N/A
Room/board/expenses: N/A
Enrollment: N/A

New York University

550 First Avenue
New York, NY 10016
school.med.nyu.edu
Private
Admissions: (212) 263-5290
Email: admissions@nyumc.org
Financial aid: (212) 263-5286
Application deadline: 10/15
Tuition: $52,600
Room/board/expenses: $15,240
Percent receiving grants: 30%
Average student indebtedness at graduation: $135,393
Enrollment: 650
men: 53%; women:
47%; minorities: 41%;
underrepresented minorities:
12%; in state: 43%
Acceptance rate: 6%
Median MCAT total score: 36
Median GPA: 3.84
Most popular undergraduate majors: biological sciences:
29%; physical sciences: 28%;
nonsciences: 18%; other: 25%
Percent of graduates entering primary-care specialties: 39.0%

Stony Brook University-SUNY

Office of Admissions
Health Science Center, L4
Stony Brook, NY 11794-8434
medicine.stonybrookmedicine.edu/
Public
Admissions: (631) 444-2113
Email: somadmissions@
stonybrookmedicine.edu
Financial aid: (631) 444-2341
Application deadline: 12/01
In-state tuition: $38,020
Out-of-state tuition: $63,180
Room/board/expenses: $11,413
Percent receiving grants: 22%
Average student indebtedness at graduation: $166,245
Enrollment: 500
men: 55%; women:
45%; minorities: 44%;
underrepresented minorities:
13%; in state: 77%
Acceptance rate: 7%
Median MCAT total score: 32
Median GPA: 3.70
Most popular undergraduate majors: biological sciences:
40%; physical sciences: 38%;
nonsciences: 22%; other: N/A
Percent of graduates entering primary-care specialties: 35.7%

University at Buffalo–SUNY[1]

155 Biomedical Education Building
Buffalo, NY 14214
medicine.buffalo.edu
Public
Admissions: (716) 829-3466
Email: jjrosso@buffalo.edu
Financial aid: N/A
Tuition: N/A
Room/board/expenses: N/A
Enrollment: N/A

University of Rochester

601 Elmwood Avenue, Box 706
Rochester, NY 14642
www.urmc.rochester.edu/
education/md/admissions
Private
Admissions: (585) 275-4542
Email: mdadmish@
urmc.rochester.edu
Financial aid: (585) 275-4523
Application deadline: 10/15
Tuition: $50,900
Room/board/expenses: $16,500
Percent receiving grants: 66%
Average student indebtedness at graduation: $139,314
Enrollment: 435
men: 48%; women:
52%; minorities: 41%;
underrepresented minorities:
15%; in state: 58%
Acceptance rate: 5%
Median MCAT total score: 33
Median GPA: 3.72
Most popular undergraduate majors: biological sciences:
32%; physical sciences: 19%;
nonsciences: 25%; other: 24%
Percent of graduates entering primary-care specialties: 37.0%

Yeshiva University (Einstein)

1300 Morris Park Avenue
Bronx, NY 10461
www.einstein.yu.edu
Private
Admissions: (718) 430-2106
Email: admissions@
einstein.yu.edu
Financial aid: (718) 862-1813
Application deadline: 11/01
Tuition: $53,142
Room/board/expenses: $17,350
Percent receiving grants: 44%
Average student indebtedness at graduation: $152,316
Enrollment: 793
men: 53%; women:
47%; minorities: 31%;
underrepresented minorities: 11%;
in state: 44%
Acceptance rate: 4%
Median MCAT total score: 33
Median GPA: 3.78
Most popular undergraduate majors: biological sciences:
47%; physical sciences: 15%;
nonsciences: 16%; other: 22%
Percent of graduates entering primary-care specialties: 44.0%

NORTH CAROLINA

Duke University

DUMC 3710
Durham, NC 27710
dukemed.duke.edu
Private
Admissions: (919) 684-2985
Email: medadm@mc.duke.edu
Financial aid: (919) 684-6649
Application deadline: 10/15
Tuition: $55,770
Room/board/expenses: $16,440

Percent receiving grants: 71%
Average student indebtedness at graduation: $112,249
Enrollment: 430
men: 51%; women:
49%; minorities: 54%;
underrepresented minorities:
21%; in state: 13%
Acceptance rate: 3%
Median MCAT total score: 35
Median GPA: 3.80
Most popular undergraduate majors: biological sciences:
45%; physical sciences: 29%;
nonsciences: 17%; other: 9%
Percent of graduates entering primary-care specialties: 32.0%

East Carolina University (Brody)

600 Moye Boulevard
Greenville, NC 27834
www.ecu.edu/bsomadmissions
Public
Admissions: (252) 744-2202
Email: somadmissions@ecu.edu
Financial aid: (252) 744-2278
Application deadline: 11/01
In-state tuition: $20,558
Out-of-state tuition: N/A
Room/board/expenses: $14,927
Percent receiving grants: 93%
Average student indebtedness at graduation: $59,784
Enrollment: 313
men: 50%; women:
50%; minorities: 32%;
underrepresented minorities:
16%; in state: 100%
Acceptance rate: 13%
Median MCAT total score: 28
Median GPA: 3.72
Most popular undergraduate majors: biological sciences:
33%; physical sciences: 18%;
nonsciences: 12%; other: 37%
Percent of graduates entering primary-care specialties: 54.6%

University of North Carolina-Chapel Hill

CB #7000
4030 Bondurant Hall
Chapel Hill, NC 27599-7000
www.med.unc.edu/admit/
Public
Admissions: (919) 962-8331
Email: admissions@med.unc.edu
Financial aid: (919) 962-6117
Application deadline: 11/01
In-state tuition: $20,802
Out-of-state tuition: $47,681
Room/board/expenses: $32,004
Average student indebtedness at graduation: $90,155
Enrollment: 827
men: 53%; women:
47%; minorities: 34%;
underrepresented minorities:
22%; in state: 91%
Acceptance rate: 4%
Median MCAT total score: 32
Median GPA: 3.67
Most popular undergraduate majors: biological sciences:
49%; physical sciences: 9%;
nonsciences: 20%; other: 22%
Percent of graduates entering primary-care specialties: 63.0%

Wake Forest University

Medical Center Boulevard
Winston-Salem, NC 27157
www.wakehealth.edu
Private
Admissions: (336) 716-4264
Email: medadmit@wakehealth.edu

Financial aid: (336) 716-2889
Application deadline: 11/01
Tuition: $50,300
Room/board/expenses: $24,112
Percent receiving grants: 43%
Average student indebtedness at graduation: $150,301
Enrollment: 469
men: 53%; women: 47%; minorities: 28%; underrepresented minorities: 14%; in state: 38%
Acceptance rate: 3%
Median MCAT total score: 32
Median GPA: 3.58
Most popular undergraduate majors: biological sciences: 44%; physical sciences: 23%; nonsciences: 22%; other: 11%
Percent of graduates entering primary-care specialties: 37.0%

NORTH DAKOTA

University of North Dakota[1]

501 N. Columbia Road, Stop 9037
Grand Forks, ND 58202-9037
www.med.und.nodak.edu
Public
Admissions: (701) 777-4221
Financial aid: N/A
Tuition: N/A
Room/board/expenses: N/A
Enrollment: N/A

OHIO

Case Western Reserve University

10900 Euclid Avenue
Cleveland, OH 44106
casemed.case.edu/
Private
Admissions: (216) 368-3450
Email: casemed-admissions@case.edu
Financial aid: (216) 368-3666
Application deadline: 11/01
Tuition: $57,050
Room/board/expenses: $20,658
Percent receiving grants: 55%
Average student indebtedness at graduation: $168,786
Enrollment: 864
men: 52%; women: 48%; minorities: 42%; underrepresented minorities: 10%; in state: 21%
Acceptance rate: 8%
Median MCAT total score: 36
Median GPA: 3.74
Most popular undergraduate majors: biological sciences: 32%; physical sciences: 33%; nonsciences: 20%; other: 15%
Percent of graduates entering primary-care specialties: 33.1%

Northeast Ohio Medical University[1]

4209 State Route 44
PO Box 95
Rootstown, OH 44272-0095
www.neomed.edu/
Public
Admissions: (330) 325-6270
Email: admission@neomed.edu
Financial aid: N/A
Tuition: N/A
Room/board/expenses: N/A
Enrollment: N/A

Ohio State University

200 Meiling Hall
370 W. Ninth Avenue
Columbus, OH 43210-1238
medicine.osu.edu
Public
Admissions: (614) 292-7137
Email: medicine@osu.edu
Financial aid: (614) 688-4955
Application deadline: 11/01
In-state tuition: $31,273
Out-of-state tuition: $35,947
Room/board/expenses: $10,066
Percent receiving grants: 79%
Average student indebtedness at graduation: $164,400
Enrollment: 824
men: 54%; women: 46%; minorities: 44%; underrepresented minorities: 20%; in state: 84%
Acceptance rate: 7%
Median MCAT total score: 34
Median GPA: 3.77
Most popular undergraduate majors: biological sciences: 44%; physical sciences: 29%; nonsciences: 4%; other: 23%
Percent of graduates entering primary-care specialties: 43.3%

University of Cincinnati

231 Albert Sabin Way
Cincinnati, OH 45267-0552
www.MedOneStop.uc.edu
Public
Admissions: (513) 558-7314
Email: comadmis@ucmail.uc.edu
Financial aid: (513) 558-6797
Application deadline: 11/15
In-state tuition: $32,174
Out-of-state tuition: $50,438
Room/board/expenses: $19,096
Percent receiving grants: 39%
Average student indebtedness at graduation: $168,557
Enrollment: 671
men: 51%; women: 49%; minorities: 32%; underrepresented minorities: 14%; in state: 92%
Acceptance rate: 8%
Median MCAT total score: 33
Median GPA: 3.74
Most popular undergraduate majors: biological sciences: 51%; physical sciences: 19%; nonsciences: 12%; other: 18%
Percent of graduates entering primary-care specialties: 31.9%

University of Toledo

3000 Arlington Avenue
Toledo, OH 43614
hsc.utoledo.edu
Public
Admissions: (419) 383-4229
Email: medadmissions@utoledo.edu
Financial aid: (419) 383-4232
Application deadline: 11/01
In-state tuition: $33,257
Out-of-state tuition: $63,763
Room/board/expenses: $12,468
Percent receiving grants: 16%
Average student indebtedness at graduation: $182,929
Enrollment: 714
men: 54%; women: 46%; minorities: 20%; underrepresented minorities: 5%; in state: 95%
Acceptance rate: 8%
Median MCAT total score: 30
Median GPA: 3.70
Most popular undergraduate majors: biological sciences: 54%; physical sciences: 25%; nonsciences: 6%; other: 15%
Percent of graduates entering primary-care specialties: 37.9%

Wright State University (Boonshoft)

3640 Col. Glenn Hwy
Dayton, OH 45401-1751
www.med.wright.edu
Public
Admissions: (937) 775-2934
Email: som_saa@wright.edu
Financial aid: (937) 775-2934
Application deadline: 11/15
In-state tuition: $36,086
Out-of-state tuition: $52,746
Room/board/expenses: $13,867
Percent receiving grants: 49%
Average student indebtedness at graduation: $191,779
Enrollment: 427
men: 51%; women: 49%; minorities: 29%; underrepresented minorities: 15%; in state: 89%
Acceptance rate: 7%
Median MCAT total score: 28
Median GPA: 3.73
Most popular undergraduate majors: biological sciences: N/A; physical sciences: N/A; nonsciences: N/A; other: N/A
Percent of graduates entering primary-care specialties: 49.4%

OKLAHOMA

University of Oklahoma

PO Box 26901, BMSB 357
Oklahoma City, OK 73126
www.medicine.ouhsc.edu
Public
Admissions: (405) 271-2331
Email: adminmed@ouhsc.edu
Financial aid: (405) 271-2118
Application deadline: 10/15
In-state tuition: $23,844
Out-of-state tuition: $52,926
Room/board/expenses: $20,926
Percent receiving grants: 47%
Average student indebtedness at graduation: $145,019
Enrollment: 660
men: 60%; women: 40%; minorities: 26%; underrepresented minorities: 11%; in state: 92%
Acceptance rate: 11%
Median MCAT total score: 30
Median GPA: 3.84
Most popular undergraduate majors: biological sciences: 45%; physical sciences: 25%; nonsciences: 8%; other: 22%
Percent of graduates entering primary-care specialties: 38.8%

OREGON

Oregon Health and Science University

2730 S.W. Moody Ave, CL5MD
Portland, OR 97201-3098
www.ohsu.edu/xd
Public
Admissions: (503) 494-2998
Financial aid: (503) 494-7800
Application deadline: 10/15
In-state tuition: $41,312
Out-of-state tuition: $57,856
Room/board/expenses: $19,500
Percent receiving grants: 70%
Average student indebtedness at graduation: $198,715
Enrollment: 526
men: 51%; women: 49%; minorities: 21%; underrepresented minorities: 10%; in state: 72%
Acceptance rate: 4%
Median MCAT total score: 31
Median GPA: 3.64

Most popular undergraduate majors: biological sciences: 43%; physical sciences: 10%; nonsciences: 9%; other: 38%
Percent of graduates entering primary-care specialties: 46.3%

PENNSYLVANIA

The Commonwealth Medical College[1]

Scranton, PA 18509
www.tcmc.edu/
Private
Admissions: N/A
Email: admissions@tcmc.edu
Financial aid: N/A
Tuition: N/A
Room/board/expenses: N/A
Enrollment: N/A

Drexel University

2900 Queen Lane
Philadelphia, PA 19129
www.drexelmed.edu
Private
Admissions: (215) 991-8202
Email: Medadmis@drexel.edu
Financial aid: (215) 991-8210
Application deadline: 12/01
Tuition: $53,250
Room/board/expenses: $15,516
Percent receiving grants: 27%
Average student indebtedness at graduation: $208,926
Enrollment: 1,083
men: 50%; women: 50%; minorities: 46%; underrepresented minorities: 11%; in state: 32%
Acceptance rate: 4%
Median MCAT total score: 31
Median GPA: 3.59
Most popular undergraduate majors: biological sciences: N/A; physical sciences: N/A; nonsciences: N/A; other: N/A
Percent of graduates entering primary-care specialties: 37.6%

Pennsylvania State University College of Medicine[1]

500 University Drive
Hershey, PA 17033
med.psu.edu/web/college/home
Public
Admissions: (717) 531-8755
Email: StudentAdmissions@hmc.psu.edu
Financial aid: N/A
Tuition: N/A
Room/board/expenses: N/A
Enrollment: N/A

Temple University

3500 N. Broad Street
MERB 1140
Philadelphia, PA 19140
www.temple.edu/medicine
Private
Admissions: (215) 707-3656
Email: medadmissions@temple.edu
Financial aid: (215) 707-7486
Application deadline: 12/15
Tuition: $45,822
Room/board/expenses: $13,180
Percent receiving grants: 36%
Average student indebtedness at graduation: $208,136
Enrollment: 879
men: 54%; women: 46%; minorities: 36%; underrepresented minorities: 16%; in state: 60%

Acceptance rate: 5%
Median MCAT total score: 32
Median GPA: 3.68
Most popular undergraduate majors: biological sciences: 49%; physical sciences: 14%; nonsciences: 22%; other: 15%
Percent of graduates entering primary-care specialties: 36.0%

Thomas Jefferson University (Kimmel)

1025 Walnut Street, Room 100
Philadelphia, PA 19107-5083
www.tju.edu
Private
Admissions: (215) 955-6983
Email: jmc.admissions@jefferson.edu
Financial aid: (215) 955-2867
Application deadline: 11/15
Tuition: $52,954
Room/board/expenses: $17,050
Percent receiving grants: 45%
Average student indebtedness at graduation: $178,726
Enrollment: 1,072
men: 51%; women: 49%; minorities: 31%; underrepresented minorities: 8%; in state: 46%
Acceptance rate: 4%
Median MCAT total score: 32
Median GPA: 3.69
Most popular undergraduate majors: biological sciences: 37%; physical sciences: 13%; nonsciences: 13%; other: 37%
Percent of graduates entering primary-care specialties: 40.7%

University of Pennsylvania (Perelman)

237 John Morgan Building
3620 Hamilton Walk
Philadelphia, PA 19104-6055
www.med.upenn.edu
Private
Admissions: (215) 898-8001
Email: admiss@mail.med.upenn.edu
Financial aid: (215) 573-3423
Application deadline: 10/15
Tuition: $54,378
Room/board/expenses: $20,610
Percent receiving grants: 73%
Average student indebtedness at graduation: $138,860
Enrollment: 655
men: 53%; women: 47%; minorities: 46%; underrepresented minorities: 25%; in state: 25%
Acceptance rate: 5%
Median MCAT total score: 38
Median GPA: 3.84
Most popular undergraduate majors: biological sciences: 46%; physical sciences: 13%; nonsciences: 30%; other: 11%
Percent of graduates entering primary-care specialties: 35.0%

University of Pittsburgh

401 Scaife Hall
Pittsburgh, PA 15261
www.medschool.pitt.edu
Public
Admissions: (412) 648-9891
Email: admissions@medschool.pitt.edu
Financial aid: (412) 648-9891
Application deadline: 10/15
In-state tuition: $49,634

Out-of-state tuition: $50,856
Room/board/expenses: $17,010
Percent receiving grants: 57%
Average student indebtedness at graduation: $134,564
Enrollment: 601
men: 53%; women:
47%; minorities: 50%;
underrepresented minorities:
19%; in state: 26%
Acceptance rate: 6%
Median MCAT total score: 36
Median GPA: 3.85
Most popular undergraduate majors: biological sciences:
34%; physical sciences: 21%;
nonsciences: 10%; other: 35%
Percent of graduates entering primary-care specialties: 36.0%

PUERTO RICO

Ponce School of Medicine[1]

PO Box 7004
Ponce, PR 00732
www.psm.edu
Private
Admissions: (787) 840-2575
Email: admissions@psm.edu
Financial aid: N/A
Tuition: N/A
Room/board/expenses: N/A
Enrollment: N/A

San Juan Bautista School of Medicine[1]

PO Box 4968
Caguas, PR 00726-4968
www.sanjuanbautista.edu
Private
Admissions: (787) 743-3038
Email: admissions@
sanjuanbautista.edu
Financial aid: N/A
Tuition: N/A
Room/board/expenses: N/A
Enrollment: N/A

Universidad Central del Caribe[1]

PO Box 60-327
Bayamon, PR 00960-6032
www.uccaribe.edu/medicine/
Private
Admissions: (787) 798-3001
Email: admissions@uccaribe.edu
Financial aid: N/A
Tuition: N/A
Room/board/expenses: N/A
Enrollment: N/A

University of Puerto Rico School of Medicine[1]

PO Box 365067
San Juan, PR 00936-5067
www.md.rcm.upr.edu/
Public
Admissions: (787) 758-2525
Financial aid: N/A
Tuition: N/A
Room/board/expenses: N/A
Enrollment: N/A

RHODE ISLAND

Brown University (Alpert)

222 Richmond Street, Box G-M
Providence, RI 02912-9706
med.brown.edu
Private
Admissions: (401) 863-2149
Email: medschool_admissions@
brown.edu
Financial aid: (401) 863-1142

Application deadline: 12/31
Tuition: $55,421
Room/board/expenses: $17,924
Percent receiving grants: 52%
Average student indebtedness at graduation: $126,631
Enrollment: 490
men: 48%; women:
52%; minorities: 53%;
underrepresented minorities:
23%; in state: 8%
Acceptance rate: 3%
Median MCAT total score: 33
Median GPA: 3.65
Most popular undergraduate majors: biological sciences:
43%; physical sciences: 16%;
nonsciences: 36%; other: 5%
Percent of graduates entering primary-care specialties: 38.0%

SOUTH CAROLINA

Medical University of South Carolina

96 Jonathan Lucas St, Suite 601
Charleston, SC 29425
www.musc.edu/com1
Public
Admissions: (843) 792-2055
Email: taylorwl@musc.edu
Financial aid: (843) 792-2536
Application deadline: 11/02
In-state tuition: $37,911
Out-of-state tuition: $64,366
Room/board/expenses: $13,340
Percent receiving grants: 41%
Average student indebtedness at graduation: $193,379
Enrollment: 725
men: 58%; women:
42%; minorities: 26%;
underrepresented minorities:
17%; in state: 88%
Acceptance rate: 15%
Median MCAT total score: 30
Median GPA: 3.71
Most popular undergraduate majors: biological sciences:
53%; physical sciences: 16%;
nonsciences: 0%; other: 31%
Percent of graduates entering primary-care specialties: 35.7%

University of South Carolina[1]

6311 Garners Ferry Road
Columbia, SC 29208
www.med.sc.edu
Public
Admissions: (803) 216-3625
Email: admissions@
uscmed.sc.edu
Financial aid: N/A
Tuition: N/A
Room/board/expenses: N/A
Enrollment: N/A

SOUTH DAKOTA

University of South Dakota (Sanford)

1400 W. 22nd Street
Sioux Falls, SD 57105
www.usd.edu/med/md
Public
Admissions: (605) 677-6886
Email: md@usd.edu
Financial aid: (605) 677-5112
Application deadline: 11/15
In-state tuition: $29,942
Out-of-state tuition: $66,228
Room/board/expenses: $17,331
Percent receiving grants: 78%
Average student indebtedness at graduation: $138,034

Enrollment: 235
men: 53%; women: 47%;
minorities: 8%; underrepresented
minorities: 3%; in state: 94%
Acceptance rate: 15%
Median MCAT total score: 29
Median GPA: 3.74
Most popular undergraduate majors: biological sciences:
46%; physical sciences: 9%;
nonsciences: 14%; other: 31%
Percent of graduates entering primary-care specialties: 38.6%

TENNESSEE

East Tennessee State University (Quillen)

PO Box 70694
Johnson City, TN 37614
www.etsu.edu/com
Public
Admissions: (423) 439-2033
Email: sacom@etsu.edu
Financial aid: (423) 439-2035
Application deadline: 11/15
In-state tuition: $33,079
Out-of-state tuition: $63,357
Room/board/expenses: $11,048
Percent receiving grants: 49%
Average student indebtedness at graduation: $150,133
Enrollment: 289
men: 58%; women:
42%; minorities: 16%;
underrepresented minorities: 6%;
in state: 96%
Acceptance rate: 5%
Median MCAT total score: 29
Median GPA: 3.75
Most popular undergraduate majors: biological sciences:
44%; physical sciences: 32%;
nonsciences: 6%; other: 18%
Percent of graduates entering primary-care specialties: 44.6%

Meharry Medical College[1]

1005 D. B. Todd Jr. Boulevard
Nashville, TN 37208
www.mmc.edu/education/som/
Private
Admissions: (615) 327-6223
Email: admissions@mmc.edu
Financial aid: N/A
Tuition: N/A
Room/board/expenses: N/A
Enrollment: N/A

University of Tennessee Health Science Center

910 Madison Avenue, Suite 1002
Memphis, TN 38163
www.uthsc.edu/Medicine/
Public
Admissions: (901) 448-5559
Email: diharris@uthsc.edu
Financial aid: (901) 448-5568
Application deadline: 11/15
In-state tuition: $36,278
Out-of-state tuition: $68,708
Room/board/expenses: $19,380
Percent receiving grants: 39%
Average student indebtedness at graduation: $155,676
Enrollment: 667
men: 60%; women:
40%; minorities: 26%;
underrepresented minorities:
14%; in state: 96%
Acceptance rate: 15%
Median MCAT total score: 30
Median GPA: 3.69
Most popular undergraduate majors: biological sciences:
46%; physical sciences: 22%;
nonsciences: 12%; other: 20%

Percent of graduates entering primary-care specialties: 52.6%

Vanderbilt University

1211 22nd Ave. South and 201
Light Hall
Nashville, TN 37232-2104
medschool.vanderbilt.edu/
mdadmissions
Private
Admissions: (615) 322-1786
Email:
mdadmissions@vanderbilt.edu
Financial aid: (615) 322-2145
Application deadline: 11/02
Tuition: $49,092
Room/board/expenses: $18,539
Percent receiving grants: 74%
Average student indebtedness at graduation: $123,022
Enrollment: 429
men: 52%; women:
48%; minorities: 40%;
underrepresented minorities:
23%; in state: 17%
Acceptance rate: 4%
Median MCAT total score: 36
Median GPA: 3.87
Most popular undergraduate majors: biological sciences:
25%; physical sciences: 21%;
nonsciences: 10%; other: 44%
Percent of graduates entering primary-care specialties: 36.2%

TEXAS

Baylor College of Medicine

1 Baylor Plaza
Houston, TX 77030
www.bcm.edu
Private
Admissions: (713) 798-4842
Email: admissions@bcm.tmc.edu
Financial aid: (713) 798-4612
Application deadline: 11/02
Tuition: $18,518
Room/board/expenses: $25,047
Percent receiving grants: 37%
Average student indebtedness at graduation: $107,650
Enrollment: 738
men: 52%; women:
48%; minorities: 55%;
underrepresented minorities:
16%; in state: 88%
Acceptance rate: 4%
Median MCAT total score: 35
Median GPA: 3.84
Most popular undergraduate majors: biological sciences:
24%; physical sciences: 29%;
nonsciences: 5%; other: 42%
Percent of graduates entering primary-care specialties: 52.0%

Texas A&M Health Science Center

8447 State Highway 47
Bryan, TX 77807-3260
medicine.tamhsc.edu
Public
Admissions: (979) 436-0237
Email: admissions@
medicine.tamhsc.edu
Financial aid: (979) 436-0199
Application deadline: 10/01
In-state tuition: $16,432
Out-of-state tuition: $29,532
Room/board/expenses: $14,014
Percent receiving grants: 39%
Average student indebtedness at graduation: $111,443
Enrollment: 794
men: 52%; women:
48%; minorities: 47%;
underrepresented minorities:
16%; in state: 96%
Acceptance rate: 15%

Median MCAT total score: 30
Median GPA: 3.67
Most popular undergraduate majors: biological sciences:
48%; physical sciences: 15%;
nonsciences: 9%; other: 30%
Percent of graduates entering primary-care specialties: 40.8%

Texas Tech University Health Sciences Center

3601 Fourth Street
Lubbock, TX 79430
www.ttuhsc.edu/som/
Public
Admissions: (806) 743-2297
Email: somadm@ttuhsc.edu
Financial aid: N/A
Application deadline: 10/01
In-state tuition: $17,045
Out-of-state tuition: $30,145
Room/board/expenses: $15,290
Percent receiving grants: 78%
Average student indebtedness at graduation: $123,908
Enrollment: 628
men: 56%; women:
44%; minorities: 12%;
underrepresented minorities:
12%; in state: 89%
Acceptance rate: 12%
Median MCAT total score: 32
Median GPA: 3.60
Most popular undergraduate majors: biological sciences:
39%; physical sciences: 20%;
nonsciences: 9%; other: 32%
Percent of graduates entering primary-care specialties: 40.1%

University of Texas Health Science Center-Houston

6431 Fannin Street
MSB G.400
Houston, TX 77030
https://med.uth.edu
Public
Admissions: (713) 500-5116
Email:
ms.admissions@uth.tmc.edu
Financial aid: (713) 500-3860
Application deadline: 10/01
In-state tuition: $18,354
Out-of-state tuition: $30,454
Room/board/expenses: $15,910
Percent receiving grants: 27%
Average student indebtedness at graduation: $95,453
Enrollment: 960
men: 57%; women:
43%; minorities: 42%;
underrepresented minorities:
22%; in state: 95%
Acceptance rate: 10%
Median MCAT total score: 32
Median GPA: 3.79
Most popular undergraduate majors: biological sciences:
54%; physical sciences: 21%;
nonsciences: 6%; other: 19%
Percent of graduates entering primary-care specialties: 29.4%

University of Texas Health Science Center-San Antonio

7703 Floyd Curl Drive
San Antonio, TX 78229-3900
som.uthscsa.edu
Public
Admissions: (210) 567-6080
Email:
medadmissions@uthscsa.edu
Financial aid: (210) 567-2635
Application deadline: 10/01
In-state tuition: $18,630

Out-of-state tuition: $33,037
Room/board/expenses: $17,329
Average student indebtedness at graduation: $117,223
Enrollment: 860
men: 53%; women: 47%; minorities: 42%; underrepresented minorities: 24%; in state: 91%
Acceptance rate: 11%
Median MCAT total score: 32
Median GPA: 3.77
Most popular undergraduate majors: biological sciences: 52%; physical sciences: 16%; nonsciences: 14%; other: 18%
Percent of graduates entering primary-care specialties: 38.7%

University of Texas Medical Branch–Galveston[1]

301 University Boulevard
Galveston, TX 77555-0133
www.som.utmb.edu/
Public
Admissions: (409) 772-6958
Email: somadmis@utmb.edu
Financial aid: N/A
Tuition: N/A
Room/board/expenses: N/A
Enrollment: N/A

University of Texas Southwestern Medical Center

5323 Harry Hines Boulevard
Dallas, TX 75390
www.utsouthwestern.edu/
Public
Admissions: (214) 648-5617
Email: admissions@utsouthwestern.edu
Financial aid: (214) 648-3606
Application deadline: 10/01
In-state tuition: $18,593
Out-of-state tuition: $31,693
Room/board/expenses: $22,362
Percent receiving grants: 60%
Average student indebtedness at graduation: $96,300
Enrollment: 953
men: 54%; women: 46%; minorities: 47%; underrepresented minorities: 15%; in state: 86%
Acceptance rate: 10%
Median MCAT total score: 34
Median GPA: 3.85
Most popular undergraduate majors: biological sciences: 33%; physical sciences: 35%; nonsciences: 14%; other: 18%
Percent of graduates entering primary-care specialties: 44.4%

UTAH

University of Utah

30 N. 1900 E.
Salt Lake City, UT 84132-2101
medicine.utah.edu
Public
Admissions: (801) 581-7498
Email: deans.admissions@hsc.utah.edu
Financial aid: (801) 581-6499
Application deadline: 11/01
In-state tuition: $34,789
Out-of-state tuition: $65,011
Room/board/expenses: $9,492
Percent receiving grants: 73%

Average student indebtedness at graduation: $148,117
Enrollment: 369
men: 56%; women: 44%; minorities: 17%; underrepresented minorities: 5%; in state: 77%
Acceptance rate: 9%
Median MCAT total score: 29
Median GPA: 3.72
Most popular undergraduate majors: biological sciences: 39%; physical sciences: 18%; nonsciences: 8%; other: 35%
Percent of graduates entering primary-care specialties: 37.9%

VERMONT

University of Vermont

E-126 Given Building
89 Beaumont Avenue
Burlington, VT 05405
www.uvm.edu/medicine/admissions/
Public
Admissions: (802) 656-2154
Email: medadmissions@uvm.edu
Financial aid: (802) 656-5700
Application deadline: 12/15
In-state tuition: $34,719
Out-of-state tuition: $58,759
Room/board/expenses: $10,794
Percent receiving grants: 60%
Average student indebtedness at graduation: $178,055
Enrollment: 465
men: 50%; women: 50%; minorities: 29%; underrepresented minorities: 10%; in state: 30%
Acceptance rate: 5%
Median MCAT total score: 31
Median GPA: 3.75
Most popular undergraduate majors: biological sciences: 37%; physical sciences: 17%; nonsciences: 38%; other: 8%
Percent of graduates entering primary-care specialties: 43.0%

VIRGINIA

Eastern Virginia Medical School

721 Fairfax Avenue
PO Box 1980
Norfolk, VA 23501-1980
www.evms.edu
Public
Admissions: (757) 446-5812
Email: mclendm@evms.edu
Financial aid: (757) 446-5804
Application deadline: 11/15
In-state tuition: $32,004
Out-of-state tuition: $57,802
Room/board/expenses: $13,953
Percent receiving grants: 10%
Average student indebtedness at graduation: $193,785
Enrollment: 576
men: 56%; women: 44%; minorities: 35%; underrepresented minorities: 12%; in state: 52%
Acceptance rate: 5%
Median MCAT total score: 31
Median GPA: 3.55
Most popular undergraduate majors: biological sciences: 36%; physical sciences: 27%; nonsciences: 17%; other: 20%
Percent of graduates entering primary-care specialties: 52.0%

University of Virginia

PO Box 800793
McKim Hall
Charlottesville, VA 22908-0793
www.medicine.virginia.edu/education/medical-students/admissions
Public
Admissions: (434) 924-5571
Email: SOMADM@virginia.edu
Financial aid: (434) 924-0033
Application deadline: 11/02
In-state tuition: $47,118
Out-of-state tuition: $57,044
Room/board/expenses: $21,452
Percent receiving grants: 68%
Average student indebtedness at graduation: $128,292
Enrollment: 620
men: 54%; women: 46%; minorities: 37%; underrepresented minorities: 19%; in state: 52%
Acceptance rate: 11%
Median MCAT total score: 35
Median GPA: 3.85
Most popular undergraduate majors: biological sciences: 43%; physical sciences: 17%; nonsciences: 9%; other: 31%
Percent of graduates entering primary-care specialties: 35.4%

Virginia Commonwealth University

PO Box 980565
Richmond, VA 23298-0565
www.medschool.vcu.edu
Public
Admissions: (804) 828-9629
Email: somume@hsc.vcu.edu
Financial aid: (804) 828-4006
Application deadline: 10/15
In-state tuition: $32,260
Out-of-state tuition: $47,612
Room/board/expenses: $14,500
Percent receiving grants: 50%
Average student indebtedness at graduation: $162,529
Enrollment: 845
men: 52%; women: 48%; minorities: 42%; underrepresented minorities: 12%; in state: 54%
Acceptance rate: 5%
Median MCAT total score: 30
Median GPA: 3.65
Most popular undergraduate majors: biological sciences: 34%; physical sciences: 20%; nonsciences: 8%; other: 38%
Percent of graduates entering primary-care specialties: 46.7%

Virginia Tech Carilion School of Medicine[1]

2 Riverside Circle
Roanoke, VA 24016
www.vtc.vt.edu/
Public
Admissions: (540) 526-2560
Email: VTCAdmissions2015@carilionclinic.org
Financial aid: N/A
Tuition: N/A
Room/board/expenses: N/A
Enrollment: N/A

WASHINGTON

University of Washington

PO Box 356350
Seattle, WA 98195
www.uwmedicine.org/admissions
Public
Admissions: (206) 543-7212
Email: askuwsom@uw.edu
Financial aid: (206) 685-9229
Application deadline: 10/15
In-state tuition: $32,370
Out-of-state tuition: $61,356
Room/board/expenses: $16,341
Percent receiving grants: 73%
Average student indebtedness at graduation: $151,116
Enrollment: 938
men: 46%; women: 54%; minorities: 23%; underrepresented minorities: 8%; in state: 91%
Acceptance rate: 5%
Median MCAT total score: 31
Median GPA: 3.68
Most popular undergraduate majors: biological sciences: 61%; physical sciences: 8%; nonsciences: 15%; other: 15%
Percent of graduates entering primary-care specialties: 54.3%

WEST VIRGINIA

Marshall University (Edwards)

1600 Medical Center Drive
Huntington, WV 25701-3655
musom.marshall.edu
Public
Admissions: (800) 544-8514
Email: warren@marshall.edu
Financial aid: (304) 691-8739
Application deadline: 11/01
In-state tuition: $20,086
Out-of-state tuition: $47,736
Room/board/expenses: $14,560
Percent receiving grants: 55%
Average student indebtedness at graduation: $172,324
Enrollment: 289
men: 63%; women: 37%; minorities: 17%; underrepresented minorities: 7%; in state: 63%
Acceptance rate: 7%
Median MCAT total score: 28
Median GPA: 3.63
Most popular undergraduate majors: biological sciences: 51%; physical sciences: 15%; nonsciences: 14%; other: 20%
Percent of graduates entering primary-care specialties: 45.6%

West Virginia University

1 Medical Center Drive
Morgantown, WV 26506-9111
medicine.hsc.wvu.edu/students
Public
Admissions: (304) 293-2408
Email: medadmissions@hsc.wvu.edu
Financial aid: (304) 293-3706
Application deadline: 11/01
In-state tuition: $28,134
Out-of-state tuition: $55,107
Room/board/expenses: $15,216
Percent receiving grants: 54%
Average student indebtedness at graduation: $164,789

Enrollment: 421
men: 54%; women: 46%; minorities: 18%; underrepresented minorities: 5%; in state: 61%
Acceptance rate: 5%
Median MCAT total score: 29
Median GPA: 3.75
Most popular undergraduate majors: biological sciences: 55%; physical sciences: 22%; nonsciences: 5%; other: 18%
Percent of graduates entering primary-care specialties: 46.3%

WISCONSIN

Medical College of Wisconsin

8701 Watertown Plank Road
Milwaukee, WI 53226
www.mcw.edu/acad/admission
Private
Admissions: (414) 955-8246
Email: medschool@mcw.edu
Financial aid: (414) 955-8208
Application deadline: 11/01
Tuition: $45,067
Room/board/expenses: $9,500
Percent receiving grants: 65%
Average student indebtedness at graduation: $176,135
Enrollment: 817
men: 56%; women: 44%; minorities: 31%; underrepresented minorities: 30%; in state: 47%
Acceptance rate: 7%
Median MCAT total score: 31
Median GPA: 3.78
Most popular undergraduate majors: biological sciences: 41%; physical sciences: 18%; nonsciences: 9%; other: 32%
Percent of graduates entering primary-care specialties: 34.4%

University of Wisconsin–Madison

750 Highland Avenue
Madison, WI 53705-2221
www.med.wisc.edu/education
Public
Admissions: (608) 263-4925
Email: medadmissions@med.wisc.edu
Financial aid: (608) 262-3060
Application deadline: 11/01
In-state tuition: $24,944
Out-of-state tuition: $34,841
Room/board/expenses: $20,066
Percent receiving grants: 39%
Average student indebtedness at graduation: $145,720
Enrollment: 697
men: 51%; women: 49%; minorities: 24%; underrepresented minorities: 13%; in state: 80%
Acceptance rate: 5%
Median MCAT total score: 32
Median GPA: 3.76
Most popular undergraduate majors: biological sciences: 62%; physical sciences: 13%; nonsciences: 10%; other: 15%
Percent of graduates entering primary-care specialties: 44.9%

INSTITUTIONS THAT GRANT THE DOCTOR OF OSTEOPATHIC MEDICINE (D.O.) DEGREE

ARIZONA

A.T. Still University of Health Sciences-Mesa[1]
5850 E. Still Circle
Mesa, AZ 85206
www.atsu.edu/soma/index.htm
Private
Admissions: (866) 626-2878
Email: admissions@atsu.edu
Financial aid: N/A
Tuition: N/A
Room/board/expenses: N/A
Enrollment: N/A

Midwestern University[1]
19555 N. 59th Avenue
Glendale, AZ 85308
www.midwestern.edu
Private
Admissions: (623) 572-3215
Email: admissaz@midwestern.edu
Financial aid: N/A
Tuition: N/A
Room/board/expenses: N/A
Enrollment: N/A

CALIFORNIA

Touro University California
1310 Club Drive
Vallejo, CA 94592
www.tu.edu
Private
Admissions: (707) 638-5270
Email: steven.davis@tu.edu
Financial aid: (707) 638-5280
Application deadline: 03/15
Tuition: $48,770
Room/board/expenses: $19,488
Percent receiving grants: 14%
Enrollment: 540
men: 56%; women:
44%; minorities: 39%;
underrepresented minorities: 2%;
in state: 75%
Acceptance rate: 6%
Median MCAT total score: 30
Median GPA: 3.49
Most popular undergraduate
majors: biological sciences:
56%; physical sciences: 16%;
nonsciences: 7%; other: 21%
Percent of graduates entering
primary-care specialties: 61.0%

Western University of Health Sciences
309 E. Second Street
Pomona, CA 91766-1854
prospective.westernu.edu/
index.html
Private
Admissions: (909) 469-5335
Email: admissions@westernu.edu
Financial aid: (909) 469-5350
Application deadline: 02/01
Tuition: $52,255
Room/board/expenses: $18,790
Percent receiving grants: 10%
Average student indebtedness at
graduation: $239,680
Enrollment: 1,315
men: 54%; women:
46%; minorities: 49%;
underrepresented minorities: 7%;
in state: 69%
Acceptance rate: 7%
Median MCAT total score: 27
Median GPA: 3.59
Most popular undergraduate
majors: biological sciences:
55%; physical sciences: 13%;
nonsciences: 23%; other: 9%

Percent of graduates entering
primary-care specialties: 55.9%

COLORADO

Rocky Vista University
8401 S. Chambers Road
Parker, CO 80134
www.rvu.edu/aboutCOM.asp
Private
Admissions: (720) 875-2800
Email: admissions@rvu.edu
Financial aid: (720) 875-2800
Application deadline: 03/15
Tuition: $48,578
Room/board/expenses: $15,950
Percent receiving grants: 22%
Average student indebtedness at
graduation: $222,607
Enrollment: 623
men: 57%; women:
43%; minorities: 16%;
underrepresented minorities: 6%;
in state: 41%
Acceptance rate: 7%
Median MCAT total score: 28
Median GPA: 3.63
Most popular undergraduate
majors: biological sciences:
81%; physical sciences: 10%;
nonsciences: 4%; other: 5%
Percent of graduates entering
primary-care specialties: 45.4%

FLORIDA

Nova Southeastern University
3200 S. University Drive
Fort Lauderdale, FL 33328
medicine.nova.edu
Private
Admissions: (954) 262-1101
Email: hpdops@nova.edu
Financial aid: (954) 262-7439
Application deadline: 03/01
Tuition: $46,140
Room/board/expenses: $29,889
Percent receiving grants: 12%
Average student indebtedness at
graduation: $224,685
Enrollment: 980
men: 58%; women:
42%; minorities: 43%;
underrepresented minorities:
19%; in state: 65%
Acceptance rate: 10%
Median MCAT total score: 28
Median GPA: 3.55
Most popular undergraduate
majors: biological sciences:
43%; physical sciences: 26%;
nonsciences: 17%; other: 14%
Percent of graduates entering
primary-care specialties: 58.0%

ILLINOIS

Midwestern University[1]
555 31st Street
Downers Grove, IL 60515
www.midwestern.edu
Private
Admissions: (630) 515-6171
Email: admissil@midwestern.edu
Financial aid: N/A
Tuition: N/A
Room/board/expenses: N/A
Enrollment: N/A

IOWA

Des Moines University[1]
3200 Grand Avenue
Des Moines, IA 50312
www.dmu.edu/do/
Private
Admissions: (515) 271-1499
Email: doadmit@dmu.edu
Financial aid: N/A
Tuition: N/A
Room/board/expenses: N/A
Enrollment: N/A

KENTUCKY

University of Pikeville
147 Sycamore Street
Pikeville, KY 41501
www.upike.edu
Private
Admissions: (606) 218-5409
Email:
kycomadmissions@upike.edu
Financial aid: (606) 218-5407
Application deadline: 02/01
Tuition: $40,120
Room/board/expenses: $0
Percent receiving grants: 28%
Average student indebtedness at
graduation: $165,086
Enrollment: 479
men: 58%; women:
42%; minorities: 18%;
underrepresented minorities: 6%;
in state: 47%
Acceptance rate: 7%
Median MCAT total score: 24
Median GPA: 3.48
Most popular undergraduate
majors: biological sciences:
65%; physical sciences: 5%;
nonsciences: 13%; other: 17%
Percent of graduates entering
primary-care specialties: 72.1%

MAINE

University of New England
11 Hills Beach Road
Biddeford, ME 04005
www.une.edu/com/
Private
Admissions: (800) 477-4863
Email: gradadmissions2@une.edu
Financial aid: (207) 602-2404
Application deadline: 02/01
Tuition: $52,435
Room/board/expenses: $12,500
Percent receiving grants: 17%
Average student indebtedness at
graduation: $236,444
Enrollment: 592
men: 50%; women:
50%; minorities: 16%;
underrepresented minorities: 5%;
in state: 15%
Acceptance rate: 7%
Median MCAT total score: 28
Median GPA: 3.56
Most popular undergraduate
majors: biological sciences:
47%; physical sciences: 26%;
nonsciences: 12%; other: 14%
Percent of graduates entering
primary-care specialties: 59.0%

MICHIGAN

Michigan State University (College of Osteopathic Medicine)
A308 E. Fee Hall
East Lansing, MI 48824
www.com.msu.edu
Public
Admissions: (517) 353-7740
Email:
com.admissions@hc.msu.edu
Financial aid: (517) 353-5188
Application deadline: 12/01
In-state tuition: $41,790
Out-of-state tuition: $88,784
Room/board/expenses: $17,356
Percent receiving grants: 33%
Average student indebtedness at
graduation: $202,022
Enrollment: 1,234
men: 57%; women:
43%; minorities: 24%;
underrepresented minorities: 7%;
in state: 87%
Acceptance rate: 9%
Median MCAT total score: 28
Median GPA: 3.56
Most popular undergraduate
majors: biological sciences:
74%; physical sciences: 8%;
nonsciences: 5%; other: 13%
Percent of graduates entering
primary-care specialties: 79.3%

MISSISSIPPI

William Carey University College of Osteopathic Medicine[1]
498 Tuscan Avenue
Hattiesburg, MS 39401
www.wmcarey.edu/departments/
college-osteopathic-medicine
Private
Admissions: (601) 318-6235
Email: wcucom@wmcarey.edu
Financial aid: N/A
Tuition: N/A
Room/board/expenses: N/A
Enrollment: N/A

MISSOURI

A.T. Still University of Health Sciences-Kirksville[1]
800 W. Jefferson Street
Kirksville, MO 63501
www.atsu.edu/kcom/index.htm
Private
Admissions: (866) 626-2878
Email: admissions@atsu.edu
Financial aid: N/A
Tuition: N/A
Room/board/expenses: N/A
Enrollment: N/A

Kansas City University of Medicine and Biosciences[1]
1750 Independence Avenue
Kansas City, MO 64106-1453
www.kcumb.edu/
Private
Admissions: (800) 234-4847
Email: admissions@kcumb.edu
Financial aid: N/A
Tuition: N/A
Room/board/expenses: N/A
Enrollment: N/A

NEW JERSEY

Rowan University
1 Medical Center Drive
Stratford, NJ 08084-1501
www.rowan.edu/som
Public
Admissions: (856) 566-7050
Email: somadm@rowan.edu
Financial aid: (856) 566-6008
Application deadline: 02/01
In-state tuition: $40,886
Out-of-state tuition: $62,866
Room/board/expenses: $14,120
Average student indebtedness at
graduation: $158,306
Enrollment: 643
men: 53%; women:
47%; minorities: 54%;
underrepresented minorities:
16%; in state: 97%
Acceptance rate: 5%
Median MCAT total score: 28
Median GPA: 3.54
Most popular undergraduate
majors: biological sciences:
53%; physical sciences: 13%;
nonsciences: 2%; other: 32%
Percent of graduates entering
primary-care specialties: 52.1%

NEW YORK

New York Institute of Technology[1]
Old Westbury
Northern Boulevard
Long Island, NY 11568
www.nyit.edu
Private[1]
Admissions: (516) 686-3747
Email: comadm@nyit.edu
Financial aid: N/A
Tuition: N/A
Room/board/expenses: N/A
Enrollment: N/A

Touro College of Osteopathic Medicine
230 W. 125th Street
New York, NY 10027
www.touro.edu/med
Private
Admissions: (212) 851-1199
Email: admissions.tourocom@
touro.edu
Financial aid: (212) 851-1199
Application deadline: 04/01
Tuition: $45,950
Room/board/expenses: $20,365
Percent receiving grants: 0%
Average student indebtedness at
graduation: $200,940
Enrollment: 545
men: 52%; women:
48%; minorities: 52%;
underrepresented minorities:
17%; in state: 41%
Acceptance rate: 5%
Median MCAT total score: 29
Median GPA: 3.33
Most popular undergraduate
majors: biological sciences:
42%; physical sciences: 16%;
nonsciences: 29%; other: 13%
Percent of graduates entering
primary-care specialties: 49.0%

OHIO

Ohio University

Grosvenor Hall
Athens, OH 45701
www.oucom.ohiou.edu
Public
Admissions: (740) 593-4313
Email: ou-hcom@ohio.edu
Financial aid: (740) 593-2158
Application deadline: 02/01
In-state tuition: $32,806
Out-of-state tuition: $47,048
Room/board/expenses: $14,132
Percent receiving grants: 33%
Average student indebtedness at
graduation: $185,678
Enrollment: 610
men: 54%; women:
46%; minorities: 21%;
underrepresented minorities:
16%; in state: 97%
Acceptance rate: 5%
Median MCAT total score: 27
Median GPA: 3.64
Most popular undergraduate
majors: biological sciences:
60%; physical sciences: 20%;
nonsciences: 10%; other: 10%
Percent of graduates entering
primary-care specialties: 56.1%

OKLAHOMA

Oklahoma State University

1111 W. 17th Street
Tulsa, OK 74107-1898
healthsciences.okstate.edu
Public
Admissions: (918) 561-8421
Email: sarah.quinten@okstate.edu
Financial aid: (918) 561-8278
Application deadline: 02/01
In-state tuition: $24,094
Out-of-state tuition: $46,225
Room/board/expenses: $18,000
Percent receiving grants: 21%
Average student indebtedness at
graduation: $184,682
Enrollment: 430
men: 57%; women:
43%; minorities: 30%;
underrepresented minorities:
21%; in state: 92%
Acceptance rate: 20%

Median MCAT total score: 26
Median GPA: 3.67
Most popular undergraduate
majors: biological sciences:
57%; physical sciences: 15%;
nonsciences: 4%; other: 24%
Percent of graduates entering
primary-care specialties: 56.8%

PENNSYLVANIA

Lake Erie College of Osteopathic Medicine

1858 W. Grandview Boulevard
Erie, PA 16509
www.lecom.edu
Private
Admissions: (814) 866-6641
Email: admissions@lecom.edu
Financial aid: (814) 866-6641
Application deadline: 04/01
Tuition: $30,380
Room/board/expenses: $13,100
Percent receiving grants: 36%
Average student indebtedness at
graduation: $176,883
Enrollment: 2,241
men: 60%; women:
40%; minorities: 27%;
underrepresented minorities: 7%;
in state: 35%
Acceptance rate: 10%
Median MCAT total score: 27
Median GPA: 3.48
Most popular undergraduate
majors: biological sciences:
70%; physical sciences: 12%;
nonsciences: 12%; other: 6%
Percent of graduates entering
primary-care specialties: 67.9%

Philadelphia College of Osteopathic Medicine[1]

4170 City Avenue
Philadelphia, PA 19131
www.pcom.edu
Private
Admissions: (800) 999-6998
Email: admissions@pcom.edu
Financial aid: N/A
Tuition: N/A
Room/board/expenses: N/A
Enrollment: N/A

TENNESSEE

Lincoln Memorial University (DeBusk)

6965 Cumberland Gap Parkway
Harrogate, TN 37752
www.lmunet.edu/dcom/
admissions
Private
Admissions: (800) 325-0900
Email:
dcomadmissions@lmunet.edu
Financial aid: (423) 869-7107
Application deadline: 03/15
Tuition: $44,320
Room/board/expenses: $14,108
Percent receiving grants: 4%
Enrollment: 822
men: 56%; women:
44%; minorities: 27%;
underrepresented minorities:
12%; in state: 27%
Acceptance rate: 10%
Median MCAT total score: 25
Median GPA: 3.43
Most popular undergraduate
majors: biological sciences:
57%; physical sciences: 13%;
nonsciences: 16%; other: 14%
Percent of graduates entering
primary-care specialties: 63.5%

TEXAS

University of North Texas Health Science Center

3500 Camp Bowie Boulevard
Fort Worth, TX 76107-2699
www.hsc.unt.edu
Public
Admissions: (800) 535-8266
Email:
TCOMAdmissions@unthsc.edu
Financial aid: (800) 346-8266
Application deadline: 10/01
In-state tuition: $19,022
Out-of-state tuition: $34,710
Room/board/expenses: $16,588
Percent receiving grants: 54%
Average student indebtedness at
graduation: $126,881
Enrollment: 927
men: 51%; women:
49%; minorities: 44%;

underrepresented minorities:
15%; in state: 95%
Acceptance rate: 15%
Median MCAT total score: 28
Median GPA: 3.62
Most popular undergraduate
majors: biological sciences:
75%; physical sciences: 3%;
nonsciences: 8%; other: 14%
Percent of graduates entering
primary-care specialties: 63.9%

VIRGINIA

Edward Via College of Osteopathic Medicine-Virginia and Carolinas

2265 Kraft Drive
Blacksburg, VA 24060
www.vcom.vt.edu
Private
Admissions: (540) 231-6138
Email: admissions@vcom.vt.edu
Financial aid: (540) 231-6021
Application deadline: 02/15
Tuition: $42,500
Room/board/expenses: $0
Percent receiving grants: 31%
Enrollment: 1,374
men: 48%; women:
52%; minorities: 27%;
underrepresented minorities:
13%; in state: 33%
Acceptance rate: 8%
Median MCAT total score: 25
Median GPA: 3.55
Most popular undergraduate
majors: biological sciences:
55%; physical sciences: 14%;
nonsciences: 14%; other: 17%
Percent of graduates entering
primary-care specialties: 61.0%

WASHINGTON

Pacific Northwest University of Health Sciences[1]

200 University Parkway
Yakima, WA 98901
www.pnwu.edu/college-of-
osteopathic-medicine-com/
Private
Admissions: (509) 452-5100

Email: admission@pnwu.edu
Financial aid: N/A
Tuition: N/A
Room/board/expenses: N/A
Enrollment: N/A

WEST VIRGINIA

West Virginia School of Osteopathic Medicine

400 N. Lee Street
Lewisburg, WV 24901
www.wvsom.edu
Public
Admissions: (800) 356-7836
Email:
admissions@osteo.wvsom.edu
Financial aid: (800) 356-7836
Application deadline: 02/15
In-state tuition: $21,650
Out-of-state tuition: $51,400
Room/board/expenses: $14,980
Percent receiving grants: 13%
Average student indebtedness at
graduation: $236,931
Enrollment: 815
men: 53%; women:
47%; minorities: 22%;
underrepresented minorities: 6%;
in state: 33%
Acceptance rate: 9%
Median MCAT total score: 24
Median GPA: 3.49
Most popular undergraduate
majors: biological sciences:
51%; physical sciences: 11%;
nonsciences: 13%; other: 26%
Percent of graduates entering
primary-care specialties: 70.0%

NURSING

Here you'll find information on the 503 nursing schools with master's or doctoral programs accredited by either the Commission on Collegiate Nursing Education or the Accreditation Commission for Education in Nursing. Two hundred seventy-three schools responded to the U.S. News survey, which was conducted in the fall of 2014 and early 2015. Nursing schools or programs that did not respond have abbreviated entries.

KEY TO THE TERMINOLOGY

1. A school whose name has been footnoted with the numeral 1 did not return the U.S. News statistical survey; limited data appear in its entry.

N/A. Not available from the school or not applicable.

Admissions. The admissions office phone number.

Email. The address of the admissions office. If instead of an email address a website is listed, the website will automatically present an email screen programmed to reach the admissions office.

Financial aid. The financial aid office phone number.

Application deadline. For fall 2016 enrollment. "Rolling" means there is no deadline; the school acts on applications as they are received. "Varies" means deadlines vary according to department or whether applicants are U.S. citizens or foreign nationals.

Degrees offered. Master's, Ph.D. and Doctor of Nursing Practice (DNP)

Tuition. For the 2014-15 academic year for master's, Ph.D. and Doctor of Nursing Practice programs. Doesn't include fees.

Credit hour. The cost per credit hour for the 2014-15 academic year.

Room/board/expenses. For the 2014-15 academic year.

Enrollment. Full-time and part-time, including master's, Ph.D. and DNP

candidates, for fall 2014.

Minorities. Full-time and part-time master's, Ph.D. and DNP minority enrollment percentage for fall 2014. Reflects the share of students who are black or African-American, Asian, American Indian or Alaskan Native, Native Hawaiian or other Pacific Islander, Hispanic/Latino or two or more races. The minority percentage was reported by each school.

Acceptance rates. Percentage of applicants who were accepted among those who applied for fall 2014 admission to master's, Ph.D. or DNP nursing programs.

Nursing programs offered in 2014. Areas of specialization include administration, case management, clinical nurse leader, clinical nurse specialist, community health/public health, education, forensic nursing, generalist, health management & policy, health care systems, informatics, nurse anesthesia, nurse-midwifery, nurse practitioner, adult-gerontology acute care nurse practitioner, adult-gerontology primary care nurse practitioner, adult nurse practitioner, family nurse practitioner, pediatric primary care nurse practitioner, psychiatric-mental health nurse practitioner–across the lifespan, research, school nursing, other majors, combined nurse practitioner/clinical nurse specialist, dual majors.

ALABAMA

Auburn University
102 Miller Hall
Auburn University, AL 36849
www.auburn.edu/academic/nursing/
Public
Admissions: (334) 844-4700
Email: gradadm@auburn.edu
Financial aid: (334) 844-4634
Application deadline: N/A
Degrees offered: master's
In-state tuition: full time: $8,586; part time: $477/credit hour
Out-of-state tuition: full time: $25,758
Room/board/expenses: $12,178
Full-time enrollment: 3
men: 0%; women: 100%;
minorities: 0%; international: 33%
Part-time enrollment: 105
men: 5%; women: 95%;
minorities: 17%; international: 1%
Acceptance rate (master's): 52%
Specialties offered: education, nurse practitioner, nurse practitioner: family, dual majors

Auburn University-Montgomery[1]
PO Box 244023
Montgomery, AL 36124
Public
Admissions: N/A
Financial aid: N/A
Tuition: N/A
Room/board/expenses: N/A
Enrollment: N/A

Jacksonville State University
700 Pelham Road N
Jacksonville, AL 36265-1602
www.jsu.edu/nursing/index.html
Public
Admissions: (256) 782-5268
Email: info@jsu.edu
Financial aid: (256) 782-8399
Application deadline: N/A
Degrees offered: master's
In-state tuition: full time: $349/credit hour; part time: $349/credit hour
Out-of-state tuition: full time: $698/credit hour
Room/board/expenses: $6,985
Full-time enrollment: 12
men: 17%; women: 83%;
minorities: 25%; international: 17%
Part-time enrollment: 39
men: 0%; women: 100%;
minorities: 46%; international: 0%
Acceptance rate (master's): 53%
Specialties offered: community health/public health, education, other majors

Samford University
800 Lakeshore Drive
Birmingham, AL 35229
www.samford.edu/nursing/
Private
Admissions: (205) 726-2047
Email: amaddox@samford.edu
Financial aid: (205) 726-2905
Application deadline: N/A
Degrees offered: master's, DNP

Tuition: full time: $23,490; part time: $762/credit hour (master's); full time: $23,490; part time: $762/credit hour (DNP)
Room/board/expenses: $12,100 (master's); $12,100 (DNP)
Full-time enrollment: 250 (master's); 34 (DNP)
men: 20%; women: 80%;
minorities: 18%; international: 0%
Part-time enrollment: 8 (master's); 27 (DNP)
men: 23%; women: 77%;
minorities: 17%; international: 0%
Acceptance rate (master's): 68%
Acceptance rate (DNP): 84%
Specialties offered: administration, education, health management & policy health care systems, nurse anesthesia, nurse practitioner, nurse practitioner: family

Spring Hill College[1]
4000 Dauphin Street
Mobile, AL 36608
Private
Admissions: N/A
Financial aid: N/A
Tuition: N/A
Room/board/expenses: N/A
Enrollment: N/A

Troy University-Montgomery
College View Building
Troy, AL 35082
www.troy.edu/healthandhumanservices
Public
Admissions: (800) 551-9716
Email: admit@troy.edu
Financial aid: (800) 414-5756
Application deadline: 05/01
Degrees offered: master's, DNP
In-state tuition: full time: $365/credit hour; part time: $365/credit hour (master's); full time: $365/credit hour; part time: $365/credit hour (DNP)
Out-of-state tuition: full time: $730/credit hour (master's); full time: $730/credit hour (DNP)
Room/board/expenses: $1,505 (master's); $1,505 (DNP)
Full-time enrollment: 70 (master's); 8 (DNP)
men: 17%; women: 83%;
minorities: 22%; international: 0%
Part-time enrollment: 183 (master's); 37 (DNP)
men: 14%; women: 86%;
minorities: 33%; international: 0%
Acceptance rate (master's): 89%
Acceptance rate (DNP): 92%
Specialties offered: clinical nurse specialist, informatics, nurse practitioner: family

University of Alabama
Box 870358
Tuscaloosa, AL 35487-0358
nursing.ua.edu/index.html
Public
Admissions: (205) 348-5921
Email: gradschool@ua.edu
Financial aid: (205) 348-6756
Application deadline: 04/01
Degrees offered: master's, DNP

In-state tuition: full time: $9,826; part time: $354/credit hour (master's); full time: $9,826; part time: $354/credit hour (DNP)
Out-of-state tuition: full time: $9,826 (master's); full time: $9,826 (DNP)
Room/board/expenses: $4,400 (master's); $4,400 (DNP)
Full-time enrollment: 58 (master's); 41 (DNP)
men: 15%; women: 85%; minorities: 36%; international: 1%
Part-time enrollment: 87 (master's); 178 (DNP)
men: 14%; women: 86%; minorities: 36%; international: 0%
Acceptance rate (master's): 56%
Acceptance rate (DNP): 63%
Specialties offered: case management, clinical nurse leader, nurse practitioner: family, nurse practitioner: psychiatric-mental health, across the lifespan

University of Alabama–Birmingham
1530 Third Avenue S
Birmingham, AL 35294-1210
www.uab.edu/nursing/home/
Public
Admissions: (205) 975-7529
Email: sonstudaffairs@uab.edu
Financial aid: (205) 934-8223
Application deadline: 09/01
Degrees offered: master's, Ph.D., DNP
In-state tuition: full time: $476/credit hour; part time: $476/credit hour (master's); full time: $476/credit hour; part time: $476/credit hour (Ph.D.); full time: $476/credit hour; part time: $476/credit hour (DNP)
Out-of-state tuition: full time: $476/credit hour (master's); full time: $1,118/credit hour (Ph.D.); full time: $476/credit hour (DNP)
Room/board/expenses: $5,400 (master's); $5,400 (Ph.D.); $5,400 (DNP)
Full-time enrollment: 616 (master's); 18 (Ph.D.); 14 (DNP)
men: 17%; women: 83%; minorities: 20%; international: 1%
Part-time enrollment: 1,020 (master's); 27 (Ph.D.); 123 (DNP)
men: 13%; women: 87%; minorities: 20%; international: 0%
Acceptance rate (master's): 66%
Acceptance rate (Ph.D.): 56%
Acceptance rate (DNP): 88%
Specialties offered: clinical nurse leader, community health/public health, education, health management & policy health care systems, informatics, nurse anesthesia, nurse practitioner: adult-gerontology acute care, nurse practitioner: adult-gerontology primary care, nurse practitioner: family, nurse practitioner: pediatric primary care, nurse practitioner: psychiatric-mental health, across the lifespan, dual majors

University of Alabama–Huntsville
301 Sparkman Drive
Huntsville, AL 35899
uah.edu/nursing
Public
Admissions: (256) 824-6198
Email: deangrad@uah.edu
Financial aid: (256) 824-6212

Application deadline: 04/01
Degrees offered: master's, DNP
In-state tuition: full time: $655/credit hour; part time: $655/credit hour (master's); full time: $340/credit hour; part time: $340/credit hour (DNP)
Out-of-state tuition: full time: $1,471/credit hour (master's); full time: $340/credit hour (DNP)
Room/board/expenses: N/A
Full-time enrollment: 62 (master's); 8 (DNP)
men: 16%; women: 84%; minorities: 21%; international: 3%
Part-time enrollment: 180 (master's); 63 (DNP)
men: 13%; women: 87%; minorities: 18%; international: 1%
Acceptance rate (master's): 53%
Acceptance rate (DNP): 67%
Specialties offered: administration, clinical nurse specialist, nurse practitioner, nurse practitioner: adult-gerontology acute care, nurse practitioner: family

University of Mobile
5735 College Parkway
Mobile, AL 36613
www.umobile.edu/nursing
Private
Admissions: (251) 442-2270
Email: driley@umobile.edu
Financial aid: (251) 442-2239
Application deadline: N/A
Degrees offered: master's
Tuition: full time: $502/credit hour; part time: $502/credit hour
Room/board/expenses: N/A
Full-time enrollment: 7
men: 14%; women: 86%; minorities: 71%; international: 29%
Part-time enrollment: 5
men: 0%; women: 100%; minorities: 100%; international: 0%
Acceptance rate (master's): N/A
Specialties offered: administration, education

University of North Alabama[1]
223 Stevens Hall
Florence, AL 35632
Public
Admissions: N/A
Financial aid: N/A
Tuition: N/A
Room/board/expenses: N/A
Enrollment: N/A

University of South Alabama[1]
5721 USA Drive N, Room 3068
Mobile, AL 36688-0002
Public
Admissions: N/A
Financial aid: N/A
Tuition: N/A
Room/board/expenses: N/A
Enrollment: N/A

ALASKA

University of Alaska–Anchorage[1]
3211 Providence Drive
Anchorage, AK 99508-8030
Public
Admissions: N/A
Financial aid: N/A
Tuition: N/A
Room/board/expenses: N/A
Enrollment: N/A

ARIZONA

Arizona State University
500 N. Third Street
Phoenix, AZ 85004
nursingandhealth.asu.edu/
Public
Admissions: (480) 727-0262
Email: Michael.Mobley@asu.edu
Financial aid: (855) 278-5080
Application deadline: 12/15
Degrees offered: master's, Ph.D., DNP
In-state tuition: full time: $10,610; part time: $758/credit hour (master's); full time: $10,610; part time: $758/credit hour (Ph.D.); full time: $10,610; part time: $758/credit hour (DNP)
Out-of-state tuition: full time: $19,530 (master's); full time: $19,530 (Ph.D.); full time: $19,530 (DNP)
Room/board/expenses: $12,118 (master's); $12,118 (Ph.D.); $12,118 (DNP)
Full-time enrollment: 10 (master's); 17 (Ph.D.); 133 (DNP)
men: 9%; women: 91%; minorities: 29%; international: 3%
Part-time enrollment: 19 (master's); 25 (Ph.D.); 46 (DNP)
men: 13%; women: 87%; minorities: 30%; international: 0%
Acceptance rate (master's): 83%
Acceptance rate (Ph.D.): 71%
Acceptance rate (DNP): 54%
Specialties offered: education, nurse practitioner, nurse practitioner: adult-gerontology primary care, nurse practitioner: family, nurse practitioner: pediatric primary care, nurse practitioner: psychiatric-mental health, across the lifespan, research, other majors

Grand Canyon University[1]
3300 West Camelback Road
Phoenix , AZ 85061
Private
Admissions: N/A
Financial aid: N/A
Tuition: N/A
Room/board/expenses: N/A
Enrollment: N/A

Northern Arizona University
NAU Box 15035
Flagstaff, AZ 86011
Public
Admissions: N/A
Financial aid: N/A
Application deadline: N/A
Degrees offered: master's, DNP
In-state tuition: full time: $435/credit hour; part time: $435/credit hour (master's); full time: $435/credit hour; part time: $435/credit hour (DNP)
Out-of-state tuition: full time: $1,102/credit hour (master's); full time: $1,102/credit hour (DNP)
Room/board/expenses: N/A
Full-time enrollment: 17 (master's)
men: 18%; women: 82%; minorities: 18%; international: 0%
Part-time enrollment: 136 (master's); 22 (DNP)
men: 16%; women: 84%; minorities: 25%; international: 0%
Acceptance rate (master's): 74%
Acceptance rate (DNP): 100%

Specialties offered: generalist, nurse practitioner

University of Arizona
1305 N. Martin Avenue
Tucson, AZ 85721-0203
www.nursing.arizona.edu/
Public
Admissions: (520) 626-3808
Email: studentaffairs@nursing.arizona.edu
Financial aid: (520) 621-1858
Application deadline: 12/15
Degrees offered: master's, Ph.D., DNP
In-state tuition: full time: $766/credit hour; part time: $766/credit hour (master's); full time: $775/credit hour; part time: $775/credit hour (Ph.D.); full time: $766/credit hour; part time: $766/credit hour (DNP)
Out-of-state tuition: full time: $1,539/credit hour (master's); full time: $775/credit hour (Ph.D.); full time: $1,539/credit hour (DNP)
Room/board/expenses: N/A
Full-time enrollment: 150 (master's); 19 (Ph.D.); 165 (DNP)
men: N/A; women: N/A; minorities: 30%; international: 0%
Part-time enrollment: 247 (master's); 48 (Ph.D.); 131 (DNP)
men: N/A; women: N/A; minorities: 32%; international: 0%
Acceptance rate (master's): 45%
Acceptance rate (Ph.D.): 89%
Acceptance rate (DNP): 67%
Specialties offered: administration, generalist, nurse practitioner, nurse practitioner: adult-gerontology acute care, nurse practitioner: family, nurse practitioner: pediatric primary care, nurse practitioner: psychiatric-mental health, across the lifespan, research

University of Phoenix[1]
4615 E. Elwood Street
Phoenix, AZ 85040
Private
Admissions: N/A
Financial aid: N/A
Tuition: N/A
Room/board/expenses: N/A
Enrollment: N/A

ARKANSAS

Arkansas State University–Jonesboro
PO Box 910
State University, AR 72467-0069
www.astate.edu/college/conhp
Public
Admissions: (870) 972-2031
Email: www.astate.edu/college/graduate-school/
Financial aid: (870) 972-2310
Application deadline: 02/01
Degrees offered: master's, DNP
In-state tuition: full time: $244/credit hour; part time: $244/credit hour (master's); full time: $244/credit hour; part time: $244/credit hour (DNP)
Out-of-state tuition: full time: $621/credit hour (master's); full time: $621/credit hour (DNP)
Room/board/expenses: N/A
Full-time enrollment: 98 (master's)
men: N/A; women: N/A; minorities: 14%; international: 0%

Part-time enrollment: 99 (master's); 4 (DNP)
men: N/A; women: N/A; minorities: 11%; international: 0%
Acceptance rate (master's): 39%
Acceptance rate (DNP): 86%
Specialties offered: administration, clinical nurse specialist, education, nurse anesthesia, nurse practitioner: family

Arkansas Tech University[1]
Dean Hall 224
402 West O Street
Russellville, AR 72801
Public
Admissions: N/A
Financial aid: N/A
Tuition: N/A
Room/board/expenses: N/A
Enrollment: N/A

University of Arkansas
Room 324
Graduate Education Building
Fayetteville, AR 72701
nurs.uark.edu/
Public
Admissions: (479) 575-4883
Email: admissions.uark.edu/
Financial aid: (479) 575-3806
Application deadline: N/A
Degrees offered: master's, DNP
In-state tuition: full time: $388/credit hour; part time: $388/credit hour (master's); full time: $388/credit hour; part time: $388/credit hour (DNP)
Out-of-state tuition: full time: $388/credit hour (master's); full time: $388/credit hour (DNP)
Room/board/expenses: $17,128 (master's); $17,128 (DNP)
Full-time enrollment: 3 (master's); 25 (DNP)
men: 4%; women: 96%; minorities: 14%; international: 0%
Part-time enrollment: 22 (master's); 20 (DNP)
men: 5%; women: 95%; minorities: 10%; international: 0%
Acceptance rate (master's): 100%
Acceptance rate (DNP): 78%
Specialties offered: clinical nurse specialist, education, generalist, nurse practitioner, nurse practitioner: adult-gerontology acute care

University of Arkansas for Medical Sciences[1]
4301 W. Markham Street
Slot 529
Little Rock, AR 72205-7199
Public
Admissions: N/A
Financial aid: N/A
Tuition: N/A
Room/board/expenses: N/A
Enrollment: N/A

University of Central Arkansas
201 Donaghey Avenue
Conway, AR 72035
Public
Admissions: (501) 450-3120
Email: rschlosser@uca.edu
Financial aid: (501) 450-3410
Application deadline: N/A
Degrees offered: master's, DNP

In-state tuition: full time: $240/
credit hour; part time: N/A
(master's); full time: $243/credit
hour; part time: N/A (DNP)
Out-of-state tuition: full time: $240/
credit hour (master's); full time:
$486/credit hour (DNP)
Room/board/expenses: $5,778
(master's); $5,778 (DNP)
Full-time enrollment: 2 (master's)
men: 50%; women: 50%;
minorities: 0%; international: 0%
Part-time enrollment: 154
(master's); 11 (DNP)
men: 6%; women: 94%;
minorities: 13%; international: 0%
Acceptance rate (master's): 94%
Acceptance rate (DNP): N/A
Specialties offered: clinical
nurse leader, education, nurse
practitioner, nurse practitioner:
adult-gerontology primary care,
nurse practitioner: adult, nurse
practitioner: family

CALIFORNIA

Azusa Pacific University[1]
Graduate Center
Azusa, CA 91702-7000
Private
Admissions: N/A
Financial aid: N/A
Tuition: N/A
Room/board/expenses: N/A
Enrollment: N/A

Brandman University[1]
16355 Laguna Canyon Road
Irvine, CA 92618
Private
Admissions: N/A
Financial aid: N/A
Tuition: N/A
Room/board/expenses: N/A
Enrollment: N/A

California Baptist University
8432 Magnolia Avenue
Riverside, CA 92506
www.calbaptist.edu/academics/
schools-colleges/school-nursing/
Private
Admissions: (877) 228-8877
Email: graduateadmissions@
calbaptist.edu
Financial aid: (951) 343-4236
Application deadline: 08/01
Degrees offered: master's
Tuition: full time: $22,944; part
time: $717/credit hour
Room/board/expenses: $7,662
Full-time enrollment: 65
men: 22%; women: 78%;
minorities: 51%; international: 5%
Part-time enrollment: 111
men: 15%; women: 85%;
minorities: 56%; international: 0%
Acceptance rate (master's): 55%
Specialties offered: clinical nurse
specialist, education, health
management & policy health care
systems, nurse practitioner:
family

California State University-Chico
400 W. First Street
Chico, CA 95929-0200
www.csuchico.edu/nurs
Public
Admissions: (530) 898-6880
Email:
graduatestudies@csuchico.edu

Financial aid: (530) 898-6451
Application deadline: 11/01
Degrees offered: master's
In-state tuition: full time: $6,738;
part time: $3,906
Out-of-state tuition: full time:
$15,666
Room/board/expenses: $11,200
Full-time enrollment:
men: N/A; women: N/A; minorities:
N/A; international: N/A
Part-time enrollment: 23
men: 4%; women: 96%;
minorities: 22%; international: 0%
Acceptance rate (master's): 85%
Specialties offered: administration,
education

California State University-Dominguez Hills
1000 East Victoria Street
Carson, CA 90747
www4.csudh.edu/son/
Public
Admissions: (310) 243-3645
Email: admit@csudh.edu
Financial aid: (310) 243-3691
Application deadline: 06/01
Degrees offered: master's
In-state tuition: full time: $6,738;
part time: $3,906
Out-of-state tuition: full time:
$9,714
Room/board/expenses: $24,716
Full-time enrollment: 31
men: 16%; women: 84%;
minorities: 68%; international: 0%
Part-time enrollment: 258
men: 9%; women: 91%; minorities:
59%; international: 0%
Acceptance rate (master's): 76%
Specialties offered: administration,
clinical nurse leader, clinical
nurse specialist, education, nurse
practitioner, nurse practitioner:
family

California State University-Fresno[1]
2345 E. San Ramon Avenue
Fresno, CA 93740-8031
Public
Admissions: N/A
Financial aid: N/A
Tuition: N/A
Room/board/expenses: N/A
Enrollment: N/A

California State University-Fullerton[1]
800 N. State College Boulevard
Fullerton, CA 92834
Public
Admissions: N/A
Financial aid: N/A
Tuition: N/A
Room/board/expenses: N/A
Enrollment: N/A

California State University-Long Beach[1]
1250 Bellflower Boulevard
Long Beach, CA 90840
Public
Admissions: N/A
Financial aid: N/A
Tuition: N/A
Room/board/expenses: N/A
Enrollment: N/A

California State University-Los Angeles
5151 State University Drive
Los Angeles, CA 90032-8171
www.calstatela.edu/academic/
hhs/nursing
Public
Admissions: (323) 343-3901
Email: admission@calstatela.edu
Financial aid: (323) 343-6260
Application deadline: 11/30
Degrees offered: master's, DNP
In-state tuition: full time: $7,610;
part time: $4,780 (master's); full
time: $15,182; part time: N/A (DNP)
Out-of-state tuition: full time:
$16,538 (master's); full time:
$21,878 (DNP)
Room/board/expenses: $12,750
(master's)
Full-time enrollment: 178 (master's)
men: 13%; women: 87%;
minorities: 69%; international: 0%
Part-time enrollment:
men: N/A; women: N/A; minorities:
N/A; international: N/A
Acceptance rate (master's): 46%
Acceptance rate (DNP): N/A
Specialties offered: education,
nurse practitioner: adult-
gerontology acute care, nurse
practitioner: adult-gerontology
primary care, nurse practitioner:
family, nurse practitioner:
psychiatric-mental health, across
the lifespan

California State University-Sacramento[1]
6000 J Street
Sacramento, CA 95819-6096
Public
Admissions: N/A
Financial aid: N/A
Tuition: N/A
Room/board/expenses: N/A
Enrollment: N/A

California State University-San Bernardino[1]
5500 University Parkway
San Bernadino, CA 92407
Public
Admissions: N/A
Financial aid: N/A
Tuition: N/A
Room/board/expenses: N/A
Enrollment: N/A

California State University-San Marcos[1]
333 S. Twin Oaks Valley Road
San Marcos, CA 92096
Public
Admissions: N/A
Financial aid: N/A
Tuition: N/A
Room/board/expenses: N/A
Enrollment: N/A

California State University-Stanislaus[1]
One University Circle
Turlock, CA 95382
Public
Admissions: N/A
Financial aid: N/A
Tuition: N/A

Room/board/expenses: N/A
Enrollment: N/A

Charles R. Drew University of Medicine and Science[1]
1731 E. 120th Street
Los Angeles, CA 90059
Private
Admissions: N/A
Financial aid: N/A
Tuition: N/A
Room/board/expenses: N/A
Enrollment: N/A

Dominican University of California[1]
50 Acacia Avenue
San Rafael, CA 94901
Private
Admissions: N/A
Financial aid: N/A
Tuition: N/A
Room/board/expenses: N/A
Enrollment: N/A

Holy Names University
3500 Mountain Boulevard
Oakland, CA 94619
www.hnu.edu/academics
Private
Admissions: (510) 436-1317
Email: lgibson@hnu.edu
Financial aid: (510) 436-1327
Application deadline: N/A
Degrees offered: master's
Tuition: full time: $928/credit hour;
part time: $928/credit hour
Room/board/expenses: $11,608
Full-time enrollment: 8
men: 25%; women: 75%;
minorities: 50%; international:
13%
Part-time enrollment: 103
men: 15%; women: 85%;
minorities: 69%; international: 2%
Acceptance rate (master's): 55%
Specialties offered: administration,
case management, education,
informatics, nurse practitioner,
nurse practitioner: family

Loma Linda University[1]
School of Nursing Admissions
Office
Loma Linda, CA 92350
Private
Admissions: N/A
Financial aid: N/A
Tuition: N/A
Room/board/expenses: N/A
Enrollment: N/A

Mount St. Mary's College[1]
10 Chester Place
Los Angeles, CA 90007
Private
Admissions: N/A
Financial aid: N/A
Tuition: N/A
Room/board/expenses: N/A
Enrollment: N/A

Point Loma Nazarene University
3900 Lomaland Drive
San Diego, CA 92106
www.pointloma.edu/experience/
academics/schools-departments/
school-nursing
Private
Admissions: (619) 563-2856

Email: gradinfo@pointloma.edu
Financial aid: (619) 849-2847
Application deadline: master's
Degrees offered: master's
Tuition: full time: $715/credit hour;
part time: $715/credit hour
Room/board/expenses: N/A
Full-time enrollment: 5
men: N/A; women: N/A; minorities:
100%; international: 0%
Part-time enrollment: 90
men: N/A; women: N/A; minorities:
49%; international: 1%
Acceptance rate (master's): 97%
Specialties offered: clinical nurse
specialist, generalist

Samuel Merritt University
3100 Summit Street, 3rd Floor
Oakland, CA 94609
www.samuelmerritt.edu/nursing
Private
Admissions: (510) 869-6511
Email:
admission@samuelmerritt.edu
Financial aid: (510) 869-6511
Application deadline: 11/01
Degrees offered: master's, DNP
Tuition: full time: $1,215/credit
hour; part time: $1,215/credit hour
(master's); full time: $1,052/credit
hour; part time: $1,052/credit
hour (DNP)
Room/board/expenses: N/A
Full-time enrollment: 364
(master's); 16 (DNP)
men: 21%; women: 79%;
minorities: 64%; international: 0%
Part-time enrollment: 48
(master's); 9 (DNP)
men: 25%; women: 75%;
minorities: 51%; international: 0%
Acceptance rate (master's): 32%
Acceptance rate (Ph.D.): N/A
Acceptance rate (DNP): 67%
Specialties offered: case
management, nurse anesthesia,
nurse practitioner, nurse
practitioner: family

San Diego State University[1]
Hardy Tower, Room 58
San Diego, CA 92182-4158
Public
Admissions: N/A
Financial aid: N/A
Tuition: N/A
Room/board/expenses: N/A
Enrollment: N/A

San Francisco State University[1]
Burk Hall, Room 371
San Francisco, CA 94132
Public
Admissions: N/A
Financial aid: N/A
Tuition: N/A
Room/board/expenses: N/A
Enrollment: N/A

San Jose State University
Health Building 420
San Jose, CA 95192-0057
www.sjsu.edu/nursing/
Public
Admissions: (408) 283-7500
Email: graduate@sjsu.edu
Financial aid: (408) 283-7500
Application deadline: 11/01
Degrees offered: master's, DNP

In-state tuition: full time: N/A; part time: N/A
Out-of-state tuition: full time: N/A
Room/board/expenses: N/A
Full-time enrollment:
men: N/A; women: N/A; minorities: N/A; international: N/A
Part-time enrollment: 44 (master's)
men: 11%; women: 89%; minorities: 66%; international: 0%
Acceptance rate (master's): 88%
Acceptance rate (DNP): N/A
Specialties offered: administration, education

Sonoma State University[1]
1801 E.Cotati Avenue
Rohnert Park, CA 94928
Public
Admissions: N/A
Financial aid: N/A
Tuition: N/A
Room/board/expenses: N/A
Enrollment: N/A

University of California–Davis
4610 X Street, Suite 4202
Davis, CA 95817
www.ucdmc.ucdavis.edu/nursing/
Public
Admissions: (916) 734-2145
Email: BettylreneMooreSON@ucdmc.ucdavis.edu
Financial aid: (916) 734-4120
Application deadline: 01/15
Degrees offered: master's, Ph.D.
In-state tuition: full time: $19,578; part time: N/A (master's); full time: $11,220; part time: $5,610 (Ph.D.)
Out-of-state tuition: full time: $31,823 (master's); full time: $26,322 (Ph.D.)
Room/board/expenses: $14,107 (master's); $14,107 (Ph.D.)
Full-time enrollment: 52 (master's); 33 (Ph.D.)
men: 19%; women: 81%; minorities: 41%; international: 2%
Part-time enrollment:
men: N/A; women: N/A; minorities: N/A; international: N/A
Acceptance rate (master's): 54%
Acceptance rate (Ph.D.): 17%
Acceptance rate (DNP): N/A
Specialties offered: nurse practitioner, nurse practitioner: family, other majors

University of California–Irvine[1]
252 Berk Hall
Irvine, CA 92697
Public
Admissions: N/A
Financial aid: N/A
Tuition: N/A
Room/board/expenses: N/A
Enrollment: N/A

University of California–Los Angeles
760 Tilverton Avenue
Factor Building 2-256
Los Angeles, CA 90095-1702
nursing.ucla.edu
Public
Admissions: (310) 825-9193
Email: rflenoy@sonnet.ucla.edu
Financial aid: (310) 825-2583
Application deadline: 12/01
Degrees offered: master's, Ph.D.

In-state tuition: full.time: $19,578; part time: N/A (master's); full time: $11,220; part time: N/A (Ph.D.)
Out-of-state tuition: full time: $31,823 (master's); full time: $26,322 (Ph.D.)
Room/board/expenses: $13,794 (master's); $13,794 (Ph.D.)
Full-time enrollment: 325 (master's); 65 (Ph.D.),
men: 15%; women: 85%; minorities: 46%; international: 4%
Part-time enrollment:
men: N/A; women: N/A; minorities: N/A; international: N/A
Acceptance rate (master's): 46%
Acceptance rate (Ph.D.): 59%
Specialties offered: clinical nurse leader, clinical nurse specialist, community health/public health, generalist, nurse practitioner, nurse practitioner: adult-gerontology acute care, nurse practitioner: adult-gerontology primary care, nurse practitioner: family, nurse practitioner: pediatric primary care, research, combined nurse practitioner/clinical nurse specialist

University of California–San Francisco
2 Koret Way, #N-319X
San Francisco, CA 94143-0602
nursing.ucsf.edu/
Public
Admissions: (415) 476-4801
Email: judy.martin-holland@ucsf.edu
Financial aid: (415) 476-4181
Application deadline: 02/01
Degrees offered: master's, Ph.D.
In-state tuition: full time: $24,792; part time: $14,875 (master's); full time: $16,449; part time: $9,869 (Ph.D.)
Out-of-state tuition: full time: $37,037 (master's); full time: $31,551 (Ph.D.)
Room/board/expenses: $20,484 (master's); $20,484 (Ph.D.)
Full-time enrollment: 395 (master's); 120 (Ph.D.),
men: 15%; women: 85%; minorities: 43%; international: 4%
Part-time enrollment:
men: N/A; women: N/A; minorities: N/A; international: N/A
Acceptance rate (master's): 32%
Acceptance rate (Ph.D.): 65%
Specialties offered: clinical nurse specialist, community health/public health, nurse-midwifery, nurse practitioner, nurse practitioner: adult-gerontology acute care, nurse practitioner: adult-gerontology primary care, nurse practitioner: family, nurse practitioner: pediatric primary care, nurse practitioner: psychiatric-mental health, across the lifespan

University of San Diego
5998 Alcala Park
San Diego, CA 92110
www.sandiego.edu/nursing
Private
Admissions: (619) 260-5906
Email: grads@sandiego.edu
Financial aid: (619) 260-2234
Application deadline: 11/01
Degrees offered: master's, Ph.D., DNP

Tuition: full time: $1,345/credit hour; part time: $1,345/credit hour (master's); full time: $1,375/credit hour; part time: $1,375/credit hour (Ph.D.); full time: $1,375/credit hour; part time: $1,375/credit hour (DNP)
Room/board/expenses: $12,000 (master's); $12,000 (Ph.D.); $12,000 (DNP)
Full-time enrollment: 161 (master's); 48 (Ph.D.), 65 (DNP)
men: 14%; women: 86%; minorities: 44%; international: 1%
Part-time enrollment: 44 (master's); 39 (Ph.D.), 2 (DNP)
men: 9%; women: 91%; minorities: 32%; international: N/A
Acceptance rate (master's): 27%
Acceptance rate (Ph.D.): 33%
Acceptance rate (DNP): 46%
Specialties offered: administration, clinical nurse leader, clinical nurse specialist, informatics, nurse practitioner, nurse practitioner: adult-gerontology primary care, nurse practitioner: family, nurse practitioner: pediatric primary care, nurse practitioner: psychiatric-mental health, across the lifespan, research

University of San Francisco
2130 Fulton Street
San Francisco, CA 94117-1080
www.usfca.edu/nursing/
Private
Admissions: (415) 422-6681
Email: nursing@usfca.edu
Financial aid: (415) 422-2020
Application deadline: N/A
Degrees offered: master's, DNP
Tuition: full time: $1,209/credit hour; part time: $1,209/credit hour (master's); full time: $1,209/credit hour; part time: $1,209/credit hour (DNP)
Room/board/expenses: N/A
Full-time enrollment: 399 (master's); 94 (DNP)
men: 17%; women: 83%; minorities: 54%; international: 1%
Part-time enrollment: 117 (master's); 44 (DNP)
men: 17%; women: 83%; minorities: 47%; international: 2%
Acceptance rate (master's): 53%
Acceptance rate (DNP): 79%
Specialties offered: administration, clinical nurse leader, nurse practitioner, nurse practitioner: family, nurse practitioner: psychiatric-mental health, across the lifespan

West Coast University[1]
1477 S. Manchester Avenue
Anaheim, CA 92802
Private
Admissions: N/A
Financial aid: N/A
Tuition: N/A
Room/board/expenses: N/A
Enrollment: N/A

Western University of Health Sciences[1]
309 E. Second Street
Pomona, CA 91766-1854
Private
Admissions: N/A
Financial aid: N/A
Tuition: N/A
Room/board/expenses: N/A
Enrollment: N/A

COLORADO

American Sentinel University[1]
2260 South Xanadu Way
Suite 310
Aurora, CO 80014
Private
Admissions: N/A
Financial aid: N/A
Tuition: N/A
Room/board/expenses: N/A
Enrollment: N/A

Aspen University[1]
720 South Colorado Boulevard
Denver, CO 80246
Private
Admissions: N/A
Financial aid: N/A
Tuition: N/A
Room/board/expenses: N/A
Enrollment: N/A

Colorado State University-Pueblo
2200 Bonforte Boulevard
Pueblo, CO 81001
ceeps.colostate-pueblo.edu/nursing/
Public
Admissions: (719) 549-2462
Financial aid: (719) 549-2753
Application deadline: 04/15
Degrees offered: master's
In-state tuition: full time: $249/credit hour; part time: N/A
Out-of-state tuition: full time: $741/credit hour
Room/board/expenses: N/A
Full-time enrollment: 40
men: N/A; women: N/A; minorities: 25%; international: 0%
Part-time enrollment:
men: N/A; women: N/A; minorities: N/A; international: N/A
Acceptance rate (master's): 49%
Specialties offered: education, nurse practitioner, nurse practitioner: adult-gerontology acute care, nurse practitioner: family, nurse practitioner: psychiatric-mental health, across the lifespan

Regis University
3333 Regis Boulevard
Denver, CO 80221-1099
regis.edu/RHCHP/Schools/Loretto-Heights-School-of-Nursing.aspx
Private
Admissions: (303) 458-4344
Email: healthcare@regis.edu
Financial aid: (303) 458-4126
Application deadline: 01/05
Degrees offered: master's, DNP
Tuition: full time: $620/credit hour; part time: $620/credit hour (master's); full time: $825/credit hour; part time: $825/credit hour (DNP)
Room/board/expenses: N/A
Full-time enrollment: 308 (master's); 51 (DNP)
men: 7%; women: 93%; minorities: 27%; international: 4%
Part-time enrollment: 263 (master's)
men: 6%; women: 94%; minorities: 24%; international: 0%
Acceptance rate (master's): 78%
Acceptance rate (DNP): 86%
Specialties offered: administration, education, generalist, nurse practitioner, nurse practitioner: family

---

University of Colorado
13120 E. 19th Avenue
Box C288
Denver, CO 80262
www.ucdenver.edu/academics/colleges/nursing/Pages/default.aspx
Public
Admissions: (303) 724-1450
Email: amy.schlueter@ucdenver.edu
Financial aid: (303) 724-8039
Application deadline: N/A
Degrees offered: master's, Ph.D., DNP
In-state tuition: full time: $560/credit hour; part time: $560/credit hour (master's); full time: $525/credit hour; part time: $525/credit hour (Ph.D.); full time: $560/credit hour; part time: $560/credit hour (DNP)
Out-of-state tuition: full time: $1,020/credit hour (master's); full time: $1,020/credit hour (Ph.D.); full time: $1,020/credit hour (DNP)
Room/board/expenses: $21,936 (master's); $21,936 (Ph.D.); $21,936 (DNP)
Full-time enrollment: 294 (master's); 34 (Ph.D.), 17 (DNP)
men: N/A; women: N/A; minorities: 18%; international: 1%
Part-time enrollment: 103 (master's); 4 (Ph.D.), 30 (DNP)
men: N/A; women: N/A; minorities: 15%; international: 0%
Acceptance rate (master's): 85%
Acceptance rate (Ph.D.): 60%
Acceptance rate (DNP): 78%
Specialties offered: administration, clinical nurse specialist, health management & policy health care systems, informatics, nurse-midwifery, nurse practitioner, nurse practitioner: adult-gerontology acute care, nurse practitioner: adult-gerontology primary care, nurse practitioner: family, nurse practitioner: pediatric primary care, nurse practitioner: psychiatric-mental health, across the lifespan, dual majors

University of Colorado-Colorado Springs
1420 Austin Bluffs Parkway
Colorado Springs, CO 80933-7150
www.uccs.edu/
Public
Admissions: (719) 255-4424
Email: asilvasm@uccs.edu
Financial aid: (719) 255-3460
Application deadline: 06/15
Degrees offered: master's, DNP
In-state tuition: full time: $11,898; part time: $4,451 (master's); full time: $11,898; part time: $4,451 (DNP)
Out-of-state tuition: full time: $20,052 (master's); full time: $20,052 (DNP)
Room/board/expenses: $11,020 (master's); $11,020 (DNP)
Full-time enrollment: 15 (master's); 9 (DNP)
men: 4%; women: 96%; minorities: 17%; international: 4%
Part-time enrollment: 133 (master's); 18 (DNP)
men: 7%; women: 93%; minorities: 18%; international: 0%
Acceptance rate (master's): 24%
Acceptance rate (DNP): 65%

Specialties offered: education, nurse practitioner, nurse practitioner: adult-gerontology acute care, nurse practitioner: adult-gerontology primary care

University of Northern Colorado

Gunter 3080
PO Box 125
Greeley, CO 80639
Public
Admissions: N/A
Email: gradsch@unco.edu
Financial aid: N/A
Application deadline: N/A
Degrees offered: master's, Ph.D., DNP
In-state tuition: full time: $9,774; part time: $543/credit hour (master's); full time: $10,746; part time: $597/credit hour (Ph.D.); full time: $578/credit hour (DNP)
Out-of-state tuition: full time: $18,684 (master's); full time: $21,420 (Ph.D.); full time: $578/credit hour (DNP)
Room/board/expenses: N/A
Full-time enrollment: 1 (master's); 2 (Ph.D.); 2 (DNP)
men: 20%; women: 80%; minorities: 20%; international: 20%
Part-time enrollment: 42 (master's); 40 (Ph.D.); 52 (DNP)
men: 12%; women: 88%; minorities: 10%; international: 1%
Acceptance rate (master's): 67%
Acceptance rate (Ph.D.): 93%
Acceptance rate (DNP): 81%
Specialties offered: clinical nurse leader, education, nurse practitioner, nurse practitioner: family

CONNECTICUT

Fairfield University

1073 North Benson Road
Fairfield, CT 06824
www.fairfield.edu/nursing
Private
Admissions: (203) 254-4184
Email: gradadmis@fairfield.edu
Financial aid: (203) 254-4125
Application deadline: 12/31
Degrees offered: master's, DNP
Tuition: full time: $850/credit hour; part time: $850/credit hour (master's); full time: $950; part time: $950 (DNP)
Room/board/expenses: N/A
Full-time enrollment: 1 (master's); 35 (DNP)
men: 8%; women: 92%; minorities: 14%; international: 0%
Part-time enrollment: 87 (master's); 71 (DNP)
men: 14%; women: 86%; minorities: 21%; international: 0%
Acceptance rate (master's): 62%
Acceptance rate (DNP): 70%
Specialties offered: nurse anesthesia, nurse practitioner, nurse practitioner: family, nurse practitioner: psychiatric-mental health, across the lifespan

Quinnipiac University

275 Mount Carmel Avenue
Hamden , CT 06518
www.quinnipiac.edu/nursing
Private
Admissions: (203) 582-8672
Email: graduate@quinnipiac.edu
Financial aid: (203) 582-8588

Application deadline: 04/30
Degrees offered: master's, DNP
Tuition: full time: $920/credit hour; part time: $920/credit hour (master's); full time: $920/credit hour; part time: $920/credit hour (DNP)
Room/board/expenses: N/A
Full-time enrollment: 63 (DNP)
men: 13%; women: 87%; minorities: 14%; international: 2%
Part-time enrollment: 110 (DNP)
men: 11%; women: 89%; minorities: 21%; international: 1%
Acceptance rate (master's): N/A
Acceptance rate (DNP): 72%
Specialties offered: nurse anesthesia, nurse practitioner, nurse practitioner: adult-gerontology acute care, nurse practitioner: family

Sacred Heart University

5151 Park Avenue
Fairfield, CT 06825
www.sacredheart.edu/academics/collegeofhealthprofessions/academicprograms/nursing/
Private
Admissions: (203) 365-7619
Email: gradstudies@sacredheart.edu
Financial aid: (203) 371-7980
Application deadline: 02/15
Degrees offered: master's, DNP
Tuition: full time: $750/credit hour; part time: $750/credit hour (master's); full time: $900/credit hour; part time: $900/credit hour (DNP)
Room/board/expenses: N/A
Full-time enrollment: 6 (master's); 13 (DNP)
men: 5%; women: 95%; minorities: 32%; international: 0%
Part-time enrollment: 70 (master's); 33 (DNP)
men: 10%; women: 90%; minorities: 27%; international: 0%
Acceptance rate (master's): 34%
Acceptance rate (DNP): 86%
Specialties offered: nurse practitioner, nurse practitioner: family

Southern Connecticut State University[1]

501 Crescent Street
New Haven, CT 6515
Public
Admissions: N/A
Financial aid: N/A
Tuition: N/A
Room/board/expenses: N/A
Enrollment: N/A

University of Connecticut

231 Glen Brook Road
Storrs, CT 06269-2026
nursing.uconn.edu/
Public
Admissions: (860) 486-1968
Email: nursingadmissions@uconn.edu
Financial aid: (860) 486-2819
Application deadline: 02/01
Degrees offered: master's, Ph.D., DNP
In-state tuition: full time: $12,202; part time: $678/credit hour (master's); full time: $12,202; part time: $678/credit hour (Ph.D.);

full time: $12,202; part time: $678/credit hour (DNP)
Out-of-state tuition: full time: $31,674 (master's); full time: $31,674 (Ph.D.); full time: $31,674 (DNP)
Room/board/expenses: N/A
Full-time enrollment: 48 (master's); 10 (Ph.D.); 13 (DNP)
men: 8%; women: 92%; minorities: 20%; international: 3%
Part-time enrollment: 92 (master's); 26 (Ph.D.); 22 (DNP)
men: 6%; women: 94%; minorities: 18%; international: 0%
Acceptance rate (master's): 67%
Acceptance rate (Ph.D.): 77%
Acceptance rate (DNP): 100%
Specialties offered: clinical nurse leader, clinical nurse specialist, nurse practitioner, nurse practitioner: adult-gerontology acute care, nurse practitioner: adult-gerontology primary care, nurse practitioner: family, other majors, combined nurse practitioner/clinical nurse specialist

University of Hartford

200 Bloomfield Avenue
West Hartford, CT 06117-1599
www.hartford.edu/enhp/academics/health/default.aspx
Private
Admissions: (860) 768-4371
Email: gradstudy@hartford.edu
Financial aid: (860) 768-4296
Application deadline: N/A
Degrees offered: master's
Tuition: full time: $520/credit hour; part time: $520/credit hour
Room/board/expenses: N/A
Full-time enrollment:
men: N/A; women: N/A; minorities: N/A; international: N/A
Part-time enrollment: 125
men: 8%; women: 92%; minorities: 18%; international: 1%
Acceptance rate (master's): 86%
Specialties offered: administration, community health/public health, education

University of St. Joseph[1]

1678 Asylum Avenue
West Hartford, CT 06117-2791
Private
Admissions: N/A
Financial aid: N/A
Tuition: N/A
Room/board/expenses: N/A
Enrollment: N/A

Western Connecticut State University[1]

181 White Street
Danbury, CT 6810
www.wcsu.edu/nursing/graduate/
Public
Admissions: N/A
Financial aid: N/A
Tuition: N/A
Room/board/expenses: N/A
Enrollment: N/A

Yale University

100 Church Street S
PO Box 9740
New Haven, CT 06536-0740
nursing.yale.edu/
Private
Admissions: (203) 737-1793
Email: melissa.pucci@yale.edu
Financial aid: (203) 737-1790

Application deadline: 11/01
Degrees offered: master's, Ph.D., DNP
Tuition: full time: $35,755; part time: $23,732 (master's); full time: $37,600; part time: N/A (Ph.D.); full time: N/A; part time: $23,732 (DNP)
Room/board/expenses: N/A
Full-time enrollment: 247 (master's); 17 (Ph.D.)
men: 11%; women: 89%; minorities: 23%; international: 5%
Part-time enrollment: 18 (master's); 45 (DNP)
men: 22%; women: 78%; minorities: 30%; international: 2%
Acceptance rate (master's): 28%
Acceptance rate (Ph.D.): 8%
Acceptance rate (DNP): 38%
Specialties offered: health management & policy health care systems, nurse-midwifery, nurse practitioner, nurse practitioner: adult-gerontology acute care, nurse practitioner: adult-gerontology primary care, nurse practitioner: family, nurse practitioner: pediatric primary care, nurse practitioner: psychiatric-mental health, across the lifespan, research, dual majors

DELAWARE

University of Delaware

25 N. College Avenue
Newark, DE 19716
www.udel.edu/nursing/index.html
Public
Admissions: (302) 831-2129
Email: gradadmissions@udel.edu
Financial aid: (302) 831-2126
Application deadline: 03/01
Degrees offered: master's, Ph.D.
In-state tuition: full time: $731/credit hour; part time: $731/credit hour (master's); full time: $731/credit hour; part time: $731/credit hour (Ph.D.)
Out-of-state tuition: full time: $731/credit hour (master's); full time: $731/credit hour (Ph.D.)
Room/board/expenses: N/A
Full-time enrollment: 13 (master's); 3 (Ph.D.);
men: 6%; women: 94%; minorities: 25%; international: 0%
Part-time enrollment: 120 (master's); 2 (Ph.D.);
men: 7%; women: 93%; minorities: 25%; international: 0%
Acceptance rate (master's): 80%
Acceptance rate (Ph.D.): 0%
Specialties offered: administration, clinical nurse specialist, nurse practitioner, nurse practitioner: adult-gerontology primary care, nurse practitioner: family, research, other majors

Wesley College[1]

120 N. State Street
Dover, DE 19901
Private
Admissions: N/A
Financial aid: N/A
Tuition: N/A
Room/board/expenses: N/A
Enrollment: N/A

Wilmington University[1]

320 N. DuPont Highway
New Castle, DE 19720-6491
Private
Admissions: N/A
Financial aid: N/A
Tuition: N/A
Room/board/expenses: N/A
Enrollment: N/A

DISTRICT OF COLUMBIA

The Catholic University of America

600 Michigan Avenue NE
Washington, DC 20064
nursing.cua.edu/
Private
Admissions: (800) 673-2772
Email: cua-admissions@cua.edu
Financial aid: (202) 319-5307
Application deadline: 07/15
Degrees offered: master's, Ph.D., DNP
Tuition: full time: $40,200; part time: $1,600/credit hour (master's); full time: $40,200; part time: $1,600/credit hour (Ph.D.); full time: $40,200; part time: $1,600/credit hour (DNP)
Room/board/expenses: $15,902 (master's); $15,902 (Ph.D.); $15,902 (DNP)
Full-time enrollment: 50 (master's); 3 (Ph.D.); 2 (DNP)
men: 9%; women: 91%; minorities: 25%; international: 5%
Part-time enrollment: 69 (master's); 62 (Ph.D.); 37 (DNP)
men: 9%; women: 91%; minorities: 36%; international: 2%
Acceptance rate (master's): 65%
Acceptance rate (Ph.D.): 70%
Acceptance rate (DNP): 78%
Specialties offered: nurse practitioner, nurse practitioner: adult-gerontology primary care, nurse practitioner: family, nurse practitioner: pediatric primary care

Georgetown University[1]

St. Mary's Hall
Washington, DC 20057
Private
Admissions: N/A
Financial aid: N/A
Tuition: N/A
Room/board/expenses: N/A
Enrollment: N/A

George Washington University

900 23rd Street NW
Washington, DC 20037
nursing.gwu.edu
Private
Admissions: (571) 553-0138
Email: sonadmit@gwu.edu
Financial aid: (202) 994-6822
Application deadline: 02/15
Degrees offered: master's, DNP
Tuition: full time: $920/credit hour; part time: $920/credit hour (master's); full time: $920/credit hour; part time: $920/credit hour (DNP)
Room/board/expenses: N/A
Full-time enrollment: 37 (master's); 1 (DNP)
men: 3%; women: 97%; minorities: 34%; international: 0%

Part-time enrollment: 373
(master's); 108 (DNP)
men: 9%; women: 91%; minorities:
27%; international: 1%
Acceptance rate (master's): 72%
Acceptance rate (DNP): 67%
Specialties offered: administration,
education, nurse-midwifery,
nurse practitioner, nurse
practitioner: adult-gerontology
primary care, nurse practitioner:
family

Howard University

516 Bryant Street NW
Washington, DC 20059
healthsciences.howard.edu/
education/schools-and-
academics/nursing-allied-health
Private
Admissions: (202) 806-7460
Email: tammi.damas@howard.edu
Financial aid: (202) 806-2820
Application deadline: 07/01
Degrees offered: master's
Tuition: full time: $29,090; part
time: $1,700/credit hour
Room/board/expenses: $18,213
Full-time enrollment: 14
men: 21%; women: 79%;
minorities: 100%; international:
7%
Part-time enrollment: 29
men: 10%; women: 90%;
minorities: 100%; international:
0%
Acceptance rate (master's): 100%
Specialties offered: education,
nurse practitioner, nurse
practitioner: family

FLORIDA

Barry University[1]

11300 NE Second Avenue
Miami Shores, FL 33161-6695
Private
Admissions: N/A
Financial aid: N/A
Tuition: N/A
Room/board/expenses: N/A
Enrollment: N/A

Florida A&M University[1]

103 Ware-Rhaney Building
Tallahassee, FL 32307
Public
Admissions: N/A
Financial aid: N/A
Tuition: N/A
Room/board/expenses: N/A
Enrollment: N/A

Florida Atlantic University (Lynn)

777 Glades Road
Boca Raton, FL 33431
nursing.fau.edu/
Public
Admissions: (561) 297-6261
Email: kasmer@fau.edu
Financial aid: (561) 297-3530
Application deadline: 06/01
Degrees offered: master's, Ph.D.,
DNP
In-state tuition: full time: $304/
credit hour; part time: $304/
credit hour (master's); full time:
$304/credit hour; part time: $304/
credit hour (Ph.D.); full time: $304/
credit hour; part time: $304/credit
hour (DNP)

Out-of-state tuition: full time: $928/
credit hour (master's); full time:
$928/credit hour (Ph.D.); full time:
$928/credit hour (DNP)
Room/board/expenses: $10,518
(master's); $10,518 (Ph.D.);
$10,518 (DNP)
Full-time enrollment: 18 (Ph.D.);
35 (DNP)
men: N/A; women: N/A; minorities:
64%; international: 4%
Part-time enrollment: 393
(master's); 34 (Ph.D.); 31 (DNP)
men: N/A; women: N/A; minorities:
35%; international: 3%
Acceptance rate (master's): 35%
Acceptance rate (Ph.D.): 73%
Acceptance rate (DNP): 66%
Specialties offered: administration,
clinical nurse leader, education,
nurse practitioner, nurse
practitioner: adult-gerontology
primary care, nurse practitioner:
family, research, other majors

Florida Gulf Coast University

10501 FGCU Boulevard S
Fort Myers , FL 33965
www.fgcu.edu/CHPSW/Nursing/
index.html
Public
Admissions: (239) 590-1095
Email: admissions@fgcu.edu
Financial aid: (239) 590-7920
Application deadline: 12/15
Degrees offered: master's
In-state tuition: full time: $6,932;
part time: N/A
Out-of-state tuition: full time:
$28,170
Room/board/expenses: $8,359
Full-time enrollment: 18
men: N/A; women: N/A; minorities:
N/A; international: N/A
Part-time enrollment:
men: N/A; women: N/A; minorities:
N/A; international: N/A
Acceptance rate (master's): N/A
Specialties offered: nurse
anesthesia, nurse practitioner,
nurse practitioner: adult-
gerontology primary care, nurse
practitioner: family

Florida International University

11200 S.W. Eighth Street
Miami, FL 33199
cnhs.fiu.edu/nursing/graduate/
index.html
Public
Admissions: (305) 348-7733
Email: gordony@fiu.edu
Financial aid: (305) 348-2333
Application deadline: 02/15
Degrees offered: master's, Ph.D.,
DNP
In-state tuition: full time: $13,783;
part time: N/A (master's); full time:
$9,073; part time: N/A (Ph.D.); full
time: $11,277; part time: N/A (DNP)
Out-of-state tuition: full time:
$24,873 (master's); full time:
$19,994 (Ph.D.); full time: $20,351
(DNP)
Room/board/expenses: N/A
Full-time enrollment: 308
(master's); 9 (Ph.D.); 9 (DNP)
men: 34%; women: 66%;
minorities: 80%; international: 2%
Part-time enrollment: 50
(master's); 15 (Ph.D.); 17 (DNP)
men: 22%; women: 78%;
minorities: 84%; international: 0%

Acceptance rate (master's): 37%
Acceptance rate (Ph.D.): 67%
Acceptance rate (DNP): 55%
Specialties offered: nurse
anesthesia, nurse practitioner,
nurse practitioner: adult-
gerontology primary care,
nurse practitioner: family,
nurse practitioner: pediatric
primary care, nurse practitioner:
psychiatric-mental health, across
the lifespan, research

Florida Southern College[1]

111 Lake Hollingsworth Drive
Lakeland, FL 33801-5698
Private
Admissions: N/A
Financial aid: N/A
Tuition: N/A
Room/board/expenses: N/A
Enrollment: N/A

Florida State University

102 Vivian M. Duxbury Hall
Tallahassee, FL 32306-4310
nursing.fsu.edu/
Public
Admissions: (850) 644-1328
Email: jfinney@admin.fsu.edu
Financial aid: (850) 644-0539
Application deadline: 04/15
Degrees offered: master's, DNP
In-state tuition: full time: $479/
credit hour; part time: N/A
(master's); full time: $479/credit
hour; part time: N/A (DNP)
Out-of-state tuition: full time:
$1,111/credit hour (master's); full
time: $1,111/credit hour (DNP)
Room/board/expenses: N/A
Full-time enrollment: 53 (DNP)
men: N/A; women: N/A; minorities:
0%; international: 0%
Part-time enrollment: 17 (master's);
10 (DNP)
men: N/A; women: N/A; minorities:
30%; international: 0%
Acceptance rate (master's): N/A
Acceptance rate (DNP): 81%
Specialties offered: education,
nurse practitioner, nurse
practitioner: family, other majors

Jacksonville University[1]

2800 University Boulevard N
Jacksonville, FL 32211
Private
Admissions: N/A
Financial aid: N/A
Tuition: N/A
Room/board/expenses: N/A
Enrollment: N/A

Keiser University[1]

1900 W. Commercial Boulevard
Suite 100
Fort Lauderdale, FL 33309
www.keiseruniversity.edu/
Private
Admissions: N/A
Financial aid: N/A
Tuition: N/A
Room/board/expenses: N/A
Enrollment: N/A

Nova Southeastern University

3200 S. University Drive
Fort Lauderdale, FL 33328
www.nova.edu/nursing
Private
Admissions: (954) 262-1975
Email: www.nova.edu/nursing
Financial aid: (954) 262-3380
Application deadline: N/A
Degrees offered: master's, Ph.D.,
DNP
Tuition: full time: $650/credit
hour; part time: $650/credit hour
(master's); full time: $750/credit
hour; part time: $750/credit hour
(Ph.D.); full time: $850; part time:
$850 (DNP)
Room/board/expenses: N/A
Full-time enrollment: 2 (master's);
1 (Ph.D.);
men: 33%; women: 67%;
minorities: 33%; international: 0%
Part-time enrollment: 339
(master's); 45 (Ph.D.); 36 (DNP)
men: 10%; women: 90%;
minorities: 65%; international: 0%
Acceptance rate (master's): 36%
Acceptance rate (Ph.D.): 25%
Acceptance rate (DNP): 47%
Specialties offered: education,
health management & policy
health care systems, informatics,
nurse practitioner, nurse
practitioner: family, research

University of Central Florida

12201 Research Parkway
Suite 300
Orlando, FL 32826-3298
www.nursing.ucf.edu/
Public
Admissions: (407) 823-2766
Email: gradnurse@ucf.edu
Financial aid: (407) 823-2827
Application deadline: 02/16
Degrees offered: master's, Ph.D.,
DNP
In-state tuition: full time: $359/
credit hour; part time: $359/
credit hour (master's); full time:
$359/credit hour; part time: $359/
credit hour (Ph.D.); full time: $359/
credit hour; part time: $359/credit
hour (DNP)
Out-of-state tuition: full time:
$1,183/credit hour (master's); full
time: $1,183/credit hour (Ph.D.);
full time: $1,183/credit hour (DNP)
Room/board/expenses: $9,758
(master's); $9,758 (Ph.D.); $9,758
(DNP)
Full-time enrollment: 13 (master's);
14 (Ph.D.); 20 (DNP)
men: 11%; women: 89%;
minorities: 32%; international: 0%
Part-time enrollment: 171
(master's); 5 (Ph.D.); 77 (DNP)
men: 10%; women: 90%;
minorities: 25%; international: 0%
Acceptance rate (master's): 47%
Acceptance rate (Ph.D.): N/A
Acceptance rate (DNP): 49%
Specialties offered: administration,
clinical nurse specialist,
education, nurse practitioner,
nurse practitioner: adult-
gerontology primary care, nurse
practitioner: family, research

University of Florida

PO Box 100197
Gainesville, FL 32610-0197
nursing.ufl.edu/
Public
Admissions: (352) 273-6436
Email: sbradley@ufl.edu
Financial aid: (352) 273-6115
Application deadline: 12/31
Degrees offered: master's, Ph.D.,
DNP
In-state tuition: full time: $528/
credit hour; part time: $528/
credit hour (master's); full time:
$528/credit hour; part time: $528/
credit hour (Ph.D.); full time: $528/
credit hour; part time: $528/credit
hour (DNP)
Out-of-state tuition: full time:
$1,253/credit hour (master's); full
time: $1,253/credit hour (Ph.D.);
full time: $1,253/credit hour (DNP)
Room/board/expenses: $15,610
(master's); $15,610 (Ph.D.);
$15,610 (DNP)
Full-time enrollment: 27 (master's);
16 (Ph.D.); 115 (DNP)
men: 8%; women: 92%;
minorities: 27%; international: 3%
Part-time enrollment: 30
(master's); 16 (Ph.D.); 144 (DNP)
men: 9%; women: 91%; minorities:
27%; international: 5%
Acceptance rate (master's): N/A
Acceptance rate (Ph.D.): 58%
Acceptance rate (DNP): 44%
Specialties offered: clinical
nurse leader, education, nurse-
midwifery, nurse practitioner,
nurse practitioner: adult-
gerontology acute care, nurse
practitioner: adult-gerontology
primary care, nurse practitioner:
family, nurse practitioner:
pediatric primary care, nurse
practitioner: psychiatric-mental
health, across the lifespan

University of Miami

PO Box 248153
Coral Gables, FL 33124-3850
www.miami.edu/sonhs/
index.php/sonhs/
Private
Admissions: (305) 284-4325
Email: nursinggrad@miami.edu
Financial aid: (305) 284-2270
Application deadline: 04/01
Degrees offered: master's, Ph.D.,
DNP
Tuition: full time: $40,700; part
time: $20,350 (master's); full time:
$1,790/credit hour; part time:
$1,790/credit hour (Ph.D.); full
time: $933/credit hour; part time:
$933/credit hour (DNP)
Room/board/expenses: $26,040
(master's); $26,040 (Ph.D.);
$26,040 (DNP)
Full-time enrollment: 88 (master's);
24 (Ph.D.); 19 (DNP)
men: 28%; women: 72%;
minorities: 51%; international: 6%
Part-time enrollment: 77 (master's);
1 (Ph.D.); 16 (DNP)
men: 15%; women: 85%;
minorities: 82%; international: 2%
Acceptance rate (master's): 25%
Acceptance rate (Ph.D.): 40%
Acceptance rate (DNP): 25%
Specialties offered: education,
informatics, nurse anesthesia,
nurse practitioner, nurse
practitioner: adult-gerontology
acute care, nurse practitioner:
adult-gerontology primary care,
nurse practitioner: family

University of North Florida[1]

1 UNF Drive
Jacksonville, FL 32224-2673
www.unf.edu/brooks/nursing/
Public
Admissions: N/A
Financial aid: N/A
Tuition: N/A
Room/board/expenses: N/A
Enrollment: N/A

University of South Florida

12901 Bruce B. Downs Boulevard
Tampa, FL 33612-4766
health.usf.edu/nursing/index.htm
Public
Admissions: (813) 974-3831
Email: cvisovsk@health.usf.edu
Financial aid: (813) 974-4700
Application deadline: 02/03
Degrees offered: master's, Ph.D., DNP
In-state tuition: full time: $348/credit hour; part time: $348/credit hour (master's); full time: $348/credit hour; part time: $348/credit hour (Ph.D.); full time: $348/credit hour; part time: $348/credit hour (DNP)
Out-of-state tuition: full time: $772/credit hour (master's); full time: $772/credit hour (Ph.D.); full time: $772/credit hour (DNP)
Room/board/expenses: $9,400 (master's); $9,400 (Ph.D.); $9,400 (DNP)
Full-time enrollment: 129 (master's); 17 (Ph.D.); 36 (DNP) men: 15%; women: 85%; minorities: 66%; international: 7%
Part-time enrollment: 717 (master's); 20 (Ph.D.); 51 (DNP) men: 11%; women: 89%; minorities: 66%; international: 4%
Acceptance rate (master's): 55%
Acceptance rate (Ph.D.): 67%
Acceptance rate (DNP): 59%
Specialties offered: clinical nurse leader, community health/public health, education, nurse anesthesia, nurse practitioner, nurse practitioner: adult-gerontology acute care, nurse practitioner: adult-gerontology primary care, nurse practitioner: family, nurse practitioner: pediatric primary care, dual majors

University of Tampa

401 W. Kennedy Boulevard
Tampa, FL 33606-1490
www.ut.edu/nursing/
Private
Admissions: (813) 253-6211
Email: admissions@ut.edu
Financial aid: (813) 253-6219
Application deadline: N/A
Degrees offered: master's
Tuition: full time: $558/credit hour; part time: $558/credit hour
Room/board/expenses: $9,624
Full-time enrollment: men: N/A; women: N/A; minorities: N/A; international: N/A
Part-time enrollment: 145 men: 14%; women: 86%; minorities: 16%; international: 1%
Acceptance rate (master's): 50%
Specialties offered: administration, education, generalist, informatics, nurse practitioner: adult-gerontology primary care,

nurse practitioner: family, nurse practitioner: pediatric primary care, other majors

GEORGIA

Albany State University[1]

504 College Drive
Albany, GA 31705
Public
Admissions: N/A
Financial aid: N/A
Tuition: N/A
Room/board/expenses: N/A
Enrollment: N/A

Armstrong State University[1]

11935 Abercorn Street
Savannah, GA 31419
Public
Admissions: N/A
Financial aid: N/A
Tuition: N/A
Room/board/expenses: N/A
Enrollment: N/A

Brenau University

500 Washington Street SE
Gainesville, GA 30501
www.brenau.edu/healthsciences/department-of-nursing/
Private
Admissions: (770) 534-6100
Email: admissions@brenau.edu
Financial aid: (770) 534-6152
Application deadline: 12/31
Degrees offered: master's, DNP
Tuition: full time: $594/credit hour; part time: $594/credit hour (master's); full time: $936/credit hour; part time: $936/credit hour (DNP)
Room/board/expenses: N/A
Full-time enrollment: 4 (DNP) men: 25%; women: 75%; minorities: 50%; international: N/A
Part-time enrollment: 57 (master's); 4 (DNP) men: 10%; women: 90%; minorities: 44%; international: N/A
Acceptance rate (master's): 42%
Acceptance rate (DNP): 20%
Specialties offered: N/A

Clayton State University

2000 Clayton State Boulevard
Morrow, GA 30260
www.clayton.edu/health/nursing
Public
Admissions: (578) 466-4108
Email: www.clayton.edu/graduate
Financial aid: (678) 466-4185
Application deadline: 11/15
Degrees offered: master's
In-state tuition: full time: $385/credit hour; part time: $385/credit hour
Out-of-state tuition: full time: $385/credit hour
Room/board/expenses: N/A
Full-time enrollment: 13 men: 0%; women: 100%; minorities: 85%; international: 0%
Part-time enrollment: 21 men: 5%; women: 95%; minorities: 86%; international: 0%
Acceptance rate (master's): 75%
Specialties offered: administration, education

Emory University

1520 Clifton Road, NE
Atlanta, GA 30322-4207
www.nursing.emory.edu/
Private
Admissions: (404) 727-7980
Email: son-admit@listserve.cc.emory.edu
Financial aid: (404) 712-8456
Application deadline: 01/15
Degrees offered: master's, Ph.D., DNP
Tuition: full time: $40,400; part time: $1,683/credit hour (master's); full time: $37,800; part time: $2,100/credit hour (Ph.D.); full time: $30,294; part time: $1,683/credit hour (DNP)
Room/board/expenses: $14,640 (master's); $14,640 (Ph.D.); $14,640 (DNP)
Full-time enrollment: 199 (master's); 25 (Ph.D.); 4 (DNP) men: 8%; women: 92%; minorities: 23%; international: 1%
Part-time enrollment: 20 (master's); 2 (Ph.D.); 2 (DNP) men: 21%; women: 79%; minorities: 38%; international: 0%
Acceptance rate (master's): 89%
Acceptance rate (Ph.D.): 26%
Acceptance rate (DNP): N/A
Specialties offered: health management & policy health care systems, nurse-midwifery, nurse practitioner, nurse practitioner: adult-gerontology acute care, nurse practitioner: adult-gerontology primary care, nurse practitioner: family, nurse practitioner: pediatric primary care, other majors, dual majors

Georgia College & State University

231 W. Hancock Street
CBX 063
Milledgeville, GA 31061
www.gcsu.edu/nursing/index.htm
Public
Admissions: (478) 445-6289
Email: grad-admit@gcsu.edu
Financial aid: (478) 445-5149
Application deadline: 01/13
Degrees offered: master's, DNP
In-state tuition: full time: $318/credit hour; part time: $318/credit hour (master's); full time: $318/credit hour; part time: $318/credit hour (DNP)
Out-of-state tuition: full time: $318/credit hour (master's); full time: $318/credit hour (DNP)
Room/board/expenses: N/A
Full-time enrollment: 44 (master's); 17 (DNP) men: 8%; women: 92%; minorities: 20%; international: 0%
Part-time enrollment: 40 (master's) men: 8%; women: 93%; minorities: 23%; international: 0%
Acceptance rate (master's): 80%
Acceptance rate (DNP): 91%
Specialties offered: education, nurse practitioner, nurse practitioner: family

Georgia Regents University

997 St. Sebastian Way
EG 1030
Augusta, GA 30912
www.gru.edu/nursing
Public
Admissions: (706) 737-1524
Email: admissions@gru.edu
Financial aid: (706) 737-1524

Application deadline: 02/01
Degrees offered: master's, Ph.D., DNP
In-state tuition: full time: $483/credit hour; part time: $483/credit hour (master's); full time: $391/credit hour; part time: $391/credit hour (Ph.D.); full time: $453/credit hour; part time: $453/credit hour (DNP)
Out-of-state tuition: full time: $1,181/credit hour (master's); full time: $1,127/credit hour (Ph.D.); full time: $453/credit hour (DNP)
Room/board/expenses: $5,150 (master's); $5,150 (Ph.D.); $5,150 (DNP)
Full-time enrollment: 292 (master's); 6 (Ph.D.); 45 (DNP) men: N/A; women: N/A; minorities: 23%; international: 0%
Part-time enrollment: 31 (master's); 6 (Ph.D.); 63 (DNP) men: N/A; women: N/A; minorities: 25%; international: 0%
Acceptance rate (master's): 45%
Acceptance rate (Ph.D.): 0%
Acceptance rate (DNP): 41%
Specialties offered: clinical nurse leader, nurse anesthesia, nurse practitioner, nurse practitioner: adult-gerontology acute care, nurse practitioner: family, nurse practitioner: pediatric primary care, nurse practitioner: psychiatric-mental health, across the lifespan, research

Georgia Southern University

PO Box 8158
Statesboro, GA 30460
chhs.georgiasouthern.edu/nursing/
Public
Admissions: (912) 478-5384
Email: gradadmissions@georgiasouthern.edu
Financial aid: (912) 478-5413
Application deadline: 03/01
Degrees offered: master's, DNP
In-state tuition: full time: $327/credit hour; part time: N/A (master's); full time: $462/credit hour; part time: N/A (DNP)
Out-of-state tuition: full time: $1,155/credit hour (master's); full time: $462/credit hour (DNP)
Room/board/expenses: $9,752 (master's)
Full-time enrollment: 35 (master's); 36 (DNP) men: 11%; women: 89%; minorities: 30%; international: 0%
Part-time enrollment: men: N/A; women: N/A; minorities: N/A; international: N/A
Acceptance rate (master's): 59%
Acceptance rate (Ph.D.): N/A
Acceptance rate (DNP): 95%
Specialties offered: nurse practitioner, nurse practitioner: family, nurse practitioner: psychiatric-mental health, across the lifespan

Georgia State University

PO Box 3995
Atlanta, GA 30303
snhp.gsu.edu
Public
Admissions: (404) 413-2500
Email: admissions@gsu.edu
Financial aid: (404) 413-2600
Application deadline: 03/01

Degrees offered: master's, Ph.D., DNP
In-state tuition: full time: $368/credit hour; part time: $368/credit hour (master's); full time: $368/credit hour; part time: $368/credit hour (Ph.D.); full time: $368/credit hour; part time: $368/credit hour (DNP)
Out-of-state tuition: full time: $1,229/credit hour (master's); full time: $1,229/credit hour (Ph.D.); full time: $1,229/credit hour (DNP)
Room/board/expenses: $13,342 (master's); $13,342 (Ph.D.); $13,342 (DNP)
Full-time enrollment: 70 (master's); 6 (Ph.D.); 1 (DNP) men: 5%; women: 95%; minorities: 39%; international: 8%
Part-time enrollment: 185 (master's); 21 (Ph.D.); 10 (DNP) men: 11%; women: 89%; minorities: 41%; international: 0%
Acceptance rate (master's): 60%
Acceptance rate (Ph.D.): 55%
Acceptance rate (DNP): 44%
Specialties offered: administration, clinical nurse leader, clinical nurse specialist, informatics, nurse practitioner, nurse practitioner: adult-gerontology acute care, nurse practitioner: adult-gerontology primary care, nurse practitioner: adult, nurse practitioner: family, nurse practitioner: pediatric primary care, nurse practitioner: psychiatric-mental health, across the lifespan

Kennesaw State University[1]

1000 Chastain Road
Kennesaw, GA 30144-5591
Public
Admissions: N/A
Financial aid: N/A
Tuition: N/A
Room/board/expenses: N/A
Enrollment: N/A

Mercer University[1]

3001 Mercer University Drive
Atlanta, GA 30341
nursing.mercer.edu/
Private
Admissions: N/A
Financial aid: N/A
Tuition: N/A
Room/board/expenses: N/A
Enrollment: N/A

South University[1]

709 Mall Boulevard
Savannah, GA 31406
Private
Admissions: N/A
Financial aid: N/A
Tuition: N/A
Room/board/expenses: N/A
Enrollment: N/A

Thomas University[1]

1501 Millpond Road
Thomasville, GA 31792
Private
Admissions: N/A
Financial aid: N/A
Tuition: N/A
Room/board/expenses: N/A
Enrollment: N/A

University of North Georgia[1]

82 College Circle
Dahlonega, GA 30597
Public
Admissions: N/A
Financial aid: N/A
Tuition: N/A
Room/board/expenses: N/A
Enrollment: N/A

University of West Georgia

1601 Maple Street
Carrollton, GA 30118
nursing.westga.edu/index.php
Public
Admissions: (678) 839-1390
Email: tziglar@westga.edu
Financial aid: (678) 839-6421
Application deadline: 06/01
Degrees offered: master's
In-state tuition: full time: $6,482;
part time: $270/credit hour
Out-of-state tuition: full time:
$25,264
Room/board/expenses: $8,532
Full-time enrollment: 19
men: 21%; women: 79%;
minorities: 21%; international: 0%
Part-time enrollment: 68
men: 4%; women: 96%;
minorities: 25%; international: 1%
Acceptance rate (master's): 79%
Specialties offered: clinical nurse
leader, education, other majors

Valdosta State University[1]

S. Walter Martin Hall
Valdosta, GA 31698-0130
Public
Admissions: N/A
Financial aid: N/A
Tuition: N/A
Room/board/expenses: N/A
Enrollment: N/A

HAWAII

Hawaii Pacific University

45-045 Kamehameha Highway
Kaneohe, HI 96744
www.hpu.edu
Private
Admissions: (808) 236-5847
Email: DKNIGHT@HPU.EDU
Financial aid: (866) 225-5478
Application deadline: 04/15
Degrees offered: master's
Tuition: full time: $1,205/credit
hour; part time: $1,205/credit
hour (master's)
Room/board/expenses: $13,500
Full-time enrollment: 33
men: N/A; women: N/A; minorities:
N/A; international: 15%
Part-time enrollment: 9
men: N/A; women: N/A; minorities:
N/A; international: 0%
Acceptance rate (master's): 72%
Specialties offered: nurse
practitioner, nurse practitioner:
family

University of Hawaii-Manoa

2528 McCarthy Mall
Honolulu, HI 96822
www.nursing.hawaii.edu/home
Public
Admissions: (808) 956-8544
Email: graduate.education@
hawaii.edu
Financial aid: (808) 956-7251
Application deadline: N/A
Degrees offered: master's, Ph.D.,
DNP
In-state tuition: full time: $870/
credit hour; part time: $870/
credit hour (master's); full time:
$870/credit hour; part time: $870/
credit hour (Ph.D.); full time: $870/
credit hour; part time: $870/credit
hour (DNP)
Out-of-state tuition: full time:
$1,652/credit hour (master's); full
time: $1,652/credit hour (Ph.D.);
full time: $1,652/credit hour (DNP)
Room/board/expenses: $13,284
(master's); $13,284 (Ph.D.);
$13,284 (DNP)
Full-time enrollment: 133
(master's); 10 (Ph.D.); 11 (DNP)
men: N/A; women: N/A; minorities:
62%; international: 1%
Part-time enrollment: 60
(master's); 39 (Ph.D.); 13 (DNP)
men: N/A; women: N/A; minorities:
66%; international: 0%
Acceptance rate (master's): 55%
Acceptance rate (Ph.D.): 81%
Acceptance rate (DNP): 100%
Specialties offered: administration,
clinical nurse specialist,
community health/public health,
nurse practitioner, nurse
practitioner: adult-gerontology
primary care, nurse practitioner:
family, other majors, dual majors

IDAHO

Boise State University

1910 University Drive
Boise, ID 82537-1840
hs.boisestate.edu/nursing/news/
Public
Admissions: (208) 426-3903
Email:
gradcoll@boisestate.edu
Financial aid: (800) 824-7017
Application deadline: 03/01
Degrees offered: master's, DNP
In-state tuition: full time: N/A; part
time: $600/credit hour (master's);
full time: N/A; part time: $600/
credit hour (DNP)
Out-of-state tuition: full time: N/A
Room/board/expenses: N/A
Full-time enrollment: 1 (DNP)
men: N/A; women: 100%;
minorities: N/A; international: N/A
Part-time enrollment: 41 (master's);
18 (DNP)
men: 17%; women: 83%;
minorities: 12%; international: N/A
Acceptance rate (master's): 68%
Acceptance rate (DNP): 95%
Specialties offered: nurse
practitioner, nurse practitioner:
adult-gerontology acute care,
nurse practitioner: adult-
gerontology primary care

Idaho State University

921 S. 8th Avenue, Stop 8101
Pocatello, ID 83209-0101
www.isu.edu/nursing
Public
Admissions: (208) 282-2325
Email: profnurs@isu.edu
Financial aid: (208) 282-2756

Application deadline: N/A
Degrees offered: master's, Ph.D.,
DNP
In-state tuition: full time: $3,867;
part time: $387/credit hour
(master's); full time: $3,867; part
time: $387/credit hour (Ph.D.);
full time: $3,867; part time: $387/
credit hour (DNP)
Out-of-state tuition: full time:
$7,734 (master's); full time: $7,734
(Ph.D.); full time: $9,663 (DNP)
Room/board/expenses: N/A
Full-time enrollment: 5 (master's); 7
(Ph.D.); 26 (DNP)
men: 24%; women: 76%;
minorities: 5%; international: 0%
Part-time enrollment:
men: N/A; women: N/A; minorities:
N/A; international: N/A
Acceptance rate (master's): N/A
Acceptance rate (Ph.D.): 100%
Acceptance rate (DNP): 85%
Specialties offered: education,
nurse practitioner: family, nurse
practitioner: psychiatric-mental
health, across the lifespan

Northwest Nazarene University[1]

623 S. University Boulevard
Nampa, ID 83686
Private
Admissions: N/A
Financial aid: N/A
Tuition: N/A
Room/board/expenses: N/A
Enrollment: N/A

ILLINOIS

Aurora University[1]

347 S. Gladstone Ave.
Aurora, IL 60506
Private
Admissions: N/A
Financial aid: N/A
Tuition: N/A
Room/board/expenses: N/A
Enrollment: N/A

Benedictine University

5700 College Road
Lisle, IL 60532
www.ben.edu/college-of-
education-and-health-services/
nursing-health/faculty-staff.cfm
Private
Admissions: (630) 366-2981
Email: online.ben.edu/msn/
masters-in-nursing
Financial aid: (630) 829-6415
Application deadline: 12/05
Degrees offered: master's
Tuition: full time: $620/credit hour;
part time: $620/credit hour
Room/board/expenses: N/A
Full-time enrollment:
men: N/A; women: N/A; minorities:
N/A; international: N/A
Part-time enrollment: 375
men: 5%; women: 95%;
minorities: 21%; international: 0%
Acceptance rate (master's): 100%
Specialties offered: administration,
education

Blessing-Rieman College of Nursing

PO Box 7005
Quincy, IL 62305-7005
Private
Admissions: (217) 228-5520
Email: admissions@brcn.edu
Financial aid: (217) 228-5520
Application deadline: N/A

Degrees offered: master's
Tuition: full time: N/A; part time:
$500/credit hour
Room/board/expenses: N/A
Full-time enrollment:
men: N/A; women: N/A; minorities:
N/A; international: N/A
Part-time enrollment: 19
men: 5%; women: 95%;
minorities: 0%; international: 0%
Acceptance rate (master's): N/A
Specialties offered: administration,
education

Bradley University[1]

1501 W. Bradley Avenue
Peoria, IL 61625-0001
Private
Admissions: N/A
Financial aid: N/A
Tuition: N/A
Room/board/expenses: N/A
Enrollment: N/A

Chamberlain College of Nursing

3005 Highland Parkway
Downers Grove, IL 60515
www.chamberlain.edu
Private
Admissions: (888) 556-8226
Financial aid: (888) 556-8226
Application deadline: N/A
Degrees offered: master's, DNP
Tuition: full time: $15,600; part
time: $650/credit hour (master's);
full time: $13,500; part time: $750/
credit hour (DNP)
Room/board/expenses: N/A
Full-time enrollment: 3,502
(master's); 352 (DNP)
men: 9%; women: 91%; minorities:
27%; international: 0%
Part-time enrollment: 1,461
(master's); 139 (DNP)
men: 7%; women: 93%;
minorities: 32%; international: 0%
Acceptance rate (master's): 98%
Acceptance rate (DNP): 100%
Specialties offered: administration,
education, health management
& policy health care systems,
informatics, nurse practitioner,
nurse practitioner: family, other
majors

DePaul University

990 W. Fullerton Avenue
Chicago, IL 60613
csh.depaul.edu/departments/
nursing/
Private
Admissions: (773) 325-7315
Email: graddepaul@depaul.edu
Financial aid: (312) 362-8610
Application deadline: N/A
Degrees offered: master's, DNP
Tuition: full time: $670/credit
hour; part time: $670/credit hour
(master's); full time: $670/credit
hour; part time: $670/credit hour
(DNP)
Room/board/expenses: N/A
Full-time enrollment: 284
(master's); 45 (DNP)
men: 16%; women: 84%;
minorities: 22%; international: 2%
Part-time enrollment: 26
(master's); 10 (DNP)
men: 3%; women: 97%;
minorities: 33%; international: 3%
Acceptance rate (master's): 89%
Acceptance rate (DNP): 100%
Specialties offered: generalist,
nurse anesthesia, nurse
practitioner, nurse practitioner:
adult-gerontology primary care,
nurse practitioner: family

Elmhurst College[1]

190 Prospect Avenue
Elmhurst, IL 60126
Private
Admissions: N/A
Financial aid: N/A
Tuition: N/A
Room/board/expenses: N/A
Enrollment: N/A

Governors State University[1]

1 University Parkway
University Park, IL 60466-0975
www.govst.edu/
Public
Admissions: N/A
Financial aid: N/A
Tuition: N/A
Room/board/expenses: N/A
Enrollment: N/A

Illinois State University

Campus Box 5810
Normal, IL 61790-5810
nursing.illinoisstate.edu/
Public
Admissions: (309) 438-2181
Email: admissions@ilstu.edu
Financial aid: (309) 438-2231
Application deadline: 04/01
Degrees offered: master's, Ph.D.,
DNP
In-state tuition: full time: $360/
credit hour; part time: $360/
credit hour (master's); full time:
$360/credit hour; part time: $360/
credit hour (Ph.D.); full time: $360/
credit hour; part time: $360/credit
hour (DNP)
Out-of-state tuition: full time: $747/
credit hour (master's); full time:
$747/credit hour (Ph.D.); full time:
$747/credit hour (DNP)
Room/board/expenses: $9,814
(master's); $9,814 (Ph.D.); $9,814
(DNP)
Full-time enrollment: 6 (master's)
men: 33%; women: 67%;
minorities: 0%; international: 0%
Part-time enrollment: 68
(master's); 22 (Ph.D.); 14 (DNP)
men: 9%; women: 91%; minorities:
5%; international: 0%
Acceptance rate (master's): 38%
Acceptance rate (Ph.D.): 100%
Acceptance rate (DNP): 100%
Specialties offered: administration,
clinical nurse leader, nurse
practitioner: family

Lewis University

1 University Parkway
Romeoville, IL 60446
www.lewisu.edu/academics/
nursing/
Private
Admissions: (815) 836-5610
Email: grad@lewisu.edu
Financial aid: (815) 836-5263
Application deadline: 10/01
Degrees offered: master's, DNP
Tuition: full time: $760/credit
hour; part time: $760/credit hour
(master's); full time: $750/credit
hour; part time: $750/credit hour
(DNP)
Room/board/expenses: $9,750
(master's); $9,750 (DNP)
Full-time enrollment: 12 (master's)
men: 8%; women: 92%;
minorities: 25%; international: 0%

Part-time enrollment: 321 (master's); 13 (DNP) men: 6%; women: 94%; minorities: 29%; international: 0%
Acceptance rate (master's): 49%
Acceptance rate (DNP): 81%
Specialties offered: administration, clinical nurse specialist, education, nurse practitioner, nurse practitioner: adult-gerontology primary care, nurse practitioner: family, school nursing, other majors, dual majors

Loyola University Chicago

6525 North Sheridan Road
Chicago, IL 60626-5385
www.luc.edu/nursing
Private
Admissions: (312) 915-8902
Email: gradapp@luc.edu
Financial aid: (773) 508-7704
Application deadline: 06/01
Degrees offered: master's, Ph.D., DNP
Tuition: full time: $1,020/credit hour; part time: $1,020/credit hour (master's); full time: $1,020/credit hour; part time: $1,020/credit hour (Ph.D.); full time: $1,020/credit hour; part time: $1,020/credit hour (DNP)
Room/board/expenses: N/A
Full-time enrollment: 134 (master's); 27 (Ph.D.); 6 (DNP) men: 5%; women: 95%; minorities: 13%; international: 1%
Part-time enrollment: 220 (master's); 7 (Ph.D.); 8 (DNP) men: 6%; women: 94%; minorities: 21%; international: 0%
Acceptance rate (master's): 73%
Acceptance rate (Ph.D.): 100%
Acceptance rate (DNP): 86%
Specialties offered: administration, clinical nurse specialist, informatics, nurse practitioner, nurse practitioner: adult-gerontology acute care, nurse practitioner: adult-gerontology primary care, nurse practitioner: family, research, other majors, combined nurse practitioner/ clinical nurse specialist

McKendree University

701 College Road
Lebanon, IL 62254
www.mckendree.edu/ academics/info/nursing-health/ nursing/index.php
Private
Admissions: (618) 537-6576
Email: graduate@mckendree.edu
Financial aid: (618) 537-6828
Application deadline: N/A
Degrees offered: master's
Tuition: full time: $420/credit hour; part time: $420/credit hour
Room/board/expenses: N/A
Full-time enrollment: 4 men: 0%; women: 100%; minorities: N/A; international: 0%
Part-time enrollment: 74 men: 5%; women: 95%; minorities: 14%; international: 0%
Acceptance rate (master's): 42%
Specialties offered: administration, education, other majors, dual majors

Millikin University

1184 W. Main Street
Decatur, IL 62522
www.millikin.edu/ academics/cps/nursing
Private
Admissions: (217) 424-6210
Email: admis@millikin.edu
Financial aid: (217) 424-6317
Application deadline: N/A
Degrees offered: master's, DNP
Tuition: full time: $725/credit hour; part time: $725/credit hour (master's); full time: $828/credit hour; part time: $828/credit hour (DNP)
Room/board/expenses: N/A
Full-time enrollment: 21 (master's); 12 (DNP) men: N/A; women: N/A; minorities: 15%; international: 3%
Part-time enrollment: 23 (master's); 3 (DNP) men: N/A; women: N/A; minorities: 12%; international: 0%
Acceptance rate (master's): 48%
Acceptance rate (DNP): 90%
Specialties offered: clinical nurse leader, education, nurse anesthesia

Northern Illinois University[1]

1240 Normal Road
DeKalb, IL 60115
Public
Admissions: N/A
Financial aid: N/A
Tuition: N/A
Room/board/expenses: N/A
Enrollment: N/A

North Park University[1]

3225 W. Foster Avenue
Chicago, IL 60625-4895
Private
Admissions: N/A
Financial aid: N/A
Tuition: N/A
Room/board/expenses: N/A
Enrollment: N/A

Olivet Nazarene University[1]

3601 Algonquin Road
Rolling Meadows, IL 60008
Private
Admissions: N/A
Financial aid: N/A
Tuition: N/A
Room/board/expenses: N/A
Enrollment: N/A

Resurrection University[1]

1431 N. Claremont Avenue
Chicago, IL 60622-`
Private
Admissions: N/A
Financial aid: N/A
Tuition: N/A
Room/board/expenses: N/A
Enrollment: N/A

Rush University

600 S. Paulina Suite 1080
Chicago, IL 60612-3873
www.rushu.rush.edu/servlet/ Satellite?c=RushUnivLevel1Page& cid=1204497838852&pagename=
Private
Admissions: (312) 942-7110
Email: con_admissions@rush.edu

Financial aid: (312) 942-6523
Application deadline: 01/02
Degrees offered: master's, Ph.D., DNP
Tuition: full time: $999/credit hour; part time: $999/credit hour (master's); full time: $999/credit hour; part time: $999/credit hour (Ph.D.); full time: $999/credit hour; part time: $999/credit hour (DNP)
Room/board/expenses: N/A
Full-time enrollment: 275 (master's); 4 (Ph.D.); 78 (DNP) men: 15%; women: 85%; minorities: 28%; international: 0%
Part-time enrollment: 118 (master's); 32 (Ph.D.); 490 (DNP) men: 9%; women: 91%; minorities: 22%; international: 0%
Acceptance rate (master's): 54%
Acceptance rate (Ph.D.): 50%
Acceptance rate (DNP): 75%
Specialties offered: clinical nurse leader, clinical nurse specialist, community health/public health, generalist, health management & policy health care systems, nurse anesthesia, nurse practitioner, nurse practitioner: adult-gerontology acute care, nurse practitioner: adult-gerontology primary care, nurse practitioner: family, nurse practitioner: pediatric primary care, nurse practitioner: psychiatric-mental health, across the lifespan, research, other majors

Southern Illinois University-Edwardsville

Campus Box 1066
Edwardsville, IL 62026-1066
www.siue.edu/nursing/
Public
Admissions: (618) 650-3705
Email: tburrel@siue.edu
Financial aid: (618) 650-3880
Application deadline: 07/18
Degrees offered: master's, DNP
In-state tuition: full time: $2,513; part time: $1,675 (master's); full time: N/A; part time: $13,000 (DNP)
Out-of-state tuition: full time: $6,283 (master's)
Room/board/expenses: N/A
Full-time enrollment: 71 (master's) men: 35%; women: 65%; minorities: 11%; international: N/A
Part-time enrollment: 181 (master's); 21 (DNP) men: 8%; women: 92%; minorities: 12%; international: N/A
Acceptance rate (master's): 57%
Acceptance rate (DNP): 100%
Specialties offered: administration, education, nurse anesthesia, nurse practitioner, nurse practitioner: family

St. Anthony College of Nursing

5658 E. State Street
Rockford, IL 61108-2468
sacn.edu
Private
Admissions: (815) 395-5476
Email: angelataillet@sacn.edu
Financial aid: (815) 395-5089
Application deadline: N/A
Degrees offered: master's, DNP
Tuition: full time: $848/credit hour; part time: $848/credit hour (master's); full time: $848/credit hour; part time: $848/credit hour (DNP)

Room/board/expenses: N/A
Full-time enrollment: 1 (master's) men: 0%; women: 100%; minorities: 0%; international: 0%
Part-time enrollment: 56 (master's); 14 (DNP) men: 6%; women: 94%; minorities: 24%; international: 0%
Acceptance rate (master's): 100%
Acceptance rate (DNP): 100%
Specialties offered: clinical nurse leader, clinical nurse specialist, education, nurse practitioner: adult-gerontology primary care, nurse practitioner: family, other majors

St. Francis Medical Center

511 N.E. Greenleaf Street
Peoria, IL 61603
www.sfmccon.edu/
Private
Admissions: (309) 655-2596
Email: janice.farquharson@ osfhealthcare.org
Financial aid: (309) 655-4119
Application deadline: 09/15
Degrees offered: master's, DNP
Tuition: full time: $10,548; part time: $586/credit hour (master's); full time: $10,548; part time: $586/credit hour (DNP)
Room/board/expenses: $3,300 (master's); $3,300 (DNP)
Full-time enrollment: 10 (master's) men: 10%; women: 90%; minorities: 20%; international: 0%
Part-time enrollment: 228 (master's); 25 (DNP) men: 8%; women: 92%; minorities: 5%; international: 0%
Acceptance rate (master's): 98%
Acceptance rate (DNP): 100%
Specialties offered: administration, clinical nurse leader, clinical nurse specialist, education, nurse practitioner, nurse practitioner: psychiatric-mental health, across the lifespan, other majors

St. Xavier University

3700 W. 103rd Street
Chicago, IL 60655
www.sxu.edu/academics/ colleges_schools/son/index.asp
Private
Admissions: (773) 298-3053
Email: graduateadmission@ sxu.edu
Financial aid: (773) 298-3070
Application deadline: 06/01
Degrees offered: master's
Tuition: full time: $880/credit hour; part time: $880/credit hour
Room/board/expenses: $13,660
Full-time enrollment: 119 men: 10%; women: 90%; minorities: 29%; international: 0%
Part-time enrollment: 126 men: 5%; women: 95%; minorities: 33%; international: 0%
Acceptance rate (master's): 59%
Specialties offered: administration, clinical nurse leader, education, nurse practitioner, nurse practitioner: family, dual majors

University of Illinois-Chicago

845 South Damen Avenue
MC 802
Chicago, IL 60612
nursing.uic.edu
Public
Admissions: (312) 996-7800

Email: conapply@uic.edu
Financial aid: (312) 996-3126
Application deadline: N/A
Degrees offered: master's, Ph.D., DNP
In-state tuition: full time: $19,680; part time: $13,120 (master's); full time: $19,680; part time: $13,120 (Ph.D.); full time: $21,704; part time: $14,470 (DNP)
Out-of-state tuition: full time: $31,678 (master's); full time: $31,678 (Ph.D.); full time: $33,870 (DNP)
Room/board/expenses: N/A
Full-time enrollment: 360 (master's); 41 (Ph.D.); 41 (DNP) men: 9%; women: 91%; minorities: 25%; international: 8%
Part-time enrollment: 280 (master's); 25 (Ph.D.); 177 (DNP) men: 10%; women: 90%; minorities: 29%; international: 1%
Acceptance rate (master's): 46%
Acceptance rate (Ph.D.): 61%
Acceptance rate (DNP): 81%
Specialties offered: administration, generalist, nurse-midwifery, nurse practitioner, nurse practitioner: adult-gerontology acute care, nurse practitioner: adult-gerontology primary care, nurse practitioner: family, nurse practitioner: pediatric primary care, nurse practitioner: psychiatric-mental health, across the lifespan, research, school nursing, other majors, dual majors

University of St. Francis

500 Wilcox Street
Joliet , IL 60435
www.stfrancis.edu/academics/ college-of-nursing
Private
Admissions: (800) 735-7500
Email: admissions@stfrancis.edu
Financial aid: (866) 890-8331
Application deadline: 03/01
Degrees offered: master's, DNP
Tuition: full time: N/A; part time: $724/credit hour (master's); full time: N/A; part time: $735/credit hour (DNP)
Room/board/expenses: N/A
Full-time enrollment: 90 (master's); 16 (DNP) men: 8%; women: 92%; minorities: 38%; international: 0%
Part-time enrollment: 293 (master's); 16 (DNP) men: 9%; women: 91%; minorities: 29%; international: 0%
Acceptance rate (master's): 40%
Acceptance rate (DNP): 39%
Specialties offered: administration, education, nurse practitioner: family, nurse practitioner: psychiatric-mental health, across the lifespan

INDIANA

Anderson University[1]

1100 E. Fifth Street
Anderson, IN 46012
Private
Admissions: N/A
Financial aid: N/A
Tuition: N/A
Room/board/expenses: N/A
Enrollment: N/A

Ball State University
2000 W. University Avenue
Muncie, IN 47306
www.bsu.edu/nursing
Public
Admissions: (765) 285-9130
Email: nursing@bsu.edu
Financial aid: (765) 285-5600
Application deadline: 01/09
Degrees offered: master's, DNP
In-state tuition: full time: $315/credit hour; part time: $315/credit hour (master's); full time: $315/credit hour; part time: $315/credit hour (DNP)
Out-of-state tuition: full time: $530/credit hour (master's); full time: $530/credit hour (DNP)
Room/board/expenses: $10,530 (master's); $10,530 (DNP)
Full-time enrollment: 11 (master's) men: 0%; women: 100%; minorities: 0%; international: 0%
Part-time enrollment: 350 (master's); 18 (DNP) men: 6%; women: 94%; minorities: 7%; international: 0%
Acceptance rate (master's): 65%
Acceptance rate (DNP): N/A
Specialties offered: administration, education, nurse practitioner, nurse practitioner: family

Bethel College[1]
1001 Bethel Circle
Mishawaka, IN 46545
Private
Admissions: N/A
Financial aid: N/A
Tuition: N/A
Room/board/expenses: N/A
Enrollment: N/A

Goshen College[1]
1700 South Main Street
Goshen, IN 46526
Private
Admissions: N/A
Financial aid: N/A
Tuition: N/A
Room/board/expenses: N/A
Enrollment: N/A

Indiana State University
749 Chestnut Street
Terre Haute, IN 47809-1937
www.indstate.edu/nursing/
Public
Admissions: (812) 237-3005
Email: Gina.Atterson@indstate.edu
Financial aid: (812) 237-2215
Application deadline: N/A
Degrees offered: master's, DNP
In-state tuition: full time: $475/credit hour; part time: $475/credit hour (master's); full time: $475/credit hour; part time: $475/credit hour (DNP)
Out-of-state tuition: full time: $475/credit hour (master's); full time: $475/credit hour (DNP)
Room/board/expenses: N/A
Full-time enrollment: men: N/A; women: N/A; minorities: N/A; international: N/A
Part-time enrollment: 277 (master's); 23 (DNP) men: 1%; women: 99%; minorities: 26%; international: 0%
Acceptance rate (master's): 81%
Acceptance rate (DNP): 90%
Specialties offered: administration, education, nurse practitioner, nurse practitioner: family

Indiana University East[1]
2325 Chester Boulevard
Richmond, IN 47374
www.iue.edu/nursing/msn
Public
Admissions: N/A
Financial aid: N/A
Tuition: N/A
Room/board/expenses: N/A
Enrollment: N/A

Indiana University-Kokomo[1]
2300 S. Washington Street
Kokomo, IN 46904
Public
Admissions: N/A
Financial aid: N/A
Tuition: N/A
Room/board/expenses: N/A
Enrollment: N/A

Indiana University-Purdue University-Fort Wayne
2101 E Coliseum Blvd.
Fort Wayne, IN 46805
Public
Admissions: N/A
Financial aid: N/A
Application deadline: N/A
Degrees offered: master's
In-state tuition: full time: N/A; part time: N/A
Out-of-state tuition: full time: N/A
Room/board/expenses: N/A
Full-time enrollment: 3 men: 0%; women: 100%; minorities: 0%; international: 0%
Part-time enrollment: 79 men: 8%; women: 92%; minorities: 11%; international: 0%
Acceptance rate (master's): 100%
Specialties offered: N/A

Indiana University-Purdue University-Indianapolis
1111 Middle Drive
Indianapolis, IN 46202-5107
nursing.iu.edu
Public
Admissions: (317) 274-0003
Email: tlabney@iu.edu
Financial aid: (317) 274-5920
Application deadline: 02/15
Degrees offered: master's, Ph.D., DNP
In-state tuition: full time: $489/credit hour; part time: $489/credit hour (master's); full time: $489/credit hour; part time: $489/credit hour (Ph.D.); full time: $489/credit hour; part time: $489/credit hour (DNP)
Out-of-state tuition: full time: $1,421/credit hour (master's); full time: $1,421/credit hour (Ph.D.); full time: $1,421/credit hour (DNP)
Room/board/expenses: $20,062 (master's); $20,062 (Ph.D.); $20,062 (DNP)
Full-time enrollment: 44 (master's); 12 (Ph.D.); 5 (DNP) men: 15%; women: 85%; minorities: 23%; international: 2%
Part-time enrollment: 287 (master's); 45 (Ph.D.); 31 (DNP) men: 9%; women: 91%; minorities: 14%; international: 1%
Acceptance rate (master's): 61%
Acceptance rate (Ph.D.): 100%

Acceptance rate (DNP): 100%
Specialties offered: administration, clinical nurse specialist, education, nurse practitioner, nurse practitioner: adult-gerontology acute care, nurse practitioner: adult-gerontology primary care, nurse practitioner: family, nurse practitioner: pediatric primary care, nurse practitioner: psychiatric-mental health, across the lifespan

Indiana University-South Bend[1]
1700 Mishawaka Avenue
South Bend, IN 46634
www.iusb.edu/nursing/index.php
Public
Admissions: N/A
Financial aid: N/A
Tuition: N/A
Room/board/expenses: N/A
Enrollment: N/A

Indiana Wesleyan University[1]
4201 S. Washington Street
Marion, IN 46953
Private
Admissions: N/A
Financial aid: N/A
Tuition: N/A
Room/board/expenses: N/A
Enrollment: N/A

Purdue University-Calumet[1]
2200 169th Street
Hammond, IN 46323
Public
Admissions: N/A
Financial aid: N/A
Tuition: N/A
Room/board/expenses: N/A
Enrollment: N/A

Purdue University-West Lafayette
502 N. University Street
West Lafayette, IN 47907-2069
www.nursing.purdue.edu/
Public
Admissions: (765) 494-9116
Email: admissions@purdue.edu
Financial aid: (765) 494-5050
Application deadline: N/A
Degrees offered: master's, DNP
In-state tuition: full time: $9,208; part time: $329/credit hour (master's); full time: N/A; part time: N/A/credit hour (Ph.D.); full time: $9,208; part time: $329/credit hour (DNP)
Out-of-state tuition: full time: $28,010 (master's); full time: $28,010 (DNP)
Room/board/expenses: N/A
Full-time enrollment: 32 (master's); 2 (DNP) men: 0%; women: 100%; minorities: 21%; international: 0%
Part-time enrollment: 6 (master's); 18 (DNP) men: 0%; women: 100%; minorities: 4%; international: 4%
Acceptance rate (master's): 100%
Acceptance rate (DNP): 100%
Specialties offered: nurse practitioner, nurse practitioner: adult-gerontology primary care, nurse practitioner: pediatric primary care

University of Indianapolis
1400 E. Hanna Avenue
Indianapolis, IN 46227
uindy.edu/nursing
Private
Admissions: (317) 788-3216
Financial aid: (317) 788-3217
Application deadline: 04/15
Degrees offered: master's, DNP
Tuition: full time: $672/credit hour; part time: $672/credit hour (master's); full time: $690/credit hour; part time: $690/credit hour (DNP)
Room/board/expenses: N/A
Full-time enrollment: men: N/A; women: N/A; minorities: N/A; international: N/A
Part-time enrollment: 280 (master's); 6 (DNP) men: 6%; women: 94%; minorities: 12%; international: 0%
Acceptance rate (master's): 55%
Acceptance rate (DNP): 100%
Specialties offered: administration, education, nurse-midwifery, nurse practitioner, nurse practitioner: adult-gerontology primary care, nurse practitioner: family, other majors

University of Southern Indiana
8600 University Boulevard
Evansville, IN 47712-3596
www.usi.edu/health/nursing
Public
Admissions: (812) 465-7140
Email: graduate.studies@usi.edu
Financial aid: (812) 464-1767
Application deadline: 02/01
Degrees offered: master's, DNP
In-state tuition: full time: $425/credit hour; part time: $425/credit hour (master's); full time: $475/credit hour; part time: $475/credit hour (DNP)
Out-of-state tuition: full time: $741/credit hour (master's); full time: $791/credit hour (DNP)
Room/board/expenses: $4,140 (master's); $4,140 (DNP)
Full-time enrollment: 110 (master's); 6 (DNP) men: 11%; women: 89%; minorities: 8%; international: 0%
Part-time enrollment: 321 (master's); 44 (DNP) men: 12%; women: 88%; minorities: 8%; international: 0%
Acceptance rate (master's): 55%
Acceptance rate (DNP): 61%
Specialties offered: administration, clinical nurse specialist, education, nurse practitioner, nurse practitioner: adult-gerontology acute care, nurse practitioner: family, nurse practitioner: psychiatric-mental health, across the lifespan

University of St. Francis
2701 Spring Street
Fort Wayne, IN 46808
nursing.sf.edu/
Private
Admissions: (260) 399-8000
Email: gradschool@sf.edu
Financial aid: (260) 399-8000
Application deadline: 05/01
Degrees offered: master's
Tuition: full time: $830/credit hour; part time: $830/credit hour (master's)

Room/board/expenses: N/A
Full-time enrollment: 34 men: N/A; women: N/A; minorities: 21%; international: 0%
Part-time enrollment: 60 men: N/A; women: N/A; minorities: 12%; international: 0%
Acceptance rate (master's): 92%
Specialties offered: nurse practitioner, nurse practitioner: family

Valparaiso University[1]
LeBien Hall 103
Valparaiso, IN 46383
Private
Admissions: N/A
Financial aid: N/A
Tuition: N/A
Room/board/expenses: N/A
Enrollment: N/A

IOWA

Allen College[1]
1825 Logan Avenue
Waterloo, IA 50703
Private
Admissions: N/A
Financial aid: N/A
Tuition: N/A
Room/board/expenses: N/A
Enrollment: N/A

Briar Cliff University[1]
3303 Rebecca Street
Sioux City, IA 51104
Private
Admissions: N/A
Financial aid: N/A
Tuition: N/A
Room/board/expenses: N/A
Enrollment: N/A

Clarke University[1]
1550 Clarke Drive
Dubuque, IA 52001
Private
Admissions: N/A
Financial aid: N/A
Tuition: N/A
Room/board/expenses: N/A
Enrollment: N/A

Grand View University[1]
1200 Grandview Avenue
Des Moines, IA 50316
Private
Admissions: N/A
Financial aid: N/A
Tuition: N/A
Room/board/expenses: N/A
Enrollment: N/A

Kaplan University[1]
1801 East Kimberly Road
Suite 1
Davenport, IA 52807
Private
Admissions: N/A
Financial aid: N/A
Tuition: N/A
Room/board/expenses: N/A
Enrollment: N/A

Mount Mercy University
1330 Elmhurst Drive NE
Cedar Rapids, IA 52402
www.mtmercy.edu/master-science-nursing
Private
Admissions: (319) 363-1323
Email: tom@mtermcy.edu

Financial aid: (318) 363-8213
Application deadline: 12/01
Degrees offered: master's
Tuition: full time: $550/credit hour;
part time: $550/credit hour
Room/board/expenses: N/A
Full-time enrollment: 50
men: 4%; women: 96%;
minorities: 6%; international: 0%
Part-time enrollment: 11
men: 0%; women: 100%;
minorities: 9%; international: 0%
Acceptance rate (master's): 90%
Specialties offered: administration,
community health/public health,
education

University of Iowa

101 Nursing Building
Iowa City, IA 52242-1121
www.nursing.uiowa.edu/
Public
Admissions: (319) 335-1525
Email: admissions@uiowa.edu
Financial aid: (319) 335-1450
Application deadline: 02/01
Degrees offered: master's, Ph.D.,
DNP
In-state tuition: full time: $14,720;
part time: $9,816 (master's); full
time: $8,252; part time: $5,508
(Ph.D.); full time: $17,088; part
time: $11,400 (DNP)
Out-of-state tuition: full time:
$31,064 (master's); full time:
$25,134 (Ph.D.); full time: $34,832
(DNP)
Room/board/expenses: $14,592
(master's); $14,592 (Ph.D.);
$14,592 (DNP)
Full-time enrollment: 8 (Ph.D.);
98 (DNP)
men: 16%; women: 84%;
minorities: 14%; international: 1%
Part-time enrollment: 13 (master's);
19 (Ph.D.); 76 (DNP)
men: 13%; women: 87%;
minorities: 8%; international: 1%
Acceptance rate (master's): N/A
Acceptance rate (Ph.D.): 90%
Acceptance rate (DNP): 76%
Specialties offered: administration,
clinical nurse leader, nurse
anesthesia, nurse practitioner,
nurse practitioner: adult-
gerontology primary care,
nurse practitioner: family,
nurse practitioner: pediatric
primary care, nurse practitioner:
psychiatric-mental health, across
the lifespan, research

KANSAS

Fort Hays State University[1]

600 Park Street
Hays, KS 67601-4099
Public
Admissions: N/A
Financial aid: N/A
Tuition: N/A
Room/board/expenses: N/A
Enrollment: N/A

MidAmerica Nazarene University[1]

2030 E. College Way
Olathe, KS 66062
Private
Admissions: N/A
Financial aid: N/A
Tuition: N/A
Room/board/expenses: N/A
Enrollment: N/A

Pittsburg State University[1]

McPherson Building
Pittsburg, KS 66762-7500
Public
Admissions: N/A
Financial aid: N/A
Tuition: N/A
Room/board/expenses: N/A
Enrollment: N/A

University of Kansas

Mail Stop 2029
3901 Rainbow Boulevard
Kansas City, KS 66160
nursing.kumc.edu
Public
Admissions: (913) 588-1619
Email: soninfo@kumc.edu
Financial aid: (913) 588-5170
Application deadline: 12/01
Degrees offered: master's, Ph.D.,
DNP
In-state tuition: full time: $14,915;
part time: $8,872 (master's); full
time: $14,915; part time: $8,872
(Ph.D.); full time: $14,195; part
time: $8,872 (DNP)
Out-of-state tuition: full time:
$14,195 (master's); full time:
$14,690 (Ph.D.); full time: $15,775
(DNP)
Room/board/expenses: N/A
Full-time enrollment: 8 (master's);
18 (Ph.D.); 20 (DNP)
men: 13%; women: 87%;
minorities: 15%; international: 0%
Part-time enrollment: 149
(master's); 21 (Ph.D.); 141 (DNP)
men: 6%; women: 94%;
minorities: 15%; international: 0%
Acceptance rate (master's): 100%
Acceptance rate (Ph.D.): 100%
Acceptance rate (DNP): 89%
Specialties offered: administration,
clinical nurse specialist,
community health/public health,
informatics, nurse-midwifery,
nurse practitioner, nurse
practitioner: adult-gerontology
primary care, nurse practitioner:
family, nurse practitioner:
psychiatric-mental health, across
the lifespan, research

Washburn University-Topeka

1700 SW College Avenue
Topeka, KS 66621-1117
www.washburn.edu/sonuk
Public
Admissions: (785) 670-1525
Email:
shirley.dinkel@washburn.edu
Financial aid: (785) 670-2773
Application deadline: 03/15
Degrees offered: master's, DNP
In-state tuition: full time: $427/
credit hour; part time: $427/credit
hour (master's); full time: $518/
credit hour; part time: $518/credit
hour (DNP)
Out-of-state tuition: full time: $738/
credit hour (master's); full time:
$518/credit hour (DNP)
Room/board/expenses: $8,000
(master's); $8,000 (DNP)
Full-time enrollment: 18 (master's)
men: N/A; women: N/A; minorities:
N/A; international: N/A
Part-time enrollment: 91 (master's);
15 (DNP)
men: N/A; women: N/A; minorities:
N/A; international: N/A
Acceptance rate (master's): 43%
Acceptance rate (DNP): 100%

Specialties offered: clinical nurse
leader, nurse practitioner, nurse
practitioner: adult-gerontology
primary care, nurse practitioner:
family

Wichita State University[1]

1845 Fairmount
Wichita, KS 67260-0041
Public
Admissions: N/A
Financial aid: N/A
Tuition: N/A
Room/board/expenses: N/A
Enrollment: N/A

KENTUCKY

Bellarmine University[1]

2001 Newburg Road
Louisville, KY 40205
Private
Admissions: N/A
Financial aid: N/A
Tuition: N/A
Room/board/expenses: N/A
Enrollment: N/A

Eastern Kentucky University[1]

521 Lancaster Avenue
Richmond, KY 40475-3102
Public
Admissions: N/A
Financial aid: N/A
Tuition: N/A
Room/board/expenses: N/A
Enrollment: N/A

Frontier Nursing University

PO Box 528
Hyden, KY 41749
www.frontier.edu/
Private
Admissions: (606) 672-2312
Email: admissions@frontier.edu
Financial aid: (859) 899-2516
Application deadline: N/A
Degrees offered: master's, DNP
Tuition: full time: $520/credit
hour; part time: $520/credit hour
(master's); full time: $550/credit
hour; part time: $550/credit hour
(DNP)
Room/board/expenses: $16,200
(master's); $21,600 (DNP)
Full-time enrollment: 856
(master's); 102 (DNP)
men: 5%; women: 95%;
minorities: 15%; international: 0%
Part-time enrollment: 520
(master's)
men: 4%; women: 96%;
minorities: 18%; international: 0%
Acceptance rate (master's): 35%
Acceptance rate (DNP): 53%
Specialties offered: nurse-
midwifery, nurse practitioner,
nurse practitioner: family

Murray State University

121 Mason Hall
Murray, KY 42071
www.murraystate.edu/
nursing.aspx
Public
Admissions: (270) 809-3779
Email: msu.graduateadmissions@
murraystate.edu
Financial aid: (270) 809-2546
Application deadline: 11/01

Degrees offered: master's, DNP
In-state tuition: full time: N/A; part
time: N/A (master's); full time:
$584/credit hour; part time: N/A
(DNP)
Out-of-state tuition: full time: N/A
(master's); full time: $855/credit
hour (DNP)
Room/board/expenses: N/A
Full-time enrollment: 29 (master's);
43 (DNP)
men: 29%; women: 71%;
minorities: 10%; international: 1%
Part-time enrollment: 8 (master's);
6 (DNP)
men: 36%; women: 64%;
minorities: N/A; international: N/A
Acceptance rate (master's): N/A
Acceptance rate (DNP): 45%
Specialties offered: nurse
anesthesia, nurse practitioner,
nurse practitioner: family

Northern Kentucky University[1]

Nunn Drive
Highland Heights, KY 41099
healthprofessions.nku.edu/
Public
Admissions: N/A
Financial aid: N/A
Tuition: N/A
Room/board/expenses: N/A
Enrollment: N/A

Spalding University[1]

851 S. Fourth Street
Louisville, KY 40203-2188
Private
Admissions: N/A
Financial aid: N/A
Tuition: N/A
Room/board/expenses: N/A
Enrollment: N/A

University of Kentucky

315 College of Nursing Building
Lexington, KY 40536-0232
academics.uky.edu/ukcon/pub/
Pages/Default.aspx
Public
Admissions: (859) 323-5108
Email: conss@uky.edu
Financial aid: (859) 257-3172
Application deadline: 02/15
Degrees offered: Ph.D., DNP
In-state tuition: full time: N/A; part
time: N/A (master's); full time:
$11,312; part time: $596/credit
hour (Ph.D.); full time: $14,748;
part time: $787/credit hour (DNP)
Out-of-state tuition: full time: N/A
(master's); full time: $24,664
(Ph.D.); full time: $34,078 (DNP)
Room/board/expenses: N/A
Full-time enrollment: 40 (Ph.D.);
99 (DNP)
men: 10%; women: 90%;
minorities: 13%; international: 3%
Part-time enrollment: 6 (Ph.D.);
58 (DNP)
men: 11%; women: 89%;
minorities: 8%; international: 0%
Acceptance rate (Ph.D.): 100%
Acceptance rate (DNP): 90%
Specialties offered: clinical nurse
specialist, health management
& policy health care systems,
nurse practitioner, nurse
practitioner: adult-gerontology
acute care, nurse practitioner:
adult-gerontology primary care,
nurse practitioner: adult, nurse
practitioner: family, nurse
practitioner: pediatric primary

care, nurse practitioner:
psychiatric-mental health, across
the lifespan, research

University of Louisville

555 S. Floyd Street
Louisville, KY 40292
louisville.edu/nursing/
Public
Admissions: (502) 852-4957
Email: gradadm@louisville.edu
Financial aid: (502) 852-5511
Application deadline: 10/01
Degrees offered: master's, Ph.D.
In-state tuition: full time: $11,326;
part time: $630/credit hour
(master's); full time: $11,326; part
time: $630/credit hour (Ph.D.)
Out-of-state tuition: full time:
$23,568 (master's); full time:
$23,568 (Ph.D.)
Room/board/expenses: $8,370
(master's); $8,370 (Ph.D.)
Full-time enrollment: 72 (master's);
17 (Ph.D.);
men: 10%; women: 90%;
minorities: 10%; international: 4%
Part-time enrollment: 36
(master's); 1 (Ph.D.)
men: 8%; women: 92%;
minorities: 5%; international: 0%
Acceptance rate (master's): 47%
Acceptance rate (Ph.D.): 73%
Specialties offered: education,
nurse practitioner, nurse
practitioner: adult-gerontology
acute care, nurse practitioner:
adult-gerontology primary care,
nurse practitioner: family, nurse
practitioner: psychiatric-mental
health, across the lifespan

Western Kentucky University

1906 College Heights Boulevard
Bowling Green, KY 42101-1036
www.wku.edu/nursing/index.php
Public
Admissions: (270) 745-2446
Email: graduate.admissions@
wku.edu
Financial aid: (270) 745-2755
Application deadline: 03/01
Degrees offered: master's, DNP
In-state tuition: full time: $515/
credit hour; part time: $515/credit
hour (master's); full time: $620/
credit hour; part time: $620/credit
hour (DNP)
Out-of-state tuition: full time: $691/
credit hour (master's); full time:
$775/credit hour (DNP)
Room/board/expenses: N/A
Full-time enrollment: 12 (master's);
7 (DNP)
men: 16%; women: 84%;
minorities: 5%; international: 0%
Part-time enrollment: 144
(master's); 53 (DNP)
men: 8%; women: 92%;
minorities: 6%; international: 0%
Acceptance rate (master's): 56%
Acceptance rate (DNP): 71%
Specialties offered: administration,
education, nurse practitioner,
nurse practitioner: family, nurse
practitioner: psychiatric-mental
health, across the lifespan

LOUISIANA

Grambling State University[1]
1 Cole Street
Grambling, LA 71245
Public
Admissions: N/A
Financial aid: N/A
Tuition: N/A
Room/board/expenses: N/A
Enrollment: N/A

Louisiana State University Health Sciences Center[1]
1900 Gravier Street
New Orleans, LA 70112
nursing.lsuhsc.edu/default.aspx
Public
Admissions: N/A
Financial aid: N/A
Tuition: N/A
Room/board/expenses: N/A
Enrollment: N/A

Loyola University New Orleans
Stallings Hall, Room 202
New Orleans, LA 70118
css.loyno.edu/nursing
Private
Admissions: (800) 488-6257
Email: nursing@loyno.edu
Financial aid: (504) 865-3231
Application deadline: 12/31
Degrees offered: master's, DNP
Tuition: full time: $818/credit hour; part time: $818/credit hour (master's); full time: $818/credit hour; part time: $818/credit hour (DNP)
Room/board/expenses: N/A
Full-time enrollment: 316 (master's); 70 (DNP)
men: 10%; women: 90%;
minorities: 29%; international: 0%
Part-time enrollment: 89 (master's); 54 (DNP)
men: 8%; women: 92%;
minorities: 43%; international: 0%
Acceptance rate (master's): 75%
Acceptance rate (DNP): 47%
Specialties offered: administration, nurse practitioner: family

McNeese State University
Hardtner Hall Room 102
Lake Charles, LA 70609
www.mcneese.edu/nursing/graduate
Public
Admissions: (337) 475-5504
Email: admissions@mcneese.edu
Financial aid: (337) 475-5068
Application deadline: N/A
Degrees offered: master's
In-state tuition: full time: N/A; part time: N/A
Out-of-state tuition: full time: N/A
Room/board/expenses: N/A
Full-time enrollment: 22
men: 18%; women: 82%;
minorities: 9%; international: 0%
Part-time enrollment: 135
men: 24%; women: 76%;
minorities: 16%; international: 0%
Acceptance rate (master's): N/A
Specialties offered: administration, education, nurse practitioner, nurse practitioner: psychiatric-mental health, across the lifespan

Northwestern State University of Louisiana
1800 Line Avenue
Shreveport, LA 71101-4653
nursing.nsula.edu
Public
Admissions: (318) 357-6171
Email: belle@nsula.edu
Financial aid: (318) 357-5961
Application deadline: N/A
Degrees offered: master's, DNP
In-state tuition: full time: $10,009; part time: $5,245 (master's); full time: $10,009; part time: $5,245 (DNP)
Out-of-state tuition: full time: $16,152 (master's); full time: $16,152 (DNP)
Room/board/expenses: N/A
Full-time enrollment: 14 (master's)
men: 7%; women: 93%;
minorities: 36%; international: 0%
Part-time enrollment: 221 (master's); 17 (DNP)
men: 14%; women: 86%;
minorities: 17%; international: 0%
Acceptance rate (master's): 97%
Acceptance rate (DNP): 90%
Specialties offered: administration, education, nurse practitioner, nurse practitioner: adult-gerontology acute care, nurse practitioner: adult-gerontology primary care, nurse practitioner: family, nurse practitioner: pediatric primary care

Our Lady of the Lake College[1]
7434 Perkins Road
Baton Rouge, LA 70808
Private
Admissions: N/A
Financial aid: N/A
Tuition: N/A
Room/board/expenses: N/A
Enrollment: N/A

Southeastern Louisiana University
SLU Box 10835
Hammond, LA 70402
Public
Admissions: N/A
Financial aid: N/A
Application deadline: N/A
Degrees offered: master's, DNP
In-state tuition: full time: $5,551; part time: $395/credit hour (master's); full time: $5,551; part time: $395/credit hour (DNP)
Out-of-state tuition: full time: $18,115 (master's); full time: $18,115 (DNP)
Room/board/expenses: $7,100 (master's); $7,100 (DNP)
Full-time enrollment: 19 (master's)
men: 0%; women: 100%;
minorities: 21%; international: 0%
Part-time enrollment: 119 (master's); 31 (DNP)
men: 13%; women: 87%;
minorities: 19%; international: 0%
Acceptance rate (master's): 97%
Acceptance rate (DNP): 100%
Specialties offered: education, nurse practitioner

Southern University and A&M College[1]
P.O. Box 11784
Baton Rouge, LA 70813
Public
Admissions: N/A
Financial aid: N/A
Tuition: N/A
Room/board/expenses: N/A
Enrollment: N/A

University of Louisiana-Lafayette
411 E Saint Mary Boulevard
Lafayette, LA 70503
www.louisiana.edu/
Public
Admissions: (337) 482-6965
Email: gradschool@louisiana.edu
Financial aid: (337) 482-6506
Application deadline: 06/30
Degrees offered: master's, DNP
In-state tuition: full time: $5,010; part time: $408/credit hour (master's); full time: $5,010; part time: $408/credit hour (DNP)
Out-of-state tuition: full time: $17,410 (master's); full time: $17,410 (DNP)
Room/board/expenses: $8,566 (master's)
Full-time enrollment: 25 (master's); 7 (DNP)
men: 6%; women: 94%;
minorities: 22%; international: 0%
Part-time enrollment: 97 (master's); 11 (DNP)
men: 18%; women: 82%;
minorities: 11%; international: 0%
Acceptance rate (master's): 49%
Acceptance rate (DNP): 33%
Specialties offered: education, nurse practitioner, nurse practitioner: family, nurse practitioner: psychiatric-mental health, across the lifespan

MAINE

Husson University
1 College Circle
Bangor, ME 4401
www.husson.edu/school-of-nursing
Private
Admissions: (207) 941-7166
Email: johnsont@husson.edu
Financial aid: (207) 941-7156
Application deadline: 06/30
Degrees offered: master's
Tuition: full time: $531/credit hour; part time: $531/credit hour
Room/board/expenses: $9,304
Full-time enrollment: 27
men: 4%; women: 96%;
minorities: 7%; international: 0%
Part-time enrollment: 3
men: 0%; women: 100%;
minorities: 0%; international: 0%
Acceptance rate (master's): 79%
Specialties offered: education, nurse practitioner, nurse practitioner: family, nurse practitioner: psychiatric-mental health, across the lifespan

St. Joseph's College[1]
278 Whites Bridge Road
Standish, ME 04084-5263
Private
Admissions: N/A
Financial aid: N/A
Tuition: N/A
Room/board/expenses: N/A
Enrollment: N/A

University of Maine
5724 Dunn Hall
Orono, ME 04469-5724
www.umaine.edu/nursing/
Public
Admissions: (207) 581-3291
Email: graduate@maine.edu
Financial aid: (207) 581-1324
Application deadline: N/A
Degrees offered: master's
In-state tuition: full time: $418/credit hour; part time: $418/credit hour
Out-of-state tuition: full time: $1,310/credit hour
Room/board/expenses: $11,360
Full-time enrollment: 22
men: 5%; women: 95%;
minorities: 9%; international: 9%
Part-time enrollment: 3
men: 33%; women: 67%;
minorities: 0%; international: 0%
Acceptance rate (master's): 100%
Specialties offered: education, nurse practitioner, nurse practitioner: pediatric primary care

University of Southern Maine
96 Falmouth Street
Portland, ME 04104-9300
Public
Admissions: N/A
Financial aid: N/A
Application deadline: N/A
Degrees offered: master's, DNP
In-state tuition: full time: N/A; part time: N/A
Out-of-state tuition: full time: N/A
Room/board/expenses: N/A
Full-time enrollment: 120 (master's)
men: N/A; women: N/A; minorities: 12%; international: N/A
Part-time enrollment: 77 (master's); 4 (DNP)
men: N/A; women: N/A; minorities: 14%; international: N/A
Acceptance rate (master's): N/A
Acceptance rate (DNP): N/A
Specialties offered: education, nurse practitioner, nurse practitioner: adult-gerontology primary care, nurse practitioner: family, nurse practitioner: psychiatric-mental health, across the lifespan

MARYLAND

Bowie State University
14000 Jericho Park Road
Bowie, MD 20715-9465
Public
Admissions: (301) 860-3415
Email: ddavis@bowiestate.edu
Financial aid: (301) 860-3549
Application deadline: N/A
Degrees offered: master's
In-state tuition: full time: $8,928; part time: $6,696
Out-of-state tuition: full time: $16,176
Room/board/expenses: $12,760
Full-time enrollment: 72
men: 13%; women: 88%;
minorities: 21%; international: 7%
Part-time enrollment: 95
men: 7%; women: 93%;
minorities: 22%; international: 14%
Acceptance rate (master's): N/A
Specialties offered: N/A

Coppin State University (Fuld)[1]
2500 W. North Avenue
Baltimore, MD 21216-3698
Public
Admissions: N/A
Financial aid: N/A
Tuition: N/A
Room/board/expenses: N/A
Enrollment: N/A

Johns Hopkins University
525 N. Wolfe Street
Baltimore, MD 21205-2100
nursing.jhu.edu
Private
Admissions: (410) 955-7548
Email: jhuson@jhu.edu
Financial aid: (410) 955-9840
Application deadline: 01/01
Degrees offered: master's, Ph.D., DNP
Tuition: full time: $29,020; part time: $1,451/credit hour (master's); full time: $40,626; part time: $2,257/credit hour (Ph.D.); full time: $34,656; part time: $1,444/credit hour (DNP)
Room/board/expenses: N/A
Full-time enrollment: 69 (master's); 31 (Ph.D.); 15 (DNP)
men: 4%; women: 96%;
minorities: 31%; international: 13%
Part-time enrollment: 209 (master's); 3 (Ph.D.); 25 (DNP)
men: 5%; women: 95%;
minorities: 27%; international: 0%
Acceptance rate (master's): 50%
Acceptance rate (Ph.D.): 39%
Acceptance rate (DNP): 54%
Specialties offered: clinical nurse specialist, community health/public health, nurse practitioner: adult-gerontology acute care, nurse practitioner: adult-gerontology primary care, nurse practitioner: family, nurse practitioner: pediatric primary care, nurse practitioner: psychiatric-mental health, across the lifespan

Notre Dame of Maryland University[1]
4701 North Charles Street
Baltimore, MD 21210
Private
Admissions: N/A
Financial aid: N/A
Tuition: N/A
Room/board/expenses: N/A
Enrollment: N/A

Salisbury University
1101 Camden Avenue
Salisbury, MD 21801-2195
www.salisbury.edu/nursing/welcome
Public
Admissions: (410) 543-6161
Email: admissions@salisbury.edu
Financial aid: (410) 543-6165
Application deadline: 04/15
Degrees offered: master's, DNP
In-state tuition: full time: N/A; part time: $608/credit hour (master's); full time: N/A; part time: $608/credit hour (DNP)
Out-of-state tuition: full time: N/A
Room/board/expenses: N/A
Full-time enrollment: 2 (master's); 12 (DNP)
men: 21%; women: 79%;
minorities: 29%; international: 0%

Part-time enrollment: 10 (master's);
9 (DNP)
men: 0%; **women:** 100%;
minorities: 37%; **international:** 0%
Acceptance rate (master's): N/A
Acceptance rate (DNP): 57%
Specialties offered: education,
health management & policy
health care systems, nurse
practitioner, nurse practitioner:
family

Stevenson University

100 Campus Circle
Owings Mills, MD 21117
www.stevenson.edu/
graduate-professional-studies/
graduate-programs/nursing/
Private
Admissions: (443) 352-4030
Email: www.stevenson.edu/
admissions-aid/
Financial aid: (443) 334-3200
Application deadline: N/A
Degrees offered: master's
Tuition: full time: $610/credit hour;
part time: $610/credit hour
Room/board/expenses: N/A
Full-time enrollment:
men: N/A; **women:** N/A; **minorities:**
N/A; **international:** N/A
Part-time enrollment: 151
men: 5%; **women:** 95%;
minorities: 38%; **international:** 0%
Acceptance rate (master's): 69%
Specialties offered: administration,
education, other majors

Towson University[1]

8000 York Road
Towson, MD 21252
Public
Admissions: N/A
Financial aid: N/A
Tuition: N/A
Room/board/expenses: N/A
Enrollment: N/A

Uniformed Services University of the Health Sciences

4301 Jones Bridge Road
Bethesda, MD 20814
www.usuhs.edu/gsn/index.html
Public
Admissions: (301) 295-1055
Financial aid: N/A
Application deadline: 12/31
Degrees offered: master's, Ph.D.,
DNP
In-state tuition: full time: N/A; part
time: N/A
Out-of-state tuition: full time: N/A
Room/board/expenses: N/A
Full-time enrollment: 28 (master's);
14 (Ph.D.); 131 (DNP)
men: 48%; **women:** 52%;
minorities: 25%; **international:** 0%
Part-time enrollment: 8 (Ph.D.)
men: 38%; **women:** 63%;
minorities: 25%; **international:** 0%
Acceptance rate (master's): 100%
Acceptance rate (Ph.D.): 100%
Acceptance rate (DNP): 89%
Specialties offered: clinical nurse
specialist, nurse anesthesia,
nurse practitioner, nurse
practitioner: psychiatric-mental
health, across the lifespan,
research, other majors

University of Maryland-Baltimore

Suite 516
Baltimore, MD 21201-1579
www.nursing.umaryland.edu
Public
Admissions: (410) 706-0501
Email: admissions@
son.umaryland.edu
Financial aid: (410) 706-7347
Application deadline: N/A
Degrees offered: master's, Ph.D.,
DNP
In-state tuition: full time: $641/
credit hour; part time: $641/credit
hour (master's); full time: $662/
credit hour; part time: $662/
credit hour (Ph.D.); full time: $662/
credit hour; part time: $662/credit
hour (DNP)
Out-of-state tuition: full time:
$1,178/credit hour (master's); full
time: $1,178/credit hour (Ph.D.);
full time: $1,178/credit hour (DNP)
Room/board/expenses: N/A
Full-time enrollment: 315
(master's); 21 (Ph.D.); 41 (DNP)
men: 14%; **women:** 86%;
minorities: 37%; **international:** 4%
Part-time enrollment: 404
(master's); 34 (Ph.D.); 146 (DNP)
men: 7%; **women:** 93%;
minorities: 33%; **international:** 1%
Acceptance rate (master's): 53%
Acceptance rate (Ph.D.): 48%
Acceptance rate (DNP): 40%
Specialties offered: clinical nurse
leader, clinical nurse specialist,
community health/public health,
education, informatics, nurse
anesthesia, nurse practitioner,
nurse practitioner: adult-
gerontology acute care, nurse
practitioner: adult-gerontology
primary care, nurse practitioner:
adult, nurse practitioner: family,
nurse practitioner: pediatric
primary care, nurse practitioner:
psychiatric-mental health,
across the lifespan, research,
school nursing, combined
nurse practitioner/clinical nurse
specialist

MASSACHUSETTS

American International College[1]

1000 State Street
Springfield, MA 01109
Private
Admissions: N/A
Financial aid: N/A
Tuition: N/A
Room/board/expenses: N/A
Enrollment: N/A

Boston College

Cushing Hall
Chestnut Hill, MA 02467
www.bc.edu
Private
Admissions: (617) 552-2613
Email: kathy.hutchinson@bc.edu
Financial aid: (617) 552-2613
Application deadline: 12/01
Degrees offered: master's, Ph.D.
Tuition: full time: $25,200; part
time: $7,200 (master's); full time:
$24,000; part time: $7,200 (Ph.D.)
Room/board/expenses: $11,300
(master's); $11,300 (Ph.D.)
Full-time enrollment: 163
(master's); 22 (Ph.D.);
men: 10%; **women:** 90%;
minorities: 10%; **international:** 2%

Part-time enrollment: 64
(master's); 2 (Ph.D.)
men: 15%; **women:** 85%;
minorities: 20%; **international:** 5%
Acceptance rate (master's): 58%
Acceptance rate (Ph.D.): 75%
Specialties offered: clinical nurse
specialist, forensic nursing,
nurse anesthesia, nurse
practitioner, nurse practitioner:
adult-gerontology primary
care, nurse practitioner: family,
nurse practitioner: pediatric
primary care, nurse practitioner:
psychiatric-mental health, across
the lifespan, other majors

Curry College[1]

1071 Blue Hill Avenue
Milton, MA 02186
Private
Admissions: N/A
Financial aid: N/A
Tuition: N/A
Room/board/expenses: N/A
Enrollment: N/A

Elms College[1]

291 Springfield Street
Chicopee, MA 01013
Private
Admissions: N/A
Financial aid: N/A
Tuition: N/A
Room/board/expenses: N/A
Enrollment: N/A

Emmanuel College[1]

400 The Fenway
Boston, MA 02115
Private
Admissions: N/A
Financial aid: N/A
Tuition: N/A
Room/board/expenses: N/A
Enrollment: N/A

Endicott College[1]

376 Hale Street
Beverly, MA 01915
Private
Admissions: N/A
Financial aid: N/A
Tuition: N/A
Room/board/expenses: N/A
Enrollment: N/A

Fitchburg State University

160 Pearl Street
Fitchburg, MA 01420-2697
Public
Admissions: (800) 705-9692
Email:
admissions@fitchburgsatte.edu
Financial aid: (978) 665-3156
Application deadline: N/A
Degrees offered: master's
In-state tuition: full time: $167/
credit hour; part time: $167/
credit hour
Out-of-state tuition: full time: $167/
credit hour
Room/board/expenses: N/A
Full-time enrollment:
men: N/A; **women:** N/A; **minorities:**
N/A; **international:** N/A
Part-time enrollment: 26
men: 0%; **women:** 100%;
minorities: 4%; **international:** 0%
Acceptance rate (master's): 33%
nursing

Framingham State University[1]

100 State Street
Framingham, MA 01701
Public
Admissions: N/A
Financial aid: N/A
Tuition: N/A
Room/board/expenses: N/A
Enrollment: N/A

MCPHS University[1]

179 Longwood Avenue
Boston, MA 02115
www.mcphs.edu/academics/
schools/school%20of%20nursing
Private
Admissions: N/A
Financial aid: N/A
Tuition: N/A
Room/board/expenses: N/A
Enrollment: N/A

MGH Institute of Health Professions

36 First Avenue
Boston, MA 02129-4557
www.mghihp.edu/nursing
Private
Admissions: (617) 726-3177
Email: admissions@mghihp.edu
Financial aid: (617) 726-9549
Application deadline: 01/01
Degrees offered: master's, DNP
Tuition: full time: $1,136/credit
hour; part time: $1,136/credit hour
(master's); full time: $1,136/credit
hour; part time: $1,136/credit
hour (DNP)
Room/board/expenses: N/A
Full-time enrollment: 321
(master's); 4 (DNP)
men: 14%; **women:** 86%;
minorities: 20%; **international:** 1%
Part-time enrollment: 21 (master's);
41 (DNP)
men: 11%; **women:** 89%;
minorities: 8%; **international:** 0%
Acceptance rate (master's): 51%
Acceptance rate (DNP): 53%
Specialties offered: nurse
practitioner, nurse practitioner:
adult-gerontology acute care,
nurse practitioner: adult-
gerontology primary care,
nurse practitioner: family,
nurse practitioner: pediatric
primary care, nurse practitioner:
psychiatric-mental health, across
the lifespan

Northeastern University[1]

123 Behrakis Health Sciences
Center
Boston, MA 2115
Private
Admissions: N/A
Financial aid: N/A
Tuition: N/A
Room/board/expenses: N/A
Enrollment: N/A

Regis College[1]

235 Wellesley Street
Weston, MA 2493
Private
Admissions: N/A
Financial aid: N/A
Tuition: N/A
Room/board/expenses: N/A
Enrollment: N/A

Salem State University- South Campus[1]

352 Lafayette Street
Salem, MA 1970
Public
Admissions: N/A
Financial aid: N/A
Tuition: N/A
Room/board/expenses: N/A
Enrollment: N/A

Simmons College

300 The Fenway
Boston, MA 02115
www.simmons.edu/snhs
Private
Admissions: (617) 521-2651
Email: snhs@simmons.edu
Financial aid: (617) 521-2001
Application deadline: 12/01
Degrees offered: master's, DNP
Tuition: full time: $1,246/credit
hour; part time: $1,246/credit hour
(master's); full time: $1,234/credit
hour; part time: $1,234/credit
hour (DNP)
Room/board/expenses: N/A
Full-time enrollment: 94 (master's)
men: 4%; **women:** 96%;
minorities: 31%; **international:** 0%
Part-time enrollment: 141
(master's); 12 (DNP)
men: 6%; **women:** 94%;
minorities: 23%; **international:** 0%
Acceptance rate (master's): 75%
Acceptance rate (DNP): N/A
Specialties offered: nurse
practitioner, nurse practitioner:
family

University of Massachusetts- Amherst

Arnold House
Amherst, MA 01003-9304
www.umass.edu/nursing
Public
Admissions: (413) 545-0722
Email: gradadm@grad.umass.edu
Financial aid: (413) 545-0801
Application deadline: 12/15
Degrees offered: master's, Ph.D.,
DNP
In-state tuition: full time: $750/
credit hour; part time: $750/
credit hour (master's); full time:
$110/credit hour; part time: $110/
credit hour (Ph.D.); full time: $750/
credit hour; part time: $750/credit
hour (DNP)
Out-of-state tuition: full time: $750/
credit hour (master's); full time:
$414/credit hour (Ph.D.); full time:
$750/credit hour (DNP)
Room/board/expenses: $3,920
(Ph.D.)
Full-time enrollment: 2 (master's);
23 (Ph.D.); 67 (DNP)
men: N/A; **women:** N/A; **minorities:**
27%; **international:** 12%
Part-time enrollment: 51 (master's);
36 (Ph.D.); 146 (DNP)
men: N/A; **women:** N/A; **minorities:**
29%; **international:** 6%
Acceptance rate (master's): 84%
Acceptance rate (Ph.D.): 73%
Acceptance rate (DNP): 78%
Specialties offered: clinical nurse
leader, community health/public
health, nurse practitioner, nurse
practitioner: adult-gerontology
primary care, nurse practitioner:
family, nurse practitioner:
psychiatric-mental health, across
the lifespan, research

University of Massachusetts-Boston

100 Morrissey Boulevard
Boston, MA 02125-3393
www.umb.edu/academics/cnhs
Public
Admissions: (617) 287-6400
Email: bos.gadm.umb.edu
Financial aid: (617) 287-6300
Application deadline: 03/01
Degrees offered: master's, Ph.D., DNP
In-state tuition: full time: $15,038; part time: $626/credit hour (master's); full time: $15,038; part time: $626/credit hour (Ph.D.); full time: $15,038; part time: $626/credit hour (DNP)
Out-of-state tuition: full time: $29,112 (master's); full time: $29,112 (Ph.D.); full time: $29,112 (DNP)
Room/board/expenses: N/A
Full-time enrollment: 42 (master's); 15 (Ph.D.)
men: 18%; women: 82%; minorities: 25%; international: 16%
Part-time enrollment: 134 (master's); 25 (Ph.D.); 43 (DNP)
men: 8%; women: 92%; minorities: 22%; international: 1%
Acceptance rate (master's): 60%
Acceptance rate (Ph.D.): 55%
Acceptance rate (DNP): 90%
Specialties offered: clinical nurse specialist, nurse practitioner: adult-gerontology primary care, nurse practitioner: family

University of Massachusetts-Dartmouth

285 Old Westport Road
Dion Building
North Dartmouth, MA 02747-2300
www.umassd.edu/nursing
Public
Admissions: (508) 999-8604
Email: graduate@umassd.edu
Financial aid: (508) 999-8643
Application deadline: 03/15
Degrees offered: master's, Ph.D., DNP
In-state tuition: full time: $2,071; part time: $86/credit hour (master's); full time: $2,071; part time: $86/credit hour (Ph.D.); full time: $2,071; part time: $86/credit hour (DNP)
Out-of-state tuition: full time: $8,099 (master's); full time: $8,099 (Ph.D.); full time: $8,099 (DNP)
Room/board/expenses: $11,069 (master's); $11,069 (Ph.D.); $11,069 (DNP)
Full-time enrollment: 1 (Ph.D.); men: 0%; women: 100%; minorities: 0%; international: 0%
Part-time enrollment: 30 (master's); 32 (Ph.D.); 53 (DNP)
men: 6%; women: 94%; minorities: 10%; international: 0%
Acceptance rate (master's): 100%
Acceptance rate (Ph.D.): 78%
Acceptance rate (DNP): 91%
Specialties offered: clinical nurse specialist, community health/public health, generalist, nurse practitioner: adult-gerontology primary care

University of Massachusetts-Lowell[1]

3 Solomont Way
Lowell, MA 1854-5126
Public
Admissions: N/A
Financial aid: N/A
Tuition: N/A
Room/board/expenses: N/A
Enrollment: N/A

University of Massachusetts-Worcester[1]

55 Lake Avenue N
Worcester, MA 01655
Public
Admissions: N/A
Financial aid: N/A
Tuition: N/A
Room/board/expenses: N/A
Enrollment: N/A

Worcester State University

486 Chandler Street
Worcester, MA 01602
www.worcester.edu/Graduate-Programs
Public
Admissions: (508) 929-8127
Email: gradadmissions@worcester.edu
Financial aid: (508) 929-8056
Application deadline: 06/15
Degrees offered: master's
In-state tuition: full time: $150/credit hour; part time: $150/credit hour
Out-of-state tuition: full time: $150/credit hour
Room/board/expenses: N/A
Full-time enrollment: 2
men: 0%; women: 100%; minorities: 0%; international: 100%
Part-time enrollment: 112
men: 8%; women: 92%; minorities: 18%; international: 0%
Acceptance rate (master's): 63%
Specialties offered: community health/public health, education

MICHIGAN

Andrews University[1]

Marsh Hall
Berrien Springs, MI 49103-0640
Private
Admissions: N/A
Financial aid: N/A
Tuition: N/A
Room/board/expenses: N/A
Enrollment: N/A

Eastern Michigan University[1]

3111 Marshall Building
Ypsilanti, MI 48197
Public
Admissions: N/A
Financial aid: N/A
Tuition: N/A
Room/board/expenses: N/A
Enrollment: N/A

Ferris State University

200 Ferris Drive
Big Rapids, MI 49307
www.ferris.edu/HTMLS/colleges/alliedhe/Nursing/homepage.htm
Public
Admissions: (800) 433-7747
Financial aid: (231) 591-2110
Application deadline: N/A
Degrees offered: master's
In-state tuition: full time: $522/credit hour; part time: $522/credit hour
Out-of-state tuition: full time: $768/credit hour
Room/board/expenses: N/A
Full-time enrollment:
men: N/A; women: N/A; minorities: N/A; international: N/A
Part-time enrollment: 98
men: 13%; women: 87%; minorities: 10%; international: 0%
Acceptance rate (master's): 83%
Specialties offered: administration, education, informatics

Grand Valley State University

301 Michigan Street NE
Grand Rapids, MI 49503-3314
www.gvsu/kcon
Public
Admissions: (616) 331-2025
Email: admissions@gvsu.edu
Financial aid: (616) 331-3234
Application deadline: N/A
Degrees offered: master's, DNP
In-state tuition: full time: $614/credit hour; part time: $614/credit hour (master's); full time: $690/credit hour; part time: $690/credit hour (DNP)
Out-of-state tuition: full time: $804/credit hour (master's); full time: $911/credit hour (DNP)
Room/board/expenses: $8,200 (master's); $8,200 (Ph.D.); $8,200 (DNP)
Full-time enrollment: 7 (master's); 48 (DNP)
men: 15%; women: 85%; minorities: 7%; international: 2%
Part-time enrollment: 7 (master's); 49 (DNP)
men: 11%; women: 89%; minorities: 14%; international: 0%
Acceptance rate (master's): N/A
Acceptance rate (DNP): 95%
Specialties offered: administration, clinical nurse leader, nurse practitioner: adult-gerontology primary care, nurse practitioner: adult, nurse practitioner: pediatric primary care

Madonna University

36600 Schoolcraft Road
Livonia, MI 48150-1173
www.madonna.edu/academics/departments/nursing-graduate/
Private
Admissions: (734) 432-5667
Email: grad@madonna.edu
Financial aid: (734) 432-5663
Application deadline: 01/02
Degrees offered: master's, DNP
Tuition: full time: $640/credit hour; part time: $640/credit hour (master's); full time: $640/credit hour; part time: $640/credit hour (DNP)
Room/board/expenses: $8,610 (master's); $8,610 (DNP)

Michigan State University

A117 Life Sciences Building
East Lansing, MI 48824-1317
nursing.msu.edu
Public
Admissions: (517) 353-4827
Email: nurse@hc.msu.edu
Financial aid: (517) 353-5940
Application deadline: N/A
Degrees offered: master's, Ph.D., DNP
In-state tuition: full time: $646/credit hour; part time: $646/credit hour (master's); full time: $646/credit hour; full time: $646/credit hour (Ph.D.); full time: $646/credit hour; part time: $646/credit hour (DNP)
Out-of-state tuition: full time: $1,269/credit hour (master's); full time: $1,269/credit hour (Ph.D.); full time: $1,269/credit hour (DNP)
Room/board/expenses: $10,062 (master's); $10,062 (Ph.D.); $10,062 (DNP)
Full-time enrollment: 65 (master's); 11 (Ph.D.); 11 (DNP)
men: 13%; women: 87%; minorities: 10%; international: 3%
Part-time enrollment: 110 (master's); 3 (Ph.D.)
men: 9%; women: 91%; minorities: 11%; international: 0%
Acceptance rate (master's): 39%
Acceptance rate (Ph.D.): 100%
Acceptance rate (DNP): 100%
Specialties offered: clinical nurse specialist, nurse anesthesia, nurse practitioner, nurse practitioner: adult-gerontology primary care, nurse practitioner: family

Northern Michigan University[1]

2301 New Science Facility
Marquette, MI 49855
Public
Admissions: N/A
Financial aid: N/A
Tuition: N/A
Room/board/expenses: N/A
Enrollment: N/A

Oakland University

428 O'Dowd Hall
Rochester, MI 48309-4401
www.oakland.edu/nursing
Public
Admissions: (248) 370-3167
Email: gradmail@oakland.edu
Financial aid: (248) 370-2550
Application deadline: N/A
Degrees offered: master's, DNP
In-state tuition: full time: $15,294; part time: $637/credit hour (master's); full time: $15,294; part time: $637/credit hour (DNP)

Full-time enrollment: 5 (master's); 4 (DNP)
men: 11%; women: 89%; minorities: 22%; international: 22%
Part-time enrollment: 252 (master's); 37 (DNP)
men: 11%; women: 89%; minorities: 19%; international: 2%
Acceptance rate (master's): 45%
Acceptance rate (DNP): 61%
Specialties offered: administration, education, nurse practitioner, nurse practitioner: adult-gerontology acute care, nurse practitioner: adult-gerontology primary care, dual majors

Saginaw Valley State University

7400 Bay Road
University Center, MI 48710
www.svsu.edu/nursing/
Public
Admissions: (989) 964-6096
Email: gradadm@svsu.edu
Financial aid: (989) 964-4103
Application deadline: N/A
Degrees offered: master's, DNP
In-state tuition: full time: $498/credit hour; part time: $498/credit hour (master's); full time: $547/credit hour; part time: $547/credit hour (DNP)
Out-of-state tuition: full time: $949/credit hour (master's); full time: $1,004/credit hour (DNP)
Room/board/expenses: N/A
Full-time enrollment: 1 (master's); 4 (DNP)
men: 0%; women: 100%; minorities: 0%; international: 0%
Part-time enrollment: 53 (master's); 31 (DNP)
men: 17%; women: 83%; minorities: 6%; international: 1%
Acceptance rate (master's): 77%
Acceptance rate (DNP): 100%
Specialties offered: administration, clinical nurse leader, education, nurse practitioner: family

Spring Arbor University[1]

106 E. Main Street
Spring Arbor, MI 49283
Private
Admissions: N/A
Financial aid: N/A
Tuition: N/A
Room/board/expenses: N/A
Enrollment: N/A

University of Detroit Mercy

4001 W. McNichols Road
Detroit, MI 48221-3038
healthprofessions.udmercy.edu/programs/nursing/index.htm
Private
Admissions: (313) 993-1245
Email: admissions@udmercy.edu
Financial aid: (313) 993-3350
Application deadline: 02/15
Degrees offered: master's, DNP

Out-of-state tuition: full time: $24,648 (master's); full time: $24,648 (DNP)
Room/board/expenses: $8,895 (master's); $8,895 (DNP)
Full-time enrollment: 107 (master's); 3 (DNP)
men: 24%; women: 76%; minorities: 8%; international: 3%
Part-time enrollment: 80 (master's); 31 (DNP)
men: 8%; women: 92%; minorities: 18%; international: 1%
Acceptance rate (master's): 17%
Acceptance rate (DNP): 77%
Specialties offered: nurse anesthesia, nurse practitioner, nurse practitioner: adult-gerontology acute care, nurse practitioner: adult-gerontology primary care, nurse practitioner: adult, nurse practitioner: family, nurse practitioner: pediatric primary care

Tuition: full time: $894/credit hour; part time: $894/credit hour (master's); full time: $894/credit hour; part time: $894/credit hour (DNP)
Room/board/expenses: N/A
Full-time enrollment: 15 (master's) men: 27%; women: 73%; minorities: 20%; international: 0%
Part-time enrollment: 120 (master's); 15 (DNP) men: 10%; women: 90%; minorities: 30%; international: 1%
Acceptance rate (master's): 37%
Acceptance rate (DNP): 80%
Specialties offered: clinical nurse leader, clinical nurse specialist, education, health management & policy health care systems, nurse anesthesia, nurse practitioner, nurse practitioner: family

University of Michigan-Ann Arbor

400 N. Ingalls
Ann Arbor, MI 48109-0482
nursing.umich.edu/
Public
Admissions: (734) 763-5237
Email: umsn-mastersadmissions@med.umich.edu
Financial aid: (734) 764-6690
Application deadline: 03/01
Degrees offered: master's, Ph.D., DNP
In-state tuition: full time: $19,980; part time: $1,110/credit hour (master's); full time: $19,980; part time: $1,110/credit hour (Ph.D.); full time: $19,980; part time: $1,110/credit hour (DNP)
Out-of-state tuition: full time: $41,130 (master's); full time: $41,130 (Ph.D.); full time: $41,130 (DNP)
Room/board/expenses: $13,504 (master's); $13,504 (Ph.D.); $13,504 (DNP)
Full-time enrollment: 129 (master's); 37 (Ph.D.); 6 (DNP) men: 13%; women: 87%; minorities: 11%; international: 9%
Part-time enrollment: 159 (master's); 6 (Ph.D.); 21 (DNP) men: 7%; women: 93%; minorities: 12%; international: 1%
Acceptance rate (master's): 68%
Acceptance rate (Ph.D.): 63%
Acceptance rate (DNP): 92%
Specialties offered: clinical nurse specialist, health management & policy health care systems, informatics, nurse-midwifery, nurse practitioner: adult-gerontology acute care, nurse practitioner: adult-gerontology primary care, nurse practitioner: adult, nurse practitioner: family, nurse practitioner: pediatric primary care, research, combined nurse practitioner/clinical nurse specialist, dual majors

University of Michigan-Flint

303 E. Kearsley Street
Flint, MI 48502-1950
www.umflint.edu/nursing
Public
Admissions: (810) 762-3171
Email: graduate@umflint.edu
Financial aid: (810) 762-3444
Application deadline: 08/01
Degrees offered: master's, DNP

In-state tuition: full time: $9,261; part time: $515/credit hour (master's); full time: $9,261; part time: $515/credit hour (DNP)
Out-of-state tuition: full time: $13,878 (master's); full time: $13,878 (DNP)
Room/board/expenses: $8,706 (master's); $8,706 (DNP)
Full-time enrollment: 15 (master's); 124 (DNP) men: 11%; women: 89%; minorities: 26%; international: 1%
Part-time enrollment: 1 (master's); 62 (DNP) men: 11%; women: 89%; minorities: 24%; international: 2%
Acceptance rate (master's): N/A
Acceptance rate (DNP): 78%
Specialties offered: nurse anesthesia, nurse practitioner, nurse practitioner: adult-gerontology acute care, nurse practitioner: adult-gerontology primary care, nurse practitioner: family, nurse practitioner: psychiatric-mental health, across the lifespan

Wayne State University

5557 Cass Avenue
Detroit, MI 48202
nursing.wayne.edu/
Public
Admissions: (313) 577-8141
Email: gradadmissions@wayne.edu
Financial aid: (313) 577-2100
Application deadline: N/A
Degrees offered: master's, Ph.D., DNP
In-state tuition: full time: $1,040/credit hour; part time: $1,040/credit hour (master's); full time: $1,040/credit hour; part time: $1,040/credit hour (Ph.D.); full time: $1,040/credit hour; part time: $1,040/credit hour (DNP)
Out-of-state tuition: full time: $1,698/credit hour (master's); full time: $1,698/credit hour (Ph.D.); full time: $1,698/credit hour (DNP)
Room/board/expenses: $9,133 (master's); $9,133 (Ph.D.); $9,133 (DNP)
Full-time enrollment: 59 (master's); 18 (Ph.D.); 55 (DNP) men: 7%; women: 93%; minorities: 24%; international: 12%
Part-time enrollment: 135 (master's); 5 (Ph.D.); 47 (DNP) men: 7%; women: 93%; minorities: 32%; international: 2%
Acceptance rate (master's): 40%
Acceptance rate (Ph.D.): 55%
Acceptance rate (DNP): 53%
Specialties offered: clinical nurse specialist, community health/public health, education, nurse-midwifery, nurse practitioner, nurse practitioner: adult-gerontology primary care, nurse practitioner: adult, nurse practitioner: family, nurse practitioner: pediatric primary care, nurse practitioner: psychiatric-mental health, across the lifespan, research, other majors, combined nurse practitioner/clinical nurse specialist

Western Michigan University

1903 West Michigan Avenue
Kalamazoo, MI 49008-5200
www.wmich.edu/nursing/
Public
Admissions: N/A
Email: ask-wmu@wmich.edu
Financial aid: (269) 387-6000
Application deadline: N/A
Degrees offered: master's
In-state tuition: full time: $514/credit hour; part time: $514/credit hour
Out-of-state tuition: full time: $1,089/credit hour
Room/board/expenses: $8,943
Full-time enrollment: 12 men: 8%; women: 92%; minorities: 17%; international: 0%
Part-time enrollment: 3 men: 0%; women: 100%; minorities: 0%; international: 0%
Acceptance rate (master's): N/A
Specialties offered: clinical nurse leader, education

MINNESOTA

Augsburg College[1]

2211 Riverside Avenue S
Minneapolis, MN 55454
Private
Admissions: N/A
Financial aid: N/A
Tuition: N/A
Room/board/expenses: N/A
Enrollment: N/A

Bethel University[1]

3900 Bethel Drive
St. Paul, MN 55112
Private
Admissions: N/A
Financial aid: N/A
Tuition: N/A
Room/board/expenses: N/A
Enrollment: N/A

Capella University[1]

225 South 6th Street
9th Floor
Minneapolis, MN 55402
Private
Admissions: N/A
Financial aid: N/A
Tuition: N/A
Room/board/expenses: N/A
Enrollment: N/A

College of St. Scholastica

1200 Kenwood Avenue
Duluth, MN 55811-4199
www.css.edu/academics/school-of-nursing.html
Private
Admissions: (218) 733-2240
Email: geoadmin@css.edu
Financial aid: (218) 723-6000
Application deadline: 12/15
Degrees offered: master's, DNP
Tuition: full time: $785/credit hour; part time: $785/credit hour (master's); full time: $785/credit hour; part time: $785/credit hour (DNP)
Room/board/expenses: $16,116 (master's); $16,116 (DNP)
Full-time enrollment: 39 (master's); 64 (DNP) men: 13%; women: 87%; minorities: 10%; international: 0%

Part-time enrollment: 29 (master's); 32 (DNP) men: 13%; women: 87%; minorities: 13%; international: 0%
Acceptance rate (master's): 30%
Acceptance rate (DNP): 45%
Specialties offered: informatics, nurse practitioner, nurse practitioner: adult-gerontology primary care, nurse practitioner: family, nurse practitioner: psychiatric-mental health, across the lifespan

Metropolitan State University[1]

730 Hennepin Avenue
Minneapolis, MN 55403-1897
Public
Admissions: N/A
Financial aid: N/A
Tuition: N/A
Room/board/expenses: N/A
Enrollment: N/A

Minnesota State University-Mankato[1]

College of Graduate Studies and Research
Mankato, MN 56001
ahn.mnsu.edu/nursing/
Public
Admissions: N/A
Financial aid: N/A
Tuition: N/A
Room/board/expenses: N/A
Enrollment: N/A

Minnesota State University-Moorhead[1]

202 Murray Commons
Moorhead, MN 56563
Public
Admissions: N/A
Financial aid: N/A
Tuition: N/A
Room/board/expenses: N/A
Enrollment: N/A

St. Catherine University

2004 Randolph Avenue
Mail #F-22
St. Paul, MN 55105-1794
www2.stkate.edu/nursing/home
Private
Admissions: (651) 690-6933
Email: graduate_study@stkate.edu
Financial aid: (651) 690-6607
Application deadline: N/A
Degrees offered: master's, DNP
Tuition: full time: $719/credit hour; part time: $719/credit hour (master's); full time: $911/credit hour; part time: $911/credit hour (DNP)
Room/board/expenses: N/A
Full-time enrollment: 135 (master's); 15 (DNP) men: 5%; women: 95%; minorities: 13%; international: 1%
Part-time enrollment: 6 (master's); 10 (DNP) men: 6%; women: 94%; minorities: 19%; international: 0%
Acceptance rate (master's): 65%
Acceptance rate (DNP): 88%
Specialties offered: education, nurse practitioner, nurse practitioner: adult-gerontology primary care, nurse practitioner: adult, nurse practitioner: pediatric primary care

University of Minnesota-Twin Cities

308 Harvard Street SE
Minneapolis, MN 55455
www.nursing.umn.edu/
Public
Admissions: (612) 625-7980
Email: sonstudentinfo@umn.edu
Financial aid: (612) 626-0302
Application deadline: 12/31
Degrees offered: Ph.D., DNP
In-state tuition: full time: $15,458; part time: $1,288/credit hour (Ph.D.); full time: $927/credit hour; part time: $927/credit hour (DNP)
Out-of-state tuition: full time: $23,680 (Ph.D.); full time: $927/credit hour (DNP)
Room/board/expenses: N/A
Full-time enrollment: 32 (Ph.D.); 284 (DNP) men: N/A; women: N/A; minorities: 11%; international: 1%
Part-time enrollment: 11 (Ph.D.); 50 (DNP) men: N/A; women: N/A; minorities: 18%; international: 2%
Acceptance rate (Ph.D.): 67%
Acceptance rate (DNP): 70%
Specialties offered: administration, clinical nurse specialist, community health/public health, informatics, nurse anesthesia, nurse-midwifery, nurse practitioner, nurse practitioner: adult-gerontology primary care, nurse practitioner: family, nurse practitioner: pediatric primary care, nurse practitioner: psychiatric-mental health, across the lifespan, research, other majors

Walden University[1]

100 Washington Avenue South
Suite 900
Minneapolis, MN 55401
Private
Admissions: N/A
Financial aid: N/A
Tuition: N/A
Room/board/expenses: N/A
Enrollment: N/A

Winona State University-Rochester[1]

859 30th Avenue SE
Rochester, MN 55904
Public
Admissions: N/A
Financial aid: N/A
Tuition: N/A
Room/board/expenses: N/A
Enrollment: N/A

MISSISSIPPI

Alcorn State University[1]

15 Campus Drive
Natchez, MS 39122-8399
Public
Admissions: N/A
Financial aid: N/A
Tuition: N/A
Room/board/expenses: N/A
Enrollment: N/A

Delta State University

PO Box 3343
1003 West Sunflower Road
Cleveland, MS 38733-3343
www.deltastate.edu/
school-of-nursing/
Public
Admissions: (662) 846-4700
Email: grad-info@deltastate.edu
Financial aid: (662) 846-4670
Application deadline: 02/01
Degrees offered: master's, DNP
In-state tuition: full time: $6,012;
part time: $334/credit hour
(master's); full time: $6,012; part
time: $334 (DNP)
Out-of-state tuition: full time:
$6,012 (master's); full time: $6,012
(DNP)
Room/board/expenses: N/A
Full-time enrollment: 27 (master's);
17 (DNP)
men: 20%; women: 80%;
minorities: 25%; international: 0%
Part-time enrollment: 7 (master's);
4 (DNP)
men: 9%; women: 91%; minorities:
55%; international: 0%
Acceptance rate (master's): 100%
Acceptance rate (DNP): 91%
Specialties offered: administration,
education, nurse practitioner,
nurse practitioner: adult-
gerontology primary care,
nurse practitioner: family, nurse
practitioner: psychiatric-mental
health, across the lifespan

Mississippi University for Women

1100 College Street MUW-910
Columbus, MS 39701-5800
www.muw.edu/nslp
Public
Admissions: (662) 329-7106
Email: www.muw.edu/graduates/
admission
Financial aid: (662) 329-7145
Application deadline: 02/01
Degrees offered: master's, DNP
In-state tuition: full time: $5,640;
part time: $314/credit hour
(master's); full time: $5,640; part
time: $314/credit hour (DNP)
Out-of-state tuition: full time:
$15,360 (master's); full time:
$15,360 (DNP)
Room/board/expenses: $6,381
(master's); $6,381 (DNP)
Full-time enrollment: 37 (master's);
3 (DNP)
men: 20%; women: 80%;
minorities: 20%; international: 0%
Part-time enrollment: 6 (master's);
1 (DNP)
men: 14%; women: 86%;
minorities: 71%; international: 0%
Acceptance rate (master's): 51%
Acceptance rate (DNP): 70%
Specialties offered: nurse
practitioner, nurse practitioner:
adult-gerontology acute care,
nurse practitioner: family, nurse
practitioner: psychiatric-mental
health, across the lifespan

University of Mississippi Medical Center[1]

2500 N. State Street
Jackson, MS 39216-4505
Public
Admissions: N/A
Financial aid: N/A
Tuition: N/A
Room/board/expenses: N/A
Enrollment: N/A

University of Southern Mississippi

118 College Drive
PO Box 5095
Hattiesburg, MS 39406-5095
www.usm.edu/nursing
Public
Admissions: (601) 266-4369
Email: Karen.Coats@usm.edu
Financial aid: (601) 266-4813
Application deadline: 03/01
Degrees offered: master's, Ph.D.,
DNP
In-state tuition: full time: $10,470;
part time: $7,566 (master's); full
time: $10,470; part time: $7,566
(Ph.D.); full time: $10,470; part
time: $7,566 (DNP)
Out-of-state tuition: full time:
$19,040 (master's); full time:
$19,040 (Ph.D.); full time: $19,040
(DNP)
Room/board/expenses: $8,719
(master's); $8,719 (Ph.D.); $8,719
(DNP)
Full-time enrollment: 93 (master's);
11 (Ph.D.); 46 (DNP)
men: 23%; women: 77%;
minorities: 17%; international: 0%
Part-time enrollment: 18 (master's);
11 (Ph.D.); 9 (DNP)
men: 18%; women: 82%;
minorities: 34%; international: 0%
Acceptance rate (master's): 64%
Acceptance rate (Ph.D.): 100%
Acceptance rate (DNP): 100%
Specialties offered: nurse
anesthesia, nurse practitioner,
nurse practitioner: adult-
gerontology primary care,
nurse practitioner: family, nurse
practitioner: psychiatric-mental
health, across the lifespan,
research, other majors

William Carey University

498 Tuscan Avenue
Hattiesburg, MS 39401
www.wmcarey.edu/schools/
school-nursing
Private
Admissions: N/A
Financial aid: (601) 318-6486
Application deadline: N/A
Degrees offered: master's, Ph.D.
Tuition: full time: $340/credit
hour; part time: $340/credit hour
(master's); full time: $410/credit
hour; part time: $410/credit hour
(Ph.D.)
Room/board/expenses: $1,440
(master's); $1,440 (Ph.D.)
Full-time enrollment: 48 (master's);
35 (Ph.D.)
men: 2%; women: 98%;
minorities: 43%; international: 0%
Part-time enrollment: 35
(master's); 41 (Ph.D.)
men: 9%; women: 91%; minorities:
49%; international: 0%
Acceptance rate (master's): 96%
Acceptance rate (Ph.D.): 100%
Specialties offered: administration,
case management, education,
generalist, dual majors

MISSOURI

Central Methodist University[1]

411 Central Methodist Square
Fayette, MO 65248
Private
Admissions: N/A
Financial aid: N/A
Tuition: N/A
Room/board/expenses: N/A
Enrollment: N/A

Cox College[1]

1423 N Jefferson Avenue
Springfield, MO 65802
Private
Admissions: N/A
Financial aid: N/A
Tuition: N/A
Room/board/expenses: N/A
Enrollment: N/A

Goldfarb School of Nursing at Barnes-Jewish College[1]

4483 Duncan Avenue
St. Louis, MO 63110
Private
Admissions: N/A
Financial aid: N/A
Tuition: N/A
Room/board/expenses: N/A
Enrollment: N/A

Graceland University[1]

1401 W. Truman Road
Independence, MO 64050-3434
Private
Admissions: N/A
Financial aid: N/A
Tuition: N/A
Room/board/expenses: N/A
Enrollment: N/A

Maryville University of St. Louis

650 Maryville University Drive
St. Louis, MO 63141
www.maryville.edu/hp/nursing/
Private
Admissions: (314) 529-9350
Email: admissions@maryville.edu
Financial aid: (314) 529-9360
Application deadline: N/A
Degrees offered: master's
Tuition: full time: $755/credit hour;
part time: N/A
Room/board/expenses: N/A
Full-time enrollment: 15
men: 13%; women: 87%;
minorities: 13%; international: 13%
Part-time enrollment: 147
men: 7%; women: 93%;
minorities: 13%; international: 0%
Acceptance rate (master's): 83%
Specialties offered: nurse
practitioner, nurse practitioner:
adult, nurse practitioner: family,
nurse practitioner: pediatric
primary care

Missouri Southern State University[1]

Health Sciences Building 243
Joplin, MO 64801
Public
Admissions: N/A
Financial aid: N/A
Tuition: N/A
Room/board/expenses: N/A
Enrollment: N/A

Missouri State University[1]

Professional Building
Suite 300
Springfield, MO 65897
Public
Admissions: N/A
Financial aid: N/A
Tuition: N/A
Room/board/expenses: N/A
Enrollment: N/A

Missouri Western State University[1]

4525 Downs Drive
Murphy Hall, Room 309
St. Joseph, MO 64507
Public
Admissions: N/A
Financial aid: N/A
Tuition: N/A
Room/board/expenses: N/A
Enrollment: N/A

Research College of Nursing[1]

2525 E. Meyer Boulevard
Kansas City, MO 64132
Private
Admissions: N/A
Financial aid: N/A
Tuition: N/A
Room/board/expenses: N/A
Enrollment: N/A

Southeast Missouri State University

1 University Plaza
Cape Girardeau, MO 63701
semo.edu/nursing
Public
Admissions: (573) 651-2590
Email: admissions@semo.edu
Financial aid: (573) 651-2253
Application deadline: 04/01
Degrees offered: master's
In-state tuition: full time: $258/
credit hour; part time: $258/
credit hour
Out-of-state tuition: full time: $482/
credit hour
Room/board/expenses: $8,432
Full-time enrollment: 12
men: 0%; women: 100%;
minorities: 17%; international: 0%
Part-time enrollment: 12
men: 8%; women: 92%;
minorities: 0%; international: 0%
Acceptance rate (master's): 38%
Specialties offered: education,
nurse practitioner, nurse
practitioner: family

St. Louis University

3525 Caroline Mall
St. Louis, MO 63104-1099
nursing.slu.edu
Private
Admissions: (314) 977-2500
Email: www.slu.edu
Financial aid: (314) 977-
Application deadline: N/A
Degrees offered: master's, Ph.D.,
DNP
Tuition: full time: $1,030/credit
hour; part time: $1,030/credit
hour (master's); full time: $1,030/
credit hour; part time: $1,030/
credit hour (Ph.D.); full time:
$1,030/credit hour; part time:
$1,030/credit hour (DNP)
Room/board/expenses: N/A

Full-time enrollment: 166
(master's); 16 (Ph.D.); 4 (DNP)
men: 16%; women: 84%;
minorities: 16%; international: 6%
Part-time enrollment: 270
(master's); 13 (Ph.D.); 32 (DNP)
men: 10%; women: 90%;
minorities: 16%; international: 0%
Acceptance rate (master's): 75%
Acceptance rate (Ph.D.): 83%
Acceptance rate (DNP): 100%
Specialties offered: clinical nurse
leader, nurse practitioner, nurse
practitioner: adult-gerontology
acute care, nurse practitioner:
adult-gerontology primary
care, nurse practitioner: family,
nurse practitioner: pediatric
primary care, nurse practitioner:
psychiatric-mental health, across
the lifespan

University of Central Missouri

UHC 106A
Lee's Summit, MO 64063
www.ucmo.edu/nursing
Public
Admissions: N/A
Financial aid: (660) 543-8266
Application deadline: N/A
Degrees offered: master's
In-state tuition: full time: $276/
credit hour; part time: $276/
credit hour
Out-of-state tuition: full time: $552/
credit hour
Room/board/expenses: $7,828
Full-time enrollment: 3
men: 33%; women: 67%;
minorities: N/A; international: N/A
Part-time enrollment: 137
men: 5%; women: 95%;
minorities: 5%; international: 0%
Acceptance rate (master's): N/A
Specialties offered: education,
nurse practitioner, nurse
practitioner: family

University of Missouri

Columbia, MO 65211
nursing.missouri.edu
Public
Admissions: (573) 882-0277
Email: nursing@missouri.edu
Financial aid: (573) 882-7506
Application deadline: 03/01
Degrees offered: master's, Ph.D.,
DNP
In-state tuition: full time: $422/
credit hour; part time: $422/
credit hour (master's); full time:
$422/credit hour; part time: $422/
credit hour (Ph.D.); full time: $422/
credit hour; part time: $422/credit
hour (DNP)
Out-of-state tuition: full time: $422/
credit hour (master's); full time:
$422/credit hour (Ph.D.); full time:
$422/credit hour (DNP)
Room/board/expenses: N/A
Full-time enrollment: 2 (master's);
18 (Ph.D.); 24 (DNP)
men: 5%; women: 95%;
minorities: 18%; international: 7%
Part-time enrollment: 57
(master's); 25 (Ph.D.); 156 (DNP)
men: 9%; women: 91%; minorities:
8%; international: 0%
Acceptance rate (master's): 83%
Acceptance rate (Ph.D.): 67%
Acceptance rate (DNP): 78%
Specialties offered: administration,
clinical nurse specialist,
education, generalist, nurse
practitioner, nurse practitioner:
family, nurse practitioner:
pediatric primary care, nurse

practitioner: psychiatric-mental health, across the lifespan, research, other majors, combined nurse practitioner/clinical nurse specialist, dual majors

University of Missouri-Kansas City
2404 Charlotte
Kansas City, MO 64108
www.umkc.edu/nursing
Public
Admissions: (816) 235-1111
Email: admit@umkc.edu
Financial aid: (816) 235-1154
Application deadline: 12/15
Degrees offered: master's, Ph.D., DNP
In-state tuition: full time: $343/credit hour; part time: $343/credit hour (master's); full time: $343/credit hour; part time: $343/credit hour (Ph.D.); full time: $343/credit hour; part time: $343/credit hour (DNP)
Out-of-state tuition: full time: $343/credit hour (master's); full time: $343/credit hour (Ph.D.); full time: $343/credit hour (DNP)
Room/board/expenses: N/A
Full-time enrollment: 9 (master's); 4 (Ph.D.); 37 (DNP)
men: 36%; women: 64%; minorities: 16%; international: 0%
Part-time enrollment: 186 (master's); 47 (Ph.D.); 106 (DNP)
men: 8%; women: 92%; minorities: 16%; international: 0%
Acceptance rate (master's): 84%
Acceptance rate (Ph.D.): 84%
Acceptance rate (DNP): 99%
Specialties offered: education, nurse practitioner, nurse practitioner: adult-gerontology primary care, nurse practitioner: family, nurse practitioner: pediatric primary care, nurse practitioner: psychiatric-mental health, across the lifespan, other majors

University of Missouri-St. Louis
1 University Boulevard
St. Louis, MO 63121
www.umsl.edu/divisions/nursing/
Public
Admissions: (314) 516-6066
Financial aid: (314) 516-5526
Application deadline: 02/15
Degrees offered: master's, Ph.D., DNP
In-state tuition: full time: $415/credit hour; part time: $415/credit hour (master's); full time: $415/credit hour; part time: $415/credit hour (Ph.D.); full time: $415/credit hour; part time: $415/credit hour (DNP)
Out-of-state tuition: full time: $1,024/credit hour (master's); full time: $1,024/credit hour (Ph.D.); full time: $1,024/credit hour (DNP)
Room/board/expenses: $11,731 (master's); $11,731 (Ph.D.); $11,731 (DNP)
Full-time enrollment: 1 (Ph.D.); men: 0%; women: 100%; minorities: 100%; international: 100%
Part-time enrollment: 207 (master's); 22 (Ph.D.); 11 (DNP)
men: 3%; women: 97%; minorities: 15%; international: 0%
Acceptance rate (master's): 38%
Acceptance rate (Ph.D.): 100%
Acceptance rate (DNP): 100%

Specialties offered: community health/public health, education, nurse practitioner, nurse practitioner: adult-gerontology primary care, adult, nurse practitioner: family, nurse practitioner: pediatric primary care, nurse practitioner: psychiatric-mental health, across the lifespan, research

Webster University
470 East Lockwood Avenue
St. Louis, MO 63119
www.webster.edu/arts-and-sciences/departments/nursing/index.html
Private
Admissions: (800) 753-6765
Email: admit@webster.edu
Financial aid: (800) 983-4623
Application deadline: N/A
Degrees offered: master's
Tuition: full time: $665/credit hour; part time: $665/credit hour
Room/board/expenses: $10,600
Full-time enrollment: men: N/A; women: N/A; minorities: N/A; international: N/A
Part-time enrollment: 133 men: 3%; women: 97%; minorities: 17%; international: 1%
Acceptance rate (master's): 89%
Specialties offered: education, other majors

MONTANA

Montana State University
PO Box 173560
Bozeman, MT 59717-3560
www.montana.edu/nursing/
Public
Admissions: (406) 994-2452
Email: admissions@montana.edu
Financial aid: (406) 994-2845
Application deadline: 02/15
Degrees offered: master's, DNP
In-state tuition: full time: $267/credit hour; part time: $267/credit hour (master's); full time: $267/credit hour; part time: $267/credit hour (DNP)
Out-of-state tuition: full time: $867/credit hour (master's); full time: $867/credit hour (DNP)
Room/board/expenses: $8,380 (master's); $8,380 (DNP)
Full-time enrollment: 9 (master's); 32 (DNP)
men: N/A; women: N/A; minorities: 7%; international: 0%
Part-time enrollment: 19 (master's); 14 (DNP)
men: N/A; women: N/A; minorities: 3%; international: 0%
Acceptance rate (master's): 100%
Acceptance rate (DNP): 46%
Specialties offered: clinical nurse leader, education, nurse practitioner, nurse practitioner: family, nurse practitioner: psychiatric-mental health, across the lifespan

NEBRASKA

Bryan College of Health Sciences[1]
5035 Everett Street
Lincoln, NE 68506
Private
Admissions: N/A
Financial aid: N/A
Tuition: N/A

Room/board/expenses: N/A
Enrollment: N/A

Clarkson College
101 S. 42nd Street
Omaha, NE 68131-2715
www.clarksoncollege.edu/about/
Private
Admissions: (402) 552-2796
Email: Admissions@clarksoncollege.edu
Financial aid: (402) 552-2470
Application deadline: 11/01
Degrees offered: master's, DNP
Tuition: full time: $512/credit hour; part time: $512/credit hour (master's); full time: $721/credit hour; part time: $721/credit hour (DNP)
Room/board/expenses: N/A
Full-time enrollment: 224 (master's); 3 (DNP)
men: 13%; women: 87%; minorities: 30%; international: 0%
Part-time enrollment: 184 (master's)
men: 13%; women: 87%; minorities: 30%; international: 0%
Acceptance rate (master's): 43%
Acceptance rate (DNP): 80%
Specialties offered: administration, education, generalist, nurse anesthesia, nurse practitioner, nurse practitioner: adult-gerontology primary care, nurse practitioner: family

College of St. Mary[1]
7000 Mercy Road
Omaha, NE 68106
Private
Admissions: N/A
Financial aid: N/A
Tuition: N/A
Room/board/expenses: N/A
Enrollment: N/A

Creighton University
2500 California Plaza
Omaha, NE 68178
nursing.creighton.edu/
Private
Admissions: (402) 280-2703
Email: nursing@creighton.edu
Financial aid: (402) 280-2351
Application deadline: N/A
Degrees offered: master's, DNP
Tuition: full time: $780/credit hour; part time: $780/credit hour (master's); full time: $780/credit hour; part time: $780/credit hour (DNP)
Room/board/expenses: N/A
Full-time enrollment: 62 (master's); 71 (DNP)
men: 5%; women: 95%; minorities: 5%; international: 2%
Part-time enrollment: 93 (master's); 112 (DNP)
men: 10%; women: 90%; minorities: 12%; international: 0%
Acceptance rate (master's): 51%
Acceptance rate (DNP): 42%
Specialties offered: administration, clinical nurse leader, nurse practitioner, nurse practitioner: adult-gerontology acute care, nurse practitioner: adult-gerontology primary care, nurse practitioner: family, nurse practitioner: pediatric primary care, other majors

Nebraska Methodist College
720 N. 87th Street
Omaha, NE 68114
Private
Admissions: (402) 354-7202
Email: admissions@methodistcollege.edu
Financial aid: (402) 354-7225
Application deadline: N/A
Degrees offered: master's, DNP
Tuition: full time: $698/credit hour; part time: $698/credit hour (master's); full time: $770/credit hour; part time: $770/credit hour (DNP)
Room/board/expenses: $7,174 (master's); $7,174 (DNP)
Full-time enrollment: 98 (master's); 12 (DNP)
men: 4%; women: 96%; minorities: 6%; international: 0%
Part-time enrollment: 38 (master's)
men: 8%; women: 92%; minorities: 13%; international: 0%
Acceptance rate (master's): 83%
Acceptance rate (DNP): 50%
Specialties offered: administration, education, nurse practitioner, nurse practitioner: family

Nebraska Wesleyan University[1]
5000 St. Paul Avenue
Lincoln, NE 68504-2794
Private
Admissions: N/A
Financial aid: N/A
Tuition: N/A
Room/board/expenses: N/A
Enrollment: N/A

University of Nebraska Medical Center[1]
985330 Nebraska Medical Center
Omaha, NE 68198-5330
Public
Admissions: N/A
Financial aid: N/A
Tuition: N/A
Room/board/expenses: N/A
Enrollment: N/A

NEVADA

University of Nevada-Las Vegas[1]
4505 Maryland Parkway
Las Vegas, NV 89154-3018
Public
Admissions: N/A
Financial aid: N/A
Tuition: N/A
Room/board/expenses: N/A
Enrollment: N/A

University of Nevada-Reno
1664 North Virginia Street
Reno, NV 89557-0042
Public
Admissions: N/A
Financial aid: N/A
Application deadline: N/A
Degrees offered: master's, DNP
In-state tuition: full time: $511/credit hour; part time: $511/credit hour (master's); full time: $800/credit hour; part time: $800/credit hour (DNP)
Out-of-state tuition: full time: N/A (master's); full time: $800/credit hour (DNP)

Room/board/expenses: N/A
Full-time enrollment: 26 (master's); 10 (DNP)
men: N/A; women: N/A; minorities: N/A; international: N/A
Part-time enrollment: 51 (master's); 12 (DNP)
men: N/A; women: N/A; minorities: N/A; international: N/A
Acceptance rate (master's): N/A
Acceptance rate (DNP): N/A
Specialties offered: clinical nurse leader, education, nurse practitioner, nurse practitioner: adult-gerontology acute care, nurse practitioner: family, nurse practitioner: psychiatric-mental health, across the lifespan, dual majors

NEW HAMPSHIRE

Franklin Pierce University[1]
40 University Drive
Rindge, NH 03461
Private
Admissions: N/A
Financial aid: N/A
Tuition: N/A
Room/board/expenses: N/A
Enrollment: N/A

Rivier University
420 S. Main Street
Nashua, NH 03060
www.rivier.edu/academics.aspx?menu=76&id=521
Private
Admissions: (603) 897-8507
Email: admissions@rivier.edu
Financial aid: (603) 897-8510
Application deadline: N/A
Degrees offered: master's
Tuition: full time: N/A; part time: N/A (master's)
Room/board/expenses: N/A
Full-time enrollment: 4 men: 25%; women: 75%; minorities: 25%; international: 0%
Part-time enrollment: 112 men: 6%; women: 94%; minorities: 8%; international: 0%
Acceptance rate (master's): 50%
Specialties offered: community health/public health, nurse practitioner, nurse practitioner: adult-gerontology primary care, nurse practitioner: family, nurse practitioner: psychiatric-mental health, across the lifespan, other majors

University of New Hampshire[1]
Hewitt Hall, 4 Library Way
Durham, NH 03824-3563
Public
Admissions: N/A
Financial aid: N/A
Tuition: N/A
Room/board/expenses: N/A
Enrollment: N/A

NEW JERSEY

College of New Jersey[1]
PO Box 7718
Ewing, NJ 08628-0718
Public
Admissions: N/A
Financial aid: N/A
Tuition: N/A
Room/board/expenses: N/A
Enrollment: N/A

College of St. Elizabeth[1]

2 Convent Road
Morristown, NJ 07960
Private
Admissions: N/A
Financial aid: N/A
Tuition: N/A
Room/board/expenses: N/A
Enrollment: N/A

Fairleigh Dickinson University[1]

1000 River Road, H-DH4-02
Teaneck, NJ 07666
Private
Admissions: N/A
Financial aid: N/A
Tuition: N/A
Room/board/expenses: N/A
Enrollment: N/A

Felician College[1]

262 S. Main Street
Lodi, NJ 07644-2117
felician.edu/
Private
Admissions: N/A
Financial aid: N/A
Tuition: N/A
Room/board/expenses: N/A
Enrollment: N/A

Kean University[1]

1000 Morris Avenue
Union, NJ 07083-7131
www.kean.edu/academics/
college-natural-applied-health-
sciences/school-nursing
Public
Admissions: N/A
Financial aid: N/A
Tuition: N/A
Room/board/expenses: N/A
Enrollment: N/A

Monmouth University

400 Cedar Avenue
West Long Branch, NJ 07764
www.monmouth.edu/
school-of-nursing-health/
department-of-nursing.aspx
Private
Admissions: (732) 571-3443
Email: gradadm@monmouth.edu
Financial aid: (732) 571-3463
Application deadline: 07/15
Degrees offered: master's, DNP
Tuition: full time: $1,004/credit
hour; part time: $1,004/credit
hour (master's); full time: $1,004/
credit hour; part time: $1,004/
credit hour (DNP)
Room/board/expenses: N/A
Full-time enrollment: 12 (master's)
men: 0%; women: 100%;
minorities: 33%; international: 0%
Part-time enrollment: 278
(master's); 14 (DNP)
men: 8%; women: 92%;
minorities: 36%; international: 0%
Acceptance rate (master's): 98%
Acceptance rate (DNP): 86%
Specialties offered: administration,
education, forensic nursing, nurse
practitioner, nurse practitioner:
adult-gerontology primary care,
nurse practitioner: family, nurse
practitioner: psychiatric-mental
health, across the lifespan, school
nursing

Ramapo College of New Jersey[1]

505 Ramapo Valley Road
Mahwah, NJ 07430
Public
Admissions: N/A
Financial aid: N/A
Tuition: N/A
Room/board/expenses: N/A
Enrollment: N/A

Richard Stockton College of New Jersey[1]

PO Box 195
Pomona, NJ 08240
Public
Admissions: N/A
Financial aid: N/A
Tuition: N/A
Room/board/expenses: N/A
Enrollment: N/A

Rutgers, The State University of New Jersey-Camden

213 North Third Street
Camden, NJ 08102
nursing.camden.rutgers.edu/
Public
Admissions: N/A
Financial aid: (856) 225-6039
Application deadline: 12/25
Degrees offered: DNP
In-state tuition: full time: $17,184;
part time: $706/credit hour
Out-of-state tuition: full time:
$25,944
Room/board/expenses: $12,354
Full-time enrollment: 5
men: 0%; women: 100%;
minorities: 20%; international: 0%
Part-time enrollment: 10
men: 0%; women: 100%;
minorities: 30%; international: 0%
Acceptance rate (DNP): 78%
Specialties offered: N/A

Rutgers, The State University of New Jersey-Newark/ New Brunswick

180 University Avenue
Newark, NJ 07102
nursing.rutgers.edu
Public
Admissions: (973) 353-5293
Email:
snRecruiter@sn.rutgers.edu
Financial aid: (973) 972-4376
Application deadline: 04/01
Degrees offered: master's, Ph.D.,
DNP
In-state tuition: full time: $745/
credit hour; part time: $745/
credit hour (master's); full time:
$745/credit hour; part time: $745/
credit hour (Ph.D.); full time: $745/
credit hour; part time: $745/credit
hour (DNP)
Out-of-state tuition: full time:
$1,081/credit hour (master's); full
time: $1,081/credit hour (Ph.D.);
full time: $1,081/credit hour (DNP)
Room/board/expenses: $1,020
(master's); $1,020 (Ph.D.); $1,020
(DNP)
Full-time enrollment: 61 (master's);
15 (Ph.D.); 167 (DNP)
men: N/A; women: N/A; minorities:
45%; international: 2%

Part-time enrollment: 493
(master's); 21 (Ph.D.); 274 (DNP)
men: N/A; women: N/A; minorities:
49%; international: 3%
Acceptance rate (master's): 45%
Acceptance rate (Ph.D.): 76%
Acceptance rate (DNP): 84%
Specialties offered: clinical nurse
leader, health management &
policy health care systems,
informatics, nurse anesthesia,
nurse-midwifery, nurse
practitioner, nurse practitioner:
adult-gerontology acute care,
nurse practitioner: adult-
gerontology primary care,
nurse practitioner: adult, nurse
practitioner: family, nurse
practitioner: pediatric primary
care, nurse practitioner:
psychiatric-mental health, across
the lifespan, research, school
nursing, other majors

Seton Hall University

400 S. Orange Avenue
South Orange, NJ 07079
www.shu.edu/search.cfm?q=
College%20of%20Nursing
Private
Admissions: (973) 761-9107
Email: thehall@shu.edu
Financial aid: (800) 222-7183
Application deadline: 04/01
Degrees offered: master's, Ph.D.,
DNP
Tuition: full time: $1,100/credit
hour; part time: $1,100/credit hour
(master's); full time: $1,100/credit
hour; part time: $1,100/credit hour
(Ph.D.); full time: $1,100/credit
hour; part time: $1,100/credit
hour (DNP)
Room/board/expenses: N/A
Full-time enrollment: 51 (master's);
5 (Ph.D.);
men: 14%; women: 86%;
minorities: 52%; international: 0%
Part-time enrollment: 134
(master's); 30 (Ph.D.); 23 (DNP)
men: 11%; women: 89%;
minorities: 22%; international: 0%
Acceptance rate (master's): 85%
Acceptance rate (Ph.D.): 20%
Acceptance rate (DNP): 80%
Specialties offered: administration,
case management, nurse
practitioner, nurse practitioner:
adult-gerontology acute care,
nurse practitioner: adult-
gerontology primary care, nurse
practitioner: pediatric primary
care, research, school nursing,
dual majors

St. Peter's University[1]

Hudson Terrace
Englewood Cliffs, NJ 7632
Private
Admissions: N/A
Financial aid: N/A
Tuition: N/A
Room/board/expenses: N/A
Enrollment: N/A

Thomas Edison State College[1]

101 West State Street
Trenton, NJ 08608
Public
Admissions: N/A
Financial aid: N/A
Tuition: N/A
Room/board/expenses: N/A
Enrollment: N/A

William Paterson University of New Jersey[1]

300 Pompton Road
Wayne, NJ 7470
Public
Admissions: N/A
Financial aid: N/A
Tuition: N/A
Room/board/expenses: N/A
Enrollment: N/A

NEW MEXICO

New Mexico State University

1335 International Mall, HSS110
Las Cruces, NM 88003-8001
schoolofnusing.nmsu.edu
Public
Admissions: (575) 646-3121
Email: admissions@nmsu.edu
Financial aid: (575) 646-4105
Application deadline: 07/15
Degrees offered: master's, Ph.D.,
DNP
In-state tuition: full time: $3,936;
part time: $221/credit hour
(master's); full time: $3,936; part
time: $221/credit hour (Ph.D.);
full time: $3,936; part time: $221/
credit hour (DNP)
Out-of-state tuition: full time:
$13,838 (master's); full time:
$13,838 (Ph.D.); full time: $13,838
(DNP)
Room/board/expenses: $8,100
(master's); $8,100 (Ph.D.); $8,100
(DNP)
Full-time enrollment: 7 (master's);
5 (DNP)
men: 33%; women: 67%;
minorities: 42%; international: 0%
Part-time enrollment: 17 (master's);
32 (Ph.D.); 49 (DNP)
men: 15%; women: 85%;
minorities: 47%; international: 1%
Acceptance rate (master's): 80%
Acceptance rate (Ph.D.): 82%
Acceptance rate (DNP): 64%
Specialties offered: administration,
clinical nurse specialist,
community health/public health,
generalist, nurse practitioner,
nurse practitioner: adult-
gerontology primary care,
nurse practitioner: family, nurse
practitioner: psychiatric-mental
health, across the lifespan

University of New Mexico[1]

MSC09 5350
Albuquerque, NM 87131-0001
Public
Admissions: N/A
Financial aid: N/A
Tuition: N/A
Room/board/expenses: N/A
Enrollment: N/A

NEW YORK

Adelphi University[1]

1 South Avenue
Garden City, NY 11530-0701
Private
Admissions: N/A
Financial aid: N/A
Tuition: N/A
Room/board/expenses: N/A
Enrollment: N/A

American University of Beirut

3 Dag Hammarskjold Plaza
New York, NY 10017
aub.edu.lb/~webson
Private
Admissions: (961) 137-4374
Email: admissions@aub.edu.lb
Financial aid: (961) 137-4374
Application deadline: 04/01
Degrees offered: master's
Tuition: full time: $727/credit hour;
part time: $727/credit hour
Room/board/expenses: $12,978
Full-time enrollment: 4
men: 25%; women: 75%;
minorities: 0%; international: 25%
Part-time enrollment: 56
men: 23%; women: 77%;
minorities: 0%; international: 5%
Acceptance rate (master's): 87%
Specialties offered: administration,
clinical nurse specialist,
community health/public health,
other majors, dual majors

Binghamton University-SUNY

PO Box 6000
Binghamton, NY 13902-6000
www.binghamton.edu/dson
Public
Admissions: (607) 777-2151
Email: gradadmission@
binghamton.edu
Financial aid: (607) 777-2428
Application deadline: 02/15
Degrees offered: master's, Ph.D.,
DNP
In-state tuition: full time: $10,370;
part time: $432/credit hour
(master's); full time: $10,370; part
time: $432/credit hour (Ph.D.); full
time: $21,310; part time: $888/
credit hour (DNP)
Out-of-state tuition: full time:
$20,190 (master's); full time:
$20,190 (Ph.D.); full time: $38,980
(DNP)
Room/board/expenses: N/A
Full-time enrollment: 78 (master's);
12 (Ph.D.); 4 (DNP)
men: 22%; women: 78%;
minorities: 16%; international: 11%
Part-time enrollment: 60
(master's); 24 (Ph.D.); 11 (DNP)
men: 12%; women: 88%;
minorities: 15%; international: 3%
Acceptance rate (master's): 80%
Acceptance rate (Ph.D.): 100%
Acceptance rate (DNP): 0%
Specialties offered: clinical nurse
specialist, community health/
public health, education, forensic
nursing, nurse practitioner, nurse
practitioner: adult-gerontology
primary care, nurse practitioner:
family, nurse practitioner:
psychiatric-mental health, across
the lifespan, other majors

College of Mount St. Vincent[1]

6301 Riverdale Avenue
Riverdale, NY 10471
Private
Admissions: N/A
Financial aid: N/A
Tuition: N/A
Room/board/expenses: N/A
Enrollment: N/A

College of New Rochelle[1]
29 Castle Place
New Rochelle, NY 10805-2308
Private
Admissions: N/A
Financial aid: N/A
Tuition: N/A
Room/board/expenses: N/A
Enrollment: N/A

Columbia University
630 West 168th Street
Mailbox 6
New York, NY 10032
nursing.columbia.edu/
Private
Admissions: (212) 305-5756
Email: nursing@columbia.edu
Financial aid: (212) 305-8147
Application deadline: 01/02
Degrees offered: master's, Ph.D., DNP
Tuition: full time: $1,366/credit hour; part time: $1,366/credit hour (master's); full time: $1,766/credit hour; part time: $1,766/credit hour (Ph.D.); full time: $1,766/credit hour; part time: $1,766/credit hour (DNP)
Room/board/expenses: $24,000 (master's); $24,000 (Ph.D.); $24,000 (DNP)
Full-time enrollment: 209 (master's); 29 (Ph.D.); 18 (DNP)
men: 13%; women: 87%; minorities: 36%; international: 4%
Part-time enrollment: 232 (master's); 1 (Ph.D.); 10 (DNP)
men: 7%; women: 93%; minorities: 40%; international: 2%
Acceptance rate (master's): 82%
Acceptance rate (Ph.D.): 35%
Acceptance rate (DNP): 100%
Specialties offered: nurse anesthesia, nurse-midwifery, nurse practitioner, nurse practitioner: adult-gerontology acute care, nurse practitioner: adult-gerontology primary care, nurse practitioner: family, nurse practitioner: pediatric primary care, nurse practitioner: psychiatric-mental health, across the lifespan, research

CUNY-Hunter College
695 Park Avenue
New York, NY 10010
www.hunter.cuny.edu/nursing
Public
Admissions: (212) 396-6049
Email: gradadmissions@hunter.cuny.edu
Financial aid: (212) 772-4820
Application deadline: 04/01
Degrees offered: master's, DNP
In-state tuition: full time: $9,650; part time: $405/credit hour (master's); full time: $12,740; part time: $535/credit hour (DNP)
Out-of-state tuition: full time: $17,840 (master's); full time: $20,760 (DNP)
Room/board/expenses: N/A
Full-time enrollment: 3 (master's); 3 (DNP)
men: 17%; women: 83%; minorities: 33%; international: 0%
Part-time enrollment: 530 (master's); 30 (DNP)
men: 16%; women: 84%; minorities: 54%; international: 2%
Acceptance rate (master's): 39%
Acceptance rate (DNP): 38%
Specialties offered: administration, clinical nurse specialist, community health/public health, nurse practitioner, nurse practitioner: adult-gerontology primary care, nurse practitioner: psychiatric-mental health, across the lifespan

CUNY-Lehman College[1]
250 Bedford Park Boulevard
West Bronx, NY 10468-1589
Public
Admissions: N/A
Financial aid: N/A
Tuition: N/A
Room/board/expenses: N/A
Enrollment: N/A

CUNY-Staten Island[1]
2800 Victory Boulevard
Building 5S, Room 213
Staten Island, NY 10314
Public
Admissions: N/A
Financial aid: N/A
Tuition: N/A
Room/board/expenses: N/A
Enrollment: N/A

Daemen College[1]
4380 Main Street
Amherst, NY 14226-3592
www.daemen.edu/
Private
Admissions: N/A
Financial aid: N/A
Tuition: N/A
Room/board/expenses: N/A
Enrollment: N/A

Dominican College
470 Western Highway
Orangeburg, NY 10962
www.dc.edu/gradnursing
Private
Admissions: (845) 848-7800
Email: admissions@dc.edu
Financial aid: (845) 848-7818
Application deadline: N/A
Degrees offered: master's
Tuition: full time: N/A; part time: $815/credit hour
Room/board/expenses: N/A
Full-time enrollment: 22
men: 5%; women: 95%; minorities: 36%; international: N/A
Part-time enrollment: 39
men: 8%; women: 92%; minorities: 44%; international: N/A
Acceptance rate (master's): N/A
Specialties offered: nurse practitioner

D'Youville College
320 Porter Avenue
Buffalo, NY 14201-9985
www.dyc.edu/academics/nursing/
Private
Admissions: (800) 777-3921
Email: graduateadmissions@dyc.edu
Financial aid: (716) 829-7500
Application deadline: N/A
Degrees offered: master's, DNP
Tuition: full time: N/A; part time: N/A (master's)
Room/board/expenses: N/A
Full-time enrollment: 32 (master's); 1 (DNP)
men: 15%; women: 85%; minorities: 6%; international: 33%
Part-time enrollment: 138 (master's); 9 (DNP)
men: 11%; women: 89%; minorities: 10%; international: 39%
Acceptance rate (master's): N/A
Acceptance rate (DNP): N/A
Specialties offered: N/A

Excelsior College[1]
7 Columbia Circle
Albany, NY 12203-5159
Private
Admissions: N/A
Financial aid: N/A
Tuition: N/A
Room/board/expenses: N/A
Enrollment: N/A

Keuka College[1]
141 Central Avenue
Keuka Park, NY 14478
asap.keuka.edu/programs/ms-nursing/
Private
Admissions: N/A
Financial aid: N/A
Tuition: N/A
Room/board/expenses: N/A
Enrollment: N/A

Le Moyne College
1419 Salt Springs Road
Syracuse, NY 13214
www.lemoyne.edu/nursing
Private
Admissions: (315) 445-5444
Email: nursing@lemoyne.edu
Financial aid: (315) 445-4400
Application deadline: 08/01
Degrees offered: master's
Tuition: full time: $663/credit hour; part time: $663/credit hour
Room/board/expenses: N/A
Full-time enrollment:
men: N/A; women: N/A; minorities: N/A; international: N/A
Part-time enrollment: 28
men: 18%; women: 82%; minorities: 7%; international: 0%
Acceptance rate (master's): 100%
Specialties offered: administration, education, informatics, other majors

LIU Brooklyn[1]
1 University Plaza
Brooklyn, NY 11201-8423
Private
Admissions: N/A
Financial aid: N/A
Tuition: N/A
Room/board/expenses: N/A
Enrollment: N/A

LIU Post[1]
720 Northern Boulevard
Brookville, NY 11548
Private
Admissions: N/A
Financial aid: N/A
Tuition: N/A
Room/board/expenses: N/A
Enrollment: N/A

Mercy College
555 Broadway
Dobbs Ferry, NY 10522
www.mercy.edu/health-and-natural-sciences/
Private
Admissions: (877) 637-2946
Email: admissions@mercy.edu
Financial aid: (877) 637-2946
Application deadline: N/A
Degrees offered: master's
Tuition: full time: $814/credit hour; part time: $814/credit hour
Room/board/expenses: $12,690
Full-time enrollment: 5
men: 20%; women: 80%; minorities: 80%; international: 0%
Part-time enrollment: 181
men: 9%; women: 91%; minorities: 64%; international: 0%
Acceptance rate (master's): 76%
Specialties offered: administration, education

Molloy College
1000 Hempstead Avenue
Rockville, NY 11571-5002
www.molloy.edu/academics/graduate-programs/graduate-nursing
Private
Admissions: (516) 323-4014
Email: admissions@molloy.edu
Financial aid: (516) 323-4200
Application deadline: 04/15
Degrees offered: master's, Ph.D., DNP
Tuition: full time: $980/credit hour; part time: $980/credit hour (master's); full time: $1,100/credit hour; part time: $1,100/credit hour (Ph.D.); full time: $1,100/credit hour; part time: $1,100/credit hour (DNP)
Room/board/expenses: N/A
Full-time enrollment: 17 (master's)
men: 12%; women: 88%; minorities: 76%; international: 0%
Part-time enrollment: 536 (master's); 36 (Ph.D.); 6 (DNP)
men: 7%; women: 93%; minorities: 54%; international: 0%
Acceptance rate (master's): 67%
Acceptance rate (Ph.D.): 100%
Acceptance rate (DNP): 100%
Specialties offered: clinical nurse specialist, education, nurse practitioner, nurse practitioner: adult-gerontology primary care, nurse practitioner: family, nurse practitioner: pediatric primary care, nurse practitioner: psychiatric-mental health, across the lifespan, other majors, dual majors

Mount St. Mary College[1]
330 Powell Avenue
Newburgh, NY 12550
Private
Admissions: N/A
Financial aid: N/A
Tuition: N/A
Room/board/expenses: N/A
Enrollment: N/A

New York University
726 Broadway, 10th Floor
New York, NY 10003
www.nursing.nyu.edu
Private
Admissions: (212) 998-5317
Email: admissions.nursing@nyu.edu
Financial aid: (212) 998-4444
Application deadline: N/A
Degrees offered: master's, Ph.D., DNP
Tuition: full time: $36,192; part time: $18,096 (master's); full time: $36,192; part time: $18,096 (Ph.D.); full time: $36,192; part time: $18,096 (DNP)
Room/board/expenses: $31,542 (master's); $31,542 (Ph.D.); $31,542 (DNP)
Full-time enrollment: 34 (master's); 12 (Ph.D.); 6 (DNP)
men: 10%; women: 90%; minorities: 27%; international: 25%
Part-time enrollment: 584 (master's); 21 (Ph.D.); 32 (DNP)
men: 9%; women: 91%; minorities: 35%; international: 2%
Acceptance rate (master's): 68%
Acceptance rate (Ph.D.): 48%
Acceptance rate (DNP): 80%
Specialties offered: administration, education, informatics, nurse-midwifery, nurse practitioner, nurse practitioner: adult-gerontology acute care, nurse practitioner: adult-gerontology primary care, nurse practitioner: family, nurse practitioner: pediatric primary care, nurse practitioner: psychiatric-mental health, across the lifespan, research, dual majors

Pace University
861 Bedford Road
New York, NY 10038
www.pace.edu/lienhard/
Private
Admissions: (212) 346-1531
Email: gradnyc@pace.edu
Financial aid: (914) 773-3751
Application deadline: 03/01
Degrees offered: master's, DNP
Tuition: full time: $1,070/credit hour; part time: $1,070/credit hour (master's); full time: N/A; part time: $18,370 (DNP)
Room/board/expenses: N/A
Full-time enrollment: 1 (master's)
men: 0%; women: 100%; minorities: 100%; international: 0%
Part-time enrollment: 396 (master's); 47 (DNP)
men: 7%; women: 93%; minorities: 49%; international: 0%
Acceptance rate (master's): 70%
Acceptance rate (DNP): 85%
Specialties offered: clinical nurse leader, education, nurse practitioner, nurse practitioner: adult-gerontology acute care, nurse practitioner: family

Roberts Wesleyan College
2301 Westside Drive
Rochester, NY 14624
www.roberts.edu/graduate-nursing-programs.aspx
Private
Admissions: (585) 594-6686
Email: gradnursing@roberts.edu
Financial aid: (585) 594-6391
Application deadline: N/A
Degrees offered: master's
Tuition: full time: $757/credit hour; part time: N/A
Room/board/expenses: N/A
Full-time enrollment: 66
men: 3%; women: 97%; minorities: 12%; international: 14%
Part-time enrollment:
men: N/A; women: N/A; minorities: N/A; international: N/A
Acceptance rate (master's): 76%
Specialties offered: administration, education

The Sage Colleges[1]
65 1st Street
Troy, NY 12180
Private
Admissions: N/A
Financial aid: N/A
Tuition: N/A
Room/board/expenses: N/A
Enrollment: N/A

St. John Fisher College
3690 East Avenue
Rochester, NY 14618
www.sjfc.edu/academics/nursing/
about/index.dot
Private
Admissions: (585) 385-8161
Email: www.sjfc.edu/admissions/
graduate/
Financial aid: (585) 385-8042
Application deadline: N/A
Degrees offered: master's, DNP
Tuition: full time: $825/credit
hour; part time: $825/credit hour
(master's); full time: $1,155/credit
hour; part time: $1,155/credit
hour (DNP)
Room/board/expenses: N/A
Full-time enrollment: 8 (master's);
16 (DNP)
men: 0%; women: 100%;
minorities: 21%; international: 4%
Part-time enrollment: 109
(master's); 8 (DNP)
men: 9%; women: 91%; minorities:
11%; international: 1%
Acceptance rate (master's): 39%
Acceptance rate (Ph.D.): N/A
Acceptance rate (DNP): 60%
Specialties offered: clinical nurse
specialist, nurse practitioner,
nurse practitioner: adult-
gerontology primary care, nurse
practitioner: family

St. Joseph's College[1]
206 Prospect Ave.
Syracuse, NY 13203
Private
Admissions: N/A
Financial aid: N/A
Tuition: N/A
Room/board/expenses: N/A
Enrollment: N/A

Stony Brook University-SUNY
Health Science Center
Stony Brook, NY 11794-8240
nursing.stonybrookmedicine.edu/
Public
Admissions: (631) 444-3554
Email:
Karen.Allard@stonybrook.edu
Financial aid: (631) 444-2111
Application deadline: 01/15
Degrees offered: master's, DNP
In-state tuition: full time: $10,370;
part time: $432/credit hour
(master's); full time: $888/credit
hour; part time: $888/credit hour
(DNP)
Out-of-state tuition: full time:
$20,190 (master's); full time:
$1,624/credit hour (DNP)
Room/board/expenses: $7,718
(master's); $7,718 (DNP)
Full-time enrollment: 38 (master's);
7 (DNP)
men: 9%; women: 91%; minorities:
62%; international: 2%
Part-time enrollment: 598
(master's); 55 (DNP)
men: 8%; women: 92%;
minorities: 36%; international: 6%

Acceptance rate (master's): 57%
Acceptance rate (Ph.D.): N/A
Acceptance rate (DNP): 70%
Specialties offered: education,
nurse-midwifery, nurse
practitioner, nurse practitioner:
adult-gerontology primary care,
nurse practitioner: pediatric
primary care, nurse practitioner:
psychiatric-mental health, across
the lifespan, other majors

SUNY Downstate Medical Center
450 Clarkson Avenue, Box 22
Brooklyn, NY 11203-2098
www.downstate.edu
Public
Admissions: (718) 270-4744
Email:
admissions@downstate.edu
Financial aid: (718) 270-2488
Application deadline: 10/30
Degrees offered: master's
In-state tuition: full time: $11,370;
part time: $432/credit hour
Out-of-state tuition: full time:
$20,190
Room/board/expenses: N/A
Full-time enrollment: 15
men: N/A; women: N/A; minorities:
N/A; international: N/A
Part-time enrollment: 209
men: N/A; women: N/A; minorities:
N/A; international: N/A
Acceptance rate (master's): 21%
Specialties offered: clinical nurse
specialist, nurse anesthesia,
nurse-midwifery, nurse
practitioner, nurse practitioner:
family

SUNY Polytechnic Institute
PO Box 3050
Utica, NY 13504
sunyit.edu/programs/
graduate/nur/
Public
Admissions: (315) 792-7347
Email: graduate@sunyit.edu
Financial aid: (315) 792-7210
Application deadline: 07/15
Degrees offered: master's
In-state tuition: full time: $432/
credit hour; part time: $432/
credit hour
Out-of-state tuition: full time: $841/
credit hour
Room/board/expenses: $12,250
Full-time enrollment: 51
men: 18%; women: 82%;
minorities: 12%; international: 2%
Part-time enrollment: 165
men: 6%; women: 94%;
minorities: 15%; international: 0%
Acceptance rate (master's): 45%
Specialties offered: administration,
education, nurse practitioner: adult-
gerontology primary care, nurse
practitioner: family

SUNY Upstate Medical Center[1]
750 East Adams Street
Syracuse, NY 13210-2375
Public
Admissions: N/A
Financial aid: N/A
Tuition: N/A
Room/board/expenses: N/A
Enrollment: N/A

University at Buffalo-SUNY
103 Wende Hall
3435 Main Street
Buffalo, NY 14214
nursing.buffalo.edu
Public
Admissions: (716) 829-2537
Email: nursing@buffalo.edu
Financial aid: (716) 645-8232
Application deadline: 05/01
Degrees offered: master's, Ph.D.,
DNP
In-state tuition: full time: $10,370;
part time: $432/credit hour
(master's); full time: $10,370; part
time: $432/credit hour (Ph.D.); full
time: $31,965; part time: $888/
credit hour (DNP)
Out-of-state tuition: full time:
$20,190 (master's); full time:
$20,190 (Ph.D.); full time: $58,470
(DNP)
Room/board/expenses: $11,144
(master's); $11,144 (Ph.D.);
$11,144 (DNP)
Full-time enrollment: 8 (Ph.D.);
55 (DNP)
men: 37%; women: 63%;
minorities: 27%; international: 8%
Part-time enrollment: 5 (master's);
19 (Ph.D.); 108 (DNP)
men: 14%; women: 86%;
minorities: 20%; international: 3%
Acceptance rate (master's): N/A
Acceptance rate (Ph.D.): 60%
Acceptance rate (DNP): 67%
Specialties offered: health
management & policy health care
systems, nurse anesthesia, nurse
practitioner, nurse practitioner:
adult-gerontology primary care,
nurse practitioner: family, nurse
practitioner: psychiatric-mental
health, across the lifespan,
research

University of Rochester
601 Elmwood Avenue
Rochester, NY 14642
son.rochester.edu/
Private
Admissions: (585) 275-2375
Email: son_admissions@
urmc.rochester.edu
Financial aid: (585) 275-3226
Application deadline: 03/01
Degrees offered: master's, Ph.D.,
DNP
Tuition: full time: $23,256;
part time: $1,292/credit hour
(master's); full time: $23,256; part
time: $1,292/credit hour (Ph.D.);
full time: $23,256; part time:
$1,292/credit hour (DNP)
Room/board/expenses: $12,901
(master's); $12,901 (Ph.D.);
$12,901 (DNP)
Full-time enrollment: 6 (master's);
17 (Ph.D.)
men: 17%; women: 83%;
minorities: 30%; international: 4%
Part-time enrollment: 166
(master's); 1 (Ph.D.); 20 (DNP)
men: 13%; women: 87%;
minorities: 11%; international: 1%
Acceptance rate (master's): 71%
Acceptance rate (Ph.D.): 100%
Acceptance rate (DNP): 100%
Specialties offered: clinical nurse
leader, health management &
policy health care systems,
nurse practitioner, nurse
practitioner: adult-gerontology
acute care, nurse practitioner:
adult-gerontology primary
care, nurse practitioner: family,

nurse practitioner: pediatric
primary care, nurse practitioner:
psychiatric-mental health, across
the lifespan, research

Wagner College[1]
1 Campus Road
Staten Island, NY 10301
Private
Admissions: N/A
Financial aid: N/A
Tuition: N/A
Room/board/expenses: N/A
Enrollment: N/A

NORTH CAROLINA

Duke University
Box 3322 Medical Center
Durham, NC 27710-3322
nursing.duke.edu
Private
Admissions: (877) 415-3853
Email: SONAdmissions@
dm.duke.edu
Financial aid: (877) 344-4680
Application deadline: 12/01
Degrees offered: master's, Ph.D.,
DNP
Tuition: full time: $1,495/credit
hour; part time: $1,495/credit hour
(master's); full time: $48,922; part
time: $2,765/credit hour (Ph.D.);
full time: $1,495/credit hour; part
time: $1,495/credit hour (DNP)
Room/board/expenses: $16,440
(master's); $16,440 (Ph.D.);
$16,440 (DNP)
Full-time enrollment: 146
(master's); 27 (Ph.D.); 47 (DNP)
men: 15%; women: 85%;
minorities: 20%; international: 5%
Part-time enrollment: 345
(master's); 130 (DNP)
men: 11%; women: 89%;
minorities: 20%; international: 2%
Acceptance rate (master's): 38%
Acceptance rate (Ph.D.): 33%
Acceptance rate (DNP): 46%
Specialties offered: administration,
case management, education,
health management & policy
health care systems, informatics,
nurse anesthesia, nurse
practitioner, nurse practitioner:
adult-gerontology acute care,
nurse practitioner: adult-
gerontology primary care,
nurse practitioner: family, nurse
practitioner: pediatric primary
care, research, other majors

East Carolina University
Library, Allied Health and
Nursing Building
Greenville, NC 27858
www.ecu.edu/nursing/
Public
Admissions: (252) 744-6477
Email: gradnurs@ecu.edu
Financial aid: (252) 328-6610
Application deadline: 03/15
Degrees offered: master's, Ph.D.,
DNP
In-state tuition: full time: $207/
credit hour; part time: $207/credit
hour (master's); full time: $4,595;
part time: $2,659 (Ph.D.); full time:
$207/credit hour; part time: $207/
credit hour (DNP)
Out-of-state tuition: full time: $811/
credit hour (master's); full time:
$15,372 (Ph.D.); full time: $811/
credit hour (DNP)

Room/board/expenses: $10,720
(master's); $10,720 (Ph.D.);
$10,720 (DNP)
Full-time enrollment: 97 (master's);
2 (Ph.D.); 52 (DNP)
men: 12%; women: 88%;
minorities: 22%; international: 0%
Part-time enrollment: 347
(master's); 26 (Ph.D.); 23 (DNP)
men: 10%; women: 90%;
minorities: 21%; international: 0%
Acceptance rate (master's): 35%
Acceptance rate (Ph.D.): 42%
Acceptance rate (DNP): 56%
Specialties offered: administration,
clinical nurse specialist,
education, nurse anesthesia,
nurse-midwifery, nurse
practitioner, nurse practitioner:
adult-gerontology primary care,
nurse practitioner: family

Gardner-Webb University
PO Box 7286
Boiling Springs, NC 28017
www.gardner-webb.edu/
academics/areas-of-study/
nursing/index
Private
Admissions: (704) 406-4723
Email: gradschool@
gardner-webb.edu
Financial aid: (704) 406-4247
Application deadline: 01/15
Degrees offered: master's, DNP
Tuition: full time: $413/credit
hour; part time: $413/credit hour
(master's); full time: $682/credit
hour; part time: $682/credit hour
(DNP)
Room/board/expenses: N/A
Full-time enrollment: 214
(master's); 34 (DNP)
men: 6%; women: 94%;
minorities: 12%; international: 1%
Part-time enrollment:
men: N/A; women: N/A; minorities:
N/A; international: N/A
Acceptance rate (master's): 68%
Acceptance rate (DNP): N/A
Specialties offered: administration,
education, nurse practitioner,
nurse practitioner: family, dual
majors

Queens University of Charlotte[1]
1900 Selwyn Avenue, MSC 1433
Charlotte, NC 28274
www.queens.edu/
Private
Admissions: N/A
Financial aid: N/A
Tuition: N/A
Room/board/expenses: N/A
Enrollment: N/A

University of North Carolina-Chapel Hill
Carrington Hall, CB #7460
Chapel Hill, NC 27599-7460
nursing.unc.edu/
Public
Admissions: (919) 966-4260
Email: nursing@unc.edu
Financial aid: (919) 962-8396
Application deadline: 12/31
Degrees offered: master's, Ph.D.,
DNP
In-state tuition: full time: $13,693;
part time: $10,288 (master's); full
time: $8,693; part time: $6,520
(Ph.D.); full time: $13,693; part
time: $10,288 (DNP)

Out-of-state tuition: full time: $30,904 (master's); full time: $25,904 (Ph.D.); full time: $30,904 (DNP)
Room/board/expenses: $16,520 (master's); $16,520 (Ph.D.); $16,520 (DNP)
Full-time enrollment: 121 (master's); 44 (Ph.D.); 32 (DNP)
men: 9%; women: 91%; minorities: 30%; international: 9%
Part-time enrollment: 94 (master's); 2 (Ph.D.); 10 (DNP)
men: 5%; women: 95%; minorities: 18%; international: 0%
Acceptance rate (master's): 64%
Acceptance rate (Ph.D.): 57%
Acceptance rate (DNP): 57%
Specialties offered: administration, clinical nurse leader, education, informatics, nurse practitioner, nurse practitioner: adult-gerontology primary care, nurse practitioner: family, nurse practitioner: pediatric primary care, nurse practitioner: psychiatric-mental health, across the lifespan, research, other majors, dual majors

University of North Carolina-Chapel Hill (School of Public Health)[1]

135 Dauer Drive
Chapel Hill, NC 27599
Public
Admissions: N/A
Financial aid: N/A
Tuition: N/A
Room/board/expenses: N/A
Enrollment: N/A

University of North Carolina-Charlotte

9201 University City Boulevard
Charlotte, NC 28223-0001
nursing.uncc.edu
Public
Admissions: (704) 687-5503
Email: graduateschool.uncc.edu
Financial aid: (704) 687-7010
Application deadline: 02/02
Degrees offered: master's, DNP
In-state tuition: full time: $4,008; part time: $3,006 (master's); full time: $4,008; part time: N/A (DNP)
Out-of-state tuition: full time: $17,000 (master's); full time: $17,000 (DNP)
Room/board/expenses: N/A
Full-time enrollment: 133 (master's); 11 (DNP)
men: 18%; women: 82%; minorities: 15%; international: 1%
Part-time enrollment: 75 (master's)
men: 1%; women: 99%; minorities: 17%; international: 0%
Acceptance rate (master's): 36%
Acceptance rate (DNP): 75%
Specialties offered: administration, community health/public health, education, nurse anesthesia, nurse practitioner, nurse practitioner: adult-gerontology acute care, nurse practitioner: family

University of North Carolina-Greensboro

PO Box 26170
Greensboro, NC 27402-6170
nursing.uncg.edu
Public
Admissions: (336) 334-5596
Financial aid: N/A
Application deadline: N/A
Degrees offered: master's, Ph.D.
In-state tuition: full time: $4,641; part time: N/A (master's); full time: $4,641; part time: N/A (Ph.D.)
Out-of-state tuition: full time: $18,090 (master's); full time: $18,090 (Ph.D.)
Room/board/expenses: $7,400 (master's); $7,400 (Ph.D.)
Full-time enrollment: 227 (master's); 30 (Ph.D.)
men: 17%; women: 83%; minorities: 19%; international: N/A
Part-time enrollment: 43 (master's); 5 (Ph.D.)
men: 38%; women: 63%; minorities: 29%; international: N/A
Acceptance rate (master's): 67%
Acceptance rate (Ph.D.): 67%
Specialties offered: administration, education, nurse anesthesia, nurse practitioner, nurse practitioner: adult-gerontology primary care, research

University of North Carolina-Wilmington[1]

601 S. College Road
Wilmington, NC 28403-5995
Public
Admissions: N/A
Financial aid: N/A
Tuition: N/A
Room/board/expenses: N/A
Enrollment: N/A

Western Carolina University-Cullowhee[1]

1459 Sand Hill Road
Candler, NC 28715
Public
Admissions: N/A
Financial aid: N/A
Tuition: N/A
Room/board/expenses: N/A
Enrollment: N/A

Winston-Salem State University[1]

601 S. Martin Luther King Jr. Drive
Winston-Salem, NC 27110
www.wssu.edu/school-health-sciences/departments/nursing/default.aspx
Public
Admissions: N/A
Financial aid: N/A
Tuition: N/A
Room/board/expenses: N/A
Enrollment: N/A

NORTH DAKOTA

North Dakota State University

NDSU Dept. 2820
Fargo, ND 58108
www.ndsu.edu/nursing/
Public
Admissions: N/A
Financial aid: N/A
Application deadline: 02/28
Degrees offered: master's, DNP

In-state tuition: full time: N/A; part time: N/A (master's); full time: $346/credit hour; part time: N/A (DNP)
Out-of-state tuition: full time: N/A (master's); full time: N/A/credit hour (DNP)
Room/board/expenses: N/A
Full-time enrollment: 33 (DNP)
men: N/A; women: N/A; minorities: N/A; international: N/A
Part-time enrollment: 7 (master's); 6 (DNP)
men: N/A; women: N/A; minorities: N/A; international: N/A
Acceptance rate (master's): N/A
Acceptance rate (DNP): 22%
Specialties offered: education, nurse practitioner, nurse practitioner: family

University of Mary

7500 University Drive
Bismarck, ND 58504-9652
Private
Admissions: (701) 355-8030
Email: marauder@umary.edu
Financial aid: (701) 355-8142
Application deadline: 02/01
Degrees offered: master's, DNP
Tuition: full time: $530/credit hour; part time: $530/credit hour (master's); full time: $530/credit hour; part time: $530/credit hour (DNP)
Room/board/expenses: N/A
Full-time enrollment: 16 (master's); 34 (DNP)
men: 14%; women: 86%; minorities: 14%; international: 0%
Part-time enrollment: 4 (master's); 2 (DNP)
men: 0%; women: 100%; minorities: 0%; international: 0%
Acceptance rate (master's): N/A
Acceptance rate (DNP): 41%
Specialties offered: nurse practitioner, nurse practitioner: family

University of North Dakota

Box 9025
Grand Forks, ND 58202
nursing.und.edu/
Public
Admissions: (701) 777-4535
Email: questions@gradschool.und.edu
Financial aid: (701) 777-3092
Application deadline: N/A
Degrees offered: master's, Ph.D., DNP
In-state tuition: full time: N/A; part time: N/A
Out-of-state tuition: full time: N/A
Room/board/expenses: N/A
Full-time enrollment:
men: N/A; women: N/A; minorities: N/A; international: N/A
Part-time enrollment: 234 (master's); 24 (Ph.D.); 10 (DNP)
men: N/A; women: N/A; minorities: 6%; international: N/A
Acceptance rate (master's): N/A
Acceptance rate (Ph.D.): N/A
Acceptance rate (DNP): N/A
Specialties offered: clinical nurse specialist, community health/public health, education, nurse anesthesia, nurse practitioner, nurse practitioner: adult-gerontology primary care, nurse practitioner: family, nurse practitioner: psychiatric-mental health, across the lifespan, research

OHIO

Capital University[1]

1 College and Main
Columbus, OH 43209-2394
Private
Admissions: N/A
Financial aid: N/A
Tuition: N/A
Room/board/expenses: N/A
Enrollment: N/A

Case Western Reserve University

10900 Euclid Avenue
Cleveland, OH 44106-4904
fpb.case.edu/
Private
Admissions: (216) 368-2529
Email: admissionsfpb@case.edu
Financial aid: (216) 368-0517
Application deadline: 03/01
Degrees offered: master's, Ph.D., DNP
Tuition: full time: $1,818/credit hour; part time: $1,818/credit hour (master's); full time: $1,660/credit hour; part time: $1,660/credit hour (Ph.D.); full time: $1,818/credit hour; part time: $1,818/credit hour (DNP)
Room/board/expenses: $23,680 (master's); $23,680 (Ph.D.); $6,025 (DNP)
Full-time enrollment: 165 (master's); 28 (Ph.D.); 104 (DNP)
men: 16%; women: 84%; minorities: 15%; international: 9%
Part-time enrollment: 117 (master's); 16 (Ph.D.); 60 (DNP)
men: 12%; women: 88%; minorities: 19%; international: 1%
Acceptance rate (master's): 70%
Acceptance rate (Ph.D.): 79%
Acceptance rate (DNP): 90%
Specialties offered: administration, education, informatics, nurse anesthesia, nurse-midwifery, nurse practitioner, nurse practitioner: adult-gerontology acute care, nurse practitioner: adult-gerontology primary care, nurse practitioner: family, nurse practitioner: pediatric primary care, nurse practitioner: psychiatric-mental health, across the lifespan, research, other majors, combined nurse practitioner/clinical nurse specialist, dual majors

Cedarville University

251 N. Main Street
Cedarville, OH 45314
www.cedarville.edu/Academics/Nursing.aspx
Private
Admissions: (800) 233-2784
Email: admissions@cedarville.edu
Financial aid: (877) 233-2784
Application deadline: N/A
Degrees offered: master's
Tuition: full time: $536/credit hour; part time: $536/credit hour (master's)
Room/board/expenses: $6,350
Full-time enrollment: 33
men: 6%; women: 94%; minorities: 15%; international: 0%
Part-time enrollment: 20
men: 10%; women: 90%; minorities: 10%; international: 0%
Acceptance rate (master's): 59%
Specialties offered: community health/public health, nurse practitioner: family

Cleveland State University

2121 Euclid Avenue
RT 1416
Cleveland, OH 44115-2214
www.csuohio.edu/nursing
Public
Admissions: (216) 687-5411
Email: graduate.admissions@csuohio.edu
Financial aid: (216) 687-5411
Application deadline: 01/04
Degrees offered: master's
In-state tuition: full time: $531/credit hour; part time: $531/credit hour
Out-of-state tuition: full time: $541/credit hour
Room/board/expenses: N/A
Full-time enrollment:
men: N/A; women: N/A; minorities: N/A; international: N/A
Part-time enrollment: 49
men: 6%; women: 94%; minorities: 24%; international: N/A
Acceptance rate (master's): 84%
Specialties offered: clinical nurse leader, education, forensic nursing, other majors

Franciscan University of Steubenville[1]

1235 University Boulevard
Steubenville, OH 43952
Private
Admissions: N/A
Financial aid: N/A
Tuition: N/A
Room/board/expenses: N/A
Enrollment: N/A

Kent State University

Henderson Hall
Kent, OH 44242
www.kent.edu/nursing
Public
Admissions: (330) 672-7911
Email: bsn@kent.edu; msn@kent.edu
Financial aid: N/A
Application deadline: 02/01
Degrees offered: master's, Ph.D., DNP
In-state tuition: full time: $485/credit hour; part time: $485/credit hour (master's); full time: $485/credit hour; part time: $485/credit hour (Ph.D.); full time: $485/credit hour; part time: $485/credit hour (DNP)
Out-of-state tuition: full time: $827/credit hour (master's); full time: $827/credit hour (Ph.D.); full time: $827/credit hour (DNP)
Room/board/expenses: $5,008 (master's); $5,008 (Ph.D.); $5,008 (DNP)
Full-time enrollment: 36 (master's); 21 (Ph.D.); 8 (DNP)
men: 22%; women: 78%; minorities: 9%; international: 32%
Part-time enrollment: 420 (master's); 7 (Ph.D.); 27 (DNP)
men: 11%; women: 89%; minorities: 14%; international: 1%
Acceptance rate (master's): 67%
Acceptance rate (Ph.D.): 31%
Acceptance rate (DNP): 81%
Specialties offered: clinical nurse specialist, education, health management & policy health care systems, nurse practitioner, nurse practitioner: adult-gerontology acute care, nurse practitioner: adult-gerontology

primary care, nurse practitioner: family, nurse practitioner: pediatric primary care, nurse practitioner: psychiatric-mental health, across the lifespan, dual majors

Lourdes University

6832 Convent Boulevard
Sylvania, OH 43560
Private
Admissions: (800) 878-3210
Email: gradschool@lourdes.edu
Financial aid: (419) 824-3732
Application deadline: 01/12
Degrees offered: master's
Tuition: full time: $650/credit hour; part time: $650/credit hour
Room/board/expenses: $8,200
Full-time enrollment: 92
men: 14%; women: 86%;
minorities: 16%; international: 1%
Part-time enrollment: 29
men: 3%; women: 97%;
minorities: 7%; international: 0%
Acceptance rate (master's): 84%
Specialties offered: clinical nurse leader, education, nurse anesthesia

Malone University[1]

515 25th Street NW
Canton, OH 44709
Private
Admissions: N/A
Financial aid: N/A
Tuition: N/A
Room/board/expenses: N/A
Enrollment: N/A

Mount Carmel College of Nursing[1]

127 S. Davis Avenue
Columbus, OH 43222
Private
Admissions: N/A
Financial aid: N/A
Tuition: N/A
Room/board/expenses: N/A
Enrollment: N/A

Mount St. Joseph University

5701 Delhi Road
Cincinnati, OH 45233
www.msj.edu/academics/
divisions-departments/
division-of-health-sciences/
department-of
Private
Admissions: (513) 244-4531
Financial aid: (513) 244-4418
Application deadline: N/A
Degrees offered: master's, DNP
Tuition: full time: $595/credit hour; part time: $595/credit hour (master's); full time: $620/credit hour; part time: $620/credit hour (DNP)
Room/board/expenses: $8,710 (master's); $8,710 (DNP)
Full-time enrollment: 91 (master's)
men: 20%; women: 80%;
minorities: 26%; international: 0%
Part-time enrollment: 56 (master's); 15 (DNP)
men: 6%; women: 94%;
minorities: 8%; international: 0%
Acceptance rate (master's): 87%
Acceptance rate (DNP): 100%
Specialties offered: administration, clinical nurse leader, education, generalist

Ohio State University

1585 Neil Avenue
Columbus, OH 43210
nursing.osu.edu/
Public
Admissions: (614) 292-4041
Email: nursing@osu.edu
Financial aid: (614) 292-8595
Application deadline: 12/31
Degrees offered: master's, Ph.D., DNP
In-state tuition: full time: $723/credit hour; part time: $723/credit hour (master's); full time: $723/credit hour; part time: $723/credit hour (Ph.D.); full time: $723/credit hour; part time: $723/credit hour (DNP)
Out-of-state tuition: full time: $1,850/credit hour (master's); full time: $1,850/credit hour (Ph.D.); full time: $723/credit hour (DNP)
Room/board/expenses: $785 (master's) $785 (Ph.D.); $785 (DNP)
Full-time enrollment: 450 (master's); 16 (Ph.D.); 33 (DNP)
men: 15%; women: 85%;
minorities: 15%; international: 1%
Part-time enrollment: 150 (master's); 7 (Ph.D.); 32 (DNP)
men: 13%; women: 87%;
minorities: 17%; international: 0%
Acceptance rate (master's): 58%
Acceptance rate (Ph.D.): 86%
Acceptance rate (DNP): 60%
Specialties offered: administration, clinical nurse leader, clinical nurse specialist, community health/public health, health management & policy health care systems, nurse-midwifery, nurse practitioner, nurse practitioner: adult-gerontology acute care, nurse practitioner: adult-gerontology primary care, nurse practitioner: adult, nurse practitioner: family, nurse practitioner: pediatric primary care, nurse practitioner: psychiatric-mental health, across the lifespan, research, other majors, dual majors

Ohio University[1]

Grover Center E365
Athens, OH 45701-2979
Public
Admissions: N/A
Financial aid: N/A
Tuition: N/A
Room/board/expenses: N/A
Enrollment: N/A

Otterbein University[1]

1 Otterbein College
Westerville, OH 43081
Private
Admissions: N/A
Financial aid: N/A
Tuition: N/A
Room/board/expenses: N/A
Enrollment: N/A

University of Akron[1]

209 Carroll Street
Akron, OH 44325-3701
Public
Admissions: N/A
Financial aid: N/A
Tuition: N/A
Room/board/expenses: N/A
Enrollment: N/A

University of Cincinnati

3110 Vine Street
Cincinnati, OH 45221-0038
nursing.uc.edu/
Public
Admissions: (513) 558-3600
Email: nursing1@uc.edu
Financial aid: (513) 556-9171
Application deadline: N/A
Degrees offered: master's, Ph.D., DNP
In-state tuition: full time: $15,414; part time: $758/credit hour (master's); full time: $15,414; part time: $758/credit hour (Ph.D.); full time: $15,414; part time: $758/credit hour (DNP)
Out-of-state tuition: full time: $27,156 (master's); full time: $27,156 (Ph.D.); full time: $27,156 (DNP)
Room/board/expenses: N/A
Full-time enrollment: 229 (master's); 21 (Ph.D.); 10 (DNP)
men: 17%; women: 83%;
minorities: 3%; international: 2%
Part-time enrollment: 1,343 (master's); 9 (Ph.D.); 36 (DNP)
men: 11%; women: 89%;
minorities: 22%; international: 0%
Acceptance rate (master's): 45%
Acceptance rate (Ph.D.): 53%
Acceptance rate (DNP): 76%
Specialties offered: administration, nurse anesthesia, nurse-midwifery, nurse practitioner, nurse practitioner: adult-gerontology acute care, nurse practitioner: adult-gerontology primary care, nurse practitioner: family, nurse practitioner: pediatric primary care, nurse practitioner: psychiatric-mental health, across the lifespan, research, other majors

University of Toledo

3000 Arlington Avenue, MS1026
Toledo, OH 43614
www.utoledo.edu/nursing/
index.html
Public
Admissions: (419) 383-5841
Email: admitnurse@utoledo.edu
Financial aid: (419) 530-8700
Application deadline: 12/15
Degrees offered: master's, DNP
In-state tuition: full time: $13,164; part time: $549/credit hour (master's); full time: $16,560; part time: $690/credit hour (DNP)
Out-of-state tuition: full time: $23,500 (master's); full time: $23,785 (DNP)
Room/board/expenses: $7,770 (master's); $7,770 (DNP)
Full-time enrollment: 68 (master's); 13 (DNP)
men: 20%; women: 80%;
minorities: 17%; international: 0%
Part-time enrollment: 172 (master's); 16 (DNP)
men: 9%; women: 91%; minorities: 6%; international: 1%
Acceptance rate (master's): 51%
Acceptance rate (DNP): 59%
Specialties offered: clinical nurse leader, education, nurse practitioner, nurse practitioner: adult, nurse practitioner: family, nurse practitioner: pediatric primary care

Urbana University[1]

101 Miller Hall
Springfield, OH 45505
Private
Admissions: N/A
Financial aid: N/A
Tuition: N/A
Room/board/expenses: N/A
Enrollment: N/A

Ursuline College

2550 Lander Road
Pepper Pike, OH 44124
www.ursuline.edu
Private
Admissions: (440) 449-4200
Email: graduateadmissions@ursuline.edu
Financial aid: (440) 449-4200
Application deadline: 12/31
Degrees offered: master's, DNP
Tuition: full time: $973/credit hour; part time: $973/credit hour (master's); full time: $973/credit hour; part time: $973/credit hour (DNP)
Room/board/expenses: N/A
Full-time enrollment: 146 (master's); 8 (DNP)
men: 7%; women: 93%;
minorities: 20%; international: 1%
Part-time enrollment: 125 (master's); 5 (DNP)
men: 4%; women: 96%;
minorities: 29%; international: 0%
Acceptance rate (master's): 86%
Acceptance rate (DNP): 100%
Specialties offered: clinical nurse specialist, generalist, nurse practitioner, nurse practitioner: adult-gerontology primary care, nurse practitioner: family

Wright State University

3640 Colonel Glenn Highway
Dayton, OH 45435-0001
nursing.wright.edu
Public
Admissions: (937) 775-5700
Email: admissions@wright.edu
Financial aid: (937) 775-5405
Application deadline: 08/24
Degrees offered: master's, DNP
In-state tuition: full time: $12,788; part time: $577/credit hour (master's); full time: $15,014; part time: $695/credit hour (DNP)
Out-of-state tuition: full time: $21,724 (master's); full time: $23,992 (DNP)
Room/board/expenses: $7,438 (master's); $7,438 (DNP)
Full-time enrollment: 143 (master's); 6 (DNP)
men: 12%; women: 88%;
minorities: 13%; international: 1%
Part-time enrollment: 109 (master's); 12 (DNP)
men: 12%; women: 88%;
minorities: 10%; international: 1%
Acceptance rate (master's): 77%
Acceptance rate (DNP): 36%
Specialties offered: administration, clinical nurse specialist, education, nurse practitioner, nurse practitioner: adult-gerontology acute care, nurse practitioner: family, nurse practitioner: pediatric primary care, nurse practitioner: psychiatric-mental health, across the lifespan, school nursing, other majors

Xavier University

119 Cohen Center
Cincinnati, OH 45207
www.xavier.edu/nursing
Private
Admissions: (513) 745-3301
Email: xuadmit@xavier.edu
Financial aid: (513) 745-3142
Application deadline: 01/15
Degrees offered: master's, DNP
Tuition: full time: $600/credit hour; part time: $600/credit hour (master's); full time: $760/credit hour; part time: $760/credit hour (DNP)
Room/board/expenses: N/A
Full-time enrollment: 68 (master's)
men: 19%; women: 81%;
minorities: 15%; international: 0%
Part-time enrollment: 185 (master's), 4 (DNP)
men: 6%; women: 94%;
minorities: 17%; international: 0%
Acceptance rate (master's): 93%
Acceptance rate (DNP): 80%
Specialties offered: administration, clinical nurse leader, education, forensic nursing, generalist, informatics, nurse practitioner: family, school nursing, other majors

Youngstown State University[1]

1 University Plaza
Youngstown, OH 44555
Public
Admissions: N/A
Financial aid: N/A
Tuition: N/A
Room/board/expenses: N/A
Enrollment: N/A

OKLAHOMA

Northeastern State University[1]

600 N. Grand Avenue
Tahlequah, OK 74464
academics.nsuok.edu/
healthprofessions/
DegreePrograms/Graduate/
NursingEducationMSN.aspx
Public
Admissions: N/A
Financial aid: N/A
Tuition: N/A
Room/board/expenses: N/A
Enrollment: N/A

Oklahoma Baptist University[1]

111 Harrison Avenue
Oklahoma City, OK 73104
Private
Admissions: N/A
Financial aid: N/A
Tuition: N/A
Room/board/expenses: N/A
Enrollment: N/A

Oklahoma City University

2501 N. Blackwelder
Oklahoma City, OK 73106
Private
Admissions: (405) 208-5094
Email: gadmissions@okcu.edu
Financial aid: (405) 208-5848
Application deadline: N/A
Degrees offered: master's, Ph.D., DNP
Tuition: full time: N/A; part time: N/A (master's)

Room/board/expenses: N/A
Full-time enrollment: 16 (master's);
9 (Ph.D.); 15 (DNP)
men: 30%; women: 70%;
minorities: 3%; international: 15%
Part-time enrollment: 3 (master's);
27 (Ph.D.); 63 (DNP)
men: 11%; women: 89%;
minorities: 1%; international: 0%
Acceptance rate (master's): N/A
Acceptance rate (Ph.D.): N/A
Acceptance rate (DNP): N/A
Specialties offered: administration,
education, nurse practitioner,
nurse practitioner: family

Southern Nazarene University[1]
6729 NW. 39th Expressway
Bethany, OK 73008-2605
Private
Admissions: N/A
Financial aid: N/A
Tuition: N/A
Room/board/expenses: N/A
Enrollment: N/A

University of Oklahoma Health Sciences Center[1]
PO Box 26901
Oklahoma City, OK 73190
Public
Admissions: N/A
Financial aid: N/A
Tuition: N/A
Room/board/expenses: N/A
Enrollment: N/A

OREGON

Oregon Health and Science University[1]
3455 S.W. U.S. Veterans
Hospital Road
Portland, OR 97239-2941
Public
Admissions: N/A
Financial aid: N/A
Tuition: N/A
Room/board/expenses: N/A
Enrollment: N/A

University of Portland
5000 N. Willamette Boulevard
Portland, OR 97203
nursing.up.edu/
Public
Admissions: (503) 943-7107
Email: gradschl@up.edu
Financial aid: (503) 943-7311
Application deadline: 01/15
Degrees offered: DNP
In-state tuition: full time: $1,070/
credit hour; part time: $1,070/
credit hour
Out-of-state tuition: full time:
N/A (master's); full time: $1,070/
credit hour
Room/board/expenses: N/A
Full-time enrollment: 51
men: 12%; women: 88%;
minorities: 10%; international: 0%
Part-time enrollment:
men: N/A; women: N/A; minorities:
N/A; international: N/A
Acceptance rate (DNP): 71%
Specialties offered: nurse
practitioner, nurse practitioner:
family

Alvernia University[1]
400 St. Bernardine Street
Reading, PA 19607
Private
Admissions: N/A
Financial aid: N/A
Tuition: N/A
Room/board/expenses: N/A
Enrollment: N/A

Bloomsburg University of Pennsylvania[1]
3109 McCormick Center
for Human Services
Bloomsburg, PA 17815-1301
Public
Admissions: N/A
Financial aid: N/A
Tuition: N/A
Room/board/expenses: N/A
Enrollment: N/A

California University of Pennsylvania[1]
250 University Avenue
California, PA 15419
Public
Admissions: N/A
Financial aid: N/A
Tuition: N/A
Room/board/expenses: N/A
Enrollment: N/A

Carlow University[1]
3333 Fifth Avenue
Pittsburgh, PA 15213
Private
Admissions: N/A
Financial aid: N/A
Tuition: N/A
Room/board/expenses: N/A
Enrollment: N/A

Cedar Crest College
100 College Drive
Allentown, PA 18104
www.cedarcrest.edu/ca/
academics/nursing/index.shtm
Private
Admissions: (610) 606-4666
Email: unleashed.cedarcrest.edu/
Financial aid: (610) 606-4602
Application deadline: N/A
Degrees offered: master's
Tuition: full time: $772/credit hour;
part time: $772/credit hour
Room/board/expenses: N/A
Full-time enrollment:
men: N/A; women: N/A; minorities:
N/A; international: N/A
Part-time enrollment: 23
men: 13%; women: 87%;
minorities: 4%; international: 0%
Acceptance rate (master's): 64%
Specialties offered: administration,
education

Chatham University[1]
Woodland Road
Pittsburgh, PA 15232
Private
Admissions: N/A
Financial aid: N/A
Tuition: N/A
Room/board/expenses: N/A
Enrollment: N/A

Clarion University- Edinboro University
1 Morrow Way
Slippery Rock, PA 16057
www.clarion.edu/academics/
colleges-and-schools/
venango-college/
school-of-health-science
Public
Admissions: (814) 676-6591
Email: gradstudies@clarion.edu
Financial aid: (814) 393-2315
Application deadline: 10/01
Degrees offered: master's
In-state tuition: full time: $499/
credit hour; part time: $499/
credit hour
Out-of-state tuition: full time: $529/
credit hour
Room/board/expenses: N/A
Full-time enrollment: 21
men: 10%; women: 90%;
minorities: 0%; international: 0%
Part-time enrollment: 71
men: 13%; women: 87%;
minorities: 1%; international: 0%
Acceptance rate (master's): 79%
Specialties offered: nurse
practitioner, nurse practitioner:
family

DeSales University
2755 Station Avenue
Center Valley, PA 18034-9568
www.desales.edu/home/
academics/divisions-
departments/department-of-
nursing-and-health
Private
Admissions: (610) 282-1100
Email:
gradadmissions@desales.edu
Financial aid: (610) 282-1100
Application deadline: N/A
Degrees offered: master's, DNP
Tuition: full time: N/A; part time:
$790/credit hour (master's); full
time: N/A; part time: $1,090/credit
hour (DNP)
Room/board/expenses: N/A
Full-time enrollment: 26 (master's);
24 (DNP)
men: 2%; women: 98%;
minorities: 10%; international: 0%
Part-time enrollment: 53 (master's)
men: 6%; women: 94%;
minorities: 2%; international: 0%
Acceptance rate (master's): 74%
Acceptance rate (DNP): 70%
Specialties offered: administration,
clinical nurse leader, clinical
nurse specialist, education, health
management & policy health care
systems, nurse practitioner,
nurse practitioner: adult-
gerontology acute care, nurse
practitioner: family, dual majors

Drexel University
Bellet Building
Philadelphia, PA 19102-1192
www.drexel.edu/cnhp/
academics/graduate/gradNursing
Private
Admissions: (215) 895-6172
Email: randall.c.deike@drexel.edu
Financial aid: (215) 571-4531
Application deadline: 05/01
Degrees offered: master's, Ph.D.,
DNP
Tuition: full time: $861/credit
hour; part time: $861/credit hour
(master's); full time: $1,123/credit
hour; part time: $1,123/credit hour
(Ph.D.); full time: $861/credit hour;
part time: $861/credit hour (DNP)

Room/board/expenses: N/A
Full-time enrollment: 63 (master's);
8 (DNP)
men: 35%; women: 65%;
minorities: 20%; international: N/A
Part-time enrollment: 1,173
(master's); 71 (DNP)
men: 11%; women: 89%;
minorities: 21%; international: 2%
Acceptance rate (master's): 49%
Acceptance rate (Ph.D.): N/A
Acceptance rate (DNP): 44%
Specialties offered: administration,
clinical nurse leader, education,
nurse anesthesia, nurse
practitioner, nurse practitioner:
adult-gerontology acute care,
nurse practitioner: adult-
gerontology primary care,
nurse practitioner: adult, nurse
practitioner: family, nurse
practitioner: pediatric primary
care, nurse practitioner:
psychiatric-mental health, across
the lifespan, other majors

Duquesne University
600 Forbes Avenue
Pittsburgh, PA 15282-1760
www.duq.edu/academics/
schools/nursing
Private
Admissions: (412) 396-6550
Email: nursing@duq.edu
Financial aid: (412) 396-6607
Application deadline: 03/01
Degrees offered: master's, Ph.D.,
DNP
Tuition: full time: $1,077/credit
hour; part time: $1,077/credit hour
(master's); full time: $1,077/credit
hour; part time: $1,077/credit hour
(Ph.D.); full time: $1,077/credit
hour; part time: $1,077/credit
hour (DNP)
Room/board/expenses: N/A
Full-time enrollment: 97 (master's);
34 (Ph.D.); 34 (DNP)
men: 9%; women: 91%; minorities:
15%; international: 1%
Part-time enrollment: 55
(master's); 17 (Ph.D.); 2 (DNP)
men: 9%; women: 91%; minorities:
22%; international: 1%
Acceptance rate (master's): 82%
Acceptance rate (Ph.D.): 83%
Acceptance rate (DNP): 90%
Specialties offered: education,
forensic nursing, nurse
practitioner, nurse practitioner:
family

Gannon University[1]
109 University Square
Erie, PA 16541-0001
www.gannon.edu/
Private
Admissions: N/A
Financial aid: N/A
Tuition: N/A
Room/board/expenses: N/A
Enrollment: N/A

Gwynedd Mercy University[1]
1325 Sumneytown Pike
Gwynedd Valley, PA 19437-0901
www.gmercyu.edu/academics/
graduate-programs/nursing
Private
Admissions: N/A
Financial aid: N/A
Tuition: N/A
Room/board/expenses: N/A
Enrollment: N/A

Holy Family University
9801 Frankford Avenue
Philadelphia, PA 19114
www.holyfamily.edu/
choosing-holy-family-u/
academics/schools-of-study/
philadelphia-sch
Private
Admissions: (267) 341-3327
Email: gradstudy@holyfamily.edu
Financial aid: (267) 341-3233
Application deadline: N/A
Degrees offered: master's
Tuition: full time: $704/credit hour;
part time: $704/credit hour
Room/board/expenses: N/A
Full-time enrollment:
men: N/A; women: N/A; minorities:
N/A; international: N/A
Part-time enrollment: 58
men: 10%; women: 90%;
minorities: 17%; international: 0%
Acceptance rate (master's): 75%
Specialties offered: administration,
community health/public health,
education, generalist

Immaculata University[1]
1145 King Road
Immaculata, PA 19345-0500
Private
Admissions: N/A
Financial aid: N/A
Tuition: N/A
Room/board/expenses: N/A
Enrollment: N/A

Indiana University of Pennsylvania
Johnson Hall, Room 210
1010 Oakland Avenue
Indiana, PA 15705
www.iup.edu/rn-alliedhealth/
Public
Admissions: (724) 357-2222
Email: graduate-admissions@
iup.edu
Financial aid: (724) 357-2218
Application deadline: N/A
Degrees offered: master's, Ph.D.
In-state tuition: full time: $478/
credit hour; part time: $478/credit
hour (master's); full time: $502/
credit hour; part time: $502/credit
hour (Ph.D.)
Out-of-state tuition: full time: $717/
credit hour (master's); full time:
$753/credit hour (Ph.D.)
Room/board/expenses: $11,346
(master's); $11,346 (Ph.D.)
Full-time enrollment: 7 (master's)
men: 0%; women: 100%;
minorities: 0%; international: 86%
Part-time enrollment: 32
(master's); 34 (Ph.D.);
men: 3%; women: 97%;
minorities: 3%; international: 0%
Acceptance rate (master's): 75%
Acceptance rate (Ph.D.): 30%
Specialties offered: administration,
education

La Roche College
9000 Babcock Boulevard
Pittsburgh, PA 15237-5898
www.laroche.edu/Academics/
Academic_Divisions/Education_
and_Nursing_Division/NURSING/
Private
Admissions: (412) 536-1266
Financial aid: (412) 536-1125
Application deadline: N/A
Degrees offered: master's
Tuition: full time: $660/credit hour;
part time: $660/credit hour
Room/board/expenses: N/A

Full-time enrollment: 7
men: 0%; women: 100%;
minorities: 0%; international: 0%
Part-time enrollment: 6
men: 0%; women: 100%;
minorities: 0%; international: 0%
Acceptance rate (master's): N/A
Specialties offered: administration,
education

La Salle University
1900 W. Olney Avenue
Philadelphia, PA 19141-1199
www.lasalle.edu/snhs/
Private
Admissions: (215) 951-1322
Email: dillonp@lasalle.edu
Financial aid: (215) 951-1070
Application deadline: N/A
Degrees offered: master's, DNP
Tuition: full time: $845/credit
hour; part time: $845/credit hour
(master's); full time: $900/credit
hour; part time: $900/credit hour
(DNP)
Room/board/expenses: N/A
Full-time enrollment:
men: N/A; women: N/A; minorities:
N/A; international: N/A
Part-time enrollment: 344
(master's); 21 (DNP)
men: 16%; women: 84%;
minorities: 28%; international: 1%
Acceptance rate (master's): 66%
Acceptance rate (DNP): 86%
Specialties offered: administration,
clinical nurse leader, clinical nurse
specialist, community health/
public health, nurse anesthesia,
nurse practitioner: nurse
practitioner: adult-gerontology
primary care, nurse practitioner:
family, school nursing

Mansfield University of Pennsylvania[1]
G24 South Hall
Mansfield, PA 16933
Public
Admissions: N/A
Financial aid: N/A
Tuition: N/A
Room/board/expenses: N/A
Enrollment: N/A

Millersville University of Pennsylvania[1]
127 Caputo Hall
Millersville, PA 17551
Public
Admissions: N/A
Financial aid: N/A
Tuition: N/A
Room/board/expenses: N/A
Enrollment: N/A

Misericordia University[1]
301 Lake Street
Dallas, PA 18612
Private
Admissions: N/A
Financial aid: N/A
Tuition: N/A
Room/board/expenses: N/A
Enrollment: N/A

Moravian College
1200 Main Street
Bethlehem, PA 18018
moravian.edu/nursing
Private
Admissions: (800) 441-3191
Email: admissions@moravian.edu
Financial aid: (610) 861-1330
Application deadline: N/A
Degrees offered: master's
Tuition: full time: $779/credit hour;
part time: $779/credit hour
Room/board/expenses: N/A
Full-time enrollment:
men: N/A; women: N/A; minorities:
N/A; international: N/A
Part-time enrollment: 64
men: 5%; women: 95%;
minorities: 2%; international: 0%
Acceptance rate (master's): 79%
Acceptance rate (Ph.D.): N/A
Acceptance rate (DNP): N/A
Specialties offered: administration,
clinical nurse leader, education,
nurse practitioner, nurse
practitioner: adult-gerontology
acute care, nurse practitioner:
adult-gerontology primary care

Neumann University[1]
1 Neumann Drive
Aston, PA 19014-1298
Private
Admissions: N/A
Financial aid: N/A
Tuition: N/A
Room/board/expenses: N/A
Enrollment: N/A

Pennsylvania State University- University Park
201 Health and Human
Development E
University Park, PA 16802-1589
www.nursing.psu.edu/
Public
Admissions: (814) 865-5471
Email: admissions.psu.edu/
Financial aid: (814) 865-6301
Application deadline: 11/30
Degrees offered: master's, Ph.D.,
DNP
In-state tuition: full time: $18,816;
part time: $784/credit hour
(master's); full time: $14,112; part
time: $784/credit hour (Ph.D.);
full time: $14,112; part time: $784/
credit hour (DNP)
Out-of-state tuition: full time:
$32,180 (master's); full time:
$24,138 (Ph.D.); full time: $24,138
(DNP)
Room/board/expenses: $12,510
(master's); $12,510 (Ph.D.);
$12,510 (DNP)
Full-time enrollment: 66 (master's);
8 (Ph.D.); 2 (DNP)
men: 13%; women: 87%;
minorities: 14%; international: 4%
Part-time enrollment: 73
(master's); 7 (Ph.D.); 9 (DNP)
men: 10%; women: 90%;
minorities: 7%; international: 0%
Acceptance rate (master's): 48%
Acceptance rate (Ph.D.): 33%
Acceptance rate (DNP): 85%
Specialties offered: administration,
education, nurse practitioner,
nurse practitioner: adult-
gerontology acute care, nurse
practitioner: adult-gerontology
primary care, nurse practitioner:
adult, nurse practitioner: family

Robert Morris University
6001 University Boulevard
Moon Township, PA 15108
www.rmu.edu/Undergraduate/
AcademicOfferings/Nursing
Private
Admissions: (800) 762-0097
Email: graduateadmissionsoffice@
rmu.edu
Financial aid: (412) 397-6250
Application deadline: 05/01
Degrees offered: master's, DNP
Tuition: full time: N/A; part time:
$480/credit hour (master's); full
time: N/A; part time: $870/credit
hour (DNP)
Room/board/expenses: N/A
Full-time enrollment:
men: N/A; women: N/A; minorities:
N/A; international: N/A
Part-time enrollment: 54
(master's); 109 (DNP)
men: 17%; women: 83%;
minorities: 12%; international: 0%
Acceptance rate (master's): 100%
Acceptance rate (DNP): 61%
Specialties offered: nurse
practitioner, nurse practitioner:
adult-gerontology primary care,
nurse practitioner: family, nurse
practitioner: psychiatric-mental
health, across the lifespan

Temple University
1801 North Broad Street
Philadelphia, PA 19140
cph.temple.edu/nursing/home
Public
Admissions: (215) 707-4618
Email: tunurse@temple.edu
Financial aid: (215) 204-2244
Application deadline: 02/14
Degrees offered: DNP
In-state tuition: full time: $831/
credit hour; part time: $831/
credit hour
Out-of-state tuition: full time:
$1,143/credit hour (DNP)
Room/board/expenses: $13,455
Full-time enrollment: 14
men: 7%; women: 93%;
minorities: 57%; international: 0%
Part-time enrollment: 44
men: 14%; women: 86%;
minorities: 59%; international: 0%
Acceptance rate (DNP): 47%
Specialties offered: nurse
practitioner: adult-gerontology
primary care, nurse practitioner:
family

Thomas Jefferson University
901 Walnut Street, 8th Floor
Philadelphia, PA 19107
www.jefferson.edu/nursing
Private
Admissions: (215) 503-1040
Email: erin.finn@jefferson.edu
Financial aid: (215) 955-2867
Application deadline: 01/02
Degrees offered: master's, DNP
Tuition: full time: $1,054/credit
hour; part time: $1,054/credit
hour (master's); full time: $1,054/
credit hour; part time: $1,054/
credit hour (DNP)
Room/board/expenses: N/A
Full-time enrollment:
men: N/A; women: N/A; minorities:
N/A; international: N/A
Part-time enrollment: 416
(master's); 29 (DNP)
men: 12%; women: 88%;
minorities: 35%; international: 1%

Acceptance rate (master's): 85%
Acceptance rate (DNP): 65%
Specialties offered: clinical nurse
specialist, community health/
public health, informatics, nurse
anesthesia, nurse practitioner,
nurse practitioner: adult-
gerontology acute care, nurse
practitioner: adult-gerontology
primary care, nurse practitioner:
family, nurse practitioner:
pediatric primary care, other
majors, dual majors

University of Pennsylvania
420 Guardian Drive
Philadelphia, PA 19104-6096
www.nursing.upenn.edu
Private
Admissions: (215) 898-4271
Email: admissions@
nursing.upenn.edu
Financial aid: (215) 898-8191
Application deadline: 06/01
Degrees offered: master's, Ph.D.
Tuition: full time: $36,620;
part time: $1,535/credit hour
(master's); full time: $28,890; part
time: $1,848/credit hour (Ph.D.)
Room/board/expenses: $25,926
(master's); $25,926 (Ph.D.)
Full-time enrollment: 203
(master's); 55 (Ph.D.)
men: 16%; women: 84%;
minorities: 25%; international: 6%
Part-time enrollment: 333
(master's); 3 (Ph.D.)
men: 10%; women: 90%;
minorities: 22%; international: 0%
Acceptance rate (master's): 55%
Acceptance rate (Ph.D.): 29%
Specialties offered: administration,
clinical nurse specialist, nurse
anesthesia, nurse-midwifery,
nurse practitioner, nurse
practitioner: adult-gerontology
acute care, nurse practitioner:
adult-gerontology primary
care, nurse practitioner: family,
nurse practitioner: pediatric
primary care, nurse practitioner:
psychiatric-mental health, across
the lifespan, other majors, dual
majors

University of Pittsburgh
Victoria Building
Pittsburgh, PA 15261
www.nursing.pitt.edu/
Public
Admissions: (412) 624-6910
Email: sao50@pitt.edu
Financial aid: (412) 624-7488
Application deadline: 05/01
Degrees offered: master's, Ph.D.,
DNP
In-state tuition: full time: $36,480;
part time: $992/credit hour
(master's); full time: $36,480; part
time: $992/credit hour (Ph.D.); full
time: $36,480; part time: $992/
credit hour (DNP)
Out-of-state tuition: full time:
$42,072 (master's); full time:
$42,072 (Ph.D.); full time: $42,072
(DNP)
Room/board/expenses: N/A
Full-time enrollment: 120
(master's); 34 (Ph.D.); 83 (DNP)
men: 20%; women: 80%;
minorities: 8%; international: 6%
Part-time enrollment: 69
(master's); 6 (Ph.D.); 106 (DNP)
men: 86%; women: 14%;
minorities: 10%; international: 2%

Acceptance rate (master's): 30%
Acceptance rate (Ph.D.): 55%
Acceptance rate (DNP): 80%
Specialties offered: administration,
clinical nurse leader, clinical nurse
specialist, informatics, nurse
anesthesia, nurse practitioner,
nurse practitioner: adult-
gerontology acute care, nurse
practitioner: adult-gerontology
primary care, nurse practitioner:
adult, nurse practitioner: family,
nurse practitioner: pediatric
primary care, nurse practitioner:
psychiatric-mental health, across
the lifespan

University of Scranton
800 Linden Street
Scranton, PA 18510
www.scranton.edu/nursing
Private
Admissions: (570) 941-4416
Email: cgce@scranton.edu
Financial aid: (570) 941-7700
Application deadline: N/A
Degrees offered: master's
Tuition: full time: $940/credit hour;
part time: $940/credit hour
Room/board/expenses: N/A
Full-time enrollment: 28
men: 32%; women: 68%;
minorities: 11%; international: 0%
Part-time enrollment: 50
men: 8%; women: 92%;
minorities: 16%; international: 0%
Acceptance rate (master's): 37%
Specialties offered: clinical nurse
specialist, nurse anesthesia,
nurse practitioner, nurse
practitioner: family

Villanova University
800 Lancaster Avenue
Villanova, PA 19085-1690
www1.villanova.edu/villanova/
nursing.html
Private
Admissions: (610) 519-4000
Email: gotovu@villanova.edu
Financial aid: (610) 519-4010
Application deadline: N/A
Degrees offered: master's, Ph.D.,
DNP
Tuition: full time: $812/credit
hour; part time: $812/credit hour
(master's); full time: $1,009/credit
hour; part time: $1,009/credit
hour (Ph.D.); full time: $1,375/
credit hour; part time: $1,375/
credit hour (DNP)
Room/board/expenses: $17,260
(master's); $17,260 (Ph.D.);
$17,260 (DNP)
Full-time enrollment: 127
(master's); 38 (Ph.D.); 16 (DNP)
men: 14%; women: 86%;
minorities: 10%; international: 8%
Part-time enrollment: 94
(master's); 22 (Ph.D.)
men: 9%; women: 91%; minorities:
13%; international: N/A
Acceptance rate (master's): 77%
Acceptance rate (Ph.D.): 62%
Acceptance rate (DNP): 100%
Specialties offered: administration,
education, nurse anesthesia,
nurse practitioner, nurse
practitioner: adult-gerontology
primary care, nurse practitioner:
family, nurse practitioner:
pediatric primary care, research

Waynesburg University

51 West College Street
Waynesburg, PA 15370
www.waynesburg.edu/graduate/
graduate-majors/nursing
Private
Admissions: (724) 743-7612
Email: sstoneci@waynesburg.edu
Financial aid: (724) 852-3208
Application deadline: N/A
Degrees offered: master's, DNP
Tuition: full time: $620/credit
hour; part time: $620/credit hour
(master's); full time: $740/credit
hour; part time: $740/credit hour
(DNP)
Room/board/expenses: N/A
Full-time enrollment: 2 (master's)
men: 0%; women: 100%;
minorities: 0%; international: 0%
Part-time enrollment: 125
(master's); 42 (DNP)
men: 9%; women: 91%; minorities:
4%; international: 0%
Acceptance rate (master's): 100%
Acceptance rate (Ph.D.): N/A
Acceptance rate (DNP): 73%
Specialties offered: administration,
education, informatics, other
majors, dual majors

West Chester University of Pennsylvania[1]

222 Sturzebecker Health
Sciences Center
West Chester, PA 19383
Public
Admissions: N/A
Financial aid: N/A
Tuition: N/A
Room/board/expenses: N/A
Enrollment: N/A

Widener University[1]

One University Place
Chester, PA 19013-5892
Private
Admissions: N/A
Financial aid: N/A
Tuition: N/A
Room/board/expenses: N/A
Enrollment: N/A

Wilkes University[1]

109 S. Franklin Street
Wilkes-Barre, PA 18766
Private
Admissions: N/A
Financial aid: N/A
Tuition: N/A
Room/board/expenses: N/A
Enrollment: N/A

York College of Pennsylvania[1]

York, PA 17405
Private
Admissions: N/A
Financial aid: N/A
Tuition: N/A
Room/board/expenses: N/A
Enrollment: N/A

PUERTO RICO

Universidad del Turabo[1]

P.O. Box 3030
Gurabo, PR 00778-3030
Private
Admissions: N/A
Financial aid: N/A
Tuition: N/A
Room/board/expenses: N/A
Enrollment: N/A

University of Puerto Rico[1]

Box 365067
San Juan, PR 00936-5067
Public
Admissions: N/A
Financial aid: N/A
Tuition: N/A
Room/board/expenses: N/A
Enrollment: N/A

RHODE ISLAND

Rhode Island College

600 Mount Pleasant Avenue
Providence, RI 02908-1991
www.ric.edu/nursing/
Public
Admissions: N/A
Financial aid: (401) 456-8033
Application deadline: N/A
Degrees offered: master's
In-state tuition: full time: $8,928;
part time: $372/credit hour
Out-of-state tuition: full time:
$17,376
Room/board/expenses: N/A
Full-time enrollment: 8
men: 25%; women: 75%;
minorities: 25%; international: 0%
Part-time enrollment: 75
men: 9%; women: 91%; minorities:
9%; international: 1%
Acceptance rate (master's): N/A
Specialties offered: community
health/public health, nurse
anesthesia, nurse practitioner:
adult-gerontology acute care,
nurse practitioner: adult-
gerontology primary care

University of Rhode Island

White Hall
Kingston, RI 02881-2021
web.uri.edu/nursing/
Public
Admissions: (401) 874-2872
Email: gradadm@etal.uri.edu
Financial aid: (401) 874-9500
Application deadline: 04/15
Degrees offered: master's, Ph.D.,
DNP
In-state tuition: full time: $11,532;
part time: $641/credit hour
(master's); full time: $11,532; part
time: $641/credit hour (Ph.D.); full
time: $11,532; part time: $641/
credit hour (DNP)
Out-of-state tuition: full time:
$23,606 (master's); full time:
$23,606 (Ph.D.); full time: $23,606
(DNP)
Room/board/expenses: N/A
Full-time enrollment: 54 (master's);
4 (Ph.D.); 4 (DNP)
men: N/A; women: N/A; minorities:
13%; international: 3%
Part-time enrollment: 31 (master's);
16 (Ph.D.); 26 (DNP)
men: N/A; women: N/A; minorities:
14%; international: 0%

Acceptance rate (master's): 91%
Acceptance rate (Ph.D.): 100%
Acceptance rate (DNP): 91%
Specialties offered: administration,
education, nurse practitioner:
adult-gerontology acute care,
nurse practitioner: adult-
gerontology primary care, nurse
practitioner: family, research,
combined nurse practitioner/
clinical nurse specialist

SOUTH CAROLINA

Charleston Southern University[1]

9200 University Boulevard
North Charleston, SC 29406
Private
Admissions: N/A
Financial aid: N/A
Tuition: N/A
Room/board/expenses: N/A
Enrollment: N/A

Clemson University

524 Edwards Hall
Clemson, SC 29634
www.clemson.edu/hehd/
departments/nursing/
Public
Admissions: (864) 656-3195
Email: grdapp@clemson.edu
Financial aid: (864) 656-2280
Application deadline: 03/01
Degrees offered: master's
In-state tuition: full time: $9,496;
part time: $638/credit hour
Out-of-state tuition: full time:
$19,724
Room/board/expenses: $9,888
Full-time enrollment: 65
men: 14%; women: 86%;
minorities: 11%; international: 0%
Part-time enrollment: 17
men: 6%; women: 94%;
minorities: 24%; international: 0%
Acceptance rate (master's): 86%
Specialties offered: administration,
clinical nurse specialist,
education, nurse practitioner,
nurse practitioner: adult-
gerontology primary care, nurse
practitioner: family

Medical University of South Carolina

99 Jonathan Lucas Street
Charleston, SC 29425
musc.edu/nursing
Public
Admissions: (843) 792-7408
Email: hudsonly@musc.edu
Financial aid: (843) 792-2536
Application deadline: 03/15
Degrees offered: master's, Ph.D.,
DNP
In-state tuition: full time: $24,348;
part time: $835/credit hour
(master's); full time: $24,348; part
time: $835/credit hour (Ph.D.); full
time: $24,348; part time: $835/
credit hour (DNP)
Out-of-state tuition: full time:
$28,659 (master's); full time:
$28,659 (Ph.D.); full time: $28,569
(DNP)
Room/board/expenses: N/A
Full-time enrollment: 15 (master's);
11 (Ph.D.); 143 (DNP)
men: 6%; women: 94%;
minorities: 18%; international: 0%
Part-time enrollment: 9 (master's);
54 (Ph.D.); 66 (DNP)
men: 5%; women: 95%;
minorities: 29%; international: 0%

Acceptance rate (master's): 14%
Acceptance rate (Ph.D.): 54%
Acceptance rate (DNP): 50%
Specialties offered: education,
generalist, nurse practitioner,
nurse practitioner: adult-
gerontology primary care,
nurse practitioner: family, nurse
practitioner: pediatric primary
care, research

University of South Carolina

1601 Greene Street
Columbia, SC 29208
www.sc.edu/nursing
Public
Admissions: (803) 777-7412
Email: sburgess@mailbox.sc.edu
Financial aid: (803) 777-8134
Application deadline: 02/01
Degrees offered: master's, Ph.D.,
DNP
In-state tuition: full time: $581/
credit hour; part time: $581/credit
hour (master's); full time: $581/
credit hour; part time: $581/credit
hour (Ph.D.); full time: $581/credit
hour; part time: $581/credit hour
(DNP)
Out-of-state tuition: full time:
$1,183/credit hour (master's); full
time: $1,184/credit hour (Ph.D.);
full time: $1,184/credit hour (DNP)
Room/board/expenses: N/A
Full-time enrollment: 37 (master's);
7 (Ph.D.); 14 (DNP)
men: 9%; women: 91%; minorities:
16%; international: 0%
Part-time enrollment: 75
(master's); 4 (Ph.D.); 44 (DNP)
men: 12%; women: 88%;
minorities: 20%; international: 0%
Acceptance rate (master's): 87%
Acceptance rate (Ph.D.): 67%
Acceptance rate (DNP): 76%
Specialties offered: administration,
nurse practitioner, nurse
practitioner: adult-gerontology
acute care, nurse practitioner:
family, nurse practitioner:
psychiatric-mental health, across
the lifespan, research

SOUTH DAKOTA

National American University

925 29th Street SE
Watertown, SD 57201
www.national.edu/programs/
school-nursing
Private
Admissions: (877) 398-0118
Email: graduateadmissions@
national.edu
Financial aid: (855) 459-3629
Application deadline: 11/30
Degrees offered: master's
Tuition: full time: $470/credit
hour; part time: $470/credit hour
(master's)
Room/board/expenses: N/A
Full-time enrollment: 1
men: 0%; women: 100%;
minorities: 0%; international: 0%
Part-time enrollment: 14
men: 0%; women: 100%;
minorities: 36%; international: 0%
Acceptance rate (master's): N/A
Specialties offered: administration,
case management, education,
informatics

South Dakota State University

SNF 217
Brookings, SD 57007
www.sdstate.edu/nurs/index.cfm
Public
Admissions: (605) 688-4181
Email:
sdsu_gradschool@sdstate.edu
Financial aid: (800) 952-3541
Application deadline: 04/15
Degrees offered: master's, Ph.D.,
DNP
In-state tuition: full time: $301/
credit hour; part time: $301/credit
hour (master's); full time: $301/
credit hour; part time: $301/credit
hour (Ph.D.); full time: $301/credit
hour; part time: $301/credit hour
(DNP)
Out-of-state tuition: full time: $559/
credit hour (master's); full time:
$559/credit hour (Ph.D.); full time:
$559/credit hour (DNP)
Room/board/expenses: $9,000
(master's); $9,000 (Ph.D.);
$9,000 (DNP)
Full-time enrollment: 1 (master's); 1
(Ph.D.); 23 (DNP)
men: 8%; women: 92%;
minorities: 0%; international: 0%
Part-time enrollment: 60
(master's); 25 (Ph.D.); 87 (DNP)
men: 8%; women: 92%;
minorities: 7%; international: 0%
Acceptance rate (master's): 85%
Acceptance rate (Ph.D.): 100%
Acceptance rate (DNP): 55%
Specialties offered: administration,
clinical nurse leader, clinical
nurse specialist, education, nurse
practitioner, nurse practitioner:
family, nurse practitioner:
pediatric primary care, nurse
practitioner: psychiatric-mental
health, across the lifespan,
research

TENNESSEE

Belmont University

1900 Belmont Boulevard
Nashville, TN 37212
www.belmont.edu/gradnursing/
Private
Admissions: (615) 460-6107
Email: bill.nichols@belmont.edu
Financial aid: (615) 460-6403
Application deadline: 05/01
Degrees offered: master's, DNP
Tuition: full time: $1,085/credit
hour; part time: N/A (master's);
full time: $1,160/credit hour; part
time: N/A (DNP)
Room/board/expenses: N/A
Full-time enrollment: 37 (master's);
6 (DNP)
men: 7%; women: 93%;
minorities: 7%; international: 0%
Part-time enrollment: 20 (master's)
men: 15%; women: 85%;
minorities: 0%; international: 0%
Acceptance rate (master's): 79%
Acceptance rate (DNP): N/A
Specialties offered: nurse
practitioner, nurse practitioner:
family

Carson-Newman University[1]

1646 Russell Avenue
Jefferson City, TN 71883
Private
Admissions: N/A
Financial aid: N/A
Tuition: N/A

Room/board/expenses: N/A
Enrollment: N/A

East Tennessee State University

Campus Box 70617
Johnson City, TN 37614-0617
www.etsu.edu/nursing
Public
Admissions: (423) 439-1000
Email: admissions@etsu.edu
Financial aid: N/A
Application deadline: N/A
Degrees offered: master's, Ph.D., DNP
In-state tuition: full time: $507/credit hour; part time: $507/credit hour (master's); full time: $507/credit hour; part time: $507/credit hour (Ph.D.); full time: $507/credit hour; part time: $507/credit hour (DNP)
Out-of-state tuition: full time: $1,258/credit hour (master's); full time: $1,258/credit hour (Ph.D.); full time: $1,258/credit hour (DNP)
Room/board/expenses: $4,600 (master's); $4,600 (Ph.D.); $4,600 (DNP)
Full-time enrollment: 45 (master's); 4 (Ph.D.); 39 (DNP)
men: 14%; women: 86%; minorities: 3%; international: 0%
Part-time enrollment: 289 (master's); 29 (Ph.D.); 28 (DNP)
men: 11%; women: 89%; minorities: 5%; international: 0%
Acceptance rate (master's): 88%
Acceptance rate (Ph.D.): 67%
Acceptance rate (DNP): 89%
Specialties offered: administration, clinical nurse leader, education, nurse practitioner, nurse practitioner: adult-gerontology primary care, nurse practitioner: family, nurse practitioner: psychiatric-mental health, across the lifespan, research

King University[1]

1350 King College Road
Bristol, TN 37620
Private
Admissions: N/A
Financial aid: N/A
Tuition: N/A
Room/board/expenses: N/A
Enrollment: N/A

Lincoln Memorial University[1]

6965 Cumberland Gap Parkway
Harrogate, TN 37752
Private
Admissions: N/A
Financial aid: N/A
Tuition: N/A
Room/board/expenses: N/A
Enrollment: N/A

Southern Adventist University[1]

PO Box 370
Collegedale, TN 37315
Private
Admissions: N/A
Financial aid: N/A
Tuition: N/A
Room/board/expenses: N/A
Enrollment: N/A

Tennessee Board of Regents[1]

1415 Murfreesboro Road
Suite 350
Nashville, TN 37217-2833
Public
Admissions: N/A
Financial aid: N/A
Tuition: N/A
Room/board/expenses: N/A
Enrollment: N/A

Tennessee State University[1]

3500 John A. Merritt Boulevard
Box 9590
Nashville, TN 37209-1561
Public
Admissions: N/A
Financial aid: N/A
Tuition: N/A
Room/board/expenses: N/A
Enrollment: N/A

Union University

1050 Union University Drive
Jackson, TN 38305
www.uu.edu/academics/son/
Private
Admissions: (731) 661-6545
Email: nursingadmissions@uu.edu
Financial aid: (731) 661-5015
Application deadline: 10/01
Degrees offered: master's, DNP
Tuition: full time: $545/credit hour; part time: $545/credit hour (master's); full time: $825/credit hour; part time: $825/credit hour (DNP)
Room/board/expenses: N/A
Full-time enrollment: 114 (master's); 92 (DNP)
men: 25%; women: 75%; minorities: 11%; international: 0%
Part-time enrollment: 8 (master's); 9 (DNP)
men: 6%; women: 94%; minorities: 12%; international: 0%
Acceptance rate (master's): 33%
Acceptance rate (DNP): 29%
Specialties offered: administration, education, nurse anesthesia, nurse practitioner, nurse practitioner: adult-gerontology primary care, nurse practitioner: family, nurse practitioner: pediatric primary care

University of Memphis (Loewenberg)[1]

610 Goodman
Memphis, TN 38152
Public
Admissions: N/A
Financial aid: N/A
Tuition: N/A
Room/board/expenses: N/A
Enrollment: N/A

University of Tennessee-Chattanooga

615 McCallie Avenue
Chattanooga, TN 37403
www.utc.edu/nursing/
Public
Admissions: (423) 425-4666
Email: gsadmin@utc.edu
Financial aid: (423) 425-4677
Application deadline: 10/01
Degrees offered: master's, DNP

In-state tuition: full time: $680/credit hour; part time: $680/credit hour (master's); full time: $521/credit hour; part time: $521/credit hour (DNP)
Out-of-state tuition: full time: $1,575/credit hour (master's); full time: $568/credit hour (DNP)
Room/board/expenses: $2,000 (master's); $2,000 (DNP)
Full-time enrollment: 82 (master's); 20 (DNP)
men: 33%; women: 67%; minorities: 14%; international: 2%
Part-time enrollment: men: N/A; women: N/A; minorities: N/A; international: N/A
Acceptance rate (master's): 32%
Acceptance rate (DNP): 100%
Specialties offered: administration, nurse anesthesia, nurse practitioner, nurse practitioner: family

University of Tennessee Health Science Center[1]

877 Madison Avenue
Memphis, TN 38163
Public
Admissions: N/A
Financial aid: N/A
Tuition: N/A
Room/board/expenses: N/A
Enrollment: N/A

University of Tennessee-Knoxville

1200 Volunteer Boulevard
Knoxville, TN 37996-4180
nursing.utk.edu
Public
Admissions: (865) 974-3251
Email: gradschool@utk.edu
Financial aid: (865) 974-1111
Application deadline: 02/01
Degrees offered: master's, Ph.D., DNP
In-state tuition: full time: $563/credit hour; part time: $563/credit hour (master's); full time: $563/credit hour (Ph.D.); full time: N/A; part time: $563/credit hour (DNP)
Out-of-state tuition: full time: $1,574/credit hour (master's); full time: $1,574/credit hour (Ph.D.)
Room/board/expenses: N/A
Full-time enrollment: 83 (master's); 6 (Ph.D.); 3 (DNP)
men: 20%; women: 80%; minorities: 5%; international: 2%
Part-time enrollment: 25 (master's); 20 (Ph.D.); 12 (DNP)
men: 11%; women: 89%; minorities: 12%; international: 0%
Acceptance rate (master's): 47%
Acceptance rate (Ph.D.): 55%
Acceptance rate (DNP): 40%
Specialties offered: administration, clinical nurse specialist, health management & policy health care systems, nurse anesthesia, nurse practitioner: family, nurse practitioner: pediatric primary care, nurse practitioner: psychiatric-mental health, across the lifespan

Vanderbilt University

464 21st Avenue S
Nashville, TN 37240-0008
www.nursing.vanderbilt.edu/
Private
Admissions: (615) 322-3800
Email: vusn-admissions@vanderbilt.edu
Financial aid: (615) 322-8986
Application deadline: 11/01
Degrees offered: master's, Ph.D., DNP
Tuition: full time: $46,605; part time: $21,510 (master's); full time: $51,678; part time: $26,730 (Ph.D.); full time: $33,460; part time: $19,120 (DNP)
Room/board/expenses: N/A
Full-time enrollment: 441 (master's); 23 (Ph.D.); 23 (DNP)
men: N/A; women: N/A; minorities: 13%; international: 1%
Part-time enrollment: 208 (master's); 8 (Ph.D.); 134 (DNP)
men: N/A; women: N/A; minorities: 14%; international: 1%
Acceptance rate (master's): 55%
Acceptance rate (Ph.D.): 41%
Acceptance rate (DNP): 72%
Specialties offered: administration, informatics, nurse-midwifery, nurse practitioner, nurse practitioner: adult-gerontology acute care, nurse practitioner: adult-gerontology primary care, nurse practitioner: family, nurse practitioner: pediatric primary care, nurse practitioner: psychiatric-mental health, across the lifespan, other majors, dual majors

TEXAS

Angelo State University

ASU Station 10902
San Angelo, TX 76909-0902
www.angelo.edu/dept/nursing/
Public
Admissions: (325) 942-2169
Email: graduate.school@angelo.edu
Financial aid: (325) 942-2246
Application deadline: 04/01
Degrees offered: master's
In-state tuition: full time: $202/credit hour; part time: $202/credit hour
Out-of-state tuition: full time: $564/credit hour
Room/board/expenses: N/A
Full-time enrollment: 32
men: 13%; women: 88%; minorities: 9%; international: 0%
Part-time enrollment: 51
men: 16%; women: 84%; minorities: 31%; international: 0%
Acceptance rate (master's): 39%
Specialties offered: education, nurse practitioner, nurse practitioner: family

Baylor University

3700 Worth Street
Dallas, TX 75246
www.baylor.edu/nursing/nursing_grad/
Private
Admissions: (214) 820-3361
Email: bu_nursing@baylor.edu
Financial aid: (254) 710-2611
Application deadline: N/A
Degrees offered: master's, DNP

Tuition: full time: $1,437/credit hour; part time: $1,437/credit hour (master's); full time: $1,437/credit hour; part time: $1,437/credit hour (DNP)
Room/board/expenses: $8,136 (master's); $8,136 (DNP)
Full-time enrollment: 5 (master's); 15 (DNP)
men: 0%; women: 100%; minorities: 20%; international: 0%
Part-time enrollment: 21 (master's); 6 (DNP)
men: 7%; women: 93%; minorities: 41%; international: 0%
Acceptance rate (master's): N/A
Acceptance rate (DNP): 63%
Specialties offered: administration, nurse-midwifery, nurse practitioner, nurse practitioner: family, other majors

Hardin-Simmons University[1]

2149 Hickory Street
Abilene, TX 79601
Private
Admissions: N/A
Financial aid: N/A
Tuition: N/A
Room/board/expenses: N/A
Enrollment: N/A

Lamar University

4400 Martin Luther King Boulevard
Beaumont, TX 77710
artssciences.lamar.edu/nursing/
Public
Admissions: (409) 880-8890
Email: gradmissions@lamar.edu
Financial aid: (409) 880-7011
Application deadline: 08/11
Degrees offered: master's
In-state tuition: full time: $4,230; part time: $235/credit hour
Out-of-state tuition: full time: $4,986
Room/board/expenses: $7,870
Full-time enrollment: men: N/A; women: N/A; minorities: N/A; international: N/A
Part-time enrollment: 60
men: 3%; women: 97%; minorities: 38%; international: 0%
Acceptance rate (master's): 42%
Specialties offered: administration, education, dual majors

Lubbock Christian University

5601 19th Street
Lubbock, TX 79407
www.lcu.edu/admissions/graduate/nursing
Private
Admissions: (806) 720-7599
Email: patricia.moulton@lcu.edu
Financial aid: (806) 720-7178
Application deadline: N/A
Degrees offered: master's
Tuition: full time: $388/credit hour; part time: $388/credit hour (master's)
Room/board/expenses: N/A
Full-time enrollment: 11
men: 0%; women: 100%; minorities: 9%; international: 9%
Part-time enrollment: 84
men: 12%; women: 88%; minorities: 31%; international: 7%
Acceptance rate (master's): 74%
nurse practitioner, nurse practitioner: family

McMurry University (Shelton)[1]

2149 Hickory Street
Abilene, TX 79601
Private
Admissions: N/A
Financial aid: N/A
Tuition: N/A
Room/board/expenses: N/A
Enrollment: N/A

Midwestern State University[1]

3410 Taft Boulevard
Wichita Falls, TX 76308
Public
Admissions: N/A
Financial aid: N/A
Tuition: N/A
Room/board/expenses: N/A
Enrollment: N/A

Prairie View A&M University

6436 Fannin Street
Houston, TX 77030
www.pvamu.edu/nursing/
Public
Admissions: (713) 797-7000
Email:
graduatenursing@pvamu.edu
Financial aid: (936) 261-1000
Application deadline: 06/01
Degrees offered: master's, DNP
In-state tuition: full time: $249/
credit hour; part time: $249/credit
hour (master's); full time: $249/
credit hour; part time: $249/credit
hour (DNP)
Out-of-state tuition: full time: $609/
credit hour (master's); full time:
$609/credit hour (DNP)
Room/board/expenses: $7,735
(master's); $7,735 (DNP)
Full-time enrollment: 82 (master's);
16 (DNP)
men: 9%; women: 91%; minorities:
89%; international: 6%
Part-time enrollment: 78 (master's)
men: 6%; women: 94%;
minorities: 94%; international: 0%
Acceptance rate (master's): 76%
Acceptance rate (DNP): 100%
Specialties offered: administration,
education, generalist, nurse
practitioner

Texas A&M University-Texarkana[1]

7101 University Avenue
Texarkana, TX 75503
Public
Admissions: N/A
Financial aid: N/A
Tuition: N/A
Room/board/expenses: N/A
Enrollment: N/A

Texas A&M International University[1]

5201 University Boulevard
Laredo, TX 78041
Public
Admissions: N/A
Financial aid: N/A
Tuition: N/A
Room/board/expenses: N/A
Enrollment: N/A

Texas A&M University-Corpus Christi

6300 Ocean Drive
Corpus Christi, TX 78412
nursing.tamucc.edu/index.html
Public
Admissions: (361) 825-2177
Email: gradweb@tamucc.edu
Financial aid: (361) 825-2338
Application deadline: 04/01
Degrees offered: master's
In-state tuition: full time: $372/
credit hour; part time: $372/
credit hour
Out-of-state tuition: full time: $734/
credit hour
Room/board/expenses: $9,197
Full-time enrollment:
men: N/A; women: N/A; minorities:
N/A; international: N/A
Part-time enrollment: 370
men: 14%; women: 86%;
minorities: 54%; international: N/A
Acceptance rate (master's): 43%
Specialties offered: administration,
education, nurse practitioner,
nurse practitioner: family

Texas Christian University

2800 W. Bowie Street
Fort Worth, TX 76019
www.harriscollege.tcu.edu
Private
Admissions: (817) 257-6726
Email: m.allred@tcu.edu
Financial aid: (817) 257-7858
Application deadline: 11/15
Degrees offered: master's, DNP
Tuition: full time: $1,340/credit
hour; part time: $1,340/credit
hour (master's); full time: $1,340/
credit hour; part time: $1,340/
credit hour (DNP)
Room/board/expenses: N/A
Full-time enrollment: 46 (master's)
85 (DNP)
men: 23%; women: 77%;
minorities: 14%; international: 0%
Part-time enrollment: 2 (master's)
8 (DNP)
men: 10%; women: 90%;
minorities: 20%; international: 0%
Acceptance rate (master's): 68%
Acceptance rate (DNP): 48%
Specialties offered: clinical nurse
leader, clinical nurse specialist,
education, nurse anesthesia

Texas Tech University Health Sciences Center[1]

3601 Fourth Street
Lubbock, TX 79430
Public
Admissions: N/A
Financial aid: N/A
Tuition: N/A
Room/board/expenses: N/A
Enrollment: N/A

Texas Woman's University

PO Box 425498
Denton, TX 76204-5498
www.twu.edu
Public
Admissions: (940) 898-3188
Email: admissions@twu.edu
Financial aid: (940) 898-3064
Application deadline: N/A
Degrees offered: master's, Ph.D.,
DNP

In-state tuition: full time: $233/
credit hour; part time: $233/
credit hour (master's); full time:
$233/credit hour; part time: $233/
credit hour (Ph.D.); full time: $233/
credit hour; part time: $233/credit
hour (DNP)
Out-of-state tuition: full time: $595/
credit hour (master's); full time:
$595/credit hour (Ph.D.); full time:
$595/credit hour (DNP)
Room/board/expenses: $7,191
(master's); $7,191 (Ph.D.); $7,191
(DNP)
Full-time enrollment: 31 (master's);
9 (Ph.D.); 7 (DNP)
men: 4%; women: 96%;
minorities: 34%; international:
21%
Part-time enrollment: 819
(master's); 90 (Ph.D.); 43 (DNP)
men: 7%; women: 93%;
minorities: 54%; international: 2%
Acceptance rate (master's): 60%
Acceptance rate (Ph.D.): 81%
Acceptance rate (DNP): 80%
Specialties offered: administration,
clinical nurse leader, education,
health management & policy,
health care systems, nurse
practitioner, nurse practitioner:
adult-gerontology acute care,
nurse practitioner: adult-
gerontology primary care,
nurse practitioner: adult, nurse
practitioner: family, nurse
practitioner: pediatric primary
care, other majors

University of Houston-Victoria[1]

3007 N Ben Wilson
Victoria, TX 77901
Public
Admissions: N/A
Financial aid: N/A
Tuition: N/A
Room/board/expenses: N/A
Enrollment: N/A

University of Mary Hardin-Baylor

900 College Street
Belton, TX 76513
umhb.edu/nursing
Private
Admissions: N/A
Financial aid: (254) 295-4515
Application deadline: 05/01
Degrees offered: master's
Tuition: full time: $775/credit hour;
part time: N/A
Room/board/expenses: N/A
Full-time enrollment: 56
men: N/A; women: N/A; minorities:
20%; international: 0%
Part-time enrollment: 2
men: N/A; women: N/A; minorities:
0%; international: 0%
Acceptance rate (master's): N/A
Specialties offered: N/A

University of Texas-Arlington

411 S. Nedderman Drive
PO Box 19407
Arlington, TX 76019-0407
www.uta.edu/nursing
Public
Admissions: (817) 272-3275
Financial aid: (817) 272-3561
Application deadline: 06/01
Degrees offered: master's, Ph.D.,
DNP

In-state tuition: full time: $9,728;
part time: $6,460 (master's); full
time: $9,728; part time: $6,460
(Ph.D.); full time: $9,728; part
time: $6,460 (DNP)
Out-of-state tuition: full time:
$16,100 (master's); full time:
$16,100 (Ph.D.); full time: $16,100
(DNP)
Room/board/expenses: $8,768
(master's); $8,768 (Ph.D.); $8,768
(DNP)
Full-time enrollment: 116 (master's);
2 (Ph.D.); 1 (DNP)
men: 10%; women: 90%;
minorities: 39%; international:
13%
Part-time enrollment: 1,409
(master's); 35 (Ph.D.); 41 (DNP)
men: 11%; women: 89%;
minorities: 45%; international: 1%
Acceptance rate (master's): 61%
Acceptance rate (Ph.D.): 16%
Acceptance rate (DNP): 61%
Specialties offered: administration,
education, nurse practitioner,
nurse practitioner: adult-
gerontology acute care, nurse
practitioner: adult-gerontology
primary care, nurse practitioner:
family, nurse practitioner:
pediatric primary care, nurse
practitioner: psychiatric-mental
health, across the lifespan,
research, other majors

University of Texas-Austin

1710 Red River
Austin, TX 78701-1412
www.utexas.edu/nursing/
Public
Admissions: (512) 471-7927
Email: tdemchuk@
mail.nur.utexas.edu
Financial aid: (512) 475-6282
Application deadline: 12/01
Degrees offered: master's, Ph.D.
In-state tuition: full time: $11,572;
part time: $4,180 (master's); full
time: $11,572; part time: $4,180
(Ph.D.)
Out-of-state tuition: full time:
$21,155 (master's); full time:
$21,155 (Ph.D.)
Room/board/expenses: $9,600
(master's); $9,600 (Ph.D.)
Full-time enrollment: 197
(master's); 22 (Ph.D.)
men: 20%; women: 80%;
minorities: 27%; international: 2%
Part-time enrollment: 53
(master's); 15 (Ph.D.)
men: 13%; women: 87%;
minorities: 24%; international: 4%
Acceptance rate (master's): 55%
Acceptance rate (Ph.D.): 38%
Specialties offered: administration,
clinical nurse specialist,
community health/public health,
nurse practitioner: family,
nurse practitioner: pediatric
primary care, nurse practitioner:
psychiatric-mental health, across
the lifespan, research, other
majors

University of Texas-Brownsville[1]

80 Fort Brown
Brownsville, TX 78520
Public
Admissions: N/A
Financial aid: N/A
Tuition: N/A
Room/board/expenses: N/A
Enrollment: N/A

University of Texas-El Paso

500 W. University Avenue
El Paso, TX 79902
nursing.utep.edu/
Public
Admissions: (915) 747-5491
Email: gradschool@utep.edu
Financial aid: (915) 747-5204
Application deadline: N/A
Degrees offered: master's, DNP
In-state tuition: full time: $419/
credit hour; part time: $419/credit
hour (master's); full time: $419/
credit hour; part time: N/A (DNP)
Out-of-state tuition: full time: $815/
credit hour (master's); full time:
$815/credit hour (DNP)
Room/board/expenses: N/A
Full-time enrollment: 114 (master's);
28 (DNP)
men: N/A; women: N/A; minorities:
63%; international: 1%
Part-time enrollment: 212
(master's)
men: N/A; women: N/A; minorities:
69%; international: 0%
Acceptance rate (master's): 55%
Acceptance rate (DNP): 100%
Specialties offered: administration,
education, nurse practitioner,
nurse practitioner: adult-
gerontology acute care, nurse
practitioner: family, nurse
practitioner: pediatric primary
care

University of Texas Health Science Center-Houston

6901 Bertner Avenue
Houston, TX 77030
nursing.uth.edu/
Public
Admissions: (713) 500-2101
Email: soninfo@uth.tmc.edu
Financial aid: (713) 500-3860
Application deadline: 04/01
Degrees offered: master's, Ph.D.,
DNP
In-state tuition: full time: $232/
credit hour; part time: $232/
credit hour (master's); full time:
$232/credit hour; part time: $232/
credit hour (Ph.D.); full time: $232/
credit hour; part time: $232/credit
hour (DNP)
Out-of-state tuition: full time: $875/
credit hour (master's); full time:
$875/credit hour (Ph.D.); full time:
$875/credit hour (DNP)
Room/board/expenses: N/A
Full-time enrollment: 180
(master's); 10 (Ph.D.); 35 (DNP)
men: 20%; women: 80%;
minorities: 46%; international: 6%
Part-time enrollment: 148
(master's); 24 (Ph.D.); 61 (DNP)
men: 15%; women: 85%;
minorities: 55%; international: 1%
Acceptance rate (master's): 64%
Acceptance rate (Ph.D.): 67%
Acceptance rate (DNP): 36%
Specialties offered: administration,
education, nurse anesthesia,
nurse practitioner, nurse
practitioner: adult-gerontology
acute care, nurse practitioner:
adult-gerontology primary
care, nurse practitioner: family,
research, dual majors

University of Texas Health Science Center-San Antonio[1]

7703 Floyd Curl Drive
San Antonio, TX 78229-3900
Public
Admissions: N/A
Financial aid: N/A
Tuition: N/A
Room/board/expenses: N/A
Enrollment: N/A

University of Texas Medical Branch-Galveston

301 University Boulevard
Galveston, TX 77555-1029
nursing.utmb.edu/
Public
Admissions: (409) 772-8205
Email: dpearro@utmb.edu
Financial aid: (409) 772-1215
Application deadline: 12/01
Degrees offered: master's, Ph.D., DNP
In-state tuition: full time: $285/credit hour; part time: $285/credit hour (master's); full time: $285/credit hour; part time: $285/credit hour (Ph.D.); full time: $285/credit hour; part time: $285/credit hour (DNP)
Out-of-state tuition: full time: $639/credit hour (master's); full time: $639/credit hour (Ph.D.); full time: $639/credit hour (DNP)
Room/board/expenses: $14,424 (master's); $14,424 (Ph.D.); $14,424 (DNP)
Full-time enrollment: 144 (master's); 20 (Ph.D.); men: 13%; women: 87%; minorities: 43%; international: 1%
Part-time enrollment: 357 (master's); 21 (Ph.D.); 31 (DNP) men: 13%; women: 87%; minorities: 55%; international: 1%
Acceptance rate (master's): 36%
Acceptance rate (Ph.D.): 86%
Acceptance rate (DNP): 59%
Specialties offered: administration, clinical nurse leader, education, nurse practitioner, nurse practitioner: adult-gerontology primary care, nurse practitioner: family, research

University of Texas-Pan American[1]

1201 W. University Drive
Edinburg, TX 78540
Public
Admissions: N/A
Financial aid: N/A
Tuition: N/A
Room/board/expenses: N/A
Enrollment: N/A

University of Texas-Tyler

3900 University Boulevard
Tyler, TX 75799
www.uttyler.edu/nursing/college/
Public
Admissions: (903) 566-7457
Email: ogs@uttyler.edu
Financial aid: (903) 566-7180
Application deadline: 02/15
Degrees offered: master's, Ph.D.
In-state tuition: full time: $5,180; part time: $3,108 (master's); full time: $5,980; part time: $3,588 (Ph.D.)

Out-of-state tuition: full time: $12,420 (master's); full time: $13,220 (Ph.D.)
Room/board/expenses: $11,552 (master's); $11,552 (Ph.D.)
Full-time enrollment: 53 (master's); 15 (Ph.D.) men: 12%; women: 88%; minorities: 29%; international: 0%
Part-time enrollment: 286 (master's); 48 (Ph.D.) men: 12%; women: 88%; minorities: 29%; international: 0%
Acceptance rate (master's): 27%
Acceptance rate (Ph.D.): 44%
Specialties offered: administration, education, nurse practitioner, nurse practitioner: family, research

University of the Incarnate Word

4301 Broadway
San Antonio, TX 78209
uiw.edu/nursing/
Private
Admissions: (210) 829-6005
Email: admis@uiwtx.edu
Financial aid: (210) 829-6008
Application deadline: N/A
Degrees offered: master's, DNP
Tuition: full time: $815/credit hour; part time: $815/credit hour (master's); full time: $840/credit hour; part time: $840/credit hour (DNP)
Room/board/expenses: $9,510 (master's); $9,510 (DNP)
Full-time enrollment: 6 (master's) men: 17%; women: 83%; minorities: 33%; international: 33%
Part-time enrollment: 35 (master's); 23 (DNP) men: 26%; women: 74%; minorities: 31%; international: 9%
Acceptance rate (master's): 87%
Acceptance rate (DNP): 100%
Specialties offered: clinical nurse leader, clinical nurse specialist, nurse practitioner: family

West Texas A&M University

Killgore Research Center
Room 102
Canyon, TX 79016
Public
Admissions: N/A
Financial aid: N/A
Application deadline: N/A
Degrees offered: master's
In-state tuition: full time: N/A; part time: N/A
Out-of-state tuition: full time: N/A
Room/board/expenses: N/A
Full-time enrollment: men: N/A; women: N/A; minorities: N/A; international: N/A
Part-time enrollment: men: N/A; women: N/A; minorities: N/A; international: N/A
Acceptance rate (master's): N/A
Specialties offered: administration, case management, education, generalist, health management & policy health care systems, informatics, nurse practitioner

Brigham Young University

400 SWKT
Provo, UT 84602
nursing.byu.edu
Private
Admissions: (801) 422-4091
Email: graduatestudies@byu.edu
Financial aid: (801) 422-4104
Application deadline: 12/01
Degrees offered: master's
Tuition: full time: $350/credit hour; part time: $350/credit hour
Room/board/expenses: $11,412
Full-time enrollment: 29 men: 34%; women: 66%; minorities: 0%; international: 0%
Part-time enrollment: men: N/A; women: N/A; minorities: N/A; international: N/A
Acceptance rate (master's): 35%
Specialties offered: nurse practitioner, nurse practitioner: family

University of Utah

10 S. 2000 E
Salt Lake City, UT 84112
nursing.utah.edu
Public
Admissions: (801) 581-3414
Email: info@nurs.utah.edu
Financial aid: (801) 585-1671
Application deadline: 01/15
Degrees offered: master's, Ph.D., DNP
In-state tuition: full time: $13,042; part time: N/A (master's); full time: $11,560; part time: N/A (Ph.D.); full time: $15,710; part time: N/A (DNP)
Out-of-state tuition: full time: $32,445 (master's); full time: $28,097 (Ph.D.); full time: $40,270 (DNP)
Room/board/expenses: $8,802 (master's); $8,802 (Ph.D.); $8,802 (DNP)
Full-time enrollment: 41 (master's); 52 (Ph.D.); 218 (DNP) men: 18%; women: 82%; minorities: 12%; international: 3%
Part-time enrollment: 11 (master's) men: 36%; women: 64%; minorities: 0%; international: 0%
Acceptance rate (master's): 100%
Acceptance rate (Ph.D.): 57%
Acceptance rate (DNP): 55%
Specialties offered: education, informatics, nurse-midwifery, nurse practitioner, nurse practitioner: adult-gerontology acute care, nurse practitioner: adult-gerontology primary care, nurse practitioner: family, nurse practitioner: pediatric primary care, nurse practitioner: psychiatric-mental health, across the lifespan, research, other majors, dual majors

Utah Valley University[1]

800 W. University Parkway
Orem, UT 84058
Public
Admissions: N/A
Financial aid: N/A
Tuition: N/A
Room/board/expenses: N/A
Enrollment: N/A

Weber State University

3875 Stadium Way
Department 3903
Ogden, UT 84408
weber.edu/nursing
Public
Admissions: (801) 626-6753
Email: rholt@weber.edu
Financial aid: N/A
Application deadline: 03/02
Degrees offered: master's
In-state tuition: full time: $428/credit hour; part time: N/A
Out-of-state tuition: full time: $428/credit hour
Room/board/expenses: N/A
Full-time enrollment: 44 men: N/A; women: N/A; minorities: N/A; international: N/A
Part-time enrollment: men: N/A; women: N/A; minorities: N/A; international: N/A
Acceptance rate (master's): N/A
Specialties offered: administration, education

Western Governors University[1]

4001 S. 700 E
Salt Lake City, UT 84107
Private
Admissions: N/A
Financial aid: N/A
Tuition: N/A
Room/board/expenses: N/A
Enrollment: N/A

Westminster College[1]

1840 S. 1300 E
Salt Lake City, UT 84105
Private
Admissions: N/A
Financial aid: N/A
Tuition: N/A
Room/board/expenses: N/A
Enrollment: N/A

Norwich University

158 Harmon Drive
Northfield, VT 05663
online.norwich.edu/degree-programs/masters/master-science-nursing/overview
Private
Admissions: (800) 460-5597
Email: msn@online.norwich.edu
Financial aid: (802) 485-2969
Application deadline: 08/15
Degrees offered: master's
Tuition: full time: $616/credit hour; part time: $616/credit hour
Room/board/expenses: N/A
Full-time enrollment: 96 men: 9%; women: 91%; minorities: 16%; international: 0%
Part-time enrollment: men: N/A; women: N/A; minorities: N/A; international: N/A
Acceptance rate (master's): 87%
Specialties offered: administration, education

University of Vermont

216 Rowell Building
Burlington, VT 5405
www.uvm.edu/~cnhs/nursing/
Public
Admissions: (802) 656-3858
Email: cnhsgrad@uvm.edu
Financial aid: (802) 656-5700
Application deadline: N/A
Degrees offered: master's, DNP
In-state tuition: full time: $591/credit hour; part time: $591/credit hour (master's); full time: $591/credit hour; part time: $591/credit hour (DNP)
Out-of-state tuition: full time: $1,493/credit hour (master's); full time: $1,493/credit hour (DNP)
Room/board/expenses: N/A
Full-time enrollment: 47 (master's); 13 (DNP) men: 13%; women: 87%; minorities: 12%; international: 0%
Part-time enrollment: 27 (master's); 4 (DNP) men: 16%; women: 84%; minorities: 3%; international: 0%
Acceptance rate (master's): 85%
Acceptance rate (DNP): 42%
Specialties offered: clinical nurse leader, nurse practitioner, nurse practitioner: adult-gerontology primary care, nurse practitioner: family

Eastern Mennonite University[1]

1200 Park Road
Harrisonburg, VA 22802
Private
Admissions: N/A
Financial aid: N/A
Tuition: N/A
Room/board/expenses: N/A
Enrollment: N/A

George Mason University

4400 University Drive
Fairfax, VA 22030-4444
chhs.gmu.edu/nursing/index.cfm
Public
Admissions: (703) 993-2400
Email: admissions@gmu.edu
Financial aid: (703) 993-2353
Application deadline: 02/01
Degrees offered: master's, Ph.D., DNP
In-state tuition: full time: $483/credit hour; part time: $483/credit hour (master's); full time: $483/credit hour; part time: $483/credit hour (Ph.D.); full time: $483/credit hour; part time: $483/credit hour (DNP)
Out-of-state tuition: full time: $1,199/credit hour (master's); full time: $1,199/credit hour (Ph.D.); full time: $1,199/credit hour (DNP)
Room/board/expenses: $16,710 (master's); $16,710 (Ph.D.); $16,710 (DNP)
Full-time enrollment: 29 (master's); 4 (DNP) men: 10%; women: 90%; minorities: 52%; international: 5%
Part-time enrollment: 109 (master's); 26 (Ph.D.); 44 (DNP) men: 7%; women: 93%; minorities: 32%; international: 3%

Acceptance rate (master's): 43%
Acceptance rate (Ph.D.): 63%
Acceptance rate (DNP): 52%
Specialties offered: administration, education, nurse practitioner, nurse practitioner: adult-gerontology primary care, nurse practitioner: family, nurse practitioner: psychiatric-mental health, across the lifespan, research

Hampton University[1]
100 E. Queen Street
Hampton, VA 23668
Private
Admissions: N/A
Financial aid: N/A
Tuition: N/A
Room/board/expenses: N/A
Enrollment: N/A

James Madison University
MSC 4305
Harrisonburg, VA 22807
jmu.edu/nursing
Public
Admissions: N/A
Email: walshmd@jmu.edu
Financial aid: (540) 568-7820
Application deadline: N/A
Degrees offered: master's, DNP
In-state tuition: full time: $434/credit hour; part time: $434/credit hour (master's); full time: $434/credit hour; part time: $434/credit hour (DNP)
Out-of-state tuition: full time: $1,135/credit hour (master's); full time: $1,135/credit hour (DNP)
Room/board/expenses: N/A
Full-time enrollment: 11 (master's)
men: 18%; women: 82%; minorities: 9%; international: 0%
Part-time enrollment: 45 (master's); 11 (DNP)
men: 23%; women: 77%; minorities: 2%; international: 0%
Acceptance rate (master's): 50%
Acceptance rate (DNP): 92%
Specialties offered: administration, clinical nurse leader, nurse-midwifery, nurse practitioner: family

Jefferson College of Health Sciences[1]
101 Elm Ave., SE
Roanoke, VA 24013
Private
Admissions: N/A
Financial aid: N/A
Tuition: N/A
Room/board/expenses: N/A
Enrollment: N/A

Liberty University
1971 University Boulevard
Lynchburg, VA 24502
www.liberty.edu/academics/arts-sciences/nursing/index.cfm?PID=188
Private
Admissions: (800) 424-9596
Email: gradadmissions@liberty.edu
Financial aid: (434) 582-2270
Application deadline: N/A
Degrees offered: master's, DNP

Tuition: full time: $520/credit hour; part time: $565/credit hour (master's); full time: $950/credit hour; part time: $950/credit hour (DNP)
Room/board/expenses: N/A
Full-time enrollment: 84 (master's); 18 (DNP)
men: 9%; women: 91%; minorities: 20%; international: 1%
Part-time enrollment: 429 (master's)
men: 10%; women: 90%; minorities: 22%; international: 0%
Acceptance rate (master's): 34%
Acceptance rate (DNP): N/A
Specialties offered: administration, education, nurse practitioner, nurse practitioner: family

Lynchburg College
1501 Lakeside Drive
Lynchburg, VA 24501
www.lynchburg.edu/nursing
Private
Admissions: (800) 426-8101
Email: admissions@lynchburg.edu
Financial aid: (434) 544-8228
Application deadline: N/A
Degrees offered: master's
Tuition: full time: $460/credit hour; part time: $460/credit hour
Room/board/expenses: N/A
Full-time enrollment: 4
men: 25%; women: 75%; minorities: 50%; international: 0%
Part-time enrollment: 21
men: 0%; women: 100%; minorities: 14%; international: 5%
Acceptance rate (master's): 86%
Specialties offered: clinical nurse leader

Marymount University
2807 N. Glebe Road
Arlington, VA 22207-4299
www.marymount.edu/academics/schools/shp
Private
Admissions: (703) 284-5901
Email: grad.admissions@marymount.edu
Financial aid: (703) 284-1530
Application deadline: 05/01
Degrees offered: master's, DNP
Tuition: full time: N/A; part time: $885/credit hour (master's); full time: N/A; part time: $885/credit hour (DNP)
Room/board/expenses: N/A
Full-time enrollment: 11 (master's); 1 (DNP)
men: 0%; women: 100%; minorities: 33%; international: 8%
Part-time enrollment: 39 (master's); 9 (DNP)
men: 2%; women: 98%; minorities: 40%; international: 0%
Acceptance rate (master's): 59%
Acceptance rate (DNP): 0%
Specialties offered: nurse practitioner, nurse practitioner: family

Old Dominion University[1]
Office of Admissions
Norfolk, VA 23529-0500
Public
Admissions: N/A
Financial aid: N/A
Tuition: N/A
Room/board/expenses: N/A
Enrollment: N/A

Radford University[1]
PO Box 6964
Radford Station
Radford, VA 24142
Public
Admissions: N/A
Financial aid: N/A
Tuition: N/A
Room/board/expenses: N/A
Enrollment: N/A

Shenandoah University
1460 University Drive
Winchester, VA 22601
www.nursing.su.edu/
Private
Admissions: (540) 665-4581
Email: admit@su.edu
Financial aid: (540) 665-4538
Application deadline: 05/01
Degrees offered: master's, DNP
Tuition: full time: $813/credit hour; part time: $813/credit hour (master's); full time: $813/credit hour; part time: $813/credit hour (DNP)
Room/board/expenses: $9,728 (master's); $9,728 (DNP)
Full-time enrollment: 20 (master's); 6 (DNP)
men: 12%; women: 88%; minorities: 27%; international: 0%
Part-time enrollment: 43 (master's); 3 (DNP)
men: 7%; women: 93%; minorities: 22%; international: 2%
Acceptance rate (master's): 78%
Acceptance rate (DNP): 100%
Specialties offered: health management & policy health care systems, informatics, nurse-midwifery, nurse practitioner, nurse practitioner: psychiatric-mental health, across the lifespan

University of Virginia
PO Box 800826
Charlottesville, VA 22908-0782
www.nursing.virginia.edu/
Public
Admissions: (434) 924-0141
Email: hysell@virginia.edu
Financial aid: (434) 924-0141
Application deadline: 11/01
Degrees offered: master's, Ph.D., DNP
In-state tuition: full time: $14,144; part time: $769/credit hour (master's); full time: $14,164; part time: N/A (Ph.D.); full time: $14,144; part time: $769/credit hour (DNP)
Out-of-state tuition: full time: $23,568 (master's); full time: $23,722 (Ph.D.); full time: $23,568 (DNP)
Room/board/expenses: N/A
Full-time enrollment: 123 (master's); 37 (Ph.D.); 20 (DNP)
men: 11%; women: 89%; minorities: 19%; international: 3%
Part-time enrollment: 165 (master's); 28 (DNP)
men: 11%; women: 89%; minorities: 17%; international: 0%
Acceptance rate (master's): 56%
Acceptance rate (Ph.D.): 67%
Acceptance rate (DNP): 69%

Specialties offered: clinical nurse leader, clinical nurse specialist, community health/public health, health management & policy health care systems, nurse practitioner, nurse practitioner: adult-gerontology acute care, nurse practitioner: family, nurse practitioner: pediatric primary care, nurse practitioner: psychiatric-mental health, across the lifespan, research, combined nurse practitioner/clinical nurse specialist

Virginia Commonwealth University
730 East Broad Street
Richmond, VA 23298
www.nursing.vcu.edu
Public
Admissions: (804) 828-5171
Email: VCU_Nurse@vcu.edu
Financial aid: (804) 828-6669
Application deadline: 02/01
Degrees offered: master's, Ph.D.
In-state tuition: full time: $10,258; part time: $570/credit hour (master's); full time: $8,464; part time: $470/credit hour (Ph.D.)
Out-of-state tuition: full time: $21,091 (master's); full time: $18,042 (Ph.D.)
Room/board/expenses: $8,692 (master's); $8,692 (Ph.D.)
Full-time enrollment: 78 (master's); 10 (Ph.D.)
men: 6%; women: 94%; minorities: 23%; international: 1%
Part-time enrollment: 148 (master's); 7 (Ph.D.)
men: 4%; women: 96%; minorities: 22%; international: 1%
Acceptance rate (master's): 46%
Acceptance rate (Ph.D.): 89%
Specialties offered: administration, nurse practitioner, nurse practitioner: adult-gerontology acute care, nurse practitioner: adult-gerontology primary care, nurse practitioner: family, nurse practitioner: psychiatric-mental health, across the lifespan

WASHINGTON

Gonzaga University
502 E. Boone Avenue
Spokane, WA 99258-0038
www.gonzaga.edu/SNHP
Private
Admissions: (509) 313-6239
Email: burdette@gonzaga.edu
Financial aid: (800) 793-1716
Application deadline: 12/31
Degrees offered: master's, DNP
Tuition: full time: $900/credit hour; part time: $900/credit hour (master's); full time: $905/credit hour; part time: $905/credit hour (DNP)
Room/board/expenses: $11,407 (master's); $11,407 (DNP)
Full-time enrollment: 391 (master's); 18 (DNP)
men: 14%; women: 86%; minorities: 15%; international: 0%
Part-time enrollment: 186 (master's); 39 (DNP)
men: 15%; women: 85%; minorities: 13%; international: 0%

Acceptance rate (master's): 82%
Acceptance rate (DNP): 90%
Specialties offered: administration, nurse anesthesia, nurse practitioner, nurse practitioner: adult-gerontology primary care, nurse practitioner: family, nurse practitioner: psychiatric-mental health, across the lifespan, other majors

Pacific Lutheran University
121st and Park Avenue
Tacoma, WA 98447-0029
www.plu.edu/nursing
Private
Admissions: (253) 535-7151
Email: admission@plu.edu
Financial aid: (253) 535-8725
Application deadline: 01/15
Degrees offered: master's, DNP
Tuition: full time: $1,130/credit hour; part time: $1,130/credit hour (master's); full time: $1,080/credit hour; part time: $1,080/credit hour (DNP)
Room/board/expenses: $8,000 (master's); $8,000 (DNP)
Full-time enrollment: 59 (master's)
men: 15%; women: 85%; minorities: 22%; international: 0%
Part-time enrollment:
men: N/A; women: N/A; minorities: N/A; international: N/A
Acceptance rate (master's): 33%
Acceptance rate (DNP): N/A
Specialties offered: administration, clinical nurse leader, education, generalist, nurse practitioner, nurse practitioner: family, dual majors

Seattle Pacific University[1]
3307 Third Avenue W
Seattle, WA 98119-1922
Private
Admissions: N/A
Financial aid: N/A
Tuition: N/A
Room/board/expenses: N/A
Enrollment: N/A

Seattle University[1]
901 12th Avenue
Seattle, WA 98122-4340
Private
Admissions: N/A
Financial aid: N/A
Tuition: N/A
Room/board/expenses: N/A
Enrollment: N/A

University of Washington
PO Box 357260
Seattle, WA 98195
nursing.uw.edu/
Public
Admissions: (206) 543-8736
Email: sonsas@uw.edu
Financial aid: (206) 543-6107
Application deadline: 01/15
Degrees offered: master's, Ph.D., DNP
In-state tuition: full time: N/A; part time: N/A
Out-of-state tuition: full time: N/A
Room/board/expenses: N/A

Full-time enrollment: 13 (master's); 44 (Ph.D.); 171 (DNP) men: 11%; women: 89%; minorities: 26%; international: 9% **Part-time enrollment:** 59 (master's); 24 (Ph.D.); 63 (DNP) men: 20%; women: 80%; minorities: 36%; international: 4% **Acceptance rate (master's):** 81% **Acceptance rate (Ph.D.):** 54% **Acceptance rate (DNP):** 67% **Specialties offered:** clinical nurse specialist, community health/ public health, informatics, nurse-midwifery, nurse practitioner, nurse practitioner: adult-gerontology acute care, nurse practitioner: adult-gerontology primary care, nurse practitioner: family, nurse practitioner: pediatric primary care, nurse practitioner: psychiatric-mental health, across the lifespan, research

Washington State University
PO Box 1495
Spokane, WA 99210
nursing.wsu.edu
Public
Admissions: (509) 324-7279
Email: cefitzgerald@wsu.edu
Financial aid: (509) 335-3942
Application deadline: 01/10
Degrees offered: master's, Ph.D., DNP
In-state tuition: full time: $17,756; part time: $888/credit hour (master's); full time: $17,756; part time: $888/credit hour (Ph.D.); full time: $17,756; part time: $888/credit hour (DNP)
Out-of-state tuition: full time: $32,778 (master's); full time: $32,778 (Ph.D.); full time: $32,778 (DNP)
Room/board/expenses: $11,276 (master's); $11,276 (Ph.D.); $11,276 (DNP)
Full-time enrollment: 6 (master's); 10 (Ph.D.); 56 (DNP) men: 13%; women: 88%; minorities: 26%; international: 6% **Part-time enrollment:** 44 (master's); 17 (Ph.D.); 53 (DNP) men: 18%; women: 82%; minorities: 18%; international: N/A **Acceptance rate (master's):** 58% **Acceptance rate (Ph.D.):** 55% **Acceptance rate (DNP):** 63% **Specialties offered:** administration, community health/public health, education, nurse practitioner, nurse practitioner: family, nurse practitioner: psychiatric-mental health, across the lifespan, research, school nursing

WEST VIRGINIA

Marshall University[1]
100 Angus E. Peyton Drive
South Charleston, WV 25303
Public
Admissions: N/A
Financial aid: N/A
Tuition: N/A
Room/board/expenses: N/A
Enrollment: N/A

West Virginia University
One Medical Drive
PO Box 9600
Morgantown, WV 26506-9600
nursing.hsc.wvu.edu/
Public
Admissions: (304) 293-5908
Email: mmmichael@hsc.wvu.edu
Financial aid: (304) 293-3706
Application deadline: 02/01
Degrees offered: master's, Ph.D., DNP
In-state tuition: full time: $8,298; part time: $461/credit hour (master's); full time: $8,298; part time: $461/credit hour (Ph.D.); full time: $8,298; part time: $461/credit hour (DNP)
Out-of-state tuition: full time: $20,970 (master's); full time: $20,970 (Ph.D.); full time: $20,970 (DNP)
Room/board/expenses: N/A
Full-time enrollment: 75 (master's) men: 9%; women: 91%; minorities: 7%; international: 0% **Part-time enrollment:** 57 (master's); 12 (Ph.D.); 24 (DNP) men: 9%; women: 91%; minorities: 10%; international: 0% **Acceptance rate (master's):** 77% **Acceptance rate (Ph.D.):** N/A **Acceptance rate (DNP):** 100% **Specialties offered:** nurse practitioner, nurse practitioner: family, nurse practitioner: pediatric primary care

West Virginia Wesleyan College[1]
59 College Avenue
Buckhannon, WV 26201
Private
Admissions: N/A
Financial aid: N/A
Tuition: N/A
Room/board/expenses: N/A
Enrollment: N/A

Wheeling Jesuit University
316 Washington Avenue
Wheeling, WV 26003
Private
Admissions: (304) 243-2359
Email: adulted@wju.edu
Financial aid: (304) 243-2304
Application deadline: N/A
Degrees offered: master's
Tuition: full time: $625/credit hour; part time: $625/credit hour
Room/board/expenses: N/A
Full-time enrollment: 9 men: 0%; women: 100%; minorities: 0%; international: 0% **Part-time enrollment:** 172 men: 13%; women: 87%; minorities: 1%; international: 0% **Acceptance rate (master's):** 94% **Specialties offered:** administration, education, nurse practitioner, nurse practitioner: family

WISCONSIN

Alverno College
300 S. 43 Street
Milwaukee, WI 53234-3922
www.alverno.edu/academics/
academicdepartments/
joannmcgrathschoolofnursing
Private
Admissions: (800) 933-3401
Email: admissions@alverno.edu
Financial aid: (414) 382-6046
Application deadline: N/A
Degrees offered: master's
Tuition: full time: $877/credit hour; part time: N/A
Room/board/expenses: N/A
Full-time enrollment: 82 men: 7%; women: 93%; minorities: 27%; international: 1% **Part-time enrollment:** 101 men: 5%; women: 95%; minorities: 27%; international: 0% **Acceptance rate (master's):** 58% **Specialties offered:** clinical nurse specialist, nurse practitioner, nurse practitioner: family, nurse practitioner: psychiatric-mental health, across the lifespan

Bellin College[1]
3201 Eaton Road
Green Bay, WI 54311
Private
Admissions: N/A
Financial aid: N/A
Tuition: N/A
Room/board/expenses: N/A
Enrollment: N/A

Cardinal Stritch University[1]
6801 N. Yates Road
Milwaukee, WI 53217-3985
Private
Admissions: N/A
Financial aid: N/A
Tuition: N/A
Room/board/expenses: N/A
Enrollment: N/A

Concordia University
12800 N. Lake Shore Drive
Mequon, WI 53097
www.cuw.edu/Programs/nursing/
index.html
Private
Admissions: N/A
Financial aid: (262) 243-4392
Application deadline: 05/01
Degrees offered: master's, DNP
Tuition: full time: $640/credit hour; part time: $640/credit hour (master's); full time: $705/credit hour; part time: $705/credit hour (DNP)
Room/board/expenses: N/A
Full-time enrollment: 148 (master's) men: N/A; women: N/A; minorities: 15%; international: 2% **Part-time enrollment:** 578 (master's); 61 (DNP) men: N/A; women: N/A; minorities: 14%; international: 0% **Acceptance rate (master's):** 69% **Acceptance rate (DNP):** 100% **Specialties offered:** education, nurse practitioner, nurse practitioner: adult-gerontology primary care, nurse practitioner: family

Edgewood College
1000 Edgewood College Drive
Madison, WI 53711
Private
Admissions: (608) 663-2294
Email: admissions@edgewood.edu
Financial aid: (608) 663-4300
Application deadline: N/A
Degrees offered: master's, DNP
Tuition: full time: $836/credit hour; part time: $836/credit hour (master's); full time: $836/credit hour; part time: $836/credit hour (DNP)
Room/board/expenses: N/A
Full-time enrollment: 11 (DNP) men: 0%; women: 100%; minorities: 0%; international: 0% **Part-time enrollment:** 61 (master's); 2 (DNP) men: 8%; women: 92%; minorities: 8%; international: 2% **Acceptance rate (master's):** N/A **Acceptance rate (DNP):** N/A **Specialties offered:** administration, education

Herzing University-Milwaukee[1]
525 N. 6th Street
Milwaukee, WI 53203
Private
Admissions: N/A
Financial aid: N/A
Tuition: N/A
Room/board/expenses: N/A
Enrollment: N/A

Marian University
45 S. National Avenue
Fond du Lac, WI 54935-4699
www.marianuniversity.edu/
nursing/
Private
Admissions: (920) 923-7650
Email: admission@
marianuniversity.edu
Financial aid: (920) 923-7614
Application deadline: N/A
Degrees offered: master's
Tuition: full time: $672/credit hour; part time: $672/credit hour (master's)
Room/board/expenses: N/A
Full-time enrollment: 57 men: 12%; women: 88%; minorities: 5%; international: 0% **Part-time enrollment:** 4 men: 25%; women: 75%; minorities: 0%; international: 0% **Acceptance rate (master's):** 100% **Specialties offered:** education, nurse practitioner, nurse practitioner: adult-gerontology primary care

Marquette University
PO Box 1881
Milwaukee, WI 53233
www.marquette.edu/nursing/
index.shtml
Private
Admissions: (414) 288-7137
Email: gradadmit@mu.edu
Financial aid: (414) 288-5325
Application deadline: 02/15
Degrees offered: master's, Ph.D., DNP

Tuition: full time: $1,025/credit hour; part time: $1,025/credit hour (master's); full time: $1,025/credit hour; part time: $1,025/credit hour (Ph.D.); full time: $1,025/credit hour; part time: $1,025/credit hour (DNP)
Room/board/expenses: $13,050 (master's); $13,050 (Ph.D.); $13,050 (DNP)
Full-time enrollment: 74 (master's); 4 (Ph.D.); 13 (DNP) men: 10%; women: 90%; minorities: 12%; international: 1% **Part-time enrollment:** 223 (master's); 27 (Ph.D.); 40 (DNP) men: 8%; women: 92%; minorities: 8%; international: 1% **Acceptance rate (master's):** 62% **Acceptance rate (Ph.D.):** 100% **Acceptance rate (DNP):** 100% **Specialties offered:** administration, clinical nurse leader, clinical nurse specialist, generalist, nurse-midwifery, nurse practitioner, nurse practitioner: adult-gerontology acute care, nurse practitioner: adult-gerontology primary care, nurse practitioner: pediatric primary care, other majors

University of Wisconsin-Eau Claire
Nursing 127
Eau Claire, WI 54702-4004
www.uwec.edu/CONHS/
index.htm
Public
Admissions: (715) 836-5415
Email: admissions@uwec.edu
Financial aid: (705) 836-3373
Application deadline: 01/01
Degrees offered: master's, DNP
In-state tuition: full time: $7,641; part time: $425/credit hour (master's)
Out-of-state tuition: full time: $16,771 (master's)
Room/board/expenses: $6,986 (master's)
Full-time enrollment: 35 (DNP) men: 9%; women: 91%; minorities: 11%; international: 0% **Part-time enrollment:** 6 (master's); 43 (DNP) men: 10%; women: 90%; minorities: 2%; international: 0% **Acceptance rate (master's):** N/A **Acceptance rate (DNP):** 91% **Specialties offered:** administration, clinical nurse specialist, education, nurse practitioner, nurse practitioner: adult-gerontology primary care, nurse practitioner: family

University of Wisconsin-Madison[1]
600 Highland Avenue
Madison, WI 53792-2455
Public
Admissions: N/A
Financial aid: N/A
Tuition: N/A
Room/board/expenses: N/A
Enrollment: N/A

University of Wisconsin-Milwaukee

1921 E. Hartford Avenue
Milwaukee, WI 53201
www.uwm.edu/nursing
Public
Admissions: (414) 229-2494
Email: rjens@uwm.edu
Financial aid: (414) 229-4819
Application deadline: N/A
Degrees offered: master's, Ph.D., DNP
In-state tuition: full time: $11,686; part time: $1,065/credit hour (master's); full time: $11,686; part time: $1,065/credit hour (Ph.D.); full time: $11,686; part time: $1,065/credit hour (DNP)
Out-of-state tuition: full time: $24,152 (master's); full time: $24,152 (Ph.D.); full time: $24,152 (DNP)

Room/board/expenses: $9,180 (master's); $9,180 (Ph.D.); $9,180 (DNP)
Full-time enrollment: 91 (master's); 76 (Ph.D.); 126 (DNP)
men: 10%; women: 90%; minorities: 14%; international: 3%
Part-time enrollment:
men: N/A; women: N/A; minorities: N/A; international: N/A
Acceptance rate (master's): 71%
Acceptance rate (Ph.D.): 88%
Acceptance rate (DNP): 96%
Specialties offered: administration, clinical nurse leader, clinical nurse specialist, community health/public health, generalist, health management & policy health care systems, informatics, nurse practitioner, nurse practitioner: family, research, dual majors

University of Wisconsin-Oshkosh

800 Algoma Boulevard
Oshkosh, WI 54901
www.uwosh.edu/con
Public
Admissions: (920) 424-1223
Email: gradschool@uwosh.edu
Financial aid: (920) 424-3377
Application deadline: 01/31
Degrees offered: master's, DNP
In-state tuition: full time: $481/credit hour; part time: $481/credit hour (master's); full time: $729/credit hour; part time: $729/credit hour (DNP)
Out-of-state tuition: full time: $988/credit hour (master's); full time: $1,236/credit hour (DNP)
Room/board/expenses: N/A
Full-time enrollment: 10 (master's); 36 (DNP)
men: 15%; women: 85%; minorities: 11%; international: 4%

Part-time enrollment: 41 (master's); 37 (DNP)
men: 3%; women: 97%; minorities: 5%; international: N/A
Acceptance rate (master's): 87%
Acceptance rate (DNP): 56%
Specialties offered: clinical nurse leader, education, nurse practitioner, nurse practitioner: family

Viterbo University[1]

900 Viterbo Drive
La Crosse, WI 54601
Private
Admissions: N/A
Financial aid: N/A
Tuition: N/A
Room/board/expenses: N/A
Enrollment: N/A

WYOMING

University of Wyoming[1]

Dept. 3065
Laramie, WY 82071
Public
Admissions: N/A
Financial aid: N/A
Tuition: N/A
Room/board/expenses: N/A
Enrollment: N/A

BUSINESS

ENGINEERING

MEDICINE